THE FACTS ON FILE
COMPANION TO

BRITISH POETRY

1900 TO THE PRESENT

JAMES PERSOON
ROBERT R. WATSON

Facts On File
An imprint of Infobase Publishing

Facts On File, Inc.
An imprint of Infobase Publishing
132 West 31st Street
New York NY 10001

Library of Congress Cataloging-in-Publication Data

The Facts on File companion to British poetry, 1900 to the present / [edited by] James Persoon, Robert R. Watson.
    p. cm.— (Companion to literature)
    The Facts on File companion to British poetry, 1900 to the present is part of a four-volume set on British poetry from the beginnings to the present.
    Includes bibliographical references (p.   ) and index.
    ISBN-10: 0-8160-6406-7
    ISBN-13: 978-0-8160-6406-9 (acid-free paper)
    I. English poetry—20th century. 2. English poetry—21st century. I. Persoon, James. II. Watson, Robert R. III. Facts on File, Inc. IV. Title: Companion to British poetry, 1900 to the present. V. Series.
    PR1225.F29 2008
    821'.909—dc22   2007047593

Facts On File books are available at special discounts when purchased in bulk quantities for businesses, associations, institutions, or sales promotions. Please call our Special Sales Department in New York at (212) 967-8800 or (800) 322-8755.

You can find Facts On File on the World Wide Web at http://www.factsonfile.com

Text design adapted by Annie O'Donnell
Cover design by Salvatore Luongo

Printed in the United States of America

VB Hermitage 10 9 8 7 6 5 4 3 2 1

This book is printed on acid-free paper and contains 30 percent postconsumer recycled content.

CONTENTS

INTRODUCTION

HOW TO USE THIS BOOK

The Facts On File Companion to British Poetry, 1900 to the Present is the last volume in a four-volume set on British poetry from its beginnings to the present. Like other volumes in the series, this one aims to provide commentary on poets and individual poems likely to be encountered by students in high school and college courses. To this end, the selection of entries was largely determined by combing through textbooks and anthologies. At the same time, we felt as editors and teachers that part of our duty was to expand the horizons of our readers—and perhaps expand the usefulness of this companion—beyond what is currently the most commonly taught. This process took the form of three approaches, which have added greatly to the length of this volume.

The first approach was to undertake a rescue mission of unfairly neglected poetry from the 20th century, especially the first half. Canons of taste change, and some previously neglected poets, such as Charlotte Mew, Elizabeth Daryush, Frances Comford, Anna Wickham, and Sylvia Townsend Warner, have rapidly rising or recovering reputations, evidenced by newly available editions of their poetry, or by new inclusions in anthologies. Others were important to movements and groupings, such as Richard Aldington and Wyndham Lewis in the history of imagism, or such key Georgian poets as W. H. Davies and Walter de la Mare. Later poets, such

as David Gascoyne, Basil Bunting, and Veronica Forrest-Thomson, are virtually unknown in American high school and college textbooks but key figures in modernist poetics. Students or general readers who begin to explore beyond what they are initially introduced to will find the entries on the lives and poems of these writers instructive and richly rewarding.

The second approach was to be broad-ranging in selecting contemporary poets for inclusion. The hundreds of poets and academics we corresponded with on the writing of entries made frequent suggestions of favorite emerging 21st-century writers to consider. Many of them became entries, such as Ingrid de Kok from South Africa, Sheenagh Pugh from Wales, and Benjamin Zephaniah from a first-generation Jamaican immigrant family in Birmingham.

The third approach, and arguably the most controversial as well as the most expansive, was to broaden the companion to include the world community of poets writing in English, minus the Americans. Thus many of the foremost poets of Canada, the Caribbean, Ireland, Northern Ireland, Scotland, Wales, Africa, India, Australia, and New Zealand have entries. The anthologies listed in the selected bibliography provided as an appendix will function as a guide to further reading for this poetry. To call poets from all these countries, regions, traditions, and cultures "British" invites controversy, as it implies that a common tradition—the result of the British imperial enterprise—unites them and their work. In a postcolonial period this is demonstrably just not so. What does unite these writers, however, is their use of English, which places them in a linguistic community.

Since most high school and college courses separate American literature from "English literature," we have followed their lead and for pragmatic reasons excluded only American poetry from this companion. Even that, however, makes for some uneasy choices. The 20th century saw such increased movement of peoples that nationality has also become fluid. The famous cases of T. S. Eliot and W. H. Auden, an American moving to Britain and an Englishman moving to America, illustrate the arbitrariness of these decisions, as Eliot invariably appears in anthologies of both British and American poetry, while Auden is firmly ensconced in British anthologies alone. We have included poems by Ezra Pound, H. D., and even Sylvia Plath in this companion, on the basis that they were written while the poets were residing over a period of years in England. But at the same time we have included biographical entries on the English-born poets Denise Levertov and Thom Gunn, even though most of their poetic lives were lived in America.

In addition to entries on poets and individual poems, there are another 40 entries on topics that provide background to help in understanding the history of poetry in the last 11 decades. Some of these are about important movements or books (imagism, surrealism, *BLAST, Georgian Poetry 1911–12, New Lines, Wheels*), some are about events (Boer War and poetry, Great War and poetry, Spanish Civil War and poetry, Irish independence), some about critical theories (feminism, Freud and psychoanalytic criticism, postcolonialism, poststructuralism), some on national poetries (contemporary black British poetry, Welsh poetry, Indian poetry), and so on. Finally, this volume indicates cross-references by setting in small capitals any term within an entry that has its own entry in the companion. For example, in the entry on H. D. explaining the influence of Ezra Pound on her work, his name would be printed, on its first appearance in the entry, as EZRA POUND, indicating that there is a separate entry on him.

OVERVIEW OF BRITISH POETRY FROM 1900 TO THE PRESENT

Summing up the varieties, histories, and developments of British poetry over the last 100 years or so is bound to be reductive, so we direct students to the critical works in the selected bibliography, but we can give an outline of their shape, and of some of the issues and controversies, here.

As the 20th century began, Victoria was still queen of England, though just barely (she died in January 1901). The empire was at its height, though there were troubling tensions both abroad and at home. British troops were not doing well in the Boer War in far-off South Africa, and an arms race with imperial Germany was heating up. At home, there were agitations by women for the right to vote, by socialists and trades unionists for a fairer distribution of the nation's wealth, and by Irish nationalists for independence. Little of this was reflected in poetry. The poet laureate at the time, succeeding Tennyson, was the abysmal placeholder Alfred Austin, a conservative journalist who produced patriotic and nostalgic poems for the newspapers. Tennyson's poetry was still the standard, but reviewers such as Edward Thomas were calling for a new poetry that purged the old Victorian rhetoric. There was already a great variety of writing going on during the first decade of the new century. The most popular poet at that moment was undoubtedly Rudyard Kipling; the most promising, William Butler Yeats; the most revered but ignored, Thomas Hardy, a ghostly visitant from another century. Gerard Manley Hopkins was as yet unknown. The Americans—Ezra Pound, T. S. Eliot, Robert Frost—had not yet arrived. Any who literally set foot in Britain did so to pay homage to a superior culture, not to challenge it. No "school" of poets dominated. Some, like John Masefield, faithfully attended Yeats at the Monday night meetings in his flat in London. Some, like William Watson and Alfred Austin, were holdovers from the recent Victorian past who sought to sustain its virtues. There were classical scholars such as Robert Bridges and A. E. Housman who wrote an academic poetry imitating Greek and Latin rhythms. There were followers of the worst of Kipling, such as the apologist for imperialism Henry Newbolt, and others, like G. K. Chesterton (and Yeats and Masefield), who wanted to write of Kipling's "manly" world of contemporary realism and vigorous action. There were craftsmen of the beautiful, such as Walter de la Mare, who could reproduce the music of Tennyson and Swinburne. There were the unabashed entertainers, such as Alfred Noyes, who commanded a large audience by self-confidently writing romantic ballads in the style of Robert Louis Stevenson's novels. There was a generation of younger writers, such as Rupert Brooke and D. H. Lawrence, who would emerge as Georgians and profoundly affect the new directions poetry would take.

The key year of change was 1912. Edward Marsh issued an anthology called *Georgian Poetry 1911–1912* and inaugurated what he hoped would be a new age and a new style. Ezra Pound invented imagism in a tea shop with H. D. (Hilda Doolittle) and Richard Aldington. And Robert Frost traveled to England, where he would soon meet Edward Thomas and they together would become the most interesting and enduring of the new "Georgian" poets. In a conventional retelling of literary history, what happened next was the emergence of two different traditions, one "English" and one "foreign." The foreign tradition, influenced by French symbolism and American practice, was led by Pound, who moved during the second decade of the 20th century from imagism to vorticism to modernism. In Eliot's words, Pound first modernized himself and then modernized all of poetry. Modernism carried the day through the 1920s and 1930s and was always in some way evident in the practice of even the most conservative of poets, such as Philip Larkin in the second half of the century. The greatest modernists were "outsiders" when compared to a "native" tradition that was English and male—the Irish (Yeats, Joyce, Beckett), the Americans (H. D., Pound, Eliot), and women (Woolf, Edith Sitwell, Cunard). The native English tradition was the movement represented by the Georgians, a movement whose greatest practitioners were killed in the Great War, such as Wilfred Owen, Edward Thomas, and Isaac Rosenberg, or maimed psychologically, such as Ivor Gurney or, arguably, Robert Graves. This tradition saw itself in a line running from Wordsworth through Hardy. This is a too simplistic reading of the situation, as can be seen when trying to label a major writer (in poetry as well as fiction) such as D. H. Lawrence, who was claimed by both the Georgians and the modernists. But it was an enduring narrative that explained the preference for formal poetry among many later English poets and a certain prejudice against modernist experimentation in verse.

In the 1930s a neoRomantic revival, led by Dylan Thomas, seemed a rebellion against the coolness and rationality of Eliot. A group calling itself the New Apocalypse announced itself, taking Thomas as their guide. It included David Gascoyne, who introduced surrealism to the repertoire of English verse. But the decade also saw the emergence of an "Auden generation" that admired Eliot, including of course W. H. Auden, Stephen Spender, Cecil Day Lewis, and Louis MacNeice. Their poetry had more overtly political and psychological themes than had appeared before in British poetry, as did the poetry of the Scottish nationalist Hugh MacDiarmid. In January 1939 Auden left England for America, Yeats died, and later that year World War II began. War themes again dominated British poetry, both in the older generations and with new writers, such as Henry Reed, Charles Causley, Alun Lewis, and Keith Douglas, the latter two killed in the war. Eliot, of course, was still writing and from 1935 to 1942 produced the marvelous *Four Quartets*. Stevie Smith achieved status as both a popular and a serious poet, from her first book in 1937 to her death in 1971.

Three years after the death of Dylan Thomas, a new movement announced itself in the 1956 anthology *New Lines,* called, appropriately enough, the Movement. It included poems by Philip Larkin, Thom Gunn, Donald Davie, Elizabeth Jennings, and Kingsley Amis, among others. Not a coherent movement as such, it was modest in aim and practice and helped to establish the idea of a line of "Englishness" in British poetry that hearkened back to Hardy and rejected the grandiosity of Yeats. Despite just four slim volumes of poems, one for each decade from the 1940s to the 1970s, Larkin earned what seems to be an enduring reputation as the greatest poet of this period. His main challenger for that title also emerged in the 1950s but was most certainly not a Movement poet: Ted Hughes seemed to have his ear attuned to D. H. Lawrence and the Americans, in his preference for free verse. He married the American Sylvia Plath in 1956; they became (after Plath's death and the revelation of her work in *Ariel*) the most celebrated and controversial literary couple of the 1960s and 1970s, and Hughes became poet laureate, succeeding John Betjeman, a poet in the mode of Larkin, in 1985. Hughes's posthumously published *Birthday Letters* (1998), poems written for Plath in the four decades following her death, was a best seller that continued to demonstrate the influence of their lives and work.

In 1972 in his influential book *Thomas Hardy and British Poetry* Donald Davie rejected the narrowly provincial "little Englandism" with which the Movement had come to be associated in favor of a more internationalist poetry with larger ambitions. Seamus Heaney's poems about his Northern Ireland farm childhood, in *Death of the Naturalist* (1966), launched a career that inspired a new generation of Irish writers (most importantly, Paul Muldoon and Eavan Boland) and led to a Nobel Prize in literature in 1995. The West Indian–born Derek Walcott had already produced in 1962 "A Far Cry from Africa," which explored his conflicted roots as a black poet from a subjugated people writing within the British literary tradition. In 1995 he was awarded the Nobel Prize in literature for *Omeros,* which transferred Homerean epic to the Caribbean. The southern hemisphere began to be listened to as well, in the work of Fleur Adcock from New Zealand and Les Murray from Australia, poets who often worked in traditional forms but added a new perspective. Within the United Kingdom itself different voices also moved to the fore; the working-class sensibilities of Tony Harrison and the feminist concerns of Ursula Fanthorpe

stood alongside the difficult, history-imbued work of Geoffrey Hill and the dazzling and witty poems of Craig Raine and James Fenton.

Upon the death of Ted Hughes in 1998, one of Larkin's literary executors, Andrew Motion, became poet laureate. However, the most powerful influences on British poetry and poets continued to be the large societal changes, inaugurated in the 1950s and 1960s, that slowly but profoundly had affected British life—the end of empire and the rise of postcolonialism, the beginning of the welfare state, the women's movement, and the devolution of power, both within and without Britain. These changes led to a surge of interest in outsider voices of all kinds that had not been heard before: working-class voices, gay voices, women's voices, black British voices, immigrant voices, postcolonial voices both overseas and within Britain, Gaelic voices within the political union of the United Kingdom. The richness, variety, and diversity of these voices have led to an explosion in the amount of poetry in the contemporary world and of its kinds, from the traditional formal lyric to Jamaican dub poetry, language poetry, performance poetry, multicultural poetry, feminist poetry, ecological poetry, and experimental poetry of all types. It will take many decades into the new millenium for this richness to sort itself out into a coherent narrative. Our greatest wish for this companion, however, is not to construct a history of poetry in the last hundred or so years nor to define its future, but rather to inspire readers, through well-written and insightful entries on poets and poems, to go to those poems for the enlightenment and pleasure they give.

James Persoon
Robert R. Watson

"ACT OF UNION" SEAMUS HEANEY
(1975) "Act of Union" is one of the most controversial poems from SEAMUS HEANEY's 1975 volume, *North*—the volume that expresses most explicitly Heaney's awkwardness at being expected by the public to be "the Irish Troubles poet." The poem consists of two sonnets: This choice of form is ironic, as the poem concerns not love but rather the symbolic rape of a weaker nation by an imperial power. Ireland is personified as female, with a bosomlike "heaving province" and a vaginalike "gash"; this weaker nation is raped by the "battering ram" of the "imperially / Male" Britain.

The poem—as Josep M. Armengol has helpfully pointed out—draws on Ireland's centuries-old *aisling* tradition. These nationalist, anti-British poems of the past are emotive and propagandist: Ireland is like an innocent virgin who is raped by an invading Briton. Heaney's use of this indigenous, straightforward genre of poems antipathetic to British involvement in Ireland has caused some critics to accuse Heaney of perpetuating an uncomplicated Irish republican discourse. This is true only on a superficial level. Heaney's male-personified Britain has caused irrevocable damage to the feminized female. But critics sometimes pass over the primacy of the decision to construct Britain as the speaker. Britain's uncomplicated iambic lines speak of his historical conquest of Ireland without celebration or even satisfaction; the alliteration that describes British power—"The battering ram, the boom burst"—

suggests a distaste for past acts of aggression. Britain realizes that colonial aggression has caused only detriment to both him and his feminized colony. The raped Ireland is left "raw," "stretchmarked," and in "pain," but Britain must contend with historical guilt and with the postcolonial legacy of sectarian conflict and international disapproval.

The British rape of Ireland has led to a sort of monstrous birth—the partitioned, paramilitary-dominated, "half-independent" Ireland. The speaker, wracked by guilt and pessimism, does not seek some future victory, but rather an end to the monstrous continuity of the conflict that his invasion caused. However, the speaker can see "No treaty" that will "salve completely" the wounds caused to the irrevocably damaged Ireland. So Heaney's poem should not be read as a simplistic rehearsal of anti-British sentiment. The poem constructs a Britain that has suffered as well as caused suffering. The speaker, Britain, craves a solution to the ancient, intractable Irish problem but sees only further bloodshed: This bleak vision articulates acutely the melancholy of 1970s Ulster, when never-ending violence and political stasis had disillusioned nearly every citizen.

BIBLIOGRAPHY
Armengol, Josep M. "Gendering the Irish Land: Seamus Heaney's 'Act of Union' (1975)." *Atlantis* 23 (2001): 7–26.
Heaney, Seamus. *North.* London: Faber and Faber, 1975.
Murphy, Andrew. *Seamus Heaney.* Plymouth, Eng.: Northcote House, 1996.

O'Donoghue, Bernard. "Seamus Heaney: *North.*" *A Companion to Twentieth-Century Poetry,* edited by Neil Roberts, 524–535. Malden, Mass.: Blackwell Publishing, 2003.

Kevin DeOrnellas

ADCOCK, FLEUR (1934–) A highly acclaimed writer, editor, and translator of poetry, Fleur Adcock has been praised for her "laconic style" ("Poem Ended by a Death"), her formally restrained voice, and a brilliant handling of unobtrusive rhyme. Her carefully crafted poems appear conversational and artless. Although her early work has been associated with THE MOVEMENT and the Group, her poetry is unique in its unsentimental and often ironical treatment of topics as diverse as romantic love, sexuality, personal and family relationships, domestic life and motherhood, death, loss, nature, women's and gender issues, national identity, and contemporary politics. Often openly autobiographical, her poems use major events and minor incidents as starting points from which to explore psychological processes or arrive at unvarnished insights into the human condition. Moreover, recollections of her native New Zealand or her numerous travels are recurrent themes in Adcock's work.

Born Karen Fleur Adcock in Auckland, New Zealand, on February 10, 1934, Fleur Adcock spent most of her childhood (1939–47) in England, where her parents worked during World War II. Back in New Zealand, Adcock attended Wellington Girls' College and studied classics at Victoria University at Wellington, where she obtained an M.A. in 1956. She married the poet Alistair Campbell in 1952 and gave birth to her two sons, Gregory and Andrew, in 1952 and 1957. She and Campbell were divorced in 1958.

Having worked for four years as assistant lecturer in classics at the University of Otago in Dunedin, Adcock returned to Wellington in 1962 to work as librarian in the Alexander Turnbull Library. After the failure of her brief marriage to the writer Barry Crump (1962–63), she decided to emigrate to England, taking her five-year-old son, Andrew, with her, while Gregory remained with his father. In England Adcock worked as librarian in the Foreign and Commonwealth Office in London and held various writing fellowships. She has been a freelance writer, editor, and translator of poetry since 1979. Her poetry has received numerous awards, including the New Zealand Book Award in 1984 and the Arts Council Writers' Award in 1988. She was honored with an Order of the British Empire (OBE) in 1996.

Adcock's debut collections *The Eye of the Hurricane* (1964) and *Tigers* (1967), written on the verge of departure, include detached invocations of an interrupted childhood in New Zealand as well as ruminations about broken relationships. Displaying an amused disillusionment with romantic love, the poet's candid and often chilly treatment of emotional issues is exemplified by "Advice to a Discarded Lover" (1967), in which the speaker describes her "dead affair" in terms of a decaying bird, refusing pity to her discarded lover as long as he is "eaten up by self-pity / Crawling with unlovable pathos." Adcock's unsentimental love poems are matched by her equally unsentimental though tender elegies, which are purged of clichéd responses, decidedly nonescapist, and bravely accepting of death: "Gone is gone forever" ("Flight, with Mountains").

While some of the poems in her third collection, *High Tide in the Garden* (1971), still tackle her voluntary exile ("On a Son Returned to New Zealand"), others focus on peaceful domestic scenes ("Saturday"), create science fiction settings with allegorical overtones ("Gas"), or explore the bizarre and often uncanny dream world of the subconscious ("Grandma," "Mornings After"). The much anthologized "Against Coupling" provides a witty argument in favor of masturbation and has been read in feminist terms.

Adcock's fourth collection, *The Scenic Route* (1974), contains a number of travel poems, evoking scenes from Adcock's journeys to places such as Nepal and Northern Ireland. Many of these poems explore the poet's ambivalent sense of national identity, for instance, "Please Identify Yourself" about her conflicting emotions during a visit to Belfast. Characterized by a vividness that stimulates the reader's sense perceptions, these poems bring to life atmosphere and mood in a few brushstrokes, while also addressing political and social contexts. Adcock's fifth collection, *The Inner Harbour* (1979), is subdivided into four sections, "Beginnings," "Endings," "The Thing Itself," and "To and Fro," the latter focusing on the emotional and personal consequences of Adcock's voluntary exile from her native country and longtime separation from her family. This collection also shows a heightened concern with women's lives and issues, as exemplified by "THE SOHO HOSPITAL FOR WOMEN" and "The Ex-Queen Among the Astronomers." Adcock's next collection, *Below Loughrigg* (1979), written during a writing fellowship in the Lake District, is concerned with place and tradition, exploring the poet's relationship to the literary heritage of the Lake poets.

Adcock's publication of her *Selected Poems* (1983) was followed by the *The Incident Book* (1986), which recalls scenes from Adcock's life as a foreign schoolgirl and outsider in Britain during World War II, and *Meeting the Comet* (1989). While the poet's love of nature has always been a central topic, Adcock's more recent work highlights ecological concerns, commenting on the willful destruction of our environment in poems such as "The Greenhouse Effect," "Wildlife," or "The Last Moa," all published in *Time Zones* (1991). Anxiety about ecological destruction is among the most pressing themes in this collection, while other topics include the death of the poet's father or contemporary politics, such as the Ceauçescu regime in Romania. Adcock's subsequent collection, *Looking Back* (1997), testifies to her increasing interest in family genealogy. While poems about her Irish ancestors' emigration to New Zealand feature in earlier collections, *Looking Back* provides a focused and chronological retelling of their stories.

Adcock has also gained a reputation as a translator of medieval Latin poetry (*The Virgin and the Nightingale: Medieval Latin Poems,* 1983; *Hugh Primas and the Archpoet,* 1994) and contemporary Romanian poetry (*Orient Express—Poems by Grete Tartler,* 1989; *Letters from Darkness—Poems by Daniela Crasnaru,* 1992). She has been editor of *The Oxford Book of Contemporary New Zealand Poetry* (1981) and *The Faber Book of 20th-Century Women's Poetry* (1987). *Poems 1960–2000,* published in 2002, was warmly received. Looking back on a lifetime of poetic creation, this collection concludes with a sequence titled *Kensington Gardens,* in which Adcock seems to announce her farewell to poetry, ending with the words "What wanted to be said is said."

BIBLIOGRAPHY

Adcock, Fleur. *Poems 1960–2000.* Newcastle upon Tyne, Eng.: Bloodaxe, 2000.

Gregson, Ian. *Contemporary Poetry and Postmodernism: Dialogue and Estrangement.* Basingstoke, Eng.: Macmillan, 1996.

Stannard, Julian. *Fleur Adcock in Context: From Movement to Martians.* New York: Edwin Mellen, 1997.

Michaela Schrage-Früh

"ADLESTROP" EDWARD THOMAS **(1915)** "Adlestrop" is not only EDWARD THOMAS's most famous and anthologized poem, but also one of the best loved poems of English literature. The title refers to the name of a small village in the county of Gloucestershire, and the speaker describes an unexpected stop at its station by the express train on which he is a passenger. Its simple but evocative depiction of a country idyll has helped establish Thomas's reputation as the quintessential English poet.

Stylistically the poem exhibits his concern with capturing the essence and vitality of real speech—an approach he shared and developed with his close friend, the American poet Robert Frost, who described such verse as having the "accent of sense." For the most part, the rhythm and meter of "Adlestrop" appear to be governed by the speaker's train of thought, rather than the traditional metrical foot. The lineation, plain diction, frequently paused sentences, and implied presence of another speaker—suggested especially by the conversational opening—are all means by which Thomas subtly gives the impression of an actual thinking and talking subject.

But the poem also features an unusual, energetic tension between such prosaic language and balladic archaisms, such as "no whit less still and lonely fair." In this way Thomas's modernity remains in touch with an English folk past. He described the poem in his notes as representing "an extraordinary silence between two periods of travel," and there is a distinctly visionary quality to it. The speaker's attention toward the picturesque, but unexceptional, English scenery is diverted by the solitary singing blackbird, who opens out into the expanse of "all the birds / Of Oxfordshire and Gloucestershire."

Thomas wrote the poem in January 1915, when he was deliberating over whether or not to fight for his country in the early stages of the Great War. This combination of folk idyll with the epiphanic moment is highly characteristic of the poet's preenlistment verse, in which he reflects on England and patriotism as concepts deserving the ultimate sacrifice.

BIBLIOGRAPHY
Harvey, Anne. *Adlestrop: An Anthology.* Phoenix Mill, Eng.: Sutton, 1999.
Kirkham, Michael. *The Imagination of Edward Thomas.* Cambridge: Cambridge University Press, 1986.
Spencer, Matthew, ed. *Elected Friends: Robert Frost and Edward Thomas to One Another.* New York: Handsel, 2003.

Tom Rogers

THE ADOPTION PAPERS JACKIE KAY (1991)

JACKIE KAY first gained real attention with *The Adoption Papers,* a series of poems based on her own experience of interracial adoption. The individual poems, published as a collection in 1991, were written between 1980 and 1990, and the whole piece was performed on BBC Radio 3 in 1990 as part of the BBC's *Drama Now* series. Her first poetry collection, *The Adoption Papers* won Kay a Scottish Arts Council Book Award, a Saltire Award, and a Forward Prize.

The inclusion of the poem in a radio drama series points to Kay's early background as a playwright, and *The Adoption Papers* is strikingly dramatic in form. Told from three narrative perspectives—daughter, adoptive mother, and birth mother—it identifies each voice in the text by a different typeface. The voices alternate unevenly as they weave in and out of the poem, and how they interact is often reflective of each narrator's role. In the opening three-stanza sequence, the adoptive mother speaks directly and reminiscently: "I always wanted to give birth." Her 12-line stanza recalls the pressure to "do that incredible natural thing / that women do" and her sense of failure at being unable to conceive. The third six-line stanza charts the brief tone of the birth mother imagining her unknown daughter: "She is twenty-six today / my hair is grey." Her words, like the connection between her and her daughter, are sparse and dislocated. Uniting these two stanzas is the

voice of the black daughter, caught between an adoptive mother she loves and a birth mother she longs to know, both of whom are white. Each of these opening stanzas begins with *I,* reflecting the clamoring voices of this poem striving to make their experiences known.

The poem deals with identity, particularly racial and genetic identity. The question of the "real" recurs, and the daughter puzzles the conundrum: "Ma mammy says she's no really ma mammy." The Glaswegian dialect raises questions about what it means to be "really" Scottish, and the casual racism of a teacher who speaks of "you people" and "your blood" prompts the anxious question *What is in my blood?* Biological imagery—"the well, the womb, the fucking seed"—is counteracted by the persistence of the papers of the title. The adoptive mother knows "I'm not a mother / until I've signed that piece of paper," and it seems that it is the document, after all, that makes her the "real mammy." Finally, a third understanding of identity is offered by the lines "the mother who stole my milk teeth / ate the digestive left for Santa." Here it is actions, rather than biology or papers, that justify the title of *mother.* As the poem develops, it is this recurrence of images and themes and the repetition of words, and occasionally of whole lines, that unites the frequently discordant voices of the text. A simple line such as "The frigid earth" can function as a metaphor for barrenness, stifled maternal instinct, and emotional trauma. In these aspects, the dramatic text of *The Adoption Papers* demonstrates its indisputable poetry.

BIBLIOGRAPHY
Jackie Kay. *The Adoption Papers.* Tarset, Eng.: Bloodaxe, 1991.

Fiona Tolan

"AGAINST DEATH" PETER REDGROVE (1959)

"Against Death" is one of PETER REDGROVE's early poems, written in 1959. In it, he struggles with man's place in the natural world, a world that science has exposed as impersonal, relentless, and lacking in any knowable meaning. As a student, Redgrove read natural sciences at Cambridge while writing poetry. The attempt to penetrate the factual surface of science in search of deeper meaning would continue to preoccupy his writing. "Against Death" explores the human knowledge of inevitable death and the need to keep this sensibility at arm's length.

The poem is in two stanzas. The description in the poem's first stanza of a couple at home frames the human need to maintain a certain distance from the realities of life and death. The second stanza shows us death up close and strives to take in the power of nature's forward press. In contrast to the 24-line first stanza of the poem, dealing with life, this curt final stanza consists of only eight lines.

Redgrove uses the impersonal terms of science where more sentimental language would be expected, and the effect is jarring. The scene he presents in the first stanza, of a couple bedding, bathing, raising children, is not cozy at all. Instead, bed is a "productive place" to "breed / Many human beings." Children are "shrill white bodies" to be taken care of until they are "let out into the world a homing of adults." The birds that live beyond the ceiling of the house mirror the human family within. They also personify life, the uncontrollable force so uncomfortable to humans. The inhabitants of the house are glad to have the birds close by, to hear their scratching above the ceiling and watch them through the windows. But they "keep no cats and dislike wet-mouthed dogs," suggesting that closer contact with the animal world is distasteful and to be avoided. But nature intrudes uninvited when a spider falls into the bath, interrupting the humans when they are most vulnerable. Associated with death, the spider's cold hard body is a contrast to the "hot bodies" of the multiplying sparrows. Insects are a recurring symbol in Redgrove's work. Congruently with the title of the poem, the spider is quickly washed down the drain and removed from consciousness.

The second stanza does not try to deny that death might occur. But it carefully says "if"—"If there should ever be a corpse in the house." Still holding away the certainty of death, the poet describes a dead body and the sound of the sparrows still scratching above the ceiling. Shunning emotion, he omits the funeral and describes the body's disposal as if it were that of a dead or unwanted animal. An impersonal "firm'd hurry it outdoors and burn it quick—." The final three lines address human emotion, acknowledging the human hope of being remembered after death—the least form of immortality. Here the poet provides the comfort sci-

ence gives. We must expect to be forgotten, he says. The demands of life "As the hot bodies of the sparrows increase each summer" will certainly overwhelm the attention of the living.

Mary Van Oeveren

"AH, ARE YOU DIGGING ON MY GRAVE?" THOMAS HARDY (1913)

First published in the *Saturday Review* on September 27, 1913, and included in THOMAS HARDY's 1914 volume of poetry *Satires of Circumstances,* this poem presents a dialogue between a deceased woman in her grave and another speaker who is not identified until the fourth of the poem's six stanzas, the one who is above digging on the woman's grave. In the opening two lines of the first three stanzas, the woman guesses the identity of the digger, only to be told by the speaker in the last four lines that her guess is wrong. The woman first guesses the digger must be her lover "planting rue" but is told by the digger that her lover believed he no longer had to be "true" to the woman now that she is dead and married a woman of wealth. Progressively diminishing her expectations, the woman next guesses the digger must be her "nearest dearest kin" and then finally her "enemy" but learns neither her kin nor her enemy believes there is any use to visit or cares enough to visit the grave.

Giving up on her guessing, the woman in the first two lines of the fourth stanza now asks, "Who is digging on my grave?" and in the remaining lines of the stanza the digger identifies himself as her "little dog." Unlike the question and answer structure of the first four stanzas, each of the final two stanzas of the poem is devoted to a single speaker. In the fifth stanza, the woman expresses her gratitude that her little dog proves "one true heart" and remains faithful to her and praises "[a] dog's fidelity" as having no equal "among human kind." The dog's reply in the final stanza undercuts the woman's brave attempt to make the most of what had been a diminishing progression of expectations about the identity of the digger: The dog explains he dug on the woman's grave merely to bury a bone and had "quite forgot / It was your resting place."

The humor of this poem relieves its progressive disillusionment and grim ironies of infidelity. Hardy draws on the ballad conventions of the voice from the grave and the pattern of questions and answers. J. O. Bailey suggests A. E. HOUSMAN's 1898 poem "Is My Team Ploughing?" as a source for Hardy's poem. Housman uses the same ballad conventions in his poem, in which a dead man asks a friend who has survived him a series of questions that leads to the revelation that the friend has married the dead man's sweetheart.

Hardy's own many cats and dogs may have helped inspire this poem. Hardy's most famous pet, the wire-haired terrier Wessex, was born a month before Hardy published "Ah, Are You Digging on My Grave?" and when Wessex died in 1926 he earned the epitaph of "Faithful, Unflinching" on his gravestone.

BIBLIOGRAPHY

Bailey, J. O. *The Poetry of Thomas Hardy: A Handbook and Commentary.* Chapel Hill: University of North Carolina Press, 1970.

Millgate, Michael. *Thomas Hardy: A Biography.* New York: Random House, 1982.

Robert R. Watson

ALDINGTON, RICHARD (1892–1962)

Born Edward Godfree Aldington in Portsmouth, England, Richard Aldington is best known as a key figure in the imagist movement although he is also recognized for his work as biographer, editor, translator, essayist, and fiction writer whose career spanned five decades.

Son of a middle-class lawyer, Aldington attended University College, but a combination of dissatisfaction with formal education (which he felt was stultifying) and his father's financial struggles caused him to quit after his first year. In 1911 he worked in London first as a clerk then as an assistant to a newspaper sportswriter before embarking on a literary career that led him in 1912 to form the imagists with EZRA POUND, F. S. Flint, and (H. D.) (HILDA DOOLITTLE). Aldington soon gained a measure of poetic fame owing to the appearance of three of his works in the influential *Poetry* magazine, to the publication of his volume *Images (1910–1915)*, and to other works in the major imagist anthologies: Pound's 1914 *Des Imagistes* and Amy Lowell's three editions of *Some Imagist Poets* (1915, 1916, and 1917). He also took on an increasingly larger role in IMAGISM; as editor of the *Egoist* he included an explanation of the term in

the June 1914 issue, and he devoted the May 1, 1915, issue to imagist poems. He also penned the preface to the 1915 imagist anthology, which contained the six points of imagism: language of common speech and exact word, creation of new rhythms, freedom of subject matter, presentation of an image, production of hard and clear poetry, and concentration as the essence of poetry. During this period Aldington's poems tended to adhere to these principles, and his main theme was the search for beauty in a world lacking it; the source of that beauty, he felt, was classical Greece and Rome, as well as Japan. Soon after, however, he moved away from tightly compressed imagistic poems, taking as models such diverse writers as Walt Whitman, Dante, Andrew Marvell, and T. S. ELIOT. Thematically the search for beauty was replaced by a focus on nature and on love, both romantic and sexual.

While his literary career soared, his personal life did likewise. Shortly after he met H. D. the two became romantically involved, taking a seven-month trip to Italy and marrying in 1913. Their first and only child was stillborn in 1915, and the marriage suffered as a result. In early 1919 Aldington and H. D. separated, finally divorcing in 1938.

As did many men of his generation, Aldington enlisted in the British army. Beginning in 1916, he saw active combat, advancing in rank from private to captain. In the process, however, he suffered "shell shock." His disgust with the war is evident in the poems in *Images of War* (1919), and his sense of postwar England as sterile manifests itself in his fiction, most tellingly in the auto-biographical novel *Death of a Hero* (1929).

This dissatisfaction led him first to retreat from London to a remote Berkshire village in 1919 and then to travel in France and Italy between 1928 and 1935. In 1935 his travels took him to the Caribbean and the United States. He alternated living in Connecticut, Hollywood (where he freelanced as a writer of film scripts), and Florida with visits to France. Three days after his divorce was finalized, he married Netta McCullough; the couple's daughter was born in France shortly after the wedding.

Regardless of where he was living, Aldington continued to produce prodigiously, with 11 volumes of poetry (as well as numerous collections), more than a dozen prose pieces, 17 translations—mostly of French and ancient Greek works—and a number of biographies, the most famous of which are *D. H. Lawrence: Portrait of a Genius, But . . .* (1950) and *Lawrence L'Imposteur: T. E. Lawrence, the Legend and the Man* (1954). This latter caused a serious decline in Aldington's popularity; because it was critical of the generally venerated Lawrence, publishers stopped printing Aldington's works and bookstores stopped selling them. Even after his death in 1962, efforts to restore his reputation to its previous stature have generally failed.

See also "ON THE MARCH."

BIBLIOGRAPHY

Aldington, Richard. *The Complete Poems of Richard Aldington.* London: Allan Wingate, 1948.

Doyle, Charles. *Richard Aldington: A Biography.* Carbondale: Southern Illinois University Press, 1989.

———, ed. *Richard Aldington: Reappraisals.* Victoria, Canada: University of Victoria Press, 1990.

Kershaw, Alister. *Richard Aldington: An Intimate Portrait.* Carbondale: Southern Illinois University Press, 1965.

Zilboorg, Caroline, ed. *Richard Aldington and H. D.: Their Lives in Letters, 1918–61.* Manchester: Manchester University Press, 2003.

Richard Iadonisi

"ALL DAY IT HAS RAINED" ALUN LEWIS (1941)   The poem that called ALUN LEWIS to the British public's attention and remains his best-known work, the subdued "All Day It Has Rained" was first published in the magazine *Horizon* and later included in his collection *Raiders' Dawn.* Ian Hamilton called it "one of the first really articulate 'war poems.'" It was written while the poet was stationed with the Corps of Engineers in Wales. "All Day" does not recount the horrors of war or bewail the shattered ideals of a generation, as does the work of the earlier generation of war poets. As did other poets of the Second World War, Lewis remained relatively tight-lipped, an indication of the deep pessimism and moral exhaustion felt by a world returned to cataclysm barely two decades after the war that failed to end all wars.

"All Day It Has Rained" captures the monotony of a long, muddy Sunday as a group of bored and moody soldiers wait quietly in their tents for the rain to end. The speaker notes, "From the first grey wakening we have found / No refuge from the skirmishing fine rain." The description of the wet landscape might seem almost pastoral ("All day the rain has glided, wave and mist and dream / Drenching the gorse and heather") were it not for the soggy canvas and sagging ropes of the tents. The poem dwells on the soldiers' petty activities—mending "dirty" socks, smoking, reading the paper—evoking the unremitting emptiness of the day. In a letter home the speaker reports that he saw a fox, a detail that suggests the aimlessness of the wait: Any minor distraction rises to the level of an event in an otherwise eventless present.

The soldiers exchange remarks about girls and indulge in some half-meant jingoistic talk of dropping bombs. But even their unspoken thoughts of comrades who have died and of the political leaders whipping up enthusiasm for the war have become as indifferent to them "as [thoughts] of ourselves or those whom we / for years have loved." Alienated from self and from loved ones in a world of twilight and rain, the soldiers find their memories so distant as to be unreal, and plans for the future unimaginable. Aware of his own atrophied emotions, the speaker realizes he can no longer cast his mind back into the world of love and normalcy. The only effort of memory he can muster to provide relief from the endless enormity of the present moment is to remember a long walk taken the day before, a trip past romping children and a friendly dog to a rocky outcropping where the poet Edward Thomas "brooded long / On death and beauty—till a bullet stopped his song." The walk, though life-affirming in its early course, ends (as all else does) with a return to thoughts of death, silencing the speaker's song as well. The tedious rain and the thought of death—the inconsiderable and the inconceivable—combine to wipe out the zone of real life in between.

BIBLIOGRAPHY

Fussell, Paul. *The Great War and Modern Memory.* New York: Oxford University Press, 1975.

Lewis, Alun. *Selected Poetry and Prose.* Edited by Ian Hamilton. London: George Allen & Unwin, 1966.

Pikoulis, John. *Alun Lewis: A Life.* Bridgend, Eng.: Poetry Wales Press, 1984.

Anne Kellenberger

ALVAREZ, A. (1929–)

As poetry critic for the London *Observer* from 1956 to 1966, A. Alvarez was instrumental in shaping public opinion of poetic value in postwar England, introducing and promoting such key British poets as TED HUGHES and THOM GUNN; American poets including Robert Lowell, John Berryman, and SYLVIA PLATH; and the European poets Zbigniew Herbert and Miroslav Holub. His Penguin anthology *The New Poetry* (1962, rev. 1966) is considered a major statement on postwar British poetry and a response to Robert Conquest's NEW LINES and THE MOVEMENT. In his introduction Alvarez describes mainstream British poetry, represented by PHILIP LARKIN, as beset by the "Gentility Principle," provincial, complacent, inhibited, timid, and inauthentic. In contrast, Alvarez champions the "Extremist School," poetry that attempts to capture extreme states of psychic disintegration in an authentic voice particularly through violent imagery. Alvarez is particularly identified with Sylvia Plath, of whom he was a close friend before her suicide in 1962. *The Savage God* (1971), which combines fiction, memoir, and literary analysis in a study of artists' suicide, opens with a portrayal of Plath and ends with an account of his own attempted suicide in 1961.

Born into a London Jewish family, Alfred Alvarez enjoyed an upper-middle-class childhood. At Oxford he helped found the Critical Society, which attempted to reinvigorate the poetry there through the influence of I. A. Richards, WILLIAM EMPSON, and the NEW CRITICISM. After graduating from Oxford, Alvarez taught as a visiting fellow at Princeton, where he became a protégé of R. P. Blackmur. He also spent three years, from 1955 to 1958, in New Mexico with a D. H. LAWRENCE Fellowship. There he met and married Ursula Barr, Lawrence's granddaughter, whom he divorced in 1961. After stepping down as poetry critic for the *Observer,* Alvarez turned to his own writing, which has included poetry, three novels, a memoir, and several works of nonfiction reflecting his personal interests and experience, including reflections on divorce, the oil industry, rock climbing, night, and professional poker.

Alvarez published his own poetry as early as 1952 and won the Vachel Lindsay Prize for Poetry from *Poetry* in 1961 but is generally thought of as a minor British poet. True to his call for "extremist" poetry, his work often concerns themes of love, alienation, separation, and death, conveyed through juxtapositions of violent and natural images. "Waking," one of a series of poems about his first marriage, for example, presents an image of birds singing, "shaking their song out, wrenching and spilling it / Out of the roots of the heart painfully singing," set against the "dawn over our bed / Where you lie with your body away, your face to the wall." In "A Cemetery in New Mexico (To Alfred Alvarez, died 1957)," which has been called one of the great 20th-century English elegies and possibly Alvarez's best poem, the opening lines also mark the tension between life and death: "Softly the dead stir, call, through the afternoon. / The soil lies too light upon them." The new poems in Alvarez's *New and Selected Poems* (2002) maintain the focus on love but turn more to the positive, sensual possibilities of the physical.

BIBLIOGRAPHY

Alvarez, A. *Beyond All This Fiddle: Essays 1955–1967.* New York: Random, 1968.

———. *New and Selected Poems.* London: Waywiser Press, 2002.

Holden, Anthony, and Frank Kermode, eds. *The Mind Has Mountains: a.alvarez@lxx.* Cambridge: Los Poetry Press, 1999.

Eric Leuschner

AMIS, KINGSLEY (1922–1995)

Kingsley William Amis was born on April 16, 1922, in Clapham, south London. He was educated at the City of London School as a scholarship boy before going up to St John's College, Oxford, where he developed a close friendship with the poet PHILIP LARKIN. During the Second World War, Amis served in the British army Royal Corps of Signals, an experience that he disliked intensely. From 1949 to 1963, Amis occupied various posts as lecturer in English studies at Swansea University College, Princeton University in New Jersey, and Peterhouse at Cambridge University. He retired from teaching in 1963 to become a full-time writer.

Amis's literary reputation was established early in his career, with the publication of his first novel, *Lucky Jim,* in 1954. Set at a provincial redbrick university in postwar England and featuring the quintessentially hapless and beleaguered protagonist Jim Dixon, *Lucky Jim* articulates with skill and precision many of the anxieties and frustrations that plagued the postwar generation of "angry young men." Amis's name quickly became synonymous with satirical middle-class social comedy, a genre at which he became proficient in such early novels as *That Uncertain Feeling* (1955), *I Like It Here* (1958), *Take a Girl Like You* (1960), and *One Fat Englishman* (1963).

Although he is far more renowned for his novels, Amis also produced a number of very lucid and expertly crafted collections of verse throughout his lengthy and multifaceted career. In *Bright November* (1947) and *A Frame of Mind* (1953)—which he wrote early in his career, before even *Lucky Jim*—and the very unromantically entitled *A Case of Samples* (1956) can be found many of the characteristics and preoccupations of the so-called Movement in British poetry of the 1950s. Using traditional forms and poetic devices and eschewing the complexity and obfuscation of the modernists, Amis's verse is (not unlike the hero—or, indeed, the antihero—of *Lucky Jim*) antibourgeois, antipretensious, antiromantic, and antisentimental. In "Wrong Words," for example, the poet rails against the propensity of "poets in a silver age" to "drench" their work with the verbal "confectionery" of elaborate "conceits" and "frantic . . . superlatives." In "A DREAM OF FAIR WOMEN" he satirizes vainglorious poets who court public attention and the posturing dilettantes who fall for it. In "Against Romanticism," he lambastes the "ingrown taste for anarchy" and "garish . . . complexities" of 20th-century neoromantic poets. In "The English Novel, 1740–1820," he reduces almost a century of British fiction to four terse lines, suggesting its blandness and unidimensionality. Later collections of poetry included *The Evans Country* (1962) and *A Look Round the Estate* (1966). In 1979 Amis gathered much of his verse in one volume, *Collected Poems 1944–1979.*

In the later phases of his career, Amis experimented with a diversity of genres of fiction, producing a spy novel (*The Anti-Death League* in 1966), a James Bond novel (*Colonel Sun* in 1968, written under the pen name *Robert Markham*), a thriller (*The Green Man* in 1969), a detective novel (*The Riverside Villas Murder* in 1973), a fantasy (*Russian Hide-and-Seek* in 1980), and a

book of short stories (*Mr Barrett's Secret* in 1993). He also continued to produce the savagely funny satirical comedies for which he was famous—*Ending Up* (1974), *Jake's Thing* (1978), *Stanley and the Women* (1984), *Difficulties with Girls* (1988). *The Old Devils* won the Booker Prize in 1986. His nonfiction works include *New Maps of Hell* (1961), *What Became of Jane Austen?* (1970), *On Drink* (1972), and his *Memoirs* (1990).

Amis was knighted in 1990. He died shortly after the publication of *The Biographer's Moustache* in 1995.

BIBLIOGRAPHY
Amis, Kingsley. *Collected Poems 1944–1979.* London: Hutchinson, 1979.
———. *Memoirs.* London: Hutchinson, 1990.
Jacobs, Eric. *Kingsley Amis: A Biography.* London: Hodder and Stoughton, 1995.

Robert G. May

"AMONG SCHOOL CHILDREN" WILLIAM BUTLER YEATS (1927)

"Among School Children" was inspired by a visit W. B. YEATS made in 1926 to St. Otteran's School, in county Waterford, Ireland. As a senate member, he served on a committee that was reviewing and evaluating the new curriculum established in a number of schools. As the poem begins, Yeats finds himself in the classroom in the company of a "kind old nun" and the staring eyes of the children. This poem is from the poet's last stage, evidenced by his reference to himself as a "smiling, sixty-year-old public man." Yeats adopts this mask to cover his perception of himself as an aging and bitter unfulfilled poet. In the schoolroom that day, he is acutely aware of the stark reality of the contrast between his advancing decrepitude and the youthful faces of the children. Finally, though, the poem offers a humanistic affirmation of life.

Noticing, at the end of the first stanza, the children staring at him, the poet immediately, and over the next three stanzas, thinks of Maud Gonne, the actress and Irish nationalist whom Yeats had loved for many years but failed to persuade to marry him. In Yeats's private mythology, Maud Gonne is associated with Helen of Troy. In Greek mythology, Helen is the offspring of Leda and Zeus, who assumed the form of a swan in order to rape Leda. Yeats imagines or recalls listening to a young Maud Gonne, she of "Ledaean body," tell him about some incident that turned her "childish day to tragedy" and believing they achieved a perfect platonic relationship through their "youthful sympathy." Looking at the children before him, Yeats wonders whether Maud Gonne ever "stood so," because despite considering Gonne as semidivine rather than an ordinary child, "even daughters of the swan can share / Something of every paddler's heritage." In a vision, the poet sees Maud Gonne "as a living child" in one of the schoolchildren standing before him. This vision gives way to an image of how Maud Gonne is now: "Hollow of cheek as though it drank the wind / And took a mess of shadows for its meat." Finding it too painful to think of his own decline—"I though never of Ledaean kind / Had pretty plumage once"—the poet's thoughts return to his presence in the classroom and his self-consciously maintained public persona, "a comfortable kind of old scarecrow" who will "smile on all that smile."

The personal visions in the first half of the poem give way to general and universal reflections in the second half. In the fifth stanza, Yeats wonders whether any mother still would think her newborn son worth the pain of her labor or the anxiety of her worries about his future if she could see him as he will look when he is 60. The poet next considers the philosophies of Plato, Aristotle, and Pythagoras and dismisses them, for all their ideas about reality, as useless: "Old clothes upon old sticks to scare a bird." Finally, in the seventh stanza, the poet concludes that, as the idealized images mothers have of their children will, the religious "images" nuns worship will "break hearts"; that the "Presences" the lover's "passion," the nun's "piety," and the mother's "affection" know will prove to be "self-born mockers of man's enterprise."

After acknowledging all these disappointments and failures, Yeats offers in the final stanza of the poem an affirmation of life as organic process, symbolized in the two central images of the chestnut tree and the dance. To answer the first of the two rhetorical questions that close the poem, the chestnut tree is not any one of its separate parts—neither leaf, blossom, nor bole—but rather is the entire organic whole. Similarly the dancer is one with the dance. The part should not be taken as the whole, even though each isolated part is integral to the whole. "Labour," the work of the moment, "is blossoming or dancing where / The body is not bruised to pleasure soul." Body and soul, youth and age, image and presence, public mask and private self, content and form, all, in the poet's final imaginative vision, are recognized as indissolubly integrated. The concluding stanza, which Yeats added to his original draft of the poem, is hopeful because it suggests that perhaps unity of being is obtainable, a point summarized by Hugh Underhill: "The ecstatic surge of [the poem's] final rhetorical questions sweeps us into a blossoming or dancing which enacts an assimilation of the human with the perfect, of the subjective with the objective, a 'unity of being' like that of the tree and its parts, or the dancer and the dance: citizenship fused with inner vision, human limitation fused with the enduring abstract perfection, world fused with otherworld."

BIBLIOGRAPHY

Underhill, Hugh. *The Problem of Consciousness in Modern Poetry*. Cambridge: Cambridge University Press, 1992.

Betsy Watson

"ANCESTOR" THOMAS KINSELLA (1972)   Belonging to a group of poems that were inspired by THOMAS KINSELLA's grandmother, this short work about the momentous meeting between an assumedly younger lyrical I and an older relative is dominated by a rather claustrophobic sense of doom. The frequent references to death and mortality as well as the extended bird metaphors create a sense of mythological destiny and mysterious kinship between the two figures tied together by blood relationship. The poem first appeared in *Notes from the Land of the Dead* (1972), which takes its title from a phrase by C. G. Jung, whose archetypal psychology influenced many poems in this collection. Later the volume appeared as *New Poems* (1973).

The opening of the poem introduces the ancestor as an older woman and a person whom the lyrical I seems to respect if not fear. The opening statement, "I was going up to say something, / and stopped," expresses both the longing to establish contact and the hesitation to do so. The only excuse the text offers for such trepidation is the description of the woman's profile as "old, and dark like a hunting bird's." The reference to a predatory animal, which as a guide to souls also functions as a symbol for the transition from life to death, already introduces the theme of death into the poem.

The second stanza expands on the bird metaphor by describing the woman as "perched" on her stool, "gripping the side of the barrier." The ominous bird / woman is presented as highly introvert, removed from the reality around her, only concerned with herself. The final line of the stanza reinforces the enigmatic nature of the ancestor, further contributing to the sense of disorientation and trepidation experienced by the lyrical I.

The disruption of the quiet moment, which marks the fourth stanza, finally draws the speaker to the attention of the ancestor, leading to a few defensive gestures of hiding the private sphere of the old woman. The final line yet again introduces a somewhat threatening moment, when the dark figure of the ancestor blocks out the light in the small passageway, again alluding to her metaphorical description as a bird of (bad) omen. The key to her desk at the same time stands for the mythic key to the other world, another reference to the land of the dead.

The last stanza finally identifies the person as an ancestor, an older relative. It also introduces an even more gloomy tone into the poem: The references to "sigh," "black heart," and "back room" all imply the impending death of the person and at the same time remind the lyrical I of his or her own mortality. The immediate surroundings all bear direct or indirect references to death and dying, in particular the "red hangings" and the word *scullery,* which evokes the image of a skull. The visit with the dying ancestor thus turns into a confrontation with death itself.

BIBLIOGRAPHY

Badin, Donatella Abbate. *Thomas Kinsella.* New York: Twayne, 1996.

John, Brian. *Reading the Ground: The Poetry of Thomas Kinsella.* Washington, D.C.: Catholic University of America Press, 1996.

Gerd Bayer

"AND THERE WAS A GREAT CALM"

THOMAS HARDY (1920)   The occasion for THOMAS HARDY's "And There Was A Great Calm" is the end of World War I, and though Hardy initially refused a request to write this poem to commemorate Armistice Day in 1920, he changed his mind when he noticed a correlation between the stillness at the end of the war and the biblical passages in Matthew 8:26 and Mark 4:29 that describe Christ's efforts to "rebuke the wind." Even after Hardy's loss of religious faith and his rejection of the repressive moral codes of Christianity, he continued to value "the religion of emotional morality and altruism that was taught by Jesus Christ" (*Life* 333). Hardy develops the calm brought about by Jesus into a metaphor that questions the loss of humanity and the futility of war, but in terms that encourage readers to remember the teachings of Christ. The narrator says in the second stanza, "Philosophies that sages long had taught / And Selflessness, were as an unknown thought" to describe the war's destruction of reason and compassion, then concludes the previous two lines with the remark "And 'Hell!' and 'Shell!' were yapped at Lovingkindness." The words *Philosophies, sages, taught, Selflessness,* and *Lovingkindness* might all be associated with Christ and his teachings and considered as a poetic device that establishes a rhetorical and spiritual context to invite readers to question the war along with the spirit of F'ity (and Hardy himself) and wonder, "Why?"

World War I brought about mass destruction, and, not surprisingly, the soldiers who fought in this war were separated emotionally from the rest of the population. Hardy, however, never experienced the war firsthand, but he spoke to German prisoners in Dorchester and wrote to others such as Captain Stair A. Gillon, who described to Hardy in detail the "high explosive shells and shrapnel over our heads." The testimonies of World War I veterans inform Hardy's poetic vision, which he develops through various 'Spirit' characters such as "Irony" and "Death," who wonders, "How? All firing stopped?" The Spirit characters in the poem utter poetic expressions such as "What? / Spoil peradventures woven of Rage and Wrong?" to suggest the close association between desire and destruction, but the poem's final line concludes the poetic narrative with a question that leaves the reader as silent and full of wonder as does the end of the war. After the Sinister Spirit retorts that war "had to be," the "Spirit of Pity whispered, Why?" The Spirit of Pity's final whisper reiterates the futility of war, which is ultimately Hardy's thematic point; the poem first describes the horrors of war, then features an explanation for such devastation by suggesting that a malicious Spirit prompted the war, and finally culminates with "Pity's" query to encourage readers to consider the futility of war, a topic that—unfortunately—seems applicable for almost any generation to ponder.

BIBLIOGRAPHY

Hardy, Florence Emily. *The Life of Thomas Hardy 1840–1928.* Hamden, Conn.: Archon, 1970.

Kermode, Frank, et al, ed. *The Oxford Anthology of English Literature.* Vol. 2, New York: Oxford University Press, 1973.

Pinion, F. B. *A Commentary on the Poems of Thomas Hardy.* New York: Barnes & Noble Books, 1976.

Roberts, Jon. "Mortal Projections: Thomas Hardy's Dissolving Views of God." *Victorian Literature and Culture* 31, no. 1 (2003): 43–66.

James Ortego

"ANNE HATHAWAY" Carol Ann Duffy (1999)

Carol Ann Duffy's "Little Red-Cap," which opens her best-selling *The World's Wife* (1999), is an allegory of the writer's escape from the lair of the Male Poet. In contrast, this sonnet celebrates the best possible love match between a man and a woman. It is in the voice of Shakespeare's wife, of whom little is recorded. The famously paltry bequest to her in Shakespeare's will, added to the fact of Anne Hathaway's being pregnant on their wedding day, kindled the assumptions that the pair had to marry and that there was little affection between them.

In this dramatic monologue, Duffy not only creates an identity for a woman who was both overshadowed by a great man and negatively depicted in history, but typically turns around the presumed stinginess of the will's notorious line "Item I gyve my wife my second best bed." Aptly using the Shakespearean sonnet's form to argue a case, we learn that the "best bed" was reserved for guests while Mr. and Mrs. Shakespeare enjoyed their lovemaking in the "next best bed." So, rather than a begrudging gift, this "second best" accrues status as their most valued emblem of marital union. The loving and loved wife expresses her remembered

sexual happiness with romantic images taken from her husband's works, "forests, castles, torchlights, clifftops, seas." Further indicating her involvement in his writing, parts of language become erotic metaphors for the inexpressible mutuality of their lovemaking: "his touch / a verb dancing." Characteristically preferring the evocations and imperfections of assonance, Duffy's sonnet does not rhyme apart from the formulaic closing couplet that seals the absolute happiness of their marriage, albeit self-consciously idealized by the art form.

Conflating the worlds of history, literature, myth, and the contemporary reader has become something of a classic device for women, but Duffy's potent irony and parody are distinguished by the "in-your-face" vernacular and sexuality that are illustrated in "Anne Hathaway." As always, such tricks appeal to both emotions and intellect, as Duffy intended.

BIBLIOGRAPHY

Duffy, Carol Ann. *The World's Wife.* London: Picador, 1999.

"'Metre Maid': Interview with Carol Ann Duffy." *Guardian Weekend,* 25 September 1999, 20–26.

Penguin Modern Poets. Vol. 2, *Carol Ann Duffy, Vicki Feaver, Elizabeth Bartlett.* Harmondsworth, Eng.: Penguin, 1995.

Jane Dowson

"ANNUS MIRABILIS" Philip Larkin (1974)

This ironic, "funny," clever, and typically Larkinesque poetic sketch, written originally in 1967 and included in Philip Larkin's final collection, *High Windows* of 1974, speaks about a "year of miracles," a Latin term traditionally connected to the year 1666 in post-Reformation England but rather arbitrarily applied by Larkin to 1963, the year that Larkin chooses to see as the beginning of the famous and notorious sexual revolution in the Western world. In contrast to the Great London fire and the plague of 1666, three different "miracles" define Larkin's annus mirabilis—"sexual intercourse," or, rather, new cultural and sexual freedom, permissiveness, and promiscuity; the end of the legal/official ban on D. H. Lawrence's celebrated "immoral" novel *Lady Chatterley's Lover;* and the release of the Beatles' first long-playing (LP) record defining a new, revolutionary sound of popular music.

Of course, this somewhat random selection of great defining moments of the second half of the 20th century is laughable in its imprecision and frivolity. Namely, sexual intercourse undoubtedly began with Adam and Eve, in the Judeo-Christian tradition, and, it seems, in Larkin's own life somewhere in 1945, while the "releases" of a long-suppressed "morally subversive" novel and the musically subversive LP record are really too culturally provincial and limited in impact to be seen as two milestones of a civilization.

Thus, Larkin decides to poke fun at such laughable "milestones," which cultural historians and sociologists try desperately to sell to the public and to history as important and defining events and moments. Thence Larkin's bracketed ironic modulations—"Which was rather late for me" and "Though just too late for me"— which give these "grave" pseudoscientific pronouncements a frivolous and deconstructive tone and meaning.

The second stanza of this four-stanza poem harkens back to the presixties period and describes it, in a very simplistic and thus laughable manner, as a world in which the interpersonal sexual and erotic relations were "a sort of bargaining" and "a wrangle for a ring," an ugly, calculated struggle for marital assurances and contracts, within a narrow-minded world of strict moral codes and taboos, rather than a spontaneous and free plunge into the world of sexual love. It was all tainted by "a shame that started at sixteen / And spread to everything."

Stanza three introduces dramatically the break of a new cultural, moral, philosophical, and theological "dawn"—the shameful uncertainties and guilt of the pre-1960s suddenly disappear and the new, exciting life is described, with a heavy dose of irony, as "a brilliant breaking of the bank, / A quite unlosable game."

In the last stanza the speaker reiterates his initial vision of the "brave new world" of the sixties, including the ludicrous precision of the year "nineteen sixty-three," with its three "great" successes, "sexual intercourse," "the end of the *Chatterley* ban," and "the Beatles' first LP." However, he does not forget to remind us, in the manner of J. Alfred Prufrock, that it was all "just too late for me."

On the whole this pointed and effective satirical poetic joke at our unrealistic glorification of certain moments and events in history, especially "our own," undoubtedly nudges us to think about ourselves with more humility and less pride and to see our own, much vaunted 21st century in a healthier and more realistic perspective, for it should be clear that all our iPods, laptops, Star Wars hardware, and other numerous technological miracles are still used only by the fallen human beings in whom the seven deadly sins still vie for dominance with the corresponding virtues. Nineteen-sixty-three is clearly one of the exciting, but also easily and justifiably forgotten landmarks of ever-evolving human history. This poem, in a typical Larkin manner, starts with the temporal and the seemingly insignificant and particular, only to take us suddenly, in its closing chords, into the spheres of the universal and the eternal. Larkin's best poetry always performs such memorable tricks.

BIBLIOGRAPHY

Larkin, Philip. *Collected Poems.* Edited by Anthony Thwaite. Rev. ed. London: Marvell Press and Faber and Faber, 1990.

———. *High Windows*: London: Faber and Faber, 1974.
Motion, Andrew. *Philip Larkin: A Writer's Life.* London: Faber and Faber, 1993.

Ivo Soljan

"ANOTHER EPITAPH ON AN ARMY OF MERCENARIES" HUGH MACDIARMID (1935)

HUGH MACDIARMID is most famous for his reinvention and reinvigoration of Scots verse, but he also wrote poems in English, especially if he had a political point to make with English rather than Scottish readers. During the 1930s he frequently wrote such poems, which were often more didactic than "poetic." One example of this kind of poetry is "British Leftish Poetry, 1930–1940," whose opening lines cite the most eminent English poets of the day, the group around W. H. AUDEN: "Auden, [LOUIS] MACNEICE, [C.] DAY LEWIS, I have read them all / Hoping against hope to hear the authentic call." He does not hear it, and the Auden group, who looked to the establishment of English letters like a gang of communists, Leftists, and radicals, looked to MacDiarmid like a middle-class social club, only slightly "leftish." The poem calls them a "tragical disappointment," akin to a bad night at the theater.

It is against this backdrop that MacDiarmid's challenge to another respected English poet, A. E. HOUSMAN, should be read. Housman's most famous war poem, commemorating the First Battle of Ypres in 1914, "AN EPITAPH ON AN ARMY OF MERCENARIES," was printed in *The Times* October 31, 1917, the eve of All Souls' Day and the third anniversary of the battle. The poem honors the British regular army, ordinary men who followed a military calling even before the war, not conscripts or wartime enlistees, and for that reason they are called "mercenaries," a literally true description, though the word has unpleasant overtones, of which Housman perhaps was hoping to cleanse it. They "took their wages and are dead" ends its first stanza, and they "saved the sum of things for pay" ends the second.

MacDiarmid, with his internationalist sentiments, reacted strongly to Housman and to this oft-reprinted poem, calling its sentiments a "God-damned lie." For him "They were professional murderers and they took / Their blood money and impious risks and died." Despite the anger boiling throughout the poem, and through much of MacDiarmid's most overtly political poetry, there is a softening in the last couplet, a sliver of redemption possible (else how could one still have hope in politics?): "In spite of all their kind some elements of worth / With difficulty persist here and there on earth."

BIBLIOGRAPHY

James Persoon. *Modern British Poetry, 1900–1939.* New York: Twayne, 1999.

James Persoon

"ANTHEM FOR DOOMED YOUTH" WIL-FRED OWEN (1917)

Published posthumously in 1920, this is one of several famous poems written during WILFRED OWEN's stay at Craiglockhart War Hospital, Edinburgh, while recovering from shell shock incurred in the First World War. Another patient at Craiglockhart at the same time was the poet SIEGFRIED SASSOON, who became Owen's friend and mentor. Owen produced a number of drafts of "Anthem for Doomed Youth," and manuscripts show Sassoon's suggested amendments, which Owen would later incorporate into the poem (such as the replacement of *Dead* with *Doomed* and *Nation* with *Anthem* in the title and a

clarifying of the possible ambiguities in the poem to ensure it could be read only as antiwar rather than anti-German).

As an example of the drafting process, the second part of the first line of the poem, a line that always began "What passing-bells," was repeatedly redrafted: from "for these who die so fast" to "for you who die in herds" to "for these dumb-dying cattle" to "for these who die as cattle." In earlier drafts Owen's views on religious ritual are also clearer—the end of the fifth line in an earlier draft reads, "from prayers nor bells" rather than "no prayers nor bells." The poem was heavily reworked by the pair and the final version is more powerful for Sassoon's involvement.

The premise of the poem is the comparison between the different treatments received, prior to their slaughter, by cattle and men. Owen compares the dying soldiers to cattle in the first line, asking how the soldiers' deaths will be commemorated. He answers his own question in the first stanza, realizing that only the sounds of war can mark the soldiers' passing, for, as denoted by the cattle comparison, the men are dying in too great a number for proper burial to take place and funeral rites to be observed. While clearly elegiac, the poem uses the imagery of Christian ritual in its depiction of death, and the religious ceremonies detailed have their roots in the Roman Catholic rites Owen had seen, both during his time in Bordeaux and at the period of his grandfather's death in Devon. The reader is asked to contrast the brutality of the death meted out on the battlefield with the decorous mourning rites Owen itemises (passing bells, orisons, prayers, choirs). Owen questions the possibility of the sanctification of such brutal deaths through dignified rituals and finds negatively.

The poem may use Christian imagery but it is not a Christian poem. Owen claims that there will be "no mockeries now" for the dead men and specifies that their orisons will be "hasty." In this antiwar poem the key lines are the seventh and eighth lines. The wail of the shells is juxtaposed with the call of the bugles and negative connotations are evident in "shrill" and "demented." "Demented" in particular carries a suggestion of utter madness, and this madness is associated with the military apparatus of war.

"Anthem for Doomed Youth" follows a fairly classic sonnet form with a standard rhyme structure. Both the octet and the sestet begin with a question; the mood of the poem moves from anger and aggressive military imagery in the octet to sadness and more gentle imagery in the sestet. The aggression in the octet is thrown into even sharper relief against the peace of the sestet by the use of noise. No sounds are described in the sestet, but the octet speaks of several unnatural sounds—"stuttering," "rattle," "shrill," "demented." The cyclical nature of war is emphasized in the first two lines, as the deaths of the soldiers are answered by their comrades' guns firing in revenge, but Owen retreats from the brutal physicality of the first stanza into the pastoral elegy of the second stanza. He is not averse to wordplay, as in *pallor* and *pall* in the 12th line, or powerfully onomatopoeic alliteration, as in the "stuttering rifles rapid rattle" in the second line. Owen was a longtime admirer of John Keats, the romantic poet, and Dominic Hibberd argues that the use of Keatsian language in this poem is evidence of Owen's romantic allegiance.

BIBLIOGRAPHY

Hibberd, Dominic. *Wilfred Owen.* London: Weidenfeld & Nicolson, 2002.

Simcox, Kenneth. *Wilfred Owen: Anthem for a Doomed Youth.* London: Woburn Press, 1987.

Stallworthy, Jon. *Wilfred Owen.* London: Oxford University Press, 1974.

Charlotte Kearns

"ARIEL" SYLVIA PLATH (1962) Much anthologized and discussed, "Ariel" has attracted a diverse number of interpretations, especially since for SYLVIA PLATH the poem was significant enough to lend its title to her last collection (*Ariel*), replacing that of *Daddy.* Different interpretations have been offered as to Plath's choice of "Ariel." Biographical interpretations provided by TED HUGHES inform that Ariel was the name of the horse on which Plath went riding. Further Ariel (meaning in Hebrew "God's lioness") is a symbolic name for Jerusalem. Finally, Ariel is the airy spirit in Shakespeare's *The Tempest.*

Elizabeth Bronfen sees the riding of the horse as "an unconditional embrace of self-expenditure," which will enable the self to be transformed "into pure energy" (92). Other scholars consider the poem as merely a suicide note (Susan Bassnett 146–147) or as a manifestation of the fusion of the creative and sexual self into an articulate female persona (Van Dyne, *Revising Life* 126). Critics such as Mary Kurtzman stress the poem's relation to Plath's interest in mysticism and cabalistic faith, unveiling in it important figures of the tarot pack (qtd. in Linda Wagner-Martin 104–105). Finally, noteworthy is Christina Britzolakis's reading of the horse riding as a "metaphor for the process of writing the poem" (*The Theatre of Mourning* 141).

Although many readings foreground the "fusion of the rider and the horse," the "transfiguration" and the "androgynous" nature of the evolutionary process of the persona that results in a state of nirvana (Strangeways 163), none of the scholars thus far has seen the way the fusion is conflated with Plath's 1962 essay "Ocean 1212-W," as well as a 1951 *Journal* entry and the way all these reverberate the Freudian oceanic feeling.

For Freud the "oceanic feeling" entails a "sensation" of "eternity," something "limitless, unbounded" (*Civilization and Its Discontents* 251). It is a feeling of "an indissoluble bond, of being one with the external world as a whole" (Ibid. 252). Not necessarily a religious feeling, and not absolutely "stigmatized as pathological" (253), it is the condition to which our ego aspires, "a shrunken residue . . . of a much more inclusive" ego (255).

In her autobiographical essay "Ocean 1212-W," Plath laments the loss of this feeling. The trauma of her brother's birth made her see "the separateness [emphasis in the original] of everything," feel "the wall of her skin," and experience the dissolution of "her beautiful fusion with the things of this world" (*Johnny Panic and the Bible of Dreams* 120). The same thread is taken up again in "Ariel," but in this case the self becomes involved in a journey toward the achievement of worldly fusion, which will culminate in the entrance "Into the red / Eye, the cauldron of morning" (*Collected Poems* 240).

Originally found in a state of immobility, a "stasis" immersed in darkness, the persona subsequently pretastes a feeling of infiniteness that the blue canopy of the sky offers: "Then the substanceless blue / Pour of tor and distances" (Ibid. 239). The persona wishes to be one with Ariel—"How one we grow"—but it seems that any available means are ineffective. The "furrow / Splits and passes"; the ground opens up in a trench as if one made by a plough, ready to receive her instead of a seed, but this simply passes before her quickly and does not allow her to be absorbed; she never manages to fuse with the horse, "The brown arc / Of the neck I cannot catch" (Ibid.).

New vistas of fusion now open up for her: "Nigger-eyes / Berries cast dark / Hooks." She can become part of the dark berries that extend their hooks ("nets" in the poem's drafts) to attract her to them, but their darkness does not seem compatible with her whiteness ("white Godiva"), and the creativity they offer is not real, since they are substanceless, mere "shadows." (Plath associates the shedding of blood with creativity. See "The blood jet is poetry," "Kindness" in Collected Poems, 269.) "Something else / Hauls [her] through air" (Ibid.). Now a new means of fusion becomes visible: A mode of "unpeeling," a sort of disintegration will lead to a phoenixlike process of regeneration that will simultaneously involve a regression to primordial states of worldly fusion.

"Dead hands" and "dead stringencies" are cast off. The self "Foam[s] to wheat"; it becomes a "glitter of seas" summoned to enjoy a new sort of generativity, which makes current domesticity and motherhood fade away: "The child's cry / Melts in the wall" (Ibid.). ("Wheat" strongly recalls Ceres [Demeter], productivity and fertility, and the sea, for Plath is often maternal [Johnny Panic and the Bible of Dreams 117].) The self now becomes an "arrow," a sharp, pointed object that will be microinjected in the things of the world and achieve the much coveted union. In its new form, the self will be transfigured into "dew," which will permeate everything, dissolving so that it will acquire a new state; "suicidal," annihilating the self but only to enable transfiguration ultimately to facilitate the entrance into the sun, "the cauldron of the morning" (Collected Poems 240), and be fused with it.

The self's wish for fusion with "the things of this world" as shown in "Ariel," incited by the brother's birth, has been inactive for 28 years, but now in 1962, when single motherhood overwhelmed her, when the "walls of her skin" emphasized her loneliness amid the infiniteness of the world, it is looked upon as a welcome solution. It is not pure coincidence that "Ariel" and "Ocean 1212-W" were written at approximately the same time. It is not by mere chance that "Ariel" lent its name to the whole collection. The regression to the oceanic feeling and fusion with the world were what the self was longing for. The essay mourns the loss, but the poem offers the solution. The melancholia inherent in the essay gives way to the "working out" of the loss ("Mourning and Melancholia") in the poem.

Back in 1951, as her # 89 Journal entry shows, Plath managed to achieve a similar fusion, when the sun "seeped into every pore satiating every querulous fiber of [hers] into a great glowing golden peace" (Journals 74). Stretching on a rock, as if on an altar, she is "raped deliciously by the sun, filled full of heat from the impersonal and colossal god of nature" (Ibid.). Filled by and with him is a welcome feeling, not necessarily masochistic. (Rape, deriving from Latin rapere, meaning "seize" or "snatch," does not necessarily denote an enforced sexual act but could be connoting the possession, the seizing of the self by another.) Sun-full, she becomes part of nature and "arises shining from the centuries of love, clean and satiated from the consuming fire of [the sun's] casual and tireless desire" (Ibid.). But alas, the union was not meant to last, and now (1962) the self aspires to another solution, which is to be brought about by "the riding" of Ariel, the "writing," the harnessing of the "imaginative creative" spirit on paper. Plath quotes the poet W. H. AUDEN's statement that unlike Caliban, which is "the natural bestial projection," Ariel is "the creative imaginative" one (Journals 180). It is only through the writing of the poem that the self will don the arrowlike quality of her stylus, become a writing self who will be able to harness the world, fuse with it, and enjoy the essence of things.

BIBLIOGRAPHY

Britzolakis, Christina. Sylvia Plath and the Theatre of Mourning. Oxford: Oxford University Press, 1999.

Peel, Robert. Writing Back: Sylvia Plath and Cold War Politics. Madison, N.J.: Fairleigh Dickinson University Press, 2002.

Strangeways, Al. Sylvia Plath. The Shaping of Shadows. Madison, N.J.: Fairleigh Dickinson University Press, 1998.

Van Dyne, Susan. *Revising Life: Sylvia Plath's Ariel Poems.* Chapel Hill: University of North Carolina Press, 1993.

Nephie Christodoulides

"ARISTOCRATS" KEITH DOUGLAS (1943)

KEITH DOUGLAS wrote "Aristocrats" at Enfidaville, Tunisia, probably in May and June 1943. The poem was published posthumously, in 1946, in *Alamein to Zem Zem*, an account of Douglas's experiences as a tank commander in North Africa during World War I. An alternate version of the poem, probably written later, is entitled "Sportsmen."

"Aristocrats" aptly captures Douglas's attitude toward the war. From his point of view, the conflict is an opportunity for glory, and the soldiers involved, whether they die heroes or fools, all will become "aristocrats"—heroes in the judgment of historians. The epigraph to the poem, supposedly the last words of the Roman emperor Vespasian, supports that idea by suggesting that death translates the emperor—and, to an extent, the soldiers—into the divine.

The first two stanzas present ironically humorous responses to an enemy attack. Confronted with his own mortality in a way that banishes all pleasant thoughts of England ("the shires"), one soldier simply "puts the pipe back in his mouth" in the first stanza in a stereotypical act of British forbearance. The second stanza describes the mortal wounding of Peter, whose leg is blown away by a tank and whose only response is "It's most unfair, they've shot my foot off."

With the third stanza, the speaker of the poem laments the deaths of his comrades as he wonders how one can think of them and not weep. However, at this point Douglas undercuts the sobriety of the poem. He points out that, ironically, although all of the dead will be remembered in legendary terms—like "Unicorns, almost"—many simply are fools. "Each, fool and hero, will be an immortal," the speaker comments.

Finally, in the last stanza the speaker who contemplates these dead comrades claims that he hears "a hunting horn" instead of the gunfire that killed them. He compares their efforts to failures at cricket (the "cricket pitch") or horseback riding (by referring to "drop fences" used in a horse race). The language Douglas uses in this final stanza is drawn from the radio code his own regiment, the Sherwood Rangers, used in North Africa. But Douglas seems to go a step further to suggest that equating these activities with warfare, that glorifying both fools and heroes equally in war, devalues the very nature of glory. Transforming even the fools into mythic terms makes wartime glory no better than the glory earned in a cricket match or a horse race.

Douglas's inspiration for "Aristocrats" was the death of one of his superiors in Tunisia, Lt. Col. J. D. Player. Player left £3,000 to the Beaufort hunt. He probably was the model for the description of the soldier in the first stanza, and the reference to the hunting horn in the last line of the poem also alludes to him (as well as to the epic *Song of Roland*).

While "Aristocrats" does not exhibit the grisly brutality of much of Douglas's poetry, the poem remains characteristic of its author. Douglas himself seemingly had an unquenchable thirst for martial glory and did not want that glory devalued.

BIBLIOGRAPHY
Douglas, Keith. *Complete Poems.* Edited by Desmond Graham. Oxford: Oxford University Press, 1978.
Graham, Desmond. *Keith Douglas 1920–1944.* London: Oxford University Press, 1974.
Press, John. "Poets of World War II." In *British Writers,* edited by Ian Scott-Kilvert. Vol. 7, 421–450. New York: Scribner's, 1984.

Ben Robertson

"ARMISTICE DAY" CHARLES CAUSLEY (1957)

CHARLES CAUSLEY published "Armistice Day" in 1957 as part of his collection entitled *Union Street.* As does much of Causley's poetry, "Armistice Day" relies heavily on the ballad form. Each of its six stanzas is a quatrain, rhyming *abab,* and they exhibit definite musicality in a tightly constructed form. Although Causley admired the war poetry of SIEGFRIED SASSOON, his own poetry has none of the shocking imagery of Sassoon's. Influenced by the British romantic poets, Causley aspired to recreate war experiences in more muted terms. In fact, "Armistice Day," with its vivid descriptions of Starry, Oxo, and Kitty, seems almost humorous. As the poem unfolds, however, Causley's tone evolves into sober lamentation.

Armistice Day falls on November 11, the day on which World War I officially ended. On this day of remembrance, the British traditionally honor their lost countrymen with a ceremony held at the Cenotaph in London. The Cenotaph, essentially an empty tomb, is located just off Parliament Square, where Causley indicates his narrative takes place. The ceremonies on Armistice Day involve two minutes of silence at 11:00 in the morning, the official time that the war ended. Hence, the "sea-bell eleven exploding" establishes the specific time for the poem, and since the speaker hears "No sound from the city," the moment of silence has begun. The military bands are dressed sharply in "royal array" as they play ceremonial music, but the speaker and his friends are not properly attired for the occasion.

Having established the solemn setting, Causley has the poem's narrator describe his companions to explain why their clothing does not match the occasion. Here Causley characteristically uses navy slang, for which he supplies his own footnotes. The speaker's friend Starry, for example, wears "pusser's flannel," which Causley explains simply is a "naval-issue shirt." Oxo wears "ducks" (a "white duck-suit"), and Kitty wears a "pneumonia-suit" (a type of jumpsuit a sailor would wear while painting a ship). At this point Causley makes it clear that these three men are dead. Their clothing is inappropriate, not because they have been negligent, but because these are the items they wore when their ship was sunk. Starry now is "Rubbed . . . by the regular tide"; Oxo has on the clothing he wore as he "ditched" in the English Channel; and Kitty remembers his "abandon-ship station" as he watches the Armistice Day ceremony. In clothing these sailors with such irregularity, Causley captures the haphazard unexpectedness of wartime death.

For the last two stanzas the speaker directly addresses his companions and lays the blame for their deaths on the "black captain," who, with seeming lack of emotion, makes "appalling decisions" in the navy headquarters in Whitehall. The final stanza is even more telling, for here the speaker turns inward and claims that "stiff sea-horses" stare into his eyes. Worse, he actually stands alone to watch the ceremony, and when it ends, "the city moves on" with frightening indifference to the fact that even the speaker himself is dead.

BIBLIOGRAPHY

Causley, Charles. *Collected Poems 1951–2000*. Rev. ed. London: Picador, 2000.

Chambers, Harry, ed. *Causley at 70*. Calstock, Eng.: Peterloo Poets, 1987.

Scannell, Vernon. *Not without Glory: Poets of the Second World War*. London: Woburn Press, 1976.

Schmidt, Michael. *A Reader's Guide to Fifty Modern British Poets*. New York: Barnes & Noble, 1979.

Summerfield, Geoffrey. *Worlds: Seven Modern Poets*. Harmondsworth, Eng.: Penguin Education, 1974.

Ben Robertson

ARMITAGE, SIMON (1963–)

Simon Armitage is poet, novelist, essayist, lyricist, and broadcaster. He was born in the small town of Marsden in West Yorkshire; much of his work draws on Northern English culture. He attended Portsmouth University, where he studied geography and later completed an M.A. at Manchester University exploring the impact of television violence on young children. While working as a probation officer for Greater Manchester, he published his first book of poems, *Zoom!* (1989), which went on to win the Eric Gregory Prize; the *Times Literary Supplement* described the collection as "postmodern, post-industrial, and steeped in the culture of the last decade." The volume included several poems drawing on his experiences of working for the prison service; he continued to work as a probation officer until 1994. Subsequent collections of poetry followed in 1992 (*Xanadu* and *Kid*), 1993 (*Book of Matches*), and 1995 (*The Dead Sea Poems*). He continued a busy schedule of poetry readings and journalism throughout this time. In 1997 he published a sequence of poems based around constellations entitled *Cloudcuckooland*.

In 1999 he edited the poetry anthology *Short and Sweet: 101 very short poems* and was also appointed as the Millennium Poet for Britain. The resulting commission was his 1,000-line poem entitled *Killing Time*. The poem, which was broadcast on British television and radio as well as being published by Faber, ranges over various news stories from the last year of the millennium, including the London nail bombing, the shooting at a school in Colorado, and the rail crash at Paddington station. Armitage frequently uses simple diction only to unravel the cliché he evokes, and the punning title of his millennial poem is typical in this respect. *Selected Poems* (2001) was published by Faber two years later and collects work from his first six volumes. Three collections have followed since: *The Universal Home Doctor* (2002), *Travelling Songs* (2002), and *Tyrannosaurus Rex versus the Corduroy Kid* (2006).

A sense of place is key to many of poems, and Armitage has explored the travel writing genre throughout his career. In 1996 he published with Glyn Maxwell *Moon Country,* a travelogue-cum-journal describing the pair's trip to Iceland following in the footsteps of W. H. AUDEN and Christopher Isherwood. *All Points North* (1998) is a collection of essays describing his own West Yorkshire but situates Armitage himself "on the border, between two states."

Armitage has published two novels, *Little Green Man* (2001) and *The White Stuff* (2004). Both are set in the Yorkshire Pennines memorialized in his poems. *Little Green Man* centers on a 30-something protagonist, Barney, who struggles with an autistic son, while *The White Stuff* details a couple's struggle to conceive. These were in general poorly received, leaving the *Guardian* reviewer to comment, "It is possible to write fiction without poetry, but the result is as exciting as pasta without sauce."

He has also written widely for television and theater, updating Euripides for his play *Mister Heracles* (2000) and collaborating with the director Brian Hill for docudrama films such as *Song Birds*. He also completed an opera libretto for Stuart McRae's *The Assassin Tree* in 2006. Translation continues to be an important part of his work—in 2006 he published a new version of *Sir Gawain and the Green Knight* (London: Faber and Faber, 2006).

His appealing and popular verses have perhaps suffered critical neglect precisely because of their immediate impact. His style is informed by those of PHILIP LARKIN and TED HUGHES, and he edited a selection of Hughes's verse in 2000. His interest in regional Britain also suggests affinities with poets such as TONY HARRISON. His work is absent from studies such as *British Poetry Since 1940* edited by Neil Corcoran (New York: Longman, 1993), although in 1998 he edited with Robert Crawford *The Penguin Book of Poetry from Britain*

and Ireland since 1945. In 1995 Keith Tuma characterized his work as hampered by the "wilfully provincial and anti-intellectual" stance of Philip Larkin. However, his version of Homer's *Odyssey* (2006), originally written for broadcast on BBC Radio, was well received, and he was named one of four judges for the Man Booker Prize later on in the year. He has enjoyed large popularity throughout his career, and his poems are regularly taught in British schools. His continued success makes him one of the most widely read poets writing in Britain today.

See also "HOMECOMING" "'KID' Simon Armitage," and "NOVEMBER."

BIBLIOGRAPHY
Tuma, Keith. "Who Needs Neo-Augustanism? On British Poetry." *Contemporary Literature* 34, no. 4, 718–736.

William May

"AN ARUNDEL TOMB" PHILIP LARKIN (1956/ 1964)

PHILIP LARKIN's "An Arundel Tomb" first appeared in his 1964 collection, *The Whitsun Weddings*. While it possesses many of the poetic qualities for which Larkin has been celebrated (dour clarity, traditional versification, plain language, English iconography) and while this poem can be regarded as an example of the type of writing produced by the poets associated with THE MOVEMENT, "An Arundel Tomb" departs somewhat in mood and theme from the middle-class, secular, rational, and empirical aims of the Movement's aesthetic. In the first place, in a temper unusual for Larkin, this poem considers appreciatively—without his customary irony or condescension—the possibility, at least, of an eternal, conjugal love (something Larkin himself never achieved).

The poem begins with a description of an actual tomb (in Chichester Cathedral, West Sussex) that bears upon it the sculpted likenesses of the earl of Arundel (in his "jointed armour") and his wife (in "stiffened pleat"), lying side by side, holding hands, with "that faint hint of the absurd— / The little dogs under their feet." In its seven iambic tetrameter sextets, rhymed *abbcac,* the poet meditates on the emblematic nature of the couple's pose, on the seasonal cycles and the awesome "lengths and breadths / Of time" the tomb has endured, on the unanticipated disparities between the "then" of the couple's feudal demesne and the "now" of tourists who "come up the paths," and on the palpable "untruth" of the aristocratic couple's frozen attitude in contrast to the live emotions they must have felt in their real, historical selves.

In the last stanza, the speaker concludes that their "stone fidelity . . . has come to prove / Our almost-instinct almost true: / What will survive of us is love." The poem's very last line conveys a syrupy sentiment while, just before it, back-pedaling mightily to temper that sentimentality, the speaker installs not one, but two, resisting *almosts*. They signal a struggle of reason over emotion. The speaker's repetition of *almost* implies (1) that human beings possess not the instinct itself, but something *very nearly* like a natural impulse toward fidelity and love and (2) that the symbolic representation of the sculpted couple's enduring love is, at best, only *virtually* true (not *patently* so). Despite the speaker's cavils, the overall mood of the poem—established by its Gothic topic, its couched premise of a transcendent good for all humanity, and its visual imagery luminously supplied so as to recreate "a sharp tender shock"—is uncharacteristically epiphanic—and un-Larkin-like in a neoromantic way.

BIBLIOGRAPHY

Motion, Andrew. *Philip Larkin: A Writer's Life*. London: Noonday Press, 1994.

Shaw, Robert B. "Philip Larkin: A Stateside View." *Poetry Nation* 6 (1976): 100–109.

Swarbrick, Andrew. *Out of Reach: The Poetry of Philip Larkin*. New York: Palgrave Macmillan, 1997.

Twaite, Anthony. *Larkin at Sixty*. London: Faber and Faber, 1982.

R. Victoria Arana

"AS I WALKED OUT ONE EVENING" W. H. AUDEN (1937)

W. H. AUDEN's nursery rhyme–like poem "As I Walked Out One Evening" turns the prosaic scene of an evening walk into a meditation on the transience of love in the face of time. With his characteristic honesty Auden grasps both the majesty of the lover's yearning and its insignificance, the poem both cynical and tender as Auden punctures love's pretensions with a reminder of human futility. In the dialogue between a lover and the clocks of the city, the doomed grandiosity of the lovers' claims is cruelly contrasted with the mocking of the clock bells.

The poem begins with the narrator embarking on a walk down Bristol Street. He compares the crowds to "fields of harvest wheat," suggesting both the crowdedness of the city street and the ultimate fate of the crowds, who, as will the wheat, will be reaped in their season. The narrator overhears a lover by the river under a railway arch pledging a love that will have "no ending," for his lover is "The Flower of the Ages / And the first love of the world." As in Auden's "Lullaby," where "Certainty, fidelity / On the stroke of midnight pass," the lover's promise is answered by the clocks of the city, their "whirr and chime" reminding that time is a deceiver and cannot be conquered. The clock bells do more than just remind, however; they seem also to take a perverse pleasure in their eight-and-a-half-stanza (it is 8:30 perhaps?) exposition of how time will erode the lovers' bliss. The lover's chant is overwhelmed by the clocks' prolixity, as they toll the miseries of all too finite life. "In headaches and in worry / Vaguely life leaks away," the clocks say, mocking the lovers with the knowledge that this moment under the railway arch will soon give way to mundane cares, that the quickened life of evening passion will dull with the passing of time. The clocks end their disquisition with "You shall love your crooked neighbor / With your crooked heart," adding a final note of cynicism that grants a version of love, but a version drained of innocence. The lovers are allowed their moment but only in diminished, earthly form.

The childlike meter of the poem throughout reinforces the contrast between innocence and cynicism, the meaning of the words standing in marked contrast to their sound. Even the absurdity of lines such as "The glacier knocks in the cupboard, / The desert sighs in the bed" is more taunting than playful, invoking childhood only to serve notice that it has passed. In the 12th verse, the poem explicitly invokes nursery rhymes— "the Lily-white Boy is a Roarer / And Jill goes down on her back"—but locates them in the "land of the dead" from the previous verse, as if even childhood has no place in Auden's city.

Nature, in contrast, does have a place in the city, in the form of the river that brims beneath the lovers' feet.

Water in various forms constitutes an important motif throughout. The lover sings that he will love until "the river jumps over the mountain / And the salmon sing in the street." Water later becomes a mirror as the clocks tell the lover, "Stare, stare in the basin / And wonder what you've missed," as if water is an unyielding counterpoint to human life on the surface. Glaciers, snow, tears, the water in a basin, and even the image of life "leaking away" all reinforce the sense of life's inevitable flow, leading on to the final image of the river. Finally, the lovers have gone and the clocks are silent, leaving only the "deep river" running on, indifferent to both lovers and time. Nature becomes not a sublime home for the human spirit, but a memento mori, a reminder that both lovers and the city will fall. The juxtaposition of river, lovers, and surrounding city—though the river is below the lovers, the arch of the railway forms the canopy above—also points to another theme: that human love, despite its poetry, is part of neither nature nor the city, but rather flashes briefly, futilely, between the two.

The poem conveys a sense of striking loneliness, even amid a city filled with crowds, lovers, trains, and clocks. The lover's song is only overheard, but the lovers themselves remain invisible; meanwhile, the narrator is himself not a lover, but a disinterested observer, and the poem begins and ends with his solitary ramble. Part of the pathos of the poem results from this remove. The narrator cannot take comfort in the fleeting bliss of the lover, cannot claim for himself their momentary respite; for him the bells chime the insignificance and swiftness of our passing, and the river wending through the city carries away the last echoes of human love.

BIBLIOGRAPHY

Fleissner, Robert F. "Auden's 'As I Walked Out One Evening.'" *Explicator* 2005 64, no. 1 (Fall): 48–50.

Gopnik, Adam. "The Double Man: Why Auden Is an Indispensable Poet of Our Time." *New Yorker,* 78, no. 28 (September 2002): 86–91.

Hecht, Anthony. *The Hidden Law: The Poetry of W. H. Auden.* Cambridge, Mass.: Harvard University Press, 1993.

Aaron S. Rosenfeld

"AS THE TEAM'S HEAD BRASS" EDWARD THOMAS (1915) EDWARD THOMAS opted to leave this

poem untitled but considered calling it "The Last Team"—a name that reflects its foreboding depiction of a way of life fatally threatened by a distant war. Known by the opening words of its first line, the poem depicts the speaker's observation of a team of horses ploughing a field of charlock, and his intermittent conversation with the ploughman, as he sits "amongst the boughs of a fallen elm." This physical limbo reflects the indecision that reduces him to the role of observer, in contrast to the active ploughman, who represents the ongoing necessity of a traditional and productive way of life. All of Thomas's verse was written in his last two years, during wartime, and this poem, composed in May 1915, conveys the poet's continuing inner debate over whether or not to enlist in the army.

Unlike other famous "war poets," such as WILFRED OWEN and SIEGFRIED SASSOON, Thomas wrote no poetry while on, or after, active service in France—he was killed just a month after joining his battery on the front line. He did not therefore go through the same process of rapid disillusionment, after initial idealism, upon experiencing the horrors of trench warfare. His attitude, rather, was more ambivalent from the outset; he was inclined toward the patriotic cause but also acutely aware of the personal risks that fighting for it involved—a response evident in the speaker's stark appraisal of his dilemma: "If I could only come back again I should. / I could spare an arm. I shouldn't want to lose / A leg."

The plain unadorned speech, in creative tension with the expected measure of blank verse, is highly characteristic of Thomas's style. It was partly influenced by the poetics of Robert Frost but also emerged out of his long development as a prose writer. He often based his writings on the carefully recorded real conversations that filled his notebooks. He was concerned with chronicling the overlooked life and language of common people, believing that simple country dwellers exhibited a past way of life that partly explained the fulfillment he himself had found through contact with nature. This sense of a shared humanity, belonging to the uncomplicated life of the land, is evident in the natural exchange between the two characters of the poem. As his reviewing and book commissions became affected by the conflict, Thomas turned increasingly to journalism and wrote a number of articles describing the war's influence on rural communities and agriculture. The poem reflects his concern with the social and political consequences of the military campaigns, especially its influence on the countryside, which was, for him, the essence of England. The ploughman reporting that "a good few" from the area have left for the front and the inevitable scaling down of farming operations clearly depict a community, and an industry, in rapid decline.

The poem features a wealth of subtle suggestive symbolism, also characteristic of Thomas, which contributes to the poem's dark unsettling undertones. There is the fallen tree, which cannot be removed until the war's end has spared the necessary labor. The horses' "head brass" refers to the decorative medallion on their harnesses, and there is the ironic implication of a military charge with their slow stumbling approach as if to tread him down. Some of the symbolism, however, lends itself to more optimistic explanations. The poem is framed by the apparently incidental disappearance and reappearance of two lovers, which can be seen to propose nature's potential for rebirth. One of the most significant lines is the ploughman's remark that "if we could see all all might seem good," which may be construed as naïvely trusting or the poem's ultimate affirmation of providence. Either way it illustrates how this accessible, but interpretively rich, poem defies a straightforward reading.

BIBLIOGRAPHY

Cooke, William. *Edward Thomas: A Critical Bibliography.* London: Faber, 1970.

Motion, Andrew. *The Poetry of Edward Thomas.* London: Chatto & Windus, 1991.

Smith, Stan. *Edward Thomas.* London: Faber, 1986.

Tom Rogers

"AT THE TOURIST CENTER IN BOS-TON" MARGARET ATWOOD (1968)

"At the tourist center in Boston" was published in *The Animals in That Country* (1968). MARGARET ATWOOD likes to explore issues of Canadian identity and culture, including how humans and the environment interact with each other. *The Animals in That Country* looks closely at how

humanity interprets itself through the spaces that we create.

In "At the tourist center in Boston" Atwood specifically examines, as her title implies, the tourist center in Boston, Massachusetts. It is through the lens of something as incongruous as a tourist center that Atwood examines her native land from the other side of the border, and what she sees distresses her: "Saskatchewan / is a flat lake, some convenient rocks / where two children pose with a father / and the mother is cooking something / in immaculate slacks by a smokeless fire, / Her teeth white as detergent." Here Canada has been stripped of personality. The tourist map advertising her country sanitizes the place and its people, giving no hint as to what is actually there.

Atwood questions what the map shows her: "Whose dream is this, I would like to know: / is this a manufactured / hallucination, a cynical fiction, a lure / for export only?" Her own memory is of "cities, also slush, / machines and assorted garbage," not the picture-perfect country of the tourist advertisement.

BIBLIOGRAPHY

Atwood, Margaret. *Selected Poems: 1965–1975.* Boston: Houghton Mifflin, 1976.

Howells, Coral Ann, ed. *The Cambridge Companion to Margaret Atwood.* Cambridge: Cambridge University Press, 2006.

J. J. Pionke

ATWOOD, MARGARET (1939–)

Born in Ottawa, Canada, Margaret Atwood is a literary celebrity who has changed the face of Canadian literature almost single-handedly. She began writing at the age of five but stopped at the age of eight for unknown reasons. At 16 she took up her pen again and veered sharply away from what had been her career goal at the time of being a botanist. As a child growing up when Canadian students read almost no Canadian literature, Atwood felt very isolated as a writer and reader in her homeland. Determined to be a writer, in 1957 she enrolled in the honors program of English language and literature at Victoria College at the University of Toronto. While she was at the University of Toronto, she had several short stories and poems published, and in 1961, the year she graduated, her first book of poetry, *Double Persephone* (1961), won the University of Toronto E. J. Pratt Medal. Atwood went on to attend Radcliffe College, the woman's college at Harvard University, and earned her M.A. there. She then went to Harvard University's main campus to work on her Ph.D. and completed her coursework but never finished her dissertation.

In between her M.A. and the start of Ph.D. work, Atwood took time off and returned to Canada, where she started working on her first novel, which remains unpublished. She also traveled to France and England in 1964, the first of many such trips. In between working on novels, she wrote short stories and poetry. Starting in 1966, she began publishing regularly.

Atwood's works are primarily concerned with Canada and what it means to be Canadian. *The Journals of Susanna Moodie* (1970) is one of the earliest and best examples of her work that explores and discovers the Canadian psyche. Atwood's writings are not solely centered on Canada, though the country tends to be the main focus. In *The Handmaid's Tale* (1985), one of her most famous works and winner of numerous awards, the focus is on a postapocalyptic United States that has become every feminist's nightmare. Her work is often controversial and is widely taught in women's studies classes across the globe. She writes in English and in French, and her work has been translated into a wide variety of languages, including Urdu, Greek, Hebrew, and Japanese.

In addition to poetry and fiction, she has worked with prose, radio, television, film, cartoons, and political satire. She has labored tirelessly to raise awareness for various social causes, including the environment, feminism, and human rights. The recipient of numerous honorary degrees, Atwood continues to write and maintains a healthy pace of lectures and book signings across Canada and the United States with occasional forays into Europe. She lives with her husband, the author Graeme Gibson, in Toronto.

See also "AT THE TOURIST CENTER IN BOSTON," "THE WOMAN WHO COULD NOT LIVE WITH HER FAULTY HEART."

BIBLIOGRAPHY

Cooke, Nathalie. *Margaret Atwood: A Biography.* Toronto: ECW Press, 1998.

Howells, Coral Ann, ed. *The Cambridge Companion to Margaret Atwood.* Cambridge: Cambridge University Press, 2006.

J. J. Pionke

"AUBADE" PHILIP LARKIN (1977)

PHILIP LARKIN's "Aubade" appeared in the *Times Literary Supplement* for December 23, 1977, shortly after it was written, toward the end of Larkin's life, during the long drought of inspiration when he feared that poetry had left him. It is perhaps his greatest poem, and certainly one of the most profound and moving considerations of death in English poetry, on a level with D. H. LAWRENCE's "THE SHIP OF DEATH" and DYLAN THOMAS's "DO NOT GO GENTLE INTO THAT GOOD NIGHT."

An *aubade* is literally a "dawn song," a literary genre popular in medieval courtly love poetry, in which the lover mourns the coming of dawn because then he must leave his beloved—its most famous example today is probably Romeo and Juliet's scene in bed the morning after their marriage as they argue about whether dawn has really arrived and Romeo must really depart. In contrast to the medieval aubade, or Shakespeare's use of it, Larkin is quite alone in his poem. A further irony of Larkin's aubade is that the coming of the dawn is welcome to this speaker, as it should dispel the fears of death that night brings. The poem's last stanza suggests the dawn does perhaps give some comfort, but it is also true that while the speaker begins to notice the ordinary world beginning "to rouse" (as "work has to be done"), it is the "rented" world, inhabited by us temporarily, that rouses; the sky is "white as clay"; and postmen "like doctors go from house to house"—all lines with overtones of death, mitigating whatever comfort dawn might have conferred.

The poem consists of five stanzas, each of 10 lines, in careful iambic pentameter of 10 syllables each, and just as carefully rhymed, though the enjambing or running of lines across the line breaks disguises the rhymes when the poem is read aloud. This disguising of rhyme gives the poem the feel of authentic interior monolog while making it clear that the poem is also a carefully constructed artifact, aware of itself as a poem.

"Aubade" famously begins, "I work all day, and get half-drunk at night," a line that in its bluntness seems to strip away the sympathetic pretensions we often have about ourselves, reminiscent of other blunt openings in Larkin's later poems, such as "Groping back to bed after a piss" ("SAD STEPS" from 1968) and "Love again: wanking at ten past three" ("Love Again" from 1979). Lines such as these work toward maintaining the Larkin persona of the "loser" for whom things never quite work out, who never gets the girl or the fame or the money, unlike his more successful classmate, KINGSLEY AMIS. But in their crudity and admission of such unheroic, if common, pastimes as drunkenness, pissing, and masturbation (especially in a bespectacled, middle-aged, bald librarian, not a dashing black-leather-jacket-wearing THOM GUNN or TED HUGHES), they are a kind of profile in courage, or at least honesty, and move the darker side of our humanity forward to receive some of its poetic celebration.

As is usual with Larkin's poetry, the lines seldom require explication to understand the basic sense of the poem; the language is both simple and memorable. In the first stanza the subject is announced, that in the night, waiting for dawn, the poet sees "what is really always there: / Unresting death, a whole day nearer now." Stanza 2 describes the fear accompanying this thought, and the reason for it: "Not to be anywhere, / And soon." The dropping of the phrase *and soon* to the following line lends the suddenness of surprised and frightened after-thought to the previous lines' more measured and rhythmically controlled statement of the fear. The third stanza rehearses the arguments of religion and logic, which try to dispel fear of death, but they are dismissed—religion is "that vast moth-eaten musical brocade" and rationality is "specious." The fourth stanza eschews even the benefit of courage—and contains a powerful antidote to those who might accuse the poet of being a gloomy pessimist, a worrier: "Most things may never happen: this one will." The line gains a sorrowful irony from earlier Larkin poems in which the poet has hoped for something wonderful to happen, but it does not.

"Slowly light strengthens," the fifth stanza begins, signaling coming dawn and the end of the poem. Standing "plain as a wardrobe" is "what we know, / Have always known, know that we can't escape, / Yet can't accept. One side will have to go." Death, where the "one side"

has to go, is linked to work, which "has to be done"; to postmen, who have to "go from house to house"; to doctors, who have to make their rounds to the sick and dying. There is really no answer to the fear of the poem, not religion, philosophy, courage, friends, drink, or even work. Most things never happen; this one simply and inevitably will.

BIBLIOGRAPHY

Thwaite. Anthony, ed. *Philip Larkin: Collected Poems.* New York: Farrar, Straus, Giroux, 1988.

Regan, Stephen. *Philip Larkin: An Introduction to the Variety of Criticism.* New York: Macmillan, 1992.

Rosen, Janice. *Philip Larkin: His Life's Work.* Ames: University of Iowa Press, 1989.

James Persoon

AUDEN, W. H. (WYSTAN HUGH AUDEN) (1907–1973)

Arguably the most important English poet of the twentieth century, Auden was also the first to produce work wholly of that century, undeniably modern in tone and content and yet comfortable in its relations to a tradition it perceives as persisting and present (rather than, as for his immediate modernist precursors, irretrievably fragmented or lost). His early poetry found a mode of expression and a body of images that seemed, to his contemporaries, to articulate fully the contradictory, unanchored experiences of post–First World War England. There are, however, several Audens after this initial phase (which is itself divided and critically contested), all redefining and reworking the preceding periods differently, so that Auden in his entirety is a poet difficult to categorize and consistently problematic in terms of conventional literary histories. He offers not a unified corpus of work, but a series of fundamentally liberal provisional statements and arguments, always susceptible to future modification or contradiction.

His early works articulate disconnection, alienation, and threat as registers of social and psychological discontent, drawing on a cultural climate of anxiety that they describe and seek symbolic expression for, but necessarily fail to summarize or explain. Later, geographically displaced, Auden's style shifts register to a more conventionally coherent mode, conversational and argumentative, didactic and meditative, tending to the philosophically reassuring. His metrical range encompasses mastery of virtually every available English form and many others imported from diverse sources; his translations and versions of foreign language texts offer an eclectic but refreshing reading experience. His dramatic and libretto work, his extensive reviewing and lecturing, and his essay writing add further complicating dimensions to the Auden canon, which is also muddied by his own editing, rewriting, and occasional suppression of earlier poems, and his own shifts of political and moral persuasion, which are, at least, honestly documented, if presenting obstacles to critics searching for a consistent position.

Born in York to upper-middle-class Anglican parents and raised in the West Midlands near Birmingham, Auden encountered the landscapes of the northern industrial communities as a child, and reworked such experiences in his earliest poems. He remained attracted to the north throughout his life, drawing in his poetry on the rhythms and images of Icelandic sagas and translating in 1965 the diaries of the Swedish writer Dag Hammerskjold. He was educated at Gresham's School in Norfolk and at Oxford, where he initially studied natural science, switching to English at the end of his first year. He graduated with a third-class degree in 1928 but had already, in June 1927, sent a sheaf of poems to T. S. ELIOT, then editor at Faber's. Eliot returned the poems with some favorable comments; three years later Auden sent a new selection, which Eliot accepted. *Poems* was published in 1930 and inaugurated the movement of English verse embodied in the group christened by Samuel Hynes "the Auden Generation," a poetry expressing a desire for political and ethical commitment but tempering that expression by a sometimes calculated vagueness, influenced by (but not always developing or adequately responding to) the already canonical works of 1920s MODERNISM, and immersed in its age but seeking always some kind of escape from that age, in figures of poetic responsibility that belong elsewhere in cultural history. Symptomatically the other poets of "the Auden group" (which included STEPHEN SPENDER, LOUIS MACNEICE, and C. DAY LEWIS) sought a leader (nominally found in Auden himself) who provided what Adrian Caesar has called "an illusion of author-ity," while seeking for themselves poetic roles as leaders of the community.

Auden's position within what now appears as a crisis of political and moral faith in English poetry in the 1930s is complex and contradictory. He worked through the 1930s in various schoolteaching posts and for the G. P. O. film unit (to which he famously contributed the poem "Night Mail" for the film of the same title in 1935). His earliest poems exploit the rhetoric of warfare and espionage, anxieties about borders and frontiers, languages of distrust and betrayal, to articulate a sense of what in "The Secret Agent" (1928) he describes as "trouble coming." His major work of the period, *The Orators* (1932), expresses through a series of monologues and lyrics what he called the "failure" of a "revolutionary hero" and explores "the question of leadership in our time" in poetry difficult with uncertainty. It offered poetic responses to modernity that remain cryptic and provisional, and depicted, in Stan Smith's words, an "opaque and baffling" world, suggesting that Auden's only real leadership qualities were sheer poetic aptitude and intellectual authority. As Edward Mendelson puts it, "He was often most divided when he appeared most committed."

Auden never fully committed himself to a political role or identity. His one real flirtation with a life of commitment and action, a brief sojourn with the International Brigade in the Spanish civil war in 1937, ended with his ignominious return to England a few weeks later, reluctant to discuss the experience. It was followed, unsurprisingly, by his reversion to the Anglicanism of his childhood, a rediscovery of religious faith that more or less ended his notional political commitment. His major work of this period, the magnificent "Spain" (1937) (another poem subject to subsequent suppression and alteration), seeks to locate the contemporary political arena ("today the struggle") within the immense contexts of human history. It offers a vision of human progress influenced (if not wholly persuaded) by Marxist models of history and implicates poetry itself as part of this necessary process, a cultural product simultaneously influencing and influenced by history. Spain, the challenge and opportunity it posed to Auden and his generation, becomes a "choice," a space in which commitment (to a cause never clearly articulated) can be tested.

By 1939 in "IN MEMORY OF W. B. YEATS," Auden had more or less abandoned politics as an appropriate arena for the poet, asserting in this poem that "poetry makes nothing happen." After an increasingly exotic series of excursions to Berlin (in 1928, partly in search of sexual freedoms unavailable to homosexual men in England), Iceland (1936), and China (1938), Auden and his longtime collaborator Christopher Isherwood decided in 1939 to emigrate to the United States, sailing on January 19, nine months before the outbreak of war. In the first major poem of his American period, "SEPTEMBER 1, 1939," Auden looked back on the thirties as "a low, dishonest decade" and asserted individual over communal desire: "Not universal love / But to be loved alone." "All I have is a voice," the poet laments, "to undo the folded lie." The poem's real agenda, however, is to deconstruct this individuality and this "voice," asserting instead the power of history (signified in the declarative authority of its titular date), the public intruding into the private, shared needs thwarting individual desires.

In America Auden settled into an expatriate bohemian lifestyle in New York, renting an apartment at 7 Middagh Street in Brooklyn in a building shared with, among others, Benjamin Britten and Peter Pears, "Gipsy" Rose Lee, Golo Mann (son of the German novelist Thomas Mann), and the American writer Carson McCullers and establishing a long-term but frequently fraught relationship with Chester Kallman, with whom he later moved to the Lower East Side. Auden had previously married Erika Mann, another Mann daughter, in 1935, to secure her a British passport; later in life he proposed to the German philosopher Hannah Arendt. His homosexuality, which veered between the apparently promiscuous and the (reluctantly) chaste, was the motivation behind a series of powerful love lyrics, some of which were republished after the success of "Funeral Blues" (1936) in Mike Newell's 1994 film *Four Weddings and a Funeral*. The major poems he produced in America offered an increasingly sophisticated, but also mellowing, series of responses to questions concerning, for example, in the collection *The Shield of Achilles* (1955), the status of art ("THE SHIELD OF ACHILLES"), the social and psychological effects of landscapes ("Bucolics"), and the relations of social and individual

guilt analyzed through the daily structure of the Offices of the Church (Horae Canonicae). Such works developed in Auden's mature voice an authoritative, didactic tone but courted criticism from those who felt that, in the words of his biographer Humphrey Carpenter, he was "declining into a 'comfy' middle age."

Through the 1950s Auden and Kallman divided their time between New York and Ischia, in the Italian Mezzogiorno, with Auden engaged on lecturing tours in the United States and Europe. In 1956 Auden was elected professor of poetry at Oxford, a post involving lecturing commitments in England. In 1958 the couple moved to Kirchstetten in Austria, a small village 30 miles west of Vienna, where their taste for wine and opera, and Auden's preference for a northern European climate, could be indulged. The house at Kirchstetten inspired the long sequence "Thanksgiving for a Habitat" (1962–63). Through the 1960s he published the collections *Homage to Clio* (1960), *About the House* (1965), *City without Walls* (1969), and *Epistle to a Godson* (1972). A collection of essays, *The Dyer's Hand,* was published in 1962. Throughout the 1950s and 1960s Auden cowrote and translated with Kallman libretti for operas including *The Rake's Progress* (1951, with Igor Stravinsky) and *The Magic Flute* (1956)—just as in the 1930, he had cowritten with Christopher Isherwood dramatic works such as *The Dog Beneath the Skin* (1935) and *The Ascent of F6* (1936). Auden died of a heart attack in a hotel in Vienna in 1973. *Thank You, Fog,* his last collection, was posthumously published in 1974. *Collected Poems,* edited by Auden's literary executor Edward Mendelson, appeared in 1976.

Auden's legacy resides in works that follow his own early attempts to write a poetry of commitment or elaborate responses to and revisions of his own later styles and themes. THE MOVEMENT and "group" poets of the 1950s (including PETER PORTER and ROY FULLER) and the "Hitchin school" of the 1970s (including PETER SCUPHAM) are perhaps his clearest inheritors, but his influence can be found in writers as different as the American John Ashbery and the Leeds poet TONY HARRISON. The poetry he produced after 1939 seems less burdened by the social and historical demands upon the earlier work to which the poet both had to, and yet seemed unable to, respond. His later work seeks to render "universal" themes in personal terms, while the earlier had struggled, in its public-school slang, its carefully vague elisions, its indeterminacies of reference, to make private experience somehow public. While the temptation is to ascribe such a reversal to differences between England and America, or to Auden's declaration of religious faith, his abiding concerns transcend such shifts of perspective or location and constitute an extended inquiry into the possibility, desirability, and nature of poetic language in the modern world—he meditates on this theme in the "unwritten poem" *Dichtung und Wahrheit* (1959). His earlier work can be seen as the difficult beginnings of a quest for a language and a form in which contemporary experience could be appropriately rendered. The answers he found were, perhaps, more ideological than aesthetic, concerned more with seeking poetic inspiration in a prevailing gratitude for the ordinary than with seeking the true function of poetry. The best of his "middle period" poems, such as "MUSÉE DES BEAUX ARTS" (1938), the long poem "New Year Letter" (1940), and "IN PRAISE OF LIMESTONE" (1948), achieve an imposing synthesis of complex thought, careful expression and deftly-handled form that is wholly Auden's own.

See also "AS I WALKED OUT ONE EVENING," "THIS LUNAR BEAUTY," "THE UNKNOWN CITIZEN."

BIBLIOGRAPHY

Carpenter, Humphrey. *W. H. Auden—a Biography.* London: Allen & Unwin, 1981.
Mendelson, Edward. *Early Auden.* London: Faber & Faber, 1981.
———. *Later Auden.* London: Faber & Faber, 1986.
Smith, Stan. *W. H. Auden.* Oxford: Blackwell, 1985.
———, ed. *The Cambridge Companion to W. H. Auden.* Cambridge: Cambridge University Press, 2004.

John Sears

"AUSTRALIA" A(LEC) D(ERWENT) HOPE (1939)

Though written in 1939, A(LEC) D(ERWENT) HOPE's poem "Australia" was not included in his first collection of poetry *The Wandering Islands,* published in 1955 and comprising poems produced between 1938 and 1953; not until the publication of *Collected Poems 1930–1965* (1966) was it included as part of Hope's canonical oeuvre. "Australia" is one of the very few early poems Hope composed about his native country, and it has often been taken as a conveyance of the "antinationalist" character of Hope's poetry, fostered by its radical opinions about the question of "Australianness" in the 1950s and 1960s. Hope himself made reference to the poem as one he "wrote in a disgruntled mood when I came back from England" and one that still "follows me round like a bad smell." Hope has evoked in his memoir *Chance Encounters* (1992) that after his arrival in England he felt "oddly at home, as though not observing a foreign country but returning from a long absence, picking up what I had always known," and comments such as this have advanced the idea that Hope was always quite suspicious of finding any value in Australian literature and society. It is quite often that poets who are also critics have their poetry analyzed in terms of their critical views: Hope's criticism of the Jyndiworobak movement and its rejection of the English literary tradition has traditionally biased the analysis of "Australia" as a negative poem that rejects aborigine culture and exalts European, or Anglo, literary traditions. Quite on the contrary, Hope's approach to his native country and its nascent literary tradition is never quite as clear-cut: While he sees it as a place defined by "drab green and desolate grey," as an authentic wasteland, the identification with this "Nation of trees" and its hidden possibilities surfaces here and there throughout the poem.

"Australia" is not only an analysis of the country itself, but also of its cultural traditions. Hope asserts that although it is considered to be a "young country," it is not and identifies the land with a woman "beyond her change of life, a breast still tender but within the womb is dry." The analogy of land and literature often found in Hope's critical thought also appears here in the deterioration of the native land, also understood as a degradation of the soil of Australian literature. The attack on those parasites, those "second-hand Europeans" who feed off the land, seems to have been traditionally quite lost in the analysis of the poem; Hope, however, compares Australia's "five cities" (Sydney, Melbourne, Adelaide, Perth, and Hobart) to five "teeming sores" draining the land, in a "vast parasite robber-state" that exploits the land and its possibilities.

The final two stanzas somehow "redeem" the poem, since while at its beginning it acknowledged Australia's lack of a cultural background "without songs, architecture, history," Hope still expects some kind of prophet to arise from the "waste," "some spirit which escapes / The learned doubt, the chatter of cultured apes / Which is called civilization over here." Apparently the speaker returns home from England in hopes of finding some kind of redemption for Australia and for its letters. This last assertion is consistent with Hope's view of the English classics as essential to the growth of a new, Australian literature, one that should escape "the lush jungle of modern thought" and grow off a rich English tradition, while acknowledging the rich raw materials of the land.

BIBLIOGRAPHY
Lesser, David. *The Whites of Their Eyes: Profiles by David Lesser*. St Leonards, N.S.W.: Allend & Unwin, 1999.
Zawacki, Andrew. "A. D. Hope (1907–2000)." *British Writers: Supplement VII*, edited by Jay Parini. New York: Scribner's, 2002.

Carmen Méndez García

"AUSTRALIA 1970" JUDITH WRIGHT (1970)

This poem appeared in JUDITH WRIGHT's collection *Shadow* (1970), which mostly featured a tone of acceptance rather than the highly polemic expression of Wright's previous works. "Australia 1970," however, can be considered an exception. It addresses two significant issues surrounding colonialism in Australia: the loss of the natural, untouched wilderness of Aboriginal land, referred to in the poem as the "wild country," and the self-destructive ignorance of colonialists, who are also dependent on the natural habitat they affect. The first four quatrains address the "wild country" as an animal about to become extinct: Their dramatic imperatives and emotional enjambment are neatly concluded with end-stopped rhymes, which provide a realistic structure in which the emotional expression finds full effect. The two concluding quatrains, linked by the half-rhyme *us–dust,* portray the paradoxical behavior of the colonialists.

The poet addresses the "wild country" with imperatives; its "death" is a foregone conclusion, yet should be resisted with dignity and pride. Four threatened species of native Australia set examples as to how this may be achieved; the Australian "wild country" and its animal species are thus personified as martyrs. The eaglehawk is praised for its resistance to the last in the face of death: "dangerous till the last breath's gone, / clawing and striking." The land is beseeched to follow the example of the soldier-ant, which "mindless and faithful" carries on regardless, despite the immediate threat. It is called upon to "stay obstinate; stay blind," sacrificing itself for the sake of tradition. The "wild country" is also encouraged to bring harm upon its "conquerors." The tigersnake is praised for its expression of hatred and arousal of fear in its enemy. The concluding quatrain praises natural phenomena that can be lethal to mankind: "the scoring drought, the flying dust, / the drying creek, the furious animal."

The paradoxical ambivalence of the poet's position is clear throughout the poem and reflected in a comment Wright made prior to its publication. "The landscape lost its character. The aborigines lived with the landscape and every bit of it had meaning for them. We couldn't accept any of their meanings. . . . You have to be yourself and at the same time come to terms with something that you have robbed of its original meaning." Indeed, the poet, while mourning the loss of the "wild country," as a non-Aboriginal Australian herself belongs to the "conquerors," demonstrating this affiliation through the pronouns *us* and *we*. The poet also calls upon nature to resist and even to cause harm to her people, by "cursing" its "captor," filling the "killer's dreams / with fear like suicide's invading stain," and reducing the "living soil," the colonist's source of agricultural wealth, to "naked poverty." All that is truly native to the land is praised for its potential resistance and aggression: "that they oppose us still; / that we are ruined by the thing we kill."

BIBLIOGRAPHY
Scott, W. N. *Focus on Judith Wright*. Brisbane: University of Queensland Press, 1967.
Walker, Shirley. *The Poetry of Judith Wright*. Melbourne: Edward Arnold, 1980.

Wendy Skinner

AVANT-GARDE Tension between the "mainstream" and the "avant-garde" (both contested terms) was a notable feature of British poetry for the last three decades of the 20th century and continues to be so. This tension, and its continual localized eruption into often bad-tempered controversy, remains a subtext in a large number of seemingly innocent (or not so innocent) critical debates, so a basic understanding of it is essential to an understanding of British poetry. However, one sin that nearly all critics and commentators commit (and that this short summary can hardly hope to avoid) is to distort the varied and complicated reality through the generalizations they assert. As a result, it is important to read a wide range of poetry from a number of sources, and to base one's own position on the reading of poetry in preference to the doctrines of critics, whose affiliations may not be apparent and whose judgments may therefore be misleading.

Avant-garde originated in the 19th century among European artists and critics as a term for art that was both aesthetically and politically radical. In principle, this also broadly defines British avant-garde poetry, but applying the definition in practice is very difficult, and the history of the avant-garde is a series of arguments as much as it is a literary tradition. For example, some have seen *avant-garde* as synonymous with *modernist,* while others consider MODERNISM to have been absorbed by the poetic mainstream. Meanwhile, both formal innovation and political radicalism have occurred in poetries that are not usually called avant-garde. Alongside its theoretical definition, the avant-garde is delineated at least in part by the history of its institutions—in particular by its tradition of publication in small presses and magazines, and of hostility to the literary establishment.

Historically speaking, the first avant-garde in British poetry was the modernism represented by EZRA POUND, T. S. ELIOT, and their peers early in the century. Their outspoken assault on the Georgian poetry of the day, allied with their doctrine of formal innovation (Pound said, "Make it new"), was a classically combative piece of avant-gardism. However, for all Pound's stated enthusiasm for Italian futurism—a genuinely radical artistic movement—his own view of both literature and politics was one that remained deeply committed to tradition. On the one hand, he went back to the Provençal troubadours and the Anglo-Saxons for literary models. On the other, his notorious support for fascism and anti-Semitism found its "authority" in history, whereas the futurist F. T. Marinetti's support for fascism was at least avant-garde in being based on a rejection of history and tradition. Eliot, like Pound, was more interested in the development of tradition than in its destruction, as his famous essay "Tradition and the Individual Talent" shows.

From the start, then, practical usage of the term *avant-garde* has been problematic and usually inexact: It has typically been applied to any literary group or movement that seems formally innovative and / or oppositional. But there are good reasons why it should have begun with a connection to modernism.

Because the avant-garde is theoretically interested in opposition to, and subversion of, the established order, it is particularly well disposed to disjunctions of the sort habitually performed in modernism, whether these be at the macrolevel (refusing to give a single coherent narrative, a moral viewpoint; challenging the identity or authority of the poet, the text, or the lyric subject) or at the microlevel (rejecting rhyme and meter, traditional syntax, or even the sentence itself as a linguistic unit; using techniques such as word collage and parataxis, preferring associative connections between ideas to logical argument as a model for the poem). In fact although some or all of these features remain more or less radical in terms of the general culture, because avant-garde poets have used them so heavily they have become the features that define whether a poem is avant-garde. As a result, by the end of the century a poem's status as avant-garde was determined largely by the presence of absence of specific stylistic features, rather than solely by any underlying or motivating theoretical position. Aside from specific formal devices, *avant-garde* has come to seem synonymous with *experimental*—though this term too is politically loaded and can only be defined in the most approximate terms as "refusing established literary forms and methods"—with the political content of avant-gardism often eclipsed or annihilated by such formal preoccupations. This is perhaps an inevitable development: A movement that began as hostility to tradition (and in particular to the empty formalisms committed by traditions in the name of culture) in the end became its own formal tradition. This paradox begins to show why a bipolar model of British poetry ("mainstream" versus "avant-garde") is inadequate, and why an intransigent hostility to the establishment (which had its origins in particular historical circumstances) becomes untenable as a long-term creed.

Eliot's success in penetrating and dominating the literary establishment, Pound's rather more indirect success in influencing it, and their less than revolutionary attitudes to the literary tradition made them poor figureheads for later avant-gardists, who typically prefer to trace a line of influence to other early modernists such as HUGH MACDIARMID, BASIL BUNTING, and DAVID JONES, and later modernists such as David Gascoyne and W. S. GRAHAM. Avant-garde critics assert the importance of such figures in contrast to their perceived marginalization in mainstream accounts. It is important to realize that such assertions involve the staking of claims in contested ground, for instance, in the case of Graham, whose importance was being recognized by mainstream critics well before the end of the century. But it is true that any self-consciously avant-garde poetry remained basically marginalized until at least the early 1960s (and, arguably, throughout the period). At that time the contentiously named British poetry revival—the single biggest growth period in British avant-garde poetry—began, influenced by early modernism and especially by American examples.

Poets associated with the revival include Bob Cobbing, Ian Hamilton Finlay, Gael Turnbull, ROY FISHER, Lee Harwood, Michael Horovitz, Christopher Logue, Jeff Nuttall, Tom Raworth, and particularly Eric Mottram. Mottram's controversial editorship of *Poetry Review* (the UK Poetry Society's official magazine and therefore the establishment organ par excellence) saw avant-garde poets receive more attention than ever before, yet ended acrimoniously in a way that served to entrench the mainstream–avant-garde conflict for the next three decades.

These poets' work assimilated a range of influences including the Beat poets, the Black Mountain and New York schools, and individual figures such as William Carlos Williams. Typically their work was published in low-circulation magazines and in editions from small presses, often operated by other avant-garde poets.

This pattern reflects the uneasy ambivalence with which the avant-garde has regarded the poetry world. On the one hand such marginalization has been seen as a scandal (by pro-avant-garde commentators) or a consequence of their limited appeal (by anti–avant-garde commentators); on the other, the avant-garde's lack of commerce with the mainstream has been depicted as a necessary and even deliberate aspect of its oppositional stance.

Although the 1960s and 1970s were the heyday of the small press and the avant-garde poetry scene, since that time a stable tradition has been steadily developing. New influences (particularly the L=A=N=G=U=A=G=E school) and younger poets continue to make their presence felt, but a number of family characteristics persist. These include not only formal features like those listed, but also an interest in theory and philosophy (especially philosophy of language) expressed in experimental and nontraditional forms and hostility to literary values as traditionally understood. The former can lead to aridity, as if theory preceded the poem, but also generates some fascinating technical experiments, such as an interest in writing processes that defuse or deny the poet's or subject's agency. These include found poems, aleatory poems (written according to randomly generated decisions), and poems written according to predetermined rules. It is true that the novelty of such processes does not guarantee the literary value (however determined) of the result, but, as any other formal constraint, they can serve as fruitful devices. Moreover avant-gardists might point to the mainstream lyric's continued absorption in the individual subject as a significant limitation paralleling the avant-garde's absorption in language. In both cases a strength is also a weakness.

More problematic is the avant-garde's fundamental opposition to traditional literary value. On the one hand, in practice few poets are "all avant-garde" just as few are wholly traditional, so to be an avant-garde poet does not necessarily imply a hostility to the nonmodernist poetic tradition. On the contrary, many avant-garde poets are at least as well read as their mainstream counterparts. On the other hand, the avant-garde's ultimate origin is in a radical political and aesthetic movement whose opposition to traditional culture was one of principle. In particular, traditional artistic effects were considered factitious and misleading elements of an oppressive cultural system. This means, for example, that the standards by which the mainstream judges lyric poetry are simply no longer valid in the eyes of an avant-garde critic.

In theory, this means that the avant-garde–mainstream conflict in British poetry ought to be unbridgeable, since the two sides believe in incompatible literary values. No wonder the critics cannot agree about the relative merits of the work. In practice, however, since the mainstream–avant-garde dichotomy is a gross simplification, so too is the suggestion that there is not, and cannot be, fruitful commerce between them. Nevertheless their adherence to different literary criteria is the basis of the conflict between mainstream and avant-garde poets and critics: At the root of all the often trivial and personalized exchanges are some sincerely held and artistically serious disagreements about literary value. While this means that ultimately both sides ought to be accommodated within the wider poetry world on the grounds that poets and critics are allowed to have different tastes, it is important to recognize a paradoxical tension here between a critic's theoretical commitments and her responses to an individual work. On the one hand a critic's poetic taste is partly determined by her view of avant-garde versus mainstream values, not by a merely subjective reaction to a poem. On the other, her response to an individual poem should be informed, but not driven, by her theoretical commitments: The poem, rather than theory, remains the prime focus of interest (though some avant-gardists might here argue that poem and theory are indistinguishable). Meanwhile the incompatibility of avant-garde and mainstream values goes some way to explaining the puzzlement with which the two sides view each other's work, and the fact that debate between the two sides tends to take place on a relatively informal level in reviews and magazines, rather than through works of serious criticism aiming to consider the two strands together.

The central figure in the British avant-garde in the second half of the century was J. H. PRYNNE, who has been described by John Kinsella as "possibly the most significant English poet of the late 20th century," but whose preeminence has made him, for others, the representative of an elitist and obscure poetry. Kinsella himself has written poetry on each side of the mainstream–avant-garde line, while others, such as TOM LEONARD, have written poetry that addresses avant-garde concerns while remaining easily accessible to a mainstream audience. Some other significant avant-garde poets other than those mentioned include Caroline Bergvall, Kelvin Corcoran, Andrew Crozier, BARRY MACSWEENEY, Rod Mengham, Douglas Oliver, Maggie O'Sullivan, and Iain Sinclair. A number of anthologies, such as Michael Horovitz's *Children of Albion* (Penguin, 1969), Andrew Crozier and Tim Longville's *A Various Art* (Carcanet, 1994), and Iain Sinclair's *Conductors of Chaos* (Picador, 1996), have made selections of avant-garde work widely available. Keith Tuma's *Twentieth Century British and Irish Poetry* (Oxford University Press, 2001) makes a highly controversial selection of both mainstream and avant-garde British poets available to a U.S. readership. A survey of the reviews and subsequent discussions of this anthology in a number of places (including *Poetry Review*), much of which can be found on the Internet, serves as an introduction to the basic pattern, and vitriol, of the mainstream–avant-garde conflict.

Tony Williams

B

"BABY SITTING" GILLIAN CLARKE (1978)

"Baby Sitting" is divided into two 10-line stanzas: The first offers a physical description of the child for whom the speaker is caring; the second describes the abandonment that the baby will feel if she wakes to a stranger. Clarke offers an assessment of the child's future that concludes with the prediction that abandonment will become an inescapable facet of her life.

The speaker of "Baby Sitting" is a mother, but the child she is caring for is not hers: It is the wrong baby, but not wrong in the sense that there is anything defective about the baby. As the speaker says, "She is a perfectly acceptable child." The sitter sees the child for what she is without the colorations that accompany being a mother to one's own child. The list of physical features, the snuffly nose of a baby with a cold, the "Roseate, bubbling sleep," would be cute if the child were her own daughter. But the speaker dreads the possibility of the child's awakening with her nose streaming "disgustingly" with a breath that "will fail to enchant" her.

Although she is a caregiver for the baby, it is obvious that the child is not loved by the sitter: "I don't love / This baby." But not to love does not mean to hate. There is a neutral tone in the stanza, even in the description of the baby's imagined response to waking with a stranger over her bed. There is an absence of maternal tenderness for this child, replaced with a fear that the baby will wake and, not recognizing the face of the sitter, will "shout / Her hot midnight rage." Being a mother herself, the speaker knows how the child may react and is "afraid of her."

In the second stanza, the speaker elaborates on the child's feeling of abandonment, occasioned on this instance by being left with a sitter but played forward unfolding in images of a woman betrayed by her lover or a wife losing her husband to death. The speaker understands the massiveness of abandonment, the terror, the "loss of dignity" it provokes. Clarke offers a bleak prophecy of the cold world the baby will face as a woman: the cold lover in "lonely / Sheets," the woman who waits for her husband to die in the terminal ward of a hospital—the ultimate abandonment.

Clarke smoothly returns to the present baby, with the line "As she rises sobbing from the monstrous land." The line can refer to the actions of both the woman rising from her husband's side after his death and the child waking from a bad dream peopled with monsters. What both find, the woman and the baby, is no comfort in this world great enough to ease the grief of abandonment: the woman experienced enough to know that abandonment is final, the child young enough to think that all absences are abandonings.

The poem ends with the baby seeking comfort in the shape of a breast and the milk it provides. The speaker notes sadly that the comfort will not be found. There is an air of resignation in the repeated use of the word *will* throughout the poem. *Will* is used seven times (an additional two instances of *will* with *not*), lending the speaking the oracular tone of a sibyl.

32

The speaker knows what the child will feel when she awakens in the middle of the night. Not only does she have her own children and know that she will be of little comfort to a waking baby, she has the experience of a woman, an adult who suffered abandonments, great and small, in her own life. In the final line, the word *not* is added, but the certainty of the relationship between sitter and child does not change; it is only confirmed. The crying of a baby that triggers milk production in a breast-feeding mother will not produce the same results in the sitter. The comfort of a midnight feeding cannot be offered to the child.

Clarke concludes the poem with the repetition of "It will not come. It will not come." Not only will the milky comfort not be forthcoming to the waking baby, it will not be forthcoming to her as she experiences grief in her adult life, either. The poet indicates that even when others are present, the loneliness of abandonment exists and comfort cannot be found.

Patricia Bostian

"BAGPIPE MUSIC" LOUIS MACNEICE (1937)

"Bagpipe Music," perhaps LOUIS MACNEICE's best known poem, is both a scathing portrait of economically depressed Scotland and a frenetic romp through the cultural ephemera of the era. The reeling "broadsheet ballad" meter of its verses is juxtaposed with mordant imagery—in the words of D. B. Moore, the poem has an "Irish mixture of ferocious gaiety and jaunty despair" (64). Hurried rhymes such as *Blavatsky* and *taxi* are the kind one might hear roared out in a pub song. The poem's willy-nilly tumble evokes the common man battered by bourgeois pretension and economic privation.

Against the backdrop of economic and political futility, the characters scattered through the poem suffer both everyday and outré mishaps. John Macdonald takes a "corpse" home with him and, when it comes to life, clubs it with a poker and sells "its eyes for souvenirs . . . its blood for whiskey"; Mrs. Carmichael has a fifth child and says to the midwife, "Take it away; I'm through with overproduction." While Mrs. Carmichael and the rest suffer their calamities, the rich and powerful, whose "halls are lined with tiger rugs and their walls with heads of bison," remain blithely, drunkenly oblivious.

The poem is written in quatrains of rhyming couplets, with a couplet refrain. Repeated throughout are couplets that begin "It's no go . . . ," followed by "All we want is . . ." (for example, "It's no go the Yogi-Man, it's no go Blavatsky / All we want is a bank balance and a bit of skirt in a taxi"). The contrast between what is "no go" and what is wanted suggests not only class distinctions, but also a distinction between mundane, immediate needs and more exotic or rarefied pastimes. Thus spiritualism, represented by Blavatsky, is a "no go," as are merry-go-rounds, rickshaws, government grants, elections, the Herring Board, and the Bible. What *is* wanted is a bit of lewd romp, a sugar stick to quiet the baby, or a cigarette. When MacNeice writes, "It's no go your maidenheads, it's no go your culture / All we want is a Dunlop tyre and the devil mend the puncture," the implication is that the speaker wants the tyre *now* and will not trouble himself over the possibility of "puncture"—neither of tyre nor of maidenhead. Still the poem ends on the futility of trying to make the day pause long enough to seize it: The glass (or barometer) may be falling "hour by hour," but even "if you break the bloody glass you won't hold up the weather."

Despite the poem's cacophony, it is organized around a strong central voice that speaks for working-class frustration. We see MacNeice operating in a rich vernacular that captures the fleeting rapture of mockery, invective, and defiance. The bagpipe music of the title seems to play an exuberant reel in the background, as bleakness is answered with the sheer abandon of bitter and funny words unleashed.

BIBLIOGRAPHY

Brown, Richard Danson "'Your Thoughts Make Shape Like Snow': Louis MacNeice on Stephen Spender." *Twentieth Century Literature: A Scholarly and Critical Journal* 48, no. 3 (Fall 2002): 292–323.

Moore, D. B. *The Poetry of Louis MacNeice.* Leicester, Eng.: Leicester University Press, 1972.

Ramazani Jahan, Richard Ellman, and Robert O'Clair, eds. *Norton Anthology of Modern and Contemporary Poetry.* 3rd ed. New York: Norton, 2003.

Aaron S. Rosenfeld

BAGPIPE MUZAK, GLASGOW 1990 LIZ LOCHHEAD (1991)   The title *Bagpipe Muzak, Glasgow*

1990 signals an echo of "BAGPIPE MUSIC" (1937), a well-known poem written by the 20th-century British poet and playwright LOUIS MACNEICE (1907–63). Both poems are tongue-in-cheek political commentaries on the historic moments that prompted their production. MacNeice's poem layers pre–World War II Western social attitude toward materialism over other philosophical concerns: "It's no go the Yogi-man, it's no go Blavatsky, / All we want is a bank balance and a bit of skirt in a taxi." "Yogi-man" is a reference to Hinduism, and "Blavatsky" is the founder of theosophy, a branch of what is known as "the ancient wisdom." LIZ LOCHHEAD's poem exposes the political machination occurring in Glasgow when the notion of Scottish Devolution was under serious consideration but had not yet become a reality: "It's all go the PR campaign and a radical change of image— / Write Saatchi and Saatchi a blank cheque to pay them for the damage." These lines refer to a public relations company, whose posters assisted Margaret Thatcher to her first win of the prime minister's seat in 1979. As the preceding excerpts demonstrate, an oppositional recurring refrain appears in each poem, although it is disproportionate. MacNeice uses "It's no go . . ." 17 times in "Bagpipe Music" while Lochhead employs "It's all go . . ." only eight times in *Bagpipe Muzak, Glasgow 1990*. The reader senses each poet expresses the irony of his or her respective topics in reverse terms.

Although patterned after it, *Bagpipe Muzak, Glasgow 1990* is neither a mockery of, nor an homage to MacNeice's poem. Instead, according to Keith Tuma, Lochhead's poem concerns itself with "ridiculing the debased rhetoric" of middle-class politicians who fail to recognize or acknowledge the contradictory images that Lochhead sees existing on Glasgow's city streets. Glasgow was a drug-infested, decaying major industrial city when declared European City of Culture in 1990. Lochhead considers the designation an appalling joke and voices her derision: "Aye it's Retro Time for Northern Soul and the whoop and the skirl o' the saxes. / All they'll score's more groundglass heroin and venison filofaxes. / . . . in the Metropolis of Culture."

Underlying the humor in *Bagpipe Muzak, Glasgow 1990* are the poet's resentment and frustration over the pre–Scottish devolution political status quo, British governmental rule by the Westminster parliament in London, England. The poem ends on a threat: "So— watch out Margaret Thatcher and tak' tent Neil Kinnock / Or we'll tak' the United Kingdom and brekk it like a bannock." Margaret Thatcher was the United Kingdom's Conserative prime minister (1979–90); one of her opponents, Neil Kinnock, was leader of the Labour Party (1983–92), and a bannock is a round, flat bread about an inch and a half thick and the size of a dinner plate, usually made of oatmeal, pease meal, or bere (barley) meal and baked on a girdle.

BIBLIOGRAPHY

Carson, Reed. "Blavatsky Net—Theosophy." Available online. URL: http://www.blavatsky.net/. Accessed May 11, 2008.

Lochhead, Liz. "Bagpipe Muzak, Glasgow 1990." In *Anthology of Twentieth-Century British and Irish Poetry*. Oxford: Oxford University Press, 2001.

MacNeice, Louis. "Bagpipe Music." Available online. URL: http://www.poemhunter.com/p/m/poem.asp?poet=6633&poem=27619. Accessed May 11, 2008.

Tuma, Keith, ed. *Anthology of Twentieth-Century British and Irish Poetry*. Oxford: Oxford University Press, 2001.

Katherine Gannett

"THE BANK CLERK" R. S. THOMAS (1970)

R. S. THOMAS's large output includes several tributes to fellow writers, particularly Welsh ones. This is one: a memorial to the Anglo-Welsh poet Vernon Watkins (1906–67). While the poem never names Watkins, it uses his profession as a bank clerk as an extended metaphor for describing his relationship to Wales and his poetic craft.

The poem begins with a negation that signals its priorities. Rather than listening to "the shillings" as we would expect of a bank cashier, Watkins instead hears "the clinking of the waves" on the Gower coast, near his home on the Pennard cliffs. The transfer of the epithet *clinking* from the coins to the waves implies that Watkins found value not in money, but in the natural world. Such inversion of financial and spiritual values is commonplace in Thomas's poetry, making Watkins an ideal subject for Thomas's purposes. The first stanza concludes with a continuation of the numismatic conceit, as Watkins converts the clinking waves into poetry, offering his customers "the rich change / Of his mind" in exchange for their "dry cheques." Repetition here of affricate sounds (*rich, change, coinage, language, cheques*) and more traditional alliteration (*customers* and *counter, rich* and *real*) suggest the poetic heritage of *cynghanedd* shared by Thomas and Watkins, the chiming pattern of alliteration and internal rhyme used in Welsh-language poetry. The aural repetition also links *language* with true riches. Language is of lasting value, "real coinage," in contrast to the arbitrarily assigned values of the monetary economy. The older sense of *real* as "regal" indicates that the coins of language might bear royal authority. Though shillings carry the queen's image, language has a higher (perhaps divine) source.

Thomas's purposes are confirmed in the second stanza, which describes poetry writing in a series of unfolding images, again drawn from accountancy and the sea. Thus the clerk creates poetry as if he were "wrestling" joyfully with a "sum" in the bank, just as Watkins would sometimes balance accounts in an elaborate and humorous mock-ritual. The poetic wrestling is confirmed as playful when it is described as occurring "with the sea's / Care," before the imagery circles back to its basis in accountancy, noting how the careful sea "Tots itself" on "the blank sand." These related images present Watkins's career, his love of nature, and his poetic craft as an integrated whole that challenges those who think solely in financial terms. His integration fits him for a more thorough day of reckoning, since he has "balanced honourably / His accounts" at his death. Having established Watkins as an ideal, the poem addresses a final rhetorical question to those who grumble about the cost of poetry, to "Clerks" and "businessmen." Both they and the reader are called to account with a closing second-person challenge: "what about you?"

This sermonic sting in the poem's tail embodies the prophetic strain often heard in Thomas's poetry, linking him also with a priestly predecessor and metaphysical poet like George Herbert. By using Watkins's financial career as an elaborate organizing conceit, Thomas shows the metaphysical turn of mind associated with poetic ancestors like Herbert and John Donne. The abrupt concluding question, similarly, is like the dramatic ending to a Herbert poem, drawing the reader into the poem's spiritual quest. Though ostensibly a memorial for Watkins, the poem simultaneously demonstrates Thomas's wider concerns: with Wales, nature, and poetry, but also with right living and metaphysics.

BIBLIOGRAPHY
Norris, Leslie, ed. *Vernon Watkins, 1906–1967.* London: Faber and Faber, 1970.
Shepherd, Elaine. *R. S. Thomas: Conceding an Absence: Images of God Explored.* Basingstoke, Eng.: Macmillan, 1996.

Tim McKenzie

BARKER, GEORGE (1913–1991)

George Granville Barker was born in Loughton, Essex, the third of six children of George Barker and Marion Frances Taaffe Barker. He was raised in Chelsea in London, received a Catholic education, and left school at 14.

Barker published *Thirty Preliminary Poems* (1933) when he was just 20, followed by *Poems* (1935). These early volumes reflect the Latinate diction and inverted syntax popular at this time. He married his childhood sweetheart, Jessica Woodward, in 1935. The advent of SURREALISM in 1936 influenced the style of his next three volumes, in which the political ethics of war was to predominate: *Calamiterror* (1937), *Elegy on Spain* (1939), and *Lament and Triumph* (1940). A teaching post briefly took the couple to Japan in 1939 just as the war in England began. They left in 1940 for America, escaping the later attack on Hiroshima. This phase produced the Pacific Sonnets.

The years 1940–43 were spent in America, where Barker had an affair with the Canadian Elizabeth Smart. The conflict between his attraction to Smart and his reluctance to leave his Catholic marriage to Woodward resulted in emotional trauma to all parties, portrayed in *Eros in Dogma* (1944): "My tall dead wives with knives in their breasts / gaze at me, I am guilty, as they roll / like derelicts in my tempests."

This period of personal turmoil produced some of his most outstanding love poetry.

Barker's devotion to Catholicism wavered in 1947 when he approved the abortion of his new girlfriend, Betty Cass (Cashenden Cass). Conflict with his religion came to the fore in *The True Confession of George Barker* (1950), a long autobiographical poem modeled on François Villon's *Le Testament,* and his most controversial work because of its transgressions into blasphemy. The volume *News of the World* (1950) signaled a simplification of diction that was to continue through the remainder of his work.

While in America in 1958 Barker began a brief association with the Beats but decided their poetry was too vulgar. In 1959 Barker returned to England with his new love, Dede Farrelly, but felt alienated from British poetry, which had remained formal in style. In 1960 the couple moved to Rome, where Barker found the Italian culture and backdrop of Catholicism congenial.

In 1964 he met Elspeth Langlands, and this fifth relationship produced a long period of settled life. Poems engaging with the bleak Norfolk landscape are typical of his poetry in this period, most notably in the volume *At Thurgaton Church* (1969), inspired by Thomas Gray's "Elegy in a Country Churchyard." The economic and political trauma of the Thatcher years is explored in *Anno Domini* (1983), a long poem in prayer style.

Throughout his poetic career, which spanned 58 years and 20 volumes, Barker wrote a large number of elegies and sonnets to family, friends, and other poets. The most characteristic features of his poetry are his use of internal and beginning rhyme, his wit and eloquence, and his Byronic blend of charisma and anarchy.

BIBLIOGRAPHY

Barker, George. *The Dead Seagull.* 1950. London: John Lehmann, 1950.

———. *Essays.* London: MacGibbon & Lee, 1970.

Corcoran, Neil. *English Poetry since 1940.* London and New York: Longman, 1993.

Fraser, Robert. *The Chameleon Poet: A Life of George Barker.* London: Jonathan Cape, 2001.

Smart, Elizabeth. *By Grand Central Station I Sat Down and Wept.* London: Editions Poetry, 1945.

Hillary Barker

"BASE DETAILS" SIEGFRIED SASSOON (1918)

In the hands of an unskillful poet, irony turns to mere sarcasm, a crude verbal device that is more suited to the rhetorical needs of a truculent 12-year-old than of a thoughtful adult. What, then, are we to make of "Base Details," a poem that *aims* to be sarcastic, to explore the aesthetic possibilities of incivility? SIEGFRIED SASSOON was definitely not "unskillful"; he was capable of the nuanced ironies of, say, "GLORY OF WOMEN" and helped give English poetry a straightforwardness that let it work through the ideological train wreck that occured when Victorianism met modernity. But, as capable as he was of wielding language with a surgeon's skill, Sassoon was equally able to inflict blunt force trauma with words. In much the same way that surrealists completely upset the rules of logic to attack a culture that used logic to justify modern warfare, "Base Details" uses rudeness as a strategem for attacking the gentility that sent a generation to the decidedly ungenteel trenches.

The poem typifies the stylistic strengths, as well as the weaknesses, that characterize Sassoon's most familiar poems. In 1917, he had published *The Old Huntsman and Other Poems,* a gathering of prewar lyricism and war verse that alternately romanticized combat and depicted war's horrors. While some of its poems ("To His Dead Body" and "'They,'" for instance) are prototypical (that is, disillusioned) Sassoon, others distinctly are not: "To Victory" and "The Kiss" might well have been written by a romantic who had never seen combat. But Sassoon's artistic vision cleared over the next year, resulting in the aesthetically focused collection that includes "Base Details." His breakthrough volume, *Counter Attack and Other Poems,* commences with a series of realistic poems that brutally depict the horrors of war; their purpose, it may be argued, is to make noncombatants aware of what they have got soldiers into ("the hell where youth and laughter go," he called it in "Suicide in the Trenches"). These poems, including "Prelude: The Troops," the title work, and "The Rear-Guard," seek to remedy the romantic versions of warfare put forth by such writers as RUPERT BROOKE and Sassoon himself in earlier poems. In these introductory verses, Sassoon pities his fellow soldiers; these are among the works from which Sassoon's friend WILFRED OWEN drew inspiration before besting them with his own work. But the focus of the volume changes, from sympathetic depictions of trench soldiers to verbal eviscerations of the noncombatants who put them on the line and now refuse to recognize their own complicity in the slaughter of the Great War. Poems like "Glory of Women," "Fight to a Finish," and "The Fathers" verbally assault women, journalists, and elderly clubmen for their homicidal cluelessness, a poetic drubbing that makes its point by overkill: Sassoon has many different enemies, and he *will* give all of them their vitriolic due. Overall *Counter Attack,* then, does not sympathize nearly so much as confront: That is, the "counter attack" of the title is not of doomed English troops against German, but of combatants against noncombatants. For this purpose the tonal limitations of "mere sarcasm" are more useful than the nuances of irony. Irony and other forms of wit connote decent behavior, a stance Sassoon violently avoids since warmongering noncombatants have proved themselves indecent.

"Base Details" illustrates Sassoon's confrontational technique. He divides the military world into two camps—combatants and staff officers—to travesty the "scarlet Majors at the Base," who "speed glum heroes up the line to death." "If I were fierce, and bald, and out of breath," it begins, ironically proposing a sympathetic identification that the remaining lines' horrified comedy explodes. Sassoon works with implied comparisons. His typical base officer is "out of breath" because he is comfortable and out of shape, at odds with trench soldiers, who constantly face deaths that would render them "out of breath" in their own way. The officers are "scarlet" because their uniforms feature that color and also because they are flabby and breathless, unlike line soldiers, who turn scarlet when their blood pours out. Throughout "Base Details" maintains its furious tone, refusing any deference to the officers, who live "in the best hotel," "guzzling and gulping" well out of harm's way.

While Sassoon seems merely angry that base officers avoid potential personal harm, he is enraged that they send line soldiers to their deaths and then claim to know what the war is really like. "Reading the Roll of Honour," Sassoon's scarlet major says, "Yes, we've lost heavily in this last scrap." He has taken no chances but shamelessly uses the pronoun *we* to align himself with "the glum heroes" whom officers like him martyr by the millions. He gets no sympathy from Sassoon because he

deserves none; instead, the major gets the sarcastic contempt he has earned. Sassoon's cruel unfairness extends to the poem's last line. Base officers always die in their own cozy beds, it says, condemning them to a coward's doom. His distinctly rude poem sabotages a code of civil behavior that had formed an ideological foundation for senseless war. However civil Sassoon, a gentleman by birth and a captain by rank, might have wished to be, widespread slaughter and equally widespread ignorance made civility a thing of the past.

Jimmy Dean Smith

"BAVARIAN GENTIANS" D. H. LAWRENCE (1929)

The feast of St. Michael on September 29 symbolizes the end of summer and prepares for the darker days to come. D. H. LAWRENCE's poem, written not long before his death and published posthumously in *Last Poems* (1932), begins with a reminiscence of that day. The fact that not everyone has "gentians in his house in Soft September" emphasizes the flowers' uniqueness and points to a premonition of death, since Lawrence composed this particular poem while seriously ill with tuberculosis in the Alps of southern Germany.

The poem begins as a celebration of the physical beauty of gentians—a poignantly ambivalent image. As a "torch-flower" it guides the speaker toward death but represents on the other hand life in full bloom and the world that has to be left behind. Lawrence associates the gentian with the myth of Persephone in the second stanza: Pluto, ruler of the underworld in classical mythology, abducted his bride from the earth. According to the cycle of vegetation, Persephone was allowed to return each spring but had to descend again in the autumn.

The major part of the poem is dominated by the striking image of darkness and the color blue as Lawrence moves on to connect the deep-blue flowers with his own imminent departure. Yet he seems to look forward, rather than dread his journey "down the darker and darker stairs." He proclaims, "Reach me a gentian, give me a torch!" with a readiness to descend into the unknown. The prospect of death is therefore seen as part of a natural process of renewal.

The poem itself is informed by recurring rhythms where a conventional rhetoric of fiction no longer applies. Repetition is the organizing principle. The first two lines, which set the poem's mood, are emphasized by repeated *s* sounds. In the second and third stanzas Lawrence uses recurring words as well as repetitions of sounds: alliteration (*dark, day*), assonance (*blaze, pale*), consonance (*daze, Dis*), and rhyme (gloom, *groom*). He furthermore supports the effect achieved with the repetition of syntax (*big and dark, ribbed and torch-like*).

Lawrence lets the poem pulse with its own life by using free verse. It was Walt Whitman above all who made him feel that poetry did not have to rhyme or be written in regular meter. By shortening and lengthening lines Lawrence controls the poem's pace, constructing sequences of rhythmic units. Besides the prosody of these lines, where one seems to echo the other, the poem ceaselessly circles back to its initial images while elaborating them, leading the reader through a blue, dark web to where life and death embrace.

BIBLIOGRAPHY

Chaudhuri, Amit. *D. H. Lawrence and "Difference."* Oxford: Clarendon Press, 2003.
Forsyth, Neil. "D. H. Lawrence's 'Bavarian Gentians': A Miltonic Turn toward Death." *Etudes de Lettres* 4 (1992): 83–100.
Murfin, Ross C. *The Poetry of D. H. Lawrence: Texts and Contexts.* Lincoln: University of Nebraska Press, 1983.
Sagar, Keith. "The Genesis of 'Bavarian Gentians.'" *D. H. Lawrence Review* 8 (1975): 47–53.

Andrea Heiflmaier

BAXTER, JAMES KEIR (1926–1972) The legend of James K. Baxter looms larger than his substantial literary output. Poet, postman, alcoholic, odd-job man, and barefoot prophet, Baxter had a personality that dominated New Zealand literature after World War II. Though he remains a minor figure internationally, in New Zealand he is alternately reviled and revered.

Born near Dunedin, New Zealand, Baxter inherited from his family a concern for the world (his father was a conscientious objector in World War I) and a love of poetry. With parental encouragement, his first book was published at age 18. The poems in *Beyond the Palisade* (1945), as is Baxter's other early poetry, are assured, rhetorical, and allusive. Drawing often on the New Zealand landscape, it demonstrates a personal romantic mythology much concerned with loss, "the fallen heart that does not cease to fall" ("Wild Bees," 1953).

In 1944 Baxter commenced his erratic student career at Otago University. During the next five years, he moved regularly, living in stints as a student and itinerant worker, but always as a poet. In Christchurch, he befriended many of New Zealand's established artists and writers, and in 1948, he married a fellow writer, Jacqueline Sturm. The couple moved to Wellington, where Baxter enhanced his considerable poetic reputation with success as a critic and playwright.

By the mid-1950s, Baxter appeared to have attained respectability. He worked as a teacher and civil servant, attended Alcoholics Anonymous, completed his B.A., and had a collection, *In Fires of No Return* (1958), published by Oxford University Press in London. Yet several tumultuous events intervened, including Baxter's first separation from his wife, his conversion to Roman Catholicism, and a UNESCO-sponsored trip to India. In response, his 1960s poetry assumed an increasingly prophetic and public role, though, paradoxically, this was often expressed in a conversational mode. Thus savage ballads against the Vietnam War are joined by the *Pig Island Letters* (1966), which compress the poet's personal experience into epistolary form to comment on the lovelessness of New Zealand ("Pig Island"), where only Love's "walking parody" is valued.

In 1966 Baxter returned with his family to Dunedin as the University Creative Writing Fellow. His output in prose and verse was typically prodigious and popular, again mixing humorous ballads (including the notorious "Small Ode on Mixed Flatting") with pared down monologues. The fellowship proved exhausting, however, and in 1968 Baxter believed that God had called him to establish a community for the disaffected at Hiruharama (Jerusalem), a remote settlement in New Zealand's North Island. The motivations for this popular and controversial community mixed Catholic, countercultural, and Māori values, as did the poems that followed. In his new guise as bearded prophet, Baxter produced some of his best poetry, notably the sonnets of unrhymed couplets in *Jerusalem Sonnets* (1970) and *Autumn Testament* (1972). Arranged deftly from the incidents of daily communal life, these understated "Baxterian sonnets" posit the love of God and community as remedies to the soullessness of urban New Zealand.

Nonetheless the austere realities of communal life took their toll. While visiting Auckland in October 1972, Baxter died of a heart attack. His body was returned to Hiruharama for a Catholic requiem and *tangi* on Māori land, in a funeral that drew people from all walks of life. His varied poetic corpus continues to attract a similar range of readers for the way it uses personal experience to hallow the universals of human experience: love, loss, faith, and death.

BIBLIOGRAPHY

McKay, Frank. *The Life of James K. Baxter.* Auckland, New Zealand: Oxford University Press, 1990.

Oliver, W. H. *James K. Baxter: A Portrait.* Wellington, New Zealand: Port Nicholson Press, 1983.

Weird, J. E., ed. *James K. Baxter: Collected Poems.* Wellington, New Zealand / New York: Oxford University Press, 1979.

Tim McKenzie

BEER, PATRICIA (1919–1999)

Patricia Beer, poet, literary critic, and novelist, was born in Exmouth, Devon, into a Plymouth Brethren family. Her early years spent in this extremely conservative and evangelical fundamentalist Christian sect created a strong influence on her later adult voice as a poet, a reaction to the strong value the Brethren place on hymns and perhaps also to the expected role of silence in women in the group's meetings. Beer describes this aspect of her childhood at length in her 1968 autobiography *Mrs. Beer's House.* In a 1993 interview with Clive Wilmer, Beer specifies that she decided to become a poet at the age of eight, as a result of being "abnormally terrified of dying" as a child as a result of the circumstances of her upbringing. At the time, the promise of fame through poetry enabled her to feel more comfortable with the concept of eternity.

However, Beer would not begin to write immediately upon this revelation. She went on to study at Exeter University and Oxford and would eventually teach English literature in Italy. It was not until her stay in Italy that she began writing, at the age of 28. Her early work, composed during the 1950s, was originally classified in the neoromantic style of post–World War II Britain, though as her poetry developed she would become influenced by both THE MOVEMENT and contemporary critics (she herself noted that she was only able to produce her best work after choosing to ignore such critics' opinions). Beer returned to her homeland to become a professor of English literature at Goldsmith's College, London, publishing three volumes of verse, *Loss of the Magyar, The Survivors,* and *Just Like the Resurrection.* As her literary success increased, she left her position at Goldsmith's in 1968 to become a full-time writer, settling with her second husband, Damien Parsons, an architect, in Upottery near Honiton in the Devon countryside. She would remain living in Devon for the rest of her life, and the region's rural and bucolic landscape plays an important role in much of her writing, as does the cadence of its speech, which has been linked to the spoken quality of her poetic voice.

As Beer's style moved away from new romanticism and the Movement, she continued to change her use of poetic structure and form, influenced as much by literary history as the world immediately surrounding her. Literary figures, both fictional and nonfictional, are often incorporated into her poetry, and her 1993 volume *Friend of Heraclitus* includes both a series of sonnets based on her native region of England and examples of modern imagism. Beer's early works embraced simile and personae, while later poems utilized metaphor and, influenced by Gerard Manley Hopkins, a move away from strict meter. Clive Wilmer has noted that "Beer depicts a familiar, everyday world that often seems on the point of settling, unaware, into attitudes of transcendence. An ironic tone of voice, however, is usually there to hold this possibility at bay." Indeed Beer's style, often informal, wry, and colloquial, navigates well the waters of spirituality as only that of one who has been divested of her early fundamentalist beliefs can. Yet she steers clear of the "confessional" tone associated with religious commentary and avoids full rhyme in reaction to the hymns of her youth. As is particularly evidenced in her final collection, *Autumn,* which deals with her own bout with serious illness, Beer's work is mired in the reality of mortality—illness, aging, death—and the haunting of familial influence, with a unique charm added through her deftly administered dry irony.

In addition to her poetry, autobiography, and the novel *Moon's Ottery*, Beer is well known for her extensive literary criticism and reviews. In the last 30 years of her life Beer wrote for the *Listener,* the *Times Literary Supplement,* the *London Review of Books,* and *PN Review.* The best examples of her criticism have been collected in *As I Was Saying Yesterday,* published posthumously in 2002. The volume's editor, Sarah Rigby, has observed that "her casual, almost gossipy tone, her caustic humour and her attentiveness to odd (but searingly illustrative) details of a book were an integral part of the way she wrote and thought about literature." While Beer's critical tone can be enjoyably, almost painfully honest at times, it also reflects her unbiased and generally compassionate treatment of the work of others. Above all, it reflects her lifelong relationship with own work. As the novelist Patricia Duncker, also Beer's niece, has said, "I hugely admire her ruthless imagination. There is a real ice-queen chill in her writing. And she taught me a commitment to excellence: never be sloppy, go to the sixth, seventh, eighth revision, leave your best scenes on the cutting-room floor. Work work work."

See also "FOOTBINDING" and "GRAVE DOUBTS."

BIBLIOGRAPHY

Beer, Patricia. *As I Was Saying Yesterday: Selected Essays and Reviews.* Edited by Sarah Rigby. Manchester, Eng.: Carcanet, 2002.
———. *Collected Poems.* Manchester, Eng.: Carcanet, 1988.
———. *Mrs. Beer's House.* London: Macmillan, 1968.
Wilmer, Clive. "In Conversation with Patricia Beer." *PN Review* 19, no. 5 (1993): 43–45.

Caroline Kimberley

BENNETT, LOUISE (1919–)

Louise Bennett, affectionately called "Miss Lou" by her countrymen, is often noted as the most important Jamaican poet of the Twentieth century. Born to a middle-class Kingston family, Bennett was raised by her mother, a seamstress, after her father died and received a traditional colonial education. Bennett's first paid public performance would occur shortly after her graduation from high school in a 1938 Christmas concert orga-

nized by the promoter Eric Coverley, who would later become her husband in 1954. She followed this performance with radio readings and the publication of her first book, *Jamaica Dialect Verses* (1942); her poetry would become a weekly feature in the Kingston newspaper the *Gleaner* in 1943. Upon receiving a British Council scholarship in 1945 to attend the Royal Academy of Dramatic Art in London (where she would be the only black female student), Bennett would go on to develop her skills at public performance through work at the BBC, in the English theater, and as a singer and actress in New York City throughout the following decade. After making her return to Jamaica in 1955, she applied her skills as drama officer and director at the Jamaica Social Welfare Commission, which allowed her to explore further her interest in Jamaican culture. Her tenure at the Social Welfare Commission overlapped in part with her years as an instructor of drama and folklore at the University College of the West Indies from 1955 to 1969. She also maintained her interest in public performance through public readings, theater, radio, and television, including a radio show, *Miss Lou's Views* (1965–82), and *Ring Ding,* a children's television show that ran from 1970 to 1982. While Bennett is not well known outside her home country, her work has earned extensive recognition in Jamaica and the Caribbean, where her awards include a Member of the British Empire MBE (1960), the Norman Manley Award for Excellence in the Arts (1972), the Order of Jamaica (1974), the Musgrave Gold Medal from the Institute of Jamaica (1978), and an honorary D.Litt from the University of the West Indies (1983).

As Denise DeCaires Narain has noted, "Bennett's poetry . . . is often cited as marking the birth of an 'authentic' West Indian poetry" (51). Unlike other Caribbean authors such as Una Marson and Claude McKay, Bennett writes solely in Creole. While originally this made her poetry difficult to categorize in a country still marked by colonial influence (Angela Smith points out that "in *The Independence Anthology of Jamaican Literature* published in 1962, Bennett's work was placed in the 'Miscellaneous' section, rather than under poetry"), Bennett's work is now a source of national pride and is included in the Jamaican primary and secondary school curriculum. By using dialect in a humorous, yet socially aware way, Bennett's verse embraces traditional Jamaican culture and folklore in a manner that provides a subversive and empowering alternative to dominant poetic norms. Her work both validates the importance of Jamaican heritage and invalidates the cultural superiority of the British linguistic influence, establishing a level playing field for the variety of social influences in her homeland. By co-opting English poetic forms used in the education of Jamaican children, Bennett reclaims the Creole mind and language from the effects of colonialism, in a move of postcolonial irony that has been compared to that of Yeats and Walcott.

Bennett is noteworthy for her use of persona (expressed almost exclusively in the form of dramatic monologues), her appropriation of traditional poetic forms and language from English and American usage, and her embrace of the empowering voice of women in the cultural transmission of an oral tradition. Elizabeth Wheeler has acknowledged the cultural emphasis on the male voice in public performance throughout the West Indies and the corresponding negative portrayal of female characters in poetry crafted by men, positing that Bennett provides a strong contrast to this (139–140). As such Bennett's poetry, rooted in her own public performance, can be seen as a cultural precursor to reggae and dub poetry and the work of younger female poets such as Jean Breeze. Additionally while often set in the domestic, working-class sphere, "Bennett's poems provide a fascinating catalogue of current events over an extended period (roughly the 1940s to the early 1970s); read alongside more conventional, historical accounts of the period, her poems offer distinctive and insightful comments from the 'marginal' perspective of 'ordinary Jamaicans'" (DeCaires Narain 60). This is exemplified in Bennett's signature 1966 collection *Jamaica Labrish,* a volume divided into four sections: City Life, War-Time, Politics, and Jamaica—Now An' Then. Additionally she published *Selected Poems* in 1982, and in 1988 her composition "You're Going Home Now," featured in the movie *Milk and Honey,* was nominated by the Academy of Canadian Cinema and Television as best original song. Most recently she received the honorary degree of doctor of letters from York University, Toronto, Canada, in 1998

(she has occasionally resided in Canada), and in 2001 Jamaica appointed Bennett as a member of the Order of Merit for her distinguished contribution to the development of the nation's arts and culture. To this day Bennett defends her lifelong decision to write in the Creole of her homeland, arguing, "I have always believed that English itself is a dialect. It is a beautiful language, but it is alive and changing and we must not be afraid of change. If Chaucer were alive today we wouldn't be able to understand him and he wouldn't be able to understand us, but we would both be speaking this glorious, living language" (Wilmot 55).

See also "COLONIZATION IN REVERSE," "PASS FI WHITE."

BIBLIOGRAPHY

DeCaires Narain, Denise. *Contemporary Caribbean Women's Poetry: Making Style.* London: Routledge, 2002.

Ramazani, Jahan. *The Hybrid Muse: Postcolonial Poetry in English.* Chicago: University of Chicago Press, 2001.

Smith, Angela. "Long Memoried Women: Oodgeroo Noonuccal and Jamaican Poet, Louise Bennett." *Australian Literary Studies* 16, no. 4 (1994): 77–91.

Wheeler, Elizabeth. "Riddym Ravings: Female and National Identity in Jamaican Creole Poetry." In *Imagination, Emblems, and Expressions: Essays on Latin American, Caribbean, and Continental Culture and Identity,* edited by Helen Ryan-Ransom, 139–154. Bowling Green, Ohio: Bowling Green State University Popular Press, 1993.

Wilmot, Cynthia. "The Honorable Miss Lou." *Americas* 35, no. 1 (1983): 55.

Caroline E. Wiebe Kimberly

BEOWULF TRANSLATED BY SEAMUS HEANEY **(2000)** *Beowulf* is a 3,182-line poem that was composed sometime between the mid-seventh and 10th centuries. It was composed in the English vernacular, but the language has so changed from then to now that modern readers would find it difficult to make out more than a word or two of the poem here and there. Students and scholars have been translating this poem for centuries; as a staple in most British and American school curricula as the first English epic the poem has pride of place in many English literature classes. However, the debate over exactly *how* to translate the poem is significant. Generally there are two camps: those who favor linguistic accuracy and those who favor poetic integrity. A prime example from the first camp is E. Talbot Donaldson's 1966 prose translation, which sacrifices all attempts at poetic recreation entirely. Examples from the latter are Kevin Crosley Holland's 1968 translation and Roy Luizza's 2000 contribution. When the Irish poet SEAMUS HEANEY was commissioned by W. W. Norton, the leading literary anthology publisher, to craft a new translation of *Beowulf,* many assumed that his translation would prioritize the poetics over the language. While some critics do argue that this is the case, many more laud the poet for creating an accurate, lyrical, vibrant translation of the ancient poem that infuses it with a new life—and a place on the best-seller lists.

Seamus Heaney's *Beowulf* was finally published in 2000, but he had first been approached by the editors of the *Norton Anthology of English Literature* in the mid-1980s. Heaney had been interested in the rhythms and themes of Old English poetry from the beginning of his poetic career. In the introduction to his translation of *Beowulf,* he notes that "certain lines in the first poem of my first book conformed to the requirements of Anglo-Saxon metrics" (xxiii). This was the often-anthologized "DIGGING" from *Death of Naturalist* (London: Faber and Faber, 1966). Thus Heaney was a natural fit for this project. Nevertheless he found it slow going, "like trying to bring down a megalith with a toy hammer," as he described it (xxiii). Perseverance prevailed, and Heaney was eventually able to complete his translation for Norton, and it appeared in the revised seventh edition, as well as in popular hardback release. In early 2000, it won the Whitbread Prize for book of the year, narrowly beating J. K. Rowling's *Harry Potter and the Prisoner of Azkaban.*

Heaney's approach to translating *Beowulf* centered on his desire to preserve what he called the "forthright delivery" of the unknown poet. In the poem's lines he heard the sounds of his Ulster uncles, the "big voiced Scullions" (xxvii). These were men who could command the attention of a roomful of listeners with a quiet *so* and infuse the most prosaic of utterances with a poetic seriousness and timbre. To invoke these men, Heaney chose to translate the poem's opening, *Hwæt!* as simply "So." Other translators have traditionally

seen this word as a loud call to ears, a commanding *Listen!* or even a biblical *Hark!* Preserving the style of the original poet also extended to Heaney's ability to keep a sense of the original Old English metrics. In Anglo-Saxon poetry, a poetic line is defined by two half-lines, each containing two stresses in one of a limited variety of patterns. The two half-lines, separated by a caesura, are joined through alliteration on the stressed syllables. Heaney's translation often attempts to preserve both the rhythm and the alliteration, albeit not within strict Anglo-Saxon metrical rules. For example, note the alliterative consistency in the following passage describing Grendel's voraciousness:

> he grabbed and **m**auled a **m**an on his bench,
> **b**it into his **b**one-lappings, **b**olted down his
>   **b**lood
> and gorged on him in **l**umps, **l**eaving the body
> utterly **l**ifeless. (ll. 740–743)

Heaney's ability to preserve this aspect of the original poem, while using modern English syntax and vocabulary, marks his translation as a significant achievement not only in translation, but in poetry itself. Heaney's text is not simply a translation, but a poem in its own right.

Critical reaction to Heaney's translation has been generally positive. For example, Tom Shippey, a leading Anglo-Saxonist and Tolkein expert, reviewed the poem quite favorably in the *Times Literary Supplement,* telling readers, "Like it or not, Heaney's *Beowulf* is the poem now" (Shippey, 9). However, the work is not without its detractors. Howell Chickering, while acknowledging the talent of the poet, especially in rendering the poem's dramatic speeches, finds fault with Heaney's "sudden drops into the chummily colloquial" (Chickering, 168) and his "Ulsterisms," such as his preservation of the Old English verb *Þolian* (to suffer) as the Irish word *thole* in the first lines of the poem. In his introduction, Heaney cites this and other instances of using Irish colloquialisms as a representation of his connection with the poem and a way of finding his Irish heritage within this most English of poems.

Seamus Heaney will not be the last scholar or poet to translate *Beowulf.* As translations are as much a product of the present as a representation of the past, future generations will need to recreate the poem again and again. Even so, it is likely that these future translators will turn to Heaney's work as a worthy example of what a talented poet can do with a classic, epic work of ancient literature.

BIBLIOGRAPHY

Chickering, Howell. "Beowulf and 'Heaneywulf.'" *Kenyon Review* 24, no. 1 (winter 2002): 160–178.

Donaldson, E. Talbot: *Beowulf: A New Prose Translation.* Norton Critical Editions. New York: W. W. Norton, 1966.

Heaney, Seamus. *Beowulf: A New Verse Translation.* Bilingual edition. New York: Farrar, Straus & Giroux, 2000.

Shippey, Tom. "*Beowulf* for the Big Voiced Scullions." *Times Literary Supplement,* 1 October 1999, 9–10.

Rachel Anderson

BERRY, JAMES (1924–   )

James Berry, one of the most distinct voices of British-Caribbean writing, was born in the coastal village of Boston, Jamaica. At the age of 17 he decided to embark on a journey to America, where he grew increasingly uneasy about the way in which black communities were treated by the American and local governments. As a result he returned to Jamaica four years later, only to leave again for London soon after that.

Berry arrived in London in 1948, only two years after the BBC started broadcasting its celebrated *Caribbean Voices* program and eight years before the publication of Sam Selvon's novel about Caribbean communities in London titled *Lonely Londoners* (1956). Caribbean writing at the time was predominantly concerned with exploring the region's violent past. An example of this writing is the Barbadian poet EDWARD KAMAU BRATHWAITE's trilogy *Rights of Passage, Masks,* and *Islands* (1967–69), now collected into one volume titled *The Arrivants: A New World Trilogy* (1973). The trilogy's central premise is a spiritual journey into the past that ends in the third book with a promise of a new beginning whereby poets will be "making with their rhythms something torn and new."

Similarly many of Berry's poems center around the idea of travel. He explains the importance of the concept in his first book, *Bluefoot Traveller* (1976), which is a collection of British-Caribbean poetry featuring work by Berry, Faustin Charles, and A. L. Hendriks, among others. In the title poem "Bluefoot Traveller," the speaking voice urges "Bluefoot," the man whose feet are bruised by walking barefoot along too many roads searching for a new home, to "walk again."

Indeed Berry's work as a whole is centrally concerned with notions of place and identity, intending to explore the role of immigrant communities in British society. Very early on in his writing career he observed that in Britain, "there is no nourishing atmosphere for the development of black distinctiveness." As a response his works not only aim to give voice to black British communities, but also seek to articulate various intercultural connections. His poem "The Coming of Yams and Mangoes and Mountain Honey," for example, describes a London market of Caribbean food— "chocho, okra, sweetsop, sorrel"—as if "Caribbean hills have moved / and come to London."

Berry has contributed greatly to the British-Caribbean tradition. He published numerous volumes of poetry, including *When I Dance* (1988), for which he received the Signal Poetry Award in 1989. In 1990 he was awarded the very prestigious Order of the British Empire (OBE) for services to poetry, while his children's books such as *The Future-Telling Lady: And Other Stories* (1993) are widely considered as part of the canon of children's literature. In his introduction to *News for Babylon: The Chatto Book of Westindian-British Poetry* (1984), a collection of poems that he edited, Berry draws our attention to the book's attempt to offer "a people's voice with its anguishes, its struggles and its celebrations." His own work is an embodiment of this great variety of British-Caribbean writing of the contemporary period.

See also "FROM LUCY: ENGLAN' LADY."

BIBLIOGRAPHY

Berry, James. *Bluefoot Traveller.* London: George G. Harrap, 1981.

———. *Chain of Days.* Oxford: Oxford University Press, 1985.

———, ed. *News for Babylon: The Chatto Book of Westindian-British Poetry.* London: Chatto & Windus and Hogarth Press, 1984.

Polina MacKay

BETJEMAN, JOHN (1906–1984) The poet laureate Sir John Betjeman was a prolific radio and television personality who promoted traditional "Englishness" in architecture, religion, and landscape. He was born near Highgate in London on August 28, 1906, as the only child of Ernest Betjemann, a well-off cabinet maker, whose name he would change into *Betjeman* during World War I to make it less German. Notwithstanding his academic neglect, Betjeman remains one of the most popular of "contemporary" poets. The reasons for his ongoing popularity are manifold: His poetry is readily understandable, rooted in common perceptions of a recognizably English social world and landscape; it is nostalgic and ironic at the same time; and he uses traditional meters and rhyming quatrains with which most readers feel familiar.

Betjeman's autobiographical blank verse sequence *Summoned by Bells* (1960) outlines the development of his sensibility as a poet: "Childhood is measured out by sounds and smells / And sights, before the dark of reason grows" (38). The poem develops progressively, from Betjeman's private-sector education as a boarder at the Dragon School, Oxford, from 1917 to 1920; to childhood memories of magic seaside holidays at Trebetherick in Cornwall; his suffering from school bullying as a boarder at Marlborough College; and his boyhood experience of World War I. A quirky otherness is established early, as when he writes about Archibald the teddy bear, who would accompany Betjeman all his life and was one reason why he later became "the teddy bear of the nation" himself. From 1925 onward Betjeman attended Magdalen College, Oxford, and his autobiography depicts his reveling in the social life there at the center of the "literary set," until he is finally sent down for failing a divinity exam. Laughter, carnivalesque fun, was Betjeman's means of gaining group acceptability among gentlemen, and his special sense of humor is the secret of his populist personality.

After working as a schoolteacher and private secretary, he started writing for the *Architectural Review* in October 1930 and in 1933, briefly, also became a film critic on the *Evening Standard*. In 1932 his first book of poems, *Mount Zion,* was published by an old Oxford friend, Edward James, but attracted little attention. Its most famous poem, "Death in Leamington" (*Collected Poems* 1), makes the bleak claustrophobia of its content aesthetically pleasing through the soothing rhythm and rhyme: "She died in the upstairs bedroom / By the light of the ev'ning star / That shone through the plate glass window / From over Leamington Spa."

In 1932, Betjeman married Penelope Chetwode, daughter of Field Marshal Lord Chetwode, who did not approve of him, and subsequently rented Garrards Farm in Uffington, where they lived from 1934 till 1945 with their children (Paul, born 1937; Candida, born 1942). Betjeman's second book was *Ghastly Good Taste,* a commentary on architecture, published in 1934. Betjeman was the advocate of Victorian ecclesiastical architecture (Gothic revival), but also one of the first commentators to promote the work of Le Corbusier. This idiosyncratic mixture of the conservative and the postmodern characterizes not only his art criticism, but also his poetry. In January 1935 he left the *Architectural Review* and started working with Shell, writing advertisements and producing the Shell Guides to the counties of Cornwall (1935) and Devon (1936). Betjeman contributed to Shell slogans such as "The Severn bores but Shell exhilarates," and he was a proponent of the contemporary marketing of self-perpetuating "Englishness." Around this time began an association with the BBC, which was to continue for the rest of his life. His next book of poetry, *Continual Dew,* appeared in 1937. This humorous collection, bound like an old-fashioned prayer book with lavishly decorated pages, engravings, and art nouveau, made Betjeman known as a poet to a somewhat wider circle. In one of its poems, "Slough," he openly states what he hated in contemporary England, namely, standardization, ugliness, and greed: "Those air-conditioned, bright canteens, / Tinned fruit, tinned meat, tinned milk, tinned beans / Tinned minds, tinned breath" (*Collected Poems* 22).

At the outbreak of war in September 1939, Betjeman joined the Uffington Observer Corps, and between 1941 and 1943 he became a cultural attaché to the British ambassador in Ireland, living with his family in Dublin. Much later it was revealed that the Irish Republican Army (IRA) had planned to assassinate him as a spy but on reading his poetry had decided otherwise. Further volumes of poetry appeared during the next years: *Old Lights for New Chancels* (1940), which includes the scathing piece about English wartime hypocrisy "IN WESTMINSTER ABBEY," and *New Bats in Old Belfries* (1945), with poems such as "Henley on Thames" evoking a particularized vision of England, embodied in the river, houseboat, bridge, and evening mist of the English landscape. These finely registered particularities are a shared cultural knowledge that for Betjeman meant "Englishness." Not at all unaware of modernist verse experiments, Betjeman consciously chose old-fashioned couplets and blank verse with iambic rhythms for most of his poems, exploiting their satirical possibilities, as in "A Subaltern's Love Song": "Miss J. Hunter Dunn, Miss J. Hunter Dunn, / Furnished and burnish'd by Aldershot sun" (CP 105).

Returning to Uffington in 1943, Betjeman resumed his work with the Ministry of Information, continued to write books reviews, and broadcasted regularly for the BBC. He joined the British Council in 1944. The family eventually settled in Wantage in 1951, and by the mid-1950s Betjeman had become a well-known radio and television personality, commenting on architecture and campaigning to save Victorian architecture and buildings, such as. St. Pancras Station in London. *A Few Late Chrysanthemums* was published in 1952, but Betjeman's reputation as a poet was still restricted to a fairly small circle of admirers. He achieved celebrity with the appearance of his *Collected Poems* in 1958 and his verse autobiography, *Summoned by Bells* (1960), which both were best sellers. In 1969 he was knighted, and when C. DAY LEWIS died in 1972 he was made poet laureate.

His broadcasting career continued during the 1960s and 1970s with documentaries such as *Metroland* and *A Passion for Churches*. For Betjeman, the Anglican Church was a signifier of good old and decent Englishness in a Europe threatened by fascism and communism alike. His Christianity was based on a charitable, humorous, and nondogmatic core of faith, a kind of tolerant ecumenicism. Betjeman's poetry does not so much conform to convention as profoundly unsettle ingrained assumptions about masculinity, Englishness, and Christianity.

His last book of new poems, *A Nip in the Air,* was published in 1974. Betjeman's subject matter had come to encompass postmodern concerns such as environmentalism, communitarianism, and consumerism. In his later years, he began to suffer from Parkinson's disease, and a number of strokes reduced his mobility. Sir John Betjeman died at Trebetherick on May 19, 1984, and was buried in the nearby church of St. Enodoc.

BIBLIOGRAPHY

Betjeman, John. *Collected Poems.* Compiled and with an introduction by the earl of Birkenhead. Enlarged ed. London: John Murray, 1980.

Brown, Dennis. *John Betjeman.* Plymouth, Eng.: Northcote House, 1999.

Gardner, Kevin J. "Anglicanism and the Poetry of John Betjeman." *Christianity and Literature* 53 (2004): 361–383.

Hillier, Bevis. *John Betjeman: New Fame, New Love.* London: John Murray, 2002.

Press, John. *John Betjeman.* Harlow, Eng. Longman, for the British Council, 1974.

Schröder, Leena Kore. "Heterotopian Constructions of Englishness in the Work of John Betjeman." *Critical Survey* 10 (1998): 15–34.

Stanford, Derek. *John Betjeman.* London: Neville Spearman, 1961.

Thwaite, Anthony. *Poetry Today: A Critical Guide to British Poetry 1960–1995.* London and New York: Longman, 1996.

Heike Grundmann

BHATT, SUJATA (1956–)

Sujata Bhatt was born into a traditional Gujarati Brahmin family of intellectuals at Ahmadabad, India. Her father was a virologist and her mother studied Gujarati, Sanskrit, and English literature at university. She spent her childhood in Pune with her relatives around. Growing up with a grandfather as a writer and two uncles as poets, Sujata started writing her own poetry at the age of eight. Though her native tongue is Gujarati, she chooses to write poems in English. This is due to her early education in an English school at Pune, but it also results from her experience of studying in the United States. She first went to New Orleans at the age of five and returned to India three years later. When Sujata was 12, she followed her family to move to the United States again.

Graduating from Goucher College with a double major in English and philosophy, she continued writing poetry between jobs and travel in Europe. With the hope of finding a job at a university, she attended the Writers' Workshop at the University of Iowa. After receiving her M.F.A. degree, she married the German writer Michael Augustin and moved to Germany.

Her first published collection, *Brunizem* (1988), made her one of the most promising young poets and won her the Commonwealth Poetry Prize. Poems like "Search for My Tongue" and "A Different History" show her reflection on her experience in India, North America, and Europe. She used the mixture of English and Gujarati in the poems to explore the meaning and value of the multiple influences to which she had been exposed.

The subsequent collections, *Monkey Shadows* (1991), *The Stinking Rose* (1995), *Augatora* (2000), depict a world with broader horizons. While poems like "Nanabhai Bhatt in Prison" and "Genealogy" still focus on her Indian heritage, her poetic strength is also palpable in her European and American poems such as "Mozartstrasse 18" and "Walking across the Brooklyn Bridge, July 1990." In *A Colour for Solitude* (2002), Sujata Bhatt investigates the life and experiences of the German poet Rilke; his wife, Clara; and the female painter Paula Modersohn-Becker. Though her Indian tradition does not appear in this book, the focus on the situation and voice of women is the same.

Sujata Bhatt now lives in Germany with her husband and daughter. Her most recent work is *Pure Lizard* (2006).

BIBLIOGRAPHY

Carcanet Press. "Sujata Bhatt in Conversation with Vicki Bertram." Available online. URL: http://www.carcanet. co.uk/cgi-bin/scribe?showdoc=4;doctype=interview. Accessed on June 20, 2006.

Paterson, Don, and Charles Simic, eds. *New British Poetry.* Saint Paul, Minn.: Graywolf Press, 2004.

He Ning

BINYON, ROBERT LAURENCE (1869–1943)

Robert Laurence Binyon was born on August 10, 1869, in Lancaster, England, the son of an Anglican clergyman. Raised in a family of modest means, the young Binyon won a scholarship to St. Paul's School, where he twice won the Milton Prize for poetry. An aspiring poet, he read widely and was an ardent admirer of Browning and Arnold. He continued to pursue his early literary tastes and contemplative habits of mind during his career at Trinity College, Oxford, where (as did Arnold) he won the Newdigate Poetry Prize and took degrees in classics and literature. Following his graduation in 1892, Binyon began a long career at the British Museum, first working in the area of printed books and later moving to the art collection; he ultimately rose to the position of keeper of the Department of Prints and Drawings.

Binyon's first volume of poetry, *Lyric Poems,* was published in 1894. He continued to publish poems throughout his career but also built a reputation as an important art critic, publishing essays on a variety of subjects including Blake, Japanese prints, English landscape painting, and Indian art. He cultivated friendships with many of the leading literary figures of the day, notably W. B. YEATS and EZRA POUND, but his personal demeanor and poetic tastes were more attuned to the late Victorian ethos and his tone of mind more scholarly and staid.

In 1904 Binyon married Cicely Margaret Powell, with whom he had three daughters, and lived quietly in London, publishing approximately one book every year, alternating between poetry and art criticism. But in 1915, Binyon responded to the outbreak of World War I by volunteering as an orderly in the Red Cross and served on the front lines in France. After the war, he continued his work at the museum and expanded his speaking commitments, lecturing frequently on the art of India, Persia, and the Far East. Mourning the loss of "wholeness" from modern life, Binyon invited his readers "to contemplate the creative achievements of another hemisphere" to enrich their "ideas on life and on the art of living." In 1933 he accepted an invitation to succeed T. S. ELIOT as Norton Professor of Poetry at Harvard University and retired from his post at the British Museum. He continued to travel and lecture widely in the years before his death in March 1943.

During the final decade of his life, Binyon undertook a terza rima translation of Dante's *Divine Comedy,* the kind of technical challenge he found absorbing. He also advanced his own aesthetic views by editing *The Golden Treasury of Modern Lyrics,* a successor volume to Palgrave's influential anthology, which favors poems with a late romantic sensibility. David Perkins groups Binyon with his friend ROBERT BRIDGES and other Edwardian poets whom he classifies as cultivated traditionalists. Frequently praised as dignified, elegant, and highly crafted, Binyon's verse is generally thought to lack the energy and imaginative force that would recommend him to readers who do not share his sensibilities. He remains, however, an impressive figure, a monument to the sincere and lifelong pursuit of beauty, culture, and understanding.

BIBLIOGRAPHY

Binyon, Laurence. *The Spirit of Man in Asian Art.* Cambridge, Mass.: Harvard University Press, 1935.

Hatcher, John. *Laurence Binyon: Poet, Scholar of East and West.* Oxford: Clarendon Press, 1995.

Perkins, David. *A History of Modern Poetry: From the 1890s to the High Modernist Mode.* Cambridge, Mass.: Harvard University Press, 1976.

Anne Kellenberger

BIRDS, BEASTS AND FLOWERS D. H. LAWRENCE (1923)

The work contained within D. H. LAWRENCE's poetic cycle *Birds, Beasts and Flowers* is critically regarded as among his finest verse. In his most consciously planned book of poetry, most of the poems were composed during an artistically fertile period spent in Italy between the spring of 1920 and the fall of 1921. Lawrence rounded out the volume with poems written during his travels to Ceylon and New Mexico. Much of the success of the poetry composing *Birds, Beasts and Flowers* stems from its author's new and uncompromising aesthetic vision.

For D. H. Lawrence, "the business of art is to reveal the relation between man and his circumambient universe, at the living moment." Lawrence further delineated his poetic ambitions in his "Poetry of the Present," an essay in which he argued for a particular kind of poetry quite different from the "treasured gem-like lyrics of Shelley and Keats." His antithetical poetry of the "immediate present" or "living moment" would stand in opposition to the polished and elegantly symmetrical verse of the romantic tradition, for Lawrence found these qualities inhibiting and equated strict regard for formalistic concerns with stagnation, decay, and death.

The poetry Lawrence was interested in writing was vibrantly charged, and protean; it defied classification and form. Perhaps no better examples of this aesthetic exist than in the mature verse of Lawrence's *Birds, Beasts and Flowers.*

Focusing on flora and fauna, Lawrence investigates his notion of the "blood-self" or "blood-consciousness." After reading widely in anthropological texts such as Sir James Frazer's *Exogamy and Totemism,* Lawrence became convinced of the viability of his own theory of the "blood-self": that the blood actually functions as a seat of instinctual perception. However, according to Lawrence, the development of Western civilization along the lines of rationalism and Enlightenment terms has served to silence the important perceptions and knowledge of ourselves and our world once provided by this faculty in our distant, ancestral past. In *Birds, Beasts and Flowers,* Lawrence sets about the business of attempting to recover this lost vital connection. As Sandra Gilbert observes, Lawrence's purpose in the creation of *Birds, Beasts and Flowers* "was ultimately two-fold: first to explore the inhuman otherness of animals and plants, and second, to bring to consciousness that unconscious participation in natural process which makes man like birds, beasts, and flowers." Indeed the driving force behind much of the poetry is the tension that Lawrence creates between our expectations and his execution.

Eschewing anthropomorphization, Lawrence's animals in the best poetry of *Birds, Beasts and Flowers* represent a kind of ineffable, perhaps ultimately unattainable, ideal of vitality and freedom that we may have once possessed but have long relinquished. Lawrence refuses to anthropomorphize because he aims to show the myriad, presumably "simple," things that we cannot know with our intellect alone. Animals do not primarily function to provide the observer with an opportunity for relaxation and capricious musings on the quaintness of nature. Through his complex and ambivalent encounters with the natural world and its inhabitants, Lawrence insists that we have lost touch with an important part of ourselves and have replaced it with a kind of pale, ineffectual cerebrality. This cold cerebrality leads us to lash out and destroy other life as in such works as "SNAKE" and "Fish." For Lawrence, we lack the requisite knowledge to make sense of our environment as a result of the foothold of intellection over older and more earth-bound forms of spirituality. From his attempt to construct a naturalistic religion based on primitive Aztec lore to his vision of a utopian society called Rananim, Lawrence's religious quest closely parallels his poetic struggle.

In "Fish," for example, Lawrence's poetic voice marvels at the rapturous vitality of the creature darting effortlessly along, immersed in the very element of life itself. "The waters wash, / You wash in oneness." The fish seems to exhibit such unrestrained vigor that the speaker says, "Your life a sluice of sensation along your / sides." It is difficult not to detect the underlying note of envy, if not outright jealousy, with which Lawrence's poetic persona muses on the fish's rather inviting existence. The fish is imagined to be on a free and unfettered journey, unencumbered by human concerns. The observer seems to admire and look upon with awe the very characteristics of the animal that make it most distinctly not human, a kind of quintessential otherness beyond our grasp. Whether the water rises and inundates the earth or sinks into dark and unknown, primordial crevasses, the fish shall remain a potent and viable force. The fish can be viewed as a physical incarnation of Lawrence's poetic doctrine. Only an ostensibly simple beast, it is constantly moving and changing. Undaunted by the potentially dangerous currents, the animal nimbly manipulates them, leading the speaker to conclude, "The waters wash, / You wash in oneness." Like Lawrence's lofty, if sometimes misunderstood, vision of a new kind of poetic expression capable of capturing so much more energy and vitality than previously conceivable, the fish moves quite naturally in its habitat and "never emerges." In *Birds, Beasts and Flowers,* Lawrence proposed to be an unbounded poetic visionary, free to "wash in oneness / and never emerge."

BIBLIOGRAPHY

Gilbert, Sandra. *Acts of Attention: The Poems of D. H. Lawrence.* Carbondale: Southern Illinois University Press, 1990.

Hobsbaum, Philip. *A Reader's Guide to D. H. Lawrence.* London: Thames and Hudson, 1981.

Laird, Holly. *Self and Sequence: The Poetry of D. H. Lawrence.* Charlottesville: University Press of Virginia, 1988.

Marshall, Tom. *The Psychic Mariner: A Reading of the Poems of D. H. Lawrence.* New York: Viking 1970.

Murfin, Ross. *The Poetry of D. H. Lawrence: Texts and Contexts.* Lincoln: University of Nebraska Press, 1983.

Justin Williamson

BIRTHDAY LETTERS Ted Hughes (1998)

Prior to the 1998 publication of *Birthday Letters,* TED HUGHES was known in America primarily for his famously failed marriage to the American confessional poet SYLVIA PLATH, who committed suicide in 1963, shortly after Hughes left her for Assia Wevill. Hughes had an established position as a poet in England, publishing numerous books of poetry and poetic translations of classic literature, and was named poet laureate in 1984, a lifelong appointment in England. The controversy surrounding his divorce of Plath and her subsequent suicide prompted a war of criticism against Hughes, but he was notoriously silent about his relationship to Plath. That silence was broken in 1998, 10 months before his death, with the monumental publication of the 88 poems of *Birthday Letters.* Composed over the 35 years since Plath's death, the poems of *BL* are addressed almost entirely to Plath and are Hughes's most deeply personal, most readily accessible poetry. *BL* captures Hughes's struggle to understand and explain his role(s) in his relationship with Plath and presents a portrait of a man trapped in myth, a man fated to remain in a world surrounded by Plath's legend and his own complex connection to that legend.

Although the poetry in *BL* was written over 35 years, the poems are arranged more or less chronologically by subject, charting their near-mythical introduction ("St. Botolph's"), their courtship and hasty wedding ("A Pink Wool Knitted Dress"), honeymoon ("Your Paris," "You Hated Spain," "Fever"), their years of marriage together, and the events leading up to and beyond Plath's suicide. "Fulbright Scholars," the first poem in *BL,* recounts Hughes's first possible memory of Plath: He recalls looking at a British newspaper picture of "that year's intake / Of Fulbright Scholars," and wondering whether he might meet any of their number. "Fulbright Scholars" is remarkable for its lack of certainty: Hughes does not specifically recall seeing Plath in the picture, only "Maybe I noticed you. / Maybe I weighed you up." He remembers seeing the picture, recalling, "No doubt I scanned particularly / The girls," an indication of his reputation as a philanderer. He *seems* to remember buying a fresh peach from a street vendor—"Was it then I bought a peach? That's as I remember"—despite his possession of Plath's numerous journals, the only source Hughes uses throughout *BL* is his memory, a source that from this first poem is tentative at best. This lack of certainty functions as a rhetorical device, an echo of the mysticism and mythology that fascinated Hughes and Plath, and in "Fulbright Scholars," Hughes begins to reveal his perspective of the Hughes/Plath mythology that had fascinated, attracted, and repelled scholars and critics for more than 30 years.

The Hughes/Plath mythology consists of several components, each of which emerges throughout *BL*: Hughes's and Plath's shared obsession with astrology and fate; her genius and ambition, which conflicted with his own drive and brilliance; her relationship to her dead father; her mania; and his inability to understand her. Hughes's introduction to Plath was nearly mythical, well documented in the biographies listed later and in the 2003 film *Sylvia*, and Hughes makes no effort to demythologize: The first 25 lines of "St. Botolph's" contain his recollection of the stars and planets the night they met, ending, "That day the solar system married us / Whether we knew it or not." He describes his "first sight" of Plath, and their legendary meeting: "You meant to knock me out / With your vivacity." He ends the poem recalling the significant moment she bit his cheek, drawing blood: "That was to brand my face for the next month. / The me beneath it for good." Hughes believed fate had put the two together, that the stars alone were responsible for their tragic relationship. Even in "Dreamers," the only poem in *BL* that directly refers to Assia Wevill, Hughes and Plath act merely as fated participants in a drama staged by the stars: "[Wevill] sniffed us out. The fate she carried / Sniffed us out." He later says of meeting Wevill that fate "Requisitioned you and me and her, / Puppets for its performance." It was the stars that placed Hughes and Plath together; it was the stars that tore them apart.

Hughes's unwillingness to claim agency for his actions has not gone unnoticed by his critics: Bere calls this "sense of inevitability . . . questionable, even objectionable." Only on rare occasions does Hughes imply that he was in any way responsible for his failed marriage. In "Epiphany," Hughes relates how he deliberated over purchasing a fox cub on the day their daughter was born: "What would we do with an unpredictable, / Powerful, bounding fox?" Hughes describes this as a temptation, a challenge to succeed or fail, a test that symbolized much more, although only later did he recognize this decision as monumental: He claims if he had grasped that the challenge of the fox "Is what tests a marriage and proves it a marriage— / I would not have failed the test." Yet because he did not understand how difficult marriage was, much more work than caring for a fox, "I failed. Our marriage had failed." This is the strongest statement of agency Hughes is willing to make in *BL*. More often, Hughes blames the stars ("Dreamers"), the voice of the muse ("Fishing Bridge"), Plath's ambition ("Wuthering Heights"), her mother ("Ouija"), and especially her father, the ghost who haunted Plath until her death.

Throughout *BL*, Hughes likes to link himself and Plath to different mythologies and famous literary texts, often subverting the myth or blending multiple stories into one poetic thread. In "Setebos," Hughes places himself and Plath in Shakespeare's *The Tempest*: "Who could play Miranda? / Only you. Ferdinand—only me." Ariel (a spirit-being in *Tempest* that Plath used extensively in her poetry) "entertained us," while Caliban led them to "The sweetest, the freshest, the wildest." The first half of "Setebos" records the idyllic life Hughes and Plath wanted: writing, living, and loving together, becoming myth and legend. "Then," says Hughes, "the script overtook us." Instead of the magical beauty of Prospero's island, their reality lay in another myth: "I heard the Minotaur / Coming down its tunnel-groove." Otto Plath appears, again the antagonist, as "King Minos, / Alias Otto." Plath is romanticized as the sacrifice to the monster created by her father; Hughes was reduced to a pitiful, hunted fox, "hearing the cry / Now of hounds."

Hughes's conflicting struggle to understand and perform his role appears early in *BL* and continues throughout. In "Caryatids (2)," the third poem in the book, Hughes talks of their early life, when there was

"Time in plenty / To test every role." Hughes's role was complicated by Plath's indistinct expectations for him—"Visit" states, "I did not know I was being auditioned / For the male lead in your drama." Plath's leading man, however, was required to perform a dual role, that of lover *and* father.

Otto Plath died when Sylvia was eight, and she is described as never getting over his death. His presence permeates *BL*; Hughes uses him to symbolize death, as in "Isis," or to symbolize the mania that drove Plath's ambition and that eventually led her to commit suicide. Hughes projects the image of a tumultuous marriage of three partners—Hughes, Plath, and the mortal memory of Plath's father. "Black Coat" is like a scene out of a horror film—Plath's father's ghost emerges from the sea as Ted's back is turned, and while Plath watches with her "inbuilt double exposure," the ghost and Hughes become one: "The body of the ghost and me the blurred see-through / Came into single focus." When Plath looked at Hughes, she saw both her lover and her father.

This theme is expanded in "A Picture of Otto," the only poem in the book addressed to Plath's father. Plath's "inbuilt double exposure" led to confusion regarding her husband: "She could hardly tell us apart in the end." Her own poetry leads credence to this statement—see her famous poem "Daddy." Hughes describes the grip Otto Plath had on his daughter—"I understand—you never could have released her. / I was a whole myth too late to replace you"—and on himself, directly alluding to WILFRED OWEN's "Strange Meeting." Ironically after Plath's death, it is Hughes alone in the surreal afterlife with Otto Plath: "Inseparable, here we must remain." After a legendary beginning, and several years of sustaining one another, Hughes was left alone with their two children and with the ghost of Plath's father.

Above anything else, *BL* is Hughes's final attempt to preserve the Hughes / Plath mythology into eternity. Although Hughes claims that his role constantly shifted in his relationship to Plath, his poetry consistently represents his role in the mythology as the protagonist; Plath is the tragic hero, her father the antagonist. Hughes paints a portrait of himself as young and naïve, certainly not to be held responsible for Plath's suicide.

If blame you must, says Hughes, blame Otto. In "Portraits," Hughes describes a portrait that a friend painted of Plath. In the finished portrait, the shadowing over her shoulder took the viewers by surprise, for there in the portrait, so it appeared, was "a cowled / Humanoid of raggy shadows." Plath was bound in—and by—art, "alone there, pregnant, unprotected / In some inaccessible dimension," trapped "Where that creature had you, now, to himself." Although Hughes claims he could not protect Plath against the monster of Plath's "new-fired idol brilliance," *BL* consists of 88 such portraits, each a different perspective, each trapping Plath with her demons, each perpetuating the mythology in which Hughes wanted so desperately to participate. While Hughes purports to be a mere scribe of the Hughes / Plath legend, the mythology he attempts to perpetuate in *BL* is not hers, but his.

BIBLIOGRAPHY

Bere, Carol. "Owning the Facts of His Life: Ted Hughes's Birthday Letters." *Literary Review* 41 (1998): 556–561.

Bertram, Vicki. "The Intimate Authority of Ted Hughes's *Birthday Letters*." In *Gendering Poetry: Contemporary Women and Men Poets*, 137–156. London: Pandora Press, 2005.

Middlebrook, Diane. *Her Husband: Hughes and Plath—a Marriage.* New York: Viking Press, 2003.

Wagner, Erica. *Ariel's Gift: Ted Hughes, Sylvia Plath, and the Story of* Birthday Letters. New York: Norton, 2001.

Williamson, Alan. "A Marriage between Writers: *Birthday Letters* as Memoir and as Poetry." *American Poetry Review* 27 (1998): 11–13.

Chad Cripe

"BLACKBERRY-PICKING" SEAMUS HEANEY (1965)

Appearing in Heaney's first book, *DEATH OF A NATURALIST,* this poem, along with "EARLY PURGES," introduces an important theme to that book and much of Heaney's later work: the death of a childish romanticism and the birth of a more realistic view of life. The poem is dedicated to Philip Hobsbaum, a lecturer in English at Queen's University, Belfast, who in 1963 organized a creative writing workshop, which met at his home, that included then-students SEAMUS HEANEY and MICHAEL LONGLEY. The Group, as it came to be known, did not publish a journal but instead worked from sheets of poems, given in advance to Hobsbaum to duplicate. It is from these sheets that we can derive April 1965 as a date for "Blackberry-Picking," which was then published in Heaney's first collection in 1966.

The poem consists of 24 lines of iambic pentameter couplets. The rhymes are often slant, as in *sweet/it, pots/boots, byre/fur, cache/bush*. The poem breaks into two stanzas, similarly to a sonnet with an octet and sestet reflecting a break in the poet's thought. In this case, the first part of the poem describes the picking of the berries, while the second describes the futile effort to preserve them. Like many of Heaney's poems, "Blackberry-Picking" is full of monosyllabic nouns: *clot, knot, cans, pots, blobs, pricks, byre, fur, cache, bush, flesh*, and *rot*.

The descriptions of the first part of the poem are mouth-watering: "You ate that first one and its flesh was sweet / Like thickened wine." But there is also an undercurrent of pain, loss, and even violence, as the pickers' hands "peppered / With thorn pricks, our palms sticky as Bluebeard's" evoke the sufferings of Christ and of the maidens killed by the husband of one of the most grisly of Grimm's fairy tales. This theme is made more explicit in the second part of the poem, with the cache of berries quickly developing a "rat-grey fungus" as it ferments and sours. The boy in the poem, like the six-year-old of "Early Purges," has his innocence compromised: "Each year I hoped they'd keep, knew they would not."

BIBLIOGRAPHY

Allen, Michael, ed. *Seamus Heaney. New Casebooks*. New York: St. Martin's Press, 1997.

Heaney, Seamus. *Death of a Naturalist*. London: Faber and Faber, 1966. Available online. URL: http://chaucer.library. emory.edu/irishpoet/overview. Accessed December 10, 2007.

James Persoon

BLAST Eds. Ezra Pound and Wyndham Lewis

In June 1914, six months before the outbreak of the Great War, a new periodical shook London like a bomb. *BLAST*, with its "violent pink" cover, its giant typeface, its abstract art, and its strident manifestos, quickly became the talk of the town. *BLAST*'s editor, Wyndham Lewis, who called himself "a novelist, painter, sculptor, philosopher, draughtsman, critic, politician, journalist, essayist, pamphleteer, all rolled into one," was hailed as the leading voice of a new movement called vorticism. Lewis initially advertised *BLAST* as a quarterly journal, but when England joined the fighting in the First World War, Lewis was enlisted as a British bombardier. As a result, *BLAST 2* was not published until over a year later, in July 1915. It was the second and last issue of the rebel periodical, as the energy of the vorticist movement was soon entirely engulfed by the current of World War I.

Inside the pages of *BLAST*, poems by Ezra Pound join essays by Ford Madox Hueffer (later Ford Madox Ford) and Lewis's play *Enemy of the Stars*. Rebecca West's feminist short story "Indissoluble Matrimony" stands amid the many manifestos by Gaudier Brzeska, Pound, and Lewis himself. There are plates of original visual artwork by Lewis, Brzeska, and Jacob Epstein. What drew this eclectic group of artists together was, in large part, their collective reaction to the *Futurist Manifesto*, by F. T. Marinetti, published in 1909.

Like the futurists, *BLAST*'s contributors thought that it is more demanding and more rewarding "to make than to copy." Artists of both movements sought to break with "the triumph of the commercial mind in England, Victorian 'liberalism' . . . the Royal Academy, and so on" and create art that was challenging, virile, and provocative. Lewis claimed *BLAST* to be a cure for the "bad hang-over from the puerile literary debauchery" of the Victorian period.

However, Marinetti's *Futurist Manifesto* also took a decidedly anti-British tone. He accused the English of "snobbery and intellectual indolence," prompting the English poet Richard Aldington to remark; "Mr. Marinetti has been reading his new poems to London— London is vaguely alarmed and wondering whether it ought to laugh or not." Wyndham Lewis did not wonder, but in response to Marinetti's futurist *"Putsch"* he organized what he laughingly dubbed a "counterputsch." He opened the Rebel Arts Center, which became a gathering place for a group of artists who represented "all branches of the new art, sculpture, painting, poetry." This group, many of whom contributed to *BLAST*, became known as the vorticists.

The vorticists differentiated themselves from the futurists in their belief that England could provide the inspiration for "a movement towards art and imagination" and believed such a movement "could burst up [in England], from this lump of compressed life, with more force than anywhere else." They also differed in their relationship to cultural and literary history. Marinetti's *Futurist Manifesto* called "to demolish museums, libraries, fight against moralism, feminism, and all opportunistic and utilitarian cowardices," but the vorticists were not willing to dismiss the past entirely so readily. They had a different way of articulating the value they placed on the present, modern moment. They insist, "Our vortex is not afraid of the past—it has forgotten its existence." The contributors to *BLAST* wanted to create an intellectual art that took an electrified energy from the present moment. They claimed to "stand for the reality of the present, not for the sentimental future or the sacripant past . . . the present its art" and believed that "all the energized Past that is capable of living into the future is pregnant in the vortex *now*."

What exactly was the vortex? Different contributors to *BLAST* articulate it in different ways. Ezra Pound called it "the use of, or belief in the use of the primary pigment," or a way of writing that was bold and undiluted. He also referred to it as a center of a field of energy, or "a radiant node, a cluster . . . what I must perforce call a vortex from which and through which and into which ideas are constantly rushing." The artist Gaudier Brzeska described vorticism as a new way of feeling and representing emotions through visual arts. He asserts, "I shall derive my emotions solely from the arrangement of surfaces. I shall present my emotions by the arrangement of surfaces and lines by which they are defined." Lewis's own description of the vortex is perhaps the clearest. He compared it to the funnel of a whirlpool, explaining, "at the heart of the whirlpool is a great silent place where all the energy is concentrated. And there, at the point of concentration, is the Vorticist."

The manifestation of the vorticist ideal is *BLAST*, a magazine quite unlike any other, full of the energy and audacity these artists esteemed. The magazine's first and most famous issue is a book that measures 12 inches tall, nine inches wide, and nearly an inch thick. Its cover seeks to convey a kind of concentrated power

with the one word, **BLAST**, sprawled diagonally in giant three-inch-tall, one-inch-thick, black letters across a "violent pink" background. Wyndham Lewis described it as "the puce monster" and laughingly admitted that its appearance was "not unlike a phonebook."

The pages encompassed by this violent pink cover are equally aggressive. The title to the first entry in *BLAST* is the magazine's rallying cry, "Long Live the Vortex!" It shouts, "Long live the great art vortex that has sprung up in the centre of this town!" and its most strident claims burst from the page in all capital letters. The vorticists declare, "WE NEED THE UNCONSCIOUSNESS OF HUMANITY—their stupidity, animalism and dreams," and proclaim, "WE ONLY WANT THE WORLD TO LIVE, and to feel it's [*sic*] crude energy flowing though us."

Having issued this literary call to arms, *BLAST* presents several manifestos outlining their collective intentions. The first manifesto is a 16-page harangue that presents a baffling list of things to be alternately "Blasted" and "Blessed." It begins:

BLAST First (from politeness) **ENGLAND**
CURSE ITS CLIMATE FOR ITS SINS AND
   INFECTIONS
DISMAL SYMBOL, SET round our bodies,
               of effeminate lout within.

Among the things the vorticists "blast" are England's climate, "fussiness," France, sensationalism, snobbery (which is what they call a "disease of femininity"), and British "humour." They blast "years 1837–1900" in their entirety and finally present a full page that solely comprises names to be blasted. While most of the names listed will be unrecognizable to today's readers, the list also includes such entries as "The Countess of Warwick," "Captain Cook," "The Post Office," and "Cod Liver Oil."

Among those things "Blessed" are England's ships, seafarers, and ports. They bless the "Hairdresser" ("He attacks Mother Nature for a small fee"), and the previously "blasted" English humor. It also blesses the once blasted France for its "BUSHELS of VITALITY to the square inch." While all this cursing and praising may seem cryptic and even, at times, contradictory, it does form a distinct and important pattern. The blastings and blessings demonstrate the vorticists' passion for all that is virile, challenging, and energetic, as well as their loathing of all that is passive, facile, or lethargic.

BLAST's second manifesto is a seven-part treatise. The first part contains 10 points. First, they establish themselves "Beyond Action and Reaction." They claim to occupy opposite extremes with "adolescent clearness" and fight vehemently for one side, then the other. They call themselves "Primitive Mercenaries in the Modern World" and claim to "set Humour at Humour's throat" and to "Stir up Civil War among peaceful apes." Finally, they aver they "only want Humour if it has fought like Tragedy" and "only want Tragedy if it can clench its side-muscles like hands on it's [sic] belly, and bring to the surface a laugh like a bomb." As does the first manifesto, the second in BLAST (as well as those that follow) insists on the importance of aiming for extremes. They accepted nothing marred by compromise, compromised to mediocrity, or faded into pallor. They used only what Pound called the "primary pigment" to create a more vibrant art world.

The longer pieces in BLAST are no less strident. Pound's poem "Salutation the Third" jeers at the literary critics of his day, calling them "gagged reviewers" and snarling: "HERE is the taste of my BOOT, / CARESS it, lick off the BLACKING." Ford Madox Ford's piece "The Saddest Story" later became his well-known tale The Good Soldier. The visual art challenges the viewer with bodies composed only of shadows at sharp angles, machinelike woodcuts with names like Flight, and visual meditations on modernist subjects like "Radiation." Rebecca West's "Indissoluble Matrimony" tells a rather vicious story of a husband who drowns his wife only to return home to find her "[lying] on his deathbed." An invective against the institution of marriage, West's story is both bawdy and wickedly satirical. As did all the pieces in BLAST it sought to shock its readers out of an easy complacency.

Soon, however, another force shook England (and all of Europe), which decimated a generation of England's men and dealt a deathblow to the vorticist movement. Within six months of the publishing of BLAST, England became involved in a global conflict that would claim more than 10 million lives. The BLAST artist Gaudier Brzeska enlisted with the French army. He fought with the same passion that marked BLAST's manifestos, and with little regard for his own safety. He received a decoration for bravery before being killed in the trenches in June 1915. Ford Madox Heuffer served as a lieutenant in a Welsh regiment. During the Battle of the Somme, in 1916, Ford was shell-shocked and was eventually sent home an invalid. In 1919, he changed his name to Ford Madox Ford, repudiating his German heritage.

Wyndham Lewis himself was conscripted as a British bombardier soon after the war began. His First World War service included two years spent on the western front as a battery officer from 1916 to 1918. Even BLAST's intrepid printer, William Henry Leveridge, enrolled in a volunteer regiment where he served from October 1914 until the end of the war. Needless to say, the conscription of editor, printer, and contributors slowed the production of BLAST to a near standstill. By working with Ezra Pound from afar, Lewis was able to produce one more issue of the magazine (BLAST 2) in 1915. However, that was to be the last issue.

The war ended what was best in the vorticist movement. England's apathy had been cured, but the militant fervor once admired and employed by the vorticists was replaced by a postwar weariness and a bitterness that would linger even to the outbreak of a second world war. After the war, Lewis continued to write and in these later writings commented on BLAST's literary contribution: "It cracked jokes, attached to it was a technical mumbo-jumbo to rattle and hoodwink the fashionable crowd"; he sighed, "Some recent scholarly disquisitions on 'the Vorticist aesthetic' miss the fun and haphazardness of the original." Indeed BLAST's legacy is the excitement it evokes. It is a work that is provocative, defiant, and witty. It challenges its readers to value extremes, to push themselves to the outer limits of intellectual thought, and to reach into the very center of the world's energy to produce art.

BIBLIOGRAPHY

Leveridge, Michael E. "The Printing of BLAST." Wyndham Lewis Annual 2000 (2000): 20–31.

Lewis, Wyndham. BLAST 2. Santa Rosa, Calif.: Black Sparrow Press, 2000.

————. *Blasting and Bombardiering.* Berkeley and Los Angeles: University of California Press, 1967.

Rose, R. K. "Pound and Lewis: The Crucial Years." *Agenda: Wyndham Lewis Special Issue* 7, no. 3–8, no. 1 (autumn–winter 1969–1970): 117–133.

Sala, Annamaria. "Some Notes on Vorticism and Futurism." *Agenda: Wyndham Lewis Special Issue* 7, no. 3–8, no. 1 (autumn–winter 1969–1970): 156–162.

Ann Hoff

BLUNDEN, EDMUND (1896–1974) Edmund Blunden once described himself as a "harmless young shepherd in a soldier's coat." As a poet, Blunden was a traditionalist, a pastoralist with an intense love for and knowledge of the English countryside. Blunden was decidedly not a modernist as many of his contemporaries, such as ROBERT GRAVES, were. On another level, the defining event of Blunden's life was his service as an officer during the First World War. In this role he was a shepherd to the young soldiers entrusted to his care on the western front.

Born in London on November 1, 1896, Blunden with his family moved from the city to the Kent countryside, an environment that shaped his outlook and his writing. He joined the army at age 18 in 1915 and was sent to France in the following year and stayed in France until 1918, when he was assigned to train soldiers in England. In 1920, Blunden published a collection of pastoralist poems, *The Waggoner,* and became assistant editor and writer for *Atheneum* magazine in 1920. In 1922 a collection of previously published poems was published as *The Shepherd.*

From 1924 to 1927 Blunden taught English literature at the University of Tokyo. While there he wrote *Undertones of War,* accompanied by a set of 19 (later 21) poems including "Vlamertinghe: Passing the Chateau, July 1917." A prose work, *Undertones* has been described as one of the finest poems of the war. It shares honors with SIEGFRIED SASSOON's *George Sherston Trilogy* and Robert Graves's *Goodbye to All That* as the finest accounts of life in the British army during the war. The years after his return from Japan were a busy time for Blunden; in addition to teaching, he published a collection of poems in 1930 (*The Poems of Edmund Blunden*) and another (*Poems*) 10 years later. In each case, his twin preoccupations, the war and the beauty of the countryside, were well represented. In 1931 Blunden was made a fellow of Merton College at Oxford, where he stayed until the early 1940s.

Blunden's activities and influence went beyond his own verse. In 1931 he edited an edition of WILFRED OWEN's poems; 23 years later he performed the same service for the poems of IVOR GURNEY, another soldier-poet of the First World War. As a teacher at Oxford, he tutored KEITH DOUGLAS, who would establish his own reputation as a poet during the Second World War. In addition, Blunden wrote appreciations of Clare, Keats, and Shelley. Working several years for the *Times Literary Supplement,* he wrote hundreds of reviews in the period after he left Oxford. In addition to working for the *TLS,* he published a book of poems, *Shells by a Stream* (1944), during the war and another, *After Bombing,* in 1949. Blunden returned to Japan in the late 1940s and then moved to Hong Kong, where he taught until 1960. This decade saw his last two printed collections, *A Hong Kong House: Poems 1951–1962* and *Eleven Poems* published in 1965. The 1967 death of Sassoon, Blunden's oldest and closest friend, marked the beginning of his rapid decline. At his funeral in 1974, several survivors of the First World War laid a wreath made of Flanders poppies, much like those he described in his poem about Vlamertinghe almost 60 years before.

When discussing THE GREAT WAR AND POETRY, Blunden is neither as well known nor highly regarded as others such as Owen, Graves, Sassoon, or ISAAC ROSENBERG. His style has been called archaic and very formal. He did, however, present in a sensitive and articulate way issues that were touched lightly or not at all by the other soldier-poets. He is not as sharp or direct as Sassoon and Graves but his context is wider. He sees all of war's effects, mourning the damage to the landscape as well as that done to human beings.

BIBLIOGRAPHY

Blunden, Edmund, *Overtones of War: Poems of the First World War.* London: Duckworth, 1996.

————, *Selected Poems.* Manchester, Eng.: Carcanet Press, 1982.

————. *Undertones of War.* London: Collins, 1965.

Fussell, Paul, *The Great War and Modern Memory.* New York: Oxford University Press, 1975.

Webb, Barry. *Edmund Blunden: A Biography*. New Haven, Conn.: Yale University Press, 1990.

Robert Stacy

BOER WAR (1899–1902) AND POETRY

There were two Boer wars, one from December 16, 1880, to March 23, 1881, and the second from October 11, 1899, to May 31, 1902, both between the British and the settlers of Dutch origin (called Boers, Afrikaners, or Voortrekkers) in the area that is now South Africa, which put an end to the two independent republics that they had founded, Transvaal and Orange Free State. The British made an attempt to take possession of Transvaal in 1877, but the Boers successfully resisted and secured a limited form of independence after defeating local imperial forces in a series of fights during the Transvaal Revolt or First Boer War of 1880–81.

With the discovery of gold in Transvaal, thousands of British and other settlers emmigrated to the Cape Colony. The city of Johannesburg became a poorly built town nearly overnight as the *uitlanders* (outlanders or foreigners, the name given to these settlers) poured in and settled near the mines. Though the uitlanders rapidly outnumbered the Boers, they remained a minority in the Transvaal as a whole. The Boers, irritated by the uitlanders' presence, denied them voting rights and taxed the gold industry heavily. As a response, the uitlanders and the British mine owners put pressure to overthrow the Boer government.

Transvaal's refusal to grant the uitlanders citizenship increased tension between the two sides, and the tension reached a peak when an uitlander uprising, the privately organized Jameson raid in Johannesburg, failed in 1895. Transvaal resisted British demands, with both sides preparing for war by mid-1899. When the attempt to improve rights for Britons failed, this was used to justify a major military buildup as several major British colonial leaders, the Cape Colony governor Sir Alfred Milner, British Colonial Secretary Joseph Chamberlain, and mining owners such as Alfred Beit, Barney Barnato, and Lionel Philips, favored annexation of the Boer republics. They were confident that the Boers would be quickly defeated so they tried to accelerate events to lead to war between the two sides.

War was declared on October 11, 1899, and the Boers struck first by invading Cape Colony and Natal Colony between October 1899 and January 1900. This was followed by some early Boer military successes against General Redvers Buller. The Boers were able to besiege the towns of Ladysmith, Mafeking, and Kimberley. As food began to grow scarce after a few weeks, siege life became very difficult for both the defending soldiers and the civilians in the cities of Mafeking, Ladysmith, and Kimberley. The middle of December was also very difficult for the British army. In a period known as Black Week (December 10–15, 1899), the British suffered a series of devastating losses at Magersfontein, Stormberg, and Colenso.

On February 14, 1900, British troops commanded by Field Marshal Lord Roberts began to gain ground against the Boers. Meanwhile, Buller succeeded in defeating Botha's forces north of Colenso, allowing the relief of Ladysmith the day after Cronje surrendered. Roberts then advanced into the two republics, capturing Bloemfontein, the capital of the Orange Free State, on March 13 and Pretoria, the capital of the Transvaal, on June 5, 1900.

The British believed the war to be over; however, the Boers met at a new capital of the Orange Free State, Kroonstad, and planned a guerrilla campaign to hit the British supply and communication lines. Roberts, joined by troops under the command of Buller, advanced against them and broke their last defensive position at Bergendal on August 26. Kruger sought asylum in Portuguese East Africa (modern Mozambique), as did some dispirited Boers. However, the hard core of the Boer fighters under Botha easily broke back into the Transvaal. By September 1900 the British were in control of both republics, except for the northern part of Transvaal. As a guerrilla style of warfare, the Boer commandos were sent to their own districts with the order to act against the British. The Boer commandos in the western Transvaal were very active after September 1901.

The last of the Boers surrendered in May 1902 and the war ended with the Treaty of Vereeniging in the same month. The British gave £3,000,000 to the Boers for reconstruction. The Union of South Africa was established in 1910. The treaty ended the existence of the Transvaal and the Orange Free State as Boer republics and placed them within the British Empire. In the war 75,000 people lost their lives—22,000 British soldiers, 6,000–7,000 Boer soldiers, 20,000–28,000 Boer civilians and perhaps 20,000 black Africans.

In order to analyze the poetry of this period, it would be helpful to group the poets writing on the theme of war: The first group includes the poets who glorify the war though they had not taken part in it, the second group includes the noncombatants who were against the war, and the third group includes the ordinary Tommys (the name given to English soldiers) who fought in the war, experienced the bloodshed, and wrote about the events from firsthand experience.

From the first group, Henry Newbolt's "Vitai Lampada" was typical of the war poems of the 1890s. Newbolt's poem uses the hearty rallying cry to a batter in a cricket game as his metaphor for British pluck in war: "The river of death has brimmed his banks / And England's far, and Honour a name / But the voice of a schoolboy rallies the ranks / 'Play up! play up! and play the game!'" The aim of such poetry was to fill the heart of the reader with pride and show how bravery, a bravery learned on the playing fields of the English public school, separated the Englishman from his rivals on the battlefield. The poem was hugely popular with soldiers and public alike when it was published in 1898. Alfred Austin, the new poet laureate of the country after the death of Tennyson, was another who firmly believed in England's supremacy over other nations; he showed the forces of the empire as modern knights in his poem "Alfred's Song."

But by this time a new kind of war poem was beginning to attract the attention of readers, one shaped by humanitarian opposition to war. RUDYARD KIPLING was medically unfit to enlist for the war, so he traveled to South Africa to help distribute the supplies bought with the funds raised by the song in which he popularized the everyman army figure of Tommy Atkins—a lovable rogue doing his duty for queen and country. When he witnessed the difficulties brought upon the troops through poor leadership and training in South Africa, Kipling became disillusioned with the old aggressive imperialism that had brought about the conflict.

THOMAS HARDY, too, was disappointed with the events in Transvaal because he did not support the idea of war though he did not completely disagree with the policies of the empire. Hardy went to Southampton to see the troops off. In his poem "The Departure" (later titled "Embarcation") published in the *Daily Chronicle* on October 25, 1899, he captured the emotions on the faces of the people on the ships and at the quayside—excitement mixed with foreboding. His poem "DRUMMER HODGE" is about an unnamed soldier who has died in an unknown land far away from his home as the victim of a conflict beyond his understanding. Another of Hardy's poems about the Boer War, "A Christmas Ghost-Story," was published in the *Westminster Gazette* on December 23, 1899. The ambiguous ghost could be either a Boer or a Briton. In this poem Hardy shows a commitment to ordinary, unheroic values. The ghosts of soldiers killed in battle return home proud of their deeds in war, but they come across "a senior soul-flame" who shows them that they are remembered by their loved ones because of affection, not because of their sacrifice for queen and country. Hardy, through these poems, became an early model for the poets of the Great War.

Others on the home front who were even more active against the war were William Watson, who wrote verse criticizing the policies during this war, and A(LFRED) E(DWARD) HOUSMAN, who became critical of the war after losing a brother to it. T.W.H. Crosland's poem "Slain," published in 1899, was one of the most effective critical poems of this period.

As Britain had sent soldiers who were literate to the battlefield for the first time, those who were fighting at the front were able to put their experiences down on paper. Much of the poetry was based upon the traditional army songs that went back decades, or upon Kipling's hugely popular and memorable verse. Readers were fascinated by these works, too, because though not of the highest poetic order, they resulted from firsthand experience.

BIBLIOGRAPHY
Doyle, Arthur Conan. *The Great Boer War*. London: Smith, Elder, 1900.
Farwell, Byron. *The Great Anglo-Boer War*. New York: Harper & Row, 1976.

Pakenham, Thomas. *The Boer War.* New York: Random House, 1979.

Van Wyk Smith, M. *Drummer Hodge: The Poetry of the Anglo-Boer War (1899–1902).* Oxford: Clarendon Press, 1978.

Sema Taskin

BOLAND, EAVAN (1944–)

Eavan Boland is one of the leading voices in contemporary Irish poetry. She has published many collections of poems, influenced a generation of young writers, and contributed to critical conversations about nationalism, feminism, and contemporary poetics. Although much of her work negotiates questions of Irish identity, Boland works in California, where she directs the creative writing program at Stanford University. She has also been writer in residence at Trinity College and at University College, Dublin. Currently a member of the Irish Arts Council and the Irish Academy of Letters, Boland is a regular reviewer for the *Irish Times.* Her nine books of poetry are *Against Love Poems* (2001), *The Lost Land* (1998), *An Origin Like Water: Collected Poems 1967–1987* (1996), *In a Time of Violence* (1994, winner of the Lannan Award), *Outside History: Selected Poems 1980–1990* (1990), *The Journey* (1986), *Night Feed* (1982), *In Her Own Image* (1980), and *The War Horse* (1975).

In 1995 Boland published a prose memoir, *Object Lessons: The Life of the Woman and the Poet in Our Time,* which has been influential in shaping critical conversations about the role of the poet in relation to the poetry he or she produces. All of the essays in *Object Lessons* trace the experiential implications of being simultaneously a woman and a poet in contemporary Ireland. Before Boland arrived on the scene, Ireland's literature and nationalist politics had included women in poetry primarily as symbolic objects, not as speaking subjects. That is, in Irish cultural history, particularly its literature, female figures had been presented as mere caricatures of real women. For instance, a popular caricature was the folkloric figure of the *spéirbhhean,* a young rape victim who stands for the invaded nation that must be restored to its former purity as a young virgin. In this image the woman serves a doubly limited, and limiting, role: She is useful as a sexual object to male invaders, and she is useful as a muse to male freedom fighters. Rarely were women depicted outside these oversimplified, romanticized caricatures. Often in Irish literary history even the relationship between poet and poetry was represented as a gendered dynamic between a male writer and a female muse, and this equation troubled Boland. What happens, she asked, when the poet is a woman whose vision points her away from the very idea of a passive, objectified muse? In questioning the literary association of nationalism and the female muse, Boland has challenged the parameters of Irish literary convention.

It is due in part to *Object Lessons* that Boland's name has been attached to the feminist movement, particularly to the feminist goal of theorizing the gender politics of literary canons that have excluded women as authors and as sentient voices. As her compatriot SEAMUS HEANEY, Boland is interested in exploring the influence of locale, geography, and nation on a writer's poetics. But she has also made it a point to embrace the personal experiences of real women and the domestic settings thereof. Moreover, Boland has written not just about women whose stories had been untold, but also about the women whose work as wives and mothers in 20th-century suburbs had been previously considered an inappropriate subject for poetry.

To classify some topics as more "poem-worthy" than other topics was, Boland has argued, a sort of romantic heresy. Boland believed that women's domestic suburban lives were worthy subjects indeed, and she deliberately crowded her poems with ordinary things—laundry dials, stockpots, cradles. Her poems consistently equate the mother's work of procreation with the poet's power: the female imagination. In poems about family and parenting Boland revisits the ancient tribal ideal as a repository for culture itself. For Boland the activity of child rearing is emblematic of larger cultural projects, such as the theorizing of legacy and the regenerating of human history. Of her early parenting years, Boland says, "I was there with two small children in a house and I could see what was potent and splendid and powerful happening every day in front of me and I wanted to express that."

One of the ways she has expressed the powerful splendor of the ordinary was to revisit the same ancient mythology that had excluded and distorted the experience of women. Trained as a classicist at Trinity College, Boland was well versed in the great stories of Greek legend, and she often approached her contemporary subject matter through a matter-of-fact, almost passionless subversion of a familiar myth. Boland has been married since 1969 and is the mother of two children; maternal sacrifice becomes the prompt for several poems that allude to the Ceres/Persephone myth but that repossess the myth in new ways. The most famous of these poems is "THE POMEGRANATE," in which a suburban mother meditates on the future of her teenaged daughter. In the Greek myth, a distraught mother tries to reclaim her beloved daughter. But in Boland's version of the myth, the mother wisely tries to let her daughter go.

Born in 1944 to privileged upper-class parents, Boland spent most of her childhood in New York and London. Her father was a diplomat; that meant that although he literally represented Ireland, he and his family would live abroad. At age six Boland moved with her family to London, where she experienced for the first time the anti-Irish sentiment that gave her an acute sense of political otherness. She did not return to Ireland until she was 14. When she did, she discovered that she was an outsider in her own land, and this was a realization that prompted an ongoing intellectual consideration of what it meant to be in exile. As she learned more about Irish literary history, she began questioning the exile of the sentient woman writer.

Two of Boland's essays in particular have mapped out the argument with which Boland has become associated in literary circles: "A Kind of Scar; the Woman Poet in the National Tradition" (first a LIP pamphlet in Ireland and later "Outside History" in *Object Lessons*) and "The Woman, The Place, The Poet" (*Georgia Review,* 1990). Together these essays made a case for Boland's literary project: to reclaim literary history for those women whom Irish literary history had forgotten and displaced. Specifically Boland challenged the form of Irish nationalism whose hollow rhetoric and caricatured, totemic female figures had rendered her, as a woman, "an outsider in my own national literature, cut off from its archive, at a distance from its energy."

When Boland objected that Irish literary history had fused the feminine and the national, a fusion that had resulted in an oversimplification of both, she was alluding to all of the traditional avatars for Mother Ireland, including the Cailleach Bhéarra (the beleaguered Old Mother of Irish folklore), the Sean Bhean Bhocht (the "poor old woman"), and *Cathleen ni Houlihan* (W. B. Yeats and Augusta Gregory's 1902 play, which allegorized Ireland both as the long-suffering old woman and as the beautiful young virgin, or *spéirbhean*). In all of these legends Ireland figures as a victimized old matriarch who calls upon her sons to rise up against the invader so that she might be redeemed of colonial violation and be restored to her purity once more. In this political metaphor, *purity,* a metonym for the female physical state of *virginity,* acts as a representation of Irish sovereignty. The call to restorative purity was also the call to Irish autonomy in land, language, and religion. Thus historically the Sean Bhean Bhocht had been invoked by the Irish against the hegemonic and imperialist powers of colonizing England.

Boland, deeply engaged in the many potential symbologies of maternity, was intrigued by the notion of exploring the emblematic relationship between her own feminine experience and the matriarch of her national past. Yet the Sean Bhean Bhocht of Irish lore was the ultimate projection of objectification. Ireland had represented itself as an old woman in need of a rescue, a rescue that would merely exchange one passive position for another. Boland, in her quest to reclaim the humanity and agency of this oversimplified mother figure, argued that even as mothers must be perpetually connected to their children, they must also engage in a long journey of renunciation. Mothers must let their children be who they are; they cannot expect them to be like them, or, indeed, like one another. Boland therefore criticizes a narrowly nationalist conception of a united Ireland. Her work celebrates diversity, community, and complexity. She is consistently drawn to the notion of the margin, the border space, where the untold stories of shadowy figures represent more than the melancholy failures of history. They represent the powerful transformation from personal experience into communal awareness.

Throughout Boland's work is the notion that language, a powerful weapon, can wound and scar. These wounds and scars permanently change the identity of those who suffer them. The aforementioned essay, "A Kind of Scar," borrows its title from a phrase in "Mise Éire," one of the poems in *The Journey* (1986). In the poem the speaker observes that a new language "is a kind of scar / and heals after a while / into a passable imitation / of what went before." A scar is by definition *not* what went before; it is rather the permanent sign of a wound, a visible semiotic that has been made flesh *on* flesh, a retelling of both the pain and the healing. Boland may distrust language and may recognize in its elisions and absences the many disenfranchisements of history, yet she respects its power to create and recreate experience. "I don't write a poem to express an experience," she says. "I write it to experience the experience." Her myth making is fully grounded in the experiences that have been omitted from the history of her nation. Tellingly her myth making does not oppose national history. But it does draw on, and depart from, national history. Her favorite images, the wound and the scar, reflect her vision of the body politic, not as a single unblemished entity, but as a collection of hurts.

Boland has famously said that while she considers herself a feminist, she does not consider herself a feminist poet. Boland defines feminism as a political movement and as a commitment to activism on behalf of women and men who have been marginalized by inequity. As such, feminism is an ideology, not an aesthetic. The reason Boland does not consider herself a feminist poet is that, for her, the very substance of poetry is aesthetic. Believing that poetry begins where certainty ends, she argues that her aesthetic engagement—choices toward ambiguity, darkness, memory, and symbology—is outside the purview of ethics, or ideology. She acknowledges that the distinction between *feminist* and *feminist poet* is a fine one, emphasizing that her feminism has helped her to define herself as a writer in ways she would not have been able to do otherwise; yet Boland clearly wants to preserve the epistemic space of writing the poem, the process that has neither ideology nor project. When Boland says that her feminism "stops at the margins of the poem, at the edge of the act of writing it," she is suggesting that both the writing and the reading of poetry must be more than the sum total of a political position. Her poetry occupies the very interstices she has sought to write about—the liminal space between mute images and speaking lives.

See also "The Dolls Museum in Dublin," "Fond Memory," "Mise Eire," "That the Science of Cartography Is Limited," "The War Horse," "The Women."

BIBLIOGRAPHY

Auge, Andrew. "Fracture and Wound: Eavan Boland's Poetry of Nationality." *New Hibernia Review* 8, no. 2 (summer 2004): 121–141.

Boland, Eavan. *In a Time of Violence*. New York: W. W. Norton, 1994.

———. *Object Lessons: The Life of the Woman and the Poet in Our Time*. New York: W. W. Norton, 1995.

———. *Outside History: Selected Poems 1980–1990*. New York: W. W. Norton, 1990.

Kirkpatrick, Kathryn, ed. *Border Crossings: Irish Women Writers and National Identities*. Tuscaloosa: University of Alabama Press, 2000.

Rhoda Janzen

BRATHWAITE, EDWARD KAMAU

(1930–   ) Forever compared to and held in false competition with Derek Walcott, Kamau Brathwaite (born Lawson Edward Brathwaite, later self-identified as Edward Kamau Brathwaite, and now publishing as Kamau Brathwaite) is deeply deserving of consideration in his own right. Impressively published in several disciplines and genres and recipient of major international awards and fellowships, Kamau Brathwaite has spent his poetic career developing his theory of nation language and recording it in his poetry. Deeply committed to recording the "history of the voice" that speaks in the Caribbean island nations, his poetry captures the language of the Caribbean experience.

Born in 1930 in Bridgetown, Barbados, Brathwaite was educated at Harrison University in Barbados; Pembroke College, Cambridge, from which he graduated with honors in history in 1953; and the University of Sussex, from which he earned a Ph.D. in 1968 with a dissertation titled and later published, as (Oxford University Press, 1971) *The Development of Creole Society in Jamaica 1770–1820*. He has continued to publish essays and lectures more closely affiliated with history and sociology than with literature throughout his career, including *Folk Culture of the Slaves in Jamaica* (New

Beacon, 1970), *Contradictory Omens: Cultural Diversity and Integration in the Caribbean* (Savacou, 1974), and *History of the Voice: The Development of Nation Language in Anglophone Caribbean Poetry* (New Beacon, 1984).

However, Brathwaite is known primarily for his internationally recognized poetry. He began publishing literature (short stories and poetry) and literary criticism in *Bim,* a journal edited by Frank Collymore dedicated to West Indian writing, in the 1950s, but his breakthrough in poetry occurred in 1967, with the Oxford publication of *Rights of Passage.* This volume of poetry was the first third of a trilogy eventually issued in one volume by Oxford as *The Arrivants* (1973), which draws deeply from Brathwaite's experiences as an officer in the Ministry of Education in Ghana, where he worked from 1955 to 1962. Oxford later published his Bajan trilogy, which comprised *Mother Poem* (1977), *Sun Poem* (1982), and *X/Self* (1987). He has earned from his poetic efforts the Cholmondely Prize (1970), Guggenheim Fellowships (1972 and 1983), a Fulbright Fellowship (1983), and the Neustadt International Prize for Literature (1994).

Always Brathwaite's poetry seeks to encode within it a distinctly Caribbean or Bajan experience, and he seems to agree with Orlando Patterson that Sisyphus supplies the appropriate mythos here: The experience is characterized by progress followed by setback. Nowhere is this more apparent to Brathwaite than in the colonial educational system. In *Sun Poem* he writes that "to learn was a / wave up the slope of the beach and slipping back down to dark water." Pleased that the formerly enslaved inhabitants of the islands receive schooling, he lambastes the educational system for what it does and does not teach the children. He has lamented on several occasions that "the hurricane does not howl in pentameters," yet the literature offered him as part of his colonial education in Barbados included nothing but British writers. He has pointed out in "English in the Caribbean" (1979) the paradox that he and his classmates learned more "about English kings and queens than . . . about our own national heroes," that they can recite poetry about snow but not about hurricanes. Brathwaite's poetry calls the schools factories, prisons, and cells; desks become gas chambers, and students are the "black hostage[s] / of verbs" under

the tutelage of "Chalkstick the teacher" (in *Mother Poem*).

In order to break free of the limiting and insufficient language taught to them, Brathwaite encourages peoples of the Caribbean to use what he terms nation language. Detailed in *The History of the Voice,* nation language is essentially what the people actually speak, a mixture of English and patois strongly influenced by African models of language and by the African aspects of their experiences. "It may be in English," Brathwaite writes, "but often it is in an English which is like a howl, or a shout, or a machine-gun, or the wind, or a wave." Unrecognized by the colonial authorities, this particular language has been submerged and unrecorded in the written records of the Caribbean; therefore there are no authorities to which Brathwaite can refer in this history. Instead he urges his (Caribbean) readers to create their own authorities.

Creating an authoritative, published record of this language has been one of Brathwaite's most profound achievements in his poetry. He has identified *X/Self* as his "biggest effort" in inscribing nation language. In this poetry collection the Caribbean protagonist writes a letter in the poem "X/Self's Xth Letters from the Thirteen Provinces" (which appears in the 1992 collection *Middle Passages* as "Letter Sycorax"), a poem Brathwaite identified as entirely in nation language. X/Self writes this letter "guess what! pun a computer o / kay?" Despite the success inherent in using a computer to write, however, X/Self still laments the inadequacy of the written word to approximate his speech and, more importantly, his thoughts. While he fears that he cannot "get nutten really rite," he actually achieves an important milestone, in that he accurately records his voice.

Having recorded the voice of the Caribbean in nation language, Brathwaite further celebrates his linguistic breakthrough with *SHAR: Hurricane Poem* (1990) by uncovering the "syllabic intelligence" in which to record the voice of the hurricane, perhaps the most defining experience of the Caribbean and the one that he frequently lamented was inexplicable within the confines of the English language. In this poem, Brathwaite employs a technique he identified at a conference in his honor in 1992 as "video poetics" and in

Middle Passages (1992) as "Sycorax video style." His video poetics relies upon varying fonts and formats, especially unusually large character size, available on personal computers (Brathwaite's own computer is named Sycorax), to add visual and rhythmic emphasis to the sounds in the poetry. To read *Shar* is visually and orally to sense the rhythms of the hurricane, inspired by hurricane Gilbert, which, in 1988, ripped the roof off Brathwaite's Jamaican home and instigated a mud slide that damaged his personal library.

Still writing and affiliated with the Comparative Literature Department of New York University, Brathwaite has more recently published *Roots* (University of Michigan Press, 1993); *Dream Stories* (Longman, 1994); *Words Need Love Too* (House of Nehesi, 2000); *Ancestors,* a longer, revised version of the Bajan Trilogy (New Directions, 2001); and *Born to Slow Horses* (Wesleyan Poetry, 2005).

BIBLIOGRAPHY
Brathwaite, Kamau. *Roots.* Ann Arbor: University of Michigan Press, 1993.
Brown, Stewart, ed. *The Art of Kamau Brathwaite.* Brigend, Wales: Seren, 1995.
World Literature Today 68, no. 4 (autumn 1994). Special issue devoted to Kamau Brathwaite.

Michelle DeRose

"BREAK OF DAY IN THE TRENCHES"
ISAAC ROSENBERG (1916) "Break of Day in the Trenches" was written from the battlefield trenches in France in June 1916. ISAAC ROSENBERG's ironic skepticism is apparent from the opening of the poem. The beginning of day, so often associated with new life and opportunities, opens instead on another day in which violence and death are everywhere. As is true in much of Rosenberg's war poetry, the horrors of war are much more understated than they are in the works of many of the other poets of World War I. This understated quality in fact makes the process of war all the more horrific. It is as if Rosenberg has become so inured to death and trench life that events that would horrify the average person pass almost unnoticed.

Such an attitude appears in the image of the rat, for instance. Unlike the average person, who would be terrified and disgusted if a rat ran over his or her hand, Rosenberg seems unconcerned. Rats are so common in that environment that Rosenberg does not think twice about its appearance. More important, though, because of their association with death, the prevalence of the rats in the trenches is a constant reminder of death's ever-present possibility. In the Judeo-Christian world, human beings are believed to be the highest of God's creatures, while creatures like rats are among the lowest. In this poem, however, their roles are largely reversed. The rat even becomes a creature to be envied. As Rosenberg notes, the rat has a freedom of movement denied the human beings, who are trapped below ground and forced to live like rats in burrows but who cannot leave these burrows, burrows that often become their coffins. Furthermore the rat, this perceived lowly creature, has a longer life expectancy than do the humans; as Rosenberg remarks to the rat, the men are "less chanced than you for life." While under normal circumstances the men's life expectancy would be many times that of a rat, in this world of violence and death it is a fraction of what it would be otherwise. The rat's "cosmopolitan sympathies" also becomes a crucial element in the poem. On the one hand, the rat demonstrates the basic similarity of the English and German soldiers. To the rat, they are the same, and thus, Rosenberg implies, perhaps there is in fact no difference between them—no difference worth killing one another over in any case. The rat's "cosmopolitan sympathies," though, signify something even more chilling. In the rat's very indifference to the English and German soldiers, Rosenberg emphasizes the profound indifference of the natural world to the human world and to human suffering and tragedy.

In this poem Rosenberg's is an utterly modernist view of the universe in which no Judeo-Christian God watches over the welfare of humanity. This absence of God had already been implied earlier in the poem when Rosenberg referred to its being "the same old Druid Time as ever"—thus the Judeo-Christian worldview is not in effect in the world of the trenches. This world moves to a different time altogether from that of the Judeo-Christian world. Also underscoring the indifference of the natural world in the poem is Rosenberg's description of the landscape between the opposing armies: "the sleeping green between." This lyric representation sounds more like a pastoral scene than a battlefield and shows the separation between the human and natural worlds. The descriptive term *sleeping* adds to this effect, suggesting not just normal sleep but also death, the sleep from which one never wakes.

The indifference of nature is further reinforced by references to the poppy. The poppy, along with the rat, is a crucial image in the poem, and one of its primary roles is as an image of natural beauty that contrasts with the death and destruction of war. The very fact that poppies appear in the midst of this environment demonstrates the separation between the natural world and the human world. In addition, Rosenberg refers to "poppies whose roots are in man's veins," thus showing not only a separation and indifference to the human world in general but to human suffering in particular since Rosenberg implies that the poppies gain their sustenance from the ground of the battlefields, a ground into which human blood freely flows. Similarly poppies are traditionally images commemorating the dead, and this role runs throughout the background of the poem as they remind the reader of the numerous lives lost and yet to be lost. The poppies also become associated with the soldiers themselves, not connecting the human and naturals worlds but rather, as in the reversal of roles that occurs with the rat, minimizing the usual high place of human beings in the Judeo-Christian world by making the men of no more import than poppies that "drop, and are ever dropping." The men, like the poppies, are dropping around Rosenberg. After the attack, his poppy behind his ear, like his own life, is safe—for the moment, although the dust that whitens the poppy (and presumably himself as well) shows just how tentative such safety is. "Break of Day in the Trenches" is Isaac Rosenberg's most famous poem, and its controlled narrative detachment and profound statement about the nature of human existence make it one of the most important commentaries on life in World War I.

BIBLIOGRAPHY

Liddiard, Jean. *Isaac Rosenberg: The Half Used Life.* London: Victor Gollancz, 1975.

Maccoby, Deborah. *God Made Blind: Isaac Rosenberg, His Life and Poetry.* Northwood, Eng.: Symposium Press, 1999.

John Peters

BRIDGES, ROBERT (1844–1930) Robert Seymour Bridges was born on October 23, 1844, in the village of Walmer, in the county of Kent, England. He was sent to school at Eton and then to Corpus Christi College, Oxford. It was during his time at Oxford University that Bridges became good friends with Gerard Manley Hopkins. The two remained in contact after their university education, and Bridges was later to edit and publish Hopkins's complete poetic works in 1918, 30 years after the death of his friend, thereby allowing Hopkins, relatively unknown as a poet until then, to achieve the reputation he has had ever since.

Following his university education, Bridges worked as a medical doctor at St. Bartholomews, Great Ormond Street, and at the Great Northern Hospitals in London. Upon his retirement in 1882, he moved to Yattendon in the countryside. He married Monica Waterhouse in 1884; with her he had three children, Elizabeth, Margaret, and Edward. Elizabeth became a poet herself; most of her work was published under her married name of ELIZABETH DARYUSH.

Bridges's first book of poetry was published in 1873, and *The Growth of Love,* a collection of sonnets, followed in 1876. He was always interested in prosody and published two works on the subject: *Milton's Prosody* (1893) and *John Keats* (1895). Bridges was not particulary well known during his lifetime, yet his contribution to English poetry was significant. Not only was he responsible for publishing the work of Hopkins; he also cofounded the Society for Pure English, together with Walter Raleigh and Henry Bradley, and was made poet laureate in 1913. The work generally considered to be his greatest is his *Testament of Beauty* (1929), a philosophical poem on the evolution of the human soul. In this work he continued his experiment with a meter based on syllables rather than on accents, which has first appeared in his collection of 1925: *New Verse.* His poem "LONDON SNOW" has also become a landmark of English literature. Some of his poems were set to music by such composers as Hubert Parry, Gustav Holst, and Gerald Finzi. After moving to Yattendon upon his retirement, Bridges remained in rural seclusion there and then at Boar's Hill, Oxford, where he died on April 21, 1930. He is buried in Yattendon.

BIBLIOGRAPHY
Catherine Phillips: *Robert Bridges: A Biography*. Oxford:
    Oxford University Press, 1992.

Wendy Skinner

BROOKE, RUPERT (CHAWNER) (1887–1915)

Called by W. B. YEATS "the most handsome man in England," Rupert Brooke was born on August 3, 1887, the second son of the housemaster of School Field, Rugby, and his wife, Ruth Cotterill, in Rugby, Warwickshire. His father taught classics at Rugby School, and as a child Brooke was immersed in English poetry, twice winning the school poetry prize. In 1906 he entered King's College, Cambridge, and became friends with G. E. Moore, Lytton Strachey, Maynard Keynes, Roger and Leonard Fry, and other members of the future Bloomsbury Group.

In 1910, upon his father's sudden death, Brooke became a deputy housemaster at Rugby for a short time, later giving it up to subsist on an allowance from his mother. In 1909 he became a full member of the Fabian Society. During 1911 he worked on a thesis on the playwright John Webster and Elizabethan drama; spent the spring in Munich, Germany; and traveled Italy. In England he was known as a leader of a group of young "Neo-pagans," who slept and swam naked outdoors, embracing a religion based on nature. Over the course of 1911, despite his secret engagement to Noel Olivier, a schoolgirl six years his junior, Brooke embarked on a love relationship with Ka Cox, a fellow Fabian committee member. In 1912, Ka Cox gave birth to a stillborn child. From 1913 to 1914 Brooke wandered through North America and the South Seas and depicted his impressions in his *Letters from America* (1916). He spent three months on Tahiti, wrote some of his finest poems there, and had an affair with a local woman, commemorated in "Tiare Tahiti."

Returning to England he strengthened his friendship with Winston Churchill and the Asquith family. At the outbreak of World War I, Brooke took a commission in Churchill's Royal Navy division. He joined the Dardanelles expedition but did not see any action. He died of septicemia as a result of a mosquito bite—or, according to some sources, of food poisoning—on a hospital ship off Skyros Island in the Aegean Sea on April 23, 1915. He was buried on the island, his early death mourned publicly by prominent figures like Henry James and Winston Churchill, then First Lord of the Admiralty.

Brooke's entire reputation as a war poet rests on only five "war sonnets" while his actual war experience consisted of one day of limited military action with the Hood Battalion during the evacuation of Antwerp. Consequently, his "war sonnets" resonate with generalized sentiments on themes like the purpose of existence and romantic death—reflecting the mindset of many (but not all) young Englishmen in 1914. They exhibit an enthusiasm that most soldiers and poets eventually lost. Another poet, CHARLES HAMILTON SORLEY, severely critical of those who sentimentalized the war, said of Brooke's poetry, "He has clothed his attitudes in fine words: but he has taken the sentimental attitude." Sorley too was killed in 1915, so he did not live to see the brutal poetry of WILFRED OWEN, SIEGFRIED SASSOON, and ISAAC ROSENBERG. Some critics doubt that Brooke would have written the sonnets or continued to write other poems in a similar vein later in the war.

Brooke was acclaimed at first as the "war poet" who inspired patriotic enthusiasm in the early months of the Great War; however, it is not easy to imagine how Brooke's poetry would have changed in theme, tone, and imagery had he lived through the war. Critics like JON STALLWORTHY note that "England at that time needed a focal point for its griefs, ideals and aspirations," and the public valedictory in the *Times* (April 26, 1915) by Winston Churchill, the First Lord of the Admiralty, acknowledged the symbolic role of poet/bard that Brooke had assumed—that of FRANCES CORNFORD's "young Apollo, golden haired." The symbolism and sentiment surrounding his persona eventually evolved into his enduring myth of the young and beautiful fallen warrior of classical and romantic tradition.

Brooke's popular appeal began to wane after the publication of Siegfried Sassoon's hard-hitting depiction of the war's reality and the poems of Wilfred Owen (1893–1918), who was killed in the trenches barely a week before the war ended. In France writers returning home from the horrors of trench warfare created such artistic and literary movements as dada and SURREALISM.

In England the neoromanticism of Brooke and his fellow poets was replaced by the nausea and despair of the modernists and T. S. ELIOT's expression of meaninglessness in *The Waste Land.* Brooke's chivalry became a literary anachronism and he is now chiefly valued for his lighter verse and for the Tahiti poems, while his "war sonnets" are generally held up as examples of the initial naiveté of the establishment at the beginning of World War I.

See also "GRANTCHESTER," "THE SOLDIER."

BIBLIOGRAPHY

Cross, Tim. *The Lost Voices of World War I.* London: Bloomsbury, 1988.

Delany, P. *The Neo-Pagans: Friendship and Love in the Rupert Brooke Circle.* London: Macmillan, 1987.

Hale, Keith, ed. *Friends and Apostles: The Correspondence of Rupert Brooke and James Strachey 1905–1914.* New Haven, Conn., and London: Yale University Press, 1998.

Hassall, Christopher Vernon. *Rubert Brooke: A Biography.* 1964. London: Faber and Faber, 1972.

Lehmann, John. *Rupert Brooke, His Life and His Legend.* London: Weidenfield, 1980.

Marsh, Edward. *The Collected Poems, by Rupert Brooke with an Introduction by Gavin Ewart.* London: Macmillan, 1992.

Silken, Jon, ed. *The Penguin Book of First World War Poetry.* London: Penguin, 1981.

Divya Saksena

BROWN, GEORGE MACKAY (1921–1996)

To understand George Mackay Brown's art, the reader must appreciate its deep rootedness in the poet's place of birth. Orkney looms large in all of his writings, its lore, language, history, and myth, providing Brown with most of the material he used in his 50 years as a professional writer. Brown was born and lived all his life in Stromness, a small town on Mainland, the largest of the Orkney Islands, situated off the northern coast of Scotland. Except for his student years at Newbattle Abbey and Edinburgh University, as a protégé of EDWIN MUIR, Brown rarely left Orkney. He returned time and again to the matter of Orkney as inspiration for his work, often evoking its Viking heritage and the influence of the mysterious Neolithic settlers who predated the Norsemen. The other abiding influence on his work is his Roman Catholicism—he converted at the age of 40, after years of reflection.

Brown's background was poor. His father, John Brown, was a postman, and his mother, Mhairi Mackay Brown, worked in a hotel. Brown attended the local school, Stromness Academy, where he discovered his talent for writing in the weekly "compositions" set by his English teacher. A bout of tuberculosis ended his schooling and led to his becoming a writer, since he was scarcely fit for a regular job. From the early 1940s, he earned a living as a professional writer, often publishing his work in the local newspaper, for which he continued to write until a week before his death.

Brown's first verse publication, *Loaves and Fishes,* appeared in 1959. It set the tone for the volumes that followed at regular intervals for the next 35 years. He considers, in traditional verse forms, the lives of the islanders, focusing on the rituals and rhythms of the seasons as experienced by the Orcadian farmers and fishermen among whom he made his living. A later volume celebrates them explicitly in its title, *Fishermen with Ploughs.* Just as Brown saw himself in the traditional mold of the "maker," the poet who was an intrinsic part of the community, so his vision of the world celebrated the timeless nature of rural life on Orkney's islands in poetry untouched by the influence of his more experimental contemporaries.

A typical poem from this early collection is "Elegy," in which Brown interweaves the rituals of the agricultural calendar with those of the Christian faith. The opening stanza illustrates much of the essence of Brown's art:

> The Magnustide long swords of rain
>   Quicken the dust. The ploughman turns
>   Furrow by holy furrow
>   The liturgy of April.
>   What rock of sorrow
>   Checks the seed's throb and flow
> Now the lark's skein is thrown
>   About the burning sacrificial hill?

The use of *Magnustide* for "spring" not only locates the poem in Orkney, where the medieval cathedral of St. Magnus dominates the capital town of Kirkwall, but also evokes the peculiarly Scandinavian ambience of the place. The ploughman's work is expressed in religious terms, and the reference to the seed introduces a central image in Brown's work. The sower and the seed, with its obvious Christian connotations, was a defining concept in Brown's work. As he said himself, it "seemed to illuminate the whole of life for me . . . from the most primitive breaking of the soil to Christ himself with his parables of agriculture and the majestic symbolism of his passion, death and resurrection."

The rich Viking heritage of the Orkney islands—which were in Norway's possession until 1470—is a constant presence in Brown's work. The raw material offered by the medieval *Orkneyinga Saga* is sensitively exploited by Brown in many of his best poems, and at greater length in his novel *Magnus.* One of his later poems, "Tryst on Egilsay," demonstrates his narrative gift and his ability to evoke the harsh world of the ancient earls. The poem uses first-person voices to retell the story of the martyrdom of Magnus at the hands of his cousin Hakon. Here Hakon reveals his ambition:

> This can never be good, a cloven earldom.
> Bad governance, the folk
> Fallen into faction, insolence, orisons.
> I too would have a sheaf carved on the lintel.
> Therefore to Egilsay we have sailed,
> The prows of my eight ships beaked like falcons.

This shows a mature Brown, no longer reliant on rhyme, but still strongly attached to the powerfully rhythmic and alliterative tradition of the ancient bards. To read George Mackay Brown is to experience an uncompromising vision of island life. His autobiography is entitled *For the Islands I Sing,* and although he will always be associated with his beloved Orkney, his work has a quiet authority that will ensure it is appreciated far beyond those shores.

BIBLIOGRAPHY

Bevan, Archie, and Brian Murray, eds. *The Collected Poems of George Mackay Brown.* London: John Murray, 2005.

Bold, Alan. *George Mackay Brown.* Edinburgh: Oliver and Boyd, 1978.

Fergusson, Maggie. *George Mackay Brown: The Life.* London: John Murray, 2006.

Murray, Rowena, and Brian Murray. *Interrogation of Silence: The Writings of George Mackay Brown.* London: John Murray, 2004.

Spear, Hilda, ed. *George Mackay Brown—a Survey of His Work and a Full Bibliography.* Lampeter, Eng.: Edward Mellen Press, 2000.

Rob Spence

BUNTING, BASIL (1900–1985)

BUNTING, BASIL (1900–1985) Sailor, conscientious objector, diplomat, and intelligence agent, the modernist poet Basil Bunting lived a life of extraordinary adventure. As Bunting's autobiographical long poem *Briggflatts* (1965) suggests, however, no events in his life defined him as consummately as his encounters with language and his sustained conversations with living and dead peers about how best to approach the world. The title of the poem—the name of a historically important small Quaker community in northern England that was home to his young lover—situates Bunting as a Northumbrian sympathetic to the dissenting Quaker worldview.

Bunting grew up amid the coal mining culture of the North. His mother was the daughter of a coal-mine manager, and his father—a histologist who compared animals' lymph glands in his free time—made a living as a physician for local coal miners. From his father, Bunting learned to attend to the concrete specificity of organic forms and to appreciate the music of one of his Northumbrian artistic precursors, William Wordsworth. Bunting was first exposed to Quaker silence, wherein, in Makin's words, one can "hear what [one does] not already know" (209), when his parents sent him to a Quaker boarding school. There hidden behind bookshelves, he discovered a book of poetry by Walt Whitman. Whitman's influence informs *Briggflatts* in the "recurrencies" and "variety" of vowel and consonant sounds that Quartermain says knit words into far richer song than the verse produced by invariable British meter.

In 1919 after a punishing year in prison for refusing to fight in World War I—details of which appear in his first sonata, *Villon* (1925)—Bunting discovered his mentor, EZRA POUND. Pound's work confirmed Bunting's conviction that poems ought chiefly to be musical compositions. Pound further contributed to Bunting's poetics by encouraging him to develop his craft by translating and juxtaposing different poetries. In the years between the wars, Bunting learned Persian, so he could read the 10th-century Persian poet Firdosi's epic; completed inventive translations of poetry; and, adopting the ode as his trademark short form because of its association with song and another musical form, the sonata, as his long form, experimented with lyric form, rhythm, and sound. After service in Iran, during World War II and afterward—as interpreter, intelligence officer, and journalist—and 13 years of silence during which he was unable to secure any but the most tedious of newspaper jobs, Bunting produced his modernist masterpiece, *Briggflatts*.

Bunting would insist that *Briggflatts* is an aural composition created by carefully arranging the multifarious consonant and vowel sounds, to which he danced for an entire life, into short, rhythmic lines. *Briggflatts* is the account of a Northumbrian poet taking his own measure by way of comparison and contrast with past and present alternative selves. Among those alternative selves are a host of Northumbrian seekers, including sixth- and seventh-century Welsh war poets, saints from the Celtic Catholic Church, rats, lizards, a marauding murdered 10th-century Viking, and a 20th-century stone mason from the Quaker town of Briggflatts.

See also "THE COMPLAINT OF THE MORPETHSHIRE FARMER."

BIBLIOGRAPHY

Bunting, Basil. *Complete Poems.* New York: New Directions Books, 2000.

Forde, Victoria. *The Poetry of Basil Bunting.* Newcastle upon Tyne, Eng.: Bloodaxe Books, 1991.

Makin, Peter. *Bunting: The Shaping of His Verse.* Oxford: Clarendon Press, 1992.

Quartermain, Peter. "'To Make Glad the Heart of Man': Bunting, Pound and Whitman." In *Sharp Study and Long Toil,* edited by Richard Caddel and Peter Lewis, *Durham University Journal* special issue (March 1995), 54–70.

Robin Calland

"BYZANTIUM" WILLIAM BUTLER YEATS (1933)

"Byzantium," drafted in 1930 and published in W. B. YEATS's 1933 collection *The Winding Stair and Other Poems,* is a response to T. Sturgis Moore's criticism of "Sailing to Byzantium." Yeats's second poem about the holy city that was the seat of the Eastern Roman Empire exalts the unity of being he finds in Byzantium during the reign of Justinian in the sixth century. The verses also attempt to do in words what Eastern Orthodox iconography does in paint, that is, to express the ineffable in a way that manifests the presence of unspeakable mystery in the physical world while communicating its existence beyond the mundane. In *A Vision,* Yeats's treatise on the cycles of history, he discusses Byzantium as a place in which the ideal union, or coinherence, of opposites existed briefly. The capital city for him is a place in time and simultaneously beyond time, at least for the moment during which Hagia Sofia was built; the city was then a whole, poised in a perfection that is necessary to but also alien to the human condition around it.

The speaker of "Sailing to Byzantium" longs to be gathered into unchanging eternity and expresses his desire in the first person, as if he were having a vision of what is to come. The speaker of "Byzantium," in contrast, sees the metropolis that epitomizes the conjunction of the temporal and the eternal as an entity in his line of sight. The "unpurged images" of the opening line hint at perfection: They are sufficient to themselves and require no artist to present them. These forms are neither natural nor shaped but exist in undisputable simplicity. The immediate temporal setting of the poem suggests a time that is neither one thing nor another. Twilight is not day and not night but mixes the two seamlessly. Midnight can be blindingly bright, almost like daylight, during the full moon, which is Phase 1 in the system of *A Vision,* or it can be completely dark, the opposite of daylight, during the new moon, which is Phase 15 in Yeats's scheme of history. Both phases are as near to perfection as anything human can hope to be, and Byzantium belongs in both categories. Similarly the "starlit or moonlit dome" of line 5 can be the ceiling of Hagia Sofia or the sky itself. It can be both, coinciding mysteriously in the holy place that is an emblem of the unified civilization that built it. This mystery and the cupola itself have an impervious simplicity beyond the complexities that have troubled the speaker of the poem. Also, in the opening stanza, the images of the "cathedral gong" and the "night-walkers' song" hint at the coexistence of opposites like the religious and the worldly and suggest that the two may be necessary to the whole, just as Crazy Jane tells the bishop that fair and foul are near relations that need each other.

Likewise the mummy of the second stanza is neither a physical being nor a specter but a miracle of immortality in itself, a preserved body removed from the confusion found in day-to-day fleshly living. The mummy may be the form the body takes when it is out of time, the form the speaker of "Sailing to Byzantium" seeks. The golden bird of stanza 3 of "Byzantium" is the golden bird of the fourth stanza of Yeats's first Byzantium poem. Some believe that the bird, even though it is artificial, represents the speaker's soul, and like the mummy, the bird is a miracle since it looks like a living bird in spite of its immortality. A further representation of immortality is the flame in stanza 4, which is the holy fire of "Sailing to Byzantium"; its gold is not of human creation. The fire, which the background of Byzantine mosaics recreate, burns eternally without human intervention. It will not harm the body as an ordinary fire does, but it can purge the human person. The dance, for Yeats, is a symbol of purgation since it represents the unity of actor and action. That which is utterly itself, such as the images of the first line, has no need of purification, but that which is complex must be refined to attain and experience perfection.

The final stanza of "Byzantium" implies that however attractive stasis is to human beings, it is not possible in a world of flesh and blood for anyone to remain in that perfection. People must return to the arena of human endeavor with all its unattractive confusion and artistic artificiality, which the poem calls "the gong-tormented sea." The sea, a traditional symbol of life, intimates the variety and chaos of the human condition, and the gong, the call of immortality, no longer offers the comfort it did in the first stanza of the poem. Here the gong reminds the speaker of his unattainable goal, remaining in the unity of Byzantium while still alive. At the end of the second poem, the speaker sails away from the holy city he had crossed the sea to visit because he cannot yet enter fully into quiet, refined perfection.

One of the ways in which "Byzantium" delineates the stasis that Yeats equates with perfection is through a paucity of verbs: Verbals occur throughout the work to give the impression of movement. In addition to repeating the images of "Sailing to Byzantium," the second poem contains verbal repetition; the words *complexity* and *blood,* for example, each occur three times in the course of the poem. Recurring words imply the timelessness of ritual, which seems never to change. The patterned words and images of "Byzantium" become a mosaic that represents and evokes the mystery of unity of being, and this poem, like the Byzantine liturgy, is a mystery that is easily seen but not entirely apprehended.

BIBLIOGRAPHY

Ellmann, Richard. *The Identity of Yeats.* London: Macmillan, 1954.

Masson, David I. "Word and Sound in Yeats' 'Byzantium.'" *ELH* 20 (1953): 136–160.

O'Donnell, William H. *The Poetry of William Butler Yeats: An Introduction.* New York: Ungar, 1986.

Porter, Kevin J. "The Rhetorical Problem of Eternity in Yeats' Byzantium Poems." *Yeats-Eliot Review* 4 (1996): 10–17.

Stallworthy, Jon. *Vision and Revision in Yeats' Last Poems.* Oxford: Clarendon Press, 1969.

Karen Rae Keck

C

CAMPBELL, ROY (1901–1957) Roy Campbell was born to a prominent family in Durban, Natal, South Africa: His grandfather had helped to found the city, and his physician father had fought in the Zulu War. Campbell's immediate surroundings were elite, yet South Africa's rugged lands, on which he hunted and rode horses, also shaped him. He later reflected this upbringing in his reactionary attitude toward other writers and intellectuals, as well as in his physical exploits, which included bullfighting, working as a deckhand on a whaler, and serving in the British army during World War II. Poetically Campbell cultivated a sense of tradition, an ethos of aristocratic excellence, and an admired technical control. However, these qualities also earned the poet his detractors. The American poet John Ciardi decried his "storm-trooper arrogance," along with the "violence" of his verse and its worldview. His mind and style, Ciardi opines, "is all sledgehammers."

Certainly Campbell was never mistaken for a quiet poet. The publication of his first work, *The Flaming Terrapin* (1924), with its exuberant, visionary tone, shocked a poetry world still pessimistic after World War I. With mythic daring the 23-year-old poet imagined a giant tortoise pulling Noah's ark through the flooded world. The animal's "stormy back" maintained the "clean / System of active things" that eventually bred "men who do great deeds." The poem, whose characters also include "old Plutocracy" and "Patriotism," allegorically represented modern lassitude, and

he attributed its rhetorical vigor to the influence of the Zulu language. Campbell's classmates had nicknamed their energetic peer "Zulu" shortly after he entered Oxford University in 1918; his friend WYNDHAM LEWIS would variously depict Campbell's memorable personality in his fiction. At Oxford Campbell studied French poets such as Baudelaire and English Renaissance writers. He also visited Paris and Provence in the early 1920s, further discovering Rimbaud and Valéry. These writers, and places, were to exert profound influence on Campbell's writing. He married the art student Mary Garman in 1922, although his father thought him impulsive and temporarily withheld financial support. The newlyweds had to live more austerely in northern Wales, where Campbell wrote *The Flaming Terrapin,* even as the couple's first daughter was born. He nevertheless managed to take part in London's literary scene, befriending EDITH SITWELL and T. S. ELIOT. Despite their very different poetic styles and temperaments, Campbell found in Eliot a kindred spirit. Reviewing his work in 1926, Campbell praised his "powerful mind," which (as he saw it) condemned the "drifting industrialised herds" and "sham ideals of the crowds."

Campbell also had a penchant for making enemies. After returning with his family to South Africa, in 1926 he cofounded the magazine *Voorslag* (Whiplash). However, it provoked many readers, and Campbell shortly left his native country in disgust. *The Wayzgoose* emerged from this disappointing homecoming, and the satire's couplets skewer alleged provincialism—"In fair Banana Land we lay our scene," begins the poem in mock-archaism. Campbell published the poem only in 1928, after he had returned to England. Unfortunately he was just as disenchanted there. Despite benefiting from the kindness of writers and literati such as Sir Harold Nicolson and Virginia Sackville-West, Campbell found their sophistication, affluence, and socialist sympathies to be intolerable. He sneers in a 1928 essay at the honest, homely Georgian writers, whom he dubbed "prophets of Domestic Comfort," while one epigram denigrates "all the clever people" of the Bloomsbury circle. With a second child now in tow, Campbell moved his family again, this time to Provence.

Campbell responded better, personally and professionally, to southern Europe. He purged his English bitterness in another satirical poem, *The Georgiad* (1931), which followed the publication of *Adamastor*, a more lyrical volume featuring "The Zulu Girl," "Autumn," and other poems for which Campbell is best known. The American poet and critic Allen Tate praised their "genuine center of feeling," previously unknown in Campbell's work, and the "lucidity" the author sought is also apparent in his next volume, *Flowering Reeds* (1933). Clearly at home in Provence, Campbell found inspiration in the native poet Mistral, as well as in his beloved French poets. He also published the prose works *Taurine Provence* (1932) and *Broken Record* (1932), his first autobiography, which reveals a knack for self-promotion and narrative exaggeration. The Campbells moved to Spain and converted to Roman Catholicism in 1935. (A falling out with neighbors necessitated their leaving Provence.) Toledo's severe beauty, made famous by El Greco, and strong tradition of Catholic mysticism heightened Campbell's spirituality, as reflected in the poetry of *Mithraic Emblems* (1936). The outbreak of the Spanish Civil War further intensified these feelings: The poem "Hot Rifles" speaks of Toledo as now "hammered on the Cross"; the sacred city now suffers at the hands of Leftist aggressors.

Their lives regularly endangered, the Campbells endured the political "Terror" that overtook Spain. As he tells it, Campbell protected the Carmelite archives, including the works of the order's patron, St. John of the Cross, when militiamen burned the nearby monastery and killed 17 monks. Campbell vowed to translate the saint's rapturous mystical poetry if saved from the strife. Eventually he rendered these poems with ease, "as if I were being helped," and they proved to be among his most popular translations, along with versions of Baudelaire. He and his family escaped to England, though Campbell returned as a war correspondent in 1937. He became convinced that Franco's nationalist forces were defending a noble feudal Christian tradition against communism, and he defended them by writing *Flowering Rifle* (1939), an epic poem that stridently recounts the fight for Spain. The English poet STEPHEN SPENDER, who as most writers did favored the republican side, said the poem made him "feel physically sick." Although reactionary by nature, Campbell in later years may have regretted his more extreme views. In his epic he defended Franco's killing of the poet Federico García Lorca, yet later he translated Lorca's verse and wrote an appreciative critical study (1952). He chose not to include *Flowering Rifle* in his first volume of *Collected Poems* (1949): it was reprinted only posthumously, in revised form.

Following Franco's victory, Campbell lived again in Toledo from 1939 to 1941, after which he served the British cause in World War II as an air-raid warden and soldier. (His knowledge of African languages benefited the Allied forces.) The trench slang of *Talking Bronco* (1946), comprising mainly war poems, fails to conceal a general diminishment in Campbell's poetic powers. However, he still succeeds in his elegiac sonnet to the great Portuguese poet Luis de Camões, who also "Wrestled hardships into forms of beauty." After the war Campbell worked in England as a journalist, lecturer, translator, and producer for the BBC. *Light on a Dark Horse* (1951), his second autobiography, was stronger than the first and well received. The Campbells moved in 1952 to a farm in Portugal, where they lived and worked happily. In 1957 he oversaw a second volume of *Collected Poems* and completed *Portugal*, a literary survey. Campbell was intermittently at work on a history of the Spanish Civil War, "to correct the Kremlin-crazy liars in England." Returning from Holy Week in Toledo and Seville, the Campbells suffered a blown-out tire in southern Portugal, which caused an accident fatal to the poet. A third volume of *Collected Poems* was published in 1960.

BIBLIOGRAPHY

Alexander, Peter. *Roy Campbell: A Critical Biography.* Oxford: Oxford University Press, 1982.

Campbell, Roy. *Collected Works.* Edited by Peter Alexander, Michael Chapman, and Marcia Leveson. 4 vols. Craighall, South Africa: Ad. Donker, 1985–88.

Ciardi, John. "Muscles and Manners." *Nation* 181, no. 24 (December 1955): 515–516.

Parsons, D. S. J. "Roy Campbell." In *Dictionary of Literary Biography.* Vol. 20, *British Poets, 1914–1945,* edited by Donald E. Stanford, 92–102. Detroit: Gale Research, 1983.

Smith, Rowland. *Lyric and Polemic: The Literary Personality of Roy Campbell.* Montreal: McGill-Queen's University Press, 1972.

Tate, Allen. "Roy Campbell's Poetry." *New Republic* 66 (March 1931): 133.

Brett Foster

"CANAL BANK WALK" Patrick Kavanagh (1958)

In 1955, while recovering in Dublin from the removal of a cancerous lung, PATRICK KAVANAGH experienced what he considered to be the turning point in his poetic life. Sitting on the banks of the canal, he experienced an epiphanic kind of rebirth, which he would speak of afterward in baptismal terms. In *Self Portrait*, his 1964 TV interview memoir, he claimed that "in this moment of daring I became a poet." This experience was the foundation for a new personal mythology, no longer confined to the distinction between rural and urban but beginning to move toward a notion of a more unified world. The canal served as an ideal image for this new view, itself a kind of synthesis of the natural and the human, two common features of the country and the city. His return to the sonnet form in these later poems is central to the overall project. Though he experimented with the form throughout his career, earlier examples such as "Inniskeen Road: July Evening" were often more focused on the explicitly rural and on peasant stereotypes, a limiting mode away from which he saw this new phase moving.

"Canal Bank Walk" became Kavanagh's poetic marker for the onset of this change, filling it with illustrations of newly realized mediation. The imagery in the poem is balanced between the natural and human-based, reflecting the new realization of unity. The breeze floating between and around "the couple kissing on an old seat" commingles the ideas of old and new. The "bird gathering materials for the nest for the Word" revives a traditional romantic notion of nature as the birthplace of poetry, but in this case it takes an "Eloquently new" shape. Throughout the poem, the waters of the canal double as images of cleansing and continuity—the notion that repetition of habit is "the will of God" brings about the conclusion that the world is constantly new and fresh, always part of the immediate. It is this constant "unworn" quality that is celebrated here. The natural is appealed to again in the sense of being antiartificial—the obvious implication for Kavanagh is the ability to produce a more genuine poetry. To be possessed of "ad lib," the ability "to pray unselfconsciously with overflowing speech," not only provides for the possibility of this type of ideal poetry, but also allows a personal approach in the refusal to limit the self. A certainty that this poetry will serve as an honor to the soul by being "a new dress woven / From green and blue things" springs from an almost environmentalist tone—clearly the sanctity of nature as an inspirational entity is to be revered, but also understood in a nonmaterial sense. The soul is wrapped in the natural at the end of the poem but is also embracing intangible truths—"arguments that cannot be proven." As with the epiphany on the bank of the canal, Kavanagh seems to be searching for a way to connect smaller and larger contexts by finding places where nature and the individual can coexist.

BIBLIOGRAPHY

Kavanagh, Patrick. *Collected Poems.* New York: Norton, 1973.

———. *Self Portrait.* Dublin: Dolemen Press, 1964.

Quinn, Antoinette. *Patrick Kavanagh: A Critical Study.* Syracuse, N.Y.: Syracuse University Press, 1991.

Patrick McCarty

CANNAN, MAY WEDDERBURN (1893–1973)

The first president of the Female Writers' Club, May Cannan published poems, a novel, and memoirs. Her father was dean of Trinity College, Oxford, and the family home was frequently visited by writers such as RUDYARD KIPLING, Sir Walter Raleigh, and T. E. Lawrence. Her aspirations to train as an actress were thwarted by the First World War, and her fiancé, Bevil Quiller-Couch, son of the renowned academic Sir Arthur, tragically died of influenza in 1919. Consequent broken dreams recur throughout her writing. *The Lonely Generation* (1934), a novel whose central character is a young girl growing up in 1914, records how Cannan and her contemporaries' golden days of books and pastoral landscapes were blasted by the outbreak of war. *Grey Ghosts and Voices* (1976) consists of a sequence of personal reminiscences that are more overtly autobiographical.

The first-person pronoun that dominates the slim poetry volume *In War Time* (1917) slips between the seemingly intimate and the more universal articulation of human endurance in the face of extremity. *The Splendid Days* (1919), dedicated to Bevil, was well reviewed and is considered Cannan's best collection. Many poems are tinged with the tragedy of war's losses and the felt emptiness of life afterward but always offer spiritual consolation in tidy rhymes. The grief expressed in "Lamplight" or "Since they have died" can seem awkwardly sentimental and uncritical of nationalistic propaganda: "There's a scarlet cross on my breast, my Dear, / And a torn cross with your name" (December 1916). Cannan imbibed patriotic rhetoric when she worked at the Clarendon Press publishing war propaganda, and for MI5 in Paris during the war. "I Dreamed" presents a vision of an angel riding along with the cry "for England Victory." When it was read in a crowded cathedral service by the bishop of Newcastle, he was inundated by requests for the source. Cannan's expressed views on women's roles are conventional, and the title of "The Ballad of the Independent Woman" is ironic, for the speaker is glad to give up her autonomy for marriage: "But I'm not so independent now—/ But I don't mind, since it's you." "Women Demobilised," written July 1919, insists that women will never forget the men who died in wartime. *The House of Hope* (1923), dedicated to her father, received letters of appreciation; one admirer was Percival Slater, whom she married in 1924. The selection in Catherine Reilly's war poetry anthology *Scars upon My Heart* represents Cannan's range. The posthumous *The Tears of War*, compiled by her great-niece, contains extracts from Cannan's prose, correspondence and poetry with some unpublished verses that had been left in a handwritten notebook.

See also "ROUEN."

BIBLIOGRAPHY

Fyfe, Charlotte, ed. *The Tears of War: The Love Story of a Young Poet and a War Hero.* Upavon, Eng.: Cavalier, 2000.

Reilly, Catherine, ed. *Scars upon My Heart: Women's Poetry and Verse of the First World War.* London: Virago, 1981.

Jane Dowson

"CARRICKFERGUS" LOUIS MACNEICE (1938)

LOUIS MACNEICE's poem "Carrickfergus" is neither a nostalgic evocation of the poet's boyhood home, nor a poem about the loss of home; rather, it is an oddly ambivalent meditation on being suspended between, never quite at home, never quite elsewhere. From the poem's inception, origins and destinations are ambiguous and shifting. The poem moves from Belfast to Carrickfergus, to Dorset in England, where MacNeice went to school. The town of Carrickfergus is conspicuously wedged between a personal past and future. As does "STAR-GAZER," the poem focuses on a moment in time that is not complete in itself, that hints at the inevitability of befores and afters.

The poem begins, "I was born in Belfast between the mountain and the gantries / To the hooting of lost sirens and the clang of trams." The first *between* in the poem separates pastoral Ireland from industrial Ireland with its "hooting" sirens and trams. The sense of betweenness is doubled by the gantries, which stand between ships and shore. The next lines shift the site of reminiscence from Belfast to Carrickfergus, where MacNeice's father was appointed rector of the Church of Ireland when MacNeice was two. Despite its lack of picturesqueness, MacNeice maintained in an interview with the BBC that he always kept "an affection for this really rather drab looking harbor." Typically this acknowledgment of the city's shortcomings does not prevent MacNeice from offering a double-edged tribute to its quiddities. In Carrickfergus, MacNeice is both alienated and at home, wishing, in a sense, he could be *worse* off. He writes, "I was the rector's son, born to the anglican order, / Banned for ever from the candles of the Irish poor." Like MacNeice, the city itself is between, a seaport that links Ireland to England. The divisions of class and religion suggested by the relation between Ireland and England, Protestant and Catholic, constitute the backdrop to MacNeice's meditation on place. The residential homes of the Scotch-Irish are contrasted with the slums of the Irish Quarter. But it is not simply an economic or religious divide. In fact, the divide goes all the way back to the Norman conqueror, who "walled this town against the country / To stop his ears to the yelping of his slave." Walled in like the Norman conquerors he references, MacNeice is both insider and outsider.

The sense of betweenness is also reinforced by other ironic images of thwarted motion. Though the poem is filled with boats, steamers, trams, and trains, these vehicles become images not of motion but of suspension. As do the "little boats" jammed by mud, they speak of confinement and immobilization. Later in the poem, MacNeice writes, "Somewhere on the lough was a prison ship for Germans / A cage across their sight." The quick shift from a ship that is "somewhere"—that is, nowhere in particular—to the perceiving subjects who would look out from inside such a vehicle, is a familiar one in MacNeice's work, where consciousness is frequently anchored in transitional spaces. The prison boat, an image of transportation that does not transport, opposes the "Carlisle train," which carries the young MacNeice to school in England. Yet even this image of the train is immediately followed by an invocation of inescapable continuity: "I thought that the war would last forever and sugar / Be always rationed."

If it is a convention to imagine human affairs as ephemeral and nature as permanent, MacNeice reverses the formulation. Here war and degradation are the constant, and nature in pristine form is conspicuously absent or corrupted throughout. Thus we are also given numerous images of the ugly human world intruding on nature: Carrickfergus's "brook ran yellow from the factory stinking of chlorine." Then with the onset of World War I, a military camp "grew from the ground," as if in parody of nature. In England as well,

the war intrudes: "Across the hawthorn hedge the noise of bugles / Flares across the night."

The poem includes stylistic elements that reinforce the sense of stasis and suspension. Rhymes are amplified by assonances and near-rhymes. For example, the rhyme of *trams* and *jams* in the second and last lines of the first quatrain is echoed by *gantries* and *Antrim* at the end of the first and third lines. Similarly the second stanza has line endings of *castle, salt, houses,* and *halt*— *salt* emerges out of *castle,* the *s* sound links *houses* to the previous two words, and then the *h* leads into the final *halt.* These echoes bind the poem together, giving it the surface sheen of a still life.

The point of view and tone—that of a plainspoken eavesdropper on his own observations—are characteristic of MacNeice. A bemused, purposefully childlike detachment governs the voice, setting up a distance between MacNeice and his own experience. The poem ends with MacNeice at school in Dorset, "a puppet world of sons" insulated, as the prison boat, from the larger world. The school is "far from the mill girls, the smell of porter, the salt mines / And the soldiers with their guns." The world that one might join, however compromised, is forever behind glass, like the stars from the train in his poem "STAR-GAZER" or snow framed in a window. It is precisely this suggestion of quietism that STEPHEN SPENDER criticized in MacNeice. Still it is unfair to say that MacNeice's poetry of separation is withdrawal. Michael Kirkham captures this dialectic nicely: "If MacNeice's sense of things is too 'metaphysical' to be rendered by mere transcription of the world, it is also too personal and ambiguous to equip him for the part of oracle or commentator" (543). Then less out of uncertainty than out of a fierce desire to record the logic of perception, MacNeice fixates on the tensions that govern the act of seeing. It is in the interstice that MacNeice is most comfortable, because it is there that the world becomes visible.

BIBLIOGRAPHY
BBC Recorded Interview with Louis MacNeice. Sound File Online. Available online. URL: http://www.bbc.co.uk/ northernireland/learning/getwritingni/ram/macneice_ carrickfergus.ram. Accessed December 4, 2005.
Brown, Richard Danson. "'Your Thoughts Make Shape Like Snow': Louis MacNeice on Stephen Spender." *Twentieth*

Century Literature: A Scholarly and Critical Journal 48, no. 3 (fall 2002): 292–323.

Kirkham, Michael. "Louis MacNeice's Poetry of Ambivalence." *University of Toronto Quarterly* 56, no. 4 (summer, 1987): 540–556.

Stallworthy, Jon. *Louis MacNeice: A Biography.* New York: Norton, 1995.

Aaron S. Rosenfeld

"CARRICK REVISITED" Louis MacNeice (1945)

While on leave in Ireland from his job at the BBC in the months immediately following the end of the Second World War in Europe, Louis MacNeice, finding himself "in a topographical frame," revisited the terrain of his childhood, and of his earlier autobiographical poem, "Carrickfergus" (1936). The months MacNeice spent in Ireland after V-E Day with his wife, Hedli, who was recovering from an enlarged heart, proved fruitful creatively; his radio play, *The Dark Tower*, dates from the same period. "Carrick Revisited" presents the same locale as "Carrickfergus" in a different light; the earlier poem recorded a child's impressions, based on a young man's memories, of a place both familiar and terrifying, while the speaker in "Carrick Revisited" is the same man, older and more experienced, relating not the memories themselves, but the impressions created by those memories.

The impression of Carrickfergus created by the eponymous poem is static, and the only motion tends to be related to violence. While "The Chichesters knelt in marble," "The brook ran yellow from the factory stinking of chlorine." The atmosphere evoked is at once rigid and toxic. In the later poem, meanwhile, the Norman castle is "as plumb assured / As thirty years ago," suggesting that the landscape has changed little, but indeed it is as if an entirely different location is described: "But the green banks are as rich and the lough as hazily lazy / And the child's astonishment not yet cured." Robyn Marsack writes that the "astonishment voiced in this poem bridges gulfs: between childhood and adulthood, one war and another, catching the surprise of attachment to that from which so much subsequent experience had alienated him" (Marsack 76). Indeed the poem's shifting rhyme scheme, which changes from one stanza to the next, indicates a more fluid understanding of and attitude toward his childhood home.

Though the speaker is surprised to find pleasant things in Carrickfergus, he is by no means ready to forgive everything, and the attitude of the poem remains ambivalent. The turn occurs in the penultimate stanza, when MacNeice shifts his gaze inward: "Torn from birth from where my fathers dwelt, / Schooled from the age of ten to a foreign voice." This stanza reflects what Terence Brown calls MacNeice's "spiritual hyphenation" (Brown 14); for the Northern Irish Protestant from an Anglican religious family with native Irish roots and nationalist political opinions who was educated, lived, and worked in England, his homecoming to "the red Antrim clay" evokes the same bitterness that his being sent away to Dorset did in "Carrickfergus." For MacNeice, "the pre-natal mountain is far away" and is always out of reach.

BIBLIOGRAPHY

Brown, Terence. *Louis MacNeice: Sceptical Vision.* Dublin: Gill & Macmillan, 1975.

Grennan, Eamon. "'In a Topographical Frame': Ireland in the Poetry of Louis MacNeice." In *Facing the Music,* 192–207. Omaha, Nebr.: Creighton University Press, 1999.

MacNeice, Louis. *Collected Poems.* New York: Oxford University Press, 1967.

Marsack, Robyn. *The Cave of Making: The Poetry of Louis Macneice.* Oxford: Clarendon Press, 1982.

Stallworthy, Jon. *Louis MacNeice.* New York: W. W. Norton, 1995.

Michael Moir

CARSON, CIARAN (1948–)

Ciaran Carson was born in Belfast, Northern Ireland. Carson's parents shared a love of the Irish language and made an effort to cherish and preserve the native Irish tongue in their own home. Young Ciaran grew up bilingual, speaking Irish at home and English at school, becoming finely attuned to the mysteries and idiosyncrasies of both languages. Carson's father was a postman who used his intimate knowledge of Belfast streets to introduce his children to the urban mythology of crumbling buildings, winding streets, and boxy factories. The traditions of the *seanachie,* or storyteller, and Belfast's rich history were themes that later resurfaced in Carson's own poetry and prose.

He attended Queen's University in Belfast, where he would later return in 2003 as a professor of poetry and director of the SEAMUS HEANEY Centre. In addition to teaching, Carson was a musician, worked in the Civil Service, and acted as Northern Ireland Arts Council's traditional arts officer for 21 years.

Carson is one of the rare writers who move as fluidly through prose as they do through poetry. Over time he has experimented with rhyme, meter, line length, narrative structures, and even Japanese forms. As a musician, Carson was particularly interested in and inspired by traditional Irish music, ballads, and instruments, such as the tin whistle and *bodhrán* drum. The rhythms of traditional Irish music, improvisational *ceilis,* and the singing and dancing of audiences fed into Carson's emerging style. His work depicts objects, people, places, and characters through variegated viewpoints with distinct, concrete, unflinching detail. He is particularly known for his sense of dialect, slang, and voice, as well as the history that permeates everyday details.

Carson's connection to Belfast is an important part of his identity as a writer. Ireland's tragic and violent political history, commonly called "the Troubles," has its epicenter in Belfast. The conflicts between Catholic and Protestant, Falls and Shankill, and Irish nationalism and the desire to keep Northern Ireland part of Britain all feed into Carson's work. He often describes the tensions in the North as well as the buildings and families caught in the crossfire. Other themes include separation, surveillance, loyalty, fear, love, history, etymology, and topography.

Carson's poetry and prose have been honored by numerous organizations and awards. His publications include *The New Estate* (1976), *The Irish for No* (1987), *Belfast Confetti* (1989), *First Language* (1993), *The Twelfth of Never* (1998), *The Star Factory* (1998), *Shamrock Tea* (2001), and *Breaking News* (2003). He currently lives in Belfast with his wife, the fiddle player Deirdre Shannon, and their children. Carson, as do his fellow Belfast poets MICHAEL LONGLEY and MEDBH McGUCKIAN, continues to investigate, stretch, and reimagine the boundaries of contemporary poetry.

BIBLIOGRAPHY

Carson, Ciaran. *Belfast Confetti.* Loughcrew, Ire.: Gallery Press, 1989.

———. *Breaking News.* Winston-Salem, N.C.: Wake Forest University Press, 2003.
Corcoran, Neil. *After Yeats and Joyce: Reading Modern Irish Literature.* Oxford: Oxford University Press, 1997.
Laskowski, David. "Inventing Carson: An Interview." *Chicago Review* 45, no. 3/4 (1999): 92–100.
Vance, Norman. *Irish Literature since 1800.* London: Pearson Education, 2002.

Tara Prescott

CAUSLEY, CHARLES (1917–2003)

Charles Stanley Causley is known in literary circles primarily for the war poetry that resulted from his six years in the Royal Navy during World War II. However, he also wrote children's stories and verse. By the time he died in 2003, he had produced dozens of books, edited still others, and written several successful one-act plays and libretti.

Causley was born in Launceston, Cornwall, on August 24, 1917. He was educated at Launceston College, and he later attended Peterborough Training College. He served in the Royal Navy from 1940 to 1946, and his experiences during this period proved fruitful in terms of inspiring poetic composition. In his own words, "the wartime experience was a catalytic one." His war poetry constantly emphasizes the tragedy and the waste of human life, both of which he had witnessed firsthand at war and in the slow death of his own father due to the older man's experiences during World War I.

After his service in the navy, Causley returned to Cornwall, where he taught school until 1976. During this time, he also began writing in earnest and produced his first collection, *Farewell, Aggie Weston,* in 1951. Subsequent works include *Survivor's Leave* (1953), *Union Street* (1957), *Underneath the Water* (1968), *Johnny Alleluia* (1961), *Six Women* (1973), *Secret Destinations* (1984), and children's books like *Figgie Hobbin* (1970), *Dick Whittington: A Story from England* (1976), *Jack the Treacle Eater* (1987), and *The Merrymaid of Zennor* (1999).

Causley has been honored widely for his literary achievements. In 1967, he was awarded the Queen's Gold Medal for Poetry; in 1986, he was appointed commander of the Order of the British Empire; in

1990, he received the Ingersoll/T. S. Eliot Award; in 2000, he was awarded the Heywood Hill Literary Prize; and in 2001, the Royal Society of Literature named him a Companion of Literature.

The first poetry Causley memorized was by SIEGFRIED SASSOON. Causley's poetic vision, however, was tempered by the British romantic poets so that he did not create the kind of visceral poetry that Sassoon had written. Influenced by the work of John Clare and other romantic poets like John Keats, Causley's war poetry evades direct confrontation with the grisly aspects of warfare in favor of a romanticized ideal. His poetry sometimes explores the implications of Christianity, for example, and often delights in employing the slang Causley had learned as a sailor—fingers as "grabhooks" or rum as "stagger juice."

Unlike many of his contemporaries, Causley preferred more traditional poetic forms to experimentation. He was deeply attached to his native county and drew upon Cornish folk traditions to craft his own ballads. Indeed he is credited with inspiring renewed interest in the ballad form and its reliance on narrative and on regular meter and rhyme scheme. As a result, his poetry exhibits careful attention to the musicality of language. Causley's image-laden style has been compared with the styles of such poets as THOMAS HARDY, W. H. AUDEN, JOHN BETJEMAN, and A(LFRED) E(DWARD) HOUSMAN.

See also "ARMISTICE DAY."

BIBLIOGRAPHY

Causley, Charles. *Collected Poems 1951–2000*. Rev. ed. London: Picador, 2000.

Chambers, Harry, ed. *Causley at 70*. Calstock, Eng.: Peterloo Poets, 1987.

Scannell, Vernon. *Not without Glory: Poets of the Second World War*. London: Woburn Press, 1976.

Schmidt, Michael. *A Reader's Guide to Fifty Modern British Poets*. New York: Barnes & Noble, 1979.

Summerfield, Geoffrey. *Worlds: Seven Modern Poets*. Harmondsworth, Eng.: Penguin Education, 1974.

Ben Robertson

"THE CENOTAPH" CHARLOTTE MEW (1921)

Even within the seemingly simple title of CHARLOTTE MEW's first published poem about World War I, one can locate the tension and ambivalence that pervade the piece. A cenotaph—an empty tomb intended to memorialize the fallen—attempts to create a permanent site for something that is always missing: the bodies of the dead.

In the first two lines of this short poem, the speaker refers to the "measureless fields," where "only yesterday the wild, sweet, blood of wonderful youth was shed." The actual locations of death will remain unmarked and unknown, while the great monument featuring "Victory, winged, with Peace, winged too, at the column's head" will preside over a busy market square in England. Importantly the first-person collective voice declares the intention to build the monument; throughout her poetry, Mew uses this voice when describing acts that are distasteful or shameful, such as, in this case, the construction of a column that can never capture the true losses of war.

The poem then slips back into an implied third-person voice as the speaker acknowledges that the cenotaph is built for the surviving "watchers," who experience war not as physical battles but as the "thrust of an inward sword" from which they have "more slowly bled." In other words, the monument is a place for women to leave flowers as well as "the small, sweet, twinkling country things" that represent those who have died. The ambivalence of the poem emerges again in the description of the paradoxically "desolate, passionate hands" that leave behind reminders of the missing loved ones. The flowers and women beside the empty grave lead to the speaker's frustrated observation "It is all young life." Mew, by this time in her late forties, visited young war wives as a part of the home-front volunteer efforts to boost morale, so the acts of waiting and mourning became terribly familiar to her.

While the speaker realizes that some will be taken aback at the festive appearance of the monument surrounded by young women and colorful flowers, she insists that "God is not mocked and neither are the dead." The speaker finishes the poem by wondering how the market square can again be home to "Every busy whore's and huckster's face / As they drive their bargains," for there also "is the Face / Of God: and some young, piteous, murdered face." Can the masses continue their normal—and corrupt—operations while the ghosts of those who died in battle look on? The cenotaph thus remains an empty tomb and an unanswered question, a marketplace stage on which will play out the best and worst elements of human response to war.

BIBLIOGRAPHY

Fitzgerald, Penelope. *Charlotte Mew and Her Friends.* London: Collins, 1984.

Persoon, James. *Modern British Poetry, 1900–1939.* New York: Twayne, 1999.

James Persoon

"CHANNEL FIRING" Thomas Hardy (1914)

"Channel Firing" was first published in the May 1914 *Fortnightly Review,* a few months before the outbreak of World War I; Thomas Hardy also included the poem in his 1914 collection of poetry, *Satires of Circumstances.* The channel firing referred to by the title and by God in line 10 ("It's gunnery practice out at sea") is the British fleet's firing of naval guns on the English Channel in the months prior to World War I. In a letter she wrote soon after Hardy finished the poem, Hardy's second wife, Florence, identified the setting for the poem as the churchyard containing the Hardy family graves, saying, "The buried people at Stinsford hear the guns being fired at Portsmouth." Hardy also would have heard the sound of the 12-inch guns at Max Gate, his Dorchester home two miles from Stinsford Church and eight miles from the Channel. Looking back on the poem soon after the outbreak of World War I, Hardy termed it "prophetic," even though he admitted that "nobody was more amazed than he" when the war actually broke (*Life* 365–366).

There are four speakers in the poem's nine iambic tetrameter quatrains, which rhyme *abab.* The narrator is one of three "skeleton" speakers, along with another unnamed skeleton and Parson Thirdly, whose comments are quoted by the narrator. Speaking between the narrator's opening exposition and his two companions' later comments is God, whose four-stanza speech is the longest in the poem.

The narrator addresses and explains to the living world how when "your great guns" shook "all our coffins as we lay," the graveyard residents "sat upright" in the belief that "Judgement-day" had arrived. The image of the awakened skeletons sitting upright in their coffins at first may seem meant to be terrifying, especially coupled with the "drearisome" howling of dogs so familiar to gothic literature of horror, but the irony, especially evident in a second reading of the poem, that it is the skeletons who are disturbed by the living, rather than the other way around, along with the narrator's anticlimactic further list of responses to the guns by other nonhuman creatures—a mouse drops its "altar-crumb," a worm goes back into its mound, and the parish cow drools—reflect Hardy's wry humor. The narrator, however, is innocent of Hardy's irony, and of Hardy's criticism of war. The narrator does not blame the living for disturbing the peace of the churchyard, for shaking the coffins or breaking the chancel window squares, excusing them for being "unawares" of the consequences of their actions. The word *unawares* reverberates throughout the poem in a deeper sense than the narrator realizes, though; for Hardy, as he worked out most particularly while writing *The Dynasts* several years earlier, the chance for world improvement depends upon the "unconscious Will of the World," which largely is the sum of all the individual human wills, "growing aware of Itself" and "ultimately, it is to be hoped, sympathetic" (*Life* 335). It is remaining "unawares" along with the advanced technology of warfare that results in the progressively worse state, as God later affirms in "Channel Firing," of "All nations striving strong to make / Red war yet redder."

The God who tells the skeletons that Judgment Day has not arrived, that it was only the Channel firing that awoke them, is not the conventional Christian God of love and mercy. Instead he taunts and teases the skeletons and shows little sympathy for mankind. He is not so much cruel as ironic, a jokester. At first, God seems to be reassuring the skeletons when he tells them the actual cause of their awakening and states that it is "just as before you went below; / The world is as it used to be:" Occurring at the end of the stanza and with the full colon, the apparent reassurance is held for a pause, before being undercut by God's ironic explanation that the world situation continues to be as bad, not as good, as it was before; that nations continue to wage war and to be "Mad as hatters" and "do no more for Christés sake / Than you who are helpless in such matters." Hardy's God not only mixes a cliché and an archaism in the exuberance of his speech, but also laughs aloud over the thought of all those who would "have to scour / Hell's floor for so much threatening" if it were Judgment Day, adding, "Ha, ha. It will be warmer when I blow the trumpet." God's afterthought that he might cancel Judgment Day because "you are men, / And rest eternal sorely need" is more teasing than compassionate but at least reveals more consideration that those behind the Channel firing who "unawares" awoke the cemetery inhabitants.

Just as the skeletons did not blame the living for disturbing their sleep, they do not reflect upon or judge the personality or ways of the God they have just heard speak. Instead, after they all lie back in their coffins again, one turns his thoughts to the future, wondering, "Will the century ever saner be," only to be answered, in a wonderfully humorous as well as sad line, "And many a skeleton shook his head." Finally, Parson Thirdly, looking back on his life, perhaps silently reflecting upon hearing a God who turned out to be quite different from the one about whom he had preached or upon the little effect the church has had on the state of the world, says he wished he "had stuck to pipes and beer" rather than "preaching forty year."

After the quaint humor associated with the meek skeletons and the dark irony of God's speech, the final stanza of "Channel Firing" is lyrical and solemn. The great guns have begun again, "Roaring their readiness to avenge," sounding "as far inland as Stourton Tower, / Camelot, and starlit Stonehenge." The repeated *st* and *t* sounds recreate the effect of the explosive gunfire echoing through the sites of past civilizations: Alfred Tower near the town of Stourton, commemorating Alfred the Great's defeat of Viking invaders in 876; Camelot, the legendary site of King Arthur and the Knights of the Round Table; and Stonehenge, the prehistoric ruins on the Salisbury Plain. As the sound of the gunnery practice echoes "far inland" and "disturb[s] the hour" as well as the monuments of the distant historic past, the present situation is contemplated within the context of the rise and fall of civilizations throughout immemorial time.

BIBLIOGRAPHY

Bailey, J. O. *The Poetry of Thomas Hardy: A Handbook and Commentary.* Chapel Hill: University of North Carolina Press, 1970.

Hardy, Florence Emily. *The Life of Thomas Hardy.* Hamden, Conn.: Archon, 1970.

Millgate, Michael, ed. *Letters of Emma and Florence Hardy.* Oxford: Oxford University Press, 1996.

Robert R. Watson

"THE CHERRY TREES" EDWARD THOMAS (1916)

The manuscripts of Edward Thomas indicate that he composed "The Cherry Trees" in early May 1916, the year before his death at the Battle of Arras in northern France. The poem appeared posthumously in 1917, under the pseudonym *Edward Eastaway,* in a volume entitled *Poems.*

While "The Cherry Trees" is no more than a quatrain, the poem is a carefully crafted text that exhibits close attention to detail. The poem is a single, balanced sentence, whose four lines rhyme *abab.* The text functions as an epitaph commemorating the many soldiers killed in World War I, and its use of the imagery of cherry petals falling on a road is reminiscent, in its close attention to that specific image, of the style associated with the Japanese haiku. Thomas begins the poem with a personification of the trees that "bend over" to drop their petals. The poet thus establishes the setting as late spring—when flower petals drop—and reiterates that setting in the fourth line with a reference to the "early May morn." By situating the primary image of the poem in the early morning and in the spring, Thomas evokes a sense of newness and rejuvenation that he reaffirms in the third line with a reference to a wedding.

However, Thomas undercuts the positive imagery by adding strongly contrasting ideas that give the poem a negative tone in general. In the second line, he describes the petals as falling "on the old road where all that passed are dead," and in the last line, the speaker of the poem laments that "there is none to wed" on the beautiful spring morning. The landscape Thomas describes is devoid of human life, and the only evidence of humanity's existence—the "old road"—is being reclaimed by nature. On one level, this poem emphasizes the continuity and indifference of nature, which pursues its perennial cycles without regard to human existence. Simultaneously, however, the poem laments the destructiveness of a war that terminates so many innocent lives. The cherry petals are symbolic tears that blanket the countryside as the trees bend under the oppressive weight of grief.

This poem provides a good illustration of Thomas's interest in the English countryside. Influenced by the English romantic poets and especially by his friend Robert Frost, Thomas devoted much of his poetry to nature and to the individual's place within the natural world. He was acutely aware of the disjunction between nature and the individual, and "The Cherry Trees" captures the ambiguity of humanity's role. Although Thomas does not mention war directly in the poem, his reference to the dead and to the void left by their absence connects the text with the conflict in which Thomas himself was to lose his life.

BIBLIOGRAPHY

Cooke, William. *Edward Thomas: A Critical Biography 1878–1917*. London: Faber and Faber, 1970.

Motion, Andrew. *The Poetry of Edward Thomas*. London: Routledge, 1980.

Thomas, Edward. *The Collected Poems of Edward Thomas*. Edited and introduction by R. George Thomas. Oxford: Clarendon Press, 1978.

———. *The Diary of Edward Thomas 1 January–8 April 1917*. Introduction by Roland Gant. Andoversford, Eng.: Whittington Press, 1977.

Thomas, R. George. *Edward Thomas: A Portrait*. Oxford: Clarendon Press, 1985.

Ben Robertson

"CHOICES" ELIZABETH JENNINGS *A SENSE OF THE WORLD* (1958)

In "Choices," ELIZABETH JENNINGS echoes the sentiments of Frost's "The Road Less Traveled." The narrator is outside, looking in, reflecting on choices she has made and the road she has decided not to take. At the same time, Jennings suggests that it may well be that those inside are reflecting on choices they have made as well.

In nine rhyming couplets, the speaker watches the couple inside the house, perhaps at dinnertime. The couple is so "deep in tenderness / They cannot speak a word of happiness." The neighborhood speaks of suburban comfort: a "cared-for lawn," a roof that is their own, a dog barking. The speaker indicates that she has "designed a way to live" and she "clothed in confusion, set their choices by."

Jennings herself made the choice to write, giving up a steady librarian position to do so. Unmarried, and with little financial assistance, she was often impoverished, occasionally having to sell her books and manuscripts. Inside the room the couple are warm in a "patch of light," while outside, with her breath "warming the air," she watches as the day closes and her shadow lengthens. The tone of the poem changes as inside "one looks up." She continues with the pronoun *he,* suggesting that it is the husband who sees her standing outside. Maybe the narrator is spying on an old flame who has married someone else.

Feeling her watching, he opens the window and stares at her. Maybe he is regretting the choices he made as well, or at the least wondering how his life could be different if he stepped out into the dark night, away from the patch of light. The speaker describes the man as seeming to urge her darkness into the room, perhaps to let a little of her otherness into his comfortable, predictable suburban life. The poem ends with the sentence "We need each other's need." Whether the speaker and the man know each other from a previous relationship, or her spying is random, "Choices" is clearly about people who have chosen a path and who, at least momentarily, acknowledge that there were other directions their lives could have taken.

BIBLIOGRAPHY

Bradley, Jerry. "Elizabeth Jennings." In *The Movement: British Poets of the 1950s*, 87–100. New York: Twayne, 1993.

Gerlinde, Gramang. *Elizabeth Jennings: An Appraisal of Her Life As a Poet, Her Approach to Her Work, and a Selection of the Major Themes of Her Poetry*. Lewiston, N.Y.: Edwin Mellen Press, 1995.

Schmidt, Michael. *Lives of the Poets*. New York: Knopf, 1998.

Patricia Bostian

"CHURCH GOING" PHILIP LARKIN (1955)

One of the best poems by PHILIP LARKIN, published in his 1955 volume, *The Less Deceived,* "Church Going" is, as the title indicates, not about the traditional religious experience of attending a church service, but about a touristy activity, such as visiting museums or brass rubbing, simply a "collector's" experience—adding one more church to one's list of cultural activities. The persona of the poem, a bike-riding tourist, perhaps the poet himself, visits different churches, explores their historical and cultural riches, and thus creates a personal "collection" of the artistic treasures of the British world.

"Once I am sure there's nothing going on / I step inside"—thus begins the peregrination of this typically shy and awkward Larkinesque figure. The reader feels very much a part of this peregrination; we are right there, together with the observer, in yet "another church," an obvious, if rather dubious, cultural milestone; a seemingly useless place without vitality, visibly empty and sad, with Larkin or his traveling persona snooping around and trying to be "cultured" by the experience.

Once in the church, the observer's eye roams around, from object to object, from the matting, seats, and "little books," to the wilted flowers, "some brass and stuff," and a "small neat organ." Absolutely nothing there is exceptional or exciting; it is a boring little holy place. The tourist's "reverence" is simply "awkward," as he takes off his cycle clips, an old-fashioned piece of biking paraphernalia that clearly defines the church visitor as a fastidious and awkward person. And then, emboldened by the "musty" emptiness of the church and the absence of the authorities, the churchgoer touches the sacred objects somewhat reverently, moves around, and even "mounts" the lectern, from which God's word is usually pronounced. His voice betrays him there, and, too loud in this silent world, it "pronounces" a very significant and symbolic phrase—"Here endeth."

This richly ironic phrase will reverberate throughout the rest of this seven-stanza poem. What is it that "here endeth"? Just a biblical verse, a prayer, or the human search for the meaning of life? The time-revered religious practices, devotions, and all institutionalized religion? The beauty of the old, but "useless," churches of the British world? The visitor's retreat from the church follows some usual steps: "Back at the door / I sign the book, donate an Irish sixpence." So we are in Ireland? This geographical hint broadens the horizons of the poem. The final thought before stepping out is that "the place was not worth stopping for," a typically Larkin melancholic, cynical, disappointing conclusion.

But then, surprisingly, with the third stanza, the poem moves from the "light" and introductory descriptive mode into a much more serious, contemplative, philosophical, and theological, mode. It grows into a breath-taking exploration of the meaning of the organized religion, with its buildings, customs, ceremonies; of the destiny of the modern world distancing itself increasingly from the mystical and mythological experiences of the past; of the ultimately totally uncertain and open traits of human spirituality and human visions in general. The rather pathetic and grotesque figure with the cycle clips becomes suddenly a thinking human being in search of the answers to some very important questions. Significantly these new and intense thoughts have been provoked by a small, insignificant, and pathetic church, which "was not worth stopping for." "Yet stop I did," says the speaker, and this stopping acquires an important human dimension; it provokes numerous essential spiritual and philosophical questions: "When churches fall completely out of use," what shall then be their uses? Empty buildings that have lost their important functions crop up in Larkin's poetry in many places. "Shall we avoid them as unlucky places?" worries the churchgoer. This interesting archetypal idea of the holy places, as opposed to the cursed or unlucky places, enters the poem here full force, and the reader becomes keenly aware of the material aspects of the world, of the powerful physical, of the places and the things, in powerful conjunction with what we call the spiritual, the metaphysical, of the body and the spirit, of the ultimate and infinite complexity and the unity of the universe.

In the fourth stanza, the churchgoer continues this imaginative exploration of the possible "uses" of these ubiquitous, and increasingly unused, objects known as churches, temples, places of worship. Superstition is one obvious answer, and the poem's persona imagines some "dubious women" making "their children touch a particular stone," for good luck, health, or a spiritual revelation. Here, quite dramatically, if unwarranted, a cynical and positivist "knowledge" creeps in, and the presumably scientifically empowered speaker tells us that "superstition, like belief, must die, / And what remains when disbelief has gone?" The answer is bleak, defeating, and disturbing—"Grass, weedy pavement, brambles, buttress, sky, / A shape less recognisable each week, / A purpose more obscure." Whether this is Larkin's own voice, or that of his scientifically minded philosophical persona mocked by Larkin, it is hard to say. Larkin is a fine master of disguise, for, of course, the questions always remain: Is the liturgical, organized religion really so profoundly different from what we term superstition? Is not an enormous part of every religion, even of those that pride themselves on the absence of the sacred objects and the graven images, inevitably and profoundly material? Is not even the word of God as much matter as it is spirit?

In the sixth stanza, something like real and touching love for this poor little material symbol of our human spirituality and our constant efforts to define ourselves in all our perplexing complexity enters both gently and powerfully this poem. "Bored, uninformed," as he sees himself and honestly confesses, the speaker senses somehow that this little church, "this accoutred frowsty barn," however unimportant and even cheap, speaks yet about a profound human desire and need. He proclaims, with obvious warmth and something that sounds like a trembling voice, "It pleases me to stand in silence here."

There is a profound, mysterious attraction here that makes the speaker linger on and tremble emotionally in the presence of a beautiful, simple mystery.

The finale, stanza seven, begins with some truly touching and profound words of religious proportions: "A serious house on serious earth it is, / In whose blent air all our compulsions meet," and it continues, in this beautifully solemn style, to the very apotheosis of human "hunger in himself to be more serious" and of finding a sacred place "proper to grow wise in." The final line surprises us with a paradoxical thought that the wisdom of that holy place is also guaranteed by the "so many dead" who have preceded us in both life and death and who "lie round" that little insignificant church. This, ultimately exciting and meaningful, dramatic journey from a dutiful, but bored and somewhat

grotesque churchgoer, a rather indifferent collector of cultural and historical "trophies," to a man trembling with powerful spiritual discovery and potential, a man who, as Hamlet, in his final, short, and most important speech in the whole play, finds the ultimate wisdom in humility and the acceptance of the verdict of the numerous centuries of human spirituality, is a veritable triumph of Larkin's poetic mind and imagination. It is a beautiful lesson in patience, openness, and sincere desire to receive a revelation. As in any physical pilgrimage, the physical fact of "church going" in this poem prepares the mind for the miracle of insight through spiritual pilgrimage, a journey of the mind and the soul. The highly skillful rhyme scheme, which is one of the hallmarks of all Larkin's poetry, passes in this masterpiece nearly unnoticed, as the thought pattern and the spiritual journey are powerfully in the creative forefront, as they keep the reader fully spellbound.

BIBLIOGRAPHY
Larkin, Philip. *The Less Deceived.* Hessle, Eng.: Marvell Press, 1955.
Motion, Andrew. *Philip Larkin: A Writer's Life.* London: Faber and Faber, 1993.

Ivo Soljan

"THE CIRCUS ANIMALS' DESERTION" W. B. YEATS (1939)

The penultimate poem in W. B. YEATS's posthumously published final collection, *Last Poems* (1939), "The Circus Animals' Desertion" is largely a portrait of the artist as an old man. Yeats's biographer, R. F. Foster, notes that a draft of a rejected last stanza for this poem was found on Yeats's desk after he died (638). Age, decrepitude, and artistic impotence are central themes in this poem, which begins in bewilderment and despair. Yet its final lines turn surprisingly hopeful as the speaker-poet recommits himself to a poetry of embodied emotion, recognizing that the willed creativity of his youth is not antithetical to the production of poetry: "I must lie down where all the ladders start / In the foul rag and bone shop of the heart." At *its* heart, "The Circus Animals' Desertion" is a poem about creating poetry, and about poetry's demands, its beauty, and its toll. In this, one of his last great poems, Yeats reexamines his own work and calls it to account.

Earlier titles for this poem included "Despair" and "On the Lack of a Theme," both titles that Foster sees as "reflecting his [Yeats's] current preoccupation with the effort to find inspiration by an act of will" (636). The poem depicts the artist's struggle with impending death, the reality of which is made clear by his own aging body and by his sudden inability to create. He is now "but a broken man," who "sought a theme and sought for it in vain . . . daily for six weeks or so." At a loss, the poet dazedly declares that "I must be satisfied with my heart," but quickly turns to point out, "Winter and summer till old age began / My circus animals were all on show." Until age set in, the poet could easily turn out the well-trained figures of his imagination. Yeats sets up the heart—here connected with old age, the failing body, and failing mind—against the career-long commitment to the ageless, eternal dream of poetic creation.

Section 2 of the poem extends and deepens the reader's understanding of the poet's feeling of loss at having to "be satisfied with my heart." Here Yeats turns our attention to his past artistic product, focusing on the dynamic characters of Irish myth, which he reinvigorated through dramatic reimaginings: Oisin, Cathleen ni Houlihan, and Cuchulain. As the poet describes his artistic development, we begin to understand that the dreams—the poetry—stand in for emotional connections outside the dream world. Ultimately, he admits, "Players and painted stage took all my love / And not those things that they were emblems of."

However, to understand these lines fully it is important to recognize that in the central section of "The Circus Animals' Desertion" Yeats turns his attention not to other lyric poems but to two plays and a narrative poem. The idea of "character isolated by a deed" connects to some of Yeats's ideas about tragic drama, which also infused his lyric poetry. At the climax of a Yeatsian drama, the hero, mired in the temporal world, is united with the eternal through a gesture of passionate significance—such as when "Cuchulain fought the ungovernable sea." While the story of Cuchulain contains "heart mysteries," the poet tells us "it was the dream itself enchanted me: / Character isolated by a deed / To engross the present and dominate memory."

"The Circus Animals' Desertion" restates an idea that Yeats raises in other poems (such as "EASTER 1916"): The act of creation is the poet's passionate, eternal gesture. In committing himself to the dream of poetry, the poet has hoped to become eternal through his works. But now he recognizes that these are but "old themes"; their loss reminds the poet that while his creations may be immortal, he himself is not.

At this powerful moment of self-recognition, Yeats suddenly turns the dichotomy back on itself. As the third section of the poem begins, the speaker asks,

> Those masterful images because complete
> Grew in pure mind but out of what began?
> A mound of refuse or the sweepings of a street,
> Old kettles, old bottles, and a broken can,
> Old iron, old bones, old rags, that raving slut
> Who keeps the till.

This litany of inanimate objects culminates in an image of insanity—the terrifying obverse of the "pure mind." The missing "ladder" the poet mentions has previously given him an escape from what Richard F. Peterson calls "the refuse of the heart" (185), but it is here nonetheless where "all ladders start / In the foul rag and bone shop of the heart." The poet's decision to accept the heart—set aside in pursuit of poetic creation—ultimately enables that body to reinvigorate the creativity that he feared was lost.

"The Circus Animals' Desertion" is about loss, but it is also about another new kind of writing and a new kind of self-dramatization. The old themes are no longer viable or even accessible, but inspiration still exists, expressed in the very existence of the poem itself. Yeats does combine the very lack of a theme and the rags and bones to create another poem and in so doing asserts the tragic will that seemed to be gone. "The Circus Animals' Desertion" presents a poet-hero transformed by his own passionate gesture of poetic creation: one who recognizes the sources of artistic creation for what they are and continues to create nonetheless.

BIBLIOGRAPHY
Finneran, Richard J., ed. *The Collected Poems of W. B. Yeats.* New York: Scribner Paperback Poetry, 1996.

Foster, R. F. *W. B. Yeats: A Life*. Vol. 2, *The Arch-Poet*. Oxford: Oxford University Press, 2003.

Peterson, Richard F. *William Butler Yeats*. Boston: Twayne, 1982.

Mary Wilson

CLARKE, AUSTIN (1896–1974)

Born in Dublin, Austin Clarke had a life as uneven as his texts; both were marked by bad patches and shining moments. When he started at University College, Dublin (UCD), in 1912, he was initially awestruck and intimidated, but his time there gave him the chance to engage enthusiastically with English and Irish literature. He worked with some of the Irish literary greats, for example, Thomas MacDonagh. It was while he was at UCD that Clarke was first influenced and inspired by W. B. YEATS. This led to the attachment to Gaelic prosody, myths, and legends that characterizes his poetry.

Little is known about his family, and although he was ashamed of his father as he was growing up, his father's death in 1919 was a contributory factor to Clarke's first breakdown. After graduating with a masters' degree from UCD, Clark became an English lecturer there. In 1917 he published his first book of narrative poetry, *The Vengeance of Fionn*. This book was so popular it quickly went to a second edition. In 1920 Clarke married Lia Cummins, a marriage that lasted two years.

Unfortunately Clarke lost his position at UCD in 1921 and the following year he made the drastic move to London, where he lived until 1937 working as a literary journalist. In 1929 Clarke was made assistant editor of the *Argosy* magazine. By the time he returned to Ireland not only did he have a new wife, Nora Walker, but several published collections of poetry, including *The Cattledrive in Connaught* and *Pilgrimage and Other Poems*. Despite the growing success of his poetry, Clarke was insulted by Yeats, who omitted Clarke from his 1936 *Oxford Book of Modern Verse*. Clarke's professional life did not suffer, and he remained a vibrant part of the Irish literati through his associations with numerous writers and his role in the founding of the Irish Academy of Letters.

Clarke's return to Ireland was not victorious. In 1938 he suffered a second breakdown, this one stemming from a personal crisis, which led to a 17-year hiatus in the poetry that up to this point had seemed unstoppable. The breakdown is rumored to have been caused, in part, by a particularly personal poem that he was writing. The poem, *Memnesyone Lay in the Dust*, eventually published in 1966, is very personal and full of autobiographical reminiscing. During his break from poetry Clarke wrote several verse plays and a novel and helped to found the Lyric Theatre Company.

Clarke returned to poetry in 1955 and the change in the poetry was phenomenal. In 1952–53 Clarke was president of the Irish Academy of Letters. In 1966 Dublin University conferred upon him the honorary degree Litt. D. (doctor of letters) and in 1968 he was awarded the Gregory Medal. Clarke's life remained bumpy and he suffered two heart attacks, in 1959 and 1964, respectively. His *Collected Poems* was published posthumously in 1974. This huge book covers poetry from all stages of his career and stands as a memorial to a prolific writer.

BIBLIOGRAPHY

Austin, Clarke. *Collected Poems*. Dublin: Dolmen, 1974.

Halpern, Susan. *Austin Clarke, His Life and Works*. Atlantic Highlands, N.J.: Humanities Press, 1974.

Claire Norris

CLARKE, GILLIAN (1937–)

Clarke began her career as a freelance writer and a news researcher in the 1960s while her children were young. She first began publishing her poetry in the 1970s in Welsh journals such as *Poetry Wales*, and she began to be included in English and Irish magazines after the release of her 1971 chapbook *Snow on the Mountain*. In addition to her writing, Clarke is a teacher. She was appointed to a lecturer position in art history at Gwent College of Art and Design, in Newport, Wales. Clarke also edited the *Anglo-Welsh Review* from 1975 to 1984.

In 1977 Clarke's first volume of poems, *The Sundial*, was published to much acclaim, and she was catapulted to the status of preeminent female Welsh poet. Her early poems are brief lyrics on the cycle of life: birth, love, death, and so on. These early lyrics became hallmarks of Clarke's poetry. In them she develops a nationalism, celebrating her Welsh homeland through the lyrical evocation of family and domesticity. There is a feminism that is not strident or harsh and is not a criticism of woman's domestic sphere and its importance. The poems such as "Catrin" and "Foghorns," and "The Sundial" about her children, insist upon the importance of motherhood as a feminist experience.

The title poem in her second collection ruminates on the domestic life of women in a rural community. The poem's 43 stanzas move through the day in the life of the speaker as she contends with domestic chores, incorporating reflections of her female ancestors and their lives. The poem is intended as a letter to the men in her family; it is the speaker's "apologia, / my letter home from the future." Clarke has described the poem as an "epic to housework" and the poem focuses on both Clarke's Welshness and her celebration of the work of her female progenitors, which is often overlooked and demeaned.

Her poems become more nationalistic and political in *Letting in the Rumour* (1989). In poems such as "Fires on Llŷn," she addresses the issue of the increase of property values in Wales preventing local residents from buying homes, but opening the market to the British to buy Welsh land. The line "three English boys throw stones" is an echo of past violence and suppressed Welsh rage that threatens to ignite. After a weary day, the speaker of the poem says, "Through binoculars we see / distant windows curtained in flame": What appears to be the fulfillment of the prophecy of violence reveals itself to be the reflection of the setting sun in the windows. In "Borders" there is more criticism of the changes being introduced to the countryside of Wales. The speaker "feels foreign in my own country" as she finds fewer establishments where Welsh is understood. She says of the British: "They came for the beauty / but could not hear it speak."

In Clarke's introduction to the long poem "Cofiant," in *Letting in the Rumour, cofiant* means "biography." In the 19th century, hundreds of these biographies were written about preachers and included biographical material about their lives and samples of their writings and ended with elegies. Clarke's poem is based on her great-great-grandfather Thomas Williams's 1887 cofiant written by Williams's eldest son. The poem is told in the first person and comprises a multitude of voices

like the poem "The King of Britain's Daughter" in the 1993 volume of the same name. Where "The King of Britain's Daughter" relies on Welsh myth to ground the nationalism of Wales, "Cofiant" does so by exploring the political nature of the family—its relationships, its power struggles, its failures and successes. Both poems are nationalistic, but the center of "The King of Britain's Daughter" is mythological family, and in "Cofiant," the poet's family.

While attending the first Hay-on-the-Wye Literary Festival in 1990, where the theme "Border: Fatherland, Motherland" was presented, Clarke was immediately impressed with the way the theme related not only to the border where mother and father come together in one's own psyche, but to the border in Wales dividing the country into two languages. Deeper reflection began to produce what would be *The King of Britain's Daughter*. The poems in that volume are based in part on the stories of Branwen and the giant Bendigeidfran, from the *Mabinogion*, and the story of King Lear and his daughter Cordelia, told by Shakespeare. The poem was commissioned as an oratorio for the festival but became a more personal piece of introspection as Clarke wove the stories of Branwen and Cordelia with her own. The epic nature of *The King of Britain's Daughter* is compared to that of GEOFFREY HILL's "MERCIAN HYMNS" (1971) and John Montague's *The Rough Fields* (1972).

In 1998 Clarke published *Five Fields,* a volume that is still firmly located on Welsh soil and exploring the life of the rural Welsh (which she and her husband as sheep farmers share). Her net is cast farther, however, in this collection, grappling with the war in Bosnia in such poems as "Letters from Bosnia" and "Snow." Other poems confront the war in Europe more indirectly, couching the atrocities and anxieties in rural and domestic imagery. "THE FIELD MOUSE" employs the metaphor of summer haymaking and the death of small animals under the plow's sweep. The poems in *Five Fields* offer the language and natural imagery for which Clarke is known. In the opening image of "Barn," a "wheelbarrow slumps, a lake of rust in its lap." The collection concludes with a translation of part of William Langland's *Piers Plowman*.

Clarke's poetry, unrhymed and of varying lengths and meters, often seems spontaneous, yet Clarke herself has commented on her poetry as being influenced by traditional Welsh verse. She often employs a seven-syllable line and *cynghanedd* alliteration, a complex system involving internal rhyme and elaborate forms of alliteration. This is a tradition that Gerard Manley Hopkins says shaped his experimental poetry as well.

Collected Poems was released in 1997 and was followed by *Nine Green Gardens* (2000), a volume commissioned by the Aberglasne Gardens, and *Owain Glyn Dwr* (2000), a tribute to the Welsh hero who rebelled against the British occupation in the 15th century. She also published *The Animal Wall,* a children's book, in 1999. *Making the Beds for the Dead* (2004) is Clarke's most recent publication. It is a highly structured compilation that includes, along with her characteristic examinations of Wales and domestic matters, poems on the Iraqi conflict and meditations on the foot and mouth disease that struck European farms so forcefully. Gillian Clarke is one of Wales's best-loved poets. She continues to write and teach creative writing to both children and adults.

See also "BABY SITTING," "A DIFFICULT BIRTH, EASTER 1998," "MALI," "OCTOBER."

BIBLIOGRAPHY

Adams, Sam. "Weaving a Cymric Web? A Perspective on Contemporary Anglo-Welsh Poetry." In *Comparative Criticism.* Vol. 19, *Literary Devolution: Writing in Scotland, Ireland, Wales and England,* 117–133. Cambridge: Cambridge University Press, 1998.

Clarke, Gillian. "The King of Britain's Daughter." In *How Poets Work.* Edited by Tony Curtis, 122–136. Bridgend, Eng.: Seren, 1996.

"An Interview with Gillian Clarke." In *Common Ground: Poets in a Welsh Landscape.* Bridgend, Eng.: Seren, 1985.

Kerrigan, John. "Divided Kingdom and the Local Epic: *Mercian Hymns* to *The King of Britain's Daughter.*" *Yale Journal of Criticism* 13, no. 1 (2000): 3–21.

Peach, Linden. "Wales and the Cultural Politics of Identity: Gillian Clarke, Robert Minhinnik, and Jeremy Hooker." *Contemporary British Poetry: Essays in Theory and Criticism,* edited by James Acheson and Romana Huk, 373–396. Albany: State University of New York Press, 1996.

Pykett, Lyn. "Women Poets and 'Women's Poetry': Fleur Adcock, Gillian Clarke, and Carol Rumens." In *British Poetry from the 1950s to the 1990s: Politics and Art,* edited by Gary Day and Brian Docherty, 253–267. New York: St. Martin's Press, 1997.

Smith, K. E. "The Poetry of Gillian Glarke." In *Poetry in the British Isles: Non-Metropolitan Perspectives,* edited by Hans-Werner Ludwig and Lothar Fietz, 267–280. Cardiff: University of Wales Press, 1995.

Thurston, Michael. "'Writing at the Edge': Gillian Clarke's Cofiant." *Contemporary Literature* 44, no. 2 (summer 2003): 275–300.

Patricia Bostian

CLASS IN BRITAIN   A survey of British poetry and politics during the 20th century not only emphasizes the extent to which class dictated who would write and read poetry, but also highlights class as the continued way readers elevate some writers over others. JOHN BETJEMAN's poem "IN WESTMINSTER ABBEY" famously celebrated the British nation as one characterised by "Free speech, free passes, class distinction, / Democracy and proper drains." Yet the century that saw two world wars and the collapse of the British Empire also challenged many of those distinctions or else made them redundant.

The 1900s saw the formation of the Labour Party, a political group claiming to offer the working people of a heavily industrialized nation representation for the first time. This new presence threatened the increasingly beleaguered middle classes, memorably recorded in Hilaire Belloc's "The Garden Party" as "The People in Between," who look "underdone and harassed." After the First World War, which had not only seen a shrinking in Britain's colonies but the collapse of royal dynasties around the world, the certainties of Edwardian tradition seemed increasingly unstable.

When, after the 1918 Reform Act, working men and women older than 30 were permitted to vote, this previously unheard group redrew the political map. With all classes now part of the electorate, class and social difference became politicized; all subsequent prime ministers would be made and broken by their ability to define then appeal to various sections of society. If Marxist theories of labor and capital informed the Labour movement at this time, the Tory Party looked to Darwinism to prove that traditional hierarchies and inherited privilege were a political as well as an evolutionary fact.

The interwar years saw the continuing rise of the working-class Labour Party, fueled in the part by the collapse of the Liberals in 1914. The party's focus on trade unions for laborers led to an increasingly politically savvy working class, and the 1920s were typified by workers' strikes and other industrial actions. The conservative response to this was to attempt to challenge Britain's notion of its own tripartite class structure, with Prime Minister Stanley Baldwin arguing that there was no such thing as class: that the country was only made of individuals. Yet if British society was as egalitarian as Baldwin suggested, W. H. AUDEN's depiction of the country's "solitary agents" and "insufficient units" in "Consider this and in our time" suggested an increasingly divided nation. Auden's own popularity at this time was revealing, in the same way that his subsequent domination of critical accounts of 1930s literature continues to highlight our own preconceptions about the period. As Adrian Caeser notes in *Dividing Lines: Poetry, Class and Ideology in the 1930s,* the popularity of Auden today over poets like DYLAN THOMAS can be attributed to his appeal to modern liberal middle-class values. While Auden adopts the omniscient position of the "hawk" or the "helmeted airmen" in the poem, his association with the Cambridge-educated elite of C. DAY LEWIS, STEPHEN SPENDER, and LOUIS MACNEICE points to a more earthly position of privilege than his poem's perspective admits. Other 1930s poetry, such as STEVIE SMITH's ironic attack on "The Suburban Classes" in her poem of the same name, suggests a British intelligentsia increasingly anxious about the sprawl of the middle classes, an anxiety that is explored in John Carey's classic polemic of MODERNISM and class, *The Intellectuals and the Masses* (1988).

If 1930s literature saw the reestablishment of the educated elite in poetry, and largely disparaging portraits of the middle class in novels such as George Orwell's *Keep the Aspidistra Flying* (1936), the onset of war in 1939 demanded a political rhetoric that denied any such divisions. Winston Churchill remarked on the "rapid effacement" of class difference early in 1939, but if, as he argued, the war did promote an increasing sense of social community, postwar Britain seemed skeptical of its legacy. In 1944, the Butler Education Act preserved the public school system (meaning, in Britain, the elite private boarding schools), ensuring another generation of wealthy children a safe passage from their boardinghouses to Oxbridge. This proved to be the final undoing of Churchill's government, and Clement Atlee's energetic Labour Party soon took control; in a comparatively short period, they were able to establish the National Health Service and limit the powers of the hereditary peers in the House of Lords. The wave of socialist measures brought in during the postwar years,—not to mention the dismantling of the ornately British hierarchy of the Raj with the withdrawal from India in 1947,—suggested a nation seeking to replace its colonial rule with civic welfare. The Tory Party, meanwhile, was sidelined as the party of property and privilege.

As Britain sat entranced watching the coronation of Elizabeth II in 1952, class warriors and analysts seemed to fall silent, even if those households unable to afford a television might have questioned this myth of national participation in a media event. In 1959, the then prime minister, Harold Macmillan, could declare that the class war was over without fearing a cry of dissent. As if to underline the fact, Britain's most celebrated writers from the 1950s and 1960s, PHILIP LARKIN and KINGSLEY AMIS, passed through Oxbridge but from state-funded grammars rather than public school, suggesting an age of increased social mobility. Larkin's "CHURCH GOING," a poem celebrating the everyman and his bicycle clips, becomes the archetypal statement of the Pylon poets precisely through its evocation of a middle-class Middle England. Yet, tellingly, his evocation of his university experience in his novel *Jill* (1946) points to an education that emphasizes rather than erodes class differences—he records his protagonist's alienation on arriving in Oxford to hear the "self-parodying Southern coo." Meanwhile, the poet and novelist Allan Sillitoe defended his groundbreaking representations of working-class Nottingham as portraits of individuals rather than veiled political statements.

Throughout the 1950s and 1960s, language use increasingly became a defining characteristic of British class, with institutions like the BBC continuing to uphold the "standard" of Received Pronounciation. The working-class poet TONY HARRISON recalls being denied a main part in *Macbeth* at this time because of his Leeds accent. This debate effectively made the very tool of poetry into a self-conscious class barometer, perhaps best seen in Harrison's autobiographical poetry recalling his parent's response to his work—"How you became a poet's a mystery!" The Scottish poet DOUGLAS DUNN also helped create a republican working-class voice through collections such as *Barbarians* (1979). His poem "The Competition" recalls how he was marked as a "poor boy, who should shut up" from early on in his life.

If the liberalizing government of the 1960s suggested a newly permissive society, legalizing abortion and homosexuality, that very same permissiveness proved the victim of its own success. The increasing strength of the trade unions was cemented when Arthur Scargill was appointed leader of the National Union of Mineworkers in 1974. The political power accorded the unions by the left-wing government proved catastrophic, leading to the "Winter of Discontent," which saw union strikes and utility cuts taking the country to a standstill. It was from this political crisis point that Margaret Thatcher emerged as leader of the Conservative Party. In her 12 years as prime minister, she attempted to undo what she saw as the British culture of dependency encouraged by liberal governments. In practical terms, this meant abolishing the power of the trade unions and supporting the rights of "individuals" and "consumers." As had Stanley Baldwin before her, she argued that there was no such thing as society. There were only individual men and women, and families. Her isolationist rhetoric co-opted American individualism with the language of economics and nostalgia for what she termed "Victorian" values. Although her dismantling of British heavy industry during the 1980s led to mass unemployment among the poorest strata of society, huge economic investment and the growth of yuppie culture prompted her subsequent reelection. Poetry's stance on this refashioned Britain was largely critical; SIMON ARMITAGE's first collection, *ZOOM!* (1989), introduces him mock-threateningly as someone who "lived with thieves in Manchester." Thatcher's rhetoric meanwhile struggled to eliminate class as a political issue, suggesting a cultural Britain that could take in both "Princess Di and the football hooligan" as CAROL ANN DUFFY's poem "Translating the English, 1989" records. Thatcher handed over to her successor, John Major, the myth of the classless society. His own political rhetoric made direct use of Larkin's churchgoing men with their bicycle clips to evoke a notion of Britain as an archaic village idyll. Yet from Thatcher's time onward, politicians have been increasingly wary about using terms such as *classless, underclass,* or *upper class.* The debate now continues in the veiled nouns of *citizens, honest people,* or *consumers.*

Yet if the massive increase in homeowning and an increasingly debt-ridden culture have made material assets a less reliable indicator of social status, political and social life in Britain continues to be bound up in class-consciousness. The National Lottery was founded in 1992, most of the proceeds directed toward national heritage or arts schemes. Many attacks on the lottery in the media have argued that this in essence has amounted to an arts tax on the poorest workers in Britain, a politically expedient way to charge a minimum-wage earner for the refurbishing of the Royal Opera House. TED HUGHES's death in 1999 opened up the post of poet laureate. Tony Harrison's response to media speculation that he would be asked to run took the form of a poem calling for the monarchy to be abolished and celebrating his freedom to "blast and bollock" Tony Blair and his government. The "class distinction" that Betjeman saw as endemic to British life then has proved a stubborn myth to rebut; if anything, Britain has demonstrated in both its poetry and its politics that it is the very symbiotic nature of class that has made it such a pervasive social and economic barometer.

BIBLIOGRAPHY

Adonis, Andrew, and Stephen Pollard. *A Class Act: The Myth of Britain's Classless Society.* London: Penguin, 1998.

Cannadine, David. *Class in Britain.* London: Penguin, 2000.

Carey, John. *The Intellectuals and the Masses.* London: Faber, 1992.

William May

"COLONIZATION IN REVERSE" LOUISE BENNETT (1957)

Originally published in the collection *Anancy Stories and Dialect Verse*, "Colonization in Reverse" has become LOUISE BENNETT's most commonly cited piece of poetry. Referenced as a touchstone in a variety of articles, on subjects as far ranging as literature, visual culture, and art, this work reflects Bennett's ongoing interest in finding the personal in the political, of looking at the working-class experience of major historical events and cultural shifts. "Colonization in Reverse" uses Bennett's typical humor and dialect verse to offer wry commentary on the sudden influx of hundreds of thousands of Jamaicans to British cities following World War II, a reaction to the postwar labor shortage.

As with many of Bennett's other poems, the verse is spoken as a dramatic monologue, directed to "miss Mattie" in an exuberant tone of postcolonial shock that: "Jamaica people colonizin / Englan in Reverse." This move is one that will "turn history upside dung!", co-opting the history of the colonizer's influence, commonly taught to Jamaican schoolchildren at the time, for the unique goals and purposes of the colonized people. With Bennett's typical ironic humor, she casually notes that the goal of these expatriates "Is fe get a big-time job / An settle in de mother lan." Bennett's joke here is on England, symbolic "mother" of Jamaica, her abandoned or unwanted child, and on whom the responsibility of parenthood has suddenly come home to roost. This cultural "turnabout" has resulted in a massive influx of immigrants whereby "jamaica live fe box bread / Out a English people mout'."

With its exploration of the social, economic, and cultural implications of "Colonization in Reverse," Bennett's poem echoes many of the concerns of 21st-century America over the rising tide of immigration and foreign labor. However, there is an important key difference between the two scenarios from a political standpoint: Under the impetus of obligations laid upon England by colonial rule, the Jamaicans are only exercising their full rights as citizens of that empire. Thus, as any other British citizen may, upon arriving in "De seat a de Empire," "Some will settle down to work / An some will settle fe de dole." When Bennett's narrator focuses her sights on "Jane," a friend who has chosen the latter of the two options, her tone is harsh: "For all day she stay popn Aunt Fan couch / An read love-story book." Her depiction calls to mind the comparable level of relaxation among British colonists made possible by Jamaican native labor and that leisure now possible for Jamaican immigrants due to British labor and

labor laws. Ultimately in many ways Bennett's tone is sympathetic to the English cause; after all, "Dem face war an brave de worse." But now the colonized is beating the colonizer at his own game, and the narrator can only be left "wonderin how dem gwine stan / Colonizin in reverse."

BIBLIOGRAPHY
Narain, Denise deCaires. *Contemporary Caribbean Women's Poetry: Making Style.* London, Routledge, 2002.
Ramazani, Jahan. *The Hybrid Muse: Postcolonial Poetry in English.* Chicago: University of Chicago Press, 2001.

Caroline Kimberly

"THE COMPLAINT OF THE MORPETHSHIRE FARMER" Basil Bunting (1930)

In this ballad from Basil Bunting's *First Book of Odes* (1965), the richness of the Northumberland farmer's song compensates for the fact that wealthy landowners "have made" Northumberland "a bare land." Bunting spotlights the song-making of the farmer—and, perhaps, his own poetic debt to Northumberland's oral tradition of balladry—with a primary narrator who appears only long enough to introduce the "song" he has heard a "farmer / muttering."

The source of infertility in the poem is the landed gentry, who have chased yeoman farmers off the land for generations. They have enclosed common areas, designated huge chunks of land as wild hunting areas for the wealthy, and charged exorbitant rents to farmers for the remaining limited grazing land. But if landowners have "spoiled" the countryside by transforming it into a lonely, uncultivated, and "overgrown" refuge for doomed grouse, the farmer's fertile song reflects a contrasting vision of community, heterogeneity, and order. Directly addressing his lost sheep and the house previously inhabited by the ears and eyes of his family, he laments his forced withdrawal from the network of relationships that sustain him. Humans, the farmer knows, make life possible by implementing generous order. He meets, therefore, the disorder unleashed by landowners who will not let farmers keep the land productive with a song that exemplifies inclusive structure. Although the second stanza complains that those left behind will hear the grouse "but not" the cow, the onomatopoeic last two lines of the stanza itself suggest that "the flurry of the grouse," the "lowing of the kye," and the voices of those who call a cow a "kye" can all occupy the same space.

The farmer adheres to the formula for the ballad—quatrains of alternating lines of four and three beats and a rhyme scheme of *abcb*—just enough to make the reader aware of the alterations he makes to the form. He substitutes, for instance, a three-beat line for the traditional four-beat first line in the seventh, eighth, and 10th stanzas, all of which address the shrinking of the farmer's world. Moreover, as Robinson warns, the ballad has rhythm, but do not expect predictable iambs. Look instead, for instance, for sequences of stressed syllables ("where the sweet grass might grow") and alternating iambs and trochees ("a straw bed and a hind's wages"). The farmer maintains the tradition of rhyme between the final stressed syllables of lines 2 and 4 of each quatrain, but the effect of that rhyme is dispersed by the more complex play of consonance, assonance, and alliteration throughout the poem. One of the most suggestive instances of consonance takes place in the third line of the eighth stanza, in which the unstressed last two syllables of *Northumberland's* are followed by the stressed syllables *bare land.* The progression from -*berland* to *bare land,* which is followed by the line "for men have made it so," drives home the farmer's argument that poor stewardship has corrupted, perhaps irrevocably, his homeland.

BIBLIOGRAPHY

Robinson, Peter. "Bunting's Ballads." In *Sharp Study and Long Toil: Basil Bunting Special Issue,* edited by Richard Caddel and Peter Lewis. *Durham University Journal* special issue. (March 1995), 85–99.

Robin Calland

CONSTANTINE, DAVID (1944–) A

prolific poet, novelist, and translator of German and French literature, David Constantine was born in Salford in 1944 and educated at Wadham College, Oxford. His academic career included periods teaching German language and literature at Durham and Oxford before becoming a freelance writer in 2000. He has written a biography of Sir William Hamilton (*Fields of Fire,* 2001), an academic study of travel in ancient Greece, a novel (*Davies,* 1985), and a collection of short fiction. His translations include versions of major texts by Goethe, Kleist, Enzensberger, Michaux, and Jaccottet. Several of his collections and translations have won prizes, notably the Southern Arts Literature prize for *Madder* (1987) and the European Poetry Translation prize for his translation of Hölderlin's *Selected Poems* (revised edition, 1996). He edits the journal *Modern Poetry in Translation.*

His own poetry is erudite and sometimes complex in its deft interweavings of personal experience with nods to English and European literary traditions—"I write about what I know something about," he has stated, suggesting the importance of grounding poetry in the certainties of the knowable, of finding accurate analogies for the specificities of experience: "All I can ever do is say what things are like," he writes in "Fulmars," the penultimate poem in *Something for the Ghosts* (2002), his most recent collection, which examines the apparent immateriality of language and memory in contrast with the evident solidity of human experience and suffering, describing the ghosts of different histories who "flit like snowflakes, drift like mist" through the collection. *Caspar Hauser: A Poem in Nine Cantos* (1994) relates a version of the life of the famous 19th-century "child of nature," a foundational myth of modern times, through a powerful and effective mixture of lyric and epic forms. As befits a writer so deeply involved in analyzing relations between languages, form itself is one of Constantine's abiding preoccupations. In the "Note" to his translation of Kleist's writings, he states: "True style—the shape and rhythm of a poetic line or of a prose sentence—is never an extra. It is integral and essential," and elsewhere he states that he has "a horror of shapelessness in poetry." Form and style are, for Constantine, vehicles for the sustaining of cultural memories that he sees as a politically vital dimension of the power of literature; "Poetry wants to witness; it is instinctive," he has stated, and it is toward this politically motivated task that his own writings and translations are constantly oriented.

BIBLIOGRAPHY

Constantine, David. *Collected Poems.* Tarset, Eng.: Bloodaxe, 2004.

———, ed. and trans. *Selected Writings: Heinrich von Kleist.* London: J. M. Dent, 1997.

John Sears

CONTEMPORARY "BLACK" BRITISH POETRY

Although a handful of best-selling "black" British novelists backed by powerful publishing houses (like Andrea Levy and Zadie Smith) are the individual "black" British writers reaching the widest audiences, the numbers of "black" British poets receiving popular and critical acclaim grow each day. The British public flocks in ever-increasing numbers to hear this new poetry read or performed in community centers, bookshops, schools, public venues, festivals, and the streets—in part for the upbeat tone of the poetry, in part for the entertainment value of the productions, which are often amplified and accompanied (as in dub or rap) by dynamic drumming or musical accompaniment of one sort or another, sometimes even by rave-style (dance-hall) sound systems and dramatic lighting.

Eclectic poetry anthologies (for instance, *BURNING words/flaming IMAGES* [1996]; *Bittersweet: Contemporary Black Women's Poetry* [1998]; *Empire Windrush: Fifty Years of Writing about Black Britain* [1998]; *The Fire People: A Collection of Contemporary Black British Poets* [1998]; *Voice Memory Ashes: Lest We Forget* [1999]; and *IC3: The Penguin Book of New Black Writing in Britain* [2000]), once the primary outlet for young "black" British poets, are giving way to themed anthologies as well as to coherent, slim volumes of verse published by major British publishing enterprises (Picador, Bloodaxe, Penguin, Virago) or by smaller, "black"-owned publishing companies (Peepal Tree Press, Angela Royal Publishing, SAKS Publications, Bogle L'Ouverture Press, and Allison & Busby).

While their works are immensely diverse in form, subject matter, and tone, the latest generation of "black" British poets, for the most part, share in a spirit that has been celebrated across the British Isles not only by other young "black" Britons, who pay handsomely to attend public events, but also by the reigning establishment, which has sought to honor outstanding individual artists with high honors, including the Order of the British Empire (famously offered to and declined by BENJAMIN ZEPHANIAH; and accepted by SuAndi, the novelist Buchi Emecheta, and other contemporary "black" British writers). Zephaniah, SuAndi, and other "black" British poets—including Chris Abani, John Agard, Patience Agbabi, Joan Anim-Addo, Moniza Alvi, Valerie Bloom, Malika Booker, Jean "Binta" Breeze, Jean Buffong, Bernardine Evaristo, Martin Glynn, Linton Kwesi Johnson, Anthony Joseph, Peter Kalu, JACKIE KAY, MIMI KHALVATI, E. A. Markham, Karen McCarthy, Leone Ross, Lemn Sissay, GRACE NICHOLS, Dorothea Smartt, Maud Sulter—have achieved national and international recognition in recent years for their artistic activism and their contributions to a renaissance of interest in poetry as a medium of communitarian discourse. Their artistic success is in step with declared national political aspirations and is not, in comparison to the (American) black arts movement of the 1960s and 1970s, the result of a revolutionary countermovement. As Zephaniah does, these poets reserve the right to speak out against government policies when they choose, and they do so; and, as Zephaniah, they appreciate and accept the financial support of arts agencies and community-funded organizations (e.g., the British Council, the Arts Council England, the British Museum, the Arvon Foundation, b3 media, the South East London Community Foundation, the BBC).

Literary critics and scholars have noted several trends of feeling in these new bodies of verse: a robust sense of entitlement to the benefits of nationally protected civil liberties and an appreciation of them, a constructive outlook on importunate social problems such as bigotry and racism, and a positive and optimistic attitude toward a "reinvented Britain" that "black" Britons can comfortably call home. Despite these shared cultural objectives and AVANT-GARDE social commitments, contemporary "black" British poets do not constitute a consolidated aesthetic movement. Rather, the emergence of "black" British poetry has many points of origin in the world and many sources of inspiration: Caribbean dub and reggae; African belief systems and spirituality; Indian subcontinental, Near Eastern, and Persian lyricism; the hugely various prosodic legacies of English, Irish, Scottish, Welsh, and American poetics; African, Asian, and Western verse forms; African American jazz and blues rhythms and iconographies; and a host of specific poetic practices, experiments, and influences from around the world. As a result, the voices and styles of contemporary "black" poets in Britain vary impressively. The term *"black" British*—useful politically in Britain during the late 1970s and 1980s as an umbrella designation for immigrant populations from Africa, the Caribbean, and "the East" and their descendants—is today felt, especially by artists and writers, to be wanting as a practical descriptor of cultural realities, for the poetries as well as the people themselves are increasingly of mixed heritage.

Although Lauri Ramey's helpful categories for grouping the sensibilities of "black" British poets—*urban griots* and *trickster figures*—do not embrace the range of nostalgic lyricisms that connect some contemporary "black" British poets to, say, Indian cultural backgrounds (Amiti Grech, Joyoti Grech, and Raman Mundair) or Persian ones (Mimi Khalvati), Ramey's tags can help readers to examine the projects and devices of British poets of African and Caribbean heritage. According to Ramey, the *urban griots* "narrate contemporary Britain as a citified and diverse diasporic village, partly defined by its external connections. The poets using trickster identities . . . hold up British culture to a mirror, providing knowing reflection and pinpoint critique" (110–111). Ramey's categories may not be stable, but they do distinguish the impetus *to chronicle* the present serious state of affairs from the impetus *to poke fun* at social pretentiousness and bad behavior. Patience Agbabi is a brilliant urban griot in her tour-de-force set of seven sestinas ("Seven Sisters" in *Transformatrix*, 2000), in each of which she evokes the lifestyle of a different young "black" woman; she is a trickster figure in "The Wife of Bafa," her hilarious Nigerian-inspired send-up of Chaucer's "The Wife of Bath" (in *Transformatrix*). Grace Nichols is an urban griot in reciting the life in England of her dislocated, tropical Fat "black" Woman (*The Fat Black Woman's Poems*, 1984); she is also a trickster figure who vividly (and humorously) appropriates the panoply of cosmogonic situations into which the poet laureate TED HUGHES placed his famous Crow—thus making her Fat Black Woman just as archetypal as her predecessor's compelling figure of

élan vital. In *Connecting Medium* (2001), Dorothea Smartt captures the feelings of Caribbean immigrants to England in a griotlike, incantatory field of words; in her Medusa series (in the same volume), Smartt ingeniously transforms the Greek myth, implying that it has always been about strong "black" women, who embody the Medusa mythos to this day. In her versified novel *The Emperor's Babe,* set in Roman times (A.D. 211), Bernardine Evaristo is an urban griot, describing the lives of a multiethnic group of characters who inhabit a far-flung outpost of empire, Londinium; she is a trickster figure, too, in fashioning a story in which juicy cultural and linguistic anachronisms provocatively connect the life and times of two widely separate historical eras (then and now). Zepahniah's *City Psalms* (1992) and nearly all of the poems in *Too Black, Too Strong* (2001) are dazzling urban tirades, sharply critical of those who run the world, but no one who knows PHILIP LARKIN'S "THIS BE THE VERSE" (*TBTS,* 30) can miss the tricky moves in Zephaniah's "This Be The Worst," a poem that luminously parodies Larkin's crude abuse of "your mum and dad" so as to indict "those lords and priests" who historically have ruined more than just "you"; the poem ends with a warning to the reader to "start thinking for yourself." These few examples can only begin to suggest in what diverse ways "black" British poets are engaging contemporary realities while employing wit and imagination to underscore the intellectual independence of their own cosmopolitan analyses of global as well national problems.

Contemporary "black" British poets in various ways announce that we inhabit an era of "broadband cosmopolitanism," where new technologies "are helping to produce a borderless world in which an individual has choice and can select from different values, cultures, and languages" and where, more and more, the resultant "cosmopolitan vision recognizes the values of local cultures, but opens them to everyone" (Skrzeszewski, 14, 15). Such descriptions of this new imaginary (cyber cosmopolitanism) call to mind numerous poems in Lemn Sissay's anthology *The Fire People*—particularly Chris Abani's "Rambo 3" (9–10), Lorraine Griffith's "Diary of Poette" (37–41), as well as Maud Sulter's eulogy for James Baldwin titled "Delete and Enter" (in *Zabat,* 73–74) and Zephaniah's "The One Minutes of

Silence" (in Newland's *IC3,* 142). These and many other similarly motivated poems remind us that, whatever their complaints, present-day "black" British poets tend to admit that they love Britain, criticize it because they do, and ardently desire "the 'project' to work" (Zephaniah, *TBTS,* 14).

Patience Agbabi's poetry (like Zephaniah's) is a galloping, hip commentary on postmodern Britain and the global community. Her slim heteroglossic volume *Transformatrix* contains a wide spectrum of monologic poems, each of which sounds out a denunciation of political and social injustice, prejudice, and utopian (or apocalyptic) expectations for planet Earth. "UFO Woman" (the lead poem) ends with the following "broadband cosmopolitan" stanza: "So, smart casual, I prepare for lift off, / in my fibre-optic firefly Levis, / my sci-fi hi-fi playing *Revelations* / and my intergalactic mobile ON. / Call me. I'll be surfing the galaxy / searching for that perfect destination" (17). Despite the strip searches, incarcerations, hostilities, and so forth, that Agbabi's poetic personae suffer daily, they reject silence. Agbabi's poetry criticizes the injustices in the metropolitan centers and the postcolonial spaces equally harshly, and her rap rhythms resonate with a trenchant observation also made by Richard W. Miller, the social philosopher, who wrote: "A political system that cannot be a basis for the reasonable expectation of civic loyalty is unjust" (43).

A similar kind of cosmopolitanism inhabits the poems of Dorothea Smartt, whose volume *Connecting Medium* commemorates her world travels—to Portugal, Lagos, downtown Manhattan, Harlem, the West Indies, and the Gambia. *Connecting Medium* celebrates Smartt's knowledge and sharp-eyed assessments of the world. Her poems on Medusa (envisioned here as a tremendous present-day "black" woman with snaky dreadlocks) form a brainy poetic sequence that shockingly pulverizes the Euro-Greek myth and rewrites it from a contemporary, Afro-British woman's perspective. Smartt's poetry is cosmopolitan as well as feminist, in a form that Ali Rattansi identifies as "non-essentialist" and representative of "post-national and transnational heterogeneous publics" (615).

No summary account of contemporary "black" British poets can be complete without mentioning such tours de force as Bernardine Evaristo's versified quasi-autobiographical verse novel *Lara,* Jackie Kay's hard-hitting *Off Colour,* Lemn Sissay's stormy *Morning Breaks in the Elevator,* and SuAndi's stoical *There Will Be No Tears;* nor would it be complete without some recognition that even "white" poets—including the renowned Scottish poet CAROL ANN DUFFY—are sounding the same themes, ironically, and from an empathic "black" cosmopolitan British perspective (see, for example, "Originally" and "Translating the English" in *The Other Country,* 7, 11).

BIBLIOGRAPHY

Arana, R. Victoria. "Black American Bodies in the Neo-Millennial Avant-Garde Black British Poetry." *Literature and Psychology* 48, no. 4 (2002): 47–80.

———. "The 1980s: Retheorizing and Refashioning British Identity." In *Write Black, Write British,* 230–240. London: Hansib, 2005.

Ball, John Clement. *Imagining London: Postcolonial Fiction and the Transnational Metropolis.* Toronto: University of Toronto Press, 2004.

Dabydeen, David, and Nana Wilson-Tagoe. *Reader's Guide to West Indian and Black British Literature.* London: Hansib, 1997.

Donnell, Alison, ed. *Companion to Contemporary Black British Culture.* London: Routledge, 2002.

Duffy, Carol Ann. *The Other Country.* London: Anvil Press Poetry, 1990.

Evaristo, Bernardine. *The Emperor's Babe.* London: Penguin, 2001.

———. *Lara.* London: TunbridgeWells, Eng.: Angela Royal, 1997.

Innes, C. L. *A History of Black and Asian Writing in Britain: 1700–2000.* Cambridge: Cambridge University Press, 2002.

Kay, Jackie. *Off Colour.* Newcastle upon Tyne, Eng.: Bloodaxe, 1998.

King, Bruce. *The Oxford English Literary History.* Vol. 13, *The Internationalization of English Literature. (1948–2000).* Oxford: Oxford University Press, 2004.

McLeod, John. *Postcolonial London: Rewriting the Metropolis.* London: Routledge, 2004.

Miller, Richard W. "Cosmopolitanism and Its Limits." *Theoria,* August 2004: 39–53.

Nasta, Susheila. *Writing across Worlds: Contemporary Writers Talk.* London: Routledge, 2004.

Newland, Courttia, and Kadija Sesay, eds. *IC3: the Penguin Book of New Black Writing in Britain.* London: Hamish Hamilton, 2000.

Procter, James. *Dwelling Places: Postwar Black British Writing.* Manchester: Manchester University Press, 2003.

Ramey, Lauri. "Contemporary Black British Poetry." In *Black British Writing,* edited by R. Victoria Arana and Lauri Ramey, 109–136. New York: Palgrave Macmillan, 2004.

Rattansi, Ali. "Dialogues on Difference: Cosmopolitans, Locals and 'Others' in a Post-National Age." *Sociology* 38, no. 3 (2004): 613–621.

Sandhu, Sukhev. *London Calling: How Black and Asian Writers Imagined a City.* London: HarperCollins, 2003.

Sesay, Kadija. *Write Black, Write British: From Post Colonial to Black British Literature.* London: Hansib, 2005.

Sissay, Lemn. *Morning Breaks in the Elevator.* Edinburgh: Payback Press, 1999.

Skrzeszewski, Stan. "From Multiculturalism to Cosmopolitanism: World Fusion and Libraries." *Feliciter* (Canadian Library Association) 1 (2004): 14–16.

Smartt, Dorothea. *Connecting Medium.* Leeds, Eng.: Peepal Tree Press, 2001.

SuAndi. *There Will Be No Tears.* Manchester, Eng.: Pankhurst Press, 1995.

Sulter, Maud. *Zabat: Poetics of a Family Tree.* Hebden Bridge, Eng.: Urban Fox Press, 1989.

Zephaniah, Benjamin. *City Psalms.* Newcastle upon Tyne, Eng.: Bloodaxe Books, 1992.

———. *Too Black, Too Strong.* Newcastle upon Tyne, Eng.: Bloodaxe Books, 2001.

R. Victoria Arana

CONTEMPORARY WELSH POETRY IN ENGLISH

A brief glance at the development of English-language Welsh poetry since the mid-20th century is a useful reminder of the way so many critical overviews of British poetry are distorted by focusing on London. The situation in Wales is no pale imitation of the London scene but emerged in a different space with different pressures and stimuli. Primary among these is the presence of a contemporary Welsh-language poetry rooted in ancient traditions. English language poetry in Wales could not help, from its inception, being hyperconscious of language and linguistic play—and hence ripe for experiment. This is the poetry on which I focus here.

It could be said that modern Welsh poetry in English started with DYLAN THOMAS, who rebelled against the Auden-inflected empiricism of 1930s English poetry with a surreal, determinedly "Celtic" excess and an emphasis on breath and body in performance that influenced the Beat poets. Thomas fell from grace in Britain during the cultural retrenchments of the 1950s and 1960s but returned indirectly through the passion for international poetry—especially that of the Beats and the L=A=N=G=U=A=G=E poets—that fueled the British poetry revival of the 1960s and 1970s.

This was the writing that electrified a young Peter Finch fleeing from convention in Cardiff: "The Anglo-Welsh Poetry anthology of the [1960s] was *Dragons and Daffodils, Contemporary Anglo-Welsh Verse.* . . . Its content was so tight buttoned, so worthy, so introvertedly provincial. No confidence, no flair. Where else could I go but the avant garde?" The hybrid term *Anglo-Welsh* is the key to the "introvertedly provincial." Wales may have a venerable tradition of poetry—but it is in the Welsh, not the English, language. For centuries, lacking the legal, governmental, or educational institutions that guarantee national identity, it has had a distinctive identity that has been defined through that tradition. Wales may be known as "the land of song," but in the 1960s that "song" was trammeled in its cultural freight. There were problems for writers in the monoglot English communities that sprang up with nineteenth-century industrial expansion. Finch scathingly summarizes the standard reaction: to adopt the sober, reflective verse of a pared-down English empiricism, then label it "Welsh" by adding stereotypical content such as miners and industrial tragedies, or farmers and sheep, or (here) the national symbols of dragon and daffodil; Finch, however, aflame with the Beats, rejected the lot: "Sod this, I had no history or reputation to get mashed. I could do what I wanted."

Finch has had a huge impact on the poetry scene. In 1966 he established the influential poetry magazine *second aeon,* in Cardiff, publishing work by everyone who was anyone on the international scene: Burroughs, Ginsberg, Bukowski, and the British experimenters PETER PORTER, Bob Cobbing, PETER REDGROVE. Cut-ups, concrete, found, sound, visual, open-field: all were there—with Welsh poetry. In his *British Poetry 1964–84,* Martin Booth assesses *second aeon* as "the most important magazine of the period," even claiming that "the demise of Finch's astounding enterprises led to the showdown of the art. A central cog had seized . . .

the decline and rot set into British verse soon after." Richard Kostelanetz's *Dictionary of the Avant-Gardes* claims that "since the early 1970s, Finch has been the principal innovator in Welsh poetry . . . He deserves a Welsh knighthood."

In 1975 the Arts Council of Wales (ACW) appointed Finch to manage Oriel, their new specialist bookshop and art gallery. As an employee he could no longer access ACW grants and *second aeon* closed. The closure may have been a setback for radical British poetry, but, before cutbacks forced its demise in 1998, Oriel was a center for small press book fairs and launches, lectures, talks, debates, and workshops. Welsh writers in both languages read there with concrete and sound poets like EDWIN MORGAN and Bob Cobbing, the Merseybeat poets, and international women writers like MARGARET ATWOOD and Jeni Couzyn.

Finch provided access to information, networks, and resources from within Cardiff and helped set up Cabaret 246, a dadaesque performance phenomenon with writers like Ifor Thomas, John Harrison, and Topher Mills playing domestic appliances and setting poems on fire. Cabaret 246 was associated with Adventures in Creative Writing, Chris Torrance's Beat-inspired night classes at the university from 1976 to 2001. Current writers are still indebted to the project. The example of Mills's Red Shark poetry press motivated Richard Davies to set up Wales's most dynamic publishing company, Parthian Books, itself a vigorous publisher of nontraditional poetry.

lloyd robson, a Parthian poet, sounds wistful: "i feel guilty that i haven't taken on the mantle from topher & finchy & that lot. i organised the golden cross reading which at the time, i was told, was the first thing for years to get a decent audience, & then the slam thing happened with regular events organised by kerry-lee powell & steve prescott. then me, steve & chris brooke organised the 'sampler:' readings, but since then it's all died a death." But Finch himself thinks otherwise: "London commercial publishers are continuing to find Welsh material and Welsh authors acceptable. Welsh publishers are better supported by the state now than they have ever been. There is much more literary interest and activity than I can ever remember. . . . The post-colonial cultures of recently politically-devolved Scotland, Northern Ireland and Wales have seen poetry in those countries boom." Finch is now chief executive of *Yr Academi Gymreig,* the Welsh National Literature Promotion Agency and Society for Writers. He has grown complacent about neither writing nor language.

In 2000 Wales voted for limited devolution and Cardiff began to transform itself from capital to center of government. Cultural activity has blossomed and what was once known as "Anglo-Welsh" poetry seems increasingly defined by the confidence and flair that Finch yearned for in the 1960s. There is, for example, David Greenslade, an accomplished, prolific writer (more than 20 volumes), who is highly praised in experimental poetry magazines such as *Angel Exhaust* and *Terrible Work.* Take his splendid oddball "Peas" with its coded Welsh subtext: "Peas. Knuckle dusters. Boxing gloves. Ever worn a set? Ever shelled a pod? Cut a peastick.? In your face. Crazy all the time. That's peas! Coming on strong; bursting at the seams; trying to run the government; held back by lousy bits of constitutional string. Why should they forgive? Or dry up their tears?"

Literature festivals and readings by poets of every description are hosted by Swansea's Dylan Thomas Centre. The Beat-influenced John Goodby and Chris Ozzard read there, as do younger Welsh writers like Clare Potter, whose blues style and delivery are inspired by seven years living and working in New Orleans. Newport and Cardiff have vibrant poetry scenes.

The acclaimed novelist Richard Gwyn writes prose meditations like "Dusting":

> Dust is verbal. Billions of particles of god knows what, collecting on every surface, in every corner. Breeding bugs which, under the microscope, become grotesque and terrifying monsters. Dust that accumulates unnoticed and invisible until such time as it is noticed, and then suddenly you hear yourself observe that you had never realised quite how dusty this house was. . . . medieval dust, Roman dust, good old Celtic sunset dust. Scoop it up and flog it off in coloured glass. Pagan dust, rhino dust, dinosaur dust. Millenium dust. Dust brushed by the saints. Christ dust. Buddha dust. The dust of our ancestors. Dust: if it weren't a metaphor for oblivion it could be a happy verb.

Cardiff-based Viki Holmes sounds more American: "the city continues much as it did before you went away. lights / sparkle in the trees / and it's almost picturesque, you might say. people, there are many / people here . . ." ("postcard #1: winter wonderland").

As elsewhere, locality and regional voices are being revalued: robson's *cardiff cut* explores the dingy delights of a run-down Cardiff in its street slang. Mike Jenkins writes Merthyr dialect; Stephen Knight has a volume of Swansea dialect poems—and declares both local and international credentials in his tongue-in-cheek title *The Sandfields Baudelaire.* The first stanza of a delectable *villanelle* runs, "IssFair wuz-honourCaw-munlarz-Satdee: / doorjums, toff yapples, goalfish. Lie kytold, / wee wenhonourGhosetrayn, mean Bare vully" ("The Heart of Saturday Night").

Ian Davidson has a different approach to the recognition of difference in North Wales. His own work consciously addresses ideas of time and place. About American influences he says, "It was much later that I came to realise that many of the 'Americans' whose ideas were part of the mixture of influences I got, were first and second generation immigrants to America. Their background was linguistically complex, and far more like the linguistic complexity of my experience in Wales than that of growing up in 'PHILIP LARKIN' country . . . or the historically determined 'poetry of place' from Wales." He engages in more formally exploratory work—as does Zoë Skoulding, with whom he co-edits the splendid (and very cheap) *Skald* magazine. Davidson feels himself deeply rooted in North Wales but has only now started to be published there. Claiming that "there is no 'authentic' language usage within Wales which can reflect the experience of all its citizens," he argues that "a poetry that can provide a critique of this situation, of thinking with it, of providing within one poem a variety of perspectives and positions, can begin to reflect cultural condition." Skoulding's "Uruk" serves as an excellent example:

> To deconflict an airspace
> you have to think in four dimensions,
>   three you know
> then all the trajectories.

The new dynamism of the Welsh poetry scene can be traced in *Poetry Wales,* run since 1997 by the fiery environmentalist poet ROBERT MINHINNICK, who, like Peter Finch, Ian Davidson, Wendy Mulvey, Viki Holmes, lloyd robson, and David Greenslade, among others, is attracted to international poetry, especially of the Americas. As they do, too, he accuses his mainstream contemporaries of "prescriptive writing which tells people what Wales or Welshness is." Minhinnick publishes international work from the United States to Japan, Argentina to India, from a wider Europe—and, of course, from Wales. The multiple-award-winning Minhinnick, described as "the leading Welsh poet of his generation" in the *Sunday Times,* serves as a marker for the future. He, as is Peter Finch, is moving into and changing, the mainstream. For all of these writers the old conservatism acts as a spur. Some may win prizes, some may disappear, but all would agree with Minhinnick that though "most people think of writing as a hobby . . . it's not. It's a life commitment or it's nothing." It is an adventure—and there is not a daffodil in sight.

BIBLIOGRAPHY

Conran, Tony. *Frontiers in Anglo-Welsh Poetry.* Cardiff: University of Wales Press, 1997.

Gregson, Ian. *The New Poetry of Wales.* Cardiff: University of Wales Press, 2007.

Gwyn, Richard, ed. *The Pterodactyl's Wing: Welsh World Poetry.* Cardigan, Eng.: Parthian, 2003.

Meredith, Christopher, and Tony Curtis, eds. *Re-imagining Wales. Literary Review* 44, no. 2 (2001).

PeterFinch (and poetry in Wales). Available online. URL: http://www.peterfinch.co.uk. Accessed January 10, 2007.

Wack, Amy et al., eds. *Oxygen: New Poets from Wales.* Bridgend, Eng.: Seren, 2000.

Jeni Williams

"THE CONVERGENCE OF THE TWAIN (*LINES ON THE LOSS OF THE 'TITANIC'*)"

THOMAS HARDY (1912)   The SS *Titanic* sank on April 15, 1912, while crossing the Atlantic. Because the British passenger liner, the largest and most luxurious in its time, was considered unsinkable, the ship failed to have enough lifeboats for its passengers, resulting in the deaths of 1,513 of the 2,224 people aboard, including two of THOMAS HARDY's own acquaintances. Hardy completed his "occasional" poem within a week of the disaster, on April 24, 1912, and first published it in a souvenir program for the "Dramatic and Operatic Matinée in Aid of the 'Titanic' Disaster Fund," given at Covent Garden Theatre on May 14. Hardy revised and expanded the poem for publication in the June issue of the *Fortnightly Review* and included it in his 1914 collection of poetry, *Satires of Circumstance*.

The poem is typographically impressive: The stanzas look the same on the printed page, two short lines followed by a final longer third line, but also are numbered consecutively in Roman capitals, providing a visual representation of repetition with progression, even before the poem is read. A closer look at the first five stanzas reinforces this initial visual impression: Each is a sentence, complete in itself. In each of these stanzas, the first two lines describe the above-sea pride in the ship's majesty and the passengers' wealth, in contrast with the undersea indifference to such "vaingloriousness." Reading then reveals the stanzas to be concrete, or picture, poems, with the first two short lines representing the ship floating on top of the longer bottom line, the ocean into which the *Titanic* sank. Undersea, "cold currents" thread ("thrid") through the "steel chambers" that above sea were lit with "salamandrine fires" (salamanders were once believed to have been created from fire). The mirrors that above sea reflected the opulence of the passengers' jewelry are the undersea crawling place of the "indifferent" "seaworm," and the sparkling jewels themselves "lie lightless" and "black" undersea. Finally, the question asked by the "dim moon-eyed fishes" seeing the "gilded gear" on the bottom of the sea—"What does this vaingloriousness down here?"—leads to the answer given in the second half of the poem.

The first five stanzas (6–10) of the second half of the poem focus simultaneously on the *Titanic*'s being fitted out for its maiden voyage and the creation of the iceberg that will sink the ship. Although throughout these stanzas the two entities are "for the time far and dissociate" from each other, the impending doom of their eventual joining is signaled by the way the sentence begun in stanza 6 runs over into stanza 7 and the sentence begun in stanza 9 runs over into stanza 10, only

to be completed in stanza 11, the final stanza of the poem. Only stanza 8 is a self-contained sentence. The vertical above- and below-sea contrasts in the first five stanzas shift into horizontal here-and-there creations in the second five stanzas. The short first two lines of each stanza depict the human "fashioning" of the ship in terms suggesting a godlike creation, making a "creature of cleaving wing" that grows "In stature, grace, and hue." The long third lines of the stanzas reveal the underlying forces that will destroy the ship, not only the iceberg but also its creator, "the Immanent Will that stirs and urges everything." The Immanent Will is the blind drive of the universe that operates beyond human realization and without regard for human desires, ambitions, or assertions. It becomes especially manifest when it seems to be working against the individual or collective human will.

The final stanza of the poem presents the collision to which the preceding five stanzas were building. "No mortal eye" could foresee the "intimate welding" of the ship and iceberg

> Till the Spinner of the Years
> Said "Now!" And each one hears,
> And consummation comes, and jars two
>   hemispheres.

The description of the collision as a "consummation" picks up on the earlier imagery of the iceberg's being prepared as "a sinister mate" for the ship, the possible pun on *wedding* in the reference to the future "intimate welding" of the iceberg and ship, and the two creations being "twin halves of one august event," as well as on the fact that the *Titanic* was making its maiden voyage. To regard the tragedy as a marriage is an irony appropriate to the amoral Immanent Will. The dispassionate and mechanical objectivity of the poem's title displays a similar disregard for the human loss suffered during the sinking of the *Titanic*. This is not to say that Hardy did not himself sympathize with the loss and suffering, but in "The Convergence of the Twain" he adopts, to refer to Hardy's earlier epic drama *The Dynasts*, the cosmic points of view of the Spirit Ironic in the first half of the poem and of the Spirit of the Years, who sees that events are governed by the Immanent Will, in the second half, but not the compassionate view of the Spirit of Pities.

BIBLIOGRAPHY

Bailey, J. O. *The Poetry of Thomas Hardy: A Handbook and Commentary*. Chapel Hill: University of North Carolina Press, 1970.

Robert R. Watson

"THE COOL WEB" ROBERT GRAVES (1926)

The last poem published in *Poems (1914–1926)* by ROBERT GRAVES deals with language in its dual aspects, on the one hand its structuring and ordering function, and on the other the constraints it exerts on human experience. The poem mourns the loss of emotional immediacy in our linguistically shaped response to the world, at the same time stating the necessity of language for the preservation of human sanity. Graves poses the question whether poetry should be written out of emotional intensity alone or from a standpoint of intellectual detachment. He questions both extremes yet does not find a real compromise.

The poem contrasts concrete images in the first two stanzas with abstract argument in the last two stanzas. Childhood speechlessness in stanza 1 is set against an adult world conditioned by language in stanza 2. The two stages in human development are compared through the parallel repetition of four sensory impressions: tactile ("how hot the day is"), olfactory ("how hot the scent is of the summer rose"), visual ("how dreadful the black wastes of evening sky"), and auditory ("how dreadful the tall soldiers drumming by"). The undifferentiated perception of children is represented through repetition of the indirect question "how" and the monosyllabic simplicity of the sensory data—hot, tall, dark—an effect heightened by the regular iambs and the rhyming couplets at the end of each stanza. The children's reaction to these stimuli is initially described from an adult perspective negatively— "Children are dumb to say how hot the day is." Yet Graves also attempts to express truthfully the children's perspective. Their senses are exposed to the direct impact of experience, the vague but intense feelings caused by the simple but concrete impressions of the color, height, sound, and smell of the world.

The second stanza contrasts the experience of children with that of adults ("But we have speech"), who can interpret verbally the quality of the four impressions: the day is "angry," the smell of the rose "cruel," the night "overhanging," and the effect of the soldiers "fright." All phenomena are subsumed under anthropomorphic explanations, whereby the power (the "spell") of the immediate impression is broken: "We spell away the soldiers and the fright." The pun of "spell away" implies the magic possibilities of language (to place under a spell), but also the linguistic destruction of the enchanting and threatening might of things through their being put into words, through explanation and clarification of an objective "meaning" (to spell something out). Language can heighten the mystic or mythological aspects of reality, but it can also conquer and destroy them through intellectual abstraction. The subservience of the world to the linguistically able person is shown syntactically by the shift of *day, rose, sky,* and *soldiers* from the subject position in the first stanza to the object position of sentences where the subject is a defining *we*. The monosyllabic half-rhymes *chill, dull, spell* give an onomatopoeic impression of the "hushing" of emotions that would be overwhelming without a distancing language.

The remaining two stanzas switch from the concrete and imaginative to the abstract; from things such as the rose, night, and heaven to terms such as *language, joy, fear, self-possession,* and *death*. The metaphor of the "cool web of language," which winds us in, is reshaped into the metaphor of the cold sea, in which we drown. In our "retreat from too much joy or too much fear" into the security of language, we "die" through our own "volubility." Our enmeshment in the web of language, which "cools" our emotional response to reality, turns into a suffocation; we "coldly die" in the "brininess" of the sea of words. Language serves as a protection against joy and pain, yet its isolating function against the full heat of sensory impressions anesthetizes the emotions and deadens the soul.

The last stanza shows the other extreme state, the state of speechlessness in adults. We also "die" when we refuse the protective impersonality of words. "Throwing off language and its watery clasp" endangers human identity. Without the mediation of reality through a consciousness shaped by language, the chaotic onset of impressions and the intensity of our experiences of love and death would cause madness, as a shell-shocked, traumatized, and neurotic poet such as Graves knew. Naove openness ("the wide glare of the children's day") toward an overwhelming reality would lead to insanity: "We shall go mad no doubt and die that way."

Graves states the aporetic or paradoxical situation of the poet, who depends on language, yet is also afraid of losing touch with the origin of his emotions. There is no solution to this dilemma, but poetry must be written between these two extremes of primordial involvement with reality on the one hand and intellectual detachment on the other. We must choose between a world of abstract verbiage and madness. And yet the poem itself shows that language is so omnipresent that even a state of speechlessness can only be communicated through language; it is impossible to transcend our world of words. Derrida's dictum "il n'y a pas dehors texte" (there is nothing outside the text) applies: There is no escape from language.

BIBLIOGRAPHY

Day, Douglas. *Swifter than Reason: The Poetry and Criticism of Robert Graves.* Durham: University of North Carolina Press, 1963.

Graves, Robert. *The Complete Poems in One Volume,* edited by Beryl Graves and Dunstand Ward. London: Penguin, 2003.

Hühn, Peter. *Geschichte der englischen Lyrik.* Vol. 2. *Von der Viktorianischen Epoche bis zur Gegenwart.* Tübingen and Basel: Francke, 1995.

Kersnowski, Frank L. *The Early Poetry of Robert Graves: The Goddess Beckons.* Austin: University of Texas Press, 2002.

Kirkham, Michael. *The Poetry of Robert Graves.* London: Athlone Press, 1969.

Stewart, Jack F. "Graves's 'The Cool Web.'" *Explicator* 45 (1986): 49–50.

Heike Grundmann

COPE, WENDY (1945–)

Born to a 60-year-old department store manager and a wife three decades younger, both high-school dropouts, Wendy Mary Cope was educated at boarding schools and given instruction in piano and violin. As Gerry Cambridge has noted, her unusual background prevented her from fitting in with any social class or group at Oxford, where she read history. However, her position as an outsider would later stand her in good stead as a writer of satiric light verse. Despite battles with depression, Cope earned a B.A. from St. Hilda's College in 1966 and a diploma in education from Westminster College a year later. She then taught primary school in London for 17 of the next 19 years. Since 1986 she has made her living from her writing, including one four-year stint as the television critic for *Spectator.*

Cope began writing poetry in her late twenties after her father died, became depressed, and sought help from a therapist. Psychoanalysis put her in touch with her feelings, gave her confidence in her own private view of situations, and prepared her for the process of unearthing "surprises" from her psyche, as she told one interviewer. Within a few years, little magazines began publishing Cope's bitterly funny poems about failed relationships with men, as well as the witty parodies of famous male poets that she signed with the pseudonym *Jason Strugnell.* Her first poetry collection, MAKING COCOA FOR KINGSLEY AMIS (1986), contained sections devoted to both types of poems, mostly in rhymed and metered forms, plus a third section whose lone four-line poem explained that the book's title had originated in a dream. While provoking mixed reactions from critics, Cope's poems have been embraced by the British public: *Making Cocoa* and its successor, *Serious Concerns* (1992), have each sold more than 100,000 copies, and a 1998 BBC Radio poll pronounced Cope the listeners' choice to become Britain's next poet laureate. In her third collection, *If I Don't Know* (2001), Cope shifted her thematic focus from the failure of heterosexual relationships to the transience of domestic happiness, reflecting her 1994 move to Winchester, Hampshire, to live with the poet and critic Lachlan Mackinnon. The volume also contained a long narrative poem in rhymed couplets about an unloved child who grows up to be a teacher; while ambitious in its scope, it has been judged as less successful than Cope's shorter lyrics.

If I Don't Know was shortlisted for the Whitbread Poetry Award; Cope's other honors include a Cholmondeley Award (1987) and the Michael Braude

Award from the American Academy of Arts and Letters (1995). In addition to her slim poetic output, Cope has authored two children's books and edited five anthologies, including *The Funny Side: 101 Humorous Poems* (1998) and *Heaven on Earth: 101 Happy Poems* (2001).

See also "THE WASTE LAND LIMERICKS."

BIBLIOGRAPHY

Cambridge, Gerry. "Wendy Cope (1945–   )." In *British Writers: Supplement VIII*, edited by Jay Parini, 67–84. New York: Scribner's, 2003.

Gioia, Dana. "The Two Wendy Copes." In *Barrier of a Common Language: An American Looks at Contemporary British Poetry*, 64–70. Ann Arbor: University of Michigan Press, 2003.

Julie Kane

CORNFORD, FRANCES (1886–1960)

It is likely that every opening sentence about Frances Cornford will note her famous family: She was the granddaughter of Charles Darwin; the daughter of Sir Francis Darwin, the Cambridge botanist; the wife of Francis Cornford, the Cambridge classicist and translator of Plato; the mother of JOHN CORNFORD, the poet killed at 21 in the Spanish Civil War. Less well known is that her mother, Ellen Crofts, was a great-niece of William Wordsworth. As both a Darwin and a Wordsworth, she was heir to two of the most noteworthy and iconic figures of the 19th century, who often were seen to be in opposition to each other. Her obliteration for a while in our literary histories was prefigured in her own life by the disappearance even of her first name, which she shared initially with her father and then with her husband. To prevent household confusion with her husband, she was known by her initials, *FCC*, for *Frances Crofts Cornford* (and he was known as *FMC*, for *Francis MacDonald Cornford*).

She celebrated her famous family later in life in a small poem called "Family Likeness." It is a typical poem by Cornford, focusing on a domestic moment, seen from the maternal eye. She recalls how for "half a century now" she has noticed, "under the shaggy or the baby brow," both the old and young members of her family looking "through microscope or at a picture-book." The family likeness she captures is a particular look, of "quick, responsive, curious delight" (the triple adjective is a common Cornford poetic device), whose sight she has always "blessed." The poem's superficial qualities make Cornford appear a comfortably middle-class prefeminist poet: the polite and self-effacing diction; the stability and comfort of rhyme; the "poetic feel" of such a synecdoche as *brow*; the happy aliveness of babies; the implied warm relationship between mother and child, which has us imagining them reading a picture book together in the nursery at bedtime; the honoring of the old, who are not feeble but rather a more hearty *shaggy*; the honoring of intelligence, in both science and art (*microscope* and *picture*); and the conventional call upon religion in the last line, through the word *blessed*, which earlier in her life would have been used in a secular way or ironically.

Read this way, one sees why Cornford has disappeared from the canon, which gave her a place through the 1950s, especially in the anthologies edited by Louis Untermeyer. Most anthologists since the 1960s have favored the new and the ground-breaking, which Cornford's work was not, except in her belated eschewing of Georgian poetic diction and strong, regular rhythms. Her most famous anthology pieces, unfortunately, are her quatrain for RUPERT BROOKE, "YOUTH," and her frequently parodied triolet "To a Fat Lady seen from a Train," a piece of juvenilia whose tone fights with its intention, creating a misunderstanding that caused her much grief. She is also known for "The New-Born Baby's Song," an eight-line poem that shows Cornford's gift for clever, compact evocations of sentiment, which ends, however, with the surprising couplet "But I could bite my mother's breast, / And that made up for all the rest"—an ending too biting to anchor a greeting card line.

That biting quality in apparent even in "Family Likeness," implicit in its rhetorical structure. Though the poem overtly does nothing but praise, the position of the poet is curiously buried. She makes her appearance only in the middle, in the fourth line's "I," surrounded early and late by images of the family. This may represent being in the bosom of the family, except that her own breast gives suckle and comfort but receives only a bite. The bite here, the price she pays for the good of the family, is her retreat to the middle, a kind of suffocation in domestic duty. Even the locution "for half a century I have seen it now" suggests the in-betweenness or halfway quality of her status in the poem. She is the instrument of the family's blessing, balanced at its fulcrum, surrounded by the very young or the very old. And though the poem does not explicitly say so, the family sounds quite male: the "shaggy brow" of age does not square with concepts of female beauty, and the sexless infants indifferent to song, sun, or skies, intent only on their goal-directed hunger, suggest (in the conventional cultural gender categories) male drive rather than female relatedness. In a metaphorical view, she is halfway between Darwin and Wordsworth. She is a poet, but a very practical, clear-headed one, who prefers the precise observation of small moments (such as Darwin's finches) to grand Wordsworthian pronouncements. As a Darwin, she is firmly ensconced in Cambridge academic life (SIEGFRIED SASSOON said he could not imagine her outside Cambridge), yet not formally educated, schooled instead by a Wordsworthian aliveness to her surroundings. She mitigates each predecessor's genius, taking something from the father and something from the mother, as all children must do. Read this way, a subtle complexity enters the poetry. Neither conventionally maternal nor overtly feminist, poems such as "The New-Born Baby's Song" and "Family Likeness" stand the poet in an uncomfortable spot, celebrating that which is at one and the same time debilitating and worthy. Mother to three sons and two daughters, Cornford had a life punctuated by three periods of depression. The first, after the death of her mother, lasted three years, after which she suddenly recovered, returned to Cambridge from Switzerland, and reentered society with a renewed, almost manic, energy at age 20. She and her cousin Gwen Darwin Raverat became close to Rupert Brooke and the group that gathered around him, named the Neo-Pagans by Virginia Stephen for their flouting of Victorian conventions. The Second episode of extended depression occurred in 1917, when Christopher was born just a year after her oldest son, John. This period ended two years later, in 1919, when Frances was 33. The next decade and a half were fruitful for her; she published volumes of poetry in 1923, 1928, and 1934, when the third and longest depression struck, lasting six years, during which she stayed in bed at home and was

unable to write or even see her children. She made a sudden recovery in 1940—at the fall of France, the family story goes—and from that time to the end of her life was not troubled by depression again. She produced five more volumes: *Poems from the Russian* (1943); *Travelling Home* (1948); *Collected Poems* (published in 1954, when she was 68, and including new poems from 1948 to 1953); and *On a Calm Shore* (1960) and *Fifteen Poems From the French* (1976), both published posthumously.

BIBLIOGRAPHY

Dowson, Jane, ed. *Frances Cornford: Selected Poems*. London: Enitharmon Press, 1996.

Raverat, Gwen. *Period Piece*. New York: Norton, 1952.

Rogers, Timothy. "Frances Cornford." *London Magazine*, August–September 1992: 101–112.

James Persoon

CORNFORD, JOHN (1915–1936) Rupert

John Cornford, the oldest son of Francis and FRANCES CORNFORD, was born in 1915, the same year his namesake, RUPERT BROOKE, died. Cornford began writing poetry at an early age: An instructor sent some of his poems for comment to W. H. AUDEN and T. S. ELIOT. Both poets took the time to respond encouragingly to the work of someone so young. Eliot and Auden, as well as ROBERT GRAVES, Louis Aragon, and William Blake, were significant influences.

Cornford joined the Communist Party in 1933, shortly before going up to Cambridge. As a student, he excelled in his studies while engaging in political activity and writing essays defining the role of poetry in life, particularly politics. He noted that Eliot's descriptions of a disintegrating society were brilliant, but he had failed to perform a satisfactory analysis (presumably based on Marxist orthodoxy). He also attacked STEPHEN SPENDER's poetry as being fashionably rather than substantially revolutionary. Only nine of Cornford's poems from this time survive. Most (such as "Keep Culture Out of Cambridge" and "Sergei Mironovich Kirov") were political. Two, however, one untitled and the other, "Sad Poem," describe his feelings of pain upon ending a relationship with the woman who had borne him a son.

In August 1936 he became the first Englishman to go to fight for the republicans in the Spanish Civil War.

Wounded in early fall 1936, he returned to Britain to enlist recruits. At the end of the year he was serving on the front lines with the International Brigades and was killed leading a unit that was covering a retreat while under assault by the nationalists. He died either on or the day after his 21st birthday and his body was never found. He wrote three poems on his first tour in Spain. Two, "Full Moon at Tierz" and "A Letter from Aragon," are based upon his military experience. Both poems, but particularly the latter with its refrain, "This is a quiet sector of a quiet front," capture the drudgery and fear that infantry on the line experienced. His third poem, "To Margot Heinemann," distills the thoughts of a man in love who also performs what he considers to be his duty even though that pursuit requires their perhaps permanent separation.

It is impossible to guess how Cornford's poetry would have evolved or whether he would have continued to write poetry. As he became more skilled as a poet, he seemed to lose interest in it as something apart from revolutionary politics. As did his contemporaries, V.G. Kiernan and Bernard Knox, he might have pursued other fields altogether. What remains is a small, intense body of work that captures the voice of a period when many poets believed themselves to be part of a revolutionary struggle.

BIBLIOGRAPHY

Galassi, Jonathan, ed. *Understand the Weapon, Understand the Wound: Selected Writings of John Cornford.* Manchester, Eng.: Carcanet, 1976,

Sloan, Pat, ed. *John Cornford, a Memoir.* Dunfermline, Eng.: Borderline Press, 1938.

Stansky, Peter, and William Abrahams. *Journey to the Frontier: Two Roads to the Spanish Civil War.* Chicago: University of Chicago Press, 1983.

Robert Stacy

"CORPSE-DAY" OSBERT SITWELL (1919) This poem was OSBERT SITWELL's first contribution to the newly founded mouthpiece of the Labour Party, the *Daily Herald,* in post–World War I London. Although the editors of the *Herald* were socialists, many contributors at this time were young intellectuals who had become radicals as a result of the Great War. Osbert Sitwell, while not a socialist in the strict sense, contrib-

uted poetry arising from his own disillusionment with and contempt for the ruling classes. The Great War poet SIEGFRIED SASSOON was appointed literary editor of the paper, and on July 19, 1919, he published Sitwell's poem, "Corpse-Day."

This poem is a bitter statement arising from Osbert Sitwell's own experiences in the First World War. In this poem, Sitwell attacks those whom he considers to be warmongers, among them Winston Churchill. Sitwell believed that the Great War lasted as long as it did and sacrificed so many lives because of politicians who attempted to make the public believe that the war was for the good, and that they had right on their side. "Corpse-Day" bitterly strikes at those who hold this view, and instead of celebrating the end of the war, this poem expresses shame and pity for the tremendous suffering and grief caused by the war.

The poem opens with a description of dusk and the scents of midsummer flowers and trees in the wind. Despite the apparent beauty of this image, dusk or evening is a trope of death and loss, and the scents on the wind are caused by bruised and battered flowers. The first line of the poem associates evening with the earth: "Dust floated up from the earth beneath." The earth beneath is reminiscent of graves, and in the second section of the poem the image of graves becomes clearer, as "Up from the earth there rose / sounds of great triumph and rejoicing."

It would appear that the dead are celebrating the end of the war. However, in the next section of the poem the focus shifts to an image of Christ watching the victory celebrations from heaven. Christ is disturbed by other sounds: "The continuous weeping of widows and children / which had haunted Him for so long." The poem emphasizes that the victory celebrations are most joyful in Christian countries, yet Christ himself is the only one able to hear the noises of grief and loss.

In this poem the fireworks of the peace celebrations are paralleled with the rockets and shells of the war. The prosperity and joy of 1919 are built upon the bones of corpses, and Sitwell satirizes the so-called Christianity of a country that could send so many to their deaths. Christ looks into the city and sees his image in many churches. But he sees how his image has been changed again and again over time "so as to make war more easy," until it is no longer the face of Christ that is worshipped but the face of Moloch, the god who demands sacrifice.

BIBLIOGRAPHY

Sitwell, Osbert. *The Collected Satires and Poems of Osbert Sitwell.* London: Duckworth, 1931.

Hazel Atkins

"CRAZY JANE TALKS WITH THE BISHOP" W. B. YEATS (1931)

The Crazy Jane series makes up the first seven poems in W. B. YEATS's "Words for Music Perhaps," a collection of tightly rhymed verses drawing on the forms of ballads, Irish peasant poetry, and the songs of Shakespeare's fools. Crazy Jane, the speaker of the series, is not crazy at all: Her name stems from her status as an outsider. As an independent and radical figure, she speaks both for Yeats's version of Irish nationalism and for his philosophy of love.

Crazy Jane's implied interlocutor and nemesis throughout the series is the Bishop. The Bishop has earned her enmity by enforcing an orthodox sexual morality and exiling her lover, Jack the Journeyman, with whom, he says early in the series, she "lived like beast and beast" ("Crazy Jane and the Bishop").

In "Crazy Jane Talks with the Bishop," the antagonistic positions of the interlocutors become clear. The Bishop speaks first, reminding Crazy Jane of her mortality and urging her to repentance, saying, "Live in a heavenly mansion, / Not in some foul sty." The Bishop urges Jane (and the reader) to eschew the "foul sty" of transient, animal sexual love, as it is inferior to the "heavenly mansion" of Christian purity.

Jane refuses, responding that the Bishop misunderstands the nature of love and that his vision of heaven is incomplete. She accuses him of drawing a false dichotomy: "'Fair and foul are near of kin, / And fair needs foul,' I cried," and points out the biological truth "Love has pitched his mansion in / The place of excrement." Jane's response shows that the Bishop's "heavenly mansion" is not heavenly—or not purely heavenly—at all: The genitals' dual use for reproduction and excretion becomes her evidence that love

must have a "foul" component. The "foul" is not necessarily repellent or evil; instead, it is an undeniable aspect of human experience. The Bishop's refusal to acknowledge the importance of the "foul" renders his heaven sterile, making it no heaven at all. Jane ends with the lines "nothing can be sole or whole / That has not been rent," arguing that the loss of virginity is necessary to make a person complete. A love that is simultaneously sexual and spiritual has a frightening potential for destruction, but it makes the lover whole, allowing her access to the multifaceted "heavenly mansion" that the Bishop cannot imagine.

BIBLIOGRAPHY

Ellman, Richard. *Yeats: The Man and the Masks.* New York: Macmillan, 1948.
MacNeice, Louis. *The Poetry of W. B. Yeats.* London: Oxford University Press, 1941.
Rosenthal, M. L., and Sally M. Gall. "The Evolution of William Butler Yeats's Sequences II (1929–38)." In *Critical Essays on W. B. Yeats,* edited by Richard J. Finneran, 224–245. Boston: G. K. Hall, 1986.

Rachel Trousdale

"THE CREMATION OF SAM McGEE" ROBERT WILLIAM SERVICE (1907)

A folksy ballad with a surprise ending and an eminently approachable narrative voice, "The Cremation of Sam McGee" introduces itself by opening a window onto the foreign, frozen world of the North:

> There are strange things done in the midnight
>   sun
> By the men who moil for gold;
> The Arctic trails have their secret tales
> That would make your blood run cold;
> The Northern lights have seen queer sights,
> But the queerest they ever did see
> Was that night on the marge of Lake Lebarge
> I cremated Sam McGee.

Its irrepressible rhythm and rhyme, its lilting ballad stanza and grisly plot twists, are all perfectly representative of ROBERT WILLIAM SERVICE's Yukon poetry, a poetry that is ridiculously easy to recite and almost as easy to memorize. Even in this first stanza, there is a sample of Service's love of language, where the unusual word *moil* takes the place of *toil,* lending the poem an exotic sound to accompany the strange landscape and supernatural events.

The story itself, fit for a campfire as well as a corner table in the saloon, is one that takes us on the trail with the intrepid gold rush narrator and his unfortunate companion, as "On a Christmas day we were musing our way over the Dawson trail. / Talk of your cold! Through the parka's fold it stabbed like a driven nail." Homely metaphors and an infusion of natural images allow readers to hunker down with the gold miner in the "long, long night, by the lone firelight, while the huskies, round in a ring, howled out their woes to the homeless snows," in a climate where the men all work incredibly hard, overcoming impossible odds to survive, and tell their story to the yet unknowing world. Ultimately this poetry earned Service a reputation as the quintessential Canadian frontier poet. The sensual detail and raw, gripping narrative of death and cold make an unforgettable combination as Sam McGee's frozen corpse torments the narrator until he fulfills his promise to cremate the body if McGee dies along the trail, for "a promise made is a debt unpaid, and the trail has its own stern code."

BIBLIOGRAPHY

Hirsch, Edward. "A Structural Analysis of Robert Service's Yukon Ballads." *Southern Folklore Quarterly* 40 (1976): 125–140.

Marshall, Ian. "When East Meets West: Strategies of Enclosure in Robert Service's 'The Cremation of Sam McGee.'" *South Dakota Review* 30, no. 1 (1992): 96–103.

Jo Miller

CROW TED HUGHES (1970)   In 1962 a book of engravings by Leonard Baskin was published with an introduction by TED HUGHES, in which he singled out for comment Baskin's depiction of a dead crow. Baskin then invited Hughes to "make a book with him simply about crows," a project that eventually developed into the *Crow* series of poems. Hughes was already established as a nature poet, but his poetic voice gained new range, new urgency, and raucousness from the conjunction of Baskin's visual stimuli, his strange, unbeautiful, lumpy-bodied crow-people; of crow and raven myth from the old and new worlds; and of real life crow attributes such as adaptation to city life, bold curiosity, an omnivorous diet of scraps and carrion, and a formidable set of survival skills.

To this mix Hughes added his interest in sacred texts such as the Tibetan Book of the Dead, classical myth, and modern interpretations of myth such as ROBERT GRAVES's *The White Goddess,* Paul Radin's *The Trickster,* and Carl Jung's *The Archetypes and the Collective Unconscious.* Hughes was also influenced by the writings of Vasko Popa and other contemporary Eastern European poets, whose politically aware works give a "fresh and urgent" inflection to the themes of disaster and survival. *Crow* is also deeply concerned with what Hughes diagnosed as the perilously sick state of Western civilization, now dwindled into a "nationalistic, humanistic outlook" while still dominated by reductive, unduly constraining scientific parameters and Judeo-Christian beliefs. Out of this mix of influences and concerns poured the execrations, catalogs of disasters, invocations, squawks of despair, and crude jokes that make up *Crow.*

In writing these poems, Hughes had in mind an extensive storyline, to which Crow's songs were to be attached. Hughes's myth starts after the universe has been created, when God ("the man-created, broken-down, corrupt despot of a ramshackle religion") experiences a recurrent nightmare of a hand attacking and overcoming him in fight. Eventually God makes this nightmare being speak: It mocks him and his creation, especially man, "who has completely mismanaged his gifts and destroyed himself and the world." God challenges the hand to do better, and after some disastrous experiments it produces Crow, who becomes half-man after a series of exploits.

Unknown to him, Crow's quest is to discover the true, imprisoned female creator deity, but he bungles every meeting with her—or, according to another account, finally integrates his "almost humanity" and unites with his goddess bride. This mythic narrative was not published alongside the *Crow* poems, although it appears on the jacket of the recorded version, and Hughes often spoke of it (not altogether consistently) in interviews and at poetry readings. Seven new poems were added to the second edition of *Crow* and Hughes brought other poems to bear on the narrative in public readings. Thus the exact boundaries of *Crow* are indeterminable: Should it be considered the original publication, or the extended series of poems published as *Crow,* or the whole set of poems that Hughes from time to time nominated, alongside his mythic narrative?

Hughes came to regret the publication of *Crow* as an unfinished work, but he had found it hard to complete this project along the lines of his narrative; the narrative itself, particularly its ending, does not seem to have been fully worked out. Whether in their first or expanded edition, the *Crow* poems by no means cover the span of his story, clustering more toward its nightmarish start. *Crow* emphasizes problems, confrontations, battles and other disasters, clumsy experiments, and deliberate sabotage. Its relationships sometimes involve glee or awe but more commonly evoke shock and anguish. Robinson proposes that the myth itself precluded the celebratory ending that Hughes had planned, for in it Crow is given two incompatible roles, that of a heroic adventurer who can learn from his experiences, become almost human, and achieve integration (in Jungian terms, individuate), and that of the immortal trickster who provokes, taunts, and wrecks, an agent for chaos and also for change within human consciousness but in himself changeless (in Jungian terms, the trickster archetype). Such incompatibility becomes acute in those poems where Crow meets the feminine as mother earth, as birth mother, or as sexual being. When Crow is portrayed as trickster, it is impossible for him to achieve the connectedness of loving relationship.

While some of Hughes's statements about the *Crow* poems insist on this mythic context, others encourage a reading of the book as self-sufficient, with the story only a means of engendering the published work; Hughes says, for instance, that the Crow story is "not really relevant to the poems as they stand." Unaware of the mythic framework, the book's first critics responded to the poems "as they stand," and many of them did not like what they read. Critics regretted Hughes's shift of subject matter away from more traditional nature poetry to confronting and sometimes savage depictions of human folly and destructiveness. Hughes's language was deplored, its lack of lyricism, its flat colloquialisms, the bathetic endings to poems such as "Crow and the Birds" ("Crow spraddled head-down in the beach-garbage, guzzling a dropped ice-cream") or "A Horrible Religious Error" ("Beat the hell out of it, and ate it"). Some found the collection disturbing as a celebration of violence. Calvin Bedient accused Hughes of nihilism, saying that the book was "the croak of nihilism itself." In terms of both themes and language, Hughes was considered to be in danger of wasting his talents as a nature poet in a nasty, ugly dead end.

Much of this criticism stems from a misperception of Hughes's method of attack. A dominant theme in these poems, evident without recourse to the missing mythic narrative, is an attack on culturally dominant Western ways of thinking that, according to Hughes, have shut down imaginative possibilities, reduced truth to externalities, and diminished human sensitivity, morality, and capacity to love. In effect this is a Blakean attack on the scientific and religious underpinnings to contemporary technological and ecological disaster, in particular to do with war, and all the political, social, sexual, psychological, and spiritual ills that beset the modern world. To accuse him of nihilism is thus to mistake the doctor for the disease. The emphasis of Hughes's first critics on negativity can be regarded as a mark of his success in evoking for critical scrutiny the nihilism permeating twentieth-century Western culture.

Nevertheless, Hughes's hostile critics have a point. In poems such as "In Laughter," it is hard to read the details of violent death as other than celebratory. Crow is not a sensitive human being who has attained inner calm: He is a bird who eats carrion, an amoral trickster who enjoys mischief making, whatever its cost, exulting in disconnection and dissonance. A few poems like "Littleblood" stand out as lyrical evocations of connectedness, and "Crow's Undersong" can be read as praise of the Jungian anima, tender, tentative, and speechless, but such moments are rare amid the cacophany, and Hughes's faithfulness to ancient mythic representations of the feminine as goddess, tomb, womb, and poetic muse can also be read as misogynistic.

In its use of biblical and less familiar mythic material, and in its portrayal of the wreckage of Western civilisation, *Crow* revisits the territory of T. S. ELIOT's

THE WASTE LAND, but with far less promise of revival and renewal. "Crow on the Beach" is the book's sardonic homage to Matthew Arnold's "Dover Beach," with Crow able to grasp something of the sea's "ogreish outcry and convulsion" but too small-brained to achieve Arnoldian melancholy. "A Horrible Religious Error" revisits D. H. LAWRENCE'S "SNAKE," now not "earth-golden" but "earth-bowel brown"; not portentous of Satan, sin, and death or of reemerging pre-Christian religion, but instead a lump of feces eaten by the unfastidious crow. This poem embodies the paradoxical challenge of the work as a whole: Is it a celebration of violent energy for its own sake, with Crow as amoral trickster, or is it furiously grieving, mocking, and tearing away at a millennia-long deception that human beings have practiced on themselves, a call for its readers to notice, be shocked, and change?

BIBLIOGRAPHY

Faas, Ekbert. *Ted Hughes: The Unaccommodated Universe.* Santa Barbara, Calif.: Black Sparrow Press, 1980.

Hughes, Ted. *Crow, from the Life and Songs of the Crow.* London: Faber, 1970.

Robinson, Craig. *Ted Hughes as Shepherd of Being.* New York: St. Martin's Press, 1989.

Alice Mills

CUBISM Cubism constitutes one of the most critical breakthroughs for the development of art in the 20th century, formulating a new way of seeing and representation for artists. The product of the creative partnership of the Frenchman Georges Braque (1882–1963) and Spanish-born Pablo Picasso (1881–1973), cubism's influence on modern art cannot be overstated. It is perhaps the most influential and original art movement of the 20th century. Although it was born in France, cubism became the first truly international or transnational art movement, embraced by artists regardless of nationality or ideology as an entirely new and wholly modern mode of representation.

Although the canon of artists beyond Picasso and Braque identified as cubists is relatively small—the Frenchmen Fernand Léger (1881–1955) and Robert Delaunay (1885–1941) and the Spaniard Juan Gris (1887–1927)—there is hardly a major artist of the early 20th century who was not influenced by cubism in some way, and many of the significant movements that followed such as futurism, Orphism, and Russian constructivism would have been inconceivable without it. Even artists such as the Dutchman Piet Mondrian (1872–1944) and the Russian Kasimir Malevich (1878–1935), who experimented with cubism before moving in a different direction, could not have developed the ideals and forms of the movements for which they are known, respectively—de Stijl and suprematism—were it not for their earlier encounters with cubism.

Predominantly a movement in the visual arts, cubism also attracted a number of poets as practitioners and proponents. Most notable among those were Guillaume Apollinaire, André Salmon, and Pierre Reverdy. Apollinaire and Salmon were both art critics on influential newspapers such as *L'Intransigeant, Le Temps,* and *Le Journal* and wrote for the journals *Les Soirées de Paris and Montjoie!* Apollinaire's book, *The Cubist Painters: Aesthetic Meditations,* first published in 1913, however, is valuable more for the author's insights into contemporary painting than into cubism per se.

Cubism is yet another AVANT-GARDE art movement that derived its name from an offhand pejorative remark. The term was coined when the critic Louis Vauxcelles wrote in a review of an exhibition of Braques's work that Braque "reduces everything, places and figures and houses, to geometrical schemes, to cubes." This remark was a response to overhearing the painter Henri Matisse refer to Braque's "little cubes" on seeing his painting *Houses at L'Estaque* at the 1908 Salon d'Automne.

Cubism abandons the perceptual realism based on linear perspective that had dominated Western painting since the Renaissance. Illusionism was rejected in favor of a more conceptual approach to representation that attempted to capture something more fundamental and thus more "real" than mere visible appearance. It reduces the visible subject to its constituent parts, identifying the fragment as the common denominator in both visual perception and the representation of things. Although direct influences have been difficult to confirm, cubism has been associated with contemporary developments in science, specifically those regarding Einstein's theories of relativity and the space-time continuum, and the molecular subdivision of matter. It has commonly been considered the antithesis of expressionism—reflecting rational investigation as opposed to intuitive expression. Expressionism and cubism, the two dominant strains of early modern art, are frequently presented in terms of the clash of classical and romantic sensibilities that goes back to antiquity and the debate over the proper relationship between the Apollonian and Dionysian forces at work in man and society in Western thought.

As many of their contemporaries did, Picasso and Braque sought a new form of art that was to them more authentic, more direct, and thus, more "real." They were drawn to many of the same sources as their contemporaries, rejecting the artifice and illusionism of the Western tradition since the Renaissance. Specifically they drew on the simple directness and abstract, underlying geometrical forms found in so-called primitive sculpture from Africa, Oceania, and Iberia that was appearing in exhibitions around Europe. From closer to home, they drew on the structured paintings of the postimpressionist painter Paul Cézanne, who transformed his subject into a composition of colorful patches "woven" together into a harmonious tapestry of paint on the surface of the canvas.

Cubism's impact on British poetry was facilitated, as were so many modern movements, by EZRA POUND. Several cubist techniques are to be found in imagist poetry, such as the tendency to focus on ordinary objets, the foregrounding of isolated details, and the vizualisation of the essence of an object. Cubist-influenced painting and poetry were linked and shaped anew under vorticism, Pound's futuristic alternative to IMAGISM, which demanded a transforming modern explosion in the arts that was meant to start a whirl of artistic creation. In terms of the visual arts, vorticism represented an original variant of elements borrowed from cubism. Pound's most obviously vorticist poem is "Dogmatic Statements on a Game of Chess: Theme for a Series of Pictures," whose angular shapes and abrupt movements could described a vorticist painting. The poetry magazine BLAST, produced by WYNDHAM LEWIS and Pound to "blast" old conceptions of art (but which unfortunately appeared in only two issues during 1914–15, when Britain was being blasted quite enough in the Great War), reflected cubist influence with its typographical and visual experiments. Early practitioners included T(HOMAS) E(RNEST) HULME, RICHARD ALDINGTON, H. D. (HILDA DOOLITTLE), and Herbert Read.

Cubism arguably changed the trajectory of the visual arts in the 20th century. What began as an intense personal artistic collaboration between two artists investigating the problem of representation gave rise to developments that were to be essentially iconoclastic. Cubism's rejection of perceptual realism and "significant" subject matter, the assertion of the notion that a work of art may be made from anything no matter how mundane the material or object and does not depend on craftsmanship or permanence, effectively undermined the Western fine arts traditions, setting contemporary art on an entirely different course.

BIBLIOGRAPHY
Cooper, Douglas, and Gary Tinterow. *The Essential Cubism: Braque, Picasso, and Their Friends.* New York and London: G. Braziller in association with the Tate Gallery, 1984.

Fry, Edward. *Cubism.* New York: McGraw-Hill, 1966.

Harrison, Charles, Francis Frascina, and Gill Perry. *Primitivism, Cubism, Abstraction: The Early Twentieth Century.* New Haven, Conn.: Yale University Press, 1993.

Rosenblum, Robert. *Cubism and Twentieth-Century Art.* Rev. ed. New York: Abrams, 1984.

Rubin, William. *Picasso and Braque: Pioneering Cubism.* New York: Museum of Modern Art, 1989.

Zelevansky, Lynn, ed. *Picasso and Braque: A Symposium.* New York: Museum of Modern Art, 1992.

Rachel Smith

CUNARD, NANCY (1896–1965)

Nancy Cunard was a modernist poet and political activist with a radical disregard for social propriety. Her poetry has its roots in British modernist experimentation and the traditional English prosody she learned from governesses and elite boarding schools. The British AVANT-GARDE—EZRA POUND, C. DAY LEWIS, T. S. ELIOT; and EDITH SITWELL, for instance—gave Cunard social and artistic environments wherein she could repudiate the stuffiness of her aristocratic upbringing. Indeed she published some of her first poems in *Wheels*—an avant-garde anthology she co-edited with Edith Sitwell. In her first books of poetry—*Outlaws* (1921) and *Sublunary* (1923)—Cunard experiments with free verse but generally deploys more traditional sonnets or iambic rhythms. The wandering, melancholic speakers of these poems often describe the painful compensations of social exile.

Expatriate 1920s Paris enabled Cunard to refine her poetry and embark upon the collaborative projects so integral to her adult cultural achievement. Her involvement there with surrealists who sought to use unorthodox juxtapositions to articulate the unconscious coincided with the writing of *Parallax* and two other fine poems: "Simultaneous" (1930) and "In Provins" (1930). In these innovative poems unmarked by Cunard's earlier formal rigidity, travelers use fragmented images to explore the overlapping of and gaps between past and present. Cunard's position in Paris at the center of international networks of writers and artists also enabled her to initiate cooperative artistic production by opening her own press in 1928. The Hours Press printed works by, among others, expatriate American and British modernists.

The shift from the aesthetics of the 1920s to the politics of the 1930s found Cunard fighting tyranny through more collective literary projects. Cunard's *Negro* anthology (1934)—for which she coordinated submissions from 150 writers and intellectuals, two-thirds of whom were black—documented the cultural triumphs and sociopolitical nightmares of Africans in diaspora. The rise of fascism catapulted the passionately antifascist Cunard to Spain, where she reported on the Spanish Civil War for the Associated Negro Press and the *Manchester Guardian*. Cunard also raised money for the republican cause by publishing a series of poems by international poets called *Poets of the World Defend the Spanish People* (1937). She followed that project with the publication of *Authors Take Sides on the Spanish War* (1937)—the first known attempt to effect political change by presenting the opinions of writers en masse. Cunard coordinated another anthology of poems in support of the French resistance during World War II, but neither she nor her career ever rebounded from the defeat of the republicans by Franco. "To Eat To-Day" (1938), a poem juxtaposing the hunger of men running bombing missions and the victims of their bombs, is one of numerous uncollected poems Cunard wrote in response to the Spanish conflict.

Cunard's controversial life—her published rebukes of her mother, her relationships with black men, and her associations with primitivism and communism—have made critics and historians reluctant to recognize her substantial contributions to modernist poetry, history, and art. Fortunately scholars are now beginning to grapple with the controversies and restore Cunard to modernist history.

BIBLIOGRAPHY
Benstock, Shari. *Women of the Left Bank*. Austin: University of Texas Press, 1986.
Chisholm, Anne. *Nancy Cunard: A Biography*. New York: Alfred Knopf, 1979.
Dowson, Jane, and Alice Entwistle. *A History of Twentieth-Century British Women's Poetry*. Cambridge: Cambridge University Press, 2005.
Hugh, Ford, ed. *Nancy Cunard: Brave Poet, Indomitable Rebel 1896–1965*. Philadelphia: Chilton Book Company, 1968.
Marcus, Jane. "Bonding and Bondage: Nancy Cunard and the Making of the Negro Anthology." In *Hearts of Darkness: White Women Write Race*. New Brunswick, N.J.: Rutgers University Press, 2004.

Robin Calland

CURNOW, ALLEN (1911–2001) Allen

Curnow was born in 1911 in Timaru, New Zealand, the son of an Anglican minister. Many moves to the various parishes his father served meant living in a succession of vicarages before finally moving to Christchurch. There he began working as a junior journalist for the *Christchurch Sun* in 1929–30 before moving to Auckland in order to prepare for the Anglican ministry at a theological college between 1931 and 1933. During this time his first poems were published in the university periodicals *Kiwi* and *Phoenix,* already hinting at a growing distance from his religious vocation. Though biblical imagery and allegory remained a constant element of his writing, his first collection, *Valley of Decision,* published to great acclaim in 1933, coincided with his own decision not to be ordained after all.

Instead Curnow turned to full-time writing, publishing poems, a poetic manifesto ("Poetry and Language," 1935), satires, essays, and reviews across the genres, in a variety of outlets, such as the *New Zealand Herald,* the radical periodical *Tomorrow* (1934–40), and various anthologies by the nation's leading publishing house, Caxton. Often he used pseudonyms in his more radical writings ("Whim-Wham," "Amen," "Julian"). In his volumes of poetry (*Poems 1934–36*, 1937; *Sailing or Drowning*, 1943), he developed a sharp awareness of New Zealand's striking individuality in landscape and geopolitical situation, marking him out as the unique explorer of New Zealand psyche and outlook on life.

After the war, Curnow gradually became recognized to be one of his nation's leading poets and intellectual voices, mastering a genuinely new fusion of (predominantly) English poetic traditions in tone, meter, and imagery with regional, New Zealand–specific topics and settings, thus achieving in verse what Katherine Mansfield had undertaken for prose a generation earlier. He took an active stand in many public debates, authored a number of controversial plays for stage and radio, and undertook the critical assessment of New Zealand's poetic achievements single-handedly: "Only an art well-rooted will ever spread its branches far." Though remaining intellectually committed (and personally resident in) to his native country, Curnow's work also displayed universal concerns with transnational issues such as ecology, faith, and justice, probably most impressively rendered in the highly successful collection *Trees, Effigies, Moving Objects* (1972). His main merits lie in a rare technical mastery of poetic language in his own works and in his position as mastermind of New Zealand poetry and poetology: "Whatever is true vision belongs, here, uniquely to the islands of New Zealand." An associate professorship he held at Auckland University from 1951 to 1976 and the numerous literary awards he received in the 1980s and 1990s confirm this reputation.

BIBLIOGRAPHY

Curnow, Allen. *Early Days Yet: New and Collected Poems 1941–1997*. Auckland: Auckland University Press, 1997.

Norgate, James. "Challenging Discourses in Allen Curnow's Poetry." *Journal of New Zealand Literature* 15 (1997): 75–94.

Simpson, Peter, ed. *Allen Curnow. Look Back Harder: Critical Writings 1935–1984*. Auckland: Auckland University Press, 1987.

Wright, F. W. Nielsen. *Leviathan Beached: A Brief Study of Allen Curnow*. Wellington: Cultural and Political Booklets, 1997.

Goeran Nieragden

"CUT" SYLVIA PLATH (1962) Written on October 24, 1962, the poem has attracted numerous readings, employing various critical approaches. Interpretations vary from purely autobiographical/confessional readings to psychoanalytic and feminist ones, or merely dismissals of the poem as a "playful" exercise that "commemorates a real event" (*Bitter Fame* 271). Further many scholars have noted the way SYLVIA PLATH conflates Americanness and Englishness as if wishing to stress her current hybridity, as an American residing in England. (In late 1959, Plath and TED HUGHES left America to settle down in England and in an interview with Peter Orr, Plath confessed: "Well I think that as far as language goes I'm an American. My accent's American. My way of talk is an American way of talk. I'm an old-fashioned American" (qtd in Brain 45).)

Originally the poem may seem to be revolving around a domestic incident, that is, the cutting of the persona's finger while chopping an onion. One may note the mocking tone and the way the cut finger is distanced from the persona, everytime transformed in a succession of different images. It first becomes a pilgrim scalped by Indians only to be then equated with a "turkey wattle" dripping red blood and welcoming the persona to step on it (*Collected Poems* 235).

> Little pilgrim,
> The Indian's axed your scalp
> Your turkey wattle
> Carpet rolls
>
> Straight from the heart.

All of a sudden millions of British soldiers (Redcoats) whose allegiance is dubious march out of the wound (*Collected Poems* 235).

> Out of a gap
> A million soldiers run,
> Redcoats, every one.
>
> Whose side are they on?

Subsequently the finger as if castrated by its injury becomes a "Homunculus," a little man, a term which could be directed against her husband. (That the target of "Homunculus" could be the husband is deduced from what she confided to her friend Elizabeth Compton in July 1962 after she had discovered the clandestine affair of Hughes with Assia Wevill: "Ted lies to me, he has become a little man." [170].) Thus, it becomes difficult to establish who is addressed of the following apostrophes: "Saboteur," "Kamikaze man." Is it the finger she is addressing or the husband?

The finger is then transformed in a silent Ku Klux Klan figure, or a babushka who has suddenly turned into a "trepanned" veteran. In contrast to the inherent violence of the previous apostrophes, the "trepanned veteran" is a mocking trope strongly recalling the previous "Homunculus." Although an experienced and hence worthy of respect figure, a veteran is here humiliated by being "trepanned," operated in the brain. Such operation strongly recalls the "beastly lobotomy" in Plath's unpublished version of one of her motherhood poems, "Nick and the Candlestick." As a treatment for mental disorders, lobotomy is the cutting into or across a lobe of the brain, a method tried by Egaz Moniz, a Portuguese neurologist who used the method after seeing its effectiveness on the taming of a monkey (hence "beastly"). For Plath, much like the castrated Homunculus, as well as the castrated Atlas figure in "Nick and the Candlestick," who has lost "his phallus and balls," the finger becomes a target of derision in its several metamorphoses, ultimately to be dismissed as a figure equated with a "thumb stump," cut off, incomplete, hence unwelcome.

In other readings of the poem, critics see the cutting of the finger as a "gendered moment" with the oozing blood as "emblematic female blood" that contrasts female creativity with male violence (Peel 194). Such interpretation can be furthered if we consider the dedication to Susan O'Neill Roe, Plath's nurse and main support during the difficult months of single motherhood. This female world of allegiance is strongly opposed to the male world, one that entails catastrophe, with "Kamikaze" men, "Ku Klux Klan" figures, "Saboteur[s]," and "trepanned veteran[s]" (Collected Poems 235–236).

The poem, however, can also be read as one carrying heavy "political baggage" (Peel 194), especially in light of its composition day and the intertextuality that connects it with Plath's The Bell Jar. The poem was composed on October 24, 1962, a red-letter day marking the answer of the Soviet chairman Khrushchev to President Kennedy, following the latter's demand that the Soviets remove all the missile bases and their deadly contents from Cuba. Khrushchev's answer stressed the right of the Soviet people to use "international waters and air space" as well as their determination to "protect their rights." With the American and Russian allusions, the cutting of the finger and the shedding of blood mark the dissension between the two countries and the imminent war.

The cultural significance of the poem is further accentuated by the fact that Plath wrote it on the verso of chapter 1, page 2, of The Bell Jar, which foregrounds Esther's obsession with the electrocution of the Rosenbergs on the accusation of passing the secret of the atomic bomb to the Russians. It seems that the intentional intertextuality employed by Plath once again stresses male violence manifested in the execution decision as opposed to a female world of domesticity and allegiance.

BIBLIOGRAPHY
Brain, Tracy. The Other Sylvia Plath. Essex: Pearson Education, 2001.
Hayman, Ronald. The Death and Life of Sylvia Plath. London: Heinemann, 1991.
Peel, Robert. Writing Back: Sylvia Plath and Cold War Politics. Madison, N.J.: Fairleigh Dickinson University Press, 2002.
Wagner-Martin, Linda. Sylvia Plath: A Literary Life. New York: St. Martin's Press, 1999.

Nephie Christodoulides

D

DABYDEEN, DAVID (1955–) David Dabydeen said in an interview, "One has the possibilities of inhabiting different masks intensely," and the idea of inhabiting different identities and exploring the ramifications of these hybrid identities "intensely" has formed the foundation for much of his work (Birbalsingh 181). Dabydeen seeks to uncover the Caribbean experience and explores issues of race, sexuality, and cultural hegemonies in his novels and poetry.

David Dabydeen was born in 1955 in Berbice, Guyana, where he grew up as part of the Indian-Guyanese community. In 1969, he emigrated to England to be with his father. He studied at Cambridge University and then went on to complete his Ph.D. in 18th-century literature and art at the University of London. Following his degree, Dabydeen became a research fellow at Wolfson College, Oxford University, and continued his studies at Oxford and Yale before moving on to the University of Warwick, where he is currently a professor in the Centre for Caribbean Studies.

Dabydeen is considered one of the most important immigrant writers in Britain. Strongly influenced by fellow Caribbean writers such as Samuel Selvon, Wilson Harris, EDWARD KAMAU BRATHWAITE, V. S. Naipaul, and DEREK WALCOTT, Dabydeen's novels and poetry investigate the questions of ethnic and racial experience in the Caribbean. *Slave Song (1984)*, Dabydeen's first collection of poems, which were written while he was a student at Cambridge, won the Commonwealth Prize for Literature. One year later, Dabydeen published *Hogarth's Blacks* (1985), a study of images of blacks in the 18th-century English art of William Hogarth. *Coolie Odyssey,* a second collection of poems, was published in 1988, followed quickly by his first novel, *The Intended* (1990), which won the 1992 Guyana Prize for Literature. His other creative works include the novel *Disappearance* (1992); *Turner: New and Selected Poems* (1993), a collection of poems inspired by the works of the British artist J. M. W. Turner; *The Counting House* (1996); and *A Harlot's Progress* (1999), based on the work *A Harlot's Progress,* completed by William Hogarth in 1732, in which Dabydeen constructs an identity for and builds a story around the image of Hogarth's black slave boy to confront cultural representations of slavery. Dabydeen's most recent novel, *Our Lady of Demerera,* was released by Dido Press in 2004.

Throughout his career, Dabydeen has published scholarly works on Caribbean literature and black British literature, including *The Black Presence in English Literature* (1985), *Hogarth, Walpole, and Commercial Britain* (1987), and *Black Writers in Britain 1790–1890* (1991).

BIBLIOGRAPHY

Birbalsingh, Frank, ed. "David Dabydeen: Coolie Odyssey." In *Frontiers of Caribbean Literature in English,* 167–182. New York: St. Martin's Press, 1996.

Dawes, Kwame, ed. "David Dabydeen." *Talk Yuh Talk: Interviews with Anglophone Caribbean Poets,* 196–214. Charlottesville: The University Press of Virginia, 2001.

Parry, Benita. "Between Creole and Cambridge English: The Poetry of David Dabydeen." *Kunapipi* 10, no. 3 (1988): 1–14.

Corinna McCleod

"THE DARKLING THRUSH" THOMAS HARDY (1900)

When THOMAS HARDY first published this poem as "By the Century's Deathbed" in the *Graphic* on December 29, he symbolically dated it 31st December 1900. He later included it under the new title "The Darkling Thrush" in *Poems of the Past and the Present,* his 1902 collection, in order to make it seem as though its action occurred on the final night of the 19th century. The poem, in fact, is a pastoral elegy for the dying century and arguably the first great 20th century poem.

The poem has four eight-line stanzas, each with an *ababcdcd* rhyme scheme and alternating lines of iambic tetrameter and iambic trimester meter. The first two stanzas set the winter evening scene, and the last two describe the encounter between the poem's speaker and the "aged thrush."

The first two stanzas set the scene with both literal and figurative imagery. In the first stanza, there is a gate leading to a "coppice," a thicket of small trees or shrubs, with their "tangled bine-stems." The word *tangled* is more than literally descriptive; it suggests metaphorically the ideas of confusion, of getting ensnared in complications. Reinforcing this metaphorical meaning, Terry Eagleton notes that the very "sound texture" of *tangled bine-stems* is "unmelodious" and "chock-full of muscular syllables rammed haphazardly up against each other, a cluster of sharply diverse sounds which the reader has to work especially hard at." The poem extends the imagery of the stems, observing that they "score the sky / Like strings of broken lyres." Hardy here evokes one of the central images of romantic poetry, the Eolian lyre, or wind harp, that plays musical cords in response to the wind. For the romantics, the lyre represented the natural harmony of nature and became a symbol for poetic inspiration. John Bayley cites in connection with Hardy's image Shelley's lines from "Ode to the West Wind": "Make me thy lyre, even as the forest is." The point, however, is that the lyre is broken; the 19th century ends not as it began, not with romantic springtime optimism about a new world about to be born, but with the opposite. It is winter, the death of the year and of the century, and of hope. Hardy introduces the idea of death as early as the second line of the poem, describing the personified "Frost" as "spectre-grey." The second stanza of the poem extends this metaphor of death, portraying the entire landscape as the "century's corpse outleant," with the clouds forming the "crypt" and the wind singing the "death-lament." Hardy again opposes the romantic joyous participation in the vital spirit of nature and anticipates the wasteland imagery of T. S. ELIOT that became the emblem for the early 20th-century modernists, in the lines summarizing the winter scene: "The ancient pulse of germ and birth / Was shrunken hard and dry." J. O. Bailey offers a historical context for the poem's death imagery, explaining that Hardy believed the end of the 19th century to be "a time when science and rationalist philosophies undermined man's religion and sense of divine purpose, and left man in a bleak world where basic forces were unintelligible to the mind." In this regard, Hardy must have changed the title with Matthew Arnold's earlier use of the word *darkling* in his famous passage in "Dover Beach" about the intellectual confusions brought about by the loss of faith in the mid-19th century in mind: "And we are here as on a darkling plain / Swept with confused alarms of struggle and flight, / Where ignorant armies clash by night."

The first half of "The Darkling Thrush" begins and ends with the word *I*. The landscape is framed by the solitary speaker, making the natural scene the outward projection of his inner life. The first line of the poem—"I leant upon a coppice gate"—parallels the second stanza's opening depiction: "The land's sharp features seemed to be / The Century's corpse outleant." The speaker, the landscape, and the century are all one, superimposed on each other, and all, "every spirit upon earth," the speaker says in the final line of the first half of the poem, "seemed fervourless as I."

The second half begins with an immediacy and vitality that challenges, or more precisely rises above, the somber tenor of the first half:

> At once a voice arose among
>   The bleak twigs overhead
> In a full-hearted evensong
>   Of joy illimitied.

This new voice retrospectively highlights the speaker's previous qualification that every spirit perhaps only "seemed" to share his lack of passion and draws new attention to the "household fires" that all but the wandering solitary speaker seeks at night. Still, despite the subtle clues in the first half of the poem that all might not be as "desolate" as the speaker has portrayed, the song is a surprise, breaking through, with the exception of the observation of the twigs overhead, the speaker's "bleak" view of life at the end of the century and evoking what John Hughes terms "an affect of joy which in turn passes into writing." In the second half of the third stanza, however, the speaker visually identifies the source of the song: It is an "aged thrush, frail, gaunt, and small, / In blast-beruffled plume." The speaker frames the incongruity between the thrush's visual appearance and song as a body/soul dualism, noting that the thrush "Had chosen thus to fling his soul / Upon the growing gloom." By ascribing the thrush anthropomorphically with deliberation and desperation, the speaker, despite the way the song initially and spontaneously moved him, again reasserts "the growing gloom" he described in the first half of the poem.

The first half of the final stanza encloses, and apparently limits the validity of, the thrush's soulful song with counterevidence from the surrounding material environment:

> So little cause for carolings
>   Of such ecstatic sound
> Was written on terrestrial things
>   Afar or nigh around.

The final four lines of the poem also enclose, but less clearly repudiate, the thrush's joyful affirmation, now with the inner reflection of the speaker. Seeing no reason for the thrush to sing so joyfully, the speaker reflects,

> That I could think there trembled through
>   His happy good-night air
> Some blessed Hope, whereof he knew
>   And I was unaware.

The speaker neither fully comprehends nor absolutely dismisses the "blessed Hope" voiced by the thrush's song. Hardy's capitalization emphasizes the religious promise of the "blessed Hope." Again, the title word *darkling* provides literary allusions, now to John Milton's *Paradise Lost* and to John Keats's "Ode to a Nightingale" in addition to Arnold's "Dover Beach," that contribute to the deep meaning of the poem. Milton refers to his blindness in the invocation in book 3 of *Paradise Lost* and seeks to be moved by inspiration just as "the wakeful bird / Sings darkling, and in shadiest covert hid / Tunes her nocturnal note." Deprived of outward sight, Milton asks that "celestial Light / Shine inward . . . / . . . that I may see and tell / Of things invisible to mortal sight." The speaker in Hardy's poem, however, is all too well aware that he cannot himself "see and tell / Of things invisible to mortal sight," that he is unable to see or comprehend whatever it is that has inspired the thrush to sing. The "ecstatic sound" of Hardy's thrush recalls how Keats heard a nightingale "pouring forth its soul abroad / In such an ecstasy!" Unlike the speaker in Hardy's poem, though, Keats has an imagination that enables him to share the nightingale's happiness. In "Ode to a Nightingale," the word *darkling* is associated with the human listener rather than the singing bird. Keats says, "Darkling I listen," but rather than suggesting some undesirable or deceiving blindness, the darkling state frees the listener from his mortal "sole self," making him think it would be "rich to die" in the moment of transcendence. Hardy's speaker experiences no such transcendent moment; the thrush's insight, if insight it be, remains inaccessible, in the dark. That the speaker "could think" the thrush "knew" something of which the speaker "was unaware" is far from an absolute affirmation of the "blessed Hope." Neither does the speaker openly reject the possibility.

Readers have interpreted the ambivalence of "The Darkling Thrush" various ways. As Hardy himself notes, writing under the name of his second wife in his disguised autobiography *The Life of Thomas Hardy,* the poem was "much admired" by the general public when it was first published. Many of the first readers probably admired the promise of the "blessed Hope" proclaimed by the thrush and believed that the speaker not only "could" but probably eventually *would* come to "think" the Hope to be valid. Donald Davie acknowledges this optimistic reading but suggests Hardy was writing for his audience, expressing what he thought they wanted to hear. On the other hand, readers have dismissed the Hope promised by the thrush as an illusion, interpreting the poem to be about the absence of any justification for religious faith and romantic joy in the modern world. In this reading, the speaker's "fervourless" acknowledgment that he perhaps "could think" in fact means he does not now nor ever *will* think that there is some celestial hope beyond his "terrestrial" awareness. Taken together, these two opposing interpretations of the poem—optimistic and pessimistic, spiritual and realistic—represent a characteristic Hardyan conflict between the tendency of his heart and that of his head, and to deny either fails to appreciate the rich complexity of the poem. Hardy along with the speaker in the poem may refuse to validate beliefs he has found to be intellectually unacceptable, but he does not deny that he still can be emotionally moved by them, in the words of "The Oxen," "hoping it might be so," even while knowing it is not. What is most significant about the thrush's song in the poem is not whether or not its message is true, its affirmation or denial, but the way it moves the speaker and reawakens his, and Hardy's, capacity to respond to a song of "illimited joy." This emotional response to hope may be tragic because, as Hardy wrote in his diary 20 years before he wrote "The Darkling Thrush," "The emotions have no place in a world of defect, and it is a cruel injustice that they should have developed in it," but it, more than and alongside the intellectual lack of belief, accounts for the greatness of the poem.

BIBLIOGRAPHY

Bailey, J. O. *The Poetry of Thomas Hardy: A Handbook and Commentary.* Chapel Hill: University of North Carolina Press, 1970.

Bayley, John. *An Essay on Hardy.* Cambridge: Cambridge University Press, 1978.

Davie, Donald. *Thomas Hardy and English Poetry.* New York: Oxford University Press, 1972.

Eagleton, Terry. *How to Read a Poem.* Malden, Mass.: Blackwell, 2007.

Hardy, Florence Emily. *The Life of Thomas Hardy.* 1930. Hamden, Conn.: Archon Books, 1970.

Hughes, John. *"Ecstatic Sound": Music and Individuality in the Work of Thomas Hardy.* Aldershot, Eng.: Ashgate Publishing, 2001.

Langbaum, Robert. *Thomas Hardy in Our Time.* London: Macmillan Press, 1995.

May, Charles E. "Hardy's 'Darkling Thrush': The 'Nightingale' Grown Old." *Victorian Poetry* 11, no. 1 (1973): 62–65.

Robert R. Watson

DARYUSH, ELIZABETH (1887–1977)   Elizabeth Daryush, raised in an extremely well-to-do British family, was daughter to the poet ROBERT BRIDGES, England's poet laureate (1913–30), and Mary Monica Bridges. Born in London and privately educated, Daryush was certain of her career as a poet from an early age. Her first book, *Charitessi,* was published under the name *Elizabeth Bridges* and released when she was a mere 24 years old. Her second book of poems, *Verses,* was published only five years later in 1916. After her first two books, she became known for her traditional style and intense discussion of class issues with particular attention to the wrongdoings of the rich.

In 1923, Daryush married Ali Akbar Daryush, a Persian foreign office official, and lived in Iran for four years. During this time, her work shifted noticeably. Daryush's "consistent and well-defined personal vision" earned the respect of her peers. However, there were certainly assorted reactions to her work. Some critics suggested Daryush wrote "using a language that is dead."

Through her poetry, Daryush altered her father's approach to meter. While Bridges was an advocate of writing poems that focused on the number of syllables in each line and not necessarily regular accented syllables, Daryush only counted syllables that were audible. Although never as well known as her father, Daryush published 14 books of poetry in her lifetime. Her last book, *Collected Poems,* was published only one year before she passed away. Elizabeth Daryush died in 1977 at the age of 90.

See also "STILL-LIFE."

BIBLIOGRAPHY

Contemporary Authors: New Revision Series. Vol. 3. Detroit: Gale Research, 1969.

Davie, Donald. "The Poetry of Elizabeth Daryush." *Poetry Nation* no. 5 (1975): 43–51.

"Elizabeth Daryush." *Oldpoetry.* Available online. URL: http://oldpoetry.com/authors/Elizabeth%20Daryush. Accessed February 28, 2005.

"Mildness Is No More." *Time,* 7 February 1949.

Jenny Sadre-Orafi

DAVIE, DONALD (1922–1995)

Born in Barnsley, South Yorkshire, Davie was educated at Cambridge, where he absorbed the influence of F. R. Leavis. After serving in the Royal Navy, he held a series of university positions in Trinity College, Cambridge, and Essex. In the late sixties he emigrated to the United States and became a professor at Stanford University.

Davie has been considered to be the head theorist of THE MOVEMENT, the antiromantic, antibohemian poetic group that dominated British poetry in the 1950s, in part because of his inclusion in Robert Conquest's *New Lines* anthology. With THOM GUNN, PHILIP LARKIN, ELIZABETH JENNINGS, and KINGSLEY AMIS, Davie sponsored the belief that experimentalism was not reconcilable with the English poetic scene, as attested in his critical books *Purity of Diction in English Verse* (1952) and *Articulate Energy* (1955). His "neo-Augustinian" and antiromantic stance are not, however, limited to his criticism but can also be found, most importantly, in his poetic oeuvre.

Influenced by Russian poets (especially by Pushkin, whom Davie read during his service in the war), his first volume of poetry, entitled *Poems* (1954), was followed by a series of volumes such as *Brides of Reason* (1955) and *A Winter Talent* (1957) before the first collection of his poems was made available under the title *Collected Poems, 1950–1970,* in 1972. This first anthological volume (with would be followed by a second volume in 1983) reflects Davie at his "Augustinian" best: The poems brim with studied virtuosity, accuracy, and chastisement both in subject matter and in style. *Six Epistles to Eva Hesse* (1970) marks the beginnings of experimentation with British forms that would be continued in *The Shires* (1974), a tour across the English counties, and *Three for Water Music* (1981).

In the mid-1970s, Davie began to reject his early poetic style, its philosophical nature, and its abused stylization. He also began to compare American and British literature, accusing the Movement poets of "little Englandism" and rejecting his former affiliation to it. Along with this change in critical mood, late poetry by Davie is much more experimental and exploratory and noticeably less cerebral, the mark of what Davie considered "a cautious but consistent movement towards 'freedom.'" Davie always regarded himself as a "Dissentient Voice" (the title of one of his early poems),

and his loss of confidence in English audiences must be framed within this will to dissent.

A man of letters, Davie must be read in his many facets—as a poet, as a critic, and as a thinker—since as he suggests in his early poem "The poet-scholar" "the poet-scholar cannot keep apart / the gift and the investment." His roles as a literary polemicist and critic (amounting to a total of 15 books of criticism) have often diverted attention from his verse and poetic quest, which has been recently revisited after his death in 1995.

See also "A WINTER TALENT."

BIBLIOGRAPHY

Decker, George, ed. *Donald Davie and the Responsibilities of Literature.* Manchester, Eng.: Carcanet New Press, 1983.

Gioia, Dana. *Barrier of a Common Language: An American Looks at Contemporary British Poetry.* Ann Arbor: University of Michigan Press, 2003.

Jones, Peter, and Michael Schmidt, eds. *British Poetry since 1970: A Critical Survey.* Manchester, Eng.: Carcanet Press, 1980.

Carmen Méndez García

DAVIES, W. H. (WILLIAM HENRY) (1871–1940)

Born in Newport, England, in 1871, W. H. Davies left school as a teenager to train as a carver and gilder. A voracious reader with a desire for adventure, he left his vocational training and home country to tramp across North America as a young man. A legacy from a deceased aunt kept him from utter starvation, but these were certainly lean times for Davies. In March 1899, he was permanently crippled while attempting to jump a train to Canada. He soon returned to England, where he continued a hobo existence that exposed him to the slums of industrial cities and the wretched people who inhabited such cities. Davies was writing poetry all the while, but finding a publisher proved difficult.

Finally at the age of 34 he managed to get his first collection into print. *The Soul's Destroyer* (1905) introduced several themes that would remain integral to Davies's lyrical production: an inclination for the pastoral, an identification with those existing on the fringes of society, and a preference for simplicity in diction and form. Over the next several years, he published volumes of poetry with increasing regularity: *New Poems* (1907), *Nature Poems* (1908), *Farewell to Poesy* (1910),

Songs of Joy (1911), *Foliage* (1913), and *The Bird of Paradise* (1914). While generally remembered as a poet, Davies also published several prose works, among them *The Autobiography of a Supertramp* (1908), which includes a foreword by George Bernard Shaw.

Davies's inspiration most often arose from either the beauty of nature or the sordidness of urban blight. In celebratory poems like "The Kingfisher" and "Raptures," he offers meditations (often tinged with melancholy) on the delicate, myriad wonders of the natural world. Alternatively the dismal realities of poverty and its spirit-crushing consequences come across in pieces like "Saturday Night Slums" and "Australian Bill." Davies was a far more nimble and complex poet than his posthumous reputation would suggest.

In 1923 Davies married Helen Payne, 30 years his junior and a reputed prostitute. The couple settled in Gloucestershire, where they lived until his death in 1940. His production during these years includes the collections *Secrets* (1924) and *The Loneliest Mountain* (1939). In 1929, the University of Wales awarded him an honorary degree. Despite enjoying wide popularity and a modest fame during his lifetime, Davies has the legacy of a minor poet. He is probably most remembered now for his oft-anthologized pastoral poem "Leisure." This piece includes the couplet that continues to resonate with readers living within the accelerating swirl of (post)modernity: "What is this life if, full of care, / We have no time to stand and stare?"

See also "THE RAT."

BIBLIOGRAPHY

Harlow, Sylvia. *W. H. Davies: A Bibliography*. New Castle, Del.: Oak Knoll Books, 1993.

Normand, Laurence. *W. H. Davies*. Bridgend, Eng.: Seren Books, 2003.

Jason Spangler

DAY LEWIS, C. (1904–1972) Cecil Day Lewis

gained fame first as one of the poets associated with W. H. AUDEN in the 1930s and then decades later as England's poet laureate. Day Lewis was born in Ballentubbert, Ireland, where his father, Frank Day-Lewis, was an Anglican clergyman. His mother died when the poet was only four, making him the sole recipient of his father's rather demanding affection. At Oxford his academic record was undistinguished, but there he initiated his career as a poet, paying for the printing of his first collection and seeing two poems included in *Oxford Poetry* for 1925. During his final year at Oxford he met W. H. Auden and the two jointly edited *Oxford Poetry* for 1927, coauthoring a polemical preface on the need for a new poetry. His first mature volume, *Transitional Poem,* was accepted by Leonard and Virginia Woolf's Hogarth Press in 1929.

Also while at Oxford he met and later married Mary King. To support his new family, Day Lewis took a job as a schoolteacher at Cheltenham Junior School, despite his initial lack of interest in teaching. His next book, *From Feathers to Iron* (1931), explored his thoughts and hopes as he prepared for the birth of their first child. His reputation grew as his poetry appeared in literary periodicals and Michael Roberts's 1932 anthology, *New Signatures*. Day Lewis's overtly political *The Magnetic Mountain* (1933) showed too clearly the influence of Auden, and some of the personal references in the poems suggested the existence of a cohesive Auden group, a notion that later critics dismiss.

Day Lewis's Marxism culminated in his joining the Communist Party in 1935. Weary of the conservative atmosphere and "intermittent dust-ups" at Cheltenham, Day Lewis resigned and thereafter supported himself entirely as a freelance writer. This move was made easier financially by the publication of his first mystery novel, *A Question of Proof,* under the pseudonym Nicholas Blake. Busy writing reviews, pamphlets, and introductions, as well as his own poetry, Day Lewis also poured time into political activity. In 1938 he felt the need to retrench and moved his family to the village of Musbury, dropping his relation to the party. During this period he began a 10-year-long love affair with the novelist Rosamond Lehmann. He continued to write poetry in the 1940s, but his reputation was in decline among critics. He maintained his role as a public man of letters, editing anthologies, doing readings (live and broadcast), and giving lectures on poetry at Cambridge, Oxford (as elected professor of poetry in 1951), and later Harvard.

By 1950 his marriage finally collapsed, and he surprised both wife and his lover by marrying the young Jill Balcon, a BBC actress whom he had met during a reading. The couple had two children. Day Lewis continued producing mystery novels (20 in all), considered some of the best detective fiction of the period, and in 1960 wrote an autobiography. The poetry of his last decades is polished and articulate, somewhat derivative, and characterized by a lyricism present in his earliest poetry. He accepted the office of poet laureate in 1968 and served until his death in 1972.

See also "WHERE ARE THE WAR POETS?"

BIBLIOGRAPHY

Day Lewis, C. *The Buried Day*. London: Chatto and Windus, 1960.

Day-Lewis, Sean. *C. Day-Lewis: An English Literary Life*. London: Weidenfeld and Nicholson, 1980.

Gelpi, Albert. *Living in Time: The Poetry of C. Day Lewis*. New York: Oxford University Press, 1998.

Anne Kellenberger

"DEAD MAN'S DUMP" ISAAC ROSENBERG **(1917)** ISAAC ROSENBERG's poem "Dead Man's Dump" was written in France in May 1917 and is one of his most important poems. This poem differs somewhat, however, from his other trench poems in its graphic details and searching questions. In his other trench poems, Rosenberg has a tendency to understate the scenes he describes and thus emphasize their horrific effect on him and his fellow soldiers. In "Dead Man's Dump," though, more of the graphic nature of the destruction of war makes its way to the surface of the poem. The poem begins with Rosenberg on barbed wire patrol. As the wagon rolls across the fields crushing corpses on its way, Rosenberg considers the scene. The rusty barbed wire in the wagon appears to him as "many crowns of thorns" and the rusty stakes "as sceptres old." In these images, the sacrificial nature of the soldiers and the ineffectual rule of the governments become clear. The bodies of the soldiers are both "friend and foeman," and their similarity in death emphasizes their similarity in life, thus questioning the ultimate sense of the conflict. Thereafter in the poem, Rosenberg makes no distinction between "friend and foeman" and considers their joint plight. During the course of "Dead Man's Dump," Rosenberg muses upon the dead soldiers in general and in particular, sympathizing with the group in its entirety while maintaining the individuality of each soldier by singling out the fate of specific individuals: the soldier who dies with

his brains splattering the "stretcher-bearer's face" and the soldier who dies with arms stretched out toward the wagon just before its wheels "grazed his dead face." As he does in other poems, Rosenberg adds to the horror of the scene through the deadened quality of the living soldiers' response to what they see: "What of us, who flung on the shrieking pyre, / Walk, our usual thoughts untouched." The living soldiers have seen so much death that they are largely unaffected by this scene. Even Rosenberg's own sympathy toward the dead soldiers maintains much of the detached quality exhibited in other of his trench poems, such that one of the horrors of war is the deadening of the souls of the living. In addition to his musings on the dead and living soldiers in the poem, Rosenberg turns to metaphysical subjects, as he wonders, "What fierce imaginings their dark souls lit / Earth! Have they gone into you?" and asks "their soul's sack, / Emptied of God-ancestralled essences. / Who hurled them out? Who hurled?" In these questions, Rosenberg makes clear the human responsibility for their deaths, but he also questions the responsibility of a God who would allow such tragedies to occur. Rosenberg further emphasizes his skepticism when he speaks of the dead soldiers and remarks, "The grass and coloured clay / More motion have then they." As often occurs in Rosenberg's trench poems, in these lines Rosenberg emphasizes the gulf that exists between the human and natural worlds such that nature's indifference to human suffering is unmistakable. For Rosenberg, both a benevolent nature and a loving God are far removed from carnage of the battlefield.

BIBLIOGRAPHY

Cohen, Joseph. *Journey to the Trenches: The Life of Isaac Rosenberg 1890–1918*. New York: Basic Books, 1975.

Liddiard, Jean. *Isaac Rosenberg: The Half Used Life*. London: Victor Gollancz, 1975.

Maccoby, Deborah. *God Made Blind: Isaac Rosenberg, His Life and Poetry*. Northwood, Eng.: Symposium Press, 1999.

Noakes, Vivien. *The Poems and Plays of Isaac Rosenberg*. Oxford: Oxford University Press, 2004.

Tomlinson, Charles. *Isaac Rosenberg of Bristol*. Bristol, Eng.: Bristol Branch of the Historical Association, 1982.

Wilson, Jean Moorcroft. *Isaac Rosenberg: Poet and Painter*. London: Cecil Woolf, 1975.

John Peters

DEATH OF A NATURALIST Seamus Heaney

(1966) *Death of a Naturalist* is the first published book of poems by the Northern Irish poet Seamus Heaney, and despite occasional evidence of apprenticeship, many of its poems exhibit the development of that distinctive poetic voice for which Heaney would eventually be awarded the Nobel Prize in literature in 1995. The themes of the poems themselves reflect the initiatory status of the volume. For approximately the first third of the book Heaney recollects his childhood in rural county Derry—that era of his life he refers to in his Nobel lecture as "an intimate, physical, creaturely existence."

Influenced by Ted Hughes and Patrick Kavanagh, both of whom had previously explored rural life in their poetry, Heaney exploits qualities of language that adequately render the physicality of the natural environment. His frequent use of hard consonants creates a deliberately rough texture, as in these lines from the book's opening poem, "Digging": "The cold smell of potato mould, the squelch and slap / Of soggy peat, the curt cuts of an edge." The onomatopoeia of *squelch* and *slap* is also characteristic of Heaney's early verse, as is the use of alliteration, which evinces Heaney's debt to both Gerard Manley Hopkins and Anglo-Saxon poetry. In the title poem, "Death of a Naturalist," Heaney employs these elements of language to depict a rite of passage in which he learned the disturbingly crude origin of "frogspawn"; the air is filled with "a coarse croaking that I had not heard / Before," and to the innocent child, "The slap and plop were obscene threats." The onset of sexual awakening is treated again in "Blackberry Picking," but the more general phenomenon of initiation—and the tension between youth and adulthood that it signifies—recurs throughout the book.

"Digging" is characteristic not only for its technical and stylistic attributes, but also for its subject matter. As do many of his poems, it expresses the poet's need to feel connected to his family and his culture and his simultaneous awareness that he is somehow alienated. The first two lines suggest a subtext of violence, or at least a restatement of the motto "The pen is mightier than the sword": "Between my finger and my thumb / The squat pen rests; snug as a gun." The near-chiasmus, *snug as a gun,* seems an intimation of the Troubles that would begin to plague Northern Ireland in earnest just

three years later, but the poem heads in another direction. Heaney reflects instead upon images of his father and grandfather digging, and he admires the skill with which they handle their spades. Not wanting to dissociate himself from his heritage but realizing "I've no spade to follow men like them," the poet turns back to the pen in his hand and decides, "I'll dig with it." The digging metaphor proves to be central to the rest of the volume, and to a certain extent, it has lent shape to Heaney's entire career. For Heaney, excavation symbolizes the poetic act par excellence—discovering what lies hidden beneath the surface of both individual and national consciousness. Thus for the title of his 1998 volume of selected poems, the fruit of his career's work as a poet-archaeologist, Heaney selected a phrase from his poem "Act of Union": *Opened Ground.*

Many of the most memorable poems in *Death of a Naturalist* are variations on the theme of digging or the revelation of buried truth. The description of water divination in "The Diviner" aligns closely with Heaney's understanding of poetic vocation; with professional skill and precision, the diviner draws spring water from below ground so that "its secret stations" are broadcasted. The inability of the "bystanders" in the final stanza to repeat this act suggests both the uniqueness of the poet-diviner's gift and his responsibility to serve the larger community. In "At a Potato Digging" Heaney further develops the digging metaphor while coming to terms with Ireland's troublesome past. Anticipating later poems such as *Wintering Out*'s "The Tollund Man," Heaney describes the Irish land as a goddess who demands devotion and sacrifice from her people: "Heads bow, trunks bend, hands fumble towards the black / Mother." As in "Digging," the unearthing of potatoes is portrayed as a culturally distinctive activity, but here the people's seemingly mindless religious worship of the land takes on a darker quality such that, by the end of the poem, the ground itself is accused of being "faithless."

Yet despite forays like this and in other poems into more communal themes, *Death of a Naturalist* is primarily about individual initiation and self-discovery. The final poem, "Personal Helicon," recapitulates the subject matter from the early pages of the volume, particularly the Wordsworthian idea that "The Child is Father of the Man." For the first four stanzas Heaney describes his youthful fascination with wells and the echoes and reflections they produce. In the final stanza, however, the child's love of the wells' narcissistic qualities becomes the poet's metaphor for the self-revelatory nature of his poetry: "Now," he writes, "I rhyme / To see myself, to set the darkness echoing." Helicon refers to the muses' mountain, but again, Heaney's personal source of inspiration is not the heights but the depths. While *Death of a Naturalist* may chronicle the end of childhood innocence, it also marks the birth of a remarkably talented poet whose subterranean excursions have yielded some of the best English language poetry of the last 40 years.

BIBLIOGRAPHY

Curtis, Tony, ed. *The Art of Seamus Heaney.* 4th ed. Brigend, Eng.: Seren, 2001.
Foster, Thomas C. *Seamus Heaney.* Boston: Twayne, 1989.
Heaney, Seamus. *Finders Keepers: Selected Prose 1971–2001.* New York: Farrar, Straus & Giroux, 2002.
———. *Opened Ground: Selected Poems 1966–1996.* New York: Farrar, Straus & Giroux, 1998.

Matthew Paul Carlson

"THE DEATH OF JOY GARDNER" BENJAMIN ZEPHANIAH (1996)

Early on a summer morning in 1993, six police officers burst into the home of Joy Gardner, a 40-year-old Jamaican women living in London, England. Joy Gardner had been refused permission to remain in Britain, even though her son had been born there and her mother was a legal resident. In front of her five-year-old son the officers forced her to the floor and bound her in a leather body belt and manacles, winding 13 feet of adhesive tape around her mouth to stop her screaming. She was taken to hospital in a coma but never recovered. Three of the police officers were acquitted of charges of manslaughter after claiming that Ms. Gardner was the most violent woman they had ever dealt with and that they were following routine procedures.

For many people, the death of Joy Gardner symbolized the British state's disregard for the lives of immigrants and members of ethnic minority communities, and the institutional racism that fostered it. Since 1969 there have been more than 1,000 deaths in police custody in Britain, yet not a single police officer has ever been convicted of wrongdoing.

BENJAMIN ZEPHANIAH's poem "The Death of Joy Gardner" captures both the individual inhumanity of Joy Gardner's treatment and the larger sense of historical betrayal felt by many of those with roots in Britain's former colonies: "She's illegal, so deport her / Said the Empire that brought her." We find the police officers arriving "as her young son watched TV," only to witness a few lines later "a child watch Mummy die." But if "the alien deporters" kill Joy Gardner in the name of keeping things in their proper place, the poem reminds us that Britain's colonial history is one of violent displacement: "The Bible sent us everywhere / To make Great Britain great." "'I fear as I walk the streets," the poet confides in the face of this dangerous amnesia, "That one day I just may meet / Officials who may tie my feet," just as Joy Gardner's had been.

One of the recurring ideas in Zephaniah's poetry is the often literal failure of justice to materialize for black people: "Why hide / Behind . . . robes," the poet asks Justice in "To Be Seen, To Be Done" (1996). In "The Death of Joy Gardner" this failure takes the form of the nonexistence of Joy Gardner's killers: "Nobody killed her," the poem observes ironically, yet "she never killed herself." Sadly this idea returns in "What Stephen Lawrence Has Taught Us" (2001), a poem that commemorates another high-profile death that shook confidence in the British legal system. "Why is it so official," the poem asks, "that black people are so often killed / Without killers?" Yet Zephaniah remains committed to the power of dialogue and to the pursuit of human rights through the courts: "We must talk some Race Relations / With the folks from immigration," he rhymes, while in an interview he has said that "the most positive thing for me" about the British legal system "is that in this country we can bring our own government to court, and the people at the top have to listen to the judges and to answer to them."

Tragically 10 years after the death of Joy Gardner, Zephaniah's cousin Michael Powell died while in police custody. His family continues to campaign for an independent inquiry into the circumstances of his death.

BIBLIOGRAPHY

Mills, Heather. "A Life without Joy." *Guardian,* 7 March 1999.
Zephaniah, Benjamin. *Propa Propaganda.* Newcastle upon Tyne, Eng.: Bloodaxe, 1996.

Graham MacPhee

"DECEPTIONS" PHILIP LARKIN (1950)

PHILIP LARKIN's "Deceptions," originally titled "The Less Deceived," is in essence the title poem of *The Less Deceived* (1955), the book that established his reputation. It is one of the early examples of his distinctive voice, after he gave over the poems that sounded like a pastiche of W. B. YEATS in his first book, *The North Ship* (1945). When George Hartley of Marvell Press in Hull, where Larkin had been appointed librarian in 1955, accepted the manuscript Larkin showed him that year, the title was *Various Poems,* which Hartley felt was weak. Larkin then renamed this poem "Deceptions" and used its original title to name the volume. In his subsequent two volumes, *The Whitsun Weddings* (1964) and *High Windows* (1974), he took the volume titles from each volume's chief poem without change.

The lengthy epigraph to the poem is taken from Henry Mahew's ground-breaking study *London Labour and the London Poor* (1861–62), which shocked Victorian England with its revelations of the living conditions of the poor. It gives the story, and feelings, of a young woman who was drugged and raped and then who, inconsolable for days, "cried like a child to be killed." The first stanza of Larkin's poem empathizes with the young woman's pain. It begins, "Even so distant, I can taste the grief," detailing what it must be like to be so shocked and scarred while life goes on in its ordinary way, the wheels of the street still busily turning, the sun still shining. Its light must have seemed "unanswerable and tall and wide," a light that "forbids the scar to heal, and drives / Shame out of hiding." Here light does not heal but rather keeps the wound open, when the raped woman would prefer privacy to recover herself, instead of being laid open "like a drawer of knives." The ordinariness of the image of tableware and an open drawer bespeaks the ordinariness of pain; the image of knives tells us of the piercing sharpness of new grief.

The second stanza takes a quite surprising turn. The woman is left behind: "Slums, years, have buried you. I would not dare / Console you if I could." If he can no longer help the woman with empathy, what is there left for the poem to do? The answer: look at another sufferer, the aggressor, not the victim. She was deceived—more than deceived, drugged. But he was deceived too, by his belief that his rape would yield him something. His desire has deceived him. Larkin paints the deception, drugging, and rape of the woman not as an issue of power and domination but as one of sexual desire. When the deceiver clambers, stumbles "up the breathless stair," he is full of impetuous haste—the counterpart of Shakespeare's "lust in action" from Sonnet 129. But as that sonnet tells us, as soon as that lust is fulfilled, there is no fulfillment; it is "enjoyed no sooner but despised straight."

In a brilliant last line, the rapist achieves his desire only to "burst into fulfillment's desolate attic." The image of "burst" suggests orgasm, the epitome of male sexual satisfaction, intense and brief. But this "fulfillment" of desire is desolate, deserted, empty. And it finds itself in an attic, another bare room, devoid of human connection and presence. The attic suggests what the "high windows" of the poem with that name also suggest, that there is a desire akin to religious searching here, which can become intertwined, especially for men, with sexual seeking. But the sexuality described in "HIGH WINDOWS" and in this poem is not satisfying; it is only thought to be. So this is the greatest lie of all, the bigger deception, and hence the woman Mayhew describes is "the less deceived."

By its conclusion, the poem is about male experience, not about the woman at all. The turning is deftly handled, though troubling for some readers. Sympathizing with an aggressor's pain may always be a troubling move, but it is typical of Larkin, earning him a damaged reputation in some quarters as antifeminist, racist, and conservative, and in others admiration for his willingness to violate Leftist standards of perceived correctness.

BIBLIOGRAPHY

Lerner, Laurence. *Philip Larkin.* Plymouth, Eng.: Northcote House, 1997.

Regan, Stephen. *Philip Larkin: An Introduction to the Variety of Criticism.* New York: Macmillan, 1992.

Swarbrick, Andrew. *The Whitsun Weddings and The Less Deceived by Philip Larkin.* Macmillan Master Guides, edited by James Gibson. New York: Macmillan, 1986.

Thwaite, Anthony. ed. *Philip Larkin: Collected Poems.* New York: Farrar, Straus, Giroux, 1988.

James Persoon

"DEDICATION OF THE COOK" ANNA
WICKHAM (1921)   Many of ANNA WICKHAM's poems
deal with women's attempts to fulfill several roles and
the particular conflicts of the woman artist: "If any ask
why there's no great She-Poet / Let him come live with
me and he will know it." The light syllables of this
opening line from "Dedication of the Cook" belie the
agony of a dilemma that the poet never resolved. The
rhyming couplets imitate a wife's mask of cheeriness
about her chores while the shifts between regular and
irregular iambic pentameter reconstruct the yearning
to break out of the kitchen in order to write. The central symbol of flowers for poems parodies the conventional imagery of feminine creativity, and the emotional
dilemma that they signify is far from trite: "Can I survive and be my good man's wife?" The adjacent end
rhymes *sonnet* and *bonnet* strengthen the felt opposition between what the wife wants to do and her socially
prescribed role. The exaggerated rhyme throughout
the poem also signals that the calm surface of middle-
class respectability overlays disturbing undercurrents
of repressed impulses for freedom. *Virginity* rhymed
with *have me free* conspires against the implicit restraint
of "Since I am wedded" with its weighty monosyllables
and harsh consonants. The couplet that closes each of
the two stanzas is the same except that the flowers that
"die for clammy odours of my kitchen" are transformed
into ones that "will blossom from the ashes of my
kitchen." The half-rhyme of *kitchen* and *rich in* is a
favorite device of Wickham's; here it maintains a question mark over whether the desired freedom to write
can be achieved. Matt Holland's discerning discussion
identifies her self-referential use of rhyme to convey
predictability and flat routine, the stultifying effects of
British conventionality.

Wickham is at her best in telling the story of women
whose masks of ordinariness and survival conceal a
losing battle with frustration. Read in conjunction with
poems like "Suppression"—"If you deny her right to
think, / If you deny her pride of ink"—and "Woman
and Artist," "Dedication of the Cook" resonates with
the poet's negotiation with contemporary ideals of
femininity that arguably engender the creative energy
of her work. Confronting her sense of failure in *Fragment of an Autobiography,* Wickham noted the lack of

positive role models: "There have been few women
poets of distinction." "The Fresh Start" collects together
her irresolvable tensions concerning the competing
roles of wife, mother, and artist: "Two years now I have
sat beneath a curse / And in a fury poured out frenzied
verse." "New Eve," a previously unpublished poem in
Writings, articulates the impossibility of reconciling the
"two sides of me"—"Why was I born beneath two
curses, / To bear children and to write verses?" Most
often overwhelmed by the hindrance of femaleness, on
good days the poet finds, "I can forget my skirt, / I hide
my breast beneath a workman's shirt, / And hunt the
perfect phrase" ("A Woman in Bed").

BIBLIOGRAPHY
Holland, Matt. "Anna Wickham: Fettered Woman, Free
Spirit." *Poetry Review* 78, no. 2 (1988): 44.
Smith, R. D., ed. *The Writings of Anna Wickham.* London:
Virago Press, 1984.

Jane Dowson

DE KOK, INGRID (1951–)   *Familiar Ground*
(1988), the book that established de Kok as one of her
country's finest English-language poets, consists chiefly
of lyric meditations on the interrelated personal and
political dimensions of life under apartheid, the system
of legally sanctioned racial segregation that dominated
all facets of life in South Africa from 1948 until 1994.
Much of the urge for liberation that motivated anti-
apartheid resistance in the 1980s found expression
through cultural forms, including poetry. Often this
was poetry influenced by African oral traditions and
intended for performance at the funerals, marches, and
mass rallies through which South Africans resisting
apartheid expressed their grievances and demands.

Next to many of the declamatory poems that were
performed during the climactic years of the struggle
against apartheid, de Kok's poetry seems unusually
soft-spoken. Yet its quietness does not indicate quies-
cence. Rather than shun the realm of national conflict,
de Kok's poetry alludes to it in ways that evoke its
more intimate dimensions while sidestepping its more
spectacular manifestations. A clear example of a poem
that eschews the dramatic in favor of the everyday is
"Small Passing." One theme of this brief poem is an
imagined cross-racial solidarity among mothers whose

children are at risk in a conflict-ridden land and who must contend with a willful sexist misunderstanding of the varied causes of their suffering.

In implicitly questioning the gender-coded dichotomy between the public and private spheres, a poem like "Small Passing" enacts a feminist outlook. But de Kok's poetry is not reducible to a single perspective. Moreover vantage points and ways of seeing are themselves often themes in her work. In part this is perhaps because she has often found or located herself at an angle to the mainstream: as an English speaker from a Dutch-descended family, as a lyric poet writing in the shadow of PERFORMANCE POETRY, as a female contending with patriarchy, as a white South African opposed to apartheid, as a South African émigré in Canada, and as a person returning to the South African conflict after the relative calm of her seven-year Canadian sojourn (1977–84).

Along with perspective and positioning, the relationship between familiarity and unfamiliarity is also a dominant motif in *Familiar Ground*. Often these three motifs are bound up with various manifestations of spatial, temporal, and emotional distance: distance from one's homeland, distance between the future-bound trajectory of adulthood and the receding past of remembered childhood, and distance between the repressive present of apartheid and the as-yet-to-be-realized emancipation from white supremacy. Memory is often at work in these poems, and if de Kok's poetry pays sustained attention to the nuances of spatial environments, or to the experience of growing up in one country and living in another, it also focuses attentively on the nonlinear ways in which remembrance shapes our immersion in time and in history.

The past is represented in part 1 of the book, entitled "In a Hot Country," while the present comes into focus most sharply in part 3, "A Small Passing." Along with those in parts 1 and 3, the poems in part 2, "Where there is water," are tied to a specific social geography. In the case of part 2 the geography is chiefly that of Canada, a cold northern country that as did its counterpart in the global south emerged as a nation-state from a history of conquest and colonialism. In addition to evoking specific geographies of childhood and adulthood, all three parts focus on the relationship between place and identity. Another unifying motif is an ongoing attempt to grapple with the meanings of "home" and "nation."

"Home is where the heart is," runs the opening line of the first poem in *Familiar Ground,* "To drink its water." But the startling image of the next line, "a tin can tied to a stray dog," belies the seemingly reassuring proverbialness of the first. "Home," it turns out, is a parched drought-ridden place, where longevity is common but life seems to have little point besides sluggish, lizardlike locomotion:

> Those who carry their homes on their backs
> Live for hundreds of years,
>   Moving inch by inch from birth to lagoon

Images of aridity and decay dominate this poem of return to the places of the speaker's childhood, situated in a land where the elements are hostile ("Over the path, the rocks, the tree / marauding sky, fiercer than memory") and where the light—ostensible source of life—is diseased ("In a hot country / light is a leper"), just as the body politic of the South African nation is scored by metaphorical sickness and suffering. It is to this inclement climate, this inhospitable land, that the speaker must return. Her sojourn away from the place where she grew up, "on the edge of scrub," as she notes in the next poem, has not issued in a sentimental denial of the difficulty of living in a "hot country." Instead she confronts the principal task that her homecoming demands of her:

> To return home, you have to drink its water,
> In a drought, you have to drink its water,
> Even from the courtyard well,
> The water blossoming in the gut,
> Or brackish, from a burning trough,
> Flypaper on your tongue,
> Pooling your hands,
> Bending when you drink.

In the poem's next and final section, it initially seems as if the speaker might not be up to the task of shouldering the burden of living in a hot country where the natural world crackles with menace:

Home is where the heart is:
Husk of heat on the back.
The sky enters into the skin,
The sky's red ants

Crawl over the shoulders.

And yet, in a subdued, stoical gesture, the speaker assumes the task of slaking her thirst, and of thereby reviving her bereft body. Only it is not quite water she drinks, but in an ambivalent gesture, her own dark projection into the water:

This bending body is my only body.
I bend and drink

The shadow in the water.

Some of the thematic concerns and poetic strategies of *Familiar Ground* are also present in de Kok's two subsequent volumes, *Transfer* (1997) and *Terrestial Things* (2002). Among the threads that bind all three volumes we can mention the themes of geography, migration, and home, or the relationship between personal preoccupations and the large public questions of the day. In formal terms, we can note de Kok's continued use of various modes of free narrative verse as well as an abiding concern with what she has referred to as "the formal representation of the furies, of grief, violence, and anger," and with "how [the furies] play themselves out, are reordered, in the delicacies and constraints of quite formal work."

After apartheid's official demise, de Kok sought to shed light on its tortuous legacy and on the resistance to it, especially as they played themselves out in the dramatic settings of the Truth and Reconciliation Commission's (TRC's) public hearings. The commission was charged by South Africa's first postapartheid government with the task of gathering testimony from both victimizers and victims. In televised sessions held around the country, former security and military personnel admitted—or denied—that they had engaged in brutal and extralegal acts of repression in the name of shoring up apartheid. (If they could claim a political motive for their actions and express repentence, the victimizers

could be exonerated from prosecution.) For their part, victims of those acts or the relatives of victims testified to their suffering and loss or sought clarification about or redress for crimes committed in apartheid's name.

De Kok first directed her attention to the TRC in two poems that appeared in *Transfer*, "At the Commission" and "Bandaged." The 12 poems that compose part 2 of *Terrestrial Things*, "A Room Full of Questions," also address themselves to different moments in and facets of the TRC proceedings: among them, the weeping to which the TRC's chairman, the Nobel laureate Archbishop Desmond Tutu, succumbed on the first day of hearings; the confrontation by a torture victim of his torturer; and the inability of a hardened soldier to convey adequately his shame and repentence. Three of the poems in this sequence, "Parts of Speech," "Tongue-Tied," and "The Transcriber Speaks," thematize the difficulty of expressing the horror that the poems record:

Why still believe stories can rise
with wings, on currents, as silver flares,
levitate unweighted by stones,
begin in pain and move towards grace,
aerating history with recovered breath?

Perhaps the answer to this question is found in the way that some of the poems acknowledge the problematic nature of representing and possibly appropriating the pain of others even as they try to wrestle with what de Kok has described as "this major revelatory complex mixture of truth and lying" in contemporary South Africa.

Not all of the poems in *Terrestrial Things* address themselves to matters of immediate public consequence. In part 1 of the book, "Foreign and Familiar," the poet revisits questions probed in the earlier books, such as the meanings of national affiliation and disaffiliation. De Kok has sojourned in Italy and has found in the landscapes of the Italian peninsula an intriguing counterpoint to the "far south . . . where contradictory seas crash in tidal war." (That quotation refers to the southernmost point of the African continent, Cape Agulhas, where the Atlantic and Indian Oceans meet and clash.) At peace in "the glittering Tuscan hills," the speaker of these postapartheid poems nonetheless finds that she is sometimes out of place, and memories and images of home intrude upon the idyll of "this elegant isthmus of history." Arriving in Venice, she is moved to ask, "What have we Africans to do with all this?" One answer is provided by the presence amid the tourist sites of young Senegalese men, members of Europe's immigrant underclass, embraced by the speaker as

> three of our continent's diasporic sons,
> young men in dreadlocks and caps, touting
> leather bags and laser toys in the subdued dialect
> of those whose papers are never correct,
> homeboys now in crowded high-rise rooms
> edging the embroidered city.

These young men, living on the edge in the margins of a prosperous European city, are not cast as mere victims of circumstance, adrift in foreign lands. Rather, they are the new "merchants in Venice" proclaimed by the title of the poem, the last line of which dubs them "the mobile inheritors of any renaissance." The speaker has come a long way since she evoked tentative gestures of cross-racial solidarity in *Familiar Ground*. While "stern" Tuscan cypresses "assess" her "foreignness" and "patronize the yucca / somnabulent migrant plant / its tortoise hide in better camouflage" thousands of miles to the south, in her native country, the speaker—inheritor of the privileges and alienations of white settler culture—seems finally to be at home in Africa.

That home, however, is a place in which parents have passed away, relatives and friends face the implacable passing of time, and "landscapes come to die." Moreover, outside the family circle, other tragedies have struck. While neither acquired immunodeficiency syndrome (AIDS) nor the human immunodeficiency virus (HIV) is directly named in the five poems that the book's last part comprises ("IV Freight"), it is clear from their titles and from such internal references as "viral carriers," "disease of acronyms," "orphans," and "dying ones" that the poems address themselves to the pandemic that has devastated South Africa more than any other country on Earth. Somber in mood, restrained in tone, elegiac in form, the poems enact a respectful but determined attempt to acknowledge and understand the multiple sources of suffering in contemporary South African society. One of the two TRC poems in *Transfer*,

"Bandaged," enjoins readers/auditors not to shy away from listening to the testimony of one of apartheid's victims. In so doing, the poem emphasizes—perhaps a touch reticently—poetry's role as bearer of witness:

> O listen, let us not turn away
> from seeing and hearing
> the witness speak with bowed neck

While some of de Kok's poems explicitly thematize the necessary work of healing and recovery that must take place in South Africa (e.g., "Mending"), even the poems that speak to the horrors of the AIDS crisis have a restorative quality to them inasmuch as they neither succumb to despair nor condescend to pity.

The themes of sickness, convalescence, and solidarity also feature in de Kok's most recent book of poetry, *Seasonal Fires: New and Selected Poems* (2006), her first collection to be published in the United States as well as in South Africa. Echoes of de Kok's earlier work abound here in assorted poems of place, childhood, dislocation, and remembrance. Yet the geographic reach of these new poems is wider than that of the previous collections, and the thematic terrain more varied and nuanced. We encounter some place-names for the first time—Baghdad, Malawi, Mogadishu, and Beirut, for example—and although specifically South African realities still dominate the moral and imaginative landscape of these poems, poetic ruminations on the destructiveness of war ("Pilgrimage"), on the demands of friendship ("Time to go"), or on parent-child relationships ("When Children Leave") make the overall mood of the new poems at once more global and more universally intimate in scope.

Together with some fresh formal efforts—a villanelle here, poems in couplets there—a series of novel intertextual references—to W. B. YEATS, George Seferis, William Blake, and Vincent Van Gogh—also contribute to the changed tone of these poems, as does an occasional impulse to celebrate occasions that offer tentative grounds for hope. This is notably the case in "Child Stretching," a poem that alludes to a haunting image conjured up by a poetic precursor of de Kok's, Ingrid Jonker, a fellow white South African poet based in Cape Town, who as did her younger conational, wrote tough-minded and tender lyric poetry, albeit in Afrikaans.

Jonker's best known poem, "The Child is not Dead" ("Die kind is nie dood nie"), imagines a child shot dead by the police coming back to life in outsize form and striding forth across Africa to reclaim his continent from the colonizers. In "Child Stretching," the implied white female speaker—who is looking at a photograph by Santu Mofokeng of a black rural mother getting her boychild ready for the day—thinks she recognizes the reborn child of Jonker's poem ("I think this is the boy who may grow tall / —he is already practising— / who will stride through Africa / —look at his sturdy legs— / this Vaalrand boy with his joyful stretch"), affirms the quiet quotidian strength of the parent and the promise of her offspring, and expresses a desire for kinship with them both, even as she acknowledges the potentially doubtful motives behind such a desire, as well as the stubborn difficulty of achieving such closeness in the world outside the verbal and visual texts and the hopes that they represent, frame, suggest, and contain:

> This is not my child.
> Nor is his assiduous mother my friend.
> But her loving proximity
> Makes me, here just outside the frame,
> (I know, you don't have to tell me,
> in the simplest, most suspect way),
> makes me want to be her sister,
> her child my buoyant nephew.

If poverty, suffering, and death haunt some of these pages, so do resilience, redress, and restoration. Even when they are contemplating some of the harshest realities of the contemporary world, these poems neither flinch nor give in to defeatism. Instead in the thoughtful, determined, and precise manner that has come to be an abiding and defining feature of de Kok's oeuvre, they testify modestly but tenaciously to poetry's capacity for capturing the temper of the times and for conveying terse truths about the ways in which we organize our social orders. Moreover de Kok's poems, old and new, constitute eloquent testaments to the ways in which the personal lyric can reflect upon and give shape to the dialogue between the tumultuous arenas of our worldly selves and the recondite depths of our inner lives.

BIBLIOGRAPHY

De Kok, I. J. *Familiar Ground.* Johannesburg, S.A.: Ravan Press, 1988.

———. *Seasonal Fires: Selected and New Poems.* New York: Seven Stories Press, 2006.

———. *Terrestrial Things.* Cape Town, S.A.: Kwela/Snailpress, 2002.

———. *Transfer.* Snailpress, Cape Town, S.A.: Snailpress, 1997.

Ingrid De Kok Web Page. Available online. URL: http://www.ingriddekok.co.za/interviews.html. Accesed May 3, 2008.

Interview by Erica Kelley, Erica. "Strangely tender: an interview with Ingrid de Kok." In *Scrutiny 2: Issues in English Studies in Southern Africa,* 8, no. 1 (2003): 34–38.

Pinsky, Robert. Review of *Seasonal Fires.* Available online. URL: http//www.washingtonpost.com/wp-dyn/content/article/2006/09/28/AR2006092801409.html. Accessed May 3, 2008.

David Alvarez

DE LA MARE, WALTER (1873–1956)

It has been said that Walter de la Mare is "squarely in the same world as the rest of us, but he sees deeper and further into its implications." Born at Charlton, county of Kent, on April 25, 1873, of Huguenot and Scottish descent, Walter de la Mare experienced loss at an early age. His father, James Edward de la Mare, was 62 when Walter was born and died when Walter was just four years old. After his father's death, Walter's mother, Lucy Sophia, moved the family to London. Walter was educated at St. Paul's Cathedral Choir School. Walter and his mother were very close (the name *Lucy* appears many times in de la Mare's works). At the age of 16, de la Mare began work for the Anglo-American Oil Company in London. In 1900 de la Mare began to publish in magazines such as *Black and White, The Sketch,* and *The Pall Mall Gazette.* Longmans published *Songs of Childhood* in 1902 under the pen name Walter Ramal. His first book in prose form, *Henry Brocken,* was published in 1904. In 1908 de la Mare quit his office job and officially began work as a freelance writer. He married and fathered four children and later had 11 grandchildren. Over the span of 60 years, de la Mare would publish almost 1,000 works in prose and verse form. He died on June 22, 1956, at Twickenham.

Walter de la Mare was a great admirer of Charles Dickens, Wilkie Collins, and THOMAS HARDY. Critics compared the magical, spellbinding quality of de la Mare's poetry to Coleridge's "Kubla Khan" and "Christabel." De la Mare was best known for his poetry for children, especially *Peacock Pie*. Walter de la Mare's world is a world of fantasy, fairies, moonlight, and magic. His poetic craftsmanship is subtle and delicate and is characterized by "vowel melody, and cunning rhythm, all combining to give haunting overtones, strangeness and spellbinding dreams."

Though de la Mare is best remembered for his children's poetry, he was also a profound writer of love poetry. In his poetry for adults, de la Mare exhibits "infinite tenderness." Writing between World War I and World War II, de la Mare felt and expressed a deep pessimism regarding the horrific loss of human life. Nevertheless, he had a profound love for his native England. His patriotism is expressed in his poetry as a love for the peacefulness and tranquility of England. The pessimism that de la Mare felt during this time is probably best expressed in *The Widow, Of a Son, Music, The Old Angler,* and *The Familiar.*

De la Mare was well loved by his friends and countrymen. He was gracious and remarkably kind to young writers. Furthermore he "was a poet who believed in the beauty and everlastingness of the human spirit." His talent for weaving together both magic and innocence earned for him the British Order of Merit, Companion of Honour.

When his ashes were laid to rest in St. Paul's Cathedral, hundreds of his admirers paid their respects to the most prolific, most charming of the Edwardian poets.

See also "SILVER," "THOMAS HARDY."

BIBLIOGRAPHY

Clark, Leonard. *Walter de la Mare.* New York: Henry Z. Walck, 1961.

Duffin, Henry Charles. *Walter de la Mare: A Study of His Poetry.* Freeport, N.Y.: Books for Libraries Press, 1969.

Hopkins, Kenneth. *Walter de la Mare.* London: Published for the British Council and the National Book League by Longmans, Green, 1957.

Sturgeon, Mary C. *Studies of Contemporary Poets.* Port Washington, N.Y.: Kennikat Press, 1970.

Precious McKenzie Stearns

DEVLIN, DENIS (1908–1959)

DEVLIN, DENIS (1908–1959) Denis Devlin was born in Greenock, Scotland, to Irish parents, who returned to Dublin in 1918 when he was 10. Devlin's home was happy, and, as befitted the eldest son of an Irish Catholic household, once he left school (Belvedere College), he enrolled as a seminarian at an eminent Catholic seminary, Clonliffe College, in 1926. His sojourn at Clonliffe was brief—he left in 1927—but it allowed him to study literature at University College Dublin (UCD) in a modern language course.

Devlin met and befriended Brian Coffey at UCD, and together in 1930 they published *Poems,* a collection of poetry written by both men. In this same year, Devlin graduated from UCD with his B.A. After graduating, Devlin spent some time working on his Gaelic in the Blasket Islands, before studying literature at Munich University and the Sorbonne in Paris. During this time (1930–33) Devlin met Samuel Beckett and Thomas MacGreevy. Beckett was impressed with Devlin and greatly respected his work.

These early travels were to mark a life punctuated by travel. Devlin was always greatly affected and inspired by place, and this response is prevalent in his poetry. In 1933 Devlin returned to UCD, where he received his M.A. He taught at UCD from 1933 to 1935, while he was writing a dissertation on Montaigne, teaching the literature he himself loved. But teaching was clearly not for Devlin, who left academia in 1935 to become an Irish diplomat. His career within the Irish Foreign Service was varied and distinguished. He held several important posts in Italy, England, Turkey, and the United States, including minister plenipotentiary to Italy and Turkey. He married in 1946, and his widow, Marie Caren Roden, survived him.

Despite his traveling and reputation as an international writer, Devlin remained at heart an Irishman and Irish poet. He published two collections of poems during his international traveling days, *Intercessions* in 1937 and *Lough Derg and Other Poems* in 1946. Both collections are infused by Irishness. The later *Tomb of Michael Collins* (1956) clearly embodies the influence Irish politics had on Devlin. During his time as a diplomat Devlin met St. John Pearse, and he published three collections of Pearse's poetry, which he had translated, *Rain* (1945), *Snow* (1945), and *Exile and Other Poems* (1949).

Devlin was Irish and worldly simultaneously, and his poems reflect both influences, with place and its effects remaining the dominating feature. Devlin returned to Ireland in 1959; he died in Dublin that same year. Since his death several collections of his poetry have been published, including Brian Coffey's *Collected Poems* in 1964, *The Heavenly Foreigner* in 1967, and his *Selected Poems* in 1963 edited by Allen Tate and Robert Penn Warren, whom he met while working in America. The Arts Council in Ireland awards the Denis Devlin Memorial Award, ensuring that his legacy and influence continue.

BIBLIOGRAPHY

Davis, Alex. *Broken Line: Denis Devlin and Irish Poetic Modernism.* Dublin, Ire.: Dublin Press, 2000.

Devlin, Denis. *Collected Poems.* Edited by Brian Coffey. Dublin: Dolmen, 1964.

Claire Norris

"A DIFFICULT BIRTH, EASTER 1998"

GILLIAN CLARKE (1998)   Easter, the season of rebirth, has been a frequent trope in Western poetry, both as subject and as metaphor. In GILLIAN CLARKE's "A Difficult Birth, Easter 1998," Easter Sunday serves as a metaphor that unfolds in three ways: A sheep thought to be barren gives birth, the Irish are at the brink of closing a peace deal, and Christ's resurrection is celebrated.

The couple—although it is not definitively stated in the text that the pair are a couple—are set to celebrate the imminent conclusion to the Irish peace talks. The poem works as a coda to W. B. YEATS's "Easter 1916," in which he responds to the "terrible beauty" of the rebellion set in motion. In Yeats's poem the clash between the Irish and the British for home rule has just begun—in Clarke's, the story is coming to an end. In the Easter story there are a beginning and an ending as well: Jesus's life is about to end, yet the resurrection will begin a new one. Clarke's Easter is begun with the anticipated conclusion of "eight decades" of Irish "slogg[ing] it out." Although the speaker never announces whether a deal has been reached, the poem ends with the birth of two new lives, and the renewal of hope that all will be well. This sense of renewal and rebirth, of both animal life and the life of Ireland, permeates the poem.

The celebration, a "quiet supper and bottle of wine" if the deal goes well, is postponed as an older ewe is approaching delivery. The age of the ewe is important: The speaker notes that they had believed the sheep barren as she has never given birth. The ewe seemed to be beyond the age of reproduction, infertile. Yet on this evening she is preparing a site for her delivery, instinctively "hoofing the straw." Clarke and her husband raise a small flock of sheep in West Wales. She is well versed in animal husbandry and has written many other poems about the birth of sheep. The details of the labor and assisted delivery, the water breaking, the ewe licking up the water, hoofing the straw into a resting spot, all ring true.

This delivery in stanza 3 is not an easy one, however. The lamb is stuck and cannot fit through its mother's birth canal. The male in the poem rushes to phone for veterinary assistance, but the speaker, unfazed by the turn of events, plunges her hands into the ewe, twisting the wedged lamb until it "comes / in a syrupy flood." As a woman she instinctively knows how to help the ewe and dismisses the assistance of medical men, who in their white coats "come to the women, / well meaning, knowing best, with their needles and forceps." The divide between midwifery, with its natural focus on helping the birthing female (animal or human), and the medical profession, with its emphasis on technology (at the ready with needles to repair incisions and forceps to drag the offspring forcibly from its mother), yawns wide in this stanza.

That this birth is an echo of both Christ's birth and the miracle of his resurrection lies in several images. The concluding stanza is open to being read as an allusion to the birth of Jesus as well as his death and resurrection. The animal the narrator is helping is not a cow or a horse, common farm animals, but a lamb, the symbol of Jesus's innocence and purity. The second is the final line of the poem: A second lamb is born as "the stone rolled away." The stone is a reference to the one that was rolled away from the entrance to Jesus's tomb when the women went to it on Sunday morning. And finally, the one who sees the stone rolled away is a woman, just as in the Easter story in the Gospels. The male in the poem leaves the scene, and it is the woman who delivers the lambs and who witnesses the miracle of birth.

The poem also alludes to the power of cooperative work that goes into the birthing process and how that lack of cooperation between Catholics and Protestants has resulted in violence and death. The speaker works with the ewe, sliding her hands into its body: "We strain together, harder than we dared." The pronoun used is *we*. It is only when the sheep pushes and the woman pulls that the birth of the first lamb is accomplished. Alone the sheep and the lambs would have died. Such cooperation by all parties in the peace process would be needed to secure a deal as well. The poem ends inconclusively regarding the outcome of the peace talks, but the lambs have been born successfully and the hopes are high that the birthing process of peace will be successful as well.

BIBLIOGRAPHY

Adams, Sam. "Weaving a Cymric Web? A Perspective on Contemporary Anglo-Welsh Poetry." In *Comparative Criticism*. Vol. 19, *Literary Devolution: Writing in Scotland, Ireland, Wales and England,* 117–133. Cambridge: Cambridge University Press, 1998.

Clarke, Gillian. "The King of Britain's Daughter." In *How Poets Work.* Edited by Tony Curtis, 122–136. Bridgend, Eng.: Seren, 1996.

Smith, K. E. "The Poetry of Gillian Clarke." In *Poetry in the British Isles: Non-Metropolitan Perspectives,* edited by Hans-Werner Ludwig and Lothar Fietz, 267–280. Cardiff: University of Wales Press, 1995.

Thurston, Michael. "'Writing at the Edge': Gillian Clarke's Cofiant." *Contemporary Literature* 44, no. 2 (summer 2003): 275–300.

Patricia Bostian

"DIGGING" Seamus Heaney **(1966)** This poem, written in 1964, was published in Seamus Heaney's first collection, *Death of a Naturalist* (1966). It is an early example of Heaney's concern with place, tradition, and continuity as well as with his role and identity as a Northern Irish poet. By means of the central pen/spade analogy, Heaney strives to reconcile his own identity as poet with his family tradition of physical farm labor.

The poem consists of eight sections varying from two to eight lines. It has no regular meter or rhyme scheme, although it contains occasional end rhyme (*sound–ground*), half-rhyme (*thumb–gun*), and internal rhyme (*knee–firmly*). Written in accessible language, the poem conveys a sensual impression of the physical world by means of onomatopoeia (*rasping, gravelly, squelch*), alliteration (*spade sinks, gravelly ground*), and rhythm. The "cool hardness" of the potatoes and the rough occupation of working the earth are matched by Heaney's economic style and coarse rhythm.

The two opening lines start out with a simile between the speaker's pen and a gun: "Between my finger and my thumb / The squat pen rests; snug as a gun." That the pen perfectly suits the speaker suggests that his profession is that of a writer, and the pen is likened to a gun, which implies the powerful impact writing can have. Although the reference to a gun in a Northern Irish poem might evoke the violent context of the Troubles, it must be kept in mind that this poem was written before their onset in the 1970s. All the same, by likening his pen to a gun the speaker may try to locate himself in the tradition of Irish nationalist writing and resistance. However, the image of the gun is dropped immediately when the speaker's attention is caught by the sound of a spade sinking "into gravelly ground: / My father, digging." Looking down through the window at his father gardening, the speaker is reminded of similar situations 20 years back, when his father was "Stooping in rhythm through potato drills / Where he was digging." The word *rhythm* suggests a link between the creation of poetry and the occupation of digging potato drills. The next section gives a detailed description of the father's expertise at working the land, which results in the son's retrospective admiration: "By God, the old man could handle a spade. / Just like his old man." Accordingly the speaker continues by recalling memories of his grandfather at turf digging, "going down and down / for the good turf." The craft of handling a spade has been passed down through the generations and has provided families with the necessities of food and home fuel. By emphasizing the expertise and endurance necessary for the task, Heaney pays tribute to and dignifies the easily devalued physical labor. Feeling an acute sense of "the curt cuts of an edge / Through living roots," the speaker realizes that he has departed from his family tradition: "But I've no spade to follow men like them." At this point the poem echoes the proverb that "the pen is lighter than the spade." However, in an attempt to establish a sense of continuity between his ancestors' physical and his own cultural labor, the speaker suggests a metaphorical link between spade and pen in the closing three lines: "Between my finger and my thumb / The squat pen rests. / I'll dig with it." Rather than digging for turf or potatoes, the poet will dig into the past, memorizing his forefathers' lives, exploring his cultural and family origins, and ultimately recovering his own "living roots." Viewed thus, "Digging" foreshadows Heaney's idea of the poet as archaeologist digging up and preserving a nation's history and communal roots, which he would develop in his later works, notably in his series of bog poems written throughout the 1970s.

BIBLIOGRAPHY
Andrews, Elmer. *The Poetry of Seamus Heaney: All the Realms of Whisper.* New York: St. Martin's Press, 1988.
Heaney, Seamus. *Opened Ground: Selected Poems 1966–1996.* New York: Farrar, Straus & Giroux, 1998.

Michaela Schrage-Früh

"DISABLED" WILFRED OWEN (1917)

This is one of a number of poems written by WILFRED OWEN at Craiglockhart War Hospital in Edinburgh, where he stayed for several months while recovering from shell shock incurred on the battlefields of the First World War. It depicts a severely injured, very young soldier and follows his train of thought as he compares his life before the war, as a young and handsome teenager, keen on sports and girls, with his current existence, as an almost-limbless ("his ghastly suit of grey, / Legless, sewn short at elbow"), institutionalized patient. The fields of both football and the battle are compared, notably in terms of injuries received, although the soldier seems to understand the irony in his previous desire for sporting wounds to affirm his masculinity now that the legs on which he had liked "a blood-smear" have been amputated.

Several of Owen's recurring poetic themes are present in the poem. The idea of youth in hell is made clear through the juxtaposition of "the old times, before he threw away his knees" and the present, a time where he "will never feel again how slim girl's waists are." Owen criticizes the military system that has enabled the soldier to enlist through lying about his age and shows the mental breakdown and panic gripping the young man at the realization that his life is now drastically limited ("how cold and late it is! Why don't they come?"). The influence of the romantic poets, evident in many of Owen's poems, is shown in the soldier's remembering having been told he would look "a god in kilts."

Owen would have met men such as the one described in "Disabled" and is careful to balance the immaturity of the soldier (as seen in his fantasizing and reasons for enlisting—"to please his Meg") with anger at the view of war as glamorous, a view held both by the soldier before the war and by much of the public throughout it. Like his mentor, SIEGFRIED SASSOON, whom he met at Craiglockhart, Owen is scathing about the public perception of returning soldiers, noting that the women who would have cheered the soldier as a healthy, handsome man now visit only the able-bodied men in hospital.

See also "STRANGE MEETING."

BIBLIOGRAPHY
Hibberd, Dominic. *Wilfred Owen* London: Weidenfeld & Nicolson, 2002
Stallworthy, Jon, ed. *The Complete Poems and Fragments.* Oxford: Oxford University Press, 1984.
———. *Wilfred Owen.* London: Oxford University Press, 1974.

Charlotte Kearns

"A DISUSED SHED IN CO. WEXFORD" DEREK MAHON (1975)

DEREK MAHON's best-known poem was first published in *The Snow Party* (1975), a collection obsessed by a sense of ending and loss. "A Disused Shed in Co. Wexford" is an elegy to worlds and peoples that have disappeared. A pair of travelers force open the long-locked door of a disused shed and come upon a host of a "thousand mushrooms" crowding in the darkness "Deep in the grounds of a burnt-out hotel, / Among the bathtubs and the washbasins." They have been there, the poet imagines, for "half a century," all yearning for and striving toward the light entering through a small keyhole, their only access to the real world. The historical moment of their abandonment is clearly specified as the Irish War of Independence: "They have been waiting for us in a foetor [fetid odour] / Of vegetable sweat since civil war days," when the "expropriated mycologist" departed. The war, which ended in 1922 with the treaty signed between the British government and Michael Collins's Irish Republican Army (IRA), led to the partition of Ireland into the 26 Catholic southern counties (the Free State) and the six Protestant northern counties, creating the basis for the still ongoing conflict. Protestants in the South were as marginalized as Catholics in the North, and the estate described might have been left by an Irish Ascendancy family after independence. Apart from this political reading, the mycologist (expert on fungi) could also be read as a god figure, deserting the world of suffering humanity.

The first line of the poem, "Even now there are places where a thought might grow," introduces both a pessimistic outlook and a minimal yet defiant hope in the image of growth despite reduced and exacerbated living conditions. The fungi in the dark shed are a symbol for all the lost lives that make up history, victims who yet lift their heads in desire for a recognition of their fate: "They are begging us, you see, in their wordless way, / To do something, to speak on their behalf, / Or at least not to close the door again." The mushrooms stand for the enslaved Indians in South America, who were forced to work in "Peruvian mines, worked out and abandoned" now, but also for the victims any Irish reader would associate with county Wexford, a place standing for centuries of bloody political conflict and colonial exploitation. After its use as a Viking base for incursions and trading, it became an Anglo-Norman conquest in 1169, then an English garrison loyal to the Crown; Cromwell perpetrated the massacre of Wexford there in 1649, killing 1,500 of its 2,000 inhabitants; the town also played a significant role in the disastrous rebellions of 1798 and 1916. Mahon expands the meaning of the poem to epic proportions, as the mushrooms also stand for the "lost people of Treblinka and Pompeii"; Holocaust victims in a Nazi concentration camp in Poland during World War II or the people who lost their lives in the eruption of Vesuvius in A.D. 79 appeal alike to the visitor to save them from perpetual oblivion: "Let the god not abandon us." This epic sweep is emphasized by the poem's epigraph, taken from the Greek poet George Seferis's (1900–71) *Mythistorema* (The mythical history). "Let them not forget us, the weak souls among

the asphodels" refers to Odysseus's descent to the underworld in Homer's *Odyssey* (and Seferis's adaptation of it), the asphodel the flower said to fill the plains of Hades and to be the favorite food of the dead. These dead also desire to be remembered.

Mahon's poem is dedicated to his friend James Gordon Farrell (1935–79), a novelist of Anglo-Irish descent, the title of whose most famous novel, *The Troubles* (1970), refers to the euphemism applied to the brutal partisan war that began in 1919 between Sinn Fein/IRA and the British army of occupation. The 1970s saw a new round of Troubles between Protestants and Catholics in Northern Ireland, and Mahon's poem is to be seen in this context. The cruel deformation of the victims is evoked by almost surreal images of gothic vampirism, as the mushrooms are described as "Magi, moonmen, / Powdery prisoners of the old regime, / Web-throated, stalked like triffids [carnivorous plants]." The visitors to the shed likewise seem only to intensify their helpless suffering: As they are photographed, the mushrooms react with "only the ghost of a scream / At the flashbulb firing squad we wake them with." SEAMUS HEANEY reads the mushrooms as part of the unconscious and interprets the poem as an expression of Mahon's feeling of guilt for his abandonment of his home country (cf. Seamus Heaney in Elmer Andrews, 1993, 131ff). While the poem seems to celebrate the resilience and unquenchable vitality of the oppressed, there is no avoiding the fact that the poet himself— despite his detached compassion—feels deeply complicit in the forces of repression that have so largely determined the course of history.

BIBLIOGRAPHY

Andrews, Elmer, ed. *Irish Poetry: A Collection of Critical Essays.* Basingstoke, Eng.: Macmillan, 1993.

Boisseau, Maryvonne. "'Soul, Song and Formal Necessity': Une lecture de 'A Disused Shed in Co. Wexford' de Derek Mahon." *Etudes Anglaises* 2 (2003): 162–172.

Campbell, Matthew, ed. *The Cambridge Companion to Contemporary Irish Poetry.* Cambridge: Cambridge University Press, 2003.

Donnelly, Brian, guest ed. "Derek Mahon." Journal issue no. 24. Special issue, *Irish University Review* 24 (1993).

Haughton, Hugh. "'Even now there are places where a thought might grow': Place and Displacement in the Poetry of Derek Mahon." In *The Chosen Ground: Essays on*

the *Contemporary Poetry of Northern Ireland,* edited by Neil Corcoran, 87–122. Bridgend, Eng.: Seren Books, 1992.
———. "On Sitting Down to Read 'A Disused Shed in Co Wexford' Once Again." *Cambridge Quarterly* 31 (2002): 183–198.
Kennedy-Andrews, Elmer, ed. *The Poetry of Derek Mahon.* Gerrards Cross, Eng.: Colin Smythe, 2002.
Mahon, Derek. *Selected Poems.* London: Penguin, 2006.
McDonald, Peter. *Mistaken Identities: Poetry and Northern Ireland.* Oxford: Clarendon, 1997.

Heike Grundmann

"DIVORCE" ANNA WICKHAM (1911)

The closing couplet of each of this poem's three loose stanzas is a continuing cry for a freedom that is imagined but not experienced: "I smother in the house in the valley below, / Let me out to the night, let me go, let me go." The ongoing depth of feeling that the repetition supports is embellished by the unsettling metaphors. "The dark cold winds" that "rush free" are preferable to the smothering and lonely warmth of the hearth, itself a conventional symbol of settled womanhood. The additional rhyming couplet in the poem's final section tells that the woman's secret struggle to stifle her heart's desire has become intolerable: "On the hill there is fighting, victory or quick death / In the house is the fire which I fan with sick breath." The adjacent end rhyme reinforces the felt fine line between life and death. The quick pace and extra syllables in this couplet's second line reinforce the evocation of an impulse that cannot be contained. The internal dissonance of the poem's second line, "In the close house I nurse a fire," is especially characteristic of Wickham's early work, which can seem cluttered with rhyming effects. However, it does the job of setting up a mood of unease. The fire is the literal hearth and emblematic of the wife's irrepressible urge to escape from the claustrophobia of "home."

Although an early poem, "Divorce" illustrates the troubled feminist voice and stylistic concerns that run through much of Wickham's poetry. As several poems do, it operates in conjunction with the *Fragment of an Autobiography,* which relates the unrelenting oppression in Wickham's own marriage. As here, she flexes the dramatic monologue to explore the complex psychology at work in domestic conflict. The mixture of the conversational and the lyrical imperceptibly contrasts the idealized and mythical with quotidian realities. With the reader in the position of confidant/e, sympathy is directed toward the silent suffering of women who felt trapped by social demands. "The Scapegoat," "The Dilemma," and "Envoi" articulate the warring claims of personal liberty and social restraint. "The Angry Woman" is a lengthy disclosure on gender inequalities: "If sex is a criterion for power, and never strength, / What do we gain by union?" While "Divorce" was radical in a period when women had limited legal rights, even more shocking would have been "The Revolt of Wives," which contradicts the idea that child-bearing is woman's greatest gift, goal, and pleasure. In "Marriage," civilized fighting, symptomatic of a couple's competing instincts for love and independence, is depicted as inextricable and inevitable.

BIBLIOGRAPHY
Dowson, Jane. *Women, Modernism and British Poetry 1910–39: Resisting Femininity.* Aldershot, Eng.: Ashgate, 2002.
Smith, R. D., ed. *The Writings of Anna Wickham.* London: Virago Press, 1984.

Jane Dowson

"THE DOLLS MUSEUM IN DUBLIN" EAVAN BOLAND (1994)

Dublin society was forcefully disrupted on April 24, Easter Monday, in 1916, when members of the Irish Volunteers and other dissenting brotherhoods stormed the General Post Office (GPO) and other public buildings. Their purpose was to use the GPO as the headquarters for a rebellion against the British and for Irish nationalism. Called the Easter Rising, the rebellion was quickly put down by British forces through superior numbers and discipline. That week 450 people died in Dublin, and the seven insurgents who held the GPO were among the many rebel leaders who agreed to execution to save their followers' lives. Most Dubliners, however, stayed far away from the fighting. The British triumphed then, but the struggle for an independent Irish republic was far from over.

Months after the uprising, the poet and activist W. B. YEATS glorified the events in "EASTER 1916." He instructed his fellow Dubliners that they could no longer see their city or country the same way because "All changed,

changed utterly." For Yeats the event contrasts the self-sacrifice that the Irish insurgents willingly undertook with the "polite meaningless words" spoken by British nationalists. From that contrast "a terrible beauty is born." Yeats recasts the rebels' lives into legend and their actions into symbols of courage and bravery.

Yeats was not only a scholarly influence on the Dublin poet EAVAN BOLAND but also one of her creative muses. While she mines Yeats's characteristic lyricism in "The Dolls Museum in Dublin," Boland reinterprets history and, in particular, the Easter Uprising. Specifically where Yeats mythologizes the rebel leaders and their actions, Boland looks to visual remnants of the past and tries to reconstruct history imaginatively through tangible details and unromanticized figures. Unlike Yeats, Boland rejects the clichés of Ireland as female and Irish history as male. Nor does she feverishly speak for the speechless survivors of conflict—the women and children who know the Irish experience as defeat—or turn history into man-made legends. With a determined eye, Boland reads the histories of Irish women from the women's possessions, items such as discarded dolls.

As a title, "The Dolls Museum in Dublin" conjures images of childhood innocence, playfulness, and times when life centered on family. The poem's first sentence, "The wounds are terrible," counters that cheerfulness and prompts readers to ask whose wounds, what wounds, and how did the wounds come about. The poem retells how the dolls are wounded, how their paint is old, how they have "cracks along the lips and on the cheeks / [that] cannot be fixed," how their clothing is soiled and their ivory arms "dissolved to wax." These inanimate feminine survivors were more ornament than substance, more trivial remainders of little girls' imaginations than valuable artifacts deemed worthy of keeping. Nonetheless Boland sees the dolls as complex remnants of "the present of the past" because they are children's toys rather than mythic idols.

The poet instructs readers to remember historic contexts not as unvarying rhythms but as mismatched music: Quadrilles have 6/8 or 2/4 time; waltzes are triple timed; promenades mean marching, yet none of these musical forms naturally leads to the others. She moves to romantic images of "yacht-club terraces," lamps with "copper holders," carriages, and "cobbled quays" that also have the wrong beats when used to

"recreate Easter in Dublin." Rather than Easter's bringing a pleasant spring day to honor God's redemption, violence enters Dublin as "booted officers" riding horses with "steam hissing from the[ir] flanks." The discord of incompatible musical forms fits exactly with the discord of insurrection and military conflict. Boland moves smoothly from gentle expectations to violence, from dolls in a museum to the fear children experience when war disrupts shielded lives.

The fourth verse starts with an initially confusing pronoun: *They* cannot be the British officers, their Irish mistresses, or their horses of the previous stanza because "they" are "cradled and cleaned, / held close in the arms of their owners." Boland again shifts her readers' attention to the dolls and juxtaposes their owners, the children and their mothers, with the British military. Forcefully the poem swings from military images to the dolls to the Easter altars dressed for the day "with linen" and "lilies" and "candles . . . burning and warning." Rather than the joy of Easter rituals and Christ's promise of eternal life, the next stanzas warn Dublin's celebrants of the approaching Easter Rising and degrade the patriotic appeals by which "the [British] Empire is summoning its officers."

Children "cossetting [protecting] their dolls" as they walk past the soldiers are chilled by the "carriages . . . turning back." "Twilight falls," a metaphor that suggests how the way of life exemplified by parasols, the Shelbourne Hotel bar, and "laughter and gossip on the terraces" is vanishing like the pastel sunlight. The poem returns to the present, to the Dolls Museum, where in the twilight the dolls' injuries are visible. In a syntactically perplexing sentence, the poet describes how

> Shadows
> remain on the parchment-coloured waists,
> are bruises on the stitched cotton clothes
> are hidden on dimples on the wrists.

The shadows deepen not only the dolls' figures but also the bruises and hidden specters on their wrists. These offenses emphasize how similar the dolls and their owners, children and governesses, are as they walk together "looking down." To look up is to face the (British) officers and to chance suffering terrible wounds much like those in the poem's opening line.

Now silent and terrified from what they have "seen," the dolls peer out of "the airless peace of each glass case" with "eyes wide open." They are helpless because they could not change the violence of the past, they could not warn the children and their families, and, most importantly, they cannot warn anyone of present or future brutality. They are now museum relics. Having survived their purpose as symbols of childhood and a civilized time of manners, the dolls are hostages. Time leaves today's museum visitors ignorant of what the dolls experienced, and destiny has altered the dolls' purposefulness as either messengers of joy or warning to relics of earlier history.

Far from mythologizing either an individual—as Yeats does the rebel leaders Thomas MacDonagh, John Mac-Bride, James Connolly, and Patrick Pearse—or glorifying any history of violent political struggle, Boland perceives horror through the "terrible stare" of the dolls' eyes. The dolls shut up in their display cabinets represent the same type of helplessness that occurs when people turn away from questioning, refuse to see their history through commonplace items, or deny a voice to women, the ones who live daily with the human consequences of heroic rebellions, wars, and man-made confrontations.

BIBLIOGRAPHY

Boland, Eavan. "The Dolls Museum in Dublin." In *In a Time of Violence,* 14–15. New York: W. W. Norton, 1995.

———. *Object Lessons: The Life of the Woman and the Poet in Our Time.* New York: W. W. Norton, 1996.

Hagen, Patricia L., and Thomas W. Zelman. *Eavan Boland and the History of the Ordinary.* Bethesda, Md.: Academica Press, 2003.

Lynndiane Beene

"DO NOT GO GENTLE INTO THAT GOOD NIGHT" DYLAN THOMAS (1951) Dylan Thomas wrote "Do Not Go Gentle," a poem urging men to "rage, rage against the dying of the light," in response to his father's being diagnosed with cancer. Soon after finishing it, Thomas told his friend and critic John Brinnin that he had not shown it to his father yet, "but hoped he would have the courage to read it to him very soon." The poem was not published until after his father's death.

The poet SEAMUS HEANEY calls it "one of the best villanelles in the language." As seen in the last poem he

wrote, "Prologue" for the *Collected Poems,* Thomas enjoyed the challenge of experimenting with difficult forms. He also habitually turned his gaze upon the extremes of our existence—the womb, the tomb—and often his poems manage to capture both parts of the dichotomy at once. "Do Not Go Gentle" is agonizingly clear about the emotional proximity of death, but it is also movingly faithful in its adherence to the strict form of the villanelle's highly complex structure, and in that sense, the poetry itself enacts a kind of redemption, finding something stable to believe in when the fiction of solid matter crumbles, loss is imminent, the light is fading, and we are faced with the impossibility of immortal longings.

A villanelle is a French poetic form consisting of 19 lines: five tercets followed by a quatrain, all on two rhymes. The first and third lines of the first stanza are alternately repeated as a refrain at the end of each tercet, and the two repeated lines become the final couplet of the quatrain. This repetitive form where each new stanza uses a familiar line, but uses it differently, is one that Thomas might naturally gravitate toward, as repetition with difference is elemental to his poetry, but in this highly personal poem, with its exigency in his father's illness, the surprising choice of this artificial form takes Thomas beyond the spontaneous revelations of his earlier poetry and shows his maturity as a poet, with form, diction, tone, rhyme, and rhythm all conspiring to create the poem's great depth, its power to confront mortality. Seamus Heaney describes it rather beautifully: "One of the poem's strengths is its outwardly directed address, its escape from emotional claustrophobia through an engagement with the specifically technical challenges of the villanelle. Yet that form is so much a matter of crossing and substitutions, of back-tracks and double-takes, turns and returns, that it is a vivid figure for the union of opposites, for the father in the son, the son in the father, for life in death and death in life. . . . It is a living cross-section, a simultaneously open and closed form, one in which the cycles of youth and age, of rise and fall, growth and decay find their analogues in the fixed cycle of rhymes and repetitions."

The first two stanzas, in typical Dylan Thomas fashion, plunge directly into the poem's center, exhorting a figure made universal by being called "Old age" to fight against the ending of the metaphorical "day," the "light." And these two words, as if to emphasize their own universal quality, set the rhyme for the rest of the poem, where one of these two sounds will end every line. But the exhortation against dying itself, which seems straightforward enough, is made more complex by the colloquializing twist in which *night,* normally the opposite of *light,* is made into *good night,* not the dark, scary thing under the bed after all, but a greeting, an everyday phrase with all the warm, familiar quality of the voice in it.

In the fertile ground of Thomas's imagery, the dying men of stanza two can also become the famous "wise men," who, at the end of their biblical journey, came upon the birth of the Christ Child. Interestingly the "wise men" "know dark is right," so even though they should "rage, rage" against it (the doubling of that single syllable echoing with intensity), and should not go "gentle" into it, the night of darkness is always already conjoined with the light of new beginning and the hope of human contact. In this way the poem enacts the reaching for the impossible, the fusion of opposites in sound, which is both what many of Thomas's poems are about, and, perhaps more importantly, what they *are.* With this poem as a powerful example, it may be fair to say that poetry for Thomas is simultaneously a raging against and rejoicing in both the limits and the possibilities of all human forms, social, linguistic, physical, and spiritual. The villanelle structure allows Thomas to struggle against form and at the same time use the intensity of its frame to make possible the expression of this very personal struggle, a vivid declaration of love and fear that was somehow too naked for him to read to his father without some extra measure of courage.

Repetition with difference continues in the poem as each of the central stanzas renames the men, first "wise men," then "Good men," "Wild men," and, in the final three-line stanza, "Grave men," a pun that threatens to mock and thus undo the poem's somber quality. But Thomas's characteristic abundance, by being playful even at the end, manages to give the poem more power, the way a child's ribbon found on a tombstone might intensify the solemn scene of the graveyard.

BIBLIOGRAPHY

Brinnin, John Malcolm, ed. *A Casebook on Dylan Thomas.* New York: Thomas Y. Crowell, 1960.

Davies, James A. *A Reference Companion to Dylan Thomas.* Westport, Conn., and London: Greenwood Press, 1998.

Heaney, Seamus. *The Redress of Poetry.* New York: Farrar, Straus & Giroux, 1995.

Jo Miller

DOUGLAS, KEITH (1920–1944) Scholars who write about Keith Castellain Douglas almost always mention an incident that occurred in the Middle East in 1942 while Douglas was working as a camouflage-training officer. Frustrated with the relative inactivity of his job, Douglas abandoned his post and fled, not away from the fighting, but toward the front lines where the Battle of Alamein was under way. The act of military disobedience perfectly captures the spirit of Douglas's poetry and of the man himself. Personally he was direct, confrontational, and, in EDMUND BLUNDEN's opinion, "obstinate." His strong character is mimicked in his poetry, which exhibits blunt honesty in its depiction of war.

Douglas was born in Tunbridge Wells, Kent, on January 24, 1920. He attended Christ's Hospital School and, later, Merton College, Oxford, where he was tutored by Edmund Blunden. He exhibited an early predilection for writing and published his first poem at the age of 16. At age 20 in 1940, he entered the army, served for a year in England, and then was shipped to Egypt as part of the Second Derbyshire Yeomanry regiment (known as the Sherwood Rangers). Shortly thereafter his frustration over his assignment led to the insubordination that took him to the front lines. Because the regiment had lost so many officers, Douglas's commanding officer decided not to discipline him and instead gave Douglas command of a tank. Douglas carried out his duties with alacrity (he was recommended for a military cross) until he was wounded by a mine at Zem Zem on January 15, 1943. Invalided for the time being, he was sent for six weeks to a hospital at El Ballah, Palestine, where he had the leisure to write much of what became *Alamein to Zem Zem* (published posthumously in 1946), a prose account of his experiences with desert warfare as a tank commander. The book included drawings of war scenes Douglas had witnessed, and, unlike many war memoirs, it depicted war as an extremely mobile, active engagement. Douglas continued to write poetry and published his first volume, *Selected Poems,* with J. C. Hall and Norman Nicholson in February 1943. At the end of the same year the Sherwood Rangers were sent back to England, where Douglas stayed for six months. He then participated in the D-Day invasion of Normandy but was killed by mortar fire on June 9, 1944, at the age of 24.

Douglas's early death, though unfortunate, seems somehow appropriate for a man who was fascinated by warfare and adventure. He developed an interest in guns and soldiers in his childhood, and as he grew older, he was drawn to activities that tended to encourage competition. An athletic youth, he swam, played rugby, and enjoyed horseback riding. He was rebellious in school and later had difficulty following orders in the army. He also found it difficult to maintain stable relationships with women as he struggled to express his own sense of aggressive masculinity. Indeed his zest for adventure was so great that when he received a photograph of himself as a military cadet in 1940, he decorated it with leaf work, classical columns, and the words from Horace Dulce et decorum est pro patria mori (It is sweet and proper to die for one's country). He even added a halo around his own head.

Douglas's poetry is unique in that it neither partakes of the patriotism inherent in the work of many other war poets nor engages in direct protest over the waste and pointlessness of battle. Douglas avoided touching on the political implications of war and chose not to make moral judgments on his subject. He was not interested as much in the musicality or beauty of poetry as in its ability to unsettle the reader with the stark, visceral reality of battle and its aftermath. As he once commented, he wanted to write "true things." His best known poem, for example, "VERGISSMEINNICHT" (meaning "forget me not"), describes finding a decaying German body with, at its side, a "picture of his girl" soiled with mud and gore. The grisly image of the poem aptly captures the brash but human quality that Douglas wished to evoke in his writing. It also illustrates well Douglas's ability to create strong visual imagery. A similar starkness is clear in "How to Kill," in which the speaker comments, "How easy it is to make a ghost." Another of Douglas's poems, "Simplify me when I'm dead," acts as a farewell to England and is essentially Douglas's own elegy. Douglas wrote it shortly before leaving for Africa, and even though it preceded Doug-las's war experiences, it, too, offers a grisly image as the poem's speaker imagines layers of skin and flesh being stripped away from his skeleton.

Because Douglas died so young, most of his work has been issued posthumously. *Collected Poems* appeared in 1951, *Selected Poems* was published in 1964 (edited by TED HUGHES), *Complete Poems* was issued in 1978, and *Keith Douglas: A Prose Miscellany* saw the press in 1985. Although the *Complete Poems* is a relatively slim volume of less than 150 pages, Douglas achieved—much as John Keats had more than a century earlier with a small corpus of poetry—a significant reputation. Many scholars consider him one of the most important British poets of World War II.

See also "ARISTOCRATS."

BIBLIOGRAPHY

Douglas, Keith. *Complete Poems.* Edited by Desmond Graham. Oxford: Oxford University Press, 1978.

Graham, Desmond. *Keith Douglas 1920–1944.* London: Oxford University Press, 1974.

Scannell, Vernon. *Not without Glory: Poets of the Second World War.* London: Woburn Press, 1976.

Schmidt, Michael. *A Reader's Guide to Fifty Modern British Poets.* New York: Barnes & Noble, 1979.

Shires, Linda M. *British Poetry of the Second World War.* New York: St. Martin's Press, 1985.

Ben Robertson

"DOWN, WANTON, DOWN!" ROBERT GRAVES (1933)

The poem was first published in the collection *Poems 1930–33.* Its theme, the conflict between love and lust, the dichotomy of body and mind, and the impossibility of reconciling the two, recurs obsessively in this volume. Poems in close proximity are "The Succubus," a sexual nightmare in which the copulating woman is envisaged as "gulping away your soul" and as having a "paunched and uddered carcase," and "Ulysses," where the Greek hero of the *Odyssey* is regarded as a victim at the mercy of his sexual appetite, for whom all women have become one: "Flesh had one pleasure only in the act."

The poems belong to a period in ROBERT GRAVES's life when his poetical theory and outlook on humanity had undergone a profound change due to the influence of his companion (and first muse) Laura Riding, whom he had met in 1926. After his separation from his wife, Nancy, in 1929, he and Riding had gone into exile in Mallorca, where Graves began to come to terms with his traumatic war experiences as well as with his puritanical upbringing. "My religious training developed in me a great capacity for fear—I was perpetually tortured by the fear of hell—a superstitious conscience, and a sexual embarrassment from which I have found it very difficult to free myself" (Graves, *Goodbye to All That,* 20–21). Through Riding's influence, Graves began to develop his theory of woman as a representative of a higher, transcendent reality and man as belonging to the sense-bound world. Honesty, integrity, and independence from the prejudices of "civilized" society became the goals of his poetry, yet Graves still wavered among a romantic view of love, outright disgust at human sexuality, and then rejection of both masculine romanticism and mystification of human sexuality. In 1932 their relationship became increasingly asexual, partly because of Riding's precarious health after her suicidal leap from a window, partly for ideological reasons; she rejected the sensual as detrimental to the divine, transcendent side of love and as a threat to the intellect (cf. Seymour, 213).

The brazen invocation of his own *membrum virilis* (male member = penis) in "Down, Wanton, Down!" by a speaker who has an erection in an inopportune moment clearly shows that Graves had been able to shed his priggish Protestant inheritance, and yet the disgusted rejection of the sexual urge reveals the creative tension between theory and practice, thought and feeling, mind and body. The humorous and energetic shout with which the poem begins, "Down, wanton, down! Have you no shame," is reminiscent of the manner of Shakespeare in his sonnets (Riding and Graves had analyzed the sonnet "Th'expense of spirit in a waste of shame" in their *The Survey of Modernist Poetry*) and of the metaphysical poets John Donne (compare the chiding of the morning in "The Sun Rising": "Busy old fool, unruly sun") and Andrew Marvell. It shows a Renaissance approach to sexuality that is unafraid of obscenity, and yet the use of the rather archaic word *wanton* evokes a medieval deprecation of sexuality as one of the foremost vices, namely, lust. The speaker expresses disgust at the lack of discrimination of his unruly organ in its mechanical reaction to a stimulus such as the mere "whisper of Love's name."

In the second stanza, Graves explores the connection between masculine sexuality and martial aggression by using the metaphorical field of warfare for a sexual encounter. The penis now becomes a "bombard-captain" who is blindly pursuing his goal of reaching "the ravelin and effect[ing] a breach / Indifferent what you storm or why." This is a martial image with clear sexual connotations: The penis is attacking and breaking the "ravelins" (defense mechanisms) of the castle (female body) and finally reaches the "breach" (vagina). The speaker stresses the blindness of the pursuit and again uses Renaissance terminology for the sexual climax: "So be that in the breach you die" refers to the equation of an orgasm with death common since the Middle Ages.

In the third stanza the speaker differentiates the blindness of the merely sexual (and martial) urges of the male from "Love" (with a capital *L*): "Love may be blind, but Love at least / Knows what is man and what mere beast." The duality of man who is drawn upward to heaven through his intellectual nature and pulled downward to sheer animality by his instincts was a major topic of Neoplatonic philosophy as well as court poetry (troubadours, Petrarch). Ideal Love and even "wayward Beauty," he claims, deserve "more delicacy from her squires." The archaic, chivalric language here evokes an entire code of behavior, associated for instance with the knights and squires at King Arthur's court, who had to be both, perfect warriors and perfect lovers, and for whom love meant the unselfish service and adoration of a lady who was forever out of reach as an object of sexual consummation. These attempts by human civilization at a sublimation of mere carnal desire into divine, pure love are again subverted in the following address to the penis. The speaker doubts that this "witless" organ has ever been able to live up to such a sophisticated and complex ideal of "Love," just as the intellectual (wit) and the corporeal (will) were the two opposed faculties in Renaissance philosophy of man. By claiming that the erect penis might boast with his "staunchness at the post," but not the ability "to think fine and profess the arts," he mocks the pretensions with which civilization has endowed the merely sexual. Conventions of society that sublimate brutish desire are mere fictions, attempts to domesticate what remains forever untamed.

By ending with the mocking question whether "Beauty" and "Love" are going to bow to the "bald rule of thumb" (a pun on the thumblike form of the penis) or swear loyalty to its "crown," the poem again evokes the allegorical battle of wit against will, mind against body, that occupied Graves throughout his life. Here he treats the problem in a facetious manner (the humor is emphasized by the rhyming couplets), exorcising the power of his male member merely by shooing him away: "Be gone, have done! Down, wanton, down!" But the problem of a reconciliation of the two natures of man remains, because a mere suppression of the id (sexual drives) by the ego (conscious self) and superego (morality of society) will never occur, as Sigmund Freud has taught us.

BIBLIOGRAPHY
Canary, Robert H. *Robert Graves*. Boston: Twayne, 1980.
Carter, D. N. G. *Robert Graves: The Lasting Poetic Achievement*. Totowa, N.J.: Barnes & Noble, 1989.
Graves, Robert. *Goodbye to All That: An Autobiography*. London: Cape, 1929.
Kirkham, Michael. *The Poetry of Robert Graves*. London: Athlone Press, 1969.
Seymour, Miranda. *Robert Graves: Life on the Edge*. New York: Henry Holt, 1995.

Heike Grundmann

"A DREAM OF FAIR WOMEN" KINGSLEY AMIS (1956)

"A Dream of Fair Women" appears in KINGSLEY AMIS's 1956 collection, *A Case of Samples*, along with such poems as "Wrong Words," "Against Romanticism," and "The English Novel, 1740–1820." The aggressively antiromantic, satirical, and self-reflexive wit of the works in *A Case of Samples*, of which "A Dream of Fair Women" is among the best examples, placed Amis (along with PHILIP LARKIN, THOM GUNN, and others) squarely in the vanguard of the Movement of post–Second World War British poetry.

Amis borrows the title from Tennyson's "A Dream of Fair Women," in which the poetic persona dreams that he is conversing with various beautiful but tragic heroines throughout history. Amis's poem describes a fantasy of the poetic persona—ostensibly Amis himself—that he is surrounded by a bevy of worshipful young women, or "a squadron of draped nudes," as he writes in the opening stanza. The poet describes the women as "Angels" and "Aeronauts" who see him as "their god," their very supplier of life-giving "bright oxygen." However, he appreciates them more for their physical charms than for their intelligence or wit:

"Speech," Amis writes, "fails them," unlike the fair women in Tennyson's work. These nubile figments of the poet's considerable imagination are all eager immediately to bed him, and Amis uses a number of unsubtle and arresting metaphors, laced with naughty doubles entendres, to describe their ardor: On "the barn-door target of [their] desire" he is "a crack shot"; they implore him "to sign / [Their] body's autograph-book"; and "each princess" longs for him to use his "key" to gain "entrance to her tower." Because "this is 'all a dream,'" the speaker's lascivious escapades earn him not violence or derision, but, ironically, congratulatory "cheers" and "handshake[s]" from the women's "fathers" and "brothers," and even "from the chief of police," that arbiter of public morality in the real world of flesh and blood, he gets "a nod, a wink, a leer."

Close to the end of the poem, Amis changes gears, asserting that his dream of fair women is "not 'just a dream,'" but "it is also true." The implication is that he himself has been beset by real-life fair women, "weak, / Limelighted dolls" who wish to explore with Amis, the celebrated writer and bon vivant, "the halls of theoretical delight," to compartmentalize themselves (like the "Map-drunk explorers" and "dry-land sailors" they are) inside "that small room" of vacuous celebrity fantasy rather than to find true love in the real world of "ordinary distances." In effect Amis is satirizing the shallowness and gullibility of the pseudointellectual groupies who make such fools of themselves by worshiping blindly at the altar of literary or cultural celebrity, as well as poking self-deprecating fun at his own dubious status as the object of such crazed adulation. As one of the most popular writers of his generation, Amis may have loved all the attention that was lavished upon him, but at the same time he no doubt loathed the posturing dilettantism that inevitably accompanied it.

BIBLIOGRAPHY
Amis, Kingsley. *A Case of Samples: Poems 1946–1956*. London: Gollancz, 1957.
———. *Collected Poems 1944–1979*. London: Hutchinson, 1979.

Robert G. May

"DRUMMER HODGE" THOMAS HARDY (1901)

First published in *Literature* in 1899 under the title

"The Dead Drummer" and included in THOMAS HAR-
DY's *Poems of the Past and the Present* (1901), this poem
describes the burial of a young Wessex soldier killed
in South Africa during the Boer War (1899–1902).
Drummers were soldiers usually too young to fight,
and *hodge* is a derogatory nickname for a person from
the country, equivalent to a "yokel" or a "bumpkin."
In *Tess of the d'Urbervilles,* Angel Clare at first sees all
country farm folk as the same, "personified by the
pitiable dummy known as Hodge," but after staying
at Talbothays Dairy comes to recognize them as "varied fellow creatures—beings of many minds, beings
infinite in difference." Hardy ironically "names" the
drummer *Hodge* in order to deplore the brutal impersonality of a war that took his young countryman
from home to die anonymously in a distant land.

Each of the three stanzas of this poem is numbered
in capital roman numerals, honoring the drummer
with a dignified formality denied him at his death,
when he was thrown into his grave "just as found" and
"uncoffined." In each of the six-line stanzas, the first
two lines focus on Drummer Hodge and the final four
line on the South African setting, with two lines about
the land and two lines about the sky.

The first two stanzas express the pity of the drummer's death in an alien land. Rather than use the Wessex terms he favors in so many of his other poems,
Hardy here emphasizes the foreignness of the burial
site by using South African Dutch words of the Boers:
Drummer Hodge is buried, not on downs surrounded
by pastureland, but on "a kopje-crest / That breaks the
veldt around," and "fresh from his Wessex home," the
drummer "never knew," as he did the heath near his
village, "the meaning of the broad Karoo." The stars of
the Southern Hemisphere are "foreign" and "strange."

The final stanza, however, turns from pity to sublimity, consistently with the closing consolation of a
pastoral elegy that occurs when the elegist realizes that
death means the deceased will rise to a higher, eternal
life. This turn is signaled by the stanza's initial word
Yet and by the words *for ever* in the second line, which
counters the *never* in the second stanza: "Yet portion
of that unknown plain / Will Hodge for ever be." Hardy's consolation is not the traditional Christian ascension to heaven, though, but rather the belief that the
drummer through his death eventually will become

one with the alien South African landscape through
the organic process of nature and that the "strange-
eyed constellations" that "reign" over his grave will
become "his stars eternally."

BIBLIOGRAPHY
Bailey, J. O. *The Poetry of Thomas Hardy: A Handbook and
    Commentary.* Chapel Hill: University of North Carolina
    Press, 1970.
Millgate, Michael. *Thomas Hardy: A Biography.* New York:
    Random House, 1982.

                                            Robert R. Watson

A DRUNK MAN LOOKS AT THE THISTLE
HUGH MACDIARMID (1926)   *A Drunk Man Looks at
the Thistle* is considered by many critics to be HUGH
MACDIARMID's most successful poem. It is a long, rambling work that includes more than 2,800 lines of Scots
verse. Its narrator is a man who, while walking home
from the pub after an evening of drinking, falls into a
ditch by the side of the road and finds himself looking
at a thistle plant. The poem is a record of this narrator's
thoughts, musings, and free translations of the poetry
of others, including works by the Belgian poet George
Ramaekers and the Russian poet Alexander Bok. Mac-
Diarmid's structure is loose; the poem's metrical configuration shifts from section to section, often leading
editors to divide *A Drunk Man Looks at the Thistle* into
components, adding titles and section breaks. This
does a disservice to the poem, as its strength lies in its
far-ranging unity and the recurrence of themes woven
throughout the poem. The poem's seemingly disjointed
association of ideas, suggested by the inebriation of its
narrator, allows MacDiarmid to explore the ironies he
sees in Scottish life. As the critic Alexander Scott has
written, "There is no other Scottish poem which
resolves within itself so many of the contradictions of
experience, delighting equally in the lovely and the
grotesque, the profound and the profane, finding
beauty in the terrible and terror in the trumpery"
(Scott, xix).

The poem's major theme is MacDiarmid's analysis of
the current state of Scotland within the context of its
people, its politics, and eternity. Scotland, the "thistle"
of the title, is harshly criticized in sections of the poem.
Often the cult of the Scottish poet Robert Burns is
severely mocked, yet the narrator calls out to him:

"Rabbie, wad'st thou wert here—the warld hath need, / And Scotland mair sae, o' the likes o' thee! / The whisky that aince moved your lyre's become / A laxative for loquacity" (*Drunk,* ll. 61–64). Burns is the representative of the romantic Scotland that MacDiarmid firmly rejects as old-fashioned and useless; yet Burns's status as Scotland's poet and his use of the Scots language are characteristics with which MacDiarmid has an affinity. Tied into Burns's decline into a misunderstood, sentimental icon is the image of whiskey. Throughout the poem the narrator's drunken state, acquired through substandard liquor, represents the decline of Scotland. As the previous lines state, the poor whiskey just makes for "loquacity," rather than action.

The most complex relationship that the narrator in the poem returns to time and again is that of the thistle, representing the Scottish national spirit, or Scotland itself; his wife, Jean; and the moonlight that falls on the thistle plant as the narrator lies in the ditch. One of the first places these three elements join is in the stanzas from lines 253 to 276. In this section the narrator calls out to his wife, complaining that but for her, he would be "as happy as the munelicht, withoot care" (*Drunk,* l. 254). But the thought of her, and her anger at him for his drinking, transforms him into a thistle, which in turn feeds on the moonlight, yet the moonlight denies him its freedom at the same time. This narrow condemnation, likened to the strict Scottish Presbyterianism that MacDiarmid was brought up in, is what "kills a' else wi'in its reach" (*Drunk* l. 263). This paradox leads the narrator to muse: "For ilka thing a man can be or think or dae / Aye leaves a million mair unbeen, unthocht, undune, / Till his puir warped performance is, / To a' that micht ha' been, a thistle to the mune" (*Drunk,* ll. 269–272). This movement, from the immediate to the eternal, is representative of MacDiarmid's narrative strategy throughout the poem and creates a narrative commentary on Scotland's place within history and in the present.

MacDiarmid's voice in this poem is rough, strident, and self-mocking. Underneath that, though, runs an unmistakable national pride in Scotland. Even while castigating his mother country, in its own language, for all of its failings, MacDiarmid betrays an unquenchable love for the land whose symbol is the prickly, unlovely thistle plant.

BIBLIOGRAPHY
MacDiarmid, Hugh. *A Drunk Man Looks at the Thistle.* Edinburgh: W. Blackwood, 1926.
Scott, Alexander. "MacDiarmid: The Poet." In *The Hugh MacDiarmid Anthology: Poems in Scots and English,* xvii–xxiii. London: Routledge & Kegan Paul, 1972.

Rachel Anderson

DUFFY, CAROL ANN (1955–)

Considered as one of the most representative, widely read, important, and loved poets of her time, Duffy has produced eight main collections that span 20 years since the publication of *Standing Female Nude* in 1985. It received the Scottish Arts Council book award, and her other collections also received prizes such as the Somerset Maughan for *Selling Manhattan* (1987) and the Forward and Whitbread for her fourth collection *Mean Time* (1993). She was given an Order of the British Empire (OBE) in 1995. In addition to her outstanding reputation and output, she qualifies as a major poet on account of her range and influence on other poets. She restored poetry's function as public utterance and generated new kinds of democratic expression that maintain the imaginative and linguistic qualities of her art.

Insisting on the difference between poetry and journalism in her parodic "Poet for our Times" (1990), Duffy seizes and deflates cheap tabloid jargon: "Cheers. Things is, you've got to grab attention / with just one phrase as punters rush on by." Implicitly distancing the poet from the unscrupulous commercial editor, she opposes the market pressures upon poets merely to please the crowd. Her books are full of animated voices telling their stories with a colloquialism that cuts across the demands of the verse form and places everyday language itself under the microscope. This jostling of the literary with the unpoetic, largely by imitating contemporary speech rhythms and idioms, became a feature of the period.

Duffy's trademark is her ventriloquizing through monologues and dialogues that dramatize the complexities and power relations of human interaction, frequently in the present tense. In "The Dummy," a ventriloquist's stooge speaks back to its manipulator, personifying the socially marginalized who are silenced to keep them in their place. She exploits the dramatic monologue's power to voice experience directly to the reader and thus invite sympathy where it would not be expected. The phrase "Just teach me / the right words" is both a cry for help and a rebellious threat. Where the speaker transgresses social niceties or conventions, such as the unfaithful partner ("Adultery"), an unemployed youth who is up to no good ("Education for Leisure"), or, most shockingly, a murderer who has had his way with a young girl at a fair and chucked her in the canal ("Psychopath"), their confiding appeal for understanding is unsettling. The reader is deprived of reassuring moral censure and this late 20th-century moral void becomes an aspect of the poem's subject matter.

Born in Glasgow (to Irish parents) and educated in Staffordshire, Duffy is not duly concerned with Scottish identity. She graduated in philosophy from Liverpool University and then worked in London and Manchester. Consequently a cosmopolitan urban environment informs her attention to those who are psychologically or socially alienated. She explores and exploits poetry's expressive function to give voice to Britain's outsiders, particularly criminals, foreigners, and women.

A rare poet in her working-class origin, she is interested in the role of language in oppressing or emancipating an individual. The enjoyable "Head of English" was an early jibe at the conflict between "a real live poet" and a traditionalist English school curriculum: "We don't / want winds of change about the place." "Litany" dramatizes the young girl's negotiation between the sanitized vocabulary preserved by her mother's coterie of cellophane-wrapped women and the uncensored slang of a boy in the playground. Significantly she thrills with power at reciting his forbidden swear words in the housewives' face: "Language embarrassed them." Other poems that investigate the education system are "Mrs Tilscher's Class" and "The Good Teachers." These draw on the contrasts between the poet's convent schooling and writer residencies in East London schools. (It is something of a paradox that Duffy's poems became staple examination texts on the 14–18 curriculum in schools.) "Comprehensive," referring to the state system of schools for all, interrogates the ideal of racial harmonization in the face of irrepressible and monolithic nationalism. The parallel narratives of Jewish, African, Muslim, Indian, and working-class white children present the reader with insoluble yet shared states of alienation. In "Yes, Offi-

cer," Duffy enacts how easily the police can convict a man by overwhelming him with their statements: "Without my own language, I am a blind man / in the wrong house." As for "Translating the English, 1989," the collage of voices cleverly indicates the anachronisms and contradictions in so-called British culture.

Few poets tackle the greed and injustices associated with 1980s Thatcherism as head on as Duffy in her satirical pamphlet *William and the Ex–Prime Minister* (1992). Duffy's empathy for the unemployed here, *"But there's thousands jobless! Millions! / Thanks to that narsy ole witch,"* is replicated in "Education for Leisure," "Stealing," and "Like Earning a Living." Duffy's popular collection *The World's Wife* (1999) consists of female-centered monologues that supremely resurrect silenced or marginalized women down the years. The cast of wives who "speak back" is taken from history, myth, fairy tale, and popular culture and most palpably emphasizes the power of language to make, mar, or deny human dignity and identity.

Although she is associated with contemporary dramatic monologues and caustic social dialogues, Duffy's volumes are also littered with tender love lyrics that appropriate the traditional form to a candidly contemporary location. In *Selling Manhattan,* there is a series about separation and misunderstandings, "Homesick," "Correspondents," "Telegrams," and "Telephoning Home," but the book ends with "Miles Away," one of the most affirming expressions of love, even or especially at a distance. Duffy's most frequently anthologized sonnet, "Prayer," is a monument to multifaith epiphanies that occur outside orthodox institutions. The sonnet's final line, which borrows from the daily shipping forecast on the radio, is a conspicuous example of how nonliterary but shared references are set in dialogue with high language and forms. Just as praying is taken out of its religious rituals to the unexpected moments of the mundane, so poetry implicitly bursts through traditional literary edifices. "Away and See" (1993) is a more lyrical evocation of the opportunities and limitations of language to imitate experience. The opening lines give a taste of her characteristic combinations of regular and irregular meter, varying line lengths, assonance, and internal rhyme: "Away and see the things that words give a name to, the flight / of syllables, wingspan stretching a noun. Test words."

See also "ANNE HATHAWAY," "HAVISHAM," "MRS. LAZA-RUS," "WARMING HER PEARLS," "WE REMEMBER YOUR CHILDHOOD WELL."

BIBLIOGRAPHY

Duffy, Carol Ann. *Selected Poems.* London: Penguin, 1994.

Kinnahan, Linda. "'Now I Am Alien': Immigration and the Discourse of Nation in the Poetry of Carol Ann Duffy." In *Contemporary Women's Poetry: Reading/Writing/Practice,* edited by Mark, Alison and Deryn Rees-Jones. Basingstoke, Eng.: Macmillan, 2000.

Michelis, Angelica, and Antony Rowland. *The Poetry of Carol Ann Duffy: "Choosing Tough Words."* Manchester, Eng.: Manchester University Press, 2003.

Rees-Jones, Deryn. *Carol Ann Duffy: Writers and Their Work.* Plymouth, Eng.: Northcote House, 1999.

Jane Dowson

"DULCE ET DECORUM EST" WILFRED OWEN (1917) Probably WILFRED OWEN's most famous poem, "Dulce et Decorum Est" owes much to the influence of his fellow poet, SIEGFRIED SASSOON. Owen and Sassoon met while both were patients at Craiglockhart War Hospital in Edinburgh and were recovering from shell shock (Owen was sent to Craiglockhart by an army medical board in June 1917 and did not rejoin his regiment until the end of November). Although Owen was already writing poetry, it was through his discussions with Sassoon and Sassoon's friend, the poet ROBERT GRAVES, and Sassoon's editorial suggestions when shown Owen's work that Owen's poetic style matured into that exhibited in "Dulce et Decorum Est." The poem is nearer to direct speech than much of Owen's previous work and has a more journalistic, narrative style.

Owen was in the Manchester regiment, and it is thought that the poem, which tells of a gas attack on a group of soldiers marching away from the front line toward a "distant rest," is based on a similar incident that happened to his platoon. As the soldiers march, they hear the din of the battle behind them and are suddenly subject to a gas attack. All but one of the men, in "an ecstasy of fumbling," manage to secure their safety by fitting cumbersome gas masks, and Owen uses the middle of the poem to detail the horrors of watching the man die from behind "the misty panes" of the gas mask.

The poem shifts at this point from a present tense account of a war experience to a tone of horrified recollection, which in turn gives way to a furious didacticism. The surviving men have the unpleasant task of trudging behind the wagon carrying the dying man, and this sight is used to refute the jingoistic ignorance of some poets and commentators that Owen so despised. Owen wrote to his mother, in October 1917, "the famous Latin tag [from Horace] means of course *It is sweet and meet to die for one's country. Sweet! And decorous!*" and the weak *glory/mori* rhyme does not detract from the power of the poem's ending.

Early drafts of the poem were dedicated to Jessie Pope (or, in one draft, "To a certain Poetess"), a poet writing in popular newspapers whose verse spoke of war as "the red crashing game of the fight" and whose ignorance of, or refusal to write about, the realities of war angered Owen. Written in a direct and accessible style, "Dulce et Decorum Est" was intended to counteract the overly sentimental patriotic poetry of the early part of the war, such as that written by Pope or, with more skill, RUPERT BROOKE. Owen's early war poetry had been in a similar vein to Brooke's work, but, with battlefield experience and his meetings with Sassoon, his feelings changed and his poetic articulation became more refined.

Much of the poem's success rests with its imagery. The reader is forced to reenact the scene and comprehend the raw physicality of the incident, from the bloodied feet of the bootless men "coughing like hags" to "the white eyes writing" in the gassed soldier's face. The thrust of corporeal reality is unrelenting, as blood gargles from "froth-corrupted lungs" and "innocent tongues" are pictured with "vile, incurable sores." Owen provokes a state of horrified suspense in the reader and is therefore able to deliver his lesson in the last few lines with an increased impact.

A notable image in this poem is the terrifying face of the dying or paralyzed man, a clear link to the romantic poets' influence on Owen, such as Keat's depiction of Moneta. The fixed ghostly face is a recurring image in Owen's poetry, as is the concept of soldiers as cattle (see "ANTHEM FOR DOOMED YOUTH"), shown here by the used of the word *cud.* The most powerful imagery, however, is reserved for the movements of the "drowning" man. Destined to live in "all" the poet's dreams, his actions ("stumbling . . . flound'ring . . . choking") are a sharp counterpoint to the soldiers' previous motions ("bent double . . . marched asleep . . . limped . . . drunk with fatigue") and take place "under a green sea" (i.e., chlorine gas, the inhalation of which caused a similar death to that by drowning), emphasizing the dream-like, haunting quality of the poem. The man is described as "guttering" as the flickering of life disappears, and his "drowning" is reflected in the "smothering" dreams that the poet experiences. The juxtaposition of the natural and unnatural, specifically "an ecstasy of fumbling" and the idea of "drowning" on dry land, coupled with the otherworldly reality of the poem, confirms its power.

BIBILIOGRAPHY

Hibberd, Dominic. *Wilfred Owen.* London: Weidenfeld & Nicolson, 2002.

Stallworthy, Jon, ed. *The Complete Poems and Fragments.* Oxford: Oxford University Press, 1984.

———. *Wilfred Owen.* London: Oxford University Press, 1974.

Charlotte Kearns

DUNN, DOUGLAS (1942–)

Though born and brought up in Scotland, Douglas Dunn is often associated with the English city of Hull, where he worked as a librarian with PHILIP LARKIN. Both Larkin and the city itself heavily influenced his first book, *Terry Street* (1969). From the start Dunn has been a politically committed poet—though a left-wing one, differing from Larkin in this respect. In *Terry Street* he repeatedly examines the working-class people whose neighborhood he inhabits, with great sympathy but constantly at a distance because of his nationality and education. It is as if he is looking for a place and community he can live happily in: "I want to be touched by them, know their lives, / Dance in my own style, learn something new." This utopian yearning marks Dunn's interest in the pastoral. But this early work has an elegiac tone, constantly implying that utopia is unattainable and that politics is ineffectual: "You hardly notice you have grown too old to cry out for change."

While Larkin's technically accomplished conversational style continued to inform Dunn's work throughout his career, this strain of pessimism gradually receded, so that, in a reversal of the usual pattern, his youthful cynicism gives way to an impassioned and sometimes angry idealism in later books like *Barbarians* (1979) and *St Kilda's Parliament* (1981). Rather than writing about those he feels sympathy for but is also divided from, in *Barbarians* Dunn imagines *himself* as a "barbarian in a garden," enjoying the cultural pleasures from which his nation and class have historically been excluded. He relishes the distress of a "spinster with her sewing . . . [who] begs you leave her pretty world alone," underwriting his hostility by discussing the societies that lie behind "Empires": "We worked their mines and made their histories. / *You work, we rule,* they said. We worked; they ruled."

In *St Kilda's Parliament* this fascination with social history continues but is focused more closely on Scotland and Scottishness. Poems like "An Address on the Destitution of Scotland" and "Washing the Coins" express anger at the oppression of Scottish people by the English, but also by other Scots and religious and political ideologies.

Elegies (1985), written after the death of his wife, may be Dunn's best known book. Its clarity of diction and frank, moving treatment of its subject made it hugely popular among the poetry-reading public. The book's pared-down style makes it difficult to do it justice in quotation; for a sense of its tone, see the discussion, in this volume, of "THIRTEEN STEPS AND THE THIRTEENTH OF MARCH."

Dunn is a prolific writer, who published 11 collections of poetry between 1969 and 2000, as well as short stories, television and radio plays, reviews, critical articles, and translations. He has won numerous prizes. His polished style is such that the technical skill that goes into making it is sometimes easy to overlook—again like that of Larkin. But he goes beyond Larkin most significantly in his use of that style to examine social, political, and historical circumstance.

BIBLIOGRAPHY

Crawford, Robert, and David Kinlock. *Reading Douglas Dunn.* Edinburgh: Edinburgh University Press, 1993.

Dunn, Douglas. *New Selected Poems, 1964–2000.* London: Faber and Faber, 2003.

Tony Williams

E

"EARLY PURGES" Seamus Heaney (1966)
Appearing in Seamus Heaney's first book, *Death of a Naturalist,* this poem, along with "Digging" and "Blackberry-Picking," introduces an important theme to that book and much of Heaney's later work: the death of a childish romanticism and the birth of a more realistic view, toward Ireland, politics, nature, the poet's own life and background, and his own nature. The poem is written in a modified terza rima stanza, used by Dante and Shelley to such great effect in much grander poems.

The *early purges* of the title refers most literally to the story of the poem. A young boy of six watches as a neighboring farmer, Dan Taggert, drowns kittens in a bucket of water. "The scraggy wee shits," Dan calls them roughly, when to the six-year-old, the sound of their "soft paws scraping like mad" is heartbreaking. The kittens are being purged—pests rid from the farm—and the soft-heartedness of the boy is being purged, early, at the age of six, as he intuits that to act like a man, or at least a true farm boy, he must restrain emotion and imitate Dan. It is a difficult purging of emotion, and not immediately effective. For days he "sadly hung / Round the yard, watching the three sogged remains / turn mealy and crisp as old summer dung"—and here, without punctuation, the stanza breaks, and when we pick up the completing phrase of the sentence at the beginning of the next stanza, we find that the death of sensitivity has begun: "until I forgot them."

The process is not easily completed, as the remainder of the fifth stanza tells us, as "the fear came back" whenever the boy watched Dan kill rats, rabbits, or even old hens. Through an act of will, the boy forces himself to squelch his fears with a hearty aphorism: "Still, living displaces false sentiments." The false sentiments are a sensitivity to death, when death is a natural part of living—as with the hens, for example, who now are too old to lay eggs productively but are still useful as meat, and hence have their necks rung by Dan. To feel sentimental at their deaths is to require oneself to face one's complicity as a meat eater, in the ordinary course of life. But the "sentiment" that the boy most often expresses is not just a sensitivity to animal suffering, but rather "fear"—a much stronger word. What is the boy afraid of? The poem does not explore this explicitly, but the question is implicitly asked. At the age of six, he is closer to being a kitten himself than anything useful—boys of six are not productive members of a farm—is he, too, a pest "to be kept down"? What is his "use" that protects him from savage death, from the likes of Dan Taggert? The love of his parents, or of humans for their own kind, no doubt, but the element of love or human kindness is not visibly present in the poem, except in the six-year-old's feelings, which are nowhere reflected back by the adult world, nor the "natural" world of the farmyard. So the boy grows up: "now, when shrill pups are prodded to drown, / I just shrug 'Bloody pups.'" With a small profanity, "Bloody pups," the grown-up speaker has become closer to Dan Taggert's small vulgarity "wee shits," and the process of internalizing the attitudes of the farm and the adult world seems complete.

The poem goes on a little longer, however, in this same vein, with the grown-up speaker justifying a little more his changed attitude, and one wonders, with Queen Gertrude in *Hamlet,* whether the speaker does not protest too much: "'Prevention of cruelty' talk cuts ice in town / Where they consider death unnatural." A new dichotomy is introduced, the city versus the country. It is city folk, who do not deal with animals, who are always on about animal welfare; country folk, more in touch with nature, have a sounder view. This, at least, is the sense of the lines, and even more the tone, with its dismissive bracketing of quotes around "'prevention of cruelty' talk," as well as the hard-bitten phrase *cuts ice in town,* implying that in the *real world* of the farm, where people deal with hard things, there is no place for this easy sentimentality, which will not get the ice cut. Are all these city folk vegetarians, the poem almost sneers? It ends on the flattest, hardest line of all, closing the rhyme with *town:* "But on well-run farms pests have to be kept down."

And yet, we wonder, after finishing the poem, is this truly the attitude of the grown-up speaker? Or is he still bluffing his way along, just as when as a six-year-old he tried to toughen himself up? The description of the kittens' struggle for life, their suffering, is vivid, as are those of the haunted boy hanging around the dung pile of the farmyard and the returning fears. Has all this just disappeared? If so, why can the adult speaker recall it all so precisely, so vividly, with such feeling? Furthermore, when the poem is placed in the larger political context of the centuries-long British occupation of Ireland, during which English lords were literally landlords over Irish farmers, the last line takes on a particularly harsh meaning. The "pests" from the English point of view are the Irish, who must be "kept down" by the weight of political, economic, legal, and social discrimination, in order for Ireland to be a "well-run" colony. In this respect "Early Purges" is a subtly political poem and belongs in the company of "Digging," the powerfully personal, subtly political poem that leads off *Death of a Naturalist.*

BIBLIOGRAPHY
Allen, Michael, ed. *Seamus Heaney.* New Casebooks. New York: St. Martin's Press, 1997.
Heaney, Seamus. *Death of a Naturalist.* London: Faber and Faber, 1966.
McDonald, Peter. *Mistaken Identities: Poetry and Northern Ireland.* Oxford: Oxford University Press, 1997.

James Persoon

"EASTER MONDAY" ELEANOR FARJEON (1947)

A poem written by ELEANOR FARJEON as an elegy for the poet EDWARD THOMAS, who was killed in France on Easter Monday, 1917, it is the final poem in the sonnet collection *First and Second Love,* and the only one in which Farjeon forcibly rejects the form at which she excelled. The poem contains no end rhymes and has some lines with 12 syllables, while the stanza break forms an irregular pattern of nine and five lines. Unlike DYLAN THOMAS's "DO NOT GO GENTLE INTO THAT GOOD NIGHT," in which the grief-stricken speaker remains within the strict form of a villanelle, Farjeon retains just enough similarity to a sonnet to alert the reader that in spite of her calm language, she is unable to maintain the form's rigid requirements.

The first stanza of the poem is based on the final letter Thomas wrote to Farjeon, in which he considered the Monday *before* Easter to be his own "Easter Monday." His praise of the day, and his claim that "it was such a lovely morning" (both borrowed from his letter) are therefore their own premonitions, echoed by the speaker on the Easter Monday that brings his death.

It is possible to read Thomas as a Christ figure whose farewell in the first stanza will lead to a rebirth, promised by the seeds and apple bud of the second. At the time of writing the poem, Farjeon had no official religious beliefs, and her conversion to Catholicism did not occur until late in her life. She stated, though, that she had been moving toward her religious rebirth for years. Therefore although "Easter Monday" was not written by a religious poet, the subtexts of "the eve" point not only to the night before the battle that killed Thomas, but to the spiritual experience of the poem's speaker.

BIBLIOGRAPHY
Blakelock, Denys. *Eleanor: Portrait of a Farjeon.* London: Victor Gollancz, 1966.

Farjeon, Eleanor. *Edward Thomas: The Last Four Years.* London: Oxford University Press, 1958.

———. *First and Second Love.* London: Michael Joseph, 1947.

Motion, Andrew, ed. *First World War Poems.* London: Faber and Faber, 2003.

Persoon, James. *Modern British Poetry, 1900–1939.* New York: Twayne, 1999.

Tracy Rosenberg

"EASTER 1916" WILLIAM BUTLER YEATS

(1916/1920) In the six days following Easter Sunday of 1916, Irish Republican Brotherhood insurgents held sites more symbolic than strategic throughout Dublin; they surrendered only after the British military had leveled many of the city's key buildings and killed nearly 500 Irish, mostly civilians. Over the next several weeks, 16 of the Irish leaders were executed. In a letter to Lady Gregory, W. B. YEATS wrote that the event was "brave but foolish," a sentiment shared by many Irish initially, but that "British incompetence" by way of the executions had made martyrs of its leaders. Similarly, shifting attitudes resonate in this poem but never resolve. Yeats evades commentary on the historical significance of the event, his queries in the final stanza qualifying the few declamatory remarks made earlier, and meditates instead on the tension between the personal and the public rather than the political and symbolic.

Written in the summer months following the executions, "Easter 1916" nonetheless was not published until 1920 in the *New Statesman* and a year later collected in *Michael Robartes and the Dancer*—and then only in response to British Black and Tan atrocities in Cos, Galway, and Cork (Yeats showed the poem prior to publication only with close friends and even refused to read it on a tour of the United States). Categories of "occasional poem" and "elegy" thus largely miscast "Easter 1916." Aside from its title, the poem ignores the event itself and remains ambivalent about its aftermath; the individuals mentioned are those with whom Yeats was familiar, yet they are torn from the fabric of the Rising and granted personal consideration. The poem evinces a struggle within Yeats between his personal convictions and his sense of public duty, as verified in the memorable but conflicting "terrible beauty" that is the poem's signature. If anything, "Easter 1916" serves as a retraction of "September 1913," where Yeats declares that "Romantic Ireland's dead and gone"; as have the martyrs, Yeats and Ireland itself have been "changed utterly," though not by choice.

That famous refrain—"All changed, changed utterly: / A terrible beauty is born"—acts as a resolute context against which Yeats posits his own conflicting thoughts. Interestingly the seeming oxymoron "terrible beauty" is not original to Yeats. It may be found in Standish O'Grady's *Story of Ireland* (1894), a favorite book of the younger Yeats, and similar phrasings appear in two plays by a poet and executed leader mentioned in the poem, Pádraic Pearse ("a terrible, beautiful voice that comes from the hearts of battles" in *The King*, and from *The Story of Success*, death that makes "possible the terrible beautiful thing we call physical life"). While *terrible* generally connotes "awful" or "horrible," it also acts as a positive intensifier among English-speaking Irish, suggesting a remarkable or stunning beauty. This beauty, too, is born, not reborn; despite the significance of the Easter weekend (planned by the leaders because of Jesus's blood sacrifice), Yeats indicates that this is a new Ireland emerging, not an old Ireland revived. The variance in the refrain also is noteworthy: "All" of a past Ireland is changed in the opening stanza, lives of the individuals mentioned have been "transformed" in the second stanza, and the leaders of the Rising are denied agency for the cultural shift through the passive "are changed" in the final stanza. The refrain reifies that this is not a poem of praise or tribute, but rather one of a poet's contested feelings about Irish historicomythology.

The *I* to open the poem—the pronoun recurring three times in the stanza—asserts its personal nature. While Yeats is responding to a historical event, it is the friends and acquaintances who were part of that event who matter most. These relationships, considered more intimately in the second stanza, are juxtaposed against *them* in the opening stanza: nameless people whose "polite meaningless words" betray an autonomic artifice to the Dublin preceding Easter 1916. Their everyday "motley" attire amid the "grey / Eighteenth-century houses" illustrates the dated inconsequence of life that is soon to be "changed utterly" (interestingly the familiarity and intimacy, which extend to the remembrances of four individuals in the second stanza, imply that Yeats is in the midst of the event, when he actually was in London at the time and completely unaware of the impending Rising). What confirms the personal nature of the poem are those chosen individuals: Of the four, only two—Pádraic Pearse and Thomas MacDonagh—were among the seven who signed the Proclamation of the Republic. Furthermore the attention given them reverses their importance to the Rising: "This other man" (John MacBride) receives nine lines, "that woman" (Con Markievicz) seven, "his helper" (MacDonagh) five, and "this man" (Pearse) two. James Connolly, the leader of the Irish Citizen Army, receives but a mention in the final stanza.

Markievicz, the former Constance Gore-Booth, had been a childhood friend, "young and beautiful," but revolutionary politics had made her "shrill." Pearse ran a bilingual school, St. Enda's, and was steeped in myth ("our winged horse" is an allusion to Pegasus); MacDonagh, a university teacher, had dedicated a book of poems to Yeats, who thought MacDonagh "was coming into his force." MacBride was the abusive husband of Maud Gonne, the star of Yeats's controversial nationalist play *Cathleen Ní Houlihán* (1902), whom Yeats proposed to (unsuccessfully) five times during his life; MacBride had also sexually assaulted his stepdaughter and was an alcoholic, yet he too was "transformed" by the events of the Rising, which becomes the "stone" of the third stanza. Commentators offer numerous allegoric interpretations for the stone: a symbol of the martyrs' rigidity and death, or the firmness of purpose with which they pursued independence; the philosopher's stone of Yeats's alchemical interests, or perhaps the talismanic Stone of Destiny of Tuatha de Danaan mythology. This stone now resides "in the midst of all," there forever to "trouble the living stream" of Irish life.

The philosophical third stanza disintegrates into a series of rhetorical questions in the final stanza. The mother who "names her child" may be a reference to Mother Ireland (again, from *Cathleen Ní Houlihán*). More likely it alludes to Pearse's poem "The Mother," where two sons, sent out in "bloody protest for a glorious thing," are remembered by their mother, who "will speak their names," which "were once familiar / around my dead hearth"; future "generations shall remember them / And call them blessed." Yeats, who to this point has postponed the naming of the dead, fulfills bardic duties in a balladlike final six lines; at this point, however, the naming has none of the elegiac confidence of a poem charged with nationalism. Whether England is to "keep faith" by passing a Home Rule bill or not, all has been "changed, changed utterly": the trivial "motley" to Irish "green," the faceless individuals who "dreamed and are dead" to the status of mythical heroes, and a poet who believed romantic Ireland to be "dead and gone" to one awakened by "a terrible beauty."

The four stanzas of "Easter 1916" are in trimeter with a regular *ababcdcd* rhyme scheme, though many are near-rhymes (*gibe* and *club*). There are between six and nine syllables per line; three primary stresses per line emphasize key words. Other of Yeats's poems that may be considered with "Easter 1916" include "The Rose Tree," "Sixteen Dead Men," "Three Songs to One Burden," "The O'Rahilly," and "The Statues."

BIBLIOGRAPHY
Eagleton, Terry. "History and Myth in Yeats's 'Easter 1916.'" *Essays in Criticism: A Quarterly Journal of Literary Criticism* 21 (1971): 248–260.

Foster, John Wilson. "Yeats and the Easter Rising." *Canadian Journal of Irish Studies* 11, no. 1 (1985): 21–34.

Foster, R. F. *W. B. Yeats: A Life.* Vol. 1, *The Apprentice Mage, 1865–1914.* New York: Oxford University Press, 1997.

———. *W. B. Yeats: A Life.* Vol. 2, *The Arch-Poet, 1915–1939.* Oxford: Oxford University Press, 2003.

Kiberd, Declan. *Inventing Ireland: The Literature of the Modern Nation.* Cambridge, Mass.: Harvard University Press, 1995.

Kurt Bullock

"EAVESDROPPER" MEDBH MCGUCKIAN (1982)

This poem exemplifies MEDBH MCGUCKIAN's characteristic mode of creating multiple levels of meaning by interweaving images of female and national identity. This oblique method enables her to deal with the political tension of her native Northern Ireland from a female perspective, thus complementing and at times subverting the traditionally male Irish canon and discourse. Since the poem focuses on the female poet's emerging identity in the specific Northern Irish context, it might well be read as McGuckian's poetic response to a poem like SEAMUS HEANEY's "DIGGING," which explores a similar theme from a male perspective. Initially published as "That Year," the short poem consisting of four unrhymed four-line stanzas was the opening poem of McGuckian's first book-length collection, *The Flower Master* (Oxford University Press, 1982). A slightly modified version was republished under the title "Eavesdropper" in *The Flower Master and Other Poems* (Gallery, 1993). Although it is arguably one of McGuckian's more readily accessible poems, its intricate use of rhetorical devices and images is exemplary of the poet's dense, oblique, and multilayered style.

In the first stanza the speaker addresses her younger self, a pubescent girl faced with the confusing changes of her body, starting to "play about," that is, to experiment with jewelry, the color of her hair, her first bra. However, references to "harnessing rhythm" and "shackling the breast" disrupt the experimental playfulness, suggesting that the onset of puberty terminates the child's freedom. In stanza two the speaker switches to the first person singular: "I remembered as a child the red kite / Lost forever over our heads." The kite symbolizes lost childhood, as does the "white ball / A pin-prick on the tide," an image indicating heteronomy and pain and thus echoing the vocabulary of violence introduced in stanza one. Remembering how she studied "the leaf-patterned linoleum, the elaborate / Stitches on [her] pleated bodice," the speaker recalls that "it was like a bee's sting or a bullet / Left in [her], this mark, this sticking pins in dolls." Menstruating for the first time, the girl feels injured, like a doll stuck with pins. The colors red and white serve as a recurring motif in the short poem, as suggested by the "bleach" and "henna" of the first stanza, the "red kite" and the "white ball" in the second, and the "red and white / Particles of time" in the third and fourth. White symbolizes purity and innocence, whereas red stands for blood, menstruation, and loss. While the girl's awakening sexuality initially makes her dream of romantic "curtainings and cushionings," she soon wakes up to the sobering realities of a woman's life, as implied by the poem's final line: "The grass is an eavesdropper's bed." Tellingly, the "linoleum" of stanza two evokes domestic chores, "elaborate stitches" and "sticking pins in dolls" suggest needlework, "feeding [a] child" hints at motherhood—the three traditional tasks a woman is supposed to "master" in her life. To a girl then the onset of puberty means becoming aware of restrictions and a sense of otherness.

It is noteworthy that McGuckian changed the poem's title from "That Year" to "Eavesdropper." A child's eavesdropping on a grown-up conversation and thus gaining forbidden knowledge implies the idea of a premature initiation into adulthood. Moreover in the literal sense of the term, an eavesdropper would be someone who "drops (falls) off the eaves," which hints at disillusionment. Finally, the term puns on the name *Eve*, while an alternative term for "to drop" would be "to fall." The term *eavesdropper,* then, suggests a fall from grace, the girl's awakening sexuality being represented as a child's paradise lost. A Catholic girl for the first time "eavesdropping" on her body's involuntary changes could easily feel tainted and associate her sexuality with Eve, Christianity's sinful first mother. The poem thus stages an identity crisis initiated by the girl's first awareness of her sexuality.

On careful reading, the poem simultaneously abounds with political allusions. While red and white are the two colors of the Union Jack, the color green, evoked by the "leaf-patterned linoleum" and the "grass," is traditionally associated with Ireland. The combination of the colors green, red, and white thus indicates the Ulster Catholic girl's blurred sense of national identity. Moreover the numerous references to violence, imprisonment, and blood reflect the hostile environment of the Northern Irish Troubles, which the speaker internalizes: "a bullet / Left in me." While the speaker's enmeshed sense of her own sexual and national identity results in a confusing pattern of images, this pattern points to the third aspect of her emerging identity: the artist. Most images employed in the poem reflect the domestic sphere (the linoleum floor) or refer to women's traditional occupations such as needlework (elaborate stitches) and nursing (the wet nurse). In this early poem McGuckian hints at what will become her major metaphors of poetic creation: women's traditional craft and motherhood. Moreover to harness "rhythm," to study a "pattern," and "elaborate" stitches all suggest artistic creation. The poem itself, an intricate pattern of rhetorical devices and images, particularly in its abundance of alliteration and internal rhyme, can be read as the poetic outcome of a demanding existential situation. Trying to come to terms with one's sexual and national identity triggers the creative process out of which the poem emerges.

BIBLIOGRAPHY

McGuckian, Medbh. "Drawing Ballerinas": How Being Irish Has Influenced Me as a Writer." In *Wee Girls: Irish Women's Writing*, edited by Liz Murphy, 185–203. North Melbourne, Australia: Spinifex Press, 1996.
———. *The Flower Master and Other Poems*. Loughcrew, Ire.: Gallery, 1993.
Schrage-Früh, Michaela. *Emerging Identities: Myth, Nation and Gender in the Poetry of Eavan Boland, Nuala Ní Dhomhnaill and Medbh McGuckian*. Trier, Germany: WVT, 2004.

Michaela Schrage-Früh

"AN ECLOGUE FOR CHRISTMAS" LOUIS MACNEICE (1933) LOUIS MACNEICE wrote "An Eclogue for Christmas" over the Christmas holiday in 1933. He notes in his autobiography that he "sat down deliberately to write a long poem . . . with a kind of cold-blooded passion" (MacNeice 146), and the result was this lengthy dialogue in rhymed couplets, first published in Geoffrey Grigson's *New Verse* in 1934, and again as part of a series of four eclogues in his 1935 volume, *Poems*. There are two speakers in the poem: A is an urban sophisticate looking to the country for the answers he cannot find in his cosmopolitan environment, while B is a farmer or shepherd bemoaning the increasing philistinism of rural life and the decline of the country gentry. Their conversation takes place on Christmas, of which the two speakers remind one another at the end of the poem after reciting a litany of complaints about modern industrial society.

The opening lines suggest that the Christmas season is perhaps the height of, or the reason for, the problems they describe ("A. I meet you in an evil time. / B. The evil bells / Put out of our heads, I think, the thought of everything else"). Christmas is the point around which "the jaded calendar revolves"; A retreats from "the excess sugar of a diabetic culture" in the belief that B, a rustic individual of "morose routine," is free from the constant pursuit of novelty that is "rotting the nerve of life and literature." B offers no consolation to A; rather he sees the same decay in the country that A sees in the city and recommends that A look elsewhere for answers ("Analogue of me, you are wrong to turn to me / . . . / One place is as bad as another. Go back where your instincts call"). The country and the city are afflicted by the same consumerist illness.

The decline of the West as described in MacNeice's eclogue is a common trope in the left-wing poetry of the 1930s; W. H. AUDEN, STEPHEN SPENDER, and others of MacNeice's circle wrote many similar poems. Terence Brown observes that "MacNeice is unique in this group in conveying a sense of total doom" (Brown 51). Despite his oft-expressed left-wing sympathies, MacNeice was not a true believer in the way that many of his friends and associates were; the workers' revolution is as terrifying to MacNeice as the philistinism of the urban bourgeoisie, "planked and paneled with jazz," or the conservatism of the rural aristocracy, who "cannot change" and "will die in their shoes." "The jutlipped farmer gazing over the humpbacked wall" and "the commercial traveler joking in the urinal" are one and the same. Both are "tin toys of the hawker," "not knowing that they are wound up," unwitting products of the cultures they criticize.

Indeed "An Eclogue for Christmas" is, as Robyn Marsack contends, "in the ideal/allegorical tradition, where some degree of degeneracy is presumed" (Marsack 26). Neither of the speakers argues in concrete terms, and the tone of their conversation is impressionistic, as neither holds on to a particular idea or image for more than a few lines. A and B are themselves degenerate in that they are separate parts of a divided self; Michael O'Neill and Gareth Reeves argue that "this picture of modern life as divided and fragmented . . . hints at an ideal of the complete man, where flesh and spirit, body and soul, intellect and experience, are united" (O'Neill and Reeves 65). The problem with this argument is that at the end of the poem, nothing is resolved or brought together; A and B refuse to give in to a pessimistic idealism ("the old idealist lie") and instead decide to enjoy the pleasures that their respective ways of life still afford them ("B. I will walk about the farm-yard which is replete / As with the smell of dung so with memories"), as each "cannot do otherwise." While B attempts to will the pleasant impressions of their separate lives into permanence ("Let all these so ephemeral things / Be somehow permanent like the swallow's tangent wings"), it cannot be so. There are no definitive answers for either speaker's dilemma as the poem returns to its beginning, the fact of the Christmas holiday. B bids farewell to A with the lines "Goodbye to you, this day remember is Christmas, this morn / They say, interpret it your own way, Christ is born." If A and B are two parts of an ideal man, then, there should be a reunification, but what we get is an injunction from one to the other to "interpret it your own way." The fact of individuality is all that remains; Christmas cannot mean the same thing to two different people, and the urban and rural spheres cannot join in any meaningful way.

BIBLIOGRAPHY

Brown, Terence. *Louis MacNeice: Skeptical Vision.* Dublin: Gill & Macmillan, 1975.

MacNeice, Louis. *Collected Poems.* New York: Oxford University Press, 1967.

————. *The Strings Are False.* London: Faber and Faber, 1965.

Marsack, Robyn. *The Cave of Making: The Poetry of Louis MacNeice.* Oxford: Clarendon Press, 1982.

McKinnon, William T. *Apollo's Blended Dream: A Study of the Poetry of Louis MacNeice.* New York: Oxford University Press, 1971.

O'Neill, Michael, and Gareth Reeves. *Auden, MacNeice, Spender: The Thirties Poets.* New York: St. Martin's Press, 1992.

Michael Moir

EDWARDIAN PERIOD   The Edwardian period comprises the years of the reign of King Edward VII, the eldest son of Queen Victoria, who succeeded to the throne upon her death in 1901 and ruled until his own death in 1910. The reign of Edward passed quickly enough that it had little time to denote more than a style of opulence, reflecting the love of the king for lavish parties and dressing up in uniforms. Queen Victoria had always intended for her son, when king, to become Albert I, memorializing the austere and earnest virtues of her German husband, but on her death Bertie instead assumed the name of Edward VII. He created around himself exactly the sort of life his father and mother had always disapproved of, a world of courtiers and card tables, horse races and shooting parties. The poet and aristocrat OSBERT SITWELL described the time, in which he had been a participant, as a profusion of exotic fruits: "Never had Europe seen such mounds of peaches, figs, nectarines and strawberries at all seasons, brought from their steamy tents of glass. . . . And to the rich, the show was free." *Edwardian* came to imply an expensive, excessive, exquisite surface, maintained by and for the rich. The decade seemed to lack seriousness, as if it were one long country house party. From the hindsight of the Great War (1914–18) and its destruction, the period before the war looked unforgivably naive. Its innocent virtues seemed to arise from a complacency and blindness toward what was about to happen. Edwardians (and Georgians too, those poets who wrote during the reign George V, 1910–26) were likewise increasingly dismissed as somehow responsible for a lack of foresight. Their reputations have still hardly recovered.

From the vantage point of 1957, John Osborne in *Look Back in Anger* referred to the period with disdain, though one can also detect the powerful image that Edwardian England was to project deep into the century and deep into British consciousness: "The old Edwardian brigade do make their brief little world look pretty tempting. All home-made cakes and croquet, bright ideas, bright uniforms. Always the same picture: high summer, the long days in the sun, slim volumes of verse, crisp linen, the smell of starch. What a romantic picture. Phoney too, of course. It must have rained sometimes." The poet ROY CAMPBELL satirized the period as having a weekend-picnic view of the world that issued in poems in "Ye Olde Teashoppe Style." Reading the criticism that the modernists, led by EZRA POUND and T. S. ELIOT, aimed at the Edwardians, one finds colorful and reductive epithets: the poetry of rainbows and wood smoke, cottages and ducks, happy brook and cuckoo's song. And certainly there was a willful innocence and nostalgia in the first decade of the 20th century that even its best social historian indulged. In *The Condition of England* (1909) Charles Masterman (at the time also a sitting Liberal member of Parliament and during the war the nation's first propaganda minister) lamented the loss of a rural world of "little red-roofed towns and hamlets, the labourer in the fields at noontide or evening, the English service in the old English village church," a world irrevocably passing for the majority of Britons, four-fifths of whom by then lived in cities. Masterman was aware both of the passing of this yeoman's world and of problematic new conditions underlying the pleasant aristocratic surface.

The poet laureate Alfred Austin wrote the official verse for the newly urban and suburban nation, verse that took no account of the new realities, though it betrayed some anxiety that the Victorian achievement could be maintained by the Edwardians. Austin's verse was backward-looking, to his great predecessors in office, William Wordsworth and Alfred, Lord Tennyson. While he was as aware as his contemporaries that there was a considerable falling off in his selection as the successor to Tennyson, he dutifully strove to preserve the accomplishments of the past, as in these lines from "Why England is Conservative," a poem in which he describes England as a "Mother" of "hamlets meek, and many a proud desmesne, / Blue spires of cottage smoke 'mong woodlands green." What Austin fears is political change, which may bring about the collapse of the social order and perhaps even the natural order: "And shall we barter these for gaping Throne, / Dismantled towers, mean plots without a tree?" What is most striking in the poem is how much its description of the English landscape is a denial of reality. England had already lost most of its "woodlands green" and, for four-fifths of the nation, its "hamlets meek" and "cottage smoke," which had been replaced by urban ghettos, at least throughout the industrial Midlands, where Englishmen had already been herded into "mean plots without a tree." Near the end of the century another conservative poet, PHILIP LARKIN, would express his fears about this loss of the rural pastoral in a poem called "Going, Going."

In Samuel Hynes's phrase, the "essential Edwardian mood is somber—a feeling of nostalgia for what has gone, and of apprehension for what is to come." This Hynes traces to two large and unanswered questions: "how to live in a scientific universe, and how to live with industrialism." Though most Edwardian poets, except THOMAS HARDY, did not directly address the issue of how science undermined one's confident assumption of a central place in the universe or the growing problem of the transformed economic and social basis of people's lives, they did not revert simply to nostalgia. They were extremely conscious of social issues, perhaps in reaction to the "art-for-art's-sake" aesthetic of the 1890s (itself a reaction to a Victorian sensibility that preferred "art for morality's sake"). Women's rights, the unfairness of social Darwinism, the poor condition of the cities and of workers, Irish nationalism, international belligerances, all found their expression, especially in the novel and drama, but also in poetry, especially in the poetry of RUDYARD KIPLING, and to a lesser extent in the work of other important Edwardian poets such as JOHN MASEFIELD, WALTER DE LA MARE, and ROBERT BRIDGES.

BIBLIOGRAPHY

Hynes, Samuel. *Edwardian Occasions.* New York: Oxford University Press, 1972.

———. *A War Imagined: The First World War and English Culture.* New York: Atheneum, 1991.

Millard, Kenneth. *Edwardian Poetry.* Oxford: Clarendon Press, 1991.

Sitwell, Osbert. *Great Morning.* London: Macmillan, 1948.

James Persoon

"EIGHT O'CLOCK" A(LFRED) E(DWARD) HOUSMAN (1922) A(LFRED) E(DWARD) HOUSMAN, well known for incisive wit and scholarly precision, uses several poetic devices to his advantage in this short poem in which the weight of time is felt by a person awaiting the impending doom of execution. The clock is personified, as it is able to "sprinkle the quarters on the morning town," and the clock even "tossed [the quarter-hours] down" to the people moving about below. For the speaker who "cursed his luck," however, the clock "collected . . . / Its strength and struck." Of course the clock is also used as a symbol for the concept of time. The hands of time seem to work in conjunction with the hands of the executioner—almost striking the man who is waiting on the gallows. The hands of time could also be seen as tied, since the clock was bound to announce measurements already established. Now metonymy may come into play. Does the clock stand in for the executioner or some "establishment" that kills? So much depends upon perspective here. Those who have no reason to worry about the passage of time may see the clock as playful and may enjoy hearing the chimes that are "sprinkled" about and "tossed . . . down," but those who have worries or fears may see the passage of time as painful, and the clock's announcements would thus "strike" such people differently.

Interestingly some personal information may give readers more insight into this poem. Once when young Housman was boarding at Bromsgrove School to avoid an outbreak of scarlet fever at his family residence, Fockbury House (also known as the Clock House), he stood in the churchyard for a solid hour and looked toward his home, which could be clearly seen from there. He may have called upon that memory as he wrote this poem, because time would not have tossed its hours down lightly on one who longed to be home. He had often looked upon the church spire from the windows of his home. That day in the churchyard he was bound to wonder whether or not anyone chanced to be standing there in the home windows similarly looking out toward him.

BIBLIOGRAPHY

Housman, A. E. *The Collected Poems of A. E. Housman.* New York: Holt, 1965.

Page, Norman. *A. E. Housman: A Critical Biography.* New York: Schocken Books, 1983.

Geraldine Cannon Becker

ELIOT, T. S. (THOMAS STERNS ELIOT) (1888–1965)

Thomas Sterns (T. S.) Eliot was born in St. Louis, Missouri, to a well-known Unitarian family (his grandfather founded Eliot Seminary, which eventually became Washington University in St. Louis). His early years were relatively uneventful. He attended preparatory school from 1898 to 1905, and his intelligence manifested itself in his precocious study of Latin, Greek, French, and German during these formative years. Through his parent's Unitarian connections, he gained admittance to the prestigious Milton Academy in Boston, Massachusetts, before going to Harvard, where he earned his bachelor's degree in 1909 and published a few poems in the *Harvard Advocate*. Afterwards he spent time traveling in Europe that included studies at the Sorbonne in Paris as well as Merton College, Oxford. He continued to explore languages by learning Sanskrit and Pali in order to be able to read Hindu and Buddhist scriptures in the original languages. Eliot eventually composed a dissertation on the English philosopher F. H. Bradley but failed to appear to defend his thesis in person; consequently Harvard denied him a doctorate. Nonetheless Eliot's studies allowed him to meet and interact with philosophers such as George Santayana, William James, Henri Bergson, and Bertrand Russell, and their works and ideas underpinned many of his poetic endeavors.

Eliot's personal life grew much more complex in 1915 when he married Vivien Haigh-Wood, an Oxford governess, who proved to have severe physical and psychological problems, which, in turn, exacerbated Eliot's own rather delicate emotional nature. Yet his literary career began to emerge with the 1916 publication of "THE LOVE SONG OF J. ALFRED PRUFROCK" through EZRA POUND's influence in Harriet Monroe's *Poetry Magazine*. Eliot included that poem with a few others and produced his first book, *Prufrock and Other Observations*, in 1917. By the early 1920s Pound facilitated Eliot's interaction with a wide-ranging collection of writers including W. B. YEATS, the painter and novelist WYNDHAM LEWIS, and the Italian futurist Tamaso Marinetti. Despite the literary achievement, Eliot's marriage continued to become more strained as Vivien's mental and physical health deteriorated, and an emotionally stressful visit by his mother and sister after his father's death provoked a nervous collapse. He spent three months recovering, partially at a sanitarium in Lausanne, Switzerland, and during this time he began to produce a long poem examining the spiritual malaise of post–World War I Europe that eventually became a cornerstone of the modernist movement: *THE WASTE LAND* (published 1922).

The original version of *The Waste Land* was almost twice as long, but his friend, Ezra Pound, pared material, tightening the poem's structure and making it much more enigmatic. Eliot dedicated the poem to Pound and dubbed him "il miglior fabbro"—the better craftsman. The poem, divided into five parts, found inspiration in Jessie L Weston's investigation of Grail myth in *From Ritual to Romance* (1920) along with anthropologist Sir James Frazer's analysis of vegetation myths in *The Golden Bough* (13 vols., 1890–1915). Eliot incorporated his own interests in Eastern philosophy to create a poem that investigates Western Europe's decline into spiritual aridity and the need for regeneration. Utilizing the archetypal quest motif, the poem evokes a blend of Christian, pagan, and Eastern philosophy paralleling the Grail knight's journey to heal the wounded Fisher King—a central figure in the Grail legend—whose condition produces drought and infertility in his lands. Eliot further complicated the poem with abundant erudite footnotes that often serve to obscure further the work's central symbolism rather than clarifying its content. Valerie Fletcher Eliot published a facsimile of the original poem, which includes Pound's suggested alterations, in 1971, and this text has greatly assisted those seeking to trace the development of the poem from inception to publication.

The Waste Land established Eliot as one of the leading poets of his generation, but his financial and emotional situation remained desperate. Vivien nearly died in 1923, and the strain very nearly caused Eliot to suffer another breakdown, but he managed to gain employment as an editor with the prestigious publishing firm Faber and Faber, which he would retain for the remainder of his working life. Occupational stability was followed by his quest for spiritual fulfillment. Disenchanted with his Unitarianism, Eliot began to attend Anglican services, and new verse appearing in *Poems 1909–1925* (published 1925) signaled a shift in Eliot's attitudes. This period culminated in his joining the Anglican Church and taking British citizenship in 1927. The following year (1928), he shocked many AVANT-GARDE friends with his politically conservative collection of essays *For Lancelot Andrewes*, declaring in the preface that he was a "classicist in literature, royalist in politics, and Anglo-catholic in religion." He spent the next couple of years studying the works of Dante Alighieri and William Shakespeare and writing a number of short poems including "JOURNEY OF THE MAGI"

(1927), "A Song for Simeon" (1928), "Animula" (1929), "Marina" (1930), "Triumphal March" (1931), and "Ash-Wednesday" (1930)—the latter poem seen as Eliot's Anglican-influenced response to the spiritual emptiness of *The Waste Land*.

After 1925 Eliot's marriage irrevocably deteriorated, and in 1933 he separated from Vivien, though he refused to divorce her because of his conservative Anglican beliefs. Vivien's mental health declined, and she embarrassed him a number of times by attempting dramatic reconciliations when Eliot made public appearances. She eventually was confined to a mental hospital, which Eliot did not visit, where she died in 1947.

During the 1930s and 1940s Eliot continued producing literary essays, published his ambitious poem collection *Four Quartets* (1943), and turned his hand to verse drama. The most famous of these are *Murder in the Cathedral* (1935), *The Family Reunion* (1939), and *The Cocktail Party* (1949). He also produced a book of whimsical verse for children, *Old Possum's Book of Practical Cats* (1939), later adapted by the composer Andrew Lloyd Webber into the phenomenally successful Broadway musical *Cats* (ran 1982–2000).

Eliot's success and fame gave him some measure of consolation after his earlier struggles, and his reputation as a literary critic reached its apex during the 1930s and 1940s. In 1948 the Nobel Committee awarded him that year's Nobel Prize in literature, citing him "for his outstanding, pioneer contribution to present-day poetry." Despite the award, from the late 1940s through the 1960s, Eliot wrote no more major verse; however he continued to produce literary essays and verse drama, including *The Confidential Clerk* (1953) and *The Elder Statesman* (1958). In 1957 he married his longtime secretary, Valerie Fletcher, 38 years his junior, but by all accounts enjoyed more happiness in his last seven years than at nearly any time before.

Along with his creative endeavors, Eliot gained fame as a literary critic, and he is almost single-handedly responsible for reviving interest in the previously neglected British poets of the early 17th century through his essay "The Metaphysical Poets" (1921). In the essay he elevated the works of such figures as John Donne and Andrew Marvell to a high level and denigrated the romanticism of the latter 18th and early 19th centuries. He argued that the complexity and passion exhibited in the works of Donne and his contemporaries far outshone the self-centered interests of the romantics. Though it was long regarded as a masterful work of criticism, many contemporary critics have distanced themselves from the religious and political conservatism that influenced Eliot's aesthetic judgments. Eliot also made a foray into social criticism with his 1948 essay "Notes towards a Definition of Culture." This pro-Christian, proconservatism essay defined culture as an organic entity centered on the family and further reflected Eliot's conservatism, which grew more marked after his conversion to Anglicanism.

In his early years, especially during his first marriage, Eliot was sensitive, physically frail, and, as noted, prone to psychological episodes that occasionally incapacitated him in his professional and creative pursuits. However, upon his separation from Vivien, and notably after his second marriage, to Valerie, he became something of a prankster—placing whoopee cushions in chairs and providing exploding cigars to guests. Indeed he felt honored when he discovered that American comedian Groucho Marx admired his poetry and the two kept up a correspondence for a number of years.

Despite his emotional tranquility in his last few years, Eliot's health steadily deteriorated and he died of emphysema in London January 4, 1965. His body was cremated, and his ashes interred in church of St. Michael's in East Coker with an epitaph taken from his *Four Quartets*: "In my beginning is my end. In my end is my beginning." In the years since his passing, his literary legacy has remained strong but not without reserve. A number of critics have found anti-Semitic statements, elitist attitudes, and a cold intellectualism in Eliot's work. Nonetheless in spite of those charges, critics have also noted that Eliot's complexities, such as his omission of connective and transitional material in many works, underscore his perceptive insights into human nature—especially the spiritual hollowness and intellectual aridity that dominated European consciousness after World War I. His influence on poetry and literary criticism since his time has been profound, and he remains one of the towering figures in British poetry of the 20th century.

BIBLIOGRAPHY

Ackroyd, Peter. *T. S. Eliot*. New York: Simon & Schuster, 1984.

Esty, Jed. *T. S. Eliot*. University of Illinois at Urbana-Champaign. Available online. URL: http://www.english. uiuc.edu/maps/poets/a_f/eliot/eliot.htm. Accessed November 10, 2006.

Gardner, Helen. *The Art of T. S. Eliot*. New York: Dutton, 1959.

Southam, B. C. *A Guide to the Selected Poems of T. S. Eliot*, 6th ed. Fort Washington, Pa.: Harvest Books, 1996.

Joseph Becker

EMPSON, WILLIAM (1906–1984)

The son of privileged parents, William Empson was born in North Yorkshire at the height of the Edwardian period. He was an early and avid reader, who, at age seven and a half began formal schooling at Praetoria House in Folkestone. There his love of books was soon matched by his skill in mathematics, earning him honors. He advanced to Winchester Preparatory School in 1920 and, winning firsts in the subject at all levels, continued to study mathematics at Magdalene College, Cambridge, in 1925. He was 19 years old.

English literature was just coming into its own as an academic discipline at Cambridge when Empson matriculated there. He was inspired by T. S. ELIOT to take up the Renaissance poets, particularly John Donne. Eliot and Empson's professor, I. A. Richardson, were to be lifelong influences and Empson transferred from the study of mathematics to English literature in 1928. The following year Empson received his degree, having written plays, reviews, and founding an AVANT-GARDE magazine, *Experiment*. Just as he was about to accept a Cambridge fellowship, Empson was dismissed for an infraction of housing rules.

For two difficult years (1929–31) Empson worked as a freelance writer in London, and, encouraged by T. S. Eliot and Virginia Woolf, he pursued poetry, both as author and as theorist. The next 20 years of Empson's life were a series of junkets between London and the Orient. Beginning in 1931, literature professorships that were closed to him in Britain were offered by universities in Japan and then in China. In 1931 just after he left for Tokyo University his first collection of poems, *New Signatures,* and his landmark study on the varieties of literary meaning, *The Seven Types of Ambiguity,* were published.

After teaching for three years in Tokyo, Empson returned to London, where he published *Poems* in 1935 and the following year his interpretation of a classic poetic form, *Some Versions of the Pastoral.* During the years 1937–39 Empson taught at National Peking University—until the Japanese invaded and drove him into exile. He managed to return to London and for the duration of World War II worked as a Chinese specialist for the BBC. He married Hester Crouse in 1941 and in 1947 returned to his teaching post at National Peking University. He published *The Structure of Complex Words* in 1951, one year before the Communist takeover. In 1953 Empson received his first professorial appointment on British soil: He would teach English literature at the University of Sheffield until his retirement in 1971. During his tenure there Empson published *Milton's God* (1961), a diatribe that had its origin in the seventh of Empson's *Seven Types of Ambiguity.* Empson's early rejection of Christianity had become a full repudiation of a god he saw as at once vengeful and cruel. Having been expelled by the academy, he belonged to no one "school" and openly disparaged New Critics and literary theorists in equal measure.

A missing manuscript, *The Faces of the Buddha,* was recovered in 2006. Compiled between 1930 and 1947, it is a firsthand photojournal of the Orient, and, according to his biographer, will provide the missing piece in the study of Empson's life and thought.

Empson's major legacy is that of a unique "literary critic" (a term he depised), but his poetry deserves to be better known. In 1979 50 years after being expelled from its halls, William Empson was elected honorary fellow, Magdalene College, Cambridge. That same year, five years before his death, Empson was knighted for "services to English Literature."

See also "VILLANELLE."

BIBLIOGRAPHY

Haffenden, John. Letter. *Times Literary Supplement,* 11 August 2006.

———. *William Empson: Among the Mandarins.* Vol. 1. New York: Oxford University Press, 2005.

Sale, Roger. *Modern Heroism: Essays on D. H. Lawrence, William Empson & J. R. R. Tolkien.* Berkeley: University of California Press, 1973.

Ann Hayworth

"EPIC" PATRICK KAVANAGH (1951)   Phrased as a retrospective look at PATRICK KAVANAGH's career-long struggle between the worldly and the local, this poem represents a kind of turning point in perspective—the realization of value in a new kind of provincialism. Kavanagh is looking back in this poem to the later 1930s, the period of growing conflict in Europe as well as the time in his own life that saw the ill-fated move from Inniskeen to Dublin. The tone of much of the poem is one of renunciation; what has been is not nearly as glamorous or important as it once seemed, but the reader is led to this conclusion in a roundabout way. Faced with the comparison of the rural conflict of the Duffys and old McCabe to the impending violence of the Second World War, the speaker—and by extension, the reader—is "inclined / To lose . . . faith" in the importance of the local. We are meant to scoff at these rustics along with the speaker. However, the conclusion to the poem is not the same conclusion that led Kavanagh to leave Inniskeen. The poem almost leads to a recurrence of the same mistake but is corrected. His new realization is brought on by the ghost of Homer—a kind of rural poet himself—and the benefit of hindsight; after his fall from stylish metropolitan grace, he knows where the road to Dublin really leads.

As his focus shifted from the literary expectations of the urban center back to the seemingly truer Inniskeen farmer, Kavanagh reflects on the construction of histories. The enormous importance of the "Munich bother" eventually became history, remembered and retold in stories as well as in facts and figures. The local becomes legend though—spreading from the village slowly, mediated by the poet. That Kavanagh's Homer claims to have used the common rural scene when he "made the Iliad" appeals to this sense of creative importance. However, the poem twists again at the end, leaving a sense of uncertainty in the final "Gods make their own importance." The continued contrast between worldly history and localized legends suggests that Kavanagh has decided upon the rural as the proper place for poetic inspiration. If the larger events in the world will become history solely on the basis of their perceived importance, it is for the poet to look to the smaller and mold them into legends in their own right.

BIBLIOGRAPHY

Kavanagh, Patrick. *Collected Poems.* New York: Norton, 1973.

Quinn, Antoinette. *Patrick Kavanagh: A Critical Study.* Syracuse, N.Y.: Syracuse University Press, 1991.

Patrick McCarty

"EPITAPH ON AN ARMY OF MERCENARIES" A(LFRED) E(DWARD) HOUSMAN (1922)

A(LFRED) E(DWARD) HOUSMAN masterfully uses irony in this short poem, which may have been inspired by a German press report calling British professional soldiers "mercenaries," as opposed to soldiers conscripted or drafted into battle. The poem argues that the soldiers got little "pay" in the end, especially since most of them waged war and are dead. The cutting wordplay may actually mislead some readers into thinking this poem glorifies war. However, Housman was appalled by the death of so many young men and the destruction of beautiful landscapes that might be forever scarred by war. As it had D. H. LAWRENCE and WILFRED OWEN, war left Houseman disgusted.

The men in Housman's poem seem to have fought for the pay of saving the "sum of things" for others. They heard a calling and followed through on a mission, even though the cause was said to be "abandoned" by "God." These men are depicted as doing heroic things: "Their shoulders held the sky suspended; / They stood [their ground], and earth's foundations stay." The speaker of Housman's poem seems to indicate that these soldiers fought the good fight for their country, for the ground they stood on, for those who would follow, and that the dead have been paid the wages of war.

Interestingly, another poet, HUGH MACDIARMID, wrote a response to Housman's poem, "ANOTHER EPITAPH ON AN ARMY OF MERCENARIES." The speaker in this poem takes an opposing view, saying the soldiers took "blood money" at great "risk" to themselves and others.

BIBLIOGRAPHY

Housman, A. E. *The Collected Poems of A. E. Housman.* New York: Holt, 1965.

MacDiarmid, Hugh. *Selected Poetry.* Edited by Alan Riach and Michael Grieve. New York: New Directions, 1993.

Page, Norman. *A. E. Housman: A Critical Biography.* New York: Schocken Books, 1983.

Geraldine Cannon Becker

"EPITAPHS OF WAR" RUDYARD KIPLING (1914–1918)

When World War I broke out in 1914, RUDYARD KIPLING, who had been a supporter of British imperialism, calling it the "white man's burden" in his poem "The White Man's Burden" (1899), urged his own son to join the British military. One week after his son enlisted, he was dead. Overwhelmed with grief, Kipling wrote "Epitaphs of the War" between 1914 and the end of the war in 1918.

The poem expresses the way Kipling personally encountered and experienced the profound disillusionment of World War I. Hence rather than merely celebrating the high-class officers and the bellicose politicians who occupy the ivory towers of command, it resonates with the spirit of the ordinary, unquestioning footsoldiers, who carry out the actual business of war. It also symbolizes in a profound, graphic, and bitter way the tendency of people to ignore the lessons of history and war.

In what may be a poignant personal statement of his own apparent betrayal of his son, Kipling gives to dead soldiers the following assertion: "If any question why we died, / Tell them because our fathers lied." George Orwell observed, "A humanitarian is always a hypocrite, and Kipling's understanding of this is perhaps the central secret of his power to create telling phrases." So in the epitaph for "The Dead Statesman," a political leader confesses that reality has caught up with him at last: "Now all my lies are proved untrue. / And I must face the men I slew."

There are many kinds of betrayal in human affairs, but according to Kipling, in the affairs of state, there is no greater disloyalty, no greater act of betrayal, than to send unsuspecting youths to their deaths on the basis of lies that uphold a politician's career. Here Kipling repeats the note of uncharacteristic humility and caution sounded earlier in "The Recessional" (1897). He also echoes SIEGFRIED SASSOON's criticism of the upper echelons of military power in poems like "The General" and "How to Die."

BIBLIOGRAPHY

Gilmour, David. *The Long Recessional: The Imperial Life of Rudyard Kipling.* London: John Murray, 2002.

Green, R. L., ed. *Kipling, the Critical Heritage.* New York: Barnes & Noble, 1971.

Jones. R. T., ed. *The Collected Poems of Rudyard Kipling.* Ware, Eng.: Wordsworth Poetry Library, 2001.

Divya Saksena

"ESCAPE" ROBERT GRAVES (1916) First published in the privately printed edition of *Goliath and David* in 1916 and distributed among his fellow officers, the poem gives an ironical account of ROBERT GRAVES's own escape from death in the battle of the Somme in 1916. Graves had joined the army shortly after the outbreak of the war in 1914, partly to alleviate his family's doubts about his career, partly out of boredom and the need to carve out his own identity. Because he happened to be in Wales on a holiday after he had finished school at Charterhouse, the 19-year-old Graves joined the Royal Welsh Fusiliers and traveled to France as a captain in May 1915.

Having grown up in a partly German family, Graves felt more confusion and ambivalence toward the enemy than hatred, and he replaced his crumbling Christian faith by ancient mythology. By coincidence the war poet SIEGFRIED SASSOON also belonged to the Royal Welsh Fusiliers. They struck up a friendship (Graves would later save him from court-martial), and Sassoon began to exert an influence on Graves's poetic style. Graves fought in both the infamous Battle of Loos and the Battle of the Somme, where his Fusiliers were reduced to fewer than 400 men and he suffered from mental breakdowns. In July 1916 he was badly wounded and regarded as dead. *The Times* published his obituary but later at his request inserted an announcement that he was alive. In his autobiography, *Good-Bye to All That,* Graves gives the specifics of his wounding and treatment, as well as the accompanying disorientation and emotional instability. His wounds caused a long period of convalescence, in 1916–17,

during which he published his three volumes of war poetry: *Over the Brazier, Goliath and David,* and *Fairies and Fusiliers.* In the poem he wrote about his survival, "Escape," he presents his "experience of a virtual death and rebirth as a dream in which the incidents only parody the reality" (Kirkham, 15).

The poem is a rather facetious pastiche, with the language and experience of a 20th-century soldier imposed on Greek myth. Graves uses an italicized comment to indicate the particular event that occasioned the poem: "*(August 6th, 1916.—Officer previously reported died of wounds, now reported wounded. Graves, Captain R., Royal Welch Fusiliers.).*" The poem starts *in medias res*—"But I was dead, an hour or more"—and describes his descent into the Underworld through the door guarded by the three-headed hellhound Cerberus on his way to Lethe, the river where the dead drink forgetfulness before crossing over into the Underworld. Greek mythology is humorously mixed with remnants of a soldier's reality (signpost, stretcher) and an array of symbols goes through his mind. In the "subterrene sky" of Hades, the Underworld, he sees "A Key, a Rose in bloom, a Cage with bars / And a barbed Arrow." These images seem to combine Christian mythology with pagan images: the rose (e.g., in Dante's *Divina Commedia*) an image of heavenly love and perfection, the key probably St. Peter's key to heaven, whereas the cage and arrow could refer to ancient heroic mythology, while "barbed" again reminds one of the barbed wire that cost so many soldiers their lives.

The confused mind of a man suspended between life and death sees "Lady Proserpine" as a kind nurse, who "stooping over me" clears his head and sends him back "along the track" into life. The Greek goddess Proserpine was forced to spend part of each year in the Underworld as the wife of Hades, only intermittently returning to the upper world in Henna, where Hades had first seen her. Graves manages to recreate the sounds associated with shell shock and traumatic wounding: the buzzing, roaring, and clattering of demons and the sounds of battle reverberating in his head. The runaway from hell is persecuted by "angry hosts / Of demons, heroes, and policeman-ghosts"— again a mixture of everyday reality with mythical remnants, probably from Dante's hell, where devils chase the sinners who try to escape from the pit. The desire for life and unwillingness to sacrifice himself are strong—"Life! life! I can't be dead! I won't be dead! / Damned if I'll die for anyone!"—but escape from the Underworld is obstructed by the guardian Cerberus, who stands grinning above him, obstructing the gate to the upper world. Graves ascribes three rather peculiar heads to this mythological animal, lion, lynx, and sow, perhaps representing the three aspects of trench warfare he had experienced, heroism, slyness, and wallowing in the mud.

The poem reaches a dramatic climax in the breathless attempts of the speaker to find a means of getting by the hell hound: "Quick, a revolver! But my Webley's gone, / Stolen . . . No bombs . . . no knife . . . The crowd swarms on." In panic he suddenly remembers having "some morphia that I bought on leave," which he crams into Cerberus's mouths with "army biscuit smeared with ration jam," sending the dog into a drugged sleep and enabling Graves to run back into life: "Too late! for I've sped through. / O Life! O Sun!" Graves uses here soldier's jargon: Webley, bombs, leave, ration jam ("Tickler's jam" in the first edition), and the term *crowds* could even refer to lice as in the slang of his comrades.

By depicting himself as a second Heracles, Orpheus, or cunning Odysseus, the only ancient heroes who managed to escape and return from hell, Graves attempts to make light of an experience that haunted him for the rest of his life. This humorous account of his survival—almost all of his comrades died at the Somme—shows his main techniques for grappling with the horrors of war and death: wrapping the experience into mythological images, making fun of it, while therapeutically opening the doors to his unconscious. In another war poem, "A dead Boche," these techniques fail when he describes the carcass of a dead German soldier "Big-bellied, spectacled, crop-haired / Dribbling black blood from nose and beard" in the hope that this kind of realistic poetry could serve as a "certain cure for lust of blood."

Graves was soon active again at the front lines after his physical wounds had healed and only further injuries returned him to Britain. After the war he was left shell-shocked and mentally scarred, depressed and neurotic, for the rest of his life. The last republication of "Escape" was in *Poems (1914–27)*, after which Graves eliminated it from his oeuvre.

BIBLIOGRAPHY

Kersnowski, Frank L. *The Early Poetry of Robert Graves: The Goddess Beckons.* Austin: University of Texas Press, 2002.

Kirkham, Michael. *The Poetry of Robert Graves.* London and New York: Athlone and Oxford University Press, 1969.

McPhail, Helen, and Philip Guest. *On the Trail of the Poets of the Great War: Robert Graves and Siegfried Sassoon.* Barnsley, Eng.: Pen & Sword Books, 2001.

Quinn, Patrick J. *The Great War and the Missing Muse: The Early Writing of Robert Graves and Siegfried Sassoon.* Selinsgrove, Pa.: Susquehanna University Press, 1994.

Seymour, Miranda. *Robert Graves: Life on the Edge.* New York: Henry Holt, 1995.

Thomas, William David. "The Impact of World War I on the Early Poetry of Robert Graves." *Mahalat Review* 35 (1975): 113–129.

Heike Grundmann

"EURYDICE" H. D. (HILDA DOOLITTLE) (1917)

This poem is one of H. D.'s (HILDA DOOLITTLE's) responses to the many strong male writers who surrounded her, people like D. H. LAWRENCE and EZRA POUND, who, she felt, wanted to put her and keep her in one place. While "Eurydice" continues H. D.'s early interest in Greek mythology, female speakers, and the imagery of flowers and light, it departs from her early imagist verse in its length and implied narrative, as well as in the suppressed anger that drives it. It is considered one of her most important poems of this period, a transition from her earlier "perfect imagist" poems to her late, long meditations.

Eurydice begins her response to Orpheus just after he has looked back at her and left her irrevocably in hell. While in Virgil's and Ovid's versions of the story Eurydice is given little if any voice, in H. D.'s poem, Eurydice's experience is central and continues; indeed her difference from Orpheus derives from the fact that her identity is tied to the future, while his is constituted by the backward glance. At first angry and defiant, she accuses Orpheus of "arrogance" and "ruthlessness" for awakening in her the hope of a return to earth. She sees hell not only as terrifying and horrible but also "colourless," a sort of "nothingness." She wonders why he felt the need to turn back and look at her, figuring his gaze as narcissistic: "What was it you saw in my face / The light of your own face, / the fire of your own presence?" She is especially bemused at his turn because all she had to offer was "reflex of the earth," that is, what Orpheus has as a living being and what she is deprived of ("all, all the flowers are lost; / everything is lost"). As she tries to find ways to comfort herself, she finds that had Orpheus allowed her any contact with the earth, she could have incorporated into herself "the whole of the great fragrance" and thus "dared the loss." Denied this, however, she needs to assert her being in opposition to the earth. She asserts that "such loss is no loss" and "hell is no worse" than earth. She does not, however, stop with this Satanic argument. Instead she argues that in contrast to the dark of hell, she has "more light" than Orpheus has on earth, though she cannot tell him about it because he would turn back to see her again and she would "sink into a place / even more terrible than this."

Finally, the consolation for Eurydice is her own being. She asserts her integrity and in one final beautiful image asserts that "before I am lost / hell must open like a red rose / for the dead to pass." Thus taking up the challenge of her loss, Eurydice begins to acknowledge what is hers and discovers that her loss is empowering, for it is neither like his loss nor like the loss he envisions her having, but this power, as critics have noted, is bravado. Eurydice is inextricably tied to hell; her "light," her "fervour," and her "flowers" exist only in opposition to the cold and dark of hell. H. D., perhaps herself bound by the terms of the myth she rewrites, creates a moving dramatic lyric, but one that remains in binary opposition to the canonical myth. H. D.'s interest in revising such stories develops over her career into complex neoepics like *Helen in Egypt*.

BIBLIOGRAPHY

Burnett, Gary. *H. D. between Image and Epic: The Mysteries of Her Poetics*. Ann Arbor: UMI Research Press, 1990.

Duplessis, Rachel Blau. "Romantic Thralldom in H. D." *Signets: Reading H. D.*, edited by Susan Stanford Friedman and Duplessis, 406–429. Madison: University of Wisconsin Press, 1990.

Sword, Helen. *Engendering Inspiration: Visionary Strategies in Rilke, Lawrence, and H. D.* Ann Arbor: University of Michigan Press, 1996.

Helen Emmitt

"EVERYONE SANG" Siegfried Sassoon (1919)

Siegfried Sassoon describes the composition of this poem in *Siegfried's Journey*, the concluding volume of his autobiographical trilogy. His account almost classically describes one type of creative moment, that of the "accidental" or "inspired" composition. It was a warm evening in April, he writes, and he felt logy, too absent-minded for anything but sleep. As he commenced preparing for bed, some words occurred to him, and then some lines, till at last the entire poem had come to him and he went off to bed. As many other writers and artists who have enjoyed the fruits of such inspiration, he was not entirely confident of its value. It was not till his friend John Masefield had judged "Everyone Sang" the only genuine poem celebrating the peace after the Great War that Sassoon was able himself to acknowledge its merits.

Many of the other poems in *Picture Show*, Sassoon's collection of 1919, explicitly recall the recently ended war: "Memorial Tablet," "Aftermath," "Reconciliation." But "Everyone Sang" is different because, while it certainly fits into the context of the volume as a "war poem," it is abstract enough to work equally well, better perhaps, as a description of mystical experience. "Everyone Sang" is not the kind of poem modern warfare had taught Sassoon to write, full of hard-nosed detail, but rather a symbolist lyric about liberation from fear. "My heart was shaken with tears," he writes, describing a catharsis, "and horror / Drifted away." Certainly the poem can be taken as a comment on liberation from the horrors of war. The speaker may after all have had an emotional breakthrough that let him weep away the nightmares that reminded him of his experience in combat. But the poem works equally well as a more general description of transcendence, of liberation from an old life into a new reality.

In the next several years Sassoon would turn to religion, writing in *The Heart's Journey* that a "flower has opened in my heart." But he was not yet prepared to recognize mystical liberation in April 1919, not yet prepared to state outright his recognition that the war, including his duty of commenting on the war, was indeed over and a new path opening before him. Thus he made the subject of "Everyone Sang" the release from a very specific kind of fear, denying it its mystical cast. He was not, even when inspiration rewarded him with a poem that granted him permission to get over war's horror, yet able to accept his heart's peace.

BIBLIOGRAPHY

Sassoon, Siegfried. *The Heart's Journey*. London: Heinemann, 1927.

Jimmy Dean Smith

EWART, GAVIN B(UCHANAN) (1916–1995)

Born in London in 1916, Ewart was educated at Wellington College and Christ's College, Cambridge, where he read classics and English and was taught by F. R. Leavis and I. A. Richards, among others. His first volume, *Poems and Songs,* was published in 1939, and after a pause in his poetic production that coincided with his serving in North Africa and Italy in the Royal Artillery during World War II, he published a second volume of poetry, *Londoners,* in 1964. While working in advertising and, after 1971, as a freelance writer, he managed to produce a huge amount of poems that earned him a reputation as a witty, comic writer. When only 17, Ewart published a poem ("Phallus in Wonderland") in Frey Grigson's *New Verse,* and apart from his reputation as a parodist and as an erotic writer (his book *Pleasures of the Flesh* was banned by W. H. Smith and Sons in 1966), he produced several collections for children (*The Learned Hippopotamus,* in 1986, and *Caterpillar Stew,* in 1990) and edited *The Penguin Book of Light Verse* (1980). Most of his poetry published before 1990 was collected into two books, *The Collected Ewart 1933–1980* (1980) and *Collected Poems 1980–1990* (1991).

Ewart's satiric gift and the occasional lewdness (a style he defined as "witverse") that imbues his poetry are always combined with a deep understanding and concern for the nature of humanity, sex, relationships, aging, and dying (especially in his imitations of PHILIP LARKIN's old age personas, or in his "translations" of classic poems such as Wyatt's *They Flee from Me*). Ewart's evident gift for parody and light verse, his love

of "minor" poetic forms such as epigrams, songs, limericks, or clerihews, place him in a continuum of light verse poets such as Lewis Carroll or Edward Lear, a tradition he acknowledges and updates, claiming that "light verse . . . is urbane, the product of big cities; it lives by wit and sophistication . . . it deserves to be taken seriously." This seriousness is provided not by the style of his poetry (which is a mixture of provocative language, colloquial tones, and verbal wit), but by the choice of subjects, which appear surprisingly sober (aging, sex, death, love, human compassion, and harshness), given the forms and meter he usually employs.

Showing a concern produced by his labor as a professional critic, Ewart is aware of the existence of a very diverse audience, and he tries to accommodate elements that will attract all his potential readership, be it ordinary readers, critics, or poets. Much of his production is devoted to poems about poetic forms and the creation of poetry itself. Also, his "parapoems" (a term of Ewart's, making reference to poems where "without any intention of burlesque, you use the form and diction of another poet") take other poetic voices (W. H. AUDEN, Wordsworth, Larkin, for example) and thus reveal his literary inclinations, admirations, and predilections. In all of his oeuvre Ewart goes beyond some labels that were applied to him (such as the "Laureate of Lust"), and his use of sex as a topic and satire as a pose allows him to explore in earnest deep preoccupations about humanity and life itself.

See also "THE LARKIN AUTOMATIC CAR WASH," "WILLIAM WORDSWORTH (1700–1850)."

BIBLIOGRAPHY

Delchamps, Stephen W. *Civil Humor: The Poetry of Gavin Ewart.* Madison, N.J.: Fairleigh Dickinson University Press, 2002.

Jones, Peter, and Michael Schmidt, eds. *British Poetry since 1970: A Critical Survey.* Manchester, Eng.: Carcanet Press, 1980.

Willhardt, Mark, and Alan Michael Parker, eds. *Who's Who in 20th Century World Poetry.* London: Routledge, 2002.

Carmen Méndez García

"THE EXPLOSION" PHILIP LARKIN (1970/1974)

PHILIP LARKIN's "The Explosion" first appeared at the very end of his last book, *High Windows* (1974), which also contained some of Larkin's best loved poems, including "THIS BE THE VERSE," "Going, Going," "HOMAGE TO A GOVERNMENT," and "HIGH WINDOWS." "The Explosion"—because of its cryptic denouement—has elicited a number of excellent close readings and considerable critical commentary. Its subject is ostensibly the shock, spiritual as much as physical, to the people of a mining village following a blast that killed a group of men who had been working in a mine shaft. Larkin's treatment of the incident is, for him, exceptionally tender and compassionate.

An unrhymed elegy in 25 lines of mainly eight syllables each (three are short a syllable), this poem consists of eight tristichs and a final lone line. Larkin exploits this form by playing against its stanzaic regularity in several remarkable ways. In the first four stanzas the speaker describes the sort of day it was: sunny enough to cast shadows, which ominously "pointed towards" the entrance to the mine although, presumably, no one particularly noticed that omen because it was an ordinary phenomenon. The lines of these first four stanzas are neatly end stopped and evoke a picture of the village setting and of its inhabitants, with words and images that capture a sensation of the ordinary: "Down the lane came men in pitboots / Coughing oath-edged talk and pipe-smoke"; one of the miners even "chased after rabbits; lost them; / Came back with a nest of lark's eggs." The sentimentality of that vignette is followed by a moving and increasingly blurry image of the miners, in their beards and work clothes, men who are "fathers, brothers, nicknames, laughter," passing into the mine through its "tall gates."

The fifth stanza, which describes the explosion itself, contains three short independent clauses. Two of them come to a halt before the line ends, truncating and disrupting the regularity established in the first half of the poem. The first clause refers to the explosion succinctly: "At noon, there came a tremor"; the second delivers the metonymically momentous detail that "cows / Stopped chewing for a second." The third clause emphasizes its own starkness by dropping the expected definite article before its subject: "sun, / Scarfed as in a heat-haze, dimmed." The rest of the poem is heavily enjambed, with the sense spilling over from stanza to stanza, thereby creating a dramatically different effect, beginning halfway through the poem, of an uncontainable surplus of feeling and a melding of images bordering on the surreal. Line ends are mostly unpunctuated or lapse in dashes.

Stanza six, all in italics, represents fragments of the words of a memorial service (*The dead go on before us . . . / . . . / We shall see them face to face*); that stanza is followed by the visions those words evoke in the minds of the wives and other congregants, including images of the dead miners, "Gold as on a coin, or walking / Somehow from the sun towards them, / One showing the eggs unbroken."

The last stanza, a single line, chokes emotionally on the heartbreaking image of the vibrant young man who ran after rabbits and admired the lark's nest—and cannot complete itself. As in Larkin's "AN ARUNDEL TOMB," this poem (positioned as the finale to the poet's last book) ends poignantly with the speaker pondering the luminous link that language, or art, establishes between living human beings and their yearning for immortality.

BIBLIOGRAPHY

Shaw, Robert B. "Philip Larkin: A Stateside View." *Poetry Nation* 6 (1976): 100–109.

R. Victoria Arana

EXPRESSIONISM   The term *expressionism* was probably established when the critic Louis Vauxcelles reviewed a group of paintings called *Expressionnismes* by the little known painter Julien Auguste Hervé in 1901. *Expressionism* generally refers to art that emphasizes the representation of strong feeling or emotion predominantly through the manipulation of formal elements and principles such as line, texture, color, and balance. In painting color tends to be the dominant and essential element used to embody and convey the expressive content of the composition. Expressionism focuses on the representation of subjective, interior experience and contrasts with impressionism, which ostensibly renders visible reality with a quasi-scientific objectivity. Whereas *expressionism* typically refers to developments in modern art that began in the first decade of the 20th century, the term *expressionist* is used much more widely to describe art from any period that places a premium on the representation of emotion through the treatment of the formal dimensions of the medium used. While expressionism originated from movements in the visual arts, corresponding developments soon emerged in other arts, particularly in literature and film (e.g., *The Cabinet of Dr. Caligari*, 1919).

The year 1900 marks the acceleration of the pace of artistic innovation in the West, giving birth to a fast-paced succession of movements, or "isms," in the decades to follow. Artists with strong expressionist tendencies such as the Norwegian Edvard Munch (1863–1944) and the Belgian James Ensor (1860–1949), the Frenchman Paul Sérusier (1863–1927), and the post-impressionists Paul Cézanne, Georges Seurat, Paul Gauguin, and Vincent van Gogh served as the inspiration for many of these movements, and of the expressionist movements in particular. In 1912 the critic Paul Ferdinand Schmidt explained the development of expressionism and the strong affinity it would have for Teutonic peoples in an article for *Sturm*: "Cézanne taught the simplification of tone values, Gauguin the effect of the plane, and van Gogh added the flaming luminosity of color. Maurice Denis, Vuillard, and Bonnard attempted to prepare a planar simplification in the grand style, but they lacked persuasive power. This was found by the Teutons of the north and south, Munch and Hodler."

In contrast with the visual arts, where expressionism was a significant strain of modern art, expressionism did not constitute a major movement in literature or poetry. But as in the visual arts, literary expressionism found its most fertile soil in Germany, placing a premium on emotion and interior experience, and gave birth to the periodicals *Der Sturm* (Storm) and *Die Aktion* (Action), which promoted AVANT-GARDE movements in Europe. Writing in *Der Sturm* Herwarth Walden declared, "We call the art of this century Expressionism in order to distinguish it from what is not art. We are thoroughly aware that artists of previous centuries also sought expression. Only they did not know how to formulate it." Literary expressionism is characterized by strong rhythms and disjointed syntax, discontinuity, and shifting points of reference. It rejects the perceptual realism of impressionism in favor of subjective feeling. The early phase of expressionism in poetry included the work of Georg Heym, Ernst Stadler, and Georg Trakl, the latter the best known to English readers for his moving poetry of the Great War, rivaling that of WILFRED OWEN. Expressionist poets like Franx Werfel, J. R. Becher, and Gottfried Benn represent strong but varied philosophical and political commitments, much as one finds among visual artists. August Stramm reflects a tendency toward abstraction where word formations operate independently of meaning, anticipating the birth of dadaism. Outside Germany, expressionism had a limited influence. It appears in traces in the work of W. H. AUDEN and Christopher Isherwood (who spent significant periods of time in Berlin). The greatest impact appears in theater in the work of playwrights like Eugene O'Neill, Elmer Rice, and Thornton Wilder.

BIBLIOGRAPHY

Dube, Wolf-Dieter. *Expressionists*. Translated by Mary Whittal. New York: Thames and Hudson, 1998.

Elderfield, John. *The "Wild Beasts": Fauvism and Its Affinities*. New York: Museum of Modern Art, 1976.

Gordon, Donald E. *Expressionism: Art and Idea*. New Haven, Conn.: Yale University Press, 1987.

Lloyd, Jill. *German Expressionism: Primitivism and Modernity*. New Haven, Conn.: Yale University Press, 1991.

Samuel, R., and R. H. Thomas. *Expressionism in German Life, Literature, and the Theater (1910–24)*. Cambridge: W. Heffer & Sons, 1939.

Weinstein, Joan. *The End of Expressionism: Art and the November Revolution in Germany, 1918–1919*. Chicago: University of Chicago Press, 1990.

Rachel Hostetter Smith

F

"THE FACE IN THE MIRROR" ROBERT GRAVES (1958)

Published first in 1958 in a miscellaneous collection of poems called *5 Pens in Hand,* this poem is ROBERT GRAVES's open declaration of a belated "midlife crisis." When he celebrated his 63rd birthday in 1957, he told friends that he had reached his "fateful year of the grand climacteric" (to Joshua Podro, July 24, 1957, quoted in Seymour 368), expressing the superstitious belief that this age heralded a period of change in his life. Encroaching old age was especially threatening to a poet whose work was based on his love of young women, so-called muses. He now began to wonder at what age it became indecent or impossible to write passionate erotic poetry. Physical ailments had begun to weigh heavily on him; loss of teeth, incontinence, and the fear of prostate cancer and ensuing impotence culminated in a prostate operation in 1959 that almost cost him his life.

"The Face in the Mirror" gives an easily recognizable account of Graves's facial appearance in the mirror, and it was used in a BBC television feature about the poet in honor of his *Collected Poems* (1959), showing him shaving, with his "voice over" reading the poem. The intense observation of his own face can be compared to Rembrandt's late self-portraits, in that it is "a brutal itemization of a body in decay" (Seymour 370), yet we should not think him discontent with what he seems to deprecate, as he rather depicts the face he deserves and is proud to deserve (cf. Carter, 1ff). Graves seems to follow—or rather parody—here the

tradition of Petrarchist poetry. The Italian Renaissance poet Petrarch (1304–74) had initiated the fashion not only of adoring a woman forever out of reach, but of itemizing the eyes, nose, lips, and teeth of the woman in a list (called a blazon). Graves turns the tradition upside down, emphasizing the ugliness, distortion, and decay of his own bodily features instead of their perfect beauty. He sees no eyes as brilliant and beautiful as stars, but instead "grey haunted eyes, absent-mindedly glaring / From wide, uneven orbits," stressing the lack of focus and luster and the distortion of his features. The irregularity of his face ("one brow drooping") is accounted for by his war experiences: A "missile fragment still inhering" has mutilated his appearance. This "foolish record of old-world fighting" marks him as a veteran of this "old world" and reminds readers of his traumatic experiences of World War I, as depicted in his autobiography *Good-bye to All That.* His face is not only a remnant of a foregone age, but also a rugged stone of remembrance, inscribed by the experiences that shaped Graves's life. The disturbing irregularity of his face is further stressed by varying *o* and *e* sounds, which imitate the shape of his eyes and especially by the meter of the poem, which mixes dactyls (´xxx) with trochees (´xx) and iambs (x´x). The first line of the poem could be transcribed metrically as follows: ´xxx´x/´xx´xxx´xx.

The inventory of his face gains an almost military sharpness in the additive style of the second stanza. To his "crookedly broken nose" from a rugby accident in early youth ("low tackling caused it") are added further particles of his face with the heavy brushstrokes of an expressionist painter. He accelerates the tempo of his addition by becoming more and more asyndetic (leaving out the *and*): "Cheeks, furrowed; coarse grey hair, flying frenetic; / Forehead, wrinkled and high, / Jowls, prominent; ears, large, jaw, pugilistic; / Teeth, few; lips, full and ruddy; mouth, ascetic." The heavy stress on the first syllable of each line, the cacophony of monosyllabic words, and the clash of consonants in close proximity, especially the alliterative *c* and *f* sounds, heighten the impression of a contemptuously quick enumeration of his bodily parts and gives an almost cubist impression of disintegration. The unusual rhyme words *frenetic, pugilistic,* and *ascetic,* derived from Greek and Latin roots, stress the pseudoscientific character of this description.

The last stanza returns to a more leisurely, predominantly iambic, rhythm and a reflective ironic detachment. The speaker now self-mockingly addresses his own mirror image as "the other," as a "he" "scowling derision / At the mirrored man whose beard needs my attention." The poem ends with his asking his mirror image why he "stands ready, with a boy's presumption / To court the queen in her high silk pavilion." This "queen" can be understood as the White Goddess. Graves, who believed that matriarchy was the original or natural form of society, which had only been subjected by force to patriarchal structures, regarded the White Goddess as a symbol of womanhood, at once creative, reproductive, and destructive. She is mother figure, lover figure, and witch, and men are supposed to adore her in her various manifestations on earth in the form of "muses." In an interview in 1970 Graves answered the question who the "queen in her high silk pavilion" was as follows: "She's the woman to whom I'm writing the poem, and whatever her name may be is unimportant. . . . You can't write poems unless you're in love with someone, but you don't mention the name, because it's bad manners. There are very often poems of good-bye which are very painful. They are a goodbye to love, while love is still very much in your mind—horrible."

The poem therefore could be read as deriding the folly of an old man ("boy's presumption") to continue in his adoration of the White Goddess and as a pathetic bewailing of his lack of strength for the self-imposed ordeal of muse love, a topic he also explored in "Around the Mountain." And yet the self-conscious voyeurism and humorous tone of this unashamedly autobiographical poem make us suspect the opposite. A poet who had only recently become a celebrity, who was surrounded by admiring American students at his house in Mallorca, and who would frantically pursue beautiful young women after his operation in 1959 in an attempt to prove his virility and his potency as a man and a poet seems rather to advertise himself to his next "muse" than to be haunted by his mortality. As a servant of the goddess, he has to persevere in his worship despite old age, yet as an old man he is prone to ridicule and pain.

BIBLIOGRAPHY

Canary, Robert H. *Robert Graves.* Boston: Twayne, 1980.

Carter, D. N. G. *Robert Graves: The Lasting Poetic Achievement.* Totowa, N.J.: Barnes & Noble, 1989.

Kirkham, Michael. *The Poetry of Robert Graves.* London and New York: Athlone, Oxford University Press, 1969.

Quinn, Patrick J., ed. *New Perspectives on Robert Graves.* London and Selinsgrove, Pa.: Associated University Press, Susquehanna University Press, 1999.

Seymour, Miranda. *Robert Graves: Life on the Edge.* New York: Henry Holt, 1995.

Norris, Leslie. Interview with Robert Graves. *The Listener,* 28 May 1970. BBC TV Wales. Available Online. URL: http://www.lib.byu.edu/~english/WWI/influence/graves.html. Accessed on July 20, 2006.

Heike Grundmann

FANTHORPE, U. A. (1929–)

Ursula Fanthorpe did not publish her first book of poetry until she was almost 50, but she soon arose to prominence despite her late start, to the extent that she was seriously considered for the laureateship on the death of TED HUGHES in 1998. Four years earlier she became the first woman in more than 300 years to be nominated professor of poetry at Oxford.

Born in Kent in 1929, Fanthorpe studied English at St. Anne's College, Oxford, from 1949 to 1953 and then trained for a year as a teacher at the University of London Institute of Education. She taught English at

Cheltenham Ladies' College for 16 years (1954–70) and then quit teaching to pursue a diploma in school counseling. In 1974 while working as a hospital receptionist in Bristol, she began to write poetry: "I began writing because I felt obliged to describe the strange specialness of the patients in the hospital where I worked. Neuropsychiatric disorders were new to me, and I felt the urge to tell the world. Also I wanted to resurrect the language of poetry, which moulders prosaically in hospital folders."

Her first book, *Side Effects* (1978), consisted mostly of poems that recorded the stories of patients and staff at the hospital, but it also displayed a background that was something other than that of a working-class hospital clerk. Its title poem, "NOT MY BEST SIDE," attractively wrapped around the cover of the original Peterloo edition along with a colorful reproduction of Ucello's *Saint George and the Dragon,* is a smart-alecky postmodernist take on the old legend, with each of the three principals in the painting allowed to speak. The knight proves to be part of a military-industrial complex that wants to protect jobs in the "spear- and horse-building industries"; the damsel questions whether she wants to be rescued by this boy, who, under his armor, might have acne for all she knows (while the dragon makes her feel he wants to "eat me. And any girl enjoys that"); and the dragon worries that he is not being taken seriously. Thus Fanthorpe early on established one of her characteristic tones and a feminist, anti-romantic stance.

In her next book, *Standing To* (1982), many more of these challengingly humorous poems appeared, taking loving and irreverent potshots at the canon of great literature, displaying feminist concerns, as in the four monologues that rewrite Shakespeare from a female point of view. "MOTHER-IN-LAW" is Gertrude's commentary on whether Ophelia is "top drawer" enough for her boy. In "King's daughter" Regan moans about how hard it is to be the middle child with a father as nutty as Lear and the older and younger sisters grabbing the attention. "Army wife" turns Emilia's husband, Iago, into "Jim," an "old campaigner" who "keeps his cool" while she, too, can be plopped down anywhere in the empire and, with "good servants," make a go of it. "Waiting gentlewoman" gives us the voice of a teen-aged aristocrat, a little put off by Lord and Lady Macbeth, who hopes "Daddy comes for me soon." The diction of the poems, as well as their conception, reminds one of the colloquialness of PHILIP LARKIN. Fanthorpe says she wanted to write them to see how the world of Shakespeare looked "from the woman's angle," with each of the four women just "having a chat with some usual female confidante, like a hairdresser, or a telephone."

Fanthorpe has published eight volumes of poetry with Harry Chambers's Peterloo Poets, not including a *Selected Poems* in 1986 with Peterloo/Penguin and a *Collected Poems 1978–2003* in 2005. In 1989 Fanthorpe left the hospital to pursue her writing full time. She is featured on the Peterloo Poets Web site, www.peterloopoets.com.

See also "THE PASSING OF ALFRED," "YOU WILL BE HEARING FROM US SHORTLY."

BIBLIOGRAPHY
Fanthorpe, U. A. "Observations of a Clerk." *Poetry Review* 75 (1985): 26–30.
Gilbert, Sandra M., and Susan Gubar. *The Norton Anthology of Literature by Women: The Traditions in English.* 2nd ed. New York: W. W. Norton, 1996.
Hacker, Marilyn. "Unauthorized Voices: Ursula Fanthorpe and Elma Mitchell." *Grand Street* 8 (1989): 147–164.

James Persoon

"A FAR CRY FROM AFRICA" DEREK WALCOTT (1962)

DEREK WALCOTT's meditation on cultural identity in the colonial and postcolonial world reflects his complicated family history: Born in 1930 on the Caribbean island of St. Lucia while it was still a British colony, the grandchild of two black and two white grandparents, raised speaking French-English patois while formally educated in English, Walcott writes as someone without a simple, unified cultural or national identity. "A Far Cry from Africa" explores a condition of cultural exile, the condition of someone "a far cry from" home listening with ambivalence to "a far cry from" home. The double sense of Walcott's title ("a far cry" simultaneously designates a long distance and a distant utterance) introduces a host of dualities in the poem: black and white, colonized and colonizer, Africa and Europe, most obviously, but also the tension between the abstractions of ideology and embodied, lived experience. "Statistics justify and scholars seize / The salients of colonial policy. / What is that to the white child hacked in bed? / To savages, expendable as Jews?" Walcott suggests that ideology—academic, political, and religious obfuscations of the violence that people suffer in colonial conflict—is part of the situation's brutality. He examines how rationalizations and dogmas that justify such violence achieve a life and power of their own, absorbing the suffering of others into persuasive abstractions: "The violence of beast on beast is read / As natural law, but upright man / Seeks his divinity by inflicting pain." These lines remind us of the role of religion in colonial domination, on the one hand, and show us that the pain suffered in such conflicts cannot be effaced or excused by ideology, on the other.

These dualities are especially interesting because they break down into moments of undecidability, ambivalence. The poem is sensitive enough to the real complexities of history to resist simple, easy assignments of guilt and innocence, victim and victimizer. Note the poem's beginning: "A wind is ruffling the tawny pelt / Of Africa." The wind is amoral, impersonal, beyond judgment. The Kikuyu—an east African people whose members participated in often vicious campaigns against British settlers in Kenya in the 1950s—are neither glorified nor vilified, but likened to the nonhuman "flies" that "batten upon the bloodstreams of the veldt." (*Veldt* is the Afrikaans word for an area of open, uncultivated land.) Walcott uses the passive voice, as if refusing to attribute responsibility: "Corpses are scattered through a paradise." Despite the long history of European aggression and exploitation in Africa, the poem's dominant perspective is nonpartisan, trying to find a home beyond the conflict, looking on as a distant observer who laments the loss of human agency in cycles of violence more than it adjudicates guilt and innocence.

These cycles operate in the poem's expansive sense of time and history. Historical crimes and traumas repeat, never quite finished, inflecting the present with past suffering. Walcott refers to the Jews murdered in the Holocaust and Spanish civil war (1936–39) as parts of the same long story of political violence. He even

suggests that this is not merely a modern story, but, in a vivid image in the poem's second verse paragraph, one that goes back to antiquity: "Threshed out by beaters, the long rushes break / In a white cloud of ibises whose cries / Have wheeled since civilization's dawn / From the parched river or beast-teeming plain." (Beaters are often hired by hunters to frighten animals from the brush into the open.) The ibises give a barely articulate voice to history, the fragile evidence that the past and dead are still among us. These are also the "cries" that are referred to in the poem's title—the cry of a distant past, as well as a distant place. Note that European hunters and African beaters collaborate in the scenario, less important for their specific identities or roles than for their shared participation in this ongoing historical drama. In many of his poems Walcott cultivates this profound historical sense, infusing the present with the living past. His book-length epic poem OMEROS (1990) is a rewriting of Homer's *Odyssey* (*Omeros* is the modern Greek name for *Homer*). Walcott's extraordinary project tells a story about the modern Caribbean caught up in powerful mythic and historical currents. "Art is History's nostalgia," Walcott writes (*Omeros* 228), suggesting that poetry has the responsibility to remember that which has been lost, even if this memory is too painful or complicated to be easily used by the present.

The primary ambivalence in "A Far Cry from Africa" concerns cultural affiliation. As a colony of both England and France at different times until earning independence in 1979, but one largely populated by the descendents of African slaves, St. Lucia is a fitting place to explore the complexity of postcolonial linguistic and aesthetic traditions. The poem ends with its most acute expressions of ambivalence, describing the insufficiency of both Africa and Europe for Caribbean identity: "I who am poisoned with the blood of both, / Where shall I turn, divided to the vein? / I who have cursed / The drunken officer of British rule, how choose / Between this Africa and the English tongue I love?" In his essay "What the Twilight Says," Walcott turns this impossible question into a double rejection: "Mongrel that I am, something prickles in me when I see the word 'Ashanti' as with the word 'Warwickshire,' both separately intimating my grandfathers' roots, both baptizing this neither proud nor ashamed bastard, this hybrid, this West Indian" (*What the Twilight Says*, 9). Walcott's attention to language is crucial: Especially with the atypical line break after the phrase "I who have cursed," he evokes the paradox that Shakespeare famously creates with a black character named Caliban in *The Tempest*. Enslaved and trained by Europeans who have arrived on his island, Caliban also makes language a primary issue of cultural domination: "You taught me language, and my profit on't / Is, I know how to curse. The red plague rid you / For learning me your language!" (1.2.363–365).

However, this is not exactly Walcott's sentiment. His poem claims that even if Caribbean identity exceeds both African and European, it cannot deny these roots. The poem's final questions reach an urgent pitch because they have no final answers, claiming only this difficult uncertainty and searching as a kind of home. But Walcott shows how this questioning itself can achieve a kind of affirmation, a claim to identity. In part 1 of the long poem *The Schooner Flight* (1979), he writes these frequently quoted lines, no longer a question but a hesitant answer: "I have Dutch, nigger, and English in me, / and either I am nobody, or I am a nation" (*Collected Poems 1948–1984*, 346). In "A Far Cry from Africa," Walcott articulates the struggle for this hybrid identity, a sense of self and home that neither ignores the colonial past nor lets it totally determine the present.

BIBLIOGRAPHY

Shakespeare, William. *The Tempest*. New York: Signet, 1963.
Walcott, Derek. *Collected Poems 1948–1984*. New York: Farrar, Straus & Giroux, 1986.
———. *Omeros*. New York: Farrar, Straus & Giroux, 1990.
———. *What the Twilight Says*. New York: Farrar, Straus & Giroux, 1998.

David Sherman

FARJEON, ELEANOR (1881–1965)   Eleanor
Farjeon was the only daughter of five children born to Benjamin Farjeon, a prolific Victorian novelist, and Margaret Jefferson, who was descended from several generations of American actors. This combination of literary and dramatic talent provided Farjeon with a voracious appetite for reading (which stood her in lieu of formal schooling) as well as an instinctive capacity for taking on other roles. Unfortunately her talents were largely used for an intense imaginative game shared with her older brother Harry, which she did not relinquish until she was 29. Farjeon herself later admitted that the game was "a harmful check on life itself" and that it had stunted her emotional growth almost beyond recovery. As a result although her early writings were abundant and wide-ranging, they had little lasting substance, for most of her creative energy went into her daydreams.

Farjeon was a talented writer, earning compliments on her Shakespearean sonnets from critics such as D. H. Lawrence. However, her poetry suffered from sentimentality and a failure to face issues without shying away from the truth. She had a superior ability to mimic; many scholars were fooled when *Blackwood's Magazine* published her spoof Elizabethan poems. The drawback of this ability was that she felt her work was often derivative, a judgment she made about her first collection, *Pan-Worship, and other poems* (1908). The title of her next book, *Dream-Songs for the Beloved* (1911), implies that she and her writing were still trapped in the "prolonged states of self-hypnosis" that had overwhelmed her adolescence and young adulthood. Farjeon preferred the discipline of poetic forms rather than free verse, but although this allowed her to demonstrate her cleverness, her talent never fully developed.

She published more than 80 books, many of them for children, as well as songs and musical librettos, often in conjunction with her younger brother, Herbert. Her hymn "Morning Has Broken" became a pop hit after her death. One of her sonnets, "Easter Monday," is an elegy to her fellow poet Edward Thomas, who was killed in the First World War.

BIBLIOGRAPHY

Blakelock, Denys. *Eleanor: Portrait of a Farjeon*. London: Victor Gollancz, 1966.
Colwell, Eileen H. *Eleanor Farjeon*. A Bodley Head Monograph. London: Bodley Head, 1961.
Farjeon, Annabel. *Morning Has Broken: A Biography of Eleanor Farjeon*. London: Julia Mcrae Books, 1986.
Farjeon, Eleanor. *Edward Thomas: The Last Four Years*. London: Oxford University Press, 1958.

————. *A Nursery in the Nineties.* Oxford: Oxford University Press, 1980.

Tracey Rosenberg

"THE FARMER'S BRIDE" CHARLOTTE MEW (1916)
CHARLOTTE MEW's best-known poem is "The Farmer's Bride," a wrenching monologue in which a farmer recounts the story of his failed marriage to a reluctant bride, who sleeps in the attic to get away from him. The farmer has been married for three years. At the beginning of their marriage, the bride suddenly

> turned afraid
> Of love and me and all things human;
> Like the shut of a winter's day
> Her smile went out, and 'twadn't a woman—
> More like a little frightened fay.

Even in this initial description, the farmer describes his wife as the very incarnation of alterity, defining her by what she is not—not human, not a woman, not interested in the marriage bed. Even the meter of the poem falls out of its orderly iambic tetrameter at the unexpected trochaic word *human,* as if the bride's otherworldliness were impossible to reconcile with the farmer's sense of domestic order. Instead of being human the wife is a "little frightened fay," the one kind of fairie most scared by human contact. Just as the farmer categorizes his wife as inhuman, the meter changes yet again, with two anapests whose extra syllables hurry the line: "Like the shut of a winter's day." The line itself is hurrying to its close, even as the farmer's realization sets in with swift and terrible finality: There is no hope for his marriage; he will not be able to sweet-talk his bride into the role of domestic cheer and sexual compliance that he desperately wants *her* to want.

The farmer compares his child-bride to small woodland animals whose "wild" nature is untamable, and even to nature itself: She is swift as a leveret, shy as a mouse, slight as a larch, sweet as violets. The farmer notes, "The women say that beasts in stall / Look round like children at her call." Even as the farmer bestializes the person and personifies the beasts, he implies that his world is so far from his wife's that for them there is

no language with which to communicate. Although the wife can effectively call the animals in the stable and chat with birds and rabbits, she can speak only mutely and nonverbally to men. The farmer says that when any one of "us"—meaning "us men"—approaches her, her eyes beseech "'Not near, not near!'" The fact that she will not speak to him at all testifies to her status as untamable. As the brown rabbit she resembles, she will remain a wild creature, even in the marriage cage. Moreover Mew's awkward dictive choice points to the desperation of this cage. The bride's eyes beseech the men in negative rather than positive terms; she is not interested in telling them what to do, only in telling them what not to do. This essentially passive command underscores her own sense of entrapment and passivity in a world in which men act and women react.

Mew frequently locates gender anxiety on the threshold of the church. The farmer tells us that one night "in the Fall," the wife ran away. The fall, the season that prefigures the harshness of winter, is also an analogue for the Edenic fall from grace that doomed women to be the brides of men. The girl tries to fly away from this fate, running over "seven-acre field and up-along across the down." Tellingly the farmer and his friends catch the runaway in "Church-Town," that place of symbolically sanctioned male authority that curtails female freedom.

But the poem ends with an example of what Jessica Walsh calls "poetic ambivalence toward the body." The farmer's narration breaks down into a syntactically inchoate expression of longing for his child-wife as he explains that although he has her back, he does not have her love:

> 'Tis but a stair
> Betwixt us. Oh! My God! The down,
> The soft young down of her, the brown,
> The brown of her—her eyes, her hair, her hair!

The poem gives neither the farmer nor the bride any peace. She is left fearful and trembling like the mad woman in the attic, forever out of his reach in the realm of the innocent and the insane, and he is left with the guilt of wanting to corrupt a sexual innocent. The stair that separates them homonymically refigures the bride's earlier beseeching stare, and both seem to function as symbols of insurmountable distance. Usually a stair represents movement and, by extension, the possibility of growth through ascension. But this stair/stare denies the very possibility that it seems to invite. It has gone up, but it will not come down—and the word *down* here seems self-consciously to act in terms of both spatial typology and secondary sexual characteristic. The "soft young down of her"—that is, the erotic body hair that she is beginning to develop as a nubile adult—is also the downward stair that she will never willingly traverse. Even the farmer's observations about the passage from autumn to winter turn on the very up/down movement he would like to see between him and his bride: "The blue smoke rises to the low grey sky, / One leaf in the still air falls slowly down." Outdoors nature seems to sanction the rising and falling that lead to seasonal change, but in his own house he finds stasis and loneliness.

Pleasure, in Mew's poetry, is often unattainable and always punishable. It is that untraversable stair between bedroom and attic, the reminder of where we want to go and what we must not risk. Indeed Mew experiences the human body as a kind of invidious insanity, an omnipresent black speck whose cancer must be checked by measures at once drastic and dangerous. The farmer's desire for his bride is punishable in spite of the fact that his longing for her is social as well as sexual. "What's Christmas-time," he exclaims, "without there be / Some other in the house than we!" Christmas, the season for reddening berries and the birth of babies, seems especially forlorn without the possibility of having children of his own. The farmer is thrice punished, hurt by his wife's revulsion, by his ongoing childlessness, and by the awareness that he himself is to blame for his situation. The opening lines of the poem make this clear: "I chose a maid— / Too young maybe—but more's to do / At harvest-time than bide and woo." The farmer acknowledges responsibility, since he admits that he chose a maiden too young for marriage; moreover he admits that he never took the time to court her properly, as he was busy with work.

The farmer's admission of complicity in his own unhappiness introduces the trope of confession only to renounce it, a gesture Mew makes frequently in her poetry. Indeed many critics have observed that Mew's poems seem both drawn to, and repelled by, scenes of repentance. Angela Leighton, for instance, argues that Mew's poetry was representative of a larger cultural tendency in fin de siècle women's writing in general; writers like Mew were beginning to make discursive movements away from overwrought expressions of Victorian sensibility. Instead they began moving toward a deliberate emotional restraint, a kind of "writing against the heart." Emily Dickinson's oft-cited line "Renunciation—is a piercing Virtue!" applies to most of Mew's poems. The farmer has renounced the possibility of intimacy with his bride, but there is still so much he will not say. While he is virtuous insofar as he will not force his unwilling bride to bed, both he and she pay a hefty price for what they have renounced.

The poem is heavy with the weight of what remains unsaid. The farmer renounces all speech but the bare plot of the account that he relates to us; the bride renounces sex, children, and speech. When the farmer says, "*I've* hardly heard her speak at all," the unsaid becomes more ominous than virtuous; the unsaid is always more threatening than the said, as Mew demonstrates in all her poems. If the farmer's house represents the farmer's own psychic interior, and if what happens inside that house is less important than what fails to happen, the poem maps a symbolic transformation from house of marriage to house of fiction. The farmer begins the poem with a matter-of-fact report of events but ends with an exclamation so full of longing that we infer he has nowhere to go but the house of fiction, a place in which he can at least *imagine* intimacy with his bride. The unsaid comes to represent the liminal space of the house of fiction. In this space men and women know the truth but refuse to name it. It is the space of narrative, of make-believe; it is the necessary space where imagination constitutes reality. Like the stair, this space is the structural point of connection on which nobody walks.

BIBLIOGRAPHY

Fitzgerald, Penelope. *Charlotte Mew and Her Friends*. Reading, Mass.: Addison-Wesley, 1984.
Leighton, Angela. *Victorian Women Poets: Writing against the Heart*. Charlottesville: University of Virginia Press, 1992.
Merrin, Jeredith. "The Ballad of Charlotte Mew." *Modern Philology* 95, no. 2 (November 1997): 200–217.

Mew, Charlotte. *Charlotte Mew: Collected Poems and Selected Prose.* Edited and introduction by Val Warner. New York: Routledge, 2003.

Walsh, Jessica. "'The Strangest Pain to Bear': Corporeality and Fear of Insanity in Charlotte Mew's Poetry." *Victorian Poetry,* September 2002: 217–240.

Rhoda Janzen

"THE FAT BLACK WOMAN REMEMBERS" GRACE NICHOLS (1984)

This poem is representative of GRACE NICHOLS's concern with debunking myths and stereotypes of black women, a concern that underlies *The Fat Black Woman's Poems.* The whole collection is dedicated to representing the diversity of black femininity, which cannot be reduced to conventional stereotypical notions of either womanhood or ethnicity. In this particular poem Nichols investigates a Western stereotype that is especially prevalent in the United States: the mammy, or the "Jemima" stereotype. The fat black woman remembers her mother, another black woman, as a servant and mammy, feeding the white children but having to neglect her own. "Remembering" does not have to be understood literally here; rather Nichols wants to assert a link between black women, focusing on interwoven histories, while pointing out the individualities of the black female experience.

The figure of the black mammy is one of the central myths of the Old South and still is a vivid reminder of slavery. At the end of the 19th century, the mammy was given a pseudopersonality through the characteristics and the face of "Aunt Jemima," the first advertising trademark of the company Quaker Oats. The popular phrase "as American as apple pie, baseball, and Aunt Jemima" gives evidence to the popularity of Aunt Jemima, who still features on products like maple syrup today. The first product that she was used to advertise for was a mixture of pancake batter, and one of the memories of the fat black woman is of "tossing pancakes / to heaven." She also remembers "smokes of happy hearty" but also "murderous blue laughter," an indication of the pretended joviality that is rendered to the "little white heads / against her big-aproned breasts." While the white children are having pancakes, associated with heaven, all that is left for Jemima's own children is "Satanic bread."

While there is a sense of solidarity between the two women in the poem, and an indication of a shared history, the fat black woman draws a clear line between herself and the Jemima figure, a line that cuts across gender, ethnicity, and class: "But this fat black woman ain't no Jemima," she claims, and emphasizes this in the concluding line: "Sure thing Honey / Yeah." Grace Nichols thus sums up an important notion about history: On the one hand, a shared history establishes a bond between black women over the divide of class, place, and generation; on the other, it allows for the opportunities that individual experiences offer. Black female identity, Nichols shows us again and again, covers a multitude of personalities and cannot be reduced to racist or sexist stereotypes.

BIBLIOGRAPHY
Nichols, Grace. *The Fat Black Woman's Poems.* London: Virago, 1984.

Susanne Reich

FEINSTEIN, ELAINE (1930–)

Elaine Feinstein is one of Britain's few Jewish poets. She was born in Bootle and grew up in Leicester, but both sets of grandparents were Russians from Odessa. The uncles on her mother's side were socialists and militantly atheistic, but her father's family were Orthodox in their religious practice. Her father maintained this tradition when the family moved to Leicester, becoming president of the synagogue.

Feinstein attended Cambridge University from 1949 to 1952 and returned there after her marriage. She was interested in the work of EZRA POUND, Samuel Beckett, and Allen Ginsberg and edited a magazine called *Cambridge Opinion* while living in what she describes as "a great commune of undergraduates and their friends." It was during this time that she became impatient with traditional poetry and began to associate with J. H. PRYNNE and DONALD DAVIE. They were advocates of a new style of poetry that turned away from rhyme, stanza, meter, and even narrative sense and focused instead on the way the poem sounded when read and the way it looked on the page. This period of innovation and the poets who subscribed to its philosophy later became known as the Cambridge school. It was related to changes taking place in America in response to the Vietnam War, changes that began at Black Mountain College in North Carolina with the poet and teacher Charles Olson. Feinstein was influenced by the Americans and sought to introduce their work to other British writers and students.

Although Feinstein participated in the literary developments of her day, it was also her Russian Jewish heritage that formed her poetic voice. Traditional English poets, known as THE MOVEMENT poets, depended on the use of irony to maintain a distance between writer and reader, to hint at feelings and subjects that were uncomfortable to express. Feinstein, while working as a lecturer, discovered the Russian poet Marina Tsvetayeva and translated her poems into English. She credits Tsvetayeva with showing her that it was possible to be candid without embarrassment. Feinstein's first book of poetry, *In a Green Eye* (1966), was unusual at the time for its expression of frank emotion and opinion. Her poem "Mother Love" describes a baby's bowel movement and she says that it embarrassed audiences when she first read it in public. Feinstein's poetry continues to be straightforward in its handling of emotion. TED HUGHES, one of her advocates, says that "there is nothing hit or miss, nothing for effect, nothing false. Reading her poems one feels cleansed and sharpened." Her Jewish identity adds yet another dimension to her work, a sense of "otherness," a distinct sense of her place in the world.

BIBLIOGRAPHY

Feinstein, Elaine. *Elaine Feinstein: Collected Poems and Translations*. Manchester, Eng.: Carcanet, 2002.
The Elaine Feinstein Page. Available online. URL: www.elainefeinstein.com. Accessed July 6, 2006.

Mary VanOeveren

FEMINISM AND BRITISH POETRY

When the 20th century began, women of Britain could not vote. By the time the century came to its close, women had not only earned this right, but had helped to elect a woman to the highest elected position in British government, prime minister. Women of Britain also gained the right to inherit property, the right to hold jobs once barred to them, the right to equal pay, the right to divorce, the right to prosecute for domestic abuse. Birth control became widely available, giving women greater control over their health and family planning. Transportation such as bicycles and later cars gave women unprecedented physical independence. The woman of the house ventured out and asserted that it was not exclusively a man's world.

Of course this was not a direct trajectory; women's empowerment met with ample opposition and difficulty. It was also not a struggle confined to the political realm. The poetry of Britain was often a showground of the feminist movement, and women's growing literary success was one of the most sensitive gauges of how women's struggle for equality was faring. The literary establishment also provided some of the most vitriolic reactions against feminism, serving as often as a gauge of contemporary backlash against women's advances as a gauge of their progress. Among the many texts that offer accounts of the British feminist movements, two studies offer particularly adept examinations of the nexus of political and literary feminisms in the 20th century: Gilbert and Gubar's *No Man's Land* (1988) and, more recently, Dawson and Entwistle's *A History of Twentieth Century British Women's Poetry* (2005). The latter offers a particularly useful timeline that poses historical landmarks beside literary landmarks beginning in 1901 and continuing to the century's end.

The first decade of the 20th century, or the Edwardian era, began in 1901 with the death of Queen Victoria. Lest we think that the death of Victoria prompted sudden urgency for women's rights, is important to note that discussions of women's rights were already stirring in the 1890s when the term *feminism* was imported from France. France's Marie Curie won the Nobel Prize in 1903, and in the same year in Britain the Women's Social and Political Union (WSPU) was formed. In 1905 rising impatience with conventional lobbying tactics prompted the women of the WSPU to turn to a more militant strategy. They began with street demonstrations and gradually turned toward deliberate attempts to provoke public disorder. There were attacks on public buildings; incidents of arson, bombing, and vandalizing of pillar boxes; and window smashing raids in London's West End. One of the most famous acts was the defacement of several art treasures in a London museum. This act prompted EZRA POUND and WYNDHAM LEWIS to address a section of their periodical *BLAST* (151) to suffragettes, instructing them:

IN DESTRUCTION AS IN OTHER THINGS,
STICK TO WHAT YOU UNDERSTAND.
WE MAKE YOU A PRESENT OF OUR VOTES
ONLY LEAVE WORKS OF ART ALONE.

Indeed within the literary establishment, poets, editors, and critics consistently enforced a strict divide between male and female character and creativity. The editor of *Poetry Review* went so far as to claim that the male poet had "represented woman so adequately in poetry that there seemed scarcely any call for her to represent herself" and that, despite any strides toward emancipation, "[woman's] poetry is the expression of personal moods . . . it is remarkable how seldom she may be reckoned a whole poet" (Dawson 10).

Despite such hostilities, women continued aggressive tactics to keep Women's suffrage in the forefront of British consciousness, and they developed their own significant works of art. In poetry the voices of the period included Alice Maynell—who was perhaps the epitome of the independent literary women—as well as Katherine Tynan, Mary Coleridge, Jane Barlow, Anna Bunston, and Margaret L. Woods. In 1910 Lady Margaret Sackville published *A Book of Verse by Living Women,* in whose introduction she countered, "When women have fully proved their capacity for freedom, we can begin to estimate better their capacity for poetry" (Dawson 11).

In 1910 King Edward died, and with the accession of King George V (1910–36) the Georgian era began with a great many promising developments. The influences of film, radio, magazines, as well as the English translation publications of both Freud and Jung, joined with the development of literary criticism and an increasingly literate public to offer whole new realms for women writers to enter. However, these transformations were "accompanied by reactionary backlashes, especially against women's emancipation." Of course the most significant event of the reign of King George V was the First World War. The war had a complicated effect on the women's movement. In some ways it was

emancipating—women took on men's work and pay for the first time. May Sinclair published her *Feminist Manifesto* in 1914, and women's war work—as nurses and ambulance drivers and on the home front—was widely lauded. At the end of the war in 1918 married women older than age 30 earned the right to vote and helped to elect the first women to Parliament. In 1919 the Sex Disqualification Act opened all professions except the church to women. In 1920 Oxford began conferring degrees on women, and Cambridge followed suit in 1921. Marie Stopes published *Wise Parenthood* and *Married Love* in 1918 and *Contraception* in 1923. Stopes also opened the first birth control clinic in London in 1921. In 1928 all women above the age of 21 earned the right to vote.

In other ways the effect of the First World War on women's rights was highly problematic. From the outset Britain had used disturbingly feminized propagandist rhetoric, urging men to serve "Mother England" and make the world safe for their women and children. Conservatives played on a woman's sense of "womanly duty," and many conscription posters of the day depicted women urging (and sometimes literally pushing) their men to enlistment offices. There were even poems by women (emotional appeals to patriotism) urging men to enlist. Of course when the war dragged on years longer than planned, the death tolls rose to unheard-of totals, and men returned dismembered and disfigured, they remembered that it was women who had urged them to go, that for women's sake they had sacrificed, and that women had entered the workforce in their place.

Many women writers had deeply pacifist commitments and were uncomfortable with the conflation of "motherhood" and "patriotism." Women poets were torn between urges for change and for stability, and in their writing we see mixed impulses about tradition and experiment in poetry. The academy, meanwhile, remained entrenched in the idea that *femininity* and *intellect* were binary opposites. And while women's weekly periodicals gained them public identities, they also reinforced the notion that women's writing remained on the losing end of the growing divide between "popular" (read "feminine") and "high" modernism.

Still women writers made some extremely important strides in this period. EDITH SITWELL'S *Wheels* (published annually from 1916 to 1921) sparked considerable debates over where the boundaries of morality in poetry should be drawn. Harriet Shaw Weaver served as editor of *Egoist.* Sylvia Beach established Shakespeare & Co. bookshop and lending library, Alida Moore opened Poetry Bookshop on Devonshire Street, and NANCY CUNARD'S The Hours Press put out 24 books between 1928 and 1931. Laura Riding joined Robert Graces at the Seizin Press and Dorothy Wellesley and Winnifred Bryher were patrons of Hogarth Press, Contact Publishing Company, Beaches Bookshop, and the Egoist Press. Alice Maynell continued intense creativity until her death in 1922. CHARLOTTE MEW published her first two books; Sackville and H. D. contributed *Pageant of War* and *The Sea Garden,* respectively; and Vera Brittain and Jessie Pope contributed to the canon of war poetry.

In 1939 England was once again at war with Germany and would remain so for the next six years. During the war the language of democracy, which had become more and more prevalent throughout the 1930s, developed widespread currency. It was also accompanied by a 50 percent increase in the numbers of workers belonging to trade unions between 1938 and 1948. During this time women continued to progress toward social and sexual autonomy. The Matrimonial Causes Act, the Inheritance Act, and the Education Act all had empowering effects for women. Of course they encountered resistance to their legal and personal strides through the persistent feminizing of their creativity by the conservative literary establishment. Still the Second World War offered subject matter that was gender-neutral, and some of the most candid war poems were written by women in this decade. Ada Jackson's *Behold the Jew* (1943) was tremendously successful. Other successful women poets of the 1940s included Alice Coats, E. J. Scovell, Frances Bellerby, Eva Dobell, Dorothy Ratcliffe, Edith Nesbitt, Sheila Wingfield, and Lynette Roberts.

The decades that followed the two world wars were as complex as those before. The reign of King George VI (1936–52) ended, and Queen Elizabeth II took the throne in 1952. In 1954 rationing from World War II finally ended. As in the United States, the end of the Second World War in Britain was followed by a period that disarmed the feminist movement. Fired by the upheaval of the war, the following peace yielded a gigantic surge in marriage and a massive baby boom. Some scholars argue that feminism's energies dissipated during this period. The women poets who were meeting with success in this decade—Bellerby, Sitwell, FRANCES CORNFORD, ELIZABETH DARYUSH, H. D., STEVIE SMITH, and SYLVIA TOWNSEND WARNER—had largely established themselves before the war. However, other notable names include Olga Katzin, Helen Spalding, Helen Waddell, Margaret Willy, Ursula Wood (later Vaughn Williams), Susan Miles, Joan Barton, Sheila Wingfield, ANNE RIDLER, E. J. SCOVELL, RUTH PITTER, and KATHLEEN JESSIE RAINE.

In the 1960s the feminist movement, or women's liberation movement, gained momentum once more. Civil activism that prompted protests over Suez, Cuba, Vietnam, and civil rights also prompted strides in women's rights, including the introduction of the contraceptive pill, abortion law reform, and the Family Planning Act. Amid this fury of public demonstration, some noteworthy feminist texts began circulating. Simone de Beauvoir published *The Second Sex* in 1961 and Betty Friedan published *The Feminine Mystique* in 1963. Kate Millett's *Sexual Politics* and Sheila Rowbotham's *Women's Liberation and New Politics* both appeared on the scene in 1969. Also in 1969 Stevie Smith was awarded the Queen's Medal for poetry.

Stevie Smith died just two years later in 1971. Later that year London was the scene of the first International Women's Day march. Through continued activism the 1970s saw the passage of the Sex Discrimination Act, the Domestic Violence Act (1976), and the appointment of the first female prime minister, Margaret Thatcher (1979). During this decade statutory marriage rights were set in place and an Equal Opportunity Commission was created. Amid these important gains, the literary voices on the scene included ELIZABETH JENNINGS, PATRICIA BEER, EAVAN BOLAND, and Adams. DENISE LEVERTOV published three books of poetry in this decade: *To Stay Alive, Footprints,* and *The Freeing of the Dust.*

In the 1980s and 1990s Helen Sharman became the first Briton in space, the Church of England ordained its first female deacons, and Ireland elected its first female president, Mary Robinson. Betty Boothroyd also earned the distinction of serving as the first female speaker of the House of Commons. Many of today's most distinctive female authors began to arrive on the literary scene. Elizabeth Jennings published no fewer than 13 volumes between 1980 and the year 2000. CAROL ANN DUFFY and Eavan Boland both emerged as important poets. Boland's *Object Lessons: The Life of the Woman and the Poet in Our Time* (1995) is a collection of essays of the caliber of Woolf's *A Room of One's Own.* Other notable contemporary British writers include Katie Donovan, LIZ LOCHHEAD, and Rita Ann Higgins.

In the first decade of the 21st century women continue to make advances in British literature and have truly begun to penetrate "the glass ceiling of literary authority" (Rowbotham 169). Our anthologies are notably more balanced in their inclusion of literature by women, and women of variant backgrounds. Feminism has blossomed from its initial desire to see woman have "a literature of her own" and has come to recognize that women's rights are human rights—and that they must be inclusive of theories of class and race. For instance feminism has grown to incorporate postcolonial theories and is marked by a "heightened awareness of cultural diversity" (Rowbotham 176). Similarly economic and ecological feminisms push for more global implications for women's empowerment.

BIBLIOGRAPHY

Dawson, Jane, and Alice Entwistle. *A History of Twentieth-Century British Women's Poetry.* New York: Cambridge University Press, 2005.

Dombrowski, Nicole Ann. *Women and War in the Twentieth Century: Enlisted with or without Consent.* New York and London: Routledge, 1999.

Gilbert, Sandra M., and Susan Gubar. *No Man's Land: The Place of the Woman Writer in the Twentieth Century.* Vol. 1. New Haven, Conn., and London: Yale University Press, 1988.

Rowbotham, Sheila. *A Century of Women: The History of Women in Britain and the United States.* New York: Viking, 1997.

Smith, Harold, ed. *British Feminism in the Twentieth Century.* Amherst: University of Massachusettes Press, 1990.

Ann Hoff

FENTON, JAMES (1949–)

Readers of the *New York Review of Books* recognize Fenton, a regular contributor for more than 20 years, as a consummate man of letters, writing on everything from the visual arts and Far Eastern politics to poetry and the joys of gardening. Born to an Anglican priest and his wife in the English cathedral city of Lincoln, Fenton attended choir school, Repton, and Magdalen College, Oxford, from which he was graduated with a B.A. in 1970, having read philosophy, psychology, and physiology (PPP). As an undergraduate, Fenton won the distinguished Newdigate Prize for poetry, writing a sonnet sequence (with two haiku) on the set topic of Commodore Perry's opening of Japan ("Our Western Furniture").

After college, he began his career as a journalist, first pursuing literary topics but soon turning to political affairs. In the early seventies he freelanced from Vietnam and Cambodia, and he returned in the mid-eighties as correspondent for the *Independent,* all of which became the core of his book *All The Wrong Places* (1988). A short stint as the *Guardian*'s correspondent in Germany was followed by a five-year run as the drama critic for the London *Times*; his reviews are collected in *You Were Marvellous* (1983). Elected to the professorship of poetry at Oxford in 1994, Fenton published his lectures as *The Strength of Poetry* (2001), in which he discusses many of the poets who influence his work, especially PHILIP LARKIN and W. H. AUDEN, to whom he is most often compared.

Fenton's first volume of poetry published in the United States, *Children of Exile* (1984), combines his first two volumes printed in England, themselves the compilation of his many small-press pamphlets. On both sides of the Atlantic, his early work met extravagant praise for its verbal dexterity, its range of forms and styles, and its startling subjects. Fenton draws heavily on his years abroad to write some of the most sobering and politically charged poems of our time, especially the title poem (about Southeast Asian refugees in Italy), "Dead Soldiers" (a chilling narrative in which the poet dines with Cambodian soldiers), and "A GERMAN REQUIEM" (a meditation about postwar Europe). A number of comic pieces point to another direction Fenton pursues in his work: "Letter to John Fuller," his fellow poet and former Oxford mentor, suggests they execute a suicide pact to guarantee fame: "If poets want to get their oats / The first step is to slit their throats." Fenton and Fuller later coauthored a collection of irreverent ballads and poems, *Partingtime Hall* (1987), a technical tour de force that pokes fun at sex, religion, and the state of contemporary poetry.

Fenton further explores his sense of comedy and nonsense in his next volume, *Out of Danger* (1994), and in his latest collection of words for music, *The Love Bomb* (2003). His poems in the former volume draw more and more on the performance styles of RUDYARD KIPLING, though of course Fenton is a man of the Left. In the title section, Fenton includes some surprisingly personal love lyrics, but the major part of the volume is made up of political ballads and macabre nonsense songs. The long sequence "A Manila Manifesto" updates his view of the poetry scene with more songs, prose snippets, jokes, foreign bits, and epigrams. Fenton's love of music, evident everywhere in his rhymed and metered work, finds full expression in the two librettos (along with an oratorio) collected in *The Love Bomb,* which owes as much to opera as it does to popular song and show music. A short *Introduction to English Poetry* (2002) provides a neat statement of Fenton's expansive poetic aesthetic.

BIBLIOGRAPHY

Fenton, James. *Children in Exile: Poems 1968–1984.* New York: Random House, 1984.
——. *An Introduction to English Poetry.* New York: Farrar, Straus & Giroux, 2002.
——. *The Love Bomb and Other Musical Pieces.* New York: Penguin, 2003.
——. *Out of Danger.* New York: Farrar, Straus & Giroux, 1994.
—— and John Fuller. *Partingtime Hall.* New York: Viking, 1987.

Thomas Depietro

"FERN HILL" DYLAN THOMAS (1945)

"Fern Hill," which appeared in *Deaths and Entrances,* may be DYLAN THOMAS's most famous poem, and it exemplifies many of the defining characteristics that set him apart from other poets. Here we find him defying prose logic by twisting idiomatic phrases ("happy as the heart was long"); running headlong through regular, pulsating stanzas; creating an almost tangible web of sound, rhythm, and imagery ("I ran my heedless ways, / My wishes raced through the house high hay"). And as do most of Thomas's best poems, it stirs up some of the most extreme sensations of our lives, from childhood exuberance to a stark awareness of death.

"Fern Hill" is a joyful, singing poem about childhood remembered, infused with the sense of time's passing as we see in the final three lines, now inscribed in stone at the park near Thomas's childhood home in Wales:

> Oh as I was young and easy in the mercy of his
>   means
> Time held me green and dying
> Though I sang in my chains like the sea.

Wonder, delight, and loss are inextricably entwined in these images of the child both "green" and "dying," singing "like the sea" in his chains as yet unfelt, and the poem leaves us both grieving and rejoicing in that paradox of feeling.

Beginning with the first stanza, the poem looks back at childhood—in particular at the summers the young Dylan spent at his aunt's farm called Fernhill, a retrospective shot through with the present, an enchanting, golden landscape, full of apples and animals, nature, color, and of course sounds. With the supreme confidence of youth, this "lordly" boy, "prince" of the farm world, rushes headlong through his golden "heydays" and dreamily embraces the nighttime's "dingle starry," while time lets him "hail and climb." The pastoral melody of the language colors the boy's days with an Edenic innocence and gives the poem its power to move us.

Each stanza continues with an equally confident meter in unrhymed lines full of alliteration and assonance to intensify the sense of growth and exhilaration until, in stanza 4, we come upon a scene of creation as beautiful and pure as any in literature. This triumphant vision is bound to earth by the concreteness of the warm horses but infused with spirit by "light," "spinning," and the "spell" that binds the horses upon the fields of "praise." Still, the moment in the garden cannot last, because time, the boy learns in the next stanza, allows "in all his tuneful turning so few and such morning songs." And the poet awakes in the final stanza to a fallen world, "to the farm forever fled from the childless land," which leads to the sigh at the beginning of the last movement, "Oh as I was young and easy in the mercy of his means," so different from the eagerness with which the poem began: "Now as I was young and easy under the apple boughs."

While "Fern Hill" is often praised for its achingly pure lyricism, it has also been criticized for being overly nostalgic or escapist, overly sentimental or solipsistic (the boy poet is the only human presence in the poem). Because of its remarkably simple language and childlike vision, some critics have thought it too accessible, too approachable, not as intellectually demanding as Thomas's earlier poetry. More appreciative readers have remarked on the poem's inherent romanticism, with links to Wordsworth's pastoral "Tintern Abbey," or the retrospective "Ode on Intimations of Immortality." Other readings of the poem have called attention to its Welshness, the quality of aurality and linguistic exuberance that seems to mark it as a product of the Welsh rather than the English poetic tradition. In yet another perspective, the poem has been read in its social context, written in August–September 1945, in the direct aftermath of Hiroshima and Nagasaki, and from within the stifling social sensibility of a middle-class family living at the edge of poverty.

Even as the green and golden beauty of "Fern Hill" may be one of Thomas's crowning achievements, the intense craftsmanship and almost equal carelessness with which the poem came into being are characteristic of his whole career. John Brinnin recalls seeing more than two hundred handwritten versions of "Fern Hill" when he visited Thomas in Wales, so we know that he was writing with his usual fastidious care and precision. But we also know that the first typesetting of the manuscript for *Deaths and Entrances* had already been done when Thomas belatedly sent a copy of "Fern Hill," along with this note to the publisher: "I am enclosing a further poem, "Fern Hill," not so far included in the book, which I very much *want* included as it is an *essential* part of the feeling & meaning of the book as a whole" (Ferris, 201). The publishers did insert it as the last poem in the volume, and no reading of Dylan Thomas or of English poetry would now be complete without it.

BIBLIOGRAPHY

Brinnin, John Malcolm, ed. *A Casebook on Dylan Thomas.* New York: Thomas Y. Crowell, 1960.

Davies, James A. *A Reference Companion to Dylan Thomas.* Westport, Conn., and London: Greenwood Press, 1998.

Ferris, Paul. *Dylan Thomas.* New York: Dial Press, 1977.

Jones, T. H. *Dylan Thomas.* New York: Grove Press, 1963.

Simpson, Louis. *A Revolution in Taste: Studies of Dylan Thomas, Allen Ginsberg, Sylvia Plath, and Robert Lowell.* New York: Macmillan, 1978.

Jo Miller

"FETCHING COWS" NORMAN MACCAIG (1965) "Fetching Cows" is from NORMAN MACCAIG's seventh book of poetry, *Measures* (1965), after which, with his eighth book, *Surroundings* (1966), he turned to free verse. The poem is written in stanzas of three lines, rhyming *aba*, a kind of modified terza rima (modified because the rhymes between stanzas are not interlocking) used earlier by Shelley and Dante for much grander poems. It consists primarily of description of a rural scene little enough seen in modern life but once quite common—a cow being fetched home for milking.

The poem's opening presents us with its unnamed main character, "the black one, last as usual," who we quickly realize from the title is a cow, but a cow whom the observer has some familiarity with, as she is "last as usual," described somewhat affectionately in the way a parent might describe a child's habit of being early or late to go on trips. The poem moves slowly, in its second and third lines taking our eyes along the cow's body. We move from her "black tongue," coiling around a tuft of grass to graze while she is bringing up the rear of the herd, to her feet: "I / watch her soft weight come down, her split feet spread."

Stanzas 2 and 3 give us new kinds of movement, as "the others swing and slouch; they roll." The sea nearby is suddenly mentioned for its sound—a "tired sound"— that is "almost stopping though it never stops." The mention of the sea is perhaps both literally accurate and metaphorically true. The sea is never far from pastureland in the isles of the rural highlands of the Northwest, one-half of MacCaig's heritage, his mother's side, Highlanders who were from Scalpay. The sea also replicates the motion of the cows, rolling, swinging, almost stopping in the pauses between waves but never stopping. Into this undulating motion the collie abruptly "trots" and "plops / Into the ditch." The quickness of the collie at the observer's heels contrasts with the slowness of the cows.

Stanza 4 lets us lift our eyes from the cow's feet, from the collie, from our own heels, to look at the sky, and the "wrecked sun," which "founders though its colours fly." This wonderfully unconventional description of a sunset "wrecked" makes it seem a ship on the sea of cows, the brilliant last light of day the ship's ensigns flying in the wind. The other unusual word in the description of the sunset is *founders,* which a ship may do in the ocean in a storm when it takes on water, but it is also the word used for cows and horses who eat too much green hay, their bellies bloating with gas, which kills them.

The last stanza opens with the impatient, bored collie—"There's nothing to control," since the cows move at their own speed, almost stopping but not stopping, seemingly docile. And then the poem ends quickly with a striking, perhaps controversial, image—"The black cow is two native carriers / Bringing its belly home, slung from a pole." The image is straight out of Hollywood B films, cartoons, and the picture books of MacCaig's childhood, those boys' adventure stories of explorers in the bush of darkest Africa or New Guinea coming upon "natives" carrying meat on a pole. The two natives in the image are like the black cow's front and back legs. Between them, the meat slung on the pole is like the cow's belly, bending sway-backed from its heavy load of milk, about to be delivered by and to the farmer.

By poem's end the black cow has been so particularly noticed and affectionately described that the title becomes enriched, and "Fetching Cows" is not only a literal description of the activity of retrieving cows but also a compliment to them, for their "fetching" beauty.

BIBLIOGRAPHY
McCaig, Norman. *Collected Poems.* London: Chatto and Windus, 1991.

James Persoon

FIELD, MICHAEL (KATHARINE HARRIS BRADLEY 1846–1914 AND EDITH COOPER 1862–1913)

Katharine Harris Bradley (1846–1914) and Edith Cooper (1862–1913) were the aunt and niece who used the name *Michael Field* as their pseudonym. Katharine had a good but tragic childhood, losing her father (a wealthy tobacco merchant) in 1848 and her mother to cancer in 1868. Lissie, Katharine's older sister, was bedridden after the birth of her youngest daughter, Amy. Therefore, Katharine assisted in raising and educating her nieces, Edith and Amy, as well as taking care of the household. Katharine spent some time in France studying and she passed this knowledge on to Edith, who was curious about such things. Katharine also attended Cambridge's Newnham College for women for a short time.

In 1878, the family moved to Bristol so that Katharine and Edith could attend the University College Bristol, where they were active members of the antivivisection league. Katharine published her first volume of poetry, *The New Minnesinger* (1875), under the pseudonym *Arran Leigh*. In 1881, Katharine and Edith published *Bellerophôn* under the names *Arran Leigh* and *Isla Leigh*. It met with mediocre reviews but they decided on one last name change: Michael Field. In 1884, they published *Callirrhoë and Fair Rosamund* and were Michael Field from then on. The 1880s and 1890s were good times in Victorian England and Katharine and Edith enjoyed themselves immensely in the literary world. They met and befriended many well-known Victorians, including but not limited to Oscar Wilde (1854–1900), Charles Ricketts (1866–1931), Fr. John "Dorian" Gray (1866–1934), and W. B. YEATS (1865–1939).

Robert Browning (1812–89) was attracted to their poetry and became fast friends with the Fields, as Katharine and Edith were known. Unfortunately, he divulged the secret of their identity, that they were women and writing jointly, to a reviewer, who then made mention of it in his review. This forever damaged the Fields' ability to get honest criticism they craved from the aesthete community. Their works in the beginning garnered good critical attention, but as the years passed, this critical attention declined until their works were not reviewed at all. It was not until 1905 when they published their drama *Borgia* anonymously that their work was critically reviewed favorably once more. Every drama after that was written by "the author of *Borgia*." All of their poetry was written under the *Michael Field* name, denoting that it was a very personal form of writing for them and somehow less important than their dramas, though they are remembered more for their poetry today.

Though they suffered through several tragedies during their lifetime, nothing was more life altering than the death of their dog, Whym Chow, in 1906. So traumatic was this experience that it was the final push needed to convince them to give up their Hellenistic lesbian aesthete lifestyle and become Roman Catholics in 1907. Out of this experience, they wrote a volume of poetry, *Whym Chow: Flame of Love*. It is an elegiac love poem aimed at their dog and their conversion to Roman Catholicism. Their work therefore falls into two distinct camps: works written before their conversion and works written after it.

Of the preconversion works, *Long Ago* is the most famous. In 1885, H. T. Wharton published translations of Sappho's fragments. The Fields were so moved by his translations that they decided to "extend" them and "finish" the fragments into whole poems. The poems themselves play off the translations and create quite a ribald—for Victorian England anyway—picture. Their postconversion works vary in quality as they mainly address religious issues and adoration of God. The most commonly anthologized poems are "Prologue" and "Cyclamens," both from *Underneath the Bough* (1893). Debates exist among Michael Field scholars over several topics with the main focus on the nature of their relationship. In one camp are those who believe that the Fields were in an incestuous lesbian relationship and in the other are those that believe that they were not. Three of the most hotly contested lines by both camps are "My Love and I took hands and swore, / Against the world, to be / Poets and lovers evermore" from "Prologue." Regardless of their sexuality, the Fields left behind a treasure trove of material that is open to the critical attention that body of work is finally starting to receive.

BIBLIOGRAPHY
Donoghue, Emma. *We Are Michael Field*. Bath, Eng.: Absolute Press, 1998.

Treby, Ivor. *Music and Silence: The Gamut of Michael Field*. Suffolk, Eng.: De Blackland Press, 2000.

J. J. Pionke

"THE FIELD MOUSE" GILLIAN CLARKE (1998)

Many of the poems in GILLIAN CLARKE's *Five Fields* explore the greater political and social activities of the world beyond Wales expressed in the rural environment of daily farm life. An afternoon of hay making in Wales is interrupted with unwelcome news of war in Bosnia, lending the poem an anxious, oppressive air in "The Field Mouse."

The poem begins with a reference to military activity. Military jets frequently run maneuvers over the hill country of Britain. In the first stanza, "the air hums with jets" and the grass is a snare drum, an instrument associated with armies marching. The speaker of the poem says that they, the adults, are trying to escape the news on the radio by cutting hay with the children. But images of war continue to encroach upon the day—the natural images take on bloody significance.

In stanza 2, the narrative focuses on a small mouse that has been injured by the plows. A child takes the dying mouse "through the killed flowers" to an adult to save it. As they watch, the mouse "curls in agony big as itself." The mouse may be a small creature but the pain it feels is not unlike the agony that those dying in Bosnia must feel. Clarke continues the stanza with a scene of children kneeling on the ground "staring at what we have crushed." The mouse is a metaphor for the damage that has been done to humanity in not only the Bosnian war, but all wars everywhere, where children are helpless in the face of their parents' destructive warring.

Clarke notes that in Welsh *making hay* translates into *killing the hay*. Phrases such as "the killed flowers," the "fields hurt," and "the field lies bleeding" refer not to the happy activity of preparing the hay for winter usage, but to battlefields. Animals are inevitably killed as the farm machinery moves through the tall grass where they hide their nests. Death, of both premeditated (e.g., slaughtering of animals for food) and accidental sorts, in this instance the fatal injury of a mouse, permeates farm life. Each year, though, life is renewed with the planting and growth of new crops and new offspring of livestock. Farm life is a wonderful representation of the cyclic nature of life. In "The Field Mouse," however, the death end of the cycle is prominent and there is little hope of renewal. The fields are likened to the fields of war, specifically to those in Bosnia where the most recent killing is taking place.

Not all is destroyed, however. In the final stanza, the close of the day of hay making finds "the dusk garden" filled with the animals who were not killed: "voles, frogs, a nest of mice." What should have been a long, busy, yet fun-filled summer day has been underscored with anxiety over a war that, though far away, could have serious repercussions for everyone. Newspapers and radios have been ignored, but the "rumour of pain" is present.

That night the speaker dreams of children, "their bones as brittle as mouse ribs." The death of the mouse mingles with the deaths of children in battle, and the sound of farm activities has been replaced with that of "stammering" gunfire. In the first stanza, the speaker notes that a neighbor is enriching his soil with limestone. Residue from the limestone is carried on the wind to her land, "a chance gift of sweetness." As she ponders the dream, the narrator wonders what it would be like if the neighbor were no longer a familiar friend, but a stranger intent on "wounding [the] land with stones." An ancient custom of warfare was to scatter stones in the fields of the conquered, making them nonarable. Similar is modern warfare's planting of mines in fields to prevent them from being plowed.

The land in "The Field Mouse" not only encompasses the speaker's land, but extends into the idea of nation as well. The war that took place in Bosnia, the former Yugoslavia, was waged on the basis of territory and ethnicity. The land was divided by the hatred of one ethnic group for another. Clarke concludes "The Field Mouse" wondering whether such a fate could ever occur in her country.

BIBLIOGRAPHY

Clarke, Gillian. "The Field Mouse." Gillian Clarke Web Site. Available Online. URL: www.gillianclarke.co.uk. Accessed May 20, 2005.

Patricia Bostian

FISHER, ROY (1930–) Fisher's first major publication, *City* (1961), was a collage of lyrics, diaristic fragments, and fictionalized episodes that explored the industrial decline and contemporary presence of his home city, Birmingham, England. But the city itself was never directly named, and Fisher has said that his intention was less to describe a real city than to record the subjective experience of one. Indeed throughout his career Fisher has been concerned, not with "objective" reality, society, morality, and narrative, but with the disclosure of subjective experience, particularly in its unmediated form before the imposition of language's (and society's) distorting structures. He has said that his purpose is "to somehow enact . . . the angle the world hits me at," and his scrupulous commitment to this project justifies his claim to be "a realist."

Fisher's affinity with American MODERNISM is clear. Early in his career he became associated, though not closely, with the Black Mountain poets and their techniques. He is also influenced by early European modernism, a fact that he once wryly acknowledged by calling himself "a 1905 Russian modernist." Fisher worked as a teacher and lecturer for many years and as a jazz piano player throughout much of his life. His interest in jazz is visible both thematically and stylistically in *The Thing About Joe Sullivan* (1978) and poems like "The Home Pianist's Companion." He has also collaborated extensively with visual artists and film makers.

The moral or political dimension of Fisher's work has, apart from a small output of satirical poems, been limited to a rejection of conventional language and its political commitments. It is this aspect of his work, rather than his association with Birmingham, that makes him a "provincial" poet. "I'm not interested in making a structure which has got . . . an authoritarian centre, a rule or mandate somewhere in its middle which the work will unfold and will reach," he has said. This anarchic hostility to authority reveals a typically dissident frame of mind, which might explain why he is a relatively marginal figure in British poetry, and why this status does not concern him: He is not interested in the center to which he is considered peripheral. The rejection of familiar discourses and linguistic forms also makes high demands on the reader, who is unable to use such discourses as a "way into" the work.

Fisher has been rightly associated with the AVANT-GARDE. In recent years, critics from both sides of the mainstream/avant-garde divide have achieved a growing consensus as to his importance. Fisher is best approached through *The Dow Low Drop: New and Selected Poems* (1996), which collects much (but not all) of his work up to that date.

BIBLIOGRAPHY

Fisher, Roy. *The Dow Low Drop: New and Selected Poems.* Newcastle, Eng.: Bloodaxe, 1996.

————. *Interviews through Time and Selected Prose.* Kentisbeare: Shearsman, 2000.

Kerrigan, John, and Robinson, Peter. *The Thing about Roy Fisher: Critical Studies.* Liverpool: Liverpool University Press, 2000.

Tony Williams

"FOLLOWER" SEAMUS HEANEY (1966) "Follower" pays tribute to the skill of SEAMUS HEANEY's father, a farmer who masterfully works the land to prepare it for planting; his precision allows the sod to roll "over without breaking." Such a determined struggle with the earth works as an analogy for the act of writing poetry, as the poet seeks out the seedling wealth that lies at the base of the imagination and then plots out each line of verse, "mapping the furrow exactly." Appearing in Heaney's first book, DEATH OF A NATURALIST, this poem, along with "DIGGING," introduces what will become a lasting theme in his work: the arts of agriculture and the comparative act of crafting verse. Heaney delights in the tools of craftsmanship. In "Digging," he acknowledges "I've no spade to follow men like them," the farmers. Rather, he will "dig with" his pen. What clearly fascinates him, as seen in the poem's first few stanzas, is the process by which ground, whether literal or figurative, is made fertile.

"Follower" belongs to a group of early Heaney poems that consider the value of tools (spade, plow, hammer, and pen) associated with particular generative trades (farmer, sculptor, blacksmith, and writer). In the 1969 poem "The Forge," for example, Heaney highlights the nearly mystical occupation of a village blacksmith, who works at "an altar / where he expends himself in shape and music," the anvil ringing after contact with a horseshoe. What these labors have in common is that all engage the human hand, a hand bent on creation rather than destruction. This is not to say that destruction and dissonance are not also tensions in Heaney's work. We see this even in "Follower," a poem that carefully addresses, and even slightly sidesteps, the speaker's relationship with his father. A lack of resolution closes the poem; the father "keeps / Stumbling behind" him and "will not go away."

In the fourth and fifth stanzas, Heaney describes the way a child naturally models his own desires after the patterns set before him by his father. This inclination to imitate the "expert" is confounded by youthful physical clumsiness, and the son soon realizes the impossibility of following in his father's footsteps: "I stumbled in his hob-nailed wake, / Fell sometimes on the polished sod." The compact quatrains contain lines that are propelled forward by four strong stresses each, cutting short any inclination to adhere to the longer pentameter or blank verse of English literary tradition. Hints of working with and against tradition, embedded in both meter and etymology, abound here. Notice how the tetrameter line "SomeTIMES he RODE me ON his BACK" follows a smooth iambic pattern, and yet the line that follows, "DIPPing and RISing to the plod," resists the iambic flow and in turn enacts the movement of father and son, who are sometimes in sync but more often not.

With the speaker's claim that he "wanted to grow up and plough," we have as consolation the knowledge that the adult poet has mastered turning lines of verse (from the Latin *vertere,* meaning "to turn") if not earth, as if his pen were a plough, creating stanzas that brim over with diction characterized by blunt monosyllables (*sock, sod, pluck, hob, plod*), most of which derive from Old English. His word choice captures the generative nature of the English language, the language he primarily works in, from however complicated a position as an Irish poet.

Other elements of Heaney's preoccupation with inheritance surface here. On the one hand, the first three stanzas given over to the description of his father's skillful maneuvering suggest what is laudatory about the passing down of a commitment to craftsmanship. But on the other hand, for a Northern Irish poet, less savory kinds of inheritance must also come to mind: the barbed yet bountiful heritage of the conqueror's language (English rather than Gaelic), among other things. While such concerns are quiet in "Follower," this poem subtly questions the ritual of often unquestioning acceptance connected to all forms of inheritance.

In the final stanza, the speaker describes himself as "tripping, falling, yapping," all participial rather than simple present or past forms of the verbs, reflecting the child's sense of impotence. At the close, the poem shifts ground to the adult realization that the elderly father is now the weaker figure; the roles have been reversed. As the speaker manages his "expert" lines of verse, the image of the less able father haunts him. In an interview with John Brown, Heaney comments on his father's understanding of his son's literary ambitions, "As far as he was concerned, I was in a different world and seemed to be operating in it competently enough, but we had no developed language for linking up on subjects outside the first world we'd shared." "Follower" is a tribute to that "first world" shared by father and son.

BIBLIOGRAPHY

Andrews, Elmer, ed. *The Poetry of Seamus Heaney*. Columbia Critical Guides. New York: Columbia University Press, 1998.

Heaney, Seamus. *Preoccupations: Selected Prose 1968–1978*. London: Faber and Faber, 1980.

Miller, Karl. *Seamus Heaney in Conversation with Karl Miller*. London: Between the Lines, 2000.

O'Donoghue, Bernard. *Seamus Heaney and the Language of Poetry*. Hertfordshire, Eng.: Harvester Wheatsheaf (Division of Simon & Schuster), 1994.

Parker, Michael. *Seamus Heaney: The Making of a Poet*. Iowa City: University of Iowa Press, 1993.

Meg Tyler

"FOND MEMORY" Eavan Boland (1986) One of the most representative poems of Eavan Boland's diasporic texts, describing her early sense of detachment and loneliness as an exiled child in London, is "Fond Memory." Boland's imposed exile as a young child is going to mark her whole production of poetry. At the age of five in 1950, she had to leave Ireland for England, since her father, the diplomat Frederik H. Boland, was commissioned to London, to work as the Irish ambassador to the Court of St. James. Later, she spent a few years in New York, where her father served as president of the United Nations General Assembly. Boland's return in "Fond Memory" to her memories of detachment and dislocation is a resistance mechanism to construct a fluid poetic self that is able to escape imposed restrictive ideologies. Written in tercets, the poem records the confusions and contradictions of a girl who does not know where she belongs. Feeling neither entirely English nor "authentically" Irish, Boland advocates an exiled place, "in-between" identity claims. The first verse lines are dedicated to describing London, in particular her primary school, as an uncomfortable setting. Boland starts to feel English in some interesting ways. Whereas she hardly knows her country, the history and traditions of Ireland, she is learning English culture and history in detail. She can list the English kings, name the famous battles; she knows about the royal family of Hanover, and about the Magna Carta. Nevertheless, she is not entirely English since she cannot identify the English king as her king, and therefore she cannot share the children's sorrow when the reverend mother announces that the king has died. The second part of the poem introduces us to an interesting contrast. After school the girl goes to her house (an apparently Irish homely setting) and encounters her father playing "the slow/ lilts of Tom Moore" in the piano. The literal journey by bus describes how the speaker travels from two different and antagonistic worlds: the English world (symbolized here by the convent school) and the Irish world (her house in London). Significantly enough, the girl is described as emotionally detached, as when she heard that the king had died: She does not approach her father but rather stays at a distance. On the other hand, she is trying not to cry when hearing Moore's lilts, but funnily enough not because of any sense of loss of, or nostalgia for, Ireland (which the song actually evokes), but because of the cigarette her father is smoking. Whereas the Irish emigrants would feel a highly emotional nostalgia (a fervent affection and "fondness" toward their land of birth) when hearing Moore's lilts, the girl simply feels immune to the song. In this sense,

"Fond Memory" highlights Boland's dispossession as a child who feels neither entirely English nor Irish. In order to overcome this detachment and out of her desire to belong somewhere, the child tries to identify with Moore's song: "—as much as I could think— // I thought this is my country, was, will be again." The girl senses that Moore's song, highly emotional and sorrowful ("upward-straining"), gives voice to the sufferings of the Irish people. Furthermore she identifies her painful experiences, as an exiled and unhappy girl living in London, with the emigrant Irish the song evokes. Boland's difficulties in London, in combination with the ruptures of emigration, prompt her construction of an "imaginary homeland," an anchor molded on the symbols and narratives contained in the discourses of Irish nationalism. Nevertheless, the mature poet debunks her earlier sense of identification with the Ireland of songs and poems in the last sentence of the poem: "And I was wrong." Whereas the whole poem is constructed upon very strong enjambments and long unfolding sentences that create a melancholic tone and quicken the speed as we approach the last line, this short line brings the poem to a sudden stop and creates an anticlimax. Now Boland expresses her adult sense of detachment, as a mature poet, from that construction. First of all, nationalist songs such as Moore's mainly focus on action and resistance, and as such, they are based on a damaging politics of opposition in which the English are viewed as the enemy. Second, Boland decries the eloquence of a patriotic dialect that fuses the national and the feminine and excludes women's real lives and experiences and, therefore, her own reality as a woman. Thus "Fond Memory" shows a confused child who learns "the (English) hum and score of the whole orchestra" and yearns to assimilate "the slow / lilts of Tom Moore." By showing at the end of the poem that none of them are appropriate models to follow, Boland advocates exile and the "in-between" as the best stance to adopt. In other poems such as "An Irish Childhood in England: 1961" (1986), Boland continues to draw on her early sense of detachment and loneliness as a strategic mechanism to adopt a more critical stance on Irish nationalism. This poem is constructed in similar ways to "Fond Memory." First, Boland focuses on her earlier feelings of dislocation as an exiled girl living in London. Second, she expresses her longing for assimilation into the Irish national culture. Last, Boland shows the fallacy involved in her earlier attempts to define Ireland and advocates adopting a middle position with which to counteract essentialist notions such as "Irishness" and "Englishness."

BIBLIOGRAPHY

Boland, Eavan. *The Journey and Other Poems.* Dublin: Carcanet Press, 1986.

Kupillas, Peter. "Bringing It All Back Home: Unity and Meaning in Eavan Boland's 'Domestic Interior' Sequence." In *Contemporary Irish Women Poets: Some Male Perspectives,* edited by Alexander G. González, 13–32. Westport, Conn., and London: Greenwood Press, 1999.

Malcolm, Cheryl Alexander. "The Ugly Sister Talks Back: Eavan Boland's (Re)Visions of Ireland." *Atenea* 23, no. 1 (June 2003): 9–20.

O'Connor, Mary. "Chronicles of Impeded Growth: Eavan Boland and the Reconstruction of Identity." *Post Identity* 2, no. 2. (fall 1999). Available online. URL: http://liberal arts.umercy.edu/pi/PI2.2/PI22_Oconnor.pdf. Accessed May 22, 2008.

Villar, Pilar. "Deconstruction of 'Irishness' and 'Womanhood' in Eavan Boland's Poetry: Towards a Fluid Conception of the 'Self.'" In *Towards an Understanding of the English Language: Past, Present and Future,* edited by Luis Quereda Rodríguez-Navarro, 393–410. Granada: Editorial Universidad de Granada, 2005.

Pilar Villar Argáiz

"FOOTBINDING" Patricia Beer (1993) Patricia Beer once described herself as "a rather wonky feminist," and "Footbinding" could be categorized as one of her more feminist works. The poem appeared in her second-to-last collection of poetry, *Friend of Heraclitus,* and deals with some of the most common themes of her oeuvre: familial oppression, religious hypocrisy, and cross-cultural roles of women. In particular Beer explores the development of matrilineal subjugation in the context of centuries of cultural norms, both Western and Eastern, and the near-impossibility for an individual on either side of this East/West divide to relate fully to the empowering gender roles of the other.

The juxtaposition of West and East comes about quite literally through the books Beer describes at her poem's center. On her grandmother's "small shelf of books" are both *Foxe's Book of Martyrs* and "works by missionaries who had served / In China." These latter volumes frighten the young Beer far more than the first, for "As well / As every other heathen practice, they / Described footbinding." Yet while *Foxe's* is often considered a classic Protestant text, in the eyes of those unfamiliar with the legends of Protestant martyrdom the tales therein could very well seem as viscerally "heathen" as those norms of Chinese culture that "the missionaries revelled in" detailing to their Western readers.

More explicitly and crucial to Beer's point, the cultural norm of footbinding is a gender-specific one. Read through a postcolonial gaze, these "handsome volumes, hard / With gold and angry colours" became "heavy with Empire." The Christian sense of superiority imbued in their pages emphasized the hypocrisy in religion and in Western culture alike. For Beer personally, this hypocrisy extended to her relationship with her mother and grandmother, the same women who frowned upon such Eastern practices used to control and contain the wills of foreign maidens, but who Beer surmises "planned on twisting me / Into a little lady if it killed them." It is only with the ironic detachment of adulthood that she can dryly note the ultimate disjunction in the missionaries' narration of this oppression of women by the Other: Rather than earning permanent oppression, those whose feet were successfully bound gained ultimate societal success, as with "Their family's approval . . . they married Emperors. / An aim the missionaries did not mention." In Beer's subversive feminism, sometimes it is only by working through the gender system of one's society that a woman can truly subvert that system to her own benefit.

BIBLIOGRAPHY

Beer, Patricia. *As I Was Saying Yesterday: Selected Essays and Reviews.* Edited by Sarah Rigby. Manchester, Eng.: Carcanet, 2002.
———. *Collected Poems.* Manchester, Eng.: Carcanet, 1988.
———. *Mrs. Beer's House.* London: Macmillan, 1968.
Wilmer, Clive. "In Conversation with Patricia Beer." *PN Review* 19, no. 5 (1993): 43–45.

Caroline Kimberly

"THE FORCE THAT THROUGH THE GREEN FUSE DRIVES THE FLOWER" DYLAN THOMAS (1933)

A study in contraries, as is much of DYLAN THOMAS's poetry, "The force that through the green fuse" is a stirring conjunction of images that collide and move and collide again, creating a sense of perpetual motion, both creation and destruction occurring simultaneously in nature and in the human body. Included in his first book, *18 Poems,* this poem was one of several that Thomas published in London magazines in 1933, the year that he was 18, still living in Wales, furiously composing and sending off individual poems to London editors.

When Thomas said, "All that matters" about poetry "is the eternal movement behind it, the vast undercurrent of human grief, folly, pretension, exaltation, or ignorance, however unlofty the intention of the poem," he could have been speaking directly about "The force that through the green fuse." On its surface small and unpretentious, the poem yields some of the "vast undercurrent" of humanity's struggle with time and mortality as it celebrates the energy of living and dying occurring within the same body always at the same moment. The first line's "force that through the green fuse drives the flower" can be read as a metaphor for life-giving sperm/blood/sap pulsating through the phallic green fuse/vein/stem, but that force is also, inevitably, the destroyer, time, which gives urgency, friction, and power to the moment—and makes it unrepeatable. As much of Thomas's early work is, this poem is wrapped up in the "eternal movement" between womb and tomb, and intensely involved with the mechanisms of that movement. Noting that this poem is the most famous example, James Davies calls these early poems Thomas's "process poems, his fierce sense of life in his body and his body as microcosm of the wider, natural world, a metaphor for cosmic actions" (28).

Intensely rhythmical, as if caught up in the footsteps of time, the poem's iambic pentameter beats a strong cadence through four stanzas of five lines each, with the third line of each stanza breaking conspicuously out of the set rhythm into a shortened, three- or four-syllable line. The poem ends with a truncated couplet that gives a strong sense of finality—and fatalism. The poem's regularity is both formal and thematic; the first line of each stanza introduces a subject—the "force" in the first two stanzas, then the "hand," and the "lips" in stanzas three and four—that generally performs two opposing actions, as the "force," for instance, that "drives" the green fuse, or "drives" the speaker's "green age," also "blasts the roots of trees" and is ultimately "my destroyer." In the second stanza, the force that "drives the water through the rocks" also "dries the mouthing streams" and "turns mine to wax." In stanza three, the hand that "whirls the water in the pool" also "ropes the blowing wind" and "hauls my shroud sail," again, as always, first an excitement and then a containment of substance, energy, or spirit. The image of a "shroud sail" is a characteristically intense conjunction of life and death forces, revealing one of the ways in which Thomas's poems are both concrete and abstract at the same time, invoking strong physical, sensual experience to imagine ultimately abstract possibilities.

In typical Thomas fashion, sound and rhythm carry the emotional burden of this poem. In the first three stanzas, the headlong rush of the first two lines is stopped by the third line, which calls the goodness of the stirring "force" into question. In every stanza, the short third line contains the first final punctuation, and that, together with its blunt rejection of the iambic pentameter, marks it as a place to pause and reflect on these processes of nature and life. If, in the first three stanzas, the third line is an acknowledgment of the threat within the "force," there is a marked shift in the fourth stanza, where the third, short line, rather than darkening the prospects for the human subject, surprises us by promising a kind of redemption:

The lips of time leech to the fountain head;
Love drips and gathers, but the fallen blood
Shall calm her sores.

As this stanza's first sentence ends, the "fallen blood" of the second line is becoming a "calm," soothing force, reducing the pain of the "sores" that suggest venereal sores, created as "love drips and gathers." But the sores could also be caused by the "lips of time," which "leech to the fountain head," and suck out our vitality. Because Thomas has too often been criticized as solipsistic in his concern with the mechanical processes of the human body, it is important to hear in the "fallen blood" that "shall calm her sores" the religious and social suggestion of both Christ's sacrifice, and the killed or wounded soldiers in World War I, or those in the next, impending war that seems to haunt Thomas (along with the rest of Europe) throughout the early 1930s.

The couplet that ends every stanza and the poem itself begins with the confessional phrase "And I am dumb to tell . . ." suggesting the poet/speaker's frustrating inability to voice the fear of annihilation that he feels in the face of overwhelmingly powerful life-giving and life-sapping forces. In the first stanza, for example, the poet is "dumb to tell the crooked rose / My youth is bent by the same wintry fever." In the fourth stanza, however, the move toward redemption that began with "the fallen blood" continues into the couplet, where time creates a mysterious, almost mystically satisfying cosmic vision: "And I am dumb to tell a weather's wind / How time has ticked a heaven round the stars."

The final couplet, coming as it does on the heel of this most optimistic stanza of the poem, reinforces the motion of the scythe, cutting down the speaker in his prime, and emphasizing the paralysis of his voice, unable to say the final truth that the poem insists on at the end: "And I am dumb to tell the lover's tomb / How at my sheet goes the same crooked worm." Here *sheet* echoes both the "shroud sail" of stanza three, a winding sheet for the poet's dying body, and the sailing sheet of the lover's bed, where life is engendered and celebrated as if on the breast of the sea. The personalizing of the sheet in the word *my* makes the poet's powerfully felt sense of personal, impending doom and clashing hopefulness the final note of the poem.

BIBLIOGRAPHY

Ackerman, John. *Dylan Thomas: His Life and Work.* London: Oxford University Press, 1964.

Brinnin, John Malcolm, ed. *A Casebook on Dylan Thomas.* New York: Thomas Y. Crowell, 1960.

Davies, James A. *A Reference Companion to Dylan Thomas.* Westport, Conn., and London: Greenwood Press, 1998.

Thomas, Dylan. *Selected Letters,* ed. Constantine Fitzgibbon. New York: New Directions, 1967.

Tindall, William York. *A Reader's Guide to Dylan Thomas.* New York: Noonday Press, a subsidiary of Farrar, Straus & Giroux, 1962.

Jo Miller

FORD, FORD MADOX (1873–1939)

Although primarily remembered for a handful of his novels, most notably *The Good Soldier* (1915) and the *Parade's End* tetralogy (1924–28), Ford Madox Ford (born Ford Hermann Hueffer) wrote 13 volumes of poetry. Related to D. G. and Christina Rossetti, Ford was the grandson of the pre-Raphaelite painter Ford Madox Brown. The late Victorian aesthetic of this group is the dominant influence on Ford's earliest work, and the artistically charged environment of his childhood provided a valuable literary education. With his first volume of poems, *The Questions at the Well* (1893), published under the pseudonym *Fenil Haig,* Ford could already count W. B. YEATS among his admirers.

In 1898, Ford was introduced to Joseph Conrad, and their subsequent 10-year personal and professional association was partially responsible for the development of the literary impressionism that informed Ford's later poetry. The poetics of this later work is described in Ford's preface to his first *Collected Poems* (1913). Among his claims is an assertion that poetic value is located in the quotidian. According to Ford, pastoral imagery and stylized "poetic" diction must yield, in contemporary poetry, to the urban and the conversational. Max Saunders reminds us that many of Ford's critics overlook other techniques that contribute to the conversational tone of the mature poetry, particularly his masterful handling of sentence structure and verse form. Ford's poetics made him an attractive example for many younger poets. After EZRA POUND met Ford in 1909, Pound quickly adopted Ford's claims that poetry should be at least as well written as prose, and that "good prose is just . . . conversation." That Pound recognized Ford's anticipation of so much of IMAGISM and high MODERNISM was verified when Pound included a selection from Ford in the influential *Des Imagistes* anthology. While Paul Skinner is justified in pointing out that Ford's poetry often lagged slightly behind his poetics, Ford's defense of contemporary diction and a conversational tone as the material of poetry found an audience even beyond the modernists: Robert Lowell and Kenneth Rexroth reprinted Ford's *Buckshee* sequence (1931), his best collection, in 1966. Among Ford's other notable poems are "In October 1914 [Antwerp]" (1918), considered one of the best poems about the First World War, and the unusual dramatic poem *Mr. Bosphorus and the Muses or a Short History of Poetry in Britain* (1923).

In addition to producing his own material, Ford worked extensively with English literature as a critic and editor. The founder and editor of the *English Review* and the *transatlantic review* and a dedicated critic, Ford published established acquaintances such as Henry James, H. G. Wells, James Joyce, Gertrude Stein, and THOMAS HARDY and discovered or promoted younger authors, including D. H. LAWRENCE, Jean Rhys, and Ernest Hemingway. Plagued throughout his life by romantic and financial difficulties, and during and after his life by critical neglect, Ford's work as a poet and defender of letters is increasingly being recognized as indispensable to the transition of poetry from the Edwardian to modern.

BIBLIOGRAPHY

Ford, Ford Madox. *The Ford Madox Ford Reader.* Edited by Sondra Stang. New York: Ecco, 1986.
———. *Selected Poems.* Edited and introduction by Max Saunders. New York: Routledge, 2003.
Saunders, Max. *Ford Madox Ford: A Dual Life.* 2 vols. Oxford: Oxford University Press, 1996.
Skinner, Paul. "Poor Dan Robin: Ford Madox Ford's Poetry." In *Ford Madox Ford: A Reappraisal,* edited by Robert Hampson and Tony Davenport, 79–103. International Ford Madox Ford Studies Series. Amsterdam: Rodopi, 2002.

Christopher K. Coffman

FORMAL VERSE

Formal verse is a category of poetic forms based upon longstanding literary traditions. Poems within this category typically have regulated lengths, stanza arrangements, specified meter (such as iambic pentameter), and sometimes theme and topic. These types of poems are also sometimes referred to as closed forms, and many different forms within the realm of formal verse exist. The advent of

MODERNISM at the beginning of the 20th century brought along a turning away from formal verse among some of the period's central poets. In many ways, modernism was a reaction against the highly formal Victorian era—hence, EZRA POUND's goal "to break the iamb." Still others in accordance with his mantra "Make it new" used traditional formal verse in their work but either took liberties with the conventions of the form or used them to address subjects not normally addressed with those forms. In most cases, poets strive to make old verse forms new by stretching them to their limits, sometimes raising the question of whether or not the form remains.

Among the most recognizable of the formal verse categories is the sonnet, which is a poem composed of 14 lines of iambic pentameter (lines of five iambs: an unstressed syllable followed by a stressed syllable). Sonnets are traditionally lyric poems, which convey the ideas and emotions of a single speaker. The form entered English poetry from the Italian tradition in the early 1500s and has survived through today. Among sonnets, there are two predominant formulas, the Petrarchan, or Italian, sonnet and the Shakespearean, or English, sonnet. The Petrarchan sonnet is divided into an octave (an eight-line stanza), which poses a question or problem, and a sestet (a six-line stanza), which provides the solution, and has the rhyme scheme *abbaabba cdecde* (or alternatively *cdcdcd* for the sestet). The Shakespearean variety is organized into three quatrains (four-line stanzas) positing a problem or situation with a final couplet providing the resolution. Its rhyme scheme is *abab cdcd efef gg.*

The sonnet has long been a popular form because of its compact and highly organized structure, which makes it a helpful form when dealing with large themes like love, death, and time. However, the sonnet form is highly adaptable, and poets have used it to address these large themes in imaginative ways, and they have broken some of its technical conventions as well. Such a poem is W. B. YEATS's "LEDA AND THE SWAN." The poem ultimately addresses the issue of love, death, and time, but rather than making the poem a lyric, Yeats addresses the issue through a narrative retelling of the story of Zeus's rape of Leda in the form of a swan. Neither is the poem written in iambic pentameter; instead,

the meter is irregular, mimicking the violent, chaotic scene the poem depicts. The lines are organized into two quatrains and a sestet, going against the sonnet's traditional stanzaic structures. Despite all the ways "Leda and the Swan" breaks the sonnet form, the poem is still true to the form in important ways. The poem's themes and the organization of those themes, with the first portion of the poem describing the situation and the last portion describing that to which the situation led, match the form.

Another poem that adheres to the sonnet form in these ways is R. S. THOMAS's "The Country Clergy." The first 12 lines of the poem present the problem of the simple clergymen's work's being forgotten, and the final two lines provide the resolution, explaining that it is a problem "God in his time / Or out of time will correct." Thomas addresses problems of temporality and death in this poem and even hearkens to the lyric tradition of the sonnet by writing in the first person, but limits it to the *I* of the first line. While the poem is 14 lines long, it is not broken into stanzas. Neither does it have regular, discernable meter nor rhyme scheme. By stripping the sonnet of its ornament, Thomas makes the sonnet form new to him by adapting it to his own simple, direct, and concrete style.

A form that has been made new by the subjects it is used to address rather than changing much of the actual form is the villanelle. The villanelle is a form borrowed from French poetry in the 1800s. The form typically uses a meter (though no single one is specified) and has 19 lines organized into five tercets (three-line stanzas) and an ending quatrain. The first and third lines of the initial tercet reappear as the final line of alternate tercets in the body of the poem, then again as the final couplet of the quatrain: A_1bA_2 abA_1 abA_2 abA_1 abA_2 abA_1A_2. However, these refrains may be simplified to use only the final phrase from the lines rather than an exact repetition. It was originally used as a light verse form but has since been used by many poets to address a variety of themes. Villanelles are especially helpful to poets when trying to write a poem with an obsessive tone because the two refrains become such a pervasive force in the poems.

The most famous villanelle might be DYLAN THOMAS's "DO NOT GO GENTLE INTO THAT GOOD NIGHT," which follows the traditional villanelle form almost exactly. Rather than working with a light or humorous topic, though, Thomas uses the form to write about the serious topic of his father's impending death. The highly disciplined form is used for a topic requiring much thought and gravity. The poem is written in iambic pentameter that does not scan exactly but varies the stress patterns at key phrases in the poem. The form also becomes a container of sorts for the "rage against the dying of the light" Thomas begs his father to make.

Another form from French poetry is the triolet—used in French from the 14th century but not used in English until the 1800s. It is composed of a single octave and, as the villanelle, has two rhymes and two repeated lines: ABaAabAB. The triolet also uses a meter, but none is specified. Its topic is often love. This form was not used with great frequency in the 20th century, but THOMAS HARDY's "The Puzzled Game-Birds" is an excellent example from the early 1900s.

The sestina is a more difficult form from the French tradition. It is arranged in six sestets and a final tercet called the envoy. The form requires that the last words of each line of the first sestet be repeated in the following sestets as the last words of each line, but the ordering changes every stanza: *123456, 615243, 364125, 532614, 451362,* and *246531.* In the envoy, the words are repeated within the lines and at the end: *531* at the ends of the lines, and *246* within the lines. Sestinas are notoriously difficult to write, and while they have been relegated to the ranks of exercises for creative writing students, many poets have written them with success. One such example is W. H. AUDEN's "Paysage Moralise." In this poem, Auden creates an abstract world built around his repeated words: *valleys, mountains, water, islands, cities,* and *sorrow.* The poem presents a bleak, pessimistic outlook on society of the 20th century, and Auden uses the repetition of the form to amplify that point.

A simple but quite recognizable verse form is the ballad, a narrative poem written in quatrains with an *abab, aabb,* or *abcb* rhyme scheme and a simple meter. These poems typically tell a dramatic story (sometimes a love story) and have been written in English for hundreds of years but have their origins on the Continent.

They were originally sung, and many were popular folk songs. While many popular ballads are still sung, a literary form has also developed. Poets reinvigorated the literary form in the 20th century by placing the narrative in modern contexts, as Auden does in "As I WALKED OUT ONE EVENING." In addition to retaining traditional meter and rhyme scheme, the poem relies on the typical ballad theme of love's tragic frailty but places it in a world that has seen two world wars within 30 years of each other. JAMES FENTON strays from the usual topics of the ballad in his "God, a Poem," which uses dialogue, a convention of the ballad form, to develop the character (albeit a nonexistent character) of a highly abstract being with very ordinary, concrete things.

Many more categories of formal verse exist: the pantoum (a quatrain form dependent upon repetition), the ballade (yet another French form requiring repetition and an envoy), haiku (a form borrowed from Japanese literature), and blank verse (unrhymed iambic pentameter), to name a few. Each of these forms was used by poets in the 20th century and often updated. At a time when it was fashionable to disregard traditional formal verse in favor of free verse or open form (as with experimental MODERNISM), formal verse remained alive and useful to a great number of poets into the 21st century.

BIBLIOGRAPHY

Flack, Colin, and Ian Hamilton, eds. *Poems since 1900: An Anthology of British and American Verse in the Twentieth Century.* London: Macdonald and Jane's, 1975.

Murfin, Ross, and Supryia M. Ray. *The Bedford Glossary of Critical and Literary Terms.* 2nd ed. Boston: Bedford/St. Martin's, 2003.

Preminger, Alex, and T. V. F. Brogan, eds. *The New Encyclopedia of Poetry and Poetics.* Princeton, N.J.: Princeton University Press, 1993.

Ramazani, Jahan, Richard Ellmann, and Robert O'Clair, eds. *The Norton Anthology of Modern and Contemporary Poetry.* 3rd ed. New York: W. W. Norton, 2003.

Jordan J. Dominy

FORREST-THOMSON, VERONICA (1947–1975)

Poet, literary critic, academic—Veronica Forrest-Thomson created work that has been a major influence on experimental poetry in both Britain and the United States, yet her work, outside her posthumously published book *Poetic Artifice,* has been largely neglected in works on British and American poetry. Unfortunately since she died at age 27, her promising career was cut short, but even in that short time she published several important collections of poetry, *Language-Games* and *On the Periphery,* and set the theoretical stage for the American Language Poets, especially Charles Bernstein, a poet who largely incorporated Forrest-Thomson's poetic theories into his own.

While Forrest-Thomson was a doctoral student at Cambridge, the works of Ludwig Wittgenstein were circulating widely, and she became influenced by his exploration of language, especially his concept of a language-game, which posits that words gain meaning through context, not through reference to some outside idea. Forrest-Thomson uses this idea both in her poetry, as can be seen from the title of *Language-Games,* and in her theoretical works. In her later poetry, she focuses more on the process of writing poetry than on what it means. She explores form, playing around with allusions, quotations, and odd word positions, to push the reader to rethink how to read poetry. In addition she disrupts narratives by employing formal interruptions, focusing the reader on the actual poetic artifice being used to create the effect. Take, for example, the first two lines of "The Brown Book": "But in a fairy tale the pot too can hear and see[1] / and help the hero on his way[2]." These lines seem straightforward until we look at the reference notes at the end of the poem, which suggest other readings of the lines. Number 1 points us to a note that explains, "Certainly but it can also talk." The straightforward narrative we initially see is complicated, forcing us to focus on multiple interpretative possibilities. Forrest-Thomson presents poems aware of themselves as constructed language, and that aspect of her work allows for its most important poetic innovations.

Though her poetry is interesting, her poetic theory espoused through her book *Poetic Artifice* has had more influence on later poets. In *Poetic Artifice* Forrest-Thomson is concerned with the difference between poetic language and other types of language, suggesting that poetic language functions with a different set of rules—she refers to them as artifice—and it is this difference that allows poetry to question ordinary linguistic uses. In this book she attempts and partially manages to craft a poetic theory that can accommodate a wide range of poetry from Shakespeare to the postmodernists. That is a task few others have successfully achieved.

See also "STRIKE."

BIBLIOGRAPHY

Forrest-Thomson, Veronica. *Poetic Artifice: A Theory of Twentieth-Century Poetry.* New York: St. Martin's Press, 1978.

Mark, Alison. "Veronica Forrest-Thomson: Towards a Linguistically Investigative Poetics." *Poetics Today* 20, no. 4 (1999): 655–672.

William Allegrezza

"FOR THE FALLEN" LAURENCE BINYON (1914)

ROBERT LAURENCE BINYON's most famous poem, "For the Fallen," pays tribute to those killed in action during the First World War. Unlike the famous soldier-poets of World War I, Binyon was a comfortably settled, middle-aged man working as a curator in the British Museum when hostilities broke out. In a letter from early 1915, Binyon expressed the wish that he were young enough to "be fighting in France" (Hatcher 198). At the age of 44, he volunteered as an orderly for the Red Cross, and the staid and meticulous museum official served meals, cleaned up barracks, treated wounds, and even assisted in amputations. Heartsick at the suffering he witnessed, Binyon experienced war in a way that caused a major shift in his poetic subject matter. Though not among the best of the war poets, Binyon easily escapes being among the merely sentimental.

Although he published three books of war poetry, none of the other poems in these volumes had the resonance of "For the Fallen," his most notable achievement and the poem that has received the greatest acclaim. It was composed in the early weeks of the conflict, before Binyon had been to the front, and well before most Britons understood how protracted and devastating the war would become. The first three of the poem's seven stanzas reflect the mood of patriotism that characterized the early months of the war: England, like a mother, mourns in "proud thanksgiving" for her sons lost "in the cause of the free." There is no criticism of the war; instead the lines offer a somewhat predictable tribute to the youth and promise of the soldiers: "Straight of limb, true of eye," they remained "staunch to the end." The diction of the fourth stanza, however, is more direct, universal, and impressive:

> They shall grow not old, as we that are left grow
>   old;
> Age shall not weary them, nor the years
>   condemn.
> At the going down of the sun and in the morning
> We will remember them.

This quatrain in particular took on a life of its own as the war progressed. It was read out in countless funerals and carved into memorials and monuments throughout the empire. The sense of reserved emotion and measured grief communicates in a very simple way the dignity and human pathos of the loss of so much youth and promise. The lines also catch the somber reality of those left to grow old in their absence—a point of view comprehensive enough to acknowledge both the blessings and burdens of survival. The poem's remaining three quatrains touch on the lives lost—the absence at family tables, the life's work forgone—and on the consolation that, though hidden from view, the fallen remain forever in the "innermost heart" of those who love them, "as the stars that shall be bright when we are dust." Though a somewhat conventional image, the simile of stars is particularly apt in this case: Surrounded by a night of great darkness, their enduring brightness and countless number symbolized the grief of the whole nation. "For the Fallen" was warmly received through the years of the war and set to music by Sir Edward Elgar in his *The Spirit of England*.

BIBLIOGRAPHY

Binyon, Laurence. *Collected Poems of Laurence Binyon*. London: Macmillan, 1931.

Hatcher, John. *Laurence Binyon: Poet, Scholar of East and West*. Oxford: Clarendon Press, 1995.

Anne Kellenberger

"FOUNTAIN" Elizabeth Jennings (1958) Elizabeth Jennings traveled to Italy after winning the Somerset Maugham Award for her 1955 book *A Way of Looking*. Italy provided her with much material for her poetry, and while she was there she wrote "Fountains." In a 1969 poem entitled "In Retrospect and Hope," she writes, "When I look back at my past work / I find that the poem I like best / Is one about fountains in Rome." During her stay, she developed the belief that God manifests himself in the talents of artists and began to see art as sacrament. Artistry and spirituality became almost synonymous. In "Fountain," she uses a traditional object of inspiration and meditation to reflect the sense of calm she feels while in Rome. In a *Critical Quarterly* article, Jennings said, "Art for me is that strength, that summoning fountain." The fountain in this poem serves as a symbol of both spiritualism and artistic creativity.

In a departure from Jennings's usual more form-driven poetry, "Fountain" is free form with no rhyme scheme. Many lines have a 10 to 12-syllable length, but just as many vary from four to 15 syllables, visually reproducing on the page the varied sprays of water cascading into a fountain pool.

The poem's speaker addresses both the fountain's creator and the reader throughout the poem. "Fountain" begins with a series of instructions for the design of the fountain: "Let it disturb no more at first / Than the hint of the pool predicted far in a forest." The fountain, as a stand-in for both spirituality and artistry, should not announce its presence in blaring fashion; it should arrive softly, but insistently, upon the consciousness. It is there, necessary and "elemental," existing simply as a source of everything. The reader is instructed to approach the fountain, following its noise, as if it is a waterfall, a source of refreshment, where an afternoon could be spent "staring, but never / See[ing] the same tumult twice."

As the reader moves closer to the source of the sound, the imagery moves from natural to man-made: The waterfall gives way to a piazza where "Statues are bowing down to the breaking air" created by the fountain's noise, an image that mimics the arrival of creative inspiration or a spiritual insight as it bursts onto the consciousness.

The final stanza encourages the reader to experience both the tremendous stress of the "thousand flowering sprays" and calm stillness that flowing water creates within the psyche. Jennings then pulls the reader away from the present moment of stillness to a primitive past when "we (mankind) must have felt / Once at the edge of some perpetual stream" this same awed wonder and calmness in the presence of glory.

The wild rush of water and its ensuing calmness are both needed in the life of an artist—the passion and the introspection of one's spiritual life are similar. In "Fountain," both themes are as intertwined as the jets of water spraying from the fountain itself.

BIBLIOGRAPHY

Bradley, Jerry. "Elizabeth Jennings." In *The Movement: British Poets of the 1950s*, 87–100. New York: Twayne, 1993.

Gerlinde, Gramang. *Elizabeth Jennings: An Appraisal of Her Life As a Poet, Her Approach to Her Work, and a Selection of the Major Themes of Her Poetry*. Lewiston, N.Y.: Edwin Mellen Press, 1995.

Patricia Bostian

"THE FROG PRINCE" STEVIE SMITH (1966)

The poem, from STEVIE SMITH's eponymous 1966 collection, is one of her best known and well loved; it has also come to embody many of the critical commonplaces about her work. It takes for its subject the enchanted frog prince of fairy tale, only this frog, typically for Smith, is ambivalent about "disenchantment." The frog first attacks the limitations of the fairy story narrative that never tells its readers "if they will be happier / When the changes come" and then remarks on his own quiet contentment. Smith further subverts the story's dramatic convention by questioning whether the frog's own contentment might not be a further veil, and is "part of the spell . . . to fear disenchantment." The pun on *disenchantment* is modified in the final two stanzas when he then imagines the "heavenly" times promised him when he becomes a prince. The use of archaic social slang here sets up the poem's starkly ambiguous conclusion, "Only disenchanted people / Can be heavenly." Typically in Smith's work, religious profundity is unearthed from the seemingly playful and childlike.

This decidedly subversive reworking of a literary myth suggests an affinity with female poets such as LIZ LOCHHEAD and Anne Sexton. Jan Montefiore's study of feminism and poetry groups all three poets together, suggesting that Smith's rewriting of the frog myth is characteristic of the larger genre of poetry by woman who allude to traditional fairy tales in order to substitute their own "axioms." More recently, Romana Huk has offered a poststructuralist reading of the poem arguing that Smith in fact is suggesting our own entrapment within different social codes and registers. The subject matter, the frog who is "habituated / to quiet life," also brings to mind PHILIP LARKIN's toad poems. Smith herself often performed the poem during the 1960s and once prefaced it by calling it a "religious poem," casting the frog as the agnostic who "nearly missed the chance at that great happiness" but "grew strong in time." However, the published version of the poem is rendered more comic by its accompanying illustration of the hesitant frog. These myriad interpretations finally suggest the success of poem's polysemic voice.

BIBLIOGRAPHY

Barbera, Jack, and William McBrien. *Stevie: A biography of Stevie Smith*. London: Heinemann, 1985.

Huk, Romana. *Stevie Smith: Between the Lines*. Basingstoke, Eng.: Macmillan, 2005.

Montefiore, Jan. *Feminism and Poetry: Language, Experience, and Identity in Women's Writing*. New York: Pandora, 1987.

William May

"FROM LUCY: ENGLAN' LADY" JAMES BERRY (1982)

In a lecture delivered at the Literature of the Commonwealth Festival in Manchester in 2002, the inspiring British-Caribbean writer and professor of creative writing E. A. Markham noted JAMES BERRY's use of locale in his poetry. Markham talks of Berry's poem "Old Man in New Country" with admiration for a man who has been writing for so long, and with respect for the poem's politically conscious decision not to assume ownership of the place it depicts. Indeed Berry's "Old Man in New Country" introduces the speaking voice as being both "Watutsi and Pygmy," "both leaf and flesh grinder," ambling along in a deliberately unspecified new country.

Berry's collection of poems *Lucy's Letters and Loving* (1982) is engaged in a project that aims to achieve the opposite effect: to give a sense of place through a restricted, yet well-defined lens. In these beautifully written poems, Lucy gives an account of her experiences as a West Indian immigrant in London to her friend Leela, whom she left behind. Berry explains in his introduction to *Lucy's Letters* that he was inspired by a conversation he had with a female West Indian colleague and encouraged further by another female friend, who read the first "letter" and demanded that he do "more Lucy!" Berry went away and did exactly that in a series of interconnected poems that convey Lucy's fragmented impressions of London and British life in the capital. In one of these poems, "From Lucy: Englan' a University," Lucy describes her migrant journey as a "blind date to Mother Country" where a West Indian community might flourish while its members each make their own way.

In "From Lucy: Englan' Lady," first published in the collection *Fractured Circles* (1979), which is currently out of print, Berry explores the figure of the queen (Elizabeth II) in contemporary British culture. The queen whose name is never given in the poem, which in the first instance problematically universalizes her, is described as "the lady" with whom Lucy sympathizes. At first Lucy defamiliarizes her queen, who "come[s] from dust free rooms an' velvetan' diamond" going out very rarely to wave to her subjects "like a seagull flyin' slow slow." Berry capitalizes on the required—and politically adept—detachment of the British queen from the sociopolitical status quo in the country to establish a bond between this "Englan' lady" and his own, Lucy. "Everybody expec' a show from her," Lucy sympathetically relates to her friend Leela, "like she a space touris' on earth." As all *Lucy's Letters* do, the poem ends with a proverb that builds on the already developing metaphor of the queen as a precious bird forever performing for its own: "'Bird sing sweet for its nest.'"

What separates this poem from all the other poems in *Lucy's Letters* is the celebration of a series of seemingly unshakable opposites. One of these contradictions is Berry's use of Creole to tell the story of this queen, who speaks very differently than Lucy. Since Lucy is the speaker here—her words creating an identity for England's most famous lady—the roles of Lucy and queen are subtly reversed. Which of the two is the Englan' lady?

BIBLIOGRAPHY

Berry, James. *Lucy's Letters and Loving.* London: New Beacon Books, 1982.

Polina Mackay

FULLER, ROY (1912–1991)

Roy Broadbent Fuller was born on February 11, 1912, at Failsworth, Lancashire, where he received an education of only poor quality at Blackpool High School. He left school at the age of 16 and was apprenticed to a solicitor. Fuller qualified as a solicitor in 1933 and practiced law until his retirement in 1969, never choosing to make a career of writing. He married in 1936, and in 1937 the couple's only child, John Fuller, who also became a poet and Oxford lecturer, was born. In 1938, Fuller joined the Woolwich Equitable Building Society, as assistant solicitor. He remained with the firm until his retirement from the law and rose to the position of solicitor and eventually director.

During the 1930s, Fuller was active in Leftist literary and political movements. He published his first book, *Poems,* in 1939. Fuller claimed that W. H. AUDEN was his greatest influence. He served in the Royal Navy during World War II and was stationed from 1942 to 1943 in Kenya, in East Africa, where he performed his duties as a radar mechanic. Fuller's military service in Africa provided material for the poems in his next two books, *The Middle of a War* (1942) and *A Lost Season* (1944), which are considered among the best of the poetry of the Second World War. *The Middle of a War* first attracted critical notice of Roy Fuller's poetry. *A Lost Season* is further distinguished by the poet's use of animal imagery and his concern with the effects of colonialism in Africa. Both volumes were published while Fuller was still on active military duty.

From 1944 to 1946, Fuller was posted to the Admiralty in London. After leaving military service in 1946, he returned to the practice of law. In 1957, Fuller published his masterpiece, *Brutus's Orchard.* An edition of *Collected Poems* appeared in 1962. In addition to poetry, Fuller wrote fiction, especially mystery novels, as well as books for children. From 1968 to 1973, Fuller was professor of poetry at Oxford. Other honors included service as a governor of the British Broadcasting Corporation from 1972 to 1979; he received a knighthood in 1970. Roy Fuller died of prostate cancer in 1991.

Fuller's poetry is remarkable for its emphasis on the Wordsworthian ideal of clarity. He calls for the use of a poetic "language which has no evasions." Fuller also recognized a natural affinity between poetry and science, since both deal with the mysteries of life and the essential ironies of the universe. Roy Fuller writes poetry on the edge of apocalypse; his poems reveal his suspicion that human domination of this planet may have its limits and may in fact be nearing its end. Not surprisingly, Fuller lamented the contemporary decline of the reading of poetry, a development that he blamed on the poets themselves (Ellman 837).

See also "POEM OUT OF CHARACTER."

BIBLIOGRAPHY

Austin, Allan E. *Roy Fuller.* Boston: Twayne, 1979.

Ellman, Richard, and Robert O'Clair, eds., *The Norton Anthology of Modern Poetry.* 2nd ed. New York: Norton, 1988.

Smith, Steven E. *Roy Fuller: A Bibliography.* Aldershot, Eng.: Scolar Press, 1996.

Tony Rafalowski

"FUNERAL BLUES" ("STOP ALL THE CLOCKS") W. H. AUDEN (1936)

"Funeral Blues" has four titles, owing to W. H. AUDEN's early practice of dropping the titles of poems collected into books, using instead Roman numerals indicating the order of appearance. When collected into *Poems 1931–1936* (which itself has alternative titles, as it was published by Faber & Faber as *Look, Stranger!,* to Auden's displeasure), it was given the title "XXXIV," as it was the 34th poem of 37. It originally appeared in a play, *The Ascent of F6,* which Auden and Christopher Isherwood had written together during a month's stay in Portugal in 1936. There it appeared as a song. In the *Collected Poems* (1976) it was finally titled "Funeral Blues." It is most commonly known, however, by a portion of its first line, "Stop all the clocks," which is the way it was referred to before the 1976 title.

In contrast to the complicated history of its title, the poem itself seems relatively straightforward. It is a dirge, such as one might sing at a funeral. It consists of four stanzas of four lines each, and though the lines are of various syllabic lengths, each is more or less easily broken into four beats, as required by simple 2/4 or 4/4 time. The opening lines immediately announce the excessive nature of the grief felt by the mourners: "Stop all the clocks, cut off the telephone, / Prevent the dog from barking with a juicy bone." Not only is silence demanded, even from dogs, but time itself must stand still. The next two lines quickly make plain the purpose of this exaggerated response—death—as with "muffled drum" the coffin is taken out.

The second stanza continues the theme of heightened mourning with more public displays—even the doves in the public squares are dressed for the funeral, in crepe bows, and the normally white-gloved policemen directing traffic wear black gloves. The third stanza is slightly more extreme than the second, with the dead one equated with all the compass directions, every day of the week, and every time of day. And then the fourth stanza goes the third stanza one better, raising the stakes to a debilitatingly universal grief: "The stars are not wanted now; put out every one, / Pack up the moon and dismantle the sun," finally ending in the despairing last line, "For nothing now can ever come to any good."

The last two stanzas of the poem as we now know it did not appear, however, in the original setting of the dirge as it appeared in the play *The Ascent of F6.* There the first two stanzas were followed by three more, which referred to characters in the play, concluding with a man named Gunn who will drive the hearse: "He'll open up the throttle to its fullest power / And drive him to the grave at ninety miles an hour." The ludicrous image of the hearse roaring through the streets at a ridiculously impossible high speed signals that the dirge was not meant as a genuine expression of grief, but rather as a preposterous, out-of-balance, extreme form of it. The play itself portrays a British mountaineering expedition to a fictional peak identified by the letter and number F6, as Himalayan peaks were designated by the Survey of India in the 19th century. The leading mountaineer ascending the peak F6 has a dream about his brother, a high colonial official modeled on T. E. Lawrence (Lawrence of Arabia), the great British hero of Auden's youth. The song that became "Funeral Blues" was, in its original setting, meant as an ironic overstatement of the way "great men" are overeulogized as saviors of mankind. In a second incarnation in 1937 the dirge was rewritten as a cabaret song, to fit the kinds of burlesque reviews then popular in Berlin cabarets. This, then, seems to have been the intention of the poem.

This reading of the poem, however, has been changed by a powerful popular culture moment. In the 1993 film *Four Weddings and a Funeral,* it is spoken as the eulogy in the one funeral of the title. The moment is one of the highlights of the film, when a gay character, choking back emotion, lets Auden, another "splendid bugger" (in a humorous but empowering reference to Auden's homosexuality, turning a term of derision into praise), speak for him about the loss of a lover. Here in a modern Western culture celebrating romantic love over all else, the loss is a deeply personal one, which the bereaved does not feel able to bear, so that the extreme language no longer seems a burlesque but rather the most admirable, sincere, and authentic emotion one can have at a funeral. This reading of the poem also works well, and has perhaps replaced the earlier one for modern readers.

BIBLIOGRAPHY

Mendelson, Edward, ed. *As I Walked Out One Evening: Songs, Ballads, Lullabies, Limericks, and Other Light Verse by W. H. Auden.* New York: Vintage, 1995.

———. *The English Auden: Poems, Essays and Dramatic Writings 1927–1939.* London: Faber and Faber, 1977.

James Persoon

G

GASCOYNE, DAVID (1916–2001) David Gascoyne's life as a poet is marked by several distinct periods. Successful as a very young man, he developed his early imagist style into a distinctive and quite rare example of British SURREALISM. He wrote intense religious poetry in the years around the Second World War before becoming much less prolific in middle age, when he suffered from both addiction to amphetamines and mental illness. Finally he married and resumed the life of a man of letters. Although he no longer published substantial poetic work of his own, he continued to translate and write critical prose. In addition to his poetry, Gascoyne's writings include an early autobiographical novel, a novella, criticism, and historically important journals.

Born into a middle-class family on the outskirts of London, Gascoyne became a precocious writer of poetry as an adolescent, publishing his first volume, *Roman Balcony,* in 1932 at the age of 16. He moved to Paris and became absorbed in the tumultuous artistic, cultural, and left-wing political world of the prewar years. He was heavily influenced by continental writers, including the contemporary French poets André Breton, Paul Eluard, and Pierre Jean Jouve, and the German romantic Friedrich Hölderlin, whose poems he translated in *Hölderlin's Madness* (1938), interspersed with some of his own verses. Gascoyne's introduction to this volume reveals his youthful sympathy with the romantic conception of the poet as a "seer," who seeks to catch a forbidden "glimpse of Paradise."

Gascoyne lived in Paris from 1937 to 1939 and then again in France for periods between 1947 and 1964. He introduced European ideas and poems to Britain. For example, in 1936 he translated André Breton's manifesto, *What Is Surrealism?* Gascoyne also wrote an impressive historical analysis, *A Short Survey of Surrealism.* His own collection of mainly surrealist poems, *Man's Life Is This Meat* (1936), includes poems that celebrate the work of leading surrealist painters, including "SALVADOR DALI." He left surrealism behind when he briefly became a communist, but the influence of its spontaneous methods continued to inform aspects of his work. During the war he was found unfit for military service and worked as an actor.

Critics often claim that his third volume, *Poems 1937–1942,* is his most important contribution to 20th-century British poetry. It is a profound and troubling metaphysical meditation on the lives of human beings in a world apparently devoid of spiritual consolation. In the opening sequence "Miserere," the narrator prays to a wounded and dead God who has forsaken the world: "And may we know Thy perfect darkness. / And may we into Hell descend with Thee." This theme of human suffering in the face of divine abandonment remains the center of gravity of Gascoyne's poetic work. Suffused by the interplay of darkness and vision, his poems do not merely passively express desolate psychological states but rhythmically enact them. In 1956 he wrote *Night Thoughts,* a radio play that explores the pains and paradoxes of modern urban life, its buildings, nature, noises, and its crowds of lonely human beings.

Gascoyne's late marriage occurred after he met Judy Lewis in an asylum, where he heard her reading one of his own poems, "September Sun: 1947," to his fellow patients.

BIBLIOGRAPHY

Raine, Kathleen. *Defending Ancient Springs*. London: Oxford University Press, 1967.

Schmidt, Michael. *A Reader's Guide to Fifty Modern British Poets*. London: Heinemann, 1979.

Stanford, Derek. *The Freedom of Poetry: Studies in Contemporary Verse*. London: Falcon Press, 1947.

"THE GENERAL" SIEGFRIED SASSOON (1918)

"The General" rushes along on anapests, toying with an *abab* rhyme scheme before a tercet snaps it shut. It seems a quick read, one of SIEGFRIED SASSOON's bluntest satires, and apparently endorses a simplistic ideology: "Question authority." But the poem has more serious work to do than that. In it, Sassoon examines two ways of speaking—the idiotic cheerfulness of the title character and the weary sarcasm demotic of line soldiers' charges—while developing a third language of rebellion. It is, then, not simply a particularly bitter poem, but also close companion to Sassoon's "Soldier's Declaration," his plainspoken refusal to go on accepting official lies.

As most of Sassoon's First World War satires do, "The General" reduces the world to opposed camps: combat soldiers and noncombatants, in this case, the general with his staff of "incompetent swine." Combatants have witnessed what this war, a war unlike all others, is like and face its grim realities constantly; noncombatants have not witnessed the Great War but have only imagined it through a cloud of naivete. Ironically the general staff's "plan of attack" creates the grim reality line soldiers must live, or die, with. The officer who greets footsoldiers amiably—"Good-morning; good morning!"—is particularly loathsome, a "cheery old card," as the soldiers Harry and Jack call him, whose garrulity masks ignorance. For him it might indeed be a "good morning," but for them, "slog[ging] up to Arras with rifle and pack," the morning is anything but good. They themselves understand, while the general does not, that marching to battle with full packs is a wretched business. But they will never be able to understand, and neither will the blithely incompetent general, how bad their "good morning" will turn, they because they will die at Arras, he because he is simply incapable.

The speaker gives Harry and Jack the sarcasm they have earned through combat and the general the jovially meaningless greeting his ignorance requires. General-speak is marked by idiotic good cheer, soldier-speak by reflexive irony that mocks but otherwise does not subvert the general's authority. However, the speaker, who points out the general's incompetence, goes a step further, insisting on straightforward language that clarifies where blame belongs: "Now the soldiers he smiled at are most of 'em dead" and "But he did for them both by his plan of attack." He cannot forgive his general's homicidal ignorance, versifying his act of mutiny, revealing to all his commanding officer's unfitness to serve. His vocabulary and syntax, characterized by phrases like "did for them," is soldierly, as is Harry and Jack's. The speaker has chosen what linguistic side war forces him to be on, a side that Sassoon himself would promote when he took the logical step of refusing further service.

Jimmy Dean Smith

GEORGIAN POETRY (1911–1912)

Published in December 1912, *Georgian Poetry 1911–1912* was the first in a series of five anthologies of "Georgian" poetry published by the Poetry Bookshop in London. Subsequent volumes followed in 1915, 1917, 1919, and 1922. The anthologies were edited by Edward Marsh, who was Winston Churchill's private secretary and a friend of many of the poets published in the series, and *Georgian Poetry 1911–1912* included poems by 17 poets, including RUPERT BROOKE, WALTER DE LA MARE, and JOHN MASEFIELD. The goal of this first anthology, as Marsh writes in the prefatory note, was to "help the lovers of poetry to realize that we are at the beginning of another 'Georgian Period' which may take rank in due time with the several great poetic ages of the past." According to Marsh, few of these "lovers of poetry" had time or inclination to sort through all new publications and pick out the poems and poets that were of value, so *Georgian Poetry 1911–1912* was intended to serve as a sampling—and advertisement—for the best of the new poets. All of the poems in the first volume had been published within the past two years, and most of the poets were still fairly unknown, so Marsh included a substantial bibliography of other works by the contributors.

Georgian Poetry 1911–1912 came about as the result of several poetic projects. HAROLD MONRO's foundation of the Poetry Bookshop in late 1912 achieved part of his personal goal of popularizing poetry and making it as frequently read as the newspaper. Monro established the Poetry Bookshop in an 18th-century house in Bloomsbury, and it not only published and sold poetry but provided a venue for poets to meet each other, read their own work publicly, and even lodge for months at a time. Edward Marsh and Rupert Brooke frequented this "informal guild" for poets, as Monro called it, and when the two friends came up with the idea for a poetry anthology, the Poetry Bookshop was the natural choice for a publisher. The anthology began with Brooke's idea to write a volume of highly experimental poetry under a pseudonym in order to provoke the public into taking some notice of poetry. However, Marsh convinced Brooke that the volume should be an anthology instead of a single-author work and that the poems should be less experimental in order to lure rather than shock the public. On September 20, Marsh, Brooke, Monro, W. W. Gibson, John Drinkwater, and Arundel del Re met to appoint Marsh as editor and to make a list of poets whom Marsh would later ask for contributions to the anthology. Thanks mainly to Marsh's literary and social connections, *Georgian Poetry 1911–1912* was well publicized, well reviewed, and well received. The anthology sold well enough to go into the 10th edition by May 1914, and the poets could actually be paid for their contributions, a rare occurrence at the time.

Marsh named this "Georgian period" after England's new king, George V, who ascended to the throne in 1910. In spite of Marsh's pronouncement, however, the *Georgian Poetry* anthologies did not so much announce a new literary period as create a loose grouping that later degenerated into a critical stereotype. The year following George's ascension marked the begin-

ning of a revolt in poetry: Urged on by maestros like EZRA POUND and Monro, a new generation of poets rebelled against the poetic conventions of the Edwardian decade, especially those of the mode that David Perkins calls "the Beautiful and the Agreeable." The revolt took shape in two different ways: One was the revolutionary and highly experimental poetry of writers like Pound and T. S. ELIOT that later became known as "modernist," and the other was the more moderate Georgian mode. Moreover, the term *Georgian* did not indicate a uniform, preconceived doctrine or list of guidelines for writing poetry, as the 1912 imagist manifesto did. The closest thing to a Georgian manifesto occurred in the epigraph by Dunsany that preceded *Georgian Poetry 1911–1912,* which stated that to be a poet is "to see beauty in all its forms and manifestations, to feel ugliness like a pain . . . to know Nature as botanists know a flower." Thus Georgian poetry is usually described as a vital, optimistic style that takes rural life, beauty, and nature as its primary subject matter and that avoids such topics of the modernist poets as paralysis, alienation, and the industrialized city. Also, Georgian poetry tends to privilege Englishness to an extent that excludes international influences, so compared to their modernists contemporaries who were greatly influenced by Continental and Eastern cultures and literatures, the Georgians were quite insular. In spite of these generalizations, there is still some critical divergence in the usage of the term *Georgian*: David Perkins refers to Robert Frost as the finest of the Georgian poets, in spite of the fact that Frost was an American and never appeared in any of the anthologies (although he and his family did lodge in the Poetry Bookshop for a few weeks), and Robert H. Ross appears to use the term as a descriptor for those poets—including Pound—who participated in the poetic revolt that took place in the early years of George V's reign. However, it is perhaps most useful to reserve the term for those poets who actually appeared in Marsh's anthologies, regardless of how completely they conform to the stereotypical Georgian mode.

Many of the poems in *Georgian Poetry 1911–1912* do seem to justify the stereotypes, at least initially. Often, the poems take at least their titles from the natural world, as do W. H. DAVIES's "The Kingfisher," Wilfrid

Wilson Gibson's "The Hare," and James Stephens's "In the Poppy Field." However, many of these so-called nature poems use natural imagery as a jumping-off point into other subjects, as does D. H. LAWRENCE's highly erotic "The Snapdragon." Perhaps Brooke's stereotypically Georgian poem "The Old Vicarage, Grantchester" deserves the criticism of being too insularly English, as when the poet writes, "England is the one land, I know, / Where men with Splendid Hearts may go." Many poems also focus on the minute and seemingly trivial trappings of life, as Brooke does in "Dining-Room Tea," in which the poet has a kind of epiphany as he gazes on "plate and flowers and pouring tea." However, it cannot be said that all the poets in the 1912 anthology adhered to even these vague guidelines: Some of them display a style and subject that are neither natural in origin, slight, nor pretty. For example, in Lascelles Abercrombie's poem "The Sale of Saint Thomas," the doubting disciple who according to Christian tradition was the first missionary to India fears that India is "a land of flies! where the hot soil / Foul with ceaseless decay steams into flies!" The poem is a powerful dramatization of Thomas's desire and doubt, and at the end of the poem Christ appears to send Thomas to India and admonish him that "prudence is the deadly sin." Davies's "The Heap of Rags," about a mad homeless man in London who had experienced "so many showers and not / One rainbow in the lot," also deviates from the expected Georgian mode and demonstrates more social consciousness, at least, than does the poem on the facing page, "The Kingfisher," which begins, in a more typical vein: "It was the Rainbow gave thee birth, / And left thee all her lovely hues."

The 1912 and 1915 anthologies garnered popular and critical approval, selling 15,000 and 19,000 copies, respectively, and even earning some guarded praise from T. S. Eliot, who wrote in *The Egoist* in September 1917 that although the Georgian "is a limited genre," certain poets show "extraordinary cleverness" or "a really amazing felicity and command of language." Unfortunately in the following volumes Marsh made less judicious editorial choices, including more of the weaker poets like William Kerr and John Freeman who demonstrate the shortcomings of the Georgian mode

without its accompanying strengths. Eliot changed his tune after the 1917 volume, writing in *The Egoist* in March 1918 that Georgian poetry is "inbred." Also after the 1917 volume, sales began to drop until the 1922 volume sold only 8,000 copies and the series was discontinued. The last three anthologies cast a shadow over all Georgian poetry, and the real circumstances of the rise and fall of the style have been obscured. Now Georgian poets rarely appear on the syllabi of 21st-century poetry courses, and the movement is often thought of as something that occurred before MODERNISM and that was displaced by it, although actually the two developments in poetry sprang from the same source. For the purposes of accurate literary history as well as for the Georgians themselves, it is a misfortune that the decline of Georgian poetry and the resulting critical lambasting of which Eliot was only the front-runner caused the 1912 and 1915 volumes to be grouped with Georgian poetry's weaker incarnations and lost in the shuffle. The ferocity of the modernists' reaction to the Georgian mode is understandable, however, because the Georgians were the dominant and popular poetic force in the decade from 1912 to 1922 when the modernists were struggling for recognition and often even for publication. Moreover, the Georgians' insular Englishness, frequent prettiness, accessible style, and aversion to free verse were anathema to the modernists and the New Critics who followed them, so the fate of the Georgians is clearly a case in which literary history was written by the winners.

BIBLIOGRAPHY

Marsh, Edward. *Georgian Poetry 1911–1912*. London: Poetry Bookshop, 1912. Available online. URL: http://www. theotherpages.org/poems/gp1_title.html. Accessed on April 30, 2005.

Perkins, David. *A History of Modern Poetry: From the 1890's to the High Modernist Mode*. Cambridge, Mass.: Harvard University Press, 1976.

Rogers, Timothy, ed. *Georgian Poetry 1911–1912: The Critical Heritage*. London: Routledge, 1977.

Ross, Robert H. *The Georgian Revolt: Rise and Fall of a Poetic Ideal, 1910–1922*. Carbondale: Southern Illinois University Press, 1965.

Elaine Childs

"A GERMAN REQUIEM" JAMES FENTON **(1981)** A journalist for much of his early career, JAMES FENTON almost gave up the trade after an unsuccessful stint as the *Guardian*'s German correspondent in the late seventies. In the preface to his collection of theater reviews, *You Were Marvelous* (1983), he describes a dispiriting time in Germany and the pressures of daily reporting. But Fenton's assignment abroad had one positive result: He sketched out "A German Requiem," an elegy deeply inspired by what he witnessed in a country still dealing with its troubled past.

First published as a pamphlet in 1981, "A German Requiem" opens both his English volume, *A Memory of War* (1982), and the expanded American version, *Children in Exile* (1984). This prose meditation in some ways resembles all of Fenton's political verse: He imagines the past without an ideological point of view and teases out the universal significance of a localized memory. But "A German Requiem" diverges from Fenton's other political and serious poems. Neither rhymed nor metered, the long lines bring to mind the vatic utterances in biblical verse and Eliot at his most metaphysical. Fenton's sense of paradox, of ideas in opposition, leads to some uncharacteristic difficulties in the poem—a confusion of speaker, for example—that seldom occur in his other work.

The lengthy prose epigraph from Hobbes establishes Fenton's immediate aesthetic: to capture the past through imaginative memory. And the poem proceeds as a litany not just for the dead but also for those who survive catastrophe. The first section opens with a dialectic of the concrete and abstract, of presence and absence: "It is not what they built. It is what they knocked down. / It is not the houses. It is the spaces between the houses." An indeterminate "you" joins war widows on a bus to a memorial, and the formality of the ritual in section 3 becomes part of a "solemn pact between the survivors." We learn, in the next section, that it is better to survive after all. Indeed, we are reminded, in the sixth passage, that so many died so quickly that cemeteries could not contain them all. Finally, we hear of some actual, named victims—a doctor, a professor, an uncle—and they are all the first unmistakably German figures in the poem. Fenton reminds us that the grieving also share the guilt for a time when the "world was at its darkest." But this eloquent and philosophic poem ends with the "enquirer"—one presumes the poet here—engaging in some selective forgetting in language reminiscent of the opening lines: "It is not what he wants to know. / It is what he wants not to know." After all, Fenton implies, forgetting is the art of survival.

BIBLIOGRAPHY

Fenton, James. *An Introduction to English Poetry.* New York: Farrar, Straus & Giroux, 2002.
———. *Children in Exile.* New York: Random House, 1984.
———. *You Were Marvelous.* London: Jonathan Cape, 1983.
Motion, Andrew. "An Interview with James Fenton." *Poetry Review,* June 1982, 17–23.
Spender, Stephen. "Politics and a Poet," *New Republic,* 14 May 1984, 31–33.

Thomas Depietro

"THE GLORY OF THE GARDEN" RUDYARD KIPLING **(1910)** RUDYARD KIPLING (1865–1936) is best known for his idealization of British imperialism. His 1910 poem "The Glory of the Garden" reiterates his commitment to realism and to the contribution of the ordinary man to the making and maintenance of empire:

> Our England is a garden that is full of stately
> views,
> Of borders, beds and shrubberies and lawns
> and avenues,
> With statues on the terraces and peacock's
> strutting by;
> But the Glory of the Garden lies in more than
> meets the eye.

The garden in the poem is Kipling's own at Bateman's, the 17th-century house that was his home from 1902 until his death in 1936. Kipling planted the yew hedges and rose garden. He also created the pond with a concrete floor that was shallow enough for his children and their friends to bathe and boat in. The pond features frequently in the visitor's book where the letters *FIP* after a name refer to the immortal phrase "fell in pond." The engraving on the sundial warns, "It is later than you think."

Part of the political and intellectual crisis in Kipling's time involved the domestic situation in England, and how its landscape was changing. Widespread controversy about what exemplified the "true" England grew out of the great "gardening debates" of the late 19th and early 20th centuries. Hence Kipling too observes, "The Glory of the Garden, it abideth not in words." His poem contributes to the discussion about how gardens cultivated in people certain home-oriented and domestic virtues that were disappearing. He expresses his confidence in the deep connection between the garden, "being English," and an almost outdated belief that England was pastoral, rural, founded on agriculture. There is almost a divine injunction for the maintenance of empire: "Oh, Adam was a gardener, and God who made him sees / That half a proper gardener's work is done upon his knees."

However, hopes of a permanently ideal future are dashed with the more revealing thought that "the glory of the garden lies in more than meets the eye." Such artificial perfection and order in nature are created only by hard work. The glory of a garden encompasses not just its beauty but the human effort involved in creating and maintaining that beauty. Kipling reminds his reader, "Our England is a garden, and such gardens are not made / By singing:—Oh how beautiful! and sitting in the shade."

Like gardens, empires are a source of great pleasure and reward, but they need to be carefully nurtured if they are to flourish and if control over the riotousness of nature is to be maintained. England alone might not be able to retain its vast empire. Perhaps Kipling is pointing to a future sharing of the imperial endeavor with the colonies when he concludes, "And when your back stops aching and your hands begin to harden / You will find yourself a partner in the glory of the garden."

BIBLIOGRAPHY

Gilmour, David. *The Long Recessional: The Imperial Life of Rudyard Kipling.* London: John Murray, 2002.

Green, R. L., ed. *Kipling, the Critical Heritage.* New York: Barnes & Noble, 1971.

Jones, R. T., ed. *The Collected Poems of Rudyard Kipling.* Ware, Eng.: Wordsworth Poetry Library, 2001.

Divya Saksena

"GLORY OF WOMEN" SIEGFRIED SASSOON (1918) SIEGFRIED SASSOON is famous for his misogyny. Women are not the only people who invited his wrath—journalists, politicians, and staff officers were among the many ignorant noncombatants who earned his rage—but women seem especially overrepresented in his enraged verse and prose. Whether reeling from the smugness of a "Lady" in his diaries or suffering a misinformed aunt's concern in his fictionalized autobiography, Sassoon appears to target women. "Glory of Women" is an oft-cited example of Sassoon's misogyny. While the sonnet commences with single-minded anger toward women's naivete, it turns out, in fact, to offer sympathy, a sign that Sassoon was, given the right circumstances, able to replace his rage with pity.

Like many Sassoon titles, "Glory of Women" is ironic, even sarcastic; he does not seek to glorify women but to berate them. For the poems's first 11 lines, he succeeds. Women, those lines argue, continue believing in chivalry as if the Great War were no challenge to polite conventions. They "love us [the soldiers] when we're heroes . . . / Or wounded in a mentionable place." But, as a line soldier, Sassoon knows that bullets lack manners and that they are likely to tear into an unmentionable part of a soldier's body. Chivalry limits the topics soldiers can speak about, among them the realities of war. Throughout the opening lines, Sassoon accumulates the outdated language of chivalry (*worship, crown, ardours, laurelled*) and examples of women's ignorance. At last the two modes come together; Sassoon's quotation mark makes plain his disgust: "You can't believe that British troops 'retire' / When hell's last horror breaks them."

The first section ends with the distinctly modern image of soldiers unchivalrously "trampling the terrible corpses." While the sonnet has seemed pointed toward a bitterly sarcastic conclusion, the final three lines extend its emotional range. While the public would proclaim WILFRED OWEN the war's poet of "pity," Sassoon achieves that same quality in his final image of a German mother, ignorant of her son's terrible death, "knitting socks to send" to him at the front. Owen's "DULCE ET DECORUM EST," which likewise disabuses civilians of their ignorance, once bore the title "To Jessie Pope etc." Pope had written "Socks," a poem that depicts a domestic scene similar to that concluding "Glory of Women." It is as if, his friend and fellow soldier-poet Owen having railed at Pope's ignorance, the usually enraged Sassoon felt free to change his own sonnet's direction and discover an occasion for pity rather than rage.

Jimmy Dean Smith

GLOVER, JON (1943–)   Born in Sheffield in 1943, Jon Glover received a B.A. in English and philosophy in 1965 from the University of Leeds. There he brushed shoulders with JON SILKIN and took classes with GEOFFREY HILL. His early poems were published in *Poetry & Audience,* where he was member of the board while JEFFREY WAINWRIGHT was editor of the student review. In October 1965 he married Elaine Shaver, and in *Stand* 8:1 (1966), the couple was named as "Leeds Representatives" for the magazine, but only for one issue, since Glover became a part-time lecturer in his wife's native upstate New York for a year. Upon returning to Leeds both Glovers were once again involved in *Stand* distribution and representation.

Doing extensive work on the new critics, Glover obtained his master's in philosophy from Leeds in 1969. After graduation, he moved to Bolton to take up a position teaching English at the Bolton Institute of Technology. Poems reflecting his sensitivity to American topography were published in *Stand* 10:3 (1969) "Summer by Lake Ontario" and 11:2 (1970) "The Orchards by Lake Ontario" and "Shoreline." In "Summer by Lake Ontario" the feeling of heat is transmitted by oppressiveness where "fields thicken" and then "the heat closes on each thing." Eight of the 17 lines are end-stopped, heightening the impression of containment, where even the singing of the insects "enmeshes." But another reading of the poem might be sensual, where the building tension leads to the "sunflower buds" that will "burst."

Glover's first Northern House Pamphlet, *The Grass's Time,* appeared in 1970, followed by *The Wall and the Candle* in 1982. *Our Photographs* (Carcanet 1986) were poems about the adaptation of a 19th-century Scottish immigrant to the United States. Many of the poems mentioned are included in *To the Niagara Frontier* (Carcanet 1994), which offers contrasting visions of North American and British countryside, showing Glover to be sensitive to topography and the way that it can shape people's lives. The photograph of the Quaker cemetery on the cover of the volume illustrates the poems well, and the third section of "Thirty Miles East of Niagara" quotes various sources on local history, including the Somerset Society historical marker visible on the cover: "Quaker Cemetery Society of Friends 1924 . . ." (*To the Niagara Frontier* 46). In his review of Michael Hamburger's *The Truth of Poetry* (1969) in *Stand* 11, no. 4 (1970): 52–57, Glover notes: "There is also the whole academic tradition of the study of one particular literature ('English Poetry', 'The American Novel' etc.) which is called into question implicitly by Mr. Hamburger's demonstration of the international nature of modern poetry. . . . One's understanding grows through close attention to detail." Glover's interest in war poetry led him to work with Jon Silkin on *The Penguin Book of First World War Prose* (1989) and to publish *Negotiating the Great War: Poetry and Prose of the First World War* (1998) with Palgrave.

Chairman of the North West Arts Literature Panel from 1985 to 1987, Glover is deeply committed to his region and to his teaching. He has been managing editor of *Stand* since 1998. Since editing *Making a Republic* (Carcanet/Northern House 2002) he has begun to prepare a biography of Jon Silkin.

BIBLIOGRAPHY
Glover, Jon. *To the Niagara Frontier.* Manchester, Eng.: Carcanet, 1994.

Jennifer Gilgore

"THE GODS OF THE COPYBOOK HEADINGS" RUDYARD KIPLING (1919)   The term *Copybook Headings* refers to the sayings and universal truths that were printed on the pages of schoolbooks that children read every day in RUDYARD KIPLING's times. Kipling's poem "The Gods of the Copybook Headings" addresses the educational practice of having students copy passages from great works of literature, including the Bible, in order to improve their composition and penmanship. The premise was that as they copied these sayings repeatedly, children would also internalize essential or fundamental truths about morality and life. The "gods" to which he refers are not

pagan deities but the great thinkers and philosopher-sages of the past.

In "The Gods of the Copybook Headings" fundamental truths remain unchanged. We cannot wish them away because we would rather they were not there. The poem also refers to the *Gods of the Market-place,* which represent the commercial and profit-seeking market economics that colored the imperial worldview of the British Empire based on trade and commerce. Kipling is applying the poetic term *gods* to all literary and philosophical influences—secular and humanistic—both the foolish "Market-Place" flatterers and the wise "Copybook Headings" sages. The full poem is also sometimes seen as stating the perpetual folly of mankind in forsaking the elemental truths learned in school (the gods of copybook headings) in favor of seductive, but ultimately destructive utopian teachings (the gods of the marketplace). For example,

In the Carboniferous Epoch we were promised
    abundance for all,
By robbing selected Peter to pay for collective
    Paul;
But, though we had plenty of money, there was
    nothing our money could buy,
And the Gods of the Copybook Headings said:
    'If you don't work you die.'

However, as recent criticism has begun to acknowledge, Kipling's poem is informed by his commitment to realism and to the contribution of the ordinary man to the making and maintenance of empire. It resonates with the voice of the skeptical ordinary man, the one who slogs at the routine jobs, painstakingly copying out the immortal sayings to live life by, while acknowledging that often these sayings may be hopelessly out of step with his reality.

BIBLIOGRAPHY

Gilmour, David. *The Long Recessional: The Imperial Life of Rudyard Kipling.* London: John Murray, 2002.

Green, R. L., ed. *Kipling, the Critical Heritage.* New York: Barnes & Noble, 1971.

Jones, R. T., ed. *The Collected Poems of Rudyard Kipling.* Ware, Eng.: Wordsworth Poetry Library, 2001.

Divya Saksena

GOODISON, LORNA (1947–)

Considered to be one of the finest Anglophone Caribbean poets writing today, Goodison was born in Jamaica, which she still considers her home and which continues to inspire her writing. The eighth of nine children of a lower middle-class family, Goodison was educated at St. Hugh's high school for girls. Following her graduation, she worked as a bookmobile assistant and attended the Jamaica School of Art for a year. She further developed her talents as a painter at the School of the Art Students League in New York. Upon her return to Jamaica, Goodison worked in public relations, advertising, promotions, and she occasionally worked as an artist and teacher until 1977, when she began to devote herself to her writing. She continues to draw and paint the cover designs for many of her books and has exhibited her artwork internationally. Her first poetry collection, *Tamarind Season,* was published in 1980. She gained international attention with her second collection, *I Am Becoming My Mother,* which was awarded the Commonwealth Poetry Prize (Americas Region). This collection was followed by nine other volumes, including a *Selected Poems* (1992) and most recently *Controlling the Silver* (2005). Goodison has also published two collections of short stories. Her poetry appears in the *Norton Anthology of World Masterpieces* and she was awarded the Musgrave Gold Medal from Jamaica in 1999. She has held visiting appointments at universities in Canada and the United States and is currently associate professor of English at the University of Michigan, Ann Arbor.

Goodison's poetry is distinguished by her fluent use of the rich variety of contemporary Jamaican and American English, moving fluidly between and overlapping Standard English and Jamaican Creole, while also incorporating specialized vocabulary from the visual arts, religion, and literature. Throughout her career, she has sympathetically explored themes of race, class, and gender oppression as well as women's experience, particularly motherhood and the pains and pleasures of romantic relationships. Her writing is firmly rooted in Jamaica and explores issues of colonialism, racial and cultural identity, and economics within that context. Spirituality and music are also important and recurring themes for Goodison. Despite the often dark subject matter of oppression and heartbreak, Goodison's poetry is optimistic and life-affirming, paying tribute to the resilience of the Afro-Caribbean people, particularly women, with linguistic and rhythmic dexterity, humor, awe, and wonder.

See also "GUINEA WOMAN."

BIBLIOGRAPHY
Almendarez, Ayme, Jason Hubbard, and Kara Olson. "Lorna Goodison." Voices from the Gaps: Women Artists and Writers of Color. University of Minnesota Department of English. Available online. URL: http://voices.cla.umn.edu/vg/Bios/entries/goodison_lorna.html. Accessed May 5, 2005.

Dawes, Kwame. Talk Yuh Talk: Interviews with Anglophone Caribbean Poets. Charlottesville: University Press of Virginia, 2001.

Melissa Johnson

GRAHAM, DESMOND (1940–) Born near London in 1940, Desmond Graham was educated at the University of Leeds, in the North of England. It was here that Graham met fellow British poets GEOFFREY HILL, JON SILKIN, and TONY HARRISON, whose work, informed by questions of class, history, and culture, would later influence his own. Best known as the biographer and editor of the World War II poet KEITH DOUGLAS, Graham rose to prominence as a poet in his own right in 1980, with the publication of Bloodaxe's Ten North East Poets.

Graham's poetry is manifestly concerned with the politics of place, and this theme is explored variously in his first full-length collection, The Lie of Horizons (1993). In the award-winning "Three Snapshots" sequence, as well as "Bath," "Cambridge," and "St. Pauls," England's historic locations become sites at which the past, present, and future awkwardly coalesce: Where "[t]he past is stone they sand-blast every / year" and the present "is a butcher selling meat / by the carcase, driven in from elsewhere." Despite the seriousness of Graham's insights into the effects of history and politics upon the character and development of ordinary communities, his clever wordplay and subtle use of rhyme alike serve to perpetuate the tone of sympathetic humor that characterizes this early volume.

A more somber collection than his first, The Marching Bands (1996) reflects Graham's ongoing fascination with the major international conflicts of the 20th century and their impact upon individual consciousness. In "Postwar" and "Prague" he strives to view history through the lens of the personal, exposing the problematic estrangement of traditional historical narratives from lived human experience. As well as elegies to the war poets WILFRED OWEN, Edward Thomas, and IVOR GURNEY, The Marching Bands features "The Paintings of Titus," a fictionalized poetic biography of Rembrandt's son.

Following 1999's Not Falling, Graham produced the meticulously observed and wryly comic After Shakespeare (2001), in which he imaginatively recasts classic Shakespearean characters as the colorful, and often criminal, denizens of a contemporary northern city.

If, as Graham has remarked, much of his creative life "has been devoted to anti-war writing," his more recent work exhibits a shift toward "love poetry of various kinds." This progression is illustrated in the moving Milena Poems (2004), in which the poet, inspired by the growth of his own daughter, meditates upon the experience of parenthood and the peculiar, fluctuating dependencies that are contained within the father-daughter relationship.

BIBLIOGRAPHY
Graham, Desmond. The Lie of Horizons. Bridgend, Eng.: Seren Books, 1993.

———. Milena Poems. Hexham, Eng. Flambard Press, 2004.

M. J. Waters

GRAHAM, W. S. (1918–1986) William Sydney Graham was born in Greenock, a shipbuilding town on the Clyde near Glasgow. A succinct account of his life has been given by the poet Tony Lopez, author of the first book on Graham. Having completed an engineering apprenticeship, Graham went to Newbattle Abbey College to study literature and philosophy. There he met "Nessie" Dunsmuir, later his wife and the addressee of many poems. After war work as a naval engineer on Clydeside, he lived in Cornwall; briefly in New York, London, and Paris; and then again in Cornwall, settling in 1956 near St. Ives, where he became friends with many of the abstract painters in the famous artistic community.

Graham's major books were Cage without Grievance (1942), The Seven Journeys (1944), 2nd Poems (1945),

The White Threshold (1949), *The Nightfishing* (1955), *Malcolm Mooney's Land* (1970), and *Implements in Their Places* (1977). Though his poetry is full of Scottish idiom, Scottish literary allusion, and references to border ballads, he distanced himself from the "Scottish Renaissance." He is in the modernist tradition. His poetry of the 1940s and 1950s, though very distinctive, had some features of the apocalyptic and neoromantic styles of that period, and he suffered years of critical neglect when those styles fell drastically out of fashion. But with *Malcolm Mooney's Land* his mature voice emerged: unique and instantly recognizable. Lopez notes how Graham was influenced by pre-Socratic philosophy and by Heidegger's concept of "Being-in-the-World," with its principle that we should try not to foreclose possibilities by defining them in advance, but instead create open spaces that allow them to disclose themselves. In Graham's poetry, these ideas of openness—to others and to one's own unforeseen possibilities—find many rich analogues, such as a fishing voyage at night (*The Nightfishing*) and a polar journey (*Malcolm Mooney's Land,* for which his source was the explorer Fridtjof Nansen's journals). The poetry has a marvelous power to be at once epic and intimate; philosophically sophisticated, yet simple, affectionate, vulnerable, and funny. Sometimes he invokes the reader as a presence sensed across a space, making the poem seem extraordinarily present and alive.

BIBLIOGRAPHY

Graham, W. S. *New Collected Poems.* London: Faber and Faber, 2004.

Francis, Matthew. *Where the People Are: Language and Community in the Poetry of W. S. Graham.* Cambridge: Salt, 2004.

Lopez, Tony. *The Poetry of W. S. Graham.* Edinburgh: Edinburgh University Press, 1989.

Pite, Ralph, and Hester Jones, eds. *W. S. Graham: Speaking towards You.* Liverpool: Liverpool University Press, 2004.

Richard Kerridge

"GRANTCHESTER" RUPERT BROOKE (1912)

RUPERT BROOKE's poem "Grantchester" from the anthology GEORGIAN POETRY 1911–1912 produced by HAROLD MONRO and Edward Marsh from the Poetry Bookshop in London quickly became the quintessential Georgian lyric. It is a witty, urbane poem celebrating, ironically, simple country village life, made all the more piquant to the poet by his 1912 sojourn in Berlin, where the poem was composed. The freedom of English meadows, where, unkempt, blows an "English unofficial rose," is contrasted in the poem to the regulated and stuffy life in Germany, where "tulips bloom as they are told." Brooke's broad patriotism then turns in the poem to an increasingly specific love of place—not just England but the county of Cambridgeshire, not just Cambridgeshire but the village of Grantchester, and finally not just Grantchester but the specific elm clumps and bathing pool by Brooke's residence, the Old Vicarage. Here Brooke and his circle of Cambridge friends, who included FRANCES CORNFORD, achieved a reputation for challenging Victorian social strictures by indulging in nude bathing, for which they were named "Neo-pagans" by Brooke's friend Virginia Stephen (Virginia Woolf).

Brooke includes himself and the Neo-pagans in the poem in a gently deflating way: "In Grantchester their skins are white; / They bathe by day, they bathe by night." The paradisal Grantchester is such a garden of youth and high spirits that even aging and death are treated cleanly, bravely, and with an attitude of fun by the inhabitants, who "when they get to feeling old, / They up and shoot themselves, I'm told." "I'm told" is a broad irony here, since Brooke and his comrades are these free-living, day-and-night-bathing inhabitants. Other ironies are more subtle and uncertain.

The poem ends by asking a series of questions: "Say, is there Beauty yet to find? / And Certainty? and Quiet kind?" Is there still such a haven, such an England, Brooke asks? His image for this haven in the next lines is archetypically Georgian, a meadow: "Deep meadows yet, for to forget / The lies, and truths, and pain?" In this haven, lies and pain would be forgotten, but so, significantly, would truths. What a price to pay for "Quiet" and "Certainty." Those qualities and "Beauty" are opposed to "truths," uncapitalized and plural and thus brought into doubt. Grantchester is not only an idealized England but also an idealized Childhood and Youth, the last and fast-fading certainty of a young man on the brink of adulthood. The concluding couplet of the poem repeats the questionings of the penultimate couplets in more grounded language: "Stands the Church clock at ten to three? / And is there honey still for tea?" These lines attempt to change the abstractions of the previous lines into a final image of an English summer afternoon stopped at its honey-golden moment of perfection. The clock stands at its specific time, and "still," in another of its denotations, freeze-frames the picture. Read in context, the last line is both wistful and intentionally ironic; read alone, it easily lends itself to parody. This has been a problem for Brooke with critics. Read in context, Brooke's more outrageous lines are purposely flippant, ironic in a self-mocking way. That context also includes the times, for the Great War, which followed this poem by two years, changed our own view of the decade so much that in retrospect the Georgians and all Georgian poetry have been damned for lightness, flippancy, innocence, and nostalgia. A small poem written in praise of Brooke, "YOUTH," by his close friend Frances Cornford, came after the war to stand for the inadequacy of Brooke's poetry, and indeed of Georgian poetics as a whole. Brooke's reputation is slowly reviving among critics.

BIBLIOGRAPHY
Brooke, Rupert. *The Works of Rupert Brooke.* Ware, Eng.: Wordsworth, 1999.
Delaney, Paul. *The Neo-pagans: Friendship and Love in the Rupert Brooke Circle.* London: Macmillan, 1987.

James Persoon

"GRAVE DOUBTS" Patricia Beer (1993)

One of PATRICIA BEER's later works, "Grave Doubts" appeared in her second-to-last volume of poetry, *Friend of Heraclitus.* This poem opens with a hallmark of Beer's style, a literary allusion: "Peace to Lord Hamlet, I have never heard / Gravediggers talking." However, rather than continuing an exploration of this Shakespearean reference or utilizing the dramatis personae that so often marked her early work, Beer instead continues in the first person, reflecting on a common theme of her poetic corpus—the ghostlike impact of deceased relatives on the lives of the living, and her own anxiety over death. In so doing, her title plays on both the literal and figurative meanings of the term *grave,* as well as the spiritual doubts that mark her adult life after a childhood spent in the fundamentalist Christian denomination the Plymouth Brethren.

The theme of speech, or a lack thereof, in the constricting and enclosed grave runs throughout this piece, from "the clergyman's voice," which "had had its say and gone back into its box," to the "silence of people turning to go home / And the receding mutter of an empty / Hearse." In particular, it is the gravediggers, the "taciturn caterers" who "mutely" do their job, who most affect Beer, with their power to control one's destiny in the realm of the tomb, and who will do so "without a word." While early in the poem, following a distant relative's funeral, she "thought / That they would never cross my path again," she later discovers that these same gravediggers are in control of the fate of this cousin, buried in an unpaid-for plot. It is her obligation to him as his only living relation that drives the story of this poem. In the act of buying the plot for him and recording it in verse, Beer both listens to her cousin's long-silenced voice and offers a voice for the one whom "they deafened . . . once": "Now he will hold his peace in the deadpan dark / And will not hear spade voices ever again."

BIBLIOGRAPHY
Beer, Patricia. *As I Was Saying Yesterday: Selected Essays and Reviews.* Edited by Sarah Rigby. Manchester, Eng.: Carcanet, 2002.
———. *Collected Poems.* Manchester, Eng.: Carcanet, 1988.
———. *Mrs. Beer's House.* London: Macmillan, 1968.
Wilmer, Clive. "In Conversation with Patricia Beer." *PN Review* 19, no. 5 (1993): 43–45.

Caroline Kimberley

GRAVES, ROBERT (1895–1985)

Robert Graves may be most famous for writing historical fiction and creating a mythographic approach to cultural history that has taken on a life of its own, becoming a fashionable religion of sorts. But Graves was, in fact, primarily a poet, and the activities that brought him fame were the results of his need to earn money and to clear theoretical ground for the reception of his verse. As Randall Jarrell pointed out, Graves was always a literary writer, completely prepared to abandon facts when they no longer served his mythopoetic purposes. Thus his historical fiction—most famously *I, Claudius* and *Claudius the God* (1934)—must be read carefully, *as* fiction rather than as history made over to appeal to nonspecialists. His myth books—*THE WHITE GODDESS* (1947) is the best-known example, though *The Greek Myths* (1955) may be more frequently stumbled into—should be understood as literary theory and placed alongside such works as *On English Poetry* (1922) and (with Laura Riding) *A Survey of Modernist Poetry* (1927).

Many readers have encountered Graves without ever touching upon his poetry, but for Graves himself the poetry was central. In it he approaches romanticism with a realist's eye for detail and a metaphysical's wit and technique. In one widely read poem, "THE COOL WEB," for example, Graves raises the levels of emotion and intellectualism simultaneously. In "Ulysses" and "The Succubus," he promulgates an erotic philosophy while expressing distaste for, even disgust in, the body itself. Throughout his career, he fastidiously applies traditional technique, further cooling his emotions through rigorous versifying at the very same time that he seeks out more intense emotions to cool. Graves is constantly at odds with Graves, a theme that runs throughout his verse and the criticism about him and that he acknowledges outright in his autobiographical writing.

When his reputation was secure and Graves selected his own poetry for retrospective collections, he habitually suppressed verse from his early books *Over the Brazier* (1916) and *Fairies and Fusiliers* (1917). Arguably the homoeroticism of these poems struck the later Graves as problematic (though the one poem that regularly made it past the self-censorship, "Goliath and David," can certainly be read as a lover's lament, its focus on the frailty of "David's" body well informed by the speaker's familiarity with that body). Whatever Graves's reason for such suppression, the decision had praiseworthy results, for Graves, despite his obvious talents for writing formal (that is, defiantly antimodernist) verse, did not find warfare an especially amenable subject. The problem lies in a strength: Graves, a reflexive ironist, was not shocked into responding emotionally through his verse. He lacked WILFRED OWEN's empathy, the "pity" Owen himself writes about in the posthumously published "Preface" to his col-

lected poems. And, though he was by just about any measure a better versifier than his great friend SIEG-FRIED SASSOON, his war poetry does not rise to Sassoon's level of outrage; in Graves's hand, war is an occasion for expert versifying, not for the bursts of satirical fury that help make Sassoon, the weaker technician, in the end a much better war poet.

But Graves's ironic calm helps make his *Good-Bye to All That* (1929; revised 1957) one of the masterpieces of military life writing, a volume that readers can approach from several directions even while they must approach its rival for greatness, Siegfried Sassoon's "Sherston Trilogy," from a more severely delimited perspective. Graves's book is terrible as well as terribly funny, enraged and amused, its most profound critiques of war (and two other theaters for performance of masculinities, public school and university) couched among the funniest stories. Perhaps the most amusing section is also among the most appalling: In the Battle of the Somme, Graves was declared dead and his parents informed of his tragic demise; back home, convalescing, he found himself under zeppelin attack on the streets of London, a blackly humorous episode that anticipates the surrealism of Monty Python. The memoir is remarkable for its focus as well; again and again, Graves attacks institutionalized stupidity and approves, contrary to the best practices of modernist cynicism, of heroism even in—perhaps *especially* in—the face of apocalypse. The honesty at last proved too much for Graves's friendship with Sassoon, about whose "Soldier's Declaration" (and its sequel) *Good-Bye to All That* provides one authoritative account. Nor did the book entirely please Alfred Percevel Graves, who answered his son's book with one of his own titled *To Return to All That* (1930). But, as the critic Paul Fussell argues throughout his seminal *The Great War and Modern Memory,* the First World War required that its combatants remember and interpret experience with scrupulous honesty. And it may also be argued that Graves was, after all, clearing ground for new associations by calling the old ones into question.

Following the war, a recently married Graves entered St. John's College, Oxford. His circle included JOHN MASEFIELD and T. E. Lawrence ("Lawrence of Arabia," about whom Graves wrote *Lawrence and the Arabs*

[1927]). His most important association of the decade, and for years thereafter, was with Laura Riding. Riding brought about the end to Graves's marriage to Nancy Nicolson and also cowrote seminal works of criticism with him: Besides *A Survey of Modernist Poetry,* these included *A Pamphlet against Anthologies* (1928). Although Riding and Graves were resolutely *antimodernist* in preferring traditional verse to *vers libre,* they were among the first critics to create a modernist canon, give it the name *Modernist,* and treat it with scholarly and critical acumen. Riding is also an important figure in Graves's mythopoeisis: a strong, some might say domineering, woman who imposed her will on the poet even while he submitted to her and attempted to do her honor through his verse.

Graves's association with Riding ended in rancor in the mid-1930s, and he almost immediately began an affair with Beryl Hodge, the wife of his collaborator Alan Hodge. (Their books include the usage handbook *The Reader over Your Shoulder* [1943] and the excellent social history *The Long Week-End* [1941].) Beryl Hodge and Graves married in the mid-1940s at the same time that Graves was beginning to explore his ideas of the White Goddess. The two events are not exclusive of one another. Graves's lifelong pattern of falling in love with, and submitting to, different women did not end with his marriage to Beryl Graves—who was, in fact, the submissive partner in her union with Graves, thus implicitly urging Graves on to affairs with other women—nor did his marriage end as a result. Instead Graves theorized his serial adultery, mythologizing submissiveness as a sign of true poets' doing homage to the goddess, a sort of muse who would, in return, inspire the poet to greater achievement.

Under the influence of the White Goddess—or of his ideas as they were propounded in *The White Goddess*—Graves wrote such poems as "To Juan at the Winter Solstice," a much-canonized, much-honored lyric (his love poems to the Goddess are invariably lyrics) that is barely comprehensible to the uninitiated. The poem, as Randall Jarrell wrote, was one of the loveliest in the language, but to make sense of its meaning, the reader needs a background in Gravesian myth. (The same is true of his christological novel *King Jesus* [1946], a rewardingly transgressive reconfiguration of

the Gospels that, in the end, requires some knowledge of Goddess lore.) While it may be argued that having expertise in a poet's personal mythology unfairly ostracizes the uninitiated, mounting such arguments against Graves's works without doing the same for, say, Yeats's amounts to bigotry based, in the end, on which poet happens to be the more fashionable. Graves is not as central to the canon as W. B. YEATS (nor is his personal mythology as outright weird as Yeats's), but he deserves to be a minor part of the canon.

Graves lived till he was 90, carried on affairs with younger women he called his "muses," and attracted numerous younger writers to his home in Majorca, where he passed on some of his ideas. While the White Goddess herself has not attracted other devotees, Graves's yearning for myth and struggle in life and for transcendence thereby in poetry has influenced many who came after. Till the end he maintained that he was primarily a poet and that he wrote historical fiction for money, but such self-derogation masks the real excellence of novels that may at last prove his most lasting works; the novels were, and are, popular, but Graves's scholarship and his terrific wit enliven the historical novels, making them prime specimens of the genre. Still, his poetry, minor as it is when compared with that of others, matters as well, as he links the beginning of the 20th century with its end, extending the irony and cool traditionalism of THOMAS HARDY on into the 1970s and 1980s.

See also "DOWN, WANTON, DOWN!" "ESCAPE," "THE FACE IN THE MIRROR," "THE PERSIAN VERSION," "A SLICE OF WEDDING CAKE."

BIBLIOGRAPHY

Richard Percival Graves. *Robert Graves: The Years with Laura, 1926–1940.* New York: Viking Penguin, 1990.

Miranda Seymour. *Robert Graves: A Life on the Edge.* New York: Henry Holt, 1995.

Jimmy Dean Smith

THE GREAT WAR AND POETRY The wounds left by the 8 million dead in the Great War (better known in the United States as World War I) are still visible. In northern France, war cemeteries dot the countryside, and former battle sites have been turned into memorials or museums such as Verdun, Thiepval, or the Historial in Péronne. Statistics show that the nation of France bore the heaviest burden of the war, losing 16.8 percent of its 7,891,000 soldiers and 15.8 percent of the soldiers enlisted in its colonies. Perhaps that explains why comparatively little French poetry about the war exists. Visitors to the Imperial War Museum in London can enter a reconstructed trench (although their feet do not get stuck in the mud), and other British war memorials abound, but one of the most simple and moving is the flat stone in the poet's corner of Westminster Abbey, dedicated to RICHARD ALDINGTON, ROBERT LAURENCE BINYON, EDMUND BLUNDEN, RUPERT BROOKE, WILFRID GIBSON, ROBERT GRAVES, Julian Grenfell, IVOR GURNEY, DAVID JONES, Robert Nichols, WILFRED OWEN, Herbert Read, ISAAC ROSENBERG, SIEGFRIED SASSOON, CHARLES HAMILTON SORLEY, and EDWARD THOMAS. Their poetry allows us to understand what the war was really like, from the optimistic enthusiasm of war propaganda in 1914 to the grim realities of trench warfare. Britain lost 12.5 percent of its 5,704,000 enlisted men but gave the world the "War Poets."

In September 1914 the War Propaganda Bureau in London directed by C. F. G. Masterman called a meeting of authors to ask them to foster public support for the war. EZRA POUND had already written to Harriet Monroe in a letter dated August 1914 that "the war is eating up all everybody's subconscious energy. One does nothing but buy newspapers." Coincidentally Rupert Brooke's five sonnet sequence "1914," written in the last months of 1914 and published in *New Numbers* in December, worked nicely with Masterman's intention. The first poem, "Peace," beginning, "Now, God be thanked Who has matched us with His hour," was inspired, in part, by the Christian hymn "Now Thank We All Our God." The final poem of the sequence, "THE SOLDIER," was read by the dean of St. Paul's Cathedral in the Easter Sunday morning service. Brooke's reputation was such that the British nation felt the loss when he died at the age of 27: Winston Churchill himself wrote the obituary notice for the *Times* (April 26, 1915). In the magazine Harriet Monroe edited in Chicago, *Poetry* 6:3 (June 1915), she wrote about Brooke: "It is fitting to pause a moment over this symbol of the waste of war." To measure the way propaganda can influence poetry, one might com-

pare Brooke's sequence "1914" with Gurney's "Sonnets 1917," which were dedicated to Brooke's memory. In a letter dated February 14, 1917, Gurney wrote: "These sonnets . . . are intended to be a sort of counterblast against 'Sonnets 1914', which were written before the grind of war." But Brooke was not alone in supporting the establishment with his poetry. JOHN MCCRAE, author of "IN FLANDERS FIELDS," suggested that the living must carry the torch of the dead. Other poets, such as Charles Hamilton Sorley in "To Germany" (1914) presented both sides as blind and groping. Wilfred Owen's "DULCE ET DECORUM EST" is perhaps the definitive response to war propaganda.

Wilfrid Gibson was not a soldier when his series of poems called "Battle" was published in *Poetry* 6:5 (August 1915). But for those who engaged in battle, the chances of returning alive were not good. As Brian Gardner stated about the anthology he first published in 1964 called *Up the Line to Death*, "Seventy-two poets are represented, of whom twenty-one died in action."

Some discovered their gift for poetry at the front, such as Gurney, who was otherwise a composer and musician. Isaac Rosenberg, poet and painter, also turned primarily to poetry given the conditions of army life. Edward Thomas was a literary critic until he wrote five poems between December 3 and December 7, 1914, while trying to decide whether or not to enlist, as he finally did in July 1915, even though he was a father and aged 37. Wilfred Owen had written poems in his youth, but his real poetic voice found expression when he met Siegfried Sassoon at Craiglockhart War Hospital near Edinburgh while recovering from injury in spring 1917. The friendships formed at Craiglockhart have been transcribed in Pat Barker's novel *Regeneration* (1991) and in the subsequent film *Regeneration* (1997) directed by Gillies MacKinnon.

JON SILKIN in his introduction to *The Penguin Book of First World War Poetry* suggested that there are four stages of consciousness to be found in the poetry of the Great War: (1) "a passive reflection of, or conduit for, the prevailing patriot ideas" (Brooke and Sassoon's earliest poems); (2) a protest of war "through the recreation of physical horror" (Sassoon); (3) compassion (Owen); and (4) a merging of anger and compassion "into an active desire for change" (Rosenberg). Of the

49 poets anthologized by Silkin there were only three women, suggesting that his primary focus was on poetry of the eyewitness. Those who experienced the trenches used graphic descriptions. Owen's "The Sentry" captured the stench of the trench: "What murk of air remained stank old, and sour / With fumes from whizbangs, and the smell of men." Several lines from "To Robert Nichols" by Robert Graves recall the severe conditions endured in winter: "Here by a snowbound river / In scrapen holes we shiver." Rosenberg spoke of the lice in "LOUSE HUNTING" and the rats' feasting on the corpses of both sides in "BREAK OF DAY IN THE TRENCHES": "Droll rat, they would shoot you if they knew / Your cosmopolitan sympathies." T. H. Hulme's "Trenches: St Elio" noted the elements of domestic regularity, "desultory men / Pottering over small fires, cleaning their mess-tins," contrasting sharply with the same men walking "over a dead Belgian's belly." Gurney described "books, cakes, cigarettes in a parish of famine, / And leaks in rainy times with general all-damning," the half-rhyme calling attention to the damning famine in "Laventie." Rosenberg's "DEAD MAN'S DUMP" is as factually accurate as it is unbearable: "The wheels lurched over sprawled dead / But pained them not, though their bones crunched." Sassoon in "A Working Party" noted, "three hours ago he stumbled up the trench; / Now he will never walk that road again," indicating a change from his earlier optimism: "War is our scourge, yet war has made us wise" (in "Absolution" from 1915). Sassoon's elitist background perhaps makes his poems of revolt more remarkable, such as "THE GENERAL" (1917), which suggests the incompetence of army command. His friend ROBERT GRAVES wrote along the same vein, "they hadn't one Line-officer left, after Arras, / Except a batty major and the Colonel, who drank" in "Sergeant-Major Money" (1917).

No reader can remain indifferent to this poetry or to the beauty of nature that somehow prevailed amid the carnage: "Soon the spring will drop flowers / And patient creeping stalk and leaf," wrote Richard Aldington in "In the Trenches." Rosenberg celebrated birdsong in "RETURNING, WE HEAR THE LARKS." Francis Edward Ledwidge wrote of "maternal hills" and "mingling waves of pastoral streams" in "In France." Gurney's "Laventie" remarks the town's plane trees, and "Towards Lillers" mentions "October lovely bathing with sweet air the plain" in the midst of a march and thirst and "two ditches of heart-sick men."

David Jones, who survived his time as a private soldier in the Royal Welsh Fusiliers with a leg wound (July 1916) and then trench fever (February 1918), causing his timely departure from France, did not begin writing about the war until 1927. His long poem *In Parenthesis* was published in 1937 and used myth to give shape to his experience, in ways reminiscent of Joyce's *Ulysses* and T. S. Eliot's *THE WASTE LAND*. His source text was a Welsh poem from the sixth century about the raid of 300 Celtic warriors on the Saxon kingdom of Deira, resulting in only one survivor. Praised by Herbert Read as a great epic, *In Parenthesis* was criticized by Paul Fussell for its ambiguity. JON STALLWORTHY insists that the poem should be read carefully, using the notes to the text. He provides a commentary for part 7, suggesting that Jones is trying to emphasize that 19th-century decency has been dissolved "by a new order, here represented by the 'physicist's destroying toy'" (Stallworthy, 2002, 182).

While the "War Poets" were those who experienced battle firsthand, many people who never went to the front tried their hand at verse about the war. James Longenbach described how Ezra Pound and W. B. Yeats, who spent the winters of 1913–16 at Stone Cottage, at the edge of Ashdown Forest in Sussex, were able to continue their work, keeping some distance from the war atmosphere, while writing "war poems that express a sensibility close to that of the poets who suffered in the trenches" (*Stone Cottage: Pound, Yeats, and Modernism,* 1988, xi). Pound actually submitted a piece called "War Verse" for publication in *Poetry* in 1914, but it was never printed. In it, he advised those writing verse about the war: "Be still, give the soldiers their turn" rather than "scrape your two-penny glory" (Longenbach 115). Yeats, when asked by Edith Wharton to write a poem about the war for *The Book of the Homeless,* an anthology to raise money for Belgian refugees, wrote "A Reason for Keeping Silent." He would later exclude Wilfred Owen from the *Oxford Book of Modern Verse,* which he compiled in 1936.

Many women also wrote poems about the war, often from the vantage point of active participants.

Vera Brittain, Eva Dobell, Cicely Hamilton, Winifred Letts, May Sinclair, Millicent Sutherland, Katharine Tynan, and Marjorie Wilson served as nurses. MAY WEDDERBURN CANNAN was employed in the Intelligence Service. In most cases, the women's poems protest what is seen as useless waste, and many of the poems perform exacting social criticism. Amy Lowell's "Chalks: Black, Red, White" (*Poetry* 6:6, September 1915) depicts a boy named Tommy who is playing with lead soldiers: "Tommy is a lucky boy. / Boom! Boom! Ta-ra!" but when the pitcher spills in the game, it is full of blood. ELEANOR FARJEON exclaimed in "Peace," where Peace speaks in the first person, "Nations! Whose ravenous engines must be fed / Endlessly with the father and the son." EDITH SITWELL, in "The Dancers (During a Great Battle, 1916)" noted, "The floors are slippery with blood" but "We still can dance, each night." CHARLOTTE MEW addressed the lack of recompense that memorial monuments bring in "THE CENOTAPH" with "God is not mocked and neither are the dead."

Who then should be considered a "War Poet"? While today's definition should be more inclusive than the group of soldier-poets, the question is still debated. Should poets not yet born during the conflict of 1914–18 who have chosen to write about it be included? PHILIP LARKIN depicted the atmosphere outside recruiting offices in Britain in 1914, when men were ready to enlist "grinning as if it were all / An August Bank Holiday lark" in "MCMXIV." SEAMUS HEANEY wrote "In Memoriam Francis Ledwidge" for the Irish poet who was killed by a stray shell while building a road through mud, July 31, 1917. GEOFFREY HILL's *The Mystery of the Charity of Charles Péguy* (1983) portrays the French poet who was killed the day before the official beginning of the first Battle of the Marne.

Poetry about war existed well before the Great War, but in some ways "war poetry" was consecrated as a genre through its traumas. The poet writing about war today would do well to heed the caution Rosanna Warren offers in "Mud" (2003): "It's not as simple as rhyming 'mud' and 'blood'."

BIBLIOGRAPHY

Fussell, Paul. *The Great War and Modern Memory*. Oxford: Oxford University Press, 1975.

Hibberd, Dominic, ed. *Poetry of the First World War*. London: Palgrave Macmillan, 1981.

Reilly, Catherine W., ed. *Scars upon My Heart: Women's Poetry and Verse of the First World War*. London: Virago, 1981.

Sherry, Vincent. *The Great War and the Language of Modernism*. Oxford: Oxford University Press, 2003.

Silkin, Jon, ed. *The Penguin Book of First World War Poetry*. London: Penguin, 1981.

Stallworthy, Jon. *Anthem for Doomed Youth: Twelve Soldier Poets of the First World War*. London: Constable & The Imperial War Museum, 2002.

Jennifer Kilgore

"GUINEA WOMAN" LORNA GOODISON (2000)

LORNA GOODISON chose this powerful testament to the strength of her great grandmother's cultural heritage, originally included in the collection *I Am Becoming My Mother* (1986), as the title poem for *Guinea Woman: New and Selected Poems* (2000). This free verse lyric poem with occasional irregular end rhyme depicts the African Diaspora as family history. The title refers to the speaker's great grandmother, a woman from Guinea in West Africa who has gone to live in Jamaica and work on a plantation, undoubtedly as a result of the slave trade. Although enslaved or employed at menial labor, Great Grandmother is described as regal and elegant and having special powers. Not only can she see behind her, but she can predict rain through the itching of her warts. Her grace is depicted in comparisons to a "cane stalk" and an "antelope," while her profile is described as fit to grace a "guinea coin" and her scent as "royal." These metaphors connect her African origins with her life on a cane plantation in Jamaica as well as highlighting her strength and grace.

While gazing out to sea, Great Grandmother captivates a white sailor, whose ship leaves him behind at Lucea harbor—perhaps because he refuses to leave her. Whether the relationship is consensual is not clear, but Great Grandmother gives birth to a female child. This blue-eyed child is subsequently claimed by the white man—identified as "backra" in Jamaican dialect—and reared in his household under his name. The poem describes how the white household denies the child's mixed race heritage by attempting to erase signs of her mother's Guinea origins in her scent and her walk.

While the poem as a whole highlights the powerful and enduring presence of Great Grandmother, there are indications of her oppression and lack of autonomy. Her narrow waistline is described as being "the span of the headman's hand," an image that suggests her subordinate position and the possibility that she might be subject to unwanted physical intimacy. Her relationship with the sailor is described as fated and "anchored in the unfathomable sea." Just as the sea has taken her to Jamaica and frequently draws her gaze, it takes the sailor to her. Their coupling is described in a metaphor in which her body is figured as the continent of Africa. The sailor sails up her "straits," just as the colonizers and slavers had, and the evidence of his journey is the mulatto child whose kinship to her is denied.

The last stanza of the poem addresses the speaker's great-grandmother and her descendants directly and observes the reemergence of her features and coloring in later generations of the family. It is clear that the speaker sees this as a positive trend, reversing the privileging of European features by the white sailor. While Great Grandmother may not have been able to claim her own child, the speaker proudly claims her as an ancestor.

BIBLIOGRAPHY

Almendarez, Ayme, Jason Hubbard, and Kara Olson. "Lorna Goodison." Voices from the Gaps: Women Artists and Writers of Color. University of Minnesota Department of English. Available online. URL: http://voices.cla.umn.edu/vg/Bios/entries/goodison_lorna.html. Accessed May 5, 2005.

Dawes, Kwame. Talk Yuh Talk: Interviews with Anglophone Caribbean Poets. Charlottesville: University Press of Virginia, 2001.

Melissa Johnson

GUNN, THOM (1929–2004)

Thom Gunn was recognized in the early 1950s as one of the most interesting voices of his generation. He was included as the youngest member of THE MOVEMENT in Robert Conquest's 1956 anthology New Lines, in whose introduction Conquest announced a new "Movement" in British poetry, one that valued formal structures and plain language, as opposed to the romantic and surrealist excesses of DYLAN THOMAS. By the 1970s, Gunn was often mentioned in the same breath as PHILIP LARKIN, SEAMUS HEANEY, and his friend TED HUGHES as the most important contemporary British voices, even though he had been living in America since the early 1950s. While his reputation in Britain did not continue to grow as large as that of those three, he remained for more than 50 years an important voice in English and American poetry.

Thomson William "Thom" Gunn, was born in Gravesend, England, but grew up in Hampstead, London. His parents divorced when he was 11; he and his younger brother Ander lived with his mother, until four years later, when she committed suicide by gassing herself (and was found by them, an event recounted almost 50 years later in the poem "The Gas Poker"). After two years national service (in the army), Gunn attended Trinity College, Cambridge, studying under F. R. Leavis and writing most of the poems that would be gathered in his first book, Fighting the Terms (1954). At Cambridge, he met Mike Kitay, an American, who became his lifelong partner. In 1954, Gunn left England for graduate study at Stanford University, near San Francisco, where he met Ivor Winters and J. V. Cunningham, two conservative poets who valued the classical tradition in literature. Winters was writing in syllabics, in a style shared with his correspondents in Britain, ROBERT BRIDGES and ELIZABETH DARYUSH, and this provided Gunn a transitional form as he worked toward free verse, which most Americans were writing.

From 1958 to 1966 Gunn taught at the Bay Area's other great university, the University of California at Berkeley, but then gave up academic life for full-time writing, though 10 years later he again began teaching at Berkeley, one term per year as a visiting lecturer, until he retired from teaching in 1999. Gunn's embracing of his new American identity was evident in his second book of poetry, The Sense of Movement (1957), which is divided into two halves that appear to reflect both his English heritage and his new American life. In it, he also began to move away from the English tradition of formal verse to experiment with syllabics. The often-anthologized "On the Move" from that collection, with its black-jacketed motorcyclists, contrasts sharply with the almost stuffy Englishness of Philip

Larkin's bicyclist with his pants clips in "CHURCH GOING," from the same decade.

Gunn continued to write and publish prolifically after his move to San Francisco. *My Sad Captains* in 1961 and *Touch* in 1967 continued the move toward free verse, while not abandoning the formal lyric, and the content became increasingly more open as well, with *Touch* acknowledging intimacy with a male lover and *Moly* (1971) celebrating rock music and drug use. *Jack Straw's Castle* (1976) explored darker aspects of these experiences. Then in the midst of the growing acquired immunodeficiency syndrome (AIDS) epidemic of the 1980s Gunn began to write powerful poems about illness and death, collected as *The Man with Night Sweats* (1992), which was unanimously awarded the Lenore Marshall/Nation poetry prize. Some of its poems, such as "Still Life," "The Missing," and "A Blank," have become his most frequently anthologized works.

Gregory Woods sees Gunn as "a model of the contemporary gay poet in transition," who has passed from a closeted Cambridge in the 1950s to "'post-Liberation' San Francisco"; what Gunn "hides at the outset of his career and what he reveals as the years pass" is what gives his body of work its "solid thematic unity" (230). His career, Woods argues, parallels modern gay history. Throughout his years in America, Gunn remained a perfectionist in poetry, who never entirely abandoned formal verse. His poetic voice, too, remained characteristically English, modest and almost impersonal, despite his engagement with some of the most powerful issues of his time.

BIBLIOGRAPHY

Hoffmann, Tyler B. "Representing AIDS: Thom Gunn and the Modalities of Verse. *South Atlantic Reviews* 65, no. 2 (spring, 2000): 13–39.

Kleinzahaler, August. *Thom Gunn.* London: Faber and Faber, 2007.

Woods, Gregory. *Articulate Flesh: Male Homo-Eroticism & Modern Poetry.* New Haven, Conn.: Yale University Press, 1987.

James Persoon

GURNEY, IVOR (1890–1937)　Eleven of Ivor

Gurney's poems were chosen by ANDREW MOTION for *First World War Poems* (2003), placing him in quantitative second position with SIEGFRIED SASSOON to WILFRED OWEN—a clear indicator that his reputation has changed. After years of limited attention only from specialists in the field, Gurney is now considered as one of the most important poets of the Great War. One of the contributing factors to his reevaluation was the publication of *Collected Poems* (Oxford University Press, 1982), and especially *Collected Letters* (Carcanet, 1991), which detail the experiences behind the poems. As had the poet-painter ISAAC ROSENBERG, he wrote some of the most poignant poems about trench warfare.

Born in 1890, in the town of Gloucester, and from a middle-class background, he had musical talent that was noticed early. His godfather and friend the Reverend Cheesman helped to provide funding for him to attend the Royal College of Music when he won a scholarship in 1911. By 1913 he had begun to write verse, though most of his energies still went toward musical composition (musical settings for five Elizabethan lyrics composed in 1913, published in 1920). After trying diverse positions as an organist and finding it impossible to sustain himself financially from musical engagements, he joined the Fifth Gloucester Reserve Battalion in February 1915. They landed in Le Havre in May 1916, and he soon found himself at the front from Riez Bailleul, to Richebourg-St Vaast, Aubers Bridge, Albert, Vermand, and Guemappe, Musical composition at war was difficult, so increasingly he turned his attention to poetry.

Corresponding with Marion Scott, a friend from Royal College days, he described conditions in the trenches and sent manuscripts of poems that were later collected in *Severn & Somme* (November 1917). On Good Friday, April 7, 1917, he was wounded in the upper arm and spent six weeks in a hospital in Rouen. His next assignment, in the Machine Gun Corps, had him working on the front in Ypres in August. In September he was gassed at St Julien (Passchendaele). After spending months in recovery, he was eventually discharged in October 1918. But seemingly unable to readjust to civilian life, following a series of temporary jobs, he was committed to a mental asylum in Gloucester in 1922. Concerned friends obtained his transfer to the City of London Mental Hospital at Dartford in Kent, and although his musical compositions, poems, and letters continued through the

1920s, his profitable work eventually ceased. He died at Dartford on December 26, 1937.

Severn & Somme (1917) contrasts the English countryside and home to the experience of war: The closing of "Song" pleads "Do not forget me quite, / O Severn meadows" (*Collected Poems*). In "Bach and the Sentry" the uplifted spirit of a sentry remembering music asks, "When I return, and to real music-making, / And play that Prelude, how will it happen then?" (*Severn & Somme and War's Embers,* 1987). The volume closes with five "Sonnets 1917 (To the Memory of Rupert Brooke)" (*S&S and WE*), which counter Brooke's sonnet sequence "1914," poem for poem, by portraying war while questioning the prowar rhetoric. The duty of soldiers is not something so heroic and purifying as in Brooke's "Peace" or "Safety"—Gurney speaks rather of "Pain, pain continual; pain unending" (*Collected*).

Only one other volume of poems was published during Gurney's lifetime, *War's Embers* (1919). The first collection including other unpublished work appeared in 1954: *Poems by Ivor Gurney,* edited by Edmund Blunden (Hutchinson). Even today, no one volume contains all of his poems, and there is no complete bibliography for his musical and literary work.

See also "The Silent One."

BIBLIOGRAPHY

Gurney, Ivor. *Collected Poems.* Edited by P. J. Kavanagh. Rev. ed. Manchester, Eng.: Carcanet / Fyfield, 2004.

———. *Severn & Somme and War's Embers.* Edited by R. K. R. Thornton: Ashington, Eng.: Mid Northumberland Arts Group and Manchester: Carcanet, 1987.

Lucas, John, *Ivor Gurney.* Tavistock, Eng.: Northcote House/ British Council, 2001.

Jennifer Kilgore

HANNAH, SOPHIE (1971–)

HANNAH, SOPHIE (1971–) Born in Manchester, Sophie Hannah has been hailed as "the brightest young star in British poetry" and "a genius" in the British press. She has written novels, short stories, and books for children but is most recognized for her poetry. She has received a number of awards and performs at literary festivals and schools. She holds an M.A. in creative writing from Manchester University and has taught creative writing herself.

If one tried to cluster her thematic concerns, one group of poems might be called "revenge poems," poems about horrible men or broken relationships, which are occasionally treated with sadness but more often with biting humor: "Deep down, the thing that makes you want to weep / Is knowing that you once felt sentimental / About this wholly unattractive creep" ("A Day Too Late"). Another group of poems center on houses, homes, and locations, and on the movement between those places and the opportunities that train journeys and car rides offer for human relationships. Her more recent writing adds an interest in medicine, treatment, and motherhood, often with irreverence: "Eat the wrong cheese, go on the game. It's not all doom and gloom: / Never again will baby be as safe as in your womb" ("Mother-to-be"). Hannah also writes about her role as a poet: "Call Yourself a Poet" is an ironically programmatic piece in which she affirms her professionalism as a poet. The lyrical "I" tries a number of professions but finds that each needs training, so she decides to become a poet: "Oh, how restrictive! All those rules! / While verse, my friends, is free."

Sophie Hannah, without exception, adheres to rules of prosody and rhyme in her poems, often with humorous results—"The cast consists primarily of horses— / They gallop to the ending, which of course is / A happy one, where nobody divorces" ("Summary of a Western")—and she sustains a 25-line poem on merely two rhymes ("In the Bone Densitometry Room"). Hannah is the mistress of the punch line: She often finishes on unexpected humorous twists, such as "I love / The ugly millionaire" ("Marrying the Ugly Millionaire") or on deeper insights into relationships: "What's bound to cause the rows is / that he treats houses like hotels / and she, hotels like houses" ("Hotels Like Houses").

Hannah is at her best when she combines traditional forms, such as sonnets, rondels, or villanelles, with witty contemporary contents, such as alternative medicine or the trouble involved in learning how to drive. "An Aerial View" is a modern take on the carpe diem motif and ends on "An aeroplane is just a pub that flies." One of her many sonnets is a "Philanderer's Ansaphone Message," and in her "Ghazal," written in an old Arabic verse form that abounds in melancholy, it is a traveler to Mars who is missed by a woman on Earth.

Sophie Hannah draws together profound insights into the tragedies and absurdities of contemporary life, a truly comic spirit, and a close attention to language, form, rhythm, and rhyme; it is this combination that makes her one of the most exciting contemporary British poets.

BIBLIOGRAPHY

Hannah, Sophie. *First of the Last Chances.* Manchester, Eng.: Carcanet, 2003.

———. *The Hero and the Girl Next Door.* Manchester, Eng.: Carcanet, 1995.

———. *Hotels Like Houses.* Manchester, Eng.: Carcanet, 1996.

———. *Leaving and Leaving You.* Manchester, Eng.: Carcanet, 1999.

———. *Selected Poems.* London: Penguin, 2006.

Susanne Reichl

HARDY, THOMAS (1840–1928)

Born into the lower laboring class of rural England, Thomas Hardy had modest beginnings that did not preclude the success he later enjoyed in life nor after his death. Indeed it was these common origins that would help shape his life, both personal and literary. His father, a bricklayer, and mother, a domestic servant, raised Hardy in the traditions, culture, and rituals of the English countryside that would endear themselves to Hardy and become a hallmark of his works. Of special importance were the local and family histories orally passed on to Hardy and the early experiences with church and music. Hardy's father was a passionate musician and played violin in the church choir, often including young Hardy in this experience.

Hardy's mother, who herself could read and write, enrolled Hardy in several schools during his youth. While his attendance was brief and hardly resembled a traditional, rigorous education, the experience left its mark on Hardy. He developed into a smart, sensitive (called by one biographer "morbidly sensitive"), and driven young man. Hardy studied on his own voraciously, even teaching himself Greek and Latin, in hopes of gaining acceptance into Cambridge University.

In 1856, shortly after his 16th birthday, Hardy was apprenticed as an architect, thus beginning his first professional career. During this time, he met Horace Moule, a young, gifted scholar who encouraged Hardy's studies and no doubt became a sort of mentor to the young man. As Hardy learned the skills of his apprenticed trade, he also leaned on his friendship with Moule for scholarly discussions and learning.

Moule and Hardy would remain friends for a number of years until Moule succumbed to depression and committed suicide in 1873.

Even though Hardy was learning a valuable trade, his heart was still set on a formal education. In 1862, he made the leap to London with hopes of using his skills as an architect eventually to fund his academic interests. It was here that his rural values—social, familial, and religious—encountered direct conflict with the more radical modes of thought of the era. This exposure to urban life—to culture, the educated, and of course the more unpleasant aspects (prostitution, crime, poverty)—shook the very core of his beliefs and made him question the validity of what he had previously accepted as true.

His London experience culminated into the eventual loss of his Christian faith, a constant questioning of social mores, and, perhaps most importantly, the realization that his dream of a Cambridge education was financially impossible. Not satisfied with the prospects of an architectural career, Hardy threw all his efforts into writing novels—a compromise he reached with himself upon concluding that the financial rewards of poetry, his first love, were unlikely to provide a steady income.

His first attempt, *Poor Man and the Lady,* was rejected by several publishers. *Desperate Remedies* (1870), his second effort, met with more success and he followed it up with *Under the Greenwood Tree* (1872). This moderately successful novel would help define his style and establish the pattern of his career—creating stories of vivid pastoral scenery and rural characters that were read by a predominantly urban audience.

During this period of transition from architect to novelist, Hardy met his first wife, Emma. Married in 1874, Emma enjoyed the prestige of being a successful writer's wife, a title Hardy achieved with his fourth novel, *Far from the Madding Crowd* (1873), and often helped Hardy during the composition process. However, Hardy could be cold and distant at times, ignoring his wife's own literary abilities and even engaging in suspicious relationships with other women. This, coupled with the incongruity of their religious and social beliefs, eventually created a rift between them.

This rift was further widened by Hardy's publication of *Jude the Obscure* (1895). Perhaps bolstered by the incredible critical and financial success of *Tess of the d'Urbervilles* (1891), Hardy sought to attack what he saw as some of the great social problems of his time. Hardy's treatment of love, marriage, education, religion, and gender issues profoundly hurt and embarrassed the religious and traditional Emma. It also, unfortunately, incensed the critics. Dubbed *Jude the Obscene* by one reviewer, the novel was perceived as antimarriage, antichurch, and even pornographic. Pained and confused by such a stream of critical rejection, Hardy ended his career as a novelist after 15 novels and embarked on the next career of his life: poetry.

This transition is one of the most striking features of Hardy's career. After enjoying success as a prominent novelist, Hardy, at the age of 58, published *Wessex Poems*. He continued to publish poetry until his death. In all he wrote nearly 1,000 poems, including an epic poem of the Napoleonic Wars, *The Dynasts*. His "POEMS OF 1912–1913," written after his first wife's passing, are particularly moving, elegizing her and coming to terms with the emotional gulch that had formed between them.

Hardy once commented that his works were "a plea against man's inhumanity to man—to women—to the lower animals." In this way, there is a certain social awareness in his works. Hardy was keenly sensitive to the various injuries inflicted upon the weaker members of society and to the hypocrisy of social institutions. As a witness to the assimilation of the pastoral realm of his youth into the industrial, increasingly capitalistic, and Darwinistic society of the mid- to late 1800s, Hardy offers a unique perspective of the past-turning-to-present-turning-to-future and the sometimes blatant cruelty of such progress and modernity. This can range from the mildly insensitive, as in *Under the Greenwood Tree,* when the soon-to-be replaced fiddlers of the church choir are told, "It will not be that fiddlers were bad, but that an organ was better," to the tragic, as in Jude Fawley's inevitable failure and final question, "Why did I not give up the ghost when I came out of the belly?"

Jude's question, one of being *unmade,* is a recurring theme throughout Hardy's works. Consciousness for Hardy was much more of a curse than a blessing. In the poem *Tess's Lament* the speaker wishes that "my life

unbe" and "my doings be as they were not / And gone all trace of me." It is this acute awareness of one's own suffering and helplessness that makes an *unexistence* preferable to living.

These questions and observations about the nature of consciousness—and the force that bestows humankind with such a consciousness—create much of the tension in Hardy's works. Education and experience had left Hardy bereft of any type of Wordsworthian beliefs. As much as he may have wanted to believe in a universal goodness or benevolent force behind the workings of life—and it should be noted that he did indeed want very much to see any sign that would prove this to him—he found it nearly impossible to reconcile his desire with his perceptions. What he perceived to be true was, as Angel Clare reminds us, "God's not in his heaven—All's wrong with the world." The God Hardy believes to exist, if he does exist at all, is one who is indifferent to our pain and has probably forgotten us.

His works are a reflection of his great sensitivity, the loss of an absolute truth, and the resulting internal conflict. He was not just an agnostic, but (in his own words) a "churchy" agnostic, seeming to need the social ritual that church afforded him. His seasonal migrations between London and his rural home, Max Gate, typify his struggle to reconcile his early rural influences and his later social and literary success. He believed his novels to be a plea against cruelty, yet he seemed at times coldly insensitive to the needs of those around him, and, as his first wife, Emma, said of him, "His liking for people seems quite apart from any sense of obligation to them." Labeled a pessimist by his contemporaries, a claim easily understood when one considers the terrible way Hardy often treated his fictional people, he believed himself a realist and had faith that humanity could better their lot in life. When Hardy died in 1928, his ashes were buried at Westminster Abbey and his heart laid to rest in Stinsford churchyard, a rural church with past family ties. It seems even in death, Hardy was unable to find a place in which his mind and heart could comfortably rest together.

BIBLIOGRAPHY

Gittings, Robert. *Thomas Hardy's Later Years*. Boston: Little, Brown, 1978.

————. *Young Thomas Hardy.* Boston: Little, Brown and Company, 1975.

Millgate, Michael. *Thomas Hardy: A Biography.* New York: Random House, 1982.

————. *Thomas Hardy: A Biography Revisited.* Oxford: Oxford University Press, 2004.

Tomalin, Claire. *Thomas Hardy.* New York: Penguin, 2007.

Turner, Paul. *The Life of Thomas Hardy.* Oxford: Blackwell, 1998.

Justin Vance

HARRISON, TONY (1937–)

Tony Harrison's poetry is fundamentally concerned with a particular postwar construction of Englishness nuanced by cosmopolitan experience and by an awareness of corrosive, influential historical forces, celebrating its class and gender identity even as it finds them repeatedly compromised. Undoubtedly a major English poet of the late 20th and early 21st centuries, he has in his work courted controversies made all the more urgent by the very necessity of its themes, which originate in his own identity and experience and the impact that education has had upon them. Born into a working-class family in Leeds, Harrison has led a life transformed by learning, first as a grammar school pupil and then as a scholarship student to Leeds University (where he read classics and was a contemporary of GEOFFREY HILL and JON SILKIN), and subsequently by his extended creative involvement in translation and theatrical production with cultural institutions such as the National Theatre. His work in poetry and drama constantly seeks to express a fundamental set of tensions between his class origins and the demands of the conventionally "elevated" poet (leading, in turn, to a concern with issues of gender roles and identities that informs some of his most powerful work but that also sometimes results in what Marilyn Hacker calls "masculine myopia"). Other tensions exist between his regional background (in the North of England) and the tendency for cultural institutions, imitating a key division in English society, to locate themselves in the South; between his experience of modern, postwar social and cultural contexts and his translations and reworkings of classical and medieval texts; and between the demands of poetry as an aesthetic mode of expression and as a form of social critique and commentary, or between private and public writing (Carol Rutter has argued that "Harrison's poetry is all, in some sense, public," even at its most painful moments of private confession). The measure of Harrison's success in negotiating and exploiting these conflicts is that he has made them wholly his own. No other contemporary English poet demonstrates such a range of assured cultural reference, and none has contributed more to the redefinition and reinvigoration of canonical forms and meters like the sonnet and the iambic pentameter. His poetry exploits the potentials of rhythm and rhyme in surprisingly modern ways, with a creativity verging on the Byronic, demonstrating his own statement (in an interview with Richard Hoggart) that rhyme is "actually an instrument of discovery."

Harrison's first collection, *Earth Works,* was published in 1964; it was followed six years later by *The Loiners,* which won the Geoffrey Faber Memorial prize, and whose title refers to the slang term for residents of Leeds, as well as alluding to sexuality and solitude ("loners") as constituent elements of the poetic universe of poems like "The Pocket Wars of Peanuts Joe" and "The Songs of the PWD Man." His early poetry expresses postwar experience through muscular, allusive language, drawing on classical and European reference points as well as personal memories and experiences of reading and education to extend their significance. His major sonnet sequence "The School of Eloquence," published in various collections and pamphlets through the 1970s and 1980s, establishes the tension between intensely personal experience and the public duties of poetry as Harrison's chosen ground. These 16-line or Meredithian sonnets repeatedly demonstrate Harrison's mastery of the form and offer powerful meditations on love and loss, addressing the deaths of Harrison's parents as well as his own sense of "loss" in relation to the cultures and histories they embodied. He addresses education, literacy, reading, and knowledge as social and personal forces that both divide and unite. These themes are further developed in the (in)famous *V.,* published in 1984 and object of a political furor when a reading of it was broadcast on channel 4 in 1987, an event that established Harrison in the national consciousness. *V.* confirms in its title division and opposition as paradoxical constituents of artistic unity (*V.* standing for both *versus* and *verses,* the title only offering what Jeffrey Wainwright calls "an apparent unity"). The poem is at once an extended elegy for Harrison's parents, a protest poem (written during the 1984 miners' strike, a moment of crisis in English class relations, but also a protest against other *v* words like *violence* and *vandalism*) and a lament for cultural change and loss. It has been described by Bernard Levin as "one of the most powerful, profound and haunting long poems of modern times." Harrison's subsequent television work includes *The Blasphemer's Banquet* (1989), a defense of Salman Rushdie, and *The Shadow of Hiroshima* (1995), which won the Heinemann Award in 1996.

Harrison's work for the stage includes translations or versions of plays by Molière, Racine, and Aeschylus, and he has often produced drama for performance outside conventional auditoriums—*The Trackers of Oxyrhynchus,* for example, incorporating fragments of Sophocles' *The Ichneutae,* premiered in Delphi's ancient stadium in 1988. He consistently reworks ancient texts into modern forms, reasserting the relevance to contemporary concerns of older writing and offering revision as a major and urgent function of the modern poet. He has worked on opera with Jacob Druckmann and on musical work with Harrison Birtwistle. He resisted the lure of the poet laureateship on the death of TED HUGHES in 1998 and published (again controversially, involving a public argument with the eventual incumbent ANDREW MOTION) a poem, "Laureate's Block" (2000), about the experience. His war poetry ("My images are all to do with the War," he wrote, of another war, in an early autobiographical statement [1971]) includes *A Cold Coming: Gulf War Poems* (1991) and poetry written for *The Guardian* during the war in Bosnia in 1995. His most recent collection is *Under the Clock* (2005).

See also "LONG DISTANCE," "TURNS."

BIBLIOGRAPHY

Astley, Neil, ed., *Bloodaxe Critical Anthologies.* Vol. 1, *Tony Harrison.* Tarset, Eng.: Bloodaxe, 1991.

Byrne, Sandy, ed., *Tony Harrison—Loiner.* Oxford: Oxford University Press, 1997.

Harrison, Tony. *Selected Poems.* Harmondsworth, Eng.: Penguin, 1995.

———. *Theatre Works 1973–1985.* Harmondsworth, Eng.: Penguin, 1986.

John Sears

HARWOOD, GWEN (1920–1995) Gwen

Nessie Foster was born in Taringa, Brisbane, in 1920 into an upper middle-class family and attended Brisbane Girls' Grammar School between 1933 and 1937. She developed strong interests in literature and philosophy and trained as a musician. After a brief period as a novice in the convent of Poor Clares, she became a music teacher and organist at the All Saints Church of England, Brisbane. She maintained her involvement with music and religion throughout her life and together with the inspiration she gained from German philosophy (namely, the works of Ludwig Wittgenstein and Martin Heidigger), her 12 books of poetry and prose and operatic libretti testify to the inspiration she drew from these areas.

Upon marrying the academic William Harwood in 1945, she moved to Tasmania and gave birth to four children between 1946 and 1952. A key motif of her early poetry is professors. Professor Eisenbart is used to dismantle the universals of male knowledge and authority as he capitulates to a young female presence, usually an artist, while Professor Krote, the onetime musical prodigy, implodes in self-pity and the knowledge that while he accepts his mediocrity, surrounding society does not acknowledge its mediocrity. Accompanying her themes of foregrounding the intimate, unseen moments of women's lives and this satirizing of male knowledge making is Harwood's own history of "shape-shifting" in terms of her manifold use of pseudonyms (her first poems were published as Francis Geyer, thereafter Walter Lehmann, Miriam Stone, and T. F. Kline) and her relish at play and disguises, revealed in the correspondence with Thomas Riddell published as *Blessed City* (1990). Furthermore it has been noted how her vivacity, charisma, and apparent candor at interviews exist alongside the isolated "Tassie housewife" and her rejection of being named a woman poet.

Australian literature has a tradition of anxiety regarding its universality, and Harwood is arguably an example of a poet who has created a body of work that deals with universal themes at a time when her contemporaries were engaged with the literary of the national and geographical cultural psyche. Although she migrated from the northern parts of eastern Australia to its southernmost state Tasmania, she never traveled outside Australia. The limitations of language in articulating that which lies beyond it are consistently tested in her poetry, which, Trigg offers, "engages with this problem at a grammatical level . . . at the same time invoking memory, and the irresistible power of poetry to move beyond itself . . . to suggest the possibility of a life outside language" (Trigg 5).

Feminist cultural studies have attended to Harwood beyond the framework of national and local poetic traditions of the doggedly masculinist canon of Australian poetry. Surrounded by models of independent-thinking women in both her mother and grandmother (who introduced her to poetry), Harwood offers throughout her work tributes to women's fortitude in motherhood and as artists contending with the male-dominated academy. "Home of Mercy" shows an unmarried mothers' institution, where "by two and two the ruined girls are walking," and "in the Park" a mother is left bereft of her own identity after child rearing: "To the wind she says, 'They have eaten me alive'" (*Poems*, published 1963). The irreconcilable duality of artist and mother is captured in "Burning Sappho," where "the clothes are washed, the house is clean. / I find my pen and start to write," and "Suburban Sonnet": "She practises a fugue, though it can matter / to no one now if she plays well or not" (*Poems Volume Two*, published 1968). David Malouf's review of Harwood's *Selected Poems* (1981) termed her as "the most passionate and intellectual of poets, the most openly sexual, and the most ecstatically religious" (17). *The Lion's Bride* (1981) and subsequent collections saw the emergence of a mature poetic voice that is confident and personal, marking Harwood's increased national prominence wherein she won a host of awards and honorary doctorates; her poetry is set for school curricula, and the Gwen Harwood Poetry Prize was created after her death, "in memory of a much-loved Tasmanian poet."

BIBLIOGRAPHY

Hoddinott, Alison, ed. *Blessed City: Letters to Thomas Riddell 1943*. Sydney: Collins/Angus and Robertson, 1990.

———. *Gwen Harwood: The Real and the Imagined World*. Sydney, Australia: Angus and Robertson, 1991.
Malouf, David. "Some Volumes of Selected Poems of the 1970s." *Australian Literary Studies* 10 (1981): 17.
Strauss, Jennifer. *Boundary Conditions: The Poetry of Gwen Harwood*. St. Lucia, Qld.: University of Queensland Press, 1992.
Trigg, Stephanie. *Gwen Harwood*. Melbourne: Oxford University Press, 1994.

Deirdre Osborne

"HAVISHAM" CAROL ANN DUFFY (1993)

The title makes one wonder why CAROL ANN DUFFY left out the *Miss*, which is the usual epithet of the character in Charles Dickens's *Great Expectations*. In the novel, she is a tragic figure who was jilted by her fiancé on their wedding day. Since then, she has worn her wedding clothes and kept her dust-ridden room exactly as it was when she was betrayed: The clock is set at the same time and the moldy wedding cake stares her in the face. In order to avenge herself the male sex, Miss Havisham manipulates the young Pip into falling for her beautiful ward Estella, whose frozen heart breaks the hero's. This intention to make Pip suffer presents her as a cruel character because the story is told through his voice.

Here Duffy puts the record straight, and connects Miss Havisham's misery to any woman's. The no-holes-barred vernacular, such as "Beloved sweetheart bastard," runs across the unrhymed quatrains in a style that is characteristic of Duffy's poetry in the 1980s and 1990s. Just as the title evokes the "Miss" by omitting it, the theme of the poem is the presence of what cannot be: the great expectations for a future that were dashed by disloyalty. The bitterly isolated word *spinster* explains why she cannot endure to be known as "Miss." Consumed by desire for her absent husband's body, Havisham wants to kill it because she can never return to her former self. The strength of emotion is not only presented through the harsh consonants and bitter vocabulary about "love's hate" but through the violent symbols, such as stabbing the wedding cake, which make visible the pain that cannot be verbalized. The inexpressibility of her feelings is further projected through color symbolism: green for jealousy, puce for anger, a red balloon for life "bursting in my face." The dramatic monologue asks the reader to feel sorry for the melancholy spinster who hates the fact of being one; however, it also allows us to consider whether or not she has control and choice over being stuck in the past.

BIBLIOGRAPHY

Bentley, Vicci. Interview with Carol Ann Duffy. *Magma* (winter 1994): 17–24.

Bertram, Vicki. *Gendering Poetry: Contemporary Women and Men Poets.* London: Rivers Oram Pandora Press, 2004.

Duffy, Carol Ann. *Mean Time.* London: Anvil, 1993.

Jane Dowson

H. D. (HILDA DOOLITTLE) (1886–1961)

Hilda Doolittle was born in 1886 in Bethlehem, Pennsylvania, where her father was the director of the Flower Observatory at the University of Pennsylvania; her mother had a Moravian background, which her daughter absorbed in her early years and then used in her mature writing. After graduating from Friends Central School, she attended Bryn Mawr College in 1905–6; she did not do well, although she did meet Marianne Moore, a fellow student there, and William Carlos Williams, a medical student at the University of Pennsylvania. During this time her relationship with EZRA POUND, whom she had met in 1901, blossomed. She was twice engaged to him, and his mentoring of her may have been one of the reasons for her leaving Bryn Mawr. Pound wrote a number of poems for her, collected in "Hilda's Book," and called her "dryad," one of the identities with which she played for much of her life.

In 1911, H. D. went to Europe, ostensibly for a relatively short visit, with Frances Josepha Gregg, perhaps the first woman with whom she was in love and to whom she wrote poetry. When Gregg returned, H. D. stayed on. Pound, who admired some of her poetry, introduced her to people in the London literary scene, including RICHARD ALDINGTON, whom she married on October 18, 1913. One of the most famous incidents in modern literature occurred that same year when Pound read some of H. D.'s verse and declared, "But Dryad, this is poetry." He then sent some of her poems to Harriet Monroe, the editor of *Poetry,* signed "H. D. Imagiste." The IMAGISM movement, begun by Pound,

may indeed have been at least in part based on H. D.'s poems, for they are almost precise illustrations of Pound's theories (especially after the editing Pound subjected them to). H. D., Aldington, and Pound spent time together (often at the British Museum), expressing their devotion to ancient Greece and to a spare, crystalline verse. For instance, in "Oread" (initially published in *The Egoist* in 1914), the mountain nymph expresses her view of the sea with a series of imperatives, such as "splash your great pines / on our rocks," which suggest how her environment determines her point of view.

H. D. published her first volume of verse, *Sea Garden,* in 1916. With her husband at the front in World War I, she became assistant editor of *The Egoist,* as well. At the same time that H. D.'s literary career began to take off, her personal life became quite complex. As her marriage to Aldington became more difficult, especially after the stillbirth of her child by him in 1915, she started an intense, seemingly platonic relationship with D. H. LAWRENCE, and then in 1918 began an affair with Cecil Grey, a painter with whom she lived in Cornwall for a time. In 1918, her brother Gilbert died at the front, her marriage to Aldington ended in a separation, and she became pregnant with her child by Grey, Frances Perdita Aldington. Despite a serious bout of influenza, Perdita was born in 1919.

At this time, she began the most important relationship of her life with Bryher, born Annie Winnifred Ellerman, the heiress to a shipping fortune. H. D. had met Bryher in 1918 and credited her with saving her life during the influenza and last months of her pregnancy, and though they did not live together after 1946, theirs was a lifelong bond. They traveled widely and maintained homes in London and Switzerland. Their union survived a number of relationships, including Bryher's two marriages of convenience, the first to Robert McAlmon, whose press in Paris Bryher helped bankroll, and the second to the filmmaker Kenneth Macpherson, with whom H. D. had an affair and through whom the women became interested in film. During this time, H. D. published several volumes of verse, including *The Collected Poems of H. D.* in 1925 and two novels, *Palimpsest* and *Hedylus,* as well as a verse adaptation, *Hyppolytus Temporizes.* H. D. also appeared in three films produced by the company created by Macpherson and Bryher, the most important of which is *Borderline* (1930), a film starring Paul Robeson and an indication of H. D.'s interests in the borders between cultures, races, and psychological realities. She also wrote film reviews and poetry for the Macphersons' film journal *Close Up.*

H. D. began psychotherapy in 1931 in London (she had earlier become acquainted with Havelock Ellis), and in 1933 and 1934 she had the psychoanalytic sessions with Sigmund Freud, memorialized in *Tribute to Freud* (1956). Freud helped her understand her bisexuality and her fixation on her mother. He also, she claimed, liberated her to write poetry. During the 1930s H. D. wrote a number of poems and a book for children (*The Hedgehog* [1936]) and became more and more interested in both psychoanalysis and spiritualism. By 1943, she attended lectures by Lord Hugh Dowding, a spiritualist whose discussion of messages in séances from Royal Air Force (RAF) pilots who had died led H. D. to believe that she had had such communications. She also became close to Norman Holmes Pearson, who became her editor, adviser, and finally the executor of her literary estate.

Despite having published her *Collected Poems* when she was still in her 30s, H. D. began the major phase of her work with the *Trilogy.* The first section, *The Walls Do Not Fall,* appeared in 1944; *Tribute to the Angels* in 1945; and *The Flowering of the Rod* the following year. Like T. S. ELIOT's *Four Quartets, Trilogy* is both a response to and an attempt to transcend the events of World War II. In 1946 H. D. suffered a major breakdown. Her physical health and the strain of the war were major factors in her becoming ill, and she spent some time being treated in a Swiss clinic. During the next years, she lived in hotels in Switzerland, corresponding with friends, especially Pearson, and receiving visits from Bryher. She published *By Avon River* in 1949 and began corresponding with several poets of the younger generation who admired her work, most notably Robert Duncan, whose *H. D. Book* is a penetrating appreciation of her work.

In the last decade of her life, she returned several times to the United States to visit her grandchildren (Perdita married in 1950) and to receive various awards for her work. In 1957, her *Selected Poems* appeared, followed by a novel, *Bid Me to Live (A Madrigal),* in 1960, and her Homeric epic, *Helen in Egypt,* in 1961. She suffered a stroke in June 1961 and died on September 27 in Switzerland. While for most of her career, she was known for her early imagist poems, her later works have gained significantly more attention since the 1980s, when she was discovered by feminist critics. As much work unpublished in her lifetime has appeared in print, her reputation has grown as a poet and writer who offers a modernist poetics that differs sharply from that of her male peers while remaining peculiarly and importantly modern.

See also "EURYDICE."

BIBLIOGRAPHY

DuPlessis, Rachel Blau. *H. D.: The Career of That Struggle.* Bloomington: Indiana University Press, 1986.

Friedman, Susan Stanford. *Psyche Reborn: The Emergence of H. D.* Bloomington: Indiana University Press, 1982.

Guest, Barbara. *Herself Defined: The Poet H. D. and Her World.* Garden City, N.Y.: Doubleday, 1984.

Helen Emmitt

HEANEY, SEAMUS (1939–)

Achieving critical respect and genuine popularity can be difficult at best; that Seamus Heaney has managed as much, given the fractious coincidence of his poetic emergence and the deteriorating political situation in his native Northern Ireland, remains nothing short of astounding. Heaney's poetry maintains universal scope as he interrogates all sides—political and personal, Catholic and Protestant—through mythological and allusive resonance. Heaney largely resists the pressure to engage political and cultural situations directly, choosing rather to approach this tension implicitly through legendary and historical matter, informing the present through the past. Poems that focus on a mundane object or precise image of ritual intensify into a scene of mythic proportion and transcendent awareness; Heaney simultaneously exploits the physicality of words, expends from them their layers of historical overtones. Written in the midst of turmoil, Heaney's poetry has been controversial and at times contentious, yet it has contributed significantly to the culture and politics of Ireland, inviting international interest unprecedented since the work of W. B. YEATS.

The eldest of nine children, Heaney was born on a farm called Mossbawn near Castledawson, county Derry, a rural area that remains "the country of the mind," Heaney says, and where he finds his poetic focus. He asserts the farm was "more or less emotionally and intellectually proofed against the outside world," but that did not prevent Heaney from receiving a scholarship to St. Columb's in Derry at the age of 12; from there he attended Queen's University, Belfast and St. Joseph's College of Education, Belfast, where he was trained in Latin, Irish, and Anglo-Saxon. He taught at St. Thomas's Intermediate School, Belfast, one year before accepting a lectureship at St. Joseph's College, also in Belfast, and later at Queen's University Belfast (QUB), during which time he married Marie Devlin and participated in civil rights marches. In 1970–71 he accepted a one-year lectureship at the University of California, Berkeley, then moved from Belfast to Glanmore, county Wicklow, a year later to write full-time. He held a teaching position at Carysfort College, county Dublin, from 1975 to 1981, then began teaching at Harvard University, first as a visiting professor, then as Boylston Professor of Rhetoric and Oratory (1984), and later as Emerson Poet in Residence (1996). Heaney also was named professor of poetry at Oxford (1988) and visiting Avenali Professor at the University of California, Berkeley (1999). It was while attending QUB that Heaney first published poems in *Q* and *Gorgon,* university magazines; while working at St. Thomas's, Heaney was encouraged by the headmaster and fiction author Michael MacLaverty and later was a member of "The Group," led by the poet and critic Philip Hobsbaum and whose members included DEREK MAHON, MICHAEL LONGLEY, James Simmons, and Stewart Parker. Hobsbaum sent several of Heaney's poems to Karl Miller at the *New Statesman,* and in 1964 "DIGGING," "Scaffolding," and "Storm on the Island" were published.

Heaney's early work owes homage to the pastoral elements of William Wordsworth as well as the aesthetic of PATRICK KAVANAGH, in whose writing Heaney discerned the "unregarded data of the usual life." In early poems, moments from Heaney's childhood and youth are engendered with numinosity, everyday agrarian objects invested with significance and power. This is especially true of Heaney's first collection, *DEATH OF A NATURALIST* (1966), in which we find Heaney "tripping, falling" as he trails his father in the fields in "FOLLOWER," or depicting the rituals of farm labor in "Churning Day." Single, silent figures go about their routines as in "Digging," in which the poet recalls his grandfather in the peat fields and his own father digging potatoes. Spades, pitchforks, scythes, churns, plows—all become endowed with local and universal attributes that register the glorious in the mundane. In his second collection, *Door into the Dark* (1969), these familiar portraits of locals reappear, and here the characterizations are invested with a mythical quality. Scythes wielded by farmers in the 1798 Rising, commemorated in "Requiem for the Croppies," are symbols of agrarian culture as much as they are weapons; the peasant insurrectionists battling British and Loyalist troops anticipate, too, the growing sectarian violence in Northern Ireland. Whereas *Death of a Naturalist* celebrates family kinship and resonates with the deeply felt rhythms of rural life, *Door into the Dark* begins to establish metaphors by which Heaney may confront Ireland's brutal history and tackle the contemporary political concerns in Northern Ireland.

"Bogland," appearing in *Death of Naturalist*, initiates one such metaphor to which Heaney will return time and again in his poetry: the peat bogs from which well-preserved objects are routinely unearthed. The Irish ground is a "kind, black butter" in which "every layer they strip / Seems camped on before." As the poet goes "inwards and downwards," he finds repeatedly the existence of prior cultures, and yet the "wet centre is bottomless," connoting Heaney's awareness of a geography that is rich in both history and metaphor, awaiting his excavation. Poems such as "Bann Clay" and "Relic of Potato Digging" reveal an Irish soil that claims the authority to fossilize the past and preserve the objects unearthed. In "Gifts of Rain," Heaney declares his "need / for antediluvian lore" is found in a "shared calling of the blood" of Ireland. "Tollund Man," which appears in *Wintering Out* (1972), was inspired by a book on ancient bog sacrifices; Heaney said that, upon seeing photos of Tollund Man, it was "as if I had opened a chestnut and found a truth and palpable beauty hidden inside. . . . In a flash, I realized the connections between the mutilations of that long-ago epoch with the martyrs of the Easter 1916 uprising in Ireland and all the reprisals and repercussions visited on both communities." To reveal this link, Heaney, in the second half of "Tollund Man," relates an incident overheard in childhood of four Catholic brothers who were murdered by Protestant paramilitary fighters, the "stockinged corpses / Laid out in farmyards." The juxtaposition implicit is that the "ambushed / Flesh" of the four young men is akin to that of Tollund Man, who has "dark juices working / Him to a saint's kept body." To establish further the metaphor's resonance, Heaney recognizes at the poem's end that "in the old man-killing parishes" of Iron Age Jutland, he would "feel lost, / Unhappy and at home" as he does presently in Northern Ireland.

Whereas the poems of *Death of a Naturalist* and *Door into the Dark* relished the freedom and joy of poetic creativity as revealed through portraits of locals known to Heaney in rural county Derry, *Wintering Out* grows bleak in its forbidding wariness of the sectarian violence unleashed in Ireland. The persons who inhabit the poems of *Wintering Out* are cloaked in "mizzling rain" and "smoke," vaguely distinguished, and often the forgotten specters of ages past. These are silenced figures with simple lives, resurrected, as it were, by poetry itself, such as in "The Last Mummer," "Cairn Maker," "Navvy," and "Servant Boy." Silenced language also finds voice in the poems "Anahorish" and "Broagh," written in the tradition of Irish *dinnshenchas*, or placename poems, where legends are affixed to define an etymological space, thus binding language, history, myth, and landscape. *Anahorish,* deriving from the Gaelic *Anach Fhior Uisce,* which means "place of clear water," leads Heaney to the "mound-dwellers," the first inhabitants of the land, who "go waist-deep in mist / to break the light ice" that separates the Anglicized *Anahorish* of the present from the Anach Fhior Uisce of the past.

North, Heaney's most controversial collection, appeared in 1975. It drew upon another Irish poetic convention, the *aisling,* or female personification of Ireland, in poems such as "The Bog Queen," "Bone Dreams," and "Come to the Bower," which depict torture and rape and posit colonial violence and current social conflict in mythopoetic terms. Beyond "The Bog Queen," the bog motif continues in "Grabaulle Man," "Punishment," and "Kinship," the connection between Denmark of two millennia ago and contemporary Northern Ireland established as present-day atrocity that is but part of a enduring continuum. "The Bog Queen" most notably authenticates Heaney's connection between Ireland and Denmark; the body of Moira, an aristocrat of the Viking culture that occupied much of Ireland in the 10th century, was retrieved from Belfast peat beds in the 18th century, the plait of her hair "a slimy birth-cord / of bog," suggesting the intermingling of cultures that occurred during these invasions. The Viking sequence continues in the poems "North," "Viking Dublin: Trial Pieces," and "Funeral Rites," where the pillaging, plundering Danish and Norse cultures are recognized as being absorbed eventually into the Irish landscape.

The poems of *North,* entangling culpability and misery, were, according to Heaney, "grimly executed. And I really like them because they're odd as odd and I think hard and contrary." The collection remains Heaney's most overtly political collection and received polarized criticism. Martin Dodsworth, for instance, considered *North* a "testimony to the patience, persistence and power of the imagination under duress," while Ciarán Carson referred to Heaney as "the laureate of violence—a mythmaker, an anthropologist of ritual killing." Heaney himself noted in an interview the problem of "having to conduct oneself as a poet in a situation of ongoing political violence and public expectation—a public expectation, it has to be said, not of poetry as such but of political positions variously approvable by mutually disapproving groups." In the second half of *North,* "Singing School" relates the difficulties of the artist who creates amid cultural crisis; Heaney apparently took this to heart, for *North* marks a notable turning point in his career. Stylistically Heaney himself notes the "denser" forms that are "more force-fed with words" in his initial four volumes, whereas later writing—*Field Work* (1979) and beyond—has more "plain-speaking lines" with line breaks used "more as a pacer, a timer." Heaney's short-lined quatrains give way to a longer line that provides more sustained syntax, and he appears more attentive to the spoken as opposed to printed word. Rhythmic sustenance remains focused on alliteration, assonance, and consonance, and there continues to be an emphasis on the understated association of visual and phonetic imagery.

On the heels of *North*'s burgeoning mythos, the poet's voice in *Field Work* grew more direct and engaging, allowing Heaney to be subject of the poems. There remained but modest separation from Irish issues, even so. In "After a Killing," Heaney evokes the image of "two young men with rifles on the hill, / Profane and bracing as their instruments." Drawing on a memory from his childhood in Mossbawn, Heaney recalls in "The Toome Road" meeting "armoured cars" that were "all camouflaged," transporting "headphoned soldiers standing up in turrets." Unlike the extended metaphors of *North,* the interface between poet and reader in *Field Work* is highly personal, such as in "The Strand at Lough Beg," which envisions the last minutes before death of Heaney's second cousin, Colum McCartney, who was executed while returning from a Dublin football match. Numerous of the poems are elegiac, evoking the personal loss of friends and other community members from county Derry during the extreme violence that followed Bloody Sunday in 1972. Awareness of life's entangled issues more ironically appears in the "Glanmore Sonnets," a sequence of love poems principal to the collection. Here, the earth again draws Heaney's attention as "vowels plowed into other" and "opened ground" that is "steaming"; as these "turned up acres breathe," the poet perceives "my ghosts come striding into their spring stations."

Ghostly figures haunt Heaney's succeeding collection, *Station Island* (1984), only here the spectral personages—from the hunger strikers Ciaran Nugent and Francis Hughes and Heaney's deceased cousin McCartney to the Irish novelists William Carleton and James Joyce—offer advice and evoke a sense of plurality of the self. Carleton offers the injunction "Remember everything," even as he affirms that life "is a road you travel on your own." Joyce, however, has the last word—"let go, let fly, forget"—and so permits Heaney to surpass the demands of community and tribe and so not be diverted from his own path. This transcendence

is reified in the poem "Unwinding," where a ball of twine unwinds "backwards through areas that forwarded / understanding of all I would undertake," ostensibly providing Heaney new consideration of the self in relation to the nation. Succeeding works—*The Haw Lantern* (1987), *Seeing Things* (1991), and *The Spirit Level* (1996)—offer a poetics of loss that prompts a spiritual enlightenment, one engendered in *Station Island*'s remaking of a poetic identity. Heaney's poems celebrate life's mutability. In *Haw Lantern*'s "Alphabets," the poet perceives language with childlike desire: "The letters of this alphabet were trees. / The capitals were orchards in full bloom." "Settle Bed," in *Seeing Things,* affirms that "whatever is given // Can always be reimagined." These volumes imply an imaginative power that grows ever fuller and richer—one that may even transcend the cultural legacy Heaney has confronted in earlier collections.

Heaney's latest two collections, *Electric Light* (2001) and *District and Circle* (2006), are largely informed by translations undertaken in the prior 15 years, including *The Cure at Troy* (1990, version of Sophocles' *Philoctetes*), BEOWULF (1999), and *The Burial at Thebes* (2004, version of Sophocles' *Antigone*). Heaney has said that "translations have more glamour as poems in the new language when there's more disobedience going," and that even as he pays "homage to the original," there remains the impulse "to go for a new workable poem," one that yet will "honor the original." What Heaney gains from these translations is the ability to appropriate the Greek, Roman, and Anglo-Saxon, making problematic the association between place and poetry. In "Desfina" the poet gazes upon Mount Parnassus, in Greek mythology the home of the Muses, and yet a transformation obscures the source of poetic inspiration: "Mount Parnassus placid on the skyline: / Slieve na mBard, Knock Filiocht, Ben Duan," Heaney recites, culminating with the line "We gaelicized new names for Poetry Hill." Even as Heaney returns to the rural subject matter of his first four collections, the "I" of these poems is far more mature than ever before, and the "home" of writing continues to be interrogated, not justified and romanticized. The same holds true in *District and Circle* (2006), where, although Heaney returns to earth-centered evocations and visions, reminisces of the rural Ireland of his youth, and even revisits of the Danish bogs that were the site of "Tolland Man," the inclusion of Latin and Irish words, the allusion to Dante and Greek myth, and the ecoawareness of his worldview rupture rather than sustain, any connection to Heaney's earliest work. The diverse forms within this collection—quatrains, prose poems, lyrics, free verse—also speak to an ever-expanding perception by Heaney of the universal significance of his poetic vision.

Collections of Heaney's poems can be found in *Selected Poems 1965–75* (1980), *New Selected Poems 1966–87* (1990), *Opened Ground: Poems, 1966–96* (1998). Heaney has received numerous prizes, including the Somerset Maugham Award (1967), Cholmondeley Award (1968), Duff Cooper Prize (1975), Whitbread Award (1987, 2000), and Nobel Prize in literature (1995). He is a founding director of the Field Day theater company and author of several critical essay collections: *Preoccupations* (1980), *The Government of the Tongue* (1988), *The Redress of Poetry* (1995), and *Finders Keepers* (2002).

See also "ACT OF UNION," "BLACKBERRY-PICKING," "EARLY PURGES," "MID-TERM BREAK," "TWO LORRIES," "WHATEVER YOU SAY SAY NOTHING."

BIBLIOGRAPHY

Collins, Floyd. *Seamus Heaney: The Crisis of Identity.* Newark: University of Delaware, 2003.

Corcoran, Neil. *The Poetry of Seamus Heaney: A Critical Study.* London: Faber, 1998.

O'Brien, Eugene. *Seamus Heaney and the Place of Writing.* Gainesville: University Press of Florida, 2002.

———. *Seamus Heaney: Creating Irelands of the Mind.* Dublin: Liffey Press, 2002.

Tobin, Daniel. *Passage to the Center: Imagination and the Sacred in the Poetry of Seamus Heaney.* Lexington: University Press of Kentucky, 1998.

Kurt Bullock

HEATH-STUBBS, JOHN (1918–) Born in

London, July 9, 1918, John Francis Alexander Heath-Stubbs has distinguished himself as an honored and beloved poet, a learned and formidable literary critic, a gifted translator from several languages, a judicious editor, and a highly influential anthologist. By virtue of the range, scope, quantity, quality, and creativity of his literary contributions, Heath-Stubbs has earned a place among the preeminent makers of contemporary British belles lettres. Long a resident of London, but having spent a good part of his earlier years on the Isle of Wight, in Brittany, and in rural Hampshire and Cornwall, Heath-Stubbs exhibits in his diverse literary productions urbane sophistication, scholarly learnedness, acute critical discernment, amiable wit, and an unmistakable familiarity with and love of the natural world. His writings reveal vast learning in the fields of British, American, and European literature, but he is also famous for his poetic evocation of the expressions of nature, most especially of birdsong.

Inconveniently for a man who would devote his life to study of the written word, Heath-Stubbs began having degenerative eye problems at the age of three and by 19 was blind in one eye. He lost the ability to read in 1962 and lost his sight completely in 1978. His early education was obtained in rural schools. When faced with increasing vision problems he entered Worcester College for the Blind in 1937, before continuing his formal education at Queen's College, Oxford University. Drawing upon his capacious and exacting memory and an inclination for relentless study and hard work, Heath-Stubbs has been active since the early 1940s in the production of original poetry and literary scholarship. His life and career may serve as an inspiration to the unsighted and sighted alike.

The magnitude of Heath-Stubb's literary accomplishment is frankly astonishing. As regards British literature, the grasp of his critical valuation extends to, among many others, the works of Edmund Spenser, John Milton, John Dryden, Jonathan Swift, Alexander Pope, Thomas Gray, George Crabbe, William Wordsworth, Walter Savage Landor, Percy Bysshe Shelley, Alfred, Lord Tennyson, DAVID JONES, C. DAY LEWIS, and W. H. AUDEN. He has also concerned himself with the criticism of American authors, most notably with Edgar Allan Poe, EZRA POUND, and Hart Crane. His contribution to the understanding of Augustan and romantic English poetry has been great, but it is as a critic and anthologist of modernist and contemporary British poetry that Heath-Stubbs has exerted the most significant critical influence. In 1953, he edited with David

Wright the highly influential *Faber Book of Twentieth Century Verse: An Anthology of Verse in Britain 1900–1950*. The volume, since expanded and updated a number of times, has been credited with establishing the canon of *modernism* in British poetry. He has collaborated with specialists in languages both ancient and modern to produce many translations into English, most notably, perhaps, with Peter Avery in a version of Omar Khayyam's *Rubiayat* (1979).

It is as an original poet, nevertheless, that Heath-Stubbs has made his most essential and lasting contribution to English letter, from his first collection of poetry, *Beauty and the Beast* (1943); through his epic poem *Artorius* (1973); to his most recent collection; *Pigs Might Fly* (2005). Among the most honored of contemporary British poets, Heath-Stubbs was recognized in 1988 with a Queen's Gold Medal for Poetry and an Order of the British Empire. He has been awarded a St. Augustine Cross for his contribution to the arts.

BIBLIOGRAPHY

Heath-Stubbs, John. *Artorius: A Heroic Poem in Four Books and Eight Episodes*. London: Enitharmon Press, 1973.
———. *Collected Poems 1942–1987*. Manchester, Eng.: Carcanet Press, 1988.
———. *Hindsights: An Autobiography*. London: Hodder & Stroughton, 1993.
Tolley, A. T., ed. *The Literary Essays of John Heath-Stubbs*. Manchester, Eng.: Carcanet Press, 1998.

Cliff Toliver

"HE NEVER EXPECTED MUCH" Thomas Hardy (1928)

THOMAS HARDY wrote in a diary entry, labeled "A Pessimist's Apology," that pessimism is "playing the sure game": "You cannot lose at it; you may gain. It is the only view of life in which you can never be disappointed. Having reckoned what to do in the worst possible circumstances, when better arise, as they may, life becomes child's play" (*Life* 311) In Hardy's second "In Tenebris" poem, he proposes "that if way to the Better there be, it exacts a full look at the Worst." "He Never Expected Much" provides another insight into Hardy's pessimism.

Alternatively titled "A Consideration / [A reflection] on My Eighty-Sixth Birthday," "He Never Expected Much" was written in 1926 but not published until two years later, after Hardy's death, first in the *Daily Telegraph* for March 19, 1928, and then in *Winter Words*, Hardy's eighth volume of poetry. The poem is framed as Hardy's address to the world. In the first stanza, Hardy concedes, 'Well, World, you kept faith with me" since "you have proved to be / Much as you said you were." In the second half of the first stanza Hardy remembers that even as a child he never expected "that life would all be fair." The World speaks to Hardy in the second half of the second stanza and the first half of the third, and final, stanza, saying what it repeatedly has told Hardy since his childhood revelation, that life inevitably will hurt those who "desperately" love the World and those who view the World "serenely" or with "contempt" because they do not heed the World's warning that "I do not promise overmuch, / Child; overmuch; / Just neutral-tinted haps and such." In the final lines of the poem, Hardy confirms that he and others with "minds like mine" have listened to the warning not to expect much in life and "hence" has been able to "stem such strain and ache / As each year might assign."

The most striking technical feature of the poem is the repetition in the second line of a phrase from the first line of each stanza. The second line of the first stanza repeats the phrase *kept faith with me* from the first line, which is quoted earlier. The second stanza begins by introducing the World's warning to the speaker: "'Twas then you said, and since have said, / Time since have said." In the third stanza, the World expresses its warning, repeating the word *overmuch*. J. O. Bailey suggests the repetition "gives the poem a hymn-like tone." The repetition along with the rhyme scheme—*aaabcccb*—reinforces the speaker's wearied reaffirmation of a nearly 80-year-old lesson.

The poem may seem to offer more a somber version of Hardy's diary entry about pessimism as a pragmatic "sure game" than a means to the ethical end of discovering the "way to the Better," but in Hardy's recollection that his first intimation of reduced expectations came upon him as a child when he "used to lie / Upon the leaze and watch the sky," in the description of the World's revelation emanating from "that mysterious voice you shed / From clouds and hills around," and in the World's promise of "neutral-tinted haps," "He Never Expected Much" reveals Hardy's pessimism as a mode of visionary insight, what Harold Bloom identifies as the final muting of the visionary gleam of high romantic idealism.

BIBLIOGRAPHY

Bailey, J. O. *The Poetry of Thomas Hardy: A Handbook and Commentary.* Chapel Hill: University of North Carolina Press, 1970.

Bloom, Harold. *A Map of Misreading.* New York: Oxford University Press, 1975.

Hardy, Florence Emily. *The Life of Thomas Hardy.* Hamden, Conn.: Archon, 1970.

Robert R. Watson

"HIGH WINDOWS" PHILIP LARKIN (1974)

The title poem of PHILIP LARKIN's last collection, his 1974 *High Windows,* follows a highly effective developmental pattern that is found in a number of his best pieces: from a rough, angry, and, in this case, sexually explicit, opening to a sublime religious and philosophical conclusion. This pattern was already successfully tested in his "CHURCH GOING" in *The Less Deceived,* and in "High Windows" it is applied deftly and effortlessly. The result of this rhetorical and psychological abracadabra is truly unique: A poem that runs throughout its first four stanzas as a cynical and envious muttering of an elderly man is transformed, in the final stanza, through a set of mysterious images, into a metaphysical and mystical suggestion that opens the boundaries of the poem toward infinity. The effect is powerful and truly transformative; the readers follow confidently the initial steady line of thought, only to be suddenly jolted into a very different world, the one for which the poem does not prepare them.

The poem opens with some "bad language" of a typical Larkin persona, one of those reminiscent of Browning's dramatic monologues. A man obviously past his prime observes "a couple of kids," probably in the street or in a park, and guesses that, in these new, modern times, "he's fucking her and she's / Taking pills or wearing a diaphragm." He concludes somewhat wistfully that this must be "paradise / Everyone old has dreamed of all their lives." Of course, this rough and explicit description and the use of strong images sound like an attempt to express the new exciting reality of the sexual revolution of the 1960s, both in terms of the anger at the "outrages" of the new sexual freedom and the intense envy for having missed such an opportunity, an envy articulated also in "ANNUS MIRABILIS," another celebrated poem in the same collection.

This new, exciting, sexually unrestricted reality is depicted in some interesting images of the modern world. The antiquated and no longer necessary "bonds" and "gestures," the customs, attitudes, and loyalties defining the old-fashioned and morally strict world of some earlier, "better" times, are now suddenly superfluous and "pushed to one side / Like an outdated combine harvester," an old piece of farm machinery left to rust somewhere on the farm. The new and popular toy is not something pragmatic and ultimately hard working, and thus moral, as a combine harvester, but a long slide, something one finds in amusement parks and children's playgrounds, and "everyone young" is going down this slide "to happiness, endlessly." Both *happiness* and *endlessly* are, however, ambivalent words and one can certainly detect some strong sarcasm underlining them as the speaker utters them.

And, indeed, there is no end to this game. The speaker, who is obviously in his late 50s or thereabouts, glides suddenly, through the association of ideas, to an earlier time, "forty years back," to the time of his own youth, and imagines the elderly people of that time observing the same situation and making the same statement—how free and great must be the life of the young, now that conditions have changed! The image of the slide is again there: *"He / And his lot will all go down the long slide / Like free bloody birds."* However, the starting point for these "ancient" observers is decidedly different; while the first, modern-day observer does not look at "the couple of kids" from any religiously defined perspective, and probably only from a modern and popular atheistic or agnostic standpoint, the observers "forty years back" still stick to the old pieties and biblical perspectives: *"No God any more, or sweating in the dark / About hell and that."* The same envy and desire are, however, present, although, as we, the readers, observe these observers from different historic periods, it becomes increasingly clear that all this seems to be a repetitive game, the game of "discovering" the "new," which is not new, and of envying what should not be envied. The young will be young and their dealings with each other tend to appear to the "old" as too free, shocking, sexually explicit, excitingly sinful. Thus, this whole series of the envious old man, for whom all these successive sexual "revolutions" seem to come too late, repeats an old game of nervous and envious observation of the great "long slide." The problem is, of course, that their own slide is no more; a different metaphor applies to their largely spent lives.

And, then, suddenly, the words of the fifth stanza take us unexpectedly to a very different direction. The whimpering commentary of the two generations is over, in all its repetitive poverty and desire-induced pain, and the image of the high windows, rather hazy, imprecise, without clear location and dimensions, and yet curiously sharp and suggestive, penetrates the poem and becomes fully dominant. The strongly esoteric quality of that image is stressed by the fact that these are not the real, material windows, but "the thought of high windows." The reader's attention is further sharpened by stressing just one aspect of the windows—"the sun-comprehending glass," whatever the meaning of that beautiful, but unclear phrase. How and what can and does glass comprehend? More and more profoundly than the mortals, who can only observe and yearn and not understand? And, as if all this mystery is not enough, the final two lines yield more beautiful, and paradoxically peaceful, confusion: "And beyond it, the deep blue air, that shows / Nothing, and is nowhere, and is endless." This sublime escape into the "nowhere" and "nothing" and the "endless" elevates the whole poem, which begins as an angry and envious murmur, into a sphere of crystalline freedom, freedom from the yoke of desire, sex, "taking pills or wearing a diaphragm," envy, impotence, incorrect human conclusions and surmises. Sexual freedom of the sexual revolution and all other "revolutions" is, of course, an illusion, as the only real freedom, as testified by the great gurus and spiritual leaders of the world, lies in the escape from the bonds of the self and desire. While the four stanzas of this remarkable poem belabor the vision of the world oppressed by desire

and the "joys of the body," the last stanza offers a glimpse of a pure vision of something akin to nirvana or the "peace that surpasseth all understanding," a vision of transcendence, the ultimate mystery. From the "long slide," especially as one is going down it, to "happiness," that vision is blurred and inaccessible. The thought of high windows, silence, and not words, is suggested as a blessed solution and destination.

BIBLIOGRAPHY

Larkin, Philip. *Collected Poems*. Edited by Anthony Thwaite. London: Marvell Press and Faber and Faber, 1988.

———. *High Windows*. London: Faber and Faber, 1974.

Motion, Andrew. *Philip Larkin: A Writer's Life*. London: Faber and Faber, 1993.

Ivo Soljan

HILL, GEOFFREY (1932–)

Among critics, Geoffrey Hill is ranked as one of the major British poets of the last half of the 20th century and early 21st century; his name is often mentioned alongside his contemporaries SEAMUS HEANEY, TED HUGHES, and PHILIP LARKIN. But where those three achieved a certain degree of popular recognition and acceptance, Hill and his poetry remain less well known. This is in part due to the difficulty or "inaccessibility" that his poetry has been charged with, in comparison to theirs. In his defense, Hill has steadfastly maintained that difficult poetry is the most democratic and least condescending to the intelligence of the ordinary reader. In an interview with the *Guardian* newspaper in 2002 he quoted the German philosopher Theodor Haecker's assertion that "tyrants always want a language and literature that is easily understood." His poetry, in contrast, he says, cultivates the depths of memory as a civic duty, in order to fight the debased and evasive language of so much of public life, which he calls an "oligarchy of fraud."

Hill was born in 1932 in Bromsgrove, Worcestershire, to a working-class family. His father, grandfather, and uncles were policemen. But Hill became deaf in one ear from severe mastoiditis at the age of 11 and followed an academic path, attending Keble College, Oxford, to study English. There he met the American poet Donald Hall, who asked him to submit poems for the Fantasy Poets series, publishing them in 1952. These poems were published in his first book, *For the Unfallen* (1958), a stunning beginning. At Oxford he met the poet Anthony Thwaite, who has said that when he met Hill, "I felt like Larkin when he met KINGSLEY AMIS, you know, that 'here was a talent greater than my own.'"

After Oxford, Hill became an academic, with a 1954 appointment as a lecturer at Leeds University, where he would remain for 26 years, until 1980. At Leeds he met Nancy Whittaker, whom he married in 1956. In 1958 his first book was published and the first of his four children was born. Hill did not produce another book for 10 years, *King Log* in 1968. About the difficulty in writing that he faced during that period Hill has said that it was partly giving oneself over to the duties of family and teaching, but that even more truthfully he "was simply afraid to put down the next sentence," but that since 1992 writing has come more easily to him. This perhaps coincides with his finally being treated for depression and obsessive-compulsive disorder in the early 1990s in Boston.

The poems of *King Log,* which Hill had worked on throughout the 1960s, were not like those of Hughes or Larkin or THE MOVEMENT. A poem from that collection, "Ovid in the Third Reich," places Ovid in the seemingly inappropriate position of writing love poems in the midst of horror and violence. Ovid says, "I have learned one thing: not to look down / So much upon the damned." As with so much of Hill's poetry, the line breaks allow for linguistically interesting possibilities. If one pauses at the first line break, the poem suggests perhaps that Ovid, perhaps any poet, works best when he does not look down, not writing about politics, the temporal, or the ordinary (how antipathetical to the Movement ideals of Larkin). But if one reads through the line break, the poem suggests that a poet needs to be less concerned with the lofty spiritual and transcendental—not looking down upon those less favored.

Another poem from that volume, often anthologized, "September Song," shows the same method at work. The poem memorializes the Holocaust, beginning, "Undesirable you may have been, untouchable / you were not." Again the line break surprises the reader, as *untouchable* at first seems to be in apposition to *undesirable,* a restatement of the distaste of Nazi ideology for Jewishness, but reading to the next line, the meaning is reversed: Jews were literally not untouchable. They were "reached" and "touched" in the most violent way. What starts as a comfortable abstraction becomes jarringly real. "Funeral Music" from the same volume shows another characteristic of Hill's poetry, a love of history and the dense use of allusion. It is a long sequence on the Wars of the Roses, another kind of holocaust, though a very English one, which also requires memorialization and witness to the violence.

Three years later Hill published what many consider his masterwork, *MERCIAN HYMNS* (1971). It is a sequence of 30 prose poems (Hill dislikes the term) imbued with the geography and history of Hill's childhood home in the Midlands, where Offa (757–96) was king for almost 40 years over the Anglo-Saxon kingdom of Mercia. In his note to the poem, Hill gives a sense of its theme: "The Offa who figures in this sequence might perhaps most usefully be regarded as the presiding genius of the West Midlands, his dominion enduring from the middle of the eighth century until the middle of the 20th (and possibly beyond)." The poem juxtaposes elements of eighth-century history and biography with Hill's and 20th-century England's biography.

In 1981 Hill became a teaching fellow at Emmanuel College, Cambridge, a position he left in 1988 to become University Professor of Literature and Religion at Boston University in the United States. In 1988 he also underwent a triple-bypass operation following a heart attack, married a second time (he was divorced in 1983), and was finally treated for the mental health difficulties he had suffered from all his life. His wife, Alice Goodman, is an opera librettist and Anglican priest. Critics had long noted a kind of "priestly" quality in Hill's poetry, an interest in the metaphysical, and the championing of a Catholic tradition in English poetry running through Donne, Dryden, and Hopkins, three of Hill's favorites, as well as Shakespeare's distant cousin, the Jesuit poet Robert Southwell.

Since moving to America in the 1990s, his remarriage, and his treatment with antidepressants, Hill has produced at a much greater pace—eight new books of poetry and two of criticism. Though the poetry is often imbued with the past, Hill has also written more contemporary witness poems, which he has come to call "praise songs." These are poems like those in *Speech!*

Speech! written about the Biafran War and the martyred Biafran poet Christopher Okigbo. Hill had spent some time teaching in Nigeria in the 1960s, where he met Okigbo, and was influenced by hearing religious praise songs broadcast on the radio as the idea for what his poetry could achieve in celebrating heroism.

BIBLIOGRAPHY

Alderman, Nigel, and C. D. Blanton, eds. "Pocket Epics: British Poetry after Modernism." Special Issue. *Yale Journal of Criticism* 13 (spring 2000): 1.

"A Matter of Timing: Mercian Poet Geoffrey Hill." *Manchester Guardian,* 21 September 2002, Review Section.

Potts, Robert. "The Praise Singer." *Manchester Guardian.* 10 August 2002, Review Section.

Wainwright, Jeffrey. *Acceptable Words: Essays on the Poetry of Geoffrey Hill.* Manchester, Eng.: Manchester University Press, 2006.

James Persoon

HOFMANN, MICHAEL (1957–)

Michael Hofmann was born in Freiburg, Germany, in 1957. Although he writes poetry in British English, and sometimes in variations on American English, he is in fact German. He also translates poetry and prose from German into English, including works by Ernst Junger, Franz Kafka, Wolfgang Koeppen, Joseph Roth, and Wim Wenders.

When he was a child, his family—father, mother, sister, and Hofmann himself—traveled in the United States, and as a teenager he attended boarding school in Great Britain (Edinburgh and Winchester). As an undergraduate Hofmann studied English literature and classics at Magdalen College, Cambridge, where he received his B.A. (1979) and M.A. (1984) and was trained in the techniques of literary criticism by the poetry critic Christopher Ricks.

Hofmann is a good example of an international poet. After undertaking some postgraduate work in England and Germany, Hofmann became a freelance writer living in London and married the British poet Lavinia Greenlaw. Since then he has also served as a visiting professor at the University of Michigan, and he joined the faculty of the University of Florida Department of English in 1994. He now divides his time between Britain and the United States.

He is the son of the German novelist Gert Hofmann, whose novel *The Film Explainer* he translated. Many of his poems explore the challenges of his relationship with his father: "What was the centre of your life-interests? / You said your family; your family said your work" ("The Nomad, my father"). After his father's death in 1993, the tone became gentler, although no less aware of the inherent difficulties of the father-son relationship and its particular embodiment in this case: "We all wanted to bring you things, give you things, / leave you things—to go with you in some form, I suppose" ("Epithanaton"). Hofmann's other poetic themes include travel, life in other countries, the human as sexual being, and the effect of time on people.

Apart from his father, the most important influence on Hofmann's work has been the American poet Robert Lowell, and in particular Lowell's ground-breaking collection of "confessional" poetry *Life Studies* (1959). Hofmann adopts and adapts Lowell's methods of writing lyric poetry about one's personal life, yet with a curious sense of detachment. Formally he also follows in Lowell's later footsteps by employing loose, but not shapeless, forms and a relaxed, sometimes prosaic, meter. Hoffman says that he writes "out of allegiance to certain 20th-century practitioners, in particular Lowell, Brodsky, Benn and Montale. To bring confusion to my languages and clarity to myself." He accurately pinpoints the qualifications of a strong poet: "You need a pure heart, a good ear, and a wicked vocabulary."

Before the end of the 20th century, Hofmann published five books of poems, including *Nights in the Iron Hotel* (1983), for which he won the Cholmondeley Award, and *Acrimony* (1986), which won the Geoffrey Faber Memorial Prize. His other three books of poetry are *K.S. in Lakeland: New and Selected Poems* (1990), *Corona, Corona* (1993), and *Approximately Nowhere* (1999). He has also published a collection of his critical work, entitled *Behind the Lines* (2001).

BIBLIOGRAPHY

British Council, Peter Forbes, and Ulla Montan. "Author Profile: Michael Hofmann." Available online. URL: http://www.contemporarywriters.com/authors/?p=auth142. Accessed May 2, 1008.

Hofmann, Michael, and William Logan. "A Conversation on British and American poetry." *Poetry* 184, no. 3 (June/July 2004): 212–220.

Pugh, Christopher. "Robert Lowell, Life Studies, and the Father Poetry of Michael Hofmann." *Symbiosis* 5, no. 2 (2001): 173–189.

Stannard, Julian. "'Nothing Dreamier than Barracks!'" *PN Review* 28, no. 3 (January–February 2002): 53–55.

Emily Taylor Merriman

"THE HOLLOW MEN" T. S. ELIOT (1925)

"The Hollow Men" had its origins, much as "Prufrock" and THE WASTE LAND, in the poetical effusions of T. S. ELIOT over a long period. Eliot had hoped to include the "Song for the Opheron," in which "The Hollow Men" has its essential roots, in *The Waste Land* but allowed EZRA POUND to have his way. "The Hollow Men" appeared in various revised or unrevised, truncated, or elaborated versions in WYNDHAM LEWIS's *Tyro* of April 1921 (attributed pseudonymously to Gus Krutzsch), in the *Chapbook* of November 1924, in the *Criterion* of January 1925, in the *Dial* of March 1925, and in the French periodical *Commerce* in the winter of 1924–25. Its final, and familiar, version appeared in 1925 in Eliot's *Poems 1909–1925*. At this stage "The Hollow Men" acquired a concluding choral chant, "Here we go round the prickly pear," and the two epigraphs. The fragments that were left out, "The Wind sprang up at four o'clock" and "Eyes that last I saw in tears," appear in Eliot's *Collected Poems* as "Minor Poems."

In its final version "The Hollow Men" gains a unity of design and thought much as *The Waste Land* and "Prufrock" do. Eliot reordered the fragments, added a title and epigraphs, and appended new material. A structural and conceptual simplicity, though, distinguishes "The Hollow Men" from Eliot's more ambitious verse. In contrast to the overwhelming horror of the universal predicament of man that *The Waste Land* embodies in such terrifying detail, "The Hollow Men" resorts to the simplicity of lyrical verse and symbolic comment and thus gains in intensity. A major achievement of "The Hollow Men," as also of much of Eliot's verse, was his careful cultivation of speech rhythms and verbal uses of his times as poetical idiom. Eliot's obsessive concern with the problem of time as well as his belief in literature as an embodiment of composite memories of both our past and our present also underlie the strength of "The Hollow Men."

"The Hollow Men" begins with the figures who "grope together / And avoid speech / Gathered on this beach of the tumid river," reminiscent of Dante's third and fourth cantos of the *Inferno*, which describe limbo, the first circle of hell. The figures here are unable to communicate or express themselves. What is even more important, they have nothing to communicate or express, and no intention to do so either. Also, even if attempted and achieved, such a communication would be totally futile. In his essay on Baudelaire, Eliot wrote that "it is better, in a paradoxical way, to do evil than to do nothing: at least we exist." "The Hollow Men" focuses on this absence of desire, and by implication on the denial of existence, even as we exist with an assured possibility of hope.

The symbolic significance of *guy*, the stuffed effigy or the scarecrow, lies in its indictment of humanity for existing without purpose, or without hope or desire for such a purpose. Lines such as "Shape without form, shade without colour, / Paralysed force, gesture without motion" carry the burden of the essential meaning of the poem. The recurring symbol of the eye (e. g., "Eyes I dare not meet in dreams") consistently testifies to the hollowness of the men. They avoid meeting the eyes, perhaps Christ's, that pose a spiritual challenge, even though doing so would be "the hope only / Of empty men." Their own twilight existence is marked by the fact that "there are no eyes here / In this valley of dying men."

Eliot in this poem reflects upon the men of his time and society as a whole in the postwar scenario, yet larger philosophical issues emerge out of Eliot's subtler handling of the poetical tools. The finality with which the men are characterized is made more poignant in view of the authorial conviction that life itself is not devoid of significance. Men's reluctance to seek actively ultimate meaning, grace, and spiritual order—the spiritual predicament of the postwar European civilization—appears to Eliot more culpable than anything else.

Despite Eliot's celebrated comments on the impersonal character of the poet—"The progress of an artist is a continual self sacrifice, a continual extinction of personality"—he also said that that in a poem "the poet may be concerned solely with expressing in verse [his] obscure impulse; . . . to achieve clarity for himself" and that "the creator is everywhere present and everywhere hidden."

"The Hollow Men," no wonder then, gives the impression of embodying much personal experience, intensely felt feelings of anguish, and emotional torment.

Apart from Dante, "The Hollow Men" should remind us of Guy Fawkes and the Gunpowder Plot, and Conrad's *Heart of Darkness.* Eliot tells us that the title combines elements from William Morris's "The Hollow Land," and Kipling's "The Broken Men," which presents Englishmen in the colonies loitering by the shores and hoping to communicate with passengers on the ships arriving from home for "Ah, God! One sniff of England." Shakespeare's use of "But hollow men, like horses hot at hand" in *Julius Caesar* has been mentioned as another source for the title.

BIBLIOGRAPHY

Bush, Ronald. *T. S. Eliot: A Study in Character and Style.* Oxford: Oxford University Press, 1984.

Smith, Stan. *The Origins of Modernism: Eliot, Pound, Yeats and the Rhetorics of Renewal.* Hertfordshire, Eng.: Harvester Wheatsheaf, 1994.

G. R. Taneja

"HOMAGE TO A GOVERNMENT" PHILIP LARKIN (1969)

PHILIP LARKIN's "Homage to a Government," which first appeared in his most celebrated book, *High Windows* (1974), is one of his few explicitly political poems. It is ironically titled, as the government in question is not being praised. The poem was written in 1969, just as the Labour government, in response to a financial crisis, was in the process of withdrawing the last British troops from "East of Suez."

The poem is a favorite with many readers because it is "easy to get" and amusing; it also showcases Larkin's conservative, perhaps even reactionary politics. Its main point is that Britain is ending its engagement as an empire with the Middle East (Aden in particular), taking home its troops, for the simplest and most venal of reasons—want of money. The complexities of being an occupying colonial power are put in a simple and favorable light, in a defense of empire—British troops "guarded" these places, kept them "orderly." The reasons for the disengagement are laziness and greed—"we want the money for ourselves at home."

For the speaker of the poem, this is a betrayal of what was good about the English character—duty, responsibility, moral fiber—virtues he hoped to see revived when Margaret Thatcher's Conservative government came to power. The next poem Larkin composed, according to Anthony Thwaite's chronologically organized *Collected Poems,* is another polemic against liberal socialism, especially in its educational policy, a two-line ditty titled "When the Russian tanks roll westward."

In form, the poem is written in a six-line stanza. The first three rhyme words of the stanza are repeated, in reverse order, as the rhymes of lines 4, 5, and 6. The effect of this repetition is a kind of desultory refrain, as if Larkin does not expect his complaint against the government to be heard or acted upon. Instead, there is an elegiac tone for the "England gone" of "Going, Going," also in *High Windows.*

BIBLIOGRAPHY

Regan, Stephen. *Philip Larkin: An Introduction to the Variety of Criticism.* London: Macmillan, 1992.

Thwaite, Anthony, ed. *Philip Larkin: Collected Poems.* New York: Farrar, Straus and Giroux, 1988.

James Persoon

"HOMECOMING" SIMON ARMITAGE (1997)

"Homecoming" was originally published in SIMON ARMITAGE's 1997 book of poems *Cloudcuckooland.* The majority of the volume was taken up with a sequence of poems named after constellations, and "Homecoming" takes on a particularly astronomical theme in this context. In fact, the homecoming the poem describes is largely mental rather than physical and takes place through a series of cryptic images.

The poem opens with a striking command to think "two things on their own and both at once," as if setting out a manifesto for poetic ambiguity. The two images we are then presented with are a trust game where people fall backward into another person's arms, and a family argument over a child's scuffed yellow jacket. The speaker then asks us somehow to put these images together as if creatively to reenvision our own childhood. He offers us instructions, as if drawing attention to his own use of symbolism—"these ribs are pleats . . . these arms are sleeves." Memory becomes an old coat we must put on and be ready to immerse ourselves in if we are to have any chance of reconciliation, an act that Armitage's image of the "father figure" wanting to "set things straight" suggests is the primary focus of the poem.

The verse is loosely metric but unrhymed, Armitage often breaking up the rhythm to suggest the monosyllabic confrontations between children and their parents. As is typical of Armitage, he casts himself as onlooker to this remembered scene, his relationship with his addressee apparently intimate but always ambiguous. He informs us and the poetic subject that it is "sixteen years until we meet," indicating that he has placed both of us experientially in the past. We and the poetic subject, adolescent, the suffering must then roam the old sets of childhood, attempting to find a point of return to the present via the speaker's enigmatic instruction.

BIBLIOGRAPHY

"Simon Armitage." Available online. URL: http://www.bbc.co.uk/schools/gcsebitesize/english_literature/poetarmitage/homecomingrev1.shtml. Accessed May 2, 2008.

William May

HOPE, A(LEC) D(ERWENT) (1907–2000)

Born in 1907 in Cooma, New South Wales, Australia, Hope obtained an arts degree in Sydney before getting a scholarship to Oxford University, United Kingdom, in 1932. After his stay at Oxford, he devoted his life to teaching (at the New South Wales Department of Education, Sydney Teacher's College, Melbourne University, and the National University of Canberra, where he retired as a professor of English) and writing poetry. Hope has been credited with launching the first full university course devoted to Australian literature and has been praised for his lyricism and the reflective quality of his poetry.

Although Hope had already published some verse in periodicals in the 1930s, his first book of poetry, *The Wandering Islands,* was not published until 1955. His poetic oeuvre, which spans more than a dozen volumes, includes *New Poems* (1969), *Collected Works* (1970), and *The Drifting Continent* (1979). He has also written books of essays and criticism, *The Cave and the Spring* (1965), *A Midsummer Eve's Dream* (1970), and *Native Companions* (1974), as well as the memoir *Chance Encounters* (1992) and a book-length drama, *Ladies from the Sea* (1987).

In his poetry, Hope himself acknowledged the influence of W. H. AUDEN, and his style has been compared to that of John Dryden, although he has always defended the special status of poetry and its creation, conveying that it creates "an emotion which is the feeling of the poem and not the feeling of the poet." His comparison to Dryden is probably due to Hope's use of neoclassical poetic forms and of satire, especially when dealing with the subject of new poetic forms (particularly free verse, which he considered "a very common cheap and popular substitute for poetry") or with the canon of Australian literature. Hope usually prefers fixed rhymes and rhythms, usually based on six- or four-line stanzas and strong iambics, and while dealing with a wide range of subjects (such as the effects of the Vietnam War, the structure of Australian society, love, old age, sports, or sex), he has usually been regarded as a conservative poet. His controversial status has been fueled by his vitriolic and incisive criticism: He advised strongly against the creation of an Australian canon that overvalued elements considered to be uniquely Australian, and he discredited schools such as the Jindyworobak movement, which tried to advocate aboriginal traces in Australian literature. Beyond these controversies, Hope has been considered to be Australia's most important poet, and his poetic task has won him a number of prizes, among others the Encyclopedia Britannica Award for Literature in 1965 and the Robert Frost Award for Poetry in 1976. In 1972 he was made a member of the Order of the British Empire.

See also "AUSTRALIA."

BIBLIOGRAPHY

Chevalier, Tracy, ed. *Encyclopedia of the Essay.* London: Fitzroy Dearborn, 1997.
Darling, Robert. *A. D. Hope.* New York: Twayne, 1997.

Carmen Méndez García

"HORSES" EDWIN MUIR (1924/1925) Pub-

lished in *Nation and Atheneum* and collected in *First Poems,* this poem of seven quatrains evokes a landscape in which the ordinary is imbued with a mysterious power: The speaker looks out at a team of draft horses working in a field, and they suddenly seem an extraordinary sight. He wonders whether he is experiencing a strange vision or is simply remembering his childhood picture of these beasts, which were then so much larger and more powerful than he. The heavy horses were both work animals returning at the end of the day and valiant creatures who exuded an unearthly, majestic ascendancy. Their customary task, plowing, became a heroic endeavor in which the animals transformed a field of stubble into a well-ordered plot of earth. They seemed not only like brave conquerors but also like supernatural creatures who could move while seeming to be motionless.

Their latent energy and peculiarly bright eyes belonged to the end times; the horses were more than simply a sight at the end of the day. Their bodies had an inner light, and the external light of sunset slipped from them as they approached the child the speaker was. The twilight setting of the memory adds to the sense of strangeness. The sun was going down, giving the world an unusual cast, and rain fell, producing a translucent veil. The color of the land, brown, suggests the ordinary, but the color of the horses, gold, evokes the regal. Old-fashioned words like *grange* and *bossy* transform the usual into the unusual. Just as quickly as the vision/memory came upon the speaker, it left him, and he wishes to return to this ecstasy and to the paradisiacal state in which the physical world is also the magical world.

BIBLIOGRAPHY
Knight, Roger. *Edwin Muir: An Introduction to His Work*. Addison-Wesley, 1980.

Karen Rae Keck

"THE HORSES" Edwin Muir (1955/1956)

Probably the most anthologized of Edwin Muir's works, this 53-line blank verse poem in two stanzas appeared in *Listener* and *One Foot in Eden*. It speculates about the world after a catastrophic war in which modern technologies have failed and people return to external and internal peace. At first, the quiet without the noise of tractors and radios frightens them. The outside world intrudes occasionally after the conflict when the people see a corpse-laden warship and witness a plane falling like Icarus into the ocean. However, after a while, the speaker and those with him value the silence and would not return to the world of gadgets even if these things were mysteriously restored. In contrast to the false sense of unity that modern devices like the radio gave, a true sense of unity develops as those on the farm see their circumstances as universal, rather than unique.

After the seven days of man's destruction, which parallel the seven days of God's creation, these people find they are living as their ancestors did, with animals to work for them: Their oxen pull long-unused plows. In contrast with the oxen, over which the speaker exercises ownership and dominion, the horses freely come and freely work. The arrival of the horses suggests these people now live in unity with nature as well as with humankind, since plants and animals in paradise freely gave their services to humans. The power of the horses initially frightens the speaker, but as he grows used to them, he realizes that the world, although seemingly destroyed, has been restored. Critics often emphasize the cataclysmic aspect of the poem, but it shows the end time as the advent of the heavenly kingdom in which all of creation exists in right relationship.

BIBLIOGRAPHY
Knight, Roger. *Edwin Muir: An Introduction to His Work*. Addison-Wesley, 1980.

Karen Rae Keck

HOUSMAN, A(LFRED) E(DWARD) (1859–1936)

A. E. Housman, an English scholar who often quoted Aristotle, believed that all knowledge was good, even if it was hard-won knowledge, earned with great pain. He surmised that a painful challenge could make earned knowledge more valued. Young Housman, the oldest child of seven, had a hard blow to contend with when his mother died of breast cancer on his 12th birthday while he was away visiting friends of the family. Comforted by these friends and their German governess, Sophie Becker, he did not even see his mother's funeral. Housman's father thought the funeral would be too much for the young man to bear, since he had apparently prayed for his mother to be healed. When his prayers failed, he lost his faith, as his mother had suspected that he would. The young lad knew much of hard lessons and threw himself more seriously into his studies at Bromsgrove School.

In 1877, Housman earned a scholarship to St. John's College, Oxford. Since Housman was a model scholar all his life, it may surprise readers to discover that although he excelled in most areas, garnering first class honors in classical moderations, he did not pass his final school "Greats" exam in 1881. Therefore, he left Oxford without a degree. Shortly thereafter, Housman obtained a teaching position at his old school. Continuing to study, he went back to Oxford to complete the requirements for a pass degree. One year later, he was working with his dear friend from Oxford Moses Jackson at the Patent Office in London. This job allowed Housman more time to write scholarly articles and to continue his classical research and kept him in touch with the man he had grown to love more deeply than as a friend or brother. Jackson, regardless of whether he knew of Housman's affection, could not return it in kind. Moses Jackson was married in 1889 and did not tell Housman, who only learned news of the wedding after it had taken place. Housman remained a lifelong bachelor, and knowledge of his unrequited love may add texture to many of his poems about loss or unfulfilled desires. Housman kept a journal and wrote poems, but from 1887 onward he had managed to publish at least one scholarly work in classical journals each year. With impressive publications to his credit by 1892, Housman was appointed professor of latin at University College London. Although he had applied for both the Greek and Latin chairs and would have preferred the Greek chair, he accepted the appointment. However, in 1911, Housman managed to procure a long desired position as Kennedy Professor of Latin at Cambridge University, and he moved to Trinity College. On average, Housman published three or four scholarly works a year for the rest of his life, declining honorary degrees and other such honors that could have easily been bestowed upon him.

Although scholarship and learning were of utmost importance to Housman, he became known in his own lifetime as a fine poet in good critical standing. Even though by modern standards he published very little poetry, the quality of his work immeasurably outweighs the quantity. He paid close attention to detail in his own work and the work of others. He cared little for personal opinions in criticism, instead favoring textual criticism. He spent most of his own life working with manuscripts by deceased authors who could not speak out against the literary criticism leveled upon them. Desiring to leave scholarship that would be of value to future scholars, Housman accomplished heroic feats of textual criticism and sound editing through his work with the Latin authors Manilius (5 vol.: 1903, 1912, 1916, 1920, 1930) and Lucan (1926) and the Latin poet Juvenal (1904).

A. E. Housman wanted to be known as a scholar first, then as a poet, but it is through poetry that most people come to him these days. *A Shropshire Lad,* Housman's first and most well known book of poetry, was published in 1896, and this book has never been out of print. In it, Housman calls upon his experiences of loss and uses these to his advantage, filling up the pages with the content of loss that speaks out to people across the ages and stands up to any type of criticism that comes against it, because a master scholar built the poems to last, carefully and critically weighing each new word against the last. Two of his better known poems from this first volume are "When I Was One-and-Twenty" and "To an Athlete Dying Young." Housman has been quoted as saying one purpose of poetry is to make sadness in the universe more human, and that poetry is far more physical than intellectual. Often seen as cold, distant, or aloof, Housman was thought by some to have allowed himself to be more human in his poetry than he could ever allow himself to be in person. *Last Poems* was hastily pulled together and published in 1922, and a signed copy was sent with a letter to Moses Jackson, who was on his deathbed. Although there was a sense of urgency on Housman's part to publish before Jackson perished, this collection contains some of Housman's finer logically precise sentiments encased in metaphor. Two such precise poems from this volume are "EIGHT O'CLOCK" and "EPITAPH ON AN ARMY OF MERCENARIES." After Housman's own death in 1936, his brother, Laurence Housman, published these final volumes, *More Poems,* and *Additional Poems.*

BIBLIOGRAPHY

Graves, Richard Perceval. *A. E. Housman: The Scholar Poet.* New York: Charles Scribner's Sons, 1980.

Hardcastle, Martin. *A. E. Housman.* Available online. URL: http://www.chiark.greenend.org.uk/~martinh/poems/housman.html#LPxv. Accessed May 10, 2005.

The Housman Society: Alfred Edward Housman. Available online. URL: http://www.housman-society.co.uk/. Accessed May 10, 2005.

Page, Norman. *A. E. Housman: A Critical Biography.* New York: Schocken Books, 1983.

Geraldine Cannon Becker

HUGHES, TED (1930–1998)

What better place for a poet who believed in the power of myth in life and literature to be born than a village in northern England called Mytholmroyd. That is where Ted Hughes, English poet, critic, translator, dramatist, short story writer, and children's author, was born on August 17, 1930. Christened Edward J. Hughes by his parents, Edith and William Hughes, he spent his early years in pre–World War II England in this not very prosperous area of Yorkshire peppered by defunct textile mills and mining towns, which, however, allowed Hughes, his older brother Gerald, and their friends access to forest, farmland, and moors in which to play and explore.

Although Hughes's family was working class, his father, a carpenter by trade, later owned a small corner store selling tobacco and newspapers. Family life provided Hughes a vein of stories and folklore on which to draw as a writer. His mother told stories and believed in the occult and recounted conversations she had with a deceased sister. His more taciturn father had served in World War I and suffered from recurrent nightmares about his wartime traumas. Camping, fishing, hunting, and trapping with his brother served as an escape from the narrow confines of village life and established an abiding connection with the animal world that threads through Hughes's poetry. During their excursions Hughes's brother regaled him with tales from the adventure stories he had read, especially ones about American Indians living in the wilderness. From his older sister Olwyn and several teachers Hughes learned to read and enjoy more formal literary work such as that of Shakespeare, THOMAS HARDY, T. S. ELIOT, W. B. YEATS, and Hopkins.

Upon graduation from secondary school he was awarded a scholarship to Cambridge University. After two years spent completing his national service in the Royal Air Force, in 1951 Hughes entered Pembroke College at Cambridge to study English. Already determined to devote his life to writing, he eventually switched from English to archaeology and anthropology, because he found those departments more amenable to his personal interests in folklore and primitive beliefs and more helpful to the actual practice of poetry rather than literary criticism. Hughes described a dream of a fox that appeared to him and left a bloody handprint on the paper on his desk as the sign that prompted him to switch his area of study and as the inspiration for the poem he wrote several years later called "THE THOUGHT-FOX."

For two years following his graduation Hughes worked at a variety of temporary and unsatisfactory jobs—dishwasher at a zoo, gardener, night watchman, schoolteacher, and reader for a film company At the same time he clung to the idea of making his living through writing, as difficult then as it is now. At the opening party in Cambridge for a small poetry magazine called *St. Botolph's Review* that Hughes and a group of friends from his undergraduate days had started, Hughes met SYLVIA PLATH, an American Fulbright Scholar studying English at Cambridge. Their intense and vibrant personalities were magnetically attracted to each other. Plath, moreover, was also devoted to poetry as a calling and a life. They were married in June 1956, only four months after that first meeting.

During their six-year marriage they both encouraged and supported the other's writing, sharing mutual interests in other writers, such as W. B. Yeats, Shakespeare, and D. H. LAWRENCE, as well as in spiritualism and occult activities like astrology and the Ouija board. While married to Plath, Hughes published two prize-winning books of poetry, *Hawk in the Rain* and *Lupercal,* which established him as a rising star in the world of English poetry. In addition he wrote radio plays, translations, filmscripts, and children's stories and did radio broadcasts for the BBC.

Plath as well was a prolific poet and writer during this period and published her novel *The Bell Jar,* dealing with depression and attempted suicide and based on her own experiences in her college years. They also had two children, a girl, Frieda, born in 1960 and a boy, Nicholas, in 1962. Even with a family to support they were both committed to living on what they could earn as writers. Plath had taught at Smith College in Massachusetts, her alma mater, for two semesters and Hughes for a semester at the University of Massachusetts, neither finding it possible simultaneously to teach and write with the focus and dedication required.

Shortly before the birth of their son they had moved from London to a rundown country house in Devon, England. Within a year they had agreed to a separation, because of Hughes's affair with another woman. The devastating effects of this breakdown of the marriage and a recurrence of Plath's depression led to her suicide in February 1963. During the few months between the separation and her death Plath wrote a body of poetry remarkable for both quantity and quality, as if grief and anger had released the wellspring of her creativity. Hughes was so overwhelmed by her unexpected death that his own writing languished for several years afterward. The tragedy of Sylvia Plath's death in the lives of her family was compounded by the suicide of Hughes's mistress, Assia Wevil, who killed herself and their daughter, Shura, in 1969.

While dealing with his own feelings of grief and guilt, Hughes also undertook the care and responsibility for his small children by Plath. Since she had died without a will before the divorce she sought was complete, Hughes became the sole executor of her estate, which included all of her unpublished manuscripts and journals. Although he and the children profited over the years from the critical and popular success of his first wife's writing, Hughes paid a high price in terms of his personal and literary reputation, particularly outside England. Some of the poems she was working on during the final months of her life were not published until 1965 in *Ariel*. The American edition of her novel *The Bell Jar* and a collection of letters to her mother, *Letters Home,* appeared in the seventies. Her *Collected Poems* won the Pulitzer Prize in 1982.

This dilatory publication schedule not only highlighted the defensive even secretive tone that Hughes and his family adopted about his life with Plath, it also aligned Plath's growing reputation as a writer and a feminist icon, as a woman left alone by her husband with two babies in the middle of London's worst winter in a century. The feminist movement found in the circumstances of Plath's death a representative case of the injustices women suffer in a male-dominated society. There were demonstrations against Hughes when he appeared publicly at readings and poetry conferences, vandals going so far as to scratch out the name *Hughes* from the stone on Plath's grave in Heptonstall, Yorkshire. Nevertheless, Hughes, a man of considerable charm and dynamism, was famous for his generosity and encouragement of aspiring writers. His stage presence and dramatic reading made him a successful performer and promoter of poetry on radio and in public appearances.

Ironically Hughes and Plath had built a unique partnership entwining their personal literary lives. Plath typed and submitted many of Hughes's poems for publication, including his first book of poetry, *Hawk in the Rain*. Hughes in turn advised her on new directions for writing and even after the birth of their two children shared domestic responsibilities so that she had equal time during the day to work—a practice much less common in the late 1950s and 1960s than it is now.

Both Hughes and Plath wrote with startling honesty. Hughes combined technical mastery with acute observation of the natural world and an unsentimental understanding of the connection between the animal and the human. In the collection titled CROW the crow assumes an ironic and satiric role between human and God. In a retelling of creation the crow is both observer and instrument of life and death, combining myth and religion with the brutal eat-or-be-eaten facts at the heart of life in the natural world as Hughes had observed it when he was a child.

Plath took the details of her daily life, family, friends, and troubled inner life to create vivid and equally unblinking poetry. Plath's unrelenting examination of the pain and suffering connected with her own mental illness, a difficult marriage, and the rigors and rewards of childbirth and parenting paralleled Hughes's strongly masculine point of view, dealing frequently with predation and the amorality of sex and death and rejecting both the consolations of conventional religion and the mechanistic approach of science. Both Hughes and Plath created works that marked a revitalization of poetry in America and in Britain. They combined technical mastery and sophistication with a more direct, colloquial tone to describe personal and down-to-earth subject matter in a vivid, even harrowing way.

Their poetic collaboration operates as an undercurrent in many of their poems as each alludes to themes and images from the other's work. For example, they both wrote poems called "The Rabbit Catcher." Plath's version, written in the year before her death, alludes to a D. H. Lawrence poem, "Rabbit Snared in the Night," which addresses the rabbit from the point of view of the hunter. In the Plath poem the speaker is the hunter's wife, who aligns herself with the rabbit as the prey and draws on the entwined themes of death and sexuality that are apparent in the Lawrence poem. Hughes's poem, titled "The Rabbit Catcher" and published in *Birthday Letters* in 1998, refers to both Plath and Lawrence, questioning and responding to the dead. It is, however, not necessary to know much about either Hughes or Plath to enjoy their work, but the details of their turbulent story can be traced as it animates and dramatizes their work.

Hughes married again in 1970 to Carol Orchard, a marriage that lasted until his death in 1998, but his relationship with Plath remained the defining influence on his life. Over the years Hughes bought several different residences in Yorkshire and London and a farm in Devon but maintained Court Green, the house he and Plath had bought together, as home base for himself and his family. Although Hughes won numerous awards, including the Order of the British Empire and being named poet laureate of England in 1984 and receiving the Order of Merit from the queen shortly before his death in 1998, his personal and professional reputation, especially in the United States, never quite recovered from the early tragedies. In fact his prodigious body of work culminated in the publication of two final collections of poetry: *Birthday Letters,* which won the T. S. Eliot Prize for Poetry and the Whitbread Prize, as well as becoming a best seller (an extraordinary accomplishment for a book of poems echoing the popular success of Plath's poetry), and *Howls and Whispers.* Poems in both these works deal directly with Hughes's memories of his life with Plath and its emo-

tional and poetic significance, breaking a decades-long reluctance to speak publicly about those matters.

At least from his college days when he first read ROBERT GRAVES'S *THE WHITE GODDESS,* Hughes believed that primal forces are a subterranean current in life, and that they provide inspiration and direction for his work. In his final poems Hughes describes his life with Plath as fated, mythic, something neither was able to control. Both he and Plath believed in the enlightening, even curative power of poetry, but curiously Hughes implies that the writing Plath did in the last months of her life contributed to her death. Conversely he ascribed his own declining health in the last few years of his life to effects of spending too much time writing prose. Hughes died of cancer on October 28, 1998, but the ongoing yin/yang tension in the Plath/Hughes partnership continues to vibrate in their poetry, irresolvable and irresistible.

See also "PIKE," "SECOND GLANCE AT A JAGUAR."

BIBLIOGRAPHY

Feinstein, Elaine. *Ted Hughes: The Life of a Poet.* London: Weidenfield & Nicolson, 2001.

Middlebrook, Diane. *Her Husband: Ted Hughes and Sylvia Plath—a Marriage.* New York: Penguin, 2003.

Skea, Ann. *Ted Hughes: Timeline.* Available online. URL: http://ann.skea.com/timeline.htm. Accessed July 23, 2006.

Ted Hughes (1930–1998)—by name of Edward J. Hughes. Available online. URL: http://www.kirjasto.sci.fi/thughes.htm. Accessed July 23, 2006.

Sue Garafalo

HULME, T(HOMAS) E(RNEST) (1883–1917)

The poet and essayist T. E. Hulme was born in Endon in Staffordshire, England. He was educated at Newcastle-under-Lyme High School and attended St. John's College, Cambridge. While at Cambridge Hulme succumbed to his pugnacious personality and became involved in a 1904 brawl resulting in his being expelled and continuing his studies informally in London. In 1907 Hulme went to Brussels to teach English while he learned French and German as part of his ongoing interest in philosophy. Eventually with the help of the philosopher Henri Bergson, he was readmitted to Cambridge; however, no longer stimulated by university life, he left in 1912 to work on translations of Bergson's *Introduction to Metaphysics* and Georges Sorel's *Reflections on Violence*. As many British citizens did, he answered the call to serve in World War I. He was killed while fighting with the Royal Marine Artillery near Nieuport in 1917.

Had his life consisted only of his translations, Hulme would be considered a minor academic. His fame can be traced to 1908, the year he founded an informal group known as the Poets' Club. Along with F. S. Flint and Edward Storer, Hulme was an ardent and sometimes strident critic of the conventional subject matter, ornamental verse, and expressiveness of romantic poetry in general and Georgian poetry in particular. Instead, he propounded free verse, concrete language, and the primacy of the image, as the following poem demonstrates: "Old houses were scaffolding once / And workmen whistling." His ideas, as well as his few poems, greatly influenced EZRA POUND, the imagist movement, and modern poetry.

BIBLIOGRAPHY

Hulme, T. E. *Notes on Language and Style.* Edited by Herbert Read. Seattle: University of Washington Press, 1929.

———. *Speculations: Essays on Humanism and the Philosophy of Art.* Edited by Herbert Read. London: K. Paul, Trench, Trubner, 1924.

Jones, Alun R. *The Life and Opinions of T. E. Hulme.* London: Gollancz; Boston: Beacon Press, 1960.

Roberts, Michael. *T. E. Hulme.* London: Faber & Faber, 1938.

Richard Iadonisi

"HYMN FOR HOLY DECONSECRATION" SYLVIA TOWNSEND WARNER

Despite leaving nine volumes of poetry and the posthumous publication of her *Collected Poems* (1982), SYLVIA TOWNSEND WARNER was known primarily as a novelist in her own lifetime and the subsequent feminist revival of her work has also concentrated largely on her fiction. Nevertheless Warner's poetry develops a number of themes that are crucial to a full understanding of her beliefs, both artistic and political. Her poems are significant as the product of her literary aesthetic, but also as a body of work, refined in the modernist period, that has been neglected by critics

of MODERNISM but does nevertheless contain a perhaps surprising engagement with the literary developments of its time.

"Hymn for Holy Deconsecration," as its title signals, is a subversive meditation on the freedom to be gained by the disentanglement of the individual from the Christian Church. The fact that deconsecration is envisioned as a "holy" experience points to a view of a spirituality that springs not from the orthodoxies of the church service, but from the freedom of the individual. In this aspect, the poem addresses the question of liberty beyond its engagement with religion.

The poem is composed of four stanzas, each containing two quatrains of alternately rhyming lines. The regular simplicity of this arrangement is characteristic of Warner's style. Seemingly out of step with the fragmentation and experimental discordance that were preoccupying the likes of T. S. ELIOT and EZRA POUND, Warner pays attention to rhythm and rhyme in a manner that belies the frequent complexity of her imagery and the subversive nature of much of her work.

In a diary entry of 1929 in which she outlined her poetic prejudices, Warner wrote that she favored poems that contain references to Christian faith and mythology, and her partner, Valentine Ackland, once wrote of Warner: "She has a positive horror of any form of religion, which she believes to be immeasurably dangerous and destructive." "Hymn for Holy Deconsecration" is a political and subversive poem. It works to deflate the sombre ceremony and dignity of the church. With the opening line—"The Church's own detergent"—Warner juxtaposes the domestic imagery of the housewife's cleaning products with the religious metaphor of the spotless soul. The language of advertising and consumerism pollutes religious exclamation as the poem celebrates—"O mystical emulsion!"—the marvelous cleansing properties of the (un)holy rite of deconsecration.

The poem is, furthermore, of its time; "mass devotion fails" when "industry grows urgent." Although Warner has been linked with what Jane Marcus has called "a dry, bleak English pastoral irony" rather than the metropolitanism of the modernists, here in this poem, the industrial center encroaches on the churchgoing populace of pastoral England, much as the worship of consumerism encroaches on the worship of the divine.

The poem ends with a dry and cynical humor—another characteristic of poetry that Warner professed to favor. The God the poet seeks to remove with detergent and emulsion is envisioned in the end to be the agent of that separation, choosing to "move further up the road." Despite the flippancy of this concluding line with its simple, almost childish regularity of rhyme and rhythm, it causes the poem to end on a note of not triumphant rejection of "previous consecration" and the seemingly artificial "edifice of God," but instead abandonment by "th'Eternal Father." This shift in the poet's denomination of God that occurs in the final stanza points perhaps to a regret at the loss of this father figure that is belied by the self-possessed lightness of the poem's tone.

BIBLIOGRAPHY

Harman, Claire. *Sylvia Townsend Warner: A Biography*. London: Chatto & Windus, 1989.

James, David. "Realism, Late Modernist Abstraction, and Sylvia Townsend Warner's Fictions of Impersonality." *Modernism/Modernity* 12, no. 1 (2005): 111–131.

Marcus, Jane. Introduction, "Sylvia Townsend Warner." In *The Gender of Modernism; Critical Anthology*, edited by Bonnie Kime Scott, 531–538. Bloomington and Indianapolis: Indiana University Press, 1990.

Warner, Sylvia Townsend. *Collected Poems*. Manchester, Eng.: Carcanet, 1982.

Fiona Tolan

I

IMAGISM Imagism was a style and program for writing and criticizing poetry that was articulated (some would say invented) by EZRA POUND in 1912. Pound had been in England since 1908, absorbing the influences that were to become part of his program to reform modern poetry. David Perkins in his extended two-volume history of modern poetry succinctly lists those influences: "impressionist exact notation; interest in Japanese and Chinese poetry, in which poets now remarked a spare, suggestive, visual imagery in terse forms such as haiku; the orientation of poetry in the 1890s to painting, sculpture, and other 'spatial' arts; the special attention symbolist poetry directed to imagery; T. E. HULME's plea that poetry must be precisely phrased and that the essential means to precision is metaphor; the development of free verse; the rejection of poetic diction and 'rhetoric'; the cultivation of the idiomatic and the colloquial." Though no movement springs full-blown from a poet's brain without precursors, in the case of imagism, despite the groundwork laid by Hulme and others, a movement started because Pound announced to two young poets in a London teashop, RICHARD ALDINGTON and H. D. (HILDA DOOLITTLE), that they were *imagistes*. He communicated his new term to Harriet Monroe, who used it in her November 1912 issue of *Poetry* and imagism was instantly transplanted to America. Its adherents quickly grew from H. D. and Aldington to include Amy Lowell, John Gould Fletcher, and William Carlos Williams in America, and Herbert Read and F. S. Flint in England.

Flint's "interview" with an *imagiste* in the March 1913 issue of *Poetry* (the interview was actually written by Pound, who was also the interviewee) defined imagism as the "direct treatment of the 'thing,'" using "absolutely no word that did not contribute" to the poem, and written in free verse, not according to the beat of a metronome.

Pound intimated in later years that it was for Hilda Doolittle that he founded and promoted his new movement. Pound had befriended her while at the University of Pennsylvannia (where he also met William Carlos Williams, a medical student ahead of him by two years) and for a short time had been engaged to her. When she visited England in 1911 for a summer's stay that turned into a 50-year sojourn, she looked up Pound, who immediately championed her poetry to Harriet Monroe as "objective—no slither, direct—no excessive use of adjectives, no metaphors that won't permit examination." In 1912 she and Pound and Richard Aldington, whom she married the next year, made almost daily visits to the British Museum, followed by tea shop discussions. It was thus that Pound in the British Museum tea room or in "some infernal bun-shop in Kensington," as conflictingly reported by H. D. and Aldington, found two devotees willing to be discovered and mentored. The draw for the younger pair was a devotion to everything Hellenic. Hulme had predicted that a "period of dry, hard, classical verse is coming." H. D.'s spare images written in what Flint called "unrimed cadence" became the model imagist poems. The self-promotional Pound and his followers were quickly skewered by more traditional critics and poets, including by T. S. ELIOT's friend at Harvard, Conrad Aiken, who predicted they all would disappear in 20 years. Pound himself quickly abandoned imagism when he began to feel it had been hijacked by his friend the editor of *Poetry,* Amy Lowell. He derisively referred to it as Amy-gism. However, the reinvigoration of language that the movement generated swept the field, although the movement itself did not, and in the 20 years Aiken allotted, imagism had evolved in a new direction, MODERNISM. Pound had (in Eliot's famous phrase) first "modernized himself," and then English poetry.

BIBLIOGRAPHY

Hughes, Glenn. *Imagism & the Imagists: A Study in Modern Poetry.* New York: Biblio & Tannen, 1972.

Perkins, David. *A History of Modern Poetry: From the 1890s to the High Modernist Mode.* Cambridge, Mass.: Harvard University Press, 1976.

Wilhelm, J. J. *Ezra Pound in London and Paris: 1908–1925.* University Park: Pennsylvania State University Press, 1990.

James Persoon

INDIAN POETRY The literary tradition of Indian poetry in English goes back to the 1820s, when Indian poets like Henry DeVozio (1807–31), Michael Madhusudan Dutt (1824–73), and Toru Dutt (1856–77) chose to use English for their verse. The preindependence Indo-English poetry, however, is usually considered of little value, because of its complete imitation of British postromantic literary models and lack of both individual ambitions and authenticity.

The advent of independence did not prompt Indian poets to abandon the English language, but instead renewed their confidence in its use. Agha Shadid Ali (1949–   ), whose verse makes uses of what is referred to as "chutnified English," suggested in a letter to the editor that Indian English literature can contribute to the development of the English language in a unique way: "We can do things with the syntax that will bring the language alive in rich and strange ways. . . . Behind my work, I hope, readers can sometimes hear the music of Urdu." Still, Indian poets writing in English are looked

at with suspicion by other Indian writers and critics. It is less the question of inadequacy of expression in a language other than their mother tongue that has sparked controversy than the supposed absence of nativity in Indo-English poetry as opposed to the vernacular literatures. Their motives for choosing English have usually been far more prosaic: The language of the departed imperialists has proved to be the only lingua franca of the Indian subcontinent to the present day. Writing in English thus not only carries the promise of a wider audience in the West, but is also a means of overcoming regionalism in India: "Expression in English can bring a sense of release to the Indian intellectual as he endeavours to express the deepest turns and twists of his own mind. . . . Through it he can at last communicate with his fellows in different regions of India and become more consciously a member of a nation."

For Nissim Ezekiel (1924–2004) the choice of which language to use was an obvious one. Ezekiel, of Jewish descent, grew up in Bombay speaking mainly English and little Marathi. He studied and later also taught English literature in Bombay, before moving to England to study philosophy. The title of Ezekiel's first book of poetry, *A Time to Change* (1952), must be seen as programmatic, as he "breathed life into the Indian English Poetic tradition." Steering clear of neoromanticism, Ezekiel embraced in his verse the chief characteristics of Western modernist postwar poetry. His poetry is characterized by self-scrutiny and the confusing experiences of man living in the modern world. Its depiction of urban chaos blends with that of a human center striving for reconciliation with the harsh reality of life in India: "The city wakes, where fame is cheap / And he belongs, an active fool." Being a member of the tiny Jewish community in India, Ezekiel creates poetry that often shows an ironic detachment from the Indian world. His sense of alienation and superiority, on the one hand, and his attempts to come to terms with the Indian reality, on the other, are hallmarks of Ezekiel's verse: "This is the place / where I was born. I / know it / well. It is home, / which I recognize at last / as a kind of hell / to be made tolerable." Ezekiel, who suffered from Alzheimer's disease in the last years of his life, died in January 2004.

During his lifetime Ezekiel had acted as a mentor to Dominic "Dom" Moraes (1938–2004). Moraes's career was a promising one: Born in Bombay, Moraes moved to England at the age of 16 and published his first book of poems, *A Beginning,* for which he received the Hawthornden Prize in 1958, one year later. Moraes was not only the first non-English poet to win the prize, he was also the youngest. Other collections of poetry followed—*Poems* (1960), *John Nobody* (1965), and *Beldam and Others* (1966)—but these were less successful. Concentrating more on prose, travel writing, and his journalistic career, Moraes abandoned poetry for almost 20 years. After his *Collected Poems* was published in 1987, followed by *Serendip* (1990), Moraes continued writing poetry until his untimely death in 2004. Similarly to Ezekiel's, Moraes's verse expresses estrangement from the Indian world. Moraes, who claimed to have visited every country in the world, was essentially seen as an English poet—a point of view he himself seems to have shared. In "Letter to My Mother" he writes: "Your dream is desolate. / It calls me every day / But I cannot enter it. / You know I will not return. / Forgive me my trespasses." When Moraes returned to India in 1968, his ties with England began to loosen. His rootlessness becomes visible in a poem addressed to his English friend Peter Levi: "Then you went home, all of you went home. / To high tea, Gentleman's Relish, maturity. / At the end all of you knew where you came from. / All of you now have homes, Peter, not me." When Moraes was diagnosed with cancer, he refused treatment, determined to let his life follow its natural course: "We shall leave in ways we believed / Impossible in our youth, / A little tired, but in the end, / Not unhappy to have lived."

Adil Jussawalla (1940–   ) also had his first book of poetry published at a very early age. Jussawalla was born in Bombay, left India to live in England for 13 years, and studied architecture and English at Oxford. His highly acclaimed first book of verse, *Land's End* (1962), was written almost entirely in England and Europe. His only other collection of poems, *Missing Person* (1976), was written after his return to India. Despite his somewhat meager corpus, Jussawalla's presence is influential in the Indian English literary scene. About his first poems Jussawalla said that they express "resentment at being in England" and a sense of being "washed up" in a "wasteland." More than the sense of estrangement, a character-

istic musicality combined with eloquent violence make up the greatness of his poems: "Land's End or Faith's— what must I call / This faulted coast Atlantic breakers pound? / Wave after wave explodes, hour by hour / To undermine my numbed and bulwarked ground." The poems of *Missing Person* are stylistically even more sophisticated: Modernist techniques like montage, complex allusions, unexpected shifts in style, and idiosyncratic use of language have made these poems difficult to access. *Missing Person,* in which the awakening of Jussawalla's political consciousness becomes discernible, expresses chaos, disintegration, and the futile search for meaning in an absurd world: "We're the mix / Marx never knew / would make the best / Communists. . . . / You see, / we're *Das Capital,* a dried-up well / and a big *Mein Kampf.* Also."

Contrary to Ezekiel, Moraes, and Jussawalla, Kamala Das (1934–   ), who grew up bilingual, began writing not in English, but in Malayalam. Among her books of poetry in English are *Summer in Calcutta* (1965), *The Descendants* (1967), and *Collected Poems, Volume I* (1984). Das's poetry centers on the difficulty of womanhood in India, feminism, love, and sex. Her voice, far from sensational, is maybe the most direct in Indian poetry. Resorting even to ancient Hindu myths in her verse, Das rebels against female submissiveness and the social roles of a traditional wife: "That night in her husband's arms, Radha felt / So dead that he asked, What is wrong, / Do you mind my kisses, love? / And she said, No, not at all, but thought, What is / It to the corpse if the maggots nip?" Das, who has been called an "Indian Sylvia Plath" because of the confessional character of her poetry, is extremely outspoken in the depiction of her emotional wanderings and her sexual adventures. However, the candor of her poetry is far from celebrating sexual permissiveness or gratifying lower instincts. Quite often, Das's description of the sexual act reveals her disgust with male lust and domination and the resulting female sexual subjection. "These men who call me / Beautiful not seeing / Me with eyes but with hands / And, even . . . even . . . love." The accentuation of the body and bodily functions must be seen as an artistic expression of Das's belief that love should be unconditional, comprising even bodily excretions like sweat, urine, and menstrual blood: "Gift him all, / Gift him what makes you woman, the scent of / Long hair, the musk of sweat between the breasts, / The warm shock of menstrual blood, and all your / Endless female hungers."

Similarly to Kamala Das, Eunice De Souza (1940–   ) has been compared with SYLVIA PLATH. De Souza was born to Roman Catholic parents of Goan origin. She lost her father at the age of three and tried to commit suicide as an adult: "I tidied my clothes but / left no notes. I was surprised / to wake up in the morning." Her publications include *Fix* (1979), *Women in Dutch Painting* (1988), *Ways of Belonging: New and Selected Poems* (1990), and *Selected and New Poems* (1994). De Souza's poetry is characterized by brevity and precision. Not a single word seems superfluous, a quality that has led Arvind Mehrotra to compare her verse to telegrams. Her economy in style contributes to the sharpness in her poems, which is directed against herself, her mother, and women and men alike: "Forgive me, mother, / that I left you / a life-long widow / old, alone. . . . In dreams / I hack you." The combative tone of de Souza's early poems softens a little in her later work. De Souza takes up feminist issues in her poetry, protesting against the exclusion of women from the Catholic Church, or the Indian tradition of young women's marrying at a very early age. The fury lacking in the poem "Marriages are made" is compensated with cutting irony: "My cousin Elena / is to be married. / The formalities / have been completed: / her family history examined / for T.B. and madness / her father declared solvent / her eyes examined for / squints / her teeth for cavities / her stools for the possible / non-Brahmin worm."

In addition to the writers mentioned, there is a generation of Indian English poets living permanently outside India. Among these are SUJATA BHATT and VIKRAM SETH. To name the most promising contemporary poets, for whom Ezekiel, Moraes, and others have paved the way, is difficult: Manohar Shetty, Imtiaz Dharker, or Meena Alexander should not go unmentioned. Yet, whether they can follow in their predecessors' footsteps remains to be seen.

BIBLIOGRAPHY

King, Bruce, *Modern Indian Poetry in English*. Rev. ed. Delhi: Oxford University Press, 2001.

Kurup, P. K. J. *Contemporary Indian Poetry in English*. Delhi: Atlantic, 1991.

Mehrotra, Arvind K., ed. *A History of Indian Literature in English*. London: Hurst, 2003.

———. *The Oxford India Anthology of Twelve Modern Indian Poets*. Delhi: Oxford University Press, 1992.

Arnold Leitner

"IN FLANDERS FIELDS" JOHN MCCRAE **(1915)**   In its day the most famous World War I poem was JOHN MCCRAE's "In Flanders Fields." The story of its composition and its subsequent reception share the stage with the poem itself. McCrae spent 17 nightmarish, sleep-deprived days as company surgeon on the front lines in Belgium at the second Battle of Ypres, among the bloodiest of the war. McCrae, in his own "squirrel-hole," witnessed immense suffering in the closely fought trench warfare as he dressed the wounds of hundreds of soldiers each day. Whenever the shelling let up, survivors quickly buried their comrades in a nearby field. It was during such a pause that McCrae wrote his poem.

The three-part poem is a rondeau: Its opening phrase repeats at the end of the second and third stanzas. This highly formal structure together with the poem's deliberate pace and religious diction ("If ye break faith") harmonize effectively with the image of the burial ground and its repeated "row on row" of crosses. Stanza 1 describes the makeshift cemetery—poppies springing up among the crosses while larks sing above the pounding of the guns. Here nature's vital and inexhaustible beauty contrasts with the grim finality of the soldiers' end. This contrast continues in stanza 2, when the single voice of the buried soldiers describes their lost vitality as a loss of contact with nature: "We are the dead. Short days ago / We lived, felt dawn, saw sunset glow." The final section shifts attention from the burial ground to the war, commissioning the living to continue the fight—to receive "the torch" passed from their "failing hands." If the cause is abandoned, the dead "shall not sleep, though poppies grow / In Flanders Fields." The remarkable transformation of the poppy from a symbol of sleep and forgetfulness into an icon of remembrance began with these lines, but its resonance lay in the unimaginable losses endured by its first readers.

The poem, published in *Punch* in December 1915, became an instant rallying cry and recruitment tool.

John Prescott asserts, "Everyone in the English-speaking world knew the poem." If this is an exaggeration, Paul Fussell's acknowledgment that it was "the most popular English poem of the Great War" is not. Frequently reprinted and translated, the poem has been recited in Remembrance Day ceremonies and memorized by schoolchildren throughout the British Commonwealth. Red paper poppies were ubiquitous on November 11 during much of the 20th century. Some of its lines even appear on the Canadian 10-dollar bill. As poetry, however, "In Flanders Fields" is sometimes dismissed as a sentimental anachronism. The poem's final call to arms will grate on admirers of later war poetry by WILFRED OWEN and ISAAC ROSENBERG. Paul Fussell objects to its "automatic pastoralism" as well as its "recruiting-poster rhetoric." In particular he criticizes the image of passing the torch as being "grievously" out of keeping with the pattern of imagery McCrae had previously established. Whatever the poem's flaws, contemporary readers were deeply touched by its call to keep faith with the dead.

BIBLIOGRAPHY

Fussell, Paul. *The Great War and Modern Memory*. New York: Oxford University Press, 1975.

Prescott, John. *In Flanders Fields: The Story of John McCrae*. Erin, Canada: Boston Mills Press, 1985.

Anne Kellenberger

"IN MEMORIAM [EASTER 1915]" [PHILLIP] EDWARD THOMAS (1878–1917)

In its gentle portentousness and subtle skepticism, EDWARD THOMAS's elegiac quatrain "In Memoriam [Easter 1915]," which regrets the lost promise of soldiers gone to their deaths in war, may rank among the most dramatically ironic poems in the English canon. Consisting of a single sentence of 33 words, Thomas's little poem about the Great War gains much of its impact and poignancy from the fact that the verse anticipates a magnitude of war death far greater and more personally immediate than it so early on in the "war to end all wars" undertakes to commemorate. The poem offers an image of the gathering of "flowers" in a spring "wood" by "men" for their "sweethearts." But that romantic image is overshadowed by the thought that those men, gone away to war, may themselves have been "gathered," by

death, as fallen soldiers "left thick at nightfall" on the battlefields of France. The men are now "far from home," far from rural England, away in France, in the fields of the dead. Their "sweethearts" remain in England, taken home by no men, the woodland flowers remaining unpicked. The poem's setting at "Eastertide" also allows a Christian reading, with the war-dead soldiers' sacrifice in the foreign "wood" echoing the sacrifice of Christian crucifixion, its tree, the cross, hung with its unearthly flower. The fact that Thomas tended to distance himself from organized religion, revering instead the complex wonder of the natural world, suggests that the poem's controlling reading should be as a lament for the unnatural loss of human beings in war.

Thomas's poem, with its "Easter 1915" date, calls into question very early on the participation of England in the Great War in continental Europe. Yet in July 1915, no longer a young man at the age of 37, Thomas himself enlisted as a soldier in the English army and specifically volunteered for front line duty in France. He was killed by an enemy artillery shell near Arras early Easter Monday, April 9, 1917, his Easter 1915 poem foretelling the fate of its author. Despite the pastoral romantic imagery and Christian allusion of "In Memoriam," the poem's seeming rejection of the practice of war has been seen by some critics to signal the end of a long English poetic tradition, extending through Thomas's own late Victorian and Georgian eras, that glorified the patriotic human sacrifice exacted by war, a literary tradition that the machine guns, artillery barrages, mustard gas, and anonymous carnage of early 20th-century European trench warfare made impossible to sustain.

Thomas, who was born in Lambeth, South London, had taken a degree at Oxford University in 1900 and had married and fathered a child at a young age; he spent his working life as a literary reviewer of almost a thousand books. He was the author or editor of dozens of volumes of critical prose, before he took up the writing of poetry at the age of 36. He was encouraged in his late coming to a poetic vocation by his friendship with the American poet Robert Frost, who was likewise an older man beginning a poetic career. Thomas met Frost in England in October 1913 and began writing poems in November or December 1914. With its Easter 1915 date, and Easter Sunday 1915, falling on April 4, "In Memoriam" must have been among Thomas's earliest poetic efforts. Thomas did not live to see his quatrain in print. His first book of poems, which was published under the pseudonym *Edward Eastaway* and would include "In Memoriam," was in proofs at the time of Thomas's death. His collection *Poems* appeared posthumously in October 1917, with "In Memoriam" a profound and fitting epitaph for its author. Although he was initially classed by his contemporaries as a minor Georgian poet, later critics have come to discern in Thomas's 143 poems the work of both a sensitive naturalist and a highly innovative, socially conscious literary modernist.

BIBLIOGRAPHY

Barker, Jonathan, ed. *The Art of Edward Thomas.* Bridgend, Eng.: Poetry Wales Press, 1987.

Sacks, Peter, ed. *The Poems of Edward Thomas.* New York: Handsel Books, 2003.

Thomas, R. George, ed. *The Collected Poems of Edward Thomas.* Oxford: Clarendon Press, 1978.

Cliff Toliver

"IN MEMORY OF ROBERT MAJOR GREGORY" W. B. YEATS (1918)

Robert Gregory (1881–1918) was the son of Lady Gregory, W. B. YEATS's patron and a lifelong friend. He died fighting in Italy in 1918. He had studied at Harrow and Oxford and had received training as an artist. He was a man of many talents and was noted for his versatile gifts. For Yeats, he personified Renaissance man, a model of human perfection.

Yeats's earliest tribute to the young man after his death was in prose: "I have known no man accomplished in so many ways as Major Robert Gregory. . . . His very accomplishment hid genius from many. He had so many sides: painter, classical scholar, scholar in painting and in modern literature, boxer, horseman, airman—he had the military cross and the Légion d'Honneur—that some among his friends were not sure what his work would be. To me he would always remain a great painter in the immaturity of youth, he himself the personification of the handsome youth."

First published in the *The Little Review* in 1918, "In Memory of Robert Major Gregory" appeared in the sec-

ond, enlarged edition of *The Wilde Swans at Coole,* published in 1919. "In Memory of Robert Major Gregory" is one of the four such elegies that Yeats wrote; the others are "AN IRISH AIRMAN FORESEES HIS DEATH," "Reprisals," and "Shepherd and Goatherd." The poem begins by alluding to domestic intimacies and friendship, beginning with one of the most moving openings in Yeats's verse: "Now that we're settled in our house, / I'll name the friends that cannot sup with us / Beside the fire of turf in th' ancient tower." Yeats had married Georgie Hyde-Lees recently and had set up house in Galway: "Our house" refers to Thoor Balleylee, an ancient Norman tower, not far from Lady Gregory's estate at Coole Park that Yeats had bought in 1917.

The poem goes on to name Lionel Johnson (1867–1902), John Synge (1871–1909), and George Pollexfen (1839–1910), Yeats's mother's brother, as the absent friends. All these friends, individually men of undeniable talents, had only a fraction of Gregory's gifts. Even though Lionel Johnson was learned and was a steeped in classical culture, Yeats had worried that he had become cut off from humanity. "In my library I have all the knowledge of the world that I need," he had told Yeats. Yeats believed he had dissipated his talents through alcoholism. While Johnson had turned away from life, Synge had embraced it but had fared no better. Pollexfen, who "could have shown how pure-bred horses / And solid, for all their passion, live," had grown "sluggish." Gregory alone combined the virtues that in them separately, in fact, had not been fully expressed. Only in Gregory had they found full bloom. Yeats refers to Gregory as "our Sidney." Gregory resembles Sir Philip Sidney (1554–86), the great Elizabethan poet, warrior, and scholar, in his accomplishments and early death: "Soldier scholar, horseman, he, / And all he did done perfectly / As though he had but one trade alone."

Yeats's obsessive preoccupation with the heroic characters of the past and present goes back to his earliest years. He exploits heroic characters in his work for symbolic or allegorical meaning, yet it is the heroic characters themselves who captivated his mind. A single moment, or a single action, in the life of a heroic figure reveals character: This characteristic fascinated Yeats to no end. "In Memory of Robert Major Gregory" lists unusual characters whose commitments in life were exceptionally intense, and who belonged to a "timeless order of heroism" as opposed to the commonplace world of everyday realities.

BIBLIOGRAPHY
Rajan, B. *W. B. Yeats: A Critical Introduction.* London: Hutchinson University Library, 1965.
Smith, Stan. *W. B. Yeats: A Critical Introduction.* London: Macmillan, 1990.

Gulshan Taneja

"IN MEMORY OF W. B. YEATS" W. H. AUDEN (1939)

W. H. AUDEN traveled to New York on January 26, 1939. His arrival marked the beginning of his residence in the United States of America, a residence that would result in his U.S. citizenship (beginning in 1946) and would remain essentially unbroken until he began summering in Italy nearly 10 years later. Yet Auden's emigration was not alone among changes in his life in early 1939; in fact, his appearance aboard ship in the New York harbor was but one outward, biographical indication of significant developments in his work and thought. Auden's departure from England was motivated by several factors, not least important of which was his discomfort with the public view, dating from his early association with the Oxford Group, as one of the leading figures of that group of politically engaged British authors of the 1930s. Furthermore Auden's revision of his own political and aesthetic opinions was accompanied by his search for a satisfactory theological vocabulary, one that would soon be provided by his discovery of the works of Søren Kierkegaard.

The searching and redefinition that are so apparent in Auden's late-1930s geographic, political, and intellectual biographies are reflected in his written responses to the death of W. B. Yeats. Yeats died in the south of France on January 28, 1939, a mere two days after Auden's arrival in New York. Auden heard of the event the following day and marked it with both a prose piece entitled "The Public *vs.* the Late Mr. William Butler Yeats" and the poem "In Memory of W. B. Yeats." This poem, one of the century's great elegies, is a valediction and challenge not only to Yeats the poet and to that which Yeats represented for Auden, but also to the implicit stance of many of Auden's own works of the late 1920s and the 1930s, particularly insofar as those works were informed by the romantic and modernist assumptions Auden shared with Yeats. "In Memory of W. B. Yeats" is thus most important not as an elegy for the Irish poet but as an element in Auden's continuing exploration of his own poetry's strengths, faults, and possibilities. Although Auden uses the elegy as a testing ground for his own poetics, the poem offers not a clearly defined summation of his increasingly passive and private work—as so many critical statements suggest by reducing the piece to a misreading of its famous declaration that "poetry makes nothing happen"—but rather a tentative, hesitant claim for the power of art qualified by a particularly sensitive acknowledgment of the limits and difficulties inherent in any aesthetic endeavor. This claim is accompanied and indirectly supported by a meditation on the relation between the poet and his art, and on the ability of either to persist after the poet's death.

The different versions of "In Memory of W. B. Yeats" in publication indicate Auden's continued reconsideration of the tensions explored in the poem, as well as the continued relevance of the work as an appropriate and productive piece with which to explore those tensions. The original printing of the poem, in the March 8, 1939, issue of *New Republic,* excluded the entirety of what would become section 2 in the final version. It was first collected along with several other elegiac works in the volume entitled *Another Time,* of 1940, which was, importantly, the first of Auden's books to be published first in the United States. In addition to altering the refrain and making several minor changes in punctuation, Auden decided to delete three stanzas, originally included in what would become the poem's third section, between the original printings and the later appearance in the *Collected Shorter Poems* of 1966. The deletion both clarifies the ambiguity Auden achieves and resists negating that ambiguity entirely, even in that final version with which many contemporary readers are most familiar.

In the version of the piece included in the *Collected Poems,* the poem's first section describes the death of Yeats and the fate of his work. Auden follows elegiac convention by making use of the pathetic fallacy, as evident in the second line of the refrain: "The day of his death was a dark cold day." Auden also employs an extended metaphor in this first section, comparing the poet to a nation suffering civil unrest. In these terms death occurred when "The provinces of his body revolted" and "The squares of his mind were empty." After death, however, the poet is embodied in his work, and his words live on, so that the historical poet merges with his audience when they speak of and read his poems. By this process, any poet "became his admirers" after death. At the same time that Auden uses figures to lend greater import to Yeats's death, he offers images portraying a world that persists in indifference, one in which nature and human business and suffering continue largely unaffected. These two elements—the poet's death as national and natural crisis and the poet's death as almost completely insignificant—describe a tension within which Auden explores the life of the work after the death of the author. Ultimately as his work in the mouths of his readers, the poet's language, and thereby all that is left of his person, are "scattered among a hundred cities," to "be punished under a foreign code of conscience." The poet is dissipated and in exile, and the day of his death will be thought of only by a "few thousand," although his work persists. Despite the fact that the general motion of the first section is toward a valorization of the work and diminishment of the author, the refrain at the close of the first section returns the subject of the elegy to the poem's center with a conventionally appropriate tone.

The second part of the poem is primarily a catalog of all that Yeats's poetry "survives," yet in this short section appears the famous declaration that poetry is separate from much of the world, that it "makes nothing happen." The line can be, and often is, misread as an attack on the art, at once a rejection of that political tendency in Yeats, and in Auden, and a resistance to claims for a didactic poetry. Nevertheless the section closes with Auden's clarification of his argument, that is, that poetry is "A way of happening"—a mode rather than a precipitant of action.

It is in the final section of the elegy that Auden expands on the meaning of poetry's "way of happening." In rhymed trochaic tetrameter quatrains, Auden

first lays Yeats to rest and then reinvigorates him as a model for poets. The first stanza of this section is the final farewell to Yeats, who is here called "the Irish vessel." The death of Yeats, as becomes clear in Auden's development of the poem in the second and third stanzas of this section, is accompanied not only by a figurative public unrest as was described in the poem's first section, but by literal international contention. Mere months before the conflagration of World War II, Auden writes in this poem for Yeats that "nations wait, / Each sequestered in its hate," and "the seas of pity lie / Locked and frozen." As Europe hung on the brink of war, Auden moved—those who did not admire him would say he fled—to America to rethink his politics and his art. Out of this first step, and more immediately motivated by the death of Yeats, Auden produces the final three stanzas of the poem, which clarify the important role and work of the poet. These final stanzas declare the two powers of the poet, who can both "persuade us to rejoice" and "teach the free man how to praise." These final declarations deny any strength that reductivist misreadings of the poem's second section may have offered, for Auden is clearly describing Yeats's art as an effective rhetorical and didactic tool. By extension, Auden also carves out a space in which he can practice that more private poetry toward which he was moving without betraying his faith in poetry's continued relevance or undermining the power of this "way of happening."

It is in this final affirmation of the poet's powers that Auden discovers a consolatory perspective that resolves the original motivation of the elegy. While the poem adheres in several ways to elegiac conventions, such as the aforementioned use of pathetic fallacy and the implicit declaration that mourning is both public and private, none is as essential as the conclusion, which not only celebrates Yeats's work, but finds in the cause for the celebration the thoughtful recovery from mourning. As this elegy is written by one great poet for another, it is no surprise that the consolation takes a form that verifies the validity of the poetic endeavor in the hands of the author. Furthermore, this consolation addresses the question of poetry's place in the looming European political turmoil from which some accused Auden of retreating. In the face of "the dogs of Europe" and "intellectual disgrace," Auden describes poets who will, with "verse / Make a vineyard of the curse." These poets will, following Yeats, offer an increasingly fractured world their art's way of happening, thereby teaching and persuading us to value art's sustaining order.

BIBLIOGRAPHY

Auden, W. H. *Collected Poems*. New York: Random, 1991.

Fuller, John. *W. H. Auden: A Commentary*. Princeton, N.J.: Princeton University Press, 1998.

Hecht, Anthony. *The Hidden Law: The Poetry of W. H. Auden*. Cambridge, Mass.: Harvard University Press, 1993.

Mendelson, Edward. *Later Auden*. New York: Farrar, Straus & Giroux, 1999.

Robinson, Peter. "Making Things Happen." *Cambridge Quarterly* 29, no. 3 (2000): 237–266.

Christopher Coffman

"IN PRAISE OF LIMESTONE" WYSTAN HUGH AUDEN (1948)

W. H. AUDEN wrote "In Praise of Limestone" in May 1948, while on a trip to Italy. This verse essay, composed in loose syllabic lines, praises not only limestone but the beauty of mutable, imperfect human nature.

Limestone, which makes up the landscape both of Italy and of Auden's childhood home in the Pennines in northern England, is analogous to changeable humanity because it "dissolves in water." The poem opens with a description of the "secret system of caves and conduits" worn through the stone by water, an intimate system that becomes explicitly womblike when the speaker asks, "What could be more like Mother[?]" The landscape has the same form as the human body and both produces and provides a fit "background / For her son, for the nude young male who lounges / Against a rock displaying his dildo, never doubting / That for all his faults he is loved." (Auden later toned down these lines, changing them to "her son, the flirtatious male who lounges / Against a rock in the sunlight.")

The hills and valleys of a limestone landscape are harmonious not only with the human body, but with human work: The lines "From weathered outcrop / To hill-top temple, from appearing waters to / Conspicuous fountains, from a wild to a formal vineyard, / Are ingenious but short steps" suggest that the artistic,

architectural, and agricultural work of the valley's inhabitants are small modifications of the natural world, not so much taming as reframing the valley's features. Conflicts here take place on a small scale: While the people of the limestone landscape are "rivals" for the affection of their mother, they are "never, thank God, in step." The limestone landscape is not conducive either to uniformity or to militarism.

Since, Auden suggests, man's understanding of the divine results from his experience of nature, the inhabitants of the limestone landscape are

> unable
> To conceive a god whose temper-tantrums are moral
> And not to be pacified by a clever line
> Or a good lay: for, accustomed to a stone that responds,
> They have never had to veil their faces in awe
> Of a crater whose blazing fury could not be fixed

Other landscapes—the violence of the volcano, the "infinite space" of the desert, the "monstrous forms" of the jungle—are extreme, but the limestone landscape contains nothing alien or inhuman, which, Auden suggests, is necessary to produce the absolutism of a moral God; the inhabitants of the valley instead imagine gods who, as the landscape, share the faults of humanity. These people do not deal in the extremes of either morality or immorality, and "when one of them goes to the bad, the way his mind works / Remains comprehensible." Each item on the list of possible faults ("to become a pimp / Or deal in fake jewelry or ruin a fine tenor voice / For effects that bring down the house") is a means of counterfeiting something really desirable: The "bad" of the limestone landscape still want love, and beauty, and art.

"The best and worst" of human nature, on the other hand, leave this comfortable realm. "Saints-to-be," "intendant Caesars," and sailors all leave the limestone valley in search of extremes: The saints seek the hardness of the "granite wastes," in which to contemplate disapprovingly the evanescence of love; the Caesars leave for "plains," where "there is room for armies to drill," intending to "alter" the earth and mankind; and the sailors, "the really reckless," seek the inhuman, loveless freedom of the ocean.

The poem's speaker acknowledges that, as the saints believe, love is fleeting and only death is "permanent" but affirms that limestone "calls into question / All the Great Powers assume": The small-scale beauty, mutability, and accessibility of the limestone landscape demonstrate the one-sidedness of the Caesars and the saints, for the limestone landscape demands that we look at humanity and nature simultaneously. It disturbs "the poet" (possibly a portrait of Wallace Stevens), who is "admired for his earnest habit of calling / The sun the sun, his mind Puzzle," because the statues of the Roman gods contradict his "antimythological myth": The poet's claim that the human mind can be studied independently of the physical world is unsettled by the way in which the gods simultaneously embody both the human and the natural world. The scientist, too, finds his studies of "remotest" nature disrupted by "these gamins," who pursue him "with such lively offers" of sex, again reminding us that the abstract knowledge cannot be separated from the physical.

The poem concludes with the assertion that while human beings may hope not to resemble nature, "the beasts who repeat themselves, or a thing like water / Or stone whose conduct can be predicted," preferring instead "music / Which can be made anywhere, is invisible, / And does not smell," this preference leads us away from our true natures by making us unnecessarily ashamed. In the end, while perfection is unknowable, it can be best imagined by the combination of the human, the natural, and the divine expressed by the limestone valley and its occupants:

> Dear, I know nothing of
> Either, but when I try to imagine a faultless love
>   Or the life to come, what I hear is the
>   murmur
> Of underground streams, what I see is a
>   limestone landscape.

BIBLIOGRAPHY

Auden, W. H. *Collected Poems.* Edited by Edward Mendelson. New York: Vintage, 1991.

———. *The Dyer's Hand and Other Essays.* New York: Vintage, 1968.

———. *Selected Poems.* Selected and edited by Edward Mendelson. New York: Vintage, 1989

Mendelson, Edward. *Later Auden.* New York: Farrar, Straus & Giroux, 1999.

Osborne, Charles. *W. H. Auden: The Life of a Poet.* New York: Harcourt Brace Jovanovich, 1979.

Rachel Trousdale

"IN TIME OF 'THE BREAKING OF NATIONS'" Thomas Hardy (1916)

By Thomas Hardy's own admission, his poem "In Time of 'The Breaking of Nations'" represents in verse "a feeling that moved me in 1870." Hardy expresses his former "feeling" in poetic language to affirm the continuity of life and a firm belief that love is a more consequential emotion than hate. The rural farm scene and the two lovers are metaphors that suggest that common aspects of everyday life will outlast the destructive forces of war, an idea first established by the poem's biblical allusion within the title. The phrase *the breaking of nations* alludes to God's promise to Jeremiah that "with thee will I break in pieces the nations." Hardy's allusion demonstrates the futility of disagreements that lead to war. Hardy's poem suggests that universal emotions such as love will "go onward the same," despite the destruction of war and the loss of "dynasties."

The opening scene depicts a farmer and his horse "harrowing a field," which develops into a metaphor that likens the "couch-grass" to the destruction of war, the memories of which will soon become "only thin smoke without flame." "Couch-grass" is a coarse grass that spreads rapidly and inhibits the growth of new crops, much as war prevents the growth of humanity, yet this simple scene celebrates the continuity of life. "Though Dynasties pass," the renewal of life—as the renewal of crops on a farm—will continue and eventually thwart the remembrances of war. Hardy's initial thematic concern is an affirmation of life over death, an idea he develops further through the two lovers.

During the description of the two lovers, Hardy develops the word *whisper* into a verbal metaphor that expands his earlier poetic assertion that universal emotions such as love will transform war's horrors into distant memories. The young lovers "come whispering by" immediately before the narrator claims "War's annals will fade into night," encouraging readers to consider the word *whisper* as a poetic device that emphasizes both the futility of war and the power of love. The word denotes a tender, yet barely audible sound that unites two lovers, yet at the same time suggests that the harmful memories of war will fade before the lovers' "story [will] die." Hardy's poetic metaphors remind readers that the more important aspects of life such as love will inevitably overcome war's destruction.

BIBLIOGRAPHY

Bailey, J. O. *The Poetry of Thomas Hardy: A Handbook and Commentary.* Chapel Hill: University of North Carolina Press, 1970.

Coxon, Peter W. "'In Time of 'The Breaking of Nations'": The Stalking Ploughman." *Thomas Hardy Journal* 19, no. 2 (May 2003): 45–46.

Kermode, Frank, et al., eds. *The Oxford Anthology of English Literature.* Vol. 2. New York: Oxford University Press, 1973.

James Ortego

"IN WESTMINSTER ABBEY" John Betje-man (1940)

"In Westminster Abbey" was published in John Betjeman's wartime collection of poems *Old Lights for New Chancels* (1940), at the height of England's national crisis, when the bombing of London and fear of an invasion by Nazi Germany were at their worst. The seriocomic poem is characterized by the wry mocking of a middle- and upper-class mentality that would have been regarded by many as Englishness itself. Taking the form of a lady's wartime prayer, the poem brilliantly exposes her religious and nationalist hypocrisy, which serves only selfishness and arrogance.

Her class-consciousness is exposed in the first stanza, where the speaker, while attending a church service in Westminster Abbey, not only characterizes herself as a lady, but also politely asks God to let her "take this other glove off / As the *vox humana* swells." She makes a point of mentioning that the abbey is "where England's statesmen lie" and by taking her glove off she shows God that she is well mannered, but also susceptible to the throbbing of the organ. The *vox humana* (Latin for "human voice") is an organ stop often used in churches

but here also refers ironically to human voices praying to God, especially her own voice.

The following prayer has similarities with Robert Browning's dramatic monologues, where characters expose their flaws and prejudices unaware. The lady's elegant attempt at a conversation with God turns into a highly selfish wish list: "Gracious Lord, Oh bomb the Germans. / Spare their women for Thy Sake, / And if that is not too easy / We will pardon Thy Mistake." The irony of this "prayer" is blatant, as the lady reverses the relationship between a human being and God, "pardoning" God, if he happens to kill not only German men, but also women. And of course she asks God, "Don't let anyone bomb me."

Her selfishness expands in the following stanza to a prayer for the preservation of the empire ("Keep our Empire undismembered"), for the black soldiers from Jamaica, Honduras, and Togoland who defend this empire, but of course, God should especially "protect the whites." Racial prejudice and the imperial arrogance of a country using colonized people as cannon fodder are revealed here.

In the next stanza the lady attempts to impress God with the values for which Britain stands: "Free speech, free passes, class distinction / Democracy and proper drains." The hilarious juxtaposition of British values such as democracy and class distinction, free speech and efficient plumbing exposes her arrogant stupidity. The pretense at wider humanitarian interests is punctured immediately by her asking God to spare her own fashionable private address—"Lord, put beneath thy special care / One eighty-nine Cadogan Square"—and asking him not to "let my shares go down." The jingoism of the lady is concerned not so much with the triumph of the empire as with her own petty vanities, prejudices, and personal finances. Churchgoing for this woman is not a heartfelt need in times of crisis, but an egotistical pursuit of self-gratification: "Now I'll come to Evening Service / Whensoever I have the time."

The second last stanza appears an attempt at bribery, when the lady offers God as a reward her own contribution to the war, such as sending "white feathers to the cowards" or washing "the Steps around Thy Throne." In the last stanza the poem reaches its ironic peak, when the lady gratefully says, "What a treat to hear Thy Word," whereas she obviously has not listened to any voice but her own. God is a means to let one feel better, if one has the time and can squeeze him in before rushing off to a "luncheon date." The woman's Anglicanism is blatantly hypocritical and selfish, so that one is inclined to laugh at her, but the poem is also a convincing castigation of certain British attitudes prevalent during World War II.

Betjeman is often belittled as a poet of popular, funny verse, and the poem's lightly running lines with their mixing of trochaic and iambic verse feet and somewhat irregular rhyme scheme might at first seem to confirm this characterization, but this poem is a supreme example of the way his comic wit, precision of detail, and technical perfection serve a deeper purpose. Combining the trivial and the profound, the sublime and the ridiculous, his poem becomes a voice of humanity that chastises human flaws.

BIBLIOGRAPHY

Brown, Dennis. *John Betjeman.* Plymouth, Eng.: Northcote House, with British Council, 1999.

Gardner, Kevin J. "Anglicanism and the Poetry of John Betjeman." *Christianity and Literature* 53 (2004): 361–383.

Hillier, Bevis. *John Betjeman: New Fame, New Love.* London: John Murray, 2002.

Nowak, Helge. "Britain, Britishness and the Blitz: Public Images, Attitudes and Visions in Times of War." In *War and the Cultural Construction of Identities in Britain,* edited and introduction by Barbara Korte and Ralf Schneider, 241–259. Amsterdam: Rodopi, 2002.

Schröder, Leena Kore. "Heterotopian Constructions of Englishness in the Work of John Betjeman." *Critical Survey* 10 (1998): 15–34.

Stanford, Derek. *John Betjeman.* London: Neville Spearman, 1961.

Thwaite, Anthony. *Poetry Today: A Critical Guide to British Poetry 1960–1995.* London and New York: Longman, 1996.

Heike Grundmann

"AN IRISH AIRMAN FORESEES HIS DEATH" W. B. YEATS (1919)

Often misread as a statement of despair, "An Irish Airman Foresees His Death" is a poem of heroism, as is its companion tribute, "IN MEMORY OF MAJOR ROBERT GREGORY." Written in 1918 and published in *The Wild Swans at Coole* in 1919, the soliloquylike "Irish Airman" gives voice to

and evidence of the nobility of its speaker's character in a simple and unified moment of insightful self-reflection. The man whose thoughts make up the single verse of the poem is able to look at himself as if he were outside himself, as if he were an objective observer with no reason to make himself look better or worse than he is. He is an unself-conscious man, equally honest with himself and his auditors. Detachment and balance are two traits that Yeats admires, and they are important to the system of thought he expounds in *A Vision,* a prose account of the cycles of history, which can also serve as a means of understanding the symbols Yeats uses in his poetry.

This poem's persona is a man of action, the opposite in Yeats's mythology of the poet, who creates rather than acts. The former is an artist of life itself and, as have Socrates and Jesus, has no need to put forth a corpus of words since his example speaks for itself. The poet, in contrast, is an artist of words alone. Although the man of action seems to be able to stand alone, the nationality of the warrior in the poem is important. Robert Gregory, as Yeats portrays him, is the fruit of a long tradition of Anglo-Irish Protestantism, which has shaped the country and has influenced its national character. The upper class of Ireland is ideally a caste of independent thinkers who have much in common with the Renaissance men who were both artists and soldiers and who debated whether nobility is a matter of birth or a matter of character. The speaker of "An Irish Airman" has both an aristocratic birth and an exalted character, as someone with the unity of being that Yeats so prized would. The aristocrat in Yeats's thinking stands aloof, not from people, but from self-interest, and the airman identifies, as aristocrats should, with the poor of his country. As a noble man and a nobleman, the character in the poem is both an individual and a representative of his class, and he expresses through the poem his own thinking and that of his class. As he looks to the sky, he reveals a calm in the midst of strife that suggests he is at home in that unnatural habit for man. He looks coolly but not apathetically at the circumstances that have led him to join the air force and to take his place in the battle. The speaker's reasons for joining the fight are not the ordinary motives of a man going to war; he is beyond the reach of political rhetoric and the reach of public support for the conflict. Hatred of the enemy does not motivate him; nor does love of those he protects. The people of his country will not mourn him nor rejoice at his passing. Neither law nor civic responsibility has inspired his decision to fight. Rather than seek from without, he looks within and finds the motive for joining the fray, although he knows that enlisting in the newly founded air force means that he will die. The "impulse of delight" that takes him away from his countrymen is not a whim but a consequence of the judicious way he has understood the long view of history and can see his role in the world. He does not fear death, and he does not cling to life. He can look at it and his own life with a dispassionate eye. He realizes that living longer will have no more effect in the world than his personal past has had. An unspoken assumption may be that his death will set a standard in a way that his life will not.

His attitude is balanced, so, too, the language of the poem is balanced. Grammatical structures throughout the work exhibit parallel construction. For example, lines 3 and 4 begin, "those that I fight" and "those that I guard" and end with strong verbs, *love* and *hate*. The two nouns joined by *nor* in line nine are exquisitely parallel to each other, as are the two noun phrases joined by *nor* in the following line. The two lines are structured in equipoise. The final two lines of the poem are symmetric grammatically as they express the balance with which the speaker had looked at himself and his life before giving an expression to his thoughts that seems spontaneous in the midst of its grammatically powerful sentences and unobtrusive rhyme. The 16 lines of the poem consist in four counterpoised quatrains that rhyme ABAB, another form of poetic equilibrium, and the number of lines is important because 16 is a perfect square; 16 is the square of 4, itself a square of 2. Additionally the tone of the poem is balanced: The nonchalance with which the airman reveals his thought is akin to the Renaissance ideal of *sprezzatura,* an attitude that makes the difficult seem as natural as the easy, and the ease with which the speaker faces danger heightens the comparison between Robert Gregory and Philip Sidney in "In Memory of Major Robert Gregory." The form and content of Yeats's creation embody the majesty of an ideal man of action who possesses both an unclouded vision and a clarity of purpose.

BIBLIOGRAPHY
Flaherty, Michael. *The Poetry of W. B. Yeats: A Reader's Guide to Essential Criticism.* New York: Palgrave Macmillan, 2005.
Holderidge, Jefferson. *Those Mingled Seas: The Poetry of W. B. Yeats, the Beautiful, and the Sublime.* Dublin: University of Dublin Press, 2000.
Jeffares, A. Norman. *A New Commentary on the Poems of W. B. Yeats.* Stanford, Calif.: Stanford University Press, 1984.
Peterson, Richard F. *William Butler Yeats.* Boston: Twayne, 1982.
Tindall, William York. *W. B. Yeats.* New York and London: Columbia University Press, 1966.

Karen Rae Keck

IRISH INDEPENDENCE, POETRY OF
"The Irish ought to be grateful to us," wrote David Platt, a British captain, to his wife, Jane, in May 1916. "With a minimum of casualties to the civilian population, we have succeeded in removing some third-rate poets." Platt referred to Pádraic Pearse, Thomas Mac-Donagh, and Joseph Mary Plunkett, emerging poets and among 15 executed leaders of a failed rebellion against a colonizing British presence. Platt apparently was a man still too near the incident to grasp its implication, for that Easter Rising of 1916—fueled by the words of these poets—would lead shortly to a War of Independence (1919–21) and a consequential Irish Civil War (1922–23) that would result in the partition of Ireland into a republic and a British dominion. Initiated by poetic rhetoric, the Easter Rising generated an outpouring of poetry through the next seven war-torn years and beyond that would shape the Republic of Ireland—and that resonates still in the Troubles experienced in Northern Ireland.

Pearse, MacDonagh, and Plunkett, inspired by Irish mythic legends such as the Celtic warrior Cuchulain and emboldened by past martyrs such as Robert Emmet and Wolfe Tone, became at once poetic defenders of old values and instigators of rebellion. As Declan Kiberd notes, the Irish people, "having lost belief in their own expressive powers," turned to poets such as Pearse "to do what they could not, and to teach them accordingly how to repossess their emotions." The shared cultural frustration faced by the Irish was given a spiritual and moral explanation in the words of these poets, who called for bloody sacrifice that would sanctify and cleanse. None was more outspoken—nor more self-assured in his cause—than Pearse. "I that have a soul greater than the souls of my people's masters, / I have vision and prophecy and the gift of fiery speech," wrote Pearse in "The Rebel." He believed that "millions unborn shall dwell / in the house that I shaped in my heart, the noble house of my thoughts," and that "the ripe ears" would soon "fall to the reaping hooks" ("The Fool"). Linking myth with defiance, Pearse's poetry unified the Irish past with the present and the future.

Pearse (1879–1916) was a member of the Gaelic League and edited *An Claidheamh Soluis,* a paper advocating the revival of the Irish language and culture. Believing the Irish school system raised youth to be "good Englishmen" or "obedient Irishmen," he founded his own bilingual school in county Dublin in 1908. Once supportive of home rule, Pearse grew increasingly militant upon joining the Irish Republican Brotherhood (IRB) in 1913, and his stirring speech at the funeral of Fenian O'Donovan Rossa in 1915 guaranteed his role as spokesperson for the organization. Understandably then, Pearse's later works were rich with incendiary politics: "I say to my people's masters: Beware, / Beware of the thing that is coming, beware of the risen people" ("The Rebel"). Religious rhetoric, too, was never shrouded or submerged: "In bloody protest for a glorious thing, / They shall be spoken of among their people, / The generations shall remember them, / And call them blessed" ("The Mother"). In Pearse's poetry, faith in God's kingdom becomes faith in an Irish kingdom; spiritual values superseded economic facts, and war was a natural rite of purification.

Briefly a teacher at Pearse's school, MacDonagh (1878–1916) lectured in English literature at University College, Dublin. Whereas Pearse treated heroic death overtly, MacDonagh's poetry presents death as a metaphor, not reality; for MacDonagh, poetry was a divine art, and death was simply a convention within that conception. Prophetically he writes: "His deed was a single word, / Called out alone . . . / But his songs new souls shall thrill, / The loud harps dumb, / And his deed the echoes fill / When the dawn is come" ("Of a Poet Patriot"). MacDonagh was tutored by Plunkett (1887–1916), who later joined him on the IRB's military committee. Plunkett, who negotiated for arms shipments with Germany to coincide with the revolt (the shipment was intercepted and the arms confiscated), was responsible for planning the Rising. His poetry, as does Pearse's, calls upon the past: "The hands that fought, the hearts that broke / In old immortal tragedies, / These have not failed beneath the skies, / Their children's heads refuse the yoke" ("This Heritage to the Race of Kings"). It, too, is openly belligerent. "We shall not fear the trumpets and the noise / Of battle, for we know our dreams divine," Plunkett writes in "The Little Black Rose Shall be Red at Last"—the title itself declaring the inevitability of insurrection. Plunkett, MacDonagh, and Pearse were coming into their own as poets but were overshadowed by W. B. YEATS. But whereas Yeats was once a revolutionary turned poet, these three were poets turned revolutionaries.

Their Easter Rising emerged in part from a disjointed, disheartened antiwar effort. Though more than 150,000 Irish fought voluntarily with the British—presumably for the rights of small nations, such as Belgium, and with the understood assurance of home rule for Ireland following hostilities—economic need, rather than patriotism or loyalty, was the significant reason for an Irishman to fight, and a general antipathy to the war movement pervaded Ireland. While the Continent was engaged with war, the IRB Military Council began planning rebellion. With Pearse as commander in chief and president of the provisional government, the insurgent forces established positions in Dublin factories, public buildings, parks, and most famously the Post Office, on Monday morning following Easter of 1916. In making no attempt to take the more strategic Dublin Castle or Trinity College, the rebels, as Kiberd points out, appeared as interested in the theatrics of the Rising as in the strategy of battle.

Within one week, Pearse had surrendered. While only 64 rebels and 132 British soldiers died, 318 civilians were killed, largely through British retaliatory tactics. Initially the rising left but fury and disgust in its wake; Dublin was a shambles. England overreacted, however, arresting more than 3,500 people—more than twice the number of rebels. During the first week of May, 15 rebel leaders, including Pearse, MacDonagh, and Plunkett, were executed; also arrested and shot was Francis Skeffington, a pacifist who had tried to prevent shop looting. The Irish, who felt the rebels should be treated as prisoners of war, recoiled at the British response, and soon a cult of veneration emerged that converted the poets into martyrs. The social reformer and feminist Eva Gore-Booth published *Broken Glory* in 1918, commemorating the Easter Rising; in "Heroic Death 1916" she speaks of "flawless tragic graves" in which lie "the broken dreams of Ireland" that "with Irish earth the hero's heart enfolds." In continuing Pearse's correlation of religious faith with faith in Ireland, she warns: "Ye who slay the body, how man's soul / Rises above your hatred and your scorns. / All flowers fade as the years onward roll, / Theirs is the deathless wreath—a crown of thorns."

Likewise George Russel (Æ) recalled the "high talk" he had heard from MacDonagh, how "the words were idle, but they grew / To nobleness by death redeemed." Life, Russel believed, "cannot utter words more great / Than life may meet by sacrifice" ("To the Memory of Some I Knew Who are Dead and Who Loved Ireland"). Francis Ledwidge, killed one year later in the Great War, similarly commemorated MacDonagh in an eponymous poem and of his other poet friends wrote: "The fowler came, / And took my blackbirds from their songs / . . . No more from lovely distances / Their songs shall bless me mile by mile" ("Lament for the Poets: 1916"). Other Ledwidge lamentations for Easter week included "The Blackbirds," "Tho' Bogac Ban," and "The Dead Kings."

Interestingly reverence also was paid to one leader not executed: Constance Markievicz, spared because of her gender. C. DAY LEWIS claimed her "great heart" had "died / A little not to have shared a grave" with the executed coleaders. Markievicz was "tinder / Waiting a match" whose spirit "defied / Irish prejudice, English snipers" ("Remembering Con Markievicz"). Yeats also paid tribute to Markievicz in "On a Political Prisoner." Yet ironically what Yeats later called the "finest poem" to emerge from the Rising was by Arnold Bax, who was born in London but lived in Dublin and called Ireland "home"; under the pen name *Dermot O'Byrne,* his "A Dublin Ballad—1916" was suppressed by British military authorities as seditious. British forces "swarmed in from the fatal sea / With pomp of huge artillery," writes O'Byrne, and with "haughtiness" these troops "cracked

up all the town with guns / That roared loud psalms to fire and death." Afterward once "all can sneak back into town" with "desert hearts and drunken eyes," the Irish are "free to sentimentalize / By corners where the martyrs fell." Though Yeats praised O'Byrne's ballad, no poem about the Rising is more famous than "Easter 1916," where Yeats notes that "all changed, changed utterly: / A terrible beauty is born."

"Easter 1916" is typical of a Yeats poem, where a single incident awakens the poet from the infertile mind-set of one cycle into the starker authenticity of another. Yeats, however, reverses expectations of an elegiac tribute through deferral; the martyrs are not named until the final stanza. To that point, those invoked are simply the "woman" (Markievicz), the "man" (Pearse), and the "other" (MacDonagh). All the while, Yeats poses distressing questions and registers doubts about the necessity of the Rising. He finds the hearts of these revolutionaries, "enchanted to a stone," have come to "trouble the living stream," transforming Irish life irrevocably. As one whose cultural nationalism was contested by nationalist rebellion, Yeats is forced in "Easter 1916" to reassess personal and social renewal and the use of violence toward that rebirth. Writing to Lady Gregory, Yeats claimed, "I had no idea that any public event could so deeply move me . . . and I am very despondent about the future. . . . All the work of years has been overturned." The poems of Yeats henceforth would meditate on history and violence, on the discontent of civilizations—and many would focus on that one "public event," the Rising. "O but we talked at large before / The sixteen men were shot," Yeats would write in 1921. "But who can talk of give and take, / What should be and what should not / While these dead men are loitering there / To stir the boiling pot?" ("Sixteen Dead Men"). Yeats apparently came to the conclusion that the rebel deaths were required; in a poetic conversation between Pearse and Connolly, Yeats has Pearse say, "There's nothing but our own red blood / Can make a right Rose Tree" ("The Rose Tree").

Yeats would be haunted by violent nationalism ever after. "Things fall apart; the centre cannot hold," he writes in "THE SECOND COMING," as Ireland emerged from the war of independence only to slip into civil war. Ireland had "fed the heart on fantasies," Yeats maintained, and the "heart's grown brutal from the fare" (*Meditations in Time of Civil War*). He implies that the Irish, having "pieced our thoughts into philosophy, / And planned to bring the world under a rule," discovered that "we were crack-pated when we dreamed," and "now days are dragon-ridden, the nightmare / Rides upon sleep" ("Nineteen Hundred and Nineteen"). Even his later poems find Yeats uneasy with the results of independence. In "Parnell's Funeral," Yeats indicts Eamon de Valéra, Eoin O'Duffy, and William Cosgrave, who had "failed" Ireland after independence. He remains distressed by the role of myth and folklore as well: "When Pearse summoned Cuchulain to his side, / What stalked through the Post Office? What intellect, / What calculation, number, measurement replied? ("Statues").

Ireland engaged in a three-year guerrilla war of independence in which rebels shot civil servants, bombed and raided barracks, and ambushed British forces; the British for their part terrorized republican families, executed subjects without trial, and burned out entire townships. The Irish were inspired to "burn with the holy flame" and to "go to death alone, slowly and unafraid" by Æ ("A Prisoner"). Elsewhere he declared that "the power is ours to make or mar," that "not yet fixed are the prison bars," and called upon remembrance of a past, free Ireland: "Will no one, ere it is too late, / Ere fades the last memorial gleam, / Recall for us our earlier state?" ("Twilight of Earth"). World opinion went against the British, and a 1921 treaty partitioned Ireland into 26 "Free State" counties and six Ulster counties that remained with Great Britain. That treaty resulted in a civil war caused not so much by the partition as by an "oath of allegiance" to the British Crown demanded of all political representatives of the Free State. While most who fought against the British up to 1921 did not consider the wording validation for a civil war, the year-long skirmish ended up killing more Irish than had died in the war of independence. "We prisoners are so many pieces taken, / Swept from the board, only used again / When a new game is started," wrote Joseph Campbell, a republican poet interned during the civil war, in "Chesspieces."

Campbell elsewhere notes that "the little fires" that Nature "kindles in the soul— / The poet's mood, the rebel's thought— / She cannot master, for their coal /

In other mines is wrought" ("Fires"). Those poetic fires, ignited during the Rising, the war of independence, and the civil war, have continued to burn. Many Irish poets persist in invoking Cathleen ni Houlihan, Yeats's militant personification of Ireland (Ledwidge's "August," Ewart Milne's "Evergreen"), while others call upon past Irish martyrs (DENIS DEVLIN's "The Tomb of Michael Collins," Francis Carlin's "The Ballad of Douglas Bridge"). Notably these sentiments inflame more recent poems that link the revolutionary period with the Troubles in Northern Ireland—poetry typically ripe with cynicism and disillusionment. "It took those decades crammed with guns and ballads / to sanctify the names which star that myth," writes John Hewitt of the crusade for Irish independence, "and to this day, the fierce infection pulses / in the hot blood of our ghetto-youth" ("Nineteen Sixteen, or The Terrible Beauty"). Austin Clark asserts that "the blindfold woman" should "condemn her own for treason," and that in the rising "rebel souls had lost their savings" ("Celebrations"). "Griffith Connolly, Collins, where have they brought us?" questions LOUIS MACNEICE, and elsewhere in "cantos xvi" of his *Autumn Journal* declares: "Put up what flag you like, it is too late / To save your soul with bunting." As the dead spirits of nearly a century past continue to fill the poetic voids of Ireland's present, their claim places a demand on Ireland's future. Two cultures, drawn into conflict in the Rising, the war of independence, and the civil war that followed, remain in contention, perpetually reconstructed by the words of Ireland's poets.

BIBLIOGRAPHY

Costello, Francis. *The Irish Revolution and Its Aftermath, 1916–1923: Years of Revolt.* Dublin: Irish Academic Press, 2003.

Grennon, Eamon. *Facing the Music: Irish Poetry in the Twentieth Century.* Omaha, Nebr.: Creighton University Press, 1999.

Kiberd, Declan. *Inventing Ireland: The Literature of the Modern Nation.* Cambridge, Mass.: Harvard University Press, 1995.

———. *Irish Classics.* Cambridge, Mass.: Harvard University Press, 2000.

Smith, Stan. *Irish Poetry and the Construction of Modern Identity: Ireland between Fantasy and History.* Dublin: Irish Academic Press, 2005.

Kurt Bullock

J

JENNINGS, ELIZABETH (1926–2001) Usu-
ally associated with THE MOVEMENT, a loose network of
writers in the 1950s, with whom she shares artistic
style and sensibilities, if not personal relationships,
Jennings published more than 20 volumes of poetry, as
well as anthologies and critical works. A native of
Oxford, Jennings is better known in England than in
America.

The Movement, as such, was formalized by a 1956
anthology that grouped nine poets, including Jennings,
DONALD DAVIE, THOM GUNN, and PHILIP LARKIN. What
the poets had in common were a clarity of writing, an
emotional detachment, and the use of formal poetic
elements. Like many of the poets of her generation, if
not of the Movement in particular, Jennings is a formalist, writing simply and rhythmically, eschewing
mysticism or surreal ideas. She says she was more
influenced by the poets of the 1930s and 1940s than
those of her generation, citing T. S. ELIOT, W. B. YEATS,
Wallace Stevens, W. H. AUDEN, EDWIN MUIR as her
strongest influences.

A 1956 review of *A Way of Looking* praises Jennings
for breaking the stranglehold of the *New Yorker*'s formulaic light verse. Both this reviewer and one of her
1959 *A Sense of the World,* however, criticize what they
see as her flat tonelessness and muted voice. In a 1993
interview, Jennings says she enjoys working within
form for the challenge it imposes. The form she most
frequently works within is iambic blank verse. Sometimes criticized for her staid approach to form, she is

equally found lacking when she attempts more ambitious experiments in broken verse forms in *The Mind
Has Mountains* (1966), a series of poems set in a mental
hospital. She has also been compared to Eliot and
Christina Rossetti in her handling of Christian themes
and imagery, especially in "Ash Wednesday" (*Collected
Poems, 1953–1985,* 1986).

Jennings's early works exhibits a preference for short
lyrics, rarely longer than a page. Many poems evoke a
singular experience, a meditation on art, religion, or
other poets, where the self is only incidentally mentioned. Little is gleaned about Jennings in these poems.
Even her meditations on her time in Rome are not sustained by the imagery most touring poets would use in
their travel poems. "FOUNTAIN," set in an Italian piazza,
is concerned less with an evocation of place than with
a contemplation of how the spilling water is "panicked
by no perception of ourselves." Her poems are often
meditative, rather than reflective.

Jennings's later poetry begins to break away from
the emotional detachment of the 1950s but stops
short of the confessional. Her 1964 volume, *Recover-
ies,* sets the new tone in motion with its sequence of
poems set in a hospital ward, its narrator surrounded
by the ill and dying. The volume followed a hospital
stay for stomach surgery. *The Mind Has Mountains*
gives voice to her fears in "A Depression," "Madness,"
and "The Interrogator," a poem about a psychiatrist
with whom Jennings did not get along. The poems in
this book were the result of a stay in a mental hospital

after Jennings attempted suicide in 1961. Even in their evocation of the asylum, few doors are opened to the narrator's psyche.

The theme of music and its use as a testament to God's glory predominates in *Tributes* (1989). The mysteries of Jennings's Catholicism are given space in such poems as the sequence "A Happy Death," about the passing of a Dominican priest friend, and "Psalm of Childhood." The 1998 *Praises* continues the themes of religion and mythology, and the sublimity and power of art, turning frequently to elegies in the style of Henry Vaughan, to whom she has been likened.

Flights of fancy are not beyond Jennings, however. *Growing Pains* (1975) signals a new direction for her. One example from the volume is a brilliant poem about encroaching old age: "An Abandoned Palace." In a palace emptied of all the queen's retainers, as if "the close sea had / Rolled over and entered the doors," only a rheumatic old woman, intent on finishing her embroidery, keeps the queen in her mildewed crown company. Abandoned by her heir as well as her courtiers, the queen sends out a message by carrier pigeon with the instruction "Find me." The volume contains several mediations on age and the loss of friendship. *Growing Pains* also contains many of the themes and subjects to which Jennings consistently returns: mythological characters and places, childhood, and elegies to other poets. Her poetry, with its exploration of mythology and spirituality, is now far removed from the Movement.

In *Consequently I Rejoice* (1977), she continues her meditations on Christianity with a series on the life of Christ, and she explores Islam in a poem on Sufism. The volume contains 88 meditations that trace the spiritual journey of the soul through a year's cycle. *Moments of Grace* (1980) and *Celebrations and Elegies* (1982) both include Jennings's explorations of ethics and personal responsibility.

Jennings has also published several books of poetry for children, the most recent *A Spell of Words* (1998), in which she attempts to recreate that magical world of childhood. In interviews she has said that she was a child far into her teens and praises children for seeing ideas in her poems that adults do not see. Clearly the remembered innocence of childhood is balm to an often harsh life, one that sometimes bordered on pov-

erty as depression made freelance work difficult for Jennings. Although Jennings's later poetry was sometimes criticized for its stilted and awkward language, the critic Anthony Thwaite notes her "steady and persistent contemplative gift" and applauds her career-long devotion to unsentimental lyricism.

See also "CHOICES," "MY GRANDMOTHER," "ON ITS OWN."

BIBLIOGRAPHY

Blissett, William. "Elizabeth Jennings." In *Dictionary of Literary Biography*. Vol. 27, 163–170. Detroit: Gale, 1984.

Bradley, Jerry. "Elizabeth Jennings." In *The Movement: British Poets of the 1950s,* 87–100. New York: Twayne, 1993.

Gerlinde, Gramang. *Elizabeth Jennings: An Appraisal of Her Life As a Poet, Her Approach to Her Work, and a Selection of the Major Themes of Her Poetry.* Lewiston, N.Y.: Edwin Mellen Press, 1995.

Schmidt, Michael. *Lives of the Poets.* New York: Knopf, 1998.

Patricia Bostian

JONES, DAVID (1893–1974)   David Jones was born on November 1, 1893, in England at Brockley, Kent. His father, James Jones, was Welsh and a printer's overseer, and his mother, Alice Ann Bradshaw, was from Surrey, England. The father's language was Welsh, and he introduced his son to printmaking, as well as a deep love for the myths, legends, and landscape of Wales. His maternal grandfather was a mast and block maker, and from him he learned about the river and the subtleties of ships and sailing. From his mother, who was an accomplished sketch artist, he received encouragement in his artistic endeavors. As a child he sketched animals and illustrations from boys' magazines and Old Royal Academy catalogs, and some of these were exhibited with the Royal Drawing Society when he was seven years old. In 1909, at the age of 16, Jones enrolled at the Camberwell Art School, where he was introduced to more modern, innovative trends in art. In January 1915, he enlisted with the Royal Welsh Fusiliers and was sent to the western front, where he would serve from 1915 to 1918. After demobilization, Jones received a grant to study at the Westminister School of Art in London, where he displayed an enthusiasm for English landscape watercolors and the work of William Blake. His experiences in the trenches finally made the art school environment unsuitable to his restless spirit. During a trip to Surrey in 1921, he was introduced by a friend to the sculptor and engraver Eric Gill, who had established the Guild of St. Joseph and St. Dominic at Ditchlng, which later moved to Wales, where artists were "a company of craftsmen living by their work and earning such reputation as they had by the quality of their goods." Its ideals of service and dedication made it a kind of secular order. Jones converted that year to Roman Catholicism, the theology of which would ground his life and define his poetry. According to his later writings, he did not deal in symbols, but as signs that do not stand for something else, but contain in themselves the nature of the larger thing they signify, as in the Eucharist. A year after meeting, David Jones joined Eric Gill, and Gill's eccentric spirituality, industry, and conversations clarified Jones's vision and matured him in his art. While with Gill he first attempted carpentry but then learned wood and copper engraving under the direction of Desmond Chute. He suffered from a nervous disorder brought on by his war years, and in 1934 he went as a convalescent to Palestine, where he would stay for several months. Later in life he would react strongly when remembering that time, and much of his writing and imagery would be set in the Holy Land. In 1937, he published In Parenthesis, the last major literary account by a combatant of the war, and his genius was immediately recognized by T. S. ELIOT and other established writers and critics. In 1952, he published Anathemata, a poem of 200 pages in eight parts, which W. H. AUDEN hailed as "very probably the finest long poem written in English in this century." It has no continuing narrative or plot, but in the preface Jones says, "The action of the Mass was meant to be the central theme." He reinvented religious poetry in a secular age and drew on Welsh culture and the sweeping continuities of British and human history. In 1959 he would publish a collection of writings on art and poetry, Epoch and Artist, and various poems would be published as The Sleeping Lord and Other Fragments, in 1976, and The Dying Gaul, in 1978. David Jones never married or set up household but lived with his parents, or with friends, or in rented rooms, his entire life. He died quietly in his beloved Wales in 1974.

BIBLIOGRAPHY

Perkins, David. A History of Modern Poetry: Modernism and After. Vol. 2. Cambridge, Mass.: Harvard University Press, 1987.

Ward, Elizabeth. David Jones: Mythmaker. Manchester, Eng.: Manchester University Press, 1983.

Elizabeth Tomlinson

"JOURNEY OF THE MAGI" T. S. ELIOT (1927)

This poem of 43 lines was the first of four that were eventually called "The Ariel Poems." It was followed in 1928 by "A Song for Simeon," "Animula" in the next year, and "Marina" in the next. In this period T. S. ELIOT was writing few poems but many essays and was regularly editing the Criterion. "Journey of the Magi" signals the poet's passing beyond the despair and pessimism of the poems written in the first half of the decade. Images of death and the theme of death still resonate in this work, but overtones of hope and new possibilities are introduced.

The reader experiences the journey through the memories of one magus who has returned to his home and toward the end of his life seems to remember best "the cold coming" and "the hard time." He recounts nothing of Matthew's story of the three magi in the second chapter of the gospel but remembers well a journey through an inhospitable land peopled by greedy, brutal, and unfriendly natives. The purpose for his journey and the discovery of his quest are dismissed with one line, "Finding the place; it was (you may say) satisfactory."

The first five lines were adapted from a nativity sermon by Bishop Lancelot Andrews (1555–1626). Eliot appropriates from Andrews's prose elements that now, in his poem, are to be poetic, "ordonnance, or arrangement and structure, precision in the use of words, and relevant intensity." The sermon by Andrews imposes a concrete starting point for Eliot, one that takes him toward contemplating the meaning of the journey for the magus, a pagan who sees the birth as a death for his people and his former way of life.

The images of the first stanza, all negative, give way in the second to suggestions of life and hope, yet mixed with mysterious images that confuse rather than confirm. The temperate valley, vegetation, vine leaves, and stream induce hope, but what of "three trees on the low sky," a riderless white horse, hands dicing for silver, and "feet kicking the empty wine-skins"? The magus encounters signs in nature and human behavior pointing to a crucifixion (three crosses, betrayal of Jesus for silver, and the throwing of dice by the soldiers for his cloak), the twilight of a brutal age (wine skins to be filled with new wine), and a conqueror on a white horse (images of the risen Christ in Revelation 6:1–2 and 19:11–16).

The third stanza returns to the time and place of the old man's reflections. He is at the end of his life in his native land alienated from what was once his proper place in his proper world. The birth to which he was a witness is bringing to a close the age, the dispensation in which he and his people, who are now "an alien people clutching their gods," have lived. Birth and death are not, in this case, at two ends of a cycle but constitute the same moment. It is around the theme of the end of the old dispensation that "Journey of the Magi" bears a resemblance to "A Song for Simeon." Simeon, a devout Jew, is given the privilege of seeing Jesus being presented at the temple by his parents. He too is an old man facing death and anticipating the coming suffering and sorrows of his people. He is a witness of a birth, which entails a new dispensation— also full of implications for the lives of his people. Both men show resignation and acceptance in each of the poems for their own deaths and the death of the age that each inhabits, the one as a pagan and the other, as a Jew. Both anticipate a new designation for the measurement of time, *Anno Domini*.

BIBLIOGRAPHY

Eliot, T. S. *T. S. Eliot: Collected Poems 1909–1962*. New York: Harcourt Brace, 1963.

Michael Smith

JUNG AND MYTH CRITICISM

Myth has been defined in various ways—as a story that is legendary and fabricated, an untruth, an oft-repeated tale, or that which is religious and mystical as opposed to scientific and rational. Each of these definitions has its merits, but for Carl G. Jung and the mythological critics who follow him, both the essentialist/archetypalists and the structuralists, myth is a narrative of symbols.

In formulating this definition and its implications for a culture, Jung both drew upon the work of his predecessor Sigmund Freud and differed substantially from his mentor.

In 1899 Freud published *The Interpretation of Dreams* and revolutionized the study of mental health. Freud began with the simple premise that objects in dreams have meaning. He argued that the meaning is directly related to personal experience, probably to a problem a person is attempting to resolve, and that the meaning is disguised. The purpose of such mental subterfuge, he claims, is to allow the mind to solve its problems while the body sleeps. For a person experiencing psychological illness, dreams provide a convenient means of access to the root cause of the distress. The symbols in dreams need only be deciphered through free association and their meaning will become clear.

Literary critics immediately saw the potential of Freud's method. After all, works of art function in a way quite similar to that of dreams. They evoke a complex series of emotions through the use of symbols that appear nonsensical and yet possess deep and often hidden meanings. But Freudian criticism could do little more than analyze the artist who produced such a work. It remained for Jung to make two major modifications to Freud's theory before psychoanalysis could become a useful tool for literary criticism, and those two changes take the critic right to the heart of myth.

Jung's first discovery has become practically a byword in our culture, an idea that he termed the *collective unconscious*. In his 1912 essay published in *Psychology of the Unconscious*, Jung explains how, after extensive work with a relatively young and extremely intelligent woman, he realized that the images in her dreams were not connected to any personal experience. Instead they appeared to be derived from a variety of world religions about which she claimed to have no knowledge. From this he concluded that such images were archetypes—symbols drawn from a primordial memory shared collectively by all mankind. Thus he posits the existence within each person's psyche of a personal unconscious consisting of experiences, impressions, and memories alongside a collective unconscious consisting of ancient symbols. During his lifetime, Jung identified and explored the meanings of several such archetypes, including the *anima,* or the "female" spirit within the male psyche.

Jung's second break from Freud concerned the nature of the symbol and the method of free association Freud had developed. Jung discovered, again through experiences with his patients, that free association could be used with any symbol, not necessarily those found in patients' dreams. From this he deduced that the pattern or structure of a dream had as much significance as the separate symbols. He insisted that dreams should be analyzed in their totality, referring his patients to the framework of the dreams themselves rather than allowing them to associate freely.

These two discoveries, regardless of their continued application in the field of psychoanalysis, spawned two distinct types of mythological criticism. Both sets of critics see similarities between myths found in literary narratives and the content of dreams. Essentialists or archetypalists such as Northrop Frye and Philip Wheelwright concentrate on the symbols of specific characters, settings, and objects, tracing the similarities and the transmutations of certain archetypes through cultures, historical periods, or even the body of work by an individual author. The method employed by such critics is sometimes termed *paradigmatic,* because it creates a vertical picture of the archetype that is related to but that also transcends the individual contexts of creation and imitation. ROBERT GRAVES'S THE WHITE GODDESS is an example of the method. In the book, Graves identifies the essential characteristics of the ancient matriarchal figure and illustrates how she has changed over several centuries. It is felt that the similarities reveal certain deep psychological or spiritual needs shared by humankind. The differences represent specific cultural concerns and experiences.

In contrast to this emphasis on individual archetypes, structuralists focus on the narrative aspects of myth. Vladimir Propp, for example, in *Morphology of the Folktale,* identifies 39 functions that the hero is expected to perform in a sequence of adventures. A more popular work by Joseph Campbell, entitled *The Hero with a Thousand Faces,* undertakes a similar task. This *syntagmatic* approach focuses on the effect of the order of the events, the creation of expectations, and the results of fulfilling or denying such expectations. This type of criticism has proved especially helpful in the field of narratology, which attempts to discover the way narratives are constructed and the psychological and cultural impacts of specific patterns.

Both sets of critics acknowledge that the symbols found in myths cannot be fully explained. The value of myths to a culture, akin to the value of dreams to individuals, is found in the fact that they express deep, hidden truths in ways that cannot be rationalized. This limitation on analysis and criticism has drawn fire from those critics who would like to see literary criticism achieve academic status as a scientific discipline. Critics such as Terry Eagleton and Richard Ellwood are suspicious of the intuitive, spiritual, and mystical aspects of myth interpretation. Structuralist critics hope that their work on patterns rather than symbols can achieve such scientific objectivity. However, until we can discover a means of exploring literary patterns and symbols in a quantifiable and objective fashion, myth criticism will remain a helpful tool for analysis.

BIBLIOGRAPHY

Eliade, Mircea. "Myth in the 19th and 20th Centuries." In *Dictionary of the History of Ideas,* edited by Philip P. Weiner, Vol 3. 307–318. New York: Scribner, 1973.

Frye, Northrop. *Anatomy of Criticism, Four Essays.* Princeton, N.J.: Princeton University Press, 1957.

Jung, C. G. *The Archetypes and the Collective Unconscious.* Translated by R. F. C. Hull. New York: Pantheon, 1969.

Levi-Strauss, Claude. "The Structural Study of Myth." *Journal of American Folklore* 68, no. 270 (October–December 1955): 428–444.

Segal, Robert A., ed. *Literary Criticism and Myth.* Vol. 4, *Theories of Myth.* Garland Series. New York: Garland, 1996. ·

L. Michelle Baker

K

KAVANAGH, PATRICK (1904–1967) If any 20th-century poet can be said to be the literary descendant of THOMAS HARDY, it may well be Patrick Kavanagh. Born in the rural village of Inniskeen in county Monaghan, Ireland, he spent the majority of his life struggling with the notion of being a farmer-poet, unable for the most part to satisfy his own desire for authenticity and genuine expression. The early 1930s were an especially difficult time for this sort of concern—the demand was high for a poet to fulfill the romantic vision of an Irish peasant voice. *Peasant* was already a literary word; even working a small scrap of land justified being called a farmer in the rural villages. Determined to become the poetic voice of the Irish peasantry, Kavanagh sent off a collection of poetry to George Russell (Æ), the head of the *Irish Statesman*. Russell turned down the submission but attached a note requesting further attempts. To solidify his peasant-poet status, Kavanagh walked from Inniskeen to Dublin in 1931 to meet with Russell personally. The commentary he took home from the meeting eventually led to the publication of his first collection, *Ploughman and Other Poems* (1936). The poems in the collection, centered on the peasant figure, show the symptoms of an overly sentimental touch that characterize much of his early work—the focus is ostensibly on rural farming life, but the poetry is clearly written toward the Dublin literary stereotype of the peasant. In 1938, after bowing to pressure from several Dublin literary figures, he published *The Green Fool*, a literary autobiography that was reasonably well received but broadly understood as an authentic history and not the artistic work that it was meant as.

Following on his success, Kavanagh relocated in 1939 to Dublin, where he published his longest poem, *The Great Hunger* (1942). Still focused on the stock "peasant" figure, the poem begins to break with the focus on the solitary man in a kind of archetypal approach. The character of Paddy Maguire serves as both a site for the tragic individual and a more universal illustration. The speaker in the poem is marginal, relating the events of Maguire's life sometimes as a third person and others as an omniscient voice. The speaker is also like Maguire, a farmer and gambler, with presumably similar situations in his own life. Kavanagh later dismissed the poem as a symptom of his "messianic compulsion." The shift toward a further development of his poetry—along with a gradual move away from the use of the peasant stereotype—quickly put him out of fashion. In 1952 he began work on *Kavanagh's Weekly,* a literary and political paper financed by his brother. This project was cut short by the *Leader,* a larger publication that printed inflammatory statements about Kavanagh, resulting in a lost libel suit. Near the same time, Kavanagh was diagnosed with cancer and had one lung removed as a result. It was at this point that he experienced a poetic rebirth, springing from the writing of "CANAL BANK WALK" (1958). Kavanagh claimed that "in this great moment of daring," he "became a poet." The following collection, *Come Dance with Kitty Strobling and Other Poems* (1960), saw Kavanagh move toward a more comfortable connection between farmer and poet, as well as moving beyond this distinction. At the moment he stopped searching for the peasant voice, he found his own. In "The One," Dublin's influence fades and instead "an important occasion as the Muse at her toilet / Prepared to inform the local farmers." In 1967, days before the Abbey Theatre was to open a revision of Kavanagh's novel *Tarry Flynn* (1948), he died in a Dublin hospital.

See also "EPIC."

BIBLIOGRAPHY

Kavanagh, Patrick. *Collected Poems.* New York: W. W. Norton, 1973.

———. *Self Portrait.* Dublin: Dolemen Press, 1964.

Quinn, Antoinette. *Patrick Kavanagh: A Critical Study.* Syracuse, N.Y.: Syracuse University Press, 1991.

Ryan McCarty

KAY, JACKIE (1961–)

The biography of Jackie Kay has attracted interest ever since it was fictionalized in her 1991 award-winning collection of poems, THE ADOPTION PAPERS. Kay was born in Edinburgh, Scotland, in 1961 to an absent black Nigerian father and a white Scottish mother, and was adopted at birth by a politically radical white Glaswegian couple. This experience of interracial adoption is documented in detail in *The Adoption Papers,* in which the adoptive mother dismisses racial identity, saying, "Colour matters to the nutters," but is also taught to recognize its significance: "But she says my daughter says / It matters to her." Nature and nurture compete in the poem, and identity is formed at the intersection of race, nationality, genetics, family, and official documents. Kay, who is homosexual, contests the static and restrictive label of "Black Scottish Lesbian," and the instability of a developing identity composed of many shifting elements is a unifying theme that runs throughout her work. It informs her 1993 poetry collection, *Other Lovers,* which explores relationships and Afro-Caribbean history and won the Somerset Maugham Prize. Her third poetry collection for adults, *Off Colour* (1998), addresses themes of sickness and health and was nominated for the T. S. Eliot Prize.

Kay did not begin her literary career as a poet. Interested in acting, she studied part-time at the Royal Scottish Academy of Music and Drama and read English at Stirling University, graduating in 1983. Her son Matthew was born in 1988. She moved to London with the intention of becoming a playwright. She has said she started writing "because there wasn't anybody else saying the things I wanted to say and because I felt quite isolated in Scotland and being black" (Sage 1999). Her first dramas (*Chiaroscuro,* 1986; *Twice Over,* 1989) were written for the Gay Sweatshop. This dramatic background is much in evidence in *The Adoption Papers,* which is written from three narrative perspectives and was first performed on the radio.

Kay's writing is diverse and encompasses early dramatic pieces, poetry, and, increasingly, fiction. Autobiographical beginnings developed into biographical interests with *Bessie Smith* (1997), a poetic biography of the African American blues singer. Characteristically a sequence of poems about Smith appears in *Other Lovers,* indicating Kay's habit of connecting genre and theme across her canon. Her first novel, *Trumpet* (1998), is a fictionalized account of a transvestite, loosely based on the true story of the jazz musician Billy Tipton, who lived as a man but after death was identified as female. Just as *The Adoption Papers* is a self-consciously dramatic poem, so *Trumpet* is a notably poetic novel. It contains brief snapshots of peripheral characters, which encouraged Kay to begin the short story collection *Why Don't You Stop Talking* (2002), which deals with the many faces of loneliness. Other works include a poetry documentary that later became an English National Opera libretto (*Twice through the Heart,* 1991), four collections of children's poetry, and a children's novel (*Strawgirl,* 2002), all of which point not just to Kay's versatility, but also to her enthusiasm for literature in all its forms.

BIBLIOGRAPHY

Hargreaves, Tracy. "The Power of the Ordinary Subversive in Jackie Kay's *Trumpet,*" *Feminist Review* 74, no. 1 (2003): 2–16.

Sage, Lorna, ed. *The Cambridge Guide to Women's Writing in English.* Cambridge: Cambridge University Press, 1999.

Fiona Tolan

KENNELLY, BRENDAN (1936–)

Born in Ballylongford, Ireland, and neglected by academia until recently, Kennelly has firmly established himself as one of the most popular living poets in Ireland. Since his first joint collection with Rudi Holzapfel in 1959, *Cast a Cold Eye,* he has published more than 40 books of poetry, including revised editions, selections, and translations from the Irish.

His landmark achievement is *Cromwell* (1984), a book-length sequence, in which an Everyman figure, Buffún, actively relives the violent heritage of Irish history as a nightmare. With Oliver Cromwell's Irish campaign of 1649–50 functioning as a vantage point, Buffún is hurled through time and space, ending up again and again amid the bloody details of the Northern Irish conflict. Both literally as well as metaphorically, the book strikes out for a brutal scrutiny of those oppositions and ideologically constructed strategies of exclusion that lie at the heart of any (post)colonial condition, or, rather, of any historical narrative. Cromwell, whose image has solidified into a devilish symbol of all Irish suffering caused by England, is torn out of his silenced status and given a voice. Far from minimizing cruelties or neglecting historical guilt, Kennelly attempts, nevertheless, to be fair and hear each side out. Only dialogue—listening to the many voices of the formerly silenced—he claims, can overcome hatred and allow fruitful reinterpretations of identity, in terms of both history and the self. The book traces the windings of a nightmare, and confronting Cromwell here means confronting one's own prejudices and hatreds, yet Kennelly is not fatalistic. There is hope in the end that Buffún may indeed wake, to see "the light of day and the light of night."

Kennelly's other major work, *The Book of Judas* (1991), gives voice to another controversial outcast, the very scapegoat of Western Christian civilization. As Cromwell does in the previous book, Judas here appears in many forms. Wherever betrayal is involved, even in the most apparently insignificant everyday situations, he is present. However, Kennelly violently resists labeling and oversimplifying Judas. In the moments of betrayal spelled out in this book, "Judas" is never an explanation that fully serves the betrayer or the betrayed. Where then, Kennelly asks, is the line between truth and falsehood, between the Savior and the betrayer when they kiss? In some cases, Judas may even be seen to represent a suppressed alternative truth.

Of the many other collections, two deserve special mention. In *Poetry My Arse* (1995), Kennelly investigates the status of poetry itself while following the aging poet Ace de Horner and his dog Kanooce during their strolls through Dublin. *The Man Made of Rain* (1996) sketches a surreal journey in the borderland between life and death. Kennelly's most recent and most comprehensive selection is *Familiar Strangers: New & Selected Poems 1960–2004* (2004).

Gerold Sedlmayr

KHALVATI, MIMI (1944–)

Mimi Khalvati says that she started writing poetry "by mistake and discovery" when she attended a writing workshop in 1986. She published her first book of poems three years later. Previously Khalvati worked as an actor and director in the United Kingdom and Iran, founding a women's experimental theater group and co-founding Theatre in Exile. She was born in Tehran, Iran, and immigrated to Britain at age six. She grew up on the Isle of Wight and was educated at the University of Neuchatel in Switzerland and at the Drama Centre and the School of African and Oriental Studies in London. Khalvati went back to Iran when she was 17 and returned to the United Kingdom at age 25. Currently she is coordinator of the Poetry School in London and is involved in many other poetry-related activities in Britain, the United States, and Europe. She has two grown children.

Khalvati's poetry reflects her dual heritage. Her second collection, *Mirrorwork* (1995), was inspired by Islamic mirror mosaics and the refracted light from these patterns: "We are the thought of something not itself. / Each fragment whole, each unit split." References to Persian culture and family life in Iran appear throughout her work. A sequence titled "Interiors (after Eduard Vuillard)" recalls the rooms of her family's household, with its workroom for dressmaking, the parlor, and the coexistence of work and domesticity. Her fifth book, *The Chine* (2002), is about her childhood and present life. A chine is the name used on the Isle of Wight for a valley opening to the sea. Khalvati uses it as asymbol of childhood. An earlier poem, "Shanklin Chine" (1991), is also about her childhood.

Mimi Khalvati first gained attention for a poem titled "The Bowl," which appeared in her first book of poems, *In White Ink* (1991), and describes the beauty of an actual bowl but also uses the bowl image to collect memory. Her first poems are formal in style. *In White Ink* appeared at the same time as the street-smart poetry of SIMON ARMITAGE and CAROL ANN DUFFY and is lyrically beautiful in contrast. In her later work, Khalvati favors long related sequences. Her tone is warm, affectionate, and sensual. Darkness is rare, as is anger. She has been compared to Wallace Stevens, especially in *Entries on Light* (1997), a series of untitled meditations on light, using its various qualities to approach experience and emotion. Khalvati, in an interview, says that she is "drawn to the fluidity of connections, the fragility of boundaries and how we affect or are affected by the smallest things." The miniature is a recurring theme. In a sequence from "A View of Courtyards," she describes the doll furniture and rooms that her mother created when a child as miniature versions of the English homes her daughters would later enter and inhabit. The reference is repeated in *Entries on Light,* where she says that "I love all things in miniature" and speaks of "a small world inside a large." This may also characterize her poetry as a whole. It is not large or loud. It eloquently speaks of the mysterious world, small insights gathering into a deeper view.

See also "MIRRORWORK."

BIBLIOGRAPHY

Forbes, Peter. "Mimi Khalvati." The Film and Literature Department of the British Council Web Site. Available online. URL: http://www.contemporarywriters.com/ authors/?p=auth194. Accessed 15 January 2005.

Khalvati, Mimi. *Selected Poems.* Manchester, Eng.: Carcanet Press, 2000.

Melchioretto, Valeria. "The Wolf Interview: Mimi Khalvati." The Wolf: A Quarterly Publication for Fresh New Poetry with A Bite. Available online. URL: http://www.poetropical.co.uk/wolf/three/3. Accessed 15 January 2005.

Sprackland, Jean. "The Poetryclass Interview: Mimi Khalvati." *London Times, Times Educational Supplement,* autumn 2001. Available online. URL: http://www.poetryclass.net/inter3.htm. Accessed 15 January 2005.

Mary VanOeveren

"KID" SIMON ARMITAGE (1992)

This is the eponymous poem from SIMON ARMITAGE's 1992 collection of verse, his second full-length volume of poems to be published in Britain. It is an imagined narrative by Batman's sidekick Robin, now heavily disillusioned; its popular culture reference makes it typical of Armitage's work.

In the poem, Robin informs Batman that since he was "ditched" by him he is now "taller, harder, stronger." In one of a series of puns on the Batman and Robin myth, the narrator reveals that he "let the cat out on that caper / with the married woman." The caped crusader has been revealed as an immoral fraud, and Robin has abandoned his life as a superhero sidekick for a "crew-neck jumper." The puns mount as Armitage invests cliché after cliché with newly discovered ambiguity, as in Robin's defiant statement that he's "not playing ball boy any longer." The poem emphasizes the speaker's incredulity rhythmically, too: The strict pentameters are undermined by the largely trochaic rhyming patterns, so that each of the 20 lines catapults its reader onto the next (*order/wander/yonder,* etc.). The piling up of half-rhymes suggests the narrator's new-found skepticism about his superhero, while the conversational style adds further bathos to Batman's presentation.

As Robin pictures the one he once hero worshipped reduced to eating "chicken giblets," the poem becomes a larger rumination on the human need for idols. As Robin returns to claim his title as the "real boy wonder," the reader is left to consider the paternal themes of the poem. The son uncovers the father's human fallibility only to perpetuate the myth once more for the next generation. The final accusation of "you baby" is brilliantly ambiguous here, both a generational slight on his father figure and a suggestion of a subsequent paternal failing on his part. Armitage captures the speaker's abandonment of nostalgia for a world-weary cynicism with an appealing mixture of brawny toughness and unexpressed sadness.

William May

KINSELLA, THOMAS (1928–)

Thomas Kinsella, born in Dublin in 1928, entered University College, Dublin, in 1946 to study science but left almost immediately to enter the Irish Civil Service, where he remained for almost 20 years (1946–65). He continued to study at the university at night, switching his interest to the humanities, and began to publish poems in the university magazine the *National Student.* He caught the attention of Liam Miller, whose Dolman Press published a pamphlet of his poems in 1952 (*The Starlight Eye*) and his first book, *Poems,* in 1956.

Miller suggested he translate early Irish texts for the Dolman Press. This began an important career for Kinsella as a translator as well as a poet, with *Longes Mac Unsnig* and *The Breastplate of St. Patrick* in 1954, *Thirty-Three Triads* in 1955, and the monumental *Tain* (published by Dolman Press in 1969 and Oxford University Press in 1970). In 1981 he translated three centuries of Irish poetry for *An Duanaire: Poems of the Dispossessed.* In 1986 he edited *The New Oxford Book of Irish Verse.* In 1965 he left the Civil Service for a writer-in-residence position in America at Southern Illinois University, followed by a professorship at Temple University (1970–90), where he directed Temple's study abroad program in Dublin.

Kinsella's early poems are often set in Dublin, as is the poetry of AUSTIN CLARKE, whom he edited, but another early influence was W. H. AUDEN. Kinsella rejected the idea, however, that he was principally an Irish or a Catholic poet. His essay "The Divided Mind" (1973) explores the problem of being an Anglo-Irish writer who is at home in neither tradition, not Irish nor English. He claimed Joyce as his model, not W. B. YEATS, and much of his later poetry seems more influenced by the American modernists EZRA POUND and William Carlos Williams. He started his own press in 1972, the Peppercanister Press, to publish his own work. He has published well over two dozen books of poetry.

See also "ANCESTOR," "TEARS."

BIBLIOGRAPHY

John, Brian. *Reading the Ground: The Poetry of Thomas Kinsella.* Washington, D.C.: Catholic University of America Press, 1997.

Badin, Donatella Abbate. *Thomas Kinsella.* Twayne's English Author Series. New York: Twayne, 1996.

James Persoon

KIPLING, RUDYARD (1865–1936)   Short-story writer, novelist, and poet, Kipling was born on December 30, 1865, in Bombay, India, where his father, John Lockwood Kipling, was a sculpture teacher at the Bombay School of Art and Industry. His most popular works include *The Jungle Book* (1894) and the *Just So Stories* (1902), both children's classics although they have attracted adult audiences also.

As were many English children born in the colonies, at the age of six, Kipling was sent "home" with his sister to Southsea, England, for five years. This unhappy period colors his novel *The Light That Failed* (1890), the short story "Baa Baa Black Sheep," and his autobiography, *Something of Myself* (1937). In 1878 Kipling entered United Services College, an expensive boarding school in North Devon that prepared its students for admission to military academies. Although plans for a military career were ended by his poor performance as a student as well as his weak eyesight, Kipling recalled the experience quite lightheartedly in *Stalky & Co* (1899).

From 1882 to 1887 Kipling worked in India, as a journalist in Lahore for the *Civil and Military Gazette* (1882–87) and as an assistant editor and overseas correspondent in Allahabad for the *Pioneer* (1887–89). His short stories and poems gained success in the late 1880s in England, where he was hailed as a literary heir to Charles Dickens and the unofficial poet laureate. Between 1889 and 1892, Kipling lived in London and published *Life's Handicap* (1891), a collection of Indian stories, and *Barrack-Room Ballads,* a collection of poems that included "Gunga Din." The stories written during his last two years in India were collected in *The Phantom Rickshaw* (1888).

In 1892 Kipling collaborated on a novel, *The Naulakha* (1892), with Caroline Starr Balestier, an American whom he later married. His marriage was, from all accounts, not entirely happy. He moved to Vermont in the United States for four years and spent some months in South Africa during the Boer War of 1899, before returning to England in 1902 to settle at a house called Bateman's in Burwash, Sussex. He wrote *Many Inventions* (1893), *The Jungle Book* (1894), *The Second Jungle Book* (1895), *The Seven Seas* (1896), and *Captains Courageous* (1897) during these uneasy years. *Kim,* the novel widely considered to be Kipling's best, appeared in 1901. The story, set in

India, relates the adventures of the orphaned son of a sergeant in an Irish regiment. *Puck of Pook's Hill,* a historical work for children, was published in 1906 and its sequel, *Rewards and Fairies,* in 1910.

During his lifetime Kipling refused many honors, among them the poet laureateship and the Order of Merit, but he became the first Englishman to receive the Nobel Prize in literature (1907). He was an active propagandist during the First World War, until his son was killed in action while serving as a lieutenant in the Irish Guards. As a tribute, in 1923, he published *The Irish Guards in the Great War,* a history of his son's regiment. He died on January 18, 1936, in London, and his ashes were deposited in Poet's Corner at Westminster Abbey. His autobiography, *Something of Myself,* appeared posthumously in 1937.

Kipling is often remembered—and castigated—for his idealization of British imperialism and colonial heroism in India and Burma. His glorification of the British Empire and racial prejudices, particularly in poems like "The White Man's Burden" (1899), has repelled many readers, although a note of uncharacteristic humility and caution sounds in "The Recessional" (1897). However, recent criticism has begun to acknowledge Kipling's commitment to realism and to the contribution of the ordinary man to the making and maintenance of empire. He remained essentially a journalist, and his poems often resonate with the voice of the skeptical ordinary man, the one who slogs at the routine jobs, rather than merely celebrating the high-class officers and those who occupy the ivory towers of command.

See also "Epitaphs of War," "The Glory of the Garden," "The Gods of the Copybook Headings."

BIBLIOGRAPHY

Amis, Kingsley. *Rudyard Kipling.* London: Thames and Hudson, 1975.

Gilmour, David. *The Long Recessional: The Imperial Life of Rudyard Kipling.* London: John Murray, 2002.

Green, R. L., ed. *Kipling, the Critical Heritage.* New York: Barnes & Noble, 1971.

Jones, R. T., ed. *The Collected Poems of Rudyard Kipling.* Ware, Eng.: Wordsworth Poetry Library, 2001.

Keating, Peter. *Kipling the Poet.* London: Secker and Warburg, 1993.

Ricketts, Harry. *The Unforgiving Minute: A Life of Rudyard Kipling.* London: Chatto and Windus, 1999.

Silken, Jon, ed. *The Penguin Book of First World War Poetry.* London: Penguin, 1981.

Divya Saksena

KUPPNER, FRANK (1951–   )

A writer from Glasgow, Scotland, whose extremely distinctive style is often humorous and always playful, Kuppner is often called a "postmodern" poet, because his work continually calls itself, and the identity and authority of reader, writer, and narrative, into question. His subject matter is varied, but his peculiar voice and personality tend to overwhelm this variety, so that whatever world he takes us into, it is always recognizable as a world of Kuppner's. Robert Crawford has pointed out that despite his postmodern approach and eclectic subject matter, the Kuppner brand of humor and attitude makes this poet more representative of Glaswegian culture than he might at first appear.

Kuppner's first book, *A Bad Day for the Sung Dynasty* (1984), famously consisted of a single poem in 511 quatrains, or 511 poems each of a single quatrain (it is typical of Kuppner that he leaves this question undecided). Each quatrain was an exercise in deadpan *chinoiserie,* sketching an absurd situation, a snatch of narrative or a series of gnomic non sequiturs. Chinese scholars, emperors, goddesses, bureaucrats, ladies, and concubines jostle in a chaotic stream of assassinations, trysts, and other incidents, many of which are repeated, with contradictory variations, throughout the collection. Eschewing meter, rhyme, and the ideal of authenticity that other poets take as fundamental, Kuppner piles sentence on restrained, comic sentence. Although he constantly points out the fictional and flimsy nature of the world he is creating, Kuppner manages to generate real lyrical and narrative interest by adhering mercilessly to his formal constraints. A Kuppner quatrain operates entirely according to its own principles. This is just the first:

> The elderly statesman trudges wearily over the
>   bridge;
> He was expected in the palace more than
>   twenty-five minutes ago.
> Surely that is not his penis in his hand?
> From the bedroom of a house in Germany I
>   once saw trees exactly like that.

In later books Kuppner vacillated between exploitation of the verse form he had created (of *Second Best Moments in Chinese History,* from 1997, he protested, tongue-in-cheek, "Please note that this is a completely different work, although it is formally identical and very similar in its preoccupations") and attempts to modify the style to carry a more obviously sustained narrative or meditation. The best of these are probably the long poems in *The Intelligent Observation of Naked Women* (1987). The relaxing of form to allow a line of thought to proceed across more than one quatrain—sometimes the jettisoning of quatrains altogether—makes for a less limited but also less engaging style. He has also written a free version of the *Rubaiyat of Omar Khayyam* called "In a Persian Garden," as well as novels and criticism.

Kuppner remains less well known than one would expect from the critical enthusiasm that surrounds him. A *Selected Poems* appeared in 2000, but it may be a slightly misleading means to approach his work; reading a full collection would be a better introduction.

BIBLIOGRAPHY
Crawford, Robert. *Identifying Poets: Self and Territory in Twentieth-Century Poetry.* Edinburgh: Edinburgh University Press, 1993.

Tony Williams

L

"THE LANDSCAPE NEAR AN AERO-DROME" STEPHEN SPENDER (1933)

"The Landscape Near an Aerodrome" first appeared in STEPHEN SPENDER's early collection, *Poems* (1933). Along with "THE PYLONS," this poem placed Spender in the vanguard of the so-called Pylon school of poets, which also included other Leftist British poets of the 1930s such as W. H. AUDEN, C. DAY LEWIS, and LOUIS MAC-NEICE, whose self-conscious use of modern industrial and technological imagery and symbolism often provided a satirical counterpoint to the sometimes uncritical encomia that prevailed throughout the early 20th century of industrialization and urban expansion in England.

In many of his poems, including this one, Spender's attitude toward technological progress is anything but straightforward. In the opening verse paragraphs, the poet describes an "air liner with shut-back engines" as being "more beautiful and soft than any moth / With burring furred antennae." This "huge" aircraft, the veritable embodiment of technological innovation and progress, "glides . . . across sea / And across . . . land" not harshly or noisily, but "gently" and "broadly," barely "disturbing charted currents of air."

This air liner also "Glides over suburbs," however, and from this unique vantage point "the travellers . . . can see what is being done" by "industry" in "the outskirts of this town." The same technologically advanced aerodynamic principles that have "lulled" these passengers into a false sense of comfort and security are now providing them with a bird's-eye view of "the outposts / Of work" on the "fraying edge" of the expanding city. In the third verse paragraph, Spender uses words like *frightening, mad,* and *strange* to describe the decaying, seemingly "foreign," urban cityscape. His similes are evocative and arresting: The smoking "chimneys" are "like lank black fingers / Or figures," the "unhomely . . . few houses / Moan" and "complain[], like a dog / Shut out, and shivering at the . . . moon." Whereas the "feminine land" of rural England had "indulg[ed] its easy limbs / In miles of softness," the "squat buildings" that dominate the spaces of urban England are "like women's faces / Shattered by grief."

Upon those unfortunates who live here, Spender suggests, industrialization has had a dehumanizing impact. In the "fields / Behind the aerodrome," members of the younger generation "play all day." Like a scythe or a combine harvester, they take to "hacking" up the dried "grass" that years of pollution have withered. Their "cries" are not like those of "boys," but they are "like wild birds." Their attempts to communicate with one another fail, since those feral shrieks "soon are hid under the loud city" and its inhuman, mechanical din.

Spender's perspective shifts, however, in the closing verse paragraph of the poem. As the air liner descends from the "dying sky" and touches down upon "the landscape of hysteria," the passengers can "hear the tolling bell" of a church. This bell is "louder than all those batteries, / And charcoaled towers" of industrial progress so lamented in the previous lines of the poem. Even in the face of burgeoning technology and industrialization, Spender asserts, "religion stands, the church blocking the sun." While industrialization may be having a deleterious effect upon the landscape and upon people's ability to communicate fruitfully with one another, so too do the dogmas and trappings of religion. Whatever the alternative may be to industrial expansion in England, Spender suggests, it is certainly not to look backward toward the darkness of religious complacency.

BIBLIOGRAPHY
Spender, Stephen. *Collected Poems 1928–1953*. London: Faber, 1955.
———. *Collected Poems 1928–1985*. London: Faber, 1985.

Robert G. May

LARKIN, PHILIP (1922–1985)

Born into a quite unliterary family in the city of Coventry, where his father was city treasurer, Philip Larkin rose to be perhaps the most memorable poet of his generation. Among 20th-century British poets only W. H. AUDEN and W. B. YEATS can rival him in the suppleness of their use of rhyme. When his friend JOHN BETJEMAN died in 1984, it was Larkin who was reportedly first considered as the new poet laureate of Britain, but illness caused him to pass it by, and it was offered instead to TED HUGHES.

Larkin's early life is documented in his letters to his boyhood friend, James Sutton, now in the Brynmor Jones Library at Hull University, where he spent most of his working life as the head librarian. A cartoon in one of those letters to Sutton, reprinted on the flyleaf of the *Selected Letters* (1992), shows the young Larkin alienated from his family: His father is reading a newspaper and sympathizing with the rise of Hitler in Germany and the coming "end of civilization as we know it," while his mother obliviously talks about her plans for lunch and his sister prattles on about an upcoming dance. All three are talking at once, none listening to the others, while the red-faced author sits ready to explode in the corner at a desk, his back to them, writing, presumably his letter to Sutton. The picture is one of alienation and frustration, two muses for Larkin's writing that he could draw upon all of his life.

In the autumn of 1940, Larkin went up to St. John's College, Oxford, where he spent the early years of the Second World War, while Sutton in the spring of 1941 joined the military. At Oxford, his new best friend was KINGSLEY AMIS, who shared his enthusiasm for jazz. In 1943 Larkin, upon taking his degree, was exempted from service because of his bad eyesight, and he began a series of library jobs culminating in Hull, where he remained until his retirement and death of cancer.

During the 1940s Larkin had minor successes with a book of poems, *The North Ship,* in 1945, and two novels, *Jill* in 1946 and *A Girl in Winter* in 1947. It was Amis, however, who went on to become a novelist, the profession Larkin had always wanted for himself, achieving fame and success with his first attempt, *Lucky Jim,* in 1954, a novel that, ironically, starred a thinly disguised version of Larkin as its hero, and that Larkin may have helped to write. The hero, Jim Dixon, is a bored junior academic who feels forced to flatter his boss, his girlfriend, and just about everyone he meets, but who is able to release his large store of pent-up frustrations with the fools of this world by making grimacing and mocking faces behind their backs. When *Lucky Jim* became a best seller, Larkin did not hide his jealousy of Amis, nor his morose conviction that someone else always gets "the fame and the girl and the money" ("Toads").

In 1955 Larkin published the first book of poems to give him a reputation as a poet, *The Less Deceived.* Where *The North Ship* seemed highly imitative of Yeats, the new book showed Larkin's distinctive voice emerging, especially in such poems as "DECEPTIONS," "CHURCH GOING," and "Toads." In later interviews, Larkin said he had thrown over Yeats for THOMAS HARDY, as Hardy allowed one a little more freedom to write in a lower key, not all "jacked up" as Yeats was with mythologies.

The following year Robert Conquest included Larkin in an anthology he edited, *NEW LINES,* in whose introduction he announced a new "Movement" in British poetry, one that valued formal structures and plain language. While Larkin agreed with these goals for writing, especially in reaction to the "hysterias and insincerities" of poetry written during the Second World War, he thought Conquest had gone too far in declaring a new poetry, specifying "[WILFRED] OWEN, Hopkins, Hardy, EDWARD THOMAS" as poets against whom "I don't think 'our' poetry stands up for a single second" (Motion 265). Larkin's letter to Conquest gave his own succinct list of the qualities of his poetry—"plain language, absence of posturings, sense of proportion, humour, abandonment of the dithyrambic ideal"—but averred that he did not yet have the "matter"—"a fuller and more sensitive response to life as it appears from day to day, and not only on Mediterranean holidays financed by the British Council." Larkin was well on his way to becoming the "people's poet," not an academic.

Larkin was a slow writer, however, with a demanding full-time job that he took seriously. *The Less Deceived* was a slim volume, and he would produce only two more, equally slim, one in each of the following decades. *The Whitsun Weddings* appeared in 1964. It included, along with the title poem, such often anthologized pieces as "MCMXIV," "TALKING IN BED," and "AN ARUNDEL TOMB." His final volume appeared a decade later, *High Windows* (1974), with the poems most explicitly about sex, "ANNUS MIRABILIS," "THIS BE THE VERSE," and "HIGH WINDOWS." The last two broke a taboo in serious British poetry by using the word *fuck,* not what was expected by those with only a casual acquaintanceship with the bespectacled, balding Hull librarian who would soon escort the queen around the new library building for its dedication.

When Larkin moved from his flat with the "high windows" in Pearson Park to a comfortable larger home near the university to live with his companion Monica Jones, poetry seemed to leave him. Only one great poem remained, the moving "AUBADE" published in the *Times Literary Supplement* in December 1977. His jazz columns for the *Daily Telegraph* newspaper were published as *All What Jazz* (1970). He also edited *The Oxford Book of Twentieth-Century English Verse* (1973) and a collection of essays, *Required Writing* (1983).

With the posthumous publication of the *Collected Poems,* the *Selected Letters,* and a biography by one of his literary executors, his reputation was hit by controversy, when the reviews fastened upon his conservative politics, his admiration for Margaret Thatcher, and some elitist and ill-tempered remarks in letters about women, blacks, and working-class youths who should not be at university. Reviewers treated these revelations as surprising and something of a minor scandal. The attacks were significant enough that Martin Amis, son of Kingsley Amis and a novelist in his own right, attempted a defense in the *New Yorker* but ended up defending the poetry and not the man and agreed that much of what the man said was inexcusable.

Some found the poetry offensive, too, especially a few of the never published poems, such as "Love Again," written in 1979, which, as was "Dry Point" years before, is about a not often celebrated topic, masturbation. But where the former poem hints at the activity, this one begins baldly, explicitly, slangily: "Love again: wanking at ten past three." Drunkenness too has never been a stranger to poetry, but Larkin's drink was clearly taken out of fear and weakness, as that beautiful late poem "Aubade" admits. He allowed his letters and his poetry to air his mean-spirited thoughts, his nasty feelings about women, about race, about even the then-out-of-fashion mystery writer Barbara Pym, whom he helped get published. In the poem "The Dance," for example, a colleague becomes "some shoptalking shit." A letter to another poet begins with this rude limerick on Pym:

> The chances are certainly slim
> Of finding in Barbara Pym
>   (I speak with all deference)
>   The faintest of reference
> To what in our youth we called quim.

These documents he knew would become public. He left two conflicting clauses in his will, one asking that his papers be destroyed, another giving sole discretion to his literary executors, who chose, as Larkin must have known they would, to publish. In his public life Larkin was respectable, respected, and even kindhearted, tolerating life's stupidities and intrusions when his growing fame would have allowed for more outright rudeness or more insulation. One can see this in the pained yet smiling photos he stood for with Americans whom he hardly knew when he was already dangerously ill.

Larkin's troubles with women are enumerated in his executor ANDREW MOTION's biography. The unpublished poems that another executor, ANTHONY THWAITE, prints in the *Collected Poems* detail more of this for us. The sense of failure so prevalent in the poems (and perhaps the main stuff out of which the poetry is made) is not ultimately about money or women or fame. It is about Larkin's feeling that he had failed as a human being. This gives one way to read the racist and sexist remarks that Larkin showcases in the letters. He certainly believed in the duty one owed the social fabric, to be reasonably polite and socially responsible. He also believed, as does Amis's hero Jim, that one needs to express what one feels, even if it makes its first appearance with an ugly and ignoble face. He showed that ugly face to himself first. The letters are full of inarticulate sounds—*Wow, Wow, Wow*—like an animal without speech expressing its pain. On his desk Larkin kept a picture of a gorilla at the London Zoo, mouth wide open baring its fangs and flinging out an unholy scream. The gorilla is Larkin. He imagines his future biographer complaining of being "stuck with this old fart at least a year" and then drawing the conclusion that this guy Larkin was "one of those old-type *natural* fouled-up guys." That is, it was in his nature, from the very beginning, to fail. Larkin's willingness to portray himself so unheroically is, paradoxically, a heroic action, and the poetry in that sense is heroic poetry. He is unique for not looking away from the slums inside himself. They were his muse.

See also "THE EXPLOSION," "HOMAGE TO A GOVERNMENT," "SAD STEPS."

BIBLIOGRAPHY

Larkin, Philip. *Collected Poems*. Edited and introduction by Anthony Thwaite. London: Faber and Faber, 1988.
———. *Selected Letters of Philip Larkin, 1940–1985*. Edited by Anthony Thwaite. London: Faber and Faber, 1992.
Motion, Andrew. *Philip Larkin: A Writer's Life*. New York: Farrar, Straus & Giroux, 1993.

James Persoon

"THE LARKIN AUTOMATIC CAR WASH"

GAVIN EWART (1976) One of GAVIN EWART's common subjects is the poetic "reelaboration" of well-known poems, or the parodic imitation of the style of a given poet, what Ewart called "para-poems." "The Larkin Automatic Car Wash," included originally in the collection *Be My Guest!: Poems* (1975), belongs in this category. The title tells us the poet Ewart has chosen for his satire, PHILIP LARKIN. The poem Ewart chooses to rewrite is "The Whitsun Weddings," a poem that gave Larkin his initial fame as a poet when it appeared in 1964. As a "para-poem," Ewart's burlesque should be read not as a self-contained piece of literature but rather as a reflection or distortion of the original, a kind of reading Ewart himself encouraged.

The poems follow a parallel structure, a journey where certain things are observed and where, by the end of the journey, some insight is reached. Larkin's narrator is on a train traveling through the countryside; Ewart's is driving a car through an industrial setting, the outskirts of the city, and the car wash mentioned in the title. Larkin emphasizes the traditional beauties of rural England; Ewart glorifies the car wash, its lights and technology, "the Science Fiction light" that comes "creeping through Alien and weird / as when the vegetables invade in *Dr Who*." Larkin thoughtfully observes the girls who are attending the weddings and their mixture of innocence, wonder, and change; Ewart's girls within the group of adolescents, "Six teenagers squashed in" the car, are "tall half-children" who scream "delighted to be frightened." The couples who have just married board the train, and the observer in Larkin's poem examines them. They are too happy and excited to be reflective and to ponder the meaning of happiness and married life, unlike the narrator. Ewart shares his small vehicle with a group of teenagers exhilarated by the car wash itself, which is "like cigarettes and cokes . . . their slight excitement." The teenagers' hyperactivity is contrasted with the calm, reflective stance of the poet, who wants "more . . . hours, I wanted to be caught / in that wet undergrowth by that wet shore," which serves as "an exit from our boring life, a changed environment, another place, a hideout from the searchers."

Larkin's obvious epiphany in the poem (emphasized by its taking place on Whitsun) is a most serious one, reflecting on how the course of the day has made couples of strangers who meet in a train, each of them at the beginning of a different journey but still with one common starting point. Ewart's poetic voice, however, is left with no clear epiphany, wondering whether under his adolescent load's "different hats / Spiritual experiences work in a kind of code," and wondering whether he has a code, a spiritual experience of his own.

Ewart not only parodies the subjects and structure of "The Whitsun Weddings," but also writes his poem in a 10-line stanza based on iambic pentameter, which is precisely the kind of stanza Larkin chose for his long poems. The poetic voice, however, is never Larkin's; rather, it is Ewart's skillful imitation of Larkin, in an affectionate parody that enriches our reading of the original poem as we enjoy the one inspired by it.

BIBLIOGRAPHY

Delchamps, Stephen W. *Civil Humor: The Poetry of Gavin Ewart.* Madison, N.J.: Fairleigh Dickinson University Press, 2002.

Carmen Méndez García

LAWRENCE, D. H. (1885–1930)

David Herbert Lawrence was born in Eastwood, Nottinghamshire, the fourth of five children of Arthur and Lydia Lawrence. The maternal care required by his frequent bouts of bronchitis cemented an intensely—often labeled abnormally—close relationship between mother and son. In the family "class war"—Arthur's working-class values and attitudes clashing with those conditioned by Lydia's middle-class background and aspirations—the young Lawrence, a reader, writer, and artist, was in much keener sympathy with his middle-class mother than his coal miner father. With his mother's encouragement, Lawrence gained one of the first county scholarships to Nottingham High School and attended a teachers course at Nottingham University College, qualifying in 1908. While at Nottingham University College, he began writing poems and short stories, winning the *Nottinghamshire Guardian* Christmas 1907 short story competition with "A Prelude." Although his mother's nonconformist Christian faith remained embedded in his psyche throughout his life (for example, in his essay "Hymns in a Man's Life"), at this time Lawrence began his lifelong critique of Christianity as he abandoned faith in "a personal, human God."

Illness, later diagnosed as tuberculosis, ended his career as a teacher in 1911, a time that also marked the death of his mother (December 1910), the end of his relationship with Jesse Chambers (the source for Miriam in *Sons and Lovers*), his brief engagement to Louie Burrows, and the publication of his first novel, *The White Peacock* (1911). Unlike his later fiction, this novel is quite conventional in its treatment of sexuality and interpersonal relationships; while partially autobiographical, it evades the main issues in his life, most especially becoming weaned from his mother and developing satisfactory relationships with women other than his mother. The poems Lawrence was writing at this time are also relatively conventional and oblique; a more authentically autobiographical work from this period is his first play, *A Collier's Friday Night.*

In 1912, Lawrence met Frieda Weekley, the wife of his former modern languages tutor; six weeks later, Lawrence and Frieda eloped to Germany, beginning a tempestuous love-hate relationship that fundamentally shaped Lawrence's subsequent philosophical and artistic development. Lawrence had written his first major novel, *Sons and Lovers,* before meeting Frieda, but he revised it after their relationship began, reading sections to Frieda, who would then "fight like blazes" with him about it. It was Frieda who noticed the Oedipal elements in the novel; indeed, as a former mistress of one of Freud's disciples (Otto Gross), Frieda was almost certainly the one who introduced Lawrence to Freudian thought, a significant element in his thinking from 1912 on. Lawrence found marriage to Frieda both "terrible" and "great"; their struggles were, he believed, emblematic of a major problem of his time—the establishment of a new relationship between man and woman. *LOOK! WE HAVE COME THROUGH!,* a collection of poetry published in 1917, chronicles the early days of his marriage, its triumphs and defeats, in an honest and compelling fashion.

However, while Lawrence was always concerned with telling the truth, his goals as a writer were much more substantial than just transcribing his life: Personal experience alone was not sufficient for the kind of truth he sought to convey. Instead, he worked to transform his own experience and merge it with that of others into something larger, more impersonal, and more inclusive, rooted in philosophical and psychological theory. Lawrence can be viewed as a diagnostician who saw the tensions and sicknesses of his own life as a particular instance of a larger cultural pathology; Lawrence's artistic goal was thus subversive, a critique of the values and attitudes—not only sexual attitudes but also artistic, philosophical, and political ones—that created and informed England and indeed most of Western civilization in the early 20th century and that accounted for the sickness he perceived in these civilizations. Lawrence's subversive goals led to experimentation in both subject matter and artistic style as he searched for appropriate expressive vehicles for his cultural critique. In the novels he wrote after his marriage to Frieda—most particularly *The Rainbow* (1915) and *Women in Love* (1920)—Lawrence's search for a new style in which to convey new insights led him to a technique we now recognize as characteristically modernist in its strained language, symbolic density, and structural complexity. As a poet, however, Lawrence developed a style counter to the modernist mainstream.

At the center of Lawrence's cultural critique is his deconstruction of the metaphors of mechanism—in particular the epistemological and metaphoric structure of logical positivism. In the novels, the deconstructive efforts are multifaceted, embodied in character, dialogue, and situation, as well as symbol; in the poetry, the critique operates largely through a series of alternative metaphors—metametaphors, as it were—that oppose and undo our conventional conceptual structures.

As did many artists and writers of his generation, who saw World War I as evidence of the failure of Enlightenment rationality, Lawrence looked to "primitive" societies, both past and contemporary, for alternatives. His interest in these cultures was not merely nostalgic, however; nor is his use of their myths allusional in the common sense of the word; instead, the metaphors he draws from myths and from such systems as astrology are meant not to remind us of particular stories but to invoke the kind of consciousness that originally created the myth. Aware that we can never recover belief in Persephone or Zeus, Lawrence nevertheless believed that we can recreate what may be

termed a sacramental, or ecological, consciousness, a way of "knowing in togetherness"—togetherness of body, mind, and emotions; of man and woman; of animals and plants; of Earth and stars. Poetic recreation of this way of knowing was, for Lawrence, a twofold process. First, he attempted to shatter our conventional way of knowing, the mechanistic metaphors central to contemporary Western thought; second, he attempted to substitute an alternative metaphoric structure, an epistemology of "dark knowledge."

In his mature poetry, the poetry of BIRDS, BEASTS AND FLOWERS (1923) and *Last Poems* (1932, posthumous), Lawrence most fully achieves this subversive purpose. Both collections are best read as artistic wholes rather than individual poems because both are structured by implicit journey narratives; metaphors and symbols work accretively throughout the volumes. *Birds, Beasts and Flowers* can be read as a travel book, tracing on a literal level the journey taken by the Lawrences as they explored first Italy and then New Mexico. Metaphorically, it is a journey into the underworld, an exploration of corruption, sexuality, and death, "dark" processes that are a necessary precedent to eventual growth and birth. The volume is structured around a submerged rite of passage—indeed, two rites of passage, the speaker's and the reader's. "Pomegranate," the opening poem, challenges the reader to begin exploring the "dark side" external to himself or herself. This exploration culminates in "SNAKE." At this point, the speaker, confident in his assertions, confronts the serpent in his own heart and fails his initiatory test. Throughout the second half of the volume, the speaker relearns the lessons of the first half, exploring the darknesses within himself. By the end of the collection, in "The Red Wolf," the speaker finishes his rite of passage, emerging reborn as a shamanistic figure and a true poet.

Last Poems is similarly structured around an initiation, this time an initiation into death; throughout the collection the speaker reasserts the philosophical stance that structured his earlier works. By juxtaposing the fluidity of living creatures against the sterile permanence of mechanical objects, he creates a climate in which to view death as a natural part of the universe, one more transformation in the never-ending dance of universal energy.

Since Lawrence's death of tuberculosis in 1930, his reputation has experienced numerous vicissitudes. Controversial, vital, and intensely charismatic, he was adored as a prophet and vilified as a pornographer; for several decades after his death, readers and critics found it difficult to separate the works from the sensation they caused. From the 1940s through the 1960s and beyond, D. H. Lawrence was best known as the author of *Lady Chatterly's Lover,* the novel that, along with Joyce's *Ulysses,* most successfully challenged censorship and obscenity law in both England and the United States. His novels and, to a lesser extent, his poems, were alternately excoriated as sex-sodden pornography and valorized as sacred texts of sexual liberation. Readers scoured his novels for "the good parts." Detractors and disciples alike tended to read his literary output as mere apologia for his unconventional life, which was frequently considered to be his true work of art. In the 1970s, Lawrence came under fire by feminist critics; subsequent generations of feminist scholars have revised earlier judgments, acknowledging his achievements in drawing female characters and depicting human relationships.

Since the MODERNISM of his novels assimilates easily into the dominant critical narrative of the later 20th century, Lawrence's novelistic innovation and artistry were much more readily appreciated than his poetic innovation and artistry. The sensibility that informs the poetry—a sensibility that insists on the inseparability of poetic language and scientific language, that insists on the inseparability of observer and observed, that insists on the constructed nature of all knowledge—is strikingly postmodernist. Similarly Lawrence's tendency to view the universe and the creatures that inhabit it as processes, not static entities, resonates with much more familiarity in the early 21st century than in the mid-20th; it seems that critical theory needed to catch up with Lawrence in order to appreciate his poetic achievements.

See also "BAVARIAN GENTIANS," "PIANO," "RED-HERRING," "THE SHIP OF DEATH," "TORTOISE SHOUT."

BIBLIOGRAPHY

Dyer, Geoff. *Out of Sheer Rage: Wrestling with D. H. Lawrence.* New York: North Point Press, 1997.

Gilbert, Sandra. *Acts of Attention: The Poems of D. H. Lawrence.* 2nd ed. Carbondale: Southern Illinois University Press, 1990.

Hagen, Patricia. *Metaphor's Way of Knowing: The Poetry of D. H. Lawrence and the Church of Mechanism.* New York: Peter Lang, 1995.

Patricia Hagen

"LEDA AND THE SWAN" W. B. YEATS (1924)

W. B. YEATS'S "Leda and the Swan," written 1923, was first published in the *Dial,* June 1924, and collected in *The Tower* (1928). *The Tower* was the ninth collection of Yeats's poetry. According to Yeats's biographer R. F. Foster, the book "was rapidly seen as a supreme achievement, and has been recognized as one of the key books of the 20th century" (362). The collection took its name from the actual tower, Thoor Ballylee, in which Yeats lived until 1928; the book transforms the material place into a rich symbolic resource for the poet. Throughout his career, Yeats would try to use his poetry to bridge the symbolic and imaginary world, to which he was deeply attracted, with the concrete realities of the political world in which he lived.

"Leda and the Swan" is largely a poem about the incommensurability of divine and human understanding. In it, Yeats attempts to delineate the contours of human comprehension in the face of the incomprehensible. At the same time, the poem deals directly with the violence existing in the relationship between "knowledge" and "power," seen from the position of those who are not in control. While Yeats's poems often dramatize a search or a desire for wisdom and understanding, "Leda and the Swan" demonstrates the sacrifices such wisdom may require. Structurally Yeats's use of the sonnet—a poetic form often associated with Shakespeare, consisting of 14 lines in iambic pentameter—is also significant.

The poem references the Greek myth of the rape of Leda by Zeus in the form of a swan. Leda went on to give birth to Helen, Clytemnestra, Castor, and Pollux. (Different versions of the myth have Zeus as the father of both daughters, or only of Helen.) Helen's abduction by (or elopement with) Paris would lead to the Trojan War; Clytemnestra would marry Agamemnon and, with her lover Aegisthus, murder her husband upon his return from Troy.

From the time of its publication up until the present, readers of "Leda and the Swan" have had to deal with the poem's possibly problematic linkage of sexuality and violence. Marjorie Howes notes that "contemporary critics accused Yeats of eroticizing rape and glorifying violence, but in relation to most previous poetic treatments of Leda and the swan Yeats had put the violence back into a scene that was frequently figured more as a seduction than a rape" (119–120). Indeed the close proximity of violence and eroticism is crucial to the poem. As Yeats here disturbs the traditional love sonnet by introducing violence, he also reminds his readers of the many violations that run through history while tentatively suggesting that such breaches may result in some unlooked-for access to greater understanding.

The power of the poem derives largely from the intensity of its images and from its abrupt beginning: "A sudden blow: the great wings beating still / Above the staggering girl." The poem begins by focusing on Leda's experience, emphasizing both the extremity of physical difference between woman and bird (juxtaposing *thighs* with *webs* and *nape* with *bill*) and her powerlessness in the face of his power. Together these details heighten the strangeness of similarity between the two beings when "he holds her helpless breast upon his breast." The second stanza begins to step back from a perspective entirely aligned with Leda's. It consists entirely of two two-line questions that emphasize Leda's helplessness, implying that she cannot do other than as she does. However, the speaker describes her fingers as both "terrified" and "vague," while her thighs "loosen" under the swan's "feathered glory," thus presenting the disturbing and illuminating possibility of Leda's complicity or at least lack of complete resistance. The concluding six lines of the poem shift suddenly from the immediate moment of sexual climax to the grand sweep of history: "A shudder in the loins engenders there / The broken wall, the burning roof and tower / And Agamemnon dead." Yeats thus ties the future bloodshed of the Trojan War and Agamemnon's murder—the results of actions by the two daughters produced by this union—to the personal violence of the rape itself.

Yeats breaks the iambic pentameter line sharply after "And Agamemnon dead," creating a momentary pause before the poem continues. Arguably the poem's most important move occurs in the final three and a half lines. The speaker again asks a question, though this time it is not rhetorical. The speaker wonders whether Leda—now in partial possession of divine power because she has been impregnated by a god— "put on his knowledge with his power / Before the indifferent beak could let her drop?" The connection between Leda's individual trauma and its future consequences is available to the speaker because of historical knowledge, but the poem implies that divine understanding is not bounded by time in the same way. Zeus knows the future at the time of the rape—thus his "indifference": Leda is no longer necessary to him, having fulfilled her predetermined purpose. But is it possible, the speaker asks, for Leda to have received some degree—however fleeting—of godlike understanding? This is not knowledge that Leda has sought; the vision of the future is one of destruction and death. The poem raises the issue of whether in using human beings to achieve their ends, the gods may surrender some of their mastery as well. But "Leda and the Swan" is ultimately ambiguous because of the nature of that knowledge: What Leda may now know is the extreme, transhistorical extent of her domination. Rather than clearly ameliorating the trauma of rape in some redemptive way, "knowledge" in "Leda and the Swan" remains far more vague.

BIBLIOGRAPHY
Finneran, Richard J., ed. *W. B. Yeats: The Poems*. New York: Macmillan, 1983.
Foster, R. F. *W. B. Yeats: A Life. Vol. 2, The Arch-Poet.* Oxford: Oxford University Press, 2003.
Howes, Marjorie. *Yeats's Nations: Gender, Class, and Irishness.* Cambridge: Cambridge University Press, 1996.

Mary Wilson

LEONARD, TOM (1944–) Born in Glasgow, Scotland, Leonard has always been closely identified with his home city, mainly because much of his work reproduces the sound and content of Glaswegian speech to powerful, and often extremely funny, effect. Though he may be considered a member of the AVANT-

GARDE both by his associations and through his hostility to the institutions of the mainstream, many readers usually hostile to the avant-garde are disarmed by his work's charm and apparent facility: "that's ma opinion / and having delivered it / I will now have my fucking breakfast."

In fact, the ebullient style of *Six Glasgow Poems* (1969) and *Bunnit Husslin* (1975) only appears casual: Leonard's rejection of high-sounding rhetoric and insistence on dealing with working-class concerns are both part of a complicated political and poetic commitment. American readers who have not heard a Glasgow accent might find the poems difficult to approach, but in general their difficulty to readers accustomed to standardized forms of English is part of their point. In *Six Glasgow Poems* Leonard lulls the reader into relaxing her guard: "helluva hard tay read theez init / but goes on / if yi canny unnirston thim jiss clear aff then." It is not that Leonard wants to make the work inaccessible, but that he refuses to alter it in order to meet the audience's expectations. His abiding principle is "In the beginning was the sound," a commitment to speech as the basis of language in general and poetry in particular, which motivates both the much-praised Glaswegian vernacular poems and the more experimental sound poetry he produced in the 1970s.

Intimate Voices (1984), Leonard's first selected poems, won the Scottish Book of the Year Award at the same time as being banned from the Scottish Central Region's school libraries. Before this episode and since, Leonard has voiced his contempt for the education system in both poems and prose. He has also produced a number of posters and cartoons in the tradition of political satire, including "a handy newsstand for the next bombing" and "the press as phatic communion," as well as a pamphlet, *On the Mass Bombing of Iraq and Kuwait, commonly known as The Gulf War* (1993). All of these activities reflect Leonard's left-wing politics and distrust of authority of all kinds.

The popular, comic style of Leonard's vernacular poems can serve to mask his seriousness, which manifests itself both in those poems and in work—such as *Situations Theoretical and Contemporary* (1986)—which is more familiarly avant-garde. Leonard has written eloquently on the role of language in political repression and the urgent need to extend the possibilities of poetry as a means of redressing that repression. As a result he considers Williams Carlos Williams a major figure and shows a sympathy with Williams's poetic program that is comparatively rare in Britain. His prose work may prove illuminating to American readers trying to understand the peculiar forces that have shaped British poetry. Two volumes of selected poems, *Intimates Voices* and *Access to the Silence,* form the best introduction to Leonard's poetry and critical prose.

BIBLIOGRAPHY

Tuma, Keith. *Anthology of Twentieth-Century British and Irish Poetry.* New York: Oxford University Press, 2001.

Tony Williams

"A LETTER FROM THE TRENCHES TO A SCHOOL FRIEND" CHARLES HAMILTON SORLEY (1915)

CHARLES HAMILTON SORLEY (1895–1915), with so many others of his generation, had enlisted and gone into the trenches almost straight from public school, because he felt that "noncompliance would have made life intolerable," and perhaps because he could not continue to deny the patriotic response triggered by poets like RUPERT BROOKE. As was RUDYARD KIPLING's son John, he was killed at the Battle of Loos in October 1915, aged 20. His "Letter" from the trenches at first seems to celebrate the chance of fighting in the great conflict. However, the apparent note of patriotic sacrifice, the cheerful willingness to die for one's country in order to secure a peaceful future, is abruptly offset by a more sober view of death and the young, inexperienced schoolboy's sudden confrontation of the stark realities of war.

Written just before his death, as was "WHEN YOU SEE MILLIONS OF THE MOUTHLESS DEAD," the poem suggests the massive scale of the devastation caused by the war. It emphasizes the incalculable nature of the loss of innocence and the passing of a world that can never be resurrected. Sorley gives the memories of recent schooldays an ironic twist, undercutting the note of boyish optimism that led so many young men to join up in the war effort: "I have not brought my Odyssey / With me here across the sea." As WILFRED OWEN was to observe in "DULCE ET DECORUM EST," his public school education has generated idealism but has not prepared him for the reality of war. The conflict in which the poem's narrator finds himself is no heroic war of Homeric telling, yet the heroism lies in each individual soldier, "Bard of white hair and trembling foot, / Who sang whatever God might put / Into his heart."

The poem conveys a state of mind that is like a dream or trancelike memory, with the sleep imagery as always carrying with it the undertones of death, and the implicit suggestion that not only is death inevitable in the trenches but it is the most desirable alternative for the soldiers. During his high school years at Marlborough College in England, Sorley had loved to walk and run in the hills, and as an aspiring young poet, he had written several poems about the experience. Here he blends the turgid spiritual exhaustion of the trenches with nostalgia for a lost childhood and memories of a pleasant physical exhaustion after sports or a trek at school—"And at my feet the thyme and whins, / The grasses with their little crowns / Of gold, the lovely Aldbourne downs." Yet something remains of the old schoolboy spirit and enthusiasm that energize the soldiers and keep them together: "The old war-joy, the old war-pain. / Sons of one school across the sea / We have no fear to fight—"

In its concluding section, the poem reiterates its main point, the inescapable fact that, as the heroes of *The Odyssey,* these soldiers too will die, and even if they return home, they will be permanently disfigured or maimed by the war:

> And soon, oh soon, I do not doubt it,
> With the body or without it,
> We shall all come tumbling down
> To our old wrinkled red-capped town.

Sorley's sole collection *Marlborough and Other Poems* was published posthumously in 1916 and became an instant success. He is seen as a forerunner of Siegfried Sassoon and Wilfred Owen because of his unsentimental style and matter-of-fact descriptions of the war. Thus he stands in opposition to poets like Rupert Brooke and John McCrae, as he is able to observe, interpret, and communicate the reality of war honestly and directly. Therefore, the "Letter" too concludes on a seemingly unemotional note that belies the underlying appeal for sanity and reassurance from his friend of the past:

> This from the battered trenches—rough,
> Jingling and tedious enough.
> And so I sign myself to you:
> One, who some crooked pathways knew
>
> . . .
>
> Small skill of rhyming in his hand—
> But you'll forgive—you'll understand.

BIBLIOGRAPHY

Wilson, Jean Moorcroft, ed. *The Collected Poems of Charles Hamilton Sorley.* London: Cecil Woolf, 1985.

Divya Saksena

"LETTERS & OTHER WORLDS" Michael Ondaatje (1973)

In this relatively short, yet multifaceted, poem, Michael Ondaatje explores his connection to and relationship with his father. Appearing in the collection titled *Rat Jelly* (1973), "Letters & Other Worlds" predates the publication of the book-length examination of Ondaatje's familial past, *Running in the Family* (1982), by nearly 10 years, but it already foretells the complexity and depth of Ondaatje's emotional connection to his family.

Characterized by irregular repetition and a capricious tone, "Letters & Other Worlds" creates a dichotomy of experience and recognition: The "father" of the poem is both known and unknown, a participant—sometimes comical, often tragic—in the real world, but also a frequent escapee to other worlds, characterized by drunkenness and recorded in his letters. The somber first stanzas are linked by the recurring words *fear* and *letters,* suggesting a dangerous, self-injurious quality to the father's writing. "My father's body was a globe of fear / His body was a town we never knew," the first lines of the poem following the epigraph, are echoed, transformed, and condensed in the first line of the second stanza: "My father's body was a town of fear." The second stanza also directly associates the father's letters with his fear, commenting that "his letters were a room his body scared." Despite the dubious syntax of the line, the implication is clear: The father's body, the letters, and fear are inextricably linked.

The poem's third stanza portrays the father's dying, the drowning of his mind and body in an alcoholic "wash of fluid." The next several stanzas, however, retreat from this grim tone, and both the language and subject turn lighter, with a fair element of comedy and irony mixed in. These stanzas act as a kind of flashback, a movement back in time, to the years predating the father's death. The father's drunken antics are given an exaggerated importance; his "falling / dead drunk onto the street" is said to have precipitated Ceylon's independence. In its description of the parents' rocky relationship and the outrageous, increasingly eccentric behavior of the father, the tone becomes almost lovingly understanding.

However, when the poem returns to its first subject, the lethal combination of alcohol and writing, the tone changes again, becoming less sympathetic and more bleak and macabre. In his last years, the poem relates, the father retreated alone to his room, where he stayed "until he was drunk / and until he was sober." In his room, alone except for his own drunken company, the father writes, composing the fearful letters of the first stanzas. These letters reveal the depth of his perception, his awareness of his family and friends, but also suggest his incurable division from them. Even as he writes, even as he describes normal, everyday and, thus, precious family activities, he is unable to understand or save himself. Instead, the father becomes more and more isolated, more and more reduced to a terrible "privacy," until finally he falls, the "blood searching in his head without metaphor." The creation, the act of writing, implicit in the father's letters is, ultimately, destructive; the father, who represents the artist, is destroyed by his inability to reach his family, to escape his solitude, in any way more tangible than either alcohol or writing.

BIBLIOGRAPHY
Solecki, Sam, ed. *Spider Blues: Essays on Michael Ondaatje.* Montreal: Véhicule Press, 1985.

Winter Elliot

LEVERTOV, DENISE (1923–1997) Born in Ilford, England, Denise Levertov was the author of more than 20 volumes of poetry. She was educated privately, in a culturally diverse home enlivened by many visitors and political discussions, developing both an early appreciation for the arts and literature and an appetite for political activism. She served as a nurse in London during World War II, began writing poetry in England, and emigrated to America in 1948.

Levertov was strongly influenced by her ancestry, believing that the cultural ambience of her own family had a significant impact upon her own artistic development. Her father's father was an Orthodox rabbi of Hasidic ancestry; her father, however, converted to Christianity and became an Anglican priest. Her mother descended from a Welsh tailor, teacher, and preacher, Angell Jones of Mold. Levertov paid homage to this religious heritage throughout her poetic career, continually making reference to a power beyond the self. She refers to her family connections in "Illustrious Ancestors" (*The Jacob's Ladder,* 1961): "Thinking some line still taut" between her and her relatives, she wishes to make "poems direct as what the birds said". . . mysterious as the silence when the tailor / would pause with his needle in the air."

Levertov became politicized at a young age, aware not only of her own rich cultural mix but of the troubles in continental Europe in the 1940s caused by the fear of such a cultural mix. Her parents' active role in helping Jewish refugees from Germany and Austria during World War II exposed Levertov to the horrors of war and emphasized the need to speak out against injustice. She published her first poem, "Listening to Distant Guns," in *Poetry Quarterly* by Ray Gardner, editor of Grey Wolfe Press, who continued to publish her poetry, introducing her to other British poets including Tambimutu, Alex Comfort, Nicholas Moore, and Danny Abse. This early poetry was tinged by what she refers to as "New Romanticism" in an interview with Sybill Estess, "a reaction, partly, to the daily life of wartime—the drabness and grayness of English life in the early 1940s."

Having published her first book, the *Double Image* (1946), in England, Levertov married the American writer Mitchell Goodman, emigrating to the United States in 1948 and meeting the Black Mountain poets, Robert Creeley, Cid Corman, and Robert Duncan. Profoundly influenced by the transcendental and experimental poetics of EZRA POUND and William Carlos Williams, she began to make the transition from the British neoromantic traditions to an American-born poetry that combined the sacred and the every-day. Levertov explored the politics of the Black Mountain poetics throughout her career, having some work published in *Black Mountain Review*. She particularly embraced Williams's notion that there are "no ideas but in things," a maxim she used to argue that poetry, and indeed all language, has a direct impact upon the world: "Words reverberate through the poet's life, through *my* life, and I hope through your lives, joining with the other knowledge in the mind" (*The Poet in the World,* 116).

This belief made writing for her a moral undertaking, with which she tried to impact multiple aspects of the human experience, such as love, motherhood, nature, war, the nuclear arms race, the environment, mysticism, poetry, and the role of the poet. Although refusing the label herself, Levertov is often considered a feminist, because of her exploration and politicization of women's everyday experience. Numerous early poems from her first American-published book, *Here and Now* (1956), link vision and acts of making to the domestic, maternal, and marginal roles culturally encouraged for women. She adopts a clearly female-identified voice, drawing upon traditional forms of women's making. She imagines a waiting attitude of discovery, in "Something to Wear," to be "like a woman knitting," hoping her creation will "make something from the / skein unwinding, unwinding," while the poem "Mrs. Cobweb" tells of a mad woman who makes "a collage of torn leaves," "a glass moon-reflector," and creates from the materials of her own life—"whatever she could touch, she made."

With Eyes at the Back of Our Heads (1959) established Levertov as a great American poet, and between 1959 and 1975 she joined the War Resisters League, lecturing and writing against war. She experienced an awakening through her antiwar activism, during which she perceived the war effort as part of an ideology of assimilation justifying oppression. Protesting against this ideology's manifestation in Vietnam led her to consider the oppression evident in the United States; in "The Long Way Round" she realized her concern and empa-

thy for the Vietnamese helped her "learn . . . what it is to awaken / each day Black in white America" (*Life in the Forest,* 1978).

In her later years she developed her interest in religion and spirituality, as *Candles in Babylon* (1982) and *The Stream and the Sapphire: Selected Poems on Religious Themes* (1997) testify. Living in Somerville, Massachusetts, for a number of years while teaching at Brandeis, MIT, and Tufts, she moved to Seattle in 1989 and settled close to Lake Washington in the shadow of Mt. Rainier, the views of which inspired her interest in the environment recorded in *Breathing the Water* (1987) and *The Life around Us: Selected Poems on Nature* (1997). She taught part-time at the University of Washington and as a full professor at Stanford University for the first quarter of each year as she had been doing since 1982. She introduced her own distinctive spirit and goals to the Creative Writing program, retired in 1993, but did several benefits and poetry readings a year in both the United States and Europe. Despite declining health she kept up her correspondence with other poets and friends, dying of complications due to lymphoma on December 20, 1997.

BIBLIOGRAPHY

Levertov, Denise. *A Poet in the World*. New York: New Directions Press, 1973.
———. *Selected Poems*. Newcastle upon Tyne, Eng.: Bloodaxe, 1986.
Marten, Harry. *Understanding Denise Levertov*. Columbia: University of South Carolina Press, 1988.

Catherine Bates

LEWIS, ALUN (1915–1944)

Alun Lewis is best known as a World War II poet whose work expresses the soldier-speaker's need to face the possibility of death while preserving his love for life, which the anguish and foolishness of war constantly threaten to erode. Though Lewis was never in battle, he recorded the cost of war on soldiers and on those waiting for them, capturing in realistic detail the flux of unnerving boredom, alienation, and dread in poems such as "The Departure" and "On Embarkation." But to limit an approach to Lewis to the war poems is to misperceive the artist. He wrote many poems on love, on memory and consciousness, on his encounter with other lands (notably India), and on death.

His brief life began in the small South Wales mining town of Cwmamam on July 1, 1915. Lewis felt an early desire to become a writer and grew up admiring the poetry of EDWARD THOMAS. The son of two teachers, he earned a B.A. (1935) and an M.A. (1937) in history and worked as a teacher between 1938 and 1940. During that year, despite some misgivings, he enlisted in the Royal Engineers and his interests shifted to the topic of war. His first published collection of poetry, *Raiders' Dawn and Other Poems* (1942), contains some earlier poems, but a reading public eager for the emergence of a poetic voice akin to that of earlier war poets focused on his war poetry. The book sold well. During this time, Lewis was stationed in Wales and, in 1941, married Gweno Ellis, also a schoolteacher. After his request to be transferred to the Army Education Corps was denied, Lewis joined the infantry and was commissioned as an officer. Sent to India in late 1942, he began writing verses deploring the grinding poverty and discrimination he witnessed there. During officer training and a brief hospitalization, Lewis was able to assemble enough material for a second volume of poetry, *Ha! Ha! Among the Trumpets,* which he sent to ROBERT GRAVES for comments. This collection was published by Lewis's wife after the poet's death. Offered the opportunity to stay behind lines, Lewis insisted on joining the men of his company when they were ordered into battle. His unit was dispatched to Arakan, Burma, where the poet was accidentally killed on March 5, 1944, by his own pistol. He was 28 years old.

David Perkins refers to Lewis as "a poet of major promise," and this assessment is generally shared. Although his work is sometimes criticized as sentimental (Jeremy Hooker, for example, has noted Lewis's occasional "weakness for debased romantic diction"), Lewis has retained the respect and affection of his readers long after the interest in war poetry waned. He wrote several short stories, which reflected the compassion, sensitivity, and understatement characteristic of his poetry. His thoughtful letters, to his wife and to others, have also been published.

See also "ALL DAY IT HAS RAINED."

BIBLIOGRAPHY

Hooker, Jeremy. Afterword to *Selected Poems of Alun Lewis.* London: Unwin Paperbacks, 1981.

Lewis, Alun. *Selected Poetry and Prose.* Edited by Ian Hamilton. London: George Allen & Unwin, 1966.

Perkins, David. *A History of Modern Poetry: Modernism and After.* Cambridge, Mass.: Harvard University Press, 1976.

Anne Kellenberger

LEWIS, C. S. (1898–1963)

Clive Staples Lewis, born in Belfast, later to become Northern Ireland, was the son of a police court solicitor. His mother, a graduate of Queens College in mathematics and logic, died when Lewis, who by then had thrown off his given name for *Jacksie,* was almost 10. Jack and his older brother, Warren ("Warnie"), were in boarding schools until Warren entered the Royal Military Academy and Jack entered Oxford (April 1917) to read classics. In the fall of 1917, Lewis went to war as a second lieutenant in the Somerset Light Infantry. He was wounded in the Battle of Arras in April 1918 and sent to recover in London and then Bristol in 1918. When he returned to Oxford to resume his studies in 1919, he set his sights on taking a first in classics (1920), then "Greats" (*Literae Humaniores,* further study in classics with philosophy and history, 1922), and finally English language and literature (1923).

In 1925 Lewis was elected to a fellowship in English at Magdalen College, Oxford, where he taught both English and philosophy. In 1929 he converted to theism, having been self-consciously an atheist through his youth, and then, in 1931, to Christianity. His Christian faith subsequently directed and influenced his writing, especially his fiction. By the early 1930s he was spending time with like-minded scholars, critics, and writers such as J. R. R. Tolkien, Owen Barfield, and, later Charles Williams, among others. They eventually took up the name *Inklings,* appropriated from a literary club to which Lewis and Tolkien had belonged. For more than a decade the Inklings read and criticized works in progress by various members. In 1954 Lewis was invited to take up the newly formed Chair of Medieval and Renaissance English at

Cambridge University, where he taught until the year of his death.

Lewis thought himself a poet before he finally discovered himself a scholar and man of letters. He began writing lyric poems at the age of 14 and continued doing so for most of his life. In his youth, his school vacations were much devoted to the task. While he was recovering from his war wounds in Bristol, he assembled his first collection of poems for publication, *Spirits in Bondage* (London, 1919), under the pseudonym *Clive Hamilton.* He described them as "strung around the idea . . . that nature is wholly diabolical and malevolent and that God, if He exists, is outside of and in opposition to the cosmic arrangement." The few critical reviews of the poems were tepid. Many of his later poems rise above the level of adolescent sensibilities and complaints and converge with his more mature literary, philosophical, and religious reflections. He self-consciously reveals his strengths and weaknesses as a poet in "A Confession," written in 1954. "I am so coarse, the things the poets see / Are obstinately invisible to me. / For twenty years I've stared my level best / To see if evening—any evening—would suggest / A patient etherized upon a table; / In vain. I simply wasn't able." His poetry is often a reflective exposition of philosophical ideas, historical events, imaginative literature, as well as personal experiences. Peter Kreeft observes in his short essay on Lewis (1969), "Lewis knew his poetry was too 'naïve' to be fashionable, and published few of the poems collected in his single, posthumously published volume."

In addition to his lyrical poems, collected and published a year after his death by Walter Hooper, Lewis wrote four narrative poems from around 1917 through the mid-1930s. No doubt his inspiration resulted from his interest from his early adolescence in the classical epics, the Arthurian legends, the Norse myths, and the *Faerie Queene.* His first and only published narrative, *Dymer,* occurred to him as an idea when he was 17. The title character escapes from a Platonic totalitarian state, one that is much like Lewis's public school and a bit like the experiences he later had in the army. The hero must overcome the illusions that a society projects on him and then deal with his own disillusionment, which is incapable of achieving what it seeks. The poem received attenuated praise mixed with direct criticism when it was published and reviewed in 1926. The other three poems, *Launcelot, The Nameless Isle,* and *The Queen of Drum,* were labors of love, for Lewis himself more than any possible public who might receive them.

It is as a critic and scholar rather than a poet that Lewis made his contribution to literature. His work dealt with medieval and Renaissance English literature and beyond (especially to Milton, one of his major interests). He wrote about authors and their works, almost always taking care to put them into their historical context. Because history was one of Lewis's considerable strengths, he was asked to contribute to the *Oxford History of English Literature* volume on the 16th century (excluding drama). In works such as this, Lewis's deep and broad knowledge of philosophy, theology, classics, and history serves to illuminate and unveil literary works whose form and content are now so foreign to those who speak and read the English language. He probes the ancient literary forms, such as allegory, and explicates the difficult texts, such as *The Faerie Queene,* by recreating for his readers some salient aspects of the world and the minds from which they grew. Out of this same world arose many of the elements of his own fiction.

BIBLIOGRAPHY
Hooper, Walter. *C. S. Lewis: A Companion and Guide.* New York: HarperCollins, 1996.

Michael Smith

LEWIS, GWYNETH (1959–)

The first poet laureate of Wales, Gwyneth Lewis works in both her first language, Welsh, and English. She has published six poetry collections and two nonfiction books. *Parables & Faxes,* her first collection in English, won the Aldeburgh Poetry Festival Prize and was short listed for the Forward Best First Collection; *Zero Gravity* was short-listed for the Forward Best Poetry Collection and was a Poetry Book Society Recommendation. *Y Llofrudd Iaith* (The Language Murderer) won the Welsh Arts Council Book of the Year Prize and *Keeping Mum* was short-listed in 2004.

Her fascination with her American astronaut cousin's work led variously to the poems of *Zero Gravity,* a BBC documentary of the same name; a BBC radio documentary, *The Poet and the Astronaut;* and her installation as poet in residence at Cardiff University's Physics and Astronomy Department (2005). Her 2002 National Endowment for Science, Technology and the Arts (NESTA) fellowship funded voyages between Cardiff and the ports with which it was once associated. As her 2005 poem on Swansea's National Waterfront Museum demonstrates, she deals with large, abstract questions such as language, history, passion, and science.

Lewis was selected as a Poetry Book Society Next Generation poet in 2004. Her oratorio for 600 voices, *The Most Beautiful Man from the Sea,* was performed in the Wales Millenium Centre; the six-foot letters of her inscription, "In These Stones Horizons Sing" / "Creu Gwir fel Gwydr o Ffwrnais Awen," form its extraordinary windows.

BIBLIOGRAPHY

Lewis, Gwyneth. *Cyfrif Un Ac Un yn Dri.* Cymraeg, Wales: Barddas, 1996.
———. *Keeping Mum.* Newcastle upon Tyne: Bloodaxe, 2003.
———. *Parables and Faxes.* Newcastle upon Tyne: Bloodaxe, 1995.
———. *Sonedau Redsa a Cherddi Eraill.* Llandysul, Wales: Gomer, 1990.
———. *Y Llofrudd Iaith.* Cymraeg, Wales: Barddas, 2000.
———. *Zero Gravity.* Newcastle upon Tyne: Bloodaxe, 1998.
Gwyneth Lewis Web Site. Available online. URL: www.gwynethlewis.com. Accessed May 3, 2008.

Jeni Williams

LEWIS, WYNDHAM (1882–1957)

A painter, fiction and nonfiction writer, and infrequent poet, Wyndham Percy Lewis was born on November 18, 1882, aboard a ship moored at Amherst, Nova Scotia. As the son of an American Civil War veteran and an Englishwoman, he maintained his Canadian nationality while spending his youth in England after his parents separated. He studied at the Slade School of Art in London from 1898 to 1901; there he met Augustus John. Lewis, whose associates also included EZRA POUND, was immensely influential on modernists artists at the time, especially through his association with the vorticist movement.

A frequent traveler, Lewis produced writings that reflect the influences of the places he visited. Perhaps his best known and most respected novel, *Tarr,* dramatizes the cafés and cultural life of Paris, where he spent several years.

In 1910 Lewis's poem "Grignolles (Brittany)" appeared in *The Tramp: An Open Air Magazine* II. During his lifetime, Wyndham Lewis produced one volume of poetry, *One-Way Song,* which appeared in 1933, published by Faber and Faber, and was republished in 1960 by Metheun with a foreword by T. S. ELIOT. Although Eliot claims the 1960 and 1933 texts are identical, Bradford Morrow and Bernard Lafourcade note several deletions in the later edition that eliminate references to Lewis's controversial book *The Hitler Cult.*

One-Way Song, a long satirical poem, with illustrations that appear to be by Lewis, contains five pieces: "Engine Fight-Talk," "The Song of the Militant Romance," "If So the Man You Are," "One-Way Song," and "Envoi." Calling "the manner personal and the verse incisive," a reviewer in the *Times Literary Supplement* (*TLS*) in 1934 remarked, "Throughout it the poet is speaking through a nominal mask only, and speaking with some bitterness." "If So the Man You Are" concludes by introducing the Enemy, Lewis's alter ego.

Responding to a reviewer who speculated as to the identities of Lewis's "victims" in *One-Way Song,* Lewis, writing to the editor of *New Britain,* explained, "I had better state at once, to put an end to a tense situation, that no *personalities* whatever were intended. Minds in general, not certainly any particular group of partisans, were the objects of that puppet's diatribe." Later Lewis admits that "my old crony Ezra Pound and those he has influenced" are targets of the second part of "Engine Fight Talk."

A 1960 *TLS* review noted its reissue with the T. S. Eliot introduction with a brief notice under the title "Noisy Briton," a column nearly engulfed—probably intentionally—by a review of Vincent Massey's *Speaking of Canada* (Macmillan) entitled "Quiet Canadian." The reviewer asserts that the "work contains throughout its frantic progress some passages of stunning vigor, including the celebrated If so the man you are sequence, and some rare acrobatic virtuosity in its exposition of the relation between time and personality, that great red rag."

Lewis died on March 7, 1957.

BIBLIOGRAPHY

Curtis, Anthony Samuel. "Noisy Briton." *Times Literary Supplement,* 15 April 1960, 236.

Glendinning, Alex. "Review of *One-Way Song.*" *Times Literary Supplement,* 15 March 1934, 185.

Lewis, Wyndham. *Collected Poems and Plays.* Edited by Alan Munton. New York: Routledge, 2003.

———. *One-Way Song.* London: Faber and Faber, 1933.

———. *One-Way Song.* Foreword by T. S. Eliot. London: Metheun, 1960.

———. *Rude Assignment: An Intellectual Autobiography.* Edited by Toby Foshay. Santa Barbara, Calif.: Black Sparrow Press, 1984.

———. "To the Editor of 'New Britain'," December 13, 1933: *The Letters of Wyndham Lewis.* Edited by W. K. Rose. Norfolk, Conn.: New Directions, 1963.

Morrow, Brad, and Bernard Lafourcade. *A Bibliography of the Writings of Wyndham Lewis.* Santa Barbara, Calif.: Black Sparrow Press, 1978.

Marianne Cotugno

"THE LISTENERS" WALTER DE LA MARE (1912)

WALTER DE LA MARE's life (1873–1956) straddled the Victorian, the Edwardian, and the modernist periods; his poems and short stories were immensely popular for a time between the wars but came to be regarded as old-fashioned when T. S. ELIOT and EZRA POUND began to reach fame. Although his children's poems live on in anthologies and reprints, de la Mare is now a largely marginalized author, often erroneously regarded as sentimental and deeply Victorian. But to do justice to him, one has to accept that he simply disliked the new style and subject matter of MODERNISMS and until his death in 1956, when authors such as THOM GUNN and TED HUGHES were publishing their first works, remained true to his own style. T. S. Eliot who (together with Ezra Pound) valued the originality and musicality of de la Mare, summarized his style in the poem "To Walter de la Mare" as "inexplicable mystery" (*Tribute to Walter de la Mare,* Faber and Faber, 1948).

The eerie, mysterious, and haunting character of many of his poems can be demonstrated in his most-anthologized poem, "The Listeners," published in 1912 in his eponymous first successful collection of poetry. Here the poet creates a scene and a mood that permit the reader to imagine the supernatural atmosphere created by props such as the owl, turret, moonlight, and lonely traveler, as well as a slightly archaic language (the horse "champed" the grasses, he "smote upon the door," he "spake"). The poem begins in medias res with a both simple and metaphysical question: "'Is there anybody there?' said the Traveller, / Knocking on the moonlit door." The irregular yet partly trochaic meter of these first two lines recreates the sound of the knocking by a series of light beats, showing de la Mare as not only highly lyrical, but also experimental in matters of rhythm, as closer to symbolism than Victorianism. Apart from the balladlike appearance of the poem (longer and shorter lines alternate), this departure from the classical rules of prosody through an irregular arrangement of weak and medium stresses, of rising and falling rhythm, heightens its romantic and dreamlike qualities, the silence and loneliness that it evokes (cf. Bentinck, 66).

In "The Listeners" a supernatural presence haunts the solitary Traveller, the typical speaker of many of de la Mare's poems. The poem looks and sounds deceptively simple and yet is highly enigmatic and ambiguous, capable of many interpretations, as de la Mare himself stated: "A poem may have as many different meanings as there are different minds" (*Come Hither,* xxxiii, quoted in Bentinck, 75). A horseman arriving at a deserted house in the middle of a wood knocks at the door and calls out but receives no answer. The ensuing silence is highly suggestive and is personified by "a host of phantom listeners / That dwelt in the lone house then," listening "to that voice from the world of men." The Traveller, who finally rides away, after having exclaimed, "Tell them I came, and no one answered, / That I kept my word," appears to be the only real character in the little scene, but the silence, which "surged softly backward when the plunging hoofs were gone," constitutes a mysterious opposing force. In de la Mare's world there is no emptiness, as not only is every creature inhabited by a spirit, but every house, every garden, every place retains ghosts, presences (cf. McCrosson, 58). This belief might be called superstitious or childish but on the other hand shows a closer connection to the spiritual world than most people nowadays would admit to.

Instead of merely enjoying the melancholy eeriness of the poem, generations of readers and scholars alike have tried to find a "meaning" for the Traveller, the phantom listeners, and the poem as a whole. "The difficulty lies not in finding allegorical meanings for the Traveller and the listeners, but in finding too many such meanings. Readers have seen the Traveller as God, Christ, the Holy Ghost, *a* ghost, Man, *a* man, or Walter de la Mare; the listeners have been made to stand for the powers of darkness, the riddle of life, the dead, a living household, Man, or de la Mare's schoolmates" (Gwynn and Condee, no. 26). As with Robert Browning's errant knight in his "Childe Roland to the Dark Tower Came" the quest is suggestive, yet beyond explanation. It could be read as the frustrated search of humans for "God," or a meaning for their lives: The Traveller seems not so dissimilar to Kafka's man before the law, who vainly seeks admittance all his life and only on his deathbed dimly perceives an undefined radiance emanating from beyond the gate to the law (cf. Franz Kafka, *Before the Law*). Despite its romantic or Victorian appearance the poem shows an awareness of deeper questions. When the words of the Traveller fall "echoing through the shadowiness of the still house / From the one man left awake," something of the abyss and emptiness of modern man, who no longer listens to silence, who sees the presence of spirit as an absence and is therefore lonely and homeless and vagrant, is evoked. And yet, in that he "felt in his heart their strangeness, / Their stillness answering his cry" the Traveller harks back to an in-between state that is half-romantic and half-modern and seems characteristic of de la Mare's own position within literary history.

BIBLIOGRAPHY

Bentinck, Anne. *Romantic Imagery in the Works of Walter de la Mare*. Lewiston, N.Y.: E. Mellen, 2001.

De la Mare, Walter. *The Complete Poems of Walter de la Mare*. London: Faber and Faber, 1969.

———. *Come Hither: A Collection of Rhymes and Poems for the Young of All Ages*. New York: Knopf, 1923.

Gwynn, Frederick L., and Ralph W. Condee. "De la Mare's The Listeners." *Explicator* 12, no. 26 (1954).

Hopkins, Kenneth. *Walter de la Mare*. Harlow, Eng.: Longman, Green, 1969.

Khatri, Chhote Lal. *Walter De la Mare: Poetry and Novels: An Evaluation*. Jaipur, India: Book Enclave, 2003.

McCrosson, Doris Ross. *Walter de la Mare*. New York: Twayne, 1966.

Pierson, Robert M. "The Meter of 'The Listeners.'" *English Studies: A Journal of English Language and Literature* 45 (1964): 373–381.

Whistler, Theresa. *Imagination of the Heart: The Life of Walter de la Mare*. London: Duckworth, 1993.

———. *The Life of Walter de la Mare*. London: Duckbacks, 2003.

Webpage of the Walter de la Mare Society. Available online. URL: http://www.bluetree.co.uk/wdlmsociety/. Accessed May 3, 2008.

Heike Grundmann

LITTLE GIDDING T. S. ELIOT (1942)

During the darkest days of World War II in England—years of the Blitz—T. S. ELIOT's *Four Quartets* were, according to the publisher and poet John Lehmann, "as exciting to me, as they came out, as news of great military victories." In them, Lehmann found an "attempt to map out some system of thought and feeling wide enough and deep enough for our culture to exist in"—poetry, in short, "equal to the spiritual demands of an apocalyptic age" (353–357). Yet, with the exception of *Little Gidding,* the quarters are not overtly *about* war; rather, they are religious and philosophical meditations on time, eternity, and their intersection, and the individual's attempt to find meaning in the chaos that is modern history—a history whose continuity was once again in Eliot's lifetime gravely threatened, most immediately in the form of German incendiary bombs that set Central London ablaze. As he had in the aftermath of World War I in THE WASTE LAND (1922), the epitome of literary MODERNISM, Eliot sifted the rubble for fragments that might be shored against civilization's ruins, England's, and his own. It is in this multiple sense that the *Quartets* are "patriotic poems," as he once referred to the last three (Ackroyd 264).

Four Quartets are intensely personal as well as philosophical and public poems. Each is inspired by a particular place that held both private and historical significance for Eliot, landscapes that prompted the introspection of a man "in the middle way" of life (*East Coker* 172). The first, *Burnt Norton* (1936), was written as Europe gathered its strength for round two of the "war to end all wars." Using leftover passages from *The Rock* (1934), a church pageant, and *Murder in the Cathedral* (1935), about the martyrdom of Thomas à Becket, plays in which the footsoldiers of totalitarianism intrude, Eliot pondered how time and history might be redeemed, how "at the still point of the turning world" (*BN* 62) enough consciousness might be gained to conquer time through time. But *Burnt Norton* is also local in its focus, set in a 17th-century English country estate that Eliot had visited in the company of Emily Hale, an American drama teacher with whom he had fallen in love years before when he was a graduate student in philosophy at Harvard. It was only with the composition of *East Coker* (1940), modeled on *Burnt Norton,* that he began to envision a sequence of poems that eventuated in *Four Quartets.* In this case, Eliot celebrates the small Somerset village from which his ancestor Andrew Eliot had emigrated to New England about 1669 in search of religious freedom, and in which his own ashes would be buried. *The Dry Salvages* (1941) takes its title from a dangerous group of rocks off Cape Ann, Massachusetts, where the Eliot family retreated from the summer heat of St. Louis to their vacation home at Eastern Point, Gloucester. There young Tom learned to sail and absorbed the lore of the Grand Banks fishing fleet, as well as a sense of his New England heritage.

Landscapes are but one of the devices by which Eliot imposes unity on his set of long poems. He adopted a traditional method of lending universality through a scheme of seasons and the classical elements: *Burnt Norton* (retroactively assigned) Spring/Air and Light; *East Coker* Summer/Earth; *The Dry Salvages* Autumn/Water; and *Little Gidding* Winter/Fire. Appropriately, luxuriant nature imagery permeates the *Quartets,* especially that of leaf and flower, which mark the passage of time and season and play important roles in the cumulative symbolism of the sequence. Most prominently, roses are found, in varying contexts, in all four poems; from the rose garden of *Burnt Norton* to the concluding vision of *Little Gidding,* the petals that live for but a day also prefigure eternity.

As the inclusive title *Quartets* suggests, Eliot gave shape to the whole work through a musical analogy: Each consists of five movements, as if in a string quartet, all following the same basic pattern, weaving and contrasting themes, "keys," and motifs much as the quartets of Beethoven do. Beethoven, in fact, was on Eliot's mind; for some time he had been studying the late quartets, finding in them (as he wrote to STEPHEN SPENDER) "a sort of heavenly or at least more than human gaiety . . . which one imagines might come to oneself as the fruit of reconciliation and relief after immense suffering; I should like to get something of that into verse before I die" (qtd. in Gordon 390).

Little Gidding (1942), which would prove to be Eliot's last significant poem, is the one in which he took greatest satisfaction, and the one on which he was willing to let his reputation as a poet stand or fall. It was also the one that gave him the most difficulty, in part because, while it had to stand on its own, it had to conclude the sequence, "gather[ing] up themes and images from his earlier meditations on Time's losses and Time's gains, to make the poem not only complete and beautiful in itself but the crown and completion of the exploration of man in Time he had begun in *Burnt Norton*" (Gardner 71). Moreover, ill health, domestic dislocation, and a heavy load of editorial, literary, and public service commitments, undertaken as man of letter's contribution to the war effort—these kept him from "the intolerable wrestle / With words and meanings" (*EC* 70–71), as if the nightly raids of the Luftwaffe, during which he stood fire watch on the roof of Faber and Faber in Russell Square, were not alone capable of doing so.

It was a place touched by war in another century that lent its name to the last of the *Quartets*. Little Gidding—the name drives from Anglo-Saxon *gydig* "possessed by a god"—is a tiny settlement in Huntingdonshire where a religious community was established in 1625 by Nicholas Ferrar and his family. Escaping the politics and plague of London, they dedicated themselves to a practical experiment in the devotional life, an experiment whose fame soon spread. The poets Herbert and Crashaw were among the distinguished visitors, and during the Civil War, King Charles, a previous visitor, retreated there secretly at night after the Royalist defeat at Naseby, accompanied only by his chaplain. A recently challenged tradition holds that it was partially destroyed by Cromwell's Roundheads; of the original buildings, only the chapel, repeatedly restored, remains today. Eliot visited in 1936, finding in the neglected shrine a tangible focus for themes and experiences in his own life and that of his adopted country: His search for refuge from his failed marriage and healing of his stricken conscience, his hunger for religious commitment and communion as a midlife convert to the Church of England (having been raised a Unitarian), the reconciliation of ancient political and religious strife that had determined the course of both British and American history down to the present day, and a practical response to the crisis of values now writ large in the internecine war of a culture gone mad— Lehmann's "apocalyptic age": What must be the role of a poet in such a crisis? (Compare W. H. AUDEN's "IN MEMORY OF W. B. YEATS," written on the eve of the same war: "Poetry makes nothing happen . . . it survives, / A way of happening, a mouth.")

The general pattern of movements adhered to, with variations, in *Four Quartets* has been analyzed by several critics, among them A. D. Moody, whose outline has been drawn upon in this overview. Part 1 interweaves statements of a theme, presenting the first stage of a progression toward a vision of the absolute, that of the world of experience. In *Little Gidding,* the site of the Ferrar commune at the winter solstice ("Midwinter spring") forms the concrete core for Eliot's meditation on the soul's yearning for safety and renewal, as evidenced in the lives of those who long ago retreated here, and those who today make pilgrimages to the shrine seeking something, perhaps not knowing what they seek (27). The "dark time of the year" (11) recalls the Dark Night of the Soul or "negative way" Eliot presented in the previous *Quartets* as a path to union with the love of God. The paradoxes of the physical season—the flame of sunlight on the ice of pond and ditch—correspond to the low season of the heart, when the "dumb spirit" may be stirred by "pentacostal fire" (10). As the days lengthen after the solstice, "the soul's sap quivers" (12), anticipating the thaw of April (recall the opening lines of *The Waste Land*) and the blossoming of May when the hawthorn hedges near the chapel are "white again" (24) with the "snow" of spring. The turn toward "the unimaginable / Zero summer" (19–20) figures forth the spirit's turn, and the turn from the Inferno toward Purgatorio made by Virgil and Dante in *Divine Comedy*. Yet the journey of the soul may be peripatetic since what is sought is not merely elusive but beside the point. The pilgrim's expectations about the shrine are disappointed by its mundane appearance: "the rough road . . . the pig-sty . . . the [chapel's] dull façade" with the dilapidated tomb of Nicholas Ferrar before it (28–30). So too we may be surprised to find that our purpose is "altered in fulfillment" (35), that a purpose other than our own is at work, one that may entail our death. King Charles would go to the block after his retreat to Little Gidding, and others go to "the world's end" (36) in various times and places, some even now, in an England under siege. "If you [come] this way," you must be prepared, in the words of *East Coker* (123), to "be still, and wait without hope" for the purpose to reveal itself, "to put off / Sense and notion" (42–43). Curiosity and investigation must give way to vigil, here "where prayer has been valid" (46)— Eliot's ascetic adjective sets a tone of humility and repose, yet, with an eye to its etymology, of strength and efficacy. "Valid" prayer is not so much an activity as a readiness for what comes to those who wait, a "communication . . . tongued with fire" (50–51) in the language of the saints who lived and died here where history and eternity intersect in a paradoxical "timeless moment" (52).

Part 2 ponders, in two contrasting ways, the question of what knowledge can be gained from experience. The first section, a dirgelike lyric in eight-line stanzas of trimeter couplets, contrasts with the free versification of part 1, but it develops the themes of *askesis* and purgation. The classical elements are the agents of destruction and death—"the world's end" (36)—but paradoxically they foreshadow purification and baptism that entail the death of the old life. That the "daemonic fire" Eliot referred to in his notes for this section (Gardner 169) should have a salvific effect underscores Eliot's acknowledgment of the cost of sanctification, to which he will return in the closing section of part 5. Even the air raids that produce the thick dust that settles on the sleeve of the fire watcher and the drenching fire hoses that complete the destruction of house and church ("sanctuary and choir" 76) play a role in purging a civilization in spiritual ruin, and the human soul of its sin, as a cancelled passage in Eliot's draft makes clear (Gardner 168). All is consumed by one element or another: The rose, the city, the religious retreat, the soil itself, and human toil—all are gone under the hill, to paraphrase *East Coker* (100) and must do so if the soul is to rise to the "condition of complete simplicity" (253).

What this means for Eliot himself, as a person and as a poet, is the subject of the second section of part 2, in which his experience on fire patrol becomes a hallucinated journey to a Dantesque underworld. Approximating Dante's versification by substituting alternating unrhymed masculine and feminine line endings for the *aba bcb cdc* of terza rima, Eliot creates a modern Inferno in the "disfigured street" (147) of London as the last German bomber—the "dark dove" (81)—heads back across the Channel. Now strangely silent in the "uncertain hour" before the smoke-stifled dawn, it is both the "Unreal City" of *The Waste Land* where "death had undone so many" (*WL* 63) and where the speaker stops "one I knew" to inquire of a corpse, and a circle in hell. Though Eliot stated that he intended the effect to be purgatorial (Gardner 65), he imitates canto XV of *Inferno,* one of his favorites, where Dante meets the shade of his poetic master, Brunetto Latini. In Eliot's "familiar compound ghost," almost all of the senses of *familiar,* except, perhaps,

"friendly," seem relevant: "recognizable," "overly intimate," "one of the family," "an attendant spirit," "an Inquisitor." Similarly the list of poets who have been suggested as candidates for the ghost is rich: Dante, Milton, Arnold, LaForgue, Mallarmé, and, primarily, W. B. YEATS. Yet, as lines 97–100 make clear, the dead poets speak through Eliot himself, who plays the "double part" of self-examiner. Among the features of his "thought and theory" he is "not eager to rehearse" (111) seems to be the "impersonal theory of poetry" set forth in his early manifesto, "Tradition and the Individual Talent" (1919). There he declared, as a principle of *aesthetic* (formal) criticism, that "not only the best, but the most individual parts of [a poet's] work may be those in which the dead poets, his ancestors, assert their immortality most vigorously," and that poetry "is not the expression of personality, but an escape from personality." But the poet/critic nearly a quarter-century older realizes the evasiveness of his famous dictum: "The more perfect the artist, the more completely separate in him will be the man who suffers and the mind which creates." There are not degrees of perfection, and the artist is never, in life, perfect; nor can the life and the art be completely separate. That is, the *moral* dimensions of life and art are always implicated—as the post-1919 critic who spent the next two decades working out the relevance of his religious belief for his poetic theory was forced to admit. The "impersonal theory" had served its purpose, but it is now something for which Eliot pleads forgiveness (113–116), and the needs of the future "await another voice" (119).

Yet the spirit is "unappeased," unsatisfied, with confession of the critic's shortcomings. "Peregrine [wandering] / Between two worlds become much like each other" (121–122)—Eliot echoes Arnold's "Grand Chartreuse," where one world is "dead, / The other powerless to be born"—the compound ghost finds in the desolation of war a duty to speak truth (always war's first victim). "To purify the dialect of the tribe," as Mallarmé put it, requires an unflinching self-assessment of his "lifetime's effort" (130) and of what still awaits him: "the gifts reserved for age" (129). Lines 131–143 are enriched by echoes of other poets but require little gloss in their directness. (Eliot has been faulted for not spelling out the autobiographical details of "motives late revealed" and "things ill done and done to others' harm" [140–141], but these lines are *about* confession, not confession itself, which requires private communication with God, and with those harmed.) From such a circle of self-laceration the vexed spirit has but one release: the "refining fire" of Purgatory, "Where you must move in measure, like a dancer" (144–146). From the "dead patrol" (107) of the infernal streets "the one discharge" (203) is to become, in the words of Eliot's "The Death of Saint Narcissus" (1915), "a dancer to God."

The prosaic opening of part 3 signals a return to the practical world of our relationships with others past and present—with history, with society, with those whom we know and love. Life at turns may involve "attachment" or "detachment" from our world, just as the hawthorn or the nettle may flourish or become dormant. But death lurks in "indifference," paradoxically "growing" between the phases of life (153–155). Only memory liberates us from the "prison of our days" (to recall Auden's lines on the death of Yeats), from our indifferent "servitude" (162) to history, whether recalled or dreaded—"one damned thing after another," we recite—and reveals a pattern that gives meaning to the passing parade of persons and events. History, whether of individuals of nations, may, even in the devastation of war, be "renewed, transfigured, in another pattern" (165) if we do not acquiesce in its abstraction, an unredeemable "eternal present" (to recall the problem posed at the outset of *Burnt Norton*). In testimony of an alternative possibility, Eliot quotes lines from the medieval mystic Julian of Norwich: "Sin is Behovely, but / All shall be well, and / All manner of thing shall be well" (166–168).

Eliot then explores a prime case in point, the English Civil War (which he regarded as never having been concluded), for Little Gidding itself had played a small but symbolically important part in that war. Whether among the defeated, like King Charles, who retreated at nightfall to "this place," or the victorious, like the blind Puritan poet Milton, all are, in memory, "united in the strife which divided them" (174), in that their common motive was the good of England, and in death are "folded into a single party" (191), whatever their

religious or political allegiances. (The reference to a rose in 184 reaches even further back, to the Wars of the Roses, and negatively anticipates the paradisal rose of the poem's last line.) From the defeated especially we inherit the symbol of sacrificial devotion to a cause, now purified (the drafts of these lines make clear [Gardner 207–208]) by the sacrifice of Christ, "the ground of our beseeching" (199). To attempt to "revive old factions" or "restore old policies" (185–186) would be not only to perpetuate old internecine wars in the face of a foreign threat, but to refuse the gift without which all manner of thing will not be well.

Part 4 of each *Quartet* is a short stanzaic lyric, usually rhymed, in which a prayer or vision of great religious intensity is expressed. In *Little Gidding,* the Luftwaffe's incendiary raids evoke a "fire sermon" (Smith 290), in which, paradoxically, the flames figure forth the need of purgatorial cleansing through the intervention of the Holy Spirit, the "dove descending" whose tongues of pentacostal fire alone can burn away sin and error. War itself cannot purge civilization or our despairing lives; we must choose that other pyre that redeems through an "incandescent terror" (201) devised by divine love. A hard saying, this; Eliot suggests a classical parallel, the death of Heracles. Mistakenly thinking that a love potion (really a poison given her by the centaur Nessus) would rekindle her husband's love, Deianira gave Heracles a shirt suffused with it, thereby causing him such torment that he mounted a pyre on Mt. Oeta. The parallel is intentionally inexact, for the flames of the Paraclete are not administered in error, and they are our "only hope" (204), have we but the courage to inbreathe them ("suspire"), to be consumed by them. The alternative is to become victims of our own misguided loves, the hatreds and lusts that will otherwise destroy us as individuals and as nations.

As suggested, to do justice to the richness and complexity of *Little Gidding* would require tracing the trajectory of themes and images of the preceding three poems as they come to conclusion in the last. So much the more is this the case with part 5, in which every line depends for its full import and beauty upon its resonance with all that has gone before. This is brought home in the opening lines, which echo the motto (adopted from Mary, Queen of Scots) that opens *East*

Coker and its reverse, which concludes it. In the cycles of history, in the surprising completed circles of our own lives, and in the mutually supportive structures of poetry itself, a pattern can be discerned—not only of closure but of impetus to new adventure. Beginnings and ends are locked in the figure of eternity and propel its motion, motion such as that of "the complete consort dancing together" (223), which recalls "the association of man and woman / In daucning, signifying matrimonie" of *East Coker* (28–29), a motion that in turn keeps "the time of the seasons and the constellations" (*EC* 42).

Reflecting on his own career, and conscious that it was drawing toward its conclusion, Eliot assesses the calling of the poet in "the use of poetry" (the phrase appears in the title of one of his critical volumes). "Every poem"—indeed, every movement of a quartet—"is an epitaph" (225), just as every action in the world of affairs is a step toward both death and a new beginning, If "we die with the dying" (228), we are also born with them: We take our places in the consort and derive our significance from it. The shortest moment— the day of the rose—and the longest—the 1,000 years of the yew tree (232)—"are of equal duration" in the perspective of eternity and are redeemed from meaninglessness only by "a pattern / Of timeless moments" (234–235). That is the gift of history for those who will embrace it, rather than seek to escape it, like Stephen Dedalus in *A Portrait of the Artist as a Young Man* by James Joyce, for whom history is a "nightmare" from which he is trying to wake up. For Eliot, his winter visit to the "secluded chapel" at Little Gidding was such a moment: The time past and time future of *Burnt Norton* were present to him in an eternal "now" (236– 237). For readers like Lehmann, enduring the fires of the Blitz and fearing invasion from across the English Channel, these lines had an immediacy and power well beyond their import as a philosophical meditation on time and history.

Eliot's most characteristic means of communing with the dead and of bringing them to life was quotation (or paraphrase) of his poetic masters. At the conclusion of the sequence of the *Quartets* as well as of *Little Gidding,* he turns to an anonymous 14th-century treatise on the art of contemplative prayer, *The Cloud of Unknowing*: "With the drawing of this Love and the voice of this Calling" (238). This line, set apart from the preceding section and the following coda, expresses for Eliot the conviction that the divine love that "devised the torment" of spiritual purgation is also the source of purified eros, a force that draws humanity to itself, to God, and thereby creates human history by motivating human action. As does the love of Beatrice in Dante's *Paradiso,* it carries those who answer its call to the beatific vision of eternity.

The coda that follows draws upon all four *Quartets* to summarize in a highly allusive lyric Eliot's sense of what is required of those who glimpse this vision, and what blessings attend the vigil. "A condition of complete simplicity / (Costing not less than everything)" (253–254) entails both renunciation and readiness to follow where the calling draws: "We shall not cease from exploration" (239). Paradoxically such surrender yields self-knowledge, as we "arrive where we started / And know the place for the first time" (241–242). Like "The hint half guessed, the gift half understood" of Incarnation in *The Dry Salvages* (215), the beatific vision is elusive in this life but no less real for being so, and the assurance that "all manner of thing shall be well" occurs in moments of quiet expectation, "heard, half-heard, in the stillness / Between two waves of the sea" (250–251). "We must be still and still moving" (*EC* 204) until, "at the still point of the turning world. / . . . at the still point there the dance is" (*BN* 62–63), the union of fire and rose, of time and eternity, as in the final vision of Dante's *Paradiso,* is revealed.

BIBLIOGRAPHY

Ackroyd, Peter. *T. S. Eliot: A Life.* New York: Simon & Schuster. 1984.

Gardner, Helen. *The Composition of Four Quarters.* New York: Oxford University Press, 1978.

Gordon, Lyndall. *T. S. Eliot: An Imperfect Life.* New York: W. W. Norton, 1998.

Hargrove, Nancy. *Landscape as Symbol in the Poetry of T. S. Eliot.* Jackson: University of Mississippi Press, 1978.

Lehmann, John. *In My Own Time: Memoirs of a Literary Life.* Boston: Little, Brown, 1969.

Moody, A. D. *Thomas Stearns Eliot: Poet.* Cambridge: Cambridge University Press, 1979.

Smith, Grover. *T. S. Eliot's Poetry and Plays: A Study in Sources and Meaning.* Chicago: University of Chicago Press, 1956.

David Huisman

THE LIVERPOOL POETS

When John Lennon sang about counting "4000 holes in Blackburn, Lancashire" and the man "who blew his mind out in a car" ("A Day in the Life," *Sergeant Pepper's Lonely Hearts Club Band*), he captured the peculiar poetic tone of his home city, Liverpool, in the Northwest of England. The combination of art school experimentalism, working-class irreverence, and the enthusiastic embrace of American popular and countercultures that fueled the music of the Beatles also underpins one of the other key cultural phenomena of 1960s Britain—the poetic wave known as the Liverpool Poets, comprising Adrian Henri, Roger McGough, and Brian Patten. All three grew up in and around this working-class city, whose particular combination of Irish, Welsh, Scots, Chinese, African, and Caribbean immigrants created the distinctive accent and attitude known as "scouse." By writing a poetry that could be performed as well as read, and that gloried in the anarchic humor and everyday surrealism that is so much a part of "scouse" culture, the Liverpool Poets came to represent the democratic ethos of the 1960s, which would at least soften the strict class boundaries that define British society.

Henri, McGough, and Patten gained national prominence in 1967 when the success of their anthology *The Mersey Sound* aligned them in the public mind with the vibrant music and arts scene that had emerged in Liverpool. Although each poet's voice is distinctive, all three shared a quickfire wit; a love of inversion, contradiction, and the bizarre; and an admiration for the work of American countercultural writers like Allen Ginsberg, William Burroughs, Frank O'Hara, and Charles Olson. In "Liverpool Poems," Henri relocates the gunfight at the OK Corral to the city's docks, while in "I Want to Paint" he lists "thoughts that lie too deep for tears," "A SYSTEMATIC DERANGEMENT OF ALL THE SENSES," "a new cathedral 50 miles high made entirely of pram-

wheels," and "pictures that tramps can live in" as suitable subjects to be captured on canvas. But in line with their popular ethos, the surrealism of the Liverpool Poets is always accessible because it serves a clear purpose. So Roger McGough tenderly recalls a moment of love in "A Lot of Water Has Flown under your Bridge" by transposing the awkwardness of young lovers to the room in which they make love: "When we lay together for the first time / the room smiled, / said 'excuse me,' / and tiptoed away."

The Liverpool Poets are inextricably bound to the experience and images of the 1960s, signaled by Brian Patten's "Come into the City Maud," a poem that updates Tennyson's lyric maiden by having her "wear a Mary Quant dress / And eat fish and chips alone at night." But at moments a more lasting poetic vision is discernible, as perhaps most successfully in Adrian Henri's "The Entry of Christ Into Liverpool." Here, the panoply of 20th-century history is compressed into contemporary Liverpool, where competing banners proclaim "LONG LIVE SOCIALISM" and "Keep Britain White," while "a white bird" (the popular 1960s image of the dove of peace) is "dying unnoticed in a corner." Unnoticed as the bird, the poet walks home alone with "empty chip-papers drifting round my feet."

BIBLIOGRAPHY

Coles, Gladys Mary. *Both Sides of the River: Merseyside in Poetry and Prose.* West Kirby, Eng.: Headland, 1993.
Henri, Adrian, Roger McGough, and Brian Patten. *The Mersey Sound.* Harmondsworth, Eng.: Penguin, 1967.
Wade, Stephen. *Gladsongs and Gatherings: Poetry and Its Social Context in Liverpool since the 1960s.* Liverpool: Liverpool University Press, 2001.

Graham MacPhee

LOCHHEAD, LIZ (1947–)

The Scottish writer Liz Lochhead was born Elizabeth Anne Lochhead on December 26, 1947, in Motherwell, Lanarkshire. She graduated from Motherwell's Dalziel High School and went on to study at the Glasgow School of Art (GSA). Lochhead taught art at schools in Glasgow, Scotland, and Bristol, England, after graduating from GSA in 1970. As a poet, playwright, and theatrical performer who possesses a strong, Scots-flavored, feminist voice, Lochhead holds a considerable list of published credits, including the plays *Blood and Ice* (1982), *Mary Queen of Scots Got Her Head Chopped Off* (1989), and *Perfect Days* (1998). Her first poetry collection, *Memo for Spring,* was published in 1972 and won the Scottish Arts Council Book Award that same year. In 2001, Lochhead won the Saltire Society Scottish Book of the Year Award for her script adaptation of Euripides' *Medea.* Lochhead's skillful blending of Scottish vernacular with standard English contributes to her works' sustained popularity in Scotland and elsewhere around the world. Themes repeatedly highlighted in Lochhead's work are those of identity: "'cultural identity, female identity and childhood identity in a world fraught with violence, contradictions and confusions,'" according to Lucy Kay, who quotes the scholar Susan C. Triesman's location of Lochhead on the spectrum of Scottish women writers. From Lochhead's thus defined position she explores the notion that female identity is conflated with cultural identity. As argued by Cairns Craig, when cultural identity is subsumed or "lost"—as exemplified in the case of Scotland by its most often being glossed incorrectly in the larger identity of Great Britain, England, or the United Kingdom—then it is more difficult for a female to find her own identity within her culture. Two early poetry collections, *The Grimm Sisters* (1981) and *Dreaming Frankenstein and Collected Poems* (1984), are explorations of identity that also demonstrate Lochhead's interest in folktales and popular stories as ground for arguing against and revising the values of a patriarchal culture. Liz Lochhead lives in Glasgow, Scotland, and *The Colour of Black and White: Poems 1984–2003* (2003) is her latest published poetry collection.

See also BAGPIPE MUZAK, GLASGOW 1990.

BIBLIOGRAPHY

Craig, Cairns. "From the Lost Ground: Liz Lochhead, Douglas Dunn, and Contemporary Scottish Poetry." In *Contemporary British Poetry: Essays in Theory and Criticism,* 343–372. Albany: State University of New York Press, 1996.

Kay, Lucy. "Liz Lochhead." In *Dictionary of Literary Biography.* Vol. 310, *British and Irish Dramatists since World War II,* edited by Matthew J. Bruccoli and Richard Layman, 134–142. Fourth Series. John Bull. Farmington Hills, Mich.: Thomson Gale, 2005.

Tuma, Keith, ed. *Anthology of Twentieth-Century British and Irish Poetry.* Oxford: Oxford University Press, 2001.

Katherine Gannett

"LONDON SNOW" ROBERT BRIDGES (1890)

It is rare that snow falls in large quantities in the City of London, so this poem of 1890 captures an unexpected turn of nature that produced then, and still produces for us today, an experience of surprise, magic, and even chaos. The poem is divided by end-stopped lines into four sections, each of which depicts a different stage of the twilight and dawn. The first nine lines describe the nightly snowfall; lines 10–18 portray the dazzling brilliance of the snow and its surprising effect. Lines 19–30 juxtapose the magical brilliance of the snow with the additional burden it entails for manual workers, and the final section of the poem portrays the sudden burst of activity in the morning trudge to work. The poem is constructed of alexandrines: iambic hexameters, with some irregularities. The rising meter of the poem, together with the accumulated lists of adverbs and participles in lines 3–9, imitates the lightness of the snow as well as its constant falling motion.

The poem describes most effectively two aspects of snow in a city that are just as valid today as in ROBERT BRIDGES's time: that moment of surprise upon opening the curtains on the first snowy morning of the winter and the peculiarity of snow in inspiring magical delight in the eye of the beholder while proving highly inconvenient to the everyday routine. Both aspects are illustrations of snow in a social context.

The poet employs a variety of methods in preparing the reader or listener for that moment of surprise. In the first section of the poem, the snow is ascribed qualities of a somewhat cunning, secretive, and even violent entity. Arriving "when men were all asleep," it covers the city "stealthily and perpetually." The participles of "deadening, muffling, stifling" suggest a city suffocating under the burden. The power of the snow to alter the look of the landscape completely overnight is shown by the way the tiny details of a building are eradicated: "Hiding difference, making unevenness even, / Into angles and crevices softly drifting and sailing."

Another strength of the poem is its rich sensuality. Bridges first appeals to our eyes and ears: "The eye marvelled—marvelled at the dazzling whiteness; / The ear hearkened to the stillness of the solemn air." The sudden quietness of the world due to the sound-absorbent quality of snow finds expression in lines 16–18, and our sense of taste and touch is appealed to in lines 20–21: "They gathered up the crystal manna to freeze / Their tongues with tasting, their hands with snowballing." Only unaccustomed sounds, such as the boys' squeals of delight, are to be heard. Religious imagery in the metaphor of the "crystal manna" encapsulates the falling motion of the snow as well as the sheer delight of the boys, whose longing has been stilled. This poem is perhaps the best-known of Bridges's works, perhaps because of the very universality of its subject, surprise and delight at the unexpected.

BIBLIOGRAPHY

Guerard, Albert Joseph. *Robert Bridges: A Study of Traditionalism in Poetry.* New York: Russell, 1956.

Stanford, Donald E. *In the Classic Mode: The Achievement of Robert Bridges.* Newark: University of Delaware Press, 1978.

Wendy Skinner

"LONG DISTANCE" TONY HARRISON (1981)

"Long Distance," comprising a pair of 16-line sonnets from TONY HARRISON's sequence *The School of Eloquence,* explores the historical and physical gap between Harrison and his parents, which is also the gap between the young and the old, the living and the dead. The title refers to travel (the gifts guiltily purchased "rushing through JFK as a last thought") and telephone calls, as well as to the "distance" traveled by the son in relation to his father, who, the poem implies, has (with reason) failed to "move on" since his wife's death and tries to conceal this.

The poem's double-sonnet structure allows two voices to be heard, as in a telephone conversation, which is nevertheless presented as the father's monologue framed by the son's critical commentary: "Your bed's got two wrong sides. Your life's all grouse." Harrison paraphrases and summarizes his father's voice before allowing it to speak for itself, thus establishing an uneasy balance between tolerance and impatience that colors the rest of the poem. The poem's rendering of the father's voice in italics and in dialect seems both to allow space for the father's identity and subtly to undermine it. Nearly every line of this reported speech refers to the self, implying a sustained critique of apparent self-centeredness; Harrison's own voice, by contrast, oscillates more markedly between first and the colloquial second person ("You couldn't just drop in. You had to phone"), suggesting a hesitancy about his own identity that is not shared by his father. To balance this, the father's habitual reenactments of small domestic acts of love, in the opening lines of the second sonnet, contrast markedly with the son's implicit neglect, his reluctance to listen to or give time to his father. "Long Distance" thus comes to mean the gap between father and son, embodied in the increasing difficulty of communicating that seems to lie at the poem's core.

The final quatrain reveals that the poem is written after the death of both parents, transforming its meanings again—"Long Distance" becomes a temporal metaphor, an act of remembrance, the poet recollecting his father's behavior as repeated in his own small acts of mourning: "You haven't both gone shopping; just the same, / in my new black leather phone book there's your name / and the disconnected number I still call." These acts, of course, contradict the poet's flat statement of belief, which expresses a major element of Harrison's ideology, "that life ends with death, and that is all"; his desire to communicate, to reestablish lines of contact, motivates the poem as an expression of the need for connection across the distances it describes.

BIBLIOGRAPHY

Harrison, Tony. *Selected Poems.* Harmondsworth, Eng.: Penguin, 1995.

John Sears

LONGLEY, MICHAEL (1939–)   Born in

Belfast to English parents, Michael Longley received a grammar school education in the Royal Belfast Academical Institution and studied classics at Trinity College, Dublin. Following a number of years teaching in Dublin, Belfast, and London, he worked with the Arts Council of Northern Ireland as director of literature and traditional arts. In 1991, he retired from this post in order to focus on his literary career.

Longley was one of the "Belfast Group" of poets that emerged in the troubled political atmosphere of 1960s and 1970s Northern Ireland. The Troubles was one of the chief concerns of their poetry, and the group counted SEAMUS HEANEY, DEREK MAHON, and PAUL MULDOON among its members. An interest in formal poetic technique, perhaps a result of his formalistic education, is evident in Longley's first volume of poetry, published in 1969, *No Continuing City*. However, as the volume progresses, the poems become increasingly personal. One, in particular, "In Memoriam," an elegy to his father, escapes the constraints of formality. Here Longley establishes his intent to focus on personal experience as a microcosm for universal experience: "Let yours / And other heartbreaks play into my hands." The poem anticipates the thematic focus of his second collection, *An Exploded View* (1973), upon love and death in both past and contemporary contexts. This volume is dedicated to "Derek, Seamus and Jimmy": Mahon, Heaney, and James Simmons, members of the Belfast Group. Longley writes: "We are trying to make ourselves heard . . . / Like the child who cries out in the dark," emphasizing the group's struggles to express their Northern Irish experiences through poetry.

Longley has published six further collections of poetry—*Man Lying on a Wall* (1976), *The Echo Gate* (1979), *Gorse Fires* (1991), *The Ghost Orchard* (1995), *The Weather in Japan* (2000), and *Snow Water* (2004)— in which life, death, war, nature, art, and history, among other themes, are explored. In addition to his poetry, he has published a short autobiographical volume, *Tupenny Stung* (1994); has written a range of works across the arts; and has edited poetry selections. He has received numerous awards including the Eric Gregory Award, the Whitbread Poetry Award, the Belfast Arts Award for Literature, the Hawthornden Prize, the Irish Times Irish Literature Prize for Poetry, the Queen's Gold Medal for Poetry, and the T. S. ELIOT

Prize. Currently a fellow of the Royal Society of Literature and a member of Aosdána, a prestigious affiliation of creative artists in Ireland, he lives in county Mayo with his wife, the well-known Irish critic Edna Longley.

See also "WOUNDS."

BIBLIOGRAPHY

Hogan, R., ed. *Dictionary of Irish Literature,* 2nd ed. London: Aldwych Press, 1996.

Longley, M. *Poems 1963–1983.* Dublin: Gallery Press, 1985.

Sinead Carey

LOOK! WE HAVE COME THROUGH!

D. H. LAWRENCE (1917) It seems especially appropriate that this volume of poems by a still-very-young D. H. LAWRENCE would be preceded in many editions by excerpts of a long interview with his widow, Frieda Lawrence, interviewed nearly 25 years after his 1930 death, since the poems contained in the volume are focused nearly exclusively on her and on their relationship. Although she is, literally and metaphorically, present in every poem, Lawrence as the poet often does not allow her to speak for herself. Even so, these poems are Lawrence's way of not just chronicling their early years together, but also examining, according to Fiona Becket, "his marriage, and early experiences with women" and "his own sexuality," as well as developing "a personal philosophy based on 'male' and 'female' oppositions and dualities" (*Complete Critical Guide to D. H. Lawrence* 6, 20). This collection of poems stands as a record of one of the most remarkable love affairs of the 20th century and, even more importantly, stands as a record of the inscrutabilities of an institution taken for granted but misunderstood by the multitude. In spite of the inherent difficulties of the institution, as Becket points out, these poems ultimately celebrate his marriage to the love of his life.

Lawrence's habit of utilizing natural imagery appears in these poems in abundance: Bees, dragonflies, cranberries; the Moon, the Sun, stars; the sea, rainbows, twilight, lightning, and roses all appear as profusely as the gardens of the great houses of Europe and the many homes the Lawrences occupied during their time together. In "Hymn to Priapus," this lushness takes the form of a "warm, soft country lass, / Sweet as an armful of wheat." In spite of the lushness of the imagery borrowed from their many homes, or perhaps as result of their peripatetic existence, Lawrence maintains that "between her breasts is [his] home" ("Song of a Man Who Is Loved" 78).

Frieda's strength is also a source of mystery for Lawrence. In "Ballad of a Wilful Woman" she alternates from the "wilful woman" of the title to the Madonna figure bound to her Joseph and the burden of her child to the strong survivor who, at the end, is "brewing hope from despair." In "She Looks Back" Lawrence acknowledges the sacrifice she made in giving up her children to be with him, and he describes his own pain, presumably from the guilt of his role in this tragedy, as "salt, white, burning, eating salt / In which I have writhed." He also struggles greatly with his guilt in "Meeting among the Mountains," a poem in which he gazes upon the crucified Christ (presumably in the form of a crucifix in a local church) and in which he expresses his certainty that Jesus hates him and what he did to Frieda's life. He wonders whether "the joy [he] bought was not too highly priced."

While Lawrence seems to take inspiration from the natural world and from Frieda's strength, he continues to struggle with this thing called marriage. In "Bei Hennef" he explores how their differences complement each other ("You are the call and I am the answer"), and yet, in spite of this misleading symmetry, he acknowledges, "Strange, how we suffer in spite of this!" This reality seems to paint all the corners of the relationship: While there is much to celebrate, there is still much that causes pain. In some poems, he acknowledges his cruelty to her; in other poems, he admits that she has hurt him as well. While he rejoices in her, considering her "bird-blithe, lovely / Angel in disguise" ("Lady Wife"), he also recognizes that she is "confined in the orbit of me" ("Both Sides of the Medal").

Although they live in a "bonfire of oneness" ("Wedlock"), he had earlier found himself: "I am myself at last" ("I Am Like a Rose" 45). At other times he is completely dependent on her: "If you start away from my breast, and leave me, / How suddenly I shall go down into nothing" ("Wedlock" 75). At still others, he recognizes the impossibility of two individuals' becoming one: "You are you, you are not me / And I am I, I am never you" ("Wedlock" 76). He seems completely accepting of the woman's subservient role in the relationship (she is the "mere female adjunct of what I was" ["Manifesto" 93]) at the same time he proclaims proudly, "How I depend on you utterly" ("Wedlock" 76) and "I depend on you, to keep me alive" ("Wedlock" 74).

The final picture is one of two people who share the same space, the same goals, the same path, but who fight for their own sense of self within that confined space of a "bonfire of oneness." These poems are amazingly intimate and honest, and reading them gives one a sense of being a silent witness to a great love. The greatness of their passion and respect for each other is matched only by the fierceness of their struggle. M. J. Lockwood in his *Study of the Poems of D. H. Lawrence* describes the poem "She Looks Back" in a way that can be applied to the entire collection: These poems are "produced by the action of two Wills, male and female, upon each other, out of which conflict springs all life, all human history, all art. That is, [this collection of poems] is formed out of the action of freedom upon restraint, and is not the product of either impulse alone" (65–66).

Throughout the collection, the reader can see the man and woman at times circling each other, guardedly; at other times embracing in a fierce, almost desperate attempt to become one person; at other times searching for an individual sense of self that seems to have been lost and merged into something else. In short, what Lawrence has recreated here, in as pure a form as possible, is a marriage. And a remarkable one at that.

BIBLIOGRAPHY

Becket, Fiona. *The Complete Critical Guide to D. H. Lawrence.* London: Routledge, 2002.

Lawrence, D. H. *Look! We Have Come Through!* Marazion, Eng.: Ark Press, 1959.

Lockwood, M. J. *A Study of the Poems of D. H. Lawrence: Thinking in Poetry.* London: Macmillan, 1987.

Julie White

"LOUSE HUNTING" Isaac Rosenberg (1917)

Written in France during World War I sometime between the summer of 1916 and February 1917, Isaac Rosenberg's "Louse Hunting" is a poem ostensibly about a delousing incident in which a soldier tears off his shirt and burns it because of the lice and the other men decide to join in, throwing off their clothes and dancing around the fire as they try to destroy the lice infesting their bodies. The poem is also, however, about the nature of World War I and the nature of the universe.

The poem begins "Nudes—stark aglisten" in ironic parody of Adam in Eden. Rather than paradise, the setting resembles a scene from hell, as the men dance around the fire naked, projecting grotesque shadows "like a demon's pantomime" on the walls of the trenches. At one point, a soldier rips his shirt "from his throat / With oaths / Godhead might shrink at, but not the lice." Thus in this world the God of the Judeo-Christian universe is absent and is replaced by the "supreme" lice, who have more sway over the lives of the men than does God. This world is one of evil and death, in the midst of which the men gleefully participate in this bacchanalian rite, as they try to rid themselves of the lice. Further demonstrating this godless world, Rosenberg juxtaposes the "supreme flesh" of the men with the "supreme littleness" of the lice. This "supreme flesh," which in the Judeo-Christian world is created in the image of God, is in this world engaged in a losing battle with the lice.

All of this occurs in the backdrop of World War I, the ultimate challenge to the Judeo-Christian concept of God and the universe. As a result, the demonic and grotesque scene in the poem is meant to represent the demonic and grotesque nature of the war. Furthermore the most chilling aspect of the poem is that the war is nowhere evident in it except in the mention that these men are soldiers. It is as if they have become so desensitized to the war around them that it is no longer a point of notice. In effect, they now know no other world.

BIBLIOGRAPHY

Maccoby, Deborah. *God Made Blind: Isaac Rosenberg, His Life and Poetry.* Northwood, Eng.: Symposium Press, 1999.

Noakes, Vivien. *The Poems and Plays of Isaac Rosenberg.* Oxford: Oxford University Press, 2004.

John Peters

"THE LOVE SONG OF J. ALFRED PRUFROCK" T. S. Eliot (1915)

First published in *Poetry* magazine in 1915, "Love Song" was the main poem in T. S. Eliot's first book, *Prufrock and Other Observations* (1917). Thomas Stearns Eliot created in the character of J. Alfred Prufrock the quintessential antihero in modernist literature. The poem is a dramatic monologue, in which the "you" of the first verse and we the readers are the silent listeners, as we accompany Prufrock in his chaotic, fragmented, and insignificant world characterized by isolation, alienation, loneliness, inarticulateness, and defeat. Prufrock's overwhelming question embodies the drama of the modern man whose quest for love leads to total failure.

The title of the poem reflects Eliot's signature at the time of writing it (1909–11): T. Stearns Eliot. The original title was "Prufrock among the Women." The epigraph of the poem was drawn from Dante's *Inferno,* the first book of the *Divine Comedy.* Count Guido da Montefeltro, wrapped in the flames of the eighth circle of hell, deceives himself with the idea that he can tell all to Dante because he believes that Dante cannot go back to earth; to his knowledge, nobody in hell ever has. This epigraph prepares the reader for Prufrock's total disclosure of his personal hell and casts a spell of death on the whole poem. In fact, the poem can be read as J. Alfred Prufrock's own descent into his own hell: a life of paralysis, inarticulateness, and isolation. In the end, it becomes clear that the title of the poem is ironic, since the text is not a love song but Prufrock's failure to find love. The poem can be divided into five sections: lines 1–12, lines 13–36, lines 37–69, lines 70–74, lines 75–110, and lines 111–131.

The first section (lines 1–12) functions as a prologue to Prufrock's quest. He invites the silent listener (the "you") and the reader to a journey into his inner life. It introduces the themes of death ("patient etherized upon a table") and darkness, thus reinforcing the proposition that Prufrock is descending into his personal hell. The landscape is typical of modernist writings:

desolate and often deserted landscapes, darkness, death, and solitude from the sky above to the more specific "sawdust restaurants."

The second section (lines 13–36) is wrapped around the refrain about young women "talking of Michelangelo." One gets the impression that Prufrock is a middle-aged man going through midlife crisis, who would like female company but is painfully aware that he does not belong. He looks at the young, probably upper-class women, but he feels that he cannot join because of his age and lack of virility. Instead he indulges in speculations about insignificant details using a set of objective correlatives. After the "etherized patient" and the bleak city in the first section, respectively referring to Prufrock's paralysis and desolation, the second section uses the objective correlative (a concrete object, situation, or event that conveys a specific emotion) of the "yellow fog that rubs its back upon the windowpanes / the yellow smoke that rubs its muzzle on the window-panes," generally interpreted as the image of a cat trying but unable to enter a house. Defeated, the cat leaps to the ground, eventually falling asleep. As much as Eliot is said to have admired the dignity of cats, this particular image conveys the idea of a pathetic Prufrock unable to connect with the younger women. Unable to act, as are other characters in literature (such as Shakespeare's Hamlet), he consoles himself with the repeated speculation that "there will be time" to act on his social and sexual anxiety. The repetition of the expression serves to underscore his paralysis. Moreover the women's topic is intimidating to this aging man: They are "talking of Michelangelo," who sculptured *David*, the quintessence of masculinity and beauty, qualities that Prufrock knows he does not have. Prufrock's treatment of time recalls another famous poem, "To His Coy Mistress," by the 17th-century metaphysical poet Andrew Marvell. In this poem, the speaker tells his lady that if they had eternity, he would not mind waiting; in fact, he would spend long years praising every aspect of her beauty until he conquered her. But as the second stanza of the poem suggests, time is passing fast, and soon the mistress will be old. Therefore, the speaker hastens to add, they should seize the day here and now.

In the third section (lines 37–69), Prufrock appears to justify his "indecisions" by his overwhelming awareness of his age and physical state, which would not be favorably looked on by the younger women. He has a "bald spot" in his hair (line 40), which is "growing thin" (line 41), and "his arms and legs are thin" (line 44). His anxiety about his age and sexual appeal is conveyed by the many questions that appear in this section: "Do I dare / Disturb the universe?" (lines 45–46), "So how should I presume" (line 54), and "How should I begin?" (line 69). These questions reflect Prufrock's name, a phonetic combination of *prude* and *frock,* giving the image of a man emasculated by his own priggish attitude. His paralysis in this section is also conveyed by the objective correlative of an insect "pinned and wriggling on the wall" (line 58) and by his overwhelming awareness of his insignificant life: The measure of his life is expressed through the objective correlatives of "coffee spoons" (line 51) and the ends of the cigarettes he has smoked. The repetition of *I have known* underscores the idea that his life has gone in circles without achieving much of consequence.

The fourth, short section (lines 70–74) expresses the same sense of paralysis using the objective correlative of *ragged claws,* the third animal image of the poem after the images of cat (lines 15–22) and insect (pinned for scientific study) (lines 57–58). This section constitutes Prufrock's attempt to answer his own questions in the previous section. If he tried to approach the women, he would start his introduction talking about the start of his journey. Realizing that what he would say would be worthless, he decides that it would be better to be a crab: The "ragged claws . . . / scuttling across the floors of silent seas" suggest the idea that Prufrock, paralyzed by his lack of resolve, plunges into the deeper cycles of hell, making his return even more difficult to envision.

The next section (lines 75–110) returns to Prufrock's insignificant life and his uneasiness about his sexuality. He wonders whether after "tea and cakes and ices," he has the courage and strength to "force the moment to its crisis," another reference to Andrew Marvell's "To His Coy Mistress." In the third stanza of Marvell's poem, the speaker urges his lady to "roll all our strength . . . / . . . into one ball, / and tear our pleasures with rough strife," an idea invoked by Prufrock in lines 80 and 92. The comparison to two biblical figures, John the Baptist and Lazarus, conveys the idea that even before his journey, Prufrock was already subdued. In the gospels of Matthew 14:3–11 and Mark 6:17–19, Salome, giving in to her mother's scheme to have John the Baptist killed, demands the head of John the Baptist on a silver platter as a reward from King Herod for her delightful dancing. Prufrock takes the comparison back by suggesting that he cannot even pretend to the same greatness since his greatness has flickered and he has even faced death, the "eternal Footman." The invocation of Lazarus (in the gospel of Luke 16:19–31) reiterates Guido's sense that no dead has even returned to earth, the same way Prufrock's descent into hell is irreversible. The beggar Lazarus went to heaven while the rich Dives was sent to hell. When the latter appeared to Abraham to let Lazarus return to warn his five brothers, his wish was denied.

The rest of this section focuses on Prufrock's inarticulateness or inability to communicate adequately, expressed in "That's not what I meant at all" (lines 98 and 110) and suggesting that even if, unlike the beggar Lazarus, he could go back to warn people, he might not be able to communicate his feelings at all. What is it the worth, after the insignificant elements of his life—the sunsets, the dooryards, the sprinkled streets, the novels read, the teacup, and the watching of women (lines 101–102)—to betray one's inarticulateness?

The final section (lines 111–131) exposes Prufrock's ultimate defeat. This is achieved first through the invocation of Polonius and Hamlet in William Shakespeare's *Tragedy of Hamlet: Prince of Denmark*. Even though Prufrock claims not to be Hamlet, he shares with him paralysis or the lack of action. Hamlet's paralysis is his uncertainty over the murder of his father and his many tricks to ascertain that his uncle Claudius is indeed the murderer and to make sure that he kills him at the right moment to ensure that he will go to hell. Although he eventually carries out the revenge, he also succumbs. Unlike Prufrock, however, Hamlet has the qualities of a hero, and his actions affect a whole kingdom, not just an individual. Prufrock's paralysis is

about gathering enough courage and daring "to eat a peach" (line 122). Prufrock admits being like Polonius, the old councilor in Shakespeare's *Hamlet*. Polonius is the paragon of inarticulateness (lines 115–119): He beats around the bush and is quite obtuse to the point of being "ridiculous" (lines 115–119). The invocation of Hamlet and Polonius in the same stanza foreshadows Prufrock's impending doom.

In spite of his earlier consolation that he has time, Prufrock is painfully aware that he is growing old (line 120), and in a bohemian manner, he tries to cheat aging by dressing as a young man ("bottoms of my trousers rolled") and wondering whether he should also comb his hair in a way to hide his balding spot and finally tend to his sexual desire ("eat peach"). He then dreams about mermaids, an idealized form of women but also another sign of his imminent death. In sea stories (such as the *Odyssey*), the songs of the beautiful mermaids are said to have mesmerized sailors, leading to their death. They will not sing to him, and they are elusive, but he has heard their songs. He seems to enjoy the fantasy of the daydreams "in the chambers of the sea." The use of the pronoun *we* ensures that the silent listener and we readers are in here with him. And when human voices awaken him from his daydream about the mermaids, he returns to his meaningless life, which death will also soon take.

The last six lines of the poem have been read as a sestet (six lines), as in a Petrarchan sonnet. As are Dante and Michelangelo, Petrarch is an Italian Renaissance artist, who addressed many of his poems to Laura, a woman he met once but never conquered. Unlike Petrarch, Prufrock does not even have the consolation of an idolized woman. This allusion to Petrarch's unrequited love makes Prufrock appear even more pathetic because he is so paralyzed by his inadequacy that he does not even try.

Prufrock's defeat in T. S. Eliot's "Love Song of J. Alfred Prufrock" conveys the tragedy and disillusionment of the modern man in quest of identity, love, and gratification. In his paralysis, despair, alienation, inarticulateness, and lack of love, he prefigures many characters in modernist writings such as the grotesques in Sherwood Anderson's *Winesburg, Ohio* (1919), Gatsby in F. Scott Fitzgerald's *The Great*

Gatsby (1925), and the American expatriates in Ernest Hemingway's *The Sun Also Rises* (1926), who all succumb to their inability to handle the emptiness, chaos, and meaninglessness of their lives.

BIBLIOGRAPHY:
Donoghue, Denis. *Words Alone: The Poet T. S. Eliot.* New Haven, Conn.: Yale University Press, 2000.
Moody, David A., ed. *The Cambridge Companion to T. S. Eliot.* Cambridge: Cambridge University Press, 1994.
Riquelme, John Paul. *Harmony of Dissonances: T. S. Eliot, Romanticism, and Imagination.* Baltimore: Johns Hopkins University Press, 1991.
Spurr, David. *Conflicts in Consciousness: T. S. Eliot's Poetry and Criticism.* Urbana: University of Illinois Press, 1984.

Aimable Twagilmana

M

MacCAIG, NORMAN (1910–1996) The Scottish poet Norman MacCaig was born in Edinburgh in 1910 and lived most of his life in that city, attending the Royal High School and the University of Edinburgh, where he studied classics in 1928–32. He then trained as a teacher and until 1967 worked as a primary school teacher, when he was appointed fellow in creative writing at the University of Edinburgh. During the Second World War, he was a conscientious objector, an unpopular position in wartime Britain. He objected not for political reasons but for humanitarian ones, saying once on Scottish TV (*In Verse,* April 4, 1988), "I just didn't want to shoot other people."

MacCaig's first two books, *Far Cry* (1943) and *The Inward Eye* (1946), were deeply influenced by the SUR-REALISM of the 1930s and the New Apocalypse movement of the 1940s. The latter got its name from an anthology edited in 1939 by Henry Treece and J. P. Hendry, who favored the surrealistic, muscular, apolitical style of DYLAN THOMAS, though Thomas never signed their manifesto nor appeared in either of their two New Apocalyptic anthologies. MacCaig's poems from this period can be characterized as densely packed with metaphor. Another obvious early influence was John Donne, for whom he had a lifelong love, and it might be as useful to call his early books metaphysical.

In 1955 his third book, *Riding Lights,* broke new and very different ground. He produced formal metrical verse using clear diction, preferring lucidity and ordinary language to the complexity, some would say torturedness, of his former poetry. This new poetry was very much like the poetry celebrated in 1956 by Robert Conquest in his anthology *NEW LINES,* and MacCaig could easily have been included with others to whom he has since been compared, such as PHILIP LARKIN, except for his Scottishness. All of the *New Lines* poets were English. In 1966 with the publication of *Surroundings,* his eighth book, MacCaig turned to free verse, but he never rejected the lucid style that he found in *Riding Lights.*

MacCaig's poetry alternates in location between two worlds, both Scottish—the Lowlands of his native Edinburgh and the Highlands of his mother, who was from Scalpay. During most of his life he had a second home in Assynt, in a remote area in northwestern Scotland. MacCaig also mediated in Scottish poetry between powerful influences. He was a friend, and critic, of HUGH MacDIARMID, who invented a new literary dialect for Scots verse, as well as of Sorley Maclean, who revived Gaelic verse, and yet MacCaig wrote in a simple, direct English. He became by the time of his death the "grand old man" of Scottish poetry, a mentor for many younger Scottish poets, such as LIZ LOCHHEAD, and a staple on the syllabus for Scottish schoolchildren, with such poems as "FETCHING COWS." He occupies the place in Scottish poetry that Larkin did in English poetry, the favorite poet of the people and the unofficial laureate.

BIBLIOGRAPHY

Hendry, Joy, and Raymond Ross, eds. *Norman MacCaig: Critical Essays.* Edinburgh: Edinburgh University Press, 1990.

Pritchard, Dave. The Norman MacCaig site. Available online. URL: http://www.jacobite.org.uk/maccaig. Accessed on May 3, 2008.

James Persoon

MacDIARMID, HUGH (1892–1978)

Hugh MacDiarmid was born on August 11, 1892, as Christopher Murray Grieve in the Scottish border town of Langholm. His background was not elite; his father was from a millworking family and was a postman. Young Christopher grew up in what he viewed as a paradise, however; his later lyrics on the beauties of the Scottish countryside were based on an idyllic boyhood spent roaming the hills and glens around Langholm. He stated that his "earliest impressions are of an almost tropical luxuriance of Nature" (*Lucky Poet* 219) and that his senses were awakened early by this experience. His sense of his Scottish homeland did not just originate in his immediate surroundings, however. Much of his mother's family lived in the Highlands, so on visits to them Christopher learned to appreciate the Scottish country life and the language of the Highlands, Gaelic.

Christopher's literary education started early, and close to home. When he was four, his family moved to a house in the Library Buildings in Langholm. It was behind his father's workplace, the post office, and below the town's library. Christopher would carry a large washing basket upstairs to the library and borrow the works of Nathanial Hawthorne, Ambrose Bierce, Sidney Lanier, and Mark Twain, among others. He was fascinated especially by novels of the American frontier. When he was 16, he went to the Broughton Higher Grade School, where he met George Ogilvie, a teacher of English at Broughton. Ogilvie recognized Christopher's literary talents and nurtured the young writer with support, direction, and praise. Christopher, on his end, found in Ogilvie a sympathetic receptacle for his hopes, dreams, and ambitions. By this point, Christopher had recognized his own passion for writing and hoped to make his living as a man of letters.

In 1910 Christopher was finished with his formal education. He tried to free-lance as a writer in Langholm for a bit but soon returned to Edinburgh and, with Ogilvie's help, found a job at the *Edinburgh Evening Dispatch*. He was later fired for selling off the books he reviewed for the paper. Through the next few years he worked as a journalist at various newspapers around England and Wales, changing jobs frequently on account of his drinking and disagreements with his employers. This was to be a recurring pattern throughout his life; Christopher always found "bread and butter" work to be an intrusion on what he considered his real work, his writing. In 1915, when World War I broke out, he entered the army. In 1916, however, he contracted malaria and was sent home, where he soon married a woman named Peggy Skinner. After some time spent in Marseilles he returned to Scotland in 1919 to live in Montrose. From 1919 to 1929, Christopher Murray Grieve was to have a decade of his most important literary production—and to transform himself into his literary persona, Hugh MacDiarmid.

Christopher Grieve was a writer and a poet who thought that the use of the Scots vernacular in poetry, a la Robert Burns, was nostalgic and sentimental. Hugh MacDiarmid, however, embraced Scots as the voice of Scottish nationalism and wrote poems that celebrated his homeland. It was during this period that MacDiarmid wrote what many critics feel are his finest poems, contained within his collections *Sangschaw*, *Penny Wheep*, and *A Drunk Man Looks at a Thistle*. In "Gairmscoile," a lyric found at the end of *Penny Wheep*, he expresses his feelings about the importance of the Scots language:

> It's soon', no' sense, that faddoms the herts o'men,
> And by my sangs the rouch auld Scots I ken
> E'en herts that ha'e nae Scots 'll dirl richt thro'
> As nocht else could—for here's a language rings
> Wi' datchie sesames, and names for nameless
>   things.

While Scots might have "names for nameless things," MacDiarmid was also interested in making Scotland a true name for an independent country. A fierce nationalist, MacDiarmid worked tirelessly as a national propagandist and agitator. MacDiarmid was also very interested in the Communist Party and socialist thought; in Montrose he was elected to the town council as an Independent Socialist. These two political aims were often a source of conflict in his life. In 1933 he was expelled from the Nationalist Party of Scotland because of his Communist beliefs; in 1936 the Communist Party expelled him because he would not submit to "party discipline," namely, to give up his nationalist beliefs.

In 1929 MacDiarmid moved to London to edit a radio journal, *Vox*. His tenure there was interrupted by an accident—he fell from the top deck of a London bus and sustained a concussion. By the time he was well again the journal had folded. His marriage was also ending. His wife, Peggy, refused to follow him to Liverpool, where he had found a new job; the subsequent pain of a divorce and loss of contact with his children contributed to a revival of a serious drinking problem. He was remarried quickly, however, to a Cornish woman named Valda Trevlyn. With her help, and the help of friends, they relocated to the remote island of Whalsay in the Shetlands. Life there had the benefit of being cheap, solitary, and dry—no alcohol was permitted on the island. The remoteness let MacDiarmid get back to his writing, but the poems he produced were not the political ones of the previous decade. In his 1934 collection, *Stony Limits and Other Poems,* he included both experimental poems in English and Scots lyrics. He also wrote several prose works, including his autobiography, *Lucky Poet*. In 1935 a nervous breakdown essentially ended his production of important poetic works.

MacDiarmid left the Shetlands in 1942 and settled with his wife and son at a small farm cottage near Biggar, in the Scottish Lowlands. Gradually his reputation as a major literary talent grew, and the cottage began seeing distinguished visitors and graduate students pass through its door. MacDiarmid was awarded honorary degrees from the University of Edinburgh and Trinity College Dublin and received the Fletcher of Saltoun Medal and the Foyle Poetry Prize. He died of cancer on September 9, 1978; he was buried in Langholm, the village of his birth.

See also "ANOTHER EPITAPH ON AN ARMY OF MERCENARIES," *A DRUNK MAN LOOKS AT THE THISTLE.*

BIBLIOGRAPHY

Bold, Alan. *MacDiarmid: Christopher Murray Grieve: A Critical Biography*. Amherst: University of Massachusetts Press, 1990.

Gish, Nancy K. *Hugh MacDiarmid: The Man and His Work*. London: Macmillan, 1984.

MacDiarmid, Hugh. *Lucky Poet: A Self-Study in Literature and Political Ideas*. Rev. ed. Berkeley: University of California Press, 1972.

Rachel Anderson

MacNEICE, LOUIS (1907–1963)

Poet, playwright, literary critic, translator, and journalist, Louis MacNeice seems to have fit many lifetimes into his 56 years. He described his as "a life of episodes," a life spent "isolating incidents or people or aspects of people in hope of finding something self-contained, having despaired of a self-contained world." If he did not find the world "self-contained," it is perhaps because he seems to have been fascinated with its vastness.

Born in Belfast in 1907, MacNeice was the son of a strict and distant Protestant clergymen and a former schoolteacher. As theirs were for W. B. YEATS and James Joyce, MacNeice's childhood was the well from which his writing frequently drew, and, as they did, MacNeice remembered his childhood with a mixture of wonder and despair. His childhood letters and poems reveal a wonderfully imaginative young writer, but he would later recall in *The Strings Are False,* his unfinished autobiography, that his imagination was tempered by a pervading "sense of loss because things could never be replaced." A great loss occurred early when MacNiece's mother died when he was seven years old; she had been diagnosed with a uterine fibroid tumor two years earlier, and even as an adult MacNeice believed his difficult birth had caused her illness and eventual death. He was perennially curious about his origins, and this early life-in-death association must have made such an interest difficult to indulge at times. Still, he could not help but to revisit his childhood in his poetry, for, as he wrote in "CARRICK REVISITED," even "memories I have shelved peer at me from the shelf."

After attending Marlborough College in the early twenties, MacNeice won a postmastership to Oxford in 1926. There he published his first book of poetry and met two lifelong friends, STEPHEN SPENDER (with whom he edited *Oxford Poetry*) and W. H. AUDEN (with whom he would write *Letters from Iceland* 10 years later). As many poets of his generation did, MacNeice felt engulfed by a "sense of futility, of belonging to a society without values, which the ebbing World War I had left behind." That sense of futility was exacerbated just after his graduation from Oxford when he published an unsuccessful novel and, worse still, when his wife of five years abandoned him and their 18-month-old son.

However bleak conditions may have otherwise seemed, MacNeice was beginning to gain recognition as a poet. His first successful volume of poetry, *Eclogue for Christmas,* was accepted for publication in 1933 by T. S. ELIOT (Eliot, who by then worked in a London publishing house, would eventually publish a number of volumes of MacNeice's poetry). Before the decade was out, MacNeice would publish three more volumes of poetry, a cogent book of literary criticism, two works of prose, a play, and a translation of Aeschylus's *Agamemnon.* It was at this time, in 1938, that MacNeice began an ambitious and innovative long poem that would attempt to fuse public and private. *Autumn Journal* records the events leading up to the Second World War through the lens of personal experience, emphasizing the present moment yet unable to turn away from the ominous future on the horizon. An original and prescient work, *Autumn Journal* is perhaps Mac-Neice's most celebrated poetic achievement.

This prolific period extended into the following decade as MacNeice continued writing poetry, criticism, and plays for radio and remarried and had a second child. Unable to join the military during World War II because of ill health and poor eyesight, Mac-Neice began working for the British Broadcasting Company, where he worked for nearly the rest of his life. In 1946, he befriended another well-known poet working for the BBC, DYLAN THOMAS. MacNeice would later lament Thomas's premature death in his 1953 poem *Autumn Sequel.*

MacNeice's reputation as an eminent poet and man of letters did not diminish in his lifetime: In 1957 he received an honorary doctorate from Queen's University, Belfast, and was awarded by the British government a prestigious Commander of the British Empire

(CBE) the following year. Yet despite these accomplishments, MacNeice was growing increasingly frustrated with his own work. The early 1960s began auspiciously and seemed to begin a new era for MacNeice. He published a mature volume of poetry, *Solstices,* in 1961 and delivered the Clark Lectures at Cambridge University in February 1963 (posthumously published as *Varieties of Parable*). However, after recording sound effects the following August in a cave for his radio play *Persons from Porlock,* MacNeice caught a cold that turned to pneumonia. He died on September 3, 1963, nine days before his 56th birthday. His final volume of poems, *The Burning Perch,* was published soon after.

MacNeice's poetry continued to gain a wider audience after his death. A volume of collected poems appeared in 1967, and a number of books that were devoted to his life and work, including a 1995 biography, followed. This interest shows no sign of decline. Faber and Faber published a new edition of Mac-Neice's collected poems in 2007. It is not difficult to understand why MacNeice's poetry continues to be relevant, for it is engaging and inventive and reveals a mind acutely attentive to language. Though his style changed over time, MacNeice would often suspend his poetry between two opposing poles. In "Sunday Morning," for example, MacNeice begins with a celebration of youthful disregard, only to turn soberly, suddenly in the final lines to remind readers that "there is no music or movement which secures / Escape from the weekday time. Which deadens and endures." Even the most carefree and joyful expressions cannot mute the existential nausea of the passage of time. In his late poetry MacNeice set his fascination with modern life against his deep interest in the ancient world. MacNeice, who had studied classics in college and who counted Horace among his influences even late in life, was able to juxtapose the sacredness of antiquity with the peculiarity of modernity in surprising ways. "Bulldoze all memories and sanctuaries," begins a poem with the curious ancient-modern title "New Jerusalem." Our age should not hold the past at a distance, this poem argues, but should instead collapse time to make past and present one. "So come up Lazarus," MacNeice wryly prays; "we will teach you to touch-type / And give you a police dog to navigate the rush hour." Such surprising moments appear throughout his poetry, which frequently entertains as it enjoins contemplation.

See also "BAGPIPE MUSIC," "CARRICKFERGUS," "AN ECLOGUE FOR CHRISTMAS," "STAR-GAZER."

BIBLIOGRAPHY
MacNeice, Louis. *The Collected Poems of Louis MacNeice.* Edited by E. R. Dodds. New York: Oxford University Press, 1967.
———. *Louis MacNeice: Collected Poems.* London: Faber and Faber, 2007.
———. *The Strings Are False.* Edited by E. R. Dodds. London: Faber and Faber, 1965.
Stallworthy, Jon. *Louis MacNeice.* New York: W. W. Norton, 1995.

George Micajah Phillips

MacSWEENEY, BARRY (1948–2000)

Barry MacSweeney was born in a working-class section of Newcastle upon Tyne, but much of his childhood was spent on the fells surrounding the Northumbrian village of Allenheads. Here he befriended a girl with a cleft palate whom he taught to read and write and who provided inspiration for one of his final collections, *Pearl* (1997). These early experiences helped shape much of his poetry, which frequently juxtaposes the hellish image of urban Newcastle with the unspoiled beauty of the Northumbrian countryside. On leaving school at 16 he became a cub reporter with the local newspaper, the *Evening Chronicle,* where BASIL BUNTING, one of MacSweeney's formative influences, also worked. At the same time he began attending poetry readings organized by TOM PICKARD and his wife, Connie, at the now-famous Morden Tower. MacSweeney claimed that he wrote his first poem when aged seven, but witnessing the likes of Ginsberg, Ferlinghetti, Creeley, Tom Raworth, and Bunting himself at the Morden readings helped catalyze his literary convictions. Self-consciously adopting a *poète maudit* persona, his poetry wore its influences conspicuously: Shelley, Chatterton, Rimbaud, and Jim Morrison provided MacSweeney's role models. In 1966 he moved south to study journalism at Harlow Technical College, after which he worked as a reporter and arts feature writer on various weekly and daily newspapers.

Published to great acclaim in 1968, MacSweeney's first collection, *The Boy from the Green Cabaret Tells of His Mother,* is characterized by its lyrical warmth and surprising maturity. Following the book's appearance, he achieved a kind of celebrity after his publishers nominated him for the chair of poetry at Oxford University. However, the publicity stunt backfired, causing near-irreparable damage to MacSweeney's career and reputation. Unable to secure another publishing deal, he established Blacksuede Boot Press with his then wife, the poet Elaine Randall, who later admitted that MacSweeney was already an alcoholic at the time they married. One of the poets they published was J. H. PRYNNE, who became a lifelong friend. MacSweeney continued to issue pamphlets, albeit through small presses, until 1997, when Bloodaxe published *The Book of Demons* (which includes the Pearl poems). The collection records his struggle with alcohol addiction and it reinvigorated his career. In 2000, just four weeks after the relaunch of Blacksuede, MacSweeney died in the manner of one of his poems: "One day choke on it, . . . / throat's clogged highway."

BIBLIOGRAPHY
Bush, Clive. *Out of Dissent: A Study of Five Contemporary British Poets.* London: Talus, 1997.
MacSweeney, Barry. *Wolf Tongue: Selected Poems 1965–2000.* Tarset, Eng.: Bloodaxe, 2003.

Brian Burton

"MAD COW DANCE" JO SHAPCOTT (1992)

JO SHAPCOTT's witty alter ego, "The Mad Cow," appears in a fragmented sequence of poems spanning two collections, *Phrase Book* (1992) and *My Life Asleep* (1998). In "The Mad Cow Talks Back," the Cow introduces herself with characteristic chutzpah: "I'm not mad really. It just seems that way / because I stagger and get a bit irritable." Created amid growing panic about the spread of bovine spongiform encephalopathy, or "mad cow disease," in the United Kingdom in the early nineties, this endearing character is sanguine about her affliction: "There are wonderful holes in my brain / through which ideas from outside can travel." In the upside-down order of the "idiot savant" (or wise fool), where the mute (cow) can talk and lunacy is rational, affliction becomes opportunity and decline produces growth. This carnivalesque process renders the powerless suddenly, if temporarily, powerful. The Cow's political subversiveness is compounded by her gender and the poetic medium. Shapcott explains: "She's . . . rather a feisty character, rather a terrific sort of animal, and I think I made her that way in order to redeem the idea of a 'mad cow,' which is something I get called a lot" (*The Poetry Quartets*, 1999). The poet's metamorphosis deliberately conflates one form of female disenfranchisement—madness, that is, the conventionally female malady linked with hysteria as well as lunacy—with a more literary one, the woman poet.

The riotous physicality of the "Mad Cow Dance" ("I like to dance. Bang. I love to dance. Push. / / It makes me savage and brilliant. Stomp.") celebrates female sexual energy. The assertive first-person speaker transgressively asserts her power to choose independence, partnership, or community. She boldly addresses the "sitting down reader" and warns us that we might be shocked by her bravado and language. Likewise in "The Mad Cow Tries to Write the Good Poem," she connects personal freedom with untethered creativity. Unashamedly female, performatively and pointedly she will make poetry of the lowly materials of her world: "the streaky emulsion on the walls."

BIBLIOGRAPHY

Bertram, Vicki. *Gendering Poetry: Contemporary Women and Men Poets*. London: Rivers Oram Pandora Press, 2004.

Philips, Janet. "The Shape-Shifter." *Poetry Review* 91, no. 1 (2001): 21.

The Poetry Quartets 5: Helen Dunmore, U. A. Fanthorpe, Elizabeth Jennings, Jo Shapcott. Audio Cassette. Newcastle upon Tyne, Eng.: British Council/Bloodaxe Books, 1999.

Shapcott, Jo. "I Don't Believe That Autobiography Is Necessary for Poetry." Interview with Lidia Vianu. *Desperado Literature*. Available online. URL: http://lidiavianu.script mania.com/jo_shapcott.htm. Accessed December 7, 2005.

Jane Dowson

"MADELEINE IN CHURCH" CHARLOTTE MEW (1916)

In "Madeleine in Church," a complex monologue originally published in *The Farmer's Bride*, CHARLOTTE MEW confronts the unanswered and terrifying mysteries of faith through an imperfect speaker who demands proof of God's power. The nonlinear poem represents a series of Madeleine's fragmented thoughts as she eyes the various icons and statues crowded into a Catholic church. Echoing the disordered ideological content, the stanzas and lines vary in length from quite brief to extremely long and contain no consistent metrical pattern. Madeleine's journey into the intersection of spirit and body pushes at the limits of acceptable subject matter, introducing a perspective on Christianity so unorthodox that one printer refused to set it because he deemed it blasphemous.

Reluctant to turn immediately to the imposing figure of the crucifix, Madeleine in the first of 14 stanzas kneels before a "plaster saint"—who, like her, is "not too divine." She comforts herself by thinking that the person represented, as many saints, must have struggled with faith and sin during life. Madeleine declares to the saint that "anyone can wash the paint / Off our poor faces, his and mine!" A painted woman, she makes it clear early in the poem that she has broken and rejected the rules of idealized femininity. As the poem progresses, Madeleine angrily asserts that Christ cannot know the truth of her sins from his elevated position. She thinks back on her unfaithful past, recalling her first husband's face, "gone suddenly blank and old / The hateful day of the divorce." Madeleine's adultery early in her life marked the beginning of a long string of affairs. She is not a prostitute, but she is a woman whose desires place her outside the socially acceptable feminine roles. Just as marriage does not suit her, she imagines that becoming a mother would be a wrong decision. She responds bitterly to the myth of domestic bliss and tranquility, stating forthrightly that she prefers to spend her earthly time pursuing fulfillment of earthly desires.

However, Madeleine is not without ambivalence, and a sense of conflict has plagued her for as long as she can remember. As explored in stanza 4, Madeleine as a youth regularly felt overwhelmed by the visual and physical sensations of daily life. Of adulthood, she remarks, "They are not gone, yet, the lights, the colours, the perfumes" of youth. She states in a simply phrased yet conceptually crucial line, "I think my body was my soul." Physical pleasure, then, was the only spiritual joy as well. Seeing everything through the lens of the physical, she cannot imagine a division between the body and the true "self"—for Madeleine, one is intertwined with the other. But as she has aged, she has developed a strong fear of death. Given the primacy of the physical, what will happen in death, when the soul is supposed to depart the body? To Madeleine, this question is both urgent and agonizing.

For this reason, Madeleine turns in stanza 10 to the thought of Mary Magdalene, her biblical antecedent. Mary Magdalene, in Madeleine's radical and eroticized formulation, was never asked to reject passion or lust; rather than eliminating her desire, Christ displaced that desire onto himself. Affection, passion, and lust cannot be destroyed even by Christ—they can only be properly channeled: "You can change the things for which we care, / But even You, unless You kill us, not the way." Christ appears as a tolerant and understanding lover who accepts that "she did not love You like the rest, / It was in her own way, but at the worst, the best." He shows mercy to Mary by giving her an ideal outlet for her passions. The nature of her love does not change, but its object does. Madeleine envies this method of achieving "peace . . . but passion too." Becoming Christ's lover, as Mary was, would resolve her conflicts and legitimize her desires.

Yet Madeleine knows that this path is closed to her, because Christ does not appear in a physical form to her; that knowledge returns the reader to the central issue of doubt and positivist desire for proof of Christ's power. Always grounded in the body, Madeleine theorizes that physical contact alone allowed the redemption of Mary: "She was a sinner, we are what we are: the spirit afterwards, but first, the touch." Despite her yearning, she simply cannot convince herself to sublimate her preoccupation with the physical and focus on the abstract spiritual rewards promised to virtuous women by conventional Christianity. She doubts "if there were any Paradise beyond this earth." Madeleine intends to rage against the dying of the light, but as she approaches it, she grows ever more despondent regarding the end of life. Her years on earth have passed too quickly and without fulfillment. Her misplaced desires have ended in disillusionment and decreased social status. She has aged quickly, seeing the "ghost" of her elderly mother in her mirror. She is alone again, having lost all of her lovers. In this moment of desperation, she has sought Christ's assurance regarding death, convinced the entire time that he cannot give it to her: "Tell me there will be some one. Who?/ If there were no one else, could it be You?" Recalling again how Christ never "seemed to notice me," Madeleine absorbs the silence with which her desperate plea is met. Christ, failing to give proof of his existence, offers neither comfort nor an affirmation of faith. She leaves as she arrived—in doubt. As the biographer Penelope Fitzgerald states, Mew "is willing to believe and willing to disbelieve, but not able to do either."

BIBLIOGRAPHY
Fitzgerald, Penelope. *Charlotte Mew and Her Friends.* London: Collins, 1984.
Mizejewski, Linda. "Charlotte Mew and the Unrepentant Magdalene: A Myth in Transition." *Texas Studies in Literature and Language* 26 (1984): 282–302.
Walsh, Jessica. "'The Strangest Pain to Bear': Corporeality and Fear of Insanity in Charlotte Mew's Poetry." *Victorian Poetry* 40, no. 3 (2002): 217–240.

James Persoon

MAHON, DEREK (1941–)

Following in the footsteps of James Joyce and Samuel Beckett, the Irish poet Derek Mahon is a cosmopolitan writer of exile and alienation, who expresses his strong sense of place from the position of an unattached outsider. Born in Belfast, Northern Ireland, on November 23, 1941, and educated at the Royal Academical Institution, Belfast; at Trinity College, Dublin (reading French, English, philosophy); and at the Sorbonne, Paris, he has spent much of his life traveling in North America, France, and Italy. Mahon moved to London in 1970 but now lives mainly in Dublin. He has worked as editor, screenwriter, journalist, and lecturer at a number of universities in the United States and Europe. His translations and adaptations include *High Time* and *The School for Wives* (after Molière), *The Selected Poems of Philippe Jaccottet,* Euripides' *The Bacchae,* and Racine's *Phèdre.* Mahon is regarded alongside SEAMUS HEANEY and MICHAEL LONGLEY as the leader of the resurgence of Irish poetry from the late 1960s onward.

As did other Northern Irish poets, Mahon grew up in a liberal Protestant family and was confronted with the violence of sectarian battles between Catholics and Protestants. He tried to overcome the limitations of his cultural background through traveling, and his poetry reflects his self-education, rejection of his roots, and attempt to attain impartiality. His first collection of verse was *Night-Crossing* (1968), the title referring to the crossing of the Irish Sea by mail boat. Images of migration abound, establishing a disruption of the continuities of place, identity, and culture that contrasts, for example, with the work of Seamus Heaney (cf. his essay "Poetry in Northern Ireland"). "Day Trip to Donegal" evokes, but negates the pastoral and metaphysical possibilities of the Irish landscape, climaxing in a nightmarish fantasy of disorientation. In poems such as "An Unborn Child" or "A DISUSED SHED IN CO. WEXFORD" he takes an ironic stance toward reality: Just as the child in the womb is one with the mother's body and will lose this identity through birth, the mushrooms yearn for absorption into society.

His second collection, *Lives* (1972), also deals with the central question of the self's relation to the world. In "Ecclesiastes" he rejects, but acknowledges the inescapable influence of Northern Puritanism; in "In the Aran Islands" a momentary fascination by a folk singer's evocation of romantic Ireland is abruptly destroyed. While attempts to retreat from the world ("Entropy") lead not to creativity, but to fruitless isolation, immersion in the world leads to complete control by forces outside the self, so that a balance between self and world seems utopian. In Mahon's third volume, *The Snow Party* (1975), the speaker has reached a new stage of development. In the best-known poem, "Afterlives," the poet wakes up in London and thinks he has escaped Belfast with its gunfire and violence. And yet he realizes that this liberation is only a succumbing to another fantasy, that of bourgeois self-complacency.

The Hunt by Night (1982), which includes most of the poems from *Courtyards in Delft* (1981), explores the genre of *ekphrasis,* creating idyllic scenes that are only to be shattered afterward. "Courtyards in Delft," "Girls on the Bridge," and "The Hunt by Night" are reinterpretations of and meditations on famous paintings. The first poem, "Courtyards in Delft," looks behind the idyllic stability of domestic routine in Pieter de Hooch's Dutch painting, evoking Protestant Ulster

and the Orange armies. The collection shows a growing loss of confidence in the power of art to withstand chaos, and Mahon's art approaches a Beckettian minimalism. His symbolic landscapes become even more desolate in the slim volume *Antarctica* (1985), where any notion of a stable self is abandoned, along with the possibility of knowledge and order. Mahon's most recent collection of poems, *Harbour Lights* (2005), however, is more relaxed and affirmative toward life. Redemption through women ("Calypso") is a recurring theme and Yeatsian allusions are manifold. Throughout his career, Mahon has employed many received forms of verse, often a form of iambic pentameter as well as the sprung verse of Gerard Manley Hopkins, thus escaping the chaos of his native city through lyrical form.

BIBLIOGRAPHY

Brown, Terence. "Mahon and Longley: Place and Placelessness." In *The Cambridge Companion to Contemporary Irish Poetry,* edited by Matthew Campbell, 133–148. Cambridge: Cambridge University Press, 2003.

Corcoran, Neil, ed. *The Chosen Ground: Essays on the Contemporary Poetry of Northern Ireland.* Bridgend, Eng.: Seren Books, 1992.

Donnelly, Brian, guest ed. *Derek Mahon.* Special Issue of the *Irish University Review* 24.

Kennedy-Andrews, Elmer, ed. *The Poetry of Derek Mahon.* Gerrards Cross, Eng.: Colin Smythe, 2002.

Mahon, Derek. *Selected Poems.* London: Penguin, 2006.

McDonald, Peter. "History and Poetry: Derek Mahon and Tom Paulin." In *Contemporary Irish Poetry: A Collection of Critical Essays,* edited by Elmer Andrews, 86–106. Basingstoke, Eng.: Macmillan, 1993.

———. *Mistaken Identities: Poetry and Northern Ireland.* Oxford: Clarendon, 1997.

Heike Grundmann

MAKING COCOA FOR KINGSLEY AMIS
WENDY COPE (1986)   WENDY COPE was 41 years old when her first book of poems came out from Faber and Faber in 1986. A scant 59 pages in length, bearing a sketch of a child drinking cocoa on its cover, dedicated to Cope's psychiatrist, and containing mostly rhymed and metered poems in such unfashionable forms as the double dactyl and triolet, the book seemed an unlikely

candidate for bestsellerdom. Yet over the years ahead it would sell well over a 100,000 copies, and Cope would become a literary celebrity.

According to the title poem of the collection, the unusual title occurred to Cope in a dream, "And some kind of record seemed vital. / I knew it wouldn't be much of a poem / But I love the title." Although Cope was not personally acquainted with KINGSLEY AMIS at the time, critics have observed that Cope's direct, accessible, and dryly humorous poetic voice bears comparison to that of Amis and other poets of THE MOVEMENT, particularly PHILIP LARKIN. Whether Cope was paying tribute to Amis, mocking him and the male literary establishment, or simply piggybacking on Amis's fame to get attention, as various critics have suggested, Amis took the title in good humor, showing up at the book's publication party and telling a reporter that he had enjoyed reading it.

The book showed off Cope's skills as a light verse and FORMAL VERSE poet. While many poems chronicled the course of the speaker's doomed relationships with men ("There are so many kinds of awful men— / One can't avoid them all"), those that caused the most "buzz" among readers were Cope's parodies of established male poets including T. S. ELIOT, TED HUGHES, SEAMUS HEANEY, CRAIG RAINE, and GEOFFREY HILL. Cope attributed some of the parodies to "Jason Strugnell," an invented male persona revealed to be a tasteless, drunken, lecherous, envious, and unsuccessful poet. Ironically the parodies that made Cope's reputation had been written while she was struggling and failing to get her own poems published, seeking "a way of coming to terms with what was fashionable in poetry," as she told one interviewer. As with the book's ambiguous title, it was unclear whether Cope was mocking the poets she parodied, proving she could write as well as they could to gain entry to their "club," or doing a little of both. Antifeminist or feminist, conservative traditionalist or postmodern experimentalist with techniques of gender bending, sampling, and pastiche, Cope resists easy categorization, and her first book continues to intrigue both sophisticated critics and a mass-market audience.

BIBLIOGRAPHY

Pérez Novales, Marta. "Wendy Cope's Use of Parody in *Making Cocoa for Kingsley Amis.*" *Miscelanea: A Journal of English and American Studies* 15 (1994): 481–500.

Thompson, Nicola. "Wendy Cope's Struggle with Strugnell in *Making Cocoa for Kingsley Amis.*" In *New Perspectives on Women and Comedy,* edited by Regina Barreca, 111–122. Philadelphia: Gordon and Breach, 1992.

Julie Kane

"MALI" GILLIAN CLARKE (1993) "Mali" is the fifth of seven poems in a sequence entitled "Blood," from the collection *The King of Britain's Daughter* (1993). *Mali* is a popular female name in Wales and is the name of GILLIAN CLARKE's granddaughter. The theme of the sequence is the nature of childbirth, and the joy and pain that accompany motherhood. The poem itself is a celebration of the child's birth in particular, but also of childbirth and the cyclical nature of time in general.

The structure of the poem is four stanzas of seven lines each and is roughly iambic in meter. The first line of the stanza is located in the present and directs the reader to the birth of Mali three years earlier. This first line along with the final stanza featuring the birthday party frames the event of the birth that occupies the remainder of stanza 1 and all of stanzas 2 and 3. The season is late summer, the beginning of the harvest time of the year, which is bustling with activity in preparation for the dormant, dying season of winter. The grandmother is the narrator and it is through her eyes that the reader experiences the events of the poems and whose insights are presented. It is significant to the narrator that the birth takes place as autumn approaches. Autumn is the season of a woman's life when the ability to have children of one's own diminishes as menopause nears.

Throughout the poem, the idea of seasonal/unseasonal is explored. The grandmother is driving her daughter, in labor three weeks early, to the hospital. The child is arriving too early, out of season. As she is driving, the narrator comments on the "unmistakable brim and tug of the tide / I'd thought was over." She is referring both to the "tide" of menstruation and to the "tug" of maternal instincts that are set once more into motion as her daughter's delivery nears. The menstruation is also out of season—a cyclical event that the narrator thought had ended. The women have been picking berries, and their fingers are stained purple. Apples are ripening, yet summer has not totally let go.

The berries and apples are fruit in season, but they are in contrast to the weather, which is not seasonal.

The day after the baby is born, they take her to the beach since it is still so warm. The "tide" of line 2 is now echoed by the ocean tides. Clarke again refers to "things seasonal and out of season" as they celebrate Mali's birth with a party on the beach. It is too late in the year for an ocean visit, yet the summery warmth of the day encourages such activity. The grandmother is a "latecomer at summer's festival": Summer is the season of fertility and fecundity, terms that do not apply to a grandmother. Yet, she is "hooked again" by the one-day-old baby lying under an umbrella. She is pulled again into the flow of life that a mother enters with the birth of a child. Even the sea, the narrator claims, could not drag her away from her granddaughter. Throughout "Mali" it is the sea that is the central metaphor for life and fertility.

The poem takes on a more pagan atmosphere in the final stanza, in which Mali's third birthday party takes place. The grandmother bakes the child a "cake like our house" and decorates the trees with balloons and streamers. The narrator says the old trees "blossom" with balloons—the balloons and streamers replacing the springtime flowers that are not in season in late summer. The celebration culminates at twilight with a rituallike raising of "a cup of blue ocean," candles, and "three drops of, / probably, last blood." Last blood here refers to the last menstrual blood a woman sheds from her body. The *probably* is an indicator of the unpredictability of the event of ended fertility.

There are no males in the poem, and in the "Blood" sequence there are only male children, no adult men at all. Clarke often writes about the birth of human babies and of farm animals, especially sheep, and the role of men in the process is usually minimal to nonexistent in them, as it is in "Mali." The world in which the poem is set is a female one, where the cycles of a woman's body move in time with the seasons of nature and the pull of the moon and the ocean.

The themes of the poem are of motherhood—its never-ending pull of responsibility and love, even for grandmothers; the connection of fertility to the tides of the female body and the ocean; the natural cycles of regeneration and reproduction.

Patricia Bostian

MANHIRE, BILL (1946–)

Born to publican parents in Invercargill, the southernmost city in New Zealand, Bill Manhire has earned the reputation as one of that country's brightest, most prolific poets. His volumes of poetry include *Malady* (1970), *The Elaboration* (1972), *Song Cycle* (1975), *How to Take Off Your Clothes at the Picnic* (1977), *Dawn/Water* (1979), *Good Looks* (1982), *Zoetropes: Poems 1972–82* (1984), *The Old Man's Example* (1990), *Milky Way Bar* (1991), *My Sunshine* (1996), *Sheet Music: Poems 1967–1982* (1996), *What to Call Your Child* (1999), and *Collected Poems* (2001). He is also the author of several books of fiction and criticism, as well as the editor of several anthologies. His work has earned the New Zealand Book Award for poetry four times, and in 1997, he was selected as New Zealand's first poet laureate.

During the 1960s, Manhire read and was influenced by the work of the American poets James Wright, Louis Simpson, Robert Creeley, and Robert Bly. He was also influenced by his with fellow New Zealander poet, Ian Wedde. His first step toward prominence was his inclusion in the 1973 anthology *The Young New Zealand Poets*. His work has been characterized as postmodern by some critics because of its tendency to question the boundaries between fiction and reality and its appropriation of images and motifs from popular culture and clichés. At the same time, his poetry has a romantic bent, including imagery from the natural world. Critics have also said that Manhire has as much mistrust of the language he uses in his poems as of the world he perceives and writes about. His later work is more expansive than the witty, terse writings of his early career, and this shift has been attributed to his interest in writing short fiction in the 1980s.

Manhire was educated at the University of Ontago (New Zealand) before going on to study Old Norse sagas at University College London. He currently lives in Wellington, where he directs the International Institute of Modern Letters at Victoria University of Wellington and its esteemed creative writing program.

BIBLIOGRAPHY
Jackson, MacDonald P. "Manhire, Bill." In *The Oxford Companion to New Zealand Literature,* 335–336. New York: Oxford University Press, 1998.

Leggott, Michele. "Bill Manhire." *New Zealand Electronic Poetry Centre.* University of Auckland. 2004. Available online. URL: http://www.nzepc.auckland.ac.nz/seeing voices/manhire.asp#bio. Accessed May 5, 2008.

Sharp, Iain. "An Interview with Bill Manhire." In *In the Same Room,* edited by Elizabeth Alley and Mark Williams, 15–36. Auckland: Auckland University Press, 1992.

Jordan Dominy

"A MARTIAN SENDS A POSTCARD HOME" CRAIG RAINE (1979)

The title poem of CRAIG RAINE's second collection of poetry gave its name to the Martian school, whose principal device is the transformation of the ordinary by means of improbable and yet surprisingly accurate imagery. Written from the perspective of a Martian who visits Earth and records his impressions about everyday objects and rituals on his interplanetary postcards home, this poem exemplifies the idea of the poet as unprejudiced and detached observer whose defamiliarization of the familiar helps the reader to perceive the world afresh.

The poem consists of 17 couplets without end rhyme or regular meter. Only the first couplet provides a clumsy half-rhyme (*many wings—markings*). The controlling stylistic device is metaphor. The speaker describes an array of everyday objects and activities whose meaning he fails to grasp and thus interprets by means of metaphorical association. Occasionally the objects referred to are named, but mostly it is the reader's task to establish correct metaphorical correspondences. As is appropriate in a poem about reading the world, the first three couplets are preoccupied with books: "Caxtons are mechanical birds with many wings / and some are treasured for their markings—" The initial allusion is to William Caxton, who introduced the printing press to England. According to the speaker, the effect books have on their readers is either to cause "the eyes to melt," that is, cry, or "the body to shriek without pain," that is, laugh. Although he has never "seen one fly," they remind him of birds because of their "wings," that is, pages, and their tendency to "perch on a hand."

The speaker then turns to the natural phenomena of "mist" and "rain," describing their effect on human activity ("Rain is when the earth is television") or on the landscape ("It has the property of making colours darker"). Further objects metaphorically described are cars, the concept of time, and the telephone. The poem closes with two human occupations alien to the Martian's world, the first being physical exercise, the latter being sleep, during which the humans "hide in pairs" and "read," that is, dream, "about themselves— / in colour, with their eyelids shut."

Some critics have found fault with this poem for what they consider its metaphorical inconsistency. How, for instance, would a Martian know about a historical figure like Caxton and his key role in introducing book printing to England? Moreover, although in the first three couplets the speaker is at pains to paraphrase the act of reading, he later on deliberately uses the terms *bookish* and *read,* implying that he is indeed familiar with the use and function of books. Despite such critical objections, "A Martian Sends a Postcard Home" remains the most popular poem to have emerged from the Martian school and must be credited for having reinvigorated English poetry at a time when its metaphorical impetus was urgently needed.

BIBLIOGRAPHY

Forceville, Charles. "Craig Raine's Poetry of Perception: Imagery in *A Martian Sends a Postcard Home.*" *Dutch Quarterly Review* 15, no. 2 (1985): 102–115.

Raine, Craig. *Collected Poems, 1978–99.* London: Picador, 2000.

Michaela Schrage-Früh

MASEFIELD, JOHN (1878–1967)

John Masefield's early years gave little indication he would one day become poet laureate and author of poems, novels, essays, letters, and plays. Masefield was born in Herefordshire on June 1, 1878, to middle-class parents, Edward and Caroline Masefield. The first years of his life were spent at the Victorian house called Knapp in Ledbury. When John was six, his mother died, and four years later, his father also died. An uncle, John's guardian, enrolled him in Warwick School from 1888 to 1891. At 13, Masefield ran away to become a merchant seaman. He sailed aboard the *Conway* in 1982 and the *Gilcruix* two years later. Masefield became ill during his second voyage and returned to England aboard a steamer. He then accepted a position on the

White Star liner sailing for New York. Before the ship returned to England, however, he decided to remain in New York. During the next few years, he was employed at a series of menial jobs in a bakery, livery stable, bar, and carpet mill.

While living in New York, Masefield read Chaucer, Keats, and Shelley, among others. By the time he returned to England in 1897, Masefield had produced two volumes of poems that were never published and was determined to become a writer. To earn a living, Masefield took jobs in a small office and later in a bank. He also produced a large number of essays, articles, and critical reviews during the next few years. Also during this period, Masefield made literary friends who were to influence his career profoundly. In 1900, he met W. B. YEATS and Lady Augusta Gregory. Soon he was a frequent guest at the Monday night gatherings Yeats hosted in Bloomsbury. Masefield moved to the Bloomsbury area and made the acquaintance of his neighbor, John Millington Synge, who inspired Masefield to write drama. During these years, Masefield was reading intensely and working on his first volume of poetry, *Salt-water Ballads* (1902). This volume contained one of his best-known works, "SEA FEVER." A second volume, *Ballads,* followed in 1903. Both were hugely popular and received critical acclaim and forever connected Masefield's name to poetry about the sea.

However, it was a later work, a long narrative poem called *The Everlasting Mercy* (1911), which caused Masefield notoriety. Because Masefield used direct speech and realistic language, Lord Alfred Douglas pronounced the poem "nine-tenths sheer filth." The story seems too overtly moralistic to modern audiences but retains the brilliance of Masefield's objectivity, and his clear, honest storytelling. The poem relates the experience of a young rascal who is turned from debauchery and crime by a Nonconformist preacher.

In 1903, Masefield married Constance de la Cherois Crommelin. The couple had two children, a daughter and a son. Ineligible for duty during World War I, Masefield became an orderly for the Red Cross and served in France and later on a hospital ship at Gallipoli. He turned this experience into books, *Gallipoli* (1916), *The Old Front Line* (1917), and *The Battle of the Somme* (1919). An avid letter writer, Masefield had a correspondence with Constance during the war that is noted for its realistic and candid depiction of his experiences. Several collections of Masefield's letters have been published since his death.

Masefield published plays, novels, and more than 50 books of poetry, including the long narrative poems *The Widow in the Bye Street* (1912) and *Reynard the Fox* (1919). His children's books continue to appeal to adults and children alike, and *The Midnight Folk* and *The Box of Delights* are frequently presented on television, especially during the Christmas season.

In 1930, Masefield was named poet laureate, a position he held until his death. He was also awarded, among other honors, the Order of Merit in 1935, the Hamburg Prize in 1938, the William Foyle Prize in 1961, and the National Book Prize in 1964. Masefield received honorary degrees from a number of universities including Harvard, Oxford, Aberdeen, St. Andrews, and Yale.

As MODERNISM gained popularity, Masefield's work was criticized as dated and too closely controlled by rhyme and meter, and although he had once had a large devoted following, his reputation faded. Although these observations have validity, Masefield was innovative in his diction, pioneered realism in poetry, created some of the most memorable and beautiful images of the sea in the language, and was a skilled writer of narrative verse. His work also serves as an important bridge between the great poets of the Victorian age and those of the 20th century.

Masefield died at his home, Burcote Brook, near Oxford on May 12, 1967. He was 88 years old and had developed gangrene in his foot from an infected cut. Masefield's ashes were interred in the Poets' Corner of Westminster Abbey.

BIBLIOGRAPHY

Smith, Constance Babington. *John Masefield: A Life.* New York: Macmillan, 1978.

Spark, Muriel. *John Masefield.* New York: Folcroft Library Editions, 1977.

Vansittart, Peter, ed. *John Masefield's Letters from the Front, 1915–17.* London: Franklin Watts, 1985.

Jean Shepherd Hamm

McCRAE, JOHN (1872–1918)

John McCrae was born in Guelph, Canada, on November 30, 1872, to David McCrae, a Scottish immigrant, and Janet Simpson Eckford, the daughter of a Presbyterian minister. Their three children were raised with strong traditional values. The elder McCrae was a lieutenant colonel in the Canadian militia, and young John joined the Guelph Highland Cadet Corps at age 14, later transferring to his father's militia company to train as a gunner. He obtained a scholarship to the University of Toronto, where he maintained his connection with the military, regularly attended Presbyterian services, and began to publish verse. In his third year, a bout of severe asthma interrupted his studies, but he returned to complete his bachelor's degree in biology in 1894. McCrae remained in Toronto to earn a medical degree in 1898 and accepted an internship at Johns Hopkins in 1899.

When the Boer War began, McCrae briefly set aside his medical career. Eager to enlist, he served in South Africa as the leader of an artillery battery, was decorated, and was promoted to major. Back in Canada in 1901, he accepted a fellowship in pathology at McGill University. He resigned from the military altogether in 1904 and for the next 10 years pursued a successful career as a medical doctor and researcher. In addition to his private practice, he participated actively in the medical community, serving as resident pathologist at Montreal General Hospital, among many other posts. While studying in England, McCrae was named to the Royal College of Physicians. A popular teacher and successful lecturer, he gave talks on pathology and clinical medicine in Canada and New England. He contributed more than 30 articles to journals and reference works and authored a textbook in pathology. McCrae continued writing poetry as a means of relaxation and participated in literary societies. Gregarious and open, he had a wide circle of friends.

At the outbreak of World War I, McCrae rejoined the military with some trepidation, writing, "I am going because I think every bachelor, especially if he has experience of war, ought to go." He was given charge of a field hospital in Belgium during the Second Battle of Ypres, where he saw the savagery of battle, including the first use of chlorine gas. His letters describe the prolonged physical and mental suffering. As company surgeon, McCrae treated numberless casualties, but he also helped dig graves and officiated at burial services. In May 1915, waiting for more wounded to arrive, he wrote the famous poem "IN FLANDERS FIELDS." On June 1 he was assigned to a hospital behind the lines, where he served as chief of medical services until his death. McCrae had insisted on living in a tent in solidarity with the enlisted men, rather than in an officer's hut. In mid-1917, he began having severe asthma attacks and died of pneumonia complicated by meningitis in January 1918. He did not see the end of the war but lived to know the enormous popular success of his poem.

BIBLIOGRAPHY

McCrae, John. *In Flanders Fields and Other Poems.* New York: Putnam's, 1919.

Prescott, John. *In Flanders Fields: The Story of John McCrae.* Erin, Canada: Boston Mills Press, 1985.

Anne Kellenberger

McGUCKIAN, MEDBH (1950–)

Medbh McGuckian is among the most highly acclaimed Northern Irish poets. She is, moreover, the only female poet to have gained international renown alongside an almost exclusively male generation of Northern Irish poets, including such distinguished poets as SEAMUS HEANEY, DEREK MAHON, and PAUL MULDOON. In contrast to the work of these male writers, however, McGuckian has a dense, oblique, and complex metaphorical style that has tended to confound readers and critics alike.

From the beginning, her poetry has divided her critical readership into those praising her "seductive lyricism" and those dismissing her work as "alluring sort of nonsense." Yet others have tried to make sense of the poet's notorious elusiveness and ambiguity by reading her work in the light of contemporary feminist and poststructuralist theories such as Hélène Cixous's *écriture féminine* or Derrida's *différance*. Moreover McGuckian's preference for nature and domestic imagery, which in turn metaphorically "disguises" her recurring themes of pregnancy, childbirth, and motherhood, has led many critics to categorize her work as essentially private, domestic, and exclusively con-

cerned with feminine issues. However, her multilayered poems characteristically interweave the private
and the public, viewing the violence of the Troubles
through the lens of the female body as well as through
elaborate domestic and nature images. In a cultural
environment and literary tradition in which myths of a
suffering Virgin Mary or a militant Mother Ireland still
have currency, the poet thus creates spaces in which to
interrogate and redefine conventional images of woman
and/as nation. McGuckian's poetry, then, not only
opens up a rich, unpredictable, and sensually conveyed
world of female sensibility, but provides a highly original and relevant perspective on issues of Irish identity
and Northern Irish divisions.

Medbh McGuckian was born Maeve McCaughan in
Belfast, Northern Ireland, on August 12, 1950. Born
into a Catholic family as the third of six children, she
grew up in her native city, spending her summers in
Ballycastle, her father's birthplace, a coastal town in
North Antrim. She was educated at Holy Family Primary School in Newington and the Dominican convent in Fortwilliam Park. Studying English at Queen's
University, Belfast, she obtained her B.A. in 1972 and
an M.A. in Anglo-Irish literature in 1974. Although
during her student years McGuckian was associated
with a group of Northern Irish poets including Seamus
Heaney, who taught at Queen's at the time, she at first
became a schoolteacher in English. In 1977, she
married John McGuckian, a teacher and writer. They
have three sons and a daughter and reside in Belfast.
McGuckian's work has received numerous awards and
prizes, and she was the first woman to become writer
in residence at Queen's University, Belfast (1986–88),
where she currently teaches creative writing at the Seamus Heaney Centre for Poetry.

McGuckian's poetic career was launched in 1979,
when her poem "The Flitting" won the British National
Poetry Competition. Shortly afterward, in 1980, her
first poems appeared in two pamphlets, *Single Ladies:
Sixteen Poems* and *Portrait of Joanna,* followed by her
first major collection, *The Flower Master* (1982), which
won the Ireland Arts Council Award (1982), the
Rooney Prize for Irish Literature (1982), and the Alice
Hunt Bartlett Award (1983). Through images of gardens, houses, and flowers McGuckian explores issues

of female and national identity as well as interrelations
and tensions among motherhood, traditional female
craft, and poetic creation. "The Flitting," written from
the perspective of a bomb victim, characteristically
interweaves references to children, flowers, and poems:
"I postpone my immortality for my children, / Little
rock-roses, cushioned / In long-flowering sea-thrift
and metrics." Her second collection, *Venus and the Rain*
(1984), continues and broadens this project by employing *écriture féminine* to subvert static and predictable
representations of femininity, for instance, in "The
Return of Helen," one of her numerous metapoems, in
which the speaker muses on "the wrong turnings I
make / myself take, till the path into my body / And
out of it again is a sea-place / Opening where you least
expect." Several poems allude to or rewrite canonical
Irish or British poems, notably "The Rising Out," which
responds to W. B. YEATS's famous elegy "EASTER 1916"
from the perspective of a poet and mother: "My dream
sister has gone into my blood / To kill the poet in me
before Easter."

McGuckian's third collection, *On Ballycastle Beach*
(1988), which won the 1989 Cheltenham Prize, is
more openly concerned with aspects of territory and
place. The title refers to a small coastal town on the
North Antrim coast that is simultaneously the birthplace of McGuckian's father and of the Irish nationalist
Roger Casement. Exploring the concept of home in
both personal and political terms, the collection is per-
meated by a sense of rootedness. On the other hand,
recurring images of ships and airplanes signal the
poet's mental journeys and often dreamlike flights of
the imagination. In this context, a central element is
McGuckian's embracing of European writers such as
Rilke, Mandelstam, or Tsvetaeva, a reinvigorating
experience she describes in "Balakhana": "The door I
found / So difficult to close let in my first / European
feeling which now blows about, / A cream-coloured
blossom, with a blue vigour."

Her next collection, *Marconi's Cottage* (1991), short-
listed for the Irish Times Irish Literature Prize for
Poetry in 1992, develops the themes explored in *On
Ballycastle Beach,* while using autobiographical experiences such as the impending death of her father and
the birth of her first daughter as starting points from

which to explore broader implications of death, birth, and possible rebirth in the Northern Irish context. Images of destruction and war permeate the collection, culminating in the most horrible and almost surreal image of a smashed embryo: "That dream / Of a too early body undamaged / And beautiful, head smashed to pulp, / Still grows in my breakfast cup" ("No Streets, No Numbers"). The desperate and nightmarish atmosphere evoked by such images, however, is counterbalanced by poems suggesting the possibility of rebirth and redemption through the birth of a daughter: "In the wrecked hull of the fishing-boat / Someone has planted a cypress under the ribs" ("Charlotte's Delivery").

From McGuckian's fifth collection onward, the poet sets out to explore her country's political history and present more overtly. *Captain Lavender* (1994) deals with the double theme of the death of McGuckian's father and her experiences of teaching both Catholic and Protestant political prisoners. McGuckian's sixth collection, *Shelmalier* (1999), focuses on Irish history and politics even more explicitly, exploring the failed 1798 rebellion and relating the poet's own process of learning about and coming to terms with her country's painful and violent history.

The Troubles as well as the difficult Northern Irish peace process are at the heart of McGuckian's next collection, *Drawing Ballerinas* (2001). The title poem refers to a quotation by the French painter Matisse, who, "when asked how he managed to survive the war artistically, replied that he spent the worst years 'drawing ballerinas.'" McGuckian thus implicitly answers those critics reproaching her for supposedly eschewing the civil war in her poetry. Although her poem describes one of Matisse's ballerina drawings, her description presents the dancing girl as the victim of a bomb explosion: "The body turns in, restless, on itself, / . . . / It turns over, reveals opposing versions of itself, / one arm broken abruptly at elbow and wrist, / the other wrenched downwards by the force of the turning." Significantly as the reader learns from a footnote, the poem commemorates "Ann Frances Owens, schoolfellow and neighbour, who lost her life in the Abercorn Café explosion, 1972." As this poem poignantly documents, the Troubles, though often in a disguised and defamiliarized way, are implicit in and central to McGuckian's

poetry, and their impact cannot be separated from the poet's renegotiations of femininity.

McGuckian's more recent collections, *The Face of the Earth* (2002), *Had I a Thousand Lives* (2003), and *The Book of the Angel* (2004), all highlight and explore Catholicism at the religious, the political, and the personal level. Stylistically these poems seem less intricate and more readily accessible, while maintaining a tone of moving poignancy and mature restraint. *The Face of the Earth* closes with the poem "She is in the Past, She has this Grace," awarded the 2002 Forward Prize (Best Single Poem). Dedicated to her mother, this poem captures the complex nuances of the mother-daughter relation and envisions the moment of death, when "her voice becomes an opera, / and the solitude is removed / from her body, as if my hand / had been held in some invisible place."

McGuckian's distinctive style has often been described as a kind of *écriture féminine* characterised by playfulness, ambiguity, elusiveness, and flux, by means of which she aims to subvert traditional and simplified representations of women. McGuckian's purpose, however, is not only to disrupt patriarchal discourse, but also to create a language that is "un-English" and thus subversive of the colonizers' tongue as well. Her oeuvre, then, provides a distinctly female perspective on issues of Northern Irish identity and the Troubles, while her innovative poetic style renders her one of the most compelling and original voices in contemporary poetry in English.

See also "EAVESDROPPER," "OPEN ROSE," "THE SEED-PICTURE."

BIBLIOGRAPHY

Haberstroh, Patricia Boyle. *Women Creating Women: Contemporary Irish Women Poets.* Syracuse, N.Y.: Syracuse University Press, 1996.

Schrage-Früh, Michaela. *Emerging Identities: Myth, Nation and Gender in the Poetry of Eavan Boland, Nuala Ní Dhomhnaill and Medbh McGuckian.* Trier: WVT, 2004.

Wills, Clair. *Improprieties: Politics and Sexuality in Northern Irish Poetry.* Oxford: Oxford University Press, 1993.

Michaela Schrage-Früh

"MCMXIV" PHILIP LARKIN (1960) PHILIP LARKIN'S "MCMXIV," written in 1960, first appeared in *The*

Whitsun Weddings (1964). Its distinctive title, the year 1914 written in Roman numerals, makes the poem itself look like a war monument, and indeed it is a monument to those immediate but fading prewar years. It gives a last nostalgic look at the EDWARDIAN AGE, when England was at its height as a world power, before the long, slow decline beginning with the First World War (1914–18). Its ending line, "never such innocence again," depends upon an awareness of the horror that the postwar generation would feel, embodied in the works of war poets such as WILFRED OWEN and SIEGFRIED SASSOON, a horror that then cast a pall of criticism over the prewar era as a time of complacency or, more forgivingly, innocence.

The poem is a single, loose sentence, with no main verb, consisting of a list of images connected by semicolons. Formally the poem is arranged into four eight-line stanzas; within each stanza, only the fourth and eighth lines rhyme, giving a leisurely and loose pace to the poem, until the last stanza, when the repetition of the word *Never* as the head word of three of the lines gives an increasingly measured and heavier feel to the poem, and greater closure in the last line, "Never such innocence again," than could be achieved with the minimal rhyming.

Most of the poem is filled with a lyrically beautiful, if nostalgic, evocation of Edwardian and Georgian England, which contrasts favorably, by implication, with modern England—a countryside of medieval "place-names" from the Domesday Book, William the Conqueror's 11th century survey of his new country, the fields still showing in faint lines their ancient boundaries ("fields / shadowing Domesday lines"), not the squalid cities; money counted in "farthings and sovereigns," not the modern metric 100 pennies to the pound; children named "after kings and queens," strong old English names such as *Edward* and *Henry* and *Elizabeth* and *Victoria,* not modern *Heathers* and *Scotts;* "Established names on the sunblinds" and "tin advertisements / For cocoa and twist" rather than garish neon or slick media ads. The cumulative effect is to suggest that the long continuity of England's cultural heritage, from Domesday to the Great War, is about to be abruptly lost.

An alternative view of the poem, which complicates it from being just another instance of the politically conservative Larkin's nostalgia for an earlier, simpler, more respectful and yet more commanding England, is given by Stephan Regan, who suggests that the poem is also aware of social inequalities behind the settled picture of Edwardian life, such as the "servants / With tiny rooms in huge houses," thus unsettling it. The repetition of *Never such innocence,* he argues, not only reinforces a sense of the loss of innocence, but also questions whether such innocence ever really existed, making the poem "not so much nostalgia as an awareness of the desirability and yet fallibility of national ideals" (120).

BIBLIOGRAPHY

Regan, Stephen. *Philip Larkin: An Introduction to the Variety of Criticism.* New York: Macmillan, 1992.

Swarbrick, Andrew. *The Whitsun Weddings and The Less Deceived by Philip Larkin.* Macmillan Master Guides, gen. ed. James Gibson. New York: Macmillan, 1986.

Thwaite, Anthony, ed. *Philip Larkin: Collected Poems.* New York: Farrar, Straus & Giroux, 1988.

James Persoon

"MERCIAN HYMNS" GEOFFREY HILL (1971)

Mercian Hymns, considered by many to be GEOFFREY HILL's masterwork, is a sequence of 30 poems in a kind of chanting prose—they are often called prose poems, a term that Hill rejects. They juxtapose the geography and history of Hill's childhood home in the Midlands with the reign of Offa (757–96), who was king for almost 40 years of the Anglo-Saxon kingdom of Mercia, roughly the same geographic region.

In his note to the poem, Hill gives a sense of its theme: "The Offa who figures in this sequence might perhaps most usefully be regarded as the presiding genius of the West Midlands, his dominion enduring from the middle of the eighth century until the middle of the 20th (and possibly beyond)." The poem is characteristic of Hill's love of history, his dense use of allusion, and his expectation of the reader's ability to follow the elliptical syntax of modernist practice and to know English history.

The first poem immediately shows the mix of historical and modern content, and of high and low speech. It begins with a list of Offa's titles, in the formal way that epics and genealogies do. Offa is "king of the perennial holly-groves, the riven sand-stone: over-lord of the M5: architect of the historic rampart and ditch." The sandstone and holly groves are both modern and ancient features, unchanging in the landscape of Britain. But the M5—the motorway that runs up the west side of Britain and takes holiday travelers from Bristol and Birmingham and Manchester to the Lakes District, is a decidedly modern aspect of the landscape. Yet it generally parallels Offa's kingdom. And the titles remind us that Offa put his mark on the landscape, especially Offa's ditch, which can still be seen roughly marking the old boundary between England and Wales, so that it is entirely appropriate to think of a modern domination of the landscape as an idea started by Offa—overlord of the M5. The list of titles eventually ends, and then Hill gives us the line "'I liked that,' said Offa, 'sing it again'." The offhandedness of Offa's speech here is reminiscent of another mythic figure, Crow, in TED HUGHES's *Crow* poems, who also often comments at the end of his poems with a short, blunt sentence.

For readers not conversant with English history, the source of much of the wealth of allusion in these poems, there is a need for heavy annotation, and the charge of "inaccessibility" fairly stands. But even for such readers, the majesty and excitement of Hill's verse are still evident and easily felt.

BIBLIOGRAPHY
Hill, Geoffrey. *Geoffrey Hill: New and Collected Poems.* New York: Mariner, 2000.
Wainwright, Jeffrey. *Acceptable Words: Essays on the Poetry of Geoffrey Hill.* Manchester, Eng.: Manchester University Press, 2006.

James Persoon

MEW, CHARLOTTE (1869–1928)

As is SYLVIA PLATH, Charlotte Mew is a poet whose life has often been conflated with her work, perhaps because the story of her life exerts an impact as vexed as the poems themselves. At age 59, still mourning the death of her sister the year before, Mew committed suicide by drinking Lysol, a creosote cleaning solution then used for especially stubborn household dirt. Mew cleaned herself to death. In the months before her death, Mew had become increasingly worried that the black specks she kept finding in her room and on her clothes had been responsible for the death of her sister. The specks, said a chemist, were soot, but to Mew they presented a world of risk and contagion.

It is especially troubling to consider a manner of suicide that equates the female body with a dirty room. In critical work about Mew this equation has often figured as an index of her guilt over her intense but unrequited passions for women, and as a complication of a Catholic upbringing that positioned cleanliness next to godliness. The poems themselves reflect Mew's preoccupation with unhappy domestic situations, moral indeterminacy, and the anguish of conflict between body and soul.

Mew emerged from a privileged middle-class background in the era when the eugenics movement was teaching women to take responsibility for what it called "feeblemindedness," a loose term that included all forms of insanity and developmental disability. From the widespread eugenics movement women learned that feeblemindedness descended matrilineally. If women were the carriers of mental illness, it was therefore incumbent on them to exercise reproductive restraint when there was any mental illness in their own families of origin. Such was the case with Charlotte Mew. Her oldest brother, Henry, and her youngest sister, Freda, were permanently institutionalized in an asylum for the mentally ill. Together Charlotte and her remaining sister, Anne, vowed that neither of them would marry or have children. Mew's personal experience with her own mentally ill siblings is often reflected in the content of poems that question social and biological categories of alterity. Her poem "Ken," for instance, charts a relationship between a functional speaker and the institutionalized Ken, whose eyes "look at you / As two red, wounded stars might do." The speaker says, "If in His image God made men / Some other must have made poor Ken—." Mew frequently attaches social problems, psychic distress, and human suffering to Christianity, and what starts as a eugenics poem might well become a cry against God.

Mew's decision never to marry had a profound economic impact on her life. Charlotte wrote for literary journals like the *Yellow Book* and the *Egoist* to help to support her mother and her sister Anne, but after her father died in 1899, she and her family slid so close to poverty that they were obliged to relocate, take in borders, and subsist on the plainest fare—tea and cigarettes, joked their friends. Fortunately Mew had help from friends and fellow writers. A tireless advocate on her behalf, Alida Munro, the wife of the founder of the Poetry Bookshop, worked to establish Mew among a core group of intellectually vital Georgian writers; Munro even offered to publish Mew's first book-length poetry collection, *The Farmer's Bride* (1916). (This was the only book of hers published in her lifetime; in 1929, after Mew's death, Munro brought out a second book, *The Rambling Sailor*.) Mew was also indebted to THOMAS HARDY, JOHN MASEFIELD, and WALTER DE LA MARE, who eventually managed to secure her a modest pension from the Civil List. She needed it. In London at the beginning of the 1920s she had been living in one room, running down to the basement to put a penny in the gas for hot water.

Mew was not famous in her own time, although by the time she died, Thomas Hardy had called her the "best female poet" then writing. Mew had a modest reputation. Her poetic forms were memorable and daringly innovative, and she wrote in surprising voices and dialects, some of them literally offbeat in the sense that Mew favored irregular rhythms. Her versification often jarred the reader, turning as it did on abrupt prosodic variations, clumsy feet, and curious rhymes. Structurally she was interested in repeated and monosyllabic rhymes, and in lines that were as unpredictable as the rural vernacular voices she put in her characters' mouths. Yet it is important to note that Mew never rejected FORMAL VERSE altogether. Jeredith Merrin reads Mew's recurring four-beat line as a kind of fractured love affair with the form of the ballad, whose traditional emphasis on supernatural inklings and psychological disruptions was deeply resonant to Mew. To maintain any interest in form, however loose and rebellious, was to argue that the complexity and optimism of form were too compelling to sweep aside. Like the idea of Catholic confession, form was repugnant, lurid, and fatally flawed: It became interesting to Mew only as an index of spiritual struggle and psychic complexity. Mew wrestled with form as Jacob with the angel; she did not quite believe in it, but yet she could

not ignore it either. Perhaps Mew avoided blank verse—a formal gesture surprising in a poet who favored the dramatic monologue—because she early dismissed the possibility of perfection. In other words, she favored the flawed ballad and the jerked meters precisely because she felt they were more compelling.

By all counts Mew was personally compelling, too. With her diminutive stature and her tiny number 2 shoe, she presented her work with the brio of a dynamic musical performance. Friends and acquaintances described her as famously difficult, even eccentric, citing the fact that in her later years she wore only male attire, or the fact that she endlessly gave and then revoked permission for reprints. Her eccentricities of manner clearly were formative as a basis for her critical reputation: In a letter to a friend, Virginia Woolf wrote that she thought Mew "very good and interesting and unlike anyone else."

See also "THE CENOTAPH," "THE FARMER'S BRIDE," "MADELEINE IN CHURCH," "THE QUIET HOUSE," "THE TREES ARE DOWN."

BIBLIOGRAPHY

Fitzgerald, Penelope. *Charlotte Mew and Her Friends.* Reading, Mass.: Addison-Wesley, 1984.

Leighton, Angela. *Victorian Women Poets: Writing against the Heart.* Charlottesville: University of Virginia Press, 1992.

Merrin, Jeredith. "The Ballad of Charlotte Mew." *Modern Philology* 95, no. 2 (November 1997): 200–217.

Mew, Charlotte. *Charlotte Mew: Collected Poems and Selected Prose.* Edited and introduction by Val Warner. New York: Routledge, 2003.

Walsh, Jessica. "'The Strangest Pain to Bear': Corporeality and Fear of Insanity in Charlotte Mew's Poetry." *Victorian Poetry,* September 2002, 217–240.

Rhoda Janzen

MIDDLETON, CHRISTOPHER (1926–   )

Born June 10, 1926, in Truro, Cornwall, England, Christopher Middleton has made a name for himself as a relentlessly experimental poet, a gifted translator, an essayist and literary critic of distinction, and an estimable educator. Middleton published his first collection of poetry, *Poems,* in 1944, at the age of 18. Influenced by Christopher Isherwood and W. H. AUDEN, whose lives and literary careers he would in many respects emulate, Middleton studied German and French at Merton College, Oxford University, and received his B.A. in 1951. In the early 1950s, Middleton taught English at Zurich University, while researching the work of Hermann Hesse for his dissertation. He earned his D.Phil. from Oxford in 1954 and the following year accepted a lectureship in German literature at King's College, University of London. During the next decade while teaching in London, he published English translations of short stories by the Swiss writer Robert Walser, whose work would have a significant influence upon Middleton's creative writing, and he wrote the libretto for Hans Vogt's opera *The Metropolitans* (1964). He also published collections of what still stands as his most highly regarded poetry, *Torse 3: Poems 1949–61,* for which he was awarded the first Sir Geoffrey Faber Memorial Prize in 1962, and *Nonsequences / Selfpoems* (1965), which garnered international critical notice.

In 1966, Middleton emigrated to the United States to become a professor of German at the University of Texas in Austin. He taught classes in German language and literature and in comparative literature in Austin for the next three decades, until his retirement in May 1998. His stature as an academic was recognized in 1986 when he was named the first David J. Bruton, Jr., Centennial Professor of Modern Languages at the University of Texas. In his adopted homeland, Middleton adorned himself with Native American jewelry and continued his—sometimes radical, sometimes playful—experimentation with poetic language, contributing poems to many journals and little magazines and publishing 15 collections of original poetry between 1969 and 2003. Middleton has proved himself to be an important translator of German-language authors, producing well-regarded English translations of Friedrich Nietzsche's selected letters, Walser's novels, and selected poems of Johann Wolfgang von Goethe, Friedrich Hoelderlin, and Eduard Moerike. He has also published translations of works by, among others, Gottfried Benn, Elias Canetti, Paul Celan, Guenter Grass, Lars Gustaffson, Gert Hofmann, Christoph Meckel, and Christa Wolf. His translation work earned him the Schlegel-Tieck Translation Prize. He has been a frequent contributor of criticism to literary periodicals,

and some of his critical essays are collected in *Bolshevism and Art and Other Expository Writings* (1978) and *The Pursuit of the Kingfisher* (1983). Perhaps the most representative collections of Middleton's diverse writings are *Selected Writings* (1989) and *The Word Pavilion and Selected Poems* (2001). A large collection of Middleton's papers, dating from 1954 through 2003, are housed at the Harry Ransom Humanities Research Center at the University of Texas in Austin.

BIBLIOGRAPHY

Middleton, Christopher. *Nonsequences / Selfpoems.* London: Longmans, 1965 and New York: W. W. Norton, 1965.

———. *Selected Writings.* Manchester, Eng.: Carcanet Press, 1989.

———. *The Word Pavilion and Selected Poems.* Riverdale-on-Hudson, N.Y.: Sheep Meadow Press, 2001, and Manchester, Eng.: Carcanet Press, 2001.

Cliff Toliver

"MIDSUMMER XXVII" DEREK WALCOTT (1984)

This poem occurs in the middle of DEREK WALCOTT's 54-poem sequence *Midsummer* (1984), a collection of informal, loosely constructed sonnets that vary in length, meter, and rhyme just as they vary in geographical reference points: Trinidad, St. Lucia, Boston, New York, Chicago, Columbus, Cuba, the English countryside, and other quasi-locations where the speaker seems to be floating beyond any map. Walcott's use of the idea—rather than the technical exigencies—of the sonnet sequence also puts him in fluid conversation with literary history: He is returning to an old form with a new voice and set of experiences, both drawing from and testing the boundaries of tradition. This poem scans irregularly, approximating iambic pentameter but never settling too easily into it. This formal restlessness suggests that the cultural and political conflict it describes is both new and old, part of an established pattern but taking on unique elements that need to be understood in their specificity.

From a large historical perspective, the specific shift that Walcott investigates in "Midsummer XXVII" is the one from European to North American influence over the Caribbean. The "quietly American" presence in local affairs contrasts in appearance with the highly official role of the earlier British Empire, but American power is no less insidious for this subtlety. One of the poem's principal imagistic accomplishments is to have us witness a transformation of the elemental, natural world into an industrialized and commodified one: "The sea's corrugations are sheets of zinc / soldered by the sun's steady acetylene" moves industrial and natural terms into vivid collision, and "the gray, metal light where an early pelican / coasts, with its engine off" makes the bird a kind of incoming tourist plane (as if arriving to join "eager Cessnas" waiting below). The irony is that rendered in such delicate networks of assonance and consonance (in the first of these quoted lines especially), these troubling images have a beauty that resembles the troubling allure of the American dollars that have alienated the speaker from this world. This ironic disjunction between the sensuous appeal of Walcott's language and the sharpness of his political critique culminates with the lament that "the dust / is industrial and must be suffered": The intricately arranged *s, t,* and *u* sounds create a dense sonic web, associating *industry* with *suffering* but giving us aesthetic pleasure in the experience.

The poem emphasizes language as a theme early on, with the wind "muttering the word umpire instead of empire." The line has a serious playfulness, calling attention to the subtle evasions that language can perform in imperial situations, empire's strategy of misnaming itself, and the role of the poet to name things as they are. The source of the utterance itself is obscure, emanating somehow from "that chain-link fence dividing the absent roars / of the beach from the empty ball park": Walcott makes the two spaces on each side of the fence vacant, uninhabited, suggesting how difficult it is to locate and identify the agents in cultural politics. The foreign presence that intrudes upon this world is ambiguous, refracted through scattered images: the "sheds" and "hangar" "like those of the Occupation," the "rank smell" left by the "night" (as if the night itself were a colonial force), the "American rain, / stitching stars in the sand," and, most elaborately, "the fenced-off beaches where the natives walk, / illegal immigrants from unlucky islands / who envy the smallest polyp its right to work." These last lines are the first in this remarkably unpopulated poem to refer to any actual people, and they are mentioned only

to be displaced by the "wetback crab" and "mollusc" who have more rights than they do. This poetic displacement mirrors the typical imperial displacement of native peoples from sovereignty over their lands, leaving the speaker's mix of the "fear" and "envy" toward which the poem turns at the end.

The speaker ends with an attempt to understand the displacement of his own identity, the ambiguity of an interiority that is immersed in the cultural tensions of the colonial and postcolonial worlds. Not only are his blood's "corpuscles" shifting allegiance, but, as indicated by his sly reference, so is his language: "The fealty changing under my foot" refers to the metrical foot as well as the bodily one, making this very poem a symptom of imperial influence as well as its critique. The speaker achieves an acute self-awareness of his own internal ambiguities and contradictions. In describing the world with his own poetic language, Walcott is asserting a certain kind of ownership over it, but this ownership is necessarily fragile, incomplete, and vulnerable to the economic and cultural forces it describes.

BIBLIOGRAPHY

Hamner, Robert. *Critical Perspectives on Derek Walcott.* Washington, D.C.: Three Continents Press, 1993.
Ismond, Patricia. *Abandoning Dead Metaphors: The Caribbean Phase of Derek Walcott's Poetry.* Kingston: University of the West Indies Press, 2001.
Terada, Rei. *Derek Walcott's Poetry: American Mimicry.* Boston: Northeastern University Press, 1992.

David Sherman

"MID-TERM BREAK" SEAMUS HEANEY (1966)

As many of SEAMUS HEANEY's early poems do, this 22-line lyric from his first volume of poems, DEATH OF A NATURALIST (1966), treats the theme of childhood. Heaney here draws on his own experience in having an adolescent speaker reflect on the death of his four-year-old brother, for the poet's brother, Christopher, was killed in a car accident at age four in 1953. The poem is made up of seven stanzas of unrhymed tercets with a final concluding line. The speaker describes what happens to him very simply, the emotions unfolding as they might for a boy whose schoolday is interrupted with shattering news. Typically Heaney's language reveals both a sensitivity to realities of childhood and a maturity that is incompatible with it. So while the speaker seems preternaturally aware of sounds and language, he is perhaps unable to hear the irony of one friend's saying that the boy's death "was a hard blow"; nor does the "poppy bruise" necessarily resonate for him with the "snowdrops" placed by the dead boy's bedside or with the way that poppies become associated with the fragility of young men in the poetry of World War I that Heaney admires.

The speaker remembers sitting in "the college sick bay" while the bells were "knelling" to indicate the end of classes. Taken home by a neighbor, he witnessed the reactions of the adults—his father crying, his mother "cough[ing] out angry tearless sighs," friends shaking his hand as if he were an adult. The poet reminds us that a house of grief is also a house in which life must go one, as the baby, who has no concept of loss, "cooed and laughed." Only in the fifth stanza does the "corpse" appear, but his identity is withheld. The next morning the speaker ventures upstairs to see the body in the coffin. He seems to see only details—the boy is "paler" and "wear[s] a poppy bruise" on his head but is otherwise seemingly unchanged, for "the bumper knocked him clear."

In the last line, Heaney continues his seemingly objective description—"A four foot box, a foot for every year"—but the accumulation of details is transformed. The consciousness of death, merely nascent up to this point in the teenage speaker, conjoins with that of the poet, who realizes, as does the reader, that the *break* of the title is not just that of the boy leaving school to go home in the middle of the term but of the young life brought violently and suddenly to an end. The tiny coffin speaks, more eloquently than the shocked adults, of the enormity of the loss. That the last line rhymes with the penultimate line—the only couplet in the poem—only reinforces the idea of finality, of closure. This short elegy draws together many important issues in Heaney's early poetry including the need to define oneself linguistically, culturally, and personally. Typically the poet achieves this goal by investing a simple object (in this case a coffin) with emotional significance.

BIBLIOGRAPHY

Collins, Floyd. *Seamus Heaney: The Crisis of Identity*. Newark: University of Delaware Press, 2003.

Heaney, Seamus. *Opened Ground: Poems 1966–1996*. New York: Farrar, Straus & Giroux, 1999.

Vendler, Helen. *Seamus Heaney*. Cambridge, Mass.: Harvard University Press, 1998.

Helen Emmitt

"MILKWEED AND MONARCH" PAUL MULDOON (1994)

"Milkweed and Monarch" appears in PAUL MULDOON's eighth full-length collection of poetry, *The Annals of Chile*. In many ways it is typical of his later work, combining an innovative use of poetic form with recurrent themes of death, sex, and displacement. Characteristically it also straddles America and Ireland—the two most important locations in his poems. Muldoon distances himself from the events in the poem by writing in the third person but also appears to be writing about circumstances in his own life.

In terms of its structure, the poem might be described as an extended villanelle. In total it has 25 lines, but its meandering form follows the pattern of a traditional, shorter, villanelle. For instance, it includes two repeated refrains: "As he knelt by the grave of his mother and father" and "he could barely tell one from the other—" The first of these opens the poem, signaling its elegiac nature. Although both refrains are adapted during the course of the poem, they are placed together in their original form at the end. Thus the poem's movement is circular, reflecting the lack of closure in the subject matter.

Throughout "Milkweed and Monarch" mixes the conventional with the idiosyncratic. It may be a powerful elegy, but it defies many norms of the genre. For instance, there is a strong sexual undercurrent in the poem. At his parents' graveside the speaker is blunt in asserting that he is not stricken with grief for them, but for "a woman slinking from the fur of a sea-otter." It might also seem inappropriate for him to express his arousal here, but doing so adds to an impression of sincerity.

Muldoon's exploration of cause and effect is extended in his statement concerning a single butterfly "wing-beat" triggering a hurricane. As Rachel Buxton discusses, here Muldoon appears to allude to the work of Edward Lorenz, who opened up "chaos theory" as a major area of research when he investigated weather patterns in the 1960s. As she summarizes, he found that weather systems are configured in a way that amplifies imprecisions or slight alterations, a discovery labeled "the butterfly factor" on the basis that "the movement of a butterfly's wing in Brazil could, theoretically, cause a hurricane in Texas."

As Buxton also notes, there are other references to chaos theory in Muldoon's work, and, the "chaotic" movement of a weather system might even be viewed as a metaphor for the way that his poetry works. "Milkweed and Monarch" itself seemed buoyed up by language as well as powerful subject matter. Muldoon's consonant-based rhymes—such as *reckon* with *hurricane*—are characteristic of his later style. Using these unusual rhymes, Muldoon manages to follow the exacting form of the villanelle and still sound colloquial. He also reinvigorates classic poetic images—such as cliffs and butterflies—through recontextualization.

BIBLIOGRAPHY

Buxton, Rachel. *Robert Frost and Northern Irish Poetry.* Oxford: Clarendon Press, 2004.
Kendall, Tim. *Paul Muldoon.* Bridgend, Eng.: Seren, 1996.

Jennifer Sykes

MINHINNICK, ROBERT (1952–)

Born near Neath, Wales, Robert Minhinnick is both a writer and an environmental activist. His collections of poetry include *A Thread in the Maze* (1978), *Native Ground* (1979), *Life Sentences* (1983), *The Dinosaur Park* (1985), *The Looters* (1989), *Hey Fatman* (1994), and *After the Hurricane* (2002). His *Selected Poems* was published in 1999. Early in life, he held many different jobs in industry and worked for the post office. Before taking up writing full-time, he became involved in environmental projects, and his interest in environmental issues has not waned as his career progessed. In 1984, he cofounded the Friends of the Earth Cymru. Much of his journalism and essaying deals continues to deal with environmental topics, and he earned the Welsh Arts Council Book of the Year Award for his collection of essays *Watching the Fire Eater* (1993). In 1998, he received the Chlomondeley Award.

Minhinnick credits the Welsh poet Meic Stephens as a great influence on his poetic work, in particular as the one helped him to realize the industrial landscape as one appropriate for poetry. Otherwise his poetry addresses environmental issues, the beauty of his native South Wales, and the people who live there. His poetry is characterized by his concrete, wry language and short-verse style. Minhinnick served as writer in residence for the Saskatoon Library Service in Canada from 1994 to 1995, and he became editor of *Poetry Wales* in 1997.

BIBLIOGRAPHY

"Robert Minhinnick." *Caracnet.* Manchester: Caracnet Press, 2004. Available online. URL: http://www.carcanet.co.uk/cgi-bin/scribe.cgi?author=minhinnickr. Accessed May 8, 2008.
Stephens, Meic, ed. *The New Companion to the Literature of Wales.* Cardiff: University of Wales Press, 1998.

Jordan Dominy

"MIRRORWORK" MIMI KHALVATI (1995)

"Mirrorwork" appears in a book of poems by the same name and draws its inspiration from an outdoor mural in England executed in the mirror mosaic technique traditional to Islam. It is recognized by MIMI KHALVATI as an art form from her native Iran, and she uses the mural to express her feelings about living in England and to address a departed lover. It is a long poem of alternating sequences that intersect to develop the theme of reflection.

The central image of the poem is a willow tree, a common motif, made of bits of broken mirror and focal point of the mural, which is made of plaster, paint, and broken china. The mural commemorates the silver jubilee of Queen Elizabeth II, celebrating 25 years of her reign after ascending the throne in 1952. The mirror tree in the mural duplicates the cherry tree outside Khalvati's home, framed in the window as she looks out. Khalvati personifies the cherry tree using the pronoun *she* instead of *it* when speaking of the tree. In doing so, she identifies the tree with her pain, contrasting it with the mirror tree, whose branches resemble "angels' wings, epaulettes amassing, / dripping silver."

Khalvati has designated the poem with the dedication *"for Archie,"* and presumably this is the person she is speaking to in the italic portions of the poem, recalling a love that is now lost. Speaking of the cherry tree, she says, *"I saw in her indifference yours. In her / blossoms my bitterness at England."* Throughout this poem and in many others, Khalvati relates her experience as an Iranian in England. She immigrated to Britain at age six and attended a British boarding school. She speaks in the poem of "homes / that took me in but were not mine," possibly the homes of English friends. Khalvati returned to Iran at age 17 and returned again to England at 25 to stay. It is this vantage point from which she writes the poem.

"Mirrorwork" represents an intermediate stage in the development of the poet's style. Her first book, *In White Ink,* contains poems that are traditional in format. In *Mirrorwork,* she is beginning a transition to poems consisting of long sequences that are related but not distinct. Titles disappear altogether in her third work, *Entries on Light,* and the sections relate loosely or intersect, with much less attention to cohesiveness.

BIBLIOGRAPHY

Forbes, Peter. "Mimi Khalvati." The Film and Literature Department of the British Council Web Site. Available online. URL: http://www.contemporarywriters.com/authors/?p=auth194. Accessed 15 January 2005.

Khalvati, Mimi. *Selected Poems.* Manchester, Eng.: Carcanet Press, 2000.

Mary VanOeveren

"MISE EIRE" Eavan Boland (1986) A rewriting by Eavan Boland of Patrick Pearse's poem "I Am Ireland" (1912), a prototype of the passive, patient, and sorrowful Mother Ireland. This poem is a significant illustration of how Boland subverts and deconstructs the conventional fusion of the feminine and the national, a monopoly in traditional Irish poetry. In Pearse's poem, the female speaker appears as a dispossessed and sorrowful mother, who has been betrayed and abandoned by her sons and who yearns for the appearance of "Cuchulainn the valiant" to restore her happiness. In this sense, she lacks agency and depends on a male hero to save her from the British oppression. Rather than rejecting the conventional equation "woman" and "nation," what Boland does in "Mise Eire" is to reject the ideology according to which present-day women have been silenced and oppressed as virginal, bodiless, and mythical emblems. In the Irish national tradition, the heroine Hiberna was utterly passive, and her role was almost always as a mother or a virgin. Nevertheless the worst of nationalist poetry, as Boland seems to imply in this poem, is not only that it has misrepresented women, but that, in doing so, it has structured the position of the poet in such masculine terms that it has prevented women from constructing themselves as speaking subjects. Establishing a new relationship between women and nation is therefore at the core of Boland's poetry. In "Mise Eire," the traditional national icon breaks free of the conventional text and becomes the author of her own statements. In contrast to the helpless figure of Pearse's poem, this new muse mother gains authority and advocates her right to emerge in less idealized roles. First of all, she becomes a whore, who trades sex and practices "the rictus of delight," a radical rewriting of the nationalist icon of virginal Ireland being raped by corrupted England. Second, Mother Ireland has the potential to become an émigré, forced to escape from her country on board a ship called *Mary Belle.* The name of the boat embodies the two main virtues imposed on women by patriarchal tradition: They must be like "Mary" (virginal, pure, and devoted to others), and they must also be "Belle" (attractive and beautiful). Boland invokes the patriarchal Madonna/whore dichotomy in order to create a new figure of Mother Ireland that encompasses both images: She is both the prostitute and the scarifying mother; in other words, she is a more real entity. The lexical repetition of *I am the woman* twice in the poem indicates Mother Ireland's ability to be different kinds of women at the same time. By telling the story of her nation mainly by means of her sexuality, Boland contends that Irish women poets are really empowered to write a new poetry that transforms the received national culture, and hence, their concept of national identity. Nationhood is not something to be praised by nationalist ballads and songs, but a cruel reality of dispossession and oppression: Irish women's having to survive either by selling their bodies as prostitutes or by emigrating to a new country where they could start a new life. In contrast to Pearse's poem, in "Mise Eire" the sense of defeat by Mother Ireland is not transmuted into victory by the presence of the male hero. This poem moves away from the traditional political idea that a defeated nation must be reborn as a triumphant woman. Boland shows instead a nation that has been defeated by a history of colonization and by an oppressive nationalism. The "half-dead baby" of "Mise Eire" is an emblem for a nation half-destroyed by violence and crimes, scarred and damaged by painful events such as the Great Famine and emigration.

BIBLIOGRAPHY

Auge, Andrew J. "Fracture and Wound: Eavan Boland's Poetry of Nationality." *New Hibernia Review/ Irish Éireannach Nua: A Quaterly Record of Irish Studies* 8, no. 2 (summer 2004): 121–141.

Boland, Eavan. *The Journey and Other Poems.* Dublin: Carcanet Press, 1986.

Hagen, Patricia L., and Thomas W. Zelman. "'We Were Never on the Scene of the Crime': Eavan Boland's Repossession of History." *Twentieth Century Literature* 37, no. 4 (1991): 442–453.

Meaney, Geraldine. "Myth, History and the Politics of Subjectivity: Eavan Boland and Irish Women's Writing." *Women: A Cultural Review* 4, no. 2 (1993): 136–153.

Villar, Pilar. "Eavan Boland's Rewriting of Mother Ireland: 'I Won't Go Back to It— / My Nation Displaced into Old Dactyls.'" *The Representation of Ireland/s: Images from Outside and from Within,* edited by Rosa González, 277–290. Barcelona: Promociones y Publicaciones Universitarias, 2003.

Pilar Villar Argáiz

MODERNISM   The term *modernism* is typically used as a label for the period of Western aesthetics between 1890 and 1930. It is associated with a radical break with 19th-century aesthetics and morality, and with the celebration of "newness" as an abstract ideal and virtue. Nevertheless although one can identify broad, unifying trends within modernist expression, it is impossible to come up with a tidy definition of modernism, whose diversity is acknowledged and explored by most critics today. The term covers movements or tendencies in literature and the visual arts as diverse as CUBISM, dadaism, expressionism, IMAGISM, SURREALISM, and SYMBOLISM, all of which sought to develop novel forms and means of artistic expression with the aim to shatter traditional views of art and life. By employing aesthetic principles like irrationalism, fragmentation, multiperspectivity, and "primitivism," modernism defies classical norms of beauty, chronology, and verisimilitude. In verbal and visual art, these principles took the form of experimental techniques like the collage and montage, which were influenced by the new technologies of photography and film. Much modernist art is self-reflexive, drawing attention to the constructedness of artistic representation and deliberately frustrating the reader's or viewer's desire for aesthetic truthfulness and reliability.

Modernism's ideal of aesthetic innovation must be seen as a response to the experience of living a world of radical change: in short, modernity. Virginia Woolf captured the effects of this changing world in her essay "Mr. Bennett and Mrs. Brown" (1923), where she famously stated that "on or about December 1910 . . . all human relationships shifted—those between masters and servants, husbands and wives, parents and children." Woolf here identifies two concrete events as touchstones of modernity's radical transformation of human experience: an influential exhibition of postimpressionist painting in London and the death of King Edward VII. Nevertheless although the passage is often cited to illustrate the modernist mentality, its perspective is clearly limited. Woolf's focus on events taking place in Britain not only imposes artificial geographical boundaries on a phenomenon that was, after all, European and global; the year 1910, too, diminishes the true chronological scope of the transformations to which Woolf alludes: Modernity had begun long before this date. Furthermore the changes she describes in such positive terms were not greeted in the same way by everyone; in fact, Woolf herself was aware of and feared the negative repercussions of the manifold transformations she was witnessing. In science, where Charles Darwin's evolutionary theories (*The Origin of Species* and *The Descent of Man*) had revolutionized the image of the natural world already in the second half of the late 19th century, the groundbreaking theories of Einstein, Heisenberg, and Bohr further shattered the familiar image of the universe. Technical innovations developed since the late 19th century—all types of engines and engine-driven vehicles, synthetic materials, and communication technologies—facilitated life for everyone; however, they also increased the speed of living, trapping individuals in a gigantic machine of industrial production and simultaneously reducing them to passive consumers of factory-made goods. In 1867, Karl Marx's critique of capitalism (*Das Kapital*) had provided a theoretical framework to understand the social implications of 19th-century industrialization, bringing forth new political movements and parties and inspiring social conflicts that, in the early 20th century, led to the reshaping of the political face of several European nations (e.g., the October Revolution in Russia 1917). While class conflicts rocked European societies on an internal level, imperialism, that is, the competitive expansion of countries such as Belgium, Britain, and France into Africa and India, contributed to the worldwide political tensions that overshadowed the first years of the 20th century and would ultimately climax in the experience of World War I.

Uncertainty and tension were also the results of modernity's impact on the view of the human. The technologies that were seen by some to suppress individuality dangerously were celebrated by others as models for a new, relentlessly energetic form of existence. The repudiation, by the 19th-century German philosopher Friedrich Nietzsche, of Western metaphysics and Christianity, and the principles of apocalypse, individual willpower, and nihilism central to his philosophy clearly influenced some of the more destructive strands of modernist art. At the same time, there was increasing emphasis on the individual's psychic interior. The psychoanalytical writings of Sigmund Freud and C. G. Jung claimed that the unconscious was not only crucial to human identity, but in fact a constructive factor in the maintenance of the individual's psychic health. In a literary context, psychoanalysis influenced the development of experimental forms like the stream of consciousness and automatic writing (a form of writing taking place while the writer has no rational control over himself or herself, for instance, during hypnosis). Modernists shared the general awareness at the time of what Roland Barthes would later call "the problematics of language"—the understanding that language inevitably distorted the reality it served to represent—and artists' dissatisfaction with the material available to them led to the development of novel forms and genres. Imagist and symbolist poetry, for instance, celebrated the immediacy of the image as the only means to capture experience. This

skepticism also extends to the understanding of history, which modernist artists accepted, sometimes grudgingly, as an inescapable burden and often sought to grasp and transcend by working with mythic paradigms. As a result, they often explored spatial rather than linear forms of representation, exchanging the idea of simultaneity and cyclicality for the ideal of chronological narration.

The multifaceted experience of change could be embraced positively or questioned as dangerous and destructive, and indeed, the artistic responses to the crisis-ridden experience of modernity were contradictory and diverse. There is no coherent, overarching modernist style; instead, each artefact is an aesthetic statement in its own right and needs to be measured by its own principles. Although EZRA POUND's famous motto "Make it new!" may stand as the age's unifying slogan, it was translated into art in different ways by different artists. On the one hand, the experience of modernity brought about highly political movements such as Pound's and Filippo Marinetti's futurism and its British offshoot vorticism, the latter represented above all by the author and painter Percy WYNDHAM LEWIS. Glorifying the machine as a symbol of movement and energy and war as a cathartic, purifying means of destruction of a degenerate world, these groups were fascinated by the totalitarian regimes that characterized the first half of the 20th century: Pound and Lewis ultimately took sides with fascism and Nazism, respectively. Nevertheless the ideal of total destruction as a precondition for the new can also be found on the Left of the political spectrum, where the ironic movement of Dada (founded in 1916 in Zurich, Switzerland) launched its sweeping attack against bourgeois society with provocative collages, nonsensical poems, and absurd ready-mades (everyday objects exhibited as works of art). On the other end of the spectrum, some modernist artists viewed modern life from a more conservative perspective, bemoaning the loss of spirituality in modernity and looking back at the organic societies of the Middle Ages and the Renaissance for alternatives to modern life. Both in the work of T. S. ELIOT and in that of Virginia Woolf the past is idealized as a utopian space of authentic existence untainted by the noxious effects of modernity. However, although radical and conservative modernists appear to differ in their response to modernity, they shared a sense of frustration with its streamlined mass culture from which they distanced themselves with the aid of very similar aesthetic strategies of complexity and obscurity.

Given the conflicting responses to the experience of modernity, *modernism* can only partially be a comprehensive umbrella term for the aesthetic mentality of the late 19th to early 20th century. Furthermore, the typical, artificially homogenized canon of modernism has eclipsed a whole host of other authors and artists of the period who fail to fit the framework completely. In response to this awareness, criticism has long begun to speak of *modernisms* in the plural, so as to acknowledge the many different, in fact often conflicting styles and movements that constitute this period. Rather than as one, unified movement, modernism ought to be seen in terms of smaller artistic groups, which are nevertheless united by shared concerns and artistic devices. In Britain, the most famous of these artistic cells was the London-based Bloomsbury Group, a loosely organized forum for artists and intellectuals such as the writer Virginia Woolf and her sister, the painter Vanessa Bell; the economist J. M. Keynes; and the writer and translator Lytton Strachey.

Furthermore the diversity of modernist art points to the insufficiency of the rigid time frame in which it is often seen: Not all art produced between the end of the 19th century and the 1930s is modernist in style; nor did modernism emerge in different European countries at the same time. A more rewarding as well as challenging focus, therefore, would be a formal or generic one, which transcends the limits of chronology. If the defining feature of modernism is its emphasis on formal innovation, then the term could be used to describe figures as different as John Donne (17th century), Laurence Sterne (18th century), William Blake, and Samuel Taylor Coleridge (early 19th century) and would include authors beyond the assumed limit of modernism proper (ca. 1930). This focus would also question the troubled distinction between modernism and postmodernism, which has tended to be seen as a radical departure from its predecessor. Rather than trying to work out where the two movements differ, critics today agree that these consecutive movements constitute different responses to one and the same unsettling reality; where modernism tries to transcend that world, postmodernism willingly embraces it. However, when modernism itself is understood as a long trajectory in cultural and literary history, then such distinctions fall flat, asking us instead to think in terms of continuities rather than sudden ruptures and to locate ourselves in the long historical trajectory of making the new the aim of art.

BIBLIOGRAPHY

Bradbury, Malcolm, and James McFarlane, eds. *Modernism, 1890–1930.* Harmondsworth, Eng.: Penguin, 1976.
Childs, Peter. *Modernism.* London and New York: Routledge, 2000.
Levenson, Michael, ed. *The Cambridge Companion to Modernism.* Cambridge: Cambridge University Press, 1999.

Anja Mueller-Wood

MONRO, HAROLD (1879–1932)

Monro was born to affluent Scottish parents in Brussels, Belgium. He attended prestigious schools and colleges in Cambridge and very early on started his career as editor, collector, seller, adviser, and in a general sense promoter of poetry. After his well-received first collection, *Poems* (1906), he founded the influential magazine *Poetry Review* (1911–13), later continued as the *Monthly Chapbook* (1919–25).

He is best remembered for opening in 1912 the Poetry Bookshop, which remained in business until the mid-1930s. This cramped, lively little store in the heart of "arty" Bloomsbury, London, then a hothouse of modernistic and AVANT GARDE ideas in poetry and fiction, soon became a meeting place for poetry lovers and practitioners alike. For the best part of his life, Monro actually lived above the shop (now 34–35 Boswell Street), in which poets gave regular readings and had discussions with both amateur and professional critics, and anybody broadly interested in the genre found a creative and inspiring gathering place. Several poets even lived there for periods at a time, among these WILFRED OWEN, RICHARD ALDINGTON, T. E. HULME, and Robert Frost. In the 1920s, T.S. ELIOT's loosely organized "*Criterion* Club" met there to discuss issues related to that most famous of modernistic poetry magazines.

Among the most influential editorial projects realized by Monro were the three anthologies of rebellious, innovative imagist poetry edited by EZRA POUND (1914–17) and five volumes of placid, pastoral Georgian poetry edited by Edward Marsh (1912–22). Although homosexual, Monro married twice; his second wife, Alida Klementaski, was his bookshop assistant, who ran the business while he was serving during World War I. These "forced" alliances as well as his extravagant lifestyle and growing alcoholism contributed to his untimely death of tuberculosis. This growing hardship of life is traceable throughout his own poems, which started off with elevated praise of nature (*Before Dawn,* 1911) but toward his life's end were marked by a harsh and bitter tone that dealt with topics such as loneliness, frustration, and futility (*Bitter Sanctuary,* 1933).

It is one of Monro's greatest merits to have made poetry accessible to a wider readership, and to have offered young aspiring poets a forum for publicity.

BIBLIOGRAPHY

Grant, Joy. *Harold Monro and the Poetry Bookshop* Berkeley: University of California Press, 1967.

Hibberd, Dominic. *Harold Monro.* London: Palgrave, 2000.

Monro, Harold. *Collected Poems.* Edited by Alida Monro with prefaces by F. S. Flint and T. S. Eliot. London: Cobden-Sanderson, 1933.

Woolmer, J. Howard. *The Poetry Bookshop, 1912–1935: A Bibliography.* Revere, Pa.: Woolmer/Brotherson, 1988.

Goernan Nieragden

MORGAN, EDWIN (1920–)

Born in Glasgow in 1920 to a middle-class family, Edwin Morgan has spent almost his entire life in the city and was named the city's first poet laureate in 1999. Morgan began his studies at Glasgow University in 1937 but interrupted them during World War II to serve in the Royal Army Medical Corps. He returned to Scotland when the war ended, completed his degree, and began teaching in Glasgow University's English Department.

Although he had been writing poetry since his early teens, it was not until 1952 that his first volume, *The Cathkin Braes,* was published. Since then, he has published numerous collections of his own work—*The New Divan* (1977), *From Glasgow to Saturn* (1974), *Themes on a Variation* (1988), *Virtual and Other Realities* (1997), and pamphlets of poetry with a smaller print run, such as *Tales from Limerick Zoo* (1988), as well as innumerable translations.

His work encompasses a wide variety of genres, styles, and voices. He has, on the one hand, a long-standing interest in concrete and sound poetry that began in the 1960s and is, in part, influenced by the work of the Brazilian concrete poets. On the other hand, Morgan continues to write line poetry that draws its inspiration from such varied sources as science fiction ("The First Men on Mercury," "In Sobieski's Shield"), icons of popular culture (with poems about Marilyn Monroe and Edith Piaf, for example), and the urban landscapes of his native Glasgow (in poems such as "King Billy" or "Glasgow Green"). He has also written a series of what he describes as "Instamatic Poems," short works that recount details of news reports in almost snapshot fashion, focusing on the instant and the immediate, and whose titles are made up simply of a location and date.

While it is possible to identify distinct strands within Morgan's poetry, there is also a great degree of genre overlap, perhaps nowhere more visible than in his love poetry, which frequently takes the streets of Glasgow as its backdrop but also includes voices from without the city. Although Morgan made no deliberate secret of his sexuality, it was not until the celebrations for his 70th birthday that there was public recognition of him as a gay poet, which, inevitably, led to a degree of reinterpretation of his love poetry in particular.

His output as a literary translator includes adaptations of poetry and theater from Hungarian, Russian, Italian, French, German, and other source languages into both English and Scots. Among his most notable translated works are his verse translation into Scots of Edmond Rostand's *Cyrano de Bergerac* (1992), his 2000 adaptation of Racine's *Phaedra,* and the 2002 publication of his modern English version of BEOWULF, originally published in 1952. A volume of his collected translations was published by Carcanet in 1996.

BIBLIOGRAPHY

Nicholson, Colin. *Edwin Morgan: Inventions of Modernity.* Manchester: Manchester University Press, 2002.

Thomson, Geddes. *The Poetry of Edwin Morgan.* Aberdeen: Association for Scottish Literary Studies, 1986.

Whyte, Hamish, ed. *Edwin Morgan: Nothing Not Giving Messages.* Edinburgh: Polygon, 1990.

Cristina Johnston

"MORSE" LES MURRAY (1983)

LES MURRAY's poetry is defined by linguistic and formal experimentation, a flexibility with language and sound. Crucial also to his work is the landscape of the Australian countryside, which draws on his memories of growing up in the New South Wales region of Bunyah. Considered the preeminent living Australian poet, he constructs a vernacular of place characterized by self-sufficiency, connection to the land, and a masculine strength.

"Morse," first published in the 1983 collection *The People's Otherworld,* illustrates Murray's play with sound and the centrality of the Australian landscape to his work. The poem tells the story of an isolated telegraph operator "way out back of the Outback" who must perform emergency surgery. He is able to complete the procedure successfully by telegraphing with a doctor who gives him instructions in Morse code over the line.

The first verse paragraph opens with "Tuckett. Bill Tuckett. Telegraph operator, Hall's Creek." This opening sets the irregular meter and strong alliterative pattern that make the poem so distinctive. The first verse paragraph employs alliteration within the lines, showing an echo of Anglo-Saxon alliterative verse: "but he stuck it, / quite likely liked it, despite heat, glare, dust and the lack / of diversion or doctors. Come disaster you trusted to luck." The resulting lengthening of lines serves to highlight the slow pace of life in the Outback, the quiet isolation of the telegraph operator, punctuated by moments of activity. The most distinctive feature of the poem is the end alliteration of hard *k* and *t* sounds, stopping the long lines abruptly and echoing the sound of the telegraph machine's urgent "dot dot dot."

In the second verse paragraph, Murray displays his affinity for language play with a pun: "Faced, though, like Bill Tuckett / with a man needing surgery right on the spot, a lot / would have done their dashes." *Dashes* here signifies both the "dashes" of the Morse code and the response of most people of less strength and resourcefulness when confronted with a man who needs emergency surgery: to run away. Yet Bill Tuckett, taking instruction from a doctor "up a thousand miles of wire," performs the surgery. The *thousands of miles of wire* reflects the isolation of the Outback as well as the competence and strength of the two men working to save a third. In this verse paragraph, Murray uses fewer hard sounds and more rolling sounds, *l* and *r,* to signify the smooth and steady cutting of "a safety razor blade, pioneering on into the wet." The man with the blade enters into and explores the body of another, "pioneering," much the way men who laid the wire in the Australian countryside might have. This juxtaposition of body and landscape is characteristic of Murray's distinctive sense of place and the ways in which it is embodied in experience.

Finally, in the third verse paragraph, the surgery is successful: "And the vital spark stayed unshorted." Both the spark of the telegraph machine and the life spark of the man on the table are sustained. The men are triumphant, although they imagine "a properly laconic / convalescent averring Without you, I'd have kicked the bucket" The voice of the man on the table is inserted here, contrasted with the triumphant *Yallah!* of the others around him. His vernacular expression— *kicked the bucket*—reveals both the extraordinary action that has saved his life and the everyday acceptance of a man's willingness to go to such lengths.

The final stanza is separated from the rest of the poem with a break: "From Chungking to Burrenjuck, morse keys have mostly gone silent / and only old men meet now to chit-chat in their electric / bygone dialect." Here Murray positions the Morse code as one of many languages that make up experience. It is part of the past, but in the telling of the story he preserves both the tale and the language. He makes the story of Bill Tuckett and a relic from the past part of lived experience and collective memory: "So ditditdit daah for Bill Tuckett."

BIBLIOGRAPHY

Leer, Martin. "'This Country Is My Mind': Les Murray's Poetics of Place." *Australian Literary Studies* 20 (2001): 15–42.

Matthews, Steven. *Les Murray.* New York: Manchester University Press, 2001.

Murray, Les. *The Rabbiter's Bounty: Collected Poems.* New York: Farrar, Straus & Giroux, 1991.

Janine Utell

"MOTHER-IN-LAW" U. A. FANTHORPE (1982)

One of four poems in a themed sequence, "Mother-in-law" inhabits the voice of a Shakespearean character—Gertrude, the mother of Hamlet, who married her recently deceased husband's brother—and offers a soliloquy from a female perspective. A knowledge of the play is essential to the understanding of U. A. FANTHORPE's poem; were this speech in the play, it would occur after Ophelia's death (act 4, scene 4) but before Gertrude's (act 5, scene 2). Fanthorpe writes in her introduction that she was "interested to see how the masculine world of Shakespeare's tragedies would look from the woman's angle . . . women exist in this world only to be killed, as sacrificial victims." Though the notion that Gertrude's death in the play is in some way sacrificial is debatable, such a reading is of less concern here than the subject of Gertrude's obsession (and indeed, the very occasion for the poem): Ophelia.

The opening lines of the poem exhibit Fanthorpe's incisive ironic sensibility. Not only does Gertrude begin by slandering the object of her son's affection—to call someone "Such a nice girl" is, of course, to suggest that she is little more than that—but in Fanthorpe's hands she reveals the latent interest she has in the young girl's development. "Just what I wanted," Gertrude writes, "for the boy." The conspicuous break between these two lines initially suggests that Gertrude fancies Ophelia as more than just a daughter-in-law—a more radical retelling of the play than was previously imagined—but this premise is dismissed by Fanthorpe's interpretation that Gertrude would rather exploit Ophelia as a pawn in her political calculus. If knowledge is power, then Ophelia would be a suitable partner for Hamlet, who is in line to become the king of Denmark, precisely because she possesses little of either: She runs no risk that she would "get / The ideas of their station," which would "upset / So many applecarts."

What Ophelia does possess, however, that Gertrude does not is youth—and it is for this reason that she threatens the well-known Oedipal link between the mother and the son. The negation of this threat by

Ophelia's suicide consequently infuses Gertrude's soliloquy with the elements of eulogy and allows her an opportunity to reflect on her past experiences with the young woman (several of which are corroborated by Shakespeare's play) in a way that almost strikes a note of regret at her passing. But this note never arrives—rather, in the last two lines, Fanthorpe returns to where she is most at home, in subtle, understated remarks that reveal the truth about Gertrude's desires. "I can't think who will do for the boy now," she muses. "I seem to be the only woman left round here."

BIBLIOGRAPHY

Fanthorpe, U. A. "Observations of a Clerk." *Poetry Review* 75 (1985): 26–30.

Gilbert, Sandra M., and Susan Gubar. *The Norton Anthology of Literature by Women: The Traditions in English.* 2nd ed. New York: W. W. Norton, 1996.

Benjamin Morris

MOTION, ANDREW (1952–)

Born in London and educated at University College, Oxford. Motion was appointed poet laureate in 1999 on the death of TED HUGHES. In addition to being Britain's premier contemporary poet, Motion is a highly respected academic, lecturing in English at the University of Hull (1976–81) and holding the professorship of creative writing at the University of East Anglia (succeeding Malcolm Bradbury) from 1995 until 2003. Since 2003 he has been professor in creative writing at Royal Holloway, University of London. Although principally known for his poetry, Motion is also a novelist, biographer, and critic; noted works are his biographies of PHILIP LARKIN (1993) and John Keats (1997). Furthermore he has edited *Poetry Review* (1981–83) and worked as poetry editor for Chatto & Windus publishers (London) from 1983 to 1989 and was for Faber and Faber (London) from 1989 to 1995.

Motion has been awarded numerous literary prizes, including the Newdigate Prize while at Oxford University for his poem "Inland" in 1975; the Eric Gregory Award in 1976; the Arvon Foundation/Observer International Poetry for "The Letter" in 1981; the Mail on Sunday/John Llwellyn Rhys Prize in 1984 for *Dangerous Play: Poems 1974–1984*; the Dylan Thomas Award for *Natural Causes* and the Somerset Maughm Award for *The Lamberts: George, Constance and Kit,* both in 1987; and in 1993 the Whitbread Biography Award for *Philip Larkin: A Writer's Life.* Motion became the chairman of the Arts Council of England's literature panel in 1996.

Described by Michael Schmidt as "one of the least ironic English poets of his generation" (863), Motion in his work demonstrates the influence of Larkin, Keats, and EDWARD THOMAS. Motion's work is notable for its supple and economic use of language and its remote, mournful, lamenting tone. His poetry engages with loss and regret, displaying more warmth and compassion toward humanity than many of his contemporaries. Indeed although Motion's themes are often similar to those of Larkin, he has none of Larkin's harsh cynicism.

Motion's poetry is curiously lyrical, though he avoids rhyme and conventional metrical forms; he is often described as a narrative poet, as his work often blurs the distinctions among poetry, prose poetry, and prose. It should be noted that Motion's poems are often more political than they appear; for example, "Inland" is the story of a Fenland village whose economic survival is threatened by flooding and enclosure, and his 1981 poem "Independence" is concerned with the fall of British rule in India. In 1983 his poetry took a more oblique form in *Secret Narratives,* which contained shorter poems of a far more abstract nature. *Natural Causes* (1987) was marked by further experimentation, this time with register, and *Love in a Life* (1991) displayed a further change of style, Motion this time adopting a more direct and simpler form of poetry. However, whatever style he employs, Motion always surprises with shifts in tone, voice, and style—we are never clear where exactly Motion's sympathies lie in his poems. Despite his success and prestige in the world of literature and academia, Motion had perhaps unlikely origins as a poet, the son of a brewer born into a household with no love of literature. His territory is the comfortable privileged southern England of the Home Counties; however, his work is never comfortable, and it is experimental rather than conservative. Motion's poetry is often shocking despite its gentle manner and can even resort to grim violence.

Motion has embraced his role of poet laureate with vigor and has used the role to raise the profile of poetry, often hosting or appearing on radio and television shows as spokesperson for poetry and literature. He is an active promoter of young and up-and-coming poets. Motion has produced poems on public events, including the Paddington rail disaster and the wedding of Prince Charles and Camilla Parker-Bowles. Motion is a politically active poet, lending his support (and his poetry) to organizations such as the Trade Union Congress and charities such as ChildLine.

From the mid-1980s to the present British literature has been in crisis. Changes in the production and marketing practices within the publishing industry and the increased influence of the media on the literary market have stifled the development of literature in the United Kingdom. From the 1990s onward British poetry and fiction were in decline, either caught in a trap of glib, mandatory cynicism (reading more like an exercise in critical theory than an expression of anything in particular) or lost in self-apologia. Dynamic literature in English was increasingly becoming a product of America rather than Britain. After the death of Ted Hughes, British literature lacked a figure of significant weight or substance. In this staid and shallow environment British poets and writers were increasingly seen in magazines and on chat shows as minor celebrities rather than thinkers, artists, and intellectuals. Andrew Motion's significance as a poet, writer, and ambassador for literature is that he has reinvigorated the intellectual project of literature and appears in magazines and on chat shows, but as a thinker, an artist, and an intellectual.

BIBLIOGRAPHY
Schmidt, Michael, and Simon Shaw. *The Lives of the Poets.* London: Weidenfeld and Nicolson, 1998.
Stringer, Jenny, ed. *The Oxford Companion to Twentieth Century Literature in English.* Oxford and New York: Oxford University Press, 1996.

Richard Hudson

THE MOVEMENT

In his anonymously published *Spectator* article of October 1, 1954, entitled "In the Movement," the literary editor J. D. Scott coins the term "the Movement" to describe a coterie of poets and novelists whose empirical, rational, antiromantic, and world-weary writings were beginning to transform the literary landscape of post–Second World War Britain.

Although Scott acknowledges the Movement's inherent incohesiveness and its lack of a formalized manifesto of its philosophies and aims, he points out that there are certain attributes or "signs" characteristic of its prevailing poetic sensibility. "The Movement, as well as being anti-phoney, is anti-wet," Scott writes, "sceptical, robust, ironic, prepared to be as comfortable as possible in a wicked, commercial, threatened world." The poets and novelists who composed the Movement seemed to be bound together, however informally, in a common frustration with the outworn sociopolitical preoccupations of 1930s poets such as W. H. AUDEN and STEPHEN SPENDER, as well as with the moribund neoromantic stylistic excesses of 1940s poets such as DYLAN THOMAS and EDITH SITWELL. Anathema as well to the Movement was the architectonic petrification of the imagists: "We must not," John Wain writes, "talk about 'modern poetry' as if technique and attitude had remained frozen since [EZRA] POUND." Following the publication of two influential anthologies, D. J. Enright's *Poets of the 1950s* (1955) and Robert Conquest's *NEW LINES* (1956), the names of nine writers became synonymous with the Movement: KINGSLEY AMIS, DONALD DAVIE, THOM GUNN, John Holloway, ELIZABETH JENNINGS, PHILIP LARKIN, John Wain, as well as Enright and Conquest themselves. In *The Movement* (1980), one of the most comprehensive book-length treatments of the phenomenon, Blake Morrison refers to Amis, Larkin, and Wain in particular as "the nucleus of the Movement."

Perhaps the earliest and most significant work of Movement literature is *Lucky Jim* (1954), Amis's first and most celebrated novel. The protagonist, Jim Dixon, is a beleaguered lower-middle-class lecturer in history who languishes at a nondescript redbrick university in the 1950s. Many Movement writers held such unillustrious academic posts following the Second World War, occupying that vague and frustratingly unremunerative interstitial space between studenthood and professorhood, between idealistic youthfulness and jaded adulthood. In his *Memoirs,* Amis even admits that *Lucky Jim* was inspired in large part by a visit to Larkin, who had secured a post in 1946 as assistant librarian at the then fledgling University College of Leicester. Dixon detests both the pseudointellectual posturing of his supervising professor, the aging Ned Welch, and the sneering, class-conscious snobbery of Welch's son, the dilettante artist Bertrand. Dixon's incessant interior monologue teems with vitriol against his many tormentors: He fantasises at length, for example, about flushing Welch down the cloakroom lavatory and about picking Bertrand up by the scruff of the neck and throttling him. An important turning point occurs close to the end of the novel when Dixon is finally able to externalize these thoughts by knocking Bertrand to the ground and referring to him as a "bloody old towser-faced boot-faced totem-pole on a crap reservation." Dixon's outburst, while a comedic high point of the work, also symbolizes the entire Movement's skepticism toward artistic pretensions and its outright hostility toward class hierarchies. When Christine Callaghan, Bertrand's fiancée and the object of Dixon's infatuation, bases her misgivings about Bertrand not on an assessment of his many personality defects but on her own inability to define what love is, Dixon accuses her of indulging in an "orgy of emotional self-catechising." As he has learned from painful experience, it is the pragmatic, empirical aspects of love relationships—"whether you can stick the person you love enough to marry them, and so on"—that often prove far more valuable, if far more elusive. Dixon's exasperation with Callaghan's compulsion to hyperromanticize her relationship with Bertrand reflects the Movement's analogous exasperation with the hypersentimentalized neoromantic poetry of the 1940s, and its desire to debunk it with more rational, more empirical alternatives. *Lucky Jim* culminates in Dixon's "Merrie England" lecture, in which he asserts that the Middle Ages was actually "about the most un-Merrie period in our history." Dixon's very public refusal to be co-opted by the self-mythologizing tendencies of academicians (a cynicism toward the academy that is also quite characteristic of the Movement) attracts the attention of one Julius Gore-Urquhart, an influential patron of the arts, who offers Dixon a lucrative job in London, not because Dixon has any special qualifications, but because he does not have "the disqualifications," a quality that, according to Gore-Urquhart, is "much rarer." As Dixon, the Movement must be defined not by what it is, but by what it is not. Scott refers to the Movement as "anti-phoney" and "anti-wet," but it is also antibourgeois, antipretension, antiromantic, and antisentimental, just as the hero (or, indeed, the antihero) of Amis's novel is. As Conquest writes in the preface to *New Lines*, the Movement was united in "a negative determination to avoid bad principles."

This negative determination is also very visible in Movement poetry. In "Wrong Words," a poem from his collection unromantically entitled *A Case of Samples* (1956), Amis laments the extent to which many of his predecessors have so drenched popular poetic images and conceits like "love," "death," and "life" in florid, neoromantic verbal "confectionery" that the composition of poetry itself has sunk to the level of "frantic distortion" and rote "routine." In "Against Romanticism," also from *A Case of Samples,* Amis similarly rails against the "garish" and "frantic" penchant for neoromantic extravagance in some schools of earlier 20th-century poetry. Such poets, Amis asserts, are merely satisfying "an ingrown taste for anarchy," a compulsion "to discard real time and place" for something they fool themselves into believing is "better" or more "grand." Amis, by contrast, advocates a poetry of temperance, of plain images, of surfaces unflawed by obfuscating complexity, an aesthetic that reflects the Movement's thoroughly antiromantic tastes. For example, in "This Be the Verse," an infamous poem from his collection *High Windows* (1974), Larkin demonstrates that his attitude toward the older generation is anything but reverential. "They fuck you up, your mum and dad. / They may not mean to but they do," he writes, "They fill you with the faults they had / And add some extra, just for you." On at least one level, Larkin is holding his "old-style" poetic predecessors responsible for the degradation of English poetry throughout the first half of the 20th century, and the poem calls for an escape from the aesthetic "misery" of verse that is either hyperpolitically "stern" (i.e., Auden, Spender, and the socially conscious poets of the 1930s) or hyperromantically "soppy" (i.e., Dylan Thomas, Sitwell, and the neoromantic poets of the 1940s). Notice also that "This Be the Verse" takes the form of a ballad, an implicit assertion of the Movement's desire for a return to formal traditionalism rather than a slavish adherence to modernist experimentation seemingly for its own sake. In "AUBADE," which first appeared in the *Times Literary Supplement* on December 23, 1977, Larkin once again uses a traditional form—the aubade, or *dawn song,* which has its roots in medival European literature—to examine and criticize contemporary issues. Instead of celebrating the coming of dawn, as is typical in the majority of aubades, Larkin's "Aubade" describes the dawn as a harsh and glaring flash of light that serves only to illuminate "all the uncaring / Intricate rented world" and the fact that "unresting death" is "a whole day nearer now." The poet's reference to "Religion" as "that vast moth-eaten musical brocade" and as "the anaesthetic from which none come round" is reflective of the Movement's skepticism toward systems and programs of all kinds, including religious ones, as well as its "rational" willingness to reject the "specious" shibboleths of the past, be they spiritual or artistic, when they become culturally or intellectually moribund.

It is important to remember that despite the increasing influence of the Movement in British literary circles throughout the 1950s and early 1960s, most of the writers who were thought to be associated with it flatly refused to acknowledge their participation. In a 1958 letter to William Van O'Connor, an American academic who wished to study Larkin's role in the Movement, Larkin "vehemently den[ied] any but the slenderest connection with the Movement," prophesying that many of his colleagues would be similarly tight-lipped. In a 1964 interview, Gunn refers to the Movement as a "big joke," since "none of the people had ever met each other and certainly never subscribed to anything like a programme." Even more pithily, in a 1954 letter to Larkin, Amis refers to Scott's original *Spectator* article, and by extension to the Movement itself, as "a load of bullshit." This stubborn refusal to identify oneself with a movement is not surprising, however, given the Movement's inherent "negative determination" to eschew reductionistic programs and prescriptive manifestos of all kinds.

BIBLIOGRAPHY

Amis, Kingsley. *Lucky Jim.* London: Gollancz, 1954.
Conquest, Robert, ed. *New Lines: An Anthology.* London: Macmillan, 1956.
Enright, D. J., ed. *Poets of the 1950s: An Anthology of New English Verse.* Tokyo: Kenkyusha, 1955.
Morrison, Blake. *The Movement: English Poetry and Fiction of the 1950s.* Oxford: Oxford University Press, 1980.

Scott, J. D. "In the Movement." *Spectator* 1 (October 1954): 399–400.

Robert G. May

"MRS. LAZARUS" CAROL ANN DUFFY (1999)

DUFFY's witty sequence of dramatic monologues in *The World's Wife* simultaneously models and parodies blatant feminist revisionism. Published in 1999, it stands as a lighthouse for the recovery of silenced women and questions whether the sex war is over or inexorable. As indicated in the title, her 30 "heroines," from Mrs Midas and Frau Freud to Queen Kong, are everywoman types. Enhanced by live reading, the monologues appeal to a female community, although at their crudest the balance of power is simply reversed. For example, when Eurydice announces, "But the Gods are like publishers, / usually male," she directly addresses the "girls," to exclude the male reader.

The speeches may seem ingenuous because of their entertainment value, but Duffy confronts the formulaic influences of myth in the variety of personalities and their stories. For some, troublesome partnerships are unresolved; others emerge victorious. Mrs. Lazarus is the unmentioned wife in the biblical account of the man who died but was raised to life again by Christ. According to John's gospel (chapter 10), the deed was done because Jesus wept with sympathy at the grief of Lazarus's sisters, Martha and Mary. Duffy wittily shifts the usual emphasis on the sisters' joy at being reunited with their brother to the implications for his wife.

Taking poetic licence with the original timespan of three days, Duffy presents the tragic scenario of a woman who has endured her husband's extended illness, the trauma of his death, elaborate public mourning, and private pain. An emotional intensity is heightened by the consonance, dissonance, and assonance at which the poet is so adept: "howled, shrieked, clawed / at the burial stones till my hands bled, retched." Although the twist in the familiar tale can seem farcical when we have a graphic description of the villagers accompanying "my bridegroom in his rotting shroud" to meet the wife who has moved on, Duffy reconstructs a highly charged exploration of grieving. After the phases of agonized remembering, the bereaved wife eventually reaches a place of healing, so that adjusting to Lazarus's revival is not a straightforward process. The hint that when a respectable time had elapsed, Mrs. Lazarus had found comfort with another man, the schoolteacher, raises questions about fidelity to and betrayal of the deceased that confront every bereaved partner.

BIBLIOGRAPHY

Dowson, Jane, and Alice Entwistle. *A History of Twentieth Century British Women's Poetry.* Cambridge: Cambridge University Press, 2005.

Duffy, Carol Ann. *The World's Wife.* London: Picador, 1999.

Jane Dowson

MUIR, EDWIN (1887–1959)

A native of Orkney, Edwin Muir spoke a language that was neither English nor Lowland Scots; he chose to write in English. He grew up in a society that seemed little changed from the Middle Ages to the 20th century. His mother told him traditional tales of fairies and witches as well as Bible stories, and his father, a tenant farmer, led the family in daily devotions. Life on a farm engendered a sense of the interdependence between man and animal, a theme found in many of Muir's poems, and showed him the elemental realities of existence. The physical and the spiritual coinhere in many of his works, such as "HORSES."

When he was 14, the family moved to Glasgow, where life in the industrialized world seemed to him a fall from paradise. Longing for an innocent environment is a concern in much of Muir's verse. His education in Orkney had been erratic since he often had to assist in farmwork, but he was unable to continue formal schooling in Glasgow because the family needed the income from his clerking jobs. Life in the city was harsh, and its conditions seemed degrading. Between 1902 and 1907, Muir's parents and two of his five siblings died. Muir abandoned his faith, began reading Nietzsche, and became a socialist. About 1912 he began to contribute regularly to A. R. Orage's *The New Age.* Muir became Orage's assistant in 1919, the year he married Wilhelmina (Willa) Anderson, a Shetlander who was the vice-principal of a teachers' college in London.

The couple moved to the capital, where Muir underwent psychoanalysis, through which he found a means for understanding the mythic power of his dreams.

Dreams were among the sources of his inspiration, and dream journeys recur in his oeuvre. He reviewed drama for the *Scotsman* and novels for the *Athenœum* at this time. H. L. Mencken's interest in *We Moderns* (1918), a work that Muir later repudiated, led to Muir's contributing to an American publication, the *Freeman*. London was, however, an expensive place to live, and that, as well as the Muirs' sense that they were more European than British, led to their settling in 1921 in Prague, where they became friends with Karl Capek. Together the couple translated German literature and were among the first to translate the works of Kafka into English.

At 35 while in Germany, Muir began to write poetry, a pursuit in which his wife encouraged him. *First Poems* appeared in 1925. Other volumes include *The Chorus of the Newly Dead* (1926), *Journeys and Places* (1937), *The Voyage* (1946), *The Labyrinth* (1949), and *Collected Poems 1921–1951* (1952). Some critics consider *One Foot in Eden* (1956) to be his finest collection; "THE HORSES," which appears in this volume, is among his most famous works. The traditional forms and Christian themes of his poems seem out of place among modernist poetry, but his interest in dreams and his sense of alienation from contemporary life are consonant with modernist concerns.

Muir also published three novels and a biography of John Knox (1929) as well as several volumes of essays. His 1936 *Scott and Scotland* opined that the English language and the English literary traditions were the best means for creating a national literature amid the linguistic diversity of Scotland; this book ended his friendship with HUGH MACDIARMID.

In addition to writing, Muir worked from 1941 to 1949 for the British Council, first with European refugees in Edinburgh and later as a cultural representative in Prague and in Rome. He received honorary degrees from King Charles University in Prague, the University of Edinburgh, and Cambridge. He was warden at New Battle Abbey School in Dalkeith, Scotland, from 1950 to 1955, during which time he become commander of the Order of the British Empire (CBE). In the summer of 1955 Harvard invited him to be the Charles Eliot Norton Professor; his lectures, *The Estate of Poetry,* were published posthumously. After returning to England, he settled near Cambridge and died in early 1959. His wife completed the study of ballads on which he was working at the time of his death.

BIBLIOGRAPHY
Butter, P. H. *Edwin Muir: Man and Poet.* New York: Barnes & Noble, 1967.

Muir, Edwin. *An Autobiography.* New York: William Sloane Associates, 1954.

Muir, Willa. *Belonging: A Memoir.* London: Hogarth Press, 1968.

Richman, Robert. "Edwin Muir's Journey." *New Criterion* 8 (1997): 26–33.

Karen Rae Keck

MULDOON, PAUL (1951–   )

In his poem "October 1950" Paul Muldoon ponders the circumstances surrounding his conception. Did the event take place in a room "at the top of the stairs" or, alternatively, beneath "the little stars"? This wild speculation is typical of his work, which often creates more uncertainty than clarification. "October 1950" is also typical of Muldoon's self-mythologizing. Yet, despite such playfulness, his elegant poems are often grounded in his complicated personal history.

Born in Portadown, county Armagh, Paul Muldoon was the first child of Patrick and Brigid (née Regan) Muldoon. Shortly after his birth, they moved to the nearby village of Eglish, where his two siblings, Maureen and Joseph, were born. In 1955 the family settled in Collegelands, county Armagh, where Muldoon spent most of his childhood and adolescence. Collegelands appears many times in his poetry, and there are also numerous references to the small local town, the Moy, which features in the title of his collection *Moy Sand and Gravel* (2002).

Although Muldoon left Ireland in 1986, he wrote several collections of poetry there, and his Irish background has been highly instrumental in shaping his worldview. Both his parents were from poor Catholic families, and the poet grew up with a strong awareness of social class, as well as of the sectarian divides between Catholics and Protestants in Northern Ireland. Muldoon's father worked at a variety of manual jobs—and only ever attained a basic level of literacy. His mother, however, was able to train as a teacher, achieving a level of social mobility that assisted her ambition for her children.

Muldoon also benefited from the 1947 Education Act, which enabled many more Northern Irish Catholics to pursue a secondary education. As a teenager, he attended St. Patrick's College, Armagh, where he was encouraged to read and to write poetry by a range of inspiring teachers, including Sean O'Boyle, Jerry Hicks, and Gerard Quinn. They recognized his talent and introduced him to other emergent Northern Irish writers, including SEAMUS HEANEY. He left school in 1969, then moved to Belfast to begin studying for a degree in English at Queen's University.

Although Muldoon had been in contact with Seamus Heaney before university, it was there that he established a close relationship with him. Heaney was teaching at Queen's at that time and encouraged Muldoon's writing. Muldoon's academic career was undistinguished, but, famously, his first collection, *New Weather,* was published while he was still an undergraduate—when he was only 21 years old.

After he left Queen's in 1973, Muldoon remained in Belfast and started work for BBC Northern Ireland. He also married Anne-Marie Conway, whom he had met at university. However, their marriage would end in divorce a few years later. In 1974 his mother died of cancer, a loss that he only wrote about at length much later. Muldoon stayed at the BBC in Belfast for 13 years and, after his divorce, spent several years in a relationship with the artist Mary Farl Powers. His pamphlet *The Wishbone* was dedicated to her, and she would remain an important presence in his work long after they separated.

In 1986, after his father died, Muldoon left Ulster. He resigned from his job with the BBC and won an Irish government award to spend several months in southern Ireland writing poetry. He then took up teaching appointments in England at Caius College, Cambridge, and at the University of East Anglia. In 1987 he settled in the United States with his new wife, Jean Hanff Korelitz.

Since moving to America, Muldoon has held a variety of academic posts; he has been based at Princeton University since 1990. His first child, Dorothy, was born in 1992, and his son, Asher, in 1999. His recent work has been particularly ambitious in terms of its use of poetic form and difficult subject matter. For instance, his recent long-poem "At the Sign of the Black Horse, September 1999" explores themes such as the Holocaust, the Irish diaspora, and the nature of religious faith, within a very complex formal framework.

Horse Latitudes (2006) constitutes Muldoon's 10th full-length collection of poetry. In addition, he has produced several opera libretti, children's books, and poetry pamphlets, as well as translating poetry. He has also written many song lyrics, mostly for his own band, Rackett, which was formed in 2004. His work has been very influential on other poets in Britain and the United States. In 2003 he received the Pulitzer Prize for his ninth collection, *Moy Sand and Gravel*. His receipt of this prestigious American prize might be seen as a reflection of his commitment to his new host country, and to the vibrant, cosmopolitan nature of his work.

See also "MILKWEED AND MONARCH," "QUOOF."

BIBLIOGRAPHY

Kendall, Tim. *Paul Muldoon.* Bridgend, Eng.: Seren, 1996.

Muldoon, Paul. *Poems 1968–1998.* London: Faber and Faber, 2001.

The Official Paul Muldoon Web Site. "Biography." Available online. URL: http://www.paulmuldoon.net/biography.php4. Accessed 12 July 2006.

Potts, Robert. "The Poet at Play." *Guardian,* 12 May 2001.

Wills, Clair. *Reading Paul Muldoon.* Newcastle upon Tyne, Eng.: Bloodaxe, 1998.

Jennifer Sykes

MURPHY, RICHARD (1927–)

Richard Murphy was born at his family's estate in the west of Ireland (sources differ as to whether it was in county Galway or county Mayo), although he spent much of his early childhood in Ceylon (now Sri Lanka), where his father was the last British mayor of Colombo. He was educated in a variety of English boarding schools and at 17 won a scholarship to Oxford, where he studied English under the tutelage of C. S. LEWIS. In 1948 he began work as a civil servant at Government House in the Bahamas but later returned to Oxford to complete his M.A. Murphy's first collection, *The Archaeology of Love,* was published in 1955, the year in which he married Patricia Avis. The following year saw the birth of his daughter, Emily. He and Patricia divorced in 1959.

Murphy bought and refurbished a boat, the *Ave Maria,* commemorated in the poem "The Last Galway Hooker," from which he ran a successful tourism and fishing business. This poem appeared in Murphy's second collection, *Sailing to an Island* (1963), and possesses a structural strength that typifies his often masterful handling of form. Its theme of communal history is continued in Murphy's subsequent collection, *The Battle of Aughrim* (1968), a narrative sequence that chronicles the bloodiest battle in Irish history and the establishment of the Protestant Ascendancy. Murphy's ancestors fought on both sides, and this background has given rise to his own sense of cultural ambiguity. Maurice Harmon has adroitly described Murphy as "a poet of two traditions," capturing the essence of Murphy's attempts to negotiate a path between his marginalized Anglo-Irish inheritance and his desire to be "truly Irish." Also contained in *The Battle of Aughrim* is "The God Who Eats Corn," a long poem that juxtaposes Murphy's father's retirement from the British Foreign Service with Britain's surrendering of power in Southern Rhodesia ("a pyre kindles under *Pax Britannica*"). The poem also attends to the complexities of postcolonial Irish identity, a theme that likewise dominates in *The Mirror Wall* (1989), a collection based on ancient Sri Lankan graffiti.

The recipient of numerous awards, including fellowship of the Royal Society of Literature, Murphy has been praised widely for his poetry: TED HUGHES, for instance, especially admired its classical orientation. However, it has now been some considerable time since Murphy wrote anything new, and he currently divides his time between Dublin and Durban, where his daughter Emily lives with her family.

BIBLIOGRAPHY

Harmon, Maurice. *Richard Murphy: A Poet of Two Traditions.* Dublin: Wolfhound, 1978.

Murphy, Richard. *Collected Poems.* Oldcastle, Eng.: Gallery, 2000.

———. *The Kick: A Life among Writers.* London: Granta, 2002.

Brian Burton

MURRAY, LES (1938–)

Les Murray is considered by many both in Australia and outside its borders to be the most important living poet the country has produced. He is also a significant participant in political and cultural debate there and thus has been a very controversial figure over the course of his 40-year career. Murray is committed to a specifically Australian vernacular, a spiritual and linguistic connection to the land of his birth and its many peoples. He is considered a proponent of a more traditional verse, in opposition to the modernist-influenced poets of the Generation of '68 and Hard-Edge movements.

Born in 1938 on a dairy farm in the Bunyah region of New South Wales, Murray was raised in poverty. His father, Cecil, was forced to rent the land on which they lived from his grandfather; the grandfather promised the land to Cecil upon his death, a promise that was broken, resulting in the loss of the land when Murray was an adult. Murray's childhood in Bunyah, the freedom with which he roamed the countryside, the significance of land and animal life—of the place itself—would be of vital interest to Murray in his poetry throughout his career. This place would prove to be the formative landscape for Murray's memory, his sense of his own roots, and his spiritual connection to his country. The loss of his father's land would also prove to be formative, leading Murray to feel a sympathy with the Aboriginal peoples of Australia and an anger toward those with the power to colonize and dispossess. From this foundation, he constructed a sense of himself as deeply connected to Australian history and national identity, as might be seen in poems such as "Evening Alone at Bunyah," "Thinking about Aboriginal Land Rights, I Visit the Farm I Will Not Inherit," and "The Buladelah-Taree Holiday Song Cycle."

Murray's childhood was marred by another deeply formative event in 1951. His mother, Miriam, was never able to carry a pregnancy to term after the birth of her first and only son and suffered several ectopic pregnancies and miscarriages. When Murray was 12, she became pregnant, again with an ectopic pregnancy. She began hemorrhaging, and her husband refused to call for an ambulance because he did not want people to know she was pregnant. A week later, Miriam was dead. Murray blamed himself for her death; he had always believed that her difficult labor with him made it impossible for her to carry another baby to term, a belief that was confirmed by remarks to him by his father in the madness of grief and held by him for most of his adult life. This feeling of guilt led to a lifelong depression, referred to by Murray as "the Black Dog." It was only as an adult that Murray was able to address his mother's death poetically; the three poems he composed in coming to terms with the event—"Weights," "Midsummer Ice," and "The Steel"—form the emotional core of *The People's Otherworld* (1983).

The link in Murray's mind between sex and death as a result of his mother's passing, coupled with his utter lack of social graces, made his high school years almost impossible to bear, an experience he considers in "Rock Music." On her deathbed, Miriam made Cecil promise that he would see to Murray's education; in fulfillment of this wish, Cecil sent Murray to Taree High in 1955–56, in a town miles away from the farm at Bunyah. Murray had spent years running wild in the countryside, living in a shack with no running water. He was awkward and enormous, and while he was incredibly gifted with languages and had a capacious knowledge of everything related to arts, letters, and history, he had little sense of how to relate to people his own age. He was teased mercilessly, especially by girls, and recalled years later how this caused him tremendous sexual anxiety and frustration.

It was at the University of Sydney, which he began attending on a scholarship in 1957, that Murray finally began to find a place for himself. There he met other young writers, such as Geoffrey Lehmann, who befriended him and offered him feedback on his growing body of poetry. He read voraciously, pursuing his own interests rather than attending lectures; became fascinated by Catholicism; and worked for and published in the university's magazine, *honi soit.* Throughout the early 1960s, beginning with a poem in *Bulletin* in 1961, Murray began publishing his poetry, which appeared in *Quadrant* and *Southerly.* In 1962, Murray met and married Valerie Morelli, an education student of Hungarian descent whose parents escaped Europe at the end of the Second World War. Shortly thereafter, they had two children, to be followed later by three more. Valerie would prove to be instrumental in furthering Murray's career; she supported the family with teaching jobs while raising the five children and helped him work through his blackest depressions.

Murray dropped out of the University of Sydney and got a job as a translator at Australian National University in Canberra. This allowed him to put his facility with languages to use (he was capable in French, Italian, Portuguese, Dutch, and German, as well as Scandinavian languages, Afrikaans, Malay, and Gaelic) but forced him to live in a growing city. The tension Murray felt between urban and rural life, as well as the constraints he felt working as an artist in an academic setting, began to percolate at this time and would concern him throughout his career until his move back to Bunyah in the mid-1980s. He was able to meet key figures in the Australian literary scene, however, such as Kenneth Slessor and A(LEC) D(ERWENT) HOPE, and he was becoming more prolific. In 1965, he published his first book, *The Ilex Tree,* coauthored with Geoffrey Lehmann. The collection received excellent reviews, with Vivian Smith describing the book as "the best first book of poems by really young writers to have appeared in Australia for a considerable time," and Felicity Haynes specifically noting Murray's "economy and smooth polish." It was with this collection, and Murray's first solo endeavor, *The Weatherboard Cathedral,* that critics began recognizing an important voice in Australian poetry, as well as affinities with T. S. ELIOT, W. B. YEATS, W. H. AUDEN, and Gerard Manley Hopkins.

Murray may be considered closest to Hopkins in terms of use of language and formal experimentation, as well as in terms of theme. Murray himself converted to Catholicism in 1964, and in much of his writing on his own work, he speaks of the composition of poetry itself as being a transcendent process. In a 1986 lecture, reprinted in the prose collection *The Paperbark Tree,* Murray writes, "What attracts us to art and poetry is probably, first of all, the signals it sends out that here the secret world is present; to put that another way we are drawn by the bloom of dream life that the work bears." Murray seeks to impart in his work the presence of the miraculous in everyday life.

At the same time, one might compare Murray to W. B. Yeats in his engagement with issues of national and cultural identity. Murray has always been a crucial participant in the Australian literary scene, serving as editor for *Poetry Australia* and as a reader for Angus and Robertson, one of the nation's preeminent literary publishing houses. He was also an important part of the debate surrounding the creation of an Australian republic, which ultimately culminated in the defeat of a referendum to create such a state in 1999. Murray has called for a "vernacular republic," a specifically Australian poetry rooted in the land, in spiritual values, and in a polyphony of languages and experiences that parallel the truly multicultural nature of the country that he calls "a vast texture of overlaid and overlapping poetries" in the essay "Poems and Poesies." In his work, Murray rejects a European, metropolitan, intellectualized MODERNISM for a poetry that draws together consciousness of mind, body, and emotional life.

Murray was able to return to and sustain a connection with the land that is a part of him when he purchased the family home in Bunyah in 1974 and moved back in 1986. He continued to explore his own complex origins in the verse novel *The Boys Who Stole the Funeral* (1980), which draws heavily on Aboriginal tradition, and the more recent *Subhuman Redneck Poems* (1996), which returns to the farm and his relationship with his father and for which he won the T. S. Eliot Prize. His most ambitious work, *Fredy Neptune* (1998), another verse novel, examines his own psychic pain and recovery. Murray has been writer in residence at numerous institutions, given talks and readings all over the world, and has won multiple fellowships. His most recent work is *Learning Human* (2000).

See also "MORSE," "ONCE IN A LIFETIME, SNOW."

BIBLIOGRAPHY

Alexander, Peter. *Les Murray: A Life in Progress*. New York: Oxford University Press, 2000.

Clapham, Jason. *The Poet Les Murray*. Available online. URL: www.lesmurray.org. Accessed May 8, 2008.

Hergenham, Laurie, and Bruce Clunies Ross, eds. *Poetry of Les Murray: Critical Essays*. Brisbane: University of Queensland Press, 2002.

Matthews, Steven. *Les Murray*. New York: Manchester University Press, 2001.

Janine Utell

"MUSÉE DES BEAUX ARTS" W. H. AUDEN
(1938)   Written after a stay in Brussels in December 1938 and published in *Another Time* (1940), "Musée des Beaux Arts" was inspired by a visit to the art gallery that gives the poem its title and exemplifies the poetry produced during W. H. AUDEN's transition between his 1930s "persona" and his emigration in the early 1939 to the United States. In contrast to the often cryptic, complex poems he wrote in the early 1930s, "Musée des Beaux Arts" is verbally lucid and superficially simple, its unstructured sections using ekphrastic description (the verbal description of visual images, in this case Pieter Breughel the Elder's *The Fall of Icarus,* painted ca. 1558) both to ground and to develop and illustrate its poetic meditation. The poem examines art's capacity for the unconcerned rendering of its subject matter, specifically for the dispassionate rendering of human suffering, and its ability to represent the most tragic events. These are epitomized by "the miraculous birth" and "the dreadful martyrdom," images indicating the direction of Auden's impending assertion of Christian faith while remaining indeterminate epithets that retain a significant degree of rhetorical evasion (not least in finding the poem's moral "lesson" in allusions to a painting depicting a Greek myth).

The poem exploits the triviality of everyday language in "just walking dully along" and "the sun shone / As it had to" (a line possibly imitated by Samuel Beckett for the opening of *Murphy* [1938], and reinforcing the element of absurdity in Auden's poem). But the world Auden constructs, like that of the paintings by "the Old Masters" to whom he refers, is, in contrast, one suddenly devoid of simple compulsion and laden instead with the overwhelming significance, unwitting or otherwise, of human choice and folly. The limits of the human, the poem argues, lie ultimately in the impossibility of sharing subjective experience with others. Even art cannot transcend these limits: In Breughel's painting, Icarus's fall means little to those might who witness it but do not suffer it, and the miracle of faith that the poem seeks would be precisely such a human capacity for infinite sympathy, the ability to feel as the other feels. The sheer human worldliness of the world, the "expensive delicate ship" with "somewhere to get to," offers, in Breughel's painting and, by extension, in art generally, a sobering counter to any distant intimation of the miraculous.

From its opening word, the poem (as Fuller has noted) enacts circuitousness, initiating a structure of circumlocutory delay and evasion. *About* indicates indirection as well as approximation, circulation alongside guesswork, and demands the reader's attention as to precisely what the poem will be "about." In its contrasting of the distantly spiritual with the immediately human and animal, the poem is deeply philosophical and yet studiously generalizing, lexically careful and yet superficially offhand, formally loose and yet meticulously structured. It establishes its argument in relation to a position that is both aesthetic and historical (and to a tradition of art, rather than literary, history) and moves gracefully from general observation to specific description via selected images of calculated, disinterested banality, in which, with exquisitely base honesty, "the dogs go on with their doggy life and the torturer's horse / Scratches its innocent behind on a tree." Underneath the apparent simplicity, however, everything here is working hard to contribute to the poem's argument: The dogs embody unquestioning loyalty coupled with honest, brute instinct, and, perhaps, a curiosity exceeding the human; the torturer's horse figures an innocent past in its behind, its own disconnection from its owner guaranteeing its innocence; even the tree works connotatively within the poem's barely stated but overt Christian logic. None, however, has a human capacity for tragic comprehension, a quality seemingly superfluous to the world of the poem and the painting.

Clearly the poem is invested with a degree of self-conscious, autobiographical significance. Auden's role as a literary "man of action" in the 1930s, and in the Spanish Civil War in 1937, is under severe scrutiny in the poem's questioning of art's engagement with the world it depicts. His eventual abandonment of politics, and the consequent transformation of his style, constitutes one implicit subtext of "Musée des Beaux Arts." Further elements of this poem are developed in the religious meditations of the later sequence "Horae Canonicae" (1949–54), and, in its discomfiting assertion of art's intrinsic disconnection from human suffering, "Musée" initiates what Stan Smith calls Auden's "profound unease" about human involvement in the events of the crucifixion, an unease that preoccupies all his religious poetry. The poem, then, marks an important transition in Auden's understanding of the triangular relations among art, politics, and religion, in which the previously central element—politics—is notably fading in significance.

BIBLIOGRAPHY

Fuller, John. *W. H. Auden—a Commentary.* Princeton, N.J.: Princeton University Press, 2000.

Mendelson, Edward, ed. *The English Auden: Poems, Essays and Dramatic Writings 1927–1939 by W. H. Auden.* London: Faber and Faber, 1977.

Smith, Stan. *W. H. Auden.* Oxford: Basil Blackwell, 1985.

John Sears

"MY GRANDMOTHER" Elizabeth Jennings (1961)

Elizabeth Jennings's "My Grandmother" is a poem of absences: The absence of the grandmother herself, lost to death, is the central image. The antique shop that the speaker's grandmother owned is a place with glinting surfaces. The grandmother, its owner, is in love with her reflection, or rather loves it and needs it, in a way that is not necessarily narcissistic. The importance of reflections complements the centrality of absences.

When the grandmother loses the shop to her declining health, she loses the objects that afford her a reflection of who she is. Her identity is wrapped up in the running of the shop, and upon its loss, its absence, "there's nothing then / To give her own reflection back again." Her granddaughter seems to understand intuitively the importance of the shop to her grandmother's identity. One sharp memory of her grandmother involves her refusal to go out with her because she is afraid of "be[ing] used / like antique objects." At the end of the first stanza, the narrator says that her grandmother watches her own reflection "as if to prove . . . there was no need of love." It is this lack of love, yet another absence, that perhaps frightens the granddaughter.

Upon the grandmother's death, the speaker admits to feeling no grief for that loss, only a feeling of guilt for having refused the old woman her time. She wanders through her grandmother's room and notes all the possessions that she kept after the shop's closing: items "she never used / but needed." The old woman needed her things, the reflective salvers and bowls, spoons and glass, and polished furniture to provide an image of herself. Perhaps she could not see any resemblance from her own youth in her granddaughter's face.

Along with the poem's visual imagery, which conveys a sense of loss and absence, Jennings shapes her message through her use of slant or off-rhyme and sight rhymes—rhymes that are not, but seem to be. The poem consists of four five-line stanzas with an *ababcc* rhyme scheme. However, the rhymes are frequently absent: the combinations of *put/shut* and *prove/love* are sight rhymes; *guilt/felt* and *room/come* are only close in sound, not true rhymes at all. Absence thus becomes revealed through both form and meaning.

Patricia Bostian

"MY SAD CAPTAINS" Thom Gunn (1961)

"My Sad Captains," the title poem of the volume by that same name, is one of Thom Gunn's best-known and most anthologized poems. It appeared in the second half of *My Sad Captains*, a volume that marked Gunn's movement away from strictly formal verse toward free verse. It is written in syllabics—three stanzas of six lines each, with each line consisting of seven syllables. Syllabics were favored by Gunn's mentor at Stanford, Yvor Winters; they gave the younger poet a structure by which to limit a poem and know when it is ended, a comforting halfway point before abandoning the strictures of formal verse for the wide-open American free verse of Whitman and another gay American poet he admired, Robert Duncan.

The poem's title is taken from Shakespeare's *Antony and Cleopatra*. After his defeat at Actium by Octavius, Mark Antony rouses himself to fight on, saying to Cleopatra, "I'll set my teeth / And send to the darkness all that stop me. Come, / Let's have one other gaudy night: call to me / All my sad captains; fill our bowls once more; Let's mock the midnight bell" (3, 13, 181–84). Gunn's poem opens without Antony's bravado, sounding rather the note of sadness and camaraderie in the title's three words of quotation that lead into his poem: "One by one they appear in / the darkness: a few friends." Who these friends are (a few have "historical" names) is unclear. They step into the light from the

darkness and start to shine. They are "men / who . . . lived only to / renew the wasteful force they / spent with each hot convulsion." As in the march of ghostly kings in *Macbeth,* called from the darkness, they then fade in the third stanza of the poem, only to be set in the night sky, like Greek heroes: "They withdraw to an orbit / and turn with disinterested / hard energy, like the stars."

One interpretation of the "sad captains" is that they are Gunn's poems, called to march before him in much the same way that W. B. Yeats at the end of his life calls his poems "circus animals" and commands them to march before him in a final examination ("The Circus Animals' Desertion"). Gunn's sad captains are like Antony's generals, noble, stoic, and heroic, who have been with him through many battles. But their time is ending, just as Gunn's devotion purely to classical formal verse is also ending, with this volume. The poems, as men, lived only to renew the force of their creation. That is, the only purpose of a poem, in this view, is to recreate the emotional force of the creative moment it describes. Gunn said that very few of his poems were sexual, or about sex; the *hot convulsion* of these poems' creation, however, seems clearly linked to male sexuality and generativity. They "remind" him, "distant now," of their former worth, existence, creation. Now, however, they are set in the night sky, distant earlier work that is being left behind, though still beautiful, and perhaps useful as poles by which to navigate. They are fixed and "historical," because printed and given out to the world. They are "disinterested / hard energy," hard because of their hardened formal qualities, disinterested because of their detached quality, always notable in Gunn's work. They are "apart, winnowed from failures" in that the unsuccessful poems of his earlier poetic life do not see print. They are his sad captains, perhaps not so disinterested after all, if they are sad—or perhaps it is their commander, Antony, Gunn, who is sad at their passing.

BIBLIOGRAPHY

Hennessy, Christopher. "An Interview with Thom Gunn." In *Outside the Lines: Talking with Contemporary Gay Poets.* Ann Arbor: University of Michigan Press, 2005.

James Persoon

N

"THE NAMING OF PARTS" HENRY REED (1942)

HENRY REED's best known poem, "The Naming of Parts," is considered one to the best poems of World War II. In what is seemingly a dialogue between an army training officer and a young recruit, the recruit's voice is actually in his mind rather than spoken. The first four stanzas begin with the officer's instructions to his trainees. The lines then become the recruit's thoughts as his mind keeps drifting between the lesson and the japonica, the bees, and the blossoms that abound in the garden near where he is being trained. The last stanza is composed of only the recruit's thoughts.

The beauty of the surroundings presents a distinct contrast with the harsh, sterile, and regimented world of the army. The trainer's harsh, clipped, mechanical instructions are also in contrast to the recruit's flowing, poetic thoughts. In spite of the strident interruptions to his musings, the recruit is able seamlessly to incorporate the officer's words into his thoughts. The *spring* of the weapon becomes *Spring*; the *backwards and forwards* of the rifle's bolt becomes the movement of bees as they gather nectar.

The poem's central irony is that in the midst of growth and exuberance the recruits are being trained to become part of the killing machine of the military. A good soldier, such as the officer, will become oblivious to the life around him. Allowing himself to think about the garden is a way for the recruit to maintain humanity, not to think about what he will do when he is given a working weapon with all its parts.

The incompleteness of the weapons—they have no slings or swivels—emphasizes the incompleteness of the men's lives. Inexperienced riflemen, they have no "point of balance" in handling the weapon, and metaphorically no balance in their lives. They are living regimented, mechanical lives, training to kill, separated from their families and the existence they knew. A series of sexual allusions adds an additional layer to the reading as the recruits are also living a segregated life apart from their wives and girlfriends.

The poem emphasizes the absurdity of war as it separates men from the beauty and joy of life, leading them to become insensitive and unquestioning obedient.

BIBLIOGRAPHY

O'Toole, Michael. "Henry Reed, and What Follows the 'Naming of Parts.'" In *Functions of Style,* edited by David Birch and Michael O'Toole, 12–13. London: Pinter, 1988.

Jean Hamm

NEW CRITICISM

The most important critical movement of the decades spanning the 1930s through the 1950s and into the 1960s, New Criticism generated long-lasting and major effects on literary criticism, effects that underlie even the most radical scholarship today. To say that this movement revolutionized the study of English literature and even the profession itself is not an exaggeration. With its roots in English scholars and American expatriates, including T. S. ELIOT, the movement moved to the United States and rapidly grew to dominate critical interest in literature, particularly poetry, for decades. Indeed, New Criticism enjoyed a symbiotic relationship with modern poetry, giving birth to the idea of the "close reading" and emphasizing the "form" of the individual poem above authorial intention, cultural influence, and even reader response. Yet, for a movement that sought to divorce the poem from its contiguous culture, New Criticism itself was inextricably linked to the cultural forces that produced it.

The roots of New Criticism lie not in the 20th century, but in the preceding age of the Victorians. Nineteenth-century writers and scholars, among them Matthew Arnold, popularized the idea of poetry as a particularly timeless expression of superlative human achievement, linking it not to a time or society but to a transcendent didactic purpose. During the 19th century, too, "English" as the study of literature first began to be incorporated into college curricula, beginning with universities outside England itself. Several decades later, in the 1920s, the poet T. S. Eliot further developed and transformed the idea of poetry, emphasizing in his 1919 essay "Hamlet" the idea of the "objective correlative": "a set of objects, a situation, a chain of events which shall be the formula of that particular emotion." Eliot argues that the "objective correlative" should be the "only way of expressing emotion in the form of art." In other words, as his Victorian forebears had, Eliot continued the process of dissociating poetry from any surrounding reality. Poetry, according to Eliot, should rely not upon any background information such as the poet's life or experiences, but only upon its words and form to convey its emotional message. Disapproving of Victorian poets like Tennyson, Eliot looked back to Donne and Marvell for models of successful poetic integration of "wit" and emotion.

As Eliot was writing, critics, too, increasingly turned a discerning eye on poetry, using detailed, line-by-line explications of modernist poems by Eliot, Cummings, and others in order to justify their value. In England, I. A. Richards, WILLIAM EMPSON, and F. R. Leavis advanced the idea of "close reading," stressing the crucial difference between the poem itself and any paraphrase of it. Significantly Richards juxtaposed poetry with science, arguing for a concrete system of analyz-

ing and judging poetry that might compare with the modern prestige given to scientific analysis. As part of his system, Richards rigidly separated facts and emotions, allocating to science the former and to poetry the latter. Empson, who may not really be considered a New Critic himself, nevertheless delved deeply into the idea of critical close analysis, producing detailed explications of poetry based upon grammar, diction, and syntax. As Richards and Empson, Leavis initially concentrated on poetry but eventually shifted to prose. Uniquely among these leading critics, Leavis sought to justify the novel, giving it attention equal to that he gave poetry. Ultimately, though, each of these Cambridge scholars viewed the text in isolation, focusing on its form rather than any outside influence.

While Eliot and Richards inaugurated the beginnings of the New Critical movement, the beliefs and critical concepts that defined its significant decades truly developed in the United States, with a group of teachers and poets initially known as the Fugitive poets. In the United States, southern writers, most notably William Faulkner, had initiated the "Southern Renaissance," which, in turn, produced the poets John Crowe Ransom and Allen Tate. These two poets, and their students and followers, introduced New Criticism to the United States and defined it as a critical movement. Indeed, Ransom's 1941 book *The New Criticism* gave the movement its name. In the latter half of the 1930s, the Fugitive poets—John Crowe Ransom, Allen Tate, Robert Penn Warren, and Cleanth Brooks— began to introduce the theories that ultimately composed New Criticism. Notably the movement began outside the inner circles of academia; all of these early poets/critics moved outside the centers of professional study and writing. Similarly Ransom and Tate did not utilize "close reading" to the extent that later New Critics did, relying instead upon theories of "irony," "paradox," and "tension." As the Fugitive poets evolved, they came to be known as the Southern Agrarians, a term that, by the 1930s, denoted a well-defined system of political ideals.

The Southern Agrarians criticized the side effects of modern capitalism, arguing that society as a whole suffered from problems that did not exist in the 19th century. In particular, they lauded the 19th-century South as a model of cultural connection and community; they also condemned the modern preference for science. As did I. A. Richards, the "Southern Agrarians" drew a harsh distinction between poetry and science, siding, not surprisingly, with poetry. Although the Southern Agrarian movement did not last, especially since many of its most vehement proponents relocated away from the South, some of its tenets, including the sharp differentiation between poetry and science, nonetheless imbued the developing New Criticism. Poetry, first for the Southern Agrarians and then for the New Critics, became a kind of holy grail: an answer to the problems of commercialism and capitalism, a balm for readers wounded by a world these scholars saw as both superficial and alienated. Moreover, although New Criticism differentiates itself from any political movement, some of its appeal nonetheless derived from the political climate of the United States after the Second World War and during the cold war. Because New Criticism directed the scholarly eye toward the poem and only the poem, it did not require any kind of engagement with contemporary politics or world issues, and that very disengagement with the world appealed to many disoriented liberal intellectuals.

As it matured, New Criticism moved within the critical spheres of academic influence and increasingly developed as a pedagogical strategy. Many of the poets at the heart of the early stages of American New Criticism gained more important positions in universities and publications—Ransom, for example, began the *Kenyon Review* in 1937—and carried with them the tenets of New Criticism. Their published works reflected the New Critical doctrine and initiated important changes across the entire profession. Ransom's 1938 "Criticism, Inc." argued for the professionalization of the study of English literature, an idea that the *Inc.* suggests. This professionalization assumed an almost scientific arsenal of analysis, a collection of terms and tools to investigate and explicate poetry. The New Critics consciously opposed their literary "weapons" to scientific jargon and technique. As Terry Eagleton comments, New Criticism's "battery of critical instruments was a way of competing with the hard sciences on their own in a society where such science was the dominant criterion of knowledge." But New Criticism's concrete

approach to difficult texts also signified its potential in the classroom as well as the theoretical manuscripts. Notably a good part of the immediate output of the New Critics took the form of college textbooks.

New Criticism was particularly suited for the expanding English programs across the United States during the 1940s. *Understanding Poetry,* published in 1938 by Cleanth Brooks and Robert Penn Warren, addressed the need for a critical repertoire that students—and not just rarified academics and scholars—could wield at will. Because it removes poetry from any sort of cultural or even authorial locus, a student following the methods of New Criticism needs no special knowledge, background, or even training in order to interpret a text. Indeed the text is the sole requirement for a New Critical interpretation. A New Critic must only examine the words of a text, searching for potential meaning; that meaning must be interrelated to other words throughout the poem. Other textbooks and critical commentary followed, and New Criticism quickly dominated the academic discussion of poetry during the 1940s and 1950s. Significantly New Criticism enjoyed a special relationship with modern poetry. Not only can the roots of the movement be traced to modernist writers, especially T. S. Eliot, but it is also particularly well suited for interpreting the often heavily symbolic, meaning-laden works and words of modernist poets. The in-depth, close reading approach prioritized by New Criticism resounds particularly well with the complex lines of modernist poets.

This approach to poetry is a formalist one, and the new critics themselves have sometimes been called formalists. Although the history of the new critics can be traced through T. S. Eliot and to the Victorian age, they are also directly preceded by Russian formalism, which experienced its heyday before the revolution in 1917. Russian formalism prizes a constant sense of originality and innovation in literature. As Booker notes, Russian formalists "argued that the central strategy of literature was 'defamiliarization,' or the presentation of reality in new ways that can lead to a fresh perception of the world." New Criticism similarly depended upon poetry's "organic form," a term that denotes not the overall structure of a poem, but all of its component elements interpreted both individually and within the context of the entire poem. In fact, New Critics vilified any attempt to condense a poem, lumping such summaries under the heading of "the heresy of paraphrase," a term used by Cleanth Brooks in his 1947 now-classic *The Well-Wrought Urn*. For the New Critics, a poem cannot be boiled down into a prose paraphrase; it must be read and interpreted in its entirety. New critics also attacked what they saw as two additional misinterpretations or abuses of poetry. W. K. Wimsatt and Monroe Beardsley termed these problematic approaches the *intentional fallacy* and the *affective fallacy* in two eponymous essays. The intentional fallacy assumes that what the author *intended* actually matters; for the New Critics, only the text, not in any way its author, is relevant. Similarly, the affective fallacy occurs when a reader mistakes her own response to the poem for its true message, confusing the emotional effects of the poem with its truth. At the heart of new criticism is the simple idea that nothing matters *except* the text of the poem itself—nothing, not even the author's intentions or the reader's response.

In its own time, New Criticism faced challenges from other movements, including the neo-Aristotelian Chicago school and myth criticism. Currently it has largely been eclipsed by critical methods informed by cross-disciplinary approaches and new attitudes toward history, gender, and other important textual influences and considerations. But it is hard to overestimate the lingering influence of New Criticism. If New Criticism was limited and in some respects facile, it also greatly contributed to professionalizing literary scholarship. In fact, new criticism defined literary scholarship in the first real age of professional scholars of English literature. Most importantly, even though many of the basic ideas of New Criticism have been replaced or overshadowed by new developments and theories, the tools of New Criticism—especially the close reading and the emphasis upon the significance of the content and structure of a literary work—remain vitally important to literary scholarship today.

BIBLIOGRAPHY

Baldick, Chris. *Criticism and Literary Theory 1890 to the Present.* New York: Longman, 1996.
Bertens, Hans. *Literary Theory: The Basics.* London: Routledge, 2001.
Booker, M. Keith. *A Practical Introduction to Literary Theory and Criticism.* New York: Longman, 1996.
Brooks, Cleanth. *The Well-Wrought Urn: Studies in the Structure of Poetry.* New York: Harcourt, Brace & World, 1975.
———, and Robert Penn Warren. *Understanding Poetry.* New York: Holt, Rinehart & Winston, 1960.
Eagleton, Terry. *Literary Theory: An Introduction.* Minneapolis: University of Minnesota Press, 1983.
Eliot, T. S. "Hamlet." In *Selected Prose of T. S. Eliot.* Edited by Frank Kermode. New York: Harcourt, Brace, Jovanovich, 1975.
Guerin, Wilfred L., Earle Labor, Lee Morgan, Jeanne C. Reesman, and John R. Willingham. *A Handbook of Critical Approaches to Literature.* 5th ed. New York: Oxford University Press, 2005.
Harland, Richard. *Literary Theory from Plato to Barthes: An Introductory History.* New York: St. Martin's Press, 1999.
Ransom, John Crowe. *The New Criticism.* Norfolk, Conn.: New Directions, 1941.
Rubin, Louis D., Jr. "Tory Formalists, New York Intellectuals, and the New Historical Science of Criticism." *Sewanee Review* 88 (1980): 674–683.

Winter Elliott

NEW LINES ED. ROBERT CONQUEST (1956)

Published in 1956, the *New Lines* poetry anthology collected the work of eight poets associated with THE MOVEMENT, a loosely knit group of writers working in opposition to the new romanticism prevalent during the 1930s and 1940s. Edited by Robert Conquest (1917–   ), the *New Line* poets included KINGSLEY AMIS (1922–95), DONALD DAVIE (1922–95), D. J. ENRIGHT (1920–2002), THOM GUNN (1929–2004), John Holloway (1955–99), ELIZABETH JENNINGS (1926–2001), PHILIP LARKIN (1922–85), John Wain (1925–94), and Conquest himself. *New Line*'s roster would stand for years as the unofficial membership list of the Movement, making its publication significant as a literary introduction to both the tenets of the group and its poets, many of whom who would go on to well-received careers.

In his introduction, Conquest proudly defends his anthology on the grounds that a "general tendency has once again set in," which might yield the "restoration of a sound and fruitful attitude to poetry" to countermand what he terms a "rapid collapse of public taste." This new "tendency" dismissed doctrinal and imitative approaches in favor of a more rational, almost neoclassical style of poetry. Conquest's most explicit claim of definition is that this school of poetry "submits to no great systems of theoretical constructs nor agglomerations of unconscious commands. It is free from both mystical and logical compulsions." Though the poets themselves were often uneasy about (and in some cases resistant to) being part of any kind of so-called movement at all, Conquest's grouping of them based on these general definitions is remarkably accurate.

The *New Line* poets eschew incomprehensible language and formal apparatus. In "Afternoon in Florence," Elizabeth Jennings yearns for an "image of the city tangible," a more realistic, rational view of Florence made possible only when "eyes make room for light." In "The Island" she writes, "Each brings an island in his heart to square / With what he finds," echoing Conquest's call for a shift in focus from larger conceptual constructions to smaller circles of poetic experience.

In "Maiden Name," Philip Larkin calls this dependence on romantic forms "depreciating luggage" that is "applicible to no one, / Lying just where you left it." Thom Gunn is even more direct in "Lerici" when he explains that "Shelley was drowned near here." The point of the *New Lines* poets' collective disregard for such elaborate language is that it confuses the poetic purpose.

In "Wrong Words" Kingsley Amis declares that "rhyme-words of poets in a silver age" are "too fluent, drenching with confectionery," so much so that he cannot help wondering "What has this subject / Got to do with that object?" Kingsley favors a clearer, more truthful line, one "unforced, unblurred, of real defeats." In "Remembering the Thirties" Donald Davie writes that even if the devil himself carved "his own initials on a desk," in all probability "we'd miss the point, because he spoke / An idiom too dated, Audenesque." If limited to conflated language, Davie wonders, in "Rejoinder to a Critic," "How can I dare to feel?"

In "Something Nasty in the Bookshop" Kingsley Amis asks the question that defines the alternative style presented by *New Lines*: "Should poets bicycle-pump the human heart / Or squash it flat?" The answer for Amis and his peers is the latter: a cool, lucid image devoid of the extraneous flora of neoromantic, in some cases new apocalyptic, poetry. In "On the Move,"

Thom Gunn boasts that all the necessary tools for the poet are "contained within my coat" and that the place to start is at the "pinpoint of consciousness. / I stay, or start from, here."

For the *New Lines* poets, these "here" images are very often natural ones. In "Elegy for an Estrangement," John Holloway's speaker talks of "a flowerless river skulking through a plan. / Streets of an endless town. Night falls in rain." For these poets, the human poetic experience is better communicated as an experience evoked by language rather than meticulously mapped by it. In "On the Death of a Child," D. J. Enright says of his impossible subject, "The big words fail to fit. Like giant boxes / Round small bodies." In "The Interpreters," Enright explains that "what you read on the surface of the agitated page is only an / idle dusty weed." Dwelling on "idle dusty" text is unhelpful. Instead, "somewhere / someone saves a child from a swollen river, / and really means it—" is an image of greater poetic power because it is potently alive; someone "really means it." Conquest too shows the power of the simple line in "Anthéor" with simple, but vivid imagery: "And the hot stars crackle / In a sky of ice."

In *New Lines* Conquest assembled an anthology of poets joined perhaps only by their "determination to avoid bad principles" in that they avoid a "tendency to over-intellectualise," but its influence on British verse was a call to pare down the poetry of the new romantics, which had, in Conquest's eyes, become too technical. He states in his introduction, "An intellectual skeleton is not worth much unless it is given the flesh of humanity, irony, passion or sanity." *New Lines* came about because, as Conquest concludes, "the stage needed sweeping." Conquest would produce *New Lines II* in 1963 with a much larger roster (including TED HUGHES), but this volume was met with less enthusiasm.

BIBLIOGRAPHY

Baer, William. "Robert Conquest." *Fourteen on Form: Conversations with Poets.* Jackson: University of Mississippi Press, 2004.

Bradley, Jerry. *The Movement: British Poets of the 1950s.* Ottawa: Twayne, 1985.

Conquest, Robert, ed. *New Lines.* London: Macmillan, 1956.

Morrison, Blake. *The Movement: English Poetry and Fiction of the 1950s.* Oxford: Oxford University Press, 1980.

Mottram, Eric. "The British Poetry Revival, 1960–75." In *New British Poetries: The Scope of the Possible,* edited by Robert Hampson and Peter Barry. Manchester, Eng.: Manchester University Press, 1993.

Tolley, A. T. *The Poetry of the Forties in Britain.* Ottawa: Carleton University Press, 1985.

Bradley Ricca

NICHOLS, GRACE (1950–)

Born and educated in Georgetown, Guyana, Grace Nichols worked as a newspaper journalist and as a freelance writer and started writing poetry and prose while still in Guyana. In 1977 Nichols moved to England, where she has continued writing and performing poetry.

I Is a Long Memoried Woman, her first collection of poems for adults, was published in 1983 and received the Commonwealth Prize for Poetry. The collection is a lyrical history book of the unknown black woman who has survived the Middle Passage on the slave ships. The 47 pieces focus on oppression between the races and the sexes, but much more on revolution and the survival strategies that women draw on, driven by the hope for freedom and depending on the spiritual support of African gods and goddesses, such as Ala, Ogun, or Yemanji. The volume ends on what have become Nichols's most celebrated lines: "I have crossed an ocean / I have lost my tongue / from the root of the old one / a new one has sprung" ("Epilogue").

In her second poetry collection, *The Fat Black Woman's Poems* (1984), Nichols rebels against the beauty ideal of the thin white European woman and celebrates the fat black woman in a number of serio-comic poems. Humor for Nichols has an assertive power; she does away with the black woman as the eternal victim, and her subversion of racist and sexist stereotypes shows the inextricability of the political and the private. Some poems are explicitly sexual and celebratory of the woman's sensuality, such as "Invitation": "My breasts are huge exciting / amnions of watermelon / . . . my thighs are twin seals / . . . Come up and see me sometime."

Lazy Thoughts of a Lazy Woman (1989) develops further Nichols's feminist intervention against beauty ideals in its first part. In "Wherever I hang," she deals again with the black woman who makes her home in England: "Wherever I hang me knickers / that's my home." Other poems, with titles such as "Grease" and "Dirt," use rather sensual expressions and imagery to convey the profanity of housework, and bodily functions are treated similarly: "Who it Was" rages against the shaving of armpits, "Dead Ya Fuh Tan" against people trying too hard for a suntan. "About Poems and Crotches" debunks the myth of the kiss of the muse, claiming that all poems are born though the crotch. The second part of the collection, with a stronger historical and political focus, returns to the topic of her first collection, the Middle Passage. "Beverly's Saga," dedicated to the dub poet Jean Binta Breeze and written to be performed, attacks the idea of repatriation and affirms several centuries of black presence in Britain. Other poems focus on her memories of Guyana, her childhood there and her family; on globalization; and on the Western exploitation of natural resources and labor ("There is no Centre of the Universe").

Sunris, a collection published in 1996, is inspired by Nichols's fascination with carnival and the calypso. The first section of the collection, entitled "Against the Planet," draws together a celebration of creation and a number of spiritual myths from England, China, and Greece. Part 2, "Lips of History," takes us back to the meeting of Caribbean and English influences in poems such as "Hurricane hits England" and "High Tea." "Berlin snapshots" asserts the ubiquity of history: "Everywhere ghosts / of the old military / Everywhere kisses / from the thick lips of history." Other histories are quite as inescapable: Indian, African, and Brazilian histories are inextricably connected, above all through mythology. The long title poem, "Sunris," is structured like a calypso and celebrates the freedom and the spirit of the Caribbean carnival. It is an ode to Africa, an imaginary conversation with Montezuma about the fate of his people and the impact of the colonizers. The lyrical *I* in this poem is an emancipated woman who is aware of her heritage and her manifold spiritual sources. In the end she gives herself the name *Sunris.* In the final section, "Wings," Nichols asserts that it is wings, rather than roots, that enable the migrant to pull away from the homeland and enable the homing pigeon to return.

Her latest collection to date, *Paint Me a Poem,* is the result of a one-year residency at the Tate Gallery in London. In this collection she includes her own poems, inspired by paintings and exhibits in the gallery, but also those written by children during workshops at the Tate. Even though in this collection Nichols's feminist and postcolonial agenda is not as explicit as in her other writing, she is still most inspired by women's fates, as in her poems on Andy Warhol's *Marilyn Diptych,* Hilliard's portrait of Elizabeth I, and Picasso's *Weeping Woman.* Her focus is also on the act of looking: The "Gallery-Ghost at the Tate" is a female spirit who helps visitors look at paintings: "A friend to all brush-strokes / the Gallery-Ghost / will steer you to what / she wants you to see most."

Nichols has also written and edited poetry for children. In both her adult and children's writing, she uses Standard English and Caribbean Creole and moves between the two effortlessly. Her poems have a strong rhythmic quality and lend themselves to performance. Her work so far can be characterized by an urge to subvert racist and sexist stereotypes, by an irreverence toward ideals of beauty and good behavior, and by an interest in individual and collective histories. In her efforts to write a lyrical history of the Caribbean, she has been compared to EDWARD KAMAU BRATHWAITE, but it is a distinctly female history that interests Nichols. Though these concerns stand out clearly, her poetry remains diverse—as Nichols claims there is "no poem big enough / to hold the essence / of a black woman / of a white woman / of a green woman" ("Of Course When They Ask for Poems about the 'Realities' of Black Women").

See also "THE FAT BLACK WOMAN REMEMBERS," "TROPICAL DEATH."

BIBLIOGRAPHY

Nichols, Grace. *The Fat Black Woman's Poems.* London: Virago, 1984.

———. *I Is a Long Memoried Woman.* London: Caribbean Cultural International Karnak House, 1983.

———. *Lazy Thoughts of a Lazy Woman.* London: Virago, 1989.

———. *Paint Me a Poem: New Poems Inspired by Art in Tate.* London: A&C Black, 2004.

———. *Sunris.* London: Virago, 1996.

Susanne Reich

"NORTHUMBRIAN SEQUENCE" KATHLEEN JESSIE RAINE (1952) In Bede's account of the conversion of Eadwine, king of Northumberland, he records these words: "The sparrow [being compared to the life of a man] flies in at one door and tarries for a moment in the light and heat of the hearth-fire, then flies forth into the darkness whence it came." KATHLEEN JESSIE RAINE's "Northumberland Sequence" is a commentary on this account, which serves as an epigraph to the poem. The poem's speaker is like the sparrow, answering that while worldly life is but a brief interlude, her soul's journey began before the world was made and exists beyond its end. Raine spent both world wars in Northumberland, England, which is perhaps the hearth fire that kept her warm and safe while wars raged beyond.

There is a koan in Zen Buddhism—a riddle not meant to be answered—What did your face look like before your parents were born? In "Before the World Was Made," the speaker is a woman defending her vanity and her desire by the fact that she is perpetually searching for that original face. The soul longs for its past and future beauty. In Raine's poem, the soul celebrates all the stages of its vivacious power—before, during, and after a particular incarnation. The poem is built of six sections that represent the journey of the transcendent soul being poured into the imperfect form of living things, which it overflows. Plato's philosophy indicates that there are ideal forms that exist, and on which all real forms are modeled. The ideal transcendent soul, though, breaks the imperfect mold it is poured into, then death draws it back out again.

Section 1 is the Rilkean boast that all life makes: "My journey / Circles the universe." It begins the progression from the grave into life, claiming to have passed through the grave before death even reigned. Section 2 is almost an villanelle, an illumination dance in iambic pentameter that conjures into that grave the radiance of life. In section 3, death is conquered by the sky-lines of infinite birds as they track through the earthly heavens. A few lines are shorter, only four beats, giving the section the quality of a hymn celebrating not the individual life but life itself. The Yeatsean rhetorical question that ends the section is "What gossamer desire floats out to guide / Spirit ascending and descending between grave and sky?" The section's real question is, What matters if the bird dies, if flight itself keeps flying? Section 4 is a spell for letting in both the storm that destroys life and the storm that is life. "Let in the wound, / Let in the pain, / Let in your child tonight." In section 5 the sleeper by the roman tree dreams the transcendent desire of the life force to be; only, "The dream has overflowed the tree." Finally, death comes and the bird flies out into the soul-dark night, taking nothing with it but the gossamer desire of life.

BIBLIOGRAPHY
Mill, Ralph J., Jr. *Kathleen Raine: A Critical Essay.* Grand Rapids, Mich.: Eerdmans.

Brad Bostian

"NOT MY BEST SIDE" U. A. FANTHORPE (1978)

Inspired by the Florentine painter Paolo Uccello's ca. 1455 canvas *St George and the Dragon* (there was an earlier version from 1440, but U. A. FANTHORPE is responding to the later, better-known one), "Not My Best Side" offers a lighthearted, but no less critical for it, satirical look at a famous set piece of Renaissance painting. The poem is highly celebrated as an example of 20th-century ekphrasis (Greek *ek* "out, in full" + *phrazein* "to speak"), a genre in which a work of literature responds to or represents a work of nonverbal art in verbal form, in part because it accomplishes the primary function of ekphrastic works. As each stanza is a monologue by one of the figures in the painting, the poem puts words in the painting's mouth; it allows the characters literally to "speak out." Fanthorpe deviates from a time-honored tradition of the poet's paying deference to the painter, however, by presenting these characters (the dragon, the maiden, and St. George) in cognitive dissonance with their place in the painting, each in its respective way.

The dragon, by most accounts a fearsome, deadly beast, whines that it was painted poorly: that Uccello had an "obsession with / Triangles, so he left off two of my / Feet." (Given the odd perspective of the canvas, including the horse with the "deformed neck and square hoofs," the dragon's lament is hardly unfair.) Moreover the dragon complains that he is not respected by either his conqueror (whom he calls "ostentatiously

beardless"—a shot at St. George's lack of masculinity?) or his victim, who is "so / Unattractive as to be inedible." The maiden, on the other hand, reveals that she has become attracted to the dragon—"So nicely physical," not to mention "the way he looked at me, / He made me feel he was all ready to / Eat me"—and secretly spurns her unwanted rescuer, viewing him as whisking her toward a future that is beneficial less in a romantic or chivalric than in an economic sense.

Where the dragon and the maiden set a primarily comic tone in their monologues, St. George, brash and overbearing to the point of insecurity, offers the critical turn: Having run through a list of his knightly credentials ("diplomas in Dragon / Management and Virgin Reclamation," among others), he accuses the maiden of not yielding to "the roles / That sociology and myth have designed for you." Where the sexual tension depicted in the poem had previously lain in the maiden's desire for her captor (a form of the Stockholm syndrome), it becomes clear that its true locus is in her unwillingness to be ravished by historical precedent— that is, the act of myth making sustained over centuries. The dragon, whose notable "equipment" had previously caught the maiden's eye, has vanished from the poem, has lost the battle against the colonizing presence of St. George. Organized religious modernity has tamed the unkempt, immoral wilderness. Indeed the last words of this once-rescuer, now-ravager cast an unsettling shadow over the stories that are told and retold, but told inevitably by the winners: "What, in any case, does it matter what / You want? You're in my way."

BIBLIOGRAPHY
Heffernan, James A. W. *Museum of Words: The Poetics of Ekphrasis from Homer to Ashbery.* Chicago: University of Chicago Press, 1993.

Benjamin Morris

"NOT PALACES, AN ERA'S CROWN" STEPHEN SPENDER (1933)

Written in the early 1930s and published in 1933, this strongly rhetorical poem suggests an alternative to the romantic imagery of the conservative Georgian poets, and the dead-end pessimism of THE GREAT WAR AND POETRY. STEPHEN SPENDER, then in his early twenties, favored as symbols the man-made machinery of the modern world. Influenced by his contemporaries W. H. AUDEN and Christopher Isherwood, Spender was committed to a vision in which all people were comrades working side by side for an egalitarian society. As did many young writers of the 1930s he saw socialism as an antidote to both the devastation of war and the looming specter of fascism that would spark another conflagration by the end of that decade.

For his part, the speaker of this poem is not interested in erecting monuments or preserving treasures of antique regimes, family legacies, or crumbling empires. Modern times require that youth "drink from here energy and only energy . . . / To will this Time's change." Further the mere stimulation and pleasures of the senses must be discarded, as must spiritual "dreams . . . of heaven after our world." The alternative is to focus on "flashing brass" and "the polished will / Flag of our purpose." The ensuing revolution will eliminate hunger ("Man shall spend equally") with the ultimate goal that "man shall be man." But militarism is not the answer; war is depicted as a "programme of the antique Satan," and while the speaker's "programme" is just as strenuous, its purpose is "opposite, / Death to the killers, bringing light to life."

Rhetorically, the poem works by negation, listing and then eliminating each approach that does not work. The fluid lines tend toward blank verse, in a generally iambic rhythm that varies between tetrameter and pentameter. Some of the strongest assertions are made in the lines closest to iambic pentameter, most notably "Our goal which we compel: Man shall be man."

As Shelley did, Spender believed that poets should transform external circumstance into symbolic language through their personal emotions and sensory associations. Critics, in fact, have noted a conflict apparent in Spender's poems of this period between the lyric impulse (emotional intensity and sensual pleasures) and the will to perform a duty, usually political. "Not Palaces" is often criticized as clumsy in its meshing of lyrical language and sensory imagery with political necessity. The sense and the sensibility, Spender's critics assert, are not effectively integrated, and thus the poem fails to accomplish the poet's goal of transforming external circumstances into internal truth.

What is clear, however, is the poet's passion for his convictions. In this early poem Spender powerfully asserts his position that the new generation should direct their energy toward eliminating the decadent remnants of empire, the class system, and militaristic fascism alike. The poet exhorts his comrades neither to live in the past, nor to wait for some purported heavenly afterlife, but rather to act in the moment, exercise the will, join forces, and move together toward the goal of equality.

BIBLIOGRAPHY

Spender, Stephen. *Collected Poems: 1928–1985*. Oxford: Oxford University Press, 1987.
Weatherhead, A. Kingsley. *Stephen Spender and the Thirties*. Lewisburg, Pa.: Bucknell University Press, 1975.

Amy Lemmon

"NOT WAVING BUT DROWNING" STEVIE SMITH (1957)

The story echoes the old myth of "the boy who cried wolf." As he was, the chap in STEVIE SMITH's poem was known for his larks so that when he really was in trouble, his furious gestures for help were assumed to be mere tomfoolery. What the onlookers did not realize was that such foolery had always been a cry for help. The onlookers (who include poet and reader) and the dying man are all implicated in the states of both watching and being "too far out." Where we position ourselves determines our sense of being either part of the crowd—"they said"—or the drowning outsider—"oh no no no!" The assonance of the long *o* here and in the repeated words *nobody, cold,* and *moaning* provides the main dramatic props that work on the auditory imagination to produce the mood of unspeakable despair. The casually confessional *poor chap* and *I say* along with the switch to first- and second-person pronouns appeal to an audience, so that interpretation becomes a shared activity between writer and reader. The shift from third to first person finally synthesizes the poet and the subject. Smith confessed to the personal origin of the piece: "I felt too low for words (eh??) last weekend but worked it all off in a poem . . . called 'Not Waving but Drowning'" (Letter to Kay Dick, April 25, 1953). The figurative and elliptical (*eh??*) evokes unsayable feelings that connect with the poem's 10th line, "(Still the dead one lay moaning)"; being in parenthesis, it denotes the poem's emotional center, which is beyond words. As in line 2, *Still* means unmoving, almost at peace, but also the continuous present tense of being both dead and conscious. In other words, this is the pain of being still alive and yet suffering.

The quest both to extend and to lose consciousness dominates Smith's work and a phase of acute depression culminated in a suicide attempt on July 1, 1953. Smith's writing presses upon the borders of definable poetics. Her comment "There is no very great distinction between what is poetry and what is prose" ("A Turn Outside," BBC Radio Play, May 23, 1929) indicates her irreverence for the strict literary delineations on which the fundamental origins and assumptions of genre rely. As here, the conversational idioms deflate high literary diction and the prosy lines force us to question what makes a poem. Rescuing emotion from the bin of denigrated "sentimentality" is one of Smith's major achievements: "Then also as a writer she must fail / Since art without compassion don't avail?" she stated in "Full Well I Know." Her attention to undisclosed emotional undertow is also a recurring ensign of women's poems; interestingly, the sketch that accompanies "Not Waving but Drowning" in *Collected Poems* is of a woman.

BIBLIOGRAPHY

Dick, Kay. *Ivy and Stevie.* London: Allison and Busby, 1983.

Larkin, Philip. "Stevie Goodbye." *Observer,* 23 January 1972, 28.

Lee, Hermione, ed. *Stevie Smith: A Selection.* London: Faber and Faber, 1983.

Spalding, Frances. *Stevie Smith: A Critical Biography.* London: Faber and Faber, 1988.

Jane Dowson

"NOVEMBER" Simon Armitage (1989) This poem is taken from Simon Armitage's first collection, *Zoom!* (1989), and was reprinted in his *Selected Poems* (2001). The speaker describes accompanying his friend John, who is taking his grandmother to an old people's home. In six short stanzas, Armitage records the conflicting feelings of regret, relief, and guilt felt by the pair, who have "brought her here to die." The continued use of the pronoun *we* emphasizes their complicity. The journey also provokes a more general recognition of mortality, the speaker describing the senile and frail residents of the home only to remind us that "we are almost these monsters." Old age here becomes a deforming process, making people we love into gothic parodies of themselves.

There is a typically Armitage use of colloquial language, conversational phrases like *you're shattered* used here with a renewed emphasis. The occasional use of half-rhymes—*blankets/trinkets begin/again*—emphasizes the poem's uneasy passage forward, as John and the poem's narrator return home to drink to "numb ourselves." Armitage's description of faltering communication between the pair (the speaker's sex remains a mystery throughout the poem) evokes poems by Philip Larkin, as do statements such as *we can say nothing.* The speaker's repetition of the name *John* in the poem often unsteadies the meter and carries an increasingly biblical tone, not least in the ambiguous final assertion about the "one thing we have to get, John, out of this life." The final sentence seems to point a tentative way forward for the couple in their grief, but the syntax also suggests suicide as an unspoken possibility.

The poem could be read as an indictment of modern society's treatment of the elderly, but Armitage's tone emphasizes the personal rather than the political; he fights shy of describing the old people's home itself or critiquing the institutional and social structures that have brought about the predicament in the poem.

William May

O

"OCTOBER" Gillian Clarke **(1985)** Although death is an unwelcome visitor at any point in a person's life, his visits become more frequent as adults move into their older years, the autumn of their lives. In this poem, Gillian Clarke mines the theme "Life is short and death comes to all" with a reflection on the passing of her close friend Frances Horovitz.

The season is autumn and the poem begins in a garden, setting up the natural images that will appear throughout the poem. It is a rainy day, as is suitable for the passing of a loved one. Nature should weep to mourn the loss of a splendid life one holds dear. As the year winds down to its winter dormancy, signs of decay proliferate: One of the poplars sports a "dead arm"; the leaves of the tree "tremble," as palsied hands, changing from green to gold; the lobelia is tangled and overgrown, "more brown than blue." Clarke chooses images that, although they represent the vegetable decay of autumn, are not ugly. There is a beauty about the wet dreadlocked lion and the leaves of gold. The hydrangea is fading but is still green, and there are still flowers available for the grave.

"October" opens with a stanza that does not mention death, but the scene is set beautifully with natural images of a garden in autumn that are echoed in the second stanza as the funeral is described. The stone lion, shoulders darkened with rain, appears again, transformed into stony faces, the rain mingled with tears. The lobelias, brown and trailing the statue as "dreadlocks," appear again in stanza 2 as the "slow / fall of flowers" that rain on to the casket lowered into the ground. Orcop, where the funeral takes place, is a village in Heresfordshire, England, near the border of Wales on the river Monnow, a tributary of the Wye. The poem, then, is not an abstract musing on the passing of time and the inevitability of death. It is, instead, a reflection of a particular event—the lobelias, the lion, the weight of the coffin "lighter / than hare bones," the hawthorn hedge, are images from a real setting, a real event. The event, based on the death of a friend her own age, in turn evokes a reflection of the speaker's mortality. She could be the one in the box being carried on men's shoulders.

The poem's three stanzas are located in a natural setting. Even the final stanza in which the poet is reflecting on the death of her friend and her own eventual passing takes place in the natural world. The images that race past are that of leaves showing their silvery bottoms in the wind before a storm, the eye of a robin, laurels, and hydrangeas. The images are particular throughout and create a place that the speaker has before her eyes as she writes.

Later, perhaps after the funeral, the speaker is writing, but the action is centered in the pen, as the subject herself is not reintroduced until the final two lines. The pen "runs faster than the wind[ ]" and is compared to an animal in a panic running for its life from a predator. As the pen speeds over the paper, there is no permanence to the act: As when wind passes over grass, no mark is left of its passing. The poet, at whose volition the pen moves, writes to stave off mortality but fears she will leave as little mark as the wind. But it is the act of writing that keeps her alive. Even though she feels guilty for being the one left alive when her friend is gone ("health feels like pain"), the speaker must keep writing, keep "winning ground" in the race against death.

"October" has been compared to SEAMUS HEANEY's "DIGGING." The speaker in Heaney's poem has to write, just as his father has to dig—it is part of who the men are. With his pen, he digs words, carving a meaning from his life. In similar fashion, the speaker of "October" is writing to keep ahead of death—by writing, she lives to tell more tales.

BIBLIOGRAPHY

Adams, Sam. "Weaving a Cymric Web? A Perspective on Contemporary Anglo-Welsh Poetry." In *Comparative Criticism*. Vol. 19, *Literary Devolution: Writing in Scotland, Ireland, Wales and England,* 117–133. Cambridge: Cambridge University Press, 1998.

Clarke, Gillian. "The King of Britain's Daughter." In *How Poets Work.* Edited by Tony Curtis, 122–136. Bridgend, Eng.: Seren, 1996.

Smith, K. E. "The Poetry of Gillian Glarke." In *Poetry in the British Isles: Non-Metropolitan Perspectives,* edited by Hans-Werner Ludwig and Lothar Fietz, 267–280. Cardiff: University of Wales Press, 1995.

Thurston, Michael. "'Writing at the Edge': Gillian Clarke's Cofiant." *Contemporary Literature* 44, no. 2 (summer 2003): 275–300.

Patricia Bostian

OMEROS DEREK WALCOTT (1990) DEREK WAL-

COTT's 325-page poem *Omeros,* published by Farrar, Straus & Giroux in 1990, cemented his reputation not only as the premier Caribbean poet, but also as the "very man by whom the English language lives," according to his friend and fellow Nobel Prize–winning poet Joseph Brodsky (qtd. by Bruckner). Its publication and subsequent widespread appeal are widely accepted as the catalyst for Walcott's own Nobel Prize in literature in 1992.

Titled with the Greek word for Homer and divided into seven books of multiple chapters each, with the first and final two books set in St. Lucia and the middle three in Africa, the United States, and Europe, the poem certainly appears to follow traditional epic design. The characters with whom Walcott populates this narrative poem further suggest a deliberate relationship between this poem and *The Iliad* and *The Odyssey.* One of several narrative threads woven throughout the epic is a love triangle carried out by Hector, Achille (pronounced Ah-sheel), and Helen, all St. Lucians engaged in local pursuits. Helen is serially a maid for the retired British major Plunkett and his Irish wife, Maud, and a waitress at local tourist-attracting restaurants, while Hector and Achille are fishermen until a spat between them over Helen inspires Hector to trade his boat for a transport van. Achille's dearest friend is the Homerically named Philoctete, replete with festering leg wound "from a scraping, rusted anchor" (10). Even the poetic influences Walcott identifies as sources for his prosody indicate the connection between *Omeros* and the paradigmatic epics of Western literature: He describes the poem's meter as "roughly hexametrical with a terza rima form. It's like a combination of a Homeric line and a Dante-esque design" (qtd. by Hamner 5).

Critics have taken to labeling *Omeros* as an epic, despite Walcott's own hesitancy in employing the term as a descriptor for it. Shortly after its publication, Walcott said of *Omeros,* "'I do not think of it as an epic. Certainly not in the sense of epic design. Where are the battles? There are a few, I suppose. But 'epic' makes people think of great wars and great warriors. That isn't the Homer I was thinking of. I was thinking of Homer the poet of the Seven Seas'" (qtd. by Bruckner). Walcott himself is much more likely to describe the poem as a love poem about and for his home island, St. Lucia, and in fact has called it "an act of gratitude" for that island and its inhabitants.

And immortalize the inhabitants and the island the poem certainly does. In his crucial assessment of the poem Robert Hamner has labeled it an "epic of the dispossessed," yet the poem's project as a whole appears to be (among other things) to record the quotidian lives of St. Lucia's inhabitants in such a way that readers can apprehend their epic nobility. They may be dispossessed, but the fact that they still exist testifies to their power. In book 3, Achille visits his African ancestors in a dream sequence and, while he witnesses a slave raid on his ancestral village, realizes that "they crossed, they survived. There is the epical splendour" (149). Rather than set out deliberately to ennoble his St. Lucian fellow citizens, Walcott seeks to present an accurate record of their lives. Near the close of the first book, the poet-narrator's father appears to him and advises him to immortalize local coal miners, who "like ants or angels, . . . see their native town / unknown, raw, insignificant. They walk, you write" (75). In fact, the poet-narrator, who frequently reveals significant biographical similarities to Walcott himself, considers it his duty "to give those feet a voice" (76) in the metrical feet of his poetry "because the couplet of those multiplying feet / made [his] first rhymes" (75).

Part and parcel of Walcott's celebration of St. Lucia are his admiration for and accurate record of the sea that surrounds it. For Walcott, in fact, the sea has inspired the echoes between Homer's Aegean epics and his own Caribbean island. He said in 1981 to Carol Fleming, "Here we are in the Caribbean, which is like the Aegean. . . . And we *are* a sea culture. . . . So it's very easy to make a literary thing" (10). The rhythms of Walcott's everyday life in St. Lucia, forged by the repetition of the cycles this sea, resonate with what he was taught to be Homer's world. Early in the poem the poet-narrator connects its title to his sea-culture: "*O* was the conch-shell's invocation, *mer* was / both mother and sea in our Antillean patois, / *os,* a grey bone, and the white surf as it crashes" (14). Late in the poem he writes, "When would the sails drop / from my eyes, when would I not hear the Trojan War / in two fishermen cursing in Ma Kilman's shop?" (271). And when the poet-narrator comments in retrospect on his achievement, he claims, "I sang our wide country, the Caribbean Sea" (320). The phrase *the Caribbean Sea* can act either as the second half of a compound direct object (the poet sang of the country and of the sea) or as an appositive: The wide country *is* the sea.

Omeros makes it very clear that the sea is primarily responsible for the Caribbean culture that Walcott has repeatedly described as new, raw, "not marinated in the past" (Muse 18). As both the vehicle by which most inhabitants of the Caribbean were transported from their ancestral homes and a metaphor for constant erasure and rewriting of history, the sea represents neither defeat nor victory for St. Lucians, but rather "drenche[s] every survivor / with blessing" (296). The sea represents both the pain and the promise of history in its constant renewal of the surf paired with its "never altered . . . meter" (296). The pain is that of dispossession and its attendant rupture in history as well as of the "strange, / ordinary things" that disappear when one loses "one's shore" (151). But its promise is the chance to write one's history anew, the chance to write that "epic where every line was erased / yet freshly written in sheets of exploding surf" (296).

The sea-based metaphor of coral furthers this suggestion that the sea is cause of both pain and cure. When the poet-narrator questions why he "waste[s] lines on Achille, a shade on the sea-floor" (296), in a reference to the multiple thousands who perished during the Middle Passage, he answers his own question: "Because strong as self-healing coral, a quiet culture / is branching from the white ribs of each ancestor" (296). Coral is a living, growing organism in which polyps affix themselves to the skeletons of now-dead polyps. Contemporary Caribbean culture is built atop the death and destruction through which the islands were populated with Achille's (and Walcott's) African ancestors.

The poem then reinforces this notion that the pain of wounds is mitigated by the creations of contemporary Caribbean culture and the prospect of a strong future with its return to two characters—Helen and Philoctete. When Helen, representing both Helen the character and Helen the island (Dennis Plunkett learns that the island is also named *Helen,* a reference to its colonial history and its repeated passing from British to French hands), is pregnant and unsure whether Hector or Achille fathered her as-yet-unborn child, she is "vexed with both of them" (124). Helen the woman and Helen the island reject those who vie to name and claim her future as theirs. Her child of necessity and by Helen's choice must begin to trace its history with her; the genealogy cannot be determined anywhere but in Helen—the woman and the island. She affirms what Walcott and the poem also affirm: that Caribbean history begins on the islands.

This particular dating of the onset of Caribbean history is emphasized in book 2, in which is recounted the Battle of the Saints, a naval skirmish between the French and the British in 1782. The battle is ostensibly incorporated into the poem as part of Dennis Plunkett's efforts to locate a history for Helen, "Not his, but her story. Not theirs, but Helen's war" (30). Ironically, however, Plunkett fails to connect this particular battle with Helen despite the fact that the British were victorious in it only because of the aid of their African slaves. But the poem marks this battle as the moment at which other nationalities fall away in favor of Caribbean ones. Achille's African ancestor Afolabe is present at this battle, where a "small [British] admiral . . . rename[s] Afolabe 'Achilles,' / which, to keep things simple, he let himself be called" (83). Readers know, however, in retrospect, that the final s is soon dropped, changing Achilles (Ah-kill-eez) to Achille (Ah-sheel), shading the Greek name with a patois lilt. The African and the Greek become Caribbean at the moment world powers clash over the fate of the islands. British, French, Greek, and African histories converge, and from the convergence emerges this new history and new citizen designated Caribbean.

This clash and then convergence of cultures on the island itself now offers the new Caribbean citizen, represented in Philocte, the cure for any residual wounds from the clash. Recall that Philocte sustained his leg injury from a rusted anchor, a gaping hole reminiscent of the "tree-hole, raw in the uprooted ground" (140) that Achille encounters in Africa. The hole represents the uprooted person and his inability ever to fill that particular space again, and such uprooted persons so fill the island that the poem describes it as a "self-healing island / whose every cove was a wound" (249). But a swift (a bird resembling a swallow) conveys a seed from Africa to the Caribbean in its mouth, dies, and from the seed a weed grows that, in turn, cures Philocte's wound. The cure succeeds only because of the growth the African seed undergoes on the island.

For Walcott the poet, among the maladies cured by the convergence of cultures in the Caribbean is no less than the problem of language. Often questioned for his apparent bifurcated devotion to the Caribbean as a place on the one hand and the language and literary traditions of Western Europe on the other, Walcott asserts in Omeros his right to all of the beauties of the English language, described in his earlier poem "A FAR CRY FROM AFRICA" as "the English tongue I love." Now paralleling himself with Philocte, the narrator claims, "Like Philocte's wound, this language carries its cure" (323). In Omeros Walcott lays his claim to any of the cultures that converge in the Caribbean—including the Western literary cultures represented in "all that Greek manure" (271)—as his "to make what [he] wanted of it" (272). And what Walcott makes of it in Omeros is nothing short of a stunning Caribbean poem of epic proportions.

BIBLIOGRAPHY

Bruckner, D. J. R. "The Poet Who Fused Folklore, Homer, and Hemingway." New York Times, 15 October 1990.
Fleming, Carol. "The Plays and Poems of Derek Walcott: Singing the True Caribbean." Americas 34 (1982): 8–11.
Hamner, Robert. Epic of the Dispossessed: Derek Walcott's Omeros. Colombia: University of Missouri Press, 1997.
Walcott, Derek. "The Muse of History." In Is Massa Day Dead? Black Moods in the Caribbean. Edited and introduction by Orde Coombs. New York: Anchor Books, 1974.

Michelle DeRose

"ONCE IN A LIFETIME, SNOW" LES MURRAY (1969)   LES MURRAY has been acclaimed as a poet of Australia's landscape, a poet who speaks the vernacular of that country. A significant aspect of his poetry of the landscape is the finding of the miraculous within it. The landscape is a place of memory, sometimes of cruelty, but often a place where the numinous is revealed.

"Once in a Lifetime, Snow" was first published in the 1969 collection The Weatherboard Cathedral, Murray's first solo endeavor. The title of the book is from Murray's conviction that the divine may be found in the everyday. This conviction may stem in part from Murray's conversion to Catholicism five years before the publication of the book, when he would have been composing and compiling the poems for it. As he said in a later interview, "I identified with the Eucharist. I thought, yes, the absolute transformation of ordinary elements into the divine. I know about that." "Once in a Lifetime, Snow" is characteristic of Murray's vision of the natural world as sacred, as a realm where heightened consciousness is possible. Such a moment of heightened consciousness is triggered in this poem by awakening to an unexpected snowfall; suddenly the land is transformed, and it is as though something miraculous has occurred.

The poem relies on the repetition of certain elements: light and brightness, seeing and perceiving, knowledge and mystery. Words relating to these elements are repeated throughout the text, beginning in the third stanza with the description of the cattle standing in the snow "in ghostly ground / and unaccustomed light / for miles around." Animal and human life are here joined in wonder.

The uncle, the central human figure in the poem, is transfixed and transformed by the sudden alteration of his reality. All that was known and certain has been changed: "A man of farm and fact / he stared to see / the facts of weather raised / to a mystery." The world of fact has been left behind, and mystery has been revealed. The rest of the poem is marked by a growing sense of wonder as the man experiences the world anew through his senses. His bodily experiences and sensations lead him to an ever-increasing feeling of joy at having himself reawakened: "He stooped to break the sheer / crust with delight / at finding the cold unknown / so deeply bright." The unknown is not something to be feared; nor is it something that was ever so distant. It was just below the surface of everyday life, visible in an instant, and transformative.

The body in the world and its connection to a deeper knowledge through perception and consciousness are key themes of the poem. The mind and the body join together, a process that is essential, in Murray's poetics, to the composition and appreciation of poetry. The uncle is awakened: "Perceiving this much, he scuffed / his slippered feet / and scooped a handful up / to taste, and eat." These lines are meant to echo the Eucharist, the taking in of the divine, the making sacred of the body in the world. Finally, the uncle's relationship to "fact" has been radically altered: "In memory of the fact / that even he / might not have seen the end / of reality. . . ." The ellipses indicate that while reality as the man might have known it might be different, a new reality is open to him. The line is fruitfully ambiguous. The uncle, a man of "fact," could never have anticipated the "end of reality," the end of his passive and stolid relationship to a gray and black world. At the same time, the line says he might not have seen the *end* of reality: A new reality is just beginning.

BIBLIOGRAPHY

Daniel, Missy. "Poetry Is Presence: An Interview with Les Murray." *Commonweal*, 22 May 1992, 9–12.

Leer, Martin. "'This Country Is My Mind': Les Murray's Poetics of Place." *Australian Literary Studies* 20 (2001): 15–42.

Matthews, Steven. *Les Murray*. New York: Manchester University Press, 2001.

Murray, Les. *The Rabbiter's Bounty: Collected Poems*. New York: Farrar, Straus & Giroux, 1991.

Janine Utell

ONDAATJE, MICHAEL (1943–)

Although a recent film adaptation of his novel *The English Patient* brought Michael Ondaatje a good deal of fame, it is his unique and ever-evolving style—in both poetry and prose—that garners critical recognition. Born in Sri Lanka in 1943 when it was still known as Ceylon, Michael Ondaatje eventually joined his divorced mother in England. Despite the brevity of his childhood in Ceylon, the history of his family and the country of his birth remain subjects that he returns to again and again in his writing; the autobiographical *Running in the Family* chronicles Ondaatje's investigation into his family's past, and the novel *Anil's Ghost* probes the history of war-torn Sri Lanka. Whereas his years in Sri Lanka had lasting effects on Ondaatje's writing, he does not credit the time spent in England with equal influence. Indeed Ondaatje remained in England only a few years before emigrating to Canada, where he eventually earned a B.A. at the University of Toronto. It proved a fortuitous move, one Ondaatje credits with his naissance as a poet. In Canada, Ondaatje says, he met and communicated with poets; such encounters would have been unlikely if he had remained in England. In Canada, Ondaatje first began to write poetry, and in 1967, his first volume, *The Dainty Monsters,* was published.

Much of Ondaatje's poetry is remarkable for its unusual and often violent imagery and metaphor, and his first collection is no exception. Surprising and often mythological animals dot the landscape of the first half of *The Dainty Monsters,* and the second half is peopled with equally bizarre conjunctions of people, animals, and things. Ondaatje's next published book, *The Man with Seven Toes* (1969), has a more obviously historical basis than the often legendary sources of *The Dainty Monsters,* but its emotions and language are equally unsettling and sometimes shocking. *The Man with Seven Toes,* constructed as a long narrative poem, recreates the experiences of the semihistorical figure Mrs. Eliza Fraser, shipwrecked on the Australian coast, exposed to Aborigines, and eventually returned to civilization by the convict she finally betrays.

As *The Man with Seven Toes* suggests, Ondaatje is not interested in historical veracity and does not depend upon the realities of a place or past in the construction of his works. Historical moments and figures may lend Ondaatje inspiration, but they are ultimately no more "real" than the mythological characters he appropriated in *The Dainty Monsters.* In *The Collected Works of Billy the Kid* (1970), Ondaatje—now firmly a Canadian poet—annexed an American character. *The Collected Works* continues Ondaatje's use of violent and bizarre imagery, and the book is also one of Ondaatje's most critically well-received works. The volume drew Ondaatje attention outside Canada, and it was soon published in the United States. The stage adaptations of *The Collected Works of Billy the Kid* perhaps heralded the eventual adaptation of his novel, *The English Patient,* to film.

Both *The Man with Seven Toes* and *The Collected Works of Billy the Kid* were long narrative poems, but Ondaatje had not abandoned short lyrics. In 1973, *Rat Jelly,* containing the celebrated "LETTERS & OTHER WORLDS" among other notable poems, was published. Shortly before the publication of *Rat Jelly,* in 1971, Ondaatje accepted a position at Glendon College, where he is currently a professor.

Coming through Slaughter (1976) marks a turning point for Ondaatje. As in *The Collected Works of Billy the Kid,* Ondaatje rewrites an ostensibly historical figure, the jazz musician Buddy Bolden, and both characters, Billy the Kid and Bolden, have been regarded to varying degrees as representative of the figure of the artist. But, unlike Ondaatje's earlier volumes, *Coming through Slaughter* is prose. Several collections of poetry follow, including *There's a Trick with a Knife I'm Learning to Do*

(1979), which won the Governor General's Award in 1980, and *Secular Love* (1984). In between these volumes, Ondaatje composed *Running in the Family* (1982), a memoir written after a visit to Ceylon.

In 1987, Ondaatje published another novel, *In the Skin of the Lion,* which was soon followed by the novels *The English Patient* (1992) and *Anil's Ghost* (2000). Additionally another well-received work of poetry, *The Cinnamon Peeler,* was published in 1997. Both *The English Patient* and *Anil's Ghost,* while ostensibly novels, retain much of the emphasis on language and imagery that characterize Ondaatje's poetry. Both works also deal with war as both subject and setting. As in the more violent of Ondaatje's poems, the violence and horror of both novels serve to underscore human adaptability.

Ondaatje remains an active member of the Canadian literary community. Having won numerous awards, including the Booker Prize, Michael Ondaatje is a modern-day literary chimera: a best-selling, popular author whose works can only be called literature. In addition to his own prolific and wide-ranging works of poetry and prose, Ondaatje has served as an editor of other works, including collections of Canadian writers. He and his second wife, the writer Linda Spalding, publish the literary magazine *Brick,* selections of which have been separately published in a collection of their own. Despite his acknowledged Canadian identity, Ondaatje retains roots in both of the continents in which he spent his childhood. He has family in Sri Lanka, England, Australia, and Canada, and his works continue to examine the realities of places and people in refreshing, surprising, and noteworthy ways. His versatile and innovative style marks him as one of the most significant modern writers—of *any* country.

BIBLIOGRAPHY

Pearce, Jon. "Moving to the Clear: Michael Ondaatje." In *Twelve Voices: Interviews with Canadian Poets,* 129–144. Ontario: Borealis Press, 1980.

Slopen, Beverly. Interview with Michael Ondaatje. *Publisher's Weekly* 239, no. 44 (1992): 48–49.

Solecki, Sam. *Ragas of Longing: The Poetry of Michael Ondaatje.* Ontario: University of Toronto Press, 2003.

———, ed. *Spider Blues: Essays on Michael Ondaatje.* Montreal: Véhicule Press, 1985.

Winter Elliott

"ON ITS OWN" ELIZABETH JENNINGS (1980)

Using a form familiar to her from her contemporaries in THE MOVEMENT, John Wain and THOM GUNN, ELIZABETH JENNINGS employs the Venus and Adonis stanza in "On Its Own." The Venus and Adonis stanza typically has a rhyme scheme of *abbacc*. The first two stanzas move along similar ideas and the third departs from the theme and provides closure.

The narrator of "On Its Own" dives right into her subject, needing no warm up or prelude. She is addressing a lover and telling him that if he leaves, she will experience the resulting pain again with a future lover, no doubt, yet it will not be quite the same pain. It will hurt in the same way, but at the same time differently because she, as a result of her love affair, is no longer the same person.

In both the first and second stanzas, we can see what kind of relationship it has been. Apparently stormy weather has been a frequent visitor. There have been fierce arguments "that reach the bone." There have been pain and loss. Yet the speaker says she will embrace love again, knowing its attendant messiness, its arguments and possible destructiveness. If she is sure that beyond the unhappiness lies joy, even if that joy is not quite like the happiness of past experiences, she will take it all, good and bad.

Love is a constant; "It is its own"; however, although it is always different, the play of love is the same. In the first lines of stanza 3, this metaphor of a dramatic production is evoked: "My world shall be dramatic then, / No repetitions, many acts." *Dramatic* here means a theater production. The other meaning of *dramatic,* that of excessive display of emotion, is evidently meant as well, as the stanza follows two others describing pain, arguments, and destruction, all the accompanying drama of a love affair. The same curtain rises when lovers meet, the first kiss, the desires aroused. Each act follows the script, yet the actors improvise and the play subtly leaves the script behind and becomes itself, a new production based on an old theme.

The theme of love as drama shifts again to the more violent, warlike one established in the beginning of the second stanza where the heart is laid waste and love is a destructive force. Jennings introduces two lines that reinforce the metaphor of love as war in "A few hard treaties, broken tracts, / And peace made stronger yet by pain." Although the narrator does not choose to have war spread like a battle before her, if that battle threatens her hard-won peace again, it will be "accepted but not chosen." When love comes again, she will use the knowledge she has gained "and never wish[ed] unknown."

A motif frequently found in Jennings's poetry at this point of her career is that of binaries. In another poem from *Moments of Grace,* "I Count the Moments," poetry replaces love, and it is "pain as well as passion." Another poem from *Celebrations and Elegies* (1982), "The One Drawback," presents poetry as both dark and light. For the narrator of "On Its Own," love is both the same and different. For all the pain that it can cause, she will not shrink from it but will embrace it with the knowledge that pleasure comes with pain.

BIBLIOGRAPHY

Bradley, Jerry. "Elizabeth Jennings." In *The Movement: British Poets of the 1950s,* 87–100. New York: Twayne, 1993.

Gerlinde, Gramang. *Elizabeth Jennings: An Appraisal of Her Life As a Poet, Her Approach to Her Work, and a Selection of the Major Themes of Her Poetry.* Lewiston, N.Y.: Edwin Mellen Press, 1995.

Schmidt, Michael. *Lives of the Poets.* New York: Knopf, 1998.

Patricia Bostian

"ON PASSING THE NEW MENIN GATE" SIEGFRIED SASSOON (1928)

Located in Ypres, Belgium, the Menin Gate lists the names of nearly 55,000 "missing" soldiers on the walls of a massive limestone monument. The bodies of those soldiers, who died during the ferocious action about the Ypres Salient throughout the First World War, had never been recovered and the gate was to serve as a tribute those men. At its dedication, Field Marshal Herbert Charles Onslow Plumer remarked that the memorialized soldiers "are not missing; they are here." This kind of language, which lies through euphemism and insults everybody who knows what reality the soft words seek to obscure, ran counter to the blunt honesty SIEGFRIED SASSOON, in attendance at the dedication, had developed to defend against the indecency of modern war. As the poem makes plain, he was especially grieved by the callous notion that "these intolerably nameless names," inscribed in such abundance, would prove adequate to the task of memorial. (He would, one suspects, have been equally appalled by the Vietnam Memorial Wall.)

He began composing his enraged reaction to Plumer's remarks and to the inadequacy of that memorial almost immediately. In the years following the Great War, the soldier-poet turned veteran-poet continued believing, as he had during the war, that the world divided into two camps: those who had witnessed war and therefore earned the right to speak about it and those who had kept to the rear, ensuring their own safety while losing the right the speak. "On Passing the New Menin Gate" is not the only postwar poem in which Sassoon condemns attempts to memorialize the cataclysms of the Great War; "Memorial Tablet" and "At the Cenotaph" do so as well. But the Menin Gate sonnet differs in that it ends with an image that recalls such war verse as Sassoon's "Fight to a Finish" and "Blighters," works in which soldiers turn on the crowds back home to give civilians a taste of what war is really like. Rather than enduring the eternal anonymity of the Menin Gate inscription, the 55,000 in Sassoon's concluding couplet "rise and deride this sepulchre of crime"—an image hinting at a violent settling of affairs that would, if nothing else, certainly teach old field marshals to take care with their words. Thus, "On Passing the New Menin Gate" extends Sassoon's policy of radical honesty past war's end, insisting that the lessons those 55,000 paid for not be forgotten by the war's survivors.

BIBLIOGRAPHY

Caesar, Adrian. *Taking It like a Man: Suffering, Sexuality and the War Poets: Brooke, Sassoon, Owen, Graves.* New York: Manchester University Press, 1993.

Campbell, Patrick. *Siegfried Sassoon: A Study of the War Poetry.* Jefferson, N.C.: McFarland, 1999.

Moeyes, Paul. *Siegfried Sassoon: Scorched Glory: A Critical Study.* New York: St. Martin's Press, 1997.

Thorpe, Michael. *Siegfried Sassoon: A Critical Study.* Oxford: Oxford University Press, 1966.

Jimmy Dean Smith

"ON THE MARCH" RICHARD ALDINGTON (1919)

Based on RICHARD ALDINGTON's experience with the British army in World War I, "On the March," published in the volume *Images of War,* is important because it reflects the poet's development and a number of the his key concerns. First, in it Aldington demonstrates a certain loyalty to the principles of IMAGISM that he expounded in the June 1914 issue of the *Egoist,* notably "freedom in the choice of subject," the poetic aim to "render particulars exactly and not deal in vague generalities," and free verse, which Aldington considered "a principle of [poetic] liberty." The sensual/sexual images of the speaker "run[ning] naked" and the simile comparing the beauty of berries to "the points of a young girl's breasts" (both shocking to readers raised on genteel verse) exemplify the first principle. Such descriptive phrases as "red mottled berries," "rent seas," and "heavy nailed boots" indicate the desire for particulars. The poem's varied meter and syllable lengths and the absence of rhyme indicate adherence to the principle of free verse.

Nevertheless when we juxtapose "On the March" and "Machine Guns," another poem from *Images of War,* we see the poet ranging beyond the tight compression of his imagist pieces. "Machine Guns" consists of the following lines:

> Gold flashes in the dark,
> And on the road
> Each side, behind, in front of us,
> Gold sparks
> Where the fierce bullets strike the stones.

In its precision and brevity, this poem could be mentioned in the same breath as EZRA POUND's "In a Station of the Metro." In contrast, "On the March" is less concerned with the presentation of a single coalescent image than with fusion of disparate images (berries, seas, olive gardens, and the mud of London, to name a few) into a coherent poem.

Thematically "On the March" demonstrates more maturity than some of the earlier works, which focused on the search for beauty in a world lacking it. The prevalence of philistines, Aldington feels, can no longer be of paramount importance in a world that has experienced what he once termed the "insanity" of the First World War; instead Aldington addresses his disgust with war and the utter helplessness of the soldier in a war zone. While such a poem as "Bombardment," with its speaker and his fellow soldiers "listening for the imminent crash / Which meant our death," directly illustrates these negative emotions, "On the March" is less obvious. In this poem, the dramatic situation is clearly a soldier in column observing his surroundings. The title and the final line—"Party—HALT!"—serve as a frame that establishes the inescapable presence of war; the remaining three stanzas show the speaker glorying in the beauty of "bright berries" in the morning sun and embarking on a flight of fancy that takes him into the grass, across the sea, and, ultimately, home to London. The poem thus shows the speaker's desire to find solace or "something of repose" as Aldington says in the proem to *Images of War*.

The poem can also be read fruitfully as Aldington's struggle to define himself when faced with competing impulses: the enforced identity of the hard-nosed soldier commanding troops and the gentle poet striving to create art in the midst of chaos. In this sense, the poetic self wishing to "throw away rifle and leather belt, / Straps, khaki and heavy nailed boots" is more than the ordinary war-weary soldier; it is the poet who finds the *role* of soldier to be antithetical to poetry. Thus the next line's call to "run naked across the dewy grass / Among the firm red berries" is the poetic self's desire for the freedom to write what he wants when he wants, and the wish to "sing of beauty and the women of Hellas" is the poetic longing to "sing" of anything but the war. Even the poem's musing on the landscape itself is an act meant to subvert the military and its insistence on blind obedience, which he once wrote was "vehemently and blasphemously instilled."

Last, the poem's sexuality and sensuality and its mention of "the women of Hellas" are revealing from an autobiographical perspective. While the mention of ancient Greece is a reminder of the poet's frequent use of classical Greek models and allusions, it is also a subtle homage to his wife, the poet (H. D.) HILDA DOOLITTLE and her Hellenistic tendencies. At the same time, Aldington and H. D. had a very open (if troubled) marriage, so the use of the plural *women* may mean that he not only is singing to his wife but also may be referring to Arabella Yorke, with whom he was having an affair, and possibly with Florence Fallas, with whom he had a similar relationship.

BIBLIOGRAPHY

Aldington, Richard. *Images of War.* London: Allen & Unwin, 1919.

———. *Life for Life's Sake: A Book of Reminiscences.* New York: Viking, 1941.

Zilboorg, Caroline. "'What Part Have I Now That You Have Come Together?': Richard Aldington on War, Gender, and Textual Representation." In *Gender and Warfare in the Twentieth Century: Textual Representation,* edited by Angela K. Smith, 12–32. Manchester, Eng.: Manchester University Press, 2004.

Richard Iadonisi

"OPEN ROSE" MEDBH MCGUCKIAN (1991) This poem provides an appropriation and subtle revision of the symbol of the rose, which has served to represent the Irish nation from the mid-19th century on, not least of all in the allegorical figure of Roisin Dudbh, which translates as "Black Rose" or "Dark Rosaleen." The rose, then, is a version of the female representation of Ireland so that the very title "Open Rose" implies a simultaneous revision of the image of woman and nation.

On one level, this poem focuses on the speaker's impending motherhood. This is suggested, for instance, by the moon's "long cycle / Still locked away," which alludes to the fact that a woman does not menstruate during her pregnancy. Moreover the speaker grows "into a state of unbornness," which indicates the child's impending birth, *unbornness* a circumscription for not yet born or not having given birth yet. Giving birth, then, is equated with opening up.

On a second level, the poem is about the female poet, as suggested by the various references to writing and speech. The speaker clutches the rain "like a *book*" to her body; she refers to writing *letters,* claims to "have grown inside *words,*" while the "open rose on all sides / Has *spoken* as far as it can" [my italics]. In the context of women's writing, the *moon* associated with the speaker's body suggests the female identity she aims to express in her writing. In the second stanza, "his head," which is "there when I work" and "signs my letters with a question-mark," is representative of the male writer's voice, whose overpowering and restrictive influence the woman writer needs to withstand. She thus resists his hands, which "reach for [her] like rationed air," letting him go to "become a woman, or even less, / An incompletely furnished house."

On one level, then, the "open rose" signifies the female poet's style as characterized by *openness,* that is, ambiguity, multiple meanings, and flux, by means of which one-dimensional static representations of both woman and nation can be subverted. Simultaneously the *state of unbornness* comes to denote the numberless options and possibilities of an as yet unborn Ireland. Assuming the voice of (Northern) Ireland herself speaking, MEDBH MCGUCKIAN promises renewal through the *birth* rather than the *death* of a child, thereby rejecting and revising the sacrificial Mother Ireland trope. Moreover the *state of unbornness* marks the speaker's subversion of women's one-dimensional representation in Irish literature. Rather than dissolving her own identity, the speaker celebrates the fact that neither her own nor her unborn child's identity is predictable, predetermined, or prescribed. Rather, it is like "an open rose on all sides / [speaking] as far as it can."

BIBLIOGRAPHY

Haberstroh, Patricia Boyle. *Women Creating Women: Contemporary Irish Women Poets.* Syracuse, N.Y.: Syracuse University Press, 1996.

Schrage-Früh, Michaela. *Emerging Identities: Myth, Nation and Gender in the Poetry of Eavan Boland, Nuala Ní Dhomhnaill and Medbh McGuckian.* Trier: WVT, 2004.

Wills, Clair. *Improprieties: Politics and Sexuality in Northern Irish Poetry.* Oxford: Oxford University Press, 1993.

Michaela Schrage-Früh

"OUR BOG IS DOOD" STEVIE SMITH (1950)

The title words simultaneously evoke the death of a dog and of God, but any attempt to fix a translation is unsatisfactory. As in many poems, the framework is a conversation, here between an adult and a group of children. Harnessing the antipoetic patterns of Edward Lear's nonsense verse with Gertrude Stein's exaggerated repetitions and obscure signifiers, some lines suggest an unfathomable gulf between the language and experiences of grown-ups and children; they also point to the shared human sense that language fails to communicate the hidden desires between one person and another. We are made to sympathize with the children's wish to avoid the socialization that language will produce, while recognizing that without it, they will degenerate to the savagery of animals. Although they "lisped in accents mild," they are capable of wild "pride and misery," which will inevitably destroy them. Their insistence that their words can mean what they like produces havoc among themselves: "For what was dood, and what their Bog / They never could agree" can mean the irreconcilable alienation of human consciousness; at the same time, the terminology of *crucified* and *raised* summons the fate of Christ whereby the death of God is attributable to warring religious factions. In the final verse, the psychological condition of the narrator becomes the main subject of the poem, and her divided state of mind is a familiar one in STEVIE SMITH's oeuvre. She protests the "sweetness" of walking alone beside the sea while attesting that the sea will drown "them all" but not her. We suspect that she wishes for loss of consciousness, which drowning usually means in Smith's poetry. This longed for oblivion is the result of her inability to resolve the internal tensions or to answer the questions about the disparity between the best and the worst of human behavior and experience.

Like *yippity yap* or *pad pad,* which she uses elsewhere, the phrase *bog is dood* exemplifies how Smith pushes at the boundary between linguistic and nonverbal expression; through her drawings, her references to paintings, her musicality, and her aural renditions of actions or moods, these nonverbal resonances also blur the line between adults and children or people and animals. Where to draw such lines can be construed as the central question of this and other pieces.

BIBLIOGRAPHY

Heaney, Seamus. "A Memorable Voice." In *Preoccupations: Selected Prose 1968–1978,* 199–201. London: Faber and Faber, 1980.

Pumphrey, Martin. "Play, Fantasy and Strange Laughter: Stevie Smith's Uncomfortable Poetry." *Critical Quarterly* 28, no. 3 (autumn 1986): 85–96.

Severin, Laura. *Stevie Smith's Resistant Antics.* Madison: University of Wisconsin Press, 1997.

Smith, Stevie. *Stevie Smith: Collected Poems.* London: Allen Lane, 1975.

Jane Dowson

"OUTSIDE HISTORY" EAVAN BOLAND (1990)

"Outside History" is a poem by EAVAN BOLAND focusing on those marginal voices that are occluded from Irish national accounts. Among Boland's main objectives in her poetry are to attack narrow versions of history and retell those historical events that have previously obliterated women's lives and experiences, in order to include them. That is why women's involvement in historical events such as emigration and the Great Famine becomes almost an obsession in her work. Distant from a past that, she feels, directly affects her as an Irish woman poet, Boland constantly finds the need to recover a subaltern, marginal, and oppressed reality, obliterated from official national and historical narratives. This emphasis is made explicit in "Outside History," a poem in which the image of the Great Famine is treated as a paradigm for women's history. As is recurrent in her poetry, Boland uses the constellations in order to record an Irish past that, although visible to the speaker, remains largely unnoticed by historians: "There are outsiders, always. These stars." The stars that the speaker sees in the night constellations are remote and distant from her own reality. They not only suggest the separation between present and past, but are also the starting point from which the poet can reflect on her own mortality. Time and space separate the speaker from these stars, whose light was radiated "thousands of years before" and that are located at a great distance for her. But even if her mortal condition separates Boland from mythological and starry figures such as Cassiopeia, her humanity allows her to establish a connection with the famine victims of the Irish past who, as she is, were subject to death. The speaker becomes "part of that ordeal," sharing the "darkness" of fields, rivers, and roads full of corpses as numerous as those stars in the sky. Although at first she seems to establish an astonishing proximity with those Irish women who suffered the famine, this is immediately counteracted by the speaker's assertion in the last line of the poem that "we are always too late" to correct the injustices committed by constrained versions of history. In this sense, Boland ultimately describes herself as a defeated and powerless poet who is unable to retrieve Ireland's past. The poem's emphasis on the speaker's failure when attempting to go back is in itself a subversive strategy. Boland dismantles that nationalist rhetoric that encouraged the poet to act as a representative and communal figure, speaking of Ireland's oppression. In approaching the Irish past, Boland interrogates the terms of representation. The woman poet avoids acting as an appropriate spokesperson, as someone who is able to offer more "truthful" accounts of Ireland's past. She believes that such an act runs the risk of being misrepresentative, of undermining difference, and of simplifying a subaltern reality that is heterogeneous. In this sense, Boland shows the fallacy involved in believing in the authority and the "accurate" representation of official cultural and historical accounts (whether imperialist or nationalist). Her poetry teaches us that no one can truly speak on behalf of his/her own country, that one can never entirely be an "envoy" of his/her own community. As "Outside History" exemplifies, Boland favors the movement from an apparent ability to connect with the Irish past to an ultimate impossibility to do so. The very titles of poems such as "Distances" (1990) and "What We Lost" (1990), from the same volume of poetry, draw us into those gaps that Boland encounters between past and present, recovery and representation. While Boland attempts to become a suitable spokesperson for an oppressed community, she shows that she lacks the ultimate authority to grasp the past, to recover lost voices. It is not only that these lives have been lost, but also that Boland wishes to leave them as ungraspable. Rather than becoming a loquacious representative of the Irish past, she becomes a powerless speaker who shares the wordlessness of figures like those in Virgil's Underworld.

BIBLIOGRAPHY

Foster, Thomas C. "In from the Margin: Eavan Boland's 'Outside History' Sequence." In *Contemporary Irish Women Poets: Some Male Perspectives,* edited by Alexander G. González, 1–12. Westport, Conn., and London: Greenwood Press, 1999.

Huck, Christian. "Myth/ History and the Past in the Poetry of Eavan Boland." In *Critical Ireland: New Essays in Literature and Culture,* edited by Alan A. Gillis and Aaron Kelly, 102–108. Dublin: Four Courts, 2001.

Raschke, Debrah. "Eavan Boland's *Outside History* and *In a Time of Violence*: Rescuing Women, the Concrete, and Other Things Physical from the Dung Heap." *Colby Quarterly* 32, no. 2 (June 1996): 135–142.

Riley, Jeannette E. "Becoming an Agent of Change: Eavan Boland's *Outside History* and *In a Time of Violence.*" *Irish Studies Review* 20 (autumn 1997): 23–29.

Pilar Villar Argáiz

OWEN, WILFRED (1893–1918)

Despite his brief years as a poet, Wilfred Owen's reputation as a major figure emerged quickly after his death in the last week of the Great War (World War I) and has never faltered. Though he is known chiefly as a war poet, many critics have surmised that had he survived, he would have challenged EZRA POUND, W. B. YEATS, and T. S. ELIOT in impact on postwar poetry, and perhaps strengthened an "English" tradition against the rise of MODERNISM in those years. DYLAN THOMAS claimed there were only four great influences on poets in the generation after the war—Hopkins, Yeats, Eliot, and Owen. Owen is often compared to John Keats, one of his favorite poets, both for his major accomplishment in a short life and for the sweetness and lyricism with which he writes about less-than-sweet subjects, such as death and war.

Born Wilfred Edward Salter Owen on March 18, 1893, in Oswetry, Shropshire, the county made famous by A(LFRED) E(RNEST) HOUSMAN's *Shropshire Lad* poems, Owen was educated at Birkenhead Institute and Shrewsbury Technical School, where he showed a keen interest in poetry, especially that of Shelley and Keats. His family were evangelical Anglicans. When they could not afford to send him to London University, where he was accepted, though without a scholarship as his marks were not high enough, he worked as a lay assistant to the Reverend Herbert Wigan, an evangelical Anglican pastor at Dunsden, for two years before leaving for Bordeaux, France, to teach at the Berlitz School of English. He was teaching in France when the Great War broke out and later said that it was visiting a war hospital that caused him to return to England in 1915 to enlist: "I came out in order to help these boys—directly by leading them as well as an officer can; indirectly, by watching their sufferings that I may speak of them as well as a pleader can. I have done the first." Despite his own low estimation of himself as a "pleader," his poetry is the most eloquent testament to the suffering of ordinary soldiers that the war produced.

Owen became an officer in the Artist's Rifles in 1916, fought in the bloody Battle of the Somme, and in August 1917 was sent back to England, shell-shocked, for treatment at Craiglockhart War Hospital in Edinburgh. It was at Craiglockhart that Owen grew into the greatest of the British war poets. Here he met SIEGFRIED SASSOON and ROBERT GRAVES, who both aided in his development, largely through their encouragement and admiration for his work. As had his beloved Keats, Owen produced the majority of his great work in a single year. For Keats, the *annus mirabulis* was 1819; for Owen, August 1917 until August 1918, when he returned to the front. From Keats, Owen had learned the technique of slant rhyme, in which only the final consonants match, which he later developed into pararhyme and made his own. Pararhyme is consonantal rhyme, with only the vowels varying, as in "Arms and the Boy," which rhymes *blade* with *blood* and *flash* with *flesh*. The same poem employs slant rhyme with pairs such as *teeth* and *death* or *apple* and *supple*.

Sassoon disliked the first poems Owen showed him but recognized his gifts, praising the lyricism of "Song of Songs." He later characterized their differences: "My trench sketches were like rockets, sent up to illuminate the darkness. . . . It was Owen who revealed how, out of realistic horror and scorn, poetry might be made." Owen himself characterized his role as a poet differently, saying in a phrase now become famous, "The poetry is in the pity."

The next few weeks after their first meeting were a period of rich experimentation for Owen. Sassoon's courageous outspokenness seems to have liberated him to address more realistically the horrors he had experienced at the Somme (including being blown out of a trench). He seems to have first tried out pararhyme in a sustained way (in "Has Your Soul Sipped"); he also produced a poem in Sassoon's manner, "Inspection." In this poem, a fresh new lieutenant inspects his men and is offended by a spot on one soldier's uniform, for which the soldier gets "some days 'confined to camp.'" The soldier informs his lieutenant later that the spot was actually blood, "his own." This makes no difference to the lieutenant, who counters, "Well, blood is dirt," to which the soldier answers in a lyrical couplet that is pure Owen:

"The world is washing out its stains," he said.
"It doesn't like our cheeks so red."

The colloquialness of the language and the potentially bitter irony in the situation are pure Sassoon, but the Keatsian lyricism of the couplet is something of which Sassoon's "rockets" were seldom capable. The poem uses Owen's education in a more allusive way than Sassoon was wont to do, as simple parody. The washing out of stains recalls the guilt of Lady Macbeth and a hymn favored by his extremely religious mother, "Are You Washed in the Blood of the Lamb?" Housman's dying red-cheeked Shropshire lads also lie behind these lines.

Owen was soon combining a Sassoon-like realism with his Keatsian lyricism. "ANTHEM FOR DOOMED YOUTH," one of his most often anthologized poems (for which he said Sassoon provided the title) is an early example of Owen's new style. Its first line, "What passing bells for those who die as cattle?" is a response to a patriotic war anthology he had been reading whose preface claimed that the poetry within mingled "the bugle-call of Endeavour, and the passing-bells of Death." For Owen, there are no bells for those who die as cattle. Nothing mourns them, save "the choirs,— / The shrill, demented choirs of wailing shells." The words echo Keats's "To Autumn" ("in a wailful choir the small gnats mourn"), replacing a natural image of fall in England with the mechanical wail of shells bearing death as they fall in the trenches.

Owen drafted or revised several dozen more poems in the next few months, and on New Year's Eve of 1917 wrote in a letter home, "I go out this year a Poet, my dear Mother, as which I did not enter it. I am held peer by the Georgians [Graves and Sassoon]; I am a poet's poet." Only five poems were published during his lifetime (two in the *Hydra,* the hospital newsletter he edited; three in the *Nation*). Sassoon brought out the first edition of his work, consisting of 23 poems, in 1920 (adding a 24th a year later), and it was these two dozen poems alone that established his reputation in that decade, when he became a major influence on a par with Eliot, Yeats, and Hopkins (whose poetry had also been only recently revealed by ROBERT BRIDGES's edition of 1918).

See also "DISABLED," "DULCE ET DECORUM EST," "STRANGE MEETING."

BIBLIOGRAPHY
Hibbard, Dominic. *Wilfred Owen: A New Biography.* London: Weidenfeld & Nicolson, 2002.
Owen, Wilfred. *Poems of Wilfred Owen.* Edited by Jon Stallworthy. Oxford: Oxford University Press, 1985.
Perkins, David. *A History of Modern Poetry: From the 1890s to Pound, Eliot, and Yeats.* Cambridge, Mass.: Harvard University Press, 1976.
Schmidt, Michael. *Lives of the Poets.* New York: Knopf, 1999.
Stallworthy, Jon. *Wilfred Owen.* Oxford: Oxford University Press, 1974.

James Persoon

"THE OWL" EDWARD THOMAS (1915) Before EDWARD THOMAS began writing poetry prolifically in 1914, he had written nonfictional prose about natural, countryside locations. "The Owl" is set in a rural idyll, one not unlike Steep, Hampshire, in southern England, where Thomas wrote the poem on February 24, 1915. The drama of the poem centers on the vocal intervention of an owl, a wild bird that was then common in rural England. But "The Owl" is not a nature poem, but rather a potently symbolic one. The taut, four-stanza, 16-line poem constructs a moment of revelation, when a relatively privileged Briton realizes that the Great War is one that will impact everyone, not just the soldiers currently fighting abroad.

First published under Thomas's pseudonym, *Edward Eastaway,* in the 1917 volume *Poems,* "The Owl" begins with the first-person narrator happily concluding an agreeable county walk. He desires rest, shelter—a break from the travails of his country rambles. There is no real hardship. He is "not starved," just hungry. After finding an inn, the speaker gains his yearned-for rest, luxuriating in the inn's modest coziness. The monosyllables of "food, fire, and rest" convey the simplicity of the accessible pleasures the speaker enjoys. An owl is heard crying. The sound occurs abruptly, but the effects of the bird's aural intervention are long-lived—the cry is first heard in stanza 2, but enjambment takes us into stanza 3, where the speaker outlines his reaction.

The cry is a portentous, joyless one. The repeated use of negatives underlines the speaker's realization that the owl has delivered a baleful intrusion. The owl offers "No merry note, nor cause of merriment." The owl is an often-used trope in poetry; ancient and modern poets have used this nocturnal hunter as a symbol of death and ominousness. The speaker's complacency within the pleasant, restful inn is shattered by the bird. Now "salted and sobered," the speaker is forced to think about the death and vicious nighttime violence that the owl is synonymous with; he is forced to engage mentally with the realities facing his many countrymen who are fighting in France. A slightly altered version of the poem was retitled as "Those Others." At the beginning of this poem, the rambling, leisure-enjoying man has been oblivious to the plight of "Those Others." At the end of "The Owl," the psychological afflictions—although not, as yet, the material hardships—suffered by the unfortunate military men afflict the now-melancholy speaker too. He too will have to go to war. Biographers and other critics have seized on the prescient poignancy of "The Owl." Thomas himself would soon join the ranks of the fighting Allies and would be killed on April 9, 1917.

BIBLIOGRAPHY

Cooke, William. *Edward Thomas: A Critical Biography, 1878–1917.* London: Faber and Faber, 1970.

Ferber, Michael. *A Dictionary of Literary Symbols.* Cambridge: Cambridge University Press, 1999, 146–147.

Kirkham, Michael. *The Imagination of Edward Thomas.* Cambridge: Cambridge University Press, 1986.

Longley, Edna. "(Philip) Edward Thomas." In *Oxford Dictionary of National Biography,* edited by H. C. G. Matthew and Brian Harrison, Vol. 54, 312–314. Oxford: Oxford University Press, 2004.

Thomas, Edward. *The Collected Poems of Edward Thomas.* Edited by R. George Thomas. Oxford: Clarendon Press, 1978.

Kevin DeOrnellas

"THE OXEN" THOMAS HARDY (1915) First published in the London *Times* on December 24, 1915, and collected in *Moments of Vision* (1917), "The Oxen" recalls the Dorset folk legend that at midnight each Christmas Eve oxen will kneel in their stables, recreating their role in the Nativity scene. THOMAS HARDY previously had used this legend in *Tess of the d'urbervilles* when Dairyman Crick recalls how William Dewey played the Nativity Hymn on his fiddle in order to fool a charging bull into believing it was Christmas Eve and kneeling long enough for William to escape. After hearing the story, Angel Clare remarks, "It's a curious story; it carries us back to mediaeval times when faith was a living thing!" As did Angel, Hardy remained emotionally attracted to many of the religious beliefs and traditions he had rejected intellectually. Similarly the poem's speaker still nostalgically hopes against his own present disbelief that the legend of the kneeling oxen somehow might prove to be true.

The first two stanzas of this four-stanza poem evoke a Christmas Eve when the speaker was a child, part of a "flock" sitting "in hearthside ease" with other children, readily prompted by an "elder" to imagine the oxen "all on their knees." In contrast, the last two stanzas open with the disbelief the now-adult speaker shares with the times about the fanciful legend, and by extension all past beliefs beyond the proof of reason and evidence: "So fair a fancy few would weave / In these years." Implicitly the brutal reality of World War I, along with challenges to traditional religion since Hardy's childhood such as Darwin's *The Origin of the Species,* informs the skepticism of "these years."

The tension between feeling and thought, belief and doubt, the past and the present, and the idealism of childhood and the skepticism of adulthood, intensifies the poignancy of each line in this poem. The opening pastoral scene of the speaker's unquestioning childhood faith in the legend of the oxen already subtly anticipates the skepticism made explicit in the second half of the poem: The *embers* in the hearth evoke the transience of a dying fire, an image for the burning out of the speaker's childhood faith; the children's being described as a *flock* suggests their docile obedience as well as their Christian innocence, and the idea of doubt is directly raised through the statement of its absence: "Nor did it occur to one of us there / To doubt they were kneeling there."

In the second half of the poem, the initial statement of the speaker's present intellectual consideration of the legend as mere "fancy" is followed by his wish he could still believe it to be true: If "someone" were to ask him to return on Christmas Eve to his childhood, he "feel[s]" that he "should go with him in the gloom, / Hoping it might be so." The invitation to return and the speaker's acceptance of that invitation are so conditional as to be even more fanciful than the fancy of the legend. Moreover the rural Dorset dialect and images of isolation and distance in the hypothetical invitation to return to "the lonely barton by yonder comb" (a barton is a barnyard, and a comb a valley) remove the childhood locale from the urban and turbulent "these years" of London during World War I. And finally, even if the return were made, that the journey would take place "in the gloom" offers little hope for its success. Still, the "hoping it might be so" is all the more affecting in the speaker's knowing that it cannot.

BIBLIOGRAPHY

Bailey, J. O. *The Poetry of Thomas Hardy: A Handbook and Commentary.* Chapel Hill: University of North Carolina Press, 1970.

Robert R. Watson

P

"PASS FI WHITE" Louise Bennett (1949)

This poem, one of Louise Bennett's earlier works, exemplifies her use of humor in navigating the postcolonial difficulties of establishing pride in a national Jamaican heritage. As this poem deftly shows, following the Second World War, Jamaica no longer had only the British influence to contend with, but the rising dominance of the United States in international culture. The poem opens with "Miss Jane jus hear from Merica" and goes on to contrast the reactions of Jane and her husband to their daughter's news that "she fail her exam, but / She passin dere fi white!"

An unnamed narrator, speaking in a female voice in the native island dialect, details the contents of Jane's daughter's letter. Having traveled to the States to pursue an education, the daughter confesses that "her brain part not so bright— / She couldn pass tru college." But rather than return home she has decided to remain in America, where her light skin has afforded her social opportunities that Jamaica did not: "She passin wid her work-mate-dem, / She passin wid her boss," not to mention the "nice white bwoy she love" who is oblivious to her actual background. This news alarms Jane, whose frustration with her daughter's decision to throw away this educational opportunity composes the midportion of the poem. Moreover she is also disappointed at her daughter's negation of her true heritage: "Her fambily is nayga, but / Dem pedigree is right." In Jane's mind, passing is simply taking the easy way out, rather than taking the challenging, but rewarding path offered by bettering oneself through college.

For Jane's husband, however, his daughter's ability to pass offers validation of a different kind: "Five year back dem Jim-Crow him, now / Dem pass his pickney white." Rather than considering it a source of embarrassment, he takes great pride in his daughter's ability to turn the social rules that had ostracized him on their head. However his widespread "boasting" about his daughter's being "smarter dan American" and "passing" has the potential to be taken more than one way, a double meaning around which Bennett's poem revolves. Her narrator concludes by wryly observing that those who misunderstand his words, taking *passing* as a term of educational rather than social assessment, will be sorely let down when they find out the truth: "Wait till dem fine out seh she ongle / Pass de colour bar." Bennett's implication is, of course, that Jamaicans should be embarrassed by such a lack of character, and that in order for her countrymen and countrywomen to develop a unified postcolonial state, they must embrace the potential offered by learning, not continue to play the race games established by their white colonizers.

BIBLIOGRAPHY

Ramazani, Jahan. *The Hybrid Muse: Postcolonial Poetry in English.* Chicago: University of Chicago Press, 2001.

Smith, Angela. "Long Memoried Women: Oodgeroo Noonuccal and Jamaican Poet, Louise Bennett." *Australian Literary Studies* 16, no. 4 (1994): 77–91.

Wheeler, Elizabeth. "Riddym Ravings: Female and National Identity in Jamaican Creole Poetry." In *Imagination, Emblems, and Expressions: Essays on Latin American, Caribbean, and Continental Culture and Identity,* edited by Helen Ryan-Ransom, 139–154. Bowling Green, Ohio: Bowling Green State University Popular Press, 1993.

Caroline Kimberly

"THE PASSING OF ALFRED" U. A. FAN-THORPE (1982)

As ever, in "The Passing of Alfred," originally published in her 1982 volume *Standing To,* U. A. FANTHORPE's sly ironic tone results in a mockery of what she envisions as the politics of dying. Occasioning her poem is Alfred, Lord Tennyson, the major Victorian poet whose death subscribes, if we are to take Queen Victoria's comment in the epigraph at face value, to the values and mores of how a proper passing should take place. This titular word *passing* should not be passed by lightly, however, as it suggests less an end from death than a transition: in this case, the transition from history into myth.

Clues that myth is Fanthorpe's true concern arise in a number of places: the preceding sequence of poems in the volume (titled "Stations Underground," a reversal of those characteristically British symbols of transit, London Underground Stations) that take such mythical figures as Charon, Cerberus, Anubis, and Sisyphus as their subjects, as well as her closing stanza, in which she invokes the myth of Orpheus and Eurydice. But to understand this appropriation requires an excavation of the irony she has built up in the preceding lines. The best place to start is the first line, "Our fathers were good at dying," which from the outset of the poem suggests that death is, first and foremost, a *performance*: an act that involves actors, spectators, and a stage. Carefully Fanthorpe enumerates each of these elements, peppering her lines with modifiers such as *earnest, properly, responsible,* and *methodical,* all of which quietly mock the agents who embody them.

The sharpest of these modifiers are undoubtedly those in the fourth stanza, "resigned, / Orderly, chaste, aesthetic"; they stand in stark contrast to the graphic language by which she describes the more lived—that is to say, unscripted—deaths in the lines immediately preceding. To what extent is there a spectrum, Fanthorpe asks, by which we can rate or merit the way in which an individual departs this world? A corollary to this question is, To what extent does the authenticity of the account, not least its later recollection by a third party, influence the process of our estimation? Deaths differ from births in that they do not always entail a witness—so why, Fanthorpe seems to be asking, does anyone care? Why do we "envy our fathers their decorous endings / In error?"

In these words her ironic façade splinters. The truth is that all death is "in error"; it must be, to humans unwilling or unable to comprehend the loss of a loved one, a mistake. And this truth is made more poignant by the way she must break the line to avoid the full impact of her realization. This is not to say that the dead, having passed, have passed on forever. Far from it. Rather, they become mythic figures in the minds of the living, as she notes by turning them into the figure of Euridice, the bride of Orpheus: They "fade when we turn to look in the upper air." Fade they must, Fanthorpe is saying, but at least we may watch them when they do.

BIBLIOGRAPHY

Fanthorpe, U. A. "Observations of a Clerk." *Poetry Review* 75 (1985): 26–30.

Gilbert, Sandra M., and Susan Gubar. *The Norton Anthology of Literature by Women: The Traditions in English.* 2nd ed. New York: W. W. Norton, 1996.

Benjamin Morris

PAULIN, TOM (1949–)

Despite being born in Leeds, Yorkshire, Tom Paulin grew up and spent his childhood in Belfast. Paulin's father was the headmaster of a grammar school there, and his mother was a doctor. Paulin returned in England to study at Hull University and then at Lincoln College, Oxford. After graduation he worked at the University of Nottingham as a lecturer in the English Department. He remained in this position from 1972 until 1989. During those first days in Nottingham he published several volumes of poetry, including *A State of Justice* (1977), *The Strange Museum* (1980), and *Fivemiletown* (1987). *A State of Justice* received the Somerset Maughan Award in 1978, and *The Strange Museum* won the Geoffrey Faber Memorial Prize in 1982. Paulin's first literary award, however, was granted in 1976, when he won the Eric Gregory Award.

Paulin remained at Nottingham until 1994. From 1989 onward he was a reader in poetry. During his career he was a visiting professor at the University of Virginia, a fellow in creative writing at the University of Reading, and the director of Field Day Theatre Company in Derry, Northern Ireland. Paulin is currently the G. M. Young Lecturer in English at Hertford College, Oxford. He lives in Oxford with his wife and their two sons. Paulin is well known as a poet, critic, TV pundit, broadcaster, and playwright. He has appeared on the BBC's *Newsnight Review* with some frequency.

Paulin's publications are extensive, and besides the numerous volumes of poetry, he has written nonfiction (e.g., *Ireland and the English Crisis* 1984), critical studies (e.g., *D. H. Lawrence and "Difference": The Poetry of the Present* 2003), and drama (e.g., *The Riot Act: A Version of Sophocles' Antigone* 1985). He has edited several collections of poetry, including *The Faber Book of Political Verse* (1986). Paulin was short-listed twice for the T. S. Eliot Prize, and in 2000 he received a grant from the National Foundation for Science, Technology, and the Arts. The grant funded *The Invasion Handbook* (2003), a collection of poems about World War II. His latest book, *Crusoe's Secret: The Aesthetics of Dissent* (2005), is a collection of essays focusing on the issue of dissent in English literature.

Paulin has been described several times as a "writer of conscience." His poetry has always been highly political, specifically with reference to Northern Ireland and the Troubles there, which Paulin experienced firsthand as he grew up. Despite a developing style and a shift in focus (from order in the early poems to disorder in the later poems), politics and the Northern Ireland situation maintain a pivotal role in his texts and thoughts. Paulin's political views are not restricted to Ireland, and in February 2001 the *Observer* newspaper published Paulin's "Killed in the Crossfire," which caused a sensation and incited anti-Semitic comments due to its criticisms of the Israeli situation. Paulin's body of works is already extensive and only promises to grow with time. While his style and focus may change, it is certain that the political element will remain pivotal.

BIBLIOGRAPHY

Paulin, Tom. *The Road to Inver: Translations, Versions, and Imitations 1975–2003.* London: Faber and Faber, 2004.

———. *Selected Poems 1972–1990.* London: Faber and Faber, 1993.

———. *Writing to the Moment: Selected Critical Essays.* London: Faber and Faber, 1996.

Claire Norris

PERFORMANCE POETRY   Rooted in the classical Greek verse dramas at Delphi, poetry was arguably a communal cultural activity from its inception. As a democratic art with a clear social function, it moved through the ballads of preliterate Britain to the medieval mystery plays associated with Chester or York. In the 18th century, the grammarians and the growth of print led to a bookish elitist literary practice that continued through the next century. At the start of the twentieth century, T. S. ELIOT and W. H. AUDEN attempted to restore the connections between the poet and the public with verse dramas that were stylized, intellectual, infused with literary references, and performed in London's theaterland. In the 1960s and 1970s, popular oral poetry had a renaissance with the "LIVERPOOL POETS" Roger McGough, Brian Patten, and Adrian Henri. They took comic and satirical poems accompanied by pop music and pints of beer to pubs and other community venues. Their best-selling anthology *The Mersey Sound* (1967) was never out of print. Adrian Mitchell, although not a Liverpudlian, is often associated with the group. At the end of the 1970s and into the 1980s, John Cooper Clarke, known as the "Salford Bard," gained recognition for his anarchic punk poetry, which he performed alongside bands such as the Sex Pistols and Elvis Costello. On the other hand, the Scottish poet LIZ LOCHHEAD supremely demonstrated that an "oral" poem is not necessarily an unliterary one. Her hybrid cocktails of Standard English and native dialects opened up fresh territory for JACKIE KAY and Kathleen Jamie, whose dramatizations and linguistic diversity were best experienced at live readings. During the 1990s, Ian Macmillan became established as a spokesman for industrial Yorkshire communities and the poet-comedian John Hegley developed a wide following, especially with young people. New poets along the page/stage continuum include Rita Ann Higgins and Brendan Cleary, who plundered and parodied the storytelling of their native Ireland.

At the end of the 20th century, so-called performance poetry continued to shift between the two traditions of the literary and the fiercely demotic. The former, poetry that was assimilated into literary currents and anthologies, tended to cross-fertilize literary conventions with oral traditions and techniques. For example, some poems by CAROL ANN DUFFY, GRACE NICHOLS, and SIMON ARMITAGE straddle both; they have the linguistic condensation associated with the page, but their colloquial vitality is enhanced by the performer's personality and accent. As the up-and-coming Patience Agbabi put it: "Give me a stage and I'll cut form on it / give me a page and I'll perform on it'" (Transformatrix, 2000). The end of the century also saw sound poetry continue the intellectual AVANT GARDE experiments associated with early-century high MODERNISM. Key players were Bob Cobbing, Caroline Bergvall, Peter Finch, and Maggie O'Sullivan. Often the nonverbal aspects of their work approximate the sounds of technology, musical compositions, or visual sketches. They imitate the dehumanizing prospects of scientific languages while also redefining the limits of the human.

More distinct and popular performance poetry is determined by having a public and democratic context, such as a pub, club, or community arts center. Here provocative performance poets define their art antithetically to book-based culture and employ non- or antiliterary effects. They position themselves at the margins in order to comment on social and literary mainstreams and establishments. The communal activity of a live audience, which requires the poet to communicate through gestures and colloquial voices, is essential to its forms. This kind of popular performance poetry's multivocality is often undergirded by the politics of gender, race, ethnicity, and class. It exposes how everyday vernacular often pertains to a specific class or cultural group; the manipulations of accent and dialect frequently construct and interrogate stereotypes. Famously the Guyanan-British John Agard's "Mr Oxford Don" switches between phonetic and Standard English, "but mugging de Queen's English / is the story of my life" (Mangoes and Bullets: Selected and New Poems 1972–8, 1985). Another seminal example is the Glaswegian TOM LEONARD's "this is thi six o'clock news," which parodies "the Queen's English" in the context of the mandatory received pronunciation spoken by BBC news broadcasters. The working-class voice talks back in unashamed urban dialect: "yooz doant no / thi trooth / yirsellz cawz / yi canny talk / right" (Intimate Voices, 1984).

Anglophone black and Caribbean voices emerged during the 1960s, spearheaded by EDWARD KAMAU BRATHWAITE, who was an outstanding performer of his work. These antiestablishment pioneers were documented in Michael Horowitz's anthology Children of Albion: Poetry of the Underground in Britain (1969). From the 1970s, the Jamaican-born Linton Kwesi Johnson and Guyanan-born Grace Nichols continued to plough the furrow for proclaiming black British experience in phonetic English and Creole dialects and, in Kwesi Johnson's case, with reggae beats. In the 1980s, the increasing popularity of younger Caribbean and Guyanan heritage poets, such as Merle Collins and Fred D'Aguiar, helped to boost the status of performance poetry. Alongside these, Jean Binta Breeze, Valerie Bloom, and Lemn Sissay continued the line of black British voices who vitalized poetry that was primarily for stage. The most acclaimed performer and champion of social justice is BENJAMIN ZEPHANIAH. In "Dis Poetry" he protests that "heard" poetry could also be printed but that its potency may be lost if merely read in private. At the same time, his West Indian dialect words raise vernacular language to the status of literature: "Dis poetry is not afraid of going ina book / Still dis poetry need ears fr hear and eyes fe hav a look" (City Psalms, 1992).

Along with Caribbean "dub," "Street Poetry" is the most deliberately oppositional to book culture. Its label signals its connotations with "ground level" perspectives that often expose the unjust or insubstantial rhetoric of politicians, literary publishers, or critics, and any other "them" who oppress "us" as individuals. It is expected to be subversive and ungoverned by formal conventions; anticonventionality is its trademark. The growth of such street-level poetic expression is often linked to the music industry, notably jazz or rap. Joolz Denby is such a poet, in whose work struggle is aired and nourished through her articulation of shared conflicts and cathartic entertainment. As an antidote to the intense rivalry and prize-driven culture of "mainstream" poets, poetry slams are competitions that are open to all and judged by a panel whose score is determined by the audience's response. Inevitably the delivery is crucial to the poet's success.

For all its diversity, there are some common characteristics across the subgenres of performance poetry. The contexts of performance require strategies for entertainment and interaction. The audience must be involved both intellectually and emotionally and feel on the same social rung as the poet. Often the poems cross into the performance-related disciplines of stand-up comedy, theater, punk rock, calypso or folk music, and storytelling. They may ask the audience direct questions or implicate them through rhetorical statements. The pleasure may be in humor, shock, surprise, or identification. A performance poem indicates how centrally politics affects the individual and raises matters of personal concern to the status of politics. Performance-based poetry challenges the reader to find a suitable critical terminology or system of evaluation. Arguably the conventionally readable elements, notably imagery and the so-called performable features, such as rhythm, accent, tone, and rhyme, are the fabric of all poems, regardless of whether encountered on "stage" or "page." Nevertheless it seems inappropriate to apply the terms of traditional "lit-crit" value, against which performance poetry defines itself. Its image can easily be smeared by the weaker practitioners, and yet its cultural politics are intrinsically inclusive. Not only does it elude the automatic stamp of value pertaining to a book, but it implicitly or explicitly rejects such a stamp because it smacks of commerce and elitism. Mnemonic devices, notably repetition, lists, alliteration, and rhyme, can come across as facile on the page, and performance poetry's more professional promoters would reject the assumption that "anything goes." Where its principal features are related to sound, such as assonance, puns, and melody, these effects can be a source for evaluation. However, where the poetics are tied up with minority experience or protest, simply

scrutinizing the technique can undermine the poetics of resistance. The topicality of "street poetry" changes its value from immediacy to historical documentary.

Distinctive circuits provide one means of monitoring standards. Apples and Snakes, established in 1982, was a pioneering national poetry organization that aimed to be "popular, relevant, cross-cultural and accessible to the widest possible range of people." Based at London's Battersea Arts Centre, it achieved its goals through a program of home events and through tours, community projects, writer-in residencies, and commissioned pieces. At the same time, the opportunities for contemporary writers to use information technology to record and disseminate their work mean that they can evade conventional checks on literary value. Viewed positively, the transmission through CD, television, radio, and increasingly the World Wide Web heightens the orality of all poems and rekindles the awareness of how live reading and performance resonate with both interpretative significance and enjoyment.

BIBLIOGRAPHY

Beasley, Paul, ed. *Hearsay: Performance Poems Plus.* London: Bodley Head, 1994.

Breeze, Jean Binta, Patience Agbabi, Jillian Tipene, Ruth Harrison, and Vicki Bertram. "A Round Table Discussion on Poetry in Performance." *Feminist Review* 62 (summer 1999): 24–54.

Performance Poetry. Special issue of *Critical Quarterly* 38, no. 4 (1996).

Performance Poetry. Special issue of *Poetry Review* 87, no. 3 (autumn 1997).

Poetry in Performance. Vols. 1 and 2. London: 57 Productions, CD. Available online. URL: http://www.57productions.com/. Accessed May 8, 2008.

Zumthor, Paul, Kathy Murphy-Judy, and Walter Ong. *Oral Poetry.* Minneapolis: University of Minnesota Press, 1990.

Jane Dowson

"THE PERSIAN VERSION" ROBERT GRAVES (1945/46)

First published by ROBERT GRAVES in *Poems 1938–45,* "The Persian Version" is a criticism of propaganda and the distortion of historical events by politicians and biased historians. The satire was inspired by a battle of World War II, the "Dieppe raid" of August 19, 1942, a catastrophic attempt by Allied troops to mount a major attack on the French port of Dieppe. After the raid some 3,367 men, including 2,752 Canadians, remained on the beach, dead or soon to be made prisoners. The Dieppe story made instant headlines worldwide, but because the British army's press services did not mention the part played by the second Canadian Infantry Division, it was several weeks before Canadian public opinion realized what a failure Operation Jubilee had been, and how many of its own had died in action. On the other side, German air-dropped propaganda leaflets, entitled "Dieppe," were showing photographs of Canadian POWs, casualties, abandoned Churchill tanks, and discarded equipment as proof of German superiority. Conflicting assessments of the value of the raid continue to be presented: Some claim that it was a useless slaughter; others maintain that it was necessary for the successful invasion of the Continent two years later on D day, because the raid on Dieppe had shown the importance of prior air bombings and artillery fire from ships and landing crafts to support assault troops.

Graves uses the history (or historical legend) of the Greco-Persian wars to illustrate how historical "facts" are shaped by the prejudices of national pride and political expediency. History is usually written by the winners, yet Graves shows how the defeated can also manage to rewrite the accounts given by their enemy. With the first lines of his poem, "Truth-loving Persians do not dwell upon / The trivial skirmish fought near Marathon," the Persian speaker turns upside down the "official" version transmitted to us through the account given by the Greek historian Herodotus: "There fell in the battle of Marathon on the side of the barbarians, about six thousand and four hundred men, on that of the Athenians, one hundred and ninety-two" (quoted in Nims, 334). The Battle of Marathon (490 B.C.E.) was the culmination of King Darius I of Persia's first major attempt to conquer Greece and incorporate it in the Persian Empire. As it was the first time that the Greeks had defeated the Persians on land, the victory at Marathon endowed them in a single afternoon with a faith in their destiny that enabled Greece to become the cradle of Western culture. Yet although the Battle of Marathon has traditionally been regarded as a decisive victory over the Oriental threat, modern historians

have come to doubt its importance. Doubtful is also the story of the famous race of Marathon. According to Herodotus, an Athenian soldier named Pheidippides ran from Athens to Sparta to ask for assistance before the battle, covering about 150 miles (240 km). This event was later turned into the popular legend (which first appears in Plutarch's A.D. first century *On the Glory of Athens*) that the messenger ran from Marathon to Athens, a distance of about 25 miles (40 km), where he announced the Persian defeat before dying of exhaustion. This tale became the basis for the modern marathon race, which is run over a distance of 42.195 km (26.2 miles).

Given that we generally accept the Athenian version of the battle as related by Herodotus, in which the outnumbered Athenians won a surprising victory over the Persian barbarians, Graves imagines how the Persian press release might have explained the incident. Graves proves a master at capturing the exact tone of voice of the party he wishes to lampoon. The contorted and complicated syntax, interrupted by bracketed comments and colons and semicolons, gives an ironic imitation of the style we are used to encountering in propaganda, suggesting that the art of political "spin" was alive thousands of years ago. The "Persian version" claims that they were not beaten back in a "grandiose, ill-starred attempt / To conquer Greece," but suffered defeat in a "mere reconnaissance in force," thereby turning what is commonly regarded as the expulsion of dangerous conquerors into a "trivial skirmish." The Persian speaker uses all the techniques of propaganda: flat denial of the truth of the Greek account of the battle and denigration of the importance of the whole event, as well as abstract verbiage. He derides the Greek national character by claiming that their "theatrical tradition" had embellished a victory that was won only against inferior Persian forces, whose left flank was "covered by some obsolete / light craft detached from the main Persian fleet."

Rather illogically he concludes that the Persian monarch and the Persian nation "won by this salutary demonstration" great "repute," thereby blurring the distinction between victory and defeat and glossing over the fact that thousands of soldiers had died. With deeply ironic certitude, to which the perfectly rhyming (heroic) couplets impart a sense of finality, the speaker ends: "Despite a strong defence and adverse weather / All arms combined magnificently together." The trivial magnificence of this "doublespeak" is reminiscent of Robert Southey's refrain of "The Battle of Blenheim": "'But what they fought each other for / I could not well make out; / But everybody said,' quoth he, / 'That 'twas a famous victory.'" Graves expresses here his conviction that any historical disaster can be turned into a "success."

Despite its casual and almost light-hearted tone, the poem sheds light not only on the ways history is written, but also on British propaganda wars fought in World War II. The Greeks stand for the Germans and the Persians for the British, who tried to ignore the fact that the useless Dieppe raid had cost thousands of lives, while the Germans were exploiting their "success" in propagandist pamphlets. What is perhaps most unsettling is that we do not know the truth ourselves, just as we have no means of declaring the account of Herodotus or of Plutarch about the race of Marathon to be true: Was Dieppe really necessary to end the Nazi rule over Europe? Did the Battle of Marathon really secure the foundation of Europe, saving it from Oriental deprivation and absolutism? History is a fictional narrative that has long ceased to be regarded as solid facts. Historical truth is elusive and will always be in danger from the forgeries of historians and propagandists.

BIBLIOGRAPHY

Green, Peter. *The Greco-Persian Wars.* Updated ed. Berkeley and Los Angeles: University of California Press, 1998.

Nims, John Frederick. *Western Wind: An Introduction to Poetry.* 3rd ed. New York: McGraw-Hill, 1992.

Whitaker, Denis, and Shelagh Whitaker. *Dieppe: A Firsthand and Revealing Critical Account of the Most Controversial Battle of World War Two.* Whitby, Canada: L, Cooper, 1992.

————, and ————. *Dieppe: Tragedy to Triumph.* Toronto, 1992. Available online. URL: http://www.cs.rice.edu/~ssiyer/minstrels/poems/515.html. Accessed May 8, 2008.

Heike Grundmann

"PIANO" D. H. LAWRENCE (1918)

One of D. H. LAWRENCE's most anthologized and successful short rhymed poems, "Piano" first appeared in his fourth collection, *New Poems* (1918). However, the published version of "Piano" is the fourth draft of one of Lawrence's earliest poems. Composed between 1906 and 1908 and originally entitled "The Piano," the first draft consisted of five four-line stanzas. Lawrence eliminated the first and fourth stanzas and revised the remaining stanzas.

In its published form, "Piano" is a seemingly simple, deceptively complex 12-line poem consisting of three stanzas of four lines each, employing an *AA/BB* rhyme scheme. The central image of the poem is a male listening to a woman singing to him with piano accompaniment, which is indicative of Lawrence's focus throughout all of his work on the man-woman relationship that he believed to be central to the human condition. The poem's setting is indeterminate; the speaker does not specify whether he attends a private or public performance. However, the intimate mood created by the opening line, "Softly, in the dusk, a woman is singing to me," implies that the speaker is alone with the woman.

The speaker is transported from the present into the past by the conjunction of music and memory, causing him to envision himself as a child "sitting under the piano," "pressing the small, poised feet" of his mother "as she sings." Against his will, the speaker journeys internally back to "Sunday evenings at home," where his family sings "in the cozy parlor." The power of childhood memories makes it "vain for the singer" of the present "to burst into clamor," since her music cannot match the power of "the flood of remembrance" that causes the adult male speaker to "weep like a child." The poem's focus on the mother-child relationship reflects Lawrence's unusually close relationship with his mother, who died in 1910. Significantly the memory of the speaker's mother is more powerful than the presence of the presumably young, attractive woman.

"Piano" skillfully employs contrasts and binary constructions, such as intellect/emotion, control/sentimentality, mind/body, male/female, adult/child, listening/singing, sight/memory, and smile/weep. Lawrence carefully balances these pairings, partly by beginning each stanza in the present before moving into the past. The speaker moves from the exterior (the physical) to the interior (memory and emotion) before returning in the poem's final line to the present with a physical manifestation of emotion ("I weep like a child"). Although critics have identified nostalgia and sentimentality as major themes in "Piano," a tone of negativity runs through the poem, created by language such as *In spite of myself, insidious, betrays, weeps, vain,* and *cast/down.* Lawrence's diction injects musical sounds, especially through the words *boom, tingling, tinkling,* and *burst.* The poet moves the poem to its climax by eschewing punctuation in the ninth line, accelerating the rhythm into the "great black piano appassionato." The crescendo of the music precedes a pause and the denouement of the speaker surrendering to emotion. The final message of the poem is that memories of childhood are more powerful than adulthood and the present.

BIBLIOGRAPHY

Cushman, Keith. "The Tuning of 'Piano.'" *Approaches to Teaching the Works of D. H. Lawrence,* 190–192. New York: MLA, 2001.

Gilbert, Sandra M. *Acts of Attention: The Poems of D. H. Lawrence.* Ithaca, N.Y.: Cornell, University Press, 1972.

Laird, Holly. "The Poems of 'Piano.'" *D.H. Lawrence Review* 18, nos. 2–3 (1986): 183–199.

Lockwood, M. J. *A Study of the Poems of D. H. Lawrence.* London: Macmillan, 1987.

Vries-Mason, Jillian de. *Perception in the Poetry of D. H. Lawrence.* Berne: Peter Lang, 1982.

Nathanael O'Reilly

PICKARD, TOM (1946–)

A poet, novelist, playwright, and television and radio writer, Thomas Pickard was born Thomas MacKenna on January 7, 1946, in Newcastle upon Tyne, Northumberland, England, to Nicholson and Ella MacKenna. Pickard's great-uncle, Robert Bambro (a railroad worker), and great-aunt, Catherine MacKenna Pickard (a homemaker), adopted him and changed his name to *Thomas Mariner Pickard.* Pickard attended Ruskin College, Oxford, but left school at the age of 14. In 1964, he married his first wife, Constance Davison, whom he divorced in 1978, and in 1979 he married Joanna Voit, a Polish photographer. He cofounded, with his first wife, the Morden Tower Poetry Center in 1963; there he organized readings by many influential British and American poets, most importantly Allen Ginsberg, Robert Creeley, Lawrence Ferlinghetti, Gregory Corso, and BASIL BUNTING. Between 1969 and 1973 he founded and managed the Ultima Thule Bookshop and moved to London to write radio and documentary filmscripts. In addition to his work as a poet and writer, Pickard has worked for a construction company and as a wine merchant. He divides his time between Fiend's Fell, London, and Warsaw, Poland, with his three children, Matthew, Catherine, and Kuba Mieszko.

Tom Pickard has won many literary awards, including the Northern Arts Minor Award (1965), an Arts Council of Great Britain Grant (1969 and 1973), a C. Day Lewis Writing Fellowship (1976–77), as well as an Arts Council Creative Writing Fellowship (1979–80). Pickard is commonly seen as one of the key figures of the British poetry revival movement. His poetry is influenced mainly by the American Beat poets, but Basil Bunting, whom he first met at the Poetry Center, served as his mentor and poetic father during the early years of his literary career. Pickard uses what many critics consider to be crass, bawdy, and unsophisticated language. However, his counterculture aesthetic reveals a tenderness and authenticity rarely encountered in other poets of the same generation, poets who are deemed more learned and refined. In fact, his treatments, sometimes written in dialect, of everyday subjects and themes serve as a record of British working-class life rooted in sexuality, violence, addiction, religion, and politics. Pickard's most recent collections have confirmed his status as a major figure in contemporary English poetry: *The Dark Months of May* (2004), *Hole in the Wall: New and Selected Poems* (2002), *Fuckwind* (1999), *Tiepin Eros: New and Selected Poems* (1994), *Shedding Her Skirts* (1985), and *Custom and Exile* (1986).

BIBLIOGRAPHY

Contemporary Poets. 8th ed. Detroit: St. James Press, 2004.

Sherry, Vincent B., ed. *Dictionary of Literary Biography.* Vol. 40, *Poets of Great Britain and Ireland since 1960.* Detroit: Gale, 1985.

Daniel Pantano

"PIKE" TED HUGHES (1959)

"Pike" is one of TED HUGHES's earlier poems, written before the death of his first wife, SYLVIA PLATH. It is an unself-conscious, almost religiously reverent celebration of nature's power, personified by a coolly implacable predator, the pike. The pike is nature at its most relentless. It is nature in its most basic and ruthless form, stripped of sentiment though not lacking in beauty. The fish has one purpose only—to consume and go on consuming. The overwhelming power of this drive is described by Hughes in layers of image, meaning, and story that are seamless in construction and seductive in effect.

There are several progressions contained in the poem. In succeeding stanzas, the pike Hughes describes become larger and larger. Beginning with the egg and three-inch pike in the first verse, Hughes goes on to describe three larger ones "kept behind glass"; moves on to the six-pound pike in verse 6, each two feet long; and then to the ancient fish lurking in the depths, "immense" and threatening at the end of the poem. Depth and age also increase. The pike, obviously a male symbol, is balanced against the female principle in the subterranean world of the pond. The pond grows larger, deeper, older as the poem goes on. The meaning of the pond expands to encompass civilization and history—to invoke time beyond memory. It is old enough to outlast the monastery that made it, but it is "deep as England."

Hughes places himself in the poem, so that the faceless voice of description from the first four stanzas identifies itself in the fifth verse. He tells three small stories about himself, and these also have a progressive quality. The first is of the three pike kept as aquarium fish and the shock of finding that they devour not only the small fish fed them but also each other. The second story is of finding the two large pike dead on the "willow-herb," tossed up on shore. The character of the fish is further realized in this image of a predator so determined that it literally kills itself trying to devour prey too large to swallow. In the final phase of the poet's experience, Hughes encounters his own response to the specter of nature he has admired and described.

The poet's description of the pike—its physical beauty, the lethal jaw, the constant eye—is unwavering. Likewise his presentation of the fish's environment is precise and lovely in detail. With similar courage, he shows himself "with hair frozen" in fear, overwhelmed as ancient pond and ancient pike merge into "the

dream / Darkness beneath night's darkness had freed." After his wife's death, Hughes's fascination with the predatory aspects of nature encouraged a suspicion that he himself was the predator in their relationship. But in the final stanzas of this poem, he casts himself in the role of the watched, not the watcher, fixed in the eye of an approaching threat.

BIBLIOGRAPHY

Feinstein, Flaine. *Ted Hughes: The Life of a Poet.* London: Weidenfeld and Nicolson, 2001.

Grifford, Terry, and Neil Roberts. *Ted Hughes: A Critical Study.* London: Faber and Faber, 1981.

Hughes, Ted. *New Selected Poems.* New York: Harper and Row, 1982.

Mary VanOeveren

PINTER, HAROLD (1930–)

Pinter has enjoyed worldwide acclaim as an actor, playwright, and screenwriter, but his poetry has met with considerable skepticism. Indeed his later, highly politicized poems have been dismissed as doggerel by some critics. Pinter's early poems are not controversial. In the 1950s and 1960s he wrote a wide range of largely inoffensive poems. These poems contain a wide range of themes, bodied forth through a wide range of genres and formal properties. The early poems range from topographical descriptions such as 1951's grippingly subjective account of an Irish coastal region, "The Islands of Aran Seen from the Moher Cliffs," to lyrics that often feature a speaker anxious to maintain an intimacy—1956's "Daylight" is a prime example of such a lyric. From the mid-1990s onward, Pinter's poems have appeared more frequently. Indeed in 2005, Pinter announced that he would write no more plays and would devote subsequent energies to writing poetry and to political activities.

Pinter's recent poetry articulates his combative political stances. Pinter regards British and American governments as undemocratic and savage because they pursue wars, irrespective of public unease. Pinter's very slim 2003 volume, *War,* consists wholly of poems that lambast the then-current invasion of Iraq by American-led troops, a war that Pinter insists was illegal and unnecessary. Pinter's most notorious poem was written in 1991. The theme of this poem is announced in its title, "American Football": "A Reflection upon the Gulf War." This poems attacks the 1991, American-led war on Iraq, just as the poems of *War* attack the 2003 war. In "American Football," Pinter's verse ventriloquizes an aggressive American, one celebrating the bombing of Iraqis. The vicious speaker praises God for allowing him and his countrymen to destroy Middle Eastern life: "We blew the shit right back their own ass / And out their fucking ears." The simple-minded speaker then demands a kiss from the anonymous addressee: Thus Pinter equates trigger-happy ferocity with masculine lasciviousness. The monosyllabic profanity of such verse has inspired some commentators to accuse Pinter of using his celebrity to peddle low-quality verse that articulates simplistic propaganda. Others, however, see Pinter as a brave poet who argues for unfashionable causes, submerging his own artistic urges in order to satirize and somehow thwart what is perceived to be the dominant trait in Western societies—unthinking aggression and unempathetic hostility toward others.

BIBLIOGRAPHY

Derbyshire, Harry. "Pinter as Celebrity." In *The Cambridge Companion to Harold Pinter,* edited by Peter Raby, 230–245. Cambridge: Cambridge University Press, 2001.

"Pinter to Give Up Writing Plays." BBC. 28 February 2005. Available online. URL: http://news.bbc.co.uk/1/hi/entertainment/arts/4305725.stm. Accessed May 8, 2008.

Pinter, Harold. *Various Voices: Prose, Poetry, Politics, 1948–1998.* London: Faber and Faber, 1998.

———. *War.* London: Faber and Faber, 2003.

"Harold Pinter." Available online. URL: www.haroldpinter.org/poetry/index.shtml. Accessed May 8, 2008.

Kevin DeOrnellas

PITTER, RUTH (1897–1992) Pitter's 16 serious poetry collections stretched from *First and Second Poems 1912–25* (preface by Hilaire Belloc) in 1927 to her final book, *A Heaven to Find,* in 1987. Raised in Ilford, Essex, by parents who were schoolteachers, was brought up to love poetry and writing. She started at the University of London but left to work in the War Office when World War I began. Some early poems were published in the *New Age,* the *New English Weekly,* and other experimental English journals. Her reputation rose between the wars, with *A Mad Lady's Garland* (1934; *A Trophy of Arms: Poems 1926–1935* (preface by James Stephens, 1936), which won the Hawthornden Prize in 1937; and *The Spirit Watches* (1939). Her popularity was at its height during the Second World War with poems that are acutely sensitive to social differences and personal pain but buck up the fainthearted with an optimism constituted by gentle humor, buoyant rhythms, and closed rhymes. *The Bridge: Poems 1939–1944* was published in 1945. After the war, her work continued to reach wide audiences through the radio and anthologies. *The Ermine: Poems 1942–1952* won the Heinemann Award in 1954, and in 1955, she became the first woman to earn the Queen's Medal for Poetry.

Her technical versatility and stylistic independence make Pitter difficult to position. Several poems hark back to classical models such as Horace's satires or Ovid's *Metamorphoses,* while others can be placed in a tradition of English pastoral poetry. She was also conversant with the neoromantic poems of DYLAN THOMAS and with the modernist works of T. S. ELIOT, with whom she had greater affinity after her conversion to Christianity in 1941. She was insistent that poetry maintain the common touch and often favored the regular meters of familiar forms, like the ballad or narrative, which she combined with colloquial diction that does not discard the consolations of rhyme. In many poems, tightly rhyming couplets indicate Pitter's subtle irony, often when creatures—a fly, frog, mouse, or swan, for instance—display the oddities of human behavior.

In *Ruth Pitter: Homage to a Poet,* her verse forms are commended as "those of the mainstream English poetic tradition" and consequently, "it would be possible to argue that Ruth Pitter is a man's poet." However, women are frequently the subjects of her poems, as in the satirical "Maternal Love Triumphant," which both mocks and affirms the toils and sacrifices of motherhood, or the reflective "Old, Childless, Husbandless," which is typically compassionate toward individual suffering while celebrating the strength of the human spirit. Introducing a new edition of Pitter's *Collected Poems* (1996), ELIZABETH JENNINGS sympathetically notes a desire to "express something of the secret meanings which haunt life and language . . . to find words for what seems inexpressible." In 1974 Pitter was awarded a Companion of Literature, by the Royal Society of Literature and in 1979 was named Commander of the British Empire (CBE).

BIBLIOGRAPHY

Dowson, Jane. *Women's Poetry of the 1930s: A Critical Anthology.* London: Routledge, 1996.

King, Don W. "Silent Music of Ruth Pitter." *Bulletin of the New York C. S. Lewis Society* 35 (spring 2004): 1–15.

Pitter, Ruth. *Collected Poems.* London: Enitharmon, 1996.

Russell, Arthur, ed. *Ruth Pitter: Homage to a Poet.* London, Rapp & Whiting, 1969.

Jane Dowson

PLATH, SYLVIA (1932–1963)

Sylvia Plath is undoubtedly one of the most famous of American poets, so that her inclusion in a companion to British poetry is perhaps questionable, but as do others who spent portions of their writing life in Britain, such as T. S. ELIOT, EZRA POUND, and H. D. (HILDA DOOLITTLE), she has a significant British presence. Her husband was the poet laureate of Britain, TED HUGHES, and her *annus mirabilis* (the "miracle year" that some poets have), in which she produced her greatest work, the poems collected in *Ariel* and published by her husband after her death, was the last year of her life, spent in Devon and London.

Plath was born to a middle-class family in Boston in 1932 and grew up in Winthrop, Massachusetts. Her father was a professor of biology at Boston University, who wrote a treatise on bees, which were later to appear as images in several of the important *Ariel* poems. He died in 1940 when Sylvia was eight. She won a scholarship to Smith College, where she began as an art major (her paintings, along with most of her papers, are at the Lilly Library at Indiana University). During her junior year, after winning a guest editorship at *Mademoiselle* magazine for the summer, she attempted suicide, later recorded in her novel *The Bell Jar.* The loss of her father and the suicide attempt became pieces of a powerful mythology that she articulated in "Lady Lazarus" as a cycle of death and rebirth— "One year in every ten / I manage it."

After graduation from Smith Plath won a Fulbright Fellowship for study at Cambridge University, where she remained for two years, marrying Ted Hughes in 1956. The couple returned to America for a year, during which Sylvia taught at Smith and enrolled in a creative writing seminar at Harvard taught by Robert Lowell and attended by Anne Sexton. The couple then returned to England, where her two children, Frieda and Nicholas, were born in 1960 and 1962. In the summer and fall of 1962 she discovered that her husband was having an affair; they separated and the most intense period of her writing life began, during which she wrote sometimes four or five poems in a week.

After her death by suicide in February 1963, she became an icon of the burgeoning feminist movement in England and America, and Hughes became the villain. Their lives became tabloid fare in the many biographies published about her, now well over two dozen monographs, reminiscences, and full-scale works, not to mention the criticism, which has become an industry. She is buried in Heptonstall, Yorkshire, near Hughes's birthplace, in a simple grave in the overflow of new plots outside the old medieval churchyard, under the name *Sylvia Plath Hughes.*

For the remainder of his life Hughes kept silent about their relationship, but shortly before his death he published *Birthday Letters* (1998), a chronicle of his relationship with her, which continued for the 35 years after her death, in the form of birthday poems to her. She remained a haunting presence in his life, sometimes overshadowing his own considerable work, with her powerful poems and famous life story. Her daughter Frieda Hughes, like her mother, is a painter and poet, publishing in 1998 *Wooroloo.*

See also "ARIEL," "CUT."

BIBILIOGRAPHY

Alexander, Paul. *Rough Magic: A Biography of Sylvia Plath.* New York: Penguin, 1991.

Malcolm, Janet. *The Silent Woman.* New York: Knopf, 1993.

Stevenson, Anne. *Bitter Fame: A Life of Sylvia Plath.* London: Penguin, 1989.

Wagner, Erica. *Ariel's Gift: Ted Hughes, Sylvia Plath, and the Story of Birthday Letters.* London: Faber and Faber, 2000.

Wagner-Martin, Linda. *Sylvia Plath: A Biography.* New York: St. Martin's Press, 1987.

James Persoon

"A POEM ABOUT POEMS ABOUT VIETNAM" JON STALLWORTHY (1969)

In an earlier

poem, "Letter to a Friend" (1961), JON STALLWORTHY defends his poetry's characteristically personal voice against accusations that it lacks the kind of social engagement and political commentary expected of writers during the turbulent decade of the 1960s just emerging. Rather than acting as a "looking glass" mimetically reflecting nature, his poetry functions as a "window" imaginatively looking beyond present reality, one "woven out of love's loose ends; / for my family and for my friends." This apologia can serve as a guide for reading "A Poem about Poems about Vietnam" since it too calls for a poetry based upon the authenticity of those personal windows forever framing our individual perspectives.

The poem responds to a highly publicized event that took place in 1965 at the Royal Albert Hall in London, where several prominent poets, among them Allen Ginsberg, read works opposing the war in Vietnam. This Victorian auditorium—filled to its capacity of 8,000 for this event—serves as the poem's extended metaphor for a verbal and artistic battlefield, and its lineup of literary protesters, infantrymen on its front lines: "The spotlight had you covered [thunder / from the wing]. In combat zones / and in the Circle, darkness." The powerful caesura and enjambment of this opening coupled with the prosaic diction of the "muzzles of the microphones," and the "phalanxes/ of loudspeakers" from which poetry is blared underscore the jarring discordance of the protesters' words—syllables like assault weapons within a scene of mock-warfare. Counterpoint the empty rumblings of this first stanza with the mellifluous trochaic and iambic patterns of the second, where poets like Lord Byron, W. H. AUDEN, WILFRED OWEN, and JOHN CORNFORD write of revolutions and civil wars, and we soon discern why Stallworthy's own speaker views these later-day war poets as ineffectual: "But all your cartridges were blanks / when you were at the Albert Hall." These earlier poets all wrote from the front lines of the battlefield and risked physical dangers in support of their political ideals and "to make their poem's meaning plain." Without such personal sacrifice, the antiwar poets of the first stanza, most of whom had never experienced a battle, simply wear false medals, indeed, forge their own emotional force "by numbing the nerve" that actual combatants "laid bare." To condemn the war in Vietnam without such a lived emotion is likened to silencing the dead, to suppressing their voices in order to authenticate one's own anger.

The third stanza builds upon this idea of a groundless poetic authority. Invoking John Donne—Elizabethan courtier, warrior, priest, and writer of the *Holy Sonnets*—Stallworthy underscores the importance of acknowledging a powerful literary history of English war poetry, one whose literary authenticity and emotional impact derive precisely from the highly private, personal, and thoroughly experiential details that buttress its words. Indeed the speaker's cautious emphasis on the living word is represented in his highly concrete diction and description of both Donne and Owen. The modern poet writes about the Great War from the trenches "with a rifle-butt / between his paper and the slime," while the earlier writes about erotic love by "quitting Her pillow to cut a quill." The immediacy, the physicality, and the fierce vitality that ground their poetry are here made more striking by the metonyms and synecdoche employed in each crafted exemplum. Donne's sonnets are meaningful not because they are abstracted or fashionable, but because they arise from the sheer urgency of "the pillow" of lust and love. The process of writing—"cutting the quill"—does not take place outside private reality but rather must be fashioned and honed from its very core.

Moreover each stanza's final line, ending sonorously in the punctuated echoes of the iambic tetrameter line "when you were at the Albert Hall," further stresses—through its slightly mocking rhythms—the ironic differences between the two poetic stances. The forceful injunction that "in love and war / dispatches from the front are all" is brought home by a rhetorical peroration in the poem's final stanza. A traditional quatrain, delivered in heightened poetic diction, deftly replaces the deafening technological barking of stanza 1 with the single, delicate utterance these dead poets "whisper in their sleep," namely, their authoritative literary identity: "Poet."

BIBLIOGRAPHY

Stallworthy, Jon. *The Astronomy of Love*. London: Oxford University Press, 1961.
———. *Hand in Hand*. London: Chatto and Windus/ Hogarth, 1974.

Patricia M. Feito

"POEM OUT OF CHARACTER" ROY FULLER
(1954) The speaker of "Poem Out of Character" is an aging poet who finds himself moving "from the end / To the middle of anthologies" and acknowledges that youth's great "dreams of tremendous statements" will now never be realized. With age, ambition attenuates: The poet's verse will not "warn the times" as he once believed it could. Nevertheless in imagination he still contemplates mysteries and wonders. In occasional moments he experiences "vast intimations"; the phrase alludes to Wordsworth's "Ode: Intimations of Immortality" (1803–6), which addresses similar themes of aging and the attenuation of imaginative powers. ROY FULLER's version of the romantic sublime is to invoke the beauties revealed by science. The depths of the solar system, with its four gas giants "swathed in deep / Ammoniac and methane seas," and the huge lengths of prehistoric time—"the curious, long / Years before earth was dramatized"—are a sublime counterpoint to the wreckage of contemporary society. Evolution itself presents mysteries for contemplation: The "single young" that humans raise suggests the Wordsworthian wondering child and the solitude of human existence. This grandeur of nature contrasts with the "ruined autumn scene" of mid-20th-century civilization, which is "doomed to be defaced," as all of the world's great cultures are, by the depredations of historical time.

The speaker invokes such vistas only to deny them. His own muse is small-scale and comic. His objects are "ambiguous cats and sweets and birds"—perhaps alluding to T. S. ELIOT's Old Possum's Book of Practical Cats (1939) as an exemplar of the loss of poetic ambition—and he sees the world only in fragments: "a leaf, a hair, / An inch of skin." Past the "barrier" of his style lies a world of "giantesses, gods and boys; / And lions and inhuman trees." Yet this heroic universe is beyond the limits of his ability to represent it.

On the face of it, this might be read as a lament for a bankrupt imagination, or even Fuller's own poetic testimony: the record of a transition from youthful radical to middle-aged conservative. His later poetry was written "frankly from a position of weakness," lacking any belief in its power to change the world. However, from its title onward, the poem's slippery, teasing register makes this reading problematic. The adoption of a skeptical, fragmentary poetic practice may be felt by contemporary readers to resonate with the postmodern suspicion of grand narratives and totalizing representations. It may be an aesthetic choice, rather than an admission of failure, to see the world through "tiny apertures."

BIBLIOGRAPHY
Fuller, Roy. Brutus's Orchard: Poems. London: Andre Deutsch, 1957.
Lee, V. J., ed. The Individual and His Times: A Selection of the Poetry of Roy Fuller. London: Athlone, 1982.

Barry Parsons

POEMS OF 1912–13 THOMAS HARDY (1914)
THOMAS HARDY's Poems of 1912–13 is a collection of 21 elegies for his wife, Emma, written shortly after her death. While separately the poems offer examples of the elegiac style in varied forms, the collection also works when viewed as one large elegy composed of the aggregate poems. When viewed as a cohesive work, Poems of 1912–13 shows the enormity of Hardy's sense of loss, regret, and grief over Emma's death and the decrepit state to which their marriage had been reduced by the end of her life.

While there is no clear evidence that Hardy meant for the poems to be seen collectively, one critic, William Morgan, has argued that the "circumstances of composition and publication as well as from the text of the elegy" indicate an intentional cohesiveness (499). Originally, Poems of 1912–13 appeared in Satires of Circumstance published in 1914 and contained only 18 elegies. In 1919, while he was working on his Collected Poems, Hardy added "The Spell of the Rose," "St. Launce's Revisited," and "Where the Picnic Was" (Morgan 500). The order of the original set was not changed, and the three additions were tacked on the end. Hardy continued writing elegies for and about Emma for the rest of his life, and his Collected Poems contain more than 100 (Ramazani 970). The fact that he only added those three instead of the many other elegies also lends credibility to the notion of the cohesiveness of the original sequence.

The consistent use of allusions to their courtship some 25 years prior—with Hardy's love-at-first-sight experience of seeing Emma on horseback—recurs throughout the elegies. These allusions and their inherent contrasts of time—from distant past to present and various points in between—offer the strongest unifying aspects to the series. In the first poem of the group, "The Going," Hardy begins in the present, wondering why Emma died so suddenly with no good-bye and no chance to reconcile. In the fourth stanza, however, he already begins contrasting the sense of present grief with an earlier happier time when Emma rode up to him on horseback "along the Beeny Crest, / And reining nigh me, / would muse and eye me, / while Life unrolled us its very best." Here Life is an entity serving the lovers in their desires. Emma riding her horse up to him and their flirty glances are seen as innocent, happy, and full of the excitement early courtship evokes. As brief as this happy time seems to have been in reality, it is also given only a small presence within the poem. At the start of the next stanza, the tragic status of their marriage returns to Hardy's mind as if waking from a flashback to question, "Why, then, latterly did we not speak."

While the countryside and the past serve as the residences of happiness and joy in their marriage, their home at Max Gate and even her grave symbolize the bitter and strained aspects of their marriage at the end of Emma's life. In "I Found Her Out There" Hardy writes that Emma is not buried in her favored countryside near the Atlantic but instead must live her ghostly eternity near their home: "I brought her here, / and have laid her to rest / in a noiseless nest / no sea beats near." Even after her death Hardy realizes that neither can he restore their marriage and the idealism of that earlier time, nor can Emma return to the land she loved. Thus both the living and the dead forever bear their burdens without hope of reconciliation. Instead of places like Beeny Cliff and Vallency, which Hardy uses to symbolize the Edenic place of their young love, Emma must rest in "her loamy cell." Seven of the poems, with titles like "Beeny Cliff" and "At Castle Boterel," specifically allude to the countryside and their young lives together. The poems "The Going" and "I Found Her Out There" contain elements of both places and thus both moods and contrast the dichotomy of happiness and sadness in their relationship. "The Going" describes an alley of trees near their home as a

place where the mere sight of "the yawning blankness / of the perspective sickens me." The blankness is his realization that she is not walking there as she used to. Unable to handle this reality Hardy then jumps to that pure vision of young, vivacious Emma on horseback.

The strange and sad relationship of Emma and Thomas, and his elegies, which serve multiple purposes of lament, apology, avoidance, and revision, still draw readers' interest. A recent *Times* of London article speculated, with the aid of a current medical opinion of Emma's symptoms, that she died not from gallstones and a heart attack but of syphilis, which she contracted from Hardy himself (Alberge 31). While this could have been a reason for their strained relationship, Emma's papers—found and published after her death—show that she was furious with Hardy's secularism and loss of religious belief (Knoepflmacher 1061). If the syphilis theory is correct, perhaps that sheds light on his line "Her who but lately / had shivered with pain / as at touch of dishonour" (Hardy 341). Whatever the reasons, the arch of their relationship from loving and tender to bitter and biting still holds readers' attention, especially Hardy's attempts to reconcile their love via his elegies.

In the poem "The Spell of the Rose" Hardy gives the role of narrator to Emma as she discusses how her husband, the architect, built a beautiful home for them but never planted a rose. Emma states that as the years went on, the relationship soured: "And as he planted never a rose / that bears the flower of love, / though other flowers throve / some heart-bane moved our souls to sever." Emma then sneaks into the garden one night and plants a rose in the hope that "it may end divisions dire and wry." Sadly Emma dies before the rose has a chance to grow and for the spell to take effect, thus saving their marriage. With the love and remorse Hardy displays in the elegies, maybe the spell did restore their marriage, as Emma speculates at the end of the poem: "Perhaps . . . he sees me as I was, though sees / too late to tell me so!"

Hardy—the grieving widower and regretful lover—serves as the narrative voice to most of the elegies, however; as with "The Spell of the Rose," he gives the narrative *I* over to Emma in "His Visitor" and "The Haunter." In "The Phantom Horsewoman" the narrative voice is a nonrelated observer. "The Haunter" begins with Emma's pondering on the fact that "he does not think that I haunt here nightly: / How shall I let him know / That whither his fancy set him wandering / I, too, alertly go?" Here is the voice of Hardy disguised as that of his dead wife, asking how she can communicate with the very person authoring the poem. Perhaps it is narcissism, or perhaps it is merely his attempt to make perfect their relationship, but the real-life Emma did not silently join him in his viewpoints on life and marriage. She wrote scathing critiques of her husband's irreligious notions, but here she is portrayed by Hardy as the supportive, silent wife following him in his travels. Emma points out the irony: "Now that he goes and wants me with him / more than he used to do, / Never he sees my faithful phantom / though he speaks thereto." Even in her death, Hardy does not let Emma voice her Christian-based belief in the afterlife but has her live in a sort of purgatorial haunting. The voice of Emma in "His Visitor," however, seems closer to the reality of her actual mood. She returns to their home and notices that rooms have been painted and servants replaced since she died. These changes annoy her and the poem ends when the frustrated spirit decides to return to her birthplace. These poems hold a unique position in the scope of the elegy as a form since Emma gives voice to her own husband's lament. In these poems the collection not only elegizes Emma herself, but also seems to elegize their marriage and all its problems.

The elegy as a poetic form is not based on any particular structure, but rather on the poetic mode of lament for the person or thing being remembered. Hardy's *Poems of 1912–13* take on many structures and voices to show the depth of Thomas and Emma Hardy's love and eventual struggle in their marriage. Perhaps "The Spell of the Rose" actually did work and in the *Poems of 1912–13* their love for each other was restored. Or perhaps Hardy and Emma fell into Plato's philosophical camp, realizing that the *idea* of their marriage was perfect, while the actual relationship was a poor imitation, tainted as it was with all the material flaws of life. In any case, Hardy's candor, which ranges from narcissism to raw, naked guilt, gives these poems a timelessness, a universality that makes Hardy relevant not only to early-20th-century readers, but to those of any generation.

BIBLIOGRAPHY

Alberge, Dalya. "Thomas Hardy 'Infected Wife with Syphilis.'" *Times* (London) 8 December 2006.

Hardy, Thomas. *Thomas Hardy: The Complete Poems.* Edited by James Gibson. New York: Palgrave, 2001.

Knoepflmacher, U. C. "Hardy Ruins: Female Spaces and Male Designs." *PMLA*, 105, no. 5 (October 1990): 1,055–1,070.

Morgan, William. "Form, Tradition, and Consolation in Hardy's 'Poems of 1912–13'" *PMLA*, 89, no. 3 (May 1974): 496–505.

Ramazani, Jahan. "Hardy and the Poetics of Melancholia: *Poems of 1912–13* and Other Elegies for Emma." *ELH* 58, no. 4 (winter 1991): 957–977.

Sean C. Mackey

POETRY JOURNALS

POETRY JOURNALS By their very nature, little magazines and poetry journals cost little to make or buy, have small print runs, espouse guiding editorial principles (such as only publishing specific genres or writers from particular areas), and reach a small number of subscribers or readers (usually around a few hundred). They tend to appear and disappear quickly, sometimes lasting for just one or two issues. But the history of poetry journals in Britain is very much the history of British poetry: The verse being written in the early 21st century has its roots in the little modernist magazines of the early 20th century, and the experimental poems found on the Web, which play with color and typography, owe a great debt to the journals of the literary arts published in the 1910s and 1920s.

Historically poetry was published in limited editions of books. Poets from Milton to Shakespeare to Wordsworth relied on the generosity of wealthy patrons to fund the publication and distribution of their verse. In the 19th century, an increasingly literate British population began clamoring for more—and more varied—reading materials. Their demand, coupled with a reduction in the tax on paper, led to a proliferation of newspapers and periodicals. During the Victorian era, poetry appeared alongside nonfiction and fiction in such magazines as *Punch* (1841–2002), the *Germ* (1850), *Household Words* (1850–59), and *All the Year*

Round (1859–70). This juxtaposition of poetry and prose would continue well into the rise of the little magazines and poetry journals of the 20th century.

And rise they did. Myriad, multitudinous poetry journals appeared throughout the 20th century, a phenomenon attributable to one fact: Prior to the late 19th century, the technology to print rapidly and cheaply simply did not exist. New printing presses coupled with a dramatic decrease in the cost of paper set the scene for the magazines, journals, and other periodicals that began to be published in the early 20th century. Suddenly editors and poets had a low-cost way to disseminate verse quickly and easily. In 1902, the *Times Literary Supplement* began publishing poems, reviews, and essays once a week as a supplement to the *Times* newspaper; it became a separate publication in 1914 and remains an important periodical today.

Early 20th-century poets saw journals as a way to counteract what they perceived as the stiff, unappealing poetry being published in anthologies. This diverse group of writers (later known as the modernists) not only wanted to revolutionize literary expression but also sought new ways of displaying and distributing their literary output. Ford Madox Ford edited the *English Review* (1908–37; in 1937, the journal was absorbed by the *National Review*), publishing work by W. B. YEATS and THOMAS HARDY. In 1914, the artist WYNDHAM LEWIS published the first issue of *BLAST* in London. Bright pink, the iconoclastic magazine combined visual art with heretical essays on the virtues of individual expression and unrhymed, image-based poetry. The second and final issue in 1915 extolled similar politics and published poems by EZRA POUND and T. S. ELIOT. Between 1916 and 1921, the Sitwell siblings published six volumes of *Wheels*, exclusively devoted to the "new" verse being written by such poets as Aldous Huxley.

Almost immediately magazines and journals became the major means of expression for experimental, AVANT-GARDE, antiestablishment work, and London was their epicenter. In addition to *BLAST* and *Wheels,* several other notable magazines were published there during the 1910s and 1920s. HAROLD MONRO published early work by Pound in *Poetry Review* (1912–present) and *Poetry and Drama* (1913–14). After the folding of her earlier feminist magazines, Dora Mardsen poured her radical politics into the *Egoist* (1914–19), which eventually devoted itself exclusively to imagist poetry and modernist fiction and was later edited by H. D. (HILDA DOOLITTLE) and Eliot. Founded, in part, to publish his long poem *THE WASTE LAND,* Eliot's *Criterion* (1922–39) was arguably the most important journal in London throughout its 17-year history. Lewis revolutionized the magazine as an art form for a second time with the *Enemy: A Review of Art and Literature* (1927–29), in which he criticized Pound, Joyce, and Gertrude Stein, all the while explaining his philosophy of art as a rebellious, volatile force.

During the 1930s, many little magazines and journals strengthened their affiliations with left-wing politics. At the same time, however, the *Criterion,* under Eliot's editorial eye, reined British poetry in from the experimental, innovative poetic bent of the 1920s. In each issue, Eliot wrote a short column called "Commentary," in which he ranted, raved, and raged about contemporary issues, literary and otherwise. Poets like W. H. AUDEN and C. DAY LEWIS revered Eliot, even as he developed an increasingly conservative, religious point of view. As the foremost poetic voice in England, Eliot had opinions that mattered, and the literary world tuned in to everything he had to say. Eliot published early Auden, as well as poems by Geoffrey Grigson and STEPHEN SPENDER. Grigson later gained notoriety as editor of *New Verse* (1933–39): He was outspoken in his dislike for what he considered to be the staid, stable poetry of the 1930s, including the work of EDITH SITWELL and C. Day Lewis, and saw his magazine as a haven for young, Leftist poets.

World War II tempered the gung-ho enthusiasm so evident in the journals of the 1930s. Regardless of which views the journals of the 1930s espoused, they espoused those views enthusiastically. By the 1940s, in contrast, many poetry magazines reflected the somber mood of wartime Britain itself. In 1940, Cyril Connolly began publishing *Horizon* (1940–49), with the help of Spender. This journal included poems by Auden and LOUIS MACNEICE, in addition to essays by George Orwell. *Horizon*'s editorial content proposed an "art for art's sake" attitude reminiscent of the 1890s, perhaps as an attempt to demonstrate the ability of creativity to continue despite the arrival of a second world war (Hamilton 129–33). *Kingdom Come* (1939–43) published the surrealist poetry written by the new apocalyptics, a group loosely led by Henry Treece and united in their dislike of the intellectual, reasoned poetry of Auden. Essays preaching pacifism and anarchism were also published in its pages. Spender eventually went on to edit *Encounter* (1953–67).

Several magazines that began in the 1950s, 1960s, and 1970s remain in publication today. Founded by JON SILKIN, *Stand* has been published as a quarterly magazine devoted to fiction, poetry, and essays since 1952. Both "Funeral Music," by GEOFFREY HILL, and "Sonnets from the School of Eloquence," by TONY HARRISON, debuted in its pages. Silkin believed that art should be both ethical and beautiful. Although the *London Magazine* was started in 1732 and was published somewhat sporadically throughout the 18th and 19th centuries, the 1954 revamping of the magazine, spearheaded by its editor John Lehmann, helped it reach its current position of importance in the British literary scene. Today it features poetry, photographs, fiction, and essays. *Critical Quarterly* (1959–present) publishes poetry alongside literary criticism, a testament to the importance of literary theory and criticism in the postwar world, while *Ambit* (1959–present) publishes poetry, art, and short stories. Pound helped found *Agenda,* which continues publishing poems by new writers and underrated writers from the past, in 1959. *Poetry Wales* (1965–present) naturally pays particular attention to Welsh writers, but each issue also includes work by writers from other locales. *Poetry Nation* (1973–present; now known as *PN Review*), under the editorship of Michael Schmidt, has an equally pluralistic outlook, publishing work by British, American, Australian, Indian, and Irish writers, among others. Other magazines that continue to publish today include *Modern Poetry in Translation* (begun in 1965), *Orbis* (1968–present), the *Edinburgh Review* (1969–present), *Granta* (1979–present), and the *Literary Review* (1979–present). In most cases, what began as an experimental magazine has morphed into an established, more conventional journal that publishes all types of poetry from all types of poets.

In addition to full-length anthologies, little magazines and journals helped galvanize new poetic movements and present exciting new poets to public view. HUGH MACDIARMID sparked a renaissance in Scottish poetry through his monthly, the *Scottish Chapbook* (1922–23), in which he railed against English as a language and championed writing in Scotland's native vernacular. *New Statesman* (1913–present) was one of the first journals to publish work by SEAMUS HEANEY, and George Hartley's journal *Listen* (1954–62) helped introduce PHILIP LARKIN to British readers. The *English Intelligencer* (1966–68), *Second Aeon* (1966–75), and *Shearsman* (1981–83, 1991–2005, 2005–present) were magazines at the forefront of the British poetry revival of the 1960s and 1970s. In 1971, Eric Mottram, a critic affiliated with the revivalists, was invited to edit *Poetry Review,* the magazine of the prestigious Poetry Society (founded in 1909). For the next six years, the gulf between academic poets published by conventional, established publishing houses and experimental poets published by small presses widened considerably. Traditionalists objected to the avant-garde verse, which led to the cancellation of funding for many magazines, journals, and publishing houses in the 1970s and 1980s. Despite the dire financial situation, poetry journals continued to start up and publish. *Staple* (1982–present) and *Acumen* (1985–present) remain viable magazines. *Iota* (1987–present) reads all submissions, culling each issue's selections from that pool; other magazines might solicit work from specific poets. Unlike most magazines, *SOUTH* (1990–2003; 2003–present) does not have a main editor; instead, a different editor, known as a selector, chooses poems for each issue.

Throughout the 20th century, there was great cross-fertilization between British and American poets, and the American journal *Poetry* (1912–present), perhaps the most important poetry magazine printing in English, published poems by Eliot and BASIL BUNTING, among others. Ford founded the Paris-based *Transatlantic Review* (1924–present) to publish work written in English by poets in such places as the United Kingdom, France, and the United States. In 1978, the Americans Bruce Andrews and Charles Bernstein founded *L=A=N=G=U=A=G=E Magazine* (1978–80), which spearheaded the language poetry movement that influenced many contemporary British poets, such as Ken Edwards, founder and editor of the London-based journal *Reality Studios* (1978–88).

In the late 20th and early 21st centuries, British poetry journals underwent another crucial shift, due, once again, to advances in technology. Magazines and journals began creating Internet-based components to complement or, in some cases, subsume their paper versions. Web sites allow magazines and journals to list events, advertise books, feature interviews with authors, and rapidly add or shift editorial content in real time. Poetry Kit, a Web site based in the United Kingdom, boasts more than 4 million visitors since its inception in 1998. John Kinsella moderates a popular electronic discussion board devoted to verse called *poetryetc*. Many magazines, such as *Poetry London* (1979–present) and *Open Wide Magazine* (2001–present), have a companion Web site with limited content, thereby requiring interested readers to purchase the magazine. Other magazines have shifted completely to the Web: *Sheaf Magazine* (1979–present) transitioned from print-based to solely Internet-based in 2001; the magazine is now known as *e-Sheaf*. Similarly *10th Muse* (1990–present) only occasionally publishes in hard copy but always publishes online. Other magazines, such as *Magma* (1995–present), allow readers the option of subscribing either digitally or via hard copies. But as their tangible counterparts do, electronic journals fold just as quickly as they spring up, largely for financial reasons, and what is online—or in bookshops—one day might not be there the next.

Nevertheless poetry flourishes on the Internet, where such sites as *Poetry Daily, jacket, Poemhunter,* and the *Electronic Poetry Center* transcend geographical borders to deliver poems to millions of readers. A few clicks of a mouse take us to poems both modern and ancient, traditional and experimental, all from the comfort of our chairs.

BIBLIOGRAPHY

The British Library Board. "Little Magazines." The British Library. Available online. URL: http://www.bl.uk/collections/britirish/litmag.html. Accessed May 8, 2008.

Ellis, R. J. "Mapping the United Kingdom Little Magazine Field." In *New British Poetries: The Scope of the Possible,* edited by Robert Hampson and Peter Barry, 72–103. Manchester and New York: Manchester University Press, 1993.

Hamilton, Ian. *The Little Magazines: A Study of Six Editors.* London: Weidenfeld and Nicolson, 1976.

Morrisson, Mark S. *The Public Face of Modernims: Little Magazines, Audiences, and Reception, 1905–1920.* Madison: University of Wisconsin Press, 2001. "UK Little Magazines Project." Nottingham Trent University. Available online. URL: http://www.ntu.ac.uk/acc/specialist_centres/English/uk_little_mags/index.html. Accessed May 8, 2008.

"Poetry Magazines Archive." Poetry Library. Available online. URL: http://www.poetrymagazines.org.uk. Accessed May 8, 2008.

Stephensen-Payne, Phil. "Magazines." Galactic Central. Available online. URL: http://www.philsp.com/magazines.html. Accessed May 8, 2008.

Jessica Allen

POETRY PRESSES   The 20th century saw many innovations in publishing, including the advent of book clubs and associations of booksellers, and is arguably the century in which poets themselves played the most active part in publishing. Extremely influential in the early years of the 20th century was J. M. Dent, who performed a great service for literary classics when he began the Everyman series. Dent had a vision in 1905 that he began to carry out in 1906: to print a 1,000-volume collection of literary classics that would appeal, as the name suggested, to everyone. Dent's vision of taking serious literature off the academic pedestal endured beyond his own death; the 1,000th book was printed in 1956, and the number of books in the complete booklist swelled well past the original target by the time the publisher ceased publishing new titles during the 1970s. *Everyman* was relaunched by Knopf in 1991. The new launch was international, helping take poetry and prose to an even wider audience.

Methuen Press is an example of a late 19th-century publishing firm that continues to thrive into the early 21st century. Methuen published a number of books by now-famous writers, including Henry James, Kenneth Grahame, and D. H. LAWRENCE. Methuen deserves a special credit for first rattling the shackles of censorship still lingering from the Victorian era: They faced a lawsuit after publishing Lawrence's highly sexual novel *The Rainbow* in 1915. Though Lawrence lost and all copies were gathered and burned in the United Kingdom, the novel continued to enjoy American popularity. Methuen published T. S. ELIOT's first prose book, *The Sacred Wood,* in 1920

Geoffrey Faber was a publisher who had, above all, a good sense of humor. When he bought out Lady Gwyer's share of their printing house, Faber and Gwyer, he renamed it Faber and Faber in 1929. There was, of course, no Faber other than he. This did not mean he was alone though—T. S. Eliot himself was one of Faber's directors until 1965. In addition to having a steady publisher for his own poetry, Eliot helped usher in other brilliant poets under the Faber and Faber mark, such as W. H. AUDEN, EZRA POUND, and STEPHEN SPENDER. Shortly before the resurgence of poetry popularity in the 1960s, Faber and Faber also introduced THOM GUNN, PHILIP LARKIN, SEAMUS HEANEY, and the tumultuously married poets TED HUGHES and SYLVIA PLATH. With Eliot's influence, as well as the large list of writers, Faber and Faber is widely regarded as the preeminent publisher of British poetry in the last century.

Another publisher took the *Everyman* formula to all-new heights. Allen Lane, the original creator of the press Bodley Head, had watched his famous publishing creation fading as a result of financial difficulties brought on shortly before and during the Great Depression. With the humble starting capital of only £100, Lane created Penguin Books. Penguin's idea was very simple: to offer cheap paperback reprints of books that other publishers were only selling as hardbacks. Penguin books had very colorful covers, color-coded by book type: orange and white for works of fiction, green and white for crime fiction (an increasingly popular genre with children because of *Detective Comics,* the comic book that would later introduce Batman), dark red for travel books, and blue for biographies. Penguin Books eventually adopted the orange and white trim for all of its titles, retaining the color scheme to this day. Readers may note that Allen Lane had an interesting sense of humor; the cartoonish Penguin mascot on each cover has been there since the beginning.

In 1945, Penguin began what it has become most famous for, its Penguin Classics collection. Beginning with E. V. Rieu's translation of the Homer's epic poem *The Odyssey,* Penguin's classics have flourished; in fact,

many writers consider it a point of honor (and, of course, profit) to be included in Penguin's collection. Lane's company also solidified the strength of paperback books, which quickly became regarded as more profitable than their hardback counterparts. In a way, Lane can be credited with introducing classical literature to the masses, as well as presenting yesterday's poetry to a new generation of writers. One final note about Allen Lane and Penguin Books: They effectively ended the fight against obscenity trials for literature that Methuen had begun. Appropriately circular, it ended as it had begun with D. H. Lawrence. While *The Rainbow* was burned in 1915, Penguin successfully published Lawrence's *Lady Chatterly's Lover* in 1960, 32 years after it was written.

University presses played a major part in the distribution of poetry, especially Oxford University Press, which in the early 20th century expanded internationally to Bombay, Cape Town, Melbourne, and Toronto, while its existing New York branch continued publishing British literature and poetry in America, including the first edition of G. M. Hopkin's poetry in 1918 under its Clarendon Press imprint. During cutbacks in its budget in the 1990s, the Oxford University Press gave up publishing contemporary poetry; its list was taken over by the influential Carcanet Press, started by the poet Michael Schmidt and based in Manchester. Carcanet, Faber and Faber, Bloodaxe (based in Newcastle upon Tyne), and Dufour were at century's end among the leading publishers of contemporary poetry in the United Kingdom.

Charles Elkin Mathews had the honor of being the first to publish works by W. B. YEATS—his neighbor in Bedford Park, Chiswick. Though Mathews's earlier successes were with his partner John Lane (who later went on to form the printing press the Bodley Head), Mathews published the biggest authors on his own. In addition to Yeats, he was the first publisher for ROBERT BRIDGES, James Joyce, and EZRA POUND. Yeats's sister Elizabeth was a member of the Dun Emer Guild in Ireland, set up to teach young women the related arts of bookbinding and printing. In 1904, she began, with her brother, Cuala Press. Cuala was famously the first commercial press in Ireland that worked exclusively with hand presses. Though Elizabeth often receives more credit for the creation of the press, W. B. Yeats certainly benefited from it: Cuala published more than 70 books, 48 of them his own works.

Virginia and Leonard Woolf operated a hand press machine from their home, Hogarth House in Richmond, Surrey, England, starting the Hogarth Press in 1917. Hogarth eventually relied on commercial printers as its business grew, but its most famous poem was printed by hand—T. S. Eliot's THE WASTE LAND. Though Virginia Woolf's company was arguably most well known for its post–World War Two emphasis on the works of Sigmund Freud, the New Hogarth Library Series focused on poets both national and international, including C. DAY LEWIS, Federico García Lorca, and Rainer Maria Rilke. The publisher stayed independent until 1946, when it joined the publisher Chatto and Windus.

Later in the 20th century, many British publishers had to merge (or be bought outright) with larger companies in order to survive. The largest of these acquiring companies was Random House. Begun as an American company in the early 1920s by Bennet Cerf and Donald Klopfer, it became a worldwide phenomenon. Having made headlines with their successful legal defense of Joyce's *Ulysses* in America, Random House first had impact in England when it bought out the old-guard publishing houses of Bodley Head, Chatto and Windus, Jonathan Cape, Ltd., and Virago. Though Methuen continues its primary publishing efforts on its own, its drama division was purchased by Bloomsbury Publishing in May 2006. Bloomsbury, of course, is most well known for the extremely popular *Harry Potter* series of books. Collins, a publisher known best for printing *The Chronicles of Narnia* by C. S. LEWIS, was acquired by the American Rupert Murdoch's New Corporation. Murdoch joined them with the American publisher Harper & Row, creating HarperCollins. HarperCollins, in turn, went on to acquire the publisher George Allen and Sons, whose most famous publications were *The Lord of the Rings* by J. R. R. Tolkien. Under HarperCollins, the publisher's new name became Allen and Unwin.

Macmillan Publishing was fully bought out between 1995 and 1999 by the German media giant Georg von Holtzbrinck Publishing Group, ending the Macmillan family's reign over the company. Macmillan now publishes under a variety of imprints, publishing poets as varied as Heaney, Hughes, and ELIZABETH JENNINGS. Though it has not acquired any British companies, the American company W. W. Norton expanded its publishing industry into London in the 1980s. Norton was responsible for instituting a poetry program in the 1960, and is responsible for best-selling textbook anthologies of both poetry and prose that continue to be taught on a college level.

Now in the 21st century the world of publishing continues to change and evolve. Self-publishing opportunities have become both cheaper and more numerous, and the Internet has deeply shaken the industry's conception of marketing. Print as a medium for the communication of ideas faces opposition in a world of blogs, podcasts, and file sharing.

BIBLIOGRAPHY

Anderson, Patricia, and Jonathan Rose, eds. *British Literary Publishing Houses.* Detroit: Gale Research, 1991.

Feather, John. *A History of British Publishing.* New York, Routledge Kegan & Paul 1988.

Mumby, Frank Arthur, and Ian Norrie. *Publishing and Bookselling,* 5th ed. London: Jonathan Cape, 1974.

Myers, Robin, and Michael Harris, eds. *Economics of the British Booktrade.* Cambridge: Chadwyck-Healey, 1985.

Plant, Marjorie. *The English Book Trade,* 3rd ed. London: George Allen and Unwin, 1974.

Chris Snellgrove

"THE POMEGRANATE" EAVAN BOLAND (1994)

EAVAN BOLAND's most anthologized poem, "The Pomegranate," has influenced a generation of writers, feminists, and readers. In tone the poem embraces the ordinary, recounting a familiar domestic moment even as it explores several of Boland's favorite themes—nationalism, maternity, and the use of history for life. By juxtaposing an uneventful moment in a suburban milieu against larger myths and meanings, Boland does what she does best. She embraces old myths in order to reinvent them and make them new.

One of the reasons scholars often point to this poem as representative of Boland's work is its hushed absence of event. Boland's poems frequently focus on the ordinary rather than the extraordinary, partly because

Boland believes that literature should celebrate those lives that have not been lived in the spotlight. In "The Pomegranate" the action is minimal: A mother reflects as she watches her sleeping daughter. Contributing to the quiet tone is the mother's obvious desire not to wake her daughter, and as such the very topic matter shushes us. Everything about the poem is like a whisper—small words, small lines—as if what the mother is saying is not only quiet, but deeply felt. The poem's free verse establishes a discursive associative structure, as the mother's comments freely tack back and forth between the worlds of myth and experience, and between the cold suburban exterior and the warm domestic interior.

The speaker is reflecting perhaps as much for herself as for her audience, since readers are tacitly called on to look over the mother's shoulder. The occasion creates a sure identification between the reader and the mother; it makes readers acknowledge that unlike the daughter, they are presently knowing and seeing, united with the mother in studying someone who is vulnerable, and who does not know that she is being studied. The daughter has gone to bed. Next to her are a can of Coke and a stack of teen magazines—signs of youth culture and conformity—and a plate of fruit that she took to her room but has not yet eaten. On the plate is a pomegranate. From the stairwell outside the daughter's room, the mother watches this uneventful scene; she remembers her own childhood and muses on the mythical meanings of pomegranates. These associations lead her to make an important parenting decision that becomes ironic given the ostensible lack of action in the poem. On first reading, the poem appears to capture one static moment in time (daughter inert, mother motionless). But the fact that the mother stands on the threshold, in the stairwell, signals a message of symbolic transition. Stairwells and thresholds invoke a sense of passage, and, even as they connect two spaces, so do they auger a sense of movement or change from one state to another.

Before the speaker begins describing her daughter, she calls on a Greek myth to point to the journey of initiation from childhood to adulthood, from innocence and credulous optimism to experience and sentient grief. The mother begins, "The only legend I have ever loved is / the story of a daughter lost in hell." This legend, the myth of Ceres and Persephone, explains why we have seasons, and why in particular we must have six months of dark and barren land for every six months of blooming, fecund land. The story is from Hesiod's *Theogony* (ca. 700 B.C.E.) and from the anonymous *Homeric Hymn to Demeter,* most likely written in the seventh century B.C.E. Demeter, the Greek name for Ceres, was the goddess of agriculture; it was she who made crops grow and flowers bloom. As does the mother in the poem, Ceres cherished her daughter, who seemed the very incarnation of spring: young, fresh, beautiful as the blossoms with which she is associated.

One day Persephone, gathering flowers in the meadows, heard distant thunder. The earth opened in a tremendous crack and out rolled the chariot of Pluto, or Hades, god of the underworld. Pluto abducted Persephone, whisking her back into the underworld, where he offered her a pomegranate. She accepted it and ate six of the seeds. Because her choice to eat the pomegranate was freely made, as an act of her own will, she was not allowed to return to the earth, even when her mother finally discovered her whereabouts and made the long journey to try to reclaim her. After having eaten the pomegranate, Persephone was forever changed. She would have to spend six months of every year in the dark underworld with Pluto, and only then could she rejoin her mother for six months in the old world.

Thus it was that when Persephone was with her mother, Ceres was happy and allowed spring to come to the earth. But when Persephone was with her husband in the underworld, Ceres grew so mournful that no crops would grow, and winter became the projection of her loss. This is why, says the myth, winter inevitably follows the spring: For every moment of happiness, there will be a moment of unhappiness. For every joy, there will be attendant forfeiture.

In the myth, Persephone's decision to taste the pomegranate subsumes her into the cycle of male objectification; she is kidnapped because Pluto finds her beautiful and desirable. Her consent to eat the pomegranate marks not only her passage from innocence to experience, but her tacit acquiescence to be objectified by Pluto's desire. Boland connects this passage to the biblical account of the Edenic fall, when

Eve willingly tastes the fruit of the Tree of Knowledge: "She put out her hand and pulled down / the French sound for apple." The location of *pomme* inside the word *pomegranate* makes its own symbolic journey, calling on a host of Christian associations: grace, innocence, temptation, sexual shame, and regret. Boland's diction, coupled with her pointed reference to the teen magazines that train young women in the art of self-objectification, insists on the notion of sexual initiation: "She will hold the papery flushed skin in her hand / and to her lips." The papery flushed skin of a pomegranate, tender and delicate, evokes an image of aroused genital sensitivity. For the daughter to raise the fruit to her lips, in this sense, is to participate in a lovers' consummation. Here sexual initiation is by no means the end of the journey; it is neither the denouement nor the happy ending that teen magazines often promise. Instead the sexual initiation commences a life season in which the daughter will make her decisions with will and deliberation, and in which she must sustain, if not always understand, the consequences thereof.

In the myth, Persephone, as her mother Ceres, is fated to become a mere totem of desire and passivity. Although Persephone freely eats the pomegranate seeds, she still merely accepts a sexual invitation; she does not make one. But in Boland's retelling of the myth, the totemic figures of the helpless mother and the desirable virgin become real women, women who desire and choose, sacrifice and suffer. This poem's engagement with myth making is typical of Boland's work in that the oversimplified female characters of mythology are filtered through a feminist lens that ascribes to them complex motivation and agency. The mother in the poem says that she can enter the legend anywhere—that is, she can relate both to Ceres and to Persephone. Once, as an "exiled child in the crackling dusk of the underworld," she was Persephone, and now she is Ceres. Meditatively she acknowledges that although she could warn her daughter of her fate, to "defer the grief" would be to "diminish the gift." The mother *wants* the daughter to choose her own fate, to exert agency, to bear the consequences of all the adult choices to come, even at the cost of her own grief.

The relationship between the daughter and the mother also functions as an analogue for the relationship between Ireland and its colonizing motherland, England. The nation that tests its independence and rebels against the colonizing authority is like the daughter who must and will choose to author her own decisions, and who will therefore inevitably declare her own autonomy. The mythic daughter Persephone also recalls the Irish folkloric figure of the *spéirbhhean,* a young rape victim who stands for the invaded nation that must be restored to its former purity. The innocence of the daughter in Boland's poem, however, is neither prolonged nor restored. In this way Boland radically rewrites the punch line of the myth, since the object is no longer to get the daughter back, but to let her go.

Boland's poem implies a practical use for both history and mythology. Neither history nor mythology finds its best use in warning us away from a painful course of action. The mother understands that the daughter will inevitably taste the pomegranate; the question is what her own role as a parent will be. Should she try to save her daughter, tell her what she knows in the hope of preventing her from making poor and painful decisions? The mother decides: "I will say nothing." And ironically the mother who says nothing is saying a very eloquent something: History and myth become most useful to us in the way they prepare us to embrace moral, political, and intellectual independence.

BIBLIOGRAPHY

Bennett, Karen. "The Recurrent Quest: Demeter and Persephone in Modern-Day Ireland." *Classical Modern Literature* 23, no. 1 (spring 2003): 15–32.

Boland, Eavan. *Against Love Poetry: Poems.* New York: W. W. Norton, 2001.

——— *Object Lessons: The Life of the Woman and the Poet in Our Time.* New York: W. W. Norton, 1995.

——— *Outside History: Selected Poems 1980–1990.* New York: W. W. Norton, 1990.

Hagen, Patricia L., and Thomas W. Zelman. *Eavan Boland and the History of the Ordinary.* Dublin and Bethesda, Md.: Maunsel, 2004.

Kirkpatrick, Kathryn, ed. *Border Crossings: Irish Women Writers and National Identities.* Tuscaloosa: University of Alabama Press, 2000.

Rhoda Janzen

PORTER, PETER (1929–) Peter Porter was born in Brisbane, Australia, in 1929. Following his mother's death in 1938, Porter was sent to board at the prestigious Church of England Grammar School in Brisbane, which he would later describe as an austere and harsh institution. In 1941 he was transferred to the Toowoomba Church of England Boys' Preparatory School, graduating in 1946. Porter's 1959 poem "Mr. Roberts" immortalises the principal of that school, highlighting the poet's distaste for the pompousness and rigidity typical of such institutions and their leaders.

In 1951 Porter emigrated to England, settling in London. While Porter would later describe his early years in London as difficult, the city's unique blend of social, political, and artistic ferment would nevertheless help to shape the young poet and his work. Chief among these influences was the Group, a weekly poetry discussion group that he joined in 1955. The Group was attended by prolific poets such as Martin Bell and PETER REDGROVE, both of whom would become influential figures in Porter's life.

Porter was also profoundly influenced by the poetry and sensibilities of W. H. AUDEN. Porter began to share his mentor's love of Italy, music, and art, though his poetic landscape extends well beyond this limited sphere, comprising, as the critic George Szirtes has noted, "all the apparatus of high culture . . . cats, Popes, domestic sorrow, Auden, money, conspiracies, torture chambers, concentration camps, consumer goods, sex, domesticity, agents of political oppression, seediness, dreams of welfare state Britain, corrupt institutions, great tracts of Shakespeare, the Bible and big encyclopaedias, the chatter of history as well as the chatter of the chattering classes." His dual British-Australian identity is also evident throughout his work, with poems such as "SYDNEY COVE, 1788" tracing the colonization and birth of Australia's first and largest city.

Porter's first collection of poetry, entitled *Once Bitten, Twice Bitten,* was published in 1961. Both it and the selection of poems published in the 1962 Penguin Modern Poets series were well received by critics. His second collection, *Poems Ancient and Modern,* was published in 1964, while his third, *A Porter Folio,* first appeared in 1969. In 1978 he published what many consider to be his finest collection of verse, *The Cost of Seriousness.* The poems, personal in tone, focus on the death of his first wife.

Porter has published more than 20 volumes of poetry. He has won numerous awards, including the 1988 Whitbread Prize for his collection *The Automatic Oracle,* while in 2002 he was awarded the Queen's Gold Medal for Poetry. He continues to live in London, though in recent years he has made numerous visits to Australia.

BIBLIOGRAPHY
Bennett, Bruce. *Spirit in Exile: Peter Porter and his Poetry.* Melbourne: Oxford University Press Australia, 1991.
Forbes, Peter. "Contemporary Writers: Peter Porter." British Arts Council. Available online. URL: http://www. contemporarywriters.com/authors/?p=auth210. Accessed July 16, 2006.

Emma Carmody

POSTCOLONIALISM Postcolonialism is a literary theory used to highlight issues of empire, colonization, and cultural marginalization in literature. Postcolonial theory is often applied to literatures of formerly colonized countries to investigate the way literature operates within a political, economic, and sociocultural context. Developed in part as a way to understand the effects of European imperialism, postcolonialism aids in the examination of colonial and neocolonial spaces.

When Britain began to establish colonies and spheres of influence as part of its drive for empire that reached its height in the Victorian era, it tied its nation to the futures of the territories and spaces it colonized. A colony is a region or territory controlled by another nation at a distance. When a territory becomes a colony of another nation, it becomes dependent on the colonizer; as a result, the colony's own precolonial or preimperial identity is subsumed by the colonizer. Postcolonial analysis is used as one method to help a region, territory, or marginalized people to regain a sense of identity and to grapple with the effects of colonization on their country and culture. It is also a way to study the effects of cultural hegemony. But just as colonization frequently promoted assimilation and homogenization, it is difficult to assign universal qualities to postcolonial critique as by its nature, "the field seeks to develop adequate and appropriate approaches to material that is itself diverse, hybrid, diasporic" (Ashcroft et al., 1). The language of postcolonial theory and the approaches of postcolonial analysis are constantly being examined and reexamined, defined and redefined, as students and scholars try to negotiate the complexities of colonialism and imperialism.

The term *postcolonialism* sometimes appears as *postcolonialism* and there is much debate in the field as to the use of the hyphen and the meaning the hyphenation assigns to the subject. Some scholars say that *postcolonialism* signifies the end of colonization—the time at which a nation achieves independence from its colonizer. But *postcolonialism,* a term used by other critics without the key hyphen, indicates a theoretical approach that begins from the moment of contact with the friture colonizer. So where *post-colonialism* addresses the ending and repercussions of newly independent peoples and states, *postcolonialism* indicates a focus on the advent of colonialism and the effects of being colonized, existing under colonial power, and then seeking and achieving political independence. Both *post-colonial* and *postcolonial* also examine the aftereffects of colonization—to achieve political independence as a nation or a people does not mean that culturally or economically the nation is free of its colonizer. In fact, many postcolonial writers express their frustration with the seemingly inextricable ties to the former colonizer, and their texts engage with the difficulty of becoming truly independent from a colonial power.

One might ask, "If postcolonial theory is about the colonized, then how does it apply to British literature?" At this point, a brief discussion of the theorist Georg Hegel will prove helpful. In his text *Phenomenology of Spirit,* Hegel uses the analogy of a master and slave to theorize the transfer of dependency in a relationship. According to Hegel, the role of the master is a slave to the role of the slave, meaning that the master *cannot be master* if he does not have someone to enslave. By usurping this dichotomy—by turning it upside down—Hegel demonstrates that the master becomes dependent on his slave. Hegel's analogy of the master/slave relationship became enormously influential in Marxist and existentialist movements as well as the Negritude and black consciousness movements. In the case of postco-

lonial theory, Hegel's dichotomy demonstrates how the empire became as dependent on its colony as its colony became on it. The result for Britain. in this case, was to become preoccupied with the colonial spaces and with its role as the empire "where the sun never sets."

The effects of being a hegemonic power are reflected in British literature. From the drawing rooms of Jane Austen's domestic fiction to the adventures of Rudyard Kipling's characters, empire infiltrates literature. Postcolonial theory helps to identify the anxiety and heady exuberance of Britain's imperial power. It also helps to show how Britain's national identity relied on defining itself as different from its colonized regions. Thus much of British literature that incorporates issues of empire reflects a preoccupation with ideas of enlightened British civilization against what the authors deemed to be the "darkness" on the rest of the earth. Edward Said, a theorist, calls this effect "colonial discourse."

Michel Foucault, a French philosopher, theorized that discourse is "a system of statements within which the world can be known. It is the system by which dominant groups in society constitute the field of truth by imposing specific knowledges, disciplines and values upon dominated groups." (Ashcroft et al., 42). Colonial discourse placed Europe at the center and the colonies on the periphery—in the position of marginalized cultures, races, and regions. Europe was seen, literally, as the hub around which the rest of the world revolved as spokes in the wheel. Colonial discourse became a way in which to articulate power relationships between the colonizer and the colonized. Through literature, the colonized was, literally, written into being. The colonizing power. as the one in control of print capitalism, thus created a discourse with which it engaged the rest of the world. The colonized, the object of much scrutiny in colonial discourse, could become indoctrinated by the discourse generated from the center. "Rules of inclusion and exclusion operate on the assumption of the superiority of the colonizer's culture, history, language, art, political structures, social conventions and the assertion of the need for the colonized to be 'raised up' through colonial contact" (Ashcroft et al., 42). Postcolonjal responses then address issues of identity regeneration and reformation of cultural memory.

The Nobel Prize–winning Caribbean poet DEREK WALCOTT has written one of the most anthologized examples of a postcolonial response to identity; in his poem "A Far Cry from Africa," the narrative voice asks:

I who am poisoned with the blood of both,
Where shall I turn, divided to the vein?
I who have cursed
The drunken officer of British rule, how choose
Between this Africa and the English tongue I
      love? (Il. 26–30)

Originally inspired by the Mau Mau uprisings in Kenya, this excerpt demonstrates the internal tensions of the colonized for which Walcott's works are so well known. In this passage, the speaker is torn between the need to resist British colonial rule and the desire to preserve use of the English language—and thus Walcott confronts the complexity of the colonized's position: Once having encountered the colonizer, to which identity does the colonized revert or which assume when the colonizer has been displaced? If the colonizer to an extent is responsible for creating the identity of the colonized through colonial discourse, then how does the colonized establish or reestablish his/her identity?

Another aspect of discourse theories that is applied to postcolonialism is examination of "orientalism." *Orientalism* is a term used by Edward Said and discussed in his seminal work by that same title. Said describes orientalism not as a place, but as a construct of the European imagination, used in opposition to the "occidental," or "West." Thus "the Orient" was not so much a fixed geographical space on a map as a way for the West to label and then dominate other cultures. Much writing from Great Britain during the time of empire is preoccupied with "orientalizing" the non-Westerner, and poets such as Alfred, Lord Tennyson have elements of orientalism in their writing. Tennyson's orientalism mixes with imperialist ideologies in such poems as "Akbar's Dream" (1892), in which the ruler resembles King Arthur, but whose efforts to civilize his kingdom and create an oriental Camelot fall short, and the civilizing mission of building a great kingdom is

left up to the British. The poem expresses conventional orientalist and proimperialist themes: namely, that colonized cultures—while fascinating and magical and mysterious—will always need the more rational Occidental (British) world to rescue them (Brantlinger 10).

The racism evident in orientalism is addressed through postcolonial theory that seeks to confront the socially constructed hierarchies of gender, race, culture, and history. The hybridity of the theoretical approach is one reason for postcolonialism's popularity among some scholars. Postcolonial theory also inspires discourse analysis, consideration of current political and economic movements such as "globalization"; a study of gender roles, race relations, and power relationships between nations; and draws connections among psychoanalytic, Marxist, feminist, and race discourse theories. Postcolonialism's beginnings are firmly rooted in subaltern studies and the Negritude and Creolité movements and continues to have overlap with African American studies.

BIBLIOGRAPHY

Ashcroft, Bill, Gareth Griffiths, and Helen Tiffin. *Post-Colonial Studies: The Key Concepts*. New York: Routledge, 1998.
Brantlinger, Patrick. *Rule of Darkness: British Literature and Imperialism, 1830–1914*. Ithaca, N.Y.: Cornell University Press, 1988.
Gandhi, Leela. *Postcolonial Theory: A Critical Introduction*. New York: Columbia University Press, 1998.
Said, Edward. *Orientalism*. New York: Pantheon Books, 1978.
Walcott, Derek. "A Far Cry from Africa." *The Longman Anthology of British Literature*. Vol. B, edited by David Damrosch, 1,421–1,422. 2nd compact ed. New York: Longman, 2004.

Corinna McLeod

POSTIMPRESSIONISM   The term *postimpressionism* was coined by the English art critic Roger Fry in 1910 to refer to a loosely related group of painters who represented a reaction against impressionism that would lay the foundation for MODERNISM in the early 20th century. Upon seeing Fry's London exhibition of Cézanne, for which he coined the term, Virginia Woolf was so moved that she declared that human nature had changed in December 1910. The four principal artists identified as postimpressionists are the French artists Paul Cézanne (1839–1906), Paul Gauguin (1848–1903), and Georges Seurat (1859–91) and the Dutch painter Vincent van Gogh (1853–90), who spent his last years working in France. Each of these artists experimented with impressionism and had even exhibited with the impressionists but ultimately questioned then rejected the fundamental tenets of impressionism, hence the designation postimpressionism.

Reflecting an interest in contemporary optical investigations and color theory, the impressionists attempted to record the transient effects of light on objects to capture what Claude Monet referred to as the sensation of "instantaneity" that he saw as our experience of things. The term *impressionism* famously arose from a pejorative remark made in 1974 by the critic of the Parisian journal *Charivari,* Louis Leroy, when he reviewed an exhibition of a group of largely French artists who included Cézanne, Edgar Degas, Claude Monet, Berthe Morisot, Camille Pissarro, and Pierre-Auguste Renoir, who had joined to exhibit under the name Société Anonyme des Artistes Peintres, Sculptres, Graveurs, etc. Drawing on the title of a painting by Monet, *Impression, Sunrise,* Leroy used the term *impressionist* to describe the unfinished appearance of many of the paintings characterized by a bright color palette and choppy brushwork. With its emphasis on direct observation and plein-air painting to capture the momentary and changing effects of light on objects, impressionism can be seen as a naturalist movement with a strong strain of optical realism. The illusionism and solidity of the subject are undermined, however, by the broken, painterly brushwork and use of pure color unifying the surface of the painting that reveals the work of art as an object independent of its subject. In this way impressionism bridges the perceptual realism that had dominated Western art since the Renaissance and the nonperceptual interests of most modernist movements. Over time each of the four postimpressionist artists became disaffected with the impressionist emphasis on transience and changeable phenomena, desiring, each in his own way, to produce an art of greater substance, stability, and permanence.

Rejecting the flickering dematerialization of form and ephemeral nature of impressionism, the postim-

pressionists retained the impressionist high-key color palette and preference for contemporary everyday subject matter while introducing various forms of abstraction. Each developed a distinctive style arising from a distinctive set of concerns. Together they would lay the foundation for the development of the modernist art of the early 20th century that placed a premium on the embodiment of concepts and experience through abstract and expressive form over the representation of the objective appearance of things.

In British literature, the postimpressionist influence was felt most keenly in fiction, especially in the work of Virginia Woolf, Katherine Mansfield, and Joseph Conrad. But beginning with Oscar Wilde's impressionist poetry and stretching through the 20th century, a common technique of poetry has become to paint the sensory impressions of an incident or scene with details that describe rather than interpret the impressions, sensations, and emotions of a character's mental life.

BIBLIOGRAPHY

Brettel, Richard et al. *The Art of Paul Gauguin.* Washington, D.C.: National Gallery of Art, 1988.

Nochlin, Linda. *Impressionism and Post-Impressionism 1874–1904.* Sources and Documents in the History of Art Series. Englewood Cliffs, N.J.: Prentice-Hall, 1966.

Post-Impressionism: Cross-Currents in European and American Painting 1880–1906. Washington, D.C.: National Gallery of Art, 1980.

Rewald, John. *Post-Impressionism from van Gogh to Gauguin.* 3rd ed. New York: Museum of Modern Art, 1978.

Rubin, William, ed. *Cézanne: The Late Work.* New York: Museum of Modern Art, 1977.

Sutter, Jean, ed. *The Neo-Impressionists.* Greenwich, Conn.: New York Graphic Society, 1970.

Zemel, Carol. *Van Gogh's Progress: Utopia, Modernity, and Late Nineteenth Century Art.* Berkeley: University of California Press, 1997.

Rachel Hostetter Smith

POUND, EZRA (1885–1972)

POUND, EZRA (1885–1972) Ezra Loomis Pound was born in 1885 in the small mining town of Hailey, Idaho, on what was then the edge of the burgeoning American frontier. Although Pound was proud of his family origins and did much to play up his "frontier roots," the fact is that the Pounds spent little time in Hailey and his family moved in 1887, shortly after he was born, first to Wisconsin then later to New York City and Pennsylvania in a number of what Pound would later come to see as fateful eastward journeys, away from the dusty American frontier, toward the cultured drawing rooms and libraries of London and Europe. As would many of his contemporaries, including Gertrude Stein, Robert Frost, and T. S. ELIOT, Pound would eventually choose to leave the United States and seek his literary fortunes in Europe. Although Pound's work is clearly influenced by American literature, he had a complicated relationship to his home country, and his love for the achievements of European culture was often at odds with the culture of turn-of-the-century America. Indeed during the Second World War Pound became notorious for his anti-American, and sometimes anti-Semitic, radio broadcasts, in a letter to his mother during the Great War remarked scornfully and simply that "I loathe the American state of mind." Although his opinions could at times be outright antagonistic, Pound remained, in many ways, as American as any of his contemporaries. Try as he might, Pound was always aware of his American origins, saying in 1912, "It would be about as easy for an American to become a Chinaman or a Hindoo, as for him to acquire an Englishness or a Frenchness or a Europeanness that is more than half skin deep." It is perhaps, as much as anything else, this strange admixture of American pragmatism and European high-mindedness that made Pound such an irresistible public figure, both at home and abroad, and that would go on to make him one of the most difficult, inescapable, and essential literary figures of his time.

After leaving Hailey the Pounds eventually settled near Philadelphia, and Ezra spent the majority of his childhood living an affluent but modest middle-class life in the suburbs. His early education was largely ordinary for a young man of his social standing, and from 1892 to 1901 he attended an assortment of local dame schools, public schools, and military academies, later enrolling in Hamilton College in New York and the University of Pennsylvania, where he pursued both a master's and a Ph.D. in Romance languages. It was at UPenn that Pound first met and befriended the young American poets William Carlos Williams and H. D. (HILDA DOOLITTLE), both of whom would remain life-

long friends in one capacity or another. In fact Pound would eventually go on to court Doolittle, the beautiful and spritelike daughter of a local astronomy professor, over the course of the next several years, drawing her to London and eventually launching her literary career with the publication of three of her small poems in *Poetry* magazine under the arguably effete moniker H. D. *Imagiste*. On account of his studies at UPenn Pound later took a teaching job at Wabash College in 1907. However, Pound's tenure was short-lived and he was soon expelled (with pay), after a young woman, whom Pound described only as "a girl from a stranded burlesque show," was found sleeping in his quarters. Pound, who denied any wrongdoing or manhandling, was seemingly delighted by this sudden but probably inevitable termination and quickly took the opportunity to leave both Wabash College and the America that it represented to begin his career as a poet and translator in Europe. In 1908, with his salary guaranteed for a year and $85 in his pocket, Pound sailed to Europe, first landing in Gibraltar and then moving quickly to England, where he would go on to become secretary to the poet W. B. YEATS, friend to some of the most influential figures in English letters, and enfant terrible of London's literary establishment.

Pound's arrival in London, in August 1908, however, could not have been more anticlimactic. For months, despite his best efforts, Pound remained a largely unacknowledged figure on the London literary scene. In anticipation of his arrival in London Pound had already published, at his own expense, his first collection of poems, *A Lume Spento,* or "With Tapers Quenched." The poems in this first collection, according to most critics at the time, show promise and skill, but in retrospect even Pound himself, in his preface to the 1965 edition, referred to the book as "a collection of stale creampuffs." Unfortunately Pound was right; many of the poems in the collection reveal a writer still under the influence of his academic studies, stuck in the 14th century, unable to find his own voice. Take, for example, the end of stanza 1, from the poem "Villonaud for this Yule": "(Skoal! with the dregs if the clear be gone!) / Wineing the ghosts of yester-year." The tone is grotesquely overdramatic and Pound's archaic literary pursuits are clearly an undue influence.

Even William Carlos Williams, sometime friend and critic, regarded the poems as boring academicism. Indeed it was not until his relationships, first with THOMAS EDWARD HULME and later with RICHARD ALDINGTON and the incomparable Ford Madox Hueffer, or FORD MADOX FORD, as he would be known after the war, that Pound began to make waves and develop the signature precision of language that would exemplify his work and the imagist aesthetic that he would help to create.

By 1912 Pound was already experimenting with modern poetic language and his translations of Cavalacanti show the poet developing a more contemporary, plain style of verse, more sparse and exact. Pound was on the verge of a new kind of modern poetics, one that, as he described it in "A Retrospect," required "direct treatment of the 'thing' whether subjective or objective." Although Pound is usually given credit for launching her career, one should not underestimate the influence of the young H. D. on Pound's developing poetic sensibilities. Pound's initial excitement about H. D.'s poetry stemmed in large part from the degree to which her poems seemed to conform to so many of the ideas he was already formulating, but H. D.'s poems had given him a firsthand example of the application of many of those ideas, showing him what was possible, and it was only after the publication of her three short poems that Pound began to take seriously his own imagist poetry, most notably, the now highly anthologized haikulike two-line poem "In a Station of the Metro," published in Harriet Monroe's *Poetry* magazine in 1913.

> The apparition of these faces in the crowd;
> Petals on a wet, black bough.

The scene, as Pound described it, captures what he would go on to call "the emotional and intellectual complex in an instant of time," here capturing the emotional complex of an ecstatic vision of beautiful faces in the Paris metro. Although Pound, characteristically on the lookout for something new, would soon abandon the poetic limitations of IMAGISM, the movement nonetheless had an enormous impact on the nature of poetic language, influencing among others,

William Carlos Williams, Marianne Moore, and even Wallace Stevens, whose "Thirteen Ways of Looking at a Blackbird" or "A Bowl of Peaches in Russia" may be understood to be characteristically imagist.

On April 20, 1914, Pound finally married Dorothy Shakespeare, the daughter of Olivia Shakespeare, both of whom Pound had been shamelessly courting in one form or another since he had first met them in 1909. It is in the years leading up to and after the Great War, however, that Pound began to find his true poetic voice, publishing three collections of poetry and translation, *Ripostes* (1912), *Cathay* (1915), and *Lustra* (1916), which contained some of the poet's most important and best early works, including "The Seafarer," "THE RIVER-MERCHANT'S WIFE: A LETTER," "Portrait D'une Femme," "The Garden," and "A Pact," the last of which can be best understood as Pound's reconciliation with his own poetic roots. Speaking to the American poet Walt Whitman, whose poetry he had previously dismissed, Pound says:

> We have one sap and one root—
> Let there be commerce between us.

This reconciliation was also, in some ways, Pound's declaration of poetic maturity, for the poet was now officially an international literary figure of high regard and with the successes of the imagist and vorticist movements Pound was becoming an increasingly influential figure among his contemporaries.

It was also during this time that Pound met and became fast friends with the expatriate American poet T. S. ELIOT, whose "LOVE SONG OF J. ALFRED PRUFROCK" Pound had fought hard to get published in *Poetry* magazine in 1914. As he did with so many of his other "discoveries," including the Irish novelist James Joyce, Pound would take an extremely active role in Eliot's career, famously editing his influential epic poem *THE WASTE LAND*, published in 1922, and earning himself the prefatory dedication "Il Miglior Fabbro," or "the better craftsman." Indeed for anyone who has ever looked at the manuscripts, Pound's sometimes radical changes are almost always an improvement on Eliot's original. In fact, so extensive were Pound's changes that some critics have argued that his contributions were more than merely editorial, and that the writing of *The Waste Land* may be best understood as a collaboration between the two poets. It was also in the wake of the devastation of the Great War, in which he had lost many friends, including the beloved sculptor Gaudier Brzeska, that Pound began work on his first major poetic sequence, *Hugh Selwyn Mauberly*. Published in 1920, *Hugh Selwyn Mauberly*, with its colloquial dialogue and its many references to the events of the war and the climate of the age, marked a radical break with Pound's previously aesthetically oriented poetry and set the stage for the politics and poetic experiments of *The Cantos*. Pound was growing increasingly political in the years during and after the war and the Mauberly sequence begins with a eulogy of sorts for his old self, an ode on the poet's life, who "out of key with his time," "born / In a half savage country," had attempted to wring "lilies from the acorn." In addition to marking this philosophical change the poem is a very personal response to the atrocities and disillusionments of the war, and the lives wasted, as Pound describes it:

> For an old bitch gone in the teeth
> For a botched civilization.

This is a sentiment that would be echoed in Eliot's *The Waste Land* and by many other modern poets, for whom the events of the Great War were sometimes simply too much to bear.

Shortly after the publication of *Hugh Selwyn Mauberly* and after Pound had lost his position as foreign correspondent for *Poetry* magazine, thanks in large part to the controversy caused by his translations in *Homage to Sextus Propertius* (1919), he and Dorothy decided to leave London for good. In January 1921, Pound and Dorothy moved to Paris, where they would spend the next three years. Pound's Paris years were a time of reflection and radical experimentation. Although the first drafts of Cantos I, II, and III had appeared in *Poetry* in 1917, it was in Paris that Pound composed and revised many of the early cantos, including the important and comparatively straightforward narrative rendering of Odysseus's journey to the underworld in "Canto I." Pound's epic is greatly influenced by Homer as well as Dante and begins, as so many epics before, with a journey in medias res:

> And then went down to the ship,
> Set keel to breakers, forth on the godly sea.

Odysseus's journey to hell is a critical moment in his long journey home. Likewise the publication of Pound's poem is at once a great turning point in his career and, as Pound seems to intuit, a groundbreaking moment in the history of Western literature, a new translation, and thus a new and necessary reevaluation of the role and nature of poetry in history. For the next 50 years Pound would continue to write and rewrite *The Cantos*, exploring, vilifying, and celebrating the history, politics, and culture of the world from Homer to Mussolini. Although by most standards *The Cantos* remain an unfinished work, it is nonetheless marked by a certain trajectory and form that have been described by many as loosely following the form of the *Divine Comedy*, from "Hell" to "Purgatory" to "Paradise."

The Pounds eventually left Paris in 1924 and settled in Rapallo, Italy, where they would live for the next 20 years, until Pound's arrest for treason and his subsequent incarceration in Pisa at the end of the war. Pound had been an enthusiastic supporter of Benito Mussolini and during the war had made a number of radio speeches that were highly critical of the United States. After the war, Pound was extradited to America, where, found not guilty by reason of insanity, he was placed in the custody of the doctors at St. Elizabeth's Hospital, Washington, D.C. Seeing Pound at St. Elizabeth's became a sort of rite of passage for a younger generation of poets, and Pound was visited by and lectured at length to such figures as Allen Ginsberg, Charles Olson, and Robert Lowell. Pound was released from St. Elizabeth's in 1958, thanks in large part to the efforts of Robert Frost, William Carlos Williams, and other notable literary figures, and returned to Rapallo, where he died on November 1, 1972.

BIBLIOGRAPHY
Carpenter, Humphrey. *A Serious Character: The Life of Ezra Pound*. New York: Delta, 1990.

Pound, Ezra. *The Cantos*. New York: New Directions, 1996.

———. *Selected Poems of Ezra Pound*. New York: New Directions, 1957.

Wilhelm, James J. *Ezra Pound in London and Paris, 1908–1925.* Pennsylvania: Penn State University Press, 1990.

James Hoff

"A PRAYER FOR MY DAUGHTER" WILLIAM BUTLER YEATS (1919)

W. B. YEATS's daughter, Anne Butler Yeats, was born February 24, 1919. Shortly after Anne's birth, the Yeats family moved into Thoor Ballylee, the Norman tower on Lady Gregory's land that Yeats bought and refurbished. This site is the setting in "A Prayer for My Daughter," as indicated by the imagery in the first two stanzas, and a central symbol for tradition, culture, and the soul in Yeats's later poetry. In this poem, it is from within the tower while watching her sleep peacefully during a howling storm that Yeats prays his daughter will cultivate virtues that may help her to survive the chaos of the modern world.

The first two stanzas describe the screaming, "roof-leveling" sea-wind, which Yeats dreads not only for its potential of immediate destruction but also as a symbol of the greater threat that Yeats had prophesied several months earlier in "THE SECOND COMING," the storm of anarchy that eventually would destroy civilization. "A Prayer for My Daughter" recalls the "blood-dimmed tide" of anarchy in the earlier poem in Yeats's reverie "That the future years had come, / Dancing to a frenzied drum, / Out of the murderous innocence of the sea." Despite his "great gloom," Yeats still hopes his daughter will be able to "stay" the cataclysm he had predicted in "The Second Coming."

Yeats's prayer for his daughter begins in the third stanza. First he prays, "May she be granted beauty," but not too much. Too much beauty makes others "distraught" and is an enemy of "natural kindness" and "intimacy." In the fourth stanza, Yeats offers the examples of Helen of Troy and Venus as two women who suffered because they were so beautiful. Yeats symbolically associates Helen with Maud Gonne, the woman whom Yeats long loved and who, as did Helen and Venus, lacked the ability to choose the right man to love, since she continually refused to marry Yeats. Yeats alludes to Maud Gonne even more explicitly later in the poem, when he prays that his daughter will avoid the "intellectual hatred" and "opinionated mind" that turned the voice of "the loveliest woman born" into "an old bellows full of angry wind." In the fifth stanza, Yeats implicitly contrasts his former relationship with Maud Gonne to his present relationship with Georgie Hyde-Lees, his wife of two years and the mother of his daughter, when he declares that "courtesy" is superior to beauty and is the chief virtue he hopes his daughter will learn. Yeats hopes his daughter will develop the "charm" and "glad kindness" of courtesy that will enable her to "earn" the hearts of others.

Yeats introduces in the sixth stanza the image of the laurel tree, a traditional symbol for victory that represents all of the human values that can withstand the howling, destructive wind. Yeats prays for his daughter, "May she become a flourishing hidden tree" and "0 may she live like some green laurel / Rooted in one dear perpetual place." If his daughter can find refuge in a quiet life of deep-rooted custom away from the chaotic external world, Yeats believes "her thoughts may like the linnet be," harmonious "magnanimities of sound." Also, unlike those who, as Maud Gonne has, have been "choked with hate," which is "of all evil chances chief" Yeats proclaims, "If there's no hatred of the mind / Assault and battery of the wind / Can never tear the linnet from the limb." Without hatred, Yeats's daughter will be able to recover "radical innocence," to be "self-delighting," and will learn that her soul's "sweet will is Heaven's will." Although others may "scowl" at her and "every windy quarter howl," she can "be happy still." Yeats's last hope is for his daughter to be married in ceremony, away from the "arrogance and hatred" in the "thoroughfares," since ceremony and custom are the sources of innocence and the truest beauty.

"A Prayer for My Daughter" is one of Yeats's most intricately organized meditations, although the stanza form is regular and quite simple: The rhyme scheme is *aabbcddc,* with lines 1 through 3, 5, and 8 iambic pentameter, and lines 4, 6, and 7 iambic tetrameter. Yeats used the identical stanza form for "IN MEMORY OF ROBERT MAJOR GREGORY," which reveals that in addition to being a companion poem and answer to "The Second Coming," "A Prayer for My Daughter" presents Yeats's ideal woman just as "In Memory of Major Robert Major Gregory" delineates Yeats's ideal man.

Betsy Watson

"PRETTY" STEVIE SMITH (1962)   The vehemence of her stand against parrotlike mediocrity in "Pretty" is a clue to the verve of STEVIE SMITH's refusal to be acceptable if it meant compromising her artistic individuality: "Cry pretty, pretty, pretty and you'll be able / Very soon not even to cry pretty." Associationally, she satirizes agreeable but undemanding literature which describes the frost on the ground or the mist as merely "pretty." Her quatrains resemble traditional pastorals, but they refuse the rarefied climate of poetic effects, notably rhyme. Appearing to celebrate nature, Smith mocks the trite language of consoling rural verse. Her innocuous line "This field, this owl, this pike, this pool are careless" initially reads like a conventional contrast between the complex world of humans and the carefree atmosphere of the natural world. However, she makes "careless" also a pejorative description of nature's "indifference"; that is, its lack of compassion, which in the final line is projected onto the cruelty of Human Nature. Consequently, the subject of the poem becomes the psychological state of wishing to be "delivered entirely from Humanity." This familiar death wish in Smith's works is unsettlingly presented as the "prettiest of all."

In "Cool As a Cucumber," Smith is similarly merciless towards unthinking vernacular clichés which veil any resistance to social prescriptions. She exploits the power of parody to empty the authority of literary texts or other dominant discourses which erode the voices of diverse individuals. Thus, her poetry "talks back" against controlling rhetoric which pervades social prescriptions.

BIBLIOGRAPHY

Pumphrey, Martin. "Play, Fantasy and Strange Laughter: Stevie Smith's Uncomfortable Poetry." *Critical Quarterly* 28, no. 3 (autumn 1986): 85–96.

Smith, Stevie. *Stevie Smith: Collected Poems,* London: Allen Lane, 1975.

———. *Me Again: The Uncollected Writings of Stevie Smith.* London: Virago, 1981.

Jane Dowson

PRINCE, F. T. (1912–2003)   Frank Templeton Prince was born in Kimberley, South Africa, to recent British emigrants. This fact, and his long adult residence in Southampton, England, informs Prince's reluctance to consider himself a fully South African poet. Best known for his often anthologized World War II poem, "Soldiers Bathing," Prince published verse infrequently, dedicated much time to academic pursuits, and wrote poetry unique in voice and unconcerned with prevailing literary trends, all of which explain his being one of the 20th century's most underrated poets writing in English. Nevertheless, Prince's always evolving, technically accomplished poems have earned him a small but eminent following, including the English poet GEOFFREY HILL and the American poet John Ashbery. The latter writer has repeatedly praised Prince's evasion of easy distinctions between traditional and AVANT-GARDE: "Let's leave it at this," Ashbery summarizes, "Prince is one of the best 20th-century poets."

An early nervous condition led to an inactive, isolated childhood for Prince. However, during this time he read voluminously, and growing literary interests caused him to neglect his first college subject, architecture. A family friend intervened, helping Prince to undertake study at Balliol College, Oxford University (and for a short time at Princeton University), where he was more fully exposed to the French Symbolists and MODERNIST giants such as EZRA POUND and W. B. YEATS. Another influential modernist, T. S. ELIOT, served as an advocate for the precocious 26-year-old poet, and as an editor for Faber, he arranged for the publication of Prince's *Poems* (1938). Its inaugural poem, "An Epistle to a Patron," features the long lines, involved syntax, and opulent language characteristic of the poet's early phase: "I have acquired a knowledge / Of the habits of numbers and of various tempers, and skill in setting" he writes, advertising his talents through the voice of a Renaissance architect, who creates verse with "sistering pilasters." Prince engages his South African boyhood in poems such as "The Babiantje" and "Chaka," the latter a longer, biographical monologue. He regularly employed this impersonal, research-heavy technique in poems on Edmund Burke, Michelangelo, and fellow poet RUPERT BROOKE. Only in later chapbook-length poems, *Memoirs in Oxford* (1980) and *Walks in Rome* (1987), did Prince meditate more freely on his own life. The Munich Crisis and outbreak of war overshadowed Prince's first book. In any case he seemed out of place among the more socially conscious major poets of the 1930s, W. H. AUDEN and STEPHEN SPENDER. Far from espousing their socialist or communist values, for which he never really felt sympathy, Prince instead converted to Roman Catholicism.

Prince served as an intelligence officer in England and Egypt from 1940–46. He cracked codes and translated for POWs, experiences that only enhanced his deep knowledge of Italian. In 1942 he wrote "Soldiers Bathing," which idealizes repose from warfare without ignoring the extreme violence that necessarily surrounds such moments. The poet's Christian outlook is pronounced—"some great love is over all we do"—and the ending image of a red sunset that "might have issued from Christ's breast" likely alludes to a famous image from Marlowe's *Doctor Faustus*. The poem almost immediately appeared in anthologies, but Prince himself did not publish it until 1954 in a volume of the same name. Prince married Pauline Bush in 1943 (they had two daughters), and following the war he worked for nearly three decades in England as a lecturer and professor of literature at Southampton University. In addition to a stint as dean, he was a productive Renaissance scholar, producing most notably *The Italian Element in Milton's Verse* (1954), a critical study that remains essential for students of that poet, as well as editions of Shakespeare's poems and Milton's *Samson Agonistes* and other works. Prince's scholarly stature was recognized with a Visiting Fellowship at All Soul's College, Oxford, in 1968–69, and the Clark Lectures, which he delivered at Cambridge University in 1972–73. Although he retired the following year, he subsequently accepted visiting professorships in Jamaica, the United States, and Yemen.

His third poetry collection, *Doors of Stone* (1963), joined much of his previous verse with a series of new, erudite poems. Prince remarked in a 1971 essay, "Voice and Verse," that poetic voice and tone required a "composition on a fairly large scale," a forecast of his longer poems later in the decade, as well as those collected in *Later On* (1983). These latter poems featured shorter, two- and three-beat lines on eclectic topics—one in a dog's voice, another a dialogue between Shelley and Byron that at times sounds like later Yeats, and, most successfully, "The Yüan Chên Variations," an elegant

reworking of the poetry of Po-Chu-i. Reviewing Prince's first *Collected* volume (1979), the English poet DONALD DAVIE rather testily objected to his subject's penchant for abstractions. Prince might have had this criticism in mind in 1986, when he delivered the English Association's presidential address in verse, entitled "Fragment Poetry": "the decree that poetry / Must deal in things, not thoughts, / always be physical, / Not metaphysical, is / in itself an enormous, empty, / Bad *idea*." In another discursive poem from the same year, he seeks a "personal spring / To wind us up and keep us going." Prince demonstrated just such energy late in life, releasing his retrospective *Collected Poems: 1935–1992* and continuing to write verse through the 1990s. He died on August 7, 2003, at the age of 90.

BIBLIOGRAPHY

Ashbery, John. "On the Poetry of F. T. Prince." In *Selected Prose,* edited by Eugene Richie. Ann Arbor: University of Michigan Press, 2004.

Clark, Polly. "F. T. Prince: An Appreciation." *Poetry Review* 94, no. 1 (2004): 112–115.

Devereux, Stephen. *F. T. Prince.* Grahamstown, Eng.: National English Literary Museum, 1988.

Poburko, Nicholas. "Poetry Past and Present: F. T. Prince's Walks in Rome." *Renascence* 51, no. 2 (1999): 145–163.

Prince, F. T. *Collected Poems: 1935–1992.* Riverdale-on-Hudson, N.Y.: Sheep Meadow Press, 1993.

———. "Fragment Poetry." London: English Association, 1986.

———. *The Italian Element in Milton's Verse.* Oxford: Oxford University Press, 1954.

———. "Voice and Verse: Some Problems of Modern Poetry." *English* 20 (1971): 77–83.

Rudolf, Anthony et al. "F.T. Prince: A Tribute." *PN Review* 147 (2002): 26–38.

Brett Foster

PRYNNE, J. H. (1936–)

Jeremy Prynne was born in London. One poem, "On the Matter of Thermal Packing," engages with memories of evacuation to the countryside during the war. After National Service, including time with a Polish tank regiment in Germany, he began an academic career at Cambridge, where he has lectured all his professional life. For forty years he has been widely regarded as Britain's most exacting and mysterious contemporary MODERNIST poet. A group of younger poets influenced by his work has become known as the Cambridge School.

In the early 1960s he turned to "open" poetic forms in the tradition of Anglo-American Modernism, and began publishing with small specialist presses. Mainstream publishers were not receptive to modernist poetry, and Prynne seems to have preferred small presses anyway. He continues to give them first publication of his work, perhaps because he wants a readership attuned to slower, more expansive reading. Nearly all poetry opens out in response to this, but Prynne's places formidable obstacles in the way of any other kind of reading. His work is famously "difficult," but the nature of the difficulty, whether it is intimidating or engaging, is the question. What Prynne thwarts is the reader's accustomed desire to be able to take in an initial cohesive meaning. Give that up, in favor of willingness to accept partial, provisional understanding, and the difficulty becomes a different thing. Lyrical sweeps and brilliant phrases that turn and bite can then be accepted and enjoyed again when understanding has caught up a bit.

Instead of a presiding speaker producing a continuous line of argument or narrative, Prynne sets out a field in which voices, fragments, and quotations mingle and interrupt each other. There is a principle of impersonality in this writing, even when it seems impassioned and has something urgent to say. The principle is that of drawing in fragments and specimens without attempting fully to contextualize and direct their meanings in the way that narrative representation would. A certain space is preserved around each element by the discontinuity of sense. Prynne's philosophical interest in Heidegger's concept of "Being-in-the-World" and Merleau-Ponty's phenomenology of bodily perception undoubtedly influenced his turn toward this sort of "openness." When the line of sense is interrupted, the juxtaposition of different elements becomes the source of meaning.

In Prynne's hands this modernist technique has a range that is breathtaking: really exciting in what it enables us to touch; chasteningly realistic in the way each discourse jerks us away from the last. Prynne carries the lyricism of personal hope and love to a peculiar intensity produced by the compressing effect of other discourses. He followed Charles Olson in using "open" forms to introduce historical, anthropological, and geological perspectives into his poetry and to explore connections between the material livelihood of a culture and its myths. Among the other discourses used are literary quotations, the systems vocabulary of financial markets, neurological descriptions of bodily response to stimuli, astrophysical descriptions of the behavior of stars, and, more recently, the functional terms of computer programming. Prynne writes with a sense that poetry should seize the most up-to-date developments in language, knowledge, and power. Catch-phrases and snatches of slang appear, amid advertising-speak, the tones of parents speaking to children, academic pronouncements, theology, biochemistry, and legal terminology. We constantly meet terms that need looking up. Pastoral faces the glare of biochemical analysis (*High Pink on Chrome*). A fond parental view of children in the backyard is woven around thoughts of physical dissolution and genetic inheritance ("Acquisition of Love"). Puns are used brilliantly—sometimes giving a euphoric sense of sudden lightness—to collapse together the sacred and the mundane, or small and large-scale processes. Another favorite device, with similar effects, is the description of emotional or moral phenomena as if they were material, and vice versa.

One preoccupation is with the way the self is constructed by these different processes and discourses, and what sort of vantage point poetry can find from which to contemplate this. Thresholds of the self abound in Prynne's poetry: mouths, lips, eyes, ears, skin, and, repeatedly, wounds. He frequently looks to the physical conditions that define the narrow zone in which human life is possible. Snow, with its capacity to white out life or slow it into dormancy, is a recurring presence, full of different meanings. *The Oval Window* breaks new ground for poetry with its use of the resemblance between snow and the calcite crystals in the inner ear that determine our sense of balance.

Some of Prynne's earlier work—*The White Stones*, especially—draws lyricism from ideas of release, continuity, and flow in material, intellectual, and emotional contexts. Prynne used the "open" forms, with their removal of narrative enclosure, as a gesture toward healing the distinctions between mind and body, and thought and feeling, of the Cartesian tradition: a solution to the dissociation of sensibility that troubled earlier modernists. Removing this enclosure releases a lyricism that Prynne associated, in "The Wound, Day and Night," with the idea of a material song of the world, to be "heard" in the echoes of the Big Bang that still reverberate detectably. Such release is also associated with wound and damage: the vulnerability and impermanence of bodies.

Lyricism is harder to find in the recent work. Sequences of poems appear as densely packed blocks. The poet John Wilkinson describes these as consisting of "fretwork or mesh," "the common term between textiles and electronics," and points to the scarcity of pronouns as evidence that this poetry restricts the space for human autonomy almost to vanishing. Instructions such as *select, get,* and *put,* from computer programming or, as Wilkinson suggests, from computerized market trading (*buy*), seem to address the reader—or to have occupied the place where human address should be—with sinister comedy. Part of the effect of these books results from their gesture of taking back material from earlier books in compressed form, a reason, perhaps, for new readers to start with the earlier work and progress to the harsher political vision of the later.

BIBLIOGRAPHY

Duncan, Andrew. *The Failure of Conservatism in Modern British Poetry.* Cambridge: Salt, 2003.

Jarvis, Simon. "Quality and the Non-Identical in J. H. Prynne's 'Aristeas, in Seven Years'." Available online. URL: http://jacketmagazine.com/20/pt-jarvis.html. Accessed on August 8, 2006.

Nolan, Kevin. "Capital Calves: Undertaking an Overview." Available online. URL: http://jacketmagazine.com/24/nolan.html. Accessed on October 12, 2004.

Prynne, J. H. *Poems.* Tarset, Eng.: Bloodaxe Books, 2005, and Fremantle, W.A., Australia: Fremantle Arts Centre Press, 2005.

Reeve, N. H. "Twilight Zones: J. H. Prynne's 'The Land of Saint Martin'." *English* 51 (spring 2002): 27–44. Available online. URL: http://jacketmagazine.com/24/reeve.html. Accessed on August 22, 2006.

Reeve, N. H., and Richard Kerridge. *Nearly Too Much: The Poetry of J. H. Prynne.* Liverpool: Liverpool University Press, 1995.

Wilkinson, John. "Tenter Ground." *Notre Dame Review* 22 (summer 2006): 196–207.

Richard Kerridge

PSYCHOANALYTIC LITERARY CRITICISM

The psychoanalytic literary critic Norman Holland has usefully sought to delineate the phases of an evolving psychoanalytic conception of the mind, each formulated in terms of different designated polarities, and each producing a subsequent corresponding phase of psychoanalytic literary criticism. According to this model, psychoanalytic criticism began by adapting Freud's id psychology, which emphasized the polarities conscious/unconscious and latent/manifest and their role in producing the content of wish-fulfillment dreams and other variant manifestations of repressed and sublimated libidinal energy (238).

Rooted in id psychology, this criticism was concerned with establishing the poet's source of creativity in terms of his/her neurotic negotiation of some stage of psychosexual development and with analyzing the manifest details of particular poems as the gratification of the poet's latent desires through symbolic means. Attention focused on images and other aspects of the poem that could be construed as disguised analogues of anatomical processes relating to instinctual drives, such as the production of or fascination with excrement (which Freud had analyzed in terms of regression to the anal stage of psychosexual stage of development) or of anatomical conditions, such as genital impairment or loss (which Freud had analyzed in terms of the threat of castration generated by Oedipal conflict between father and son over the desire for the mother).

This search for some master compulsion ramified throughout a poem and informing its salient details encouraged the critic to produce an allegorical reading that, by turning the poem into biographical evidence, served to validate psychoanalysis's claims to having discovered universal principles of the mind. This psychobiographical approach tended to see aspects of the poem, its structure or its pattern of constituent images, as performing unconscious functions for the poet: compensatory wish fulfillment or the symbolically controlled expression of infantile or Oedipal rage, for example. Poetic detail was reduced to a set of symptoms of pathological compulsions latent in all people but normally more successfully repressed. The poet and his/her poetry were thus too easily made use of for didactic purposes of exemplification: "Some poets do not advance much beyond the earliest and later oral phases," while in others "the preoedipal phase has been the most significant one" (A. A. Brill in Oberndorf 104). This too often entailed denigration by "exposing the secret shame of the writer and limiting the meaning of his work" (Trilling 255), as well as an aggressive desire to overmaster the poet that might itself benefit from psychoanalytic diagnosis.

In contrast to the reductive practice of those who had appropriated his model for criticism, Freud himself recognized that analysis of the poet's emotional fixations and the psychic residue of his/her infantile experiences could not, because the method was not designed to, "explain creative genius"; it could only "reveal the factors which awake it and the sort of subject matter it is destined to choose" (Freud in Felman 133). Not only did Freud assert, on some occasions, that the author should not be made to "yield" to the psychoanalyst nor the psychoanalyst "coarsen" art by subjecting it to the "substantially useless and awkward terms" developed for clinical procedures (Freud in Trilling 261), he also insisted that the interpretation of any dream image should not be reduced to the application of preordained taxonomic designations. Freud's own interpretive practice reflects his insistence on the primacy of context: where and how a particular detail fits in relation to other details, both within the dream and within the process of analysis overall. Freud's further insistence on the importance of the analysand's improvisatory free association on any constituent detail also served to emphasize variable, changing, intracontextual meanings over absolutistic, invariable meanings and thereby served also to underscore how underlying conflicts prevent straightforward utterance and necessarily produce ambiguity, contradiction, evasion, and disavowal.

The practice of looking for meanings emerging out of some recognized pattern of interrelationships and then diagnosing that pattern as evidence of a psychological syndrome or complex was too productive to abandon. But the practice of decoding images in terms of invariable symbolic equations—for example, equating D. H. LAWRENCE's "SNAKE" with the phallus and deriving its import from the poet's Oedipal conflict with his parents—began to be seen as naïve because it ignored or neglected "the intermediate strata [between consciousness and unconsciousness] of former ego-activities which may in time past have forced a particular id-content to assume a specific ego-form" (Anna Freud in Holland 239).

The second phase of psychoanalytic understanding reflected a more complex diagnostic model of the intrapsychic polarity ego and nonego, which shifted the focus from processes of disguise to processes of transformation. That is, it constituted a shift from the attempt to expose the primary process, infantile phantasy and other expressions of the instinctual drives, to the attempt to trace evidence for the secondary process of inhibition and sublimation with regard to the mechanisms responsible for the defense of the ego. The model remained a conflict model, but the emphasis turned to the ways conflicts of meaning arise whenever a desire encounters an anxiety-driven defense against yielding to it and to the effects produced by this resistance. Dream images or symptoms were analyzed as sites where desire had been about to emerge but had been suppressed, contained, deflected by means of symbolization, condensation, or displacement-substitution.

While the working methods remained much the same, the objectives and purposes to which they were put changed. "Where therapy in the first phase tried to make the unconscious conscious, therapy in the second aimed at enlarging and strengthening the ego" (240). Practitioners and literary critics alike demonstrated an increased appreciation of the need for analytical subtlety equal to the newly appreciated complexity of the dynamics of the text. With regard to both dream and poem, the objective became to determine the structural logic of its internal organization, with an emphasis on *meaning making* as an activity. This objective necessitated that more attention be paid to modalities, how, for example, homoerotic or masturbatory modes might "be informatively interwoven in the strands of [the poet's] thought and be discoverable by inspection of the underlying imagery or patterns in this thought" (Burke 119).

This shift in orientation also served to expand the range of aspects of the dream text or poetic text that might receive emphasis of attention to include tonal and rhythmic qualities that carry the burden of affect and produce mood. This shift of orientation also authorized the deployment of psychoanalytic concepts toward the objective of understanding organizational aspects of the poem as a manifest symbolic analogue of unconscious psychological negotiations. Thus evidence of Oedipal desire and conflict was not sought in the content of the poetic images for purposes of biographical diagnosis but was reconceived as a structural paradigm for all sorts of analogous triangular relationships among formal elements.

By shifting away from the poet while retaining the crucial recognition of latent unconscious pressures, the focus of psychoanalytic criticism could remain on those formal, aesthetic aspects of the poem that have been the traditional concern of literary criticism. Formal elements of the poem were conceived to represent not so much diversions that deflect the resistance of the superego, as Freud maintained, but manifestations of the ego's struggle to extend its dominance over the id. Developing an understanding of the poem as a privileged type of compromise formation, critics began to pay attention to the way that phantasy and unconscious desire or aggression were rhetorically "*figured in the text*" (Wright 32). Grammatical, syntactic, and stylistic elements could be registered as traces left by the mechanisms of defense. The most minute poetic detail (often the smaller the better) could be interpreted as a trace of the ego's strategic negotiation, translation, and containment of unconscious materials such as to effect their deflection, omission, evasion, denial, disavowal, negation, or an overcompensation that insinuates the contrary.

The objectives of the critic became less to address primary process mechanisms of symbolism, condensation, and displacement-substitution in the formation of image clusters and patterns and more to call attention to how rhythm, rhyme, diction, and other linguistic elements can function as means of censoring and containing. This orientation also capitalized on the recognition that the poet's revision of his/her poem can be more than consciously rhetorical activity whose objective is greater efficiency and enhanced power necessary to overcoming the resistance of the reader. It also can involve a special instance of resistance, disavowal, and denial that Freud designated "secondary elaboration," by which the ego tries to regain control over the id by subjecting the unruly and threatening aspects of the dream to rational reorganization in the act of verbally reciting it—smoothing it over, making it more orderly, and imposing an intelligible pattern on it by selecting out or rearranging elements in the interest of narrative coherence and the logic of cause and effect.

Secondary elaboration is both a form of revision, inasmuch as it sorts out the chaotic, and a kind of re-vision, inasmuch as it can alter the perspective on, and thereby falsify, the dream. With regard to interpretation, the subversive censorship characterizing secondary elaboration serves as a warning to any psychoanalytic literary critic so committed to "systematic thinking" that he/she risks "ignor[ing] elements that do not fit into a desired pattern. Reading shares this danger with the reporting of a dream. Boundaries shift with contextual placings of the visual material of the dream or of any symbolic medium," and this goes far to explain the rivalry of interpretations of a given text (23).

Stimulated by the renewed interest in form and style, the second phase of psychoanalytic literary criticism also tended to acknowledge the communal conventions and historical dimensions of poetry by considering how these aspects may reflect "the artist's conscious or unconscious identifications with certain groups of the collectivity in a particular historical period" (Roland 254). Under the influence of Freud's pioneering psychoanalysis of culture, *Civilization and Its Discontents* (1930), acculturation processes, and literary conventions also began to be recognized as transpersonal extensions of the superego, shaping the poem in the process of containing and regulating instinctual impulses by means of the anxiety-provoking power of cultural authorization and injunction.

The psychoanalysis of culture can perform other functions and provide other kinds of insights, as well, for the literary critic. With regard to manifest content, just as psychoanalytic theory can be usefully applied to rites, ceremonies, and contests that dramatically objectify the psychic processes governing individuals, so too can it be applied to poetic evocations or metaphoric allusions to such rites, ceremonies, and games. Thus, Kenneth Burke: "In the literature of transitional eras, for instance, we find an especial profusion of rebirth rituals, where the poet is making the symbolic passes that will endow him with a new identity" (125).

BIBLIOGRAPHY
Burke, Kennneth. "Freud—and the Analysis of Poetry." In *Psychoanalysis and Literature.* Edited by Hendrik M. Ruitenbeek. New York: Dutton, 1964.

Easthope, Antony. *Poetry and Phantasy.* Cambridge and New York: Cambridge University Press, 1989.

Felman, Shoshana. "On Reading Poetry: Reflections on the Limits and Possibilities of Psychoanalytical Approaches." In *The Literary Freud: Mechanisms of Defense and the Poetic Will,* edited by Joseph H. Smith. New Haven, Conn., and London: Yale University Press, 1980.

Holland, Norman N. "Literary Interpretation and Three Phases of Psychoanalysis." In *Psychoanalysis, Creativity and Literature: A French-American Inquiry,* edited by Alan Roland. New York: Columbia University Press, 1978.

Obendorf, Clarence P. "Psychoanalysis in Literature." In *Psychoanalysis and Literature,* edited by Hendrik M. Ruitenbeek. New York: Dutton, 1964.

Roland, Alan. "Toward a Reorientation of Psychoanalytic Literary Criticism." In *Psychoanalysis, Creativity and Literature: A French-American Inquiry,* edited by Alan Roland. New York: Columbia University Press, 1978.

Wright, Elizabeth. *Psychoanalytic Criticism: A Reappraisal.* 2nd ed. New York: Routledge, 1998.

David Brottman

PUGH, SHEENAGH (1950–) Sheenagh Pugh's publications include 10 collections of poetry and translations, two selected poems, two novels, and a critical study of fan fiction. "Crossing the Bridge" was a joint winner of the 1997 Bridport Poetry Prize; "Envying Owen Beattie" was awarded the Forward Poetry Prize for Best Single Poem of 1998; *Stonelight* won the prestigious Arts Council of Wales (ACW) Book of the Year Award (2000); *The Beautiful Lie* was short-listed for both ACW Book of the Year and the Whitbread Poetry Award (2003). *The Movement of Bodies* was a Poetry Book Society recommendation (spring 2005) and short-listed for the T. S. Eliot Prize (2005). She won the British Comparative Literature Association Translation Prize in 1985 and has gone on to translate extensively from German, French, and ancient Greek.

Pugh's writing is sharp and intelligent, fascinated by language, history, and place. A poem like "Never a Trekker" concludes in self-deprecating irony: "America's sunny side up / by nature, and good luck to them, I say, / but I'm a Celt: I can't handle hope." "The Beautiful Lie" is a complex meditation on creativity:

> if she'd said *why* did you do that,
> he'd never have denied it. She showed him
> he had a choice. I could see in his face
> the new sense, the possible. That word and
>   deed
> need not match, that you could say the world
> different, to suit you.

Pugh's *Selected Poems,* on AS-Level set text (sixth-form school students), has been reprinted twice. She lives in Cardiff and teaches creative writing at the University of Glamorgan.

BIBLIOGRAPHY
Pugh, Sheenagh. *The Beautiful Lie.* Bridgend, Wales: Seren, 2002.

———. *Beware Falling Tortoises.* Poetry Wales Press, 1987.

———. *Id's Hospit.* Bridgend, Wales: Seren, 1997.

———. *The Movement of Bodies.* Bridgend, Wales: Seren, 2005.

———. *Prisoners of Transience* (translations). Bridgend, Wales: Seren, 1985.

———. *Sheenagh Pugh: Selected Poems.* Bridgend, Wales: Seren, 1990.

———. Sheenagh Pugh Website. Available online. URL: http://www.geocities.com/sheenaghpugh. Accessed May 9, 2008.

———. *Sing for the Taxman.* Bridgend, Wales: Seren, 1993.

———. *Stonelight.* Bridgend, Wales: Seren, 1999.

Jeni Williams

"THE PYLONS" STEPHEN SPENDER (1933) "The Pylons" first appeared in STEPHEN SPENDER's early collection *Poems* (1933) and is characteristic of the poet's spare and compact but rich and evocative lyric style. "Simple and straightforward . . . clarity," the poet

writes in the introduction to his *Collected Poems* (1985), "has always been my aim."

In the opening stanza, the poet celebrates the "crumbling roads," "stone . . . cottages," and "hidden villages" of rural England, but it is clear by his use of the past tense that this celebration is a nostalgic one, a bittersweet looking back upon a country that has ceased to exist. "The secret of these hills was stone," he writes; "Now over these small hills, they have built the concrete / That trails black wire." Spender asserts in the second stanza that the enormous concrete power pylons are "bare like nude, giant girls that have no secret," an arresting simile that points to the poet's assessment of the wantonness and indecency of unfettered industrial expansion in England. The colorlessness and uniformity of the pylons, juxtaposed against the natural landscape, seem to "mock[]" the richness and vibrancy of "the valley with its gilt and evening look / And the green chestnut," draining it of its beauty and vitality "like the parched bed of a brook."

Spender's perspective on technological progress and industrialization becomes much more ambiguous in the closing two stanzas of the poem. He refers to the seemingly ubiquitous electrical grids as being "like whips of anger / With lightning's danger" that "dwarf[] our emerald country." However, he also concedes that because they tower "far above and far as sight endures," the pylons are "tall with prophesy" and possess a unique "perspective of the future." Perhaps, the poet suggests, England's transformation from rural countryside to urban cityscape is not wholly detrimental. After all, he writes, the "clouds" in the sky, whose vantage point is even higher and more encompassing than that of human beings and even of the pylons themselves, "shall lean their swan-white neck" to view with appreciation and awe these new "cities" with their modern technological advancements.

Spender's "The Pylons" inspired the nickname of the Pylon school or the Pylon poets to describe the preponderance of self-conscious and socially conscious modern industrial or technological symbolism and imagery in the work of the young Leftist British poets of the 1930s, W. H. AUDEN, C. DAY LEWIS, LOUIS MAC-NEICE, and Spender himself. See especially C. Day-Lewis's "Look west, Wystan, lone flyers" and Auden's "A Summer Night," both published in 1933, the same year as "The Pylons."

BIBLIOGRAPHY
Spender, Stephen. *Collected Poems 1928–1953*. London: Faber and Faber, 1955.
———. *Collected Poems 1928–1985*. London: Faber and Faber, 1985.

Robert G. May

"THE QUIET HOUSE" CHARLOTTE MEW (1916)

In "The Quiet House" the domestic space, as it does so frequently in the poetry of CHARLOTTE MEW, represents the unknowable psychic interior, which is contrasted with the more public and noisy spaces of auction and fair: "When we were children old Nurse used to say, / The house was like an auction or a fair / Until the lot of us were safe in bed." The auction and fair are places of publicity and joyful freedom, as in Bakhtin's notion of *carnivale,* which stands as the chronotope of change, transaction, and becoming. But the speaker gives us this brief history of noise and cheer only to take it away. We learn that the cheerful hubbub of auction and fair is a distant and metaphoric memory; moreover, it is the memory of old Nurse rather than the memory of the speaker, who apparently cannot herself remember a time when the house was like an auction or a fair. The speaker's brother, sister, and mother have all died. Her older brother Tom has been sent away for crossing the authority of the ominous, overly watchful pater familias. "Poor Father" has lost his dignity in a lawsuit and now spends most of his time indoors. The "quiet" that marks this house therefore turns on loss and failure; it is quiet not by virtue of what it has, but rather of what it lacks.

The speaker is a young woman whose life has been forever changed by a sexual encounter she had a year ago with her cousin's friend, a man she did not know and cannot now clearly remember:

To get away to Aunt's for that week-end
  Was hard enough; (since then, a year ago,
  [Father] scarcely lets me slip out of his
    sight—)
At first I did not like my cousin's friend,
  I did not think I should remember him:
  His voice has gone, his face is growing dim
And if I like him now I do not know.
  He frightened me before he smiled—
  He did not ask me if he might—
  He said that he would come one Sunday
    night,
  He spoke to me as if I were a child.

As the watchful jailor Father does, the cousin's friend seems something of a predator. His manner of seduction involves the delayed smile, which suggests a degree of artificiality that renders this sort of sexual overture both premeditated and inappropriate. He takes the tone of an adult speaking to a child, which suggests that he believes she is virginal and innocent. He makes false promises that he will come to call when it is clear that he is not planning further contact with the young woman. And, perhaps most problematically, he makes his overture without having asked the speaker's permission: "He did not ask me if he might—." Might what? Might kiss or seduce the speaker? Because the speaker's syntax wanders off in a prolix, semiincoherent flood of independent clauses, we cannot know exactly what happened between the speaker and the tardily smiling cad. The suggestion, of course, is that what transpired is too troubling to tell, and that the speaker's modesty now prevents her from narrating the details of an unwholesome seduction scene. That the last four lines of this stanza stutter over the same subject, "He . . . he . . . he . . . he," alerts us to the centrality of this experience for the speaker.

The remaining stanzas turn away from this life-changing event, beginning to trace the profound consequences on the house of the young woman's mind. Her domicile is literally quiet in the sense that few visitors come to call at her father's silent house, but clearly the speaker's mind is *unquiet,* not quiet. She says,

> everything has burned, and not quite through.
> The colors of the world have turned
> To flame, the blue, the gold has burned
> In what used to be such a leaden sky.
> When you are burned quiet through you die.

In this passage both the leaden sky and the speaker herself are imaged in terms of fire, as if she is in the last stages of turning to ash. She has imagined the year since the sexual overture as a year of continuous burning, almost to the point of total annihilation. By projecting her flame of desire—that is, her own sexual awakening—onto natural sights outside the house, she makes a gesture toward the acceptance of sexual desire as part of human nature. However, here the speaker has conflated the indoors with the outdoors, and her own unquiet mind with something larger, perhaps the notion of suffering and meaninglessness itself. The burning of "the colors of the world" also recalls the burning of hellfire and the Christian punishment for exploring sex outside the procreative bond of matrimony.

Throughout the rest of the poem redness becomes a metonym for the fire of desire and its bittersweet punishment. "Red is the strangest pain to bear," says the young woman, finding analogues for the redness of her own unquiet mind in the natural world: red leaves on budding trees, red roses that "can stab you across the street / Deeper than any knife." Even the sunlight is red to her. She sees redness all around her, in every season, both outside and inside the quiet house. The speaker's persistence in stacking similes on top of each other

tells us that she is having trouble articulating what she means; the stacked similes suggest that Mew is pointing to the conceptual failure of language itself, even as all meaning eclipses the signs we so hopefully attach to it. "And the crimson haunts you everywhere—" says the young woman. "Thin shafts of sunlight, like the ghosts of reddened swords have struck our stair / As if, coming down, you had spilt your life." In this passage the redness shifts from being a phenomenon of the physical world (leaves, roses) to being a phenomenon of the metaphysical world (a ghost). The redness metaphorically ends up once more on that important stair, struck by ghosts of swords that are now metaphorically red with human blood. Inside this double simile there is a third simile: The speaker imagines herself going down the stair, bloodied, as if she had spilled her life. The emphasis on agency in this line is curious, since one might expect that the deadly swords of sunlight would have killed the speaker against her will, rendering her a ghost on her own stair. However, what the speaker actually says is "as if, coming down, you had spilt your life." The *you* means *she.* The implication, if we take blood as a metaphor for passion, is that she finds herself complicit in having squandered her creative and sexual potential.

The poem establishes a hard binary pair, dreaming versus living. When the speaker says,

> The things that kill us seem
>   Blind to the death they give:
> It is only in our dream
>   The things that kill us live,

We infer that what are killing her is this life-changing experience of a year ago and its attendant epiphanies. The cousin's friend was inconsequential; indeed the speaker can no longer recall his face; nor does she know whether she even liked him. But the experience was enough to make her understand that pain and suffering are the great by-products of a universe indifferent both to what we forfeit and what we desire.

In the penultimate stanza the speaker resumes describing the business of living in the quiet house. She abandons her rich figurative language and constrains herself to making comments about sparrows and children and trees. Her catalog is a bleak one, bleak chiefly because things have not changed as she herself as changed. The room is shut "where Mother died," an off-limits memoriam to the way things were when Mother was alive. The world "goes on the same outside"; the trees "grow green and brown and bare," tellingly ending on a note of winter finality, not of spring optimism. The church spire is "dead," an encomium, perhaps, to the irrelevance of religion to speak to the vital core of human experience. Even the image of Father, graying in his chair, insists that the watchful authorities we have appointed to guard imagination and desire will burn to ash too. The gray days that follow in sameness will, as Father's once-wavy hair, turn white.

The last stanza suggests that the speaker's mind is unsettled, and that she has begun the journey to meet her long and final solitude, whether in mental instability or death. She confides, "To-night I heard a bell again— / Outside it was the same mist of fine rain. . . . / No one for me—." How true: There is no one for any of us; we must all open the doors of our quiet houses and look down the street as night comes on. Clearly the speaker hears these doorbells often. Her house would certainly be quiet enough for her to hear the bell, if there were a bell. But there is no caller; no matter that once he said "he would come one Sunday night." He will not come, and this is something she knows. Moreover that he should come or not come is not the point. The lamps "just lighted down the long, dim street" signal the hour of indeterminacy, the twilight hour that, like the stairway, is neither here nor there. She says that it is *herself* she goes to meet:

> I think it is myself I go to meet:
> I do not care; some day I *shall* not think; I shall
> not *be*!

Not caring, not thinking, not being—once more, Mew imagines a desired state in negative rather than positive terms, as if the ghost-red girl on the stair is entitled to be so much more than what she thinks or who she is. Relationships are not enough, and we cannot rely on identity politics to provide and sustain meaning. The marriage plot is flawed; the church plot is dead; the family plot does not satisfy. Until we can learn to accept and integrate passion in our lives, Mew implies, we will be doomed to haunt the stairs in houses that are breathlessly, portentously quiet.

BIBLIOGRAPHY
Fitzgerald, Penelope. *Charlotte Mew and Her Friends.* Reading, Mass.: Addison-Wesley, 1984.
Leighton, Angela. *Victorian Women Poets: Writing against the Heart.* Charlottesville: University of Virginia Press, 1992.
Merrin, Jeredith. "The Ballad of Charlotte Mew." *Modern Philology* 95, no. 2 (November 1997): 200–217.
Mew, Charlotte. *Charlotte Mew: Collected Poems and Selected Prose.* Edited and introduction by Val Warner. New York: Routledge, 2003.
Walsh, Jessica. "'The Strangest Pain to Bear': Corporeality and Fear of Insanity in Charlotte Mew's Poetry." *Victorian Poetry,* September 2002, 217–240.

Rhoda Janzen

"QUOOF" PAUL MULDOON (1983) According to PAUL MULDOON, the title poem of his 1983 collection, *Quoof,* is taken from his family's word for a hot water bottle. This choice reflects a fascination with language that is integral to his work. Although it was written when Muldoon lived in Belfast, this particular poem does not engage directly with "the Troubles" there at all. This might be seen as a political statement in itself, indicative of a desire not to put national politics above all else. It is certainly noteworthy that Muldoon chose to make it the title poem for a book that does engage very directly with Irish politics elsewhere.

Fourteen lines long, by Muldoon's usual standards "Quoof" might be described as a sonnet. Although it is not written in a regular meter, or to a standard sonnet rhyme scheme, it does include a characteristic "turn" between octave and sestet. First it indicates that the speaker has often taken the family word "into a strange bed," as his father would carry "a red-hot half-brick / in an old sock" back to his "childhood settle." Then the sestet transports the reader to one particular bed in a "hotel room in New York City / with a girl who spoke hardly any English." In this sense it is a poem of innocence and experience, and the comparison between father and son serves to illuminate difference more than similarity. The two men are joined by their family word, but one is pictured in an atmosphere of poverty and innocence, the other in a glamorous far-off location.

The poem's play with the idea of similarity and difference is not only reflected in the poem's sonnet turn, but also in its unusual rhymes, such as *City/yeti*. Muldoon also makes striking use of simile, for instance, with its comparison of the word *quoof* and "a sword." This weapon not only carries appropriate phallic associations but is usually linked to writing rather than speaking, in the common pairing "the pen and the sword." Although language is essential to dialogue—an alternative to violence—it can also be a bar to communication, as Muldoon points out. In characteristic Muldoonian fashion, "Quoof" appears designed to question standard assumptions.

Initially "Quoof" might seem a confessional poem, but it raises more questions than it answers and resists paraphrase, largely because of the unusual grammar in its first and third "sentences." For instance, the third sentence has no active verb in its main clause. As Tim Kendall observes, its "frozen tableau" emphasizes "the absence of human interaction." Notably the nature of this sexual relationship is typical of *Quoof.* The description of a hand on a breast, "like the smouldering one-off spoor of the yeti," is unpleasant and suggests that the woman in the poem is being used. This curt representation does warrant scrutiny. However, it should be remembered that Muldoon cannot be equated with the speaker in "Quoof" and that the poem's hard-nosed attitude is not reserved for women but represents part of a more general world-weariness.

BIBLIOGRAPHY
Kendall, Tim. *Paul Muldoon.* Bridgend, Wales: Seren, 1996.
Wills, Clair. *Improprieties: Politics and Sexuality in Northern Irish Poetry,* Oxford: Oxford University Press, 1993.

Jennifer Sykes

R

"RAIN" EDWARD THOMAS (1916) Deeply melancholic and reminiscent of the work of THOMAS HARDY, "Rain" was composed January 7, 1916, while EDWARD THOMAS was in England training as a soldier for World War I. In a letter to his mentor and fellow poet Robert Frost from Hare Hall Camp, Romford, Essex, on January 19, Thomas wrote that his old hut had been "broken up, the men separated," and that the soldiers had been "homeless for a time & rather miserable in the rain" (*Elected Friends* 114).

The sorrowful and isolated soldier prays in a bleak hut. In the night's darkness, he contemplates death. Describing the rain as wild and unpredictable, he is reminded that should he die he will no longer hear it "nor give it thanks." The rain is a symbol for life and a religious symbol. Just as in a baptism where water is used to cleanse, here the soldier feels cleansed by the rain and feels cleaner than he has since he was "born into this solitude." The loneliness he feels may result from his "birth" as a soldier, or from his original birth. He is in need of cleansing in either case and on this night feels somehow blessed by what washes away—perhaps the sins he has committed while a warrior. The speaker envies the "dead that the rain rains upon" as he imagines that they are certainly blessed. This echoes the New Testament chapter where John hears a voice from heaven say: "Write: Blessed are the dead who die in the Lord from now on." In the scripture the Spirit responds that "they will rest from their labor, for their deeds will follow them" (Revelation 14:13).

The soldier prays that "none whom once [he] loved" is either dying, perhaps as his fellow soldiers or the enemy is, or "lying still awake," as he is, "solitary" and alone. His concern is with their loneliness rather than their predicaments. He does not want anyone he loves to be in pain and listening to the rain, or even in "sympathy" for another. He does not want them to be as helpless as the cold water among broken reeds is—as helpless as he feels among those dead and dying. Thomas describes the reeds as corpselike: "all still and stiff." As the poem closes, he compares the reeds to himself, recognizing "no love which this wild rain / Has not dissolved except the love of death." It is clearly not the death of others that the soldier loves; instead he feels a strange longing for his own, as the rain has told him that it will be "perfect" and therefore "cannot . . . disappoint"—as perhaps soldiering has.

BIBLIOGRAPHY

Clive, Wilmer. "Edward Thomas: Englishness and Modernity." *PN Review* 27, no. 4 (March–April 2001): 59–64.

Thomas, Edward. *The Collected Poems of Edward Thomas.* Edited by R. George Thomas. New York: Oxford, 1978.

———. *Elected Friends: Robert Frost and Edward Thomas to One Another.* Edited by Matthew Spencer. New York: Handsel Books, 2003.

Deirdre Fagan

RAINE, CRAIG (1944–) The English poet and critic Craig Raine is best known as the progenitor of the Martian school, a poetic movement influential in

England in the late 1970s and early 1980s. The term *Martian school* was introduced by JAMES FENTON, who adopted it from Raine's prize-winning *A Martian Sends a Postcard Home* (1979). According to Fenton, the Martian poets provided an imaginatively fresh outlook on the everyday world of ordinary objects and routines by means of defamiliarization and reliance on inventive metaphors and similes. Even though the movement as such was short-lived, its pervasive achievement was to breathe new life into the metaphorical and imaginative aspects of English poetry.

Born at Shildon, county Durham, on December 3, 1944, Craig Anthony Raine was raised in a working-class household and educated at Barnard Castle School and Exeter College, Oxford. In 1968 he earned a B.A. at Oxford and read for a Ph.D. on Coleridge, a project abandoned in 1973. From 1971 to 1979 he taught at various Oxford colleges, while working as books editor for *New Review,* editor of *Quarto,* and poetry editor at the *New Statesman.* From 1981 to 1991 he was poetry editor at Faber and Faber. Since 1991 he has been a fellow of New College, Oxford. He is founder and editor of the literary magazine *Areté.* In 1972 he married Ann Pasternak Slater, an Oxford don and niece of Boris Pasternak. They have four children and reside in Oxford.

In the course of his literary career Raine has become one of England's most influential and productive contemporary poets. While his first two collections, *The Onion, Memory* (1978) and *A Martian Sends a Postcard Home* (1979), are characterized by his Martian style, *A Free Translation* (1981) and *Rich* (1984) contain a number of free translations and adaptations of poems by Dante, Marina Tsvetayeva, and others. An exploration of sexual passion and love is at the heart of these collections. In 1996 Raine published *Clay: Wherabouts Unknown* (1996), which was followed by *A la recherche du temps perdu* (1999), a long elegiac poem in which Raine comes to terms with a former lover's death of acquired immunodeficiency syndrome (AIDS). His *Collected Poems, 1978–1999* was published in 2000. Besides poetry, Raine has published a verse novel, *History: The Home Movie* (1994), which recounts 20th-century history by focusing on the histories of his and his wife's families. He also wrote two stage adaptations,

The Electrification of the Soviet Union (1986), an opera libretto after a novella by Pasternak (*The Last Summer*), and *"1953": A Version of Racine's Andromaque* (1990). His reviews and essays are collected in two anthologies, *Haydn and the Valve Trumpet* (1990) and *In Defence of T. S. Eliot* (2000).

Although Raine's oeuvre is informed by its startling use of imagery, the stance of the detached Martian observer soon gave way to a growing emphasis on emotional experience, sexual passion, and a concern with existential issues. In his poem "A Chest of Drawers" (1987), for instance, Raine effectively employs metaphor to express the inextricable link between "life and the ineffable skull / which feeds at the breast." While Raine's poetry tries to grasp life in all its incongruous facets, his view on topics such as sexuality, love, or death is often relentlessly honest and shockingly direct. Ultimately, however, his poetry is positive in its intense perception and acceptance of life's chaotic and arbitrary diversity.

See "A MARTIAN SENDS A POSTCARD HOME."

BIBLIOGRAPHY

Gregson, Ian. *Contemporary Poetry and Postmodernism: Dialogue and Estrangement.* Basingstoke, Eng.: Macmillan, 1996.

Jarniewicz, Jerzy. *The Uses of the Commonplace in Contemporary British Poetry: Larkin, Dunn and Raine.* Łódź: Wydawnictwo University, 1994.

Michaela Schrage-Früh

RAINE, KATHLEEN JESSIE (1908–2003)

Kathleen Raine is often associated with the romantic poets for her use of natural themes, sometimes archaic language and diction, and the obvious influences of Samuel Taylor Coleridge, Percy Bysshe Shelley, and William Blake. A prolific poet, Raine produced 12 volumes of poetry in the course of her writing career, the first, *Stone and Flower Poems, 1935–43,* published in 1943. Although Raine's early work frequently appeared in literary publications, she heeded the general advice of Virginia Woolf that poets should not rush into print at a young age, and the particular guidance of T. S. ELIOT that she was not ready to release a volume of her poetry. *Stone and Flower,* along with *Living in Time* (1946) and *The Pythoness* (1949), are often considered her finest works.

Raine was greatly influenced by Blake, a poet about whom she wrote several scholarly texts, including the much lauded two-volume *Blake and Tradition* (1968). She wrote additional volumes about other poets she admired, such as W. B. YEATS and Samuel Taylor Coleridge; introductions to volumes of poetry; and lectures on art and culture. Her three-volume autobiography, rereleased in 1992 as *Autobiographies,* traces Raine's development as a poet. The work is structured as a journey from innocence to experience, employing a Blakean metaphor.

Born in London, the only child to two doting parents, Raine received intellectual support from her father, a Wesleyan Methodist preacher and school housemaster, and derived a love of poetry from her mother's nurturing of her imagination. She attended Girton College, Cambridge, and received an M.A. in botany and zoology. Her poetry frequently records the visible natural world she learned about in her natural science courses. The numinous and visionary quality of her poetry, however, derived from her mentors: Blake, Jung, and Yeats.

In a time in which positivist philosophy and French existentialism were embraced in intellectual circles, Raine went against the grain and railed against materialism, widening the already growing gap between her and her colleagues at Cambridge. Her poetry was a continuance of the romantic tradition of nature experienced as personal phenomena. Both *The Pythoness* and *The Year One* (1952) exhibit the nature imagery as used by Raine in symbolic terms. The symbolism in her poems becomes more archetypal in nature as she became more affected by Jung's work with dream theory and interpretation, and as her friend EDWIN MUIR encouraged her to rely on and explore her dreams as a basis for her poetry.

Six Dreams and Other Poems (1968) is heavily invested with female archetypes that Raine initiated in *The Pythoness.* Her later volumes, from *The Lost Country* (1971) to *The Oracle in the Heart* (1980), explore the mother-daughter relationship, often relying on the Demeter-Kore myths, which are rich with fertility archetypes. In her preface to the 2001 *The Collected Poems of Kathleen Raine,* Raine mentions her travels in India, a land where she felt "home at last!" Her later poetry shows evidence of the influence of Indian philosophy with its mythological and religious subjects. The visionary Hildegard von Bingen, the Tarot, Roman Catholicism, and various other mystical subjects and writers inform both Raine's poetry and her scholarly writings. Along with friends, she founded *Temenos,* a journal devoted to the "arts of the imagination."

The title of her last volume of poetry before the *Complete Poems* was compiled sums up Raine's poetic life—*Living with Mystery*: *Poems, 1987–1991* (1992). Her rejection of materialism in favor of the mysterious life of dreams, archetypes, and mythology both pleased and irritated critics of her poetry, and since her death, there has been renewed interest in her work.

See also "NORTHUMBRIAN SEQUENCE."

BIBLIOGRAPHY
Mill, Ralph J., Jr. *Kathleen Raine: A Critical Essay.* Grand Rapids, Mich.: Eerdmans.

Brad Bostian

"THE RAT" W. H. [WILLIAM HENRY] DAVIES (1920)
W. H. DAVIES is remembered primarily for his works that celebrate nature's unerring beauty or alternatively bemoan the degraded state of the modern human condition. "The Rat," composed when the author was in his late forties, is representative of the latter. The poem consists of four stanzas, each containing two short couplets written in tetrameter. The quotation marks that enclose the work indicate that the title character is addressing the reader. Such a choice of interlocutor suggests a certain morbidity of tone and the author certainly delivers on this point.

The situation Davies relates in the poem is that of a dying woman left alone at night while family members pursue their own pleasures: "Her husband in a pothouse drinks, / Her daughter at a soldier winks." The rat is a secret companion who has obscene plans for this victim of neglect: "Now with these teeth that powder stones, / I'll pick at one of her cheekbones." Upon returning from indulging their immoral inclinations, the family will be confronted with the ghastly consequences of their selfish behavior. The sentiment is typical of Davies, whose poetry often displays empathy for, and an identification with, society's forgotten and abused.

The infusion of despair and decay into the domestic circle that marks "The Rat" is important in that it anticipates one of the hallmarks of MODERNISM. Though written a few years before T. S. ELIOT's THE WASTE LAND, Davies's poem is resonant of the "rat's alley / where the dead men lost their bones." The central theme of "The Rat," the profound absence of human empathy, also echoes in the opposite direction to the recent manifold horrors of the First World War. The poem foregrounds the increasing alienation and hopelessness that become key components of literature well beyond Davies's death in 1940.

BIBLIOGRAPHY
Davies, W. H. *The Complete Poems of W. H. Davies.* Middletown, Conn.: Wesleyan University Press, 1963.

Jason Spangler

REDGROVE, PETER (1932–) Peter Redgrove, born in England in 1932, was educated at Taunton School, Somerset, and Queen's College, Cambridge. He read natural sciences at Cambridge but was also an original member of a writing workshop started by Philip Hobsbaum, which later became known as the Group. Hobsbaum later moved to Belfast and organized students, faculty, and local writers in another incarnation of the Group that included SEAMUS HEANEY, MICHAEL LONGLEY, and PAUL MULDOON. The meetings, in which writers read and critiqued each other's work, provided a environment for growth and support and remain a subject of interest to scholars because of the many talented writers who emerged from them. Redgrove published some of his first poems in *A Group Anthology,* put together by Hobsbaum and Edward Lucie Smith in 1963.

Redgrove went on to work in advertising and in scientific journalism. He has published many books of poetry, a few novels, and two books cowritten with PENELOPE SHUTTLE. One of these is *The Wise Wound,* a study of the mythology and taboos of menstruation. His poetry is an attempt to reach beyond the abstract and technical surface of science toward a deeper meaning. In this endeavor, he explores occult, pagan, pantheistic, and Jungian ideas, and turns away from traditional Christian spirituality and image. His work is dense with physical imagery and preoccupied with the sexual and the religious.

Since 1966, he has been resident author at Falmouth School of Art, Cornwall, a locale that appears in his landscapes and seascapes. His books of poetry include *The Collector and Other Poems* (1960), *The Force and Other Poems* (1966), *Sons of My Skin: Selected Poems 1954–74* (1975), *The Weddings of Nether Powers* (1979), *The Moon Disposes: Poems 1954–1987* (1987), and *My Father's Trapdoor* (1994).

BIBLIOGRAPHY
Tuma, Keith. *Anthology of Twentieth-Century British and Irish Poetry.* Oxford: Oxford University Press, 2001.

Mary Van Oeveren

"RED-HERRING" D. H. LAWRENCE (1929) A satirical poem that juxtaposes Standard English with a working-class dialect, "Red-Herring" succinctly encapsulates many of the issues of class, social propriety, and taboo that animate D. H. LAWRENCE's novels. The poem's speaker, like Lawrence, is a man from a humble background who has "risen in the world." The son of a mining pit foreman and a former schoolteacher, Lawrence grew up in a coal-mining town in Nottinghamshire. His speaker shares this pedigree: His father worked as a collier while his mother was "cut out to play a superior rôle / in the god-damn bourgeoisie." The children of this union are therefore "in-betweens" and "non-descripts," belonging wholly neither to one class nor to the other. This in-between status is reflected in their language, which alternates between the standard and the colloquial: "Indoors we called each other *you,* / outside, it was *tha* and *thee.*" As a grown man, the speaker continues to feel an "in-betweener," caught between the trappings of his bourgeois life and a desire to be addressed in his native dialect and hence recognized as something other than a respectable middle-class citizen. The poem ends with the words of the imaginary confederate who takes the speaker aside and inveighs against the bourgeoisie in an obscenity-laced Nottinghamshire patois.

"Red-Herring" is one of more than 200 *pensées* that Lawrence wrote in 1928 and 1929, in the wake of the publication of his scandalous, banned novel *Lady Chatterly's Lover.* When Lawrence sent the manuscript of these collected *pensées* to his London agent, Scotland Yard intercepted the package and held it on the grounds of obscenity. Lawrence struggled both to regain possession of his manuscript and to rewrite the poems in a version that would be publishable. The long dashes that efface the obscenities of the poem's last verse are Lawrence's attempt both to censor himself and to parody the act of censorship. These blank spaces call on the reader to reconstruct Lawrence's obscenities: To understand the poem, we must admit that we too have access to a lexicon of rude, "low-class" language.

Matthew Bolton

REED, HENRY (1914–1986)

The poet, dramatist, critic, and journalist Henry Reed is best known for a group of poems published as *The Lessons of War.* Reed was born in Birmingham, England, on February 22, 1914. His mother, though illiterate, instilled in her son a love for folktales. His father, a bricklayer, passed on his passion for books to Henry. Reed attended King Edward VI School in his hometown and received his M.A. from the University of Birmingham in 1934. Following his graduation, Reed traveled and worked as a freelance journalist for papers such as the *Birmingham Post* and *Manchester Guardian.* In 1941, Reed joined the army and transferred to the Foreign Office the next year. While in the army, Reed published his first poems in the *Listener* and *New Statesman.*

The works of British poets during World War I are numerous and admired, yet few poems written about World War II have achieved similar status. Critics consider Henry Reed's poem "THE NAMING OF PARTS" as not only his best work, but one of the most significant poems of the Second World War. The first in a series of three—"Naming of Parts," "Judging Distances," and "Unarmed Combat"—published together, this early poem was an immediate success and remains a much anthologized selection.

After the war, Reed joined the British Broadcasting Corporation (BBC) as a radio commentator and dramatist. One of his first productions was a radio version of *Moby Dick.* During the following years, Reed gained some renown for verse-dramas such as *A Very Great Man Indeed* and *Hilda Tablet.* The material for some of the plays was gathered from research Reed did in preparation for a planned biography of THOMAS HARDY, a project he never completed. Turning to another genre, in 1946 Reed published a critical study of contemporary fiction, *The Novel Since 1939.*

During the 1950s, unable to meet the standards of his early success and unhappy over the end of his most significant homosexual relationship, Reed turned to alcohol. Although he continued to write commentary for radio and adapted between 40 and 50 plays for the BBC, he did not achieve critical acclaim. In 1964, Reed accepted a three-year teaching position in Seattle at the University of Washington.

Reed's last works of note were acclaimed translations completed during the 1970s. Some of these French and Italian dramas were broadcast on radio and some produced on stage. As his alcoholism continued to worsen, Reed spent his last years as a recluse. He died in 1986.

While Reed's reputation rests primarily on *The Lessons of War,* his extensive work as a journalist, essayist, dramatist, and translator is equally important. Reed is one of the earliest writers to make the transition from page to broadcast and to understand the importance of media, an understanding he expressed in an essay for *B.B.C. Quarterly* called "What the Wireless Can Do for Literature" (1949).

Reed is often concerned with the impact of place on the actions of individuals and with human actions at crucial moments. His work demonstrates appreciation for the dramatic, is intellectual and clever, and displays his talent for humor, even when the subject and theme are somber.

BIBLIOGRAPHY

Drakakis, John, ed. *British Radio Drama.* Cambridge: Cambridge University Press, 1981.

Hamilton, Ian. "Henry Reed." In *Against Oblivion: Some Lives of the Twentieth-Century Poets,* 212–216. London: Viking, 2002.

O'Toole, Michael. "Henry Reed, and What Follows the 'Naming of Parts.'" In *Functions of Style,* edited by David Birch and Michael O'Toole, 12–13. London: Pinter, 1988.

Reed, Henry. *Hilda Tablet and Others: Four Pieces for Radio* (includes *A Very Great Man Indeed; The Private Life of Hilda Tablet; A Hedge, Backwards; The Primal Scene, As It Were*). London: BBC, 1971.

———. *Lessons of the War.* New York: Chilmark Press, 1970.

———. *A Map of Verona.* London: Cape, 1946, and New York: Reynal, 1947.

———. *Moby Dick: A Play for Radio from Herman Melville's Novel*. London: J. Cape, 1947.
———. *The Novel since 1939*. Berlin: Cornelsenverlag, 1946.
———. *Three Plays*. New York: Grove Press, 1958.

Jean Hamm

"REQUEST TO A YEAR" JUDITH WRIGHT (1955)

This poem first appeared in JUDITH WRIGHT's collection *The Two Fires* (1955), written during the dark years of the Korean War and referring to the spark of life and love as opposed to the fire of mankind's destruction. "The atom bomb was really under my skin," said Wright once while speaking about the poems in this collection; this poem is a "request" for the necessary firmness of hand in such dark times. The poem comprises six stanzas—five quatrains and a final couplet—and the rhyme scheme is irregular until it settles in the third quatrain. The prosaic effect of the first two stanzas, introducing the personality of the great-great-grandmother, gently develops into a traditional ballad through the linking rhymes (*attitude—viewed, rock—alpenstock*). The concluding rhyming couplet, now addressing the personified year itself, briefly summarizes the poet's "request."

The image of the hand forms the central motif of the poem. It is in the hand of the great-great-grandmother that artistic talent unites with the necessary practicality of a mother; it is the point where art and life meet. The poet tells us that her great-great-grandmother was a "legendary devotee of the arts," who, however, had "little opportunity for painting pictures" as a result of her duties as mother to eight children. It is the hand of her second daughter that swiftly reacts in time with the "last-hope alpenstock" to save her brother's life, despite the highly impractical "petticoats of the day." We are informed, rather hopelessly, that "nothing, it was evident, could be done"; the great-great-grandmother was, after all, sitting "on a high rock," at an alliterated "difficult distance." The poem praises the firmness of hand possessed by the great-great-grandmother, who, in full knowledge that she cannot help her son, detaches emotion from practicality with the artist's "isolating eye" and does the little she can: She turns his fate into art. Had the son not survived the incident, he would have at least been immortalized by her sketch. The fact that the son survived because of his sister's swift reaction is added in brackets as an afterthought to the fourth quatrain, which shifts the focus of the incident away from the fate of the son and toward the female courage portrayed in the poem, symbolized by the motif of the hand. This is what the poet requests of the year: the ability she considers shared by artists and mothers to isolate and detach the savable from the nonsavable and to approach fate with a shrewd combination of calmness and creativity.

BIBLIOGRAPHY

Scott, W. N. *Focus on Judith Wright*. Brisbane: University of Queensland Press, 1967.
Walker, Shirley. *The Poetry of Judith Wright*. Melbourne: Edward Arnold, 1980.

Wendy Skinner

"RETURNING, WE HEAR THE LARKS" ISAAC ROSENBERG (1917)

"Returning, We Hear the Larks" was written in France sometime in 1917. In the poem, ISAAC ROSENBERG addresses themes that are similar to those he addresses in his other war poems. The poem opens with the men returning from night battle with the reward of still being alive but knowing that they have merely survived for today. The men are exhausted from the strain of battle and besides the comfort of still having their lives they seek only "a little safe sleep." Rosenberg emphasizes the horrors of war in this passage by showing that in the midst of war the men have become so inured to its privations that they can look forward to nothing more pleasant than the safety of sleep. Other pleasures do not even enter the realm of possibilities. Suddenly in this bleak world between war and sleep, the song of the larks imposes itself. The men experience great joy, as Rosenberg remarks, "Music showering our upturned list'ning faces." Their joy, however, will be short-lived because the song serves only as a tantalizing slice of a life from which the men are barred—a life of beauty and safety. The song of the larks is beautiful "like a blind man's dreams on the sand," but the dream, like the song, is "by dangerous tides." In this world of war, death always lurks just around the corner. The song of the larks calls the men out from the world of death to taste a world of beauty—only to thrust them back into that world of death once the song disappears.

In the appearance of the larks, perhaps more so than in any of his others poems, Rosenberg also juxtaposes the human world against the natural world. The result is a natural world indifferent to human suffering. When Rosenberg remarks, "Death could drop from the dark / As easily as song—," he represents the beauty of nature appearing in the very likeness of death. Both bombs and songs fall upon the men in the same manner, and the very fact that it could be bombs and not songs that fall at this moment suggests that the larks sing regardless of the human joy or suffering occuring within their midst. Despite the men's joy at hearing the beautiful song of the larks, Rosenberg knows that it is an illusion with only danger and death behind it. Like the girl who "dreams no ruin lies there / Or her kisses where a serpent hides," Rosenberg suggests that the emphemeral and illusionary beauty of the song of the larks only obscures the true reality of the dance with death that the men must perform each day. Thus the world in which the men exist will become that much more bleak once the song of the larks ends and they must then grapple once more with the bleak world of death and suffering.

BIBLIOGRAPHY

Liddiard, Jean. *Isaac Rosenberg: The Half Used Life.* London: Victor Gollancz, 1975.

Maccoby, Deborah. *God Made Blind: Isaac Rosenberg, His Life and Poetry.* Northwood, Eng.: Symposium Press, 1999.

John Peters

RICKWORD, EDGELL (1898–1982)   Edgell

Rickword was born in Colchester, England, on October 22, 1898. In the autumn of 1916, he enlisted in the Artists' Rifles and saw active duty as an officer in the Royal Berkshire Regiment. He was later awarded the Military Cross and was subsequently invalided out of the army after the Armistice in 1918. In October 1919, Rickword went up to Oxford University as a student of French literature. He remained at Oxford for only four terms, leaving in 1921, when he married.

In straitened financial circumstances, he gained a foothold in the literary world through the influence of several friends, including J. C. Squire, who secured publication of several of Rickword's poems in the *London Mercury.* Among these was "TRENCH POETS," the piece that remains the most anthologized of all of Rickword's many poems. His first collection, *Behind the Eyes,* was also published in 1921, and in the same year he began writing articles for the *Times Literary Supplement* (*TLS*). Among the books Rickword reviewed for the *TLS* was T. S. ELIOT's *THE WASTE LAND* (1922), a book that he found reasons to praise, but one that remained flawed in his estimate because it allowed readers no "direct emotional response" to its subject. As a direct contrast to this supposed stance, in 1924 Rickword published his first critical monograph, *Rimbaud: The Boy and the Poet.* He also remained a frequent contributor to the *TLS* until 1925, when he founded his own influential review, entitled *The Calendar of Modern Letters.* This publication remained in existence only until 1927, but many of the attitudes fostered there—political alertness and critical skepticism of both the archaic and the AVANT-GARDE in modern writing—had a noticeable impact on the development of F. R. Leavis's thought.

Rickword's second collection of poems, *Invocation to Angels,* was published in 1928, but by the 1930s his left-wing political orientation dominated much of what he wrote. It was at this time that he joined the Communist Party and founded a journal called the *Left Review* (1936–38). Between 1944 and 1947 he also edited a Communist publication, *Our Time.* Rickword's *Collected Poems* was published in 1947, and he also produced editions, anthologies, and essays on various topics until his death on March 15, 1982. His last collection of poems was published in 1981, *Twittingpan and Some Others.*

Throughout Rickword's writing there are an earnestness and determination neither to falsify nor to avoid difficult emotional matters. His criticism singles out such falsifications, evident in formal posturing or the stereotyping of situations, moods, or responses, and his verse itself strives to fuse the individuality of experience with an individuality of expression—an aim that lends his verse a startling originality, and often grim humor, as in the concluding lines from "Trench Poets," in which the narrator bids farewell to a dead fellow soldier: "He stank so badly, though we were great chums, / I had to leave him; then rats ate his thumbs."

BIBLIOGRAPHY

Hobday, Charles. *Edgell Rickword: A Poet at War.* Manchester, Eng.: Carcanet, 1989.

Holbrook, David. "The Poetic Mind of Edgell Rickword." *Essays in Criticism* 12 (1962): 273–291.

Rickword, Edgell. *Collected Poems.* Manchester, Eng.: Carcanet, 1991.

John Ballam

RIDLER, ANNE (1912–2001)

Anne Barbara Bradby Ridler was the daughter of the poet Henry Bradby, who was headmaster of Rugby School in Warwickshire where Anne was born in July 1912, and Violet Milford, the author of children's books. So it is not surprising that Ridler found herself becoming a poet, dramatist, librettist, and editor over the course of her life. She was educated at Downe House School, which became the subject of her 1967 book, *Olive Willis and Downe House: An Adventure in Education.* In 1938 she married Vivian Ridler, who worked as a printer for the University of Oxford from 1958 to 1978. They had four children, two boys and two girls, who survived her death in October 2001.

After earning a degree in journalism from King's College, London, in 1932, Ridler briefly worked for the Oxford University Press, which published her first collection of poetry, succinctly titled *Poems,* in 1939, as well as her edited collection *Shakespeare Criticism: 1919–1935,* published in 1936. In 1935 she joined the publishing firm of Faber and Faber, where she worked until 1940, becoming T. S. ELIOT's assistant while he was the company's working editor. Her experiences with Eliot were eventually documented in *Working for T. S. Eliot: A Personal Reminiscence,* published by Enitharmon in 2000. Eliot was a huge supporter of Ridler's early attempts at writing poetry. When she chose the poems included in *The Little Book of Modern Verse* for Faber and Faber in 1941, Eliot, who wrote the preface, insisted that Ridler's poem "A Letter" be included in this slim volume along with poets like Gerard Manley Hopkins, W. B. YEATS, EZRA POUND, D. H. LAWRENCE, and W. H. AUDEN. "A Letter" is an interesting poem for Eliot to have chosen for the collection, because in this poem Ridler

analyzes the discomfort she feels at first using poetic language, observing that "coming to verse, I hid my lack of ease / By writing only as I thought myself able."

The few critics who have studied Ridler's poetry note the influences upon her by Eliot, in her use of classical forms, and Auden and LOUIS MACNEICE, in her variations on those forms. In fact, in an article Ridler wrote for *T. S. Eliot: A Study of his Writings by Several Hands,* she noted "that it was Eliot who first made me despair of becoming a poet; Auden . . . who first made me think I saw how to become one" (109). Kathleen Morgan's chapter on Ridler in *Christian Themes in Contemporary Poets* notes Ridler's reliance upon specific images of the sea or river, flowers, and music to convey the poet's personal joys and sorrows that are addressed in her reflective poetry, whether she is talking about childbirth, separation from her husband because of the war, or even death. As Derek Stanford observes in *The Freedom of Poetry,* Ridler's verse "seems to achieve a greater honesty, concerning herself and her whole sex" (246), using as an example her poem "The Crab," which addresses the issue of menstruation.

After leaving Faber and Faber, Ridler continued working for them as an editor, putting together a collection of *Best Ghost Stories* in 1945. She continued the relationship with Faber and Faber when they published more of her poetry—*The Nine Bright Shiners* in 1943, *The Golden Bird and Other Poems* in 1951, *A Matter of Life and Death* in 1959, *Some Time After and Other Poems* in 1972, and *New and Selected Poems* in 1988. Faber and Faber also published several of the verse dramas that Ridler wrote—*The Shadow Factory: A Nativity Play* in 1946 (produced in 1945); *Henry Bly, and Other Plays* in 1950 (*Henry Bly* was produced in 1947); *The Trial of Thomas Cranmer: A Play,* with music by Bryan Kelly, in 1956; *Who Is My Neighbor? and, How Bitter the Bread* in 1963 (with *Who Is My Neighbor?* actually produced in 1961). The verse plays are interesting in this consideration because they expand upon the ideas concentrated in Ridler's poetry. For a variety of other publishers she edited collections of poems by Gerard Hopkins, James Thomson, Thomas Traherne, George Darby, and William Austin, as well as a second collection of essays on Shakespeare. In 1962, Ridler recorded several of her poems with commentary at Isis

Recording Studios, Oxford, England; the Library of Congress has a copy of the cassette tape.

Ridler is also known for her translations of various librettos, including Cavalli's *Rosinda* (1973), Monteverdi's *Orfeo* (1975), Cavalli's *Eritrea* (1975), Monteverdi's *The Return of Ulysses* (1978), Cesti's *Orontea* (1979), Handel's *Agrippina* (1982), Cavalli's *La Calisto* (1984), and Mozart's *Cosi fan Tutte* (1986), *Don Giovanni* (1990), and *The Marriage of Figaro* (1991).

In 1954 she received the Oscar Blumenthal Prize and in 1955 the Union League Civic and Arts Poetry Prize from *Poetry,* a magazine published by the Poetry Foundation in Chicago. In 1998 she was awarded the Cholmondeley Prize for Poetry, which is administered by the Society of Authors in England, for *Collected Poems,* published by Carcanet in 1994. Then in June 2001, just a few months before her death in October, she was made an officer of the British Empire (OBE) for her services to literature.

BIBLIOGRAPHY

Dowson, Jane. "Anne Ridler." In *Women's Poetry of the 1930s: A Critical Anthology,* 102–107. London: Routledge, 1996.

Morgan, Kathleen E. "'The Holiness of the Heart's Affections': Poetry of Anne Ridler." In *Christian Themes in Contemporary Poets: A Study of English Poetry of the Twentieth Century,* 144–153. London: SCM Press, 1965.

Ridler, Anne. *Collected Poems.* Manchester, Eng.: Carcanet, 1994.

———. "A Question of Speech." In *T. S. Eliot: A Study of His Writings by Several Hands,* edited by B. Rajan, 107–118. New York: Funk & Wagnalls, 1948.

Peggy Huey

"THE RIVER-MERCHANT'S WIFE: A LETTER" EZRA POUND, TRANSLATION OF LI PO (1915)

This powerfully translated love poem grew out of EZRA POUND's reading of Eastern poets during his period of inventing IMAGISM to reform and revitalize poetry. The poem also played a particularly important role during the Great War. During and immediately after the war, the voices of women and other noncombatants were not particularly honored, though their voices soon rose into more prominence, just as trench poetry began to move from primacy to a respected but background position. In part, no one wanted to be reminded of the soldiers' bitterness, of their sacrifice and their anger. (OSBERT SITWELL had predicted this in a poem called "The Next War": "Deaf men became difficult to talk to, / Heroes became bores.") In part, in the memorializing of the war dead, the grief and losses of the civilian world, and especially of women, could be more deeply acknowledged. One route for noncombatants to have their poetry taken seriously was found by Ezra Pound, in his translations of the Chinese war poems of Li Po (701–762), which he published as *Cathay* in 1915.

The great ideological divide that grew up in the Great War had split the world into two camps—those at the front who, it was argued, had an authentic experience that they could only tell truthfully through a sharp irony, and those at home who could not know the truth and so told and believed grandiose or sentimental illusions. Those at the front were overwhelmingly male, and those at home were women or men left behind in a "feminized" situation as noncombatants. By translating Li Po, Pound could use the correct male soldierly language to affirm a connection between man and woman that the trench poets were only allowing between comrades in arms, without having to make false claims about his own experience, as in "Song of the Bowman of Shu" and "Lament of the Frontier Guard" (poems that Pound's friend at the front, the sculptor Henri Gaudier-Brzeska, picked as especially moving to his fellow soldiers there).

He also translated poems in a female voice (which he did not send to the trenches), such as "The River-Merchant's Wife: A Letter." The speaker of the letter is in Pound's feminized situation—the one left behind. The wife describes how, in her arranged marriage, she has gradually come to desire "my dust to be mingled with yours / Forever and forever and forever." Now her lord has been gone five months, and her longing for him, though stated discreetly, is palpable. She describes the leaves falling early in autumn, and notes "the paired butterflies are already yellow with August / Over the grass in the West garden." The images of pairing and of the ending of fragile life lead naturally to the surprisingly intense and direct following line: "They hurt me." The letter ends with the wife's inquiring which route her lord will take home, for she wishes to go out to meet him. The sorrow of the wife, the obvious bonds of love and eroticism, affirm a connection between man and woman that the trench poets were only allowing between comrades in arms. These two are also meant to be in each other's arms. The focus on the wife's feelings, rather than upon descriptions of the experiences of war, allows this poem to authenticate and validate women's and noncombatants' experiences during wartime.

BIBLIOGRAPHY

Apter, Ronnie. *Digging for the Treasure: Translation after Pound.* New York: Paragon House, 1987.

Wai-lim, Yip. *Ezra Pound's Cathay.* Princeton, N.J.: Princeton University Press, 1969.

Wilhelm, J. J. *Ezra Pound in London and Paris: 1908–1925.* University Park: Pennsylvania State University Press, 1990.

James Persoon

ROSENBERG, ISAAC (1890–1918)

Isaac Rosenberg was born on November 25, 1890, in Bristol, England, the son of Jewish parents who had emigrated from Lithuania in the late 1880s. In 1897, the family moved from Bristol to the East End of London and settled in a Jewish neighborhood. Rosenberg's youth, in fact his entire life, was one of poverty. As a youth, he showed a talent for painting, but at age 14 had to give up its study for a time to apprentice as an engraver. In 1907, Rosenberg was again able to study art, attending evening classes at Birkbeck College and later at the London School of Photo-Engraving and Lithography. Over the next several years, Rosenberg would win several prizes for his work. In 1911, he quit his job as an engraver and later that year, through a sponsorship, began studying painting at the Slade School of Fine Arts. Since as early as 1905, Rosenberg had also been writing poetry, his earliest known work "Ode to David's Harp." Rosenberg became acquainted with a number of writers of the time such as ROBERT LAURENCE BINYON, EZRA POUND, Edward Marsh, T. E. HULME, and W. B. YEATS. In 1912, Rosenberg privately published his first volume of poems, *Night and Day,* which did not attract much interest. The following year, Rosenberg developed a pulmonary illness that would afflict him for some time, ultimately causing him to leave the Slade School in early 1914. At that point, he was sent to South Africa in the hope that the climate would improve his health. In 1915, Rosenberg returned to England and published another volume of poems, entitled *Youth,* which again attracted little interest. Later that year, out of work and in need of money, Rosenberg enlisted in the army and was sent to France in mid-1916. Just before leaving for France, Rosenberg arranged for the publication of *Moses: A Play.* Shortly after arriving in France, Rosenberg wrote the first of his important "trench poems": "BREAK OF DAY IN THE TRENCHES." The following year, Rosenberg wrote several more: "DEAD MAN'S DUMP," "Daughters of War," and "RETURNING, WE HEAR THE LARKS." Another of his important poems, "LOUSE HUNTING," was also written sometime during this period. During his time at the front, Rosenberg, as did his fellow soldiers, experienced illness and other hardships, so much so that he even had difficulty finding paper on which to compose his poetry. He appears to have considered many of his poems still to be in draft form, but unfortunately he never had the opportunity to revise them as he was killed in action on April 1, 1918, only about seven months before the end of the war. Rosenberg's poetry attracted little interest until the 1922 collection of his poems edited by Gordon Bottomly, and even then interest was only mild. Widespread interest in his poetry did not occur until a 1937 edition of his poems appeared. Rosenberg is best known for his trench poems and is often closely associated with the other war poets such as SIEGFRIED SASSOON, WILFRED OWEN, and IVOR GURNEY, but in reality there is a good deal of difference between Rosenberg's poetry and that of the others. The difference between Rosenberg's economic and cultural background and that of the other war poets made for a very different view of the world. The disillusionment evident in the poetry of the others does not appear in Rosenberg's poetry because Rosenberg's view of the world was already infused with skepticism before he even enlisted for duty in World War I. Certainly the difficult life Rosenberg had experienced was a major factor in his worldview. Instead of disillusionment, Rosenberg's poetry evidences a realistic attention to detail that results in a sympathy for the plight and suffering of humanity in general, as well as for the particular suffering of his fellow soldiers. Rosenberg's trench poems are also known for their detached view of the world. His ability to remove himself from the tragedies he witnessed often adds to the horrors appearing in his poems by emphasizing the deadening effect they could have on those involved but also by allowing the reader to fill in the emotional response to these tragedies. As is true of the death of his fellow war poet Wilfred Owen, Rosenberg's death almost certainly altered the course of modern poetry. One can only imagine the effect Owen and Rosenberg would have had on the history of literature had they lived, both only just coming into their maturity as poets when they were killed.

BIBLIOGRAPHY

Cohen, Joseph. *Journey to the Trenches: The Life of Isaac Rosenberg 1890–1918.* New York: Basic Books, 1975.

Liddiard, Jean. *Isaac Rosenberg: The Half Used Life.* London: Victor Gollancz, 1975.

Maccoby, Deborah. *God Made Blind: Isaac Rosenberg, His Life and Poetry.* Northwood, Eng.: Symposium Press, 1999.

Noakes, Vivien. *The Poems and Plays of Isaac Rosenberg.* Oxford: Oxford University Press, 2004.

Tomlinson, Charles. *Isaac Rosenberg of Bristol.* Bristol, Eng.: Bristol Branch of the Historical Association, 1982.

Wilson, Jean Moorcroft. *Isaac Rosenberg: Poet and Painter.* London: Cecil Woolf, 1975.

John Peters

"ROUEN" MAY WEDDERBURN CANNAN (1917)

Although it tends toward jog-trot Edwardian meters and patriotic clichés, "Rouen" testifies to the excitement that war work provided for women by affording them opportunities for travel, paid labor, or public service. The conversational repetition of *And* at the beginning of several lines evokes immediacy and the breathless wonder at new sights and sensations— whether these be "the Red-Cross barges," "the endless stream of soldiers," or "the laughter" (which crops up twice). Since MARY WEDDERBURN CANNAN was qualified in nursing and first aid, she naturally joined the Voluntary Aid Detachment (VAD) when war broke out. She was posted for four weeks in spring 1915 at Rouen, where she helped to run the canteen at the railhead, serving the soldiers with coffee and sandwiches. The insistent rhythm of the long lines imitates the potency

of memory; the mood is one of nostalgia for the camaraderie and purpose of Cannan's nursing adventures in France: "Can I forget the passage from the cool white-bedded Aid Post / Past the long sun-blistered coaches of the khaki Red Cross train?" Typically the individual voice presumes to speak for collective experience, often switching to the plural pronoun *we* or the interactive second-person refrain *can you recall?* The neatly rhyming quatrains tread a fine line between reinforcing and exaggerating the cheeriness with which each scene is remembered. In spite of the regularity of the rhythm and rhyme, which are not compromised with any enjambments, the diction is remarkably colloquial except for an odd forced and archaic elision, *o'erhead,* in verse 8. The poem is included in PHILIP LARKIN's *Oxford Book of Twentieth Century English Verse* (1973), with a note that he "found it in the Bodleian [library in Oxford] . . . and immediately knew that this was something that had to go in. It seemed to have all the warmth and idealism of the VADs in the First World War. I find it enchanting."

BIBLIOGRAPHY

Dowson, Jane, "Women's Poetry and the First World War." In *Women, Modernism and British Poetry 1910–39: Resisting Femininity.* Aldershot, Eng.: Ashgate, 2002.

Fyfe, Charlotte, ed. *The Tears of War: The Love Story of a Young Poet and a War Hero.* Upavon, Eng.: Cavalier, 2000.

Reilly, Catherine, ed. *Scars upon My Heart: Women's Poetry and Verse of the First World War.* London: Virago, 1981.

Jane Dowson

"THE RUINED MAID" THOMAS HARDY (1902)

THOMAS HARDY both makes use of the familiar ballad character of the seduced village maiden and satirizes Victorian conventional morality in this comic poem. Written as a dramatic dialogue, the poem presents the chance meeting between a nameless innocent "country girl" visiting "Town," probably London, and one of her former country acquaintances, Amelia, now a "ruined maid," a mistress or a prostitute.

Each of the poem's six quatrains begins with the visiting country girl's surprised observation of her former friend and ends with Amelia's one-line reply, or in the case of the final stanza, two-line reply. The country girl's three lines of dialogue in each of the first five stanzas contain two lines recalling Amelia's past life in the country and a third observing her changed present condition in the city. The *aabb* rhyme scheme then fits not only the final stanza's equal line division of dialogue but also, although less obviously at least at first, the contrast between country and city life, between being innocent and poor or ruined and prosperous.

In the first stanza, the visiting country girl seems the dominant one in the reunion: It is she who approaches Amelia and declares that their meeting "does everything crown!" Her surprise at finding Amelia in town hints that Amelia's life in the country would not have led anyone to expect ("Who could have supposed") Amelia to be at a place that probably represents an extravagant holiday trip for the speaker. This greeting of Amelia on the basis of the country girl's former sense of superiority gives way to the country girl's observation of Amelia's present appearance and insistence that Amelia explain "whence such fair garments, such prosperi-ty." Amelia's quiet answer—"'O didn't you know I've been ruined?' said she"—may seem to suggest some sense of shame or remorse, but as the last lines of the following quatrains continue to repeat the fact of being *ruined* and the refrain *she said,* Amelia's explanation becomes incrementally triumphant.

The second through fifth stanzas continue to contrast Amelia's past life as a poor field worker in the country with her present life as a ruined maid in the city. The country visitor recalls how Amelia was "in tatters, without shoes or socks" but now wears "gay bracelets and bright feathers three," how she once spoke in the dialect of the Dorset country folk but now her speech is fit for "high company," and how her physical labor had left her battered and made her hands into bruised "paws" but now her cheek is "delicate" and she wears lady's gloves. Amelia's final line answers become progressively triumphant: "'Yes: that's how we dress when we're ruined,' said she"; "'Some polish is gained with one's ruin,' said she"; "'We never do work when we're ruined," said she"; and "'True. One's pretty lively when ruined,' said she."

In the final quatrain, Amelia's triumph is complete. Her former acquaintance no longer begins her dialogue with *you,* which had focused attention on Amelia, but now shifts to *I* and to her wish she could trade places with Amelia: "I wish I had feathers, a fine sweeping gown, / And a delicate face, and could strut about the Town!" Amelia's two-line answer begins with the affected complacency of her new status in Town but ends with her true country voice breaking out in her declaration of the privilege of her "fallen" position: "'My dear—a raw country girl, such as you be, / Cannot quite expect that. You ain't ruined,' said she."

The Victorian moral code of respectability condemning the "fallen women" ironically clashes with the reality of the Amelia's apparent life of affluence, leisure, and elevated social graces compared to the life of drudgery and hardship endured by the virtuous country maid. Although "The Ruined Maid" is dated and apparently was written in 1866, when Hardy lived at Westhoume Park Villas in London, its actual 1902 publication, in *Poems of the Past and the Present,* Hardy's second volume of poetry and first 20th-century publication, is significant considering the critical outrage over Hardy's sympathetic portrayals of "fallen women" in his novels, especially of Tess Dureyfield and Sue Bridehead.

BIBLIOGRAPHY

Bailey, J. O. *The Poetry of Thomas Hardy: A Handbook and Commentary.* Chapel Hill: University of North Carolina Press, 1970.

Renner, Stanley. "William Acton: The Truth about Prostitution, and Hardy's Not-So-Ruined-Maid." *Victorian Poetry* 30, no. 1 (1992): 19–28.

Robert R. Watson

RUMENS, CAROL (1944–)

Starting with *A Strange Girl in Bright Colours* (1973), CAROL RUMENS has published 15 collections of poetry; she contributed to making Russian work available in translation and has been a vigorous poetry editor and critic. As did that of her contemporaries, FLEUR ADCOCK and GILLIAN CLARKE, her early work tended toward an impersonal poetic persona, and she confesses to being stifled by trying to be "literary" at the start of her career. Although often lyrical, she is primarily a cultural commentator who investigates the balance of power, whether in the realm of human relationships, social groups, or between nations. Among the more obviously public poems, "Outside Oswiecim" is a lengthy multivoiced meditation on the Holocaust that indicates Rumens' sympathy with Jewish people. She frequently pitches human rights against totalitarianism, gleaned from her residences in Britain, Prague, and Northern Ireland. At times, she blurs the line between inner and outer landscapes, often through the metaphor of her experiences. Her distaste for a certain kind of nationalism in "A Lawn for the English Family" indirectly exposes the market-driven competitiveness of Britain in the 1980s. "An Easter Garland" (*Star Whisper,* 1983) and the sequence "A Geometry-Lesson for the Children of England" (*From Berlin to Heaven,* 1989) are also anti-right-wing mid-1980s poems that disdain consumerist individualism as it became manifest in cling-film-covered suburban privacy: "The misted lights of front lounges" are offset with "the frills on bruised babies." The assonance and dissonance in these lines are features of her technical range, which manipulates conventional forms or end rhymes as easily as free verse. They fulfill her wish "to keep close to my spoken diction."

Unsure about separatist aesthetics, her poems and critical writing often present and analyze the vexed creativity of the female poet. In *Making for the Open: The Chatto Book of Post-Feminist Poetry 1964–84* (1985), she excluded the "merely self-expressive," but by the time of *New Women Poets* (1990), she welcomed the increase of published women's poetry and was more able to embrace the distinctive label *woman poet.* Her poems often examine the cost of women's unprecedented opportunities for multiple roles at the end of the 20th century. "Two Women" captures the silent strain of the many who attempt to take advantage of all available options about marriage, motherhood, education, and employment: "There's another woman / who bears her name, a silent, background face." Here we see Rumens's predilection for psychological duality, especially the contingency of private and public selves. The tragicomic poems in *The Miracle Diet* (1997) disclose women's difficult relationship with food, which is exacerbated by contemporary advertising and slimming industries.

The majority of Rumens's poems can be found in *Thinking of Skins: New and Selected Poems* (1993) and *Collected Poems* (2004). She has held several posts as writer in residence and as a creative writing tutor; she also has written a novel and three plays.

BIBLIOGRAPHY

The Poetry Quartets. Vol. 2. *Fleur Adcock, Carol Ann Duffy, Selima Hill, Carol Rumens.* Audio Cassette. Newcastle upon Tyne: British Council/Bloodaxe Books, 1998.

Pykett, Lyn. "Women Poets and 'Women's Poetry': Fleur Adcock, Gillian Clarke and Carol Rumens." *British Poetry from the 1950s to the 1990s: Politics and Art,* edited by Gary Day and Brian Docherty, 253–267. London: Macmillan, 1997.

Rumens, Carol. "As Radical as Reality." *Poetry Review* 88, no. 4 (winter 1998/99): 77–83.

———. *Collected Poems.* Tarset, Eng.: Bloodaxe Books, 2004.

———. "I Feel I Am on My Own." Interview with Lidia Vianu. 10 December 1994. Available online. URL: http://lidiavianu.scriptmania.com/carol_rumens.htm. Accessed May 10, 2008.

Jane Dowson

S

"SAD STEPS" Philip Larkin (1974) Under a romantic title, *Sad Steps,* which is an ironically applied allusion, harkening back to a celebrated Renaissance love poem (Philip Sidney's "Sonnet 31" from his sequence *Astrophel and Stella*), Philip Larkin recreates his modern-day, seemingly uneventful, prosaic, bizarre, middle-of-the-night trip to the toilet, an event that, true to the strategy in numerous other poems by this poet, connects very effectively the commonplace and the universal and transforms an insignificant, even laughable, moment of intimate individual life into a sweeping vision of humanity and life in general.

Sidney's opening lines, "With how sad steps, O Moon, thou climb'st the skies, / How silently, and with how wan a face," set a stage for some important and melancholy questions about human erotic experiences and interpersonal relationships; Larkin's moon, on the other hand, seen startlingly and unexpectedly through parted curtains as he is "groping to bed after a piss," triggers a rather different psychological and intellectual reaction and journey.

This six-stanza poem was written in the late 1960s, at the time when the global students' revolutionary fervor was shaking even the usually less excitable English academic world, including Larkin's provincial Hull, and the distant echoes of that drama are detectable in the poem, mainly in its last stanza. In it, the aging poet or speaker muses how the "hardness and the brightness" of that surprising moon remind one of "the strength and pain / Of being young" and how that youthful feeling has been lost for him, "but is for others undiminished somewhere," as life inevitably goes on. This melancholy, partly envious musing occurs at the end of a poem, as the conclusion of a rather intense mental journey provoked by the sudden sighting of the moon, a celestial body symbolic of change, growth, and diminishment; of love, romantic yearnings, dreams, aspirations. That is why, in the fourth stanza, a sublime, elevated tone enters the poem. The moon is described in exulting phrases as a "lozenge of love! Medallion of art!" and invokes gushing words and powerful visions—"O wolves of memory! Immensements!"

The fifth stanza, however, cools that romantic, comically exaggerated temperature and, with a literal slight shiver, there, in front of the window facing the moon, the poet realizes and admits that the exciting celestial body is only hard and bright and plain, even laughable, as it is first seen in stanzas 2 and 3, a surprising sight that causes a confusion of emotions and makes thoughts run in unpredictable directions through the inevitable association of ideas. Consequently, the "sad steps" traced in this poem are not profoundly sad but perhaps only partly so, primarily as they remind one of his advanced age and mortality and inability to recapture the excitement of youth. But they are also the steps of maturity and wisdom, seen, of course, from and with an ironic, even comic, distance, the steps of an aging man "groping back to bed after a piss," a thinking animal that cannot avoid the seduction of sight and thought and that is obliged and conditioned to translate every impression into expression. They are the steps of the human ever-groping mind captured poetically in a beautifully bizarre situation.

BIBLIOGRAPHY
Larkin, Philip. *Collected Poems.* Edited by Anthony Thwaite. London: Marvell Press and Faber and Faber, 1988.
———. *High Windows:* London: Faber and Faber, 1974.
Motion, Andrew. *Philip Larkin: A Writer's Life.* London: Faber and Faber, 1993.

Ivo Soljan

"SAILING TO BYZANTIUM" W. B. YEATS (1928)

"Sailing to Byzantium" led off W. B. YEATS's 1928 volume *The Tower,* a book published after he was in his sixties and his reputation already made, as a Nobel Prize winner in literature (1924) and a senator in the Irish Free State (1922–28). *The Tower* outshone the earlier work, containing some of Yeats's greatest poems, including "Sailing to Byzantium," "Nineteen Hundred and Nineteen," "LEDA AND THE SWAN," "AMONG SCHOOL CHILDREN," and the title poem, "The Tower."

In *A Vision* (1937), a system of occult symbolism that he was working on during the time of *The Tower* (a first draft was completed in 1925), Yeats identified the meaning that Byzantium held for him. First of all, it was literally the capital of the Byzantine or Eastern Roman Empire in the fifth and sixth centuries. Byzantium rose to the level of symbol for Yeats, who considered it to be the apotheosis of culture, a time when religion, art, and work were united indivisibly: "I think if I could be given a month of Antiquity . . . I would spend it in Byzantium . . . I think I could find in some little wine-shop some philosophical worker in mosaic who could answer all my questions, the supernatural descending nearer to him than to Plotinus even. . . . I think that in early Byzantium, maybe never before or since in recorded history, religious, aesthetic and practical life were one" (Rosenthal 226). As a personal symbol, Byzantium represented for Yeats the perfection of the artistic and spiritual imagination.

"Sailing to Byzantium" consists of four stanzas written in the ottava rima stanza form, that is, eight lines rhyming *ababab cc.* Most famously, this is the stanza form used by Byron in *Don Juan.* Yeats used it in "Among School Children," also from *The Tower.* The

well-known opening lines ("That is no country for old men. The young / In one another's arms, birds in the trees") announce one of its themes—age reflecting on youth. The fecundity of life associated with youth is imaged with lovely assonance and alliteration in the fourth line—"The salmon-falls, the mackerel-crowded seas." The poem then moves naturally to a more universalizing treatment of the fullness of life and the cycle of life: "Fish, flesh, or fowl, commend all summer long / Whatever is begotten, born, and dies."

The second stanza emphasizes the contrary state to youth, which is Yeats's own condition, at age 62: "An aged man is but a paltry thing, / A tattered coat upon a stick." The line continues, however, with the word *unless*—this tattered aged state is all that is left to an aged man, "unless / Soul clap its hands and sing." It is in order to sing, and to study "monuments" of "magnificence," leading to more and louder singing, that the poet sails the seas to "come/ To the Holy city of Byzantium."

The third stanza starts with a direct address, "O sages." The stanza is a kind of prayer to those wise ones in Byzantium—perhaps one of whom is Yeats's "philosophical worker in mosaic" in some little wine shop, as he muses in *A Vision* (quoted previously), for the sages are compared to the holy icons in gold mosaic on a wall. This holy, golden vision of life in Byzantium is contrasted with the speaker's own state, embodied in the tragically beautiful lines describing the human heart, "sick with desire / And fastened to a dying animal." In other poems, too, Yeats images the darker side of the human condition, in even fouler terms in "A Dialogue of Self and Soul," a poem written about the same time as "Sailing to Byzantium," defining "life" as "if it be life to pitch / Into the frog-spawn of a blind man's ditch." And in "The Tower," the poem immediately following "Sailing to Byzantium," he describes the heart and the heart's desires thus: "O heart, O troubled heart—this caricature, / Decrepit age that has been tied to me / As to a dog's tail." Our human hearts, so desirous of transcendent perfection, are tied instead to bodies, as if to frog spawn, dog tails, and dying animals.

The last stanza of the poem advances these themes, beginning with a statement about how and when one achieves perfection—"Once out of nature I shall never take / My bodily form from any natural thing." That is, we achieve it only in death and only through a kind of artistic artificiality, imaged (in the next lines) as a mechanical golden bird, "a form as Grecian goldsmiths make / Of hammered gold and gold enamelling" which is "set upon a golden bough to sing" in order to "keep a drowsy Emperor awake." Brenda Maddox suggests a possible domestic source for this arresting image of the mechanical bird. While Yeats was living in London away from his family and working on *A Vision,* his wife wrote to remind him to buy a birthday present for his son, suggesting a mechanical toy, which the boy, Michael, seemed especially interested in. Yeats went off to Harrod's department store and bought "a mechanical duck that waved its wings and chimed when pulled along on a string" (218). While other sources in Yeats's reading are more likely, this suggestion reminds us that Yeats often wove the personal with the traditional in his creation of symbols. The poem ends with the golden bird singing to "Lords and Ladies of Byzantium / Of what is past, or passing, or to come." This final line suggests the complexity of Yeats's system of thought, for even in the perfect, static, timeless, eternal, transcendent world, one still has need of movement, time, impermanence, and all the flux of life.

David Perkins, in his fine book *A History of Modern Poetry,* suggests that there are three chief qualities in Yeats's later work, after 1914. First are the creation and interweaving in his poetry of symbols, in both their public and personal meanings. Sometimes, Perkins says, "the entire poem might be described as the creation and contemplation of a symbol" (583). The symbol of "Byzantium" (as well as the poem by that title) is particularly rich in this regard. Second, his poetry involved personality and "talk." In this respect it is interesting to compare "Sailing to Byzantium" with his later poem "BYZANTIUM." In the latter, the symbol itself is "beheld and described in a mood of intense excitement," while in the earlier poem it is the speaker and not the symbol that is the primary focus, the poem generating "dramatic and human interest as the expression of an old man in a moment of emotional and intellectual crisis and choice" (590). Third is the "tendency to think in terms of antithesis," which Yeats believed corresponded to the "ultimately tragic structure of reality" (583). Some of the opposite pairings that appear in these later poems, and especially in "Sailing to Byzantium," include "nature and art, youth and age, body and soul, passion and wisdom, beast and man, creative violence and order, revelation and civilization, poetry and responsibility, and time and eternity" (596). All three of these tendencies and strategies of Yeats's poetry combine in "Sailing to Byzantium" to make it a particularly rich and satisfying work.

BIBLIOGRAPHY

Maddox, Brenda. *Yeats's Ghosts.* New York: HarperCollins, 1999.

Perkins, David. *A History of Modernist Poetry: From the 1890s to the High Modernist Mode.* Cambridge, Mass.: Harvard University Press, 1976.

Rosenthal, M. L., ed. *William Butler Yeats: Selected Poems.* 3d ed. New York: Macmillan, 1986.

James Persoon

"SALVADOR DALÍ" DAVID GASCOYNE (1935)

Salvador Dalí (1904–89) was a visual artist from Catalonia. In the mid-1930s when DAVID GASCOYNE wrote this poem, Dalí was already a leading figure in the surrealist movement. Gascoyne had met Dalí in Paris and even translated Dalí's prose work *Conquest of the Irrational* (1935). In an introduction to his 1994 *Selected Poems,* Gascoyne said of this poem, which is one of several paying homage to surrealist painters, "'Salvador Dalí' . . . does not attempt to present in verbal terms the imagery to be found in Dalí's best-known works, but to provide some sort of parallel equivalent of the personal 'mythology' his paintings embody." In other words, the poem translates some of Dalí's most important visual ideas and methods into a vivid verbal imitation.

The collection in which this poem was published, *Man's Life Is This Meat,* appeared in 1936, during the London International Surrealist Exhibition, which Gascoyne helped to organize. SURREALISM was an AVANT-GARDE artistic movement that sought to create poems and other works of art by the same kind of nonrational psychological processes operating in dreams and even in madness. Gascoyne translated André Breton, one of the French chief founders of the movement (*What Is Surrealism?* [1936]). Gascoyne's translation of Breton's definition of surrealism reads, "Pure psychic automatism by which is intended to express . . . in writing . . .

the real process of thought . . . in the absence of all control exercised by the reason and outside all moral or aesthetic preoccupations."

In his study *A Short Survey of Surrealism* (1935), Gascoyne spoke of Dalí's particular approach, which is characterized by "experimental paranoia." He explains that this is not the "persecution-mania" of the mentally ill, but a state in which an individual subject can almost instantaneously find his own obsessions or ideas illustrated by objects from the outer world. Surrealist objects show how a kind of "super-reality" exists "in the material world, objectively, as well as subjectively in the automatic thought of the unconscious." Gascoyne acknowledges the "horrors" in Dalí's work and expresses admiration for how the author of these horrors "manages to exercise a kind of clinical control over his imagination, thus preventing it from dragging him with it into domains from which it would be impossible to return."

Using this kind of controlled absurdity that resembles insanity, the poem turns on a variety of images, often conveyed by metaphor or simile, of a landscape where strange, beautiful, and terrible events unfold. Alongside the rich illogical imagery of the poem, however, there are repetitions of narrative motifs (cliffs, mirrors, children, butterflies) and undercurrents of meaning that suggest possible interpretations. Strikingly, for example, the poem features a figure named "Goliath," who becomes implicitly identified with the poem's narrator. Of course Gascoyne's own first name, *David*, is that of the young man who slays the giant Goliath in the biblical story. In this way reality, religion, and imaginative art curiously reflect each other, and the giant enemy that is the rational self hovers on the threshold of destruction. In a typically surreal scene from the poem's opening stanza, "Goliath plunges his hand into the poisoned well / And bows his head and feels my feet walk through his brain."

BIBLIOGRAPHY

Gascoyne, David. *Selected Prose 1934–1996*. Edited by Roger Scott. London: Enitharmon Press, 1998.

———. *A Short Survey of Surrealism*. London: Cobden-Sanderson, 1935.

Emily Taylor Merriman

SASSOON, SIEGFRIED (1886–1967)

Siegfried Sassoon survived the First World War by nearly 50 years. In some ways, however, he was as much a casualty of the Great War as his friend WILFRED OWEN. In the last decades of his life, Sassoon wrote about a variety of topics, some of them compellingly; for example, his verse about converting to Catholicism comprises a moving spiritual autobiography, a detailed travelogue along what he termed his "Heart's Journey." Still, Sassoon is primarily considered a Great War poet—perhaps, with the exception of Owen, *the* Great War poet. Other equally anthologized poets escaped living so many years with the war slung over their lives and careers: RUPERT BROOKE, Wilfred Owen, and ISAAC ROSENBERG by dying soldiers' deaths; ROBERT GRAVES by saying "good-bye to all that" and getting on with the work of mythography and self-mythologizing. But Sassoon remained alive, and long after his physical wounds had healed the psychic wounds he received during the war remained open for readers of anthologies to see. His war experience remains the most iconic of all soldier-poets', and, since soldier-poets' reaction to their experience was perhaps the single most important element determining the ideological shifts of the early 20th century, Sassoon's awakening to the horrors of war serves as a metaphor for the beginnings of modernity itself.

Sassoon was born to wealth and comfort, a status that eventually mortified him; the title of the first of his autobiographical novels, *Memoirs of a Fox-Hunting Man,* specifies the privilege of his prewar existence, presenting it for ridicule. In the beginning, however, his upbringing served to make of Sassoon a stunning example of young British manhood (the so-called Generation of 1914) awaiting something—*anything*—to give banal lives significance and meaning. As did millions of others, he yearned to enlist and, by proving himself in combat, to cast aside the shell of an old, sordid self. (See Brooke's "Sonnet: Peace.") Thus Sassoon sealed his reputation by joining the Sussex Yeomanry in 1914 and, the following year, the Royal Welsh Fusiliers, whose ranks included Robert Graves. Already determined to make a reputation as a poet (he had privately published before enlisting), in the war's early months Sassoon wrote unremarkably about both the shallow sporting life he had left behind ("The Old Huntsman") and his experience in combat. Even admirers are at pains to excuse the romanticism of "The Kiss" and "To Victory," poems that could have been written *before* the war, they are so devoid of realism.

In the same collection that contains those poems (*The Old Huntsman and Other Poems* [1917]), however, one finds evidence of Sassoon's personal and artistic awakening. In the trenches Sassoon had seen the reality he had hoped to see, serving honorably, even brilliantly—he was decorated for bravery—and the changes wrought in him as a poet were profound. "The Kiss" might have been written by any shallow versifier with little combat experience but plenty of enthusiasm, but "'They'" and "'Blighters'" could only have been written by the newly aroused Sassoon, his eyes opened to the horrors of war and politics. These poems, and others in Sassoon's three volumes of war verse (besides *The Old Huntsman,* they are *Counter-Attack!* [1918] and *Picture Show* [1919]) are bitter, enraged, and specific, deploying vulgar language (*frowst,* for example) and biting, sometimes ranting, sarcasm to ally Sassoon with combat soldiers and against their noncombatant enemies: women ("GLORY OF WOMEN"), the press ("Junkers"), the brass ("THE GENERAL"), and others.

Between enlisting and turning into the canonical soldier-poet, Sassoon had experienced traumas both major—being gravely wounded, for instance—and mundane. In many ways, the latter more strongly effected his rhetorical and political shift; the tedium of the trenches and the constant niggling of superior officers, for instance, helped link the onetime "foxhunting man" with the working-class soldiers who bore the brunt of poor war planning and execution. At last, Sassoon had had enough of the war's reality. In 1917, home to recover from wounds, Sassoon issued his "Soldier's Declaration," refusing to return to serve in a war that had no apparent purpose besides mass murder. While the sentiment may or may not have been noble, Sassoon's mode of protest boded ill for him: By refusing to serve, Sassoon could easily have been convicted of desertion. Through Robert Graves's actions, Sassoon was instead sent to the Craiglockhart War Hospital outside Edinburgh, Scotland, to be treated for shell shock. There he met, and greatly inspired, Wilfred Owen, before returning to service and to his bitterly realistic war verse.

After the war, Sassoon wrote nature verse in a decidedly minor key as well as verse exploring his religious yearnings. (He avoided, however, writing about his homosexuality.) Still, his most important work continued to explore the Great War and his part in it. In three volumes of autobiographical fiction collectively titled *The Memoirs of George Sherston* (besides *Fox-Hunting Man* [1928], the volumes were *Memoirs of an Infantry Officer* [1930] and *Sherston's Progress* [1936] and three volumes of autobiography, *The Old Century* [1938], *The Weald of Youth* [1942], and *Siegfried's Journey* [1945]), Sassoon's obsessive rehearsal of his shocked conversion from Victorian to modern firmly established his experience as an archetype of the 20th century. That is, the way Sassoon changed and the reasons for changing continue reverberating: His experience is that of the 20th century in a tidy little package.

See also "BASE DETAILS," "EVERYONE SANG," "ON PASSING THE NEW MENIN GATE," "WIRERS."

BIBLIOGRAPHY

Caesar, Adrian. *Taking It like a Man: Suffering, Sexuality and the War Poets: Brooke, Sassoon, Owen, Graves.* New York: Manchester University Press, 1993.

Campbell, Patrick. *Siegfried Sassoon: A Study of the War Poetry.* Jefferson, N.C.: McFarland, 1999.

Hildebidle John. "Neither Worthy nor Capable: The War Memoirs of Graves, Blunden, and Sassoon." In *Modernism Reconsidered,* edited by Robert Kiely and John Hildebidle, 1,010–1,021. Cambridge, Mass.: Harvard University Press, 1983.

Lane, Arthur E. *An Adequate Response: The War Poetry of Wilfred Owen and Siegfried Sassoon.* Detroit: Wayne State University Press, 1972.

Moeyes, Paul. *Siegfried Sassoon: Scorched Glory: A Critical Study.* New York: St. Martin's Press, 1997.

Quinn, Patrick J. *The Great War and the Missing Muse: The Early Writings of Robert Graves and Siegfried Sassoon.* Cranbury, N.J.: Susquehanna University Press, 1994.

Thorpe, Michael. *Siegfried Sassoon: A Critical Study.* Oxford: Oxford University Press, 1966.

Jimmy Dean Smith

SCOTLAND, POETRY AND

SCOTLAND, POETRY AND In 1999 the Scottish parliament was "reconvened," after a lapse of almost 300 years, following a decisive vote in favor of devolution at the United Kingdom General Election in 1997. The opening ceremony of the parliament included a reading of the poem "The Beginning of a New Song" by the Scottish poet IAIN CRICHTON SMITH, invoking a renewed sense of national confidence that takes account of Scottish cultural and linguistic diversity, where "our three-voiced country" can confidently "sing in a new world." The inclusion of poetry readings at the first meeting of the new parliament signaled the central importance of poetry in the history of 20th-century Scottish politics. Not only did 20th-century Scottish poets explore questions of cultural and political nationalism in their creative work, they actively helped to shape the politics of devolution itself.

Perhaps the most significant poetic contribution to the debate on Scottish devolution is the work of HUGH MACDIARMID, arguably Scotland's greatest 20th-century poet and one of the founders of the Scottish National Party in 1928. MacDiarmid, a lifelong Scottish nationalist and cultural agitator, was the driving force behind the "Scottish Renaissance" movement of the 1920s and 1930s. This movement was a prolific and diverse group of writers, artists, and intellectuals, whose work in many ways set the agenda for a renewed sense of Scottish national culture and political identity, in contrast to the commonly held Victorian view of Scotland as "Northern Britain" rather than a nation within the United Kingdom. MacDiarmid and other poets and writers of the period reacted against certain clichéd and, some would argue, "colonial" literary representations of Scotland as a romantic landscape or an apolitical and sentimentalized "kailyard"—stereotypes that largely ignored the reality of an increasingly urban and industrial Scotland and that suppressed the artistic potential of Scottish culture—so much so, in fact, that in 1919, T. S. ELIOT felt able to ask, "Was there a Scottish Literature?" with the emphasis firmly on the past tense.

In MacDiarmid's view many Scottish writers themselves were responsible for the stagnation of Scottish culture—those Scots he criticizes in his best-known poem, *A DRUNK MAN LOOKS AT THE THISTLE* (1926), who "stick for aye to their auld groove. . . . And deem their ignorance their glory." By contrast, MacDiarmid's

motto was "Not traditions—Precedents!" setting himself the task of galvanizing Scottish cultural and political life into action and seeking to sweep out the old stereotypes and usher in a renewed sense of national identity and purpose. Taking the typical emblem of Scotland, the thistle, in *A Drunk Man*, MacDiarmid says he wants to pull Scotland up by its roots, "And wha can say / It winna bud / And blossom tae." In working toward this aim, his stance was deliberately controversial and often contradictory. "I'll hae nae hauf-way hoose, but aye be whaur / extremes meet," he declared, and indeed this meeting of extremes spilled over into his own political activity, evident from his simultaneous membership of both the Scottish Communist Party and the Scottish National Party—which resulted in his ejection from both organizations.

As early as the 1930s, MacDiarmid argued for a parallel between "English ascendancy" in literary culture and the dominance of London in U.K. politics. Wishing to rid Scotland of "all the touts and toadies and lickspittles of the English Ascendancy," MacDiarmid is known for listing "Anglophobia" as one of his hobbies. A cultural energizer and often vitriolic polemicist, he declared that his poetry "turns its back contemptuously on all the cowardly and brainless staples of Anglo-Scottish literature—the whole base business of people who do not act but are merely acted upon"—a litany of Scottish establishment figures that includes academics, politicians, religious leaders, the teaching profession, and "almost all our writers." The suppression of other national identities within the union, MacDiarmid argued, was effected by the exclusion or marginalization of national literatures and languages, particularly Scots and Gaelic. The education system of both Scotland and England suppressed regional dialects and linguistic variants in favor of "correct English," a policy through which, MacDiarmid contended, "British arts and letters . . . have lost incalculable strength and variety." In his essay "The English Ascendancy in British Literature," published in T. S. Eliot's magazine the *Criterion* in 1931, MacDiarmid presented an argument for cultural devolution within literary studies, the need to recognize the distinctiveness of Scottish, Irish, and Welsh literatures as separate traditions to mainstream English literature. This would offer resistance to English cultural (and, by implication, political) hegemony and rebut Eliot's contention that there was "no longer any tenable important distinction to be drawn" between English and Scottish literature.

MacDiarmid's project to revive the Scottish vernacular first found expression in his early lyrics, collected in *Sangschaw* (1925) and *Penny Wheep* (1926), where he employed a new "synthetic" version of Scots, delighting in deploying old Scots words that had fallen out of popular use, many of them found by trawling the pages of Jamieson's *Etymological Dictionary of the Scottish Tongue*. In doing so, MacDiarmid sought to adapt a language steeped in agricultural life and traditions to the demands of modern experience and the aesthetic discourse of MODERNISM, arguing that Scots is "a vast storehouse of just the very subtle and peculiar effects European literature in general is assiduously seeking." *A Drunk Man,* written in Scots and partly intended as an answer to Eliot's THE WASTE LAND, which is mentioned a number of times in the poem, contemplates the nature of Scottish identity. MacDiarmid suggested that Scotland's culture was above all characterized by the idea of the "Caledonian Antisyzygy" drawn from the work of Gregory Smith, a meeting of extremes that encompassed the contradictory viewpoints of realism and fantasy—just the sort of personality trait that he identified and nurtured in his own work. MacDiarmid felt that his efforts toward a Scottish Renaissance, with its range of cultural and political implications, could perform the extraordinary task of taking "my country's contrair qualities / An' make a unity o' these."

MacDiarmid's view of the vitality and political significance of the Scottish Renaissance was not shared by all of his peers, however. The poet EDWIN MUIR, another prominent poet to emerge during the Scottish Renaissance, argued that the possibility of an autonomous Scottish literature was a nationalist dream, since in modern Scotland, there was "neither an organic community . . . nor a major literary tradition . . . nor even a faith among the people themselves that a Scottish literature is possible or desirable." Muir argued that "the prerequisite of an autonomous literature is a homogeneous language"—a language that, despite MacDiarmid's experiments in synthetic Scots, Scotland notably

lacked. For Muir, Scots was no longer a distinct language since it could no longer be used to think in, having been superseded by English as the language of the classroom and, by extension, of science, of law, and of critical discourse. Instead Scots was now confined to emotion, the language of home and hearth, and this divide between the contexts in which Scots or English were used, Muir argued, led to a fundamental division between "heart" and "head" in Scottish culture—a broken culture that did not allow for a national literature.

While acknowledging the quality of MacDiarmid's poetry, Muir did not concede that he had managed to revive Scots as a national poetic language. For Muir, only by accepting the extinction of Scots as a functional language, and by embracing the idiom of Standard English, could the Scottish poet hope truly to relate to and express contemporary experience. Indeed for Muir, a native of the Orkney Islands who was inured to the worst experiences of urban-industrial Scotland during his teenage years spent in Glasgow, Scotland had become a "sham nation," which had effectively lost its identity. While the Scots were once "a tribe, a family, a people," Muir argues in the poem "Scotland 1942" that it was nationalistic pride itself that "made us a nation, robbed us of a nation." For Muir the roots of the crisis could be traced back as far as the Reformation in the 16th century: a history of cultural stultification and needless sacrifice that "strip[ped] the peopled hill and the altar bare, / And crush[ed] the poet with an iron text."

Despite such debates and divisions, however, Mac-Diarmid's experiments with the Scots language laid the groundwork for later generations of writers who would capitalize on the political and cultural implications of linguistic diversity. Again the lack of a homogeneous language was an important issue. For instance, TOM LEONARD's satirical treatment of "BBC English" in "The Six O'Clock News" (1976) highlights the perceived hierarchy of particular dialectical registers, where "correct English" is privileged over Scottish vernacular. Leonard suggests that no one would believe the news given by a journalist speaking "lik wanna yoo scruff."

Support for the Scottish National Party (SNP) grew steadily during the 1960s, marked by the election of the first SNP candidate, Winifred Ewing, in 1968. This resurgence of popular interest in the Scottish "home rule" question led eventually to a referendum on Scottish devolution in 1979. However, despite early indications of victory, the results were disappointing for the "yes" campaign, and the case for a devolved parliament failed to attract enough votes. Later in 1979 a Conservative government, under Margaret Thatcher, was elected to power and the devolution question was once again off the mainstream political agenda for a number of years.

If devolution was no longer a central issue as far as the U.K. government was concerned, it was a subject that was still very much alive for Scottish poets in the 1980s and 1990s. As in other nations and regions within the British Isles, Scottish writers were exploring cultural and political identities, both actual and imagined; the result was a proliferation of Scottish verse that the poet EDWIN MORGAN suggests emerged directly in reaction to the failed devolution vote in 1979. Indeed, DOUGLAS DUNN's *St. Kilda's Parliament* (1981) responded to these political events with an evocation of a different kind of devolved government, the "remote democracy" of the historic community on St. Kilda, a Scottish Hebridean island perched on the outermost edge of Europe. Dunn's poem "St. Kilda's Parliament: 1879–1979" looks into the people's faces as they stand outside their parliament building, noting how each man appears "proud of his shyness and of his small life" on the island, "his eyes full of weather and seabirds." If nothing else, the poem is a reminder that devolution might be as much a state of mind as a piece of legislation.

In a different way, Edwin Morgan, an active force in Scottish culture since the 1950s, also extended his poetic experimentations in the 1980s to take account of specifically national questions. The collection *Sonnets from Scotland* (1984) took a new look at Scotland, its landscape, politics, and culture, informed in particular by Morgan's fascination with science fiction. For example, "The Coin" tells of a visit to Earth by alien explorers or archaeologists in the remote future, who find a coin inscribed with *Respublica Scotorum,* evidence that the nationalist dream of a Scottish republic came to be. Capitalizing on certain aspects of the "Caledonian Antisyzygy" idea, Morgan was able to look at

real political questions through the altered viewpoint of the fantastic, exploring Scottish identity without limitations.

While the debate over Scottish nationalism continues into the 21st century, it is certain that the vote in favor of devolution within the United Kingdom has opened up new vistas for poetry in Scotland—as it has for Wales and Northern Ireland through their own devolved assemblies. Iain Crichton Smith's vision of a "fresh and glittering and contemporary" Scotland, one that "join[s] with friendliness to all around her," is a form of cultural nationalism that invites Scots to be confident in the development of their own pluralistic culture while accepting and understanding the cultures and identities of other nations, including England. This cosmopolitan outlook is echoed by contemporary Scottish poets such as Robert Crawford and Kathleen Jamie, whose poetry explores and celebrates the possibility of a new vision of Scotland and a new kind of Scottish nationalism, one that is confident in its own multicultural identity, as well its devolved status within the United Kingdom.

Following the "yes" vote in the referendum on Scottish devolution in 1997, Jamie writes that her earlier poems, many of which dealt specifically with questions of Scottish national identity, had become "obsolete" or "historical documents" that could now be read from a different perspective. Celebrating devolution, which she describes as "a watershed" in *Jizzen* (1999), Jamie also found herself free to celebrate Scotland's cultural diversity, crowded with "a field of whaups," "a shalwar-kemeez," "a Free State, a midden, / a chambered cairn." Such optimism for the possibilities of Scottish national identity certainly links back to MacDiarmid's defense of his "multiform, multitudinous Scotland," but significantly without his accompanying stance of "Anglophobia." Ultimately devolution has underlined Scottish poetry's ability to engage with and influence the political sphere, attesting to Kathleen Jamie's belief that "poetry had a part in bringing about the new Scotland."

BIBLIOGRAPHY

Crawford, Robert. *Devolving English Literature.* 2d ed. Edinburgh: Edinburgh University Press, 2000.

———, and Mick Imlah, eds. *The New Penguin Book of Scottish Verse.* London: Allen Lane & Penguin Press, 2000.

Devine, Tom. *The Scottish Nation: A History, 1700–2000*. London: Penguin, 2001.

Jamie, Kathleen. *Jizzen*. London: Picador, 1999.

MacDiarmid, Hugh. *Selected Poems*. Manchester, Eng.: Fyfield Books, 2004.

———. *Selected Prose*. Edited by Alan Riach. Manchester, Eng.: Carcanet, 1992.

Muir, Edwin. *Scott and Scotland: The Predicament of the Scottish Writer*. Edinburgh: Polygon Books, 1982.

Louisa Gairn

SCUPHAM, PETER (1933–)

"Ghosts are a poet's working capital," writes Peter Scupham in "Prehistories I" (1975). His own poetry is heavily populated with ghosts that figure the memories constituting his recurrent themes. Scupham, born in Liverpool in 1933, has published 11 collections of poetry since 1972, each refining and developing his concerns with language, history, and literature in relation to private memory and experience. Always a poet of meticulous, studied observation, Scupham in his best poems details direct experiences (of landscape, nature, and the domestic) and achieves a powerful, idiosyncratic degree of musicality, and his work as a whole constitutes a major contribution to modern revisions of the English pastoral tradition. He is a contemporary of GEOFFREY HILL and SEAMUS HEANEY and shares many of their concerns with the expression in poetic form of the complexities of historical experience. He is a fellow of the Royal Society of Literature and a Cholmondeley Award winner.

A late developer as a writer of poetry (he claims to have begun seriously writing only after the age of 30), Scupham was educated at Emmanuel College, Cambridge, and ran the Mandeville Press in Hitchin in the 1970s and 1980s with the poet John Mole, publishing pamphlets and broadsheets. After national service, he worked as a schoolteacher in Letchworth and now runs, with Margaret Steward, a secondhand bookselling business in Norfolk. His poetry has been published by Anvil, Oxford, and Carcanet and demonstrates the influence of W. H. AUDEN and ROBERT GRAVES, as well as displaying an esoteric range of references and allusions. His use of Shakespeare in the remarkable sequence "A Midsummer Night's Dream," from *Out Late* (1986), emulates Auden's own reworking of The *Tempest* in "The Sea and the Mirror" (1942–44). He is master of a wide variety of English poetic forms, displaying a willingness to experiment and innovate and excelling at the long sequence, sharing with his fellow Hitchin poet George Szirtes a fondness for sequences of interlinked sonnets, a complex form of which "The Hinterland" (1977) is a perfect example. His language oscillates between a controlled, slightly mannered archaism and a dense but lucid complexity, "the line packed with ore at every rift," as Szirtes comments in his review of *Collected Poems*. The deeply personal poems in *Watching the Perseids* (1990) offer an extraordinarily moving meditation on death and loss, mourning the passing of his parents and their generation; in *The Air Show* (1988) Scupham explores his childhood memories of the Second World War, asserting the experience of this historical moment as formative for his poetry, "the figure in my carpet" ("War Games").

BIBLIOGRAPHY

Scupham, Peter. *Collected Poems*. Manchester, Eng.: Carcanet, 2002.

Szirtes, George. "Let Chaos Reign." *Guardian*, December 14, 2002.

John Sears

"SEA FEVER" JOHN MASEFIELD (1903)

"Sea Fever" is one of JOHN MASEFIELD's most famous poems, and one that helped enhance his reputation as "the poet of the seas." The poem is also one of his earliest pieces, published in his first volume, *Salt-Water Ballads (1903)*. Frequently anthologized, the poem reiterated the call the sea life has had on so many generations of young Englishmen. Simply stated, the poem is a declaration from a former sailor that he constantly feels the pull of the sea, calling him to sail again.

Aptly titled, each of the poem's three stanzas begins with the empathic phrase *I must go*, underscoring the speaker's feverish desire to return to the sea. This is a call from deep within himself that will "not be denied." Yet in each stanza he also makes a request, a listing of what he has found on the sea and what he asks for on his return. "All I ask," he repeats, is that those things needed to recapture the magic of the sea be there: a sailing ship, winds, the sea's mist, gulls, whales, the companionship of fellow sailors, and rest at the end of a day's work. These elements form a pool of related romantic sea images, connected with the repetition of *and,* that imitates the swirl and movement of the sea itself. Other rhythmic repetitions such as "a wild call and a clear call" and "the gull's way and the whale's way" appear in the poem.

Masefield also utilizes elements of sound, particularly alliteration, assonance, and rhyme, to add to the feeling of movement. In some printings, the poem has eight-line stanzas where the second and fourth lines and sixth and eighth lines rhyme. In other editions, the poem is printed in four-line stanzas of rhyming couplets. Assonance in the repeated phrase "And all I ask is a . . ." becomes a kind of whirlpool drawing the reader into the pool of images. At times, the complicated pattern of repetition, alliteration, and assonance adds reality to the romance of the poem, for example, in "The whale's way / where the wind's like a whetted knife." "Sea Fever" and "Cargoes" are Masefield's two most often anthologized poems, both examples of the sea poems on which Masefield's name chiefly rests.

BIBLIOGRAPHY

Smith, Constance Babington. *John Masefield: A Life.* New York: Macmillan, 1978.
Spark, Muriel. *John Masefield.* New York: Folcroft Library Editions, 1977.

Jean Shepherd Hamm

"THE SECOND COMING" W. B. YEATS (1919)

W. B. YEATS wrote "The Second Coming" in 1919 and had it published in the *Dial* in 1920 and the collection *Robartes and the Dancer* in 1921. Yeats's title highlights the prophetic nature of the poem. In fact, it announces the return of Jesus Christ, which according to the Bible, will result in the end of the world and the judgment of the dead and the living. While the second stanza shows that the poem is not about the return of Jesus, the first stanza lists signs of such a return when one thinks Matthew 24:3–44, Mark 13:3–37, Luke 21.7–36, and Revelation 6.12–17. The disciples were told that there would be earthquakes, wars, famines, and all kinds of evils such as betrayal, distress, and fear. In the same manner, the first stanza of Yeats's poem describes signs of his time that point to an impending apocalypse. Yeats articulates his vision with the help of the *gyre,* a concept suggesting that history evolves in cycles.

The fourfold repetition of the *in* sound and of *turning* twice in the first verse implies the inexorable movement of the gyre and consequently of history. Yeats further underscores the circling motion with the use of another symbol: a falcon escaping the control of the falconer as the spiral widens. The rest of the first stanza underscores this loss of control and order: war, anarchy, war, and loss of innocence triumph. The word *center* in the third verse evokes ideas such as order, government, control, and command. Its absence results in *anarchy,* used in the next verse. Constructed with two words in Greek, *an-arche, anarchy* means the opposite of order, command, or control. We say of a country that it is in anarchy when the government has collapsed and disorder has triumphed. Likewise the voice in the poem suggests that the world is out of control.

One will note the use of the passive voice in verses 4–6. This structure draws attention to the absent agents, for we are not told who unleashes anarchy, who is behind the bloodshed, and who drowns innocence. There are agents acting in the background, and the poem focuses on the dreadful result of their actions. The *anarchy, blood-dimmed tide,* and the loss of innocence express the manifold devastation of World War I and other events (such as the Russian Revolution) that dramatically altered life in Europe. Evil completely triumphs as chaos reigns, wars shed blood, and humanity loses its *innocence.* This word is from two Latin words: the prefix *in* and the verb *nocere. Nocere* means to hurt or harm, and the addition of *in* leads to the opposite meaning. The loss of innocence leads to the triumph of evil. The first stanza ends with a sense of the defeat of humanity and an overwhelming triumph of the forces of evil. The first stanza is thus a list of signs of an impending doom.

The repetition of *surely, at hand,* and *second coming* in the first three verses of the second stanza reiterates the ideas of circling and inescapability of what is about to happen. The three verses also remind us that as signs in the Bible are supposed to precede the return of Jesus, the end of the world, and the final judgment, so the signs in the first stanza are prophetic. This idea is also supported by the repetition of *second coming* in verses 10–11 and the use of the word *revelation* (a synonym of the more savant *apocalypse,* which means the revelation of what was previously hidden). The use of repetition in the first three verses of the second stanza also projects suspense, as the reader is made to wait for the revelation, finally given out in verses 12–15. It is not the return of Jesus. Instead, it is the advent of a new historical era, captured in the advent of a sphinx-like monster emerging from the Spiritus Mundi (Latin for "Spirit/Soul of the World," a universal collective unconscious) with physical strength ("lion body") and intellectual ability ("head of man") and devoid of humanity ("pitiless as the sun"), a vision that is reminiscent of the Sphinx in Sophocles' *Oedipus Rex.* The monster appears in the desert (v. 13), a desolate landscape, and a motif in modernist writings that conveys spiritual desolation. The slow movement of the monster, the fear instilled in birds of prey, the darkness that follows, and the end of 20 centuries of the Christian civilization underscore the fear inspired by the monster. It announces a new, nightmarish birth to supplant the cycle of 20 centuries of the Christian civilization. In a masterly display of poetic genius, verse 21 mimics the slow progression of the monster. Each word in the verse is monosyllabic, suggesting that the monster is lifting one foot at a time, but again in an inexorable manner. The last verse of the poem creates more suspense with a question about whether the monster is progressing toward Bethlehem, the birthplace of Jesus, whose own birth marked the beginning of the previous cycle in Yeats's view of history. Fittingly if the monster symbolizes the advent of a new historical era, it must go to the very origin of the civilization it seeks to replace.

Yeats's "The Second Coming" is one of the poems that best reflect the themes of MODERNISM such as the apocalyptic vision, desolate landscapes, man's inhumanity to man, and loss of innocence, all conveying the aftermath of World War I and other events in Europe that prompted Yeats to bemoan the devastation of war and the inhumane state of the world.

"The Second Coming" has appealed to many 20th-century writers, including the Nigerian Chinua Achebe, who used the first half of the third verse ("Things Fall Apart") as the tile of his classic novel *Things Fall Apart*

and the first four verses as the epigraph of the same novel, suggesting that British colonization of Nigeria was a monstous event that befell his native land and ushered into a confusing, brutal, and tragic cycle of Nigerian history.

BIBLIOGRAPHY
Bushrui, Suheil Badi, and Tim Prentki. *An International Companion to the Poetry of W. B. Yeats.* Savage, Md.: Barnes & Noble, 1990.
Finneran, Richard J., ed. *Critical Essays on W. B. Yeats.* Boston: G. K. Hall, 1986.

Aimable Twagilmana

"SECOND GLANCE AT A JAGUAR" TED HUGHES (1967)

"Second Glance at a Jaguar," from TED HUGHES's third book, *Wodwo* (1967), is a companion piece to "The Jaguar" from his first book, *The Hawk in the Rain* (1957). The pair were often commented upon early in his career. Ekbert Faas in an interview with Hughes made the point that "your two Jaguar poems are often interpreted as celebrations of violence," to which the poet responded with a lengthy answer, beginning, "I prefer to think of them as first, descriptions of a jaguar, second . . . invocations of the Goddess, third . . . invocations of a jaguar-like body of elemental force, demonic force" (199). As with all the animal poems written throughout Hughes's career, it is a good idea to begin by taking the poems as a description of the animal in question, even more so than with the animal poems of D. H. LAWRENCE, Hughes's mentor. As with a Lawrence poem, however, there is also much beyond physical description to notice as well, as Hughes's answer to Faas indicates.

The first jaguar poem, called simply "The Jaguar," begins with two stanzas describing a slightly seedy zoo, where apes "adore their fleas," parrots "strut / Like cheap tarts," tiger and lion are "fatigued with indolence," and most cages seem empty. It is a zoo tame enough to be "painted on a nursery wall." The real action is past all these, where a crowd gathers, mesmerized, to see a jaguar who moves as if enraged, on a "short, fierce fuse," animated "by the bang of blood in the brain." He is caged, but "there is no cage to him." The prison bars melt away against his fierce, visionary quest, a restless energy that cannot be contained: "The world rolls under the long thrust of his heel. / Over the cage floor the horizons come."

By contrast, the jaguar of the second poem is not free within his cage, but caged even if the iron bars suddenly vanished. He is trapped in his body, which seems to battle against itself, "hip going in and out of joint," on a "terrible, stump-legged waddle," "trying to grind some square / Socket between his hind legs round," his head "like the worn down stump of another whole jaguar." He is wearing his body out from the inside. He is never still, but unlike the first jaguar, it is not because he sees horizons over the cage floor; rather, it is because "at every stride he has to turn a corner / In himself and correct it." He is an image of existential man, imprisoned in a meaningless, not visionary, world, and his response is to rage at it and at himself. He is a street thug with a "blackjack tail," which he flourishes "as if looking for a target, / Hurrying through the underworld, soundless."

Another poem from *Wodwo* makes the same point— "Song of a Rat." It begins with the staccato, excited first line "The rat is in the trap, it is in the trap," where it screeches and screeches while the trap's iron jaws crumple its backbone. The rat goes on screeching "trying to uproot itself into each escaping screech"—that is, similarly to humans, who attempt through utterance, language, to free themselves from the prison of their bodies, their world, their mortality. But the rat's "long fangs bar that exit." Its own teeth, its own body, enforces the terms of the trap—they are the bars that imprison.

Against these animal poems of imprisonment, Hughes's next book, *Crow* (1971), would create a new totemic animal hero, the crow, who would not be caged or killed, a survivor, just as Hughes himself would survive the horrible personal tragedies of two of his partners' killing themselves, first his wife, SYLVIA PLATH, in 1963; and then Assia Wevill, in 1969.

BIBLIOGRAPHY

Faas, Ekbert. *Ted Hughes: The Unaccommodated Universe.* Santa Barbara, Calif.: Black Sparrow Press, 1980.

Hirschberg, Stuart. *Myth in the Poetry of Ted Hughes.* Totowa, N.J.: Barnes & Noble, 1981.

Hughes, Ted. *New Selected Poems.* New York: Harper & Row, 1982.

James Persoon

"THE SEED-PICTURE" MEDBH McGUCKIAN (1982)

Published in MEDBH McGUCKIAN's first collection, *The Flower Master* (1982), this poem is one of numerous examples in which McGuckian explores interrelations among woman, mother, and artist. In two sections with 18 unrhymed lines of varying length each, the poetic speaker relates how she creates a "portrait of Joanna" out of "beautiful seeds." That the seeds are likened to children hints at motherhood but also suggests artistic creativity. They are at once the literal seeds out of which the picture is created and the artist's creative impulses. They are also connected to words, because they "dictate their own vocabulary." Thus the poem is not merely about traditional female craftsmanship and motherhood, but simultaneously about the creation of poetry. In the same way that a child's development cannot be planned completely but can only be guided, the seeds or words, too, "capture / More than we can plan."

There is a certain "clairvoyance" involved in the creation of art that is beyond the artist's control. The idea of "seeds capturing more than we can plan" also suggests the ambiguity of words. Accordingly the names of the seeds the speaker uses for her portrait are highly evocative: "*tear-drop* apple," "*wrinkled* pepper-corns," "*pocked* peach," "*seamed* cherry stone," "black *rape*" (emphasis added). The speaker has given the portrayed Joanna "gold / Of pleasure for her lips, like raspberry grain," but she has also used "millet / For the vicious beige circles underneath" her eyes. These "vicious circles" combined with a reference to the sky's having "resolved to a cloud the length of a man" and the final allusion to women who, looking at the finished portrait, "feel their age, and sigh for liberation" suggest the entrapment of the portrayed woman both in marriage, where she lives her life in the shadow of her husband, as well as in the confinement of the seed-picture.

The artist's worrying about her "self indulgence to enclose her / In the border of a grandmother's sampler" echoes female artists' common guilt feelings about neglecting their families or household tasks for the sake of their art, as well as a concern about creating a female image that entraps or does not adequately reflect the portrayed woman's life and personality. There is the added irony that the seeds used for the picture will now never bloom; they will never become flowers, plants, or trees but will be trapped in the static image, enclosed "in the border of a grandmother's sampler." The reference to this "grandmother's sampler" evokes a female tradition of craftsmanship in which McGuckian deliberately places her own work. The craftsmanship of creating samplers was, after all, one of the few creative preoccupations with which women were traditionally allowed to break their "dullness."

BIBLIOGRAPHY

Haberstroh, Patricia Boyle. *Women Creating Women: Contemporary Irish Women Poets.* Syracuse, N.Y.: Syracuse University Press, 1996.

Schrage-Früh, Michaela. *Emerging Identities: Myth, Nation and Gender in the Poetry of Eavan Boland, Nuala Ní Dhomhnaill and Medbh McGuckian.* Trier, Ire.: WVT, 2004.

Wills, Chair. *Improprieties: Politics and Sexuality in Northern Irish Poetry.* Oxford: Oxford University Press, 1993.

Michaela Schrage-Früh

"SEPTEMBER 1, 1939" W. H. Auden (1940)

In W. H. Auden's "In Memory of W. B. Yeats," another of his seemingly contradictory poems, he declares that "poetry makes nothing happen" and yet "it survives, / a way of happening, a mouth." He concludes that poem with the exclamation that through verse, one can "let the healing fountain start . . . [and] Teach the free man how to praise." His poem "September 1, 1939" also explores what Lucia Perillo describes as the poet's "aesthetic and personal conflicts about writing a poem whose intention is to effect change in the real world" and attempts to discover what are the individual citizen's and the individual poet's power and responsibility in public tragedies such as war.

The title of this poem refers specifically to Adolph Hitler's invasion of Poland, a move most historians agree Hitler made because he believed his show of military might would quickly convince the world of his superior strength and lead to further capitulation and ultimate global domination. Hitler's invasion of Poland, however, became the first military engagement leading to World War II. In the first three stanzas of "September 1, 1939," Auden describes a speaker, "uncertain and afraid," unsure as to what exactly has created such a "low dishonest decade," when "waves of anger and fear / Circulate over the bright / And darkened lands of the earth," yet who seems certain that somehow, through "accurate scholarship" we can "unearth the whole offense" and understand what creates men like Hitler. Referring to a Jungian psychoanalytical concept, the speaker exclaims that Hitler's "huge imago" (a reference to the psychological concept of the idealized image of self) must have been created in his childhood, must have "occurred at Linz," a town near Hitler's birth. Still, the speaker indicates that knowing the origins of this evil that has created this "psychopathic god" that "drives a culture mad" leads us but to conclude that "those to whom evil is done / Do evil in return," to know that our actions have consequences upon others. With an allusion to Thucydides' account of, a defeated Athenian general who warned of the dangers of dictatorship, the speaker declares that there is a circularity to history, that words themselves, analysis of situation, and even enlightenment itself will not stop tyrants: It is our "habit forming grief: / We must suffer them all again."

Stanzas 4 through 7 explore why we must suffer and take us back to the specific setting established in the first stanza, a bar, "one of the dives / On Fifty-second Street" in New York City, a city that has the "strength of Collective Man," demonstrated by its towering skyscrapers, and to this world's specific reaction to this particular atrocity. The speaker defines this city, a representative of the whole world's "neutral air," as "blind" and "vain," populated by a collective people whose "each language pours its vain / Competitive excuse" and, in doing so, creates an "international wrong." We, individually and collectively, "cling to [our] average day" and by our "conventions conspire" and live in a "euphoric dream" afraid to wake to the reality of our lives, "lest we should see where we are, / Lost in a hunted wood." This image, straight out of children's fairy tales, continues the description of mankind as "children afraid of the night," afraid to awaken and face what we must face. The speaker nevertheless admits that each of us has an "error bred in the bone" and "craves what it cannot have / Not universal love / But to be loved alone." The allusion to Nijinsky, a 20th-century ballet dancer who suffered a nervous breakdown and thus whom the speaker describes as "mad," complicates this section, yet it leads the speaker to conclude that we are all "mad" in our craving for what Nijinsky says that Diaghilev, a Russian ballet producer, craved, to be "loved alone." This desire is at the heart of the problem the speaker describes, as it leaves us in isolation, disconnected from our fellow man and his situation. This awareness of our isolationist, neutral response to dictatorships; to the plight of our fellow man, leads the speaker to question what, if anything, then can "undo the folded lie" that we have created: "Who can release them now, / Who can reach the dead, / Who can speak for the dumb?"

If the speaker provides an answer to these questions in stanzas 8 and 9, it is at best tentative. Concluding that "all [he has] is a voice" and that "no one exists alone," the speaker admits to both the poet's power and his limitations, for while a poet may speak the words that should be heard, "the citizen or the police" must act: "We must love one another or die." We all must take some part in the action and assume responsibility for the destiny of our world. He also proclaims that while mankind in general is "defenceless under the night," nevertheless "yet, dotted everywhere, / Ironic points of light / Flash out wherever the Just / Exchange their messages." This image culminates with the speaker's hope and prayer that he can be one of the Just, and "like them" he, "beleaguered by the same / Negation and despair," *may* "show an affirming flame." By extension, then, since the speaker is no different from anyone else, "composed like them / Of Eros and dust," it *may*, therefore, be possible, he hopes, for us all indeed to understand that "no one exists alone."

After publishing "September 1, 1939," Auden questioned this poem's conclusions and changed the line "We must love one another or die" to "We must love one another and die," exclaiming that that line "is a damned lie! We must die anyway." Eventually Auden even excluded "September 1, 1939" from his *Shorter Collected Poems* and declared it "the most dishonest poem I have ever written," because it "was infected with an inaccurate dishonesty." Nevertheless the question Auden raised in this poem as to whether a poem can indeed bring about change may have been answered after the September 11, 2001, tragedy.

Immediately after the Twin Towers fell in New York City, "September 1, 1939" was excerpted at many makeshift memorials throughout New York City, an apparent and perhaps ironic light of affirmation in yet another time of great darkness and despair.

BIBLIOGRAPHY

Mendelson, Edward. *Early Auden.* New York: Viking Press, 1981.
Perillo, Lucia. "Auden's 9/1/39." *American Poetry Review,* September–October 2002.
Steinfels, Peter. "After September 11, a 62 Year Old Poem by Auden Drew New Attention." *New York Times,* 1 December 2001.

Josef Vice

SERVICE, ROBERT WILLIAM (1874–1958)

By all accounts one of the best-paid poets of all time, Robert Service lived a life as adventurous as his poetry, and in many ways as rough around the edges. Known by such affectionate epithets as the Bard of the Yukon, the Canadian Kipling, and the People's Poet, Robert Service wrote for and about the common man, especially in his battle with the elements of the frozen North. His first book of poems, *Songs of a Sourdough* (1907), reprinted in North America as *The Spell of the Yukon and Other Verses,* went on to sell more than 3 million copies, making it the most successful book of poetry of the 20th century. It included such poems as "The Shooting of Dan McGrew," "THE CREMATION OF SAM MCGEE," and "The Men That Don't Fit In." Although Service eventually published more than 1,000 poems in addition to two autobiographical works, six novels, several years of war correspondence, and other nonfiction pieces, this first book of poems is the one for which he is remembered.

Born in England to Scottish parents, Service was raised and educated in Scotland, attending the University of Glasgow until the age of 20, when he emigrated to Canada and worked for the Canadian Bank of Commerce, stationed in the Yukon for eight years. No sketch can neglect the fact that Service was never a poet's poet. He said of himself, seemingly without defensiveness: "I don't believe in pretty language and verbal felicities, but in getting as close down as I can to the primal facts of life, cutting down to the bedrock of things. . . . My idea of verse writing is to write something the everyday workingman can read and approve, the man who, as a rule, fights shy of verse or rhyme. I prefer to write something that comes within the scope of his own experience and grips him with a sense of reality." Robert Service's poems of the Yukon, continuously in print for the past 100 years, have certainly accomplished that.

BIBLIOGRAPHY

Klink, Carl G. *Robert Service: A Biography.* Toronto: McGraw-Hill Ryerson, 1976.

Lockhart, G. Wallace. *On the Trail of Robert Service.* Edinburgh: Lauth Press, Baar, Girvan, 1991.

MacKay, James. *Vagabond of Verse.* Edinburgh: James MacKay Mainstream, 1995.

Roberts, R. X. *A Bibliography of Robert William Service, 1874–1958.* Toronto: University of Toronto Press, 1976.

Service, Robert. *Collected Poems of Robert Service.* N.Y.: Penguin Group, 1989.

Jo Miller

SETH, VIKRAM (1952–)

A poet of diverse talent who is often labeled a neoformalist, Vikram Seth (whose surname rhymes with *grate*) was born into a Hindu family in Calcutta in 1952. The son of India's first female chief justice and a consultant, he was educated at Doon School, the Eton of India, and took a B.A. with honors at Corpus Christi College, Oxford. He holds master's degrees from his undergraduate college and from Stanford University. He also has a diploma in Chinese poetry from Nanjing University. He left the study of Chinese demography to write literature. His first book of poetry, *Mappings* (1980), was self-published, but he attracted both scholarly and popular attention with his 1986 novel in verse, *The Golden Gate,* a postmodern, possibly mock-epic, saga and an evocation of the Bay Area during the Silicon Valley boom. Although some consider the tale Byronic, it contains themes found in Seth's other fiction: Affection is a solider basis for marriage than is romantic love, and excessive demands destroy relationships. The verse form, the Onegin stanza, clearly shows the influence of Pushkin, and the themes of love found in *The Golden Gate, A Suitable Boy,* and *An Equal Music* suggest the influence of Tolstoi. His other books of poetry include *The Humble*

Administrator's Garden (1985), a collection of love poems, and *Beastly Tales from Here and There* (1992), poetic fables. He has translated the verse of Wang Wei, Li Bai, and Du Fu in *Three Chinese Poets* (1992), and his collected poetry appears in *The Poems 1981–1994* (1995). *All You Who Sleep Tonight* (1990) shows a range of forms, styles, and subjects, and "SOON" from this collection is considered among his finest work. Although some dismiss Seth as a competent versifier, others find in his 1990 volume the deceptive simplicity of A(LFRED) E(DWARD) HOUSMAN's *A Shropshire Lad.*

BIBLIOGRAPHY

Field, Michelle. "*Publisher's Weekly* Interviews: Vikram Seth." *Publisher's Weekly,* 10 May 1993, 46–47.

Ragavan, Amit V. "Vikram Seth." *Post-Colonial Studies at Emory University,* Spring, 1999. Available online. URL: http://www.english.emory.edu/Bahri/Seth.html. Accessed on May 10, 2008.

Karen Rae Keck

SHAPCOTT, JO (1953–)

London-born, Shapcott was educated at Trinity College, Dublin. She has held positions as a teacher or visiting professor at several British universities. Her awards include twice winning the National Poetry Competition (1985, 1992).

In *Electroplating the Baby* (1988), Shapcott started off as she meant to go on by "make[ing] free with the boundaries of realism" (introduction, *Emergency Kit*). In the poem of the title, she captures the allure of scientists' promises to break through old restrictions on human experience but is skeptical about the overreaching claims of Dr. Variot, inventor of the "electrometallurgy," which he sells in a grotesquely godlike effort to hold mortality at bay. Shapcott's "Elizabeth and Robert" sequence, which plays with the sonnet form, conflates the male-dominated literary partnerships of the Brownings, and Robert Lowell and Elizabeth Hardwick, with a modern couple. In her best-known title poem from the second volume, *Phrase Book* (1992), Shapcott demonstrates how the individual's engagement with the external world is mediated by numerous information systems. Television news flashes of the Gulf War are interpolated by extracts from an old-fashioned book of English idioms for foreigners; in the communication gap of the language barrier we have the pertinent question that only an outsider dare ask, "What's love in all this debris?" In other poems, Shapcott models this self-conscious "ex/centricity," an exaggerated and creative manufacturing of rootlessness and alienation, in order to comment on the material conditions of mainstream culture from the privileged position of marginality. Her "Mad Cow" poems parody the stereotyping of female hysterics and aesthetics (and the implicit connection between them) while "Goat" allows a free rein for both depicting and interrogating human desires. Similarly, in *My Life Asleep* (1998), several characters transcend the limits of stifling or unsatisfactory human identity and interaction, through the personae of vegetables ("Cabbage Dreams," "Parsnip Cardiology") and animals ("Pig," "Rhinoceros"). Typically Shapcott negotiates with the dual postmodern urges, to voice minority experience through the channels of the powerful and to forge alternative media for representing it. One of Shapcott's finest poems, "Motherland," finds the dictionary itself problematizing; it refuses to define the title word but falls open at "Distance. *Degree of / remoteness, interval of space,*" forcing a confrontation with the paradox of expressing what is inexpressible in recognizable words: "This country makes me say / too many things I can't say."

Her Book: *Poems 1988–1998* (2000), a compilation of Shapcott's three earlier collections, provoked positive assessments of her development and individuality. She is praised for challenging assumptions about the language, sources, verse structures, and supremacy of English literature. Shapcott has notably contributed to making European work available in translation.

See also "MAD COW DANCE."

BIBLIOGRAPHY
Kinsella, John. "Her Life Awake." *Poetry Review* 90, no. 1 (spring 2000): 81–82.

Penguin Modern Poets. Vol. 12, Helen Dunmore, Jo Shapcott, Matthew Sweeney. Harmondsworth, Eng.: Penguin, 1997.

Shapcott, Jo. "About Language and How It Works." *Poetry London* 36 (summer 2000): 36.

———, and Matthew Sweeney, eds. *Emergency Kit: Poems for Strange Times.* London: Faber and Faber, 1996.

Jane Dowson

"THE SHIELD OF ACHILLES" W. H. AUDEN (1952) W. H. AUDEN's colloquial poems of social comment are relatively few; however, "The Shield of Achilles" displays a mock-heroic denunciation of many features of civilization, and some of the stanzas refer to contemporary cruelties. The poem is most effective in its evocation of the full horror of living in a world where heroic individualism is replaced by mindless conformity, and compassion is crushed by a cynical and pitiless indifference.

In Homer's *Iliad,* book 18, Thetis, goddess and mother of Achilles, the chief Greek warrior in the war against Troy, requests Hephaestos, the god of fire, to create a new shield for Achilles. Achilles' first set of armor was confiscated by the Trojan hero Hector after he killed Patroclus, Achilles' friend, who had borrowed the armor thinking that it would frighten the Trojans away. Homer gives a detailed description of the imagery on the shield, a tableau of life in all its facets including happy scenes, such as marriages and harvests, and unhappy ones, such as gory battles and lions mauling cattle in the fields. Auden appropriates this ironic juxtaposition of idealism and realism by contrasting the scenes of happiness and peace Thetis expects to see on the shield as she watches Hephaestos put the finishing touches on the shield with the actual scenes Hephaestos creates. Moreover, Auden interpolates Thetis's expectations of scenes from the ancient world with Hephaestos's actual depictions of scenes from the brutal and impersonal modern world, such as the horror of the concentration camps in Nazi Germany.

The poem is in three sections, a triptych, with the shorter-lined stanzas of Thetis's expectations of idyllic Greek scenes offset against longer-lined stanzas of Hephaestos's depictions of the brutality of modern totalitarianism. Lyrical passages rhapsodizing over "vines and olive trees," "marble well-governed cities," and heroes out adventuring in "ships upon untamed seas" alternate with prosaic descriptions of a degenerate, debased, and depraved society, reinforced by a dull and plodding metrical scheme. In the first section, an anonymous, dispassionate army listens to a speech over a loudspeaker that uses impersonal statistics to argue that a cause is just, and the army marches off to defeat. In the second section, bored, anonymous, and impassive "officials" carry out the "dehumanizing" execution of three helpless prisoners, a parody of the Crucifixion, while a crowd of ordinary people watch passively. In the third section, a "ragged urchin" throws a stone at a bird and takes for granted "that girls are raped, that two boys knife a third"; he "has never heard of any world where promises are kept / Or one could weep because another wept."

In the final, short-lined, stanza, Hephaestos "hobble[s] away" and Thetis "crie[s] out in dismay," finally disillusioned of her romantic-heroic expectations and recognizing that her son, "the strong / Iron-hearted man-slaying Achilles," "would not live long." Auden produces an interpretation of the "modern malaise" that conveys the blankness and horror of a godless world in which heroic individualism is replaced by mindless conformity, and compassion is crushed by cynical and pitiless indifference.

Betsy Watson

"THE SHIP OF DEATH" D. H. LAWRENCE (1933)
Written in 1929 shortly before D. H. LAWRENCE's death in 1930 of tuberculosis, "The Ship of Death" first appeared in the 1933 collection *Last Poems*. Lawrence wrote several versions of this poem, with no single one being definitive. Citations in this entry are taken from the most commonly anthologized version, which begins, "Now it is autumn and the falling fruit / and the long journey towards oblivion."

"The Ship of Death" illustrates Lawrence's belief in the soul's immortality. The speaker in the poem, however, is not without trepidation and observes that "the frightened soul / finds itself shrinking, wincing from the cold." Life is misery-ridden and worth living only because death is too fearsome to face. Echoing Hamlet's "To be, or not to be" soliloquy, the speaker asks, "Can man his own quietus make / with a bare bodkin?" In other words, can suicide alleviate life's pitiful suffering? Upon reflection, the speaker declares, "Surely not so!" One should die, not through "murder, even self-murder," but with a sense of spiritual harmony that leads to "the deep and lovely quiet / of a strong heart at peace."

"The Ship of Death" is replete with metaphors, beginning with the speaker's telling the reader to prepare for the end of life, which requires building "a ship of death" for "the long journey towards oblivion." The speaker compares man with "the apples falling like great drops of dew / to bruise themselves an exit from themselves." The bruise makes mortality visible and life vulnerable, such that "already our souls are oozing through the exit of the cruel bruise." The speaker urges the reader to "be willing to die, and to build the ship / of death" that will move "upon the waters of the end / upon the sea of death." The process of dying is embodied in the dark sea that will carry the soul to the beyond. Through these metaphors the speaker indicates that care and meditation are required for the transition into the unknown.

"The Ship of Death" is emblematic of Lawrence's religious faith. As "the dark flood rises," the speaker advises the reader to fill the "little ark" "with food, with little cakes, and wine / for the dark flight down oblivion." During this metaphysical voyage, he will be "drinking the confident water from the little jug / and eating the brave bread of a wholesome knowledge." These passages are full of Christian imagery, from Noah's ark to the ritual of the sacrament. Eventually the ship is consumed, and "everything is gone, the body is gone / completely under, gone, entirely gone." After the darkness, light emerges on the horizon "out of eternity," presenting "the cruel dawn of coming back to life out of oblivion." The ship "wings home," evoking the Christian representation of heaven, and the soul returns "into her house again / filling the heart with peace," providing an account of the soul's passage to an immortal place of rest. Lawrence takes the poem full circle with this expression *heart of peace*, embracing the cyclical life-giving quality of death.

BIBLIOGRAPHY

Gilbert, Sandra M. "The Longest Journey: Lawrence's Ship of Death." In *Acts of Attention: The Poems of D. H. Lawrence*. Ithaca, N.Y.: Cornell University Press, 1972.

Lawrence, D. H. *Last Poems*. Edited by Richard Aldington. London: Martin Secker, 1933.

———. "The Ship of Death." Version One and Version Two. Edited by Ian Lancashire. Department of English, University of Toronto. Available online. URL: http://rpo.library.utoronto.ca/poem/1251.html. Accessed on July 15, 2006.

Sword, Helen. "Lawrence's Poetry." In *The Cambridge Companion to D. H. Lawrence*, edited by Anne Fernihough. Cambridge: Cambridge University Press, 2001.

Katy Masuga

SHUTTLE, PENELOPE (1947–)

A poet, novelist, and playwright, Penelope Diane Shuttle was born on May 12, 1947, in Staines, Middlesex, to Jack Frederick Shuttle, a salesman, and Joan Sheperdess Lipscombe Shuttle, a homemaker. She attended Stains Grammar School, a private preparatory school, and Matthew Arnold County Secondary School, a modern girls' school. During her examination for the general certificate of education in English, Shuttle decided against writing the required brief responses to a series of general questions and instead used the time to write on *Macbeth,* which led to a low mark and her rejection by universities. Unable to receive a university education, Shuttle spent many years employed as a secretary while feverishly working on her craft as a writer of poetry and prose. At the same time, she was frequently plagued by anorexia nervosa and agoraphobia, and at the age of 19, she suffered a nervous breakdown. Nevertheless, her talent as a writer always served as a sign of strength. She published her first poems at the age of 14 and completed her first novel at 17. In 1969, she met the British poet and novelist Peter Redgrove, whom she married in 1980. Their first and only child, Zoe Teresa Redgrove, was born in 1976. For the last 30 years, Shuttle, now widowed (Redgrove died in 2003), has been living in Falmouth, Cornwall.

Shuttle is a prolific writer. She has published more than 30 books (many written in collaboration with her husband) and won numerous literary awards, including Arts Council Awards in 1969 and 1972, the Greenwood Poetry Prize in 1972, and the E. C. Gregory Award for Poetry in 1974. Her plays have been broadcast by both BBC television and BBC radio. While she is very active in many genres, Shuttle's most memorable moments are as a poet. Shuttle's poetic force stems from her acute and intense sensitivity for the female body, as well as her piercing interpretations of erotic relationships of men and women in our modern age. Her poetry often addresses the domestic lives of women, especially motherhood, and uses its myriad facets to uncover the ineffable connection between nature with all its rhythms and manifestations—from unconscious desires and urges to the female menstrual cycle—and the intellectual and emotional world of human beings. Her most stunning treatments of the aforementioned subjects can be found in *The Hermaphrodite Album* (1973), *Autumn Piano and Other Poems* (1974), *The Orchard Upstairs* (1980), *A Leaf out of His Book* (1999), and *Adventures with My Horse* (1988). Penelope Shuttle has yet to achieve the status of a major literary figure in Britain. Nevertheless she enjoys a devoted following that continues to witness her development as a poet, novelist, and social critic.

BIBLIOGRAPHY

Shelton, Pamela L., ed. *Contemporary Women Poets.* Detroit: St. James Press, 1998.

Sherry, Vincent B., ed. *Dictionary of Literary Biography.* Vol. 40, *Poets of Great Britain and Ireland since 1960.* Detroit: Gale, 1985.

Daniel Pantano

"THE SILENT ONE" Ivor Gurney (1922–1926)

Although it seems impossible to give a precise date for this poem (George Walter suggests 1925–26; Kavanagh places it within 1922–25), it belongs to the mature period of Ivor Gurney's poetic composition following the war, while in internment, and was first published by Blunden in 1954. The manuscript is in the Gurney Archive (MS 45457) of the Ivor Gurney Collection in Gloucester Library. A shorter version of the poem exists in a notebook (MS 64.7).

With a mere 17 lines, Gurney manages to conjure up the experience of fighting by the use of sight and sound. The poem hinges on the difference between the man with the "Bucks accent" who has been silenced and the officer with "a finicking accent" so that Geoffrey Hill called it "a tone poem of the class system." In the first two lines the anaphora *who* raises the question of the identity of the dead men on the wires and rhymes also with the couplet *two / through,* laying further emphasis on the two figures hanging, with the long vowel of the rhyme reproduced again in *fool.* Things come in twos in the poem: two dead men, the conversation between two men that the poem relates, the contrast between the *I* of the poem and the *Silent One,* the double repetition of *faced, line, unbroken wires, politest/politely, accent, hole, afraid, no, retreated.* The statements themselves often have a binary structure, as in line 11: "Darkness, shot at: I smiled, as politely replied—"

The dash, which may visually recall the wires, is the dominant punctuation. In *Collected Poems* the poem has nine dashes, as it does in George Walter's selection for *Ivor Gurney* (London: Everyman, 1997). But the published text varies: There are only eight dashes and the phrase *in the afraid* is absent at the end of line 10 in *First World War Poems,* edited by ANDREW MOTION (London: Faber and Faber, 2003), and in *The Penguin Book of First World War Poetry,* edited by JON SILKIN (London: Penguin, 1981). The rhymes of the poem diminish as it progresses, though they contribute strongly to the overall meaning of the poem, as in *clothes/oaths* and *seen/screen.* About the victim, the "noble fool, faithful to his stripes," Jon Silkin wrote: "By letting the man's courage into the poem, we are made to feel compassion, but this comes through because the courage and the foolishness hold each other in check." Facing the wires, he "went / . . . and ended." According to Silkin, "The politeness or the upper-class voice is made to sound absurd by making it articulate fearful demands." *Do you think you might . . .* takes the modal form to a very uncertain register, but it is countered by the lucid judgment of the soldier, who responds negatively, yet with a smile, "'I'm afraid not, Sir.'" and the line continues with his internal clear-sighted justification.

The short syllables increase the pace as one reads, with the fast clip adding a kind of exclamation to the words: "There was no hole no way to be seen." John Lucas noticed that the danger expressed here was Gurney's own: In an early draft the officer named him. The poem closes in the anxiety of "Again retreated—a second time faced the screen." One feels that the soldier who "thought of music" would not be so lucky the second time round: Is it possible to refuse an order twice without being executed? Piers Gray links the *screen* to what is "silent on the page but in reality a barrage of terrifying noise (sound beyond sense)." Whether or not he was "sane" when he wrote this text, Gurney's talent speaks for itself.

BIBLIOGRAPHY

Gray, Piers, *Marginal Men: Edward Thomas, Ivor Gurney, J. R. Ackerley,* 83–85. London: Macmillan, 1991.

Hill, Geoffrey, "Gurney's Hobby." *Essays in Criticism* 34, no. 2 (April 1984) 112–113.

Silkin, Jon. "Out of Battle." In *The Poetry of the Great War,* 124–125. London: Ark, 1987.

Jennifer Kilgore

SILKIN, JON (1930–1997) Northern Poet, critic, translator, playwright, and founding editor of the magazine *Stand,* Jon Silkin was born in London, attended Wycliffe and Dulwich Colleges, and spent a year working as a journalist before two years' national service as a teacher in the Education Corps. During the following six years, he did manual labor in London, including a stint as a grave filler.

The first issues of *Stand* were funded by severance pay money received after he tried to start a labor union with fellow janitors. His editorial in the third issue of the magazine in 1952 insists on the pressing need for "the humanising influence of the arts." That is a characteristic of his own poetry from the very first in "Caring for Animals" from *The Peaceable Kingdom* (1954): "I ask sometimes why these small animals / With bitter eyes, why we should care for them." The poem suggests that the attention given to animals can contribute to an increase of humanity. In *The Two Freedoms* (1958), the title poem bases its reflection on the story of two birds who "broke from their cage and seemed as gold" but were then returned to captivity, where their cry "like a stab pierced / Me."

As recipient of the Gregory Fellowship in Poetry at the University of Leeds from 1958 to 1960, Silkin organized an exhibit (May–June 1959) of ISAAC ROSENBERG's paintings, poetry, and letters from the trenches. From 1960 to 1962 he completed his B.A. in English at Leeds, brought out *The Re-Ordering of the Stones* (1961; reviewed by GEOFFREY HILL in *Poetry & Audience*), found financial support to continue *Stand,* and with Andrew Gurr set up the Northern House Pamphlet Poets. Emphasizing political commitment, issue 4, number 3 of *Stand* (1961) was devoted to "The War Poets." The magazine also gave a considerable amount of space to poetry in translation, with Silkin translating poems from Hebrew into English, such as "Six Poems by Natan Zach" (*Stand* 9, no. 3 [1967]).

Silkin's role in publishing young poets can hardly be overestimated, as a cursory look at issues from the 1960s and 1970s (co-edited with Ken Smith and represented by Gene Baro in the United States) indicates. Among the poets included in Silkin's *Poetry of the Committed Individual: A "Stand" Anthology of Poetry* (1973) are Dannie Abse, John Berryman, Alexander Blok, Peter Dale, ROY FISHER, Michael Hamburger, T. W. Harrison, Geoffrey Hill, Philip Levine, Tom Raworth, César Vallejo, and Jeffrey Wainwright.

Silkin's poems from the 1950s and 1960s established his reputation. His *Flower Poems* (University of Leeds pamphlet, 1964) were read to public acclaim on BBC 3, January 2, 1964, and then were included in *Nature with Man* (1965, Geoffrey Fabor Memorial Prize). In the title poem, "Nature with Man," the first stanza shows a summer landscape, "As if the earth received / A bruise." The second stanza portrays a decomposing body, whereas the final stanza shows nature searching for man. Silkin's success resulted in a move to Newcastle in 1964, contact with Merle Brown (Denison University, Ohio, 1965), and *Poems New and Selected* (1966).

Sometimes classified as a Jewish poet (see Lawson, *Anglo-Jewish Poetry from Isaac Rosenberg to Elaine Feinstein,* 2006) Silkin readily acknowledged his creative debt to Isaac Rosenberg and tried to follow that example in writing for social awareness and social change. "Conditions" (*Stand* 9, no. 4 [1968] 52) says, "Part of me feels as though / it would like to believe" (52). Silkin's own voice was captured on the eighth record of the Argo series *The Poet Speaks* (RG 518). Reviewing the record for *Stand* in his "Recent Poetry" column, Terry Eagleton praised his "reading dramatically and commandingly" and noted that he was "more ready to talk about his poems" than other poets recorded (*Stand* 9, no. 3 [1967]: 73).

In 1968–69 Silkin taught a class on creative writing in the Writer's Workshop at the University of Iowa. During the 1970s and 1980s he brought out a new volume of poetry every couple of years: *Amana Grass* (1971), *The Principle of Water* (1974), *The Little Time-Keeper* (1976), *The Lapidary Poems* (1979), *Selected Poems* (1980), *The Psalms with Their Spoils* (1980), *Autobiographical Stanzas* (1983), *Footsteps on a Downcast Path* (1984), and *The Ship's Pasture* (1986). With his wife, Lorna Tracy, and John Wardle, Silkin edited *Best Short Stories from Stand Magazine* (1988).

In "Leeds Poets: A Select Review" JON GLOVER noted: "Silkin often approached particular places (Jerusalem, York) as the location of a historic spiritual drama" (*Stand* 5, no. 2 [2003]: 54–55). While speaking to ANTHONY THWAITE (a discussion published in *Stand* 6, no. 2 [1963]: 15), Silkin explained about his York poem: "Here is a situation of a massacre of Jews at York in 1190. At the end of the poem, an exact correspondence with what happened in York is implied with what happened in Europe in this century. And I'm asking, do we want this kind of thing to continue? If we don't then we have to change society." A truthful historical sense had to be given to war so as to prevent it.

This could be done ironically as in the poem "Defence" (published in *Stand* 6, no. 2 [1963]) and later collected in *Nature with Man*. A civil servant speaks about measures civilians should take when the blast comes, which "unlike the bombs of the previous war, / Will draw the walls out." The speaker presumes civilian survival, if only to drum up support for the coming war. "Divisions" (published in *Stand* 9, no. 1 [1967]: 6–7) uses a different shock technique, addressing the similarities of enemies in Lebanon by comparing their penises, one circumcised, one not, but both wounded.

Silkin contributed to the rising interest in war poetry with *The Penguin Book of First World War Poetry* (1979, 1981) and his study *Out of Battle* (1987). With Jon Glover he edited *The Penguin Book of First World War Prose* (1989). He also prepared an edition of WILFRED OWEN's poems, published by Penguin in 1985, but then withdrawn after a dispute about copyright by the Owen estate and JON STALLWORTHY. Commissioned to write a play, he produced a verse portrait of Joseph Gurney, a character loosely based on the poet-musician IVOR GURNEY in *Gurney* (1985). Silkin explained in the introduction that "Joseph Gurney's Salieri is his friend and fellow-musician Benjamin Critchley. Benjamin's envy of Joseph Gurney's prodigal talent is fed, painfully fed, by his admiration for it." The preoccupation with man's warring ways never left Silkin, and *The Lens-Breakers* (1992) contains "Trying to hide Treblinka," and a number of other poems focusing on issues of memory, such as "Civil War Grave, Richmond."

Silkin was elected a fellow of the Royal Society of Literature in 1986, and in 1994, after playing a key role among Leeds poets, he was appointed senior fellow in poetry at the University of Leeds. His *The Life of Metrical and Free Verse in Twentieth-Century Poetry* (1997) is an important critical work. After his death, two volumes of poems appeared: *Testament without Breath* (Cargo Press, 1998) and *Making a Republic,* edited by Jon Glover (Carcanet/Northern House, 2002). Silkin's papers, his rich correspondence with poets, and the archives of *Stand* are now housed in the Special Collections of the Brotherton Library at the University of Leeds.

BIBLIOGRAPHY

Lawson, Peter. "Jon Silkin: Post Holocaust Universalist." In *Anglo-Jewish Poetry from Isaac Rosenberg to Elaine Feinstein,* 111–138. London: Vallentine Mitchell, 2006.

Silkin, Jon. *The Life of Metrical and Free Verse in Twentieth Century Poetry.* London: Macmillan, 1997.

———. *Selected Poems.* London: Routledge & Kegan Paul, 1988.

Jennifer Kilgore

"SILVER" WALTER DE LA MARE (1913) Many poems in WALTER DE LA MARE's early collections of poetry, *Songs of Childhood* (1902) and *Peacock Pie: A Book of Rhymes* (1913), use children's language and topics. Yet conventional verse forms originating in ballad, nursery rhyme, or romantic lyric are used in ways that transcend the horizon of an audience of children. De la Mare's decision to write "children's poetry" was a conscious one: He explicitly rejected EZRA POUND's attempt to win him to the modernist movement, opting instead for his own personal alternative. Through his "magic realism," his nonsense verse in the tradition of Lewis Carroll, and a pastoral poetry suggesting deeper questions, de la Mare also eludes classification with the so-called Georgian Poets, the label often applied disparagingly to poets such as RUPERT BROOKE, W. H. DAVIES, and JOHN MASEFIELD to characterize their poetry as shallow, conventional, and sentimental. Far from using nature merely as a mirror of human sentiment, de la Mare sees the world from the standpoint of symbolism, as a "forest of signs" (Baudelaire), an enigma with unseen presences, in need of and yet beyond human decoding and interpretation.

In one of his most songlike poems in the collection *Peacock Pie,* "Silver," the personified moon sheds her mystical light on the landscape: "Slowly, silently, now the moon / Walks the night in her silver shoon." The trochees and dactyls (later modulated into iambs) enhance the slowness of movement; rhyming couplets exude a peaceful tranquility; the equipoise of the words and lines conveys the universal meditative presence of the all-embracing light. The archaic word *shoon,* meaning "shoes," here also evokes *shine*; other archaisms such as *cote* or *moveless* and inversions of word order (*casements catch, sleeps the dog, in the water gleam*) add to the poem's mystical atmosphere and musicality. The moon's translucent silvery veil is cast over the trees, the casements, a dog, white-breasted doves, the harvest mouse, and finally the fish in the water, where the liquidity of the moon beams and the water merge: Human, animal, and plant world are all united in the silvery gleam. The moon is metonymically presented through her own silvery light, and the repetition of the word *silver* 11 times in a poem of 14 lines (the length of a sonnet) gives it an incantatory, talismanic quality, while the accumulation of *s* sounds (*slowly, silently, walks, silver, shoon*) adds a slightly hissing, uncanny effect.

The poem consists of one sentence only, which has no real direction but seems a simple addition of entities. This is in keeping with de la Mare's intention of an unmediated evocation: "The mere saying of the name of a thing, the very sound of it, may more than satisfy both ear and eye. It is an incantation; and, like the thing itself, a sesame to memories beyond the exquisite immediacy of perception and recognition attained through our senses" (Walter de La Mare, "A Quiet Life," 78). The idea of words as openers to forgotten experiences is reminiscent of William Blake's *Songs of Innocence* and *Songs of Experience,* where childlike simplicity conceals ambiguity and subtlety. De la Mare rejects a Newtonian view of nature that demands scientific dissection, favoring rather a physics that takes a holistic, ecological view of the indivisibility of the universe, of a harmony and order that science can only partially reveal (cf. Bentinck, 54f.). His innocence in experience, the voice of wisdom in a child, gives his poetry a Blakeian visionary character, providing access to a reality that is normally unseen.

BIBLIOGRAPHY

Bentinck, Anne. *Romantic Imagery in the Works of Walter de la Mare.* Lewiston, N.Y.: E. Mellen, 2001.

Bremser, Martha. "The Voice of Solitude: The Children's Verse of Walter de la Mare." *Children's Literature* 21 (1993): 66–91.

De la Mare, Walter. *The Complete Poems of Walter de la Mare*. London: Faber and Faber, 1969.

———. "A Quiet Life." In *Essays by Divers Hands: Being the Transactions of the Royal Society of Literature*. 20, ed. by Gordon Bottomley, 63–83. London: Oxford University Press, 1943.

Kirkham, Michael. "Walter de la Mare." In *British Poets, 1880–1914,* edited by Donald E. Stanford, 109–131. Detroit: Thomson Gale; 1983.

Smith, William Jay. "Master of Silences: Walter De la Mare, 1873–1956." *Poetry* 91 (1957): 112–116.

Vallance, Richard. "The Sonnet as the Landscape of Mystery." The Vallance Review. Available online. URL: http://www.poetrylifeandtimes.com/valrevw12.html. Accessed May 10, 2008.

Whistler, Theresa. *The Life of Walter de la Mare*. London: Duckbacks, 2003.

Heike Grundmann

SISSON, C. H. (1914–2003)

Charles Hubert Sisson was born in a working-class neighborhood of Bristol, England. His father was a watchmaker, whose family had run a comb mill since the 18th century, and his mother hailed from generations of Westmoreland farmers. This traditional, rural heritage informs the proverbial bent in his writing, his deep commitment to the continuities of history ("the past is all we are," concludes the poem "In the Silence"), and his frequent disdain for MODERNISM and the dominant literary tastes it engendered. The late development of Sisson's poetic career partially explains his self-identification as a cultural "outsider." His first book of poems appeared only in 1961, when he was 47, and broad recognition eluded him for 13 more years, till he published *In the Trojan Ditch*. "The poetry owners cannot make me out / Nor I them," he writes there, in a tone that is more defiant than self-pitying. Sisson instead prefers plain speech, rendered in a plain style free of the "individual touch," and his poem "The Discarnation" rejects the "porridge of consciousness" that he felt absorbed many of his contemporaries. Poetry should be a by-product of the active man, he claims in his prose work *Art and Action* (1965), and the statement defends his own life choices.

In secondary school Sisson studied Latin and discovered American poets such as Emerson and Poe and, later, T. S. ELIOT and EZRA POUND. He earned an honors B.A. in philosophy and English literature at the University of Bristol, after which he continued his education in Berlin, in Freiburg, and at the Sorbonne in Paris. Recoiling from the growing fascism he observed on the Continent, he returned to England and in 1936 began a long career in the civil service, including stints in the Ministry of Labour and Department of Employment. During World War II he enlisted as a private in the British army, but the Intelligence Corps soon noted his linguistic skills and assigned him to India. This experience far from home heightened his own sense of nationality, and he began to take the Anglican faith more seriously. He treats this military experience in his first memorable poem, "On a Troopship," which broods on those "already made" absent from the front, likely directed at W. H. AUDEN, STEPHEN SPENDER, and others—poets and socialists disdained by Sisson. He, by contrast, is "practising my integrity / In awkward places." Although he and his wife, Nora Gilbertson, had two daughters during the 1940s, overall the war made Sisson's wit drier, leading to his trademark mix of patriotism and cynicism.

During the 1940s he translated Heinrich Heine, the stories of Jules Superveille, and the Roman poets, whose crisp writing and clarity of voice he sought to imitate. A volume of his Heine versions was published in 1955, two years after *An Asiatic Romance,* a satirical recollection of his time in India. Sisson praised England's civic institutions and traditions in *The Spirit of British Administration* (1959), a comparison with European systems written during a sabbatical as a government research fellow. Yet two years later he frequently mocked his fellow civil servants in his first full poetry volume, *The London Zoo*: They are lecherous in "On the Way Home," unthinking in "Victoria Station," and the title poem speaks of them as coming to London "reliable as an ant, meticulous as an owl." Sisson formally entered the Anglican Church in 1953, and around this time he completed a novel, *Christopher Homm*, which begins ironically with the protagonist's death and works backward. The Dantean prefatory poem, "In a Dark Wood," frames the book as a midlife journey. The novel was not printed till 1965, and in the same year he released the collection of poems *Numbers,* featuring "A Letter to John Donne," in which he comments upon that poet's worldly ambition and libido as well as his 17th-century theology. Sisson also developed his critical voice in *The Case of Walter Bagehot* (1972), a critique of Victorian liberalism, and *English Poetry 1900–1950: An Assessment* (1971), a contrary study that dismisses DYLAN THOMAS, D. H. LAWRENCE, and W. B. YEATS in favor of more native, "honest" poets such as THOMAS HARDY and EDWARD THOMAS.

Sisson retired from the civil service in 1973, and his next two volumes of poetry, *In a Trojan Ditch* (1974) and *Anchises* (1976), solidified his poetic reputation. These collections were more austere, and marked by increased classical and Christian presences. (By now he had translated Catullus, Ovid, Horace, and Lucretius.) DONALD DAVIE declared "The Usk" one of the great poems of the age, while another critic ranked Sisson's "The Corridor" among the major works in the English existential tradition. A large collection of essays, *The Avoidance of Literature* (1978), further enhanced this literary status. In 1980 he released his next poetry volume, *Exactions,* and a translation of Dante's *Divine Comedy,* a project that had haunted his work of the previous decade. "I think Sisson / Got it," Davie said of this translation in verses to fellow poet SEAMUS HEANEY: "Plain Dante, plain as a board, / And if flat, flat." More poems followed—*Night Thoughts* (1982–83), *God Bless Karl Mark!* (1987), *Antidotes* (1991), and *What and Who* (1994)—and collected volumes of his work appeared in 1984 and again in 1998.

A thorough man of letters, Sisson also translated Virgil's *Aeneid* and several French works by Joachim Du Bellay, Jean Racine, and La Fontaine. (His diverse translations were published together in 1986.) He also edited editions of Hardy, Poe, Swift, Christina Rossetti, and selected English sermons, and other prose works included *Anglican Essays* (1983), the "partial" autobiography *On the Look-Out* (1989), *In Two Minds: Guesses at Other Writers* (1990), *English Perspectives: Essays on Liberty and Government* (1992), and *Is There a Church in England?* (1993). Sisson's later poetry often addresses difficulties of faith, and he is an eloquent recorder of the challenges of old age. In "Gardening" he asks how

to turn "ageing sorrow" into a "biting wind / To catch me like the tangles of your hair // Gone and imagined?" He spent his final years at Moorfield Cottage, a location that led to a flourishing of natural imagery in his work. Sisson died on September 5, 2003.

BIBLIOGRAPHY

Knottenbelt, E. M. "Time's Workings: The Stringent Art of C. H. Sisson." *In Black and Gold: Contiguous Traditions in Post-War British and Irish Poetry,* edited by C. C. Barfoot, 255–275. Amsterdam: Rodopi, 1994.

Manganiello, Dominic. "C. H. Sisson's Purgatorial Dark Wood." *PN Review* 137 (2001): 15–19.

Poole, Richard. "The Poetry of C. H. Sisson." *Agenda* 22, no. 2 (1984): 32–56.

Severance, Sibyl. *Dictionary of Literary Biography.* Vol. 27, "C. H. Sisson." *Poets of Great Britain and Ireland, 1945–1960,* edited by Vincent B. Sherry, Jr., 325–332. Detroit: Gale Research, 1984.

Sisson, C. H. *Collected Poems.* Manchester, Eng.: Carcanet, 1998

———. *Collected Translations.* Manchester, Eng.: Carcanet, 1996.

Brett Foster

SITWELL, EDITH (1887–1964)

SITWELL, EDITH (1887–1964) Perpetually controversial, Edith Sitwell was a modernist AVANT-GARDE poetic innovator who, after modifying her style to respond to World War II, became a popular national poet. By Sitwell's own accounts, unhappiness at being the unloved child of a misguided marriage between aristocrats was the earliest source of her poetry. Sitwell compensated for her disappointment through the fantasy life she shared with her two younger brothers in the elaborate gardens and woods of the family estate. From the period when, according to Sitwell's poem "Colonel Fantock" (1924), Edith, Osbert, and Sacheverell "walked like shy gazelles / Among the music of the thin flower-bells" originated the most consistent elements of Edith's poetics: her designation of the natural world as her source of content, symbol, and figure and her penchant for animating nature with human wishes and feelings.

Edith's governess, Helen Rootham, made it possible for Sitwell to link her hitherto private poetic universe with contemporary European conversations about poetry. Intellectual companion and catalyst, Rootham transformed Edith's training for marriage into a passionate study of new music and poetry. Most importantly for the development of Sitwell's poetics, Rootham introduced Sitwell to the poetry of the French symbolist poets. From Rimbaud and Baudelaire, Sitwell found poetic precedents for the concept of the senses as analogous to one another—as different avenues to the same destination. Moreover, Baudelaire confirmed Sitwell's early experiences of nature as expressive presence with his idea that all sensory aspects of nature correspond to spiritual essences. The relationship between Rootham and Sitwell proved crucial for the rest of Rootham's life and a good part of Sitwell's. When Edith left home and moved into the London flat from which she launched her poetic career, Rootham accompanied her as chaperone, collaborator, and companion.

Sitwell entered the British poetry scene as a leading innovator in the avant-garde. Between 1916 and 1921, she and NANCY CUNARD co-edited the anthology *Wheels*. In doing so, the two women gave poets an opportunity to critique the literary status quo represented by the poetry published in Edward March's popular *Georgian Poetry*. Contributors to *Wheels* refused to collude with the British urge, made manifest in *Georgian Poetry,* to forget the violent disruption of World War I and prewar literary radicalism. The free verse, irregular poetic forms, and subject matter of the poems in the anthologies challenged the Georgian retreat into conventional poetic form and meter, and what Sitwell, in *Aspects of Modern Poetry* (1934), called "romantic simplicity."

Sitwell's landmark production as an avant-garde poet was *Façade* (1921–23), a synthesis of comic poems and music composed to accompany the poems. The poems themselves exemplify why Sitwell was such a central figure for the British avant-garde. Certainly, as did the works of many modernists, the poems manifest her commitment to formal techniques that make habitual aspects of language new and strange. The simultaneous play of homeoteleuton, assonance, consonance, and different kinds of rhyme (end, internal, masculine, feminine, near, and eye) exposes at once the unlikely similarities and vastly numerous and subtle differences between sounds. The various playful syncopated rhythms Sitwell obtains in *Façade* through dactylic, trochaic, anapestic, and spondaic substitution admonishes poets to do something dynamic and new within the British poetic tradition. Meanwhile, as Dowson and Laird assert, the comic content of the poems parodies the traditionally mannered, stratified, and gendered British society of Sitwell's parents. In the gleefully scrambled worlds of *Façade,* light and wind are constantly described as speaking in animal sounds. Thus these natural elements possess a vitality that is lacking in the "properly proper" "Hell" of society inhabited by the admiral and family of "En Famille." Indeed, as Dowson, invoking Bahktin, observes, *Façade* critiques British society by inviting audiences to participate in the carnivalesque pleasures of violating "proper" social boundaries. The polyphonic patchwork of vivid direct speech by a range of less than refined speakers, the attribution of animal qualities to the landscape, and the blending of near-nonsensical nursery rhyme, biblical stories, and figures from Greek pastoral and myth exemplify Sitwell's willful flouting of hierarchized cultural divisions. Despite the hurly-burly fun of nursery rhyme rhythms and the description of Queen Victoria in "Hornpipe" as a "borealic iceberg," *Façade* is haunted by depictions of stasis. Pursued by satyrs, Lily O'Grady of "Popular Song" is described finally as a "lazy lady" who is "silly and shady" in a world wherein "dust forbids the bird to sing." Although the first public performance of *Façade* in 1923 met with poor reviews, an invigoratingly successful 1926 performance secured an enduring recognition of the work's artistic achievement. In fact, Sitwell was asked to perform the work numerous more times over the course of her life.

Called, she felt, to help her nation heal from and grieve the destruction of World War II, Sitwell reinvented herself in the 1940s as a more traditional popular poet. Sitwell's poetry in this period became allegorical and apocalyptic as she mediated the nation's experience of war with a fixed and limited set of widely accessible mythical symbols of death, destruction, and rebirth. No longer using short lines and exaggerated rhythms, she now delivered consolation and descriptions of loss in long lines that were, generally, five to seven feet but could be much longer. Moreover she fashioned her trademark combinations of iambs, trochees, and anapests and complex patterns of sound into discreet rhythms befitting a prophet. Sitwell's new verse facilitated the expression of feelings about the war held by many, winning her widespread public and critical support.

Ever the provocateur, Edith Sitwell generated and is still generating powerful responses in readers. She managed unconventional looks by staging herself as an unforgettable one-of-a-kind fashion spectacle. Not, perhaps, so admirably, Sitwell responded to criticism—even of serious errors like repetition, misquotation, and plagiarism—with public retaliation. More recently, feminist scholars have found it difficult to rehabilitate the reputation of a woman who sought to secure literary legitimacy by advertising her disdain for women. Some, however, are now directing attention to the ways Sitwell negotiated the traps of gender through formal innovation.

See also "STILL FALLS THE RAIN."

BIBLIOGRAPHY

Clements, Patricia. *Baudelaire and the English Tradition.* Princeton, N.J.: Princeton University Press, 1985.

Dowson, Jane. *Women, Modernism and British Poetry, 1910–1939: Resisting Femininity.* Burlington, Vt.: Ashgate, 2002.

Glendinning, Victoria. *Edith Sitwell: A Unicorn among Lions.* London: Orion Books, 1981.

Laird, Holly. "Laughter and Nonsense in the Making and (Postmodern) Remaking of Modernism." In *The Future of Modernism,* edited by Hugh Witemeyer. Ann Arbor: University of Michigan Press, 1997.

Sitwell, Edith. *The Collected Poems of Edith Sitwell.* New York: Vanguard Press, 1968.

Robin Calland

SITWELL, OSBERT (1892–1969)

Osbert Sitwell was the second child of Baronet Sir George Sitwell and Lady Ida (née Denison). His sister, EDITH SITWELL, was five years older than he, and his younger brother, Sacheverell Sitwell, five years younger. Together these three siblings would become a significant part of the AVANT-GARDE movement in London, working closely together until Sacheverell's marriage in 1925.

Osbert's father owned a number of different houses in England, including the family estate Renishaw Hall in Derbyshire. In 1902 Sir George suffered a breakdown and chose to convalesce by traveling through Italy, where he would continue to travel and live for much of the rest of his life. While in Italy, Sir George purchased a medieval Tuscan castle called Castello di Montegufoni. Sir George had the Castello registered in Osbert's name so that the 13th-century castle became part of Osbert's inheritance upon his father's death.

Osbert was educated at Eton but failed to do particularly well there. After leaving Eton in 1912 Osbert wished to attend Christ Church, Oxford, but instead his father insisted that he enter the military. Osbert became a Guards officer in 1913. The Guards enjoyed a certain high status in London at this time, and on the eve of the First World War Osbert enjoyed a glittering Edwardian social life.

Osbert fought in the trenches in France in the Great War. It was when he was in France that Osbert first began to write poetry. Much of the poetry that originates in his experiences in the war is bitter, satiric, and "militantly pacifist."

After the "Great Catastrophe," Osbert joined his sister and brother in London and there began to devote himself to life as an artist. Together with a protégé musician, William Walton, the three Sitwells collaborated on a performance called *Façade* that consisted of 21 poems by Edith Sitwell accompanied by music. The first performance of *Façade* in 1923 received an enraged reaction from the critics. Nevertheless there were many more performances of *Façade* over the years, and it came to be hailed as a masterpiece of the avant-garde.

Osbert published two volumes of poetry: *Argonaut and Juggernaut* (1919) and *At the House of Mrs. Kinfoot* (1921). He also wrote short stories and novels, including *Before the Bombardment* (1926), a novel set in Scarborough before the German shelling of 1914. After his father's death, Osbert began an autobiography that would span five volumes.

Osbert was part of a significant group of literary artists including the Bloomsbury Group, T. S. ELIOT, EZRA POUND, WYNDHAM LEWIS, D. H. LAWRENCE, Gertrude Stein, and many others. Although his work has never become a major part of the "high modernist" canon, his writing deals with many of the same concerns that influenced the modernists: the relationship of art to politics, the effects of war, the rise of the working class, and the sacredness of art.

Osbert Sitwell never married but lived much of his life with a fellow writer, David Horner. In his later years, Osbert suffered from Parkinson's disease and withdrew from the social world of England, becoming almost a recluse at Castello di Montegufoni in Italy. He died in Italy in 1969.

See also "CORPSE-DAY."

BIBLIOGRAPHY
Pearson, John. *Façades: Edith, Osbert, and Sacheverell Sitwell.* London: Macmillan, 1978.

Hazel Atkins

"A SLICE OF WEDDING CAKE" ROBERT GRAVES (1958)

The poem was originally published under the title "Bitter Thoughts on Receiving a Slice of Cordelia's Wedding Cake" in the miscellaneous collection *5 Pens in Hand,* but after 1958 retitled "A Slice of Wedding Cake." The collection had been put together shortly before ROBERT GRAVES's first trip to America in 1958 and was harshly criticized as being threadbare by a review in *Time* magazine (Seymour 374), yet the colloquial lightness and humor of many of its poems are refreshingly new. The "Cordelia" mentioned in the original title could be either an acquaintance of Graves's or a reference to King Lear's daughter, who was cast away by her father and rejected by two prospective bridegrooms because of her lack of a dowry and who then suddenly married the only man who was still willing to woo her, the king of France. Why Graves changed the title is open to speculation; he probably intended a more general approach by omitting the name. A slice of wedding cake received after the event could signify the sense of exclusion and jealousy felt by somebody (probably a rejected suitor of the bride) who is allowed to participate in the wedding only vicariously.

Graves engages in a mock-discussion of possible reasons for the omnipresent mismatch of "lovely girls" with "impossible men": "Why have such scores of lovely, gifted girls / Married impossible men?" He rejects explanations such as "simple self-sacrifice" or "missionary endeavour" and stresses the utter incompatibility of many men with their spouses, by repeating the term *impossible* three times. The speaker—who can easily be identified here with the author—differenti-ates between the usual nastiness of men (rustic, foul-tempered, or depraved), which might be used by women to stress their own goodness in contrast ("dramatic foils chosen to show the world / How well women behave, and always have behaved"), and the characteristics that make many men "impossible": "idle, illiterate, / Self-pitying, dirty, sly." The assonance of the *i* and *y* sounds and the clash of *l* sounds here emphasize his disgust and the crooked character of these men, who are a constant embarrassment to their own wives.

Having started with a question, the poem also ends with questions, the speaker ironically asking whether "God's supply of tolerable husbands" has fallen too low, and then expressing misgivings about his own prejudiced view of gender differences: "Or do I always over-value woman / At the expense of man? / Do I? / It might be so." Despite its playful and self-mocking tone the poem treats a theme that had engaged the poet deeply for years. Graves's famous work *THE WHITE GODDESS* (1948) deals with his theory that the history of higher cultures started with matriarchy and a cult of fertility goddesses. The character of the White Goddess is ambivalent, as she is both constructive and destructive, representing love and death, ending life and renewing it in the cycle of the seasons. She can feature in Egyptian mythology as Isis (whose son Osiris is sacrificed), or as Mary, the mother of God (whose son Jesus is sacrificed), but also as the lady adored by troubadour poets and suffering Petrarchan lovers. Poetry then is the realization of an old ritual of sacrificing the king to the mother goddess, with the poet's adoration of the goddess being expressed in the writing of poetry for so-called muses, female representatives of the goddess on earth. For Graves, poetry can only be written in the state of being in love, and yet his many adulterous affairs with young "muses" look suspiciously like an act of sublimation by a poet who had been inhibited sexually through his puritanical upbringing. In 1952, when Judith Bledsoe, one of Graves's "muses," returned to Mallorca with her new fiancé, Graves attacked the man and told him he had no right to be with such a noble woman and later on probably challenged him to a duel (cf. Seymour 336). It is hard to differentiate here between the jealousy of an aging poet after the end of an affair and the righteous anger of a muse poet, serving his goddess. The idealization of women in this poem is counteracted by the irony achieved through the jumpy, bumpy rhythms and humorous alliteration: "married impossible men," "simple self-sacrifice," "fallen, in fact," "always over-value woman." There may yet be another reason for women's choosing the "wrong" men, apart from the fact that everybody must appear wrong to a poet who egotistically sees himself as the only possible choice, namely, the fascination exerted by "bad" but exciting and therefore attractive men on women, or as Oscar Wilde expressed it: "Women love men for their defects."

BIBLIOGRAPHY

Canary, Robert. H. *Robert Graves.* Boston: Twayne, 1980.

Carter, D. N. G. *Robert Graves, the Lasting Poetic Achievement.* Totowa, N.J.: Barnes & Noble Books, 1989.

Kirkham, Michael. *The Poetry of Robert Graves.* London: Athlone Press, 1969.

Seymour, Miranda. *Robert Graves: Life on the Edge.* New York: Henry Holt, 1995.

Heike Grundmann

SMITH, IAIN CRICHTON (1928–1998)

Born in Glasgow in 1928, Iain Crichton Smith was brought up in a Gaelic-speaking community on the Hebridean island of Lewis. His father died when Smith was very young, and the family was left to survive on a widow's pension. Gaelic was Smith's first language until he went to school on the mainland, where lessons were conducted in English. Educated at Aberdeen University, Smith became a schoolteacher in the 1950s and eventually settled in Oban on the west coast of Scotland. He married Donalda Logan in 1977 and in the same year retired from teaching to become a full-time writer.

Smith moved easily between Gaelic and English, writing original material in both languages and translating contemporary and historical Gaelic poetry into English, including the poem "In Praise of Ben Dorain," by the 18th-century poet Duncan Ban MacIntyre. The majority of Smith's own creative output was, however, written in English, a result of being "moulded by English history, English literature" at school and university. An affable and often self-deprecatory character,

Smith knew and socialized with a number of important Scottish poets, including EDWIN MORGAN, Sorley Maclean, HUGH MACDIARMID, GEORGE MACKAY BROWN, and NORMAN MACCAIG.

While he admired Scottish poets like MacDiarmid, Smith cited Robert Lowell and W. H. AUDEN as two particularly significant influences, admiring Lowell for his "union of the classical with the quotidian" and Auden for his "fluency" with technical form. Smith's early fascination with poetic form may be partly due to his knowledge of Gaelic poets, who used traditional formal conventions in their work. Despite this affinity, however, Smith moved increasingly toward free verse, evident from much of his later long poems such as "The White Air of March" (1972).

At times a fierce critic of Gaelic culture, Smith argues in "Poem of Lewis" (1955) that the islanders "have no place for the fine graces / of poetry." While looking back on his childhood in the essay "Real People in a Real Place" (1986), he is frustrated by his "fragmented life" growing up in Lewis. Such tensions are evident in poems such as "The Gaelic Proverb" (1994), which takes the traditional saying "Sad is the state of the house / without a child or cat" and lashes back at Gaelic culture with the anger and unhappiness of the child "who carries his house on his back / like a trapped snail," or the cat on a spinster's "narrow and infertile" lap, "as the wild sun goes down." Indeed old women appear throughout Smith's poetry as representatives of cultural barrenness and joylessness, in contrast to the surrounding landscape, its "free daffodils / wav[ing] in the valleys" ("Old Woman," 1965).

Influenced by his reading of existentialist philosophy, Smith "turned against systems"—a necessary step for both his philosophy and his art, analogous to the need for poetry to be "something not dogmatic, but provisional, and almost temporary." However, this change of outlook was dangerous, a "move out into the open sea," and it led at one stage to a nervous breakdown. Smith identified exile as part of his poetic work, tackling the unreality of metaphor and the difficulty of representing the world as it is, without resorting to pathetic fallacy or other embellishments. In contemplating the redundancy of metaphor in "Deer on the High Hills" (1962), the wild deer are likened to "debutantes" or "aristocrats" before Smith concedes, "There is no metaphor. . . . The deer step out in isolated air."

Ultimately although he struggled with his identity as a bilingual poet caught between two cultures, Smith's work is very much rooted in the experience of the Highlands and Islands landscape where he was brought up and reflects the lyrical sensitivity of traditional Gaelic poetry, while seeking to reject the more authoritarian aspects of Gaelic culture. He continued to live in the village of Taynuilt, near Oban, with his wife, Donalda, until his death in 1998.

BIBLIOGRAPHY

Cambridge, Gerry. "Iain Crichton Smith at 70: An interview." *Dark Horse,* spring 1998, 46–55. Available online. URL: http://www.star.ac.uk/darkhorse/archive/Crichton Smithinterview.pdf. Accessed May 10, 2008.

Morgan, Edwin. "The Contribution of Iain Crichton Smith." *ScotLit* 23, (winter 2000). Available online. URL: http://www.arts.gla.ac.uk/ScotLit/ASLS/ICSmith.html. Accessed May 10, 2008.

Nicholson, Colin, ed. *Iain Crichton Smith: Critical Essays.* Edinburgh: Edinburgh University Press, 1992.

Smith, Iain Crichton. *Collected Poems.* Manchester, Eng.: Carcanet, 1992.

Louisa Gairn

SMITH, STEVIE (1902–1971)

Stevie Smith's uncompromising individuality made it difficult for her to get published. She wrote prolifically but encountered rejection after rejection from publishers. In 1935, one publisher suggested that she try a novel, resulting in *Novel on Yellow Wallpaper* (1936). When her poems were printed in the *New Statesman and Nation* they attracted sufficient attention to ensure further publication of individual poems and eventually the first volume, *A Good Time Was Had by All* in 1937. After her next two collections (1938, 1942), she struggled to get her poems in journals, let alone in book form, until *Harold's Leap* (1950). This collection was followed by another vacuum before *Not Waving but Drowning* (1957), although there were always plenty of poems. The positive reception of *Selected Poems* (1962) helped her enter her most successful period, and she achieved national recognition through winning the Queen's Gold Medal for poetry in 1969. Her final collections,

The Frog Prince (1966) and *Scorpion and Other Poems* (1972), can be considered the most untethered in terms of literary conformity. In her later years, she was renowned for her live performances where she sung her poems or read them as dramatic conversation pieces in a theatrical manner. From the outset, the uniqueness of the poems aroused both admiration— SYLVIA PLATH was a self-professed "desperate Smith addict"—and skepticism. After her death, the 1980s generated fresh editions, critical biographies, and some serious articles.

Born in Hull as Florence Margaret Smith, "Stevie" lived in London with her mother, aunt, and sister from the age of three, when her father left home. She attended Palmers Green High School and then the prestigious North Collegiate School for Girls. From 1922, she was employed as secretary to the publishers Sir George Newnes and Sir Neville Pearson for 30 years. In "Childe Rolandine," the secretary typist bored with her job is a thin gloss of her frustration with routine work at Newnes's. Her notebooks from the years 1924–30 record observations from her eclectic reading of literature, theology, the classics, art, and history, along with the people she saw on her daily round, all of which became the material for her writing. In her novels, interviews, and correspondence Smith freely deprecated the narrowness of her social territory while defending the personal origin of her writing, such as "The Deserter" about her ill health, "The Stroke" in response to her aunt's fatal affliction, or the recurring invitations to death. In "A House of Mercy" the poet is both narrator—"It was a house of female habitation"— and the central character: "I was the younger of the feeble babes / And when I was a child my mother died." In "The Word," the exaggeration of the personal pronoun (My / I) through repetition both asserts and parodies the personal center of the poem.

It is tempting to seek security in searching for the persona of the poet in every poem, but ultimately it is impossible to detect one unifying authentic voice: The huge cast of characters draws upon Smith's world but is never merely autobiographical. In "Behind the Knight," the heroic mask that conceals the knight's secret anxieties is a metaphor for the stripping away of surfaces throughout Smith's work. This unrelenting psychological realism accounts for the reader's frequent unease when reading the poems. It is craftily effected in devices such as the child's voice in "Landrecie" or the candid epigrams of "Two Friends" and "Revenge." "The heart had gone out of us," a recurring sentiment, and the continually voiced death wish in her tragedies of loss, loneliness, and longing knit together a huge untidy oeuvre: "Poor human race that must feed / on pain" ("So to Fatness Comes"). The mental anguish of conflicting impulses is another recurring theme. Sometimes her subjects are casualties of their network of family, friends, and colleagues, and many poems are open-ended tragedies of male/female relations. The dramatic irony in "Drugs Made Pauline Vague" makes it one of her most poignant condensations of infidelity and deception, albeit with a complicit "other woman." In many dramas and commentaries, however, Smith dealt with the forces of socialization, particularly false ideals fed to children. The baby in "Childhood and Interruption" is enviably not "properly awake," that is, free of social contrivances. In her manipulation of hymns, nursery rhymes, myths, and fairy tales we experience their potential either to reinforce or to subvert orthodox cultural codes. In "Fafnir and the Knights" we readily switch allegiance from the chivalric knight to the dragon he is supposed to slay, as if we have always wanted to. "The After-Thought," which consists of an inner dialogue between Rapunzel and her lover, demystifies the archetypal heroism of the fairy tale, ending enigmatically with a recognizable problem of communication between men and women.

The longing to be elsewhere is a frequent impulse in Smith's people; sometimes it is presented as the consequence of cultural conditions, such as poverty, but it is also endemic of the human condition. Fantasy woods and rivers, typical of fairy tales and book illustrations, are frequently entered to flee the grimness of social circumstances or psychological states but are never utopian depictions of freedom or fulfillment. In "The Wedding Photograph," for example, getting married was a means of escape for the wife who otherwise would be stuck with her family: "Yet dared not without marrying leave home." The ideal of a happy-ever-after marriage is further exploded when we learn that the new bride intends to murder her husband. In addition to the yearning to be away and alone, Smith's other favorite ploys are in "The Wedding Photograph": the frequent "good-byes," which here are amusing in their incongruity; the poetic rhyming alongside a line of sheer prose (l. 10); the blurring of differences between animals and humans (*roam*); the interdependency of public and personal experience; the exposure of driving unconscious desires (*unsheathing*); the tragicomic tone that teases us with uncertainty about how playful and how serious are the wife's intentions, largely due to her childlike renditions of jungle danger; and the whole situation of rejecting conventional prescriptions, especially for women. The reader, as confidant/e, is required to adjudicate between the wife's dishonest behavior and the social pressures that send her to it— pressures known, of course, to the poet, who broke an engagement. *Freddy* is Smith's fictional name for the ex-fiancé, Eric Armitage; the broken engagement, partly due to her aversion to the prospective confines of suburban conventionality and partly due to her problem with an *à deux* model of sex relations, provoked the troubled poem "Freddy": "Nobody knows what I feel about Freddy." Difficulty with male intimacy is easily attributable to her rage against her "absconding and very absent pa" (*Novel on Yellow Paper,* 1936) and to the lack of any other close male family relations. As is any category, "woman poet" is too limiting (and notably rarely used of her); although ambivalent about feminism, along with any polemic, Smith often centered on female experience in her portraits and was undoubtedly conscious of gendered authorship. "Miss Snooks, Poetess" dramatizes the tendency to applaud women's unchallenging literary conformity and thus perpetuate it.

Individuality is again and again the message and medium of the sketch poems. State control and organized religion were to be feared for being overtly. In conjunction with her letters, essays, or novels, Smith's poems often refract the human significance of current affairs, such as suburban development, the hydrogen bomb, colonialism, or the repeal of capital punishment. Smith poked fun at both the stereotyping and the stereotype of Englishness in "The Hostage," "Parents," "The English," "The English Visitor," and "A British Song." Anticonventional in her cynicism toward organized religion, Stevie Smith is drawn toward a noninstitutionalized god who embodies the absolute love and companionship not encountered in human relations. This is most direct and intense in "God the Eater," which she included in a radio program broadcast on April 12, 1956. The parenthetical allusion to "men's contempt" indicates the inexpressibility of the pain, which is most likely the betrayal by her literary contemporaries, especially publishers, and by her friends. It may also refer to the unresolved bitterness of her father's betrayal in her childhood. "Mr. Over" dramatizes the search for a god inside and outside human incarnations.

The impossibility of pinning her down and her defiance of conventional literary classifications cost Smith proper critical acclaim. Nevertheless, different strands of her poetry can be positioned in mainstream literary groupings. Her strong impulse for social equality and the conversational lyrics—what W. H. AUDEN coined as "memorable speech"—align Smith with the 1930s. The inclusivity of her narrative verse, ballads, children's tunes, folk songs, and hymns also fits with the return to more oral and communal traditions in the thirties, which continued into the forties. The interplay of voices that construct shifting levels of consciousness negotiates between the modernist psychologizing of human character and the postwar neoromantic return to a fixed lyric personality, albeit unheroic. At times, her self-conscious commentary, her addresses to the reader, and her absurdist manipulations of habitual meaning-making apparatus anticipate the metalinguistics of late-20th-century postmodern play.

In the final analysis, avoidance of the demands of literary standardization is Smith's hallmark. The visual sketches, which only obliquely match particular poems, add a third dimension to a simple poetry/prose binary; their ambiguity and suggestiveness produce further indeterminacy, not just about the single poem but of the very processes of determining meaning. The personalized creatures in her light-hearted sketchbook *Some Are More Human Than Others* (1958) confront assumptions about the linear evolution of human civilization from the animal kingdom. One fundamental binary opposition that she unfixes is the literary/oral in favor of a stage/page conjunction associated with the-

ater and PERFORMANCE POETRY. Her famously eclectic intertextual allusions endow nursery rhymes, the Grimms' fairy tales, ancient legends, popular proverbial wisdom, classical and Shakespearean tragedies, biblical doctrine, Milton, William Blake, and a Renoir painting with the same status. Her pastiche and parody of literary texts and diction, coupled with prosaic commentary, investigate how much the complexity of human beings is down to the variety of languages that constitute them. The application of Bakhtin's ideas on textual politics to Smith's poetry may be hardening into some kind of orthodoxy, but they do provide a sufficiently flexible terminology for her multivocality.

See also "THE FROG PRINCE," "NOT WAVING BUT DROWNING," "OUR BOG IS DOOD," "PRETTY," "VALUABLE," "WAS HE MARRIED?"

BIBLIOGRAPHY

Lee, Hermione, ed. *Stevie Smith: A Selection*. London: Faber and Faber. 1983.

Smith, Stevie. *Me Again: The Uncollected Writings of Stevie Smith*. London: Virago, 1981.

———. *Stevie Smith: Collected Poems*. London: Allen Lane, 1975.

Spalding, Frances. *Stevie Smith: A Critical Biography*. London: Faber and Faber, 1988.

Sternlicht, Stanford, ed. *In Search of Stevie Smith*. New York: Syracuse University Press, 1991.

Jane Dowson

"SNAKE" D. H. LAWRENCE (1923)

D. H. LAWRENCE's poem "Snake," one of his most often anthologized, was written during a sojourn in Taormina, Sicily, in 1921. The poem was originally published in BIRDS, BEASTS, AND FLOWERS, a collection of verse on plants and animals offering commentary on human nature and sexuality often through anthropomorphization. This is an important technique for Lawrence, who regularly wrote of the conflict between an awareness of the world positing equality with all things and another proclaiming human superiority. "Snake" is a notable example of this dualistic tension in human perception and can thus easily be analyzed in terms of its surface content, that of man's direct relation to the physical world about him, as well as in other ways, including allegorically, as indicative of man's desire to understand and reconcile issues of life, death, and sexuality—topics on which Lawrence habitually wrote.

In the first type of reading of "Snake," Lawrence provides imagery that presents the snake as reflected through man's *natural* understanding (what Lawrence calls *blood-consciousness*) as well as through his *educated* understanding. The first mode suggests that man is an equal with the snake, whereas the second mode, which presents a Western, educated understanding, favors man as the superior being who should immediately destroy such a creature, as it is considered evil and dangerous. The speaker initially appears to reject the latter position, instead expressing how he "felt so honoured" by the arrival of the unexpected "guest in quiet" at his water trough, confessing how he "liked" him and felt "glad." Yet he questions this position as inappropriate, asking himself whether it is "cowardice," "perversity," or "humility" that prevents him from performing his proper task: namely, if he "were a man," he would "take a stick and break him now, and finish him off." The speaker ultimately acknowledges his fear of the snake but notes how his reverence of it is still greater, aligning the speaker more with the *natural* mode of being. With his decision calmly to watch the snake retreat, it appears as though this natural relation to the animal has won out, until, suddenly at the last moment, the speaker "picked up a clumsy log / And threw it at the water-trough with a clatter." This action indicates how the speaker cannot overcome his inclination toward human superiority, forcing him to listen to his "accursed human education" and denigrate the snake. However, at the last, the speaker immediately regrets this action and alludes to Samuel Taylor Coleridge's "Rime of the Ancient Mariner," in which a seaman laments his destruction of the beautiful and symbolically venerated albatross, securing his own demise at sea. Here the speaker declares, "I have something to expiate: / A pettiness," suggesting that he can only hope now to atone for his unworthy violation of nature's creature.

A second reading of "Snake" involves an allegorical interpretation of the earth as the all-powerful giver of life and death. At his water trough the speaker confronts a sexually and morbidly charged image of a snake emerging from "the burning bowels of the earth,"

which "reached down from a fissure in the earth-wall in the gloom." The speaker himself stands facing the snake, "on a hot, hot day," and "in pyjamas for the heat," suggesting his vulnerability toward the surprising and penetrating presence of the serpent. He is humbled before the creature and considers it "like a king" that has come forth from the living, burning, volcanic earth. The snake here represents an authoritative and arcane force, like that of a god or any unknown entity, provoking awe and dread in the speaker. The snake, "being earth-brown, earth-golden," is produced like excrement from the earth but also like fire as it "writhed like lightning" upon being startled by the log. At the moment in which the serpent begins to slip back into the gloomy crevice, intense fear and disgust seize the speaker as he observes the snake "put his head into that dreadful hole" and slink away into the dark opening in the earth, provoking in him "a sort of horror, a sort of protest against his withdrawing into that horrid black hole." It is precisely at this moment that the speaker takes action against his fear, a fear of death and seduction emanating from the slithering, phallic body of the snake. The earth is not only life and death giving; this image also provides a reflection on hell with its cavernous gap leading into fiery innards, coupled with the symbolic figure of the evil serpent.

Pairing the allegorical with the literal reading, one sees how the speaker's difficulty in reconciling his natural and educated tendencies evokes the Old Testament scene of the serpent in the Garden of Eden. The speaker cannot decide how to treat the snake, which at once represents the natural and also violates his educated sense of right versus wrong and good versus evil. The snake, which emerges from a dark, volatile earth, is immediately feared but simultaneously respected "like a king in exile." Lawrence seems to suggest that the way the speaker reacts will indicate his moral sense. However, it is a moral sense controlled not by his instinctual beliefs but by those given to him through his common education. The speaker's final analysis proposes that to revere the snake as an equal or more, who is "uncrowned in the underworld," would be his intuitive choice, but one that violates society's expectations. Thus in following a Christian morality, which shuns the snake as an emblem of darkness and evil, the speaker misses his "chance with one of the lords / Of life."

At the time "Snake" was written, Lawrence was also producing work on psychoanalysis, in which he discusses his concept of *blood-consciousness* and the ways in which man attempts to know the world. With this in mind, any reading of this poem (literal, allegorical, or otherwise) ought to consider the dualism between nature and knowledge that pervades Lawrence's larger body of work.

BIBLIOGRAPHY

Lancashire, Ian. "Commentary on D. H. Lawrence's 'Snake.'" Department of English, University of Toronto. Available online. URL: http://rpo.library.utoronto.ca/poem/1252.html. Accessed on June 28, 2006.

Lawrence, D. H. *Birds, Beasts and Flowers.* London: Martin Secker, 1923.

Williams, W. E. "Introduction." In *D. H. Lawrence: Selected Poems.* Harmondsworth, Eng.: Penguin Books, 1950.

Katy Masuga

"THE SOHO HOSPITAL FOR WOMEN"

FLEUR ADCOCK (1979) FLEUR ADCOCK has said she is not a "woman" poet, and even in discussing her work editing *The Faber Book of 20th Century Women's Poetry* she has disavowed the idea of "woman's poetry" and herself as part of it. However, "The Soho Hospital for Women" articulates in a compelling way the female experiences of disease and community, and through these the acceptance of mortality.

"The Soho Hospital for Women" was published in *The Inner Harbour* in 1979. The book is divided into four sections; "The Soho Hospital for Women" appears in the third, "The Thing Itself." Critics have noted certain characteristics of Adcock's style that are very visible in this text. The poem has the "laconic style" (a phrase taken from another poem from *The Inner Harbour,* "Poem Ended by Death") and colloquial language so noteworthy in Adcock's poetry. In addition, "The Soho Hospital for Women" is built around a multiplicity of perspectives as the experience of disease is cast and recast through snapshots of individual women. The position of the speaker, however, is always stable as she lives through her own experience of disease. It is this experience—the awareness of mortality and loss and the ultimate acceptance of the frailty of the body and the value of life—that creates the movement of the poem. Throughout Adcock conveys a sense of the ordinariness of disease and death. At the same time, these things are not mundane; rather, they allow for moments of epiphany.

The poem is divided into four sections. The first section opens with "Strange room, from this angle." This line highlights the defamiliarization of the ordinary that results from illness; Adcock returns to this in the final section, where the ordinary is made wondrous through acceptance of mortality and appreciation of life. The poem begins with the speaker's rejecting the sense of feminine empowerment that might result from living through disease. She is not a goddess, only a woman with "ordinary legs." Yet she will come to embrace her illness and through it be recreated.

The second section gives snapshots of the women of the hospital. Despite the emphasis on breasts, ribs, and sweaters made too loose through mastectomy, the women of the poem are not reduced to sick body parts but are given individuality through carefully selected detail. They are the "taxi-party," going for their treatment and somehow finding solidarity in their illness. Even after the speaker leaves the hospital, these women—and others—stay with her.

Adcock moves away from the physicality of illness in the third and fourth sections of the poem as the speaker is lightened by her freedom from disease and her liberation from fear. Her own body seems less than incarnate: Pain is "imagined"; her stitches "dissolve." This dephysicalization of the body is in contrast to the earthiness of the final section, where the speaker goes to the market and buys food, thinking of the meal she will prepare. This meal, in all its ordinariness, signifies a renewal. The speaker thinks of the women in the final section, and of their diseased bodies in opposition to her own "almost intact" body, as light as her shopping basket filled with necessities, with life.

BIBLIOGRAPHY

Adcock, Fleur, ed. *The Faber Book of 20th Century Women's Poetry.* London: Faber and Faber, 1987.
———. *Poems: 1960–2000.* Newcastle upon Tyne, Eng.: Bloodaxe Books, 2000.
Bleiman, Barbara, ed. *Five Modern Poets: Fleur Adcock, U. A. Fanthorpe, Tony Harrison, Anne Stevenson, Derek Walcott.* New York: Longman, 1993.

Sherry, Vincent, ed. *Dictionary of Literary Biography.* Vol. 40. *British Poets since 1960:* Detroit: Gale, 1984.

Stannard, Julian. *Fleur Adcock in Context: From Movement to Martians.* Lewiston, N.Y.: Edwin Mellen Press, 1997.

Janine Utell

"THE SOLDIER" RUPERT BROOKE (1914)

Perhaps RUPERT BROOKE's best-known work is the war sonnet sequence culminating in "The Soldier," often read as a glorification of war. His early death in 1915 canonized him as an iconic hero of the first phase of World War I, who symbolized the potential of all the gifted young people destroyed by the conflict. Brooke's personal war experience consisted of one day of limited military action with the Hood Battalion during the evacuation of Antwerp. Consequently the poem conveys highly sentimentalized themes of patriotism, romantic death, and idealism that were initially shared by many thousands of young men who blithely went into the war.

Brooke observes the sonnet form (14 lines of iambic pentameter, divided into an octave and sestet). However the octave follows the Shakespearean rhyme scheme *ababcdcd,* while the sestet follows the Petrarchan *efgefg.* He also deviates slightly from the traditional thematic divisions where the octave and sestet state or express a question or predicament and its resolution, respectively. In "The Soldier" the octave and sestet both enjoin the reader to conceptualize the blissful death of the fallen soldier. This romantic vision of death combines the ideas of spiritual purification and resurrection, Neo-pagan immortalizing of fallen epic warriors, and anglicizing a foreign soil by adding the dust of dead English soldiers to it, under the overarching theme of the superiority of English heritage and personal loyalty to it.

"The Soldier" inspired imitations as well as rejections, as, for example, "To My Mother—1916" by Rifleman Donald S. Cox, which shows a recognizable connection with Brooke's sonnet, while a "clear rebuttal" may be seen in CHARLES HAMILTON SORLEY's sonnet "WHEN YOU SEE MILLIONS OF THE MOUTHLESS DEAD." Brooke's appeal began to wane as the realities of warfare were fully understood and communicated in the acrid poems of WILFRED OWEN (1893–1918), who was machine-gunned to death, and SIEGFRIED SASSOON's visions of "the hell where youth and laugher go." Today Brooke's "war sonnets" are seen as more a naively enthusiastic self-declaration occasioned by the ups and downs of his tumultuous personal life than a call to war for his generation.

BIBLIOGRAPHY

Cross, Tim. *The Lost Voices of World War I.* London: Bloomsbury, 1988.

Marsh, Edward. *The Collected Poems, by Rupert Brooke with an introduction by Gavin Ewart.* London: Macmillan, 1992.

Divya Saksena

"SOON" VIKRAM SETH (1990)

This poem is the last of six works that compose the "In Other Voices" section of *All You Who Sleep Tonight.* Its speaker is dying of acquired immunodeficiency syndrome (AIDS), and the seven stanzas speak of the causes and effects of the new disease but end in a classically human plea: that the auditor not let the speaker die. The line is both an entreaty that a miracle happen and a request that his memory be kept alive in love. The penultimate line is a supplication to be loved even in death, while earlier in the poem, the speaker has said that his beloved knows that he is in effect already dead. Paradoxically, love, his greatest desire, has engendered the condition that puts the speaker in the odd state of being both dead and alive at the same time. AIDS has made physical the spiritual condition of modern man, and the malady eats his body as the desire for love had once devoured his spirit. Knowing that he cannot be cured and his health can only degenerate, the speaker wonders whether he can go in his enfeebled state, yet he clearly wants to live.

The sterile setting of the monologue, a metal bed in a hospital ward, contrasts with the sweat and spawn that cover the speaker's body, just as the flat tone of the poem contrasts with the desperate petition at the end. Critics have said that the regular form of the dominantly iambic trimeter lines and the *abab* rhyme scheme make this poem and much of VIKRAM SETH's poetry facile. The emotion of the diction, however, presses against the regularity of its versification to create, as Elizabeth Bishop's "One Art" does, the sense that the speaker is trying with limited success to convince himself that he can control his overwhelming pain.

BIBLIOGRAPHY

Field, Michelle. "*Publisher's Weekly* Interviews: Vikram Seth." *Publisher's Weekly,* 10 May 1993, 46–47.

Ragavan, Amit V. "Vikram Seth." *Post-Colonial Studies at Emory University,* Spring, 1999. Available online. URL: http://www.english.emory.edu/Bahri/Seth.html. Accessed on May 10, 2008.

Karen Rae Keck

SORLEY, CHARLES HAMILTON (1895–1915)

Sorley started life in Aberdeen, Scotland. Born on May 19, 1895, he was the son of William Ritchie Sorley, a professor at the University of Aberdeen, and from an early age was considered an exceptional, intellectually gifted child. In 1900 the family moved to Cambridge. From 1908 onward Sorley was educated at Marlborough College, where he was acknowledged as a skilled debater and enjoyed cross-country running in the rain, an experience that colors several of his prewar poems, including "RAIN" and "The Song of the Ungirt Runners." Winning a scholarship to University College, Oxford, in 1913, he decided to spend a year in Germany before taking up residence at Oxford. He traveled to Mecklenburg and then to the University of Jena. He was still in Germany when the First World War broke out. As were other British nationals, Sorley was detained, interned for one night at Trier, and then ordered to leave the country immediately.

Although Sorley returned to England and took up his scholarship at Oxford, the internment experience left him angered and keen to join military service. In 1914 he enlisted in the Suffolk Regiment as a second lieutenant and arrived at the western front in France on May 30, 1915, as a full lieutenant. Serving near Ploegsteert he was swiftly promoted to captain in August 1915 when he was just 20 years old. He was killed in action at the Battle of Loos on October 13, 1915, shot in the head by a sniper's bullet.

Thirty-seven complete poems and several unfinished ones were found among his effects after his death. His sole collection, *Marlborough and Other Poems,* was published posthumously in 1916 and became an instant success with at least four editions printed the same year. In his work Sorley is seen as a forerunner of SIEGFRIED SASSOON and WILFRED OWEN for his unsentimental style and matter-of-fact descriptions of the war. Thus he stands in opposition to poets like RUPERT BROOKE and JOHN MCCRAE, as he is able to observe, interpret, and communicate the reality of war honestly and directly.

BIBLIOGRAPHY

Silkin, Jon, ed. *The Penguin Book of First World War Poetry.* London: Penguin, 1981.

Wilson, Jean Moorcroft, ed. *The Collected Poems of Charles Hamilton Sorley.* London: Cecil Woolf, 1985.

Divya Saksena

SPANISH CIVIL WAR AND POETRY

In July 1936 a group of Spanish army generals launched a coup to overthrow the Spanish Republic. The Republican government had been in existence since the abdication of King Alfonso XIII five years before. The new government had been relatively stable, although troubled, but the recent elections had brought in a popular front (Leftist) government that worried many monarchists, Catholics, and ultranationalists. The July coup was a reaction by the officer corps, which shared these values that opposed the direction that the republic seemed to be taking. International intervention began at the very start. The generals received immediate assistance from Nazi Germany and Italian help was not long in coming. The Soviet Union, pledged to assist popular front governments, also began its assistance to the republic.

This war, fought from 1936 to 1939, became one of the most significant political and military events of the 1930s. Its conclusion, followed a few short months later by the opening of the Second World War, marked the end of what W. H. AUDEN called a "low, dishonest decade." In the eyes of many this war in what many considered to be the backwater of Europe took on a larger significance as a black and white struggle of good versus evil, either as a crusade against fascism and Nazism or as a crusade against communism. Unlike the dictatorships, the Western democracies (the United States, Britain, and France) worked very hard to stay aloof from this fight. At the same time that these governments pursued neutrality, many of their individual citizens (as well as those from other nations) became directly involved. Some performed military duty, enlisting in the International Brigades, a military organization of volunteers fighting as part of the Republican army. In this larger unit, there were enough British volunteers to form a separate unit, the Atlee Battalion. Others served as ambulance drivers. Still others, artists, filmmakers, or writers, served as propagandists or offered their poetry whether written back home for the cause or on the battle front. The poets included several from Britain, several of whom went to Spain, although not all of these fought or stayed for any extended period.

English poets (as well as other writers and intellectuals) during this time can be easily divided into those who favored the republic, those who favored the nationalists, and those who elected to remain neutral. The reason it is so easy to divide them into these three groups is that a survey was conducted of major literary figures in Britain during the war by W. H. Auden and STEPHEN SPENDER. Foremost of those who supported the republic were the members of the Oxford Group: Auden, Spender, LOUIS MACNEICE, and C. DAY LEWIS. Of these only Lewis never visited Spain, although he was the most committed politically of this group. Lewis, however, became less engaged as a Leftist as time went on and distanced himself from the movement. Despite this, his poem *The Nabara* was well known. It was based on a naval encounter off the northern coast of Spain when Republican trawlers ran a blockade of Nationalist and German ships.

Auden went to Spain as an ambulance driver but was there only a short time (January–March 1937). His poem *Spain* may be the best known of all of the English language poems from the war and perhaps the best. He later disavowed this poem, along with his political stand of this time. He called the poem "trash," and it does not appear in his *Collected Works*. Stephen Spender compared the outbreak of the war with the year 1848, which saw revolutions throughout Europe, and considered it opportunity to change history for the better. At the time Spender was a Communist although his ideology was beginning to change. He wrote several poems about the war (published in 1939 in the collection *Poems from Spain*) and his work was among the

best produced. He later disavowed his communism and in the 1950s and 1960s was editor of a journal that was subsidized by the American Central Intelligence Agency (CIA). While Spender always denied knowledge of this, it does show that he did move very far from his left-wing enthusiasms of the 1930s.

In addition to these well-known poets, there were several who were nearly unknown and who wrote only one or a small number of poems. There were others who not only went to Spain but fought and died there. These include Ralph Fox, Julian Bell, and JOHN CORNFORD. Cornford, a Cambridge student, was killed in the fighting at the end of 1936 at the age of 21. Fox and Bell (the nephew of Virginia Woolf) were also killed fairly early on. Another, John Lepper, wrote one of the most powerful poems of the war. His *Battle of Jarama 1937* is very close in style and effectiveness to the works of the soldier-poets of World War I. Of particular note is his description of the battlefield where death walks among the olive groves, beckoning to soldiers with his "leaden finger." In *An English War Poet,* HUGH MACDIARMID attacks SIEGFRIED SASSOON's poetry, his prose (specifically his *Memoirs of George Sherston*), and his views, stating that the cynicism and self-involvement he finds in Sassoon would have no place among the members of the International Brigades. While not a bad poem, as is much of the poetry of the war it is written to prove a particular political viewpoint. The fact is that it is Sassoon's poetry and prose about the First World War and their universality that have survived while much of the British poetry of the Spanish civil war has been forgotten.

Wall posters of the Spanish civil war for either side were everywhere, characterized by imagination and visual power. The Spanish Republic printed several of these with photographs of dead children who had been killed in the air raids that the Nationalists launched on Madrid and other cities. GEORGE BARKER wrote *Elegy on Spain,* which he described as a "dedication on the photograph of a child killed in Barcelona." This extensive poem, which opens with a description of the child, expands to a description of the war's effects in Spain and the suffering that has taken place, which Barker eventually affirms will be Spain's glory and triumph.

Tom Wintringham was a soldier, a poet, and Communist activist. A commander of the British battalion of the International Brigades, he led his troops into battle at Jarama in 1937 armed only with a silver-headed cane. He was primarily a writer of prose. Wintringham wrote mostly on military and political subjects (he was military correspondent for the *Daily Worker* and wrote a book for Home Guard training). He did, however, write poetry of uneven quality. His *Barcelona Nerves* describes life in that city, death all around, and soldiers preparing to go to the front. And at its conclusion he asserts that the experiences that can ruin others are those that he and his comrades have taken on willingly. One of his poems, *Monument*, was written in 1937. In a preachy, politicized tone so common to many of these poems, he describes the battles up to that time, the losses, and the nobility of the working-class Spaniards in facing the enemy.

There were two poets of some prominence who favored the Nationalist side seeking to destroy the Spanish Republic: ROY CAMPBELL and EDMUND BLUNDEN. Campbell, who had established himself not only as a poet but as a critic of the Bloomsbury Group (which favored the republic), had converted to Catholicism in the early to mid-1930s and the tie between Catholicism and Franco's rebellion was very close. Campbell actually fought in Spain in the Nationalist army, eventually writing an epic poem about the war from the Nationalist viewpoint, *The Flowering Rifle,* published in 1939. Among the most interesting (and in some ways puzzling) aspects of Campbell's work were his championing and translating the works of the Spanish poet Federico Garcia Lorca, who was killed in the early days of the Spanish civil war by Nationalists.

Edmund Blunden was one of the most accomplished of the First World War soldier-poets. Continuing as a poet and as a writer of prose in the 1920s and 1930s, he also took a very strong stand for the Nationalists. He was so outspoken that at the outbreak of the Second World War he had become suspect in the eyes of the government as a Nazi sympathizer. He was never prosecuted for this and was even later allowed to teach officer courses for the army during the war.

Not all poets took sides. A few remained neutral. Foremost among these was T. S. ELIOT, who stated that at least some literary people should not take a stand at all. The poet EZRA POUND also kept a neutral stance

although he would later become a very vocal supporter of Mussolini's fascism. In *Keep the Aspidistra Flying* George Orwell (who fought in the war with a pro-Republican unit and wrote about it in *Homage to Catalonia*) suggested that civilization was dying but would not die in bed—airplanes, rather, would deliver death. The Western world would go up in "a roar of high explosives." His view presented a decided contrast to Eliot's poem of the previous decade that the world would end "not with a bang but a whimper." It was the events of the 1930s, climaxed by the war in Spain, that informed not only Orwell's comment but a great deal of the poetry from this era. Much of that was the expression of a major political event that in the eyes of many of the survivors, even those who became disillusioned at the end, meant the triumph of evil and made the larger conflict inevitable.

A great portion of the significance of this poetry diminished almost immediately. Franco's triumph in Spain was followed two months later by Nazi Germany's entrance into what remained of Czechoslovakia after the 1938 Munich agreement. On the first of September 1939 the Germans invaded Poland, starting the Second World War. That greater war drove the Spanish civil war into the background. The stark issues of good and evil were no longer so abstract, as bombs were now falling in London and Berlin and not in far-away Madrid. The political issues that had brought about the war became less important as it then became a grim, total struggle for survival.

In looking at events closely, however, the tone and quantity of British poetry on the war actually started to diminish rather early on after the first flush of enthusiasm of 1936 and early 1937. For one thing, the fascists were succeeding militarily from the start and made steady progress through to the conclusion of the war. Also, some poets such as Cornford and others who were highly committed died in action with few if any to take their place. In this same time frame (specifically 1938) the Moscow purge trials in which several respected Soviet politicians and leaders were accused and convicted of treason began to alienate some sympathizers. Writers such as Stephen Spender and Arthur Koestler gave voice to that disillusionment with the Left in a book entitled *The God That Failed.*

British poetry written about or affected by the Spanish civil war cannot be compared quantitatively or qualitatively to the work of the soldier-poets of the First World War. It was still, however, a significant body of work. The Spanish civil war became a theme that captured attention, defined sides, and provided a central event in the lives of many intellectuals. Its significance was greater at the time than in retrospect. It did not have a measurable effect upon the outcome of the war. Further, it is not as good or as universal as the work of WILFRED OWEN, SIEGFRIED SASSOON, or others of the Great War. It is, however, a body of work that is of its time, one that allows us to see clearly into the political concerns and beliefs of English writers in the period between the world wars.

BIBLIOGRAPHY

Brome, Vincent. *The International Brigades: Spain, 1936–1939.* New York: Morrow, 1966. Campbell, Roy. *Collected Works.* Craighall, Eng.: A. D. Donker, 1985.

Cunningham, Valentine. *The Penguin Book of Spanish Civil War Verse.* London: Penguin Books, 1996.

Ford, Hugh D. *A Poet's War: British Poets and the Spanish Civil War.* Philadelphia: University of Pennsylvania Press, 1965.

Hynes, Samuel Lynn. *The Auden Generation: Literature and Politics in England in the 1930s.* Princeton, N.J.: Princeton University Press, 1982.

Laity, Paul. *Left Book Club Anthology.* London: Gollancz, 2001.

Lee, Laurie. *A Moment of War.* London: Viking, 1991.

Pearce, Joseph. *Unafraid of Virginia Woolf: The Friends and Enemies of Roy Campbell.* Wilmington, Del.: ISI Books, 2004.

Spender, Stephen. *World within World: The Autobiography of Stephen Spender.* New York: St. Martin's Press, 1994.

Stansky, Peter. *Journey to the Frontier: Two Roads to the Spanish Civil War.* Chicago: University of Chicago Press, 1983.

Thomas, Hugh. *The Spanish Civil War.* New York: Modern Library, 2001.

Robert Stacy

SPENDER, STEPHEN (1909–1995)

Stephen Harold Spender was born on February 28, 1909, in Hampstead, a northwestern suburb of London, where he was educated at University College School as a day pupil. His father, Edward Harold Spender, was a well-known journalist of liberal leanings. His family ancestry was English on his father's side and German-Jewish on his mother's side. The Spender family actively concealed their German-Jewish heritage from Stephen and his siblings, but when Spender eventually became aware of his background at the age of 16, that knowledge prompted a period of deep self-interrogation and self-reflection. "I began to *feel* Jewish," Spender writes, "especially during the 1930s," when Nazi anti-Semitism made its first hateful forays into European life and culture.

In 1927, Spender went up to University College, Oxford, where he befriended W. H. AUDEN, LOUIS MACNEICE, C. DAY LEWIS, and Christopher Isherwood. Auden in particular proved to be an important early influence in the work of the fledgling poet, encouraging him to compose his poetry with greater judiciousness and to revise it with greater rigor. "Auden's touch left an indelible mark," John Sutherland writes, especially on Spender's "idea of what it was to be a poet."

After leaving Oxford, Spender lived and traveled in Weimar Germany, which was at that time a European center of homosexual toleration and experimentation, an experience that broadened Spender's political, intellectual, and sexual horizons. His various travels, relationships, and experiences, particularly in Hamburg and with Isherwood in Berlin, inspired his experimental novel *The Temple*, which was abandoned in draft in 1929 but eventually published in 1988.

In 1930, Spender published his first collection of verse, *Twenty Poems.* In 1933, his second collection, *Poems,* appeared; the volume included "THE LANDSCAPE NEAR AN AERODROME" and "THE PYLONS," intense and passionate lyrics filled with images of the 20th-century industrial landscape. The latter poem inspired the nickname of the "Pylon school" to describe poets whose work engages with modern technological and industrial imagery and symbolism, a label with which Spender himself, however, was never entirely comfortable. Spender's early critical work, *The Destructive Element* (1935), emphasizes the responsibility of poets and other writers to deal thoughtfully with such "political-moral" issues in their work. It was during this time that Spender's name became associated with various radical and liberal organizations, causes, and opinions.

During the Spanish Civil War (1936–39), Spender and his friends did propaganda work in Spain for the republican loyalists, an experience that influenced poems such as "The Bombed Happiness" and "Two Armies" in part 3 of his 1939 collection *The Still Centre*. In the latter poem, for example, Spender laments how the two opposing sides of the conflict "freeze and hunger . . . Deep in the winter plain" in an ultimately meaningless effort "to destroy each other." The "two armies" become for Spender mere "tormented animals" who have come to loathe "more terribly than bullets . . . the cause and distant words / Which brought" them to Spain in the first place.

In 1939, Spender co-founded *Horizon*, a literary magazine that published works by George Orwell, Evelyn Waugh, W. H. Auden, and other leading British intellectuals of the day. Spender also co-edited the journal until 1941. "The strength of *Horizon* lay not in its having any defined cultural or political policy," Spender reflects, "but in the vitality and idiosyncrasy of the editor, Cyril Connolly," whose editorial policy seemed merely "to publish what he liked." The journal always received mixed reviews, largely due to Connolly's editorial eccentricities, but it ran for 10 solid years.

For much of the Second World War (1939–45), Spender was a member of a London branch of the newly formed National Fire Service, a nationalized system of fire brigades that was responsible for extinguishing the many conflagrations sparked by wartime air raids and bomb attacks. As Sutherland points out, however, "until the V-1 raids in mid-June 1944, there were no serious fires to fight; just the odd hit-and-run," making conditions "deadly boring for the NFS" and especially so for Spender, whose political, intellectual, and rhetorical talents were being wasted as he "sat in a fireman's barracks for three years."

Although Spender had flirted briefly with communism in the 1930s—he was even a member of the Communist Party for a few weeks, an experience he reflects upon in his very candid autobiography, *World within World* (1951)—his 1950s writing shows a wholesale rejection of communist principles in favor of a more "visionary individualism." *The Creative Element* (1953), for example, emphasizes the social role of the writer and "the creative energy of the individual." From 1953 to 1967, Spender cofounded and coedited *Encounter,* a political and literary review of decidedly anti-Communist leanings, which published the work of W. H. Auden, Philip Larkin, Kingsley Amis, and other leading poets and intellectuals of the day.

In addition to *Twenty Poems* (1930), *Poems* (1933), and *The Still Centre* (1939), Spender's published collections of verse include *Vienna* (1934), *Ruins and Visions* (1942), *Poems of Dedication* (1946), *Returning to Vienna* (1947), *The Edge of Being* (1949), *The Generous Days* (1971), and *Dolphins* (1994). Spender's work is characterized by a mix of both public and private verse, of both heartfelt poems of political protest and intensely passionate personal works addressed to various friends, colleagues, and loved ones.

Spender's most productive years as a poet culminated in the publication of his *Collected Poems 1928–1953* (1955), a volume in which Spender engages in an act of "reconsidering and . . . re-experiencing poems" he wrote over a period of 25 years, arranging them in what he calls "autobiographical order." Following *The Generous Days* (1971), Spender published a second book of *Collected Poems 1928–1985* (1985). In both collections, Spender presents what Alan Brownjohn calls "a highly selective and substantially revised body of work" from which Spender's "development as a poet may be traced in much closer detail" than in the individual books of poetry. In both collections, Spender attaches a brief but revealing introduction in which he explains the rationale behind his revisions and selections.

Spender was knighted in 1983. He died in 1995.

See also "Not Palaces, an Era's Crown"; "What I Expected."

BIBLIOGRAPHY

Spender, Stephen. *Journals 1939–1983*. London: Faber and Faber, 1985.
———. *World within World*. London: Hamish Hamilton, 1951.
Sutherland, John. *Spender: The Authorized Biography*. London: Viking, 2004.

Robert G. May

STALLWORTHY, JON (1935–) Jon Stallworthy, the son of New Zealanders, was born in London in January 1935 soon after his parents had

"rounded the Horn" on a freighter whose rudder chains snapped in a midwinter storm. From his father, Sir John Arthur Stallworthy, a gynecological surgeon and rugby enthusiast, he developed an appreciation for the physical immediacy of life as well as a respect for the "tribal values" that helped fortify his family against the narrow attitudes toward "colonials" they often met. To his mother, Margaret Howie, Stallworthy attributes his first lessons as a poet, "listening to the pulse of the voice" as she sang nursery rhymes to "the march of the iamb." This education is powerfully memorialized in his poem "Mother Tongue," where, upon the instant of her cremation, the poet hears "bone grated against stone" and "about the tongues of flame . . . a voice from heaven saying, Write."

Such conditions and legacies serve as fitting allegories for both the poet's thematic concerns and his creative process and nowhere more fully than in his most mature and original collection, A Familiar Tree (1978). Here Stallworthy combines the lyricism and intricate metric architecture of his early poems in Astronomy of Love (1961) with his growing interest in the influence of family lines and—as witnessed in later works aptly entitled Root and Branch (1969) and Hand in Hand (1974)—with the authority of one's private experience of history. In "A Letter from Berlin" from Root and Branch, Stallworthy transforms into a private letter dated 1938 an incident related to him by his father in which a famous German surgeon breaches custom by continuing to perform a vaginal hysterectomy on a patient although she has died on the table, an act that eerily presages Nazi atrocities. A Familiar Tree, spanning the years 1738–1977, traces the voyages, migrations, and movements of almost three centuries of the poet's paternal ancestors, beginning at a small parish near Oxford where missionaries and their descendants made their way to the Marquesa Islands in the South Pacific, on to New Zealand, and then back to Oxford once again. Wedding actual parish documents with the personal voices of these relatives, Stallworthy forms layers of imagery—hands, journeys, germination, trees, and branches—unified by genetic meshes from which, paradoxically, a distinctive poetic voice arises. The poem "The Almond Tree" is a culminating example of such a fusion of voices when the speaker discovers his first-born son suffers from Down's syndrome and, in a Wordsworthian inversion of perspectives, he experiences his own rebirth "fathered by my son."

But Stallworthy's life has been shaped as much by Oxford, England, where he was raised, educated, and employed, and where today he serves as professor of English literature at Oxford University, as by his colonial heritage. From 1948 to 1953 Stallworthy attended Oxford's prestigious Rugby School, where under the tutelage of T. D. Tosswill he explored the formal properties of poetic meter and versification. Adhering to his teacher's dictum of "life being more important than literature" he not only pursued a passion for rugby that would last well into his twenties, but in 1953 entered the army as a lieutenant in the Oxfordshire and Buckinghamshire Light Infantry and served in Nigeria in the Royal West African Frontier Force. Upon his return to England he entered Oxford's Magdalen College, where he took a B.A. in 1958, winning that year the Newdigate Prize for English Verse for "The Earthly Paradise." He earned a B.Litt. in 1961 working with Maurice Bowra on a thesis exploring W. B. YEATS's creative processes, a work that would later inform his critical study Between the Lines: W. B. Yeats's Poetry in the Making (1963). In 1960, Stallworthy married Gillian Waldock, with whom he had three children, Jonathan, Phillippa, and Nicolas. His successful career as a poet has been paralleled by his work as an editor for Oxford University Press (1959–77) and as an award-winning biographer. His edited works, The Oxford Book of War Poetry (1984) and The Complete Poems and Fragments of Wilfred Owen (1983), are underpinned by his highly acclaimed biographical study of the war-poet WILFRED OWEN (1974), a work that earned him the Duff Memorial Prize, the W. H. Smith Award, and the E. M. Forster Award of the American Academy of Arts and Letters.

See also "A POEM ABOUT POEMS ABOUT VIETNAM."

BIBLIOGRAPHY

Stallworthy, Jon. Rounding the Horn: Collected Poems. Manchester, Eng.: Carcanet, 1998.
———. Singing School: The Making of a Poet. London: John Murray, 1998.

Patricia M. Feito

"STAR-GAZER" LOUIS MACNEICE (1963)

"STAR-GAZER" LOUIS MACNEICE (1963)   One of LOUIS MACNEICE's last poems, "Star-gazer" is a fitting coda to his career. As many of his poems do, it combines a desire to touch the world with an acute sense of its distance. The poem begins with a memory from 42 years earlier, of "darting from side to side" to see stars framed in the windows of a moving train. But it is not simply the beauty of the "intolerably bright / Holes, punched in the sky" that is striking: The narrator also recalls having been excited "partly because / of their Latin names" and "partly because I had read in the textbooks / How very far off they were." As the train window does, the Latin names and textbooks frame his experience, heightening his appreciation even as they dilute the immediacy of the "unwonted sight." The stanza ends with the reflection that the light of the stars "had left them (some at least) long years before I was," suggesting a physical reality that existed long before the subject and his perceptive apparatus stumbled on the scene. In William McKinnon's words, for Mac-Neice, "transcendent ultimates . . . reveal themselves in phenomenal experience." This experience, however, is never quite enough. The world, as MacNeice says in "Snow," is "incorrigibly plural," yet we are singular, capable only of short-lived glimpses framed by a window.

The second stanza of "Star-gazer" continues the theme of displacement. The light that left the stars 42 years ago "will never arrive / In time for me to catch it." Not only is he too late, seeing the echo of a light that came into being before he was born, he is also too early. The poem ends with the suggestion that when that light does arrive, there may not be "anyone left alive / To run from side to side in a late night train / Admiring it and adding noughts in vain." The apocalyptic suggestion simultaneously draws our attention to the intensity of the original experience and to its inconsequentiality in the face of a world that will continue even after we have gone. "Star-gazer" becomes an elegy not only for we who pass, but for a world that surrounds us in time and space and yet will never be seen.

The casual, conversational tone and irregular end rhymes that descend through the poem create a deceptively smooth surface for MacNeice's reflections on human frailty. Terence Brown notes that MacNeice's parentheticals, as in the opening two lines and at the close of the first stanza, bespeak a desire for "accuracy at all costs," signifying his rejection of "inflated and dishonest pretension." Indeed despite the metaphysical bent of some of his work, there is also humility: In MacNeice's poems, the mundane mingles with the metaphysical, poetry with prose, and melancholy with a gentle appreciation for all that *is*. Even as he shows our distance from beauty, he reminds us of the potency of those moments (and memories) that do arrive in time. Though to the universe our noughts may be "in vain," they are not to us.

BIBLIOGRAPHY
Brown, Terence. *Louis MacNeice: Sceptical Vision.* Dublin: Gill and Macmillan, 1975.
McKinnon, William T. *Apollo's Blended Dream: A Study of the Poetry of Louis MacNeice.* Oxford: Oxford University Press, 1971.
Norton Anthology of Modern and Contemporary Poetry. 3d ed. Edited by Jahan Ramazani, Richard Ellman, and Robert O'Clair. New York: W. W. Norton, 2003.

Aaron S. Rosenfeld

STEVENSON, ANNE (1933–)

STEVENSON, ANNE (1933–)   Anne Stevenson was born in England of American parents, the philosopher Charles Stevenson and Louise Destler. Educated in America, she traveled back and forth across the Atlantic many times but has spent most of her adult life in Britain. She is not wholeheartedly claimed by the literary establishment of either country, and this may be why she is not better known.

Stevenson writes about her two countries. Her poems are of place, of landscape, of custom and relationship. They are musical, lively, and ironically affectionate. Her early poems had a formal structure, but even her latest make use of rhyme. Her father was an amateur musician and Anne herself studied music at the University of Michigan before turning to poetry. The cadence of her verse recalls the phrasing of the musical line. It flows easily and is pleasing to read. Anchoring the ethereal to earth, however, is an intellectual pithiness that surprises and satisfies the reader, providing substance along with pleasure. Stevenson's first success was in America with *Correspondences*

(1973), which relates the history of a New England family with alternating letters, prose, and poetry. Her later work is better known in Britain. Throughout her poetry, a strategy that appears in various forms is an exploration of the relationship between two opposing or related topics, sometimes using this to approach a larger truth or question. In "Living in America," she contrasts attitudes of the East Coast and West Coast in order to assess the spiritual state of American culture. "On the Edge of the Island" uses the meeting of land and sea to speak of the individual path, of choice, of longing. "Meniscus" has "the moon at its two extremes / promise and reminiscence" as she ponders the proximity of happiness and loss, distrusting her ability to see "as from mirror to distorting mirror." It is as if she is perpetually negotiating between her two identities, trying to articulate the impossibility of two truths at once, expressing what anyone who has lived in two cultures feels, "of being entirely here, yet really not being."

Stevenson is a contemporary of SYLVIA PLATH, born two months after the famous poet. It has been said that her poetry bears some resemblance to Plath's, and both women were from New England, married and living in Britain, struggling to write while raising young children. More important, however, is her role as the poet's biographer, which for a time overtook her own poetic vocation. Having already published several books of poetry, Stevenson gained attention for *Bitter Fame,* her 1989 account of Plath's life and marriage. The biography was the first to examine Sylvia's part in the failed marriage and provoked a furor of controversy at the time of its release. Although her position was later vindicated, the pain caused by the book's initial reception marked Anne and she resolved never to write another biography. Her 1990 book of poetry contains "Three Poems for Sylvia Plath," which are Plath-like in their anger and sharply rendered images. Particular is a sense of competition that emerges. Anne acknowledges Plath as "the fiercest poet of our time," but says to Sylvia in her "Letter to Sylvia Plath," "My shoulder does not like your claw."

Anne Stevenson has been married four times. She has a daughter from her first marriage, and two sons from the second. She currently lives with her hus-band, Peter Lucas, in Durham, England, at the top of one of its steepest hills. She continues to write. No longer truly American, nor wholly British, she appropriately titled her latest collection of poems *A Report from the Border* (2003). In spite of her uncertain citizenship, she has entered the public life of the British nation. A line from her poem "North Sea Off Carnoustie" graces the entrance to the Deep, a new aquatic center in the Humber estuary at Hull. Stevenson has accomplished what Plath could not. She raised her children. She survived the loss of love. She has survived the practice of her art.

BIBLIOGRAPHY
Hickling, Alfred. "Border Crossings." *Manchester Guardian,* 2 October 2004. Available online. URL: http://books. guardian.co.uk/poetry/features/0,12887,1317578,00. html. Accessed on May 30, 2006.
Stevenson, Anne. *Bitter Fame.* London: Penguin, 1989.
———. *The Collected Poems, 1955–1995.* Oxford: Oxford University Press, 1996. Available online. URL: http://www.anne-stevenson.co.uk/index.htm. Accessed May 30, 2006.

Mary VanOeveren

"STILL FALLS THE RAIN" EDITH SITWELL (1941)

EDITH SITWELL wrote the critically successful and popular poem "Still Falls the Rain" in response to the World War II bombing raids over London. No doubt the poem's solemn, vigorous sounds and rhythms, as well as the accessibility of the poem's tropes and Christian imagery, made it possible for British citizens weathering the war at home to experience the poem as an occasion to express despair and entertain hope.

Sitwell strikes a grave and commanding tone in the poem through her use of repetition and an irregular mix of iambs and trochees. Until the end of the piece when she relieves despair with a final note of hope, the speaker rhythmically reiterates the impossibility of escaping the human violence and greed that drive war with the recurring phrase *Still falls the Rain.* Refusing, nevertheless, to surrender to meaninglessness, Sitwell the poet insists upon order and cohesion by deploying rhyme and consonance throughout. A handful of lines are end rhymed with the recurring *Still falls the Rain,* and numerous lines are end rhymed with successive lines. End rhymed lines do not compromise the somber seriousness of the poem, however, because the poet often follows a relatively short poetic line with a long, complex rhyming companion line. To knit elements of the poem together further, the poet deploys consonance, repeating over the course of the poem, for instance, words that begin with *b* like *blind, blood, breed, brain,* and *baited bear.* Just as the poet appropriately marries a trochee to an iamb in the title of this poem about falling bombs, fallen man, and, ultimately, rising hopes, so does the poet marry falling trochees and rising iambs in lines throughout the poem.

Manifesting Sitwell's lifelong poetic strategy of condensing imagery and tropes and her later allegorical Christian imagery, the poem conveys meaning through a simple but rich mixture of tropes. The "dark," "black," and "blind" rain evokes both the bombs falling day after day and the benighted, materialist human mentality that results in war. Dives, Cain, and Judas—who betrayed Christ's life for the silver that purchased the "Field of Blood"—exemplify mind-sets that are motivated by avarice to sacrifice human life. The man who traded his soul for knowledge and wealth, Dr. Faustus, joins the other exemplars of greed in the poem when the speaker quotes lines that Faustus speaks in Marlowe's *Dr. Faustus* (1604): "O Ile leape up to my God: who pulles me doune." Christ, of course, is the victim of, and antidote to, such annihilating values. Tortured like the "blind and weeping bear whom the keepers beat," Christ is a vehicle by which the speaker and those who have suffered through the war can experience and grieve their own suffering. Having been a mortal "child" who lay "among beasts," he is evidence that other humans *can* overcome their violence and nurture human life. Thus in the poem's final line does his statement *Still do I love* overpower and eclipse the despair manifest in the speaker's refrain *Still falls the Rain.*

BIBLIOGRAPHY

Glendinning, Victoria. *Edith Sitwell: A Unicorn among Lions.* London: Weidenfeld, 1981.

Leader, Jennifer. "'There Never Was a War That Was Not Inward': Empathic Agency and Christian Trope in the World War II Poetry of Edith Sitwell, Kathleen Raine and Marianne Moore." *Religion and the Arts* 2, no. 1 (spring 1998): 42–68.

Sitwell, Edith. *The Canticle of the Rose: Poems 1917–1949.* New York: Vanguard, 1949.

Slateliggett, Pamela. "The Vision of Edith Sitwell: Prophecy and Sensation in Her World War II Poetry." *Language and Literature* 22 (1997): 93–102.

Robin Calland

"STILL-LIFE" ELIZABETH DARYUSH (1938) First published in ELIZABETH DARYUSH's *Verses: Sixth Book* (1938), "Still-Life" is an English sonnet written in decasyllabics. The poem is one of Daryush's most well known poems, and the poet and critic Yvor Winters noted that the poem is "one of her most brilliant successes in syllabic meter." Winters also said of the poem: "There is certainly nothing in the work of the American masters of free verse to surpass it and there is little to equal it."

The poem richly describes a youthful heiress's surroundings early in the morning. Without revealing that the subject of the poem is a young heiress until the second stanza, Daryush gives careful clues to this in her first stanza—"polished breakfast-table," "a service of Worcester porcelain," and "butter in ice." There seems to be innocence in the heiress and her lifestyle, but also ignorance of those who have far less than she—"Feeling that life's a table set to bless / Her delicate desires with all that's good." Therefore, subject matter certainly deals with social issues that Daryush was somewhat consumed with at the time. Of course the fact that she herself had a privileged background and that she struggled with this gives more depth to the poem. The poem concludes with irony in that the heiress feels her future is only filled with good. Although it is implied that it will be, it further exaggerates her lack of awareness of others' realities. Daryush's sonnet "Children of Wealth" is oftentimes referred to as the companion piece to "Still-Life" and is also considered to be another of her best poems.

BIBLIOGRAPHY

Murphy, Francis, ed. *Yvor Winters: Uncollected Essays and Reviews.* Athens, Ohio: Swallow Press, 1972.

Jenny Sadre-Orafi

"STRANGE MEETING" WILFRED OWEN
(1919) WILFRED OWEN was essentially unknown as a poet when he was killed in action at the age of 25 on November 4, 1918, just one week before Armistice. Nonetheless "Strange Meeting" was immediately hailed as one of the most powerful poems written about World War I when it was published soon after his death in the 1919 edition of EDITH SITWELL's anthology WHEELS: AN ANTHOLOGY OF VERSE and in SIEGFRIED SASSOON's 1920 collection of Owen's poems. Sassoon later called "Strange Meeting" "Owen's passport to immortality."

The poem begins with a soldier describing how he apparently escaped from battle by descending a "profound dull tunnel" to a "sullen hail" where "encumbered sleepers groaned." Probing the sleepers, the soldier is surprised when one of them springs up and seems to recognize him. The soldier knows by the awakened man's "dead smile" that they are in hell. Still, since none of the blood or sound from the guns reaches their underground location, the soldier assures his new "strange friend" that "there is no cause to mourn." The awakened man's reply completes the poem. He tells the soldier that, as he did, he strove after the "wildest beauty in the world," that he too was a poet, and that worse than his death is the loss of the truth he might have written: "I mean the truth untold / The pity of the war, the pity war distilled." Unaware of the truth of war that his poetry would have revealed, future generations will continue to wage wars. In the final lines of the poem, the awakened sleeper tells the soldier, "I am the enemy you killed, my friend": that he was the enemy soldier the soldier had bayonetted to death the day before. Now the two soldier-poets are united not only in hell, but presumably in death, as the poem ends midline with the awakened man's invitation, "Let us sleep now."

"Strange Meeting" displays both Owen's literary heritage and his innovative experimentation with language. The tunnel leading to hell draws upon classical journeys to the underworld as well as Owen's World War I experiences of trench warfare. That the tunnel dates back to "titanic wars" broadens the historical scope of the poem beyond World War I and extends Owen's lament for "the pity of war" to all wars. Owen reinforces this universal condemnation of war by never specifying World War I in the poem or the nationalities of the two soldiers. *Titanic wars* also alludes to John Keats's unfinished epic *Hyperion* and dream vision *The Fall of Hyperion.* Later the awakened poet-soldier's references to "beauty" and "truth" again evoke Keats, Owen's favorite poet. The dream-vision quality of the first soldier's experience is suggested in the poem's opening line word *seemed*—"It seemed that out of battle I escaped"—and his later description of the awakened soldier as a *vision*—"With a thousand pains that vision's face was grained." Read as a dream vision, the poem represents the soldier's descent into the depths of his own mind, where he encounters his poetic self. The irony that the new friend the soldier has just met is the very enemy whom yesterday he "jabbed and killed" is compounded by the idea that the soldier had to betray his own poetic ideals in order to accomplish his killing duty as a soldier. The first soldier's journey, then, is both mythological and psychological, yet the horrors of Owen's own trench dugout experiences, recounted in his letters, invest the literary with the truth of actuality.

The romantic poet who most informs "Strange Meeting" is not Keats, though, but Percy Bysshe Shelley. Shelley's poetry, especially his beliefs in nonviolence and the redeeming power of love and his conviction that poetry can change the world, influenced Owen profoundly and "Strange Meeting" particularly. The title of the poem is from Shelley's *The Revolt of Islam,* canto V, line 1831. Here Laon urges his followers not to seek vengeance on the surrounded enemy soldiers, who had just massacred a camp of their compatriots, and calls upon the enemy to throw down their arms, appealing to the humanity he knows exists beyond their bestiality as hired killers. Enemy and patriots gather around Laon in "a strange meeting" and march together, "a nation / Made free in love," to the Golden City, whose citizens joyfully open their gates to the new brotherhood.

The similarities between *The Revolt of Islam* and "Strange Meeting" are striking, but the subtle, ironic differences within those similarities are even more meaningful. For example, both Laon and the "enemy" soldier were stabbed—the first speared and the second bayonetted—when they gave their speeches of peace, but because the soldier in "Strange Meeting" has died of his wound, he can tell only the soldier who has awakened, and had killed, him what he "would" have said and grieve that since the truth of the pity of war will remain "untold": "Now men will go content with what we spoiled, / Or, discontent, boil bloody, and be spilled. / They will be swift with the swiftness of the tigress, / None will break ranks, though nations trek from progress." Laon's success underscores by contrast the "hopelessness" the awakened poet-soldier predicts for the future in "Strange Meeting."

Owen's technical innovations also enhance the themes of "Strange Meeting." John Middleton Murry, one of Owen's earliest reviewers, recognized that Owen's use of "assonant endings"—which EDMUND BLUNDEN later termed pararhymes—were a "discovery of genius" and especially suited to the "subterranean" tone of "Strange Meeting." A pararhyme is a slant, or partial, rhyme in which words have similar consonants before and after unlike vowels: escaped and scooped, groined and groaned, bestirred and stared. Nearly all of the end rhymes in "Strange Meeting" are pararhyme couplets, with one pararhyme triplet at the ends of lines 19–21: hair, hour, and here. There is one half-rhyme, in which only the final consonants correspond, at the ends of lines 6–7: eyes and bless. The final line of the poem stands alone, unfinished, consistently with the effects of unfulfillment produced by the pararhymes. D. S. R. Welland was one of the first critics to suggest the way "half-rhyme is perfectly suited to the inconclusive nature of much of Owen's poetry, the unanswered questions, the ghosts that are so movingly raised but never laid." Continually disappointing the readers' expectations for the perfect rhyme, the partially rhyming second word usually lower in pitch than the first word (what Welland identifies as Owen's deliberate "falling-vowel sequence"), the pararhymes in "Strange Meeting" provide a sound equivalent for the poem's theme of failure and melancholy tone.

Owen drafted a preface to the volume of poetry he had planned to publish that stated, "Above all I am not concerned with Poetry, / My subject is War, and the pity of War. / The Poetry is in the Pity." "Strange Meeting" presents Owen's most direct poetic expression of this subject and represents his hope that his poems might reach the imagination and evoke the pity of his readers in time to ensure the poem's dire prophecy of ongoing future warfare will not be fulfilled.

BIBLIOGRAPHY
Blunden, Edmund. "Memoir." In The Poems of Wilfred Owen, edited by Edmund Blunden, 3–41. London: Chatto, 1931.

Hibberd, Dominic. Owen the Poet. London: Macmillan, 1986.

———. Wilfred Owen: A New Biography. London: Weidenfeld & Nicolson, 2002.

Lane, Arthur. An Adequate Response: The War Poetry of Wilfred Owen and Siegfried Sassoon. Detroit: Wayne State University Press, 1972.

Murry, J. Middleton. "The Poet of War." Nation and the Athenaeum 28, no. 21 (1921): 705–707.

Owen, Harold, and John Bell, eds. Wilfred Owen: Collected Letters. London: Oxford University Press, 1967.

Stallworthy, Jon, ed. The Poems of Wilfred Owen. New York: W. W. Norton. 1985.

Welland, D. S. R. "Half-Rhyme in Wilfred Owen: Its Derivation and Use." Review of English Studies (New Series) 1, no. 3 (1950): 226–241.

Robert R. Watson

"STRIKE" VERONICA FORREST-THOMSON (1976)
"Strike" is a good example of the theory of poetic artifice that VERONICA FORREST-THOMSON puts forward in her posthumous theoretical book Poetic Artifice. In this poem she uses odd positioning of words, parataxis, allusions, and fantasylike events to make us rethink the reading process. In Poetic Artifice, she states, "It is only though artifice that poetry can challenge our ordinary linguistic orderings of the world, make us question the way in which we make sense of things." In this three-part poem, she employs artifice, specifically poetic tropes, for just that effect, to make us reexamine what it means to make meaning in a poem. At the same time, she explores some of her main themes, such as how we create and represent identity through language.

The beginning alerts us to problems of reference in language, problems that many Postmodern poets discuss. The title Strike is followed by an epigraph, for Bonnie, my first horse. This does not seem unusual until we read the first stanza, but the elements included in it make us rethink the title. For example, the narrator references mounting an animal and talks about a saddle, but the horse quickly transforms into a Siamese cat that only eats "strawberries and cream," and we are told that the narrator has problems with "the authorities." By the end of the first section, we are forced to reconsider the title and the epigraph. *Strike* at this point can be seen to refer to a strike, an action against an employer or authority, or it could be the striking of the horse's hoof, which in itself is odd considering that our horse has transformed into a cat, or it could be the action of the poem on the reader, a striking. Whatever our interpretation is, Forrest-Thomson makes the reader step back and consider the referential possibilities in language, especially with regard to poetic language. Every poem, according to this poet, exists in the specific language of poetry, and that language is multireferential and distinct from ordinary language practices.

Moreover this poem defies a straightforward narrative. We start with a journey motif, and we end with one, but the narrative of that journey is fragmentary and leads us through parts of the poet's identity that we are not necessarily privileged to know and leaves us in front of a "god we have not met." Throughout the poem, the narrator's disrupts the narrative with repetition, commentary, and allusions to poets like T. S. ELIOT. Especially in the last section, the narrator focuses on a journey, but a journey with a narrative that is broken, impossible, or withered. In the end "Strike" is as much a commentary on the nature of poetic meaning as it is an exploration of identity as constructed through language.

BIBLIOGRAPHY

Forrest-Thomson, Veronica. *Collected Poems and Translations.* London: Allardyce, Barnett, 1990.

Mark, Alison. "Poetic Relations and Related Poetics: Veronica Forrest-Thomson and Charles Bernstein." In *Assembling Alternatives: Reading Postmodern Poetries Transnationally,* edited by Romana Huk, 114–127. Middleton, Conn.: Wesleyan University Press, 2003.

William Allegrezza

SURREALISM Although surrealism officially began in 1924 with the publication of the *Manifeste du surréalisme,* or the *Manifesto of Surrealism,* by André Breton, the movement actually has strong roots in writers, thinkers, and movements extant years previously. Breton's definition of a movement defined by a refutation of logic and a ready assumption of the seemingly irrational owes much to such antecedents as Apollinaire, Freud, and the dadaist movement. Although in the course of time surrealism traversed the boundaries between literature and the other arts, it began as a philosophic and literary movement, one inseparable from the intellectual opportunities of contemporary Paris and the pressures and disillusionments of current events. At its most basic, surrealism denied logic and the workings of the rational mind, preferring instead the importance of the abstract and the unconscious mind.

Given its Parisian origins, not surprisingly many of surrealism's direct influences were also French writers and thinkers. Indeed, it is Guillaume Apollinaire, and not Breton, who may be credited with the actual coining of the term *surrealism.* Apollinaire, a singularly modern writer, developed an idea of "surprise," or the novel or newly invented, as central to his theories of artistic creation. This concept evolved into what Appollinaire called *le merveilleux,* or the marvelous. Appollinaire further defined his idea of an exceptional, unreal aesthetic in an article published in 1914, titled "Surnaturalisme." A few years later, Appollinaire abandoned this term in favor of what he considered a clearer word, *surréalisme.* Apollinaire's idea of surprise remained central to his somewhat vague description of surrealism. This surrealism depended on analogies, unexpected and illogical connections between real and unreal. Although Apollinaire's surrealism is, of course, different from Breton's, the two movements *do* share important similarities, including an appreciation and demand for the marvelous, and Breton himself recognized Apollinaire's heavy influence upon his own development.

Surrealism also owes much to the dadaists, and many of the eventual surrealists, especially Tristan Tzara, actually began as participants in dada. Breton was himself an enthusiastic follower of dada, although his eventual discontent with the movement's limitations perhaps stimulated the seeds of surrealism. Dada, an essentially nihilistic movement that began in Zurich, decried logic and embraced the hopelessness of reality, blaming traditional methods of thinking for World War I and other travesties. Dada rejected the external world, seeing in its descent into war the utter futility of the arts, including poetry. As did the dadaists, the surrealists rejected the external world. Instead of embracing "nothing" and assuming nihilistic attitudes, though, the surrealists sought to transform reality and desired something more rewarding than futile and toxic logic. In essence, the surrealists transcended dada, accepting its rejection of logic but declaiming its essential bleakness.

The surrealists also acknowledged influences far outside France. For example, the very different intellectuals Freud and Hegel exercised unwitting, but weighty, influence upon the early stages of surrealism. With their strong interest in *le merveilleux* and in the abandonment of traditional methods of interpreting the world, it is perhaps not surprising that Breton and the other early surrealists sought in the unruly world of dreams a way of transcending, and interpreting, ordinary reality. As Anna Balakian observes, "The simplest and most obvious influence of Freudian psychology can be found in the accounts of dreams written by practically every one of the fifty of so bona fide surrealists who contributed to the surrealist periodicals." But Freud and the surrealists, despite moments of mutual admiration, espoused very different goals; Balakian notes that the surrealists' interest in dreams "was not an observation or interpretation of the subconscious world but a colonization." Indeed where Freud saw illness or mental instability, the surrealists spotted possibility. Automatic writing became one of the techniques most readily identifiable in their published works; the idea of completely excising reality and divulging only interior states through their writing resulted in some of their most notable creations. Paul Eluard and Tristan Tzara, for example, were two of the better-known devotees of this technique. In keeping with their persistent desire to communicate the unreal, the surrealists also valued insanity, seeing not disease but an altered relationship with the world. Some surrealists, including Breton, went so far as to probe the meanings and attributes of insanity in their works, actively preferring the trappings of mental illness to

rational thought. All of these differing techniques, from an appreciation for madness to a written record of dreams, can be traced to Freud's influence, but they are also perfectly in keeping with the surrealist appreciation for the marvelous.

The German influence of Hegel was not as immediately felt as that of Freud but had definitely begun to impact the surrealists by the time the movement matured in the 1930s. Hegel's exploration of thought and the workings of the mind provided the surrealists with the ability to meld their emphasis upon the unreal, the marvelous, with the inexorable presence of the real world. If Freud's influence appeared in their creative techniques, Hegel's manifested itself in a reconciliation of those irrational techniques with lucid realism. From Hegel, the surrealists gained a renewed appreciation for the concrete "object," uniting their perception of that object with its external existence. Effectively the surrealists were not influenced by the artistic object, unlike their predecessors the romantics. Rather the object in turn was transformed, manipulated, and changed by the abstract and internal perception of the artist. Unsurprisingly, the surrealists also shared Hegel's high regard for the metaphor, seeing in this figure of speech the ultimate realization of the connection between—and supremacy of—their minds and concrete reality.

Although surrealism was eventually to have a great many famous proponents reaching across all of the arts, its influential founder is undoubtedly André Breton. Influenced at a relatively early age by Apollinaire, Breton was, for a time, one of the most enthusiastic proponents of dadaism. By 1921, however, Breton began to break away from dada, recognizing its inability to effect or promise positive change. By 1924, Breton's conception of surrealism coalesced into the publication of the *Manifeste du surréalisme*. However, despite this work's seminal nature, it was not Breton's first truly surrealist composition. Instead several years before, Breton was writing in what he eventually termed the surrealist style. Along with the poet Philippe Soupault, Breton authored the collection *Les Champs magnétiques*, or *The Magnetic Fields*, in 1920. This first experiment in automatic writing emphasized the unconscious, marvelous workings of the inner mind.

Breton's later works evidence this emphasis on the unconscious mind as well as his many influences. Although Breton himself decried novels, one of his most representative works remains his 1928 work *Nadja,* a work detailing the short-lived and entirely unsuccessful relationship between Breton and a young woman. In *Nadja,* Breton's regard for Freud's work with the insane is obvious; although the woman's insanity quickly lands her in an asylum, the work by no means depicts her as an object of pity. Instead Breton suggests the allure of Nadja's madness; her insanity, he implies, lends a freedom from concrete reality similar to that which may be found in dreams.

Just as dada's initial appeal lay in its reaction to the horrors of World War I, surrealism proved equally connected to real world events. Although Breton and other surrealists admired the German Hegel, Breton was a staunch opponent of Hitler. By 1930, Breton's *Second Manifeste du surréalisme* established the movement as one linked to the real world—despite its renunciation of the ultimate reality of that world. Indeed Breton and the other surrealists were captivated by French communism and their desire for literary transcendence transformed into a need for political change. This initial alliance between surrealism and communism, however, eventually deteriorated into antipathy.

Although Breton published collections of poems, prose, and prose poems, many in collaboration with other surrealists, including Eluard, his regard for poetry was, at times, rocky. He even abandoned poetry for years at a time, publishing instead manifestos; in contrast, other surrealists continued to produce great expanses—and sometimes excesses—of poetry. Surrealism also eagerly leapt the boundaries between literature and the other arts, for a while exercising wide influence over the visual arts; Salvador Dalí, for example, remains one of the best known surrealist painters.

British poetry was late to feel the effects of surrealism, but its influence was significant and lasting. It was introduced to England by a precocious 19-year-old, DAVID GASCOYNE, who in 1935 published *A Short Survey of Surrealism.* Gascoyne's own poetry, starting with *A Man's Life Is This Meat,* paved the way for others, including Charles Madge, Kenneth Allott, and Law-rence Durrell. EDITH SITWELL, in her long choral poem "Façade," anticipated surrealist techniques (she was accused by Virginia Woolf of reciting "sheer nonsense"). It was Sitwell's discovery and protegé, however, who most lastingly made surrealist techniques an acceptable and staple tool in British poetry—DYLAN THOMAS.

The final impact of surrealism was at least as far-reaching as its influences were widespread and variegated. The movement negotiated politics, philosophy, literature, the visual arts, and other mediums during the height of its popularity, and it continued to flourish in occasional bright blossomings throughout the globe even after Breton's death in 1966. Founded on a basic paradox—the hopeful understanding and transcendence of the logical world through an audacious exploration of the irrational, unconscious mind—surrealism produced surprising, marvelous imagery, both written and visual, that remains compelling and popular today.

BIBLIOGRAPHY

Balakian, Anna. *Literary Origins of Surrealism: A New Mysticism in French Poetry.* New York: King's Crown Press, 1947.

———. *Surrealism: The Road to the Absolute.* New York: E. P. Dutton, 1970.

Benedikt, Michael, ed. *The Poetry of Surrealism: An Anthology.* Boston: Little, Brown, 1974.

Bohn, Willard. *The Rise of Surrealism: Cubism, Dada, and the Pursuit of the Marvelous.* Albany: State University of New York Press, 2002.

Bolovan, Margaret M. "André Breton." *Dictionary of Literary Biography.* Vol. 258, *Modern French Poets,* edited by Jean-François Leroux, 72–93. Detroit, Mich.: Gale Group, 2002.

Matthews, J. H., ed. *An Anthology of French Surrealist Poetry.* Minneapolis: University of Minneapolis Press, 1966.

———. *Surrealism and the Novel.* Ann Arbor: University of Michigan Press, 1969.

Remy, Michel. "The Visual Poetics of British Surrealism." In *Surrealism: Surrealist Visuality,* edited by Silvano Levy, 157–166. New York: New York University Press, 1997.

Winter S. Elliott

"SYDNEY COVE, 1788" PETER PORTER (1964)

"Sydney Cove, 1788" first appeared in PETER PORTER'S

second collection of poems, entitled *Poems Ancient and Modern* (1964). The poem was inspired by John Cobley's book *Sydney Cove 1788,* a compilation of diary and journal extracts (among other documents) written by early settlers.

Using an unidentified first-person narrator, the poem recounts the vicissitudes of life in Australia's first colony, which, as the title suggests, was founded by the British in 1788. The poem commences with an almost satirical description of the governor mapping the newly settled territory from within his small boat, the words *round and round* evoking the image of a child at play by virtue of their close association with the popular nursery rhyme "Round and Round the Garden." This scene contrasts dramatically with the ensuing description of life within the colony, a dynamic and harsh world typified by malnutrition ("On a diet of flour, your hair comes out in your comb") and cruelty born of desperation ("A convict selling a baby for a jug of rum").

Porter uses this device throughout the poem, juxtaposing the hopefulness associated with colonialism ("Some say these oysters are the sort for pearls") with the difficult and bloody reality of everyday life ("Genocide or Jesus can't work this land"). Rapid movement from one seemingly unrelated image to another also helps to convey a sense of frontier lawlessness, of almost uncontained heterogeneity. For example, within the small, nascent world of Sydney Cove, men try to sleep with native women, Bibles wash up on the shore, and "mad sharks" roam the ocean. Even the weather is unforgiving, images such as "the blood encircled sun" conveying a strong sense of the constant threat posed by the elements.

Thus within the regularity of the three-line-stanza structure there exists a sense of virtual chaos, of an unruly environment peopled by myriad characters. This tension between form and content is summed up beautifully toward the end of the poem: "Where all is novel, the only rule's explore."

The poem finishes with two lines worthy of a romantic poet such as Wordsworth or Tennyson. Porter evokes a nighttime world in which nature and humanity (represented by the mythical "lovers") live in perfect harmony, while the use of the anachronistic word *Cantor* (Latin for "singer") anchors the scene in the romantic genre. While the final image is that of a world at peace, the reader, unable to shake off the harshness depicted throughout the poem, is actually left with a sense of the contradictory foundations upon which Australia was built.

BIBLIOGRAPHY
Bennett, Bruce. *Spirit in Exile: Peter Porter and his Poetry.* Melbourne: Oxford University Press Australia, 1991.

Emma Carmody

SYMBOLISM   While the use of symbols in literature is anything but new, Symbolism (with a capital *s*) as a literary movement can be circumscribed to a very specific time and place: France in the decades between the 1860s and the 1920s. Etymologically, the word *symbol* derives from the Greek and means "throw together" or "bind": Precisely what a symbol does is to make a concept or object stand for another. Within this general meaning of *symbol* the appearance in critical works of the word *symbolism* almost always makes reference to a specific literary movement that was born in France and extended over most of Europe and to the United States of America. The French poets Arthur Rimbaud (1854–91), Stéphane Mallarmé (1842–98), Charles Baudelaire (1821–67), Paul Verlaine (1844–96), and Paul Valéry (1871–1945) are usually recognized as the classic French symbolist authors. The name of the group was derived from the publication, in 1886, of the *Symbolist Manifesto* by Jean Moréas, and the term took over other alternative labels suggested for the group as a whole or for some members of it. Authors associated with symbolism share a distrust of realism and naturalism, the two literary currents that had dominated French (and most European) literature during the 19th century and that emphasized a scientific attitude toward existence and its representation in literature. Although often confused with decadentism because of their similar subjects and their common aestheticizing character, symbolism should rather be considered heir to the former movement. To symbolists, art needs not be a loyal reflection of reality nor recreate sordid, everyday concerns: Rather, they propose the enigmatic and ambiguous as a worthy subject of art, preferring suggestion to explanation, insinuating to reporting. Although symbolism also flourished in painting, sculpture, and drama, it is considered to be mainly a poetic movement, since many of its most defining characteristics have to do with rhyme, musicality, and other aspects traditionally connected to poetry.

The symbolist creed emphasizes indirect expression, inspiration, and illusory and visionary images, in an aesthetic turn that sees art as a way out of the familiar, mundane reality. Symbolist works can no longer be taken as a reproduction of life but rather must be understood as an evasion of it. This elusiveness is achieved through a sensual, rich language, which emphasizes the aesthetic value of the word itself, and by exploring the connotative nature of art: The purpose of aesthetic works is not to denote, to show what is there, but to connote, to suggest a transcendent reality that lies behind everyday appearances through the use of symbols, where language must be a mediator between the real and the ideal. The defamiliarization from everyday language must be achieved through a style that shares more with music and melody than with immediately preceding literary examples such as Zola: According to Valéry, "prose walks, but poetry should dance." This dance of the words, of the senses and the intellect, is achieved through experimentation, both in the layout of the words and in typographical experimentation in the page, and by stressing rhythm and musicality in poetic compositions. The limitations of fixed rhymes and well-established poetic forms are transcended through the use of free verse or "prose poems," both meters that stress musicality by escaping the constraints of canonical models of poetry: The new poetry produced by symbolist poets should be as fluid and open as music, and this necessity entails the rejection of established versification.

The symbol, alluded to by the name of the movement, makes reference to the comparison between a concrete object or term that is explicit and present in the poem and another abstract idea or concept that is merely hinted at obliquely and in a merely implicit way. The reason for symbolists to use these symbols was, according to Mallarmé, to evoke an object "little by little so as to reveal a mood," what they considered "the art of choosing an object and extracting it from an *état d'âme* [mood]." Therefore we can differentiate two kinds of symbolism: One of them is an "idiosyncratic" symbolism, highly personal and making reference to private connections between the abstract and the concrete, whose meaning is immediately evident only to the poet, the user of said symbol; since the symbol-referent connection is obliterated, the reader is often left with just a symbol and with no key of interpretation to it. Also, symbolism may work at a more general level, where specific material images are used as symbols to represent an ideal or idealized world of which the real world is but a pale shadow: This second kind of symbolism, of clear Platonic hues, transforms the poet, the creator of the symbol, into a seer, who is able to access another world and to express it through the suggestion of meanings and the generation of an adequate symbology. This transcendent side to symbolism is usually connected to mysticism, to religious feelings, and to a general strong sense of spirituality, which are fields that lend themselves easily to their expressions through symbols. Other subjects in the margins of the ineffable, such as death or eroticism, are also common in symbolist poetry, which attempts to go beyond reality into a cosmos of ideas, either in the Platonic sense or concerning emotions within the poet himself. Furthermore, according to Symons (the introducer of symbolist ideas in Great Britain, as we will see) literature through symbolism "becomes itself a kind of religion, with all the duties and responsibilities of the sacred ritual." Symbolism, then, aims at producing what is called "pure poetry," that is, the blending of images (symbols) and musicality, emphasizing the suggestiveness and the music of the words.

Because the movement is associated mainly with continental France, there are not many examples of symbolist poets in the United Kingdom, although the influence of symbolism in British poetry is undeniable. Symbolism as a literary current was introduced by the decadent poet Arthur Symons (1865–1945) in his study *The Symbolist Movement in Literature* (1899), and although Symons did attempt to introduce some symbolist elements in his poetry, considering him to be a symbolist would be pushing the label too far. Symons's interest in the study of symbolism lies, rather, in his making the movement available to the British public, and especially to a series of poets who were starting to write around the time his study was published. During the 1890s there was a general assimilation of French culture in Britain, so Symons's book should be considered within this trend of cultural absorption: Although Symons asserts that symbolism can be "seen under one disguise or another in every great imaginative writer," the best known symbolist poet in Great Britain (or rather, the one who seemed to produce consistently for the longest period work in a symbolist mood) is W. B. YEATS (1865–1939), who transformed his interest in the occult and in Irish myth and legend, and his wish to escape urbanism during his early 20s, into the idealized world of the *Celtic Twilight,* which is reflected in most of his production from those years. Both in occultism's rich symbology and in myth, Yeats was able to find inspiration to turn apart from the real world and into an imaginary landscape. Yeats also was influenced by Villiers de l'Isle-Adam's drama *Axël,* quite possibly one of the symbolist works where the Platonic idea of the world as a dream is best exposed. Yeats would have first had to contact with the French symbolist poets through Symons's book, and many of the poems included in *Sailing to Byzantium* show his interest in transcending reality through the use of symbols and dwelling in a mythical world such as Byzantium or the ancient Ireland he imagined: To Yeats, "it is only by ancient symbols . . . that any highly subjective art can escape from the barrenness and shallowness of a too conscious argument, into the abundance and depth of nature." The origin and real meaning of the symbols Yeats uses to make reference to the different aspects of this ideal world are never completely understood, as is the case with French symbolist poetry, since his intention is to suggest meanings, to provide the reader with some scarce insinuations about what lies behind the symbol, and then to allow him/her to arrive at the core of the symbol, transcending reality. Yeats believed in the magic power of the word, which enables symbols loaded with a hidden meaning to change the "other," mythic world when used in the poem. Also, these words provide symbols that compensate for the depreciated, modern world and that lead us to all those ideals pertaining to long-gone civilizations such as Byzantium.

Although finding "pure" symbolist poets in Great Britain is a difficult task (and even Yeats moved well beyond symbolism after the period we have mentioned), the importance of the symbolist movement in the British Isles can be found in its repercussions in the work of a great number of authors and in other movements. According to Michael Bell, MODERNISM was, in many ways, a second-generation symbolism, and imagist writers such as T(HOMAS) E(RNEST) HULME and EZRA POUND were seduced by the tendency found in symbolist writers such as Baudeleire and Laforge to insist on the direst aspects of reality. While deriving from the symbolist use of images, however, those images used by imagists should be analyzed as metaphors or similes that are defamiliarized so as to surprise the reader (a technique mastered by T. S. ELIOT but already used by Baudelaire). The combination of utterly unrelated images and diction used by Eliot in poems such as "THE LOVE SONG OF J. ALFRED PRUFROCK," its absence of emotion, and the pervading irony of the poem can also be traced to Laforge's style. SURREALISM, among other isms, also took some elements from symbolism (although both movements should be regarded as different in scope and interest), and in general, much of 20th-century poetry (such as that of EDITH SITWELL) shows the influence of symbolism, either in innovative technical aspects that have later become consolidated as trademarks of some kinds of poetry (free verse, musicality, and typographic innovations) or in recurring subjects that still pervade modern poetry, such as the interplay of reality, antireality, irreality, and idealism as concerned with an escape from reality.

BIBLIOGRAPHY

Bell, Michael, ed. *The Context of English Literature 1900–1930.* London: Methuen, 1980.

Chadwick, Charles. *Symbolism.* London and New York: Methuen, 1971.

Childs, Peter. *Modernism.* London: Routledge, 2000.

Carmen Méndez García

T

"TALKING IN BED" Philip Larkin (1960)

Philip Larkin's "Talking in Bed," a short, often anthologized poem, first appeared in *The Whitsun Weddings* (1964). The poem shows two people lying together side by side in bed, presumably in a couple, an unusual image for Larkin, for whom human disconnection, isolation, and longing are more often the situation and the theme. It calls to mind another Larkin couple, the married pair in "An Arundel Tomb," who also are an image of marriage, but a less than perfect one, for while they are united in death, there is no telling what the marriage in life was like.

This couple, too, is troubled by silence, as the poem opens, "Talking in bed ought to be easiest"; presumably it is not. Bed is an intimate place, where one is undressed. In bed, not only the clothing of the day but also the social masks we wear can be laid aside, hence the poem's third line, that this image of two people in bed in an emblem of honesty. Yet for these two, "more and more time passes silently," as their ears are attuned to the wind outside more than to each other, a wind full of "unrest" and dispersal. The poem asserts in a six-word, six-syllable declarative sentence, "None of this cares for us," giving perhaps the foundation for why the couple is unable to show caring and communication. If Matthew Arnold's "Dover Beach" really suggests that two people in a troubled world can at least "be true to each other" as a way to achieve some small semblance of comfort and meaning, then this is the anti–Dover Beach. The couple lies together separately, full of unrest, while one searches for words "at once true and kind."

The implication of the line is that what is "true" and what is "kind" are mutually exclusive; it is difficult to find words that are both. This is a common theme in the poetry of Larkin's avowed mentor, Thomas Hardy, for whom truth and kindness were often in conflict, in poems such as "Her Dilemma," where a woman is torn between the two. A dying man, standing in a church, asks her to say she loves him, which is untrue, but which kindness demands her to say, so that her dilemma is how to negotiate between her love of both values, truth and honesty. Hardy's woman chooses uneasily. Larkin's couple lies in silence. In fact, Larkin asks of his couple an even more modest goal in the last line, simply that they find words "not untrue and not unkind," a kind of slipperiness known to modern advertising and political language. The repeated double negatives of this line make the task seem even bleaker, tortured, and doomed.

BIBLIOGRAPHY

Hassan, Salem K. *Philip Larkin and His Contemporaries.* New York: St. Martin's Press, 1988.

Swarbrick, Andrew. *The Whitsun Weddings and The Less Deceived by Philip Larkin.* Macmillan Master Guides, edited by James Gibson. New York: Macmillan, 1986.

Thwaite, Anthony, ed. *Philip Larkin: Collected Poems.* New York: Farrar, Straus & Giroux, 1988.

James Persoon

"TEAR" THOMAS KINSELLA **(1973)** As does "ANCESTOR," this 24-stanza poem belongs to a group of texts inspired by THOMAS KINSELLA's grandmother. In the poem, the passing of a grandparent is the occasion for a meditation on death and mourning. It first appeared in *Notes from the Land of the Dead* (1972), which takes its title from a phrase by C. G. Jung. Later the volume appeared as *New Poems* (1973).

The poem gives voice to the experience of dying, to the loss of a relative, or rather, of two deaths. At the moment that the lyrical I visits his dying grandmother, the scent of her apron also takes him on a mental journey back in time and makes him remember the soothing words she once spoke when his father (her son) was shedding tears over the death of his infant daughter. In the body of the dying grandmother, the poem presents the wisdom of old age, its knowledge of death and life, but also its willingness to embrace death. The final lines of the poem evoke the pain that life causes, "unless like little Agnes / you vanish with early tears." Death, then, becomes not only part of life: It becomes an alternative to life.

This morbid desire for death, the breakdown of the body, marks the relationship between the lyrical I and the grandmother. Already in the second stanza, the theme of consumption appears in the imagery of both the shrinking heart of the lyrical I and collapsing organs of the grandmother. The poem, however, presents death not only as something to shy away from, but also as a moment that holds its own attraction. The grandmother's hair is evoked in the sixth to eighth stanzas, described as "loosened out like a young woman's," and ultimately the lyrical I is afraid that his grandmother's open mouth might "tempt" him. The allusions to (incestuous) sexual desire also resurface in the image of his consummation of his grandmother's wisdom and insight through an image that furthermore evokes the metaphor of Catholic communion: "her heart beating in my mouth!" The grandmother's physical body thus becomes consumed, not only by death but also by the growing understanding of her grandchild. The final act of physical contact, however, is postponed for after her earthly demise: "When she was really dead / I would really kiss."

The title of the poem, the tear that the father shed for his daughter, also stands as an image for the gift of understanding and empathy that the grandmother passes on to her grandchild. By evoking her compassion at the child's death through a moment of Proustian remembrance triggered by smell, she also reminds the lyrical I of the need to accept death, to cry, and to accept those who mourn.

BIBLIOGRAPHY
Badin, Donatella Abbate. *Thomas Kinsella.* New York: Twayne, 1996.
John, Brian. *Reading the Ground: The Poetry of Thomas Kinsella.* Washington: Catholic University of America Press, 1996.

Ben Robertson

"TEARS" EDWARD THOMAS **(1915)** EDWARD THOMAS wrote "Tears" in Steep on January 8, 1915. The poem appeared the year of his death in 1917 in *Poems,* published under the pseudonym *Edward Eastaway.* Thomas was killed in northern France at the Battle of Arras shortly before *Poems* was published.

The poem begins, simply, "It seems I have no tears left." With such a statement, the speaker—probably a soldier—laments his inability to express grief. Perhaps in witnessing the horrors of war, the person who speaks the lines has been so traumatized that he suppresses his angst as a defensive means of preserving his sanity. The two events he mentions that should have elicited his tears seem relatively benign. Hounds "upon the scent" and the changing of the guard at "the Tower"—presumably the Tower of London—hardly seem events that should cause such a negative emotional reaction. However, the contrast between the two events and actual wartime experience proves to be the impetus for the "ghosts" of tears that the speaker claims to shed. The 20 hounds evoke pastoral pleasure as, "like a great dragon," they flow past him into the meadow. Simultaneously they may remind him of infantry charges—gleeful advances toward martial glory that end often in failure. Combining pleasure and horror, Thomas achieves a dreamlike effect that mimics the conflicted mental state of the observer. The dragon-stream of dogs is exciting but soberingly unstoppable. The changing of the guard also embraces the idea of military glory, but the seasoned observer in the poem sees only naïve pomp that will be obliterated in the visceral reality of combat. The experienced observer realizes that these "young English country-men, / Fair-haired and ruddy, in white tunics," are doomed. In referring to the young men as *countrymen*, Thomas evokes the collective thinking of wartime patriotism, but the noble bravery of the men is, ultimately, futile. The music that accompanies their drill reveals to the speaker "truths I had not dreamed, / And have forgotten since their beauty passed." The speaker seems to disclaim the idealism of the soldiers he observes as something forgotten because it is so ephemeral.

As many of Thomas's other poems do, "Tears" uses images of England to elicit conflicting emotions in readers. While the hounds and the young men are seemingly carefree and energetic, they also participate unthinkingly in organized violence that strips them of individuality to privilege their collective purposes. The dogs are hunters that move in a "rage of gladness," and the soldiers are trained killers whose clothing and music belie their grim purpose. Although Thomas wrote "Tears" before being sent to the front during World War I, he managed to capture the conflicted state of mind of a person confronted simultaneously with idealistic patriotism and the real horror of war.

BIBLIOGRAPHY

Cooke, William. *Edward Thomas: A Critical Biography 1878–1917*. London: Faber and Faber, 1970.

Kirkham, Michael. *The Imagination of Edward Thomas*. Cambridge: Cambridge University Press, 1986.

Motion, Andrew. *The Poetry of Edward Thomas*. London: Routledge, 1980.

Thomas, Edward. *The Collected Poems of Edward Thomas*. Edited and introduction by R. George Thomas. Oxford: Clarendon Press, 1978.

Thomas, R. George. *Edward Thomas: A Portrait*. Oxford: Clarendon Press, 1985.

Ben Robertson

"THAT THE SCIENCE OF CARTOGRA-PHY IS LIMITED" EAVAN BOLAND (1994)

EAVAN BOLAND's revisionist view alters nature's pastoral quality into a haunting evocation of prior suffering and anguish, exposing the trace of colonial erasure latent in an Irish famine road. These roads, funded by an agency promoting economic development, kept at work starv-ing farmers during the Great Famine (1845–50), whose fields were devastated by the potato blight. In a structure typical of Boland's poetry, her speaker localizes her environment—here a wooded setting in Connacht, Ireland's westernmost province—and relates an event—the discovery of the obscured road. The road's remnants convert the Irish landscape, traditionally a metaphor of nationalism in Irish poetry, into a collision of the personal and the historic.

Boland claims a "duality to place": a preexisting space "closed in the secrets and complexities of history" and that same space once "experience[d] in the present." Says Boland, "[We] live not in one of the other but at the point of intersection." In "Cartography," that duality exists in the juxtaposition of the map, symbolic of historiography's master narrative, and the indistinct road, symbolic of a shrouded Irish past that continues to trouble the present. The road conjures for the poet the deprivation of the Great Famine that claimed more than 1 million lives, one-eighth of the Irish population. Yet the poet's personal knowledge of the road and its legacy is betrayed by the inability of the map to indicate such a past.

The map is, then, an "apt rending of the spherical as flat." It not only fails to "show the fragrance of balsam," "gloom of cypress," and "shading of / forest," but also neglects to inform its user of the famine's torment. As an artifact of scientific recording, the map can provide but two dimensions and thus quashes the three-dimensionality of lived experience—in this case, the Irish past. The resulting metonymy, the map demarcating through absence a silenced history, agitates the speaker. What Boland, in her opening stanza, "wish[es] to prove," then, is this: that if the map's alleged exactitude and certainty is flawed, then so must all historiography be called into question.

Boland articulates a distinction between history and the past. The "ingenious design" of the map, "which persuades a curve into a plane," is illustrative of history and its ability to carve a "masterful . . . apt rendering." For Boland, however, that rendering is problematic, for the lived experience of the past "will not be there." Her history is more personal, more felt; it requires not simply recognizing the past, but understanding that the past remains present, locked in Ireland's cultural identity. When the poet discovers the famine road, she does not simply visit the site of history but is exposed to the complexity of the past and her own vulnerability to it even now. The wounds of Ireland's past, submerged in the national psyche and obfuscated by British hegemony, remain nonetheless open and inescapable. Their complexity can be healed only through revealing and contending with the past—with the human stories of the past, which, as the famine road, remain "almost invisible to the naked eye," according to Boland. For Boland, history resides in the personal sphere, where one must contend with the presentness of the past.

The interstice between present and past is particularly germane to Irish poetry, where for centuries cultural identity has been under the threat of erasure through British colonial practices. English language assimilation, first occurring through national schools in the 1820s and 1830s, coincided with an Ordnance Survey of Ireland—an exacting cartographic rendering of the island, ostensibly for taxation purposes, but certainly with military intent as well. The mapping also changed placenames from Irish to English. That the Great Famine followed soon after cannot be lost in consideration of "Cartography," which blends the dubious precision of mapmaking with the cultural decimation of language (an Irish poet writing in English) and the physical annihilation of a populace. The trace of maltreatment, Boland reminds us, resides in the very heart of her homeland. Any ability to locate cultural identity within the historiography of national tradition requires empathy for the past: a capacity to sense, as does the poet in "Cartography," the human suffering of others both then and now.

Boland claims her poems "have to do with the unfinished business of feeling and obsession." "That the Science of Cartography Is Limited" resonates with a fascination for history, a passion for the past, and a fixation on melding the incongruities of both into a felt personal and cultural identity. Use of the famine motif is prevalent in numerous other poems in the same collection, In a Time of Violence (1994), which itself substantiates a shift in Boland's poetry from the domestic to the historicocultural. In a Time of Violence extends this theme begun in Outside History (1990) and solidi-fied in the subsequent The Lost Land (1998), one that physically renders history and the past through the concrete world, exposing the incompleteness of history, much as the map of Connacht in "Cartography" fails to reveal the story of the Famine Road. Similarly, another map, this one in "In Which the Ancient History I Learn Is Not My Own," reveals the occupation of Ireland as "the red of Empire" and "the stain of absolute possession" couched within imperialistic sovereignty. In "THE DOLLS MUSEUM IN DUBLIN," the exhibited dolls gaze mutely at the observer without disclosing the nature of their origins, much as the map of Connacht cannot speak its past. Other poems from these and other collections that may be considered along with "Cartography" include "Famine Road" (War Horse), "We Are Human History. We Are Not Natural History," "OUTSIDE HISTORY," "We Are Always Too Late" (Outside History), and "Quarantine" (The Lost Land). In each instance, Boland's poems bespeak a history that must become personal if their truth is to be revealed and understood.

BIBLIOGRAPHY

Boland, Eavan. "Imagining Ireland." In Arguing at the Crossroads: Essays on a Changing Ireland, edited by Paul Brennan and Catherine de Saint Phalle, 13–23. Dublin: New Island Books, 1997.

———. Object Lessons: The Life of the Woman and the Poet in Our Time. London: Vintage, 1996.

———. "Writing the Political Poem in Ireland," Southern Review 31, no. 3 (summer 1995): 485–498.

Consalvo, Deborah McWilliams. "An Improbable Intersection: The Motif of Famine Consciousness and Tribal Continuity in Outside History and In a Time of Violence. Notes on Modern Irish Literature 9 (1997): 27–34.

Raschke, Debrah, "Eavan Boland's Outside History and In a Time of Violence: Rescuing Women, the Concrete, and Other Things Physical from the Dung Heap. Colby Quarterly 32, no. 2 (1996): 135–142.

Kurt Bullock

"THIRTEEN STEPS AND THE THIRTEENTH OF MARCH" DOUGLAS DUNN It would be easy for a poem about the death of cancer of a loved one to descend into mawkishness or mere autobiography, vital for the writer but either uninteresting or

vulgarly sensational for the reader. DOUGLAS DUNN avoids this fate here by some elegant and unobtrusive formal constraints. The poem is built on a series of parallels and coincidences, beginning with the number 13. There are 13 steps "from door to bed"; his wife died (or was buried—on this point the poem is tastefully, and typically, reticent) on the 13th of March; the poem is written in 13 stanzas; and the number 13, of course, is considered unlucky. Similarly the poem opens with the narrator (whom, for once, we might identify with the poet) taking "tea or sherry" to the guests who visit his ill wife; it closes, "After the funeral, I had them to tea and sherry / At the Newland Park."

The poem's force lies in the narrator's understated recognition that the meaning such forms impose is illusory (in the sense of formal symmetries in the poem *and* social forms such as "having people to tea"). The guests "said it was thoughtful" for the narrator to entertain them after the funeral, but "I thought it was ironic—one last time— / A mad reprisal for their loyalty." The repetition throughout the poem of certain words and ideas—*tea, sherry, visitors, steps* and *stairs,* the number 13, the visitors' trite self-comforting utterance "Her room's so cheerful. She isn't afraid," and above all domestic duties—emphasizes the insignificance of such trivia. Yet just as their formal arrangement prevents the poem from falling into mere sentimentality, so everyday social duties serve as a crutch for the narrator while his wife is dying. His attitude toward them is ambiguous: He knows they do not matter and knows that his role as host and caregiver prevents his own love and grief from being fully expressed, but he understands that this itself may be a blessing, even though it leads to "wept exhaustions."

"Each day was duty round the clock," and the couple must steal their moments of intimacy at night: "Those times together with the phone switched off, / Remembering our lives by candlelight." For all that the poem seems to risk being too personal, it is in terms of his public role (or his escape from that role) that it is possible finally to make sense of the narrator's personal experience. And, because such moments are fugitive, already precious before death has made them finally so, the value is intensified by contrast with the mun-dane reality they impinge on: "Sad? Yes. But it was beautiful also. / There was a stillness in the world."

This simple and restrained style, using undifferentiated abstractions like *sad* and *beautiful,* is extremely risky, especially in a poem with such a subject; this is a poem likely to yield many poor imitations. However, it is clear that a high-rhetorical style would be inappropriate, and Dunn gives several sly justifications of the style and reminders of the artifice that lies behind it. For example, he notes how his wife "fought death with an understated mischief"—just as Dunn's style is understated—"turning down painkillers for lucidity"—just as Dunn turns down the use of flamboyant rhetoric, for the sake of the poem's lucidity.

BIBLIOGRAPHY

Crawford, Robert, and David Kinlock. *Reading Douglas Dunn.* Edinburgh: Edinburgh University Press, 1993.
Dunn, Douglas. *New Selected Poems, 1964–2000.* London: Faber and Faber, 2003.

Tony Williams

"THIS BE THE VERSE" PHILIP LARKIN (1974)

From the jolt of the first line—"They fuck you up, your mum and dad"—to the bare-faced admonishment of the last—"don't have any kids yourself"—"This Be The Verse" consistently refuses to offer the reader any consolations. Do your parents intend to "fuck you up"? Maybe not, but they do it anyway. Are you unique? Only because your parents have added some extra faults "just for you." Can you, then, blame your parents for the way they have treated you? No, because they were "fucked up in their turn" by their own parents, just as you will implicitly "fuck up" any children you might have. The logical conclusion to the endless bequest of misery, which "deepens like a coastal shelf," is to "get out as early as you can, / And don't have any kids yourself."

The bluntness of the poem results not just from its obscenity and frank diction but also from its form. Of the 85 words in the poem, 78 have only one syllable, whereas just two (*another* and *misery*) have three. With the exception of an initial spondee in the words *Man hands,* the iambic tetrameter is relentlessly consistent. Each of the three stanzas is a discrete sentence, and most lines contain full clauses. It does not seem to be a poem that gives us much chance to object or to argue about subtleties.

And yet, though PHILIP LARKIN called the poem "perfectly serious," he also commented that it is "funny because it's ambiguous" (Haffenden 128). The first line is not just figurative (i.e., *your parents mess you up*), but also literal (your parents have "fucked you" into being). Likewise the penultimate line, "Get out as early as you can," is not just advice to die soon; it is also a recommendation for coitus interruptus. With those winking double meanings in play, the poem is as much about sex as it is about parents, misery, and children.

Despite the poem's straightforwardness, it is difficult to say what attitude it invites us to take toward the speaker. Larkin's biographer, ANDREW MOTION, suggests that in "This Be the Verse" Larkin "gives free rein to his bitterest instincts" (Motion 411). But presented so brusquely, the speaker's bitterness teeters toward comic caricature. Perhaps it is the uneasy combination of bleakness and self-ironizing certitude that makes this one of Larkin's most memorized and even most loved poems.

BIBLIOGRAPHY

Clark, Steve. "'Get Out as Early as You Can': Larkin's Sexual Politics." In *Philip Larkin,* edited by Stephen Regan, 94–134. New York: St. Martin's Press, 1997.

Haffenden, John. *Viewpoints: Poets in Conversation with John Haffenden.* London: Faber and Faber, 1981.

Motion, Andrew. *Philip Larkin: A Writer's Life.* New York: Farrar, Strauss & Giroux, 1993.

Swarbrick, Andrew. *Out of Reach: The Poetry of Philip Larkin.* New York: St. Martin's Press, 1995.

Evan Davis

"THIS LUNAR BEAUTY" W. H. AUDEN (1930)

Richard Hoggart finds in this three-stanza, 24-line poem the influence of Laura Riding and ROBERT GRAVES on the early work of W. H. AUDEN (212), but it also demonstrates the young poet's experimenting with form to generate meaning. Humanity has long pondered the strange, preternatural beauty of the night sky: The Psalmist finds the heavens to "declare the glory of God" (19:1), God rebukes Job by asking whether he may bind the Pleiades or "loose the bands of Orion" (38:32), Dante begins and ends each of the three books of his *Divine Comedy* looking upon the heavens, and Walt Whitman concludes "A Clear Midnight" by counseling his soul to contemplate in silence the eternal themes of "night, sleep, death, and the stars" (4).

Auden creates an effect akin to an incantatory chant through his use of rhyming couplets and lines of two and three metrical feet (dimeter, trimeter). The first stanza is composed of seven lines, the second eight lines, and the final stanza nine lines. As the poem unfolds, a greater separation is achieved between our human feelings of love and sorrow and the profound emotion generated by those solemn moments spent pondering the night sky.

Charting the poem's trajectory reveals a vision that is transformed into the visionary. The night sky transcends human history, and, in a movement reminiscent of Milton's "L'Allegro" and "Il Penseroso," daytime, with its social activity, is dismissed in favor of pursuing the sublime contemplatory experiences of the solitary star-gazer. Though the beauty is ethereal, this is no activity for ghosts, but for active physical beings. And, in a move prefiguring Wallace Stevens, Auden evokes a state of pure being, an eternal moment "without human meaning / Without human feeling" (5–6).

BIBLIOGRAPHY

Hoggart, Richard, ed. *W. H. Auden: A Selection.* London: Hutchinson Educational, 1961.

Stevens, Wallace. "Of Mere Being." In *Poems by Wallace Stevens: Selected, with an Introduction,* by Samuel French Morse. New York: Vintage Books, 1959.

Whitman, Walt. "A Clear Midnight." In *Leaves of Grass with an Introduction by Roy Harvey Pearce.* Ithaca, N.Y.: Great Seal Books, 1961.

Chuck Keim

THOMAS, DYLAN (1914–1953)

Dylan Thomas lived only 39 years. In 1952, a year before he died during a reading tour in the United States, he selected 89 of his poems to be published as *The Collected Poems of Dylan Thomas.* As prologue to the collection, he finished one final lyric poem, and that was to be his last completed work. The Irish poet SEAMUS HEANEY, in a brilliant essay, sums up Dylan Thomas's contribution to modern poetry this way: "In the end, Thomas's achievement rests upon a number of strong, uniquely estranging, technically original and resonant poems, including one of the best villanelles in the language. . . . The poems are his definitive achievement. . . . No history of English poetry can afford to pass them over. Others may have written like Thomas, but it was never vice versa" (126).

His unique lyric poetry and, in particular, the live performances and famous recordings of Thomas's reading his poems struck the following generations of poets and readers as an original and exciting confluence of formal, linguistic, rhetorical, and emotional elements. The poems were originally published in several small volumes, beginning with *18 Poems* in 1934, *25 Poems* in 1936, *The Map of Love* in 1939, *Deaths and Entrances* in 1946, *26 Poems* in 1950, and *In Country Sleep and Other Poems* in 1952. (The poems appeared in different volumes and at different times in the United States and England.)

Born in South Wales in 1914 and educated only through grammar school, where his father was a schoolmaster and where he proved a completely undistinguished student, Thomas was largely occupied in his early days with being Welsh, being poor, and being a poet—the three most consistent and influential facets of Thomas's life. While he always expected that his greatest achievement would be in poetry, Thomas published in addition many short stories, a radio play, filmscripts, documentaries, and various other pieces he referred to as "hack writing," produced to ward off the omnipresent poverty in his life, including a year spent as a journalist just after leaving school.

In one of his radio broadcasts for the BBC, Thomas painted a characteristically vivid yet jumbled picture of his early life in Wales: "I was born in a large Welsh industrial town at the beginning of the Great War: an ugly, lovely town (or so it was, and is, to me), crawling, sprawling, slummed, unplanned, jerry-vill'd, and smug-suburbed by the side of a long and splendid-curving shore where truant boys and sandfield boys and old anonymous men, in the tatters and hangovers of a hundred charity suits, beachcombed, idled, and paddled, watched the dockbound boats, threw stones into the sea for the barking, outcast dogs, and, on Sat-urday summer afternoons, listened to the militant music of salvation and hell-fire preached from a soap-box" (*Quite Early,* 3). Tinged with a somewhat threatening vagrancy, this picture of idyllic childhood innocence is part of the material Thomas would draw on for the rest of his life as a poet. Indeed the most prolific period for poetry occurred in his late teens, before Thomas had begun to spend much time away from Wales. Material from the notebooks he kept in the early 1930s reappears in all of his later work, and about two-thirds of his entire corpus was composed between the ages of 16 and 20 years.

Much of his adult life, while he constantly drew on these notebooks for inspiration, Thomas was stuck in the claustrophobic pattern of looking to London as a civilized escape from the grinding poverty and isolation he felt in Wales, and to Wales as an almost idyllic escape from the alcohol and hard living he endured in London. A typical line from a 1935 letter to a friend reads: "I am only just beginning to put words together again. The poetry machine is so well oiled now it should work without a hitch until my next intellectually ruinous visit to the bowels of London" (Fitzgibbon, 163).

Thomas's last completed poem, the 1952 "Prologue," draws upon many of the images and scenes of the collected poems and so reveals some of the important threads in the fabric of his work. Beginning as it does with an ending, "This day winding down now / At God speeded summer's end / In the torrent salmon sun, / In my seashaken house / On a breakneck of rocks" gives both a playful sort of upside-down quality to the poem (and indeed the collection that it begins) but also registers the loss that the poet and reader experience simultaneous with memory and joy, as the day winds down, and the shining summer moment, full of salmon running (though *run,* of course, has become *sun*), must slip away into memory. It is a summer day, naturally, as summer in a northern climate is experienced as the shortest season, the growing season, the one that we prepare for, long for, look forward to, and then, too soon, regret its passing. Typical also is the doubling up of meaning, as this day, just at the end of summer, is "God speeded summer's end," with its echo of the archaic term of farewell *God speed* and

Christian worldview, and Eliot, formerly a Unitarian, eventually joined the Church of England and became increasingly conservative in his religious beliefs.

BIBLIOGRAPHY

Bloom, Harold ed. *T. S. Eliot's The Waste Land Modern Critical Interpretations.* New York: Chelsea House, 1986.

Childs, Donald J. *From Philosophy to Poetry: T. S. Eliot's Study of Knowledge and Experience.* New York: Palgrave, 2001.

Eliot, T. S. *The Waste Land: A Facsimile and Transcript of the Original Drafts Including the Annotations of Ezra Pound.* Edited by Valerie Eliot. New York: Harcourt, 1971.

Laity, Cassandra, and Nancy K. Gish, eds. *Gender, Desire, and Sexuality in T. S. Eliot.* Cambridge: Cambridge University Press, 2004.

Williamson, George. *A Reader's Guide to T. S. Eliot: A Poem-by-Poem Analysis.* New York: Octagon Books, 1974.

Joseph E. Becker

"THE WASTE LAND LIMERICKS" WENDY COPE (1986)

This parody of the great modernist poem THE WASTE LAND by T. S. ELIOT appeared in WENDY COPE's first poetry collection, MAKING COCOA FOR KINGSLEY AMIS (1986). In the second section of that book, Cope grouped her parodies of famous male poets including PHILIP LARKIN, TED HUGHES, and SEAMUS HEANEY under the pretense that "Jason Strugnell," a fictive male persona, had written them. However, "The Waste Land Limericks" appeared in the first section of the book, under Cope's own name, indicating that she claimed it as her own poem to a greater extent than the other parodies. Maria Pérez Novales has suggested that Cope was ridiculing Eliot in "The Waste Land Lyrics," but ridiculing herself in the Strugnell parodies.

Cope's first assault on Eliot's poem was formal: She "translated" each of his five sections of AVANT-GARDE free verse into a corresponding limerick—a light-verse form whose rollicking anapestic rhythms and childish rhymes are normally used to convey bawdy humor. In place of Eliot's serious and portentous tone, Cope adopted a breezy and upbeat voice. Condensing the densely layered mythic and literary allusions of each section into a few key terms, Cope juggled them to poke fun at Eliot's pretensions to high culture. By that process, for example, Eliot's entire "Fire Sermon" section was rendered into "The Thames runs, bones rattle,

rats creep; / Tiresias fancies a peep— / A typist is laid, / A record is played— / Wei la la. After this it gets deep."

As Nicola Thompson has observed, some modern poetry instructors have begun assigning Cope's poem as required reading together with Eliot's original. Pirated copies of Cope's poem are also circulating on the Internet, enabling general readers to have the last laugh at the modernist poem that once confounded them in English class.

BIBLIOGRAPHY

Pérez Novales, Marta. "Wendy Cope's Use of Parody in *Making Cocoa for Kingsley Amis.*" *Miscelánea: A Journal of English and American Studies* 15 (1994): 481–500.

Thompson, Nicola. "Wendy Cope's Struggle with Strugnell in *Making Cocoa for Kingsley Amis.*" In *New Perspectives on Women and Comedy,* edited by Regina Barreca, 111–122. Philadelphia: Gordon and Breach, 1992.

Julie Kane

WATKINS, VERNON (1906–1967)

Vernon Phillips Watkins was born to Welsh-speaking parents in Maesteg, Glamorgan, and spent the first years of his childhood in Bridgend and Llanelli before his father's position as a bank manager took the family to Swansea in 1913. After a year at Swansea Grammar School, Vernon was sent to Tyttenhanger Lodge, Sussex, and then to Repton School, Derbyshire. His parents obviously favored an all-English education for their son, who never learned to speak Welsh. He went on to Magdalene College, Cambridge, to read French and German but found the literature classes little to his liking. By this time, he had already resolved to become a poet, and after a powerful religious awakening he decided to leave Cambridge without taking a degree. He intended to travel abroad but lack of funds and the pressure exerted on him by his family forced him to start work as a junior clerk for a branch of Lloyds Bank in Cardiff in 1925. A nervous breakdown in 1927 led to his move back to Swansea, where he was to remain for most of his life, working as a bank clerk and shunning promotion in order to focus on his poetry.

In 1935 Watkins met DYLAN THOMAS, who encouraged him to submit some of his many poems for publication, but it was only in 1941 that his first book, *The*

Ballad of the Mari Lwyd and Other Poems, appeared. His editor at the publishing house Faber and Faber, T. S. ELIOT, appraised the volume in the following manner: "He has a remarkable command over metre and language; and there's a throb of genuine passion in almost all these poems." By that time Watkins had taken up wartime service, which eventually saw him posted to Station X, the cryptographic center at Bletchley Park, Buckinghamshire, where he met his wife-to-be Gwen (née Davies). The year 1945 saw the publication of *The Lamp and the Veil,* a volume consisting of three long poems. This was followed by *Selected Poems* and *The Lady and the Unicorn* (both 1948), *The North Sea* (translations of the German poet Heinrich Heine, 1951), *The Death Bell* (1954), *Cypress and Acacia* (1959), and *Affinities* (1962). *Fidelities* was the last volume put together by Watkins himself, appearing posthumously in 1968, and the following decade saw the publication of various selections of previously unpublished material.

In his meticulously crafted poetry Watkins attempted to create new myths, which he saw as a means of "conquering" time. In the course of his career the initial paganism he had adopted from the romantic poets developed first into neoplatonism and finally into a highly idiosyncratic Christian view of life. While his frequent references to Welsh landscapes place him firmly within the context of Welsh culture, he also had a wide knowledge of European literature, as his *Selected Verse Translations,* published posthumously in 1977, attests. After the death, in 1953, of his friend Dylan Thomas, Watkins devoted himself tirelessly to the preservation of that poet's legacy, setting up the Thomas estate for his wife and children and defending his reputation in various publications.

Watkins died of a heart attack in Seattle during a visit as professor of poetry at the University of Washington in 1967, and by that time he had made a name for himself as one of the greatest Anglo-Welsh poets.

BIBLIOGRAPHY

Roland, Mathias. *Vernon Watkins.* Cardiff: University of Wales Press, 1974.

Stephens, Meic, ed. *The Oxford Companion to the Literature of Wales.* Oxford: Oxford University Press, 1986.

Watkins, Vernon. *The Collected Poems of Vernon Watkins.* Ipswich, Eng.: Golgonooza Press, 1986.

Patrick Alasdair Gill

"WELSH LANDSCAPE" R. S. THOMAS (1952)

Since 1536 Wales has been integrated into Britain, a constitutional arrangement dominated by Wales's much larger neighbor, England. Under such circumstances, maintaining a distinctively Welsh identity has proved difficult. R. S. THOMAS's poetry regularly engages with this difficulty, as is evident in this early poem.

Despite the title's associations with painting, "Welsh Landscape" does not offer a picturesque landscape description. Rather, as in several Thomas poems of this period (e.g., "Welsh History" and "The Tree'" from 1952), it meditates on the relationship between Welsh history and the present. In Wales, the speaker insists, time is not a linear progression, where the present eclipses the events of history. Rather, layers of history settle like sedimentary deposits, so that "there is no present in Wales / . . . / There is only the past."

Fittingly, therefore, the poem is in the present tense throughout. "To live in Wales," the opening infinitive declares, "is to be conscious" that the past is alive, a consciousness delineated in a series of images drawn from Wales's scarred history. Though, temporally speaking, warfare is long past, nonetheless the "thick ambush of shadows" continues in the fields, as does the "strife in the strung woods." At dusk, "the wild sky" is colored by "spilled blood," which has also dyed Wales's "immaculate rivers." The adjectives in these images all pull historical memories into the present: The *thick* shadows, for instance, remember the thick press of battle, while the *strung* woods imply hidden archers, whose twanging bowstrings resound still above the "hum" of "tractor" and "machine." Even more, there are indications that the Welsh landscape owes its beauty to its bloody history: The rivers do not cease to be *immaculate* just because they are colored with the blood of the past.

Unspoken but implicit throughout is the fact that the bloodshed in Welsh history has often involved conflict with England. Though the poem names no historical figures, it invokes memories of men like Llewelyn the

Last and Owain Glyndŵr, leaders of uprisings against the English in the 13th and 15th centuries. Since, as the poem maintains, the past endures into the present, these conflicts presumably live on, even if the battle-grounds have changed. Hence mention of the "soft consonants" of Welsh hints at the 20th-century struggle to revivify the Welsh language. Read thus, the poem is a call to continue nationalist resistance against England.

Yet even as it apparently advances the nationalist cause, the poem retracts it in a withering closing indictment. Not only is there no present in Wales, there is "no future" either. The country's famous towers and castles are "brittle . . . relics," its ghosts "sham," and its mines "mouldering." Most scathingly, its people are "impotent," "sick with inbreeding, / Worrying the carcase of an old song."

This final dismissal of the poem's subject nation involves a delicate ambiguity, typical of Thomas's work. It could be a genuine elegy for a dying nation, or at least a frustrated lament that Wales is sickening toward nothingness in attempting to live off the dead glories of its past. Or it might be what Wintle calls "apophastic invective," designed to whip a sleeping people into nationalist uprising. However interpreted, it is certain that the poem exceeds its own title, offering a fiercer vision of Wales than is typically available in the casual landscape views.

BIBLIOGRAPHY

Merchant, W. Moelwyn. *R. S. Thomas.* Cardiff: University of Wales Press, 1989.
Wintle, Justin. *Furious Interiors: Wales, R. S. Thomas and God.* London: HarperCollins, 1996.

Tim McKenzie

"WE REMEMBER YOUR CHILDHOOD WELL" CAROL ANN DUFFY (1990)

The potency of this poem results from the absent narrative of the child, which is vividly evoked in the parents' denials, such as "Your questions were answered fully." The adult voices respond to unspecified but readily imagined charges against them; they insist that they did what was best, that the youngster enjoyed a happy and protected environment. However, the repeated *nobody's* work like T. S. ELIOT's actualizations of what is being described as not there.

The resonances of Eliot's malleability with language can often be found in CAROL ANN DUFFY's work, alongside the Browningesque dramatic monologue or the "memorable speech" of W. H. AUDEN. The chilling situations that emerge through the parents' denials may pertain to one specific individual as well as to cruelties committed against children in general. "The skidmarks of sin" consolidate various allusions to emotional and physical hurt: arguments, being locked up, a "bad" man on the moors, unanswered questions, being forced, being sent away to "firm" people. Duffy typically places evocative midsentence words at the end of a line in order to maximize their suggestiveness: "argued / with somebody else," "bigger / than you." Also characteristically, Duffy takes familiar clichés ("it ended in tears," "there was nothing to fear") and invigorates them with a significance that they had lost through overuse. As here, she exposes the way that dead phrases gloss over the complex realities of experience that are hard to express. Shifting between end and internal rhymes, Duffy achieves emphases or contrasts that reach the auditory imagination: *off the light, night; didn't occur, blur; sent you away, extra holiday.*

Each of the three-line stanzas begins with the dismissal of an implied accusation: "What you recall are impressions. We have the facts." By repeating the first-person plural pronoun they harrowingly accentuate the child's helplessness; *we* are the "they" who conspiringly contradict his or her version of a tortured upbringing. Cleverly, monosyllabic "Boom. Boom. Boom" is syntactically the speech of the parents but becomes the effect of their voices in the child's head and the fearful pounding of its heart. Certain phrases particularly connect with the reports of "false memory syndrome," which was diagnosed in children who professed to being sexually abused by their relatives. Because so many instances were recorded during the 1980s, there was a reaction against the children's confessions, and they were accused of fabricating events. The callously rhetorical question that opens the final stanza, "What does it matter now?" mimics the way such cases are forgotten by authorities and the media but never by the victims. In another poem on the same subject, "Lizzie, Six" (*Standing Female Nude*, 1985), the voice of a sex abuser is merely put alongside that of an innocent girl (who is implicitly six years old and given "six of the best"), so that the reader feels her powerlessness. More poems in *The Other Country* (1990) that deal with childhood or the presence of the past include "Originally," "Hometown," "Dream of a Lost Friend," and "M-M-Memory."

BIBLIOGRAPHY
Duffy, Carol Ann. *The Other Country*. London: Anvil, 1990.
Gregson, Ian. "Monologue as Dialogue." In *Contemporary Poetry and Postmodernism: Dialogue and Estrangement,* 97–107. Basingstoke, Eng.: Macmillan, 1996.
Stabler, Jane. "Interview with Carol Ann Duffy." *Verse* 8, no. 2 (summer 1991): 124–128.

Jane Dowson

"WHATEVER YOU SAY SAY NOTHING"

SEAMUS HEANEY (1975) One of SEAMUS HEANEY's most bitter poems, "Whatever You Say Say Nothing" appears in his 1975 *North* volume of poetry. The tone and content of the poem suggest that the speaker, and Heaney himself, was bored with the ceaseless monotony of the "Troubles," which caused almost daily killing in Ulster. Indeed the unchanging, four-line, *abab* stanzas suggest a perpetual stasis. Seeing bomb craters and machine-gun posts is no longer sensational or noteworthy, but dreary and depressing: Seeing the results of fresh hostilities seems like mere "déja-vu." The speaker is bored with foreign media representatives asking for his views about the conflict. Considerable disdain is implied against the media circus, the camera crews, and reporters who seem to exploit rather than merely relay information about the multiple atrocities.

The speaker is also bored and frustrated by the clichés that Northern Irish men and women use to deflate accusations of intellectual culpability for the violence. Polite and bland, people blame extremists for the carnage, washing their hands of any accusations of prejudice or tacit support for armed actions. On occasion, there is a fleeting moment of humor. However, humorous clauses are followed up immediately by more rueful reflections. For example, the walking-on-eggshells diplomacy necessary in strife-torn Ulster is noted with amusement: "Smoke-signals are loud-mouthed compared with us." The next line urges a more cynical,

suspicious reading of such tact: "Manoeuvrings to find out name and school" are not just diplomatic, but hostile, as the discovery of names and backgrounds will reveal the religious and tribal affiliation of an individual (in 1970s' Northern Ireland, virtually all adults had been educated at denomination-specific schools). The poem, however, is unusual for an Irish Troubles poem of its period, because its target for satire and condemnation is not sectarian extremism, but exponents of middle-of-the-road platitudes. To claim a dissociation with the violence is to be "expertly civil tongued": Expressions of antitribalism and disdain for political agitators are constructed, contrived, and insincere.

Heaney's achievement in this poem is controversial. He derides banal expressions of feckless nonpartisanship—but it is clear that the reality of the dangerous environment makes such hollow diplomacy necessary. In fact, the title is not just a tag of advice but a threat, one lifted directly from a contemporary paramilitary slogan warning against cooperation with perceived enemies. Ultimately, though, the poem retains a bleak vision of the North of Ireland, as even those who claim a rejection of tribalism—those who say, "One side's as bad as the other"—are seen to offer little more redemption than the active bigots who remark mindlessly of their enemies that "you know them by their eyes."

BIBLIOGRAPHY
Bedford, William. "To Set the Darkness Echoing." In *Seamus Heaney,* edited by Harold Bloom, 11–18. New Haven, Conn.: Chelsea House, 1986.
Heaney, Seamus. *North.* London: Faber and Faber, 1975.
Longley, Edna. "*North:* 'Inner Emigré' or 'Artful Dodger.'" In *The Art of Seamus Heaney,* edited by Tony Curtis, 65–95. Dublin: Wolfhound Press, 2001.
O'Donoghue, Bernard. "Seamus Heaney: *North.*" In *A Companion to Twentieth-Century Poetry,* edited by Neil Roberts, 524–535. Malden, Mass.: Blackwell, 2003.

Kevin DeOrnellas

"WHAT I EXPECTED" STEPHEN SPENDER
(1933) As do other selections from STEPHEN SPENDER's first book, *Poems 1933,* this poem gives a glimpse into the mind of an idealistic young writer observing the dull horrors of European life between two world wars. While readers might be tempted to see the

speaker as a once-enthusiastic soldier disillusioned in the face of war's realities, the poem was written years before Spender's service in the Spanish Civil War and World War II. Rather, the poet's disappointment during the early 1930s resulted from less literal battles waged in the trenches of male friendship, literary endeavor, and general life experience.

Heavily influenced by WILFRED OWEN and other Great War poets, the young Spender was acutely conscious that he lived "under the shadow of a war," as he writes in another poem from the same collection. He longed to be one of the "truly great" but was acutely aware of his own weaknesses and insecurities. After leaving Oxford University in 1930, Spender pursued the writer's life in Europe, where he traveled for several years with a series of male companions. His longest sojourn was spent in Berlin, where his friend Christopher Isherwood had settled amid the decadent urban life and ruinous economic state of Germany's Weimar Republic. The youth culture of Berlin—a mixture of political chaos, creative foment, and social permissiveness—made a strong impression on Spender, who immersed himself in the freewheeling life of the homosexual and artistic communities.

However, he often found his partners shallow and despaired of a meaningful mutual connection. Accordingly, "What I Expected" shows a pessimistic view of male relationships. The first stanza lists the speaker's thwarted expectations of "fighting, / Long struggles with men" resulting in his "grow[ing] strong" and "rest[ing] long." Instead, as the second stanza describes, he experiences long, ineffectual days that gradually "weaken . . . the will" and dissipate life's "brightness," barring him from more heroic undertakings. A literal source of the image of "climbing" in the first stanza might be a trip to the Bavarian Alps that Spender was forced to cancel in order to help Isherwood find a publisher for his latest novel. In general, though, the images seem to be metaphorical references to the poet's longing for camaraderie and unity with others of his generation.

The poem's form—four eight-line stanzas with a fairly consistent rhyme scheme—contributes to its doleful music. The least regular rhymes occur in the third stanza, which describes "cripples" with "limbs shaped like questions" and "the sick falling from earth"; this irregularity underscores the sense of brokenness and the speaker's regret at his inability to set things right. In the final stanza even the treasures of art ("the created poem") and nature ("the dazzling crystal") do not survive. We are left with a poignant impression: The discouraged youth, who would later fight censorship worldwide and be knighted for his literary achievements, had envisioned himself a hero but had not yet distinguished himself as a man of action and letters.

BIBLIOGRAPHY

Spender, Stephen. *Poems*. New York: Random House, 1934.
Sutherland, John. *Stephen Spender: A Literary Life.* New York: Oxford University Press, 2005.

Amy Lemmon

WHEELS: AN ANTHOLOGY OF VERSE (1916–1921)

An annual anthology of poetry published in England and edited by the poet EDITH SITWELL and her two brothers, OSBERT SITWELL and Sacheverell Sitwell. Published during the early years of the period associated with MODERNISM, *Wheels* embraced the revolutionary sensibility expressed in the dictum of modernists to "make it new." If eclectic in its subjects and formal technique, the poetry in the anthologies was selected for its experimental quality and its tendency to challenge popular social mores. According to Kathryn Ledbetter, *Wheels* "was a significant aspect of the larger war to redefine modern poetics . . . [and] became a forum for the poetic politics that led to the Modernist revolution in literature" (322). The anthologies featured poetry by the Sitwells, NANCY CUNARD, WILFRED OWEN, Aldous Huxley, Helen Rootham, Iris Tree, and others. *Wheels* achieved a measure of notoriety from reviews by famous modernists such as T. S. ELIOT and EZRA POUND, and for its inclusion of and responses to criticisms in the popular British press and in cultural journals. The first five editions (called *cycles*) were published by B. H. Blackwell, and a shorter sixth edition was published by C. W. Daniel.

The project was not only a forum for experimental writing; in addition, it served a collaborative function by defining the AVANT-GARDE literary community in terms of its complex relationship to the modern age: "Assembling her own community of poets was Sitwell's daring, even grandiose, effort to proclaim . . . her generation as one of the brilliant epochs in the history of literature" (Ledbetter 328). At once providing what Edith Sitwell termed "rhythmical expression for the heightened speed" of the 20th century and lambasting the philistinism of modern Britain, *Wheels* drew its inspiration from aesthetic movements such as SYMBOLISM, POSTIMPRESSIONISM, vorticism, and futurism (Ledbetter 323).

This inheritance resulted in poetry and design features that evoked a dangerous, outré ambience, ranging from shocking and satirical to mystical. The anthologies featured cover art from prominent English vorticists and European futurists as well as send-ups of pompous English society and abstract representations of the dehumanizing effects of new technologies and World War I. Each edition featured a diagram of a wheel inscribed with the names of the anthologized authors as well as the editors and publisher. Nancy Cunard's poem "Wheels," published in the first edition of the anthology, announces the modern sensibility and ambitious nature of the anthologies:

> I sometimes think that all our thoughts are
>   wheels
> Rolling forever through the painted world
> . . .
> Our words are turned to spokes that thoughts
>   may roll
> And form a jangling chain around the world.

The poem combines the ideal and material spheres in ambivalent and disorienting physical images that, if certain on no other point, at least suggest disillusionment with the world as a whole. Cunard's note of casual utterance ("I sometimes think . . .") and her democratic idealism assert the endurance and significance of the mind, whereas the end of the poem suggests an aesthetic ambition to write poetry in order that the poets' thoughts impact history. In its insistent use of the first-person plural (*our*), the poem also illustrates the collaborative nature of the poetic enterprise.

One tactic of *Wheels,* according to Aaron Jaffe, was to "support fictions of a common working group . . .

whether it be of *personal friendship* or of *poetic kinship*" (156). That is, while contributors to the anthology may not have directly helped shape the work of the other contributors, the editors nevertheless fostered the appearance of a close-knit community.

The journal was founded in the midst of World War I, and Kathryn Ledbetter sees in its genesis an opposition to "the attitudes of those who had created the disaster of modern society" (322). However, any political aims the anthologies may have contained were subordinated to the ambition of revolutionizing the form of poetry. As Edith Sitwell explained, "A change in the direction, imagery, and rhythms in poetry had become necessary, owing to the rhythmical flaccidity, the verbal deadness, the dead and expected patterns, of some of the poetry immediately preceding us" (Ledbetter, 323).

These aesthetic aims implicitly repudiated the aesthetics of both Victorian poetry, with its emphasis on lofty human sentiment, and the popular Georgian verse anthologies, which sought to present poetry to the masses and emphasized idyllic pastoral scenes. For the editors of *Wheels,* these sources together represented the bourgeois reading tastes of the majority of the public. In this sense *Wheels* is a modernist project insofar as it rejects popular reading tastes and embraces poetry directed toward the highly literate, specialized reader.

One literary institution against which the editors of *Wheels* revolted was F. T. Palgrave's influential *Golden Treasury* anthology (1861) of the Victorian period, which was richly engraved and dominated by the work of Lord Tennyson and other male Victorians. Perhaps the most immediate source of the Sitwells' impetus for *Wheels,* however, was the wildly popular series of anthologies called *Georgian Poetry,* published in five volumes from 1912 to 1922 and edited by Edward Marsh, which featured popular poets such as RUPERT BROOKE, W. H. DAVIES, and WALTER DE LA MARE. These anthologies, lionized by the literary establishment of the day, won accolades from conservative reviewers and sold in numbers far beyond the circulation of modernist publications like *Wheels.* The Sitwells objected to the dominance of *Georgian Poetry* on two accounts: First, they objected to the anthologies' implicit declaration of cultural value, that the poetry in the pages of *Georgian Poetry* embodied the spirit of the period. By contrast to the experimental work found in publications like *Wheels, Georgian Poetry* featured conventional pastoral work that appealed to middlebrow tastes. Second, the editors objected to the idea that poetry should be accessible to the vast majority of the reading public. As Osbert Sitwell put it, "Poetry is not, as our 'man-in-the-street' reviewers imagine, a football to be kicked down any mean, squat street by any fool who passes" (Ledbetter 324). Instead he and his siblings believed good poetry was challenging: "Every poem should give its reader's imagination a little much-needed exercise" (Ledbetter 324).

The *Wheels* anthologies were criticized along several lines. First, critics dismissed the poetry in *Wheels* as embodying self-indulgent anguish and adolescent rebelliousness. Second, the poets, and the Sitwells in particular, were attacked for the contrast between their aristocratic social backgrounds and their revolutionary sensibilities. Indeed some reviewers characterized *Wheels* as the pet project of a group of overprivileged aesthetes more interested in causing a social stir than in publishing good poetry. The late 20th-century critic Hugh Kenner embodies a later version of this dismissive attitude when he describes *Wheels* as "more or less a 'family anthology' that endured for six cycles" and rather coldly asserts that the anthologies merely served to give Edith Sitwell "a sense of existence" (158).

Last, and on a related note, the project was severely criticized for its promotional tactics. Constantly seeking ways to increase interest in the anthologies, the editors engaged in public antagonism with critics and were often accused of emphasizing "shock value" rather than work of enduring merit. The renowned critic F. R. Leavis went so far as to claim that the Sitwells, and the *Wheels* anthologies along with them, "belong to the history of publicity rather than poetry" (Jaffe 159). As Jaffe notes, such criticism ignores the satirical elements of *Wheels,* and indeed this last criticism is partly what accounts for the endurance of *Wheels* as a subject of literary interest, for if the Sitwells were determined to reject popular reading tastes, they nevertheless engaged in aggressive attempts to generate substantial attention from the popular press. In one famous episode, Edith Sitwell promised to respond to critics of the latest cycle of the anthology in the next, claiming that the critics

were "properly in for it!" (Jaffe 155). Such rhetorical salvos served the interests of both the anthology and its critics, fabricating a war in the press that served each party's interests.

Ironically this emphasis links *Wheels* to the type of poetry the editors despised. Jaffe argues that the *Georgian* and *Wheels* anthologies "shared a promotional logic that indicates a shared provenance. Promising unheard of exposure, the inexpensive, polemical anthology of contemporary poetry quickly became one of the preferred vehicles for publicity among modernist poets and their contemporaries" (137). In this way, *Wheels* was a characteristic publication of its day and provides evidence of the influence of the burgeoning advertising and publicity industries in the period.

These issues aside, the *Wheels* anthologies occupy an important place in the history of modernist publishing. Herbert Read places the Sitwells as one of "three centers of intellectual ferment" during this period, noting that they "carried on a campaign against the literary establishment" (Kenner 157–158). They played a significant role in bringing to light the work of important figures such as Nancy Cunard, Aldous Huxley, Wilfred Owen, and the Sitwells themselves. Perhaps even more importantly, the anthologies placed poetry written by women on equal ground with work by male contemporaries. The first cycle, for example, contained work by four women and five men. Jane Dowson and Alice Entwistle argue that *Wheels* challenged the gender biases of literary publication. They see in the anthologies a challenge to the notion that women's writing represents a separate literary lineage and, in its place, a "launchpad for a new generation of poets where men and women were on equal terms" (20).

BIBLIOGRAPHY

Dowson, Jane, and Alice Entwistle. *A History of Twentieth-Century British Women's Poetry.* New York: Cambridge University Press, 2005.

Eliot, T. S. "Verse Pleasant and Unpleasant." *Egoist* 5 (March 1918): 43–44.

Jaffe, Aaron. *Modernism and the Culture of Celebrity.* New York: Cambridge University Press, 2005.

Kenner, Hugh. *A Sinking Island.* New York: Alfred A. Knopf, 1988.

Ledbetter, Kathryn. "Battles for Modernism and *Wheels.*" *Journal of Modern Literature* 19, no. 2 (1995): 322–328.

Christopher (Brook) Miller

"WHEN YOU SEE MILLIONS OF THE MOUTHLESS DEAD" Charles Hamilton Sorley (1915)

Charles Hamilton Sorley (1895–1915) was killed in action at the Battle of Loos on October 13, 1915, shot in the head by a sniper's bullet when he was just 20 years old. Thirty-seven complete poems and several unfinished ones were found in his kit after his death. His sole collection, *Marlborough and Other Poems,* was published posthumously in 1916 and became an instant success. Sorley is seen as a forerunner of Siegfried Sassoon and Wilfred Owen because of his unsentimental style and matter-of-fact descriptions of the war. Thus he stands in opposition to poets like Rupert Brooke and John McCrae, as he is able to observe, interpret, and communicate the reality of war honestly and directly.

Written just before his death, "When You See Millions of the Mouthless Dead" is considered Sorley's last poem. Composed as a sonnet, in its title and opening phrase, "millions of the mouthless dead," the poem suggests the massive scale of the devastation caused by the war and emphasizes the incalculable nature of that loss. The first two lines, "When you see millions of the mouthless dead / Across your dreams in pale battalions go," indicate how the poet is haunted by horrific images of the war. As does Owen in "Strange Meeting" and "Anthem for Doomed Youth" he can "see" the dead "across your dreams" as the ghosts appear in their "pale battalions."

The lines "Say not soft things as other men have said, / That you'll remember. For you need not so" convey Sorley's realistic attitude to the war and his disillusionment with its rhetoric. Speeches of bombastic praise, with other memorials for the dead soldiers, will soon be forgotten. Here the poem reiterates the stark reality of death, for in any case the dead are beyond feeling. So praise or mourning is of no consequence to them.

In its concluding lines, the poem makes its main point, the inescapable fact that these soldiers have died, and all that remains is a memory or "a spook" of those who were once much loved. Sorley also brings home to the reader the physical horror of the deformity caused by injuries that have killed the soldiers, in that they are "mouthless"—rendered unrecognizable by their wounds and permanently silenced by them, so that

None wears the face you knew
Great death has made all his for evermore.

Divya Saksena

"WHERE ARE THE WAR POETS" C. Day Lewis (1940)

Written in response to an editorial by the *Times Literary Supplement (TLS),* "To the Poets of 1940," C. Day Lewis's trenchant poem captured the conflict between public duty and private conscience experienced by many British poets at the start of World War II. The editorial had questioned the patriotism of the country's poets, reminding them of their "duty" to sound a "trumpet call" against the threat of the Axis powers. For Lewis and other members of the 1930s generation, already chastened for writing poetry in support of Leftist political platforms, and for having turned poetry into "oratory," according to Virginia Woolf, the call to arms represented a political and aesthetic dilemma. Lewis's response deftly negotiated this conflict by envisioning the true conflict as one between all industrialized nations and poets—"They" against "Us"—thereby problematizing the very idea of war poetry.

Lewis's response to this debate was unique insofar as it was a poetic response; many poets wrote essays in reviews on this same issue. One committed Leftist, Edgell Rickword, also scolded the *TLS* for its ideological blindness: War poets must depict war "not as a temporary disease, but as the culminating criminality of a system," he wrote in "Poetry and Two Wars" (1941). Lewis's poem addressed this systematic corruption in no less damning terms, suggesting that its ideology attempted to infiltrate the very language of poetry. Nevertheless, Lewis tirelessly worked as an employee in the Ministry of Information throughout the war; he remained a believer, however, in his own 1930s political ideals, supporting the Labour Party through the postwar period. It was these "honest dreams" of social equality and justice that positioned him and like-minded poets against the "logic" of patriotism espoused by every warring nation.

Notably in the "Dedicatory Stanzas to Stephen Spender" in his translation of Vergil's *Georgics* (1940), Lewis addressed this challenge yet again ("Where are all the war poets? the fools inquire") in verse that hailed the poets of the 1930s for prophesying the coming war years. Through such revisionary tactics, Lewis managed a middle way between hypocrisy and treason, between totalitarianism and capitalism—a difficult balancing act that his poetry both lamented and embraced, called on as all poets were to "defend the bad against the worse."

BIBLIOGRAPHY

Featherstone, Simon, ed. *War Poetry: An Introductory Reader.* London: Routledge, 1995.

Gelpi, Albert. *Living in Time: The Poetry of C. Day Lewis.* Oxford: Oxford University Press, 1998.

Michael G. Devine

THE WHITE GODDESS ROBERT GRAVES **(1948)** ROBERT GRAVES (1895–1985) first learned of the hypothesis of an ancient matriarchy while researching his novel *The Golden Fleece* in 1944, but long before that he had felt the power of the goddess, in his relationship with the American poet Laura Riding (later Jackson) from 1926 to 1939. Graves's relationship with Riding was intense, both creative and destructive, and produced some of Graves's best poetry, that in which he invokes his muse. Randall Jarrell praises the "White Goddess poems" as "Graves' richest, most moving, and most consistently beautiful" works. Graves formally conceived his muse in *The White Goddess: A Historical Grammar of Poetic Myth* in 1948 and amended and enlarged the work in both 1958 and 1961. This ancient goddess has three faces—maid, mother, and crone, also understood as beauty, birth, and death. The cyclical representations of her nature are derived from the cycles of the moon, the seasons, and life. She is the one who creates the "shiver factor" in poetry, causing hairs to rise and spines to tingle. For Graves, the true poet is such through his attenuation to the White Goddess, who demands that he sacrifice himself to achieve the regeneration he seeks. He states in his foreword to the 1958 edition that "the function of poetry is religious invocation of the Muse; its use is the experience of mixed exaltation and horror that her presence excites" (x).

Graves's thesis is thus straightforward. Unfortunately the details of his argument tend to obscure this fundamental idea. To prove his point, he tries to "decode" *The Song of Amergin,* "an ancient Celtic calendar-alphabet" (Foreword ix). But before he can do so, he must first divine the tree lore disguised in the *Câd Goddeu (The Battle of the Trees).* He discovers in this poem numerous myths held in common by many ancient peoples. Graves claims that such myths were carried to the British Isles in the "second millennium B.C." by Mediterranean Sea people who had been uprooted (30). He also finds an alphabet, designated by the initial letter of each tree and identified by scholars as the Beth-Luis-Nion. Graves then uses this alphabet to decode *The Song of Amergin,* in which he finds hidden the name of a deity too holy to be spoken—Jehovah or, alternatively arranged, Apollo, the deities Graves blames for the decline of the Muse's influence in our time.

Graves argues that logical reasoning is an artificial, male, and sterile practice, akin to homosexuality, and he designates such a thought process "Apollonian" because of its origins in early Greek philosophy. Poetic thought, on the other hand, is a multiple, simultaneous process, combining past, present, and future experience with all of the poet's senses. This is a transcendent faculty, that which divides man from beast, and a precedent for prose clarity. Those who must think in a linear fashion are barbaric, and, according to Graves, such are most contemporary scholars, whose only function in interpreting poetry is to provide and clarify factual information. Contemporary criticism is thus a negative capacity that only allows the exclusion of those poems that do not accord with fact but provides no standard by which to judge those that do.

The book's critical reception has been complicated by the combination of the mysticism with which he decodes the tree alphabet and the bitter invectives he makes against contemporary scholarship. An early draft entitled "The Roebuck in the Thicket" was rejected by publishers in 1944, one of whom stated, "I have to say that it was beyond me and failed to stir any spark of interest," a reaction shared by many critics (Seymour-Smith 395). Still, *The White Goddess* has been influential upon both academic and popular culture. Harold Bloom, one of the century's most powerful literary critics, employs similar ideas of poetic regeneration brought about by the sacrifice of the old king (or former poet) in both *The Anxiety of Influence* (1973) and *A Map of Misreading* (1975). The lead songwriters of Led Zeppelin, Jimmy Page and Robert Plant, were inspired by Graves's conception of the Muse to write their legendary ballad *Stairway to Heaven*. But perhaps its most paradoxical influence has been upon the American feminist movement, many of whose leaders expressed gratitude to Graves for his work. While his reverence for the female power of regeneration pervades the book, he also charges the goddess with an oftentimes whimsical power of destruction. Likewise although he elevates woman's place in the creative process, he also restricts it, claiming, "Woman is not a poet: she is either a Muse or she is nothing" (500). However, his notion of woman writing "as a woman" probably prepared the minds of English and American readers alike to accept the idea of a *feminine ecriture,* female writing from the body, postulated by Simone de Beauvoir and Hélène Cixous.

Much of the critical response, however, has ignored the fact that his argument is a parody of the scientific method, designed to prove that the rational system of logic is fallible because it pretends to be self-sufficient. He defines his method as "proleptic" and "analeptic," by which he leaps to conclusions through intuition rather than a scientific preponderance of evidence. Graves himself acknowledges that his method will not be widely accepted by "orthodox scholars" (383), and this may account for the book's relative obscurity in today's university. Graves's thesis—that poetry springs from a principle of intuition closely aligned with feminine modes of experience and thought construction—is fairly acknowledged. His "scholarly" method is not. Perhaps this is the best evidence that we are still firmly entrenched in an Apollonian world in which, as Graves laments, money is the only arbiter of value, personal salvation is more important than the good of the community, and literal and scientific facts are the only forms of truth.

BIBLIOGRAPHY

Graves, Robert Perceval. *Robert Graves and the White Goddess, 1940–1985.* London: Weidenfeld and Nicolson, 1995.

Jarrell, Randall. "Graves and the White Goddess." *Third Book of Criticism.* N.Y.: Farrar, Straus & Giroux, 1966.

Seymour-Smith, Martin. *Robert Graves: His Life and Works.* London: Bloomsbury, 1995.

Vickery, John B. *Robert Graves and the White Goddess.* Lincoln: University of Nebraska Press, 1972.

Michelle Baker

WICKHAM, ANNA (1884–1947)

The publication of *The Writings of Anna Wickham* in 1984 released her poetry from decades of obscurity. Before the First World War she produced 900 poems in four years; many of these and much of her correspondence were destroyed during the Second World War, but 1,100 unpublished poems and five published collections remained. Born in Wimbledon as Edith Alice Mary Harper, in 1900 she emigrated with her family to Australia, where her education included two Roman Catholic convents and Sidney High School for Girls. In 1904, she returned to Britain and her marriage to Patrick Hepburn in 1906 meant relinquishing a career in opera singing. She had a stillborn child and a miscarriage before her first son, James, was born; he was followed by three more children, but her third son died of scarlet fever in 1921, aged four. When her husband died in a climbing accident in 1929, she was freed from the bonds of a turbulent marriage. Some of her remorse and guilt resulting from these family tragedies and failings fueled Wickham's social welfare work and writing, especially concerning the neglected needs of working-class mothers. She assumed the pseudonym *John Oland* for her first poetry collection *Songs* (1911). On its publication, her husband dismissed her to a private asylum, presumably to prevent further artistic activity and to muffle the troublesome sentiments expressed in her writing. Subsequently she adopted *Anna Wickham* as her professional title and published *The Contemplative Quarry* (1915), *The Man with a Hammer* (1916), and

The Little Old House (1921). *Anna Wickham: Richards Shilling Selections* (1936) included 30 new poems and her posthumous *Selected Poems* came out in 1971. She was well known in Britain, in Paris (where she became attached to Natalie Barney and the circle of women who lived on the Left Bank), and in the United States (where her reputation was at its height after the First World War).

Wickham's poems were included in *Edwardian Poetry* (1937) and *Neo-Georgian Poetry* (1937) (both edited by the poet Fytton Armstrong, under the pseudonym of *John Gawsworth*), but they have nothing of the formal restraint or agreeableness associated with either of those groupings. She was more intellectually in tune with her bohemian and AVANT-GARDE literary associates, such as T(HOMAS) E(RNEST) HULME, DYLAN THOMAS, D. H. LAWRENCE, Djuna Barnes, and EZRA POUND. Her musical training gave her an ear for rhythm and movement, although she eschewed the orthodox patterns of British poetry on account of their associations with traditionalism and because they impeded the simulation of free expression. "Examination" is a rare but loosely structured sonnet—"I write my thought in a ragged way." In "The Egoist," first published in *The Contemplative Quarry,* the speaker shifts between metrical regularity and free verse, making it clear that she can "trot in / iambs" but chooses not to. The free rhythm for the allusion to the modern day "of aeroplanes" is symptomatic of Wickham's conceptual connection between stylistic and psychological emancipation. She refers to her discovery of the "near perfect rhyme," which, in many poems, holds together the hope of happiness and the disappointments of humdrum experience. The association between old techniques and tired thought recurs throughout her work—"How can I put the liquor of new days / In the old pipes of rhyme?" ("Formalist").

Editors and literary critics did not know what to make of her. A reviewer of *The Little Old House* commented on her "lively rhythm and vigorous expression" but undermined the poems as "flung-off stanzas" and "sudden unrevised inspirations, sometimes even despising punctuation in her haste" (*TLS* August 18, 1921). In his review of *The Contemplative Quarry* in the *Egoist,* RICHARD ALDINGTON disapproved of Wickham's

tendency to ruin a perfectly good poem with "doggerel" but admired her manipulation of rhyme and conceded the logic of her arguments: "She manages to say bitter and satiric and true things with a good deal of humour (she runs the eighteenth-century trick of antithetical rhyme). . . . She wants to know what the devil women are to do with their lives."

Although hard to classify, Wickham's work draws upon recognizable literary inheritances, often the forms and myths of ballad, pastoral, fairy tale, and folk legend, which are shared across cultural echelons and groups. Many poems may best be read in conjunction with the works of other female modernists, such as CHARLOTTE MEW, May Sinclair, and SYLVIA TOWNSEND WARNER, who voice the "New Woman" preoccupations with social equality. As they do, she frequently exploits the opportunity afforded by the dramatic monologue for internal dialogue and for publicizing of the personal. "Return of Pleasure," in the free verse that Wickham associates with imaginative liberty, declares, "And I had courage even to despise form. / I thought, "I have skill to make words dance, To clap hands and to shake feet, / But I will put myself and everything I see, upon the page." Although here she implicitly conflates speaker with poet, Wickham usually distances herself from the characters, who often interrogate complex womanly, and sometimes male, psychology, as in "The Sick Assailant": "I hit her in the face because she loved me / It was the challenge of her faithfulness that moved me."

Nevertheless much of the poetry illuminates and can be illuminated by her 106-page *Fragment of an Autobiography: Prelude to a Spring Clean* (reprinted in *Writings*), which records her central preoccupation with freedom of expression. Internal conflict is Wickham's signature. Typically tension between liberty and loyalty is replicated in the deceptively simple idioms of "The Wife": "'Twere better for my man and me, / If I were free, / Not to be done by, but to be. / But I am tied." The jog-trot rhythm mimics the pedestrian routine of marriage, but the woman's death wish—"So I spend my days with the tradesmen's books / And pray for the end of life"—is a disconcerting undertow. As here, the bind was never resolved and Anna Wickham finally committed suicide at home.

BIBLIOGRAPHY

Aldington, Richard. "New Poetry," Review of *The Contemplative Quarry,* by Anna Wickham (London: Poetry Bookshop, 1915) *Egoist* 2 (June 1915): 89–90.

Jones, Jennifer Vaughan. *Anna Wickham: A Poet's Daring Life.* New York: Madison Books, 2003.

McConeghey Rice, Nelljean. *A New Matrix for Modernism: A Study of the Lives and Poetry of Charlotte Mew and Anna Wickham.* New York and London: Routledge, 2003.

Smith, R. D., ed. *The Writings of Anna Wickham.* London: Virago Press, 1984.

Jane Dowson

"THE WILD SWANS AT COOLE" W. B. YEATS (1917)

"The Wild Swans at Coole," one of W. B. YEATS's most accessible and beautiful poems, first appeared in the *Little Review* in 1917 and in the same year in Yeats's collection of the same title. The setting of the poem is Coole Park, county Galway, in Dublin, which was the home of Lady Gregory, Yeats's patron and friend.

Swans help define the main concerns in several of Yeats's major poems. Apart from "LEDA AND THE SWAN," swans occur in "Nineteen Hundred and Nineteen" ("Some moralist or mythological poet / Compares the solitary soul to a swan"); in "Baile and Aillinn" ("Two swans came flying up to him, / Linked by a gold chain each to each"), where the two lovers metamorphose into swans; and in "Coole and Ballylee, 1931" ("Another emblem there! That stormy white / But seems a concentration of the sky"). In "The Tower" the poet, as if a swan, sings his swan song ("and gather me / Into the artifice of eternity").

An absence of feeling or inability to respond emotionally is a fairly common motif in Yeats. Much as "Demon and Beast" does, "The Wild Swans at Coole" delineates a state of sterility in the emotional landscape of the poet. Whereas for Yeats, passion and beauty no longer have any immediacy and evoke no response, the swans signify beauty, passion, and joy.

> Unwearied still, lover by lover,
> They paddle in the cold
> Companionable streams or climb the air

B. Rajan points out how the birds in the poem stand for inspiration, a union of time and the timeless, and for an unearthly vitality as "their hearts do not grow old" and they find the stream companionable even though it is cold, and they "climb the air," and do not merely fly through it.

Essentially elegiac in tone, "The Wild Swans at Coole" reflects upon the problem of exhaustion of imaginative powers and connects the loss to the onset of old age. Yeats's other major preoccupation in "The Wild Swans at Coole" is with time and mutability. Yeats's swans' defiance of time is reminiscent of Keats's investing the nightingale with a timeless life ("The voice that I hear this passing night was heard / In ancient days") and provokes a saddened realization of the fragility of the human existence. But Yeats, unlike Keats, does not grant the birds certainties or finalities ("great *broken* rings") but allows them to produce an illusion of immortality.

Perhaps one can ignore Lady Gregory's insistence that Yeats counted 59 actual swans, considering that birds number, variously, 45, 47, or 59 in early drafts of the poem. The uneven number of the swans—59—has been taken to symbolize loneliness, as well as draw attention to the cyclicity of history and the cyclical nature of time, in which Yeats was deeply interested.

There may be truth in the suggestion that Yeats wrote "The Wild Swans at Coole" in despair over his inability to generate an emotional response in his own heart in the wake of Maud Gonne's rejection of his suit. Herbert Levine points out how Yeats associated Maud Gonne with a swan as early as 1897: "You only know that it is / of you I sing when I tell / of the swan in the water." But Levine's belief that each swan poem marks a stage in Yeats's exorcism of Maud Gonne seems a little too neat and mechanical.

BIBLIOGRAPHY

Rosenthal, M. L. *Running to Paradise: Yeats's Poetic Art.* New York: Oxford University Press, 1994.

Yeats, W. B. *The Poems.* Edited by Daniel Albright. London: J. M. Dent & Sons, 1990.

Gulshan Taneja

"WILLIAM WORDSWORTH (1770– 1850)" GAVIN B(UCHANAN) EWART (1976)

"William Wordsworth (1770–1850)" is another of GAVIN

B(UCHANAN) EWART's "para-poems" (poems that are written in the form and diction of a given poet but that result in a commentary, often parodic, on the short-comings or poetic failures of the original creator). While some of Ewart's "para-poems" are clearly positive and meant as homages, as is the case with ones devoted to Shakespeare, W. H. AUDEN, and PHILIP LARKIN, others such as this one on Wordsworth are irreverent and satiric.

The poem on Wordsworth takes the form of an obituary or, more specifically, an encomium, a form of poetry derived from Greek drama and public speech that extolled the virtues of a person after his or her death. The form chosen by Ewart, then, presupposes some gravity, which is not, however, found in the poem. Ewart begins by comparing Wordsworth's attitude toward nature with that of "most modern Nature Lovers," and this sets the tone for the satire of the poem. He focuses on Wordsworth's early life in the English countryside, mocking his love of some scenic spots of the Lake District that have now become identified with Wordsworth, such as Applethwaite or Yarrow, where Ewart suggests he visited "when he felt like getting pissed" (British slang for extreme drunkenness), a parody on the communion with nature that Wordsworth suggests he achieved in both places.

The second stanza shows the failure of Wordsworth's "natural" philosophical system. Ewart focuses on the romantic poet's visit to France, one of the most controversial times in Wordsworth's life, and according to Ewart, "the only time the system broke down." Wordsworth is not introduced as "young and revolutionary," but rather as a seducer who manages to make a girl pregnant, and who then flees: he wanders off "lonely as a cloud" (a reference to the title of one of Wordsworth's nature poems, celebrating the status of nature as a tutor). This dissonance between the idealistic system of thought fostered by Wordsworth and his behavior, as rather unfairly and vulgarly described by Ewart, inspires one of the many humorous lines of the poem: "from then on no man was a brother and he never again fancied republicanism or a bit of the other."

The parody continues as Wordsworth's reverential attitude toward nature is updated to take a modern, less than heroic, psychoanalytical twist: "Fountains for him were father-figures." Wordsworth's ultimate failure, then, lies for Ewart in his considering nature to be a moral guide, instead of taking messages from human beings and from actual events. To Ewart, Wordsworth "would have avoided all that guilt and loss if he had managed to give himself a less ridiculous philosophy." As with so much of the poem, half the fun is the clever, reductive rhyming, which takes a grand word such as *philosophy* and pairs it was the deflating *loss if he.*

Ewart refuses to use Wordsworth's poetic diction in his poem, employing instead a vocabulary that oscillates between the formal and the extremely colloquial. Rather than use the forms Wordsworth typically employed so supply, such as the sonnet or blank verse, Ewart chooses the heroic couplet, which is anything but heroic in his hands. The lines are of purposely clumsy rhythms and of uneven lengths, a parodic style brought to perfection earlier by the American humorist Ogden Nash.

BIBLIOGRAPHY

Delchamps, Stephen W. *Civil Humor: The Poetry of Gavin Ewart.* Madison, N.J.: Fairleigh Dickinson University Press, 2002.

Carmen Méndez García

"A WINTER TALENT" DONALD DAVIE (1957)

"A Winter Talent" lends its name to DONALD DAVIE's third volume of published poetry, *A Winter Talent and Other Poems,* 1957. A fine example of Davie's self-reflexive poetry, its three stanzas are concerned with the art of poetic creation itself, with poetry's way of meaning—and being. In scarcely 12 lines, Davie examines his poetic "talent." This does not mean, obviously, that we are to take Davie's poem as merely autobiographical; rather, it proposes a way to approach what he considers his creative powers. It is in this sense a highly personal poem, since it describes an experience of creation, exemplifying how the attempt at describing how poetry is created may become, in turn, poetry itself.

The poem, short as it is, is loaded with symbols and metaphors. The recurrence of images related to fire and heat in the three stanzas (*coal, heat, burn, firing,* etc.) and the obsessive use of the lexical field of flammable objects (*sticks, dry foliage, boats*) could be inscribed within the highly standardized convention of fire as related to creative force and to the "burning" poet and artist. However, the poet in Davie is merely the coal that lights the spill. That is, while it is the poet who consciously initiates poetic creation, his "burning" power is discreet and of a limited potency. Davie's talent seems to be, he suggests, rather limited in its scope: He is but a comforting flame in the late afternoon of the cold winter, in a period especially attractive for the arrival of "meditation on its raft of sticks," for reflection and careful elaboration.

After suggesting where he thinks his poetic talents can serve, Davie describes in the second stanza the kind of talent he does not possess. The exuberant, passionate, "quick bright talents" have the ability to compose easily, and they can "burn their boats continually" while "dispensing with coals." However, these poets produce an "unreflecting brightness" that is compared to the reflectiveness proposed in the first stanza, and they are depicted, in the last stanza, as related to a "dangerous glory." Faced with both models, Davie compares, passes judgment, and finally chooses in the last two lines. Even if he feels impressed by the talents of the poets described in the second stanza, he sticks to his way of composing and of approaching experience, claiming it is "better still to burn / Upon that gloom where all have felt a chill."

"A Winter Talent," regarded in the view of Davie's full critical and poetic oeuvre, is to be taken as a declaration of his poetic principles, not only in reference to this poem, but as applicable to his whole work. As Reed suggests, the poem "is eminently approachable and suitable as a poetic initiation to the more difficult poems that constitute the work of Donald Davie's winter talent" (48). The poem is also an example of a poem that is, in itself, a piece of theoretical criticism, showing once more that both facets of Davie, as a poet and as a critic, cannot be dissociated.

BIBLIOGRAPHY

Decker, George, ed. *Donald Davie and the Responsibilities of Literature.* Manchester, Eng.: Carcanet New Press, 1983.
Reed, John R. "Reflexive Poetry: The Winter Talent of Donald Davie." *Western Humanities Review* 19 (1965): 43–54.

Carmen Méndez García

"WIRERS" SIEGFRIED SASSOON (1918) "Wirers," from SIEGFRIED SASSOON's second published volume, *Counter-Attack and Other Poems* (1918), is an example of the kind of poem Sassoon became quickly famous for during the Great War. As is much of Sassoon's war poetry, it is short, rhymed, traditional not experimental verse, which receives its power from its bitterly antiwar tone, here presented in almost an understated way in the last line, similar to the last lines of "THE GENERAL" and "They," where, respectively, a general and a bishop are oblivious to the deaths they cause for no good purpose. Sassoon's attitude, though often called antiwar, may more accurately be called "anti-conduct-of-the-war," for his protest was aimed more at the needless loss of life and the war's prolongation than at the decision to fight. Indeed, ROBERT GRAVES, for one, saw the Sassoon who wrote "The Kiss" as a blood-and-guts fighter, not a pacifist by any means.

The poem consists of three four-line stanzas rhymed, differently, *aabb, abab,* and *abba,* perhaps to indicate something of the awkwardness of mending wire in No-Man's-Land in the dark, a tangled job made suddenly chaotic when a German flare goes off. The soldiers stand "stock-still like posts" so that movement does not get them shot, then in the darkness of the flare's dying down scramble for safety. One, "young Hughes," is hit and carried away to die. That is the cost of the mission; its success is that *we* can say the front-line wire's been safely mended." Sassoon includes himself in that emphasized *we,* placing himself with the generals and bishops who are complicit in the suffering of the common soldier. Sassoon's compassion for ordinary soldiers was unusual for one of his rank and class; officers and men did not fraternize in the British army, which despite the "band of brothers" rhetoric of Shakespeare's *Henry V* maintained a strict division between ranks. Sassoon, as did WILFRED OWEN, breached this division in his poetry, and the word *safely* in the last line of the poem has a special bite—the *wire* is safely mended, but the *wirer* was not able to mend it safely.

James Persoon

"WOMAN'S SONG" SYLVIA TOWNSEND WARNER SYLVIA TOWNSEND WARNER once wrote that she preferred poems that are "formally tight in thought and construction," and her poem "Woman's Song" exemplifies this preference. As is "Hymn for Holy Deconsecration," it is composed of four stanzas of equal length, although "Woman's Song" has a more complex, yet still regular rhyme scheme. Repetition and alliteration contribute to a close rhythm that provides the melodic aspect of this "Song."

Again, as in "Hymn for Holy Deconsecration," Warner's imagery is religious, but the exuberance of that other poem is lost. There are no exclamation marks, and no exclamatory *O* is used to punctuate the lines. Instead the simple refrain *Pray for me* recurs twice in each stanza except the last and becomes a quiet incantation and prayer. Indeed the poem is presented as a prayer, and the irony and satirical distance that are evident in other of Warner's works are entirely absent here. However, "Woman's Song" is not a reconciliation with the God that Warner largely rejected but is instead a reaching out to another form of spiritual comfort that lies entirely outside the Christian Church.

Warner's writing has been frequently dismissed in consequence of the domesticity of her themes. In this poem, the domestic is imbued with a quiet but intense power to save and reassure and seemingly stave off a crisis of dissolution. Inanimate and innocuous objects are imbued with potent properties and the home is a saving oasis of peace. For the narrative voice of the poem, the kettle is *kind* and the linen is *calm*. In contrast, God is *wrath*. The poet begs the kettle to *whisper* to avoid God's attention, and so she and the objects around her become conspirators in evading an unwelcome and censorious judgment.

Domesticity in this poem orders and tames both nature and the fears of the poet. The kitchen-bound perspective does extend beyond the walls of the home, but the meadows outside are "ranged and fallowed" as neatly as the linen in the press. There are no social pretensions in the poem. The objects that provide comfort are homely and unassuming: "brown tea-pot," "wrung dishclout," "true water from the tap." Yet underlying this elegy to harmony and safety is a pervading sense of fear. The poet refers to "going bad" in "the hour of my distress" and turns to the home to illuminate the "shades" she carries within her. These brief but insistent references to an inner darkness balance and tem-

per the sweetness of this domestic scene, hinting at a barely contained existential crisis or danger.

"Woman's Song" imbues the domestic realm with an urgency that belies the safety and familiarity of home and hearth. Just as the poem's rhyme scheme is in fact more complex than the containing refrain *Pray for me* suggests, so there are a tension and a fear underlying this superficially homely scene. In the concluding stanza, the protective boundaries of the home are opened to the possibility of both "mortality" and "eternity's solitude." The poet places the objects of the home between her and these enormities, but at the same time, the myth of the domestic is deconstructed as the fear and urgency that pervade the poem seemingly spring from within rather than from without.

The poem is intimate, forcing the reader to engage with the internal world of its speaker. It offers no guidance or reassurance, and despite the comforting domesticity and femininity of its theme, it is also imbued with doubt and anxiety. It is through this unexpected juxtaposition of fear and safety that Warner introduces a deliberately jarring note to her poem, making it something other than it first appears to be.

BIBLIOGRAPHY

Beer, Gillian. "Sylvia Townsend Warner: The Centrifugal Kick." In *Women Writers of the 1930s: Gender, Politics and History,* edited by Maroula Joannou, 76–86. Edinburgh: Edinburgh University Press, 1999.

Garrity, Jane. *Step-Daughters of England: British Women Modernists and the National Imaginary.* Manchester, Eng.: Manchester University Press, 2003.

Harman, Claire. *Sylvia Townsend Warner: A Biography.* London: Chatto & Windus, 1989.

Warner, Sylvia Townsend. *Collected Poems.* Manchester, Eng.: Carcanet, 1982.

Fiona Tolan

"THE WOMAN WHO COULD NOT LIVE WITH HER FAULTY HEART" Margaret Atwood (1978)

Popular in high school anthologies, "The woman who could not live with her faulty heart" was originally published in Margaret Atwood's *Two-Headed Poems* (1978). Atwood continues to use her tried-and-true focus of Canadian identity in both the book and this particular poem.

However, this focus takes on a new twist as she applies it to politics, the state, and herself in the case of "The woman who could not live with her faulty heart."

In this poem, Atwood examines a woman's heart. The image in the opening stanza, "I do not mean the symbol / of love, a candy shape / to decorate cakes with," implicitly tells us that she is not talking about the romantic notions of the heart. The second stanza tells us she is talking about the muscle itself that sits in the chest of every human being. Her heart, she says, beats a rhythm that is unfamiliar to most. It is a rhythm of wanting and not wanting. Atwood does not define the want but she does not need to. It is a rhythm and an ache that everyone is familiar with. By the end of the poem we learn that the only solution to stilling the ache is our death: "Long ago I gave up singing / to it, it will never be satisfied or lulled ./ One night I will say to it: / Heart, be still, / and it will."

While a singular interpretation of this poem is entirely possible, that of a personal conflict within the human heart, in the context of the rest of the anthology where it appears, the poem takes on political meaning as well. Canada is a country of dual national languages and cultures, French and English, which are often at odds with each other. This poem embodies the struggle between the two languages and the two different modes of thought that go with those languages, lying at the heart of Canada. "The woman who could not live with her faulty heart" is about Atwood herself, about the struggle in every human heart, and perhaps about the political fault lines within Canada between English and French culture as well.

BIBLIOGRAPHY

Atwood, Margaret. *Two-Headed Poems.* New York: Simon & Schuster, 1978.

Howells, Coral Ann, ed. *The Cambridge Companion to Margaret Atwood.* Cambridge: Cambridge University Press, 2006.

J. J. Pionke

"THE WOMEN" EAVAN BOLAND (1986) This poem by EAVAN BOLAND scrutinizes, disturbs, and subverts assumptions over gendered identity and the role of the poet. The conflict between femininity and being a poet is the dilemma that more clearly interests Boland. Although throughout history, literature written by women has been devalued not only in Ireland, but in many other places, this suppression has been even more pronounced in Ireland. In spite of the notable recovery made by Kelly (1987) in her anthology *Pillars of the House: An Anthology of Verse by Irish Women: From 1690 to the Present,* women's poetry in Ireland has been, until very recently, almost nonexistent. Irish women have had to overcome more boundaries in order to write than their female colleagues cross-culturally: They have had to deal with the oppressive burden of a country that adopted a figure of the woman in order to express their aspirations of liberty, their national dreams and laments, with an overwhelmingly Catholic Church and a patriarchal society (the state and other political / social institutions) that have relegated women's domain to the house with scarcely any participation in the public events. In this context, Irish women's poetry, attempting to revise the very system of poetic values that "forbade" them to be poets/subjects, has suffered great resistance. The publication of *The Field Day Anthology of Irish Writing* in 1991 reinforced the continuing problems women have had in getting their works published and recognized. The little space devoted to women writers was highly controversial because it claimed to be a comprehensive collection of Irish writing from the sixth to the twentieth century. In "The Women," Boland records the difficulty involved in being a woman *and* a poet in Ireland by focusing on a woman's split identity, a subject who is troubled by "two minds" and who inhabits "two [separate] worlds." In this poem, the speaker's artistic potential lies in her own ability to occupy an intermediate space between the habits of suburban motherhood and the habits of the writer. The first stanza draws us into a beloved "in-between" space, "neither-here-nor-there." This blurring of well-established boundaries is also perceived in the scenery that the woman speaker describes: This is a landscape of diffused lights and tenuous colors, in which the air is "tea-coloured" and the silks, as she later describes in this poem, are "stove-coloured." In this setting, shapes dissolve to the extent that the simple briar rose of Boland's garden loses its consistency and becomes silk crepe. It is in this liminal space where Boland achieves

the summit of her creative potential: "This is the time I do my work best, / going up the stairs in two minds, / in two worlds." The speaker's position in the staircase of her house situates her between these two worlds, the world of the ground floor, where she carries out her own domestic tasks, and the upper floor, where she writes her poems. Therefore, the stairwell becomes an interstitial passage between fixed identifications, *in-between* the designations of identity. Boland's employs this metaphor with a view to disturbing the conventional dichotomy man (as writer) and woman (as mother and housewife). By so doing, she occupies a space that deconstructs the symmetry of designated male and female domains, allowing her to give voice to her own creative potential. In the fourth stanza, the poet encounters a new landscape, neither openly public nor exclusively private, where different kinds of women "rise like visions" to her. The poetic muses whom the speaker chooses to follow are varied: They are middle-class workers, upper-class women, as well as prostitutes. "The Women" makes explicit Boland's desire to write not only about mothers, housewives, and suburban women, but also about a more heterogeneous range of women: "women of work" with "crewel needles," well-educated women who are free from time-consuming domestic duties, and women "of the night . . . with wide open legs." The poem ends by introducing us to a domestic world of well-established boundaries. This is a landscape "without emphasis," "linear," and "precisely planned" that stands in opposition to the multidimensional and imaginative place her poetry has previously explored. Shapes are no longer shifting, unstable, and indefinite, but well delineated. In this sense, the domestic world is presented in all its crudeness; it is an asphyxiating "hot terrain" different from the radioactive "heat" that her poetry grasped by means of "the physical force of a dissonance." By emphasizing the contrast between her own flowing imaginary world as an artist and her well-demarcated domestic world as a housewife, "The Women" ends with Boland's unresolved tension between two contrary pulls: her commitment to literature and her ordinary life (as a woman). As is typical in Boland's work, the feeling one is left with is of displacement and dislocation, of a woman who is still haunted by the contradictions of being a woman poet in Ireland.

BIBLIOGRAPHY

Boland, Eavan. *The Journey and Other Poems.* Dublin: Carcanet Press, 1986.

———. *Object Lessons: The Life of the Woman and the Poet in Our Time.* London: Vintage, 1995.

Kelly, A. A., ed. *Pillars of the House: An Anthology of Verse by Irish Women from 1690 to the Present.* Dublin: Wolfhound, 1987.

Maguire, Sarah. "Dilemmas and Developments: Eavan Boland Re-Examined." *Feminist Review* 62 (summer 1999): 58–66.

Pilar Villar Argáiz

WORLD WAR II AND POETRY   From the early days of World War II, literary critics and reviewers demanded of poets and their audience, "Where are all the war poets?" As war with Germany became inevitable, members of the literary establishment looked for soldier-poets to capture the moment, to comment on the humanity and heroism of war, to serve as a conscience for the times. "Where are all the war poets?" was a crucial question for the first half of the 1940s, asked in the pages of the *Times Literary Supplement,* where an article entitled "To the Poets of 1940," appearing on December 30, 1939, claimed, "Here we are faced with an undeniable repetition of history, with nothing original, nothing unique about it. Clearly wars and revolutions are destroying the old social order of the world. But we need not despair of the birth of a new and finer order. It is for the poets to sound the trumpet call." This language echoes the "trumpet call" issued by one of the most notable authors of the Great War, Rupert Brooke, who was held up as a model for the heroic soldier-poet doing his duty by serving his nation both in the trenches and as a voice for noble wartime ideals.

It is a critical commonplace that writers in the 1940s did not answer that "trumpet call" for war poets. The Second World War did not produce a Rupert Brooke, a soldier-poet writing verses meant to inspire a nation to service and heroism while stoically accepting one's sacrifice. Nor did it produce a Wilfred Owen, another victim, an important emergent voice cut down in his youth a few days before the war's end. Owen's poetry gained an audience among modernist writers after his death for his brutal imagery and disillusioned view toward the war; at the same time, his work was notable not for its glorification of war but for its pity toward its subjects.

In many ways, the soldier-poet of the Great War was a myth. It cannot be denied that the years 1914 to 1918 produced some of the most significant poets of the twentieth century, not just Owen but SIEGFRIED SASSOON and ISAAC ROSENBERG, whose harsh rejection of the kinds of ideals and poetic conventions deployed by Brooke made them important figures for post–World War One modernist writers. However, the soldier-poet of the Great War—the myth and the reality—was produced by some very particular circumstances that were not replicated in the Second World War. First, the landscape of the two conflicts was very different. The poetry of the First World War is characterized by a strong antipastoral quality, originating in the soldiers' experience of the trenches. The men watched the destruction of the land, the rendering of fields and farmland into bleak nightmarescapes, and because of the very nature of trench warfare, with its long periods of inactivity underground, the men had the time to reflect, witness, and write. The Second World War was much more fast-moving, much more mechanized, over many distances and through many different landscapes. Men were stationed not just in the fields of Europe but in its cities, as well as in the Middle East and in the Pacific. Second, the entry into the war, its beginnings, was different. The Great War began in the summer of 1914, the last golden flush of the EDWARDIAN PERIOD, with a sense of festival and excitement about "doing one's bit." The Second World War, on the other hand, began after a dark and stagnant period of political negotiations, including the appeasement debacle of 1938. After the invasion of Poland, from September 1939 to April 1940, Britons waited through several months referred to as "The Phoney War," when Great Britain had declared war but nothing much in the way of military action seemed to be happening. This protracted period of waiting, of resigned anticipation, created an entirely different tone for the wartime experience: There was no "trumpet call." Finally, the issue of tone is directly linked to the ideas about this war and its purpose. The generation fighting in the Second World War had experienced the depression of the 1930s, the Spanish Civil War, and the rise of fascism—and they had seen what the Great War did to their fathers, uncles, and older brothers. Members of this generation held no illusions about glorious battle and wartime heroism. They recognized that this war might be necessary, but they were resigned and stoical about their duty in it rather than inspired by lofty sentiments about the ideal of the warrior and patriotic fervor.

The place of poetry in the 1940s has always been problematic; indeed, it is only in recent years that sustained critical attention has been devoted to the period. The decade has always been difficult to define as a result of the movements that immediately preceded it. On the one hand, MODERNISM—the poetry of EZRA POUND, T. S. ELIOT, H. D. (HILDA DOOLITTLE), and others—emerged as the dominant force in literature and criticism. On the other hand, and partly in response to the trends of modernism, poets of the 1930s offered an alternative vision, one defined by political commitment (mostly Left), a documentary realism, and a turn away from the self-consciously experimental. Yet each side offered a response to the question "Where are all the war poets?" T. S. Eliot, in "A Note on War Poetry," wrote about the difficulty of wrestling with an individual response in poetry to the intensity of the war. C. DAY LEWIS, a committed Leftist poet affiliated with the group dominated by W. H. AUDEN, in his poem "WHERE ARE THE WAR POETS?" claimed that poets had no place in writing about war, "no subject for immortal verse."

Poets who had done much of their work during the 1920s and 1930s did write poetry during and responding to the Second World War. Eliot's *Four Quartets* is considered one of the great poems of the war, examining the epic struggle of the conflict from an intensely personal and spiritual perspective. H. D., living in London during the Blitz, composed *Trilogy,* in which she connects the destruction of the city by bombing to the end of civilization. Both of these responses are marked by the mythical allusions and framework, as well as the stylistic experimentation, that characterize high modernist poetry.

Some poets of the 1930s, many of whom had produced some of their finest work out of the Spanish Civil War a few years before, wrote poetry in response to the Second World War as well, although many more of them found themselves in much different circumstances. STEPHEN SPENDER, who remained in London and joined the National Fire Service, produced a number of poems about living through the Blitz. However, Auden left for the United States in 1939, a move that many considered a betrayal and that marked something of an end to his dominance on the literary scene. Many writers, including George Orwell and C. Day Lewis, went to work producing propaganda for the newly created Ministry of Information instead of spending the war years producing works of literature. The writers of the previous decade, who had been in many ways the voice of conscience for a tumultuous time, could no longer hold that mantle. Damaged by Auden's defection and their own disillusionment in Spain, these writers who had once been so committed stood on the sidelines. As Randall Swingler wrote in the May 1941 issue of *Our Time,* "The war has put an end to that literary generation. . . . Nothing is left of their imaginings but the twilight, peopled by the ghosts of literary values long defunct."

It is true that no movement or generation arose from the Second World War to match that which emerged during and after the Great War. It is also true that the years of the Second World War were not, on the surface, conducive to the production of poetry. A number of magazines shrank or ceased production during the war years because of paper shortages. Some of the most significant publications of the early twentieth century closed: *Criterion, Twentieth Century Verse, New Verse,* the *London Mercury.* A closer look, however, reveals a vital and sustained literary output throughout the war years, and the emergence of a new breed of war poet. These men were not the noble heroes of the trenches of the Great War, but men who saw combat in the deserts of the Middle East and the streets of London. Their poetry is characterized by two threads: a documentary realism influenced by Auden—poets like KEITH DOUGLAS and Alun Lewis—and a visionary surrealism influenced by Yeats and Rilke—poets like Sidney Keyes. These poets cast themselves as stoic, ironic men in the world of war trying to reclaim something of the value of humanity, however small; or as mystical prophets, delving into romantic imagery and metaphysical questions of life and death. The poetry of the war is antiheroic, simultaneously exalting the human and recognizing its debasement. It does not reject patriotism or idealism; rather, these categories have become entirely irrelevant. These poets think not of England, but of exile. They are unsentimental, skeptical, bored, and clear-eyed.

Poetry served in many ways as a comfort to men during the war, not only for those who were writing it but for those who read it. Despite the paper shortages, a number of journals continued to be published, and new ones were started. Cyril Connolly founded *Horizon* in 1940 as a way to protect and sustain "high" culture during the war years. John Lehmann produced *Penguin New Writing,* one of the most popular publications among servicemen and civilians. Tambimuttu, a colorful and indiscriminate editor, brought out *Poetry (London).* Poetry and its publication continued to flourish during the war, and numerous anthologies of poetry by servicemen came out, including Keidrich Rhys's *Poems from the Forces* (1941) and *More Poems from the Forces* (1943), and *Personal Landscape,* produced by the Anglo-Egyptian Union in Cairo from 1942 to 1945. Many men who served in the Second World War wrote poetry only during the conflict and then stopped. Many others, such as ROY FULLER, HENRY REED, and Alan Ross, had been writing before the war and continued after with careers as editors, reviewers, and academics. The most notable poets—Keith Douglas, Sidney Keyes, and ALUN LEWIS—were all killed in action.

In 1941, Keyes co-edited an anthology entitled *Eight Oxford Poets,* which included Douglas. The early work of the men showed their talent as poets, a talent that was further brought out, and cut short, by wartime experience. Douglas was killed in Normandy in 1944 after spending time fighting in Cairo; his most well-known work, *Alamein to Zem Zem,* was published posthumously. Douglas's best poems, such as "VERGISSMEINNICHT," explore the debasement of humanity that inevitably results from war. Another important work, "Simplify Me When I'm Dead," directly echoes Rupert

Brooke's "THE SOLDIER," but in the voice of the world-weary, resigned servicemen of the Second World War: "Remember me when I am dead / and simplify me when I'm dead." The poem acknowledges the indifferent world of war and the place of the individual in it, "substance or nothing."

Sidney Keyes, Douglas's classmate at Oxford, hated the army, unlike Douglas, whose feelings were more ambivalent. Keyes wrote to a friend a year before his death, "I was never bored until I joined the Army; now I am crazy with the utter futility, destructiveness and emptiness of my life, to which I see no end." His poem "War Poet," written just before he enlisted, reveals his ambivalence about his role as soldier-poet: "I am the man who groped for words and found / An arrow in my hand." A later poem, "The Foreign Gate," is more representative of Keyes's turn toward a mystical imagery, envisioning a pantheon of warriors, "the brother plucked out of a foreign sky / To lie in fields of wreckage and white marble." Keyes himself was killed in Tunisia in 1943.

Alun Lewis, a third important figure, was killed in Burma in 1944 after producing two significant books of war writing, *Raiders' Dawn* in 1942 and *Ha! Ha! Among the Trumpets* in 1944. His work focuses on the loneliness and sense of exile that are part of the soldier's experience. Lewis, who had his roots in a small Welsh mining village, wrote poems about the desire for home and love, and the tension between this desire and the reality of war, as illustrated in "ALL DAY IT HAS RAINED."

One can never know what the poets of the war years might have produced had they survived. The years after the war saw the rise of the new apocalyptic poets, including DYLAN THOMAS, whose work was characterized by the same romantic visions found in some wartime poetry. This trend was countered by the MOVEMENT of the late 1940s and early 1950s. The Movement, which counted among its adherents PHILIP LARKIN, was a call for a realistic idiom and an exploration of more everyday concerns. The poetry of the Second World War serves as an important precursor to these moments, and a critical field in its own right.

BIBLIOGRAPHY
Bergonzi, Bernard. *Wartime and Aftermath: English Literature and Background, 1939–60.* New York: Oxford University Press, 1993.

Currey, R. N. *Poets of the 1939–1945 War.* London: Longmans, Green, 1967.

Hewison, Robert. *Under Siege: Literary Life in London, 1939–45.* New York: Oxford University Press, 1977.

Knowles, Sebastian. *A Purgatorial Flame: Seven British Writers in the Second World War.* Philadelphia: University of Pennsylvania Press, 1990.

Scannell, Vernon. *Not without Glory: Poets of the Second World War.* London: Woburn Press, 1976.

Shires, Linda. *British Poetry of the Second World War.* New York: St. Martin's Press, 1985.

Janine Utell

"WOUNDS" MICHAEL LONGLEY (1973)

Published in MICHAEL LONGLEY's second collection of poetry, *An Exploded View* (1973), "Wounds" is an exploration, in blank verse, of the physical and mental wounds caused by war. Longley juxtaposes his English father's experience of the Battle of the Somme with more contemporary experiences of violence in Northern Ireland, using specific episodes as a device to provide a general commentary on the nature of war.

Longley speaks often in his poetry of the lingering impact his father's wartime experiences made. In the first stanza of "Wounds," he describes the Battle of the Somme as seen through the eyes of his father, Richard. It is a horrific scene, "a landscape of dead buttocks," an image that stays with Richard for 50 years. The shocking events of World War I left an indelible mark on his psyche, and, in later years, old hurts mingled with new, his psychological wounds remanifesting themselves in physical disease. Longley refers to him as "a belated casualty" of war. This is an idea previously explored in "In Memoriam," published in his 1969 collection *No Continuing City*. Here Longley addresses his father's illness, "In my twentieth year your old wounds woke / As cancer." These wounds, the wounds that bring about his father's death, create emotional wounds in the poet. Longley's grief, a result of his father's death, is as much a part of "Wounds" as the pain endured as a consequence of physical war wounds is. His description of a shared moment of intimacy with his father is sparse but laden with emotion, "I touched his hand, his thin head I touched," displaying the love Longley had for his father.

In the second stanza of the poem, Longley aligns his father's death with the deaths of three British soldiers and a bus conductor, the results of sectarian violence in Northern Ireland. He metaphorically buries all of these people, each in a different way a victim of war, beside one another, throwing various personal belongings into the grave in order to display the humanity of these victims: "A packet of Woodbines I throw in, / A Lucifer, the Sacred Heart of Jesus." The Sacred Heart statue emphasizes the religious conflict in Northern Ireland, the imagery of Jesus and Lucifer (which in this case refers to a brand of matches) acting in opposition to one another. Longley's sympathies are not limited to the dead only. He describes the bus conductor's killer as "a shivering boy," rather than a hardened murderer. This stresses the youth and inexperience of the boy, suggesting that the perpetrators too are the victims of war. The poem ends on this note, focuses on the boy's humanity, on his confusion and remorse: "To the children, to a bewildered wife, I think 'Sorry Missus' was what he said." This exploration of the horrors of war can be seen as a universal comment on its cruelty toward all involved. There can never be victors, only victims.

BIBLIOGRAPHY
Longley, M. *Poems 1963–1983*. Dublin: Gallery Press, 1985.

Sinead Carey

WRIGHT, JUDITH (1915–2000)

Judith Wright is not only remembered as a poet, but as a critic, short-story writer, environmentalist, and social activist for Aboriginal land rights in her native Australia. Born into a wealthy pastoral family in New South Wales, she grew up surrounded by the beauty of the Australian landscape. She decided to be a poet when she was 14, after discovering poetry at the New England Girls' School. She went on to Sydney University, where she studied philosophy, history, psychology, and English without bothering to complete a degree for any one subject.

One flaw Wright found with early twentieth-century Australian writers was that they wrote as though still in England, giving no mention to the native flora or fauna. Wright's early poetry is quite different, as it captures the imagery of Australia with its particular animals, trees, and flowers. Her first book, *The Moving Image,* was published in 1946. She develops a distinctly female voice in her second book of poetry, *Woman to Man.* Most of her anthologized poems are from these first two books of poetry, even though she would publish many more volumes in her lifetime.

At the age of 30, she met the philosopher J. P. McKinney, whom she later married. His death in 1966 perhaps caused her to write poems with a more pessimistic tone than is found in her earlier work.

Wright received several awards for her poetry, including the Grace Leven Prize in 1950, the Robert Frost Memorial Award in 1977, the Australian World Prize in 1984, and the Queen's Medal for Poetry in 1992.

She had always had an interest in conservation, helping to found the Wildlife Preservation Society of Queensland in the early 1960s and working to protect the ecology of the Great Barrier Reef. In her later years, she gave up writing poetry to devote even more time to social causes. Because of her ancestry, she felt guilt for the treatment of the Aboriginal people and worked to publicize their plight and their poetry. She edited several collections of Australian verse and helped the Aboriginal poet Oodgeroo Noonuccal get published.

Over her life, Judith Wright published more than 50 books, including a memoir, *Half a Lifetime,* in 2000, which covers her life until the 1960s. Judith Wright loved Australia and its people and was still actively involved in work to make life better for its citizens when she died of a heart attack in Canberra at the age of 85.

BIBLIOGRAPHY
Brady, Veronica. *South of My Days: A Biography of Judith Wright.* North Ryde, Australia: Angus & Robertson, 1998.
Walker, Shirley. *Flame and Shadow: A Study of Judith Wright's Poetry.* St. Lucia, Australia: University of Queensland Press, 1991.
Wright, Judith. *Collected Poems 1946–1985.* North Ryde, Australia: Angus & Robertson, 1994.

Michelle Shamasneh

Y

YEATS, W. B. (WILLIAM BUTLER YEATS) (1865–1939)

When the Irish poet W. B. Yeats died in 1939, his reputation as a poet cast a shadow with which both his contemporaries and those who followed him would have to contend. Fifty years passed between the publication of his first book of poetry, *The Wanderings of Oisin,* and that of his posthumous final collection, *Last Poems.* In this time, Yeats's life and his work show his continual engagement with his ideas of the identity of Ireland and its place in the changing world. In all of his writings, Yeats attempted to work out a dialectical philosophy, setting up opposites that would be synthesized through the heroic, transformative action of the artist. Yeats was deeply occupied with the responsibilities of art and with poetry's role in the world.

Yeats was born in Dublin in 1865 to the painter John Butler Yeats and his wife, Susan Pollexfen. The oldest of six children, four of whom survived to adulthood, Yeats grew up in both London (where his father pursued the study of art) and Sligo, where his maternal relatives lived. His family belonged lineally to the Anglo-Irish Ascendancy (the Protestant aristocracy who governed the Catholic peasant class). In 1881, the family settled again in Dublin, and at about the same time Yeats began to write poetry regularly. Yeats wrote prolifically through his life, publishing not only poetry but plays, autobiographical writings, criticism, and spiritual theory.

In 1887, Yeats joined Madame Helena Blavatsky's Theosophical Society. The Theosophists' reliance on Eastern mysticism appealed greatly to Yeats, whose early poetry demonstrates his attempts to fashion a uniquely Irish spirituality, rooted in occultism and Irish myth. Throughout his life, Yeats would attach himself to various spiritual groups, such as the Theosophists and, later, the Golden Dawn (dedicated to a Celtic revival). However, Yeats was more leader than disciple, tending to want to remake the groups in light of his own developing beliefs. Ultimately Yeats's involvement with these associations helped him to craft his own theory of universal history—a theory that found its fullest expression in 1926's *A Vision.*

In 1889, Yeats published *The Wanderings of Oisin and Other Poems.* The collection's focus on transcendent myth and mysticism foreshadows the more concentrated effort Yeats would make in his next set of poems to reinvigorate specifically Irish stories and symbol. *Oisin* reflects Yeats's interest in Indian culture and mythology; others, such as "The Stolen Child," depict a very real fairyland with influence on our own reality. While these early poems show the poet's deep longing for an escape to the heightened worlds his poetry portrays, they nonetheless refuse to assign absolute value to those worlds. James Pethica points out that "much of his best early poetry . . . turns on what would become and remain a characteristic Yeatsian tension . . . a tension between desire for the visionary or unseen, and the impulse to counter its insubstantiality with the flawed but vital realm of the actual" (xii).

526

Also in 1889, Yeats met Maud Gonne, a woman who would for him embody this tension between the ideal and the real. Gonne was the great love of Yeats's life and figures prominently in many of his most powerful poems (such as "The Folly of Being Comforted," "Adam's Curse," and "No Second Troy"). The deeply complicated and long-lasting relationship between the pair involved "spiritual marriage" (both were interested in the occult and believed in astral projections of spiritual selves across physical divides), extended estrangements, and at least one consummation. But though Yeats proposed marriage several times, Gonne always refused. Nonetheless for years the idealized image of Irish womanhood seen in Yeats's work was a synthesis of major figures out of Celtic myth (such as Cathleen ni Houlihan and Grania) and Gonne.

With the publication of *The Rose* in 1893, Yeats demonstrated again his artistic commitment to Celtic culture. He understood Irish identity to be rooted in a spiritual connection with nature; the Irish artist, in Yeats's vision, has the responsibility and the power to communicate the Irish soul to the world. "The Lake Isle of Innisfree," perhaps the poem from this collection most familiar to modern readers, does not specifically invoke the worlds of "faeries" and mythological heroes, as do several of the other poems in *The Rose.* However, the speaker's claim that the sound of "lake water lapping" echoes in his "deep heart's core" repeats the connection of the poet to transcendent nature.

In 1894, Gonne's illegitimate daughter, Iseult, was born; the child was the result of a long-standing affair with a married man, of which Yeats was unaware until 1898. Soon Yeats would turn his artistic, if not romantic, attention to another important woman in his life: In 1896 he met Lady Augusta Gregory, with whom Yeats would found the Irish Literary (later National) Theatre. Their commitment to the idea of an Irish theater—intended to engage the Irish people through sound rather than written words—was so strong that Yeats viewed his 1899 collection, *The Wind among the Reeds,* as his poetic swan song.

However, while Yeats became one of the Abbey Theatre's most-produced playwrights, he did not give up writing poetry. *In the Seven Woods* was published in 1903, and this collection contained a poem that dem-

onstrates both Yeats's changing artistic interests and his revised vision of Maud Gonne. The conversation at the center of "Adam's Curse" compares the invisible work of the poet and of women. The poem demonstrates how Yeats's theatrical work has impacted his poetry and portrays some of Yeats's disappointment in Maud's failure to live up to his ideal.

However, it was also in 1903 that Maude Gonne converted to Catholicism and married a fellow Irish activist, John MacBride. Shocked, Yeats committed himself fully to the Abbey, writing and producing several more plays—and writing almost no new poetry for about five years. ("The Folly of Being Comforted" was one of only three poems written in that span.) In 1903–04, Yeats visited the United States to give a lecture tour; his speeches were almost entirely focused on his theatrical aesthetic. In 1906, the Abbey production of *The Playboy of the Western World,* by Yeats's close friend J. M. Synge, turned into riots led by Catholic nationalists angry over Anglo-Irish "decadence" (*AM* 363); Yeats, deeply committed to Irish identity but from the quite different perspective of nostalgia for the Ascendancy, defended the company and Synge. While Yeats did favor Irish independence, it was always with oligarchic leanings. Afterward, he decided he would endeavor "to separate art from political content" (366). But politics continued to affect Yeats's own life, and concerns occasioned by political upheaval surfaced in his work nonetheless. Lady Gregory's Galway estate, Coole Park, a Yeats retreat that appears often in his poetry, was—with many other Anglo-Irish "big houses"—under threat from land reform legislation. The poetry from 1908 to 1913 reflects a nostalgia for an idealized lost world of the past; as James Pethica notes, while Yeats's style becomes more modern, the theme of "an ideal world . . . is still set as a desirable image against which the actual world . . . falls short" (xv). Also at around this time, Yeats met and became friendly with the poet EZRA POUND.

A major change in Yeats's work and life occurred in 1916. On Easter Monday of that year, a group of Irish nationalists—led by a number of Yeats acquaintances, including Maud Gonne's husband, John MacBride—took over the Dublin Post Office and declared an Irish Republic. Though the small force held out for six days, the rebellion against British rule ultimately failed and the leaders were executed for treason. "EASTER, 1916," Yeats's poetic response to the rebellion, appeared in his 1921 collection *Michael Robartes and the Dancer*. The poem dramatizes Yeats's own conflicted response to the uprising, as a result of which, he claims, "All changed, changed utterly, / A terrible beauty is born." Yeats admires the idealism of the rebels but wonders whether their sacrifice was worthwhile; simultaneously he questions the worth of his own work as a poet. Finally, he concludes that by writing the names of the leaders into his verse he, too, can change their deaths into immortal martyrdoms while still maintaining each man's individuality.

After MacBride's death, Yeats again asked Maud Gonne to marry him and was again refused. He then proposed to her daughter, Iseult, but was rejected by her as well. Finally, in 1917, Yeats married George Hyde-Lees, who was 27 years younger than the 52-year-old poet. The two had known each other before, but Yeats had never previously romanced George. While their marriage seemed to begin inauspiciously, it became an artistic partnership that ushered in a new era in Yeats's work when his wife attempted automatic writing. The messages she wrote down were ostensibly from spirits; given Yeats's lifelong interest in the occult, he drew on these spiritual communications to reinvigorate his poetic practice. While much of the poetry between 1914's *Responsibilities* and 1917's *The Wild Swans at Coole* was, in Pethica's words, full of "gloomy uncertainty and sense of creative barrenness," the latter collection inaugurated a period of "renewed joy in and celebration of the power of vision and imagination" (xvii). Some of Yeats's poetry of this time continues the self-reflexive meditations on the writing of poetry, which Yeats first investigated in "Adam's Curse," now deepened by the added problems of age.

Yeats watched the events of the Anglo-Irish War of 1919–21 and the following Irish Civil War from Thoor Ballylee, the tower in Galway that the Yeatses used as a summer home. His daughter, Anne, was born in 1919; his son, Michael, in 1921. Yeats's poetry (such as "Meditations in a Time of Civil War") continued to show an engagement with and reflection on the concerns of the world. Also around this time, Yeats was at work on *A Vision,* inspired by and written through his automatic writing with George; the system of historical change that is laid out in this book underlies the SYMBOLISM of much of Yeats's late poetry. *A Vision* theorizes a cyclical history, moving through the 28 "Phases of the Moon" from progress to decline and back again; he marks his own time as one of degeneration.

In 1923, Yeats was awarded the Nobel Prize in literature. Five years later, the collection that may be his masterpiece—*The Tower*—was published to wide acclaim. The poetry of Yeats's last years is marked by a frustration with the aging body and a need to find new inspiration to continue creating new work. The title poem of that collection illustrates the push and pull between the "heart, O troubled heart" and the "excited, passionate, fantastical / Imagination"—the dialectic between the human body and the poetry-producing soul—with which Yeats feels he must grapple. Here the poet is able to use the thing that seems to hold him back from creation—the body, "this caricature, / Decrepit age that has been tied to me / As to a dog's tail"—as the inspiration for a new creation. The poetry of this time also demonstrates an increasing interest in doubleness and in the difficulty of choice. Yeats continues to look eagerly for a revelation—as in 1920's "THE SECOND COMING"—but his poetry also demonstrates a fear of what will be released at that revelation, echoing the "terrible beauty" of the Easter Rising. As in "Easter, 1916," Yeats questions the relationship between violence and art; while personally troubled by such violence, he also suggests that aesthetic distance from the violent world might somehow impede creativity. "LEDA AND THE SWAN," for example, published in *The Tower,* depicts the mythic story of Zeus and Leda as a disturbingly vivid picture of a divine rape that breeds both the beauty of Helen and the destruction of Troy.

Yeats grew increasingly vocal about antidemocratic political leanings in his later years, even publishing in 1939 a pamphlet, "On the Boiler," promoting eugenics to improve Irish "stocks" and flirting with fascism. But he came to disown fascist ideas as the realities of their practical applications in Europe became increasingly clear. Yeats's final poems again return to the conflict between body and soul, between the temporal and mortal realm and the ageless sphere of poetry. "Politics," placed last in Yeats's final collection, *Last Poems* (1939), provides one further illustration of this Yeatsian tension. The epigraph from Thomas Mann tells us that "in our time the destiny of man presents its meanings in political terms," and yet the speaker cannot pay attention to "war and war's alarms" because, seeing a girl, he wishes "that I were young again / And held her in my arms." While the poem's tone is elegiac and wistful, the poet nonetheless succeeds in capturing this elusive object of desire within his lines.

Yeats died in the South of France on January 28, 1939, and was buried in Roquebrune. His body was reinterred, as he had wished, in Drumcliff churchyard, Sligo, nine years later. The epitaph he had written for himself in "Under Ben Bulben" (*Last Poems*) inscribed on his tombstone:

> Cast a cold eye
> On life, on death.
> Horseman, pass by!

See also "BYZANTIUM," "THE CIRCUS ANIMALS' DESERTION," "CRAZY JANE TALKS WITH THE BISHOP," "IN MEMORY OF ROBERT MAJOR GREGORY," "AN IRISH AIRMAN FORESEES HIS DEATH," "THE WILD SWANS AT COOLE."

BIBLIOGRAPHY

Ellmann, Richard. *Yeats: The Man and the Masks.* New York: W. W. Norton, 2000.

Foster, R. F. *W. B. Yeats: A Life.* Vol. 1, *The Apprentice Mage.* Oxford: Oxford University Press, 1997.

———. *W. B. Yeats: A Life.* Vol. 2, *The Arch-Poet.* Oxford: Oxford University Press, 2003.

Pethica, James. "Introduction." In *Yeats's Poetry, Drama, and Prose,* xi–xxiv. New York: Norton, 2000.

Yeats, W. B. *The Collected Works of W. B. Yeats.* Edited by Richard J. Finneran and George Mills Harper. 14 vols. New York: Scribner, 2000.

Mary Wilson

"YES, WE ARE GOING TO SUFFER, NOW" W. H. AUDEN (1938)

In the 1930s W. H. AUDEN, along with various friends in his circle such as STEPHEN SPENDER, LOUIS MACNEICE, and Christopher Isherwood, began a series of travels abroad, to Spain, Portugal, America, Canada, Germany, Belgium, France, Iceland, China, and Japan. A number of these trips resulted in travel books as well as poems. "Yes, we are going to suffer, now" is a part of a sonnet cycle that Auden wrote during one of these journeys, to China. In 1938 he and Isherwood spent three months in China after being commissioned by their American publisher, Random House, to write a travel book about Asia. The book that resulted, *Journey to a War* (1939), was a report on the Sino-Japanese War, which included sonnets that Auden had composed along the way.

The poem's title, as was Auden's usual practice, was simply a Roman numeral, in this case "XIV," as it appeared 14th in a sequence of 27 sonnets (exactly at the midpoint). This sonnet, composed in the latter half of 1938, as were most of the 27, is by far the most famous and frequently anthologized. It is also, however, the one with the most complicated history of composition. It went through at least two previous, drastically different versions. The first was titled "Air Raid"; the second, appearing only in typescript, had a different octet but contained the last six lines of the sonnet as it now stands.

The overarching theme of the entire sequence is suffering, and that word appears prominently in the first line of this poem, "Yes, we are going to suffer, now." With these opening words, however, the poem announces that it is not just the Chinese who are suffering from an air raid from the sky, but all of us—"we are going to suffer"—Westerner and Easterner alike, and not just in time of literal war. Auden universalizes the experience, in an internal, personal, Freudian way—it is our own "little natures that will make us cry." These secret, internal little demons "take us by surprise / Like ugly long-forgotten memories." It is the "private massacres" we have to watch out for, our own murdering attitudes toward others in our societies— "All Women, Jews, the Rich, the Human Race." In the first two items in this series we recognize a condemnation of sexism and racism. Then the sequence opens out, surprising us, as the Leftist Auden also stands up for the rich, and then, with even wider scope, all humans. His scope could only be wider if he included all sentient and nonsentient beings, animals, the Earth, the universe.

The final three lines of the sestet begin with a pun: "The mountains cannot judge us when we lie." Most obviously, the poem is saying that when we lie in our graves, we are beyond being judged by the things and standards of this earth. The word *lie* is a powerful one, however, in the sequence as a whole. For example, two sonnets later appear the lines "But ideas can be true although men die, / And we can watch a thousand faces / Made active by one lie." In other words, lies may fool us, and the world. This is our frail human condition. Justice, from proper judging, does not necessarily win out. The last two lines of "Yes, we are going to suffer, now" say the same thing: "We dwell upon the earth; the earth obeys / The intelligent and evil till they die."

BIBLIOGRAPHY

Mendelson, Edward, ed. *The English Auden: Poems, Essays and Dramatic Writings 1927–1939.* London: Faber and Faber, 1977.

James Persoon

"YOUTH" FRANCES CORNFORD (1908) In 1908 FRANCES CORNFORD and her cousin Gwen (Darwin) Raverat became close to RUPERT BROOKE and the group who gathered around him, named the Neo-pagans by Virginia Stephen for their flouting of Victorian convention, especially in their practice of nude bathing in the pools near Brooke's residence a few miles outside Cambridge, at Grantchester. The rather dramatic photo of Cornford from these years reprinted by Paul Delany in *The Neo-pagans: Friendship and Love in the Rupert Brooke Circle* shows her in the most undomestic of poses, hair blowing free, in a loose garment rather like a toga, falling off one shoulder, as she raises herself up from the beach like some shipwrecked amazon queen. In actuality, she had married an older but rather shy member of the group, Francis Cornford, in 1909 and was the mother of a one-year-old, Helena, when the photo was taken in 1914. The next year she saw Brooke off to the Dardaenelles, where he was to die and instantly become for several years the most famous poet of the First World War, mostly for a single poem, "THE SOLDIER." She had written a short poem for him in 1908, quite beautiful and fitting for the grand and beautiful Brooke,

only two couplets long, which began, "A Young Apollo, golden-haired / Stands dreaming on the verge of strife." Brooke was strikingly handsome, blond, and ambitious, having already starred in Edward Marsh's *Georgian Poetry 1911–1912.* The concluding couplet contained a subtle criticism, in that the young Apollo was "magnificently unprepared / For the long littleness of life." She meant the poem to indicate that Brooke, as the hero of his favorite play, *Peter Pan,* would have difficulty finding outlets for his magnificent ambitions in the ordinary world. Brooke did not like the poem, for it contains the bite that is so often there in Cornford poems that otherwise praise; he is being gently chided for not engaging the more ordinary struggles of life. As with her triolet "To a Fat Lady seen from a Train," however, her quatrain about Brooke turned back upon her, overtaken this time by events. In the aftermath of the Great War, when it came to seem a huge waste, producing a "lost generation," Rupert Brooke and "Rupert-Brookeish emotions" (in the phrase of George Orwell) were seen as the cause of the disaster. In that context, Cornford's poem for Brooke suddenly appeared particularly damning. He became a naïve and arrogant dreamer, unprepared, as was an entire generation, for the destruction of the Great War. Her small poem from 1908 looked after the war as if it, too, were naively overconfident, unable to imagine the ending of Edwardian English life. In light of Cornford's history of depression, it is apparent that the "long littleness of life" carries a more personal undercurrent of dispraise than postwar England could perceive at the time. A year after Brooke's death, she bore her second child, a son, whom she named Rupert John Cornford. As had his namesake, John became a war poet and was killed too young, in Spain in January 1937. "Youth" applies equally well to her son as to Brooke, demonstrating a surprising power of universality for such a small occasional piece.

BIBLIOGRAPHY

Delany, Paul. *The Neo-Pagans: Friendship and Love in the Rupert Brooke Circle.* New York: Free Press, 1987.
Dowson, Jane, ed. *Frances Cornford: Selected Poems.* London: Enitharmon Press, 1996.

James Persoon

"YOU WILL BE HEARING FROM US SHORTLY" U. A. FANTHORPE (1982)

While many of U. A. FANTHORPE's poems take on a conversational tone, with casual cadences and everyday language constituting her lines, this poem takes the very form of a conversation between an interviewer and an applicant for an unspecified job. Through a skillful avoidance of any identifying details, and her tacit belief that this kind of situation is exclusive to no individual, Fanthorpe creates a mood of uncertainty and anxiety that carries the poem far from its origins in human speech into one of suspenseful allegory, for the notion that this poem is conversational is called into doubt, given that the applicant him- or herself is never allowed to speak—suggesting that this poem is concerned less with entry into the workforce than with the miseries along the arduous road to political enfranchisement.

The poem does not explicitly state whether this is so, but the heart of the enfranchisement issue here is that unlike the call-and-response format of traditional worship songs, here the caller is the responder as well. The short, staccato responses (*Ah, Indeed, Quite so*) take the place of the words left in the white space, words that the reader may only infer. That this poem is essentially political in its thrust, however, does not entail its becoming a piece of propaganda; rather, it is a testament to Fanthorpe's artful suspension of her language that she never allows it so to decay. Many of the questions put to the applicants—Are they the right age? Might the public find their looks disturbing? Is their education a potential impediment to the requirements of the job?—are just vague enough to destabilize the ground on which one might respond, but just damning enough to ensure that the applicant has never had a chance. After all, the interviewer unhesitatingly remarks that in this case a stereotypical family life represents "the usual dubious / Desire to perpetuate what had better / Not have happened at all." Down that terrible line, so implied, are future interviews with the same anonymous bureaucratic machine, and the same result each time.

This nigh-Orwellian vision of the distribution of labor can, in some cases, give rise to a skepticism that threatens to become the underlying foundation of the poem: a skepticism of language itself, leading to an epistemology of despair. But Fanthorpe refuses to entertain such a notion; rather, by the third stanza the suspicion arises that this is, in fact, a wildly funny poem. "We are conscious ourselves," the interviewer deadpans, "Of the need for a candidate with precisely / The right degree of immaturity." On this point, apparently, there is some concordance; after the applicant's response returns the interviewer, "So glad we agree." In such a case as this one might go so far as to suggest that a vision of language—which allows, it must be noted, a vision of poetry—has been corrupted not by skepticism but by deep irreducible laughter, the wordless sound that communicates everything in the world.

Benjamin Morris

Z

ZEPHANIAH, BENJAMIN (1958–) In his poetry and in person Benjamin Zephaniah is refreshingly direct: "I don't have an identity crisis, and I have no wish to write to win awards," he has said, arguing instead that it is the duty of every poet "to tell it as it is" and "to question and explore the state of justice" in the world. Zephaniah's directedness and sensitivity to injustice emerge from a life that reflects the experience of many second-generation black British people growing up in an indifferent and often hostile society: He was expelled from school and spent time in jail, and he has described his younger self as "an angry, illiterate, uneducated, ex-hustler, rebellious Rastafarian." It was in prison that Zephaniah realized he could use his poetic and musical talents to fight for change, and his poetry is committed to communicating an urgent and deeply human message by speaking the language of his audience rather than that of poetic tradition. Performing at comedy clubs, concerts, and political rallies and on radio and TV, Zephaniah has become probably the best-known living poet in Britain. He has made a number of albums that combine music and poetry and has recorded with the Wailers and Sinead O'Connor among others. Alongside poetry for adults, he has written poetry for children, novels for teenagers, and plays for television and radio.

Benjamin Zephaniah was born in the Handsworth district of Birmingham in England, but his childhood was as much influenced by his Jamaican roots as by British culture. Zephaniah gained to national promi-

nence in the 1980s as one of a number of "dub poets"—a style of poetry that draws on Jamaican rhythms and speech patterns and is as much at home being performed before a live audience as being read. After years of violence by neo-Nazi thugs and deteriorating relations between the police and black communities, the 1980s saw race riots in many British cities. Zephaniah grafted a keen sense of the frustration of many young black British people with racism, unemployment, and inequality onto the rhythms of reggae, capturing a widespread mood. But his poetry has always maintained a humor and concern for human idiosyncrasy and so avoids sounding doctrinaire or ideological. In "I Have a Scheme," he comically rewrites Martin Luther King's famous "I Have a Dream" speech: "I see a time," the poet prophesies, "When words like affirmative action / Will have sexual connotations," and when the U.S. president "will stand up and say / 'I inhaled / And it did kinda nice.'"

The suppleness of Zephaniah's poetic tone is matched by the openness of his political outlook. Rather than articulating a narrow identity politics, he defines *black* in a political rather than biological sense: "When I say 'Black,'" he writes, "it means more than skin color, I include Romany, Iraqi, Indians, Kurds, Palestinians all those that are treated Black by the united white states," including the Irish and "the battered White woman." This wider sense of human solidarity over and against the artificial demarcations of nation, religion, or skin color has prompted an enduring concern with the plight of immigrants, refugees, and asylum seekers. In "We Refugees," he reminds us that we could all be refugees since "we can all be told to go, / We can be hated by someone / For being someone." It has also led him to take political stands against apartheid in South Africa, against the oppression of Palestinians, and against the Anglo-American invasion of Iraq. "The world stayed silent when the Nazis started to kill trade unionists, disabled people, gays and jews," Zephaniah writes, "and now, in the age of the global village and mass communication, the world is staying silent as the Palestinians are being annihilated."

Zephaniah's popularity with audiences who are not normally seen as poetry readers has earned him numerous plaudits, including consideration for the post of professor of poetry at Oxford University and as the national poet laureate. But Zephaniah has kept his distance from establishment circles and remains committed to the lives and experiences of ordinary communities. He attended the Bloody Sunday Inquiry into the killing of 14 Irish men by the British army and served as poet in residence in the chambers of the internationally renowned human rights lawyer Michael Mansfield. Tragically, on September 7, 2003, Zephaniah's cousin, Michael Powell, died in controversial circumstances while in police custody, and the poet has been actively involved in the campaign to establish the truth about his death.

That same year, Zephaniah's high public profile and outspokenness put him at the center of controversy when he refused the award of the Order of the British Empire (OBE) by the British government. His refusal was publicly attacked by some prominent black figures, who claimed it harmed recognition of the achievements of ethnic minorities in British public life. In response, Zephaniah has argued that acceptance of such government awards is antithetical to the critical independence of the artist: "I am not on anyone's payroll," he writes, "which means that I am free to speak my mind, as every poet should be in my humble opinion." Equally he has drawn attention to the historical amnesia signaled by the title "Order of the British Empire": "I get angry when I hear that word 'empire' [because] it reminds me of slavery," Zephaniah explains, adding that "it is because of this idea of empire that black people like myself don't even know our true names or our true historical culture." But if Zephaniah is critical of Britain's colonial past and its current support of U.S. global hegemony, he is one of the most enthusiastic promoters of multiculturalism and tolerance in contemporary Britain: "The more I travel the more I love Britain," he writes, "and it is because I love the place that I fight for my rights here."

BIBLIOGRAPHY

Kellaway, Kate. "Dread Poets Society." *Observer,* 4 November 2001.

A Poet Called Benjamin Zephaniah. Available online. URL: http://www.benjaminzephaniah.com/index.html. Accessed May 12, 2008.

Zephaniah, Benjamin. *Refugee Boy.* London: Bloomsbury, 2001.

———. *Too Black, Too Strong.* Newcastle, Eng.: Bloodaxe, 2001.

Graham MacPhee

APPENDIX I

GLOSSARY

accent The STRESS on one or another syllable, especially when poetry is read aloud.

accentual verse A system of VERSE throughout at least a portion of a poem that depends on a certain fixed number of stresses in a line of poetry; this system, however, allows for any number of unstressed syllables.

allegory Extended metaphor or symbol with at least two levels of meaning, a literal level and an implied, figurative level; an allegorical narrative tells a story and at the same time suggests another level of meaning.

alliteration Repeating consonant sounds at the beginnings of words.

allusion Making reference to something or someone, usually in an indirect manner.

anapest A metrical foot consisting of two soft stresses followed by a hard stress. See METER.

anaphora A word or phrase that is repeated at the start of successive lines of poetry.

apostrophe A turn away from the reader to address another listener.

assonance Repetition of like vowel sounds, often in stressed syllables in close proximity to each other.

ballad A narrative in VERSE; the form derives from a narrative that was sung.

blank verse Unrhymed IAMBIC PENTAMETER.

cadence The rhythm in language, a pattern that can lend a musical order to a statement.

caesura A pause within a VERSE line, usually at approximately mid point.

canon A term originally derived from the Roman Catholic Church having to do with church law, this term also refers to a body of literature that is generally accepted as exhibiting what is best or important in terms of literary art.

collagist poetry Poetry that employs the organizing element of collage or the bringing together of disparate material to create a new statement or vision.

conceit Not unrelated to the term *concept,* an unusual supposition, analogy, metaphor, or image, often clever.

connotation Meaning that is implied rather than stated directly as in DENOTATION.

consonance Repetition of identical consonant sounds, within the context of varying vowel sounds.

couplet Two VERSE lines in succession that have the same END RHYME. When the two lines contain a complete statement in themselves, they are called a closed couplet. See also HEROIC COUPLET.

534

dactyl A metrical foot consisting of a hard stress followed by two soft stresses.

denotation The literal meaning of a word or statement, the opposite of CONNOTATION.

diction Word choice, the actual language that a writer employs.

dimeter A VERSE line consisting of two metrical FEET.

dramatic monologue An address to an interlocutor (another potential speaker) who is not present; a dramatic monologue has only one actual speaker.

elegy A poem mourning someone's death.

ellipsis Part of a statement left out, unspoken.

end rhyme A rhyme at the end of a VERSE line.

end-stopped A VERSE line that pauses at its end, when no ENJAMBMENT is possible.

enjambment A VERSE line whose momentum forbids a pause at its end, thus avoiding being END-STOPPED.

epic A long poem that, typically, recounts the adventures of someone in a high style and diction; classically, the adventures include a hero who is at least partially superhuman in makeup or deed, and the events have special importance in terms of the fate of a people.

epigram A brief, witty statement, often satiric or aphoristic.

epithet A word or phrase that characterizes something or someone.

eye rhyme Agreement of words according to their spelling but not their sound.

feet See FOOT.

feminine ending A VERSE line that ends with an extra soft stress.

feminine rhyme The rhyming of two words in more than a single syllable.

figurative language Language that employs figures of speech such as IRONY, HYPERBOLE, METAPHOR, SIMILE, SYMBOL, METONYMY, etc., in which the language connotes meaning.

foot A configuration of syllables to form a METER, such as an IAMB, TROCHEE, ANAPEST, DACTYL, or SPONDEE. A line of one foot is called a MONOMETER line, of two feet a DIAMETER line, of three feet TRIMETER, of four TETRAMETER, of five PENTAMETER, of six HEXAMETER, etc.

free verse Poetry lacking a metrical pattern or patterns, poetic lines without any discernible meter.

haiku A Japanese lyric form consisting of a certain number of syllables overall and in each line, most often in a five-seven-five syllabic line pattern.

half rhyme A form of CONSONANCE in which final consonant sounds in neighboring stressed syllables agree.

heroic couplet Two successive lines of END-RHYMING IAMBIC PENTAMETER.

hexameter A VERSE line consisting of six metrical FEET.

hyperbole An exaggeration meant to emphasize something.

iamb A metrical FOOT consisting of a soft stress followed by a hard stress.

iambic pentameter A five-FOOT line with a preponderance of IAMBIC FEET.

image Language meant to represent objects, actions, feelings, or thoughts in vivid terms.

internal rhyme A RHYME within a poetic line.

masculine rhyme A RHYME depending on one hard-stressed syllable only.

metaphor An implicit comparison, best when between unlike things, made without using the words *like* or *as*.

meter An arrangement of syllables in units called FEET, such as IAMB or TROCHEE, and in numbers of feet to make a pattern, such as IAMBIC PENTAMETER; the syllables can be hard- or soft-stressed according to the type of FOOT or pattern to be employed.

metonymy The substitution of a word that represents an association with, proximity to, or attribute of a thing for the thing itself; this figure of speech is not unlike SYNECHDOCHE.

monometer A VERSE line consisting of a single metrical foot.

occasional verse VERSE written to celebrate or to commemorate a particular event.

octave An eight-line stanza of poetry also the first and larger portion of a SONNET. See OCTET.

octet An eight-line stanza of poetry See OCTAVE.

ode A lyric poem usually in a dignified style and addressing a serious subject.

onomatopoeia A word or phrase whose sound resembles something the word or phrase is signifying.

oxymoron A phrase or statement containing a self-contradiction.

paradox A statement that seems to be self-contradictory but contains a truth that reconciles the contradiction.

pastoral A poem that evokes a rural setting or rural values; the word itself derives from the Latin *pastor,* or "shepherd."

pentameter A VERSE line consisting of five metrical FEET.

persona The speaker in a poem, most often the narrator; the term is derived from the Latin word for "mask."

personification Attributing human qualities to an inanimate entity.

prosody The study of versification; the term is at times used as a synonym for METER.

quatrain A four-line stanza of a poem, also a portion of a SONNET.

rhetorical figure An arrangement of words for one or another emphasis or effect.

rhyme Fundamentally, "agreement," the term specifically indicates the sameness or similarity of vowel sounds in an arrangement of words; there can be END RHYME, INTERNAL RHYME, EYE RHYME, HALF RHYME, FEMININE RHYME, etc.

rhyme scheme The arrangement of END RHYMES in a poem, indicated when analyzing a poem with the letters of the alphabet, such as, for a poem in successive COUPLETS, AA, BB, CC, etc.

rhythm A sense of movement created by arrangement of syllables in terms of stress and time.

sestet A six-line stanza of poetry also the final large portion of a SONNET.

sestina A 36-line poem broken up into six SESTETS as well as a final stanza of three lines, the six words ending the first sestet's lines appearing at the conclusions of the remaining five sestets, in. one or another order, and appearing in the final three lines; these repeated words usually convey key motifs of the poem.

simile A comparison using the word *like* or *as.*

slant rhyme A partial, incomplete RHYME, sometimes called a half, *imperfect, near* or *off rhyme.*

sonnet A poem of 14 lines, traditionally in IAMBIC PENTAMETER, the RHYME SCHEME and structure of which can vary There are two predominant types of sonnets: the English or Shakespearean, which consists of three QUATRAINS and a final COUPLET, usually with a rhyme scheme of ABAB CDCD EFEF GG; and the Italian or Petrarchan sonnet, often with an initial OCTAVE rhyming ABBA ABBA and a concluding SESTET rhyming CDECDE. However, it is important to keep in mind that sonnet rhyme schemes can be very different from the above.

spondee A metrical FOOT comprised of two hard stresses.

sprung rhythm Lines or STANZAS made up of a preset number of hard syllabic stresses but any number of soft stresses; the effect is a rhythmic irregularity.

stanza A group of lines of poetry

stress The emphasis when reading a poem accorded to a syllable.

strophe A STANZA, or VERSE paragraph in a prose poem, derived from classical Greek drama.

syllabic verse Poetry that employs a set number of syllables in a line, regardless of STRESS.

symbol A figure of speech that means what it says literally but also connotes a secondary meaning or meanings, and which usually conveys a concept, motif, or idea.

synecdoche A figure of speech in which a part of something is meant to signify the entirety of the thing, such as a hand that is meant to suggest a sailor whose hands are used in sailing a ship (as in "all hands on deck"). See METONYMY.

synesthesia The mingling or substitution of the senses, such as when talking about a sound by mentioning a color.

tanka A Japanese VERSE form consisting of five lines, with the first and third line each containing five syllables and the rest of the lines each containing seven.

tercet A three-line STANZA grouping.

terza rima Poetry comprised of TERCETS and an interlocking RHYME SCHEME: ABA, BCB, CDC, etc.

tetrameter A VERSE line of four metrical FEET.

tone A poet's manifest attitude toward the subject expressed in the poem.

trimeter A VERSE line of three metrical FEET.

trochee A metrical FOOT consisting of a hard STRESS followed by a soft stress.

trope A figurative or rhetorical mechanism, and at times a motif.

verse A line of poetry or at times a synonym for *poetry* or *poem*.

vers libre FREE VERSE.

villanelle A 19-line poem made up of six STANZAS—five TERCETS and a final QUATRAIN—with the first tercet employing an ABA RHYME SCHEME that is then replicated in the following tercets as well as in the final two lines of the quatrain. In addition, the first and third lines are repeated in lines 6, 12, and 18, and 9, 15, and 19, respectively The poem's first and third lines, and their subsequent iterations, carry a special thematic weight, and the poem's motifs are brought together in the concluding quatrain.

voice Not unlike the poem's PERSONA, a sense of a personality or speaker's diction, point of view or attitude in a poem; voice can also simply refer to a poem's speaker.

APPENDIX II

SELECTED BIBLIOGRAPHY

ANTHOLOGIES OF POETRY

Adcock, Fleur, ed. *The Oxford Book of Contemporary New Zealand Poetry.* Oxford: Oxford University Press, 1983.

Amis, Kingsley, ed. *The New Oxford Book of Light Verse.* Oxford: Oxford University Press. 1992.

Atwood, Margaret, ed. *The New Oxford Book of Canadian Verse in English.* Oxford: Oxford University Press, 1982.

Burnett, Paula, ed. *The Penguin Book of Caribbean Verse in English.* London: Penguin, 1986.

Cosham, Ralph, ed. *Celtic Poets: Poetry by Irish, Scottish, and Welsh Poets.* Poetry in Audio, 2004.

Dharwadker, Vinay, ed. *The Oxford Anthology of Modern Indian Poetry.* Oxford: Oxford University Press, 1994.

Dowson, Jane, ed. *Women's Poetry of the 1930s: A Critical Anthology.* London: Routledge, 1996.

Gardner, Brian, ed. *The Terrible Rain: The War Poets, 1939–1945.* London: Metheun, 1966.

Gilbert, Sandra M., and Susan Gubar, eds. *The Norton Anthology of Literature by Women.* 2nd ed. New York: Norton, 1996.

Hall, Linda, ed. *An Anthology of Poetry by Women: Tracing the Tradition.* London: Cassell, 1994.

Larkin, Philip, ed. *The Oxford Book of Twentieth Century English Verse.* Oxford: Oxford University Press, 1973.

Lucie-Smith, Edward, ed. *British Poetry since 1945.* Rev. ed. London: Penguin, 1985.

MacQueen, John, and Tom Scott, eds. *The Oxford Book of Scottish Verse.* Oxford: Oxford University Press, 1989.

Maja-Pearce, Adewale, ed. *The Heinemann Book of African Poetry in English.* Oxford: Heinemann, 1990.

Minhinnick, Robert, ed. *The Adulterer's Tongue: An Anthology of Welsh Poetry.* Manchester, Eng.: Carcanet, 2003.

Morrison, Blake, and Andrew Motion, eds. *The Penguin Book of Contemporary Poetry.* New York: Penguin, 1982.

Moore, Gerald, and Ulli Beier, eds. *The Penguin Book of Modern African Poetry.* 4th ed. New York: Penguin, 1998.

Muldoon, Paul, ed. *The Faber Book of Contemporary Irish Poetry.* London: Faber and Faber, 1986.

Murray, Les, ed. *The New Oxford Book of Australian Verse.* Oxford: Oxford University Press, 1986.

O'Brian, Sean, ed. *The Firebox: Poetry in Britain and Ireland after 1945.* London: Picador, 1998.

Palgrave, Francis Turner, ed. *The Golden Treasury.* Oxford: Oxford University Press, 1986.

Procter, Stephen, Michael Schmidt, and Eleanor Crawforth, eds. *New Poetries IV.* Manchester, Eng.: Carcanet Press, 2007.

Ramazani, Jahan, Richard Ellmann, and Robert O'Clair, eds. *The Norton Anthology of Modern and Contemporary Poetry.* New York: Norton, 2003.

Reilly, Catherine W., ed. *Scars upon My Heart: Women's Poetry and Verse of the First World War.* London: Virago, 1981.

Silkin, Jon, ed. *The Penguin Book of First World War Poetry.* Harmondsworth, Eng.: Penguin, 1979.

Tuma, Keith, ed. *Anthology of Twentieth-Century British and Irish Poetry.* Oxford: Oxford University Press, 2001.

Yeats, William Butler, ed. *The Oxford Book of Modern Verse.* Oxford: Oxford University Press, 1936.

GENERAL WORKS, ON MORE THAN ONE WRITER

Baker, David, and Ann Townsend, eds. *Radiant Lyre: Essays on Lyric Poetry*. St. Paul, Minn.: Graywolf Press, 2007.

Baldick, Chris. *The Oxford English Literary History. Vol. 10, 1960–2000: The Modern Movement (1910–1940)*. Oxford: Oxford University Press, 2005.

Bergonzi, Bernard. *Heroes' Twilight: A Study of the Literature of the Great War*. New York: Coward-McCann, 1966.

———. *Reading the Thirties*. Pittsburgh: University of Pittsburgh Press, 1978.

Bloom, Harold. *The Anxiety of Influence*. New York: Oxford University Press, 1973.

———. *The Art of Reading Poetry*. New York: Harper, 2005.

Broe, Mary Lynn, and Angela Ingram. *Women's Writing in Exile*. Chapel Hill: University of North Carolina Press, 1986.

Bryan, Sharon. *Where We Stand: Women Poets on Literary Tradition*. New York: Norton, 1993.

Caesar, Adrian. *Dividing Lines: Poetry, Class, and Ideology in the 1930s*. Manchester, Eng.: Manchester University Press, 1991.

———. *Taking It Like A Man: Suffering, Sexuality, and the War Poets*. Manchester, Eng.: Manchester University Press, 1994.

Campbell, Matthew. *The Cambridge Companion to Contemporary British Poetry*. Cambridge: Cambridge University Press, 2003.

Chaudhuri, Amit. *D. H. Lawrence and "Difference": Postcoloniality and the Poetry of the Present*. Oxford: Oxford University Press, 2003.

Childs, Peter. *The Twentieth Century in Poetry*. London: Routledge, 1998.

Crawford, Fred D. *British Poets of the Great War*. Selinsgrove, Pa.: Susquehanna University Press, 1988.

Davie, Donald. *Thomas Hardy and British Poetry*. London: Routledge & Kegan Paul, 1972.

———. *Under Briggflatts: A History of Poetry in Great Britain, 1960–1988*. Chicago: University of Chicago Press, 1989.

Day, Gary, and Brian Docherty, eds. *British Poetry, 1900–1950: Aspects of Tradition*. New York: St. Martin's Press, 1995.

———. *British Poetry from the 1950s to the 1990s: Politics and Art*. London: Macmillan, 1997.

Delany, Paul. *D. H. Lawrence's Nightmare*. New York: Basic, 1978.

———. *The Neo-Pagans: Rupert Brooke and the Ordeal of Youth*. New York: Free Press, 1987.

Dowson, Jane. *Women, Modernism, and British Poetry, 1910–1939: Resisting Femininity*. London: Ashgate, 2002.

———. *Women's Writing, 1945–1960: After the Deluge*. London: Macmillan, 2004.

Dowson, Jane, and Alice Entwistle. *A History of Twentieth-Century British Women's Poetry*. Cambridge: Cambridge University Press, 2005.

Eksteins, Modris. *Rites of Spring: The Great War and the Birth of the Modern Age*. New York: Anchor, 1990.

Ford, Hugh D., ed. *A Poet's War: British Poets and the Spanish Civil War*. Philadelphia: University of Pennsylvannia Press, 1965.

Fuller, Roy. *Professors and Gods*. London: André Deutsch, 1973.

Fussell, Paul. *The Great War and Modern Memory*. Oxford: Oxford University Press, 1975.

Gervais, David. *Literary Englands: Versions of "Englishness" in English Writing*. Cambridge: Cambridge University Press, 1994.

Graham, Desmond. *The Truth of War: Owen, Blunden, Rosenberg*. Manchester, Eng.: Carcanet Press, 1984.

Gray, Robert, and Geoffrey Lehmann, eds. *Australian Poetry in the Twentieth Century*. London: Heinemann, 1992.

Gregson, Ian. *Contemporary Poetry and Postmodernism: Dialogue and Estrangement*. London: Macmillan, 1996.

Grennan, Eamon. *Facing the Music: Irish Poetry in the Twentieth Century*. Omaha, Nebr.: Creighton University Press, 1999.

Heaney, Seamus. *The Redress of Poetry*. New York: Farrar, Straus & Giroux, 1995.

Hoffpauir, Richard. *The Art of Restraint*. London and Toronto: Associated University Presses, 1991.

Hughes, Glenn. *Imagism and the Imagists: A Study in Modern Poetry*. New York: Biblo and Tannen, 1972.

Hughes, Ted. *Winter Pollen: Occasional Prose*. New York: Picador, 1994.

Hynes, Samuel. *The Auden Generation*. New York: Oxford University Press, 1972.

———. *Edwardian Occasions: Essays on English Writing in the Early Twentieth Century*. New York: Oxford University Press, 1977.

———. *A War Imagined: The First World War and English Culture*. New York: Atheneum, 1991.

James, Louis. *Caribbean Literature in English*. London: Longman, 1999.

Johnston, Dillon. *Irish Poetry After Joyce*. 2nd ed. Syracuse, N.Y.: Syracuse University Press, 1997.

———. *The Poetic Economies of England and Ireland, 1912–2000*. London: Macmillan, 2001.

Johnston, John H. *The Poet and the City.* Athens: University of Georgia Press, 1984.

Kelsall, Malcolm. *The Great Good Place: The Country House and English Literature.* New York: Columbia University Press, 1993.

Khan, Nosheen. *Women's Poetry of the First World War.* Lexington: University Press of Kentucky, 1988.

King, Bruce. *The Oxford English Literary History. Vol. 13, 1948–2000: The Internationalization of English Literature.* Oxford: Oxford University Press, 2005.

Longley, Edna. *Poetry in the Wars.* Newcastle upon Tyne, Eng.: Bloodaxe Books, 1986.

Lucas, John. *Modern English Poetry from Hardy to Hughes.* London: B. T. Batsford, 1986.

———. *The Radical Twenties: Writing, Politics, and Culture.* New Brunswick, N.J.: Rutgers University Press, 1997.

Marcus, Laura, and Peter Nicholls. *The Cambridge History of Twentieth-Century English Literature.* Cambridge: Cambridge University Press, 2005.

Millard, Kenneth. *Edwardian Poetry.* Oxford: Clarendon Press, 1991.

Montefiore, Jan. *Feminism and Poetry: Language, Experience, Identity in Women's Writing.* London: HarperCollins, 1994.

O'Neil, Michael, and Gareth Reeves. *Auden, MacNeice, Spender: The Thirties Poetry.* New York: St. Martin's Press, 1992.

Parfitt, George. *English Poetry of the First World War.* New York: Harvester Wheatsheaf, 1990.

Parker, Peter. *The Old Lie: The Great War and the Public School Ethos.* London: Constable, 1987.

Paulin, Tom. *Minotaur: Poetry and the Nation State.* Cambridge, Mass.: Harvard University Press, 1992.

———. *Writing the Moment: Selected Critical Essays, 1980–95.* London: Faber and Faber, 1998.

Pearson, John. *The Sitwells.* New York: Harcourt Brace Jovanovich, 1978.

Perkins, David. *A History of Modern Poetry: From the 1890s to the High Modernist Mode.* Cambridge, Mass.: Harvard University Press, 1976.

———. *A History of Modern Poetry: Modernism and After.* Cambridge, Mass.: Harvard University Press, 1987.

Persoon, James. *Modern British Poetry, 1900–1939.* New York: Twayne, 1999.

Press, John. *A Map of Modern English Verse.* London: Oxford University Press, 1969.

Salmon, Arthur Edward. *Poets of the Apocalypse.* Boston: Twayne, 1983.

Schmidt, Michael. *Fifty Modern British Poets: A Reader's Guide.* London: Heinemann, 1979.

———. *The Story of Poetry.* London: Weidenfeld & Nicholson, 2007.

Sewell, Frank. *Modern Irish Poetry: A New Alhambra.* Oxford: Oxford University Press, 2000.

Shires, Linda M. *British Poetry of the Second World War.* New York: St. Martin's Press, 1985.

Silkin, Jon. *Out of Battle: The Poetry of the Great War.* London: Oxford University Press, 1972.

Smith, Stan. *Inviolable Voice: History and Twentieth Century Poetry.* New York: Humanities Press, 1982.

———. *Poetry and Displacement.* Liverpool: Liverpool University Press, 2007.

Stevenson, Randall. *The Oxford English Literary History. Vol. 12, 1960–2000: The Last of England?* Oxford: Oxford University Press, 2005.

Thwaite, Anthony. *Twentieth-Century English Poetry.* London: Heinemann, 1978.

Tuma, Keith. *Fishing by Obstinate Isles: Modern and Postmodern British Poetry and American Readers.* Evanston, Ill.: Northwestern University Press, 1998.

Walsh, John Evangelist. *Into My Own: The English Years of Robert Frost.* New York: Grove Weidenfeld, 1988.

Wilhelm, J. J. *Ezra Pound in London and Paris, 1908–1925.* University Park: Pennsylvannia State University Press, 1990.

Woods, Gregory. *Articulate Flesh: Male Homo-Eroticism and Modern Poetry.* New Haven, Conn.: Yale University Press, 1987.

APPENDIX III

LIST OF CONTRIBUTORS

William Allegrezza — Indiana University Northwest

Jess Allen — Independent scholar

David Alvarez — Grand Valley State University

Rachel Anderson — Grand Valley State University

R. Victoria Arana — Howard University

Pilar Villar Argáiz — University of Granada

Hazel Atkins — University of Ottawa

L. Michelle Baker — Catholic University of America

John Ballam — Harris Manchester College, University of Oxford

Hilary Barker — University of Sheffield

Catherine Bates — University of Leeds

Gerd Bayer — University of Erlangen

Geraldine Cannon Becker — University of Maine, Fort Kent

Joseph E. Becker — University of Maine, Fort Kent

LynnDiane Beene — University of New Mexico

Matthew Bolton — Loyola School

Brad Bostian — Central Piedmont Community College

Patricia Bostian — Central Piedmont Community College

David Brottman — Iowa State University

Kurt Bullock — Grand Valley State University

Brian Burton — Open University

Robin Calland — Southern Utah University

Sinead Carey — Mary Immaculate College, University of Limerick

Matthew Paul Carlson — University of North Carolina, Chapel Hill

Emma Carmody — University of Adelaide

Elaine Childs — University of Tennessee, Knoxville

Nephie Christodoulides — University of Cyprus

Christopher K. Coffman — University of Tennessee, Martin

Marianne Cotugno — Miami University, Middletown

Chad Cripe — Grand Valley State University

Catherine Anne Davies — University College, London

Evan Davis — Hampton-Sydney College

Kevin De Ornellas — University of Ulster, Coleraine

Thomas DePietro — Independent scholar

Michelle DeRose — Aquinas College

Mike Devine — University of California, Los Angeles

Jordan J. Dominy — Florida State University

Jane Dowson — De Montfort University, Leicester

Winter Elliott — Brenau University

Helen Emmitt — Centre College

Deirdre Fagan — Quincy University

Patricia M. Feito — Barry University

Brett Foster — Wheaton College

Elizabeth Fox — Massachusetts Institute of Technology

Louisa Gairn — University of Edinburgh

Katherine Gannett — University of Northern Illinois

Sue Garafalo — ABTI University, Nigeria

Carmen Méndez García — Complutense University of Madrid

Patrick Alasdair Gill — Johannes-Gutenberg University of Mainz

Heike Grundmann — University of Heidelberg

Patricia Hagen — College of St. Scholastica

Jean Shepherd Hamm — East Tennessee State University

Ann Hayward — Grand Valley State University

He Ning — Nanjing University

Andrea Heiglmaier — University of Zurich

Ann Hoff — University of Alabama, Birmingham

James Hoff — The Graduate Center, City University of New York

Richard Hudson — Southampton Solent University

Peggy Huey — University of Tampa

David Huisman — Grand Valley State University

Richard Iadonisi — Grand Valley State University

Rhoda Janzen — Hope College

Melissa Johnson — Newberry College

Cristina Johnston — University of Aberdeen

Julie Kane — Northwestern State University of Louisiana

Charlotte Kearns — University of Leeds

Karen Rae Keck — Texas Tech University

Chuck Keim — Nazarene University College

Anne Kellenberger — California State University, Northridge

Richard Kerridge — Bath Spa University

Jennifer Kilgore — University of Caen

Caroline E. Kimberly — University of Houston, Downtown

Arnold Leitner — University of Salzburg

Amy Lemmon — Fashion Institute of Technology, State University of New York

Eric Leuschner — Fort Hays State University

Polina Mackay — University of Cyprus

Sean C. Mackey — Grand Valley State University

Graham MacPhee — West Chester University

Katy Masuga — University of Washington, Seattle

Robert G. May — Queen's University, Kingston

William May — Bath Spa University

Ryan C. McCarty — University of Kansas

Tim McKenzie — The Open Polytechnic of New Zealand

Corinna McLeod — Grand Valley State University

Emily Taylor Merriman — San Francisco State University

Christopher Brook Miller — University of Montevallo

Jo Miller — Grand Valley State University

Alice Mills — University of Ballarat

Michael Moir — Catholic University of America

Benjamin Morris — University of Cambridge

Anja Müller-Wood — Johannes-Gutenberg University of Mainz

Goernan Nieragden — University of Cologne

Claire Norris — McArthur High School

Nathanael O'Reilly — Albion College

James Ortego — Troy University, Dothan

Deidre Osborne — Goldsmiths College, University of London

Daniel Pantano — University of South Florida, Tampa

Barry Parsons — King's College London

James Persoon — Grand Valley State University

John Peters — University of North Texas

George Micajah Phillips — University of Kentucky

J. J. Pionke — Harper College

Tara Prescott — Claremont Graduate University

Tony Rafalowski — University of Missouri, Columbia

Susanne Reichl — University of Vienna

Bradley Ricca — Case Western Reserve University

Ben Robertson — Troy University

Tom Rogers — Sheffield Hallam University

Tracey S. Rosenberg — University of Edinburgh

Aaron S. Rosenfeld — Iona College

Glenda Sacks — Achva College of Education, Israel

Jenny R. Sadre-Orafi — Kennesaw State University

Divya Saksena — Middle Tennessee State University

Michaela Schrage-Früh — Johannes-Gutenberg University of Mainz

John Sears — Manchester Metropolitan University

Gerold Sedlmayr — University of Passau

Michelle Shamasneh — Georgia State University

David Sherman — New York University

Bryna Siegel — University of Rhode Island

Wendy Skinner — University of Göttingen

Jimmy Dean Smith — Union College

Michael Smith — Taylor University

Rachel Hostetter Smith — Taylor University

Christopher Snellgrove — Auburn University

Ivo Soljan — Grand Valley State University

Jason Spangler — Riverside City College

Rob Spence — Edge Hill University

Robert Stacy — Independent scholar

Precious McKenzie Stearns — University of South
   Florida, Tampa
Jennifer Sykes — Hertford College, Oxford University
Gulshan R. Taneja — University of Delhi
Sema Taskin — Bilkent University
Fiona Tolan — University of Northampton
Cliff Toliver — Missouri Southern State University
Elizabeth Tomlinson — University of Montana
Rachel Trousdale — Agnes Scott College
Aimable Twagilimana — Buffalo State College
Meg Tyler — Boston University
Janine Utell — Widener University

Justin Vance — Grand Valley State University
Mary Van Oeveren — Grand Valley State University
Josef Vice — Clark Atlanta University
Melanie Waters — University of Newcastle upon Tyne
Betsy Watson — Davenport University
Robert R. Watson — Grand Valley State University
Julianne White — University of Arizona
Jeni Williams — Trinity College, Carmarthen
Tony Williams — Sheffield Hallam University
Justin Williamson — Pearl River College
Mary Wilson — University of Massachusetts,
   Amherst

INDEX

DATE DUE

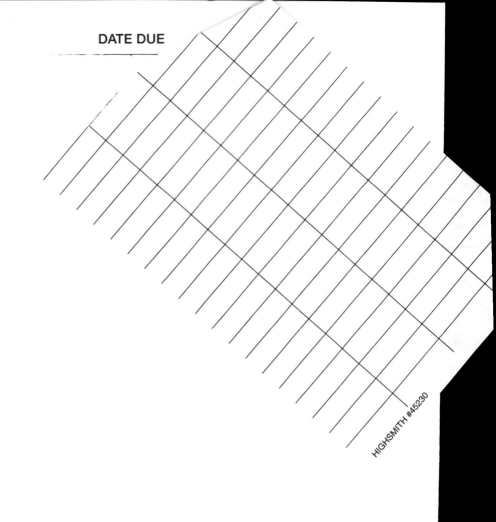